THE ENCYCLOPEDIA OF
MIDDLE EAST WARS

THE ENCYCLOPEDIA OF
MIDDLE EAST WARS

The United States in the Persian Gulf, Afghanistan, and Iraq Conflicts

VOLUME I: A–D

Spencer C. Tucker
Editor

Priscilla Mary Roberts
Editor, Documents Volume

Dr. Paul G. Pierpaoli Jr.
Associate Editor

Colonel Jerry D. Morelock, USAR (retired)
Major General David Zabecki, USAR (retired)
Dr. Sherifa Zuhur
Assistant Editors

FOREWORD BY
General Anthony C. Zinni, USMC (retired)

A B C ⬤ C L I O

Santa Barbara, California   Denver, Colorado   Oxford, England

Library of Congress Cataloging-in-Publication Data

The encyclopedia of Middle East wars : the United States in the Persian Gulf, Afghanistan, and Iraq conflicts / Spencer C. Tucker, editor ; Priscilla Mary Roberts, editor, documents volume.

    v.   cm.

  Includes bibliographical references and index.

  ISBN 978-1-85109-947-4 (hard copy : alk. paper) — ISBN 978-1-85109-948-1 (ebook)

  1. Middle East—History, Military—20th century—Encyclopedias. 2. Middle East—History, Military—21st century—Encyclopedias.
3. Middle East—Military relations—United States—Encyclopedias. 4. United States—Military relations—Middle East—Encyclopedias. 5. Persian Gulf War, 1991—Encyclopedias. 6. Afghan War, 2001—Encyclopedias. 7. Iraq War, 2003—Encyclopedias. I. Tucker, Spencer, 1937– II. Roberts, Priscilla Mary.

  DS63.1.E453 2010

  355.00956'03—dc22

2010033812

13 12 11 10 9   1 2 3 4 5

This book is also available on the World Wide Web as an ebook.
Visit abc-clio.com for details.

ABC-CLIO, LLC
130 Cremona Drive, P.O. Box 1911
Santa Barbara, California 93116–1911

This book is printed on acid-free paper ∞
Manufactured in the United States of America

*Dedicated to the brave U.S. military personnel who have given
their lives in conflicts in the Middle East, which they
and most Americans have so little understood.*

About the Editors

Spencer C. Tucker, PhD, graduated from the Virginia Military Institute and was a Fulbright scholar in France. He was a U.S. Army captain and intelligence analyst in the Pentagon during the Vietnam War, then taught for 30 years at Texas Christian University before returning to his alma mater for 6 years as the holder of the John Biggs Chair of Military History. He retired from teaching in 2003. He is now Senior Fellow of Military History at ABC-CLIO. Dr. Tucker has written or edited 36 books, including ABC-CLIO's award-winning *The Encyclopedia of the Cold War* and *The Encyclopedia of the Arab-Israeli Conflict* as well as the comprehensive *A Global Chronology of Conflict.*

Priscilla Mary Roberts received her PhD from Cambridge University and is an associate professor of history and an honorary director of the Centre of American Studies at the University of Hong Kong. Dr. Roberts has received numerous research awards and was the documents editor of *The Encyclopedia of the Cold War* and *The Encyclopedia of the Arab-Israeli Conflict,* published by ABC-CLIO. She spent 2003 as a visiting Fulbright scholar at the Institute for European, Russian, and Eurasian Studies at the George Washington University in Washington, D.C.

Contents

List of Entries

List of Maps

Preface

American contact with the Middle East began in the 18th century, when trading ships plied the Mediterranean even before the establishment of the United States. Morocco was the first country to recognize the new United States, but troubles with the Barbary States led to the Barbary Wars and the creation of the U.S. Navy. Significant U.S. involvement in the Middle East, however, did not develop until after World War II, abetted by the Arab-Israeli conflict and a growing world demand for the region's oil. Today, the Middle East remains one of the primary loci of U.S. foreign policy, including efforts to preserve the West's oil supply, halt acts of violence by terrorist organizations, and resolve the Arab-Israeli conflict. The Middle East remains perhaps the most volatile of the world's regions.

This encyclopedia is by far the most comprehensive of U.S. involvement in the region. We have chosen a somewhat looser definition of the Middle East and have thus widened the focus to include such countries as Somalia, Afghanistan, and Pakistan, which are geographically located in East Africa and Central and South Asia. The encyclopedia not only deals with military and diplomatic developments but also treats societal, political, economic, and cultural issues that undergird these. There are entries on leading individuals; overviews of the histories of the states in the region and their military establishments; wars and battles; weapons and technology; doctrines; diplomatic treaties; international organizations, including those dedicated to the perpetuation of terrorism; the Global War on Terror; and even the climate of the region.

I am especially grateful to associate editor Dr. Paul G. Pierpaoli Jr. Dr. Pierpaoli and I have worked together for the past five years on a variety of encyclopedias for ABC-CLIO but chiefly the encyclopedia project that, when completed, will have treated all of America's wars. It is both daunting and demanding, and I am grateful for

his counsel and hard work. I am also grateful to assistant editors Jerry Morelock, David Zabecki, and Dr. Sherifa Zuhur. Jerry Morelock, PhD, editor in chief of *Armchair General* magazine, is a retired U.S. Army colonel whose 36-year career included a combat tour in Vietnam, two Pentagon assignments, and the head of the History Department of the Army's Command and General Staff College. He was formerly the executive director of the Winston Churchill Memorial and Library. Major General Dr. David Zabecki, Army of the United States retried, is an honorary senior research fellow in war studies with the University of Birmingham (England) and the senior historian of the Wieder History Group. In 2003 he served in Israel as the senior security adviser of the U.S. Coordinating and Monitoring Mission, an interagency team charged with advancing the Road Map to Peace in the Middle East initiative. Sherifa Zuhur, PhD, is an expert on Middle Eastern security issues and politics. She is the director of the Institute of Middle Eastern and Islamic Studies in Carlisle, Pennsylvania, and was formerly research professor of national security affairs (Islamic and regional studies) at the Strategic Studies Institute of the Army War College. Each of the three brought a particular expertise to the project, and I am grateful for their insightful and significant contributions. All three read and edited the entire manuscript, each of them suggesting changes. U.S. policy in the region in recent years has been hotly debated both here and abroad, and some of the writers and assistant editors had strong and often conflicting viewpoints that needed to be reconciled. I carefully studied their arguments, which were sometimes strenuously advanced, and made the final decisions. I am grateful for their insight and the passion of their arguments. I am also grateful to one of this nation's most distinguished military leaders, General Anthony Zinni, U.S. Marine Corps (retired), for his splendid introduction.

Of course, such a project would not be possible without the work of many competent historians who have written the individual entries. I would like to thank them for their work. I would also like to thank Pat Carlin, director of the military history program at ABC-CLIO and the fine staff at ABC-CLIO, and especially Andrew McCormick and Maxine Taylor, who have been a great assist throughout this project. All three greatly eased what would otherwise have been a far more difficult project. As usual, I am especially grateful to Dr. Beverly Tucker for her patience and encouragement. I take full responsibility for any errors in the final copy.

Spencer C. Tucker

General Maps

MIDDLE EAST

TOPOGRAPHY OF THE MIDDLE EAST

KAZAKHSTAN

RUSSIA

Black Sea

Caspian Sea

UZBEKISTAN

GEORGIA

ARMENIA   AZERBAIJAN

TURKMENISTAN

40°N

TURKEY

AFGHANISTAN

CYPRUS   SYRIA

IRAN

LEBANON

Mediterranean
Sea

IRAQ

ISRAEL

JORDAN

30°N

KUWAIT

PAKISTAN

EGYPT

Persian Gulf

BAHRAIN

QATAR

UNITED
ARAB
EMIRATES

SAUDI
ARABIA

Arabian
Sea

Red Sea

OMAN

20°N

SUDAN

ERITREA   YEMEN

INDIAN

DJIBOUTI

OCEAN

SOMALIA

Elevation (in feet)

	10,000 +
	7,000–10,000
	5,000–7,000
	2,000–5,000
	1,000–2,000
	500–1,000
	0–500
	Below sea level

ETHIOPIA

0   100   200 mi

0 100 200 km

40°E

50°E

COALITION AGAINST IRAQ, AUGUST 2, 1990–FEBRUARY 28, 1991

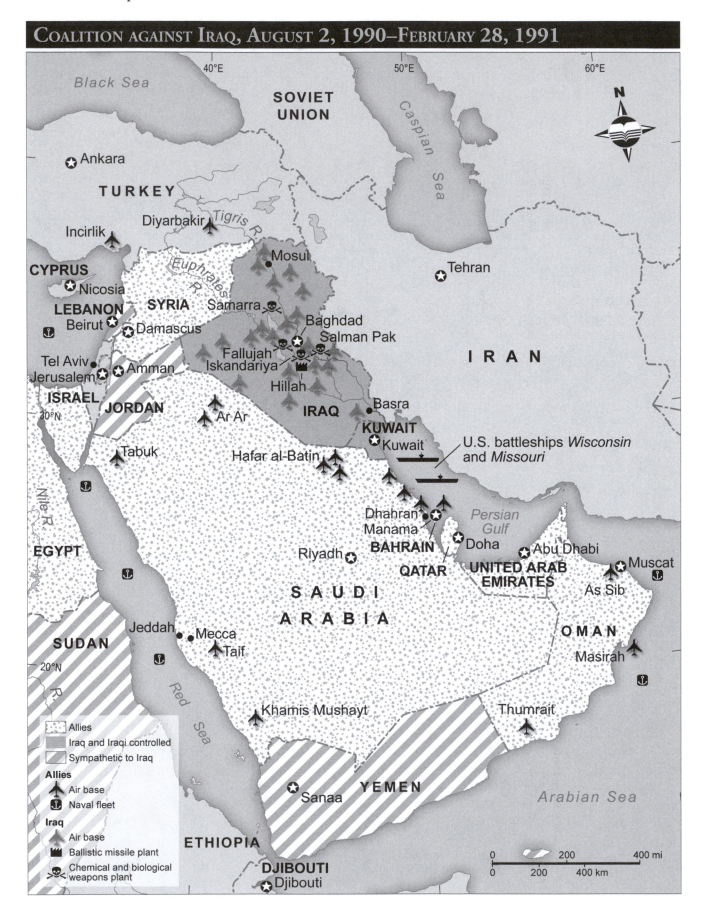

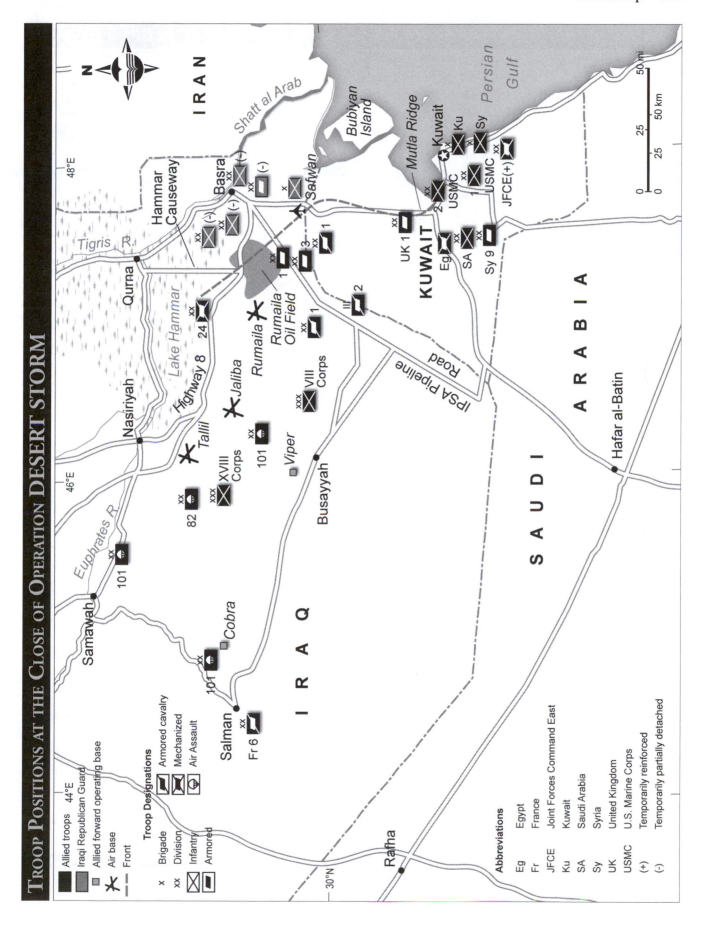

Troop Positions at the Close of Operation DESERT STORM

OPERATION ENDURING FREEDOM, 2001

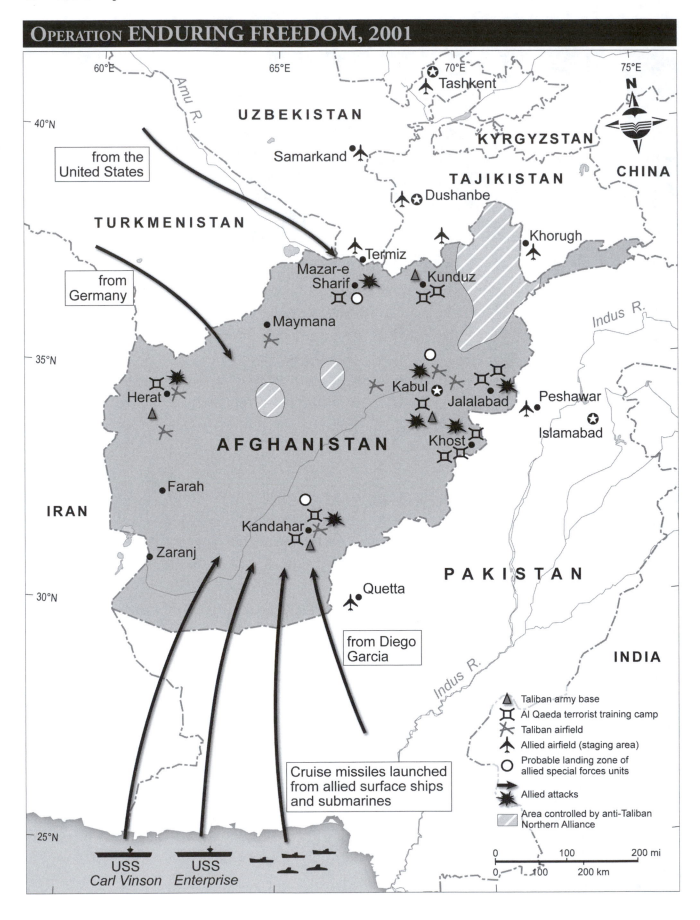

from the United States

from Germany

N

60°E

65°E

70°E

75°E

40°N

UZBEKISTAN

☆ Tashkent

✈

KYRGYZSTAN

CHINA

Samarkand ✈

TAJIKISTAN

✈ ✪ Dushanbe

TURKMENISTAN

✈ ● Khorugh

✈ Termiz

Mazar-e Sharif ●

△ Kunduz

35°N

● Maymana

Herat ●

AFGHANISTAN

✪ Kabul

Jalalabad

△

Peshawar
●

Indus R.

● Farah

Khost ●

☆ Islamabad

Zaranj ●

Kandahar ●

IRAN

PAKISTAN

30°N

✈ Quetta ●

from Diego Garcia

INDIA

Indus R.

Legend:

△ Taliban army base
✶ Al Qaeda terrorist training camp
✷ Taliban airfield
✈ Allied airfield (staging area)
○ Probable landing zone of allied special forces units
✦ Allied attacks
▨ Area controlled by anti-Taliban Northern Alliance

Cruise missiles launched from allied surface ships and submarines

25°N

USS
Carl Vinson

USS
Enterprise

0   100   200 mi
0   100   200 km

Amu R.

DISPOSITION OF FORCES ON THE EVE OF THE 2003 IRAQ WAR

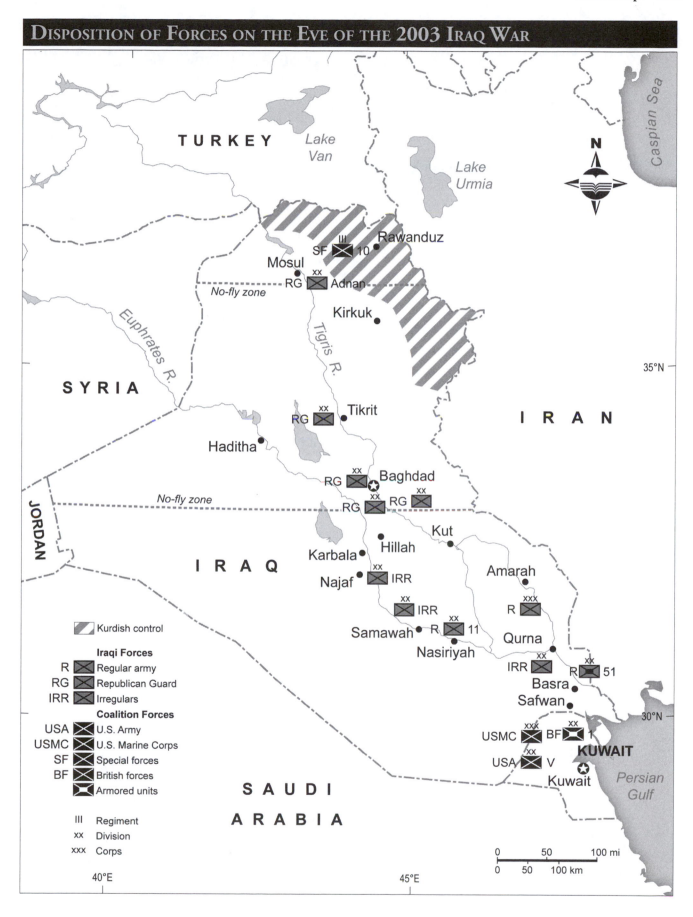

2003 IRAQ WAR

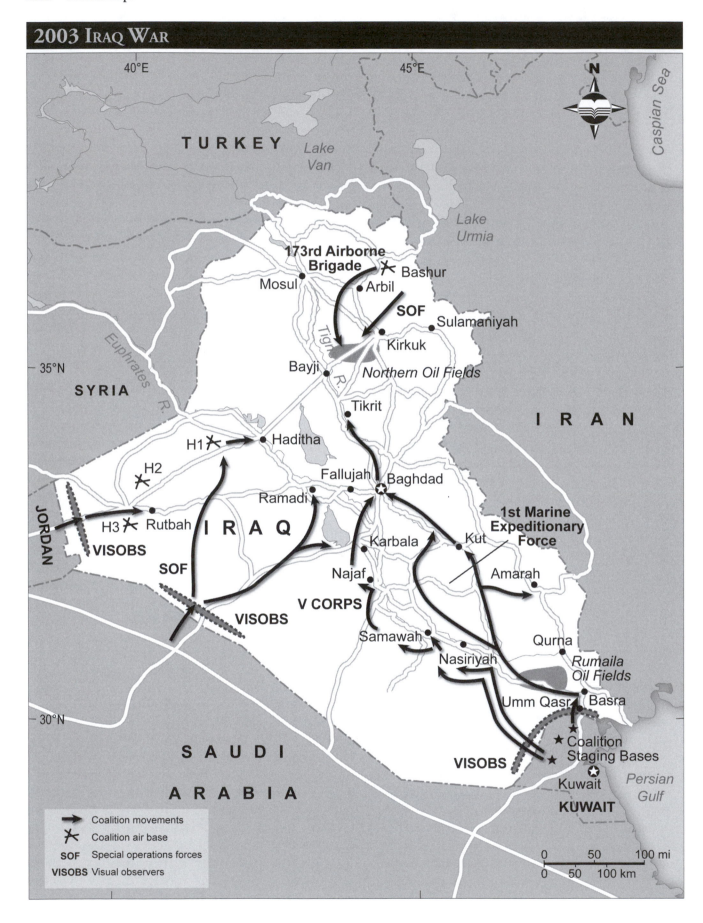

TURKEY

Lake Van

Lake Urmia

Caspian Sea

N

173rd Airborne Brigade

Mosul

Bashur

Arbil

SOF

Sulamaniyah

Kirkuk

Tigris R.

Bayji

Northern Oil Fields

SYRIA

Euphrates R.

35°N

Tikrit

IRAN

H1

Haditha

H2

Fallujah

Baghdad

Ramadi

1st Marine Expeditionary Force

JORDAN

H3   Rutbah

IRAQ

VISOBS

Karbala

Kut

Amarah

SOF

Najaf

V CORPS

VISOBS

Samawah

Qurna

Rumaila Oil Fields

Nasiriyah

SAUDI

Umm Qasr

Basra

30°N

VISOBS

Coalition Staging Bases

ARABIA

Kuwait

Persian Gulf

KUWAIT

→ Coalition movements

✈ Coalition air base

SOF   Special operations forces

VISOBS   Visual observers

| 0 | 50 | 100 mi |
| 0 | 50 | 100 km |

Introduction

Since the end of World War II the United States has had a troubled relationship with the Middle East. The superpower competition of the Cold War, the establishment of the State of Israel, the rise of militant Islam, the aggressiveness of authoritarian regimes, the dependency on Middle East oil, and a host of other factors have caused the United States to become involved in numerous regional confrontations, containments, sanctions, interventions, and wars over that period. The protection of our vital interests in the region has required a military presence and commitment that have steadily grown over that time. As former colonial powers, such as the United Kingdom, withdrew from the international policing of the region, the United States assumed that role, and that role has grown in size, complexity, and controversy.

The creation in 1980 of the U.S. Rapid Deployment Joint Task Force (RDJTF) by President Jimmy Carter acknowledged the vital national interests that we believed we had to protect and preserve from perceived Soviet threats during the Cold War. President Ronald Reagan elevated the RDJTF in 1983 to become the U.S. Central Command (CENTCOM), a full-fledged unified command. Many strategists thought that the collapse of the Soviet Union in 1991 would mark the end of the need for Central Command and that it would be eliminated or at least absorbed as a lesser command element under one of the other regional commands. The instability that came after the Cold War, however, did not see the diminishment of the threats to our interests or to the role of CENTCOM, which has actually expanded. That unified command has seen more conflict since its creation in the mid-1980s than any other of its sister regional commands during that same period.

The Middle East is the heart of an Islamic culture that stretches from North Africa to the Philippines and from Russia to Central Africa. That culture includes well over 1 billion Muslims. Global-ization has generated migrations that have expanded the locations where Muslims have settled to include North America and Europe. Holy places such as Mecca, Medina, Karbala, and Jerusalem remain the focal points of their religious belief system. This region is also the heart of the two other Abrahamic religions, Judaism and Christianity. This confluence of religious geographic and historic focal sites has resulted in long-standing tensions and conflict between East and West that have been heightened by the greater intermingling of Muslims, Jews, and Christians in the Middle East and throughout the world. This built-in source of historic cultural conflict has been exacerbated by more modern developments that have evolved over time.

Today, the importance of the Middle East is clear to most of us beyond religious implications, namely for political, security, and economic reasons. It begins with geography. The Middle East is the hinge plate of three continents. Since the establishment of the Silk Road and the East-West sea and land trade routes over the past millennium, this region has been vital to global trade and world economies. The discovery of energy resources there in the last century made the region even more strategically important. President Franklin Roosevelt foresaw this as he arranged the historic meeting in 1945 with Saudi king Abdul Aziz aboard the U.S. Navy heavy cruiser *Quincy* in the Great Bitter Lake in Egypt's Suez Canal. That meeting launched a cooperative energy and security relationship that lasts to this day, despite many strains along the way. The oil and natural gas reserves in this region remain unmatched anywhere else in the world. For these geographic and energy resource reasons, any threat that might destabilize or deny access to the Middle East has been deemed unacceptable to the United States and other world powers.

Instability and violence in the Middle East have never confined themselves to the region. On the contrary, they have drawn in international intervention and, at times, threatened global conflict between superpowers. The world's dependency on this region has made it critical to ensure free access and transit through the region's maze of sea and land choke points and to ensure and promote stability there.

Since the defeat and collapse of the Ottoman Empire at the end of World War I, the Middle East has lacked cohesion. Despite many attempts to create a regional security arrangement that would ensure stability, the nations of the region have failed to develop a credible collective security structure. Internal disputes, failed attempts at peace agreements, and disparate systems of governance have worked against regional security coherence. Security agreements and bilateral relationships with outside powers, such as the United States, have been tenuous and, at times, severely strained or quickly broken.

The lack of a consistent view on common threats and mutual interests and the political volatility of the region have made collective defense or viable alliances an illusive goal. The struggle to come to grips with modernity by religious conservatives and the rapid modernization and secularism of some elements of Middle Eastern cultures have compounded this problem as well. The West has also contributed to the regional problems by certain objectionable policies that have been met with resistance and hostility. The collective result of these factors over the last century has been the creation of an environment that has made the Middle East a breeding ground for conflict and violence, much of which I have personally witnessed and been involved in.

My first involvement in the Middle East came as a result of one of the many conflicts that have plagued this region, the Persian Gulf War in 1991. I was the deputy operations director at the U.S. European Command, and we supported CENTCOM's efforts during Operation DESERT STORM. Our supporting operation was called Operation PROVEN FORCE. Our command conducted air and special operations missions out of Turkey to attack targets in northern Iraq. We also provided Patriot missile batteries to protect Israel from the Scud attacks unleashed by Iraqi president Saddam Hussein in an operation dubbed PATRIOT DEFENDER. I was involved in the planning and coordination of these activities for our command and visited Turkey and Israel to check on the conduct of operations. It was my first exposure to the complicated politics in the region as we tried to restrain Israel from attacking Iraq, get cooperation from the Turkish government for our basing and operations needs, and adhere to the delicate command relations being established by CENTCOM with allied Muslim forces.

After the termination of hostilities, our command was again thrust into conflict in the region as Hussein attacked the Kurds in the north of Iraq after their failed revolt. I was assigned as the deputy commander and chief of staff for Operation PROVIDE COMFORT. Our mission was to rescue and return the traumatized Kurds who had fled into the mountains on the Turkish border during horrendous winter conditions and brutal Iraqi attacks. We eventually established and policed a security zone in northern Iraq that lasted until the 2003 invasion of Iraq.

Despite being assigned to the U.S. European Command, I found that the vast majority of our operational attention was focused on Middle East conflicts. Even more amazing was the fact that this came at a time when the Soviet Union was collapsing and when we did not want for important business in our own area of responsibility. It was a testimony to the chronic conflicts in the region and how they can consume and distract our attention and commitment even as other strategically critical events require our focus. For me, 1991 was only the beginning of an involvement in Middle East conflicts that would last right up to the present.

Over the years that followed, I served three tours of duty in Somalia and commanded the U.S. Marine Corps operational forces assigned to CENTCOM. I became familiar with the many war and contingency plans and participated in their development and in the exercises that followed. My command responded to several of the crises that always seemed to be part of the CENTCOM routine following the Persian Gulf War. In 1997 I became the deputy commander of CENTCOM, and the following year I was appointed as the commander in chief.

Before assuming my duties as deputy commander and commander, I read more than 50 books on the Middle East in preparation for my assignment. I had come to know the region somewhat, but I believed that there was so much more to know about the history and culture of this complex and fascinating region. I also reached out to regional experts for insights.

Like all great civilizations of the past, the ones from the Middle East had their periods of greatness and their periods of decline. What struck me was how rare periods of peace were in the region. Historical fault lines determined by religion, tribalism, or ethnicity have continued into the present, making the region prone to conflict. False borders inflicted on the region by outside imperial powers and internal struggles also continue to exacerbate their problems with identity and affiliation. It was clear to me that my tenure at CENTCOM would be interesting if the past was any indication of the future I faced.

I inherited a CENTCOM that was implementing the dual containment policy, established in the wake of the Persian Gulf War and focused on Iraq and Iran. It involved enforcing United Nations (UN) resolution sanctions on Iraq that consisted of ensuring no-fly and no-drive zones set up in the north and south of Iraq. It also required the enforcement of maritime sanctions against oil and gas smuggling. Enforcement of sanctions on Iran was also part of our mission. Iraq's lack of cooperation with the UN inspectors and the hostile action that Hussein directed against our planes resulted in several air operations striking Iraqi air defense assets and targets that could support a weapons of mass destruction (WMD) program. Iran continued hostile actions directed toward our ships until the 1997 election of President Mohammed Khatami, at which time the Iranians' hostile bridge-to-bridge communications and ship-bumping incidents ceased. They continued, however, to protect Iraqi boat-smuggling efforts that made it to their national waters.

Although Iraq and Iran were our primary concerns, other threats were growing in the region. A number of terrorist attacks occurred in the region immediately prior to, during, and immediately after my tenure. These included the Khobar Towers bombing in the eastern province of Saudi Arabia; the bombing of our embassies in Nairobi, Kenya, and Dar es Salaam, Tanzania; and the bombing of the U.S. Navy destroyer *Cole* in Aden, Yemen.

I left CENTCOM in 2000. It remained a military area of responsibility that was tense, prone to crisis, and violent. After my retirement, the September 11, 2001, terror attacks occurred, and our interventions in Afghanistan and Iraq followed. I was sent by the George W. Bush administration to engage in the Middle East peace process but once again saw it fail and degenerate into the violence of attacks and counterattacks. Recently, I went to Iraq at the request of our military commander and ambassador to conduct an independent assessment of conditions there as the United States prepared its plans for the future drawdown of forces and a handoff to the new Iraqi government.

For two decades, I have been directly or indirectly involved in the wars and violence of the Middle East as a military officer and as a diplomat. I have come to know the culture, leadership, and nature of the region. I do not agree with the inevitable "Clash of Civilizations" theory between the West and the Islamic world to which some people subscribe. However, we do seem to continuously fail to find common ground and mutual approaches to solving regional problems without resorting to the use of force, despite a strong desire on both sides to avoid conflict. I believe, however, that the strong desire for peace will eventually prevail, but it will take a degree of dedication, commitment, and political will that has been absent in the past. I am also convinced that a closer study of past conflicts is essential so as to not repeat mistakes and to better understand the causes of conflict. History, I have found, provides a great guide for the future. Too many political, diplomatic, and military leaders have attempted to do business in this region without an understanding of the past. They are thrust into this complicated environment and repeat the same mistakes of their predecessors or fail to see the depth of the complex issues that have long historic roots.

The study of the causes, conduct, and outcomes of Middle East conflicts is critically necessary for anyone who wants to understand how current attitudes and conditions have been shaped. Obviously, there have been conflicts in the region that have shaped events that have not directly involved the United States. The series of Arab-Israeli wars and conflicts that have plagued the Levant since 1948 have created an environment that has negatively impacted relations and attitudes throughout the Muslim world. These conflicts were addressed in ABC-CLIO's *Encyclopedia of the Arab-Israeli Conflict,* an excellent companion reference to this work. The *Encyclopedia of Middle East Wars: The United States in the Persian Gulf, Afghanistan, and Iraq Conflicts* serves as another excellent reference on the many conflicts in which the United States has engaged throughout this volatile region. This encyclopedia offers a superior single source for understanding the conflicts that we have been thrust into in this troubled region.

General Anthony C. Zinni USMC (Retired)

A

Abbas, Abu
Birth Date: December 10, 1948
Death Date: March 8, 2004

Leader of the Palestine Liberation Front (PLF). Abu Abbas, the nom de guerre of Muhammad Zaidan, was born in Safed, Palestine, on December 10, 1948. His family fled to Syria that same year along with 12,000–15,000 Arab residents after the Haganah attacks. In 1968 he joined the Popular Front for the Liberation of Palestine General Command (PFLP-GC) led by Ahmad Jibril. Abu Abbas disagreed with Jibril over the PFLP-GC's strong support for Syria and its failure to criticize Syrian support of the Lebanese Phalangist Party against the Palestine Liberation Organization (PLO) in Lebanon. In April 1977, Abu Abbas and Talat Yaqub left the PFLP-GC to form the PLF.

During the 1970s, Abu Abbas advocated armed struggle against Israel, chiefly in the form of attacks mounted from southern Lebanon. He was wounded in fighting during the 1982 Israeli invasion of Lebanon. The following year, when the PLF split into three factions, he led the largest pro-Iraqi group. In 1984 he became a member of the PLO Executive Committee.

On October 7, 1985, Abu Abbas masterminded the PLF's most dramatic terrorist action, the hijacking of the Italian cruise ship *Achille Lauro,* which at the time was steaming from Alexandria to Port Said, Egypt. The hijacking resulted in the death of U.S.-born Jew Leon Klinghoffer. Although the Egyptian aircraft carrying Abbas and the other three hijackers to asylum in Tunisia was diverted by U.S. aircraft to a North Atlantic Treaty Organization (NATO) air base in Sicily, the Italian government allowed the passengers to depart, and Abu Abbas escaped among them.

There was, however, much criticism of Abbas for the PLF's attempted terrorist attack on Nizamim Beach near Tel Aviv on May

Abu Abbas, leader of the Palestine Liberation Front, carried out a number of terrorist actions, including the hijacking of the Italian cruise ship *Achille Lauro*, resulting in the death of American-born Jew Leon Klinghoffer. Captured by U.S. forces in Baghdad in April 2003, he died in prison in March 2004. (AP/Wide World Photos)

30, 1990, which was designed to torpedo the possibility of PLO-Israeli peace talks. Nonetheless, the Israeli government alleged that the PLF had regularly received funding from PLO chairman Yasser Arafat. Indeed, in January 1996 the PLO agreed to provide an undisclosed sum to finance the Leon and Marilyn Klinghoffer Memorial Foundation of the U.S. Anti-Defamation League, in return for which Klinghoffer's daughters dropped a lawsuit brought against the PLO. In 1989, Abu Abbas had supported the PLO's acceptance of United Nations (UN) Security Council Resolution 242, therefore these militant actions betrayed that stance.

Following the 1993 Oslo Accords, Abu Abbas returned to Gaza. He then moved to Iraq. There was a standing U.S. warrant for his arrest, and in 2003, during the U.S.-led invasion of Iraq, he was taken into custody by U.S. forces. He died in Iraq, reportedly of natural causes, on March 8, 2004, while in U.S. custody.

SPENCER C. TUCKER

See also

Achille Lauro Hijacking; Arafat, Yasser; Palestine Liberation Organization; Terrorism

References

Alexander, Yonah. *Palestinian Secular Terrorism.* Ardsley, NY: Transnational Publishers, 2003.

Bohn, Michael K. *The Achille Lauro Hijacking: Lessons in the Politics and Prejudice of Terrorism.* Dulles, VA: Potomac Books, 2004.

Cassese, Antonio. *Terrorism, Politics and Law: The Achille Lauro Affair.* Princeton, NJ: Princeton University Press, 1989.

Nassar, Jamal R. *The Palestine Liberation Organization: From Armed Struggle to the Declaration of Independence.* New York: Praeger, 1991.

Abbas, Mahmoud
Birth Date: March 26, 1935

First prime minister of the Palestinian National Authority (PNA) and minister of the interior during March–October 2003, chairman of the Palestine Liberation Organization (PLO) since November 2004, and president of the PNA since January 2005. Mahmoud Abbas (known as Abu Mazen) was born on March 26, 1935, in Safed, Palestine. When Safed was attacked in the 1948 Israeli War of Independence, his family fled Palestine and settled in Syria. Abbas taught elementary school and then graduated from the University of Damascus and studied law in Egypt and Syria before earning a PhD in history in 1982 from the Oriental College at the People's Friendship University in Moscow.

Abbas was the director of personnel for Qatar's governmental civil service when he began his involvement in Palestinian politics in the mid-1950s. He was a founding member of Fatah. While in Qatar, Abbas began to recruit Palestinians into Fatah and also became part of the leadership of Yasser Arafat's Palestine Liberation Organization (PLO). In 1977, he led negotiations with Matityahu Peled, which resulted in the issuance of the "principles of peace" as based on a two-state solution and began dialogue with

certain Israeli left-wing and pacifist groups. Abbas had joined the Palestine National Council in 1968 and was responsible for fundraising.

Abbas assumed the leadership of the PLO's Department of Arab and International Relations from 1984 to 2000. In May 1988 he was elected chair of the division responsible for the occupied territories, succeeding Khalil al-Wazir. When PLO support for Iraq's 1990 invasion of Kuwait harmed relationships with Arab states that joined the United States–led coalition in the 1991 Persian Gulf War, it was Abbas who repaired the damage, apologizing to the Gulf states in 1993. Abbas coordinated the 1991 Madrid Conference and was a major architect of the 1993 Oslo Accords between the PLO and Israel. In 1996, Abbas was elected secretary-general of the PLO Executive Committee, headed the first session of the Israeli-Palestinian final status negotiations, led the Central Election Commission for the Palestine Legislative Council (PLC), and then was elected to the PLC in the Qalqilya district.

On March 19, 2003, Arafat appointed the more moderate and pragmatically perceived Abbas as the first prime minister of the PNA under strong pressure from Israel and the United States. However, Abbas faced divisions within the PNA and resigned from his position as prime minister on September 4, 2003, effective October 7, 2003, primarily because of a struggle over control of the PNA security forces. Ahmad Qurayya replaced him.

Following Arafat's death, Abbas became chairman of the PLO on November 11, 2004. He survived an assassination attempt at a memorial service for Arafat only three days later. His authority and attempts to reengage the Road Map to Peace (a plan to resolve the Israeli-Palestinian conflict proposed by the quartet of the United Nations, the European Union, Russia, and the United States) were challenged by most of the militant Palestinian groups, as well as by factions within the PLO and Fatah itself. On January 15, 2005, Abbas became the president of the Palestinian National Authority. A May 2005 pledge of $50 million and continued support of a free Palestinian state from the United States coupled with the Israeli withdrawal from Gaza on August 23, 2005, led Abbas to set PLC elections for January 20, 2006. However, when Hamas fared well in local elections in December 2005, Abbas sought to postpone the PLC election. He nevertheless proceeded with the January elections in which Hamas won a majority of seats in the PNA parliament. This reduced Abbas's Fatah party to a minority.

Although Abbas remained as the PNA president in agreement with Hamas, Hamas retained control of the parliament, governmental services, and the security forces in Gaza, whereas Abbas controlled parallel services in the West Bank. Israel insisted that Abbas and the PNA fulfill all agreements made prior to the 2006 elections, including the agreement to disarm Palestinian militants. The United States and certain European countries withdrew their financial support of the PNA in view of the participation of Hamas in the PNA. The financial crisis created through months of boycott of basic services and withholding of PNA salaries was expected to bring down Hamas, but that did not occur, and Abbas's leadership

Palestinian leader Mahmoud Abbas. The chairman of the Executive Committee of the Palestine Liberation Organization (PLO) since November 2004, he has been president of the Palestinian National Authority (PNA) since January 2005. (European Community)

came under challenge as he moved extralegally and in cooperation with the Israelis.

With tensions between Hamas and Fatah virtually paralyzing the PNA, Abbas called for a unity government between the two factions, which was effected in March 2007. By June, however, Abbas had dissolved the coalition government in the wake of violence between Hamas and Fatah in Gaza when Hamas preempted Fatah's plans to retake Gaza by force. This resulted in a brief period of fierce fighting between the two parties. Abbas declared a state of emergency, and on June 14 Hamas seized control of all of Gaza. Abbas's move, which denounced Hamas, resulted in the restoration of economic aid—but solely to Abbas's West Bank government—from the European Union and United States. Israel followed suit on July 1, 2007, although it restricted the transfer of funds.

Abbas refused to recognize the PNA government and appointed his own officials, including economist Salam Fayyad as prime minister. The Fayyad-Abbas government attacked Hamas sympathizers in the West Bank, and was accused of various corrupt practices there. Meanwhile it was locked in contentious peace negotiations with Israel, and Abbas several times threatened to resign if a peace deal were not arrived at "within six months." The Israeli incursion into the Gaza Strip beginning in late December 2008 and continuing into January 2009 was designed to punish the Gazan population for its support of Hamas and end militant rocket attacks on Israel.

The attack was followed by Israel elections and establishment of a right-wing Israeli government that has further widened the chasms between Fatah and Hamas, and between the PNA and Israel. In January 9, 2009, Abbas's presidential term ended, but he extended it for another year, arguing that he needed more time to better prepare the PNA for forthcoming elections. Hamas and other Palestinian groups have argued that Abbas's tenure extension was illegal under the constitution.

RICHARD EDWARDS AND SHERIFA ZUHUR

See also

Arafat, Yasser; Fatah; Hamas; Intifada, Second; Islamic Jihad, Palestinian; Palestine Liberation Organization

References

Abbas, Mahmud. *Through Secret Channels: The Road to Oslo: Senior PLO Leader Abu Mazen's Revealing Story of the Negotiations with Israel.* Reading, UK: Garnet, 1997.

Daoud, Abu. *Memoirs of a Palestinian Terrorist.* New York: Arcade Publishing, 2002.

Gelvin, James L. *The Israel-Palestine Conflict: One Hundred Years of War.* Cambridge: Cambridge University Press, 2005.

Makovsky, David. *Making Peace with the PLO: The Rabin Government's Road to the Oslo Accord.* Boulder, CO: Westview, 1996.

Pappe, Ilan. *A History of Modern Palestine: One Land, Two Peoples.* Cambridge: Cambridge University Press, 2003.

Rubin, Barry. *Revolution until Victory? The Politics and History of the PLO.* Cambridge: Harvard University Press, 1996.

Abdullah, King of Saudi Arabia
Birth Date: August 1, 1924

Saudi crown prince (1982–2005), acting ruler of Saudi Arabia (1995–2005), and king of Saudi Arabia (2005–present). Abdullah ibn Abd al-Aziz al-Saud was born in Riyadh, Saudi Arabia, on August 1, 1924. He was educated privately, chiefly at the Princes' School in the Royal Court. He became acquainted with governmental and administrative work at a young age and became mayor of Mecca in 1950.

In 1963 Abdullah assumed the post of deputy defense minister and commander of the National Guard. In 1975 he began serving as second deputy prime minister. He became the crown prince as well as first deputy prime minister in 1982 when Fahd ibn Abdul Aziz al-Saud, his half-brother, became king.

Abdullah's power increased dramatically after Fahd was incapacitated by a stroke in 1995, becoming the nation's de facto ruler. Abdullah began his formal rule when he ascended the throne on August 1, 2005. A devout Muslim, he is known in Saudi Arabia as a somewhat liberal monarch who leads a modest lifestyle. The challenges confronting him have not been easy ones, given both rising demands for reform and the activities of radical Islamic groups in the Middle East and within the borders of his own country.

Abdullah walked a diplomatic tightrope following the September 11, 2001, terrorist attacks on the United States. Although he strongly condemned the attacks, critics in the West pointed out that more of the 9/11 terrorists were Saudis than any other nationality and that Saudi Arabia was a major funding source for terrorist networks. He cooperated with international agencies in closing down numerous Islamic institutions and charitable associations, but he also had to take into account the sentiments of Saudi Arabia's very conservative population, which opposed Western criticisms of the kingdom's Islamic lifestyle and laws. Saudi Arabia had, nonetheless, provided financial support for Islamic educational institutions, including some of the madrasahs in Pakistan and Afghanistan that the West claimed to be breeding grounds for Islamic fundamentalism in many Islamic nations.

Abdullah was interested in making peace with Israel and devised a plan known as the Arab Peace Initiative in March 2002. It called for the creation of a Palestinian state in the West Bank and Gaza with its capital in East Jerusalem, in return for peace with all Arab states to be formalized in a peace treaty with Israel. Israel would then receive diplomatic recognition and exchange diplomats with all Arab states. Many in the Arab states and Israel opposed the plan, however. In January 2004, Abdullah produced an addendum to his plan that addressed the problem of Palestinian refugees. His plan still met with much skepticism.

Abdullah has not fundamentally changed the foreign policy of Saudi Arabia, and he continues to maintain cordial relations with the United States in spite of occasional strains. Having visited the United States many times before becoming ruler, Abdullah enjoyed a solid personal relationship with President George W. Bush and his immediate predecessors.

Since September 11, 2001, the Saudi government has been successful in eliminating terrorist cells operating inside Saudi Arabia that are themselves a threat to the survival of the Saudi regime. It has also eliminated from within the kingdom many sources of terrorist funding. The Saudi Arabian government has been the target of numerous attacks by Islamic militants. In May 2003, some 100 people were killed in one such attack on a compound at Riyadh.

During 2003 Iraq War operations, Abdullah did not permit U.S. forces to use Saudi air bases for coalition combat operations, but he did permit the use of Saudi Arabia's extensive command and control facilities. Tanker aircraft from these bases provided critical in-flight refueling for coalition fighter aircraft flying combat missions in Iraq. Despite ups and downs, the Saudi-U.S. relationship has remained largely unchanged under Abdullah. While Abdullah has remained rather diffident toward the Iraq War and resultant insurgency because the Saudi population overwhelmingly opposes U.S. actions in Iraq, he has been careful not to offer too much in the way of public criticism of the conflict.

Since 2004, when world oil prices began to soar, in some cases almost tripling, Abdullah has remained committed to the production and price quotas set by the Organization of Oil Exporting Countries (OPEC). In early 2008, while President George W. Bush paid a visit to Riyadh, he pointed out the difficulties that oil prices posed to the United States and the international economy. Abdullah acted to increase output and lower the price, although this action had little impact owing to a variety of other factors.

PATIT PABAN MISHRA

See also

Bush, George Walker; Saudi Arabia; September 11 Attacks; Terrorism

References

Al-Rasheed, Madawi. *A History of Saudia Arabia.* New York: Cambridge University Press, 2002.

Lippman, Thomas W. *Inside the Mirage: America's Fragile Partnership with Saudi Arabia.* New York: Westview, 2005.

Ménoret, Pascal. *The Saudi Enigma: A History.* London: Zed, 2005.

Teitelbaum, Joshua. *The Rise and Fall of the Hashemite Kingdom of Hejaz.* New York: New York University Press, 2001.

Abizaid, John Philip
Birth Date: April 1, 1951

U.S. army officer and commander in chief of the U.S. Central Command (CENTCOM) from July 7, 2003, to March 16, 2007. John Philip Abizaid was born on April 1, 1951, in Coleville, California, into a Christian Lebanese family that had emigrated to the United States in the 1880s. He graduated from the U.S. Military Academy, West Point, in 1973 and was commissioned as a second lieutenant. He served initially in a parachute regiment as platoon leader before moving to the Rangers as a company commander.

Commanders of U.S. Central Command (CENTCOM), 1983–Present

Name	Rank	Branch	Dates of Command
Robert C. Kingston	General	U.S. Army	January 1, 1983–November 27, 1985
George B. Crist	General	U.S. Marine Corps	November 27, 1985–November 23, 1988
H. Norman Schwarzkopf	General	U.S. Army	November 23, 1988–August 9, 1991
Joseph P. Hoar	General	U.S. Marine Corps	August 9, 1991–August 5, 1994
J. H. Binford Peay III	General	U.S. Army	August 5, 1994–August 13, 1997
Anthony C. Zinni	General	U.S. Marine Corps	August 13, 1997–July 6, 2000
Tommy R. Franks	General	U.S. Army	July 6, 2000–July 7, 2003
John P. Abizaid	General	U.S. Army	July 7, 2003–March 16, 2007
William J. Fallon	Admiral	U.S. Navy	March 16, 2007–March 28, 2008
Martin Dempsey (acting)	Lieutenant General	U.S. Army	March 28, 2008–October 31, 2008
David H. Petraeus	General	U.S. Army	October 31, 2008–present

Abizaid won a prestigious Olmsted Scholarship, which entitled him to study at a foreign university. After a year of training in Arabic, he enrolled in the University of Jordan–Amman in 1978. Political tension in Jordan resulted in the shutdown of the university, however, so Abizaid used the opportunity to train with the Jordanian army instead. In 1980 he earned a master of arts in Middle Eastern Studies from Harvard University.

Abizaid led a Ranger company during the U.S. invasion of Grenada in 1983. During the Persian Gulf crisis he commanded the 3rd Battalion, 325th Airborne Infantry Regiment. In 1991 the battalion was deployed in northern Iraq during Operation PROVIDE COMFORT, which immediately succeeded the end of Operation DESERT STORM. Abizaid subsequently studied peacekeeping at Stanford University's Hoover Institution and commanded the 504th Parachute Infantry Regiment of the 82nd Airborne Division before serving as assistant division commander of the 1st Armored Division in Bosnia-Herzegovina. Numerous staff appointments along the way included a tour as a United Nations observer in Lebanon and several European staff tours.

In 1997, Abizaid became commandant of cadets at West Point as a newly-promoted brigadier general. There he played a major role in reforming some of the more egregious requirements of the plebe system. Promoted to major general in 1999, Abizaid assumed command of the 1st Infantry Division, which

U.S. Army general John P. Abizaid, commander of the United States Central Command (CENTCOM), the unified combat command with responsibility for the Middle East. Abizaid held this post during 2003–2007. (U.S. Department of Defense)

contributed troops to Operation JOINT GUARDIAN, the NATO campaign in Kosovo.

Abizaid's appointment as director of the Joint Staff brought with it advancement to lieutenant general. In January 2003, he became deputy commander of the U.S. Central Command, which has responsibility for covering 27 countries of the Middle East and Central Asia. During Operation IRAQI FREEDOM, which began in March 2003, Abizaid served as deputy commander (Forward), Combined Force Command. Abizaid succeeded General Tommy Franks as CENTCOM commander when the latter retired in July 2003. At the same time, Abizaid was promoted to full (four-star) general. When he took command of CENTCOM, insurgent violence in Iraq was escalating rapidly. Abizaid had already expressed reservations about poor planning for the postwar era in Iraq and the competence of Pentagon officials in charge of the arrangements. He believed that most Iraqis would not welcome a U.S. occupation of their country and that widespread terrorism and guerrilla activity would likely follow a U.S. invasion.

Abizaid used the opportunity of his first press conference to state that the United States was now fighting a classic guerrilla insurgency in Iraq, an opinion directly opposite the views held by Secretary of Defense Donald Rumsfeld, who bristled at Abizaid's comments. The contradiction quickly made headlines and resulted in Abizaid receiving a private reprimand from Rumsfeld.

Abizaid also disagreed with the decision by Paul Bremer, head of the Coalition Provisional Authority, to disband the Iraqi Army, and he advocated rehiring select Sunni officers. Abizaid was also critical of Bremer's de-Baathification policy. In addition, Abizaid realized that the U.S. intelligence apparatus in Iraq was in total disarray. On October 1, 2003, he issued orders reorganizing intelligence operations so that in the future all reports would be passed through a single intelligence fusion center.

During the summer of 2004, Abizaid informed his superiors that a military victory in Iraq was unlikely. Instead of pursuing an elusive victory, Abizaid favored a policy of shifting the burden of the war to Iraqi security forces and minimizing the U.S. presence. Abizaid also supported research into the situation in Iraq and on the Global War on Terror. However, publicly and in interviews with the press Abizaid presented an optimistic version of events, despite having privately expressed doubts. In keeping with his public optimism, Abizaid appeared before the Senate Armed Services Committee on March 16, 2006, and gave another positive review of progress in Iraq. During a break in the proceedings, Abizaid approached Congressman John Murtha (D-Pa.), a former marine who had been highly critical of the Iraq War, and indicated to Murtha that Murtha's views were close to his own.

Abizaid's retirement as head of CENTCOM was announced in December 2006. On March 16, 2007, he was replaced by Admiral William Fallon. On May 1, 2007, Abizaid retired from his 34-year army career to take up a post as research fellow at the Hoover Institution.

PAUL W. DOERR

See also

Baath Party; Bremer, Jerry; Fallon, William Joseph; Franks, Tommy Ray; IRAQI FREEDOM, Operation; Iraqi Insurgency; PROVIDE COMFORT, Operation; Rumsfeld, Donald Henry; United States Central Command; United States Congress and the Iraq War

References

Gordon, Michael R., and General Bernard E. Trainor. *Cobra II: The Inside Story of the Invasion and Occupation of Iraq.* New York: Pantheon Books, 2006.

Ricks, Thomas E. *Fiasco: The American Military Adventure in Iraq.* New York: Penguin, 2006.

Woodward, Bob. *State of Denial: Bush at War, Part III.* New York: Simon and Schuster, 2006.

Able Danger

A highly classified military intelligence program whose leaders have claimed to have identified Muhammad Atta and three other members of the plot to hijack U.S. airliners and use them as weapons well before the September 11, 2001, terror attacks. General Hugh Shelton, the chairman of the Joint Chiefs of Staff, issued a directive in early October 1999 to establish an intelligence program under the command of the U.S. Special Operations Command (SOCOM) of the Department of Defense to be directed specifically against the Al Qaeda terrorist organization and its operatives. The commander of Able Danger was Navy captain Scott Philpott, who headed a unit of 20 military intelligence specialists and a support staff. The chief analyst of Able Danger was Dr. Eileen Priesser.

The purpose of Able Danger was to identify Al Qaeda members and neutralize them before they could initiate operations against the United States. The data-mining center was located at the Land Information Warfare Activity (LIWA)/Information Dominance Center at Fort Belvoir, Virginia. In the summer of 2000, the LIWA was transferred to Garland, Texas.

Members of this unit began intelligence operations seeking to identify Al Qaeda operatives both in the United States and abroad. Its computer analysts set up a complex computer analysis system that searched public databases and the Internet for possible terrorist cells. One of the terrorist cells so identified contained the name of Muhammad Atta and three others who were later implicated in the September 11 plot. Atta's name was supposedly placed, along with those of the others, on a chart of Al Qaeda operatives. Lieutenant Colonel Anthony Shaffer, a reserve officer attached to the Pentagon, and Able Danger's liaison with the Defense Intelligence Agency (DIA), as well as others, decided to inform the FBI about the threat posed by the Al Qaeda operatives. Three potential meetings with the FBI were postponed because of opposition from military lawyers in the Pentagon. The apparent reason for the opposition from SOCOM was fear of controversy that might arise if it were made public that a military intelligence unit had violated the privacy of civilians legally residing in the United States. Another possible reason was that the lawyers believed that the program might be violating the Posse Comitatus Act, which prohibits employing the military to enforce civil laws.

The leaders of Able Danger then decided to work their way up the military chain of command. In January 2001, the leadership of Able Danger briefed General Hugh Shelton, still the chairman of the Joint Chiefs of Staff, on its findings. Shortly afterward, the Able Danger unit was disbanded, its operations ceasing in April 2001. Defense Department lawyers had determined that the activities of Able Danger violated President Ronald Reagan's Executive Order 12333, intended to prevent the Pentagon from storing data about U.S. citizens. A direct order came from the Defense Department to destroy the database; as a result, 2.4 terabytes of information about possible Al Qaeda terrorist activities were destroyed in the summer of 2001. A chart identifying four hijackers, including Muhammad Atta, was produced by Able Danger and presented to the Deputy National Security Advisor, Jim Steinberg, but nothing came of it.

Able Danger was a classified program until its story surfaced shortly after the National Commission on Terrorist Attacks Upon the United States, or the 9/11 Commission, issued its report, which stated categorically that the U.S. government had no prior knowledge about the conspiracy that led to the September 11 attacks. Keith Phucas, a reporter for the *Norristown Times Herald* in Pennsylvania, broke the story of Able Danger on June 19, 2005, in an article titled "Missed Chance on Way to 9/11."

When the story about Able Danger became public, it erupted into a political controversy. On June 27, 2005, Representative Curt Weldon (R-Pa.), the vice chairman of the House Armed Services and House Homeland Security committees, brought the Able Danger issue into the national limelight. In a speech before the House of Representatives, Weldon accused the U.S. government of negligence in its failure to heed the information gathered by Able Danger.

Despite some lapses of information (and a tendency to blame the William J. Clinton administration for the lapses), Weldon summarized many of the features of Able Danger without disclosing its nature as a secret military intelligence initiative run from within the Department of Defense. Weldon also disclosed that the information about Able Danger had been reported to the staff of the 9/11 Commission.

Members of the 9/11 Commission responded to these charges with a series of denials. Lee H. Hamilton, former vice chair of the 9/11 Commission, admitted learning about the Able Danger program, but denied hearing anything credible about a possible identification of Atta or other skyjackers in the 9/11 plot. This argument contradicted the testimony of Shaffer that he had communicated Able Danger's findings about Atta in a meeting with the commission's executive director, Philip Zelikov, at Bagram Air Base, Afghanistan, in late 2003. Leaders of the commission then requested and obtained information about Able Danger from the Defense Department, but there had been nothing about Atta in the information provided. They also admitted that Captain Philpott had mentioned something about Atta only days before the final report came out.

This denial of prior knowledge by members of the 9/11 Commission drew the attention of Lieutenant Colonel Shaffer. In an interview on August 15, 2005, Shaffer told the story of Able Danger, and he indicated that he had been at the "point of near insubordination" over the refusal to pursue the information about Atta. Furthermore, Shaffer insisted that he had talked to the staff of the 9/11 investigation in October 2003, in Afghanistan, where his next tour of duty had taken him. Captain Philpott and civilian contractor J. D. Smith confirmed Shaffer's claim about Able Danger's awareness of Atta.

The controversy has continued because the participants have felt left out of the investigation of the events surrounding September 11. Many of them have placed their careers in jeopardy by countering the government's version. Shaffer had his security clearance revoked by the Defense Intelligence Agency (DIA) and his personal records of Able Danger destroyed. In September 2006, the Defense Department's inspector general issued a report denying that Able Danger had identified Atta by calling the testimony of witnesses inconsistent. Weldon criticized the report and investigation as incomplete. Although Weldon was an effective spokesperson in Congress who kept the story alive, his defeat in the 2006 elections deprived him of that important forum. Nevertheless, the last word has not been said about Able Danger and about whether information about Atta and others had been stored in a government database.

STEPHEN E. ATKINS

See also

Atta, Muhammad; September 11 Attacks; September 11 Commission and Report

References

Lance, Peter. *Triple Cross: How Bin Laden's Master Spy Penetrated the CIA, the Green Berets, and the FBI—and Why Patrick Fitzgerald Failed to Stop Him.* New York: ReganBooks, 2006.

McCarthy, Andrew C. "It's Time to Investigate Able Danger and the 9/11 Commission." *National Review* (December 8, 2005): 1.

Rosen, James. "Able Danger Operatives Sue Pentagon." *News Tribune* (Tacoma, WA), March 4, 2006, 6.

———. "A 9/11 Tip-Off: Fact or Fancy?: Debate Still Swirls around Claim That Secret Military Program ID'd Hijackers a Year before Attacks." *Sacramento Bee,* November 24, 2005, A1.

Shenon, Philip. "Officer Says Military Blocked Sharing of Files on Terrorists." *New York Times,* August 17, 2005, 12.

———. "Report Rejects Claim That 9/11 Terrorists Were Identified before Attacks." *New York Times,* September 22, 2006, A15.

Abrams, Creighton Williams, Jr.

Birth Date: September 15, 1914
Death Date: September 4, 1974

U.S. Army general, celebrated combat leader, and army chief of staff (1972–1974). Born in Springfield, Massachusetts, on September 15, 1914, Creighton Abrams graduated from the U.S. Military

U.S. Army general Creighton W. Abrams Jr. (1914–1974) commanded U.S. forces in the Vietnam War during 1968–1972. As chief of staff of the army during 1972–1974, Abrams worked to rebuild the army and lay the foundation for its later success. (Herbert Elmer Abrams/Center for Military History)

Academy, West Point, in 1936 and was posted to the 7th Cavalry Regiment at Fort Bliss, Texas. When World War II loomed, he volunteered for the newly formed armored force.

Abrams first rose to professional prominence as a lieutenant colonel and commander of the 37th Tank Battalion, 4th Armored Division that often spearheaded General George Patton's Third Army in the drive across Europe. He led the forces that punched through German lines to relieve the encircled 101st Airborne Division at Bastogne during the Battle of the Bulge, earned two Distinguished Service Crosses and many other decorations, and received a battlefield promotion to full colonel.

After World War II, Abrams served as director of tactics at the Armor School, Fort Knox (1946–1948); was a corps chief of staff late in the Korean War (1953–1954); and from 1960 to 1962 commanded the 3rd Armored Division in Germany, a key post during the Cold War. A year later he took command of its parent V Corps. In mid-1964 Abrams was recalled from Europe, promoted to four-star general, and made the army's vice chief of staff. In that assignment (1964–1967) he was deeply involved in the army's troop buildup for the war in Vietnam.

In May 1967 Abrams was himself assigned to Vietnam as deputy commander. In that position he concentrated primarily on improvement of South Vietnamese armed forces. When, during the 1968 Tet Offensive, those forces gave a far better account of themselves than expected, Abrams received much of the credit. Abrams formally assumed command of U.S. forces in Vietnam in July 1968. A consummate tactician who proved to have a feel for this kind of a conflict, he moved quickly to change the conduct of the war in fundamental ways. His predecessor's attrition strategy, search and destroy tactics, and emphasis on body count as the measure of battlefield success were all discarded.

Abrams instead stressed population security, the new measure of merit, as the key to success. He prescribed a "one war" approach in which combat operations, pacification, and upgrading South Vietnamese forces were of equal importance and priority. He cut back on multibattalion sweeps, replacing them with thousands of small unit patrols and ambushes that blocked communist forces' access to the people and interdicted their movement of forces and supplies. Clear-and-hold operations became the standard tactical approach, with expanded and better-armed Vietnamese territorial forces providing the "hold." Population security progressed accordingly. Meanwhile U.S. forces were incrementally withdrawn, their missions taken over by the improving South Vietnamese.

Abrams left Vietnam in June 1972 to become U.S. Army chief of staff. There he set about dealing with the myriad problems of an army that had been through a devastating ordeal. He concentrated on readiness and on the well-being of the soldier, always the touchstones of his professional concern. Stricken with cancer, Abrams died in office in Washington on September 4, 1974. But he had set a course of reform and rebuilding the U.S. Army such that General John W. Vessey, former chairman of the Joint Chiefs of Staff, could later recall: "When Americans watched the stunning success of our armed forces in Desert Storm, they were watching the Abrams vision in action. The modern equipment, the effective air support, the use of the reserve components and, most important of all, the advanced training which taught our people how to stay alive on the battlefield were all seeds planted by Abe."

LEWIS SORLEY

See also
AirLand Battle Doctrine

References
Colby, William, with James McCargar. *Lost Victory: A Firsthand Account of America's Sixteen-Year Involvement in Vietnam.* Chicago: Contemporary Books, 1989.
Palmer, General Bruce, Jr. *The 25-Year War: America's Military Role in Vietnam.* Lexington: University Press of Kentucky, 1984.
Sorley, Lewis. *A Better War: The Unexamined Victories and Final Tragedy of America's Last Years in Vietnam.* New York: Harcourt Brace, 1999.
———. *Thunderbolt: General Creighton Abrams and the Army of His Times.* New York: Simon and Schuster, 1992.
———. *Vietnam Chronicles: The Abrams Tapes, 1968–1972.* Lubbock: Texas Tech University, 2004.

Abrams, Elliott
Birth Date: January 24, 1948

U.S. attorney, foreign policy/national security official, and leader in the neoconservative movement. Elliott Abrams was born in New York City on January 24, 1948, the son of an immigration lawyer. He earned an undergraduate degree from Harvard University in 1969, an MA in international relations from the London School of Economics in 1970, and a law degree from Harvard Law School in 1973. He practiced law briefly with his father and then with a Wall Street firm but became involved in politics when he worked on Senator Henry "Scoop" Jackson's unsuccessful presidential campaign in 1976. The following year, he joined Democratic senator Daniel Patrick Moynihan's staff. He began serving as Moynihan's chief counsel, but was later elevated to chief of staff.

Despite the fact that he worked for a Democrat, the incoming Ronald Reagan administration tapped Abrams to become an assistant secretary of state, first for human rights and humanitarian affairs, and then for inter-American affairs. By now, Abrams had already begun to move to the right politically, a development that coincided with his marriage to Rachel Decter, who was the stepdaughter of Norman Podhoretz, considered the father of the modern neoconservative movement. Abrams joined the Reagan administration in 1981 and did not leave public office until 1989, at which time the Reagan administration ended.

Abrams quickly became a lighting rod for detractors of the Reagan administration's foreign policies, especially its aid to the Nicaraguan Contras and its support of oppressive regimes in Guatemala, El Salvador, and Honduras. Abrams steadfastly supported the president's position in these areas, a fact that outraged such groups as Amnesty International and Human Rights Watch. In 1985–1986, Abrams became involved in the infamous Iran-Contra Affair, which sought to skirt congressional prohibitions on funding to the Contras by clandestinely selling arms to the Iranians, the proceeds of which were funneled illegally to the Contras. The unmasking of Iran-Contra proved a great embarrassment to the White House. In 1987, Abrams, now assistant secretary of state for inter-American affairs, led the charge in declaring Panamanian dictator Manuel Noriega's regime corrupt and undemocratic, essentially making it official U.S. policy to work for his ouster.

During the official criminal investigation into Iran-Contra in 1988–1990, Abrams came under intense scrutiny for his role in the debacle and was nearly indicted on multiple felony charges. After negotiating a deal with the prosecutors, he agreed to plead guilty to two misdemeanor counts of lying to Congress. He received a $50 fine, was placed on probation for two years, and was ordered to complete 100 hours of community service. In January 1992, only days before leaving office, President George H. W. Bush pardoned Abrams, along with several other Iran-Contra figures. From 1996 to 2001, Abrams was president of the Ethics and Public Policy Center.

In January 1998, Abrams joined other fellow neoconservatives by signing the Project for a New American Century's open letter to President William Jefferson Clinton. Among other things, the letter argued forcefully for the overthrow of Iraqi dictator Saddam Hussein.

When the George W. Bush administration took office in January 2001, it wasted little time in tapping Abrams to join its retinue of neoconservatives. In June 2001, Abrams became special assistant to the president and senior director for democracy, human rights, and international organizations (National Security Council, NSC). Given his role in Iran-Contra and controversial dealings in Latin America in the 1980s, some human rights groups took umbrage at his appointment. Nevertheless, Abrams had a hand in crafting the Bush Doctrine, the neoconservatives' homage to preemptory war, and he was among those pushing consistently for regime change in Iraq.

In December 2002, Abrams became senior director for Near East and North African Affairs of the NSC; in February 2005, he became deputy national security adviser for global democracy strategy. As such, he traveled frequently with Secretary of State Condoleezza Rice and took part in the talks surrounding the July–August 2006 Israeli-Lebanon War.

In this post, Abrams once more became embroiled in controversy. Although such allegations cannot be definitively proven, Abram's detractors asserted that he has been a consistent roadblock in fostering dialogue between Israel and the Palestinian National Authority (PNA). When Hamas won a majority of parliamentary seats in the January 2006 Palestinian elections, Abrams was at the forefront of a campaign to discredit Hamas, strengthen Hamas's chief political opponent Fatah, and ultimately unseat the Hamas majority. It has been posited that the Bush administration began providing arms and other support to Fatah within days of the elections.

In addition to his many years in public service, Abrams has authored 10 books.

PAUL G. PIERPAOLI JR.

See also
Bush, George Walker; Bush Doctrine; Fatah; Hamas; Iran-Contra Affair; Neoconservatism; Rice, Condoleezza

References
Abrams, Elliott. *Close Calls: Intervention, Terrorism, Missile Defense, and "Just War" Today.* Washington, DC: Ethics and Public Policy Center, 1998.

Ricks, Thomas E. *Fiasco: The American Military Adventure in Iraq.* New York: Penguin, 2006.

Abu Daoud
Birth Date: May 16, 1937

Palestinian militant and mastermind of the Black September Organization (BSO) terrorist attack on Israeli athletes at the 1972 Munich Summer Olympics. Muhammad Daoud, more commonly known as Abu Daoud, was born in the Jerusalem community of Silwan on May 16, 1937. Little is known of his early life, but from the time he was a youth he demonstrated a penchant for militancy.

Black September refers to a violent struggle in September 1970 when Jordan's King Hussein expelled the Palestinians and the Palestine Liberation Organization (PLO) from the country. In the process, many Palestinians were killed or imprisoned before the conflict ended in July 1971. The PLO was then forced out of Jordan to Lebanon. Daoud was first an operative and then a leader of the BSO, named in commemoration of this event. The organization's original goal was to avenge the events of Black September and to gain the release of Palestinians imprisoned in Jordan.

The alleged purpose of the Munich attack was to protest the exclusion of the Palestinians from the 1972 Summer Olympic Games. Daoud planned the attack and led it during its initial phases. In response to the attacks, Israeli prime minister Golda Meir authorized, in Operation WRATH OF GOD, the assassination of those known to be responsible for the Munich massacre, and the 1973 Operation SPRING OF YOUTH, led by Ehud Barak, carried out an attack on Popular Front for the Liberation of Palestine (PFLP) headquarters in Beirut. Daoud's role in the event was well known to the Mossad Israeli intelligence agency, and he contends that it was Mossad that inflicted 13 wounds to his left wrist, chest, stomach, and jaw when he was shot at close range in a Warsaw, Poland, hotel on July 27, 1981.

Immediately following the 1972 Munich attack, Daoud went to Eastern Europe. He was arrested late that same year while leading a team into Jordan with the goal of taking hostage the Jordanian prime minister and other members of the cabinet. They were to be exchanged for Palestinians imprisoned for actions committed during Black September. Daoud was convicted and sentenced to death in March 1973. King Hussein commuted the sentence to life in prison and later released Daoud along with 1,000 other prisoners in a September 1973 general amnesty. Daoud then moved to Lebanon and remained there until the onset of the civil war in 1975, at which time he returned to Amman.

In January 1977 Daoud was arrested in Paris. Although the Jerusalem Magistrates Court issued a warrant on January 10 seeking his extradition on charges stemming from the Munich attack, a French court released him when the government of West Germany failed to expeditiously request his extradition. Daoud then returned to Jordan again. He was allowed to move from Jordan to the West Bank city of Ramallah in 1993 following the Oslo Accords. He became a member of the Palestinian National Council (PNC) in 1996, and in 1999 he publicly and unrepentantly admitted his role in the Munich attack in his book *Palestine: From Jerusalem to Munich*. In the book and interviews, Daoud claimed that his direct participation was limited to preoperation planning and to helping the eight-member commando team gain entry to the Olympic Village. The commandos were not to kill the Israeli athletes but instead were to hold them hostage in exchange for Palestinians in Israeli prisons. Daoud blamed the ensuing massacre on

the Germans. In addition to admitting his role in the Munich massacre and in the ensuing Lufthansa hijacking, Daoud also asserted that PLO chairman Yasser Arafat had granted prior approval for the Munich attack, which Arafat and others denied.

Daoud's admission led to the issuance of a German arrest warrant that resulted in the revocation of his Israeli VIP travel card. He was denied reentry into the Palestinian National Authority (PNA) territories on June 13, 1999. He protested the revocation of his VIP card and asserted that the warrant was null and void because so many years had passed since the Munich attacks. Nevertheless, he moved to Syria, the only country that would allow him residence.

RICHARD M. EDWARDS

See also

Arafat, Yasser; Meir, Golda Mabovitch; Palestine Liberation Organization; Terrorism

References

Abu Daoud. *Memoirs of a Palestinian Terrorist.* New York: Arcade, 2002.
Abu Douad [Muhammad Daoud Audeh], with Giles du Jonchay. *Palestine: De Jerusalem a Munich.* Paris: Éditions Anne Carrière, 1999.
Jonas, George. *Vengeance: The True Story of an Israeli Counter-Terrorist Team.* New York: Simon and Schuster, 2005.
Klein, Aaron. *Striking Back: The 1972 Munich Olympics Massacre and Israel's Deadly Response.* New York: Random House, 2005.
Roman, Michael. *Black September.* Orlando: Northwest Publishing, 1995.
Sayigh, Yezid. *Armed Struggle and the Search for State: The Palestinian National Movement, 1949–1993.* Oxford, UK: Clarendon, 1997.

Abu Ghraib

Prison facility located about 20 miles west of the Iraqi capital, Baghdad. Known during the regime of Saddam Hussein as an infamous place of torture and execution, Abu Ghraib prison later drew international attention when photographs of inmate abuse and reports of torture at the hands of coalition troops were made public in 2004.

Abu Ghraib, officially called the Baghdad Central Confinement Facility (BCCF) under the Hussein regime, was built by British contractors hired by the Iraqi government in the 1960s. Covering an area of about one square mile, the prison housed five different types of prisoners during the Hussein regime: those with long sentences, those with short sentences, those imprisoned for capital crimes, those imprisoned for so-called special offenses, and foreign detainees. Cells, which are about 51 square feet in area, held as many as 40 people each.

During the 1980–1988 Iran-Iraq War, the Iraqi Baathist regime used the facility to imprison political dissidents and members of ethnic or religious groups seen as threats to the central government. In particular, hundreds of Arab and Kurdish Shiites and Iraqis of Iranian heritage were arrested and housed in the BCCF; torture and executions became routine. Among the tactics used by prison guards was the feeding of shredded plastic to inmates, and it has been speculated that prisoners were used as guinea pigs for

Cell block in Abu Ghraib prison, Iraq. (U.S. Department of Defense)

Hussein's biological and chemical weapons. Although the Iraqi government kept its actions within the complex secret from Iraqi citizens and the international community alike, Amnesty International reported several specific incidents, including the 1996 execution of hundreds of political dissidents and the 1998 execution of many people who had been involved in the 1991 Shiite revolt. The prison, which contained thousands of inmates who were completely cut off from outside communication and held without conviction, was also used to house coalition prisoners of war during the Persian Gulf War.

With the 2003 U.S.-led Iraq War and subsequent fall of the Hussein government in Iraq, coalition troops took control of Abu Ghraib prison. The U.S. military used the complex for holding Iraqi insurgents and terrorists accused of anti-U.S. attacks, although by 2004 it had released several hundred prisoners and shared use of the facility with the Iraqi government. Because of the disarray in the Iraqi criminal system, many common criminals uninvolved in the war were held at the facility as well. Abu Ghraib became a household name in April 2004, when the television program *60 Minutes II* aired photographs of prisoner abuse at the hands of coalition troops. Just two days later, the photographs were posted online with Seymour Hersch's article in *New Yorker* magazine. The photos, which showed prisoners wearing black hoods, attached to wires with which they were threatened with

electrocution, and placed in humiliating sexual positions, sparked worldwide outrage and calls for the investigation and conviction of the military personnel involved.

The abuse was immediately decried by U.S. President George W. Bush and by Defense Secretary Donald Rumsfeld, who, on May 7, 2004 took responsibility for the acts occurring during his tenure. The Pentagon, which had been investigating reports of abuse since 2003, launched a further investigation into the acts documented by the photographs. Previously, detainee abuse had been investigated by U.S. Army major general Antonio Taguba, who had been given digital images of the abuse by Sergeant Joseph Darby in January 2004. Major general Taguba concluded in his 53-page report that U.S. military personnel had violated international law. More than a dozen U.S. soldiers and officers were removed from the prison as a result of the internal investigation.

More details emerged following the *60 Minutes II* broadcast. Photographs that the U.S. government would not allow to be released earlier were circulated in 2006. Most importantly, it appeared that the senior U.S. military officer, Lieutenant General Ricardo Sanchez, had authorized treatment "close to" torture, such as the use of military dogs, temperature extremes, and sensory and sleep deprivation, thus making it more difficult to locate responsibility for the general environment leading to abuse. However, in addition to charging certain troops and contractors with torture, the United States made an effort to reduce the number of detainees—estimated at 7,000 prior to the scandal's outbreak—by several thousand. However, many argued that the measures taken were not harsh enough to fit the crime, and some demanded Rumsfeld's resignation. Meanwhile, in August 2004, a military panel confirmed 44 cases of prisoner abuse at the facility and identified 23 soldiers as being responsible. Since the so-called ringleader of the operation, Army Specialist Charles Graner, was convicted and sentenced to 10 years in prison in January 2005, Abu Ghraib has twice been attacked by insurgents, who have attempted to undermine U.S. security at the facility and set prisoners free.

The United States currently holds detainees in the portion of the prison known as "Camp Redemption," built in 2004. In September 2006, the United States handed over control of Abu Ghraib to the Iraqi government. The Iraqi government holds convicted criminals in the older area known as the "Hard Site," although efforts are being made to release those who might be innocent.

JESSICA BRITT

See also

Bush, George Walker; Hussein, Saddam; Iran-Iraq War; Iraq, History of, Pre-1990; Iraq, History of, 1990–Present; Karpinski, Janis; Kurds; Miller, Geoffrey D.; Rumsfeld, Donald Henry; Taguba, Antonio Mario

References

Danner, Mark. *Torture and Truth: America, Abu Ghraib, and the War on Terror*. New York: New York Review Books, 2004.

Graveline, Christopher, and Michael Clemens. *The Secrets of Abu Ghraib Revealed*. Dulles, VA: Potomac Books, 2010.

Greenberg, Karen J., and Joshua L. Dratel, eds. *The Torture Papers: The Road to Abu Ghraib*. Cambridge: Cambridge University Press, 2005.

Strasser, Steven, ed. *The Abu Ghraib Investigations: The Official Independent Panel and Pentagon Reports on the Shocking Prisoner Abuse in Iraq*. New York: PublicAffairs, 2004.

Abu Nidal

Birth Date: May 1937
Death Date: August 16, 2002

Radical Palestinian and founder of the Fatah Revolutionary Council (FRC), also known as the Abu Nidal Organization (ANO), a notorious international terrorist group. "Abu Nidal," which translates as "the father of struggle," was the nom de guerre of Sabri Khalil al-Banna, who was born in May 1937 in Jaffa, Palestine (now Tel Aviv-Yafo), which was under the British Mandate at the time. In 1948, the Arab nations in the region rejected the United Nations (UN) Partition Plan, which ultimately led to war between Israelis and Arabs. Jaffa soon became a battle zone. During the conflict, the new Israeli government confiscated Abu Nidal's father's expansive orange groves, and Abu Nidal and his family fled to refugee camps in Gaza. He later moved on to Nablus, which was under Jordanian governance.

While in Jordan, Abu Nidal joined the Arab nationalist Baath Party. He soon landed in a Jordanian prison for his political views. When Baathists were suppressed by Jordanian King Hussein in 1957, Abu Nidal fled to Saudi Arabia. There, in 1967, he founded the Palestine Secret Organization (PSO). After the Israelis won the 1967 Six-Day War, he was jailed again, this time by the Saudis, for his radical views.

In Saudi Arabia, Abu Nidal joined Fatah, Yasser Arafat's faction within the Palestine Liberation Organization (PLO), whose stated objective was to free Palestine from Israeli control. Abu Nidal, apparently dissatisfied with certain members of Fatah who sought diplomatic solutions, including a two-state solution to the Jewish problem, left Fatah in 1973. He became enamored with the rejectionist position held by the Iraqi government, which opposed any solution to the Palestinian problem that allowed for the existence of a Jewish state. Abu Nidal soon accused the PLO of treason, formed the FRC, and became Arafat's bitter rival. Meanwhile, Fatah sentenced Abu Nidal to death in absentia.

The FRC, operating out of Iraq, burst onto the international scene on September 5, 1973, when FRC gunmen took control of the Saudi embassy in Paris. This was followed by a number of spectacular acts of violence that were remarkable primarily because they seemed to show no concern for their effect on innocent civilians. The FRC has also assassinated a number of key PLO diplomats.

In 1981, Abu Nidal switched bases from Iraq to Syria because Damascus was interested in utilizing his brand of terrorism. Just one year later, the FRC critically wounded Schlomo Argov, Israel's ambassador to the United Kingdom. The Israelis wasted no time in retaliating and, only three days later, used the failed assassination attempt as a justification to invade Lebanon and attempt to destroy the PLO there.

By the mid-1980s, Abu Nidal was considered the world's most lethal terrorist and was a top target of the U.S. Central Intelligence Agency (CIA) and other counterterrorist organizations. At the same time, he became increasingly paranoid, subjecting his followers to endless security checks and bloody purges.

In 1985 Abu Nidal moved his base to Tripoli, Libya, where he became close friends with Libyan strongman Muammar Qaddafi. As with the Syrians, Qaddafi also found many ways to employ Abu Nidal's services. After U.S. warplanes struck Tripoli in April 1986 as punishment for a West Berlin nightclub bombing, Qaddafi convinced Abu Nidal to strike the United States and Britain. The result was staggering. After a kidnapping that left 3 hostages dead, an FRC team hijacked Pan Am Flight 73 in Karachi, Pakistan, in September 1986, killing 22 people. The FRC also provided the explosives that brought down Pan Am Flight 103 en route to New York City over Lockerbie, Scotland, on December 21, 1988, killing 270 people.

The FRC was also responsible for the 1988 attack on the Greek cruise ship *City of Poros* that killed 9 people and left 80 others injured. The attack was roundly criticized in Arab circles because its savagery did not serve either the Palestinian or the Arab political cause. As a result, some theorists accused Abu Nidal of being a Mossad agent or at least being on the Israeli payroll. Some have even argued that the FRC was Arafat's supreme deception in that it allowed Arafat to pose as a moderate while Abu Nidal carried out all of the PLO's truly violent acts.

In 1999, after being expelled by Qaddafi when the Libyan leader began to mend relations with the United States, Abu Nidal returned to Iraq, where he lived in open defiance of the Jordanian government that had sentenced him to death in absentia. He was living in a Baghdad home owned by the Iraqi Mukhabbarat (Secret Service) when on August 16, 2002, he allegedly committed suicide, suffering multiple gunshot wounds, after being detained by Iraq's internal security force.

From a Western perspective, Abu Nidal's violence may have seemed to be targeted at only Israeli interests. However, most of his victims were Arabs. In fact, most of his killings were not even ideologically driven per se in that he served as a mercenary for such states as Iraq, Syria, and Libya, killing these nations' political enemies for financial gain. Abu Nidal's activities tended to put Palestinian demands in the worst possible light and diminish any hope of gaining broader international support. As a result, it should come as no surprise that the FRC was never popular among most Palestinians. Abu Nidal and the FRC were believed to have carried out some 90 terrorist attacks in 20 nations that may have killed as many as 1,000 people.

B. KEITH MURPHY

See also

Arafat, Yasser; Baath Party; Fatah; Palestine Liberation Organization; Qaddafi, Muammar; Terrorism

References

Melman, Yossi. *The Master Terrorist: The True Story of Abu Nidal.* Translated by Shmuel Himmelstein. New York: Adama, 1986.

Seale, Patrick. *Abu Nidal, a Gun for Hire: The Secret Life of the World's Most Notorious Arab Terrorist.* New York: Random House, 1992.

Tibi, Bassam. *Arab Nationalism: Between Islam and the Nation-State.* New York: St. Martin's, 1997.

Achille Lauro Hijacking
Start Date: October 7, 1985
End Date: October 10, 1985

The *Achille Lauro* was an Italian passenger liner hijacked by Palestinian terrorists in the eastern Mediterranean on October 7, 1985. Construction of the ship began at Vlissingen in the Netherlands in 1939 but was interrupted by World War II. Launched in 1946, the ship entered service in late 1947 as the *Willum Ruys.* Sold to the Italian Lauro Line in 1964, the ship was rebuilt, modernized, and returned to service in 1966, named for the former mayor of Naples. Displacing about 21,100 tons, the *Achille Lauro* could accommodate 900 passengers.

On October 7, 1985, the *Achille Lauro* was steaming from Alexandria to Port Said off the Egyptian coast when four armed

Freed hostages disembark from the passenger ship *Achille Lauro* following the surrender of their Palestinian hijackers; photographed on October 10, 1985, at Port Said, Egypt. (Bernard Bisson/Corbis Sygma)

members of the Palestine Liberation Front (PLF) led by Abu Abbas seized control, apparently in retaliation for the Israeli destruction of the Palestine Liberation Organization (PLO) headquarters in Tunis on October 1.

The terrorists had been surprised by a crew member and were forced to act prematurely, but they demanded that the *Achille Lauro* steam to Tartus, Syria, and threatened to blow up the ship if Israel did not release 50 Palestinian prisoners held in Israel. The sole casualty of the affair was U.S.-born Jewish passenger Leon Klinghoffer, who was confined to a wheelchair. Reportedly, he confronted the hijackers and was shot by them, and his body was thrown overboard.

Syrian authorities refused to allow the ship to dock, and it returned to Port Said. Following two days of negotiations, the terrorists agreed to release the ship and its passengers in return for safe conduct aboard an Egyptian airliner to Tunis. On October 10, U.S. aircraft intercepted the Egyptian plane and forced it to fly to a North Atlantic Treaty Organization (NATO) base in Sicily. Disregarding U.S. government appeals, Italian authorities released the passengers, reportedly including Abu Abbas, although he was subsequently sentenced in absentia by an Italian court to life in prison.

Some sources state that it was the close relationship between Abu Abbas and the PLO that caused the U.S. government to deny a visa to PLO chairman Yasser Arafat to enter the United States in order to speak to the United Nations (UN) General Assembly in November 1988. Abu Abbas had been a member of the PLO Executive Committee during 1984–1991. Arrested in Iraq following the U.S.-led invasion of that country in 2003, he died, reportedly of natural causes, while in U.S. custody on March 8, 2004. The other three hijackers served varying terms in Italian prisons.

On November 29, 1994, the reflagged *Achille Lauro* was steaming off the coast of Somalia when a fire broke out. All 1,090 passengers and crew abandoned ship. Other ships were soon on the scene, but 2 people died in the lifeboat transfers. The fire totally consumed the ship, and it sank on December 2.

On January 19, 1996, the PLO agreed to provide an undisclosed sum to finance the Leon and Marilyn Klinghoffer Memorial Foundation of the U.S. Anti-Defamation League. The foundation is dedicated to combating terrorism through peaceful means. In return, Klinghoffer's daughters dropped a lawsuit brought against the PLO. The *Achille Lauro* hijacking has been the subject of a 1990 television docudrama and an opera, *The Death of Klinghofffer* (1991), that appeared as a film version in 2003.

SPENCER C. TUCKER

See also

Abbas, Abu; Arafat, Yasser; Palestine Liberation Organization; Terrorism

References

Bohn, Michael K. *The Achille Lauro Hijacking: Lessons in the Politics and Prejudice of Terrorism.* Dulles, VA: Potomac Books, 2004.
Cassese, Antonio. *Terrorism, Politics and Law: The Achille Lauro Affair.* Princeton, NJ: Princeton University Press, 1989.

ACHILLES, **Operation**
Start Date: March 6, 2007
End Date: May 31, 2007

A North Atlantic Treaty Organization (NATO)–led military counterinsurgency operation in Afghanistan during March 6–May 31, 2007. In response to increased Taliban and Al Qaeda activities in the Helmand Province in southwest Afghanistan, NATO sought to expand its area of operations into the region and to disrupt a growing insurgency network there. Over the previous two years, the Taliban had launched annual campaigns in the area each spring, and NATO planners wanted to strike the insurgents before they were able undertake another springtime operation. Furthermore, poppy production in the region had expanded dramatically, and Helmand Province was responsible for as much as 40 percent of the world's total heroin production. The NATO action was also designed to suppress the narcotics trade and undermine the power of local warlords, many of whom were allied with the Taliban.

Operation ACHILLES was the largest NATO-led ground offensive in Afghanistan to date. The campaign was a follow-on to Operation VOLCANO of February 2007, during which British forces had dislodged a large Taliban force of approximately 700 fighters in 25 compounds near the Kajaki Dam in the province. The dam was one of two major hydroelectric producers in the country and the major source for irrigation for the region. However, only one of two turbine generation units were operable by the end of 2006, and the facility faced constant attack by the Taliban. An internationally-funded $100 million plan to upgrade the plant and add a third turbine had been repeatedly delayed by fighting. One of the specific goals of Operation ACHILLES was to create a secure environment for the dam to be brought up to full operational capacity. British and Australian economic and Provincial Reconstruction teams were slated to support the military effort.

NATO deployed 5,500 troops during the campaign. The majority were British, with smaller contingents from the United States, Canada, Denmark, and the Netherlands, along with 1,000 troops from the Afghan National Army. ACHILLES would be one of the largest operations undertaken by the Afghan Army and would provide coalition commanders with an assessment of the capabilities of its troops. The NATO-led forces were opposed by approximately 4,000 to 5,000 Taliban fighters. The NATO forces were initially commanded by Dutch major general Ton van Loon; British major general Jonathan "Jacko" Page assumed command of the region on May 1, 2007.

Operation ACHILLES began on March 6, 2007. The NATO-led forces moved into the more lawless northern areas in the province, including Musa Qala, Washir, Nawzad, Sangin Kajaki, and Grishk. Initially, two large Taliban compounds were attacked and captured by coalition forces near Garmsir. A combined Dutch-Afghan group, Task Force Uruzgan, was deployed along the border between the Helmand and Uruzgan provinces to block the escape route of Taliban forces. In addition, on April 30 NATO and Afghan forces attacked a large Taliban force at Gereshk, killing approximately 130 enemy fighters and forcing the Taliban from the area. Coalition forces employed air assets against the Taliban in Gereshk and surrounding villages.

Civilian casualties from the engagement led to protests among villagers in the region. Reports indicated that as many as 50 civilians were killed in the fighting. This created renewed tensions between the local populace and the NATO-led coalition. Nonetheless, by the end of May Taliban forces had been effectively removed from both Gereshk and Sangin.

The majority of fighting involved small-unit action, with bands of 10–50 Taliban fighters conducting small-scale attacks on coalition forces and posts. In most of these engagements, the NATO forces were able to use a combination of air power, precision-guided munitions, and artillery to overwhelm Taliban resistance. The Taliban also increasingly resorted to terrorist-style attacks

A leaflet drop over the mountains of southeastern Afghanistan, part of Operation ACHILLES, March 2007. The leaflets warned the Taliban not to interfere with coalition activities. (U.S. Department of Defense)

similar to those used in Iraq, including the use of improvised explosive devices (IEDs) to attack convoys and the use of car bombs, especially against Afghan police or civilian targets. During one week in April, eleven NATO troops were killed by roadside bombs, while none died in combat operations.

While the main thrust of the campaign was to destroy concentrations of Taliban fighters, the operations also included tactical air strikes and special operations forces' actions against Taliban leaders. On May 13, Mullah Dadullah, the military operational commander of the Taliban and a member of the organization's 10-member central committee, was killed in a raid by NATO forces, becoming the most senior Taliban figure killed in Afghanistan to that point. In addition, coalition air strikes were credited with killing a number of midlevel Taliban leaders during the campaign.

Operation ACHILLES ended on May 31. During the campaign, NATO leaders reported that Afghan troops performed well and undertook a number of missions independent of coalition personnel. Casualties included 19 Afghan National Army troops and 16 NATO soldiers. Taliban casualties were estimated to be between 700 and 1,000. In addition, some 39 Taliban fighters were captured. In order to support the continued presence of Afghan National Army forces, a series of bases were built by NATO engineers, and patrol stations were established throughout

the region for NATO and Afghan forces. In an effort to capitalize on the relative success of Operation ACHILLES, NATO launched a series of smaller campaigns and raids throughout the summer. One result was that the Taliban failed to mount an offensive in the spring of 2007. However, ACHILLES was unable to restore large areas of Helmand to Afghan government control, and the campaign did not significantly disrupt the region's poppy production. In addition, in 2008, the Taliban launched renewed attacks on the Kajaki Dam; nevertheless, in September, British forces were able to deliver the planned third turbine at the hydroelectric plant, and work began on dramatically increasing the facility's power output.

TOM LANSFORD

See also

Afghanistan, Coalition Combat Operations in, 2002–Present; North Atlantic Treaty Organization in Afghanistan; Provincial Reconstruction Teams, Afghanistan; Taliban

References

Bhatia, Michael, and Mark Sedra. *Afghanistan, Arms and Conflict: Armed Groups, Disarmament and Security in a Post-War Society.* New York: Routledge, 2008.

Crews, Robert D., and Amin Tarzi, eds. *The Taliban and the Crisis of Afghanistan.* Cambridge: Harvard University Press, 2008.

Guistozzi, Antonio. *Koran, Kalashnikov and Laptop: The Neo-Taliban Insurgency in Afghanistan.* New York: Columbia University Press, 2008.

Jones, Seth G. *Counterinsurgency in Afghanistan: RAND Counterinsurgency Study No. 4.* Santa Monica, CA: RAND Corporation, 2008.

Mills, Greg. *From Africa to Afghanistan: With Richards and NATO to Kabul.* Johannesburg: Wits University Press, 2007.

Addington, David
Birth Date: January 22, 1957

Attorney, government official in the Ronald Reagan and George H. W. Bush administrations, legal counsel for Vice President Richard "Dick" Cheney (2001–2005), and Cheney's chief of staff (2005–2009). David Addington was born in Washington, D.C., on January 22, 1957. He attended Georgetown University and earned a law degree from Duke University. Admitted to the bar in 1981, he served as an assistant general counsel for the Central Intelligence Agency (CIA) from 1981 to 1984. During 1984–1987, he acted as counsel for the U.S. House of Representatives' committees on intelligence and international relations. Also in 1987, he served as a special assistant to President Ronald Reagan, and then as deputy assistant until 1989. During this time, Addington suggested that Reagan's signing statements, or written statements made upon the signing of a bill into law, should exempt the president from wrongdoing in the Iran-Contra Affair.

From 1989 to 1992, Addington was special assistant to Secretary of Defense Dick Cheney. By this time he had firmly established his bona fides as a rightist Republican and a war hawk. From 1992 to 1993, he was general counsel for the Department of Defense. Addington had unusual sway over policy matters, and he became a close confidant of both Cheney and the elder Bush. Addington was reportedly deeply involved, along with Cheney, in developing contingency plans for the continuity of the U.S. government in the wake of a nuclear attack or other catastrophe. The plans Addington envisioned called for a paramount executive, in whom most power would be invested and who would work with the "cooperation" of Congress and the courts. Several sources indicate that since that time, Addington has carried with him a copy of the U.S. Constitution. Some have argued that both Addington and Cheney became obsessed by such doomsday scenarios. During 1993–2001, Addington practiced law privately and spearheaded a political action committee that attempted to lay the groundwork for a Cheney presidential campaign, which never panned out.

In 2001, Addington became Vice President Cheney's legal counsel. As such, he played a major role in setting policy during the George W. Bush administration, especially in areas pertaining to national security. After the September 11, 2001, terror attacks, Addington was the principal architect of Bush's numerous signing statements, and he helped shape U.S. policy concerning enemy combatants and detainees. He has consistently argued that the executive branch holds almost unlimited power in wartime, a stance that has angered and concerned Americans on both sides of the political spectrum. In 2002, Addington helped craft the Justice Department's opinion that in certain cases, the torture of detainees during wartime may be justifiable, and he also helped shape the Bush administration's controversial policies at the Guantánamo Bay Detainment Camp. Indeed, Addington's role in national security affairs has been so consistent and central that the magazine *U.S. News and World Report* termed him "the most powerful man you've never heard of." In 2005, when I. Scooter Libby was indicted for his role in the Valerie Plame Wilson incident, Addington took his place as Cheney's chief of staff.

In 2007, Addington, in reply to a U.S. Senate inquiry on the use of classified information, informed Senator John Kerry that the vice president's office was exempt from the U.S. National Archives' oversight of classified material because of national-security imperatives. Prior to that, he had called for the elimination of the oversight office. Addington allegedly was also involved in the Bush administration's controversial activities involving the tapping of phone calls between U.S. citizens and those abroad, which had been pursued without the requisite court orders.

In June 2008, Addington was compelled to testify under a subpoena to the House Judiciary Committee, which relentlessly grilled him about the treatment of enemy combatants and other detainees; the use of torture and questionable interrogation tactics; and the extent of executive powers in wartime. Addington remained firm in his commitment to sweeping executive powers, and saw no wrongdoing in regard to detainees and enemy combatants. In 2008, Jane Mayer published *The Dark Side: The Inside Story of How the War on Terror Turned into a War on American Ideals.* The book is a highly critical study of the George W. Bush administration, including an indictment of Addington's central role in what the author sees as the trampling of civil and constitutional liberties.

PAUL G. PIERPAOLI JR.

See also

Bush, George Walker; Cheney, Richard Bruce; Global War on Terror; Libby, I. Lewis; Wilson, Valerie Plame

References

Dean, John W. *Worse than Watergate: The Secret Presidency of George W. Bush.* Boston: Little, Brown, 2004.

Mayer, Jane. *The Dark Side: The Inside Story of How the War on Terror Turned into a War on American Ideals.* New York: Doubleday, 2008.

Adl, Sayf al-
Birth Date: April 11, 1960 or 1963

Senior Al Qaeda operative, strategic planner, and commando trainer, considered by some to be number three in the Al Qaeda hierarchy. He is currently wanted in connection with the 1998 bombings of U.S. embassies in Dar es Salaam, Tanzania, and Nairobi, Kenya. Sayf Al-Adl is a nom de guerre meaning "sword of justice." His identity has been confused with Sayf al-Din al-Ansari, a different jihadist ideologue, but he has also used the names Ibrahim al-Madani and Umar al-Sumali at different times. According to some sources and the Federal Bureau of Investigation (FBI), he is Muhammad Ibrahim Makkawi, born in Egypt on April 11, 1960 or 1963, but this point too is disputed. If he is not Makkawi, then that individual was probably killed, and there are some theories that he was a plant, or connected with the CIA. Makkawi's history is nevertheless given as that of Adl.

Makkawi/Adl has written that he turned toward Islam in the 1980s. He attained the rank of colonel in the Egyptian Army's Special Forces in 1987. That same year, he was arrested along with thousands of other Islamists who were attempting to revive the illegal Jihad Islami (Islamic Jihad) organization, a cell of which had assassinated Egyptian President Anwar al-Sadat in 1981. He was allegedly part of a plot to drive a truck bomb and an airplane into the Egyptian Parliament building, and he was imprisoned with more than 400 others from Islamic Jihadist operatives.

In 1988, Adl left for Saudi Arabia and was then based in Peshawar, Pakistan, from which he moved into Afghanistan and conducted military training for its operatives near Khost. If Adl is not Makkawi, then he may have traveled to Pakistan a year or two later. In 1992, Adl went to Khartoum and also conducted military training for Al Qaeda in vacant areas of Damazin Farms. He was part of Al Qaeda's expansion into other areas, and by then he was a member of its military committee. Subsequently, he sent an important operative into Somalia to begin activities there. In 1993 and 1994, he was engaged in activities in Somalia and wrote a letter recommending the establishment of an Al Qaeda base in southern Somalia along with a detailed description of the route from there to Nairobi, which featured tourist areas and other local sites. He may have been in Yemen in 1995 before returning to Afghanistan, where he trained commandos at the Mes Aynak camp near Kabul in 1999; he likely remained there until 2001.

During this period, Adl came to know Jordanian militant Islamist Abu Musab al-Zarqawi, helped him establish his training camp, which was near Heart, and provided points of contact for mujahideen coming from Iran into Afghanistan. A split developed among Al Qaeda leaders over the wisdom of attacking U.S. interests, and Adl was reportedly, like the Taliban's Mohammed Omar, opposed to such an operation. However, once the United States attacked Afghanistan after the September 11, 2001, terror attacks, he directed Al Qaeda operations there. He led one contingent into Iran with assistance from Gulbuddin Hekmetyar's Hizb al-Islam. From there, he planned to move back into Afghanistan to fight, while Abu Musab al-Zarqawi's group was to move into Iraq. Large numbers of both groups were arrested by Iranian authorities, and it has been asserted that Adl was still in custody or under house arrest in Iran as of 2005, along with others including the son of Osama bin Laden. He was last heard from in a 2005 memoir of Zarqawi solicited by journalist Fuad Husayn.

In Iran, Adl remained active in Al Qaeda's information activities and planning operations, perhaps in the truck-bombing of a synagogue in Djerba, Tunisia, and definitely in actions of al-Qaida

fi jazirat al-arabiyya (QAP) in Saudi Arabia. That group began publishing an Internet journal, *Muaskar al-Battar,* in December of 2003, to which Adl contributed a regular section, "Security and Intelligence Operations." In 2004, he published an Internet manual on jihadi planning ("The Base of the Vanguard") to which other Al Qaeda members contributed. Although Adl may not initially have approved of attacking the United States, he later provided the strategic rationale for it, arguing that attacking the United States on its own soil was like smashing the head of a snake. Such attacks, he continued, would lead to the emergence of a new and "virtuous" world leadership that would vindicate the downtrodden around the world.

Adl further explained how the United States could reorient its foreign policy objectives, which were costly and would lead ultimately to its defeat. U.S. objectives, as he saw them, included (1) ending the Palestinian intifada (meaning a cessation of all resistance to Israel), (2) gaining control over Hezbollah in Lebanon, (3) forcing Syria to withdraw from Lebanon, (4) promoting successful elections in Iraq, and (5) maintaining security over the oil fields in the Persian Gulf and "maritime crossing points." Jihadists engaged in a lively debate on the impact of 9/11 and the U.S.-led Global War on Terror. Adl's whereabouts remain very much in dispute.

Sherifa Zuhur

See also

Al Qaeda; Al Qaeda in the Arabian Peninsula; Al Qaeda in Iraq; Bin Laden, Osama; Dar es Salaam, Bombing of U.S. Embassy; Jihad; Nairobi, Kenya, Bombing of U.S. Embassy; Somalia, International Intervention in; Sudan

References

Combating Terrorism Center, U.S. Military Academy. "Harmony and Disharmony. Exploiting al-Qa'ida's Organizational Vulnerabilities." West Point, NY: CTC, USMA, February 2006.

Husayn, Fu'ad. *Al-Zarqawi al-jil al-thani l-il-Qa'ida.* Beirut: Dar al-Khayal, 2005.

Zabel, Sarah. "The Military Strategy of Global Jihad." *Carlisle Papers.* Carlisle, PA: Strategic Studies Institute, October 2007.

Zuhur, Sherifa. *A Hundred Osamas: Islamist Threats and the Future of Counterinsurgency.* Carlisle Barracks, PA: Strategic Studies Institute, U.S. Army War College, 2006.

Afghanistan

A landlocked nation of 252,000 square miles in South Asia with a 2008 population of 32.738 million people. Afghanistan borders Iran to the west; Turkmenistan, Uzbekistan, and Tajikistan to the north; China to the northeast; and Pakistan to the east and south. This geographically forbidding nation, almost half of which is more than 6,500 feet in elevation, with extensive desert regions and mountains exceeding 16,000 feet, has been no stranger to international intrigue throughout its long history.

Afghanistan became a center of the so-called Great Game, an imperialist rivalry between Britain and Russia, in the 19th century. The struggle ended before the turn of the century, however, with

A crowded downtown area of Kabul, Afghanistan, in November 2006. (AP/Wide World Photos)

the establishment of an independent Afghanistan that divided the regional ethnic groups in the area among Russia, British India, and Afghanistan. As elsewhere in the world, artificial borders mandated by European empires left residual problems that festered throughout the twentieth century.

The Cold War caught Afghanistan between the Soviet Union, naturally interested in a country on its southern border with ethnic connections to Soviet Central Asian republics, and the United States, which was fearful of communist expansion. The U.S. containment policy sought to encircle the Soviets and Communist Chinese with an interlocking system of alliances including the North Atlantic Treaty Organization (NATO), the Central Treaty Organization (CENTO), and the Southeast Asia Treaty Organization (SEATO); thus, Afghanistan found itself wedged between the West and the East.

After 1933, Afghanistan's king, Mohammad Zahir Shah, had tried to enhance his position by dealing with the Soviets as a counter to the British in India. Following World War II, the United States displaced Britain as the principal Western force in Asia, and Afghanistan continued to court the Soviets as a counter to perceived Western imperialism. An agreement with the Soviets in 1950 provided Afghanistan with substantial economic support and promises of oil shipments, albeit interrupted by disputes over the Pashtun border with Pakistan.

At the time, proponents of containment envisioned an interlocking system of alliances to surround the communist world.

NATO was the first in 1949 to secure Western Europe. In 1954 CENTO and SEATO surrounded the southern and eastern flanks of the communist bloc. Never fully realized, the idea was to link the three through multilateral collective security guarantees. CENTO included Pakistan, Iran, Iraq, and the linchpin, Turkey, which was also a NATO member. Pakistan was also a member of SEATO and thus tied to NATO through Turkey. Afghanistan was not included in any of these mutual-defense mechanisms.

In 1953 Mohammad Daoud Khan, a member of the Afghan royal family, became prime minister. Daoud secured a Soviet economic development loan of $3 million in 1954 that preceded a 1955 visit by Soviet leaders Nikita Khrushchev and Nikolai Bulganin, who promised another $100 million. The United States refused military aid to Afghanistan but did assist in improving the Kandahar airport. The Soviets then promised military aid and a military aircraft facility at Mazar-e Sharif. For a time, it seemed that Afghanistan was the fortunate beneficiary of Cold War rivalries.

Daoud's tenure ended in 1963, however, when Zahir resumed direct rule. The details of Daoud's fall are not entirely clear, although several factors were involved, including high inflation in the country, continued tensions with Pakistan, popular opposition to Daoud's secular government, and the king's desire to broaden participation in government.

The king ruled directly for a decade, during which time a leftist political opposition movement gained momentum, led by Babrak

AFGHAN ETHNOLINGUISTIC GROUPS

IRANIAN
- ☐ Qizilbash
- Aimak
- Baloch
- Hazara
- Pashtun
- Tajik

TURKIC
- Kyrgyz
- Turkmen
- Uzbek

OTHER
- Brahui
- Nuristani
- Sparsely populated or uninhabited

UZBEKISTAN

KYRGYZSTAN

CHINA

TAJIKISTAN

Dushanbe

TURKMENISTAN

Fayzabad

Mazar-e Sharif

Kunduz

Baghlan

35°N

Herat

Chaghcharan

Kabul

Jalalabad

Peshawar

Khyber Pass

Islamabad

AFGHANISTAN

Kandahar

Zaranj

PAKISTAN

Quetta

Multan

30°N

Sibi

Surab

Sukkur

INDIA

IRAN

Bela

65°E   70°E   75°E

0   100   200 mi
0   100   200 km

Karmal of the People's Democratic Party of Afghanistan (PDA). Political unrest and a severe drought resulted in a military coup in 1973 that placed Daoud back in power, now as head of a republic with support from Karmal. Daoud, a moderate leftist, surprised many by seeking U.S. financial aid through Mohammad Reza Shah Pahlavi of Iran. The Soviets were also providing aid; Daoud visited the Soviet Union in 1974 and again in 1977.

Daoud continued to endeavor to play the two superpowers against each other and also developed closer ties with both Iran and Saudi Arabia. By 1978, Daoud lost Karmal's support on the Left and the Islamist fundamentalists' support on the Right. That same year, Daoud's government was overthrown. Karmal and Nur Muhammad Taraki now led a new government with strong ties to the Soviets. The two Afghan leaders soon split, however, and in 1979 the Soviet Union sent troops to support Karmal. This began a bloody war of attrition for the Soviets that would not end until 1989.

Meanwhile, local tribal leaders took advantage of the turmoil, as did Islamic fundamentalists who feared that Soviet rule would result in a wholly secular regime. This dynamic forced the Soviets to back Karmal's regime with 150,000 troops and massive military aid. Sensing Soviet vulnerability, the United States provided arms and covert aid to the Afghan mujahideen (guerrilla insurrectionists). The parallel to Vietnam is not without merit. During the Vietnam War the communist powers, principally the Soviet Union and China, provided sufficient aid to the North Vietnamese and their Viet Cong allies to keep the United States bogged down in a protracted struggle until 1973. In Afghanistan, the United States ultimately supplied aid to keep the Soviets pinned down until 1989, when they gave up and withdrew. The Afghanistan-Soviet War played a sizable role in the collapse of the Soviet Union just a few years later.

After the Soviets' exit, Afghanistan was plunged into a long civil war that finally ended in 1996 when the repressive Taliban regime came to power, cultivating ties to the terrorist Al Qaeda movement. Ironically, the Taliban and Al Qaeda had received training and arms from the United States during the Afghanistan-Soviet War. The Taliban quickly went about installing an Islamic fundamentalist regime that severely repressed basic civil liberties and used frequently barbaric means to "cleanse" Afghanistan of all things secular and Western.

The country's economy was in shambles, but opposition groups were effectively stymied by the Taliban's heavy-handed rule. The Taliban's fortunes changed after the Al Qaeda–inspired terrorist attacks on the United States on September 11, 2001. The George W. Bush administration immediately demanded that the Taliban hand over Al Qaeda leader Osama bin Laden and other Al Qaeda operatives, who had sought refuge in Afghanistan, or face military reprisal. Having established a close relationship with Al Qaeda, the Taliban leaders refused, and in October 2001 the United States led a small coalition of NATO nations to invade the country and aid the indigenous Northern Alliance in defeating the Taliban and ousting it from power by year's end.

In 2002, Hamid Karzai, a prominent Pashto who was viewed favorably by the United States government, became interim president of Afghanistan. Elected in his own right in 2004, Karzai had the unenviable task of trying to rebuild his nation, keeping Taliban fighters and other Islamic extremists at bay, and maintaining a close working relationship with Washington. In the meantime, Afghanistan's economic problems proved to be quite intractable, with much of the nation mired in grinding poverty. Afghanistan is the world's major source for heroin, and Karzai has refused to get tough with opium (poppy) producers, despite much pressure from Washington, because such cultivation provides badly-needed revenue for the Afghan economy. It also is a chief source of income for the Taliban insurgency. This and other issues, especially Karzai's 2007 offer to reach out to moderate elements of the Taliban, have caused friction in the U.S.-Afghan relationship.

By 2007, however, the Taliban insurgency was clearly on the rise, despite the continued presence of NATO troops in the country working with the Afghan National Army. Karzai promised to help stem the tide of the insurgency, but he had few means with which to do this. This in turn led the United States and NATO to insert additional resources into the country to battle the insurgents. Afghanistan's future remains uncertain, with conditions not likely to improve unless the insurgency can be neutralized and the economy strengthened.

DANIEL E. SPECTOR

See also

Al Qaeda; Bin Laden, Osama; Containment Policy; ENDURING FREEDOM, Operation; Karzai, Hamid; Middle East Regional Defense Organizations; Mujahideen, Soviet-Afghanistan War; North Atlantic Treaty Organization; North Atlantic Treaty Organization in Afghanistan; Pakistan; Soviet-Afghanistan War; Soviet Union, Middle East Policy; Taliban; Taliban Insurgency, Afghanistan; United States

References

Dupree, Louis. *Afghanistan*. Princeton, NJ: Princeton University Press, 1980.
Hanson, Victor Davis. *Between War and Peace: Lessons from Afghanistan to Iraq*. New York: Random House, 2004.
Hopkirk, Peter. *The Great Game: The Struggle for Empire in Central Asia*. New York: Kodansha, 1992.
Kagan, Frederick. *Finding the Target: The Transformation of American Military Policy*. New York: Encounter, 2006.
Maley, William. *The Afghanistan Wars*. New York: Palgrave Macmillan, 2002.

Afghanistan, Climate of

The term "climate" refers to decades-long patterns of weather conditions based on average as well as minimum/maximum ranges of temperature, precipitation, atmospheric pressure, and other variables. In contrast, weather refers to daily variations in such variables. The interaction of several climate variables contributes to climatic variations in Afghanistan and elsewhere around the world. These include latitude and seasonality, altitude, maritime influence and continentality, semipermanent pressure systems, prevailing winds, ocean currents, storms, and topography. Latitude and altitude apply to regions everywhere, but other variables impact some regions more than others. For example, ocean currents are relatively insignificant for Afghanistan, which is landlocked, whereas topography plays an important role.

Afghanistan's latitude extends from 29° to 38° north, about the same as from southern New Mexico to northern Utah. Thus, it receives substantial solar radiation, but temperature and precipitation vary significantly between summer and winter. This is a latitude range prone to desert formation because of the Hadley Cell. That is, warm moist air rises at the equator to produce convectional precipitation. The drier air then descends at about 30° north and south to produce a series of deserts in both hemispheres, including the Rigestan Desert in southwestern Afghanistan.

As altitude increases, temperatures over land generally decrease at the rate of 3.3° Fahrenheit per 1,000 feet of elevation. Thus, the Rigestan Desert, with an average elevation of 3,000 feet, is about 10° cooler than deserts at the same latitude (but lower altitude), such as in Iraq and Jordan. Nevertheless, temperatures in the region can surpass 110° Fahrenheit in the summers. Elevations in the Hindu Kush mountain range vary substantially across short horizontal distances. Abrupt changes in altitude produce equally abrupt changes in climate zones. Climatologists include these mountains in the category of "Undifferentiated Highlands" due to their mosaic of climate zones.

Afghanistan's remoteness from oceans and large water bodies, which could otherwise moderate daily and annual temperature changes, makes continentality more important than the maritime influence. Thus, daily and annual temperature ranges show greater fluctuation than coastal countries such as Israel. For instance, some British and Indian troops perished from heat exhaustion during the 1839 invasion of Afghanistan, while extreme cold killed many more during their disastrous 1842 retreat.

Semipermanent pressure systems, prevailing winds, and storms are related variables that play an important role in Afghanistan. Continentality contributes to substantial heating of the Asian landmass during summer. Whereas neighboring Pakistan receives substantial rain during the summer monsoon season, Afghanistan experiences dry conditions, as northerly winds and mountains usually keep this precipitation at bay. In the winter, however, the Siberian high causes westerly winds carrying storms from the Mediterranean Sea, the Black Sea, and the Caspian Sea to veer into Afghanistan, producing substantial rain and snow throughout the Hindu Kush and its highland margins.

Topography is very important for Afghan climate zones. Moisture-laden air may blow across the northern plains without producing precipitation. When that same air rises to cross a mountain, however, rapid cooling and condensation produce orographic (mountain-induced) precipitation on the windward side. As the air mass moves down the leeward slope, however, evaporation replaces condensation in an air mass that has less water vapor. If wind direction remains relatively constant, the leeward side will experience a rain shadow of drier conditions than the windward side.

The Hindu Kush occupies a wide swath from the Tajik and Chinese borders into central Afghanistan. In the winter, deep snow often closes the high mountain passes for extended periods, and prolonged cold frequently brings military operations to a virtual halt. Summer melting, however, provides the runoff to sustain agriculture throughout numerous valleys while allowing military operations to increase in tempo.

The foothills of the Hindu Kush form two parallel U-shaped transition zones on its margins, extending from the Tajik border toward Herat in the west before looping back toward Pakistan. The inner belt exhibits characteristics of a Mediterranean climate based on average temperatures and a pattern of wet winters and dry summers. The outer belt features semiarid steppes that serve as a transition zone to the Rigestan Desert in the southwest and the edge of the Kara Kum Desert near Turkmenistan. Much of Afghanistan's production of opium poppies occurs in these steppe regions. Most of this outer belt can be classified as semiarid/hot with one exception. In the valleys between the Hindu Kush and the mountains of neighboring Waziristan, the steppes near Kabul are at higher elevations, qualifying them as semiarid/cold, like those of Kazakhstan.

Although Afghanistan is often considered a desert country, its climate is far more complicated and varied, making classification extremely difficult. Indigenous and foreign military forces alike have found that they must prepare for a wide variety of weather patterns when operating there.

CHUCK FAHRER

See also

Afghanistan, Coalition Combat Operations in, 2002–Present; Defense Meteorological Satellite Program; ENDURING FREEDOM, Operation; Topography, Afghanistan

References

Ahrens, C. Donald. *Meteorology Today*. 6th ed. Minneapolis, MN: West Publishing, 2000.

Fahrer, Chuck, and Dan Harris. "LAMPPOST: A Mnemonic Device for Teaching Climate Variables." *Journal of Geography* 103(2) (March/April 2004): 86–91.

Hammond. *Atlas of the Middle East and Northern Africa*. New York: Langenscheidt, 2006.

Pannell, Richard P. "Climatology." In *Afghanistan: Geographic Perspectives*, edited by Eugene J. Palka, 17–24. New York: McGraw-Hill, 2004.

Tanner, Stephen. *Afghanistan: A Military History from Alexander the Great to the Fall of the Taliban*. New York: Da Capo, 2003.

Afghanistan, Coalition Combat Operations in, 2002–Present

A series of U.S. and coalition military campaigns occurred against the Taliban, the Al Qaeda terrorist organization, and other anti-government and anti-Western factions in support of the Afghan government of President Hamid Karzai. In October 2001, a

U.S.-led coalition launched Operation ENDURING FREEDOM, an invasion of Afghanistan to topple the Taliban regime after its refusal to take action against Al Qaeda, which had been responsible for the September 11, 2001, terrorist attacks on the United States.

By December, U.S. forces and those of its allies had worked in conjunction with the Afghan Northern Alliance to overthrow the Taliban. A pro-Western government was then installed. Beginning in the winter of 2001–2002, coalition forces launched successive operations to expand the areas under government control and suppress a growing antigovernment insurgency.

Operation ENDURING FREEDOM and the International Security Assistance Force

Initially, allied forces were divided between two parallel missions. The first was the ongoing Operation ENDURING FREEDOM (OEF). The United States–led coalition forces were involved in direct combat and counterinsurgency operations to counter the Taliban, Al Qaeda, and powerful regional warlords. On average, the United States maintained 15,000–20,000 troops, supported by 2,000–5,000 allied forces mainly from such North Atlantic Treaty Organization (NATO) partners as the United Kingdom and Canada. In 2007, 22 countries provided troops to OEF.

The second major mission was the International Security Assistance Force (ISAF). The ISAF was created by United Nations Security Council Resolution 1386 in December 2001 and initially commanded by the United Kingdom with forces from 18 other countries. ISAF was subsequently reauthorized by a succession of UN resolutions. Its main missions were to provide security assistance for the Afghan national government, undertake reconstruction and humanitarian operations, and train Afghan security forces.

In August 2003, NATO assumed command of ISAF. At first ISAF's operations were concentrated around Kabul, but it gradually expanded its area over the next four years, taking control of provinces that had been under the geographic area of operations of OEF forces. By 2007, ISAF counted about 40,000 troops from 37 NATO and non-NATO states.

In 2007, U.S. General Dan McNeill became the first U.S. officer to command ISAF. He was succeeded by U.S. Army general David McKiernan in 2008. In October 2006, ISAF began to transition to assume command of all of Afghanistan. The majority of OEF forces, including U.S. troops, were transferred to ISAF command. By 2007, OEF had been reduced to about 8,000 troops, mainly from the U.S., who continued designated combat operations with different rules of engagement from the ISAF forces.

In both OEF and ISAF operations, combat missions were affected by national "caveats" placed on troops by their home governments. Such caveats were designed to limit casualties among the troops and typically came in one of two forms: limitations on the geographic areas where troops could be deployed, and restrictions on missions. By 2007, there were more than 100 such restrictions among the nations contributing troops. For instance, the German government limited their forces to missions in the relatively stable areas of Northern Afghanistan (with some notable exceptions for German special operations forces). Republic of Korea forces were not allowed to participate in combat operations. Such caveats dramatically reduced the flexibility of coalition operations and meant that the majority of combat missions were undertaken by U.S., Australian, British, Canadian, and Dutch forces.

Coalition operations were also constrained by the limited number of troops. The U.S.-led invasion of Iraq in March 2003 limited the number of U.S. forces available for deployment to Afghanistan. The great demands of the Iraq War also limited U.S. spending to support both combat and reconstruction efforts in Afghanistan. Allied nations faced similar constraints. For instance, the deployment of forces to Iraq by Australia, the United Kingdom, or Italy limited the forces available for Afghanistan. Other NATO partners, including Belgium, France, and Spain, had forces deployed in peacekeeping missions in the Balkans, Lebanon, and Africa, which prevented deployments to support ISAF. During a succession of NATO summits, leaders agreed in principle to increase combat forces in Afghanistan, but they were unable to secure commitments from individual states to fully meet these pledges. Nonetheless, by 2008, ISA included 50,700 troops from 40 NATO and partner countries.

The First Phase of Major Operations (2002–2004)

Following the fall of the Taliban and the Battle of Tora Bora in December 2001, the first major coalition offensive was Operation ANACONDA. It began in March 2002 when U.S.-led OEF forces launched a campaign to dislodge Taliban and Al Qaeda fighters from bases in the Shah-i-Khot Valley, south of Gardez. Insurgent forces numbered approximately 2,000 and had occupied a series of caves and bunkers in the area from which to conduct operations against Afghan government and coalition targets.

Coalition forces included 1,000 U.S. troops; 1,500 Afghan soldiers; and about 200 troops from Australia, Canada, Denmark, France, Germany, and Norway, most of them special operations soldiers. Allied forces were able to dislodge the Taliban after intense fighting that included the use of AC-130 gunships and heavy aerial bombing (more than 3,500 bombs were dropped by the end of March). Despite the considerable firepower advantage enjoyed by the coalition, the operation suffered from a lack of coordination and communication among the different units. Eight U.S. and seven Afghan soldiers died in the operation, along with an estimated 340 Taliban/Al Qaeda fighters. The majority of insurgents were able to avoid capture by coalition forces and escape into Pakistan, where they soon established new bases and from which they launched crossborder incursions into Afghanistan. The following year coalition forces conducted a smaller campaign, Operation DRAGON FURY, in the same region to prevent the reemergence of the Taliban, but it involved only minor combat.

Through the summer of 2002, the Taliban conducted small-scale raids on coalition and government targets, especially against convoys and outposts. The majority of these attacks were undertaken by small groups of 10 to 50 insurgents each and employed

A U.S. Marine Corps corporal guards a CH-53E Super Stallion helicopter in preparation for a mission in support of Operation ANACONDA in Afghanistan, March 2002. (U.S. Department of Defense)

tactics similar to those employed by the Afghans against the Soviets in the 1980s. An estimated 1,000–1,500 insurgents were actively operating in Afghanistan at the time. Insurgents fired mortars and rockets at coalition bases and convoys and set up increasingly sophisticated ambushes against patrols and convoys. In an effort to decrease the effectiveness of coalition air power, the Taliban-led forces emphasized quick, hit-and-run attacks that allowed them to disperse before they were targeted by missiles or aerial attack. The insurgents attacked both OEF and ISAF forces, in addition to Afghan security troops, government targets, and humanitarian operations.

To counter the guerrilla-style warfare, the coalition endeavored to deny the insurgents supplies and bases from which to launch attacks. U.S.-led forces initiated a series of missions to dislodge the Taliban from their bases and interdict supplies. In April 2002, U.S. troops launched Operation MOUNTAIN LION in conjunction with a British offensive, Operation PTARMIGAN, in the areas around both Gardez and Khost. Operations continued through July and were marked by minor skirmishes between coalition and insurgent forces. Afghan, Australian, U.S., and United Kingdom forces engaged a large Taliban force during Operation CONDOR, May 16–22. The bulk of the fighting was undertaken by Australian and British forces, supported by U.S. helicopters and airplanes. Meanwhile,

the British-led Operation SNIPE in May resulted in the capture and destruction of a major Taliban base that included extensive caves and a large weapons cache in southeastern Afghanistan.

In what emerged as a continuing pattern, during the later fall and winter of 2002–2003, the Taliban and Al Qaeda regrouped and prepared for new offensive action in the spring of the next year, using bases in Pakistan to resupply and train new recruits. The Taliban increasingly sought out Pakistanis and other foreign fighters to bolster its ranks. Concurrently, the coalition increased its preventative strikes against the insurgents. Allied forces attempted to disrupt the Taliban's ability to undertake large-scale operations by searching out and destroying potential bases and weapons caches.

In January 2003, intelligence indicated the presence of 60–100 Taliban fighters in a cave complex in the Adhi Ghar Mountains (which had previously served as one of the main areas of operation for the anti-Soviet mujahideen). U.S. forces conducted air strikes and cave-by-cave searches. Twenty-two insurgents were killed and 13 captured in this Operation MONGOOSE, while the U.S. had no casualties. The 300 U.S. troops involved in the attack also destroyed significant insurgent stores of weapons and explosives.

In March 2003, the U.S. launched a preemptive mission east of Kandahar concurrently with the invasion of Iraq. Operation

VALIANT STRIKE was in response to the capture of top Al Qaeda leader Khalid Sheikh Mohammed in Pakistan. Utilizing information gleaned from Mohammad's capture, some 600 coalition forces seized and destroyed three large weapons caches and captured a number of suspected Taliban fighters among villages outside of Kandahar. U.S. troops, supported by U.S. and Norwegian air units, began Operation DESERT LION the day VALIANT STRIKE ended. That four-day operation resulted in the destruction of two Taliban facilities near the coalition's main air base at Bagram.

During the late summer of 2003, U.S. forces led two campaigns designed to interdict the movement of Taliban and foreign fighters into Afghanistan. Operation WARRIOR SWEEP included U.S., Italian, and Afghan troops in the Ayubkhel Valley, one of the main supply routes for the Taliban. There, coalition forces destroyed a number of weapons caches and bases but only faced minor opposition from insurgents. WARRIOR SWEEP lasted from July into September. Meanwhile, in Operation MOUNTAIN SWEEP, U.S. Army Rangers and units of the 82nd Airborne, along with coalition special operations forces, targeted suspected Taliban hideouts and supply routes.

In September 2003, U.S. forces and Afghan national troops launched Operation MOUNTAIN VIPER following a series of attacks against Afghan security posts in the southeastern part of the country. Taliban forces were supported by warlord Gulbuddin Hekmetyar, a former anti-Taliban leader who had turned against the Karzai government. Approximately 70–100 Taliban and militia forces loyal to Hekmetyar were killed in the campaign, which lasted into December.

The growing threat from insurgents led to a parallel campaign, Operation AVALANCHE, which began in December 2003 and was the largest U.S.-led offensive since ANACONDA. More than 2,000 U.S. troops conducted strikes and patrols in eastern and southeastern Afghanistan. The operation resulted in the capture and destruction of several large weapons caches. About 20 insurgents were killed and more than 100 wounded. No coalition troops were killed.

In January 2004, the coalition initiated another preemptive offensive to disrupt the ability of the Taliban to undertake significant operations in the spring. Operation MOUNTAIN BLIZZARD included more than 1,700 armed patrols and more than 140 specific raids and search-and-destroy missions. Twenty-two insurgents were killed and scores captured, while no coalition forces were killed. The campaign also resulted in the capture and destruction of large stocks of weapons and ammunition.

MOUNTAIN BLIZZARD ended in March 2004 and was immediately followed by Operation MOUNTAIN STORM. The new offensive involved more than 13,000 coalition troops, the majority of which were U.S., and was conducted concurrently with a Pakistani offensive against the Taliban in that country's northwest provinces and with a new effort by ISAF to deploy provincial reconstruction teams in the more stable areas of Afghanistan. MOUNTAIN STORM lasted into July and was undertaken in an effort to stabilize the country ahead of the October presidential elections. Meanwhile, the Taliban and its allies increased their use of terrorist tactics, including suicide bombings and assassinations of Afghan officials and progovernment figures.

The Second Phase of Major Operations (2005–2008)

Operation LIGHTNING FREEDOM was initiated by OEF forces in December 2004 and continued through the winter of 2005. It included a succession of minor operations and was similar to earlier campaigns designed to preempt offensive action by the Taliban in the spring of 2005. However, the operation occurred at the same time as an offer of amnesty for insurgents from the Afghan government. The United States hoped to reduce its forces in Afghanistan following the legislative elections on September 18, 2005, if the amnesty was successful. However, relatively few Taliban took advantage of the offer and the organization instead increased its terrorist attacks. By the end of the year, the Afghan National Army numbered 20,000 men, of varying quality, with plans to expand their number to 70,000.

Narcotics production expanded dramatically in the post-Taliban era. By 2005, Afghanistan was the world's largest producer of opium; at least 20 percent of the population was economically dependent on poppy production, which accounted for approximately 60 percent of the country's gross domestic product. Although President Karzai declared a "jihad" against opium, efforts to suppress poppy production were resisted by some within the Afghan government for fear of alienating progovernment militia leaders. Meanwhile, the Taliban and antigovernment insurgents became increasingly involved in the narcotics trade, which they used to finance their operations. It was estimated that at least 70 percent of their expenses were paid for through drug sales. Coalition military leaders initially resisted pressure to undertake counternarcotics operations, arguing the need to instead concentrate on anti-Taliban efforts. However, in 2004, the OEF forces were authorized to conduct operations against narcotics, including the destruction of production and arresting drug traffickers and turning them over to Afghan security forces. Nonetheless, between 2005 and 2006, poppy production rose by almost 60 percent, and it continued to increase through 2007 and 2008. In October 2008, NATO agreed to increase its counternarcotics activities, following a decision by the Afghan government to take greater steps to suppress poppy production.

The Taliban and other antigovernment factions dramatically increased their attacks in 2006. During 2005 there were approximately 1,500 strikes against coalition forces, but that number rose to 5,000 the following year, while the number of roadside bombings doubled to more than 1,650 and suicide attacks increased more than 500 percent to 139. The Taliban established new bases and a new presence in regions that had not been stabilized by OEF or ISAF. In response, the coalition increasingly relied on air power to attack suspected Taliban bases and formations. During 2006, the coalition conducted more than 2,000 air strikes, the most since the initial invasion of Afghanistan. Although many of these were carried out with precision-guided weaponry, there was also a dramatic increase in the number of civilian casualties. This served to undermine popular support for both the coalition and the Afghan national government.

The coalition also launched a new series of campaigns in 2006. In April, U.S., British, and Afghan national forces initiated Operation MOUNTAIN LION in the Kunar, Nuristan, and Nangahar provinces along the northwest border with Pakistan. Although there was heavy fighting, casualties were light among both coalition and Taliban forces. Significantly, the 2,500 troops of the Afghan National Army who participated were widely praised for their performance during the offensive, which destroyed a number of Taliban bases. MOUNTAIN LION was followed by Operation MOUNTAIN THRUST, which began on June 15, 2006. The largest coalition action to date, it included more than 11,000 U.S., British, Canadian, and Afghan troops. MOUNTAIN THRUST was the first major coalition operation in the Uruzgan and Helmand provinces in southern Afghanistan. Coalition forces suffered 24 killed, while at least 1,000 Taliban were killed and more than 400 were captured. The campaign lasted into July.

In 2006, ISAF launched its first significant offensive missions. In September, NATO began Operation MEDUSA, which included about 2,000 ISAF troops from Canada, Denmark, the Netherlands, the United Kingdom, the United States, and the Afghan army. Twenty-seven coalition troops were killed, while an estimated

400–500 Taliban lost their lives. The campaign was undertaken to extend government control over rural areas near Kandahar and allow the construction of a road system. Soon after the operation ended on September 17, large numbers of Taliban returned to the area and initiated attacks on construction works. As MEDUSA ended, OEF forces, including 3,000 U.S. and 4,000 Afghan troops, launched Operation MOUNTAIN FURY in the eastern central provinces of the country. British and Canadian units also participated in the fighting in what was dubbed Operation FALCON SUMMIT. In one of the fiercest battles of the campaign, on December 5 British forces were forced to retreat under heavy fire from the Taliban before aerial support destroyed the enemy positions. On December 19, Mullah Akhtar Mohammad Osmani, the Taliban commander in the south, was killed by a NATO air assault. MOUNTAIN FURY ended on January 17, 2007. The coalition suffered 107 killed, 71 of them Afghan soldiers. The Taliban sustained more than 1,100 killed and 179 captured.

In February 2007, British forces in ISAF began Operation VOLCANO to secure territory around the Kajaki Dam in the Helmand Province. There were some 700 Taliban in 25 separate compounds around the dam. The campaign was successful, but NATO undertook a broader offensive mission to stabilize areas in the Helmand Province and remove the approximately 4,000–5,000 Taliban and antigovernment militia forces in that region. Operation ACHILLES

U.S. marines of the 2nd Battalion, 8th Marine Regiment, firing on attacking Taliban forces at Patrol Base Bracha in the Garmsir District of Helmand Province, Afghanistan, October 9, 2009. (U.S. Department of Defense)

began in March 2007 and was the largest NATO offensive operation to date. It involved 6,500 troops from Canada, Denmark, the Netherlands, the United Kingdom, the United States, and the Afghan National Army. The majority of combat involved running battles and ambushes between NATO troops and bands of 10–50 insurgents. Mullah Dadullah, the operational commander of the Taliban, was killed in a NATO attack on May 13. He was the most senior Taliban killed in Afghanistan to that time. Achilles ended on May 31. There were 34 coalition soldiers killed during the fighting and an estimated 700–1,000 Taliban casualties.

The British launched Operation PICKAXE HANDLE as a follow-on to ACHILLES. Some 2,000 NATO troops continued operations against the remaining 2,000–3,000 insurgents in Helmand. Twelve ISAF soldiers were killed and approximately 150 Taliban died. Significantly, ACHILLES and PICKAXE HANDLE preempted an anticipated large-scale Taliban offensive in the Helmand Province. In October, coalition forces engaged the Taliban in two separate battles after detecting large formations.

By 2008, there were approximately 10,000 Taliban and other antigovernment forces in Afghanistan or in bases in Pakistan. As coalition forces continued to endeavor to expand government control, more frequent clashes with insurgent forces occurred. In addition, the Taliban launched more significant operations. For instance, in June a Taliban operation against a detention facility in Kandahar freed more than 1,000 prisoners, including 400 fighters. In April, a Taliban ambush killed 10 French soldiers and wounded 21, the most significant losses suffered by France to this point in the war. In late 2008, the United States began conducting special operations forces missions and bombing of suspected Taliban bases in Pakistan in an escalation of the Afghan conflict through an effort to disrupt insurgent attacks.

By the end of 2009, coalition forces had lost 1,567 killed in Afghanistan since 2001, with 946 of these being U.S. personnel. The total for 2009 (520 coalition troops killed, of which 316 were U.S. troops) was nearly double that of the previous year (295 and 155, respectively). In addition, at least 5,500 Afghan security forces troops have been killed. Overall insurgent losses have been estimated to be between 25,000 and 30,000, with 20,000 captured. There are no reliable statistics on civilian deaths attributable to the war, but these are believed to be at least 25,000.

TOM LANSFORD

See also

ACHILLES, Operation; Casualties, Operation ENDURING FREEDOM; Hungary, Role in Persian Gulf, Afghanistan, and Iraq Wars; Italy, Armed Forces in Iraq and Afghanistan; New Zealand, Role in Persian Gulf, Afghanistan, and Iraq Wars; North Atlantic Treaty Organization in Afghanistan; Norway, Role in Persian Gulf, Afghanistan, and Iraq Wars; United Kingdom Forces in Afghanistan

References

Bhatia, Michael, and Mark Sedra. *Afghanistan, Arms and Conflict: Armed Groups, Disarmament and Security in a Post-War Society*. New York: Routledge, 2008.

Crews, Robert D., and Amin Tarzi, eds. *The Taliban and the Crisis of Afghanistan*. Cambridge: Harvard University Press, 2008.

Feickert, Andrew. *U.S. and Coalition Military Operations in Afghanistan: Issues for Congress*. Washington, DC: Congressional Research Service, 2006.

Guistozzi, Antonio. *Koran, Kalashnikov and Laptop: The Neo-Taliban Insurgency in Afghanistan*. New York: Columbia University Press, 2008.

Jones, Seth G. *Counterinsurgency in Afghanistan: RAND Counterinsurgency Study No. 4*. Santa Monica, CA: RAND Corporation, 2008.

———. *In the Graveyard of Empires: America's War in Afghanistan*. New York: Norton, 2009.

Mills, Greg. *From Africa to Afghanistan: With Richards and NATO to Kabul*. Johannesburg: Wits University Press, 2007.

Ryan, Mike. *Battlefield Afghanistan*. London: Spellmount, 2007.

Sinno, Abdulkader. *Organizations at War in Afghanistan and Beyond*. Ithaca, NY: Cornell University Press, 2008.

Afghanistan, Economic Cost of Soviet Invasion and Occupation of

On December 24, 1979, Soviet troops began an invasion of Afghanistan. The invasion and occupation of Afghanistan ended up a costly affair that lasted nearly nine years, until February 1989. The Soviets found themselves involved in a frustrating military conflict with Afghan mujahideen, resistance fighters backed primarily by the United States and Saudi Arabia.

Meanwhile, rising military expenditures, dwindling oil revenues, and an inflexible centrally planned economy had led to economic stagnation in the Soviet Union. An anemic Soviet growth rate of 1 to 1.9 percent from 1975 to 1980 fell further: from 1980 to 1985, the annual Soviet growth rate averaged between 0.6 percent and 1.8 percent. By 1980, nearly one-third of the Soviet Union's gross national product (GNP) went to capital investment, mainly in military expenditures. Soviet involvement in Afghanistan was a major catalyst for the economic malaise and eventual collapse of the Soviet Union.

While it is difficult to gauge the exact economic costs of the invasion and occupation of Afghanistan, the U.S. State Department has estimated that Soviet expenditures ran from about $3 billion per year in the early 1980s to as much as $8.2 billion per year by 1988–1989. A 1987 Central Intelligence Agency (CIA) report came up with a much higher estimate, for military costs alone, of approximately $48 billion from 1980 through 1986.

To some extent, these spiraling expenditures resulted from U.S. policy, particularly after the election of President Ronald Reagan in 1980. The so-called Reagan Doctrine, aimed at supporting anti-Soviet and anticommunist resistance movements around the world, helped to fund the mujahideen. With the support of its ally, neighboring Pakistan, the United States covertly assisted in training and equipping the mujahideen. With the insurgents now armed with heavy machine guns and U.S. Stinger antiaircraft missiles, Soviet forces suffered crippling losses. From 1980 to 1985, more than 700 Soviet aircraft were destroyed, along with more than 7,000 armored vehicles, trucks, tanks, and artillery pieces. By the mid-1980s, about 90 percent of the direct Soviet expenditures for Afghanistan went to replacing destroyed aircraft.

Additionally, the cost of training, transferring, and maintaining a total of some 120,000 Soviet occupation troops was exacerbated by defections and the black-market sales of arms to rebel insurgents. Other less-tangible economic costs of the Soviet foray into Afghanistan are more difficult to determine. The effects of an increasingly unpopular war on Soviet labor productivity and production quality was substantial. In addition, increasing drug abuse among Soviet soldiers and interethnic tensions that pitted Muslim against non-Muslim republics within the Soviet Union had negative economic repercussions for the Soviet Union. Indeed, the interethnic strife hastened the process that led to the collapse of the Soviet Union in 1991.

Even after the Soviet troop withdrawal, the cost of postoccupation support, particularly in military hardware, was estimated at $4 billion in 1989. From a nonmilitary perspective, Afghanistan also consumed an increasing percentage of Soviet foreign aid. In 1983–1984, Afghanistan received less than 10 percent of Soviet foreign aid, adding up to a total of about $1.5 billion during the first five years of the conflict. By 1991, however, Afghanistan was the recipient of 70 percent of the Soviet Union's foreign aid budget.

ANNA M. WITTMANN

See also

Afghanistan; Cold War; Mujahideen, Soviet-Afghanistan War; Reagan, Ronald Wilson; Soviet-Afghanistan War; Soviet Union, Middle East Policy

References

Arnold, Antony. *The Fateful Pebble: Afghanistan's Role in the Fall of the Soviet Empire*. Novato, CA: Presidio, 1993.

United States Central Intelligence Agency, Directorate of Intelligence. *At Cold War's End: U.S. Intelligence on the Soviet Union and Eastern Europe, 1989–1991*. Benjamin B. Fischer, ed. Reston, VA: Central Intelligence Agency, 1999.

Afghanistan, Soviet War in

See Soviet-Afghanistan War

Afghanistan Freedom Support Act of 2002

Comprehensive legislation authorizing the provision of economic, democratic, and military assistance to Afghanistan subsequent to the removal of the Taliban from power. The act was sponsored by U.S. senator Charles T. "Chuck" Hagel (R-Neb.) and passed by Congress on November 14, 2002. President George W. Bush signed the act into law on December 4, 2002.

The year 2002 witnessed the continuation of decades of violence and conflict in Afghanistan. Fighting against the Soviet Union in the 1980s and civil war during the following decade had wrought human suffering and the destruction of infrastructure throughout the country. The rise of the Taliban to power in 1996 brought further suffering to the Afghan people. These decades of constant conflict spawned the emergence of four intertwining economies. They included a war economy based on arms trafficking, looting, and black market activity; a drug economy focused on the poppy trade; a humanitarian economy driven by drought, poverty, and violence, and dependent upon foreign aid for survival; and an agricultural economy that had sustained the country prior to the civil war of the 1990s. Inherent conflicts resonated within this economic mosaic, further prohibiting any chance of stabilization and growth.

Throughout the decades of violence, the United States contributed huge amounts of aid, either directly or via international relief agencies. The 1990s witnessed the United States contributing the largest amount of assistance to Afghanistan than any other foreign provider. However, the emergence of Taliban rule from 1996 to 2001 forced the United States to contribute aid through relief agency intermediaries. Even then, the United States provided $500 million in emergency aid to the Afghan people.

The removal of the Taliban from power in late 2001 during Operation ENDURING FREEDOM and the subsequent formation of an interim government favorable to international assistance providers opened additional and more substantial avenues for the flow of aid. The U.S. complement of humanitarian assistance in fiscal year 2001 amounted to $184.3 million. Fiscal year 2002 appropriations increased to $530 million, and fiscal year 2003 funding amounted to $295.5 million. These allotments did not include military costs incurred through continued U.S. involvement in Operation ENDURING FREEDOM and other military activities.

The most significant U.S. aid legislation in the post-Taliban era, however, was the most far-reaching and targeted other than humanitarian needs, including the negative consequences stemming from the drug economy and Taliban treatment of women. The Afghanistan Freedom Support Act of 2002 authorized two major forms of assistance totaling $3.7 billion over the fiscal year 2003–2006 period. First, the economic and democratic development assistance portion of the act focused on a host of emergency humanitarian needs and economic development aid in the amount of $1.7 billion, including repatriation and resettlement of refugees and Afghans displaced internally in the country, as well as basic needs for water, food, health care, and shelter. The economic aid focused on the cultivation of a market economy with the promotion of small industry, establishment of financial institutions, development of trade relations with other countries within the region, and reconstruction efforts. Congress also recognized the impact of the drug economy by authorizing $60 million in counter-narcotics assistance over a four-year period, to include poppy eradication programs, training of Afghan enforcement agencies in drug interdiction, and the disruption of heroin production.

Assistance for political development to coincide with efforts to stabilize the Afghan economy included a $30 million outlay for national, regional, and local elections. Additional areas of aid focus included the reestablishment of such basic infrastructure elements as transportation, health, sanitation, and urban services, and the stabilization and development of the agricultural economy. The act also provided a total of $80 million to Afghan agencies responsible for providing health care and educational services to women, and for monitoring of rights for women and children. These provisions augmented the educational and health care benefits embodied in a previous authorization bill, the Afghan Women and Children Relief Act of 2001.

The second major title of the act addressed military assistance for Afghanistan. Congress made it clear that the goal of transitioning to a fully representative government in Afghanistan required U.S. support of a trained Afghan army and police force dedicated to human rights, civilian control, and a broad representation of Afghan society. Accordingly, $300 million was devoted to the core needs for developing such an army and police force: defense materials, equipment, and services; and military and counternarcotics training and education. An additional $1 billion was also authorized to expand the International Security Assistance Force responsible for peacekeeping in Afghanistan and led by the North Atlantic Treaty Organization. Military costs associated with the ongoing Operation ENDURING FREEDOM were not included in the act.

Recommendations made by the U.S. 9/11 Commission prodded Congress in 2004 to promulgate amendments to the 2002 act to strengthen the oversight and monitoring mechanisms of U.S. assistance activities in Afghanistan. The initial act and its subsequent amendments highlighted a U.S. history of active support for Afghanistan, and telegraphed a firm U.S. future commitment to the war-torn country.

MARK F. LEEP

See also

Afghanistan; ENDURING FREEDOM, Operation; International Security Assistance Force

References

Katzman, Kenneth. *Afghanistan: Post-War Governance, Security, and U.S. Policy.* Washington, DC: Congressional Research Service, September 2008.

Margesson, Rhoda, and Johanna Bockman. *Reconstruction Assistance in Afghanistan: Goals, Priorities, and Issues for Congress.* Washington, DC: Congressional Research Service, February 2003.

Afghan National Army

Military force charged with carrying out Afghanistan's national defense and the fulfillment of international mutual defense responsibilities. Active since the 1880s, the Afghan National Army (ANA) is also known as the National Army of Afghanistan. Its strength in October 2008 was about 80,000 men, although its numbers have been steadily increasing.

Afghan National Army forces and U.S. marines moving to establish a patrol base in the Garmsir District of Helmand Province in Afghanistan, October 2009. (U.S. Department of Defense)

The ANA is commanded by General Bismillah Khan Mohammadi, chief of staff since 2002, and is currently being trained by coalition forces to take the lead in land-based military operations in that country. In January 2003, slightly more than 1,700 soldiers in five *kandaks* (Pashtun for battalions) had completed the 10-week training course; by June of that year, a total of 4,000 soldiers had been trained. However, desertions have consistently plagued the ANA, with the desertion rate estimated to be some 10 percent.

At present, the ANA encompasses five corps, each serving as a regional command. The 201st Corps is based in Kabul, the 203rd Corps in Gardez, the 205th Corps in Kandahar, the 207th Corps in Herat, and the 209th Corps in Mazar-e Sharif. During 2002–2003, soldiers in the army initially received $30 per month during training, and $50 per month upon graduation; pay for trained soldiers has since risen to $120 per month. Many recruits were under 18 years of age and could not read or write, while those who spoke only Pashto experienced further difficulty because instruction was given through interpreters who spoke Farsi.

Since 2001, the United States has contributed more than $2 billion worth of military equipment and facilities to supply the ANA.

This figure will be supplemented by a further $2 billion worth of military aid, to be delivered perhaps in 2009, which will consist of 2,500 Humvees; tens of thousands of M-16 assault rifles and body armor; and the construction of a national military command center. The army's current equipment comprises a range of small arms, including the AK-47, AK-74, and M16A2 rifles, and the RPK light machine gun. The ANA also has more than 800 armored vehicles of varying types, T-55 and T-62 tanks, RPG-7 antitank weapons, and both the D-30 122-millimeter (mm) and M114 155-mm model howitzers. The basic unit in the ANA is the *kandak,* comprising 600 troops, of which at least one is mechanized and one is a tank battalion. An elite special forces unit modeled after the U.S. Army Rangers is in development, with plans to include 3,900 men in six battalions under French and U.S. tutelage. As of September 2005, 28 of the 31 ANA battalions were ready for direct combat operations and a great number had already been appropriately trained. By March 2007 almost half of the planned army of 70,000 soldiers had been raised, with 46 Afghan battalions operating alongside North Atlantic Treaty Organization (NATO) forces.

The ANA has also benefited from genial relations with India, as highlighted by the 2001 Bonn Agreement, in which governments of other nations were asked to support the rebuilding of Afghanistan. Deliveries of military goods from other nations commenced in June 2003; India has already contributed 50 four-and-a-half-ton trucks, 300 other trucks, 120 jeeps, and 15 ambulances.

Despite enjoying cordial relations with India, Afghanistan has endured fraught relations with neighboring Pakistan, and the ANA has sporadically engaged in cross-border fire exchanges with Pakistani troops. On March 2, 2007, the ANA fired rockets on a Pakistani army border post in the Kudakhel area, while in a separate incident a border clash erupted between Afghan soldiers and Pakistani troops, who overnight had seized areas in the border region of Paktika Province in the southeast of the country.

Relations between Pakistan and Afghanistan are especially strained on the issue of border security, and President Hamid Karzai has accused the Pakistanis of doing too little to restrain Islamist militants. On June 15, 2008, Karzai insisted that Afghanistan retained the right to pursue Taliban fighters who flee into Pakistan tribal regions after executing attacks in Afghanistan. Shortly thereafter, on June 21, 2008, artillery shells launched from Pakistan engaged the Afghan military and NATO troops. Karzai's threat to send Afghan troops into Pakistan in pursuit of militants has generated heated debate on cross-border military incursions and international law. In return, Pakistani prime minister Yusuf Raza Gillani responded that his country would not allow Afghan troops in, although he stressed that Pakistan wished to maintain friendly ties with Afghanistan.

Since the commencement of the ANA's collaboration with coalition forces in 2002, a number of successful military operations have been conducted. On March 7, 2007, Afghan soldiers captured the senior Taliban leader and expert bomb-maker, Mullah Mahmood, near Kandahar. Perhaps the most notable maneuver was Operation ACHILLES, executed on March 6, 2007 by the ANA and International

Approximate Troop Strength of the Afghan National Army, 2003–2009

Date	Approximate Number of Troops
September 2003	6,000
June 2004	13,400
January 2005	17,800
February 2006	26,900
June 2007	50,000
May 2008	76,600
April 2009	82,800

Security Assistance Forces (ISAF) against Taliban insurgents. Over a 24-hour period, 1,000 ANA troops and forces from Britain, Denmark, Canada, the United States, and the Netherlands successfully engaged Taliban extremist strongholds in addition to enemy compounds used as arms and ammunition storage facilities in the Garmsir area in Helmand Province, in the southwest of the country.

The ANA's goal to increase troop strength has to date proven fruitful, with figures estimated in December 2007 at 57,000. While the objective in recent years has been to bring the strength up to 70,000 troops, the Afghan defense ministry has stated that a 200,000-strong ANA would be in the interest of both Afghanistan and the international community.

K. LUISA GANDOLFO

See also

ACHILLES, Operation; Bonn Agreement; Global War on Terror; International Security Assistance Force; Karzai, Hamid; Pakistan; Pakistan, Armed Forces; Taliban Insurgency, Afghanistan

References

Dorronsoro, Gilles. *Afghanistan: Revolution Unending, 1979–2002.* London: C. Hurst, 2003.

Hodes, Cyrus, and Mark Sedra. *The Search for Security in Post-Taliban Afghanistan.* Adelphi Paper 391. Abingdon, UK: Routledge for the International Institute for Strategic Studies, 2007.

Maley, William. *The Afghanistan Wars.* New York: Palgrave Macmillan, 2002.

Rotberg, Robert I. *Building a New Afghanistan.* Washington, DC: Brookings Institution Press, 2007.

Aflaq, Michel
Birth Date: 1910
Death Date: June 29, 1989

Syrian attorney, writer, proponent of Arab Nationalism, and cofounder of the Baath Party. Michel Aflaq was born into a Greek Orthodox family in Damascus in 1910. He was educated at the Greek Orthodox Lyceum in Damascus and attended the University of Paris during 1928–1934, graduating with a degree in law. During this time, he met Salah ad-Din al-Bitar, a fellow student from Syria. Aflaq's education exposed him to the ideas of the European Enlightenment and French revolutionary periods and the rise of nationalism in the 19th century.

Returning to Damascus, Aflaq taught history and published short stories, a novel, and a play. He and Bitar flirted with Marxism for a time, but were disillusioned by Soviet support for the Franco-Syrian Treaty of 1936, which gave Syria only limited independence. They then organized Syrian students within a framework of Pan-Arab nationalism and published pamphlets. In 1941, they established the Syrian Committee to Help Iraq, sending arms and volunteers for a rebellion against British rule. The committee soon evolved into the Baath (Arab Resurrection) Party.

By 1944, the Baath Party had an office and newspaper in Damascus, and in April 1947 it adopted a constitution. Aflaq was the head of the party. The constitution asserted 3 fundamental principles and 48 articles. The fundamentals were unity and freedom for the "Arab Nation"; basic freedoms for the Arab Nation, which included freedom of speech, assembly, and religion; and repudiation of colonialism. It further declared the Baath Party was the universal Arab party that would lead a socialist revolution and secure equal rights for all, including women; an elected parliament; an independent judiciary; and a legal code based on the spirit of the times and Arab history. The constitution was profoundly secular.

In a 1940 essay, Aflaq defined nationalism as "love before everything else. It is the very same feeling that binds the individual to his family, because the fatherland is only a large household, and the nation a large family." Aflaq's ideology was an amalgam of European ideas overlaid on Arab culture. It embodied the secular nature of the Enlightenment, 19th-century European nationalism with a strong hint of Romanticism, the ideals of human rights as voiced in the French "Declaration of the Rights of Man" and the U.S. Bill of Rights, and the economic doctrines of socialism. Socialism, however, was subordinate to the needs of the state.

Aflaq and Bitar were well-respected members of the Syrian educated class, but they had to appeal to other Syrian leaders to advance their ideas. These alliances became important in Syrian politics and the development of Arab nationalism in the post–World War II period. Although Aflaq was unsuccessful in a run for parliament in 1943, the founding of the party led him to hope that he would become a national and Pan-Arab political figure. After losing a run for a seat on the constitutional assembly, he became involved in intraparty conflicts and moves to cooperate with other parties in elections.

Aflaq worked with Akram al-Hawrani, a military officer and leader of the Arab Socialist Party, to merge their parties into an Arab Socialist Baath Party to compete for power in Syria. When this failed, Aflaq went into exile in 1953. Five years later in 1958, he returned to support the union of Syria and Egypt into the United Arab Republic (UAR).

Perceiving that Egypt might dominate the smaller Syria, Aflaq again went into exile in 1959, but continued to be secretary general of the Baath Party even after its official dissolution by the UAR. When Syria seceded from the UAR in 1961, the Baath Party resumed its activities and extended them to Iraq. By the time the Baath came to power in Syria in 1966, Aflaq's influence had declined even more as he vocally opposed those who placed Syria ahead of the Pan-Arab movement. This led to his dismissal from the party and another period in exile. (In 1971 Syrian president Hafiz al-Asad sentenced Aflaq to death in absentia.)

Nevertheless, the burgeoning Iraqi Baath Party continued to recognize Aflaq as secretary general, but this did not lead to a leading political role for him when the party launched a successful coup in Iraq in 1968. In 1980, Aflaq moved to Baghdad, where he was revered as a senior statesman and Pan-Arab secretary-general of the party, but he had no actual power. With his health deteriorating, Aflaq underwent heart surgery in Paris, where he died on June 29, 1989. His death was reported in Baghdad, but ignored in Damascus.

Daniel E. Spector

See also

Arab Nationalism; Baath Party; Iraq, History of, Pre-1990; Pan-Arabism and Pan-Arabist Thought; Syria; United Arab Republic

References

Devlin, John F. *The Ba'th Party: A History from its Origins to 1966.* Stanford, CA: Hoover Institution Press, 1966.

Haim, Sylvia G., ed. *Arab Nationalism: An Anthology.* Berkeley: University of California Press, 1962.

Simons, Geoff. *Iraq: From Sumer to Saddam.* New York: St. Martin's, 1994.

Aidid, Mohammed Farrah
Birth Date: December 15, 1934
Death Date: August 2, 1996

Somali military officer, politician, and warlord. Mohammed Farrah Aidid (Aideed) was born in Beledweyne, the central region of Somalia, to the Habar Gidir clan, on December 15, 1934. The nickname "Aidid" means "rejecter of insults" and was given to him by his mother when it was imputed that he might have been conceived out of wedlock. Through family connections, Aidid learned Italian and became a member of the Italian-trained colonial police force, the Corpo di Polizia della Somalia. In 1954 the police force chose to send him to the Italian infantry school in Rome. After this, Aidid held a series of government positions in Somalia. In 1959 he returned to Italy for additional professional training. He returned to Somalia in 1960 and became an aide to Major General Daud Adbulle Hirsi, commander of the Somali National Army. After this, Aidid underwent staff training for three years at the Frunze Military Academy in Moscow.

Aidid spent five years in prison during 1969–1975 when Mohamed Siad Barre overthrew the democratic government and made himself head of state. Upon his release, Aidid served in a series of unimportant posts, but when the Ogaden War of 1977–1978 with Ethiopia began, Aidid became a brigadier general and an aide to Barre. He later became head of the Somalia intelligence service. In 1984, Aidid became Somali ambassador to India.

Throughout his regime, Barre faced significant opposition from Somalia's clans. In 1989 Aidid moved publicly into the opposition and became head of the United Somali Congress, which had been founded in Rome to oppose Barre's leadership. In this position, Aidid played a key role in forcing Barre from Mogadishu in 1991.

With Barre's removal, Somalia quickly degenerated into a state of civil war. Ali Mahdi Mohammed outmaneuvered Aidid to become president, whereupon Aidid again moved into opposition to the government. The conflict between Aidid and Ali Mahdi Mohammed divided the capital city of Mogadishu, with Aidid controlling the south and Mahdi the northern half. The ensuing civil warfare and escalating clan conflicts impoverished the nation and resulted in widespread famine, which international relief organizations and the United Nations attempted to address. By this time, many observers had begun referring to Aidid as a "warlord."

Aidid opposed the presence of United Nations troops in his nation, and his forces were responsible for the deaths of UN troops in ambushes in June 1991. These attacks and the worsening humanitarian crisis resulted in United States troops being dispatched to Somalia for Operation RESTORE HOPE, which commenced in December 1992. The United States withdrew completely from the venture after the October 3, 1993, incident that saw the shooting down of two U.S. Black Hawk attack helicopters by Somali rebels. The deaths of 18 U.S. soldiers (84 more were wounded) and hundreds of Somalis, perhaps as many as 1,500 people in all, prompted the United States to terminate the operation.

Aidid cleverly evaded capture during the Battle of Mogadishu (October 3–4, 1993), invaded Baidoa, and in September 1995 made himself president of the Somali Republic. Once he was president, however, his base began to disintegrate and his regime faced the same sort of armed internal dissent that Barre and Ali Mahdi Mohammed had endured. On August 1, 1996, Aidid was shot in the Mogadishu suburbs; he returned to his home where he died on August 2, 1996. Several prominent newspapers reported that the United States Central Intelligence Agency (CIA) or Special Operations were involved in Aidid's death.

MICHAEL BEAUCHAMP

See also

Somalia, International Intervention in

References

Bowden, Mark. *Black Hawk Down: A Story of Modern War.* 1st ed. New York: Atlantic Monthly Press, 1999.

Peterson, Scott. *Me against My Brother: At War in Somalia, Sudan, and Rwanda.* New York: Routledge, 2000.

Airborne Warning and Control System

A modified Boeing 707/320 (known in this configuration as E-3 Sentry) commercial airframe with a rotating radar dome that provides integrated command and control battle management (C2BM), all-altitude and all-weather surveillance, target detection and tracking, and early warning of enemy actions during joint, allied, and coalition operations.

The E-3's radar dome is 30 feet in diameter, 6 feet thick, and is positioned 11 feet above the fuselage by two struts. It contains a radar subsystem that permits surveillance from the earth's surface up into the stratosphere, over land or water. The radar, with a range of more than 250 miles and an identification friend or foe (IFF) subsystem, can look down to detect, identify, and track enemy and friendly low-flying aircraft by eliminating ground clutter returns that confuse other radar systems. Major subsystems in the E-3 are avionic, navigation, communications, radar, and passive detection sensors. The mission suite includes consoles that display computer-processed data in graphic and tabular format on video screens.

The radar and computer subsystems on the E-3 Sentry can gather and present broad and detailed battlefield information that includes position and tracking information of potentially hostile aircraft and ships and the location and status of friendly aircraft and naval vessels. The information can be sent to major command and control centers in rear areas or aboard ships and can also be forwarded to the president and secretary of defense in the United States. The Sentry can provide direct information for interdiction, reconnaissance, airlift, and close-air support for friendly ground forces. It also provides information for commanders of air operations so that they can gain and maintain control of the air battle and can direct fighter-interceptor aircraft to enemy targets. It can detect threats and control assets below and beyond the coverage of ground-based command and control (C2) and can exchange data with other C2 systems and shooters via data links.

As an airborne warning and control system (AWAC), the Sentry can change its flight path to meet changing mission and survival requirements. It can stay aloft for about eight hours without refueling and has in-flight refueling capability to extend its range and on-station time.

The U.S. Air Force began engineering, testing, and evaluation of the first E-3 Sentry in October 1975. In March 1977, the 552nd Airborne Warning and Control Wing (now 552nd Air Control Wing), Tinker Air Force Base, Oklahoma, received the first E-3s. The air force currently possesses 33 such aircraft. The North Atlantic Treaty Organization (NATO) obtained 17 E-3s and support equipment. The United Kingdom has 7 E-3s, France has 4, and Saudi Arabia possesses 5. Japan has 4 AWACS (Airborne Warning and Control System) housed on a Boeing 767 airframe.

Between 1977 and 1991, the E-3 Sentry registered numerous significant achievements. Air Force E-3s provided surveillance for an ongoing border dispute between North and South Yemen and assumed an ongoing commitment to support the North American Aerospace Defense Command in defense of North America. In October 1979, E-3s provided surveillance of the Korean peninsula after the assassination of President Park Chung-hee. In September 1980, U.S. Air Force E-3s began Operation EUROPEAN

The E-3 Sentry Air Warning and Control System (AWACS) can detect, identify, and track enemy aircraft from great distances and direct fighter-interceptor aircraft to the enemy targets. AWACS has been a critical tool for allied forces during the U.S. wars in the Middle East. (U.S. Department of Defense)

LIAISON FORCE (ELF) I, an eight-year deployment to Saudi Arabia during the Iran-Iraq War.

The E-3 Sentry provided airborne surveillance and battlefield management during Operation URGENT FURY, the invasion of Grenada, in November 1983; and for Operation JUST CAUSE, the invasion of Panama, in December 1989. The E-3 Sentry also provided airborne surveillance of the Caribbean Sea and Central America as part of the Department of Defense's participation in counternarcotic operations. In September 1994, the E-3 Sentry supported Operation UPHOLD DEMOCRACY, which ousted Haitian military leaders and returned the elected leader, Jean-Bertrand Aristide, to power.

After the Iraqi invasion of Kuwait in August 1991, E-3s deployed to the Persian Gulf region. When Operation DESERT STORM began on January 17, 1991, four Air Force Sentries were airborne at all times. A typical DESERT STORM E-3 mission lasted 16 to 18 hours, and each E-3 carried at least two full crews. The Sentries controlled more than 3,000 combat sorties per day and achieved a mission-capable rate of 98 percent. E-3 aircrews flew more than 7,300 combat hours with an average 91.36 percent mission-capable rate. They controlled almost 32,000 strike sorties without losing a single allied aircraft in air-to-air action and controlled 20,400 aerial refueling sorties.

After the Persian Gulf War, E-3s at Incirlik Air Base (AB), Turkey, provided surveillance support for Operation PROVIDE COMFORT and, later, Operation NORTHERN WATCH, enforcing the UN-sanctioned no-fly zone north of the 36th Parallel in Iraq. E-3 aircraft in Saudi Arabia provided postwar surveillance for Operation SOUTHERN WATCH and guided several air strikes against Iraqi targets in response to Iraqi violations of the no-fly zone imposed by the United Nations. E-3s of the United States Air Forces in Europe (USAFE) took part in Operation ALLIED FORCE against Serbia, which began on March 24, 1999.

Immediately after the terrorist attacks on the United States of September 11, 2001, Air Force E-3s were quickly airborne to patrol the airspace over the eastern United States for Operation NOBLE EAGLE, which has continued to the present. For Operation ENDURING FREEDOM, which began on October 7, 2001, U.S. Air Force and Royal Saudi Air Forces E-3s provided air surveillance and battlefield management over Afghanistan.

The air campaign for Operation IRAQI FREEDOM began on March 21, 2003. The U.S. Air Force provided six E-3s, operating from Prince Sultan AB, Saudi Arabia, and three from Royal Air Force (RAF) Akrotiri, Cyprus. The RAF also operated nine E-3s from RAF Akrotiri. The E-3s worked closely with the E-8 Joint Surveillance Target Attack Radar System (JSTARS) and RC-135 Rivet Joint aircraft throughout IRAQI FREEDOM to direct strike aircraft against emerging ground threats and to keep commanders informed of the current battlefield status. To date, E-3 Sentry crews have provided 24-hour surveillance of battle space in Iraq and Afghanistan.

The worst incident involving an E-3 Sentry occurred on April 14, 1994, during Operation PROVIDE COMFORT. Two McDonnel Douglas F-15 Eagle pilots, under the control of an E-3 Sentry, misidentified two U.S. Army Sikorsky UH-60 Black Hawk helicopters as Iraqi Mil Mi-24 "Hind" helicopters violating the no-fly zone. The two pilots fired missiles at the helicopters, destroying both and killing all 26 military and civilian personnel aboard.

The U.S. Air Force has regularly upgraded the E-3's radar systems, sensors, other electronic equipment, and mission software to improve the aircraft's network-centric capabilities. These modifications allow greater use of AWACS mission data, better access to external Web services data, an enhanced suite of battle-management tools, and improved connections to other assets throughout the airborne battle space and with battle managers on the ground.

Since its introduction in the air force inventory, the E-3 Sentry has demonstrated that it is the premier C2BM aircraft in the world through the provision of unrivaled radar surveillance and control and time-critical information on the actions of enemy forces to senior leaders.

ROBERT B. KANE

See also

DESERT STORM, Operation, Coalition Air Campaign; ENDURING FREEDOM, Operation, U.S. Air Campaign; IRAQI FREEDOM, Operation, Air Campaign; Joint Surveillance and Target Radar System Aircraft; Network-Centric Warfare; NORTHERN WATCH, Operation; PROVIDE COMFORT, Operation; SOUTHERN WATCH, Operation

References

Donald, David, ed. *US Air Force Air Power Directory*. London: Aerospace Publishing, 1992.

Knights, Michael. *Cradle of Conflict: Iraq and the Birth of Modern U.S. Military*. Annapolis, MD: Naval Institute Press, 2005.

Lambeth, Benjamin S. *Air Power against Terror: America's Conduct of Operation Enduring Freedom*. Santa Monica, CA: RAND Corporation, 2005.

Putney, Diane T. *Airpower Advantage: Planning the Gulf War Air Campaign, 1989–1991*. Washington, DC: Air Force History and Museum Programs, 2004.

Aircraft, Attack

By the late 1960s, the Middle East had become the primary arena for U.S.-Soviet competition, making its conflicts a crucible in which the contending superpowers' air warfare doctrine, tactics, and aircraft were employed, evaluated, and adjusted. While successes in air-to-air combat drew the headlines, strikes delivered by attack aircraft shaped the ground wars of the Middle East.

The Middle East's oil wealth ensured that most of the region's nations could afford their choice of aircraft and weapons platforms. Pro-West countries acquired Western-made aircraft that focused on precision weapons delivery, good range, and, after

1970, maneuverability and defensive countermeasures equipment. The cheapest and among the most versatile of these aircraft was the single-seat, single-engine, Douglas (later McDonnell Douglas) A-4 Skyhawk. Originally designed in the 1950s as a light U.S. Navy attack aircraft, the A-4 initially cost less than $1 million each. However, the advent of surface-to-air missiles (SAMs) drove the Navy to add several thousand pounds of electronic warning and countermeasures equipment, as well as engine power (the J-52-PW20). The resulting aircraft carried nearly 5,000 pounds of bombs and two AIM-9 infrared-guided Sidewinder missiles in addition to its 20-mm nose cannon. It was light, agile, and simple to fly and maintain. Once it dropped its bombs, its maneuverability proved equal to that of the Soviet-designed Mikoyan-Gurevich MiG-17 fighter. In fact, the U.S. Navy used it as a simulated adversary aircraft at the famed Fighter Weapons School in the late 1970s and 1980s. The Royal Kuwaiti Air Force had nearly 40 in its inventory when Iraq invaded the country in August 1990; 24 of them escaped and later participated in Operation DESERT STORM.

The twin-engine two-seat Grumman A-6E Intruder was the U.S. Navy's all-weather heavy bomber for most of the last four decades of the 20th century. Entering service in 1963 as the A-6A, the Intruder carried the AN/APQ-148 Norden multimode navigation and bomb-aiming radar, an inertial navigation system, and a vast array of electronic warning and countermeasures systems that were operated by the bombardier/navigator. It carried an impressive 18,000 pounds of bombs and other ordnance. Its two Pratt and Whitney J-52 nonafterburning turbojet engines provided 18,600 pounds of thrust. By 1984, the A-6E also carried the instrumentation and guidance systems to guide laser and electro-optically–guided precision weapons onto targets as well as Harpoon antiship cruise missiles. The A-6E also had a Forward Looking Infrared (FLIR) and Target Recognition and Attack, Multi-Sensor (TRAM) system. The last A-6s left naval service in 2003.

The A-6's sister attack aircraft, the Chance Vought A-7 Corsair II replaced the Skyhawk and F-105 Thunderchief in Navy and U.S. Air Force service. Like those earlier aircraft, the A-7 was a single-seat attack plane but had a more powerful and fuel-economical TF-41 P-6 turbofan engine generating over 14,500 pounds of thrust, better avionics, and electronic countermeasures equipment. It also had greater range, carried a heavier bomb load (20,000 pounds), offered more precise bomb aiming, and featured a very accurate inertial navigation system. It carried two AIM-9 AAMs for self-defense. It was also the first U.S. aircraft to have a Heads-Up-Display (HUD) to ease the pilot's cockpit workload. Entering service in 1970, the A-7's AN/APQ-116 radar and digital bombing system enabled pilots to deliver their ordnance more accurately, more than compensating for its reduced maneuverability as compared to the A-4. Its M-61 Vulcan 20-mm cannon also delivered three times the firepower of the A-4's Colt Mark 12.

This aircraft proved very successful in the Vietnam War, but the postwar period saw the introduction of better radar and electronics. The U.S. Air Force transferred all its A-7s to the Air

A U.S. Marine Corps AV-8B Harrier II of Marine Attack Squadron 513 in Operation DESERT SHIELD. (U.S. Department of Defense)

National Guard before 1976, replacing them with A-10s and, eventually, F-117s Stealth bombers. The navy retained theirs, adding improvements to accommodate lessons learned from Vietnam. By 1988, the A-7 had the more powerful and accurate AN/APQ-126 radar and an integrated digital navigation-bombing system with a projected map display system that gave the pilot the plane's precise present and future locations. U.S. Navy A-7Es saw action in the retaliatory strikes over Lebanon in 1983, in Libya in 1986, and in Operations EARNEST WILL and PRAYING MANTIS in 1987–1988. The Navy's last two A-7 squadrons participated in Operation DESERT STORM in 1991 before transitioning to McDonnell Douglas (now Boeing) F/A-18s two years later.

The U.S. Marine Corps (USMC) introduced the Hawker Siddeley Vertical/Short-Takeoff or Landing (V/STOL) AV-8A Harrier in 1970. The single-seat AV-8A is powered by a single Rolls Royce Pegasus nonafterburning turbofan engine generating 21,000 pounds of thrust. The USMC deployed about 72 AV-8As as quick-reaction, short-range light attack aircraft for immediate close air support of expeditionary operations. It carried up to 4,000 pounds of ordnance and drop tanks as well as two AIM-9 AAMs, and could be equipped with a 30-mm cannon pod. The AV-8As were used off the coast of Lebanon in 1982 but had been withdrawn from service by 1988.

These planes were replaced by the improved AV-8B Harrier II, which entered service in 1985. The AV-8B carries FLIR, the AN/

APG-65 radar; a GAU-12U 25-mm cannon; and, if it uses a short takeoff roll, up to 13,000 pounds of ordnance, including Harpoon, HARM, and Maverick missiles, as well as two AIM-120 advanced medium-range air-to-air missile (AMRAAM). If it takes off vertically, the ordnance load drops to approximately 4,000 pounds. The Harrier II served with USMC and Italian forces during Operations DESERT SHIELD, DESERT STORM, ENDURING FREEDOM, and IRAQI FREEDOM. The AV-8B Harrier II and new variants remain in British, Italian, and USMC service through 2008.

The U.S. Air Force's A-7 gave way to the Fairchild-Republic twin-engine A-10 Thunderbolt II by the late 1970s. Universally known as the Warthog, the A-10 was developed specifically for close-air support (CAS) and antitank attack. It was intended to conduct both deep strikes against Soviet-era mass tank formations and provide CAS support to army ground units. Its two GE TF-30 GE100 turbofan engines provide 9,065 pounds of thrust each and are located in armored nacelles high above the tail to protect them from runway rocks, dust, sand, and ground fire. The pilot sits in an armored "tub," and the plane's controls also have armor protection. The A-10 can take multiple direct hits from 23-mm cannon fire and even withstand hits by shoulder-fired surface-to-air missiles under some circumstances. It is equipped with a HUD; inertial navigation and precision-guided munitions instrumentation; and infrared and electronic warning and countermeasures systems. Its light wing-loading gives it exceptional maneuverability at low speed, and its GAU/8 30-mm cannon can destroy any armored vehicle in service. More importantly, it can carry up to 16,000 pounds of bombs or missiles.

The A-10 proved devastating against Iraqi tanks and air defense systems during Operations DESERT STORM and IRAQI FREEDOM as well as against Taliban units during Operation ENDURING FREEDOM. A-10 units reportedly destroyed more than 1,000 Iraqi tanks and 1,700 artillery pieces during Operation DESERT STORM, and the 60 that deployed against Iraq in 2003 proved equally effective. Some 20 squadrons, or over 400 aircraft, remained in service with U.S. Air Force and Air National Guard units as of June 2008, and the plane is expected to remain in service at least through 2026.

The Lockheed Martin F-117 Nighthawk Stealth "fighter" was the most technologically advanced U.S. attack aircraft to see service in the Middle East. The single-seat attack aircraft entered service in 1983 and first saw combat in Panama in 1989–1990 during Operation JUST CAUSE. Its design was derived from the lessons learned during the Vietnam War and the newly-emerging research into technologies that either absorbed or deflected radar signals to reduce the plane's radar cross section. As a result, its radar cross section is less than that of a single-engine Piper Cub light plane. It carries two bombs in an internal bomb bay for a total bomb load of 4,000 pounds. It is powered by two nonafterburning GE-404 turbofan engines generating 10,600 pounds of thrust each. The plane's odd angular construction reduces its radar cross section, but necessitates a computer-assisted flight system to ensure safe flight. It has a Global Positioning System (GPS) and inertial navigation system as well as bomb aiming and electronic warning systems to deliver precision weapons.

The F-117A's stealth characteristics and instrumentation made it the key strike asset during all major U.S. bombing operations from 1990 to 2003. For example, F-117s were committed against 40 percent of the key strategic targets destroyed during Operation DESERT STORM, even though they constituted less than 2 percent of the total sorties launched in that war. Unfortunately, the plane's aging technology, particularly its complicated stealth coatings, requires intensive maintenance. The last F-117As were retired from service in August 2008.

The Panavia Tornado was the predominant European-built attack aircraft to serve in Operations DESERT STORM and ENDURING FREEDOM. Designed and built by a trinational consortium consisting of British, West German, and Italian manufacturers, the twin-engine two-seater Tornado entered service in 1978. Britain also purchased an air defense variant, but Italy deployed a dozen IDS (Interdiction/Strike) variants to Saudi Arabia during Operation DESERT SHIELD and employed them during DESERT STORM. Intended as a supersonic fighter-bomber, the Tornado employs a variable-geometry-wing to provide good slow-speed maneuverability and landing characteristics without compromising supersonic performance. Its two Turbo-Union RB-199-34R afterburning turbofan engines generate 19,700 pounds of thrust. Armament includes a

Two-ship formation of Lockheed F-117A Nighthawk Stealth fighter aircraft. (U.S. Department of Defense)

single Mauser BK-27 27-mm cannon, two AIM-9 AAMs, and up to 19,800 pounds of bombs or guided munitions. The Tornado carries a full suite of electronic warning and self-defense countermeasures equipment, an integrated GPS-inertial navigation and digital weapons system, a terrain-following radar, and all-weather guidance systems for the full range of Western guided munitions. In addition to the Italian and RAF Tornado contingents, Saudi Arabia possessed 48 of the planes in service during the 1991 Persian Gulf War, employing them against Iraqi airfields and air defenses.

Britain also deployed the Fleet Air Arm's Blackburn Buccaneer attack bombers during Operation DESERT STORM. The single-seat, carrier-capable Buccaneer entered service in 1962, and the 12-plane detachment that served in DESERT STORM marked its last operational employment. It carried up to 12,000 pounds of ordnance and was equipped with electronic warning and countermeasures equipment. It could laser-designate bombs and carry a variety of air-to-ground missile systems. Its two Rolls Royce Mark 101 nonafterburning turbofans provided 22,000 pounds of thrust. The last Buccaneers were retired in 1993.

Attack aircraft employed by the U.S. opponents in the Middle East wars were primarily of Soviet design. The Sukhoi series attack

The Soviet Sukhoi Su-17 (NATO designation Fitter) fighter aircraft. (U.S. Department of Defense)

planes were the most commonly encountered attack aircraft. Initially designed and introduced into service as a fighter interceptor in 1959, the single-seat, single-engine Su-7 Fitter A proved a dangerous plane to operate. Its high landing speed and poor cockpit visibility gave it a high accident rate, and its lack of maneuverability made it a poor dogfighter when compared to the MiG-19 and MiG-21. As a result, it was quickly transitioned to a ground attack aircraft that became the first export jet fighter-bomber sold to the Soviet Union's allies. It suffered a high loss rate in Indian, Egyptian, and Iraqi service. Afghanistan had about a dozen on its airfield in late 2001 when ENDURING FREEDOM began, but none was in flying condition. The Su-7 had two 30-mm cannon in the nose and could carry up to 4,400 pounds of bombs. Its AL-7F afterburning turbojet engine provided up to 22,150 pounds of thrust, giving it good acceleration; however, the lack of electronic countermeasures equipment and poor maneuverability made it vulnerable to modern air defense systems.

The Su-17 Fitter employed a variable geometry wing to give it a lower landing speed and better maneuverability. It was also equipped with a more powerful and less maintenance intensive AL-21F-3 afterburning turbojet engine that produced 24,675

pounds of thrust. Armament was improved to 8,800 pounds of bombs and two AA-8 Aphid infrared-guided air-to-air missiles. The addition of electronics countermeasures and precision bombing equipment resulted in the designation of Su-22 for the export versions that served with the Iraqi, Afghan, and Libyan air forces. U.S. Navy F-14s shot down two Su-22s in the Gulf of Sidra in 1986, and the U.S. Air Force destroyed 19 during Operation DESERT STORM. The remainder of Iraq's 70 Su-22s fled to Iran in January 1991, just prior to the beginning of the air war.

The best ground attack aircraft in the Iraqi inventory in 1991 was the two-seat Sukhoi Su-24 Fencer. The twin-engine variable-geometry-winged attack aircraft entered Soviet service in 1972. Iraq had 25 in service when it invaded Kuwait in August 1990. The Fencer's two AL-21F-3A afterburning turbojet engines provided a total of 49,350 pounds of thrust, enabling it to carry 17,600 pounds of bombs and two AA-8 Aphid AAMs. It was also equipped with a 23-mm cannon in the nose and a primitive ground mapping radar. The Fencer was Iraq's only supersonic attack aircraft, with a top speed of Mach 2.1 in a clean configuration. More importantly, unlike Iraq's Su-7s and Su-22s, it was equipped with electronic countermeasures equipment, as well as flare and chaff pods. It could also employ the AS-7 Kerry air-to-surface missile. Eighteen of Iraq's Su-24s flew to Iran in January 1991. None now survive.

The Sukhoi Su-25 Frogfoot rounded out Iraq's ground attack force. The twin-engine single seat Frogfoot was specifically designed for CAS missions. Like the A-10, its cockpit and critical flight systems were protected by titanium armor. Its two R95Sh nonafterburning turbojet engines provide 18,960 pounds of thrust. Armament includes a 30-mm cannon and up to 9,700 pounds of bombs and guided missiles. It is also equipped with radar warning systems; chaff and flare pods; and a guidance system for the AS-7 Kerry ASM. The Afghan Air Force also had about a dozen Su-25s in its inventory at the beginning of Operation ENDURING FREEDOM, but none was in flying condition. Neither Iraq nor Afghanistan operates the Su-25 today.

Attack aircraft with crews specifically trained in bombing and precision weapons employment have been critical to the conduct of military operations since World War II. Air supremacy nets the military commander little if it does not lead to decisive strikes against key enemy positions or support forces on the ground or sea. The success of the United States and that of its allies in the Middle East largely can be attributed to the successful integration and employment of all facets of air power, in which attack aircraft play a sizable role. High technology attack aircraft have constituted a major component of western air power and will remain such for many years to come.

CARL OTIS SCHUSTER

See also

Aircraft, Bombers; Aircraft, Electronic Warfare; Aircraft, Manned Reconnaissance; DESERT SHIELD, Operation; DESERT STORM, Operation, Coalition Air Campaign; ENDURING FREEDOM, Operation, U.S. Air Campaign; IRAQI FREEDOM, Operation, Air Campaign

References

Gordon, Yefim. *Sukhoi Su-7/-17/-20/-22 Soviet Fighter and Fighter-Bomber Family.* Hersham, Surrey, UK: Ian Allan, 2004.

Green, William, and Gordon Swanborough. *The Complete Book of Fighters.* New York: Barnes and Noble Books, 1998.

Higham, Robin D., and Stephen Harris. *Why Air Forces Fail: The Anatomy of Defeat.* Lexington: University Press of Kentucky, 2006.

Kaplan, Robert D. *Hog Pilots, Blue Water Grunts: The American Military in the Air, at Sea and on the Ground.* New York: Random House, 2007.

Lambeth, Benjamin. *Moscow's Lessons from the 1982 Lebanon Air War.* Washington, DC: RAND Corporation, 1985.

Murray, Williamson, and Robert H. Scales Jr. *The Iraq War: A Military History.* Cambridge, MA: Belknap, 2005.

Nicolle, David, and Mark Styling. *Arab MiG-19 & MiG-21 Units in Combat.* Oxford, UK: Osprey, 2004.

Olsen, John. *Strategic Air Power in Desert Storm.* London: Frank Cass, 2003.

Smallwood, William L. *Warthog: Flying the A-10 in the Gulf War.* Washington, DC: Brassey's, 1993.

Winchester, Jim. *Douglas A-4 Skyhawk.* Yorkshire, UK: Pen and Sword Books, 2005.

Aircraft, Bombers

Middle Eastern nations have never acquired large numbers of specialized bombers. Regional opponents have been sufficiently close geographically that the longer ranges offered by strategic bomber aircraft were not required, and none of the combatants seriously envisioned a strategic bombing campaign.

Iraq possessed Soviet-built bombers that played no meaningful role in either Operation DESERT STORM or Operation IRAQI FREEDOM. The United States, on the other hand, committed its strategic bombers extensively in conventional roles during the Middle East wars. The United States used B-52 bombers against Iraq in the 1991 Persian Gulf War and used B-52, B-1, and B-2 bombers against terrorists in Afghanistan in 2001 and against Iraq in 2003. U.S. bombers were especially valued for their heavy payloads and ability to remain aloft for long periods.

Coalition nations in the Middle East wars did not operate dedicated bombers. The British and French, for example, used fighters capable of dropping bombs, but their aircraft are not considered bombers. Afghanistan possessed no strategic bomber aircraft at all.

Iraqi Bombers

Iraqi bombers played virtually no role in that nation's wars with the United States, principally because they were either hidden or sent to neighboring countries before hostilities began (as in the Persian Gulf War) or were destroyed on the ground in the opening air campaign. Nevertheless, Iraq possessed three types of bombers.

The Ilyushin Il-28 is a two-engine straight-wing Soviet-inspired medium bomber that used Soviet copies of the Rolls Royce Nene turbojet in nacelles under each wing. Some 3,000 Il-28s were built, and about half were exported. The Il-28 was sturdy and reliable, handled easily, and was equipped with both optical and radar bombsights. Iraq received its first Il-28s in 1958 and used them successfully against Kurdish rebels in the 1970s and against the Iranians in the 1980s during the Iran-Iraq War. In the 1990s, derelict Il-28s were parked on runways as decoys to lure American air strikes away from more important targets.

The Tupelov Tu-16 bomber (the Soviets built 1,509 between 1953 and 1963) is a swept-wing twin-engine aircraft. Iraq first received them in 1962 and used them in the June 1967 Six-Day War but not the 1973 Yom Kippur (Ramadan) War. They were used against the Kurds in the 1970s and against Iran in the 1980s. Iraq bought four H-6D bombers (a Chinese-built Tu-16) equipped with C-601 antiship missiles in 1987. The U.S. Air Force destroyed three Iraqi Tu-16s on the ground in the 1991 Persian Gulf War, and the remaining Tu-16s never flew again.

The Tu-16 had a maximum speed of 615 miles per hour (mph) and a 49,200-foot ceiling. Maximum range was 3,680 miles. It had four crew members. Armament consisted of six 23-millimeter (mm) cannon (two each in dorsal and ventral turrets and two in the tail turret). It also carried up to 24 250-pound or 18 500-pound

A U.S. Air Force Boeing B-52G Stratofortress bomber of the 1708th Bomb Wing takes off on a mission during Operation DESERT STORM. (U.S. Department of Defense)

A U.S. Air Force Northrop Grumman B-2 Spirit (also known as the Stealth Bomber). (U.S. Department of Defense)

bombs internally or two KSR-2 supersonic air-to-surface cruise missiles carried under the wing. The aircraft weighed 82,000 pounds empty and 167,100 pounds loaded.

The Tupelov Tu-22 is a swept-wing supersonic Soviet bomber with two engines on the rear fuselage on either side of the tail fin. The Tu-22 was difficult to fly and maintain and frequently crashed. Iraq ordered 16 in 1973 and had received 10 Tu-22B bombers and 2 Tu-22U trainers by 1979. They were employed against the Kurds in 1974 and suffered heavy losses against the Iranians during the Iran-Iraq War. Coalition forces destroyed the surviving Iraqi Tu-22s in 1991 during Operation DESERT STORM. The Tu-22B had three crew members. Cruise speed was 516 mph, and maximum speed was 1,000 mph. Combat radius was 1,522 miles unrefueled, and ceiling was 48,228 feet. Armament consisted of one 23-mm cannon in the tail and up to 20,000 pounds of bombs or one Kh-22 missile. The Tu-22 weighed 86,000 pounds empty and 188,495 pounds loaded.

U.S. Bombers

The United States was the only nation to operate strategic bomber aircraft during the Middle East wars.

The Boeing B-52 Stratofortress was designed in 1948 for intercontinental nuclear strikes on the Soviet Union. Boeing built 744 between 1952 and 1962 in numerous variants. Extensively used for conventional bombing during the Vietnam War, the B-52 returned to combat against Iraq in 1991. B-52s flying directly from Louisiana began Operation DESERT STORM with cruise missile attacks on Iraqi air defenses. Other B-52s pounded Iraqi troops with a total of more than 25,000 tons of bombs. In 1996 and 1998, B-52s struck Iraq with cruise missiles in punitive strikes designed to coerce the Iraqi government to abide by United Nations (UN) sanctions and weapons inspections. B-52s based in Diego Garcia provided precision close air support to coalition troops in Operation ENDURING FREEDOM in Afghanistan in 2001 and Operation IRAQI FREEDOM in Iraq in 2003. The B-52 has a maximum speed of 650 mph and a 55,773-foot ceiling. Unrefueled combat radius is 4,480 miles. The B-52 has a crew of five; carries up to 60,000 pounds of cruise missiles, bombs, and other munitions; and weighs 185,000 pounds empty and 265,000 pounds loaded.

The Rockwell B-1 Lancer resulted from the search for a new manned strategic bomber in the late 1960s. It first entered service in 1985. The swing-wing aircraft was designed to take off and land at low speed and penetrate enemy air defenses at low altitude and supersonic speeds. The B-1B force transitioned from a nuclear to a conventional strike role in 1993 and participated in the December 1998 punitive attack on Iraq. In autumn 2001, eight B-1Bs supported Operation ENDURING FREEDOM in Afghanistan. During Operation IRAQI FREEDOM in 2003, 12 B-1Bs dropped half the total number of 2,000-pound precision-guided bombs expended. With four GE F-101 engines, B-1B maximum speed is 950 mph, with a cruising speed of 600 mph and a 60,000-foot ceiling. Unrefueled range is 7,457 miles. The B-1B has a crew of four and is usually armed with 24

2,000-pound Global Positioning Satellite (GPS)-guided bombs. The aircraft weighs 190,000 pounds empty and 477,000 pounds loaded.

The Northrop B-2 Spirit ("Stealth Bomber"), a flying wing design, emerged from classified studies in the mid-1970s into stealth technology, or the use of shapes and composite materials to reduce the aircraft's visibility to enemy radar. The B-2 was originally designed to conduct nuclear strikes on the Soviet Union. Intended production was drastically curtailed (from 132 to 21) when the Cold War ended in 1991. The remaining aircraft were given the capability to deliver conventional precision-guided munitions. Six B-2s served in Operation ENDURING FREEDOM in 2001, including a mission that began in Missouri and ended in Afghanistan that lasted 44 hours. Four B-2s served in Operation IRAQI FREEDOM in 2003, dropping 583 JDAM (Joint Direct Attack Munition) precision bombs. The B-2 has a maximum speed of 475 mph and a 50,000-foot ceiling. Unrefueled range is 7,457 miles. The B-2 has a crew of two and carries up to 80 2,000-pound GPS-guided bombs. It weighs 100,000 pounds empty and 400,000 pounds loaded.

JAMES D. PERRY

See also

Aircraft, Fighters; B-2 Spirit; B-52 Stratofortress; DESERT STORM, Operation, Coalition Air Campaign; Diego Garcia; Iran-Iraq War; Iraq, Air Force; IRAQI FREEDOM, Operation, Air Campaign

References

Angelucci, Enzo. *The Rand McNally Encyclopedia of Military Aircraft, 1914–1980.* New York: Military Press, 1983.

Fredriksen, John C. *Warbirds: An Illustrated Guide to U.S. Military Aircraft, 1915–2000.* Santa Barbara, CA: ABC-CLIO, 1999.

Aircraft, Electronic Warfare

The American-led electronic warfare effort during Operations DESERT STORM (Iraq, 1991), ENDURING FREEDOM (Afghanistan, 2001), and IRAQI FREEDOM (Iraq, 2003) rendered enemy air defense and command and control systems virtually ineffective. In a campaign that involved more than destroying radars, command bunkers, and communications, coalition electronic warfare aircraft jammed sensors and communications when required and often allowed enemy systems to operate so that allied intelligence services could glean critical information about enemy operations and intentions. In effect, coalition forces controlled the electronic spectrum during those conflicts and determined whose military forces could use it and when. Their success coined a new phrase, "information dominance," to characterize superiority in the movement and use of battlefield information. Originally developed as part of an effort to defeat large armies in the field, the concept has evolved tactically in the Global War on Terror to attack terrorist groups that have a lower reliance on and less structured use of electronic warfare.

Although U.S. work in electronic warfare can be traced back to World War II, it was the experience of the Vietnam War, supplemented by Israeli lessons learned during the Yom Kippur

(Ramadan) War that drove the United States to make electronic warfare superiority a strategic and tactical imperative. In those wars, electronic warfare shortcomings cost aircraft and lives. Therefore, as America's involvement in the Middle East increased, electronic warfare aircraft constituted a key, if not numerous, component of its air operations.

Because air defense systems rely most heavily on the electronic spectrum, aircraft have become the most important assets in any electronic warfare operation. With their altitude extending their electronic signals' reach and in some cases their speed, electronic warfare aircraft are the ideal electronic warfare weapon.

Jamming radars, data links, and communications systems require intimate knowledge of the equipment and of their signals and how they are used. For most of the 1970s through Operation DESERT STORM in 1991, the United States relied on three primary electronic surveillance aircraft: the U.S. Air Force's Boeing RC-135 and the U.S. Navy's Douglas EA-3B Skywarrior and Lockheed EP-3 Shadow aircraft.

The air force aircraft is based on the C-135 Stratolifter cargo plane, itself derived from the Boeing 707 commercial airframe. Its four CF-801 turbofan engines give it a top speed of 415 knots, and it has a maximum range of more than 3,200 nautical miles. It has a three-person flight crew and up to 27 mission personnel operating the electronic surveillance equipment. First entering service in 1964, the RC-135 has remained current through several modifications over the years, and its latest variants are expected to remain in service through 2015.

The navy's EA-3B is the largest aircraft ever designed to operate from an aircraft carrier. Essentially, a modified A-3/B-66 Skywarrior bomber carrying four mission personnel and an array of electronic monitoring equipment instead of targeting systems and bombs, the EA-3 Skywarrior (affectionately called the "Whale") entered service in 1956 and served with the navy through Operation DESERT STORM, retiring from service on September 27, 1991. Its two J-59 turbojets gave it a top speed of 400 knots, and it had a maximum range of nearly 2,000 nautical miles. At peak strength,

A U.S. Air Force Lockheed Martin EP-3 Aries II electronic surveillance aircraft in flight. (U.S. Department of Defense)

the navy had three squadrons of EA-3s, but the aging aircraft began to be replaced in the late 1980s by the ES-3 Shadow.

The ES-3 Shadow was a modification of the S-3A Viking, in which electronics surveillance equipment replace the aircraft's antisubmarine warfare systems. It had a two-person flight crew and two systems operators. Advances in computer technology and data link systems enabled the Shadow to provide the same level of collection coverage as the older aircraft. The U.S. Navy had two squadrons of ES-3A aircraft in service by 1991 but never expanded the force beyond that. With a maximum speed of 410 knots and a range of 1,200 nautical miles (seven-hour endurance), ES-3s deployed in 1–2 plane detachments aboard carriers in the Persian Gulf. Only two served in Operation DESERT STORM, but detachments served aboard carriers and ashore in support of Operation SOUTHERN WATCH until 1998. However, the squadrons were decommissioned and their aircraft placed in storage on October 1, 1999.

The retirement of the ES-3 leaves the EP-3 as the navy's last remaining electronic surveillance aircraft. Similarly to the ES-3, the EP-3 was derived from an antisubmarine warfare aircraft, the P-3. The land-based EP-3 Aries is a four-engine turboprop with a four-person flight crew and up to 24 operator stations. First flying in 1969, EP-3s have flown missions in support of every U.S. contingency and combat operation in the Middle East from 1974 through 2008. Three 9-plane squadrons were operational in 1991, and two remain in commission in 2008.

The U.S. employed two electronic countermeasures aircraft during its Middle East operations, the navy's EA-6 Prowler and the air force's EF-111 Raven. Of these, the Prowler is the oldest and the only one remaining in service. Manufactured by Grumman (now Northrop Grumman Aerospace) and first entering service as an updated EA-6A in 1974, the Prowler is built around a heavily altered A-6 Intruder airframe. Its four-man crew operates a wide variety of advanced jamming and deception equipment. The control systems are operated from the cockpit, but the actual jamming/deception equipment is carried in wing pods. The pod load-out varies with the mission and targeted portion of the electromagnetic spectrum. For example, EA-6Bs operating over Iraq and Afghanistan are configured with systems that jam the frequencies over which terrorists remotely detonate their improvised explosive devices (IEDs). The U.S. Navy currently retains 12 four-plane EA-6B squadrons, and the U.S. Marine Corps retains 3 such squadrons.

The longer-ranged and faster General Dynamics/Grumman EF-111 Raven first entered service in 1981. Carrying the same electronic countermeasures avionics as the EA-6B, the Raven's first combat mission came in April 1986 when the United States conducted retaliatory air strikes against Libya for that country's involvement in a Berlin terrorist bombing. The Mach 2.5 swing-wing EF-111 has a maximum range of 1,740 nautical miles and is credited with being the only electronic warfare aircraft to have downed another fighter in combat (an Iraqi Mirage F1 on January 17, 1991). The EF-111 served through Operation DESERT STORM and was retired from service on October 1, 1998.

Finally, in September 2006 the first Boeing EA-18G Growler came off the production line, destined for the U.S. Navy. The long-awaited replacement for the EA-6B is the fourth major variant of the F/A-18 family. A derivative of the F/A-18F Super Hornet, the 2-seat Growler uses high-speed computer processing and data links to provide the same electronic warfare capabilities as the EA-6B in a supersonic (Mach 1.8) platform. Its speed and range (1,500 nautical miles) enable it to accompany strikes deep into enemy territory and conduct integral or standoff electronic jamming and other countermeasures, including air defense suppression using high-speed antiradiation missiles (HARMs). The EA-18G has the ability to conduct soft or hard kills of enemy sensor and communications systems. The first full squadron of EA-18Gs is scheduled to enter service in 2010 and replace the last EA-6B before the end of the next decade.

CARL OTIS SCHUSTER

See also

Aircraft, Bombers; Aircraft, Fighters; Aircraft, Helicopters; Aircraft, Manned Reconnaissance; Aircraft, Suppression of Enemy Air Defense; DESERT STORM, Operation; ENDURING FREEDOM, Operation; IRAQI FREEDOM, Operation

References

Fabey, Michael. "Growler Passes Milestone C," *Aerospace Daily* (Washington DC), July 19, 2007.

Finlan, Alastair. *The Gulf War, 1991.* Oxford, UK: Osprey, 2004.

Gunston, Bill. *An Illustrated Guide to Spy Planes & Electronic Warfare Aircraft.* New York: Arco, 1983.

Hewson, Robert. *Jane's Air-Launched Weapons, 2001.* London: Jane's, 2002.

Jackson, Paul, et al. *Jane's All the World's Aircraft 2005–06.* London: Jane's, 2005.

Olsen, John. *Strategic Air Power in Desert Storm.* London: Frank Cass, 2003.

Tripp, Robert. *Lessons Learned from Operation Enduring Freedom.* Santa Monica, CA: RAND Corporation, 2004.

Aircraft, Fighters

The Middle East conflicts provided the primary combat arena for the world's fighter aircraft in this period. For the United States, the Middle East was a region of constant conflict but one in which most U.S. leaders wanted to avoid involvement. However, those conflicts were also the crucible in which American air warfare doctrine, tactics, and aircraft were employed, evaluated, and evolved against that of their Soviet counterparts. This was particularly true after America replaced France as Israel's primary weapons supplier. American fighters didn't engage in aerial combat during the Arab-Israeli wars or during Israel's occupation of Lebanon, but its pilots benefited from the lessons learned in those conflicts and applied them during the 1991 Persian Gulf War and later.

The primary driver in America fighter design was its experiences in the Vietnam War. Aerial combat in that war exposed the fallacy of overreliance on guided missiles and the need for highly maneuverable fighters that provided good pilot visibility. As a result, U.S. fighter aircraft, more than those of any other nation, emphasized high thrust-to-weight ratios (the weight of engine thrust versus the aircraft's weight), composite construction materials to reduce weight, fly-by-wire flight controls to accelerate responsiveness, and the use of lift-body fuselage designs to reduce wing loading. All of these facilitated horizontal and vertical maneuverability.

America's primary fighter aircraft for most of the 1970s through mid-1980s were the McDonnell Douglas F-4 Phantom II, Grumman F-14A Tomcat, McDonnell Douglas F-15 Eagle, Lockheed Martin F-16 Fighting Falcon, and McDonnell Douglas F-18 Hornet. The first of these, the Phantom, was a Vietnam War–era aircraft that initially entered service in 1958. The twin-engine two-seater Phantom is one of the few fighters to serve in both the U.S. Air Force and the U.S. Navy. The air force version, the F-4E, carried an internal cannon and more electronic countermeasures equipment. Because of their carrier landing equipment, the U.S. Navy F-4J and U.S. Marine Corps F-4S had to carry their cannon and electronic countermeasure equipment in pods mounted in the nose and on the wings, respectively. Typically, they had to leave the centerline drop tank behind to compensate for the additional weight. All F-4 variants carried up to eight air-to-air missiles (AAMs), four radar-guided AIM-7 Sparrows, and four

AIM-9 infrared-seeking Sidewinders. Additionally, for a ground attack role, the F-4 could eschew its AAMs to carry up to 12,000 pounds of bombs, or it could carry a mixture of AAMs and bombs. Although the F-4 had good acceleration and climb rates, its heavy wing loading and poor cockpit visibility placed it at a disadvantage in low-altitude aerial dogfighting. Experienced Phantom pilots employed the plane's superior vertical performance when facing more maneuverable enemy fighters.

The F-4's replacement in U.S. Navy fighter squadrons, the twin-engine swing-wing F-14A Tomcat, first entered service in 1972. Also a two-seater, the F-14A originally was envisioned as a fighter-bomber much like the F-4, but budget cuts precluded the installation of bomb-aiming equipment. The F-14A therefore became a fleet defense fighter. It had an improved 140–nautical mile range radar and combat system that enabled it to track and engage up to six targets simultaneously. More importantly, its AIM-54 Phoenix AAMs could engage bombers at ranges up to 60 nautical miles away, over three times that of the AIM-7. Its variable geometry (VGW) or swing wing also gave it a stable and slow landing and takeoff speed, a critical consideration with carrier aircraft. However, its 52,000-pound full-load weight limited it to service aboard USS *Forrestal* and later classes of carrier. The carriers *Midway* and *Constellation* had to be modified, with a reinforced flight deck and new catapults, to handle the Tomcat.

A Grumman F-14 Tomcat prepares for refueling during Operation DESERT STORM. (U.S. Department of Defense)

The Qatari F-1 Mirage, French F-1C Mirage, U.S. Air Force F-16C Fighting Falcon, Canadian CF/A-18A Hornet, and Qatari Alpha Jet were all employed by coalition forces during Operation DESERT SHIELD. (U.S. Department of Defense)

The first upgraded F-14s were the F-14Bs that entered service in 1987. Equipped with more powerful GE F-110-400 engines, the F-14B was the first navy fighter to enjoy a thrust-to-weight ratio above 1.0:1.0. The U.S. Navy had approximately 86 F-14Bs in its inventory in 1990. The final F-14 variant, the F-14D Super Tomcat, entered service in 1991. It was equipped with the same engines as the F-14B, but its digital avionics and combat systems were lighter, faster, and more capable. It also had a glass cockpit with improved all-around vision and an infrared search and tracking system, and it had the capability of conducting attack and air defense suppression missions. It could carry up to 13,000 pounds of ordnance and drop tanks. Only 37 were produced, while another 18 F-14As were upgraded to F-14Ds. The navy employed 144 F-14s in Operation DESERT STORM. The F-14 was phased out of naval service by October 2006.

The U.S. Air Force F-15 was the second post–Vietnam War aircraft to enter service. The prototype's maiden flight came in 1972, and the production model F-15A entered service in 1976. The first improved F-15C left the production line in 1978. Powered by two Pratt and Whitney F-100 fan jet engines, the single-seat F-15 was the first American-built fighter aircraft to enjoy a thrust-to-weight ratio exceeding 1.0:1.0, giving it the best acceleration rate of any fighter in the world when it entered service. Employing a lift-body and single-piece all-around cockpit, the F-15 provided superior

pilot visibility. It also enjoyed a higher climb and turning rate than its Soviet-era opponents and was the world's first fighter to have a look-down/shoot-down capability, provided by its AN/APG-63 radar. That radar, with its supporting computer processing capability and heads-up display, enabled the pilot to sort out low-flying targets from among ground clutter. In addition to eight air-to-air missiles, the F-15 was also equipped with a 20-millimeter (mm) Vulcan cannon, firing more than 3,000 rounds per minute. The combination of its radar, weapons, and horizontal and vertical maneuverability made the F-15 one of the 20th century's most capable fighter aircraft. It first saw combat in Israeli service, where Israeli captain Moshe Melnik downed a Syrian MiG-21 over Lebanon in 1979. By the time Saddam Hussein invaded Kuwait in 1990, the U.S. Air Force had more than 800 in its active and reserve unit inventory. U.S. ally Saudi Arabia also had two 25-plane squadrons.

In 1989 the U.S. Air Force introduced a fighter-bomber version, the two-seater F-15E Strike Eagle. The all-weather F-15E is probably the world's most capable aircraft in service. Designed to replace the General Dynamics FB-111 Aardvark, the F-15E's primary mission is to serve as a long-distance all-weather attack and air-defense suppression aircraft, but it is also an equally capable fighter. Its AN/APG-70 radar can be used for aerial and surface targeting, and the plane carries Low-altitude Navigation Targeting

Infrared for Night (LANTIRN) for nocturnal attack missions. The U.S. Air Force had approximately 150 F-15Es in service during DESERT STORM.

Like the F-15, the single-seat F-16 Falcon entered production in 1976. Intended as the U.S. Air Force's economical low-technology fighter when it achieved initial operational capability, the F-16 Fighting Falcon ("Viper") is actually a high-technology single-engine aircraft. It has a 1.1:1.0 thrust-to-weight ratio, light wing loading, and a lift body, giving it exceptional acceleration and maneuverability at all altitudes and regimes. Initially a daytime fighter equipped with infrared-guided AIM-9 Sidewinder air-to-air missiles (AAMs) and capable of carrying up to 8,000 pounds of bombs, by 1989 frontline F-16Cs were all-weather aircraft carrying both radar-guided AIM-120 advanced medium-range air-to-air missile (AMRAAM) and AIM-7 Sparrow missiles as well as Sidewinders.

The F-16 employs the same F-100 engine as the F-15. It uses the AN/APG-66 radar that has less range but the same look-down/shoot-down capability as the F-15's AN/APG-63 and AN-APG-70. Late-model F-16Es carry the AN/APG-80 Actively Electronically Scanned Array Radar. The F-16's high-performance characteristics and comparatively low cost have made it the most popular jet fighter of the post–Vietnam War era, with more than 4,400 produced through 2007 and serving in the air forces of more than 40 nations.

The twin-engine single-seat McDonnell Douglas (now Boeing) F/A-18 Hornet was the last American fighter aircraft of the 20th century. Designed as an all-weather multipurpose aircraft to replace the U.S. Navy's and U.S. Marine Corps' A-4, A-7, and F-4 aircraft, it was produced as the navy's low-cost counterpart to the F-14. It has a lighter wing loading than the F-14 and uses a lift-body design, and its two F-404 engines provide 35,550 pounds of thrust in afterburner, giving the F/A-18 a thrust-to-weight ratio of 0.95:1.0 when fully loaded. Its AN/APG-73 radar and combat systems have the same range and target-handling capacity as the F-14. Armament includes a Vulcan 20-mm cannon in the nose and up to 13,000 pounds in external equipment (a combination of electronic countermeasure pods; drop tanks; bombs; AIM-7, AIM-9, and AIM-120 AMRAAMs; AGM-45 Shrike antiradiation; AGM-84 Harpoon; or AGM-85 Maverick air-to-surface missiles). The U.S. Navy employed 120 F/A-18s in DESERT STORM, as did the Canadian Air Force (24) and French Navy (24). The Canadian F-18s were F-18Ls, a land-based variant that weighs some 4,000 pounds less than its carrier-based counterpart.

The Northrup single-seat twin-engine F-5E Freedom Fighter was the oldest American-built fighter to serve in DESERT STORM. Saudi Arabia had more than 70 of them in its inventory, but they also equipped Bahrain's Air Force (12). An upgraded model of a lightweight fighter-intercept first built in 1960, the F-5E had an AN/APQ-159 20-nautical miles–range radar and two M-39 20-mm cannon in the nose and carried two AIM-7 Sparrow and two AIM-9 Sidewinder missiles. It could also carry up to 6,000 pounds of bombs or drop tanks. Its light wing loading gave comparable horizontal maneuverability to that of the Soviet Union's MiG-21, and its two J-85 jet engines gave a thrust-to-weight ratio of 0.7:1.0.

The French Dassault-built Mirage 2000 and Mirage 5 also saw service in DESERT STORM. France and Bahrain each deployed 12 single-seat single-engine Dassault Mirage 2000 fighter aircraft. The delta-winged Mirage entered service in 1984. Its high wing loading inhibited the Mirage's maneuverability, particularly at low altitude, but its fly-by-wire flight control system gave it superb flight response, and its roll rate was superior to that of all other Western-built aircraft. Its SNECMA M-53-P2 turbofan engine gives it a thrust-to-weight ratio of 0.8:1.0, the best of any European-built aircraft. The Mirage is equipped with two DEFA 30-mm cannon, two Matra 530 radar-guided and two Matra Magic missiles, or AIM-9 infrared guided AAMs. It can also carry up to 4,000 pounds of bombs or drop tanks.

The United Arab Emirates' 29 single-seat Mirage 5s also participated in the 1991 allied air campaign against Iraq. First introduced into service in 1968, it was the foundation design for the Israeli Kfir fighter. The delta-winged Mirage 5 was powered by a single SNECMA Atar 09C turbojet that provided a maximum thrust of 13,230 pounds in afterburner, giving the 29,700-pound Mirage a thrust-to-weight ratio of 0.4:1.0. Armament included two DEFA 30-mm cannon, two Matra Magic or AIM-9 Sidewinder AAMs, or up to 4,000 pounds of bombs.

Iraq and Libya have engaged U.S. fighter aircraft. The latter lost two Soviet-built Sukhoi Su-22s in 1986 when they tried to engage a flight of U.S. Navy F-14As in the Gulf of Sidra and never challenged U.S. air operations there again. The same cannot be said for Iraq. Its air force included a mixture of Soviet and Western fighter aircraft, with Soviet-era models constituting the bulk of its inventory. The oldest were its 150 Mikoyan-Gurevich MiG-21 Fishbeds (North Atlantic Treaty Organization [NATO] designation) and 40 Chinese-built F-7 variants, 1960s-vintage single-seat fighters that carried up to four AAM-2 Atoll missiles (either infrared or radar-guided variants). Equipped with a twin 23-mm cannon for dogfighting, the MiG-21's roll and turning rates were superior to the American F-4, but its thrust-to-weight ratio was only 0.6:1.0, giving an inferior acceleration and climb rate.

Iraq's 90 single-seat swing-wing Mikoyan-Gurevich MiG-23 Flogger (NATO designation) was based on Soviet design that entered production in 1972. It had a slightly higher thrust-to-weight ratio (0.7:1.0) than the MiG-21 and a better radar. Its armament included a 23-mm cannon and two radar-guided AA-7 Apex and two infrared-guided AA-8 Aphid AAMs. Its swing wing gave it a very low landing/takeoff speed, but the MiG-23's cockpit visibility and vertical maneuverability were inferior to its Western opponents.

Iraq's 25 twin-engine Mikoyan-Gurevich MiG-25 Foxbats (NATO designation) also suffered from poor cockpit visibility but had a far higher operational ceiling (72,000 versus 55,000 feet) and a top speed faster than any other aircraft the West had ever faced. It had entered Soviet service in 1964 as a high-altitude high-speed interceptor to counter America's Mach 3.5 Lockheed SR-71

The Soviet-made Mikoyan-Gurevich MiG-29 (NATO designation Fulcrum) was the Iraqi Air Force's top air-superiority fighter. (George Hall/Corbis)

Blackbird reconnaissance aircraft. Carrying four AAMs (two AA-2 Atoll and two radar-guided AA-6 Acrid), the Foxbat had a top speed above Mach 3.0, but its low thrust-to-weight ratio (only 0.41:1.0) and heavy wing loading made it much less maneuverable than any other fighter aircraft in the Middle East.

Iraq also had approximately 30 Mikoyan-Gurevich MiG-29 Fulcrums (NATO designation) in service by 1990. Iraq's only fourth-generation fighter had entered Soviet production in 1983. Designed specifically to counter the expected capabilities of the F-16 and F-18, it has a lift body, light wing loading, an airframe stressed a gravity force of up to 9, improved cockpit visibility, and a heads-up display, and most importantly, its two RD-33 turbofan engines give it a thrust-to-weight ratio of 1.13:1.0. In terms of pure aerodynamic performance, it can outmaneuver any Western aircraft vertically and horizontally. However, its cockpit visibility remains inferior to Western designs, and like all other MiGs of that era, its radars are inferior in range and tracking ability compared to Western models. Moreover, in Iraqi hands the MiG-29s did not fare well in combat against American fighter aircraft, losing over a dozen of their number without inflicting any losses.

The Iraqi Air Force was also equipped with 94 Dassault Mirage F-1 single-seat fighter-bombers, as were two coalition members' air forces, that of Qatar (12) and Kuwait (32). An upgrade of the F-1C that entered French service in 1974, Iraq's F-1EQ could carry up to 14,000 pounds of ordnance (e.g., two Exocet antiship missiles or a single missile and drop tank for antishipping missions). For aerial combat missions, it carried four infrared-guided AAMs, either French-built R-550s or American-made AIM-9Ls. It was equipped with two 30-mm cannon in the nose and Thomson-CSF Cyrano IV monopulse radar. The Cyrano IV was outranged by the American fighters' radar, but it was better than that of Iraq's Soviet-built fighters. The F-1 had a good initial turn rate, but its low thrust-to-weight ratio (0.45:1.0) placed it at a disadvantage against American-built fighters.

During America's 1982–1984 participation in the United Nations (UN) peacekeeping operation in Beirut, Lebanon, U.S. Navy F-14s flew aerial reconnaissance missions and provided combat air patrol missions over Lebanon, but the Syrian Air Force never challenged their operations. U.S. Air Force F-15s and F-16s deployed to Saudi Arabia in the late 1980s to provide air cover for

U.S. Navy ships protecting tankers from Iranian and Iraqi air and missile attack.

Iraqi president Saddam Hussein's invasion of Kuwait in August 1990 triggered Operation DESERT SHIELD, a massive U.S. and allied deployment into the Middle East. Fighter aircraft constituted the leading elements of that deployment. They had two purposes: to ensure that the incoming transport aircraft would not be intercepted and shot down and to protect the receiving airfields from Iraqi air attack. America's NATO and Arab Middle Eastern allies joined in the UN-authorized force buildup to liberate Kuwait. The primary European-built fighter was the twin-engine Panavia Tornado. A variable geometry or swing-wing two-seat aircraft similar to the American F-14, it was built by a British/Italian/West German consortium and became operational in 1979. Designed as a fighter-bomber, the Tornado IDS (Interdictor/Strike) fighter-bomber version was employed primarily for ground attack missions, but Britain's Royal Air Force deployed its Air Defense Version (Tornado ADV) to the Middle East. The Royal Air Force's Tornado F-3 ADV carried four British Skyflash, AIM-9L, or AIM-120 AMRAAMs. Entering service in 1989, only 18 F3s were built in time to participate in Operation DESERT STORM. All Tornado variants carried a 27-mm cannon in the nose. The Tornado's were effective interceptors, but their high wing loading and low thrust-to-weight ratio (0.38:1.0) limited their effectiveness in aerial combat.

The Iraqi Air Force did not challenge the allied aerial bridge that delivered troops, equipment, and supplies into Saudi Arabia. Moreover, once the coalition initiated combat operations in January 1991, American-made F-14, F-15, F-16, and F/A-18 and British Tornado aircraft enjoyed a massive superiority over Iraq's Soviet-built fighters and limited number of Mirage F-1s that were employed using Soviet-era close control intercept tactics. As a result, Operation DESERT STORM's aerial operations consisted almost entirely of offensive air strikes against Iraqi targets. The F-15E Strike Eagle and F/A-18 made their operational debut in that war, employing a wide range of precision-guided weapons to destroy high-value targets. In one highly publicized incident, a U.S. Navy F/A-18 shot down an Iraqi MiG-21 and then accurately bombed a target and shot down a second MiG-21 as it pulled away.

A decade later, these same aircraft were employed to great effect over Afghanistan during Operation ENDURING FREEDOM (2001) and alongside the Italian Tornados and French-built aircraft in the 2003 Iraq War (Operation IRAQI FREEDOM). There was no serious aerial opposition to the American-led operations in any of those campaigns, freeing the coalition's fighters to focus on ground attack and suppression of ground-based air defense systems.

CARL OTIS SCHUSTER

See also

Aircraft, Bombers; Aircraft, Electronic Warfare; Aircraft, Manned Reconnaissance; Aircraft Carriers; DESERT SHIELD, Operation; DESERT STORM, Operation; ENDURING FREEDOM, Operation, U.S. Air Campaign; Iran-Iraq War; IRAQI FREEDOM, Operation, Air Campaign

References

Aloni, Shlomo. *Arab-Israeli Air Wars, 1947–1982.* London: Osprey Books, 2001.

Green, William, and Gordon Swanborough. *The Complete Book of Fighters.* New York: Barnes and Noble Books, 1998.

Hallion, Richard P. *Storm over Iraq: Air Power and the Gulf War.* Washington, DC: Smithsonian Institution Press, 1997.

Higham, Robin D., and Stephen Harris. *Why Air Forces Fail: The Anatomy of Defeat.* Lexington: University Press of Kentucky, 2006.

Holmes, Tony. *US Navy Hornet Units in Operation Iraqi Freedom.* 2 vols. Oxford, UK: Osprey, 2004–2005.

Nicolle, David, and Mark Styling. *Arab MiG-19 & MiG-21 Units in Combat.* Oxford, UK: Osprey, 2004.

Nordeen, Lon, and David Nicolle. *Phoenix over the Nile: A History of Egyptian Air Power, 1932–1994.* Washington, DC: Smithsonian Books, 1996.

Olsen, John. *Strategic Air Power in Desert Storm.* London: Frank Cass, 2003.

Aircraft, Helicopters

Helicopters have constituted a key component of virtually all U.S. military operations since the Vietnam War, and America's involvement in the Middle East is no exception. U.S. Navy and U.S. Marine Corps operations in Lebanon during the early 1980s were heavily reliant upon helicopters, albeit primarily for logistics and antisubmarine warfare missions. More importantly, helicopters participated in every aspect of all American-led military operations in the Middle East, from the 1987 Operation PRAYING MANTIS through Operations ENDURING FREEDOM and IRAQI FREEDOM. America's opponents were slow to adopt helicopters, but Iraq had a significant fleet of Soviet- and European-made helicopters during Operation DESERT STORM in 1991. Given their importance in modern military doctrine, helicopters will remain a ubiquitous presence on America's battlefields and those of its allies for some years to come.

The primary transport helicopters employed in Lebanon were the U.S. Boeing CH-46E Sea Knight and Sikorsky CH-53D Sea Stallion twin- and single-rotor helicopters, while the single-rotor Bell AH-1S Cobra attack helicopter equipped the marine strike helicopter detachments, although they were used primarily as combat escorts for transport and combat search and rescue missions. Of these, the CH-53 Sea Stallion is probably the most famous. Best known for its involvement in the ill-fated April 1979 attempted rescue of the U.S. embassy hostages in Iran, the CH-53 is America's most powerful and longest-ranged helicopter. The early models could carry up to 32 fully armed troops or lift 12,000 pounds of cargo; the latest variant, the CH-53E Super Stallion, can lift up to 16,000 pounds of cargo and transport it more than 100 nautical miles. It can also refuel in flight from Lockheed Martin KC-130 Hercules tankers, giving it almost unlimited range.

The first CH-53A Sea Stallion entered U.S. Marine Corps service in 1967, and the latest variant, the CH-53E Super Stallion, is expected to remain in use well beyond 2015. The Super Stallion's

A CH-53E Super Stallion helicopter lands on the flight deck of the amphibious transport dock USS *Raleigh* as other ships of the task force steam in formation behind. (U.S. Department of Defense)

powerful lift capability has proven particularly useful in the thin air and high altitudes of Afghanistan. The U.S. Air Force Combat Search and Rescue (CSAR) and its other Special Operations detachments have been using specially modified Sikorsky HH-53 Pave Low helicopters—equipped with armor, refueling probes, and special electronic warning and countermeasures equipment as well as 7.62-millimeter (mm) electronic Gatling guns and other armament—since 1970. U.S. Air Force transport helicopter squadrons received the standard CH-53C. The U.S. Navy modified Sea Stallions for minesweeping, giving it the designation RH-53 (later MH-53).

The CH-46 Sea Knight has been the U.S. Navy and U.S. Marine Corps standard transport helicopter since 1964. Early models carried up to 26 fully equipped troops or 4,000 pounds of cargo, but later models could transport an additional 1,000 pounds of cargo under some conditions. Armament is optional but can include two M-60 7.62-mm or Browning M-2 .50-caliber machine guns. The U.S. Navy retired the last of its UH-46s in 2004, but the U.S. Marine Corps plans to retain its Sea Knights until they can be replaced by Bell Helicopter's MV-22 Osprey.

The Bell/Textron UH-1 Iroquois "Huey" light utility helicopter was America's first gas turbine–powered military helicopter. Entering production in 1963, it was the U.S. Army's primary troop

transport helicopter during the Vietnam War but had been supplanted in that role by the Sikorsky UH-60 Black Hawk by the mid-1980s. Its capacity was limited to six fully armed soldiers or about 2,000 pounds of cargo slung beneath it, but it could carry the same armament as the CH-46E. The U.S. Navy and U.S. Marine Corps continued to use UH-1s until 1992. Its small radar cross-section and agility made it ideal for covertly delivering small Special Forces elements near their objectives. Italy produced a license-built version called the Augusta-Bell 204 that is serving with the International Security Assistance Force, led by the North Atlantic Treaty Organization (NATO), in Afghanistan.

The U.S. Marines Corps' final Vietnam-era helicopter, the Bell AH-1 Cobra (models AH-1J and AH-1T through AH-1Z Super Cobras) attack helicopter, has been the backbone of that service's attack helicopter force since 1969. The Super Cobra variants presently in service have a top speed exceeding 190 knots, are equipped with a 3-barreled 20-mm cannon in a nose turret, and can carry two AIM-9 infrared-guided air-to-air missiles in addition to its normal load out of eight AGM-65 Maverick and AGM-114 guided air-to-surface missiles.

By the time Iraq invaded Kuwait in August 1990, the U.S. Army had five helicopters in its inventory: the Hughes OH-6 Cayuse and Bell OH-58 Kiowa reconnaissance and observation helicopters, the

Boeing Ch-47 Chinook Heavy Lift and UH-60 Black Hawk transport helicopters, and the Hughes/McDonnell Douglas AH-64 Apache attack helicopter. Of these the OH-6 was the oldest, having entered service in 1966. In the 1980s the OH-6As modified for Special Forces transport and attack were assigned to the army's elite 160th Special Operations Aviation Regiment (Airborne) as MH-6C Little Birds and AH-6Cs. They were still serving with the 160th during Operations DESERT STORM and IRAQI FREEDOM. The MH-6 can carry up to six soldiers, while the AH-6 is armed with two 7.62-mm Miniguns, two .50-caliber GAU-19 electrically driven Gatling guns, four AGM-114 Hellfire missiles, and two 70-mm rocket pods.

The OH-58 Kiowa began to replace the OH-6 in 1985. Essentially a more robust version of the venerable Bell 206 Jet Ranger, the single-rotor OH-58 was equipped with a sensor mast above its rotor so that it could detect, track, and designate targets while remaining hidden below the tree line. The OH-58C was also equipped with an infrared suppression and countermeasures system. Also, it was the U.S. Army's first helicopter to carry radar warning equipment. Early OH-58s were armed with a 7.62-mm Minigun, but the M-129 automatic grenade launcher was added after experiences in Operation PRIME CHANCE (1987–1989) in the Persian Gulf indicated a need to upgrade its weapons capabilities. It can also carry two Stinger infrared-guided missiles for air-to-air engagements. The armed

OH-58D Kiowa Warrior serves with U.S. Army Air Cavalry units in Iraq and Afghanistan, where the flexibility provided by its universal weapons pod enables local commanders to tailor its weapons load to specific missions. In addition to the Minigun and 30-mm grenade launcher, the Kiowa Warrior can carry a load of AGM-114 Hellfire missiles, two Hydra 7-tube 70-mm rocket pods, a M-296 .50-caliber machine pod, or four AIM-92 Stinger air-to-air missiles. Despite the upgrade, the helicopter's primary employment is for armed scouting and reconnaissance.

The AH-64 Apache has been the U.S. Army's attack helicopter since it replaced the AH-1 Cobra during the 1980s. The single-rotor two-seat Apache was designed originally by Hughes Aircraft, which was subsequently purchased by McDonnell Douglas. The Apache entered production in 1981 and incorporated all the lessons learned from the Vietnam War and the 1973 Yom Kippur (Ramadan) War. The two-person crew compartment and fuel tanks are armored against 23-mm antiaircraft fire, and the helicopter carries a 30-mm chain cannon for antitank engagements. Additionally, it is equipped with a helmet-mounted display that enables the gunner to aim its weapons by turning his head toward the target. The Apache is equipped with Global Positioning Systems (GPS), electronic and infrared sensing systems, and infrared suppression and countermeasures equipment.

A U.S. Army UH-60 Blackhawk flies off the drop zone of Joint Security Station War Eagle, near Baghdad, Iraq, on July 16, 2009. (U.S. Department of Defense)

The Apache first saw combat in the 1989 Operation JUST CAUSE in Panama and has served in all U.S. East African and Middle East operations since 1990. During Operations DESERT STORM and IRAQI FREEDOM, the Apache went beyond its originally intended antitank role to air defense suppression, where its low-altitude all-weather capabilities and advanced electronic sensor suite enabled it to destroy key portions of Iraq's radar network. Its versatility and robustness have made it a popular weapons system. The British Army operates a license-built Westland variant, while the Dutch Air Force owns 30 Apaches, which have deployed in 6-aircraft detachments to Iraq, Djibouti, and Afghanistan.

The twin-rotor Boeing CH-47 Chinook and single-rotor Sikorsky UH-60 Black Hawk are the U.S. Army's primary cargo and troop transport helicopters. The former has been in service since 1962, enjoying many upgrades over the years. The CH-47D constitutes the mainstay of the U.S. Army's and British Army's heavy helicopter transport squadrons. With a maximum lift capacity of 26,000 pounds, it can transport a 155-mm Howitzer, its 11-man crew, and up to 30 rounds of ammunition over 100 nautical miles in a single lift. Its navigation systems include GPS and instrumentation for all-weather flying. It has terrain-following radar to support nap-of-the-earth flying in poor visibility.

The U.S. Air Force flies the CH-47, designating it the HH-47. There is also a specially modified MH-47E serving with the U.S. Army's 160th Special Operations Aviation Regiment. The MH-47E has in-flight refueling capability, infrared suppression systems, and electronic warning equipment. It has a greater fuel capacity and range than the MH-47D. Other upgraded versions, the CH-47F and MH-47G, entered production in 2007. The newest models have upgraded avionics, more robust engine transmissions, and better high-altitude performance based on lessons learned from operations in Afghanistan.

The UH-60 Black Hawk is the U.S. Army's most numerous transport helicopter. A maritime variant, the Sikorsky SH-60 Sea Hawk, also serves with the U.S. Navy. The Black Hawk entered service in 1979 and replaced the UH-1 as the army's light transport helicopter by 1989. The Black Hawk can carry up to 11 passengers or 6,000 pounds of cargo slung below the fuselage. It also comes in command and control versions, designated the EUH-60C and EUH-60L, as well as an electronic warfare version, the EH-60C, that was employed during Operation DESERT STORM and was retired shortly thereafter. The MH-60K and MH-60L Direct Action Penetrator equip the 160th Special Operations Aviation Regiment. The MH-60s have in-flight refueling capabilities, special navigation systems, infrared warning, suppression and countermeasures equipment, and electronic sensor systems. Finally, the MH-60L carries a 30-mm chain gun, an M134D Minigun, and 70-mm rocket pods.

U.S. Army Black Hawks saw action in Somalia (1992–1993), the Persian Gulf (1987–1989), Afghanistan (2001–present), and Iraq (1991, 2003–present). The Australian Army also employed the Black Hawk in Operations ENDURING FREEDOM and IRAQI FREEDOM.

Black Hawks will remain these services' primary troop transport aircraft through 2020.

The Sikorsky SH-2 LAMPS and SH-3 Sea King were the U.S. Navy's mainstays for most of the Cold War era. Their primary mission was antisubmarine warfare and search and rescue operations, but they were used occasionally for fleet logistics. Both could carry a single Mark 44 or Mark 46 antisubmarine torpedo, while SH-3s in British service were also equipped to carry two Sea Eagle antiship cruise missiles. For search and rescue missions, the Sea King could carry an M-60 7.62-mm machine gun slung in the cargo door. These Vietnam War–era helicopter types were used in Operations EARNEST ENDEAVOR and PRAYING MANTIS, augmented by the SH-60 LAMPS II helicopters then entering service. The SH-60 eventually replaced both the LAMPS I and Sea King helicopters by 1990 and 2003, respectively. Sea Kings remained in Italian, British, and Australian service through 2005.

The single-rotor Aerospatiale SA-321 Super Frelon heavy-lift helicopter served with French and Iraqi forces during Operations DESERT SHIELD and DESERT STORM. It can carry up to 38 fully armed troops or about 10,000 pounds of cargo. The French Navy's version carried a dipping sonar, up to four antisubmarine warfare torpedoes, and two Exocet antiship cruise missiles. In French Air Force and Iraqi Air Force service, it carried a 20-mm cannon. None of Iraq's Super Frelons are operational today, and they have been retired from French service. However, China produces a license-built variant, the Z-8, for the People's Liberation Army.

The single-rotor Aerospatiale SA-330 Puma is a medium-lift transport helicopter that has served with French, Iraqi, and Kuwaiti forces as well as Britain's Royal Air Force through the 1990s. Entering service in 1968, the Puma was the French Army's primary troop transport helicopter during Operations DESERT SHIELD, DESERT STORM, and ENDURING FREEDOM. The U.S. Coast Guard also used them for search and rescue operations. It can transport up to 16 soldiers or 4,000 pounds of cargo. Armament in French and Iraqi service consisted of a coaxial 7.62-mm machine gun and side-firing 20-mm cannon. It was replaced after 1990 by the more powerful Eurocopter SA 332 Super Puma, which has better avionics and can carry more weight (24 troops or 6,000 pounds of cargo). The Netherlands deployed its Super Pumas to Iraq and Afghanistan, where they supported NATO/International Security Assistance Force operations through 2008.

The Aerospatiale SA-341F Gazelle was France's primary attack helicopter during Operations DESERT SHIELD and DESERT STORM. The attack variants were equipped with a 20-mm nose cannon and carried four HOT (Haut subsonique Optiquement Téléguidé tiré d'un tube) French-developed wire-guided antitank missiles; it was in that configuration that French forces employed them in Iraq. British forces also employed the light utility transport version to support the Special Air Service. In that role it carries four soldiers or about 2,000 pounds of cargo.

The Soviet-supplied single-rotor Mil Mi-6 Hook helicopter dominated Syria's and Iraq's helicopter forces during U.S. operations in

Members of the 82nd Airborne Division inspect a Soviet built Iraqi Mi-24D Hind assault helicopter abandoned by Iraqi forces during Operation DESERT STORM. (U.S. Department of Defense)

the Middle East. All of Iraq's were destroyed during Operations DESERT STORM and IRAQI FREEDOM, but they remain in the Syrian inventory to this day. In some cases, they installed rocket launchers and heavy machine guns and employed them as attack helicopters. However, for the most part Syria used them for rear-area transport duties. Iraq, however, employed Mi-6 helicopters in Kuwait City when it invaded Kuwait in August 1990. The Mi-6 entered Soviet service in 1957, and the later models serving in Syria and Iraq could lift up to 26,000 pounds of cargo or transport up to 61 troops.

The Soviet Mil Mi-8 Hip entered service in 1967, but Iraq did not purchase its first Hips until 1978. Slightly smaller but faster than the Hook, the Hip could carry 24 passengers or 6,600 pounds of cargo. The Iraqis employed them primarily as rear-area troop transports, but they were employed in the vertical assault role during the 1990 invasion of Kuwait. They are no longer in service in Iraq.

The Soviet Mil Mi-24 Hind constituted Iraq's only attack helicopter. Although it could carry six passengers, the Soviets intended it primarily as an attack helicopter, which was its primary role in Iraqi service. Iraq used it extensively against Iranian forces attempting to break though its lines during the 1980–1988 Iran-Iraq War, where it worked in tandem with Iraq's French-built Gazelle helicopters. Hinds are heavily armored. They can carry up to 1,100 pounds of bombs, S-24 240-mm rockets, UB-32

rocket pods, or two AT-2 Swatter wire-guided antitank missiles. They are equipped with door-mounted 7.62-mm machine guns and nose turret containing two 23-mm cannon. This is altogether a formidable array of weaponry, but the Hind sacrificed agility, maneuverability, and altitude for its firepower. It did not fare well in combat against Iranian Bell AH-1T Sea Cobras and American attack helicopters. None survived Operation IRAQI FREEDOM.

America's large helicopter inventory has enabled it to conduct vertical envelopment operations that far exceed that of any other country. For example, during Operation DESERT STORM the U.S.-led coalition conducted the world's largest mobile air assault, landing the bulk of the 101st Air Assault Division in the Iraqi Army's rear. Helicopters served a similar role in degrading air defenses and ground force cohesion during Operations ENDURING FREEDOM and IRAQI FREEDOM. The helicopter's ability to deliver troops, equipment, and weapons quickly and directly onto an objective has made them an indispensable platform for tactical operations in the difficult terrain and complex political environment of the Middle East.

CARL OTIS SCHUSTER

See also

DESERT SHIELD, Operation; DESERT STORM, Operation, Coalition Air Campaign; ENDURING FREEDOM, Operation, U.S. Air Campaign; IRAQI FREEDOM, Operation, Air Campaign

References

Bernstein, Jonathon. *AH-64 Units of Operation Enduring Freedom and Iraqi Freedom.* Oxford, UK: Osprey, 2005.

Bradbook, Roy. *Desert Storm Air Power: The Coalition and Iraqi Air Forces.* Oxford, UK: Osprey, 1991.

Dunstan, Simon. *The Yom Kippur War,* Vols. 1 and 2. Oxford, UK: Osprey, 2003.

Finlan, Alastair. *The Gulf War, 1991.* Oxford, UK: Osprey, 2003.

Jackson, Paul, ed. *Jane's All World Aircraft 2001–2002.* London: Jane's, 2002.

Jackson, Robert, ed. *Helicopters: Military, Civilian and Rescue Rotorcraft.* Berkeley, CA: Thunder Bay, 2005.

Pretty, Ronald T. *Jane's Weapons Systems, 1972–73.* London: Jane's, 1973.

Aircraft, Helicopters, Operations
DESERT SHIELD and DESERT STORM

Both coalition and Iraqi forces deployed helicopters during Operations DESERT SHIELD and DESERT STORM in 1991. Helicopters were used for transporting supplies and equipment to units in the field, in search and rescue operations to recover downed pilots and ground troops, for moving ground troops into and out of the field, for medical evacuation of wounded troops, and in a ground-attack role.

The U.S. Army also deployed helicopters in the Persian Gulf War; the majority of these helicopters moved the 101st Airmobile Division around Kuwait and southern Iraq. Attack and observation were conducted by the AH-64 Apache attack helicopter and the OH-58 Kiowa observation helicopter. The U.S. Army also deployed medium-lift helicopters, including the CH-47 Chinook, for the movement of troops and supplies.

The U.S. Marine Corps and U.S. Navy deployed helicopters as well. The Marines deployed CH-46 Sea Knight and CH-53 Sea Stallion helicopters in the logistics and troop transport role. AH-1 Cobras, Marine attack helicopters, also supported Marine forces in the Kuwait theater of operations. The Navy deployed SH-3 Sea King medium helicopters in a variety of roles, including logistical support and troop transport. Two Sea Kings were deployed on a U.S. destroyer operating in the northern Persian Gulf to act as search and rescue assets in the event coalition air crews had to ditch in the water.

The U.S. Air Force also deployed helicopters during the Persian Gulf War. MH-60 Pave Hawks and MH-53 Pave Lows were deployed to insert and extract special operations forces in and around Kuwait and Iraq. U.S. coalition partners also deployed various rotor-wing aircraft in the Gulf. French and British helicopters, operating with army and navy units, saw action in the Persian Gulf War.

On the opening night of the air campaign on January 15–16, 1991, U.S. AH-64 Apache gunships supported by MH-53 Pave Lows moved across the border into Iraq and struck two Iraqi radar sites. The resultant gap in Iraqi radar coverage allowed coalition aircraft and cruise missiles the window of opportunity to strike targets in Iraq. During the ground war, the 101st Airborne Division staged the largest airborne assault in history on February 24, 1991, when it moved forces 93 miles into Iraq to establish Forward Operating Base Cobra. From here, established elements of the 101st flew 175 miles, establishing a 50-mile front between Samawah and Nasiriyah in the Euphrates River Valley.

The Iraqis also employed helicopters. As Saddam Hussein moved his army up to the border with Kuwait in August 1990, 80 combat helicopters moved with the ground forces to support the invasion of Kuwait. During the actual invasion of Kuwait, the Iraqi military operated 160 helicopters of Soviet, French, and German manufacture.

During Operation DESERT SHIELD, coalition forces lost 13 helicopters to noncombat accidents, while 2 U.S. Army helicopters were lost in combat. The Iraqi helicopter force was largely destroyed on the ground at the commencement of the air campaign in January 1991, although 6 Iraqi helicopters were also destroyed in air-to-air engagements against coalition fighter aircraft in the opening weeks of the war. At the beginning of Operation DESERT STORM, it is estimated that 300 Iraqi fixed-wing and rotor aircraft were destroyed on the ground. During DESERT STORM, coalition forces lost just 2 helicopters.

STEVEN F. MARIN

See also

Aircraft, Helicopters; DESERT SHIELD, Operation; DESERT STORM, Operation; DESERT STORM, Operation, Coalition Air Forces; Iraq, Air Force

References

Hallion, Richard P. *Storm over Iraq: Air Power and the Gulf War.* Washington, DC: Smithsonian Institution Press, 1997.

McKinney, Mike, and Mike Ryan. *Chariots of the Damned: Helicopter Special Operations from Vietnam to Kosovo.* New York: St. Martin's, 2003.

Aircraft, Helicopters, Soviet-Afghanistan War

Helicopters were used with varying degrees of success during the 1979–1989 Soviet-Afghanistan War. Combat helicopters played a crucial role during the initial Soviet intervention in Afghanistan in late 1979 and early 1980, ferrying troops into combat and providing close air support of ground forces. Helicopters also saw extensive service in protecting supply convoys, especially given the difficult Afghan terrain and the hit-and-run tactics of the mujahideen, or Afghan resistance fighters. Later they were used to provide ground support, to cut enemy lines of communication, and to attack villages and infrastructure. It was not until the introduction of U.S.-made *Stinger* and British-manufactured *Blowpipe* shoulder-fired antiaircraft missiles in 1986 that the mujahideen were able to neutralize Soviet attack helicopters.

When the Soviets invaded Afghanistan, they used the same military tactics that they had employed in the 1968 invasion of Czechoslovakia. Motorized rifle units spearheaded offensives designed to dislodge and defeat mujahideen units while helicopter units were kept in reserve. Unable to defeat the growing insurgency, the Soviets changed their strategy and tactics. The Soviets increased the number of helicopters from some 50 in 1980 to 300 the following year. They also introduced the Mi-24 Hind attack helicopter and the Mi-8 Hip combat helicopter to the theater of operations. Eventually, the Mi-24 Hind became the main antiguerrilla weapon.

The Mi-24 Hind attack helicopter, equipped with 4-barrel machine guns and 64 57-mm rockets, proved to be particularly effective against the mujahideen, who lacked adequate air defenses. Operating in groups of two to six, flying close to the ground for protection, the Mi-24 Hind could either deliver helicopter-born troops to destroy enemy convoys or attack isolated groups of mujahideen fighters. The Mi-24 Hind attack helicopter was particularly effective when scout helicopters or air guides on the ground provided terminal control of the strike.

By 1984, the Soviets had approximately 325 helicopters based in 4 helicopter regiments in the Afghan theater of operations: the 181st Helicopter Regiment at Kunduz and Fayzabad; the 280th Helicopter Regiment at Kandahar; and the 292nd Helicopter Regiment and the 146th Helicopter Detachment at Kunduz. Of the 325 helicopters, close to one-half were the Mi-24 Hind. The large number of Hinds enabled the Soviets to change tactics to counter the increasing level of sophistication in antihelicopter tactics of the mujahideen.

The Soviets conducted many types of helicopter operations. Helicopters were used to lead airborne assaults against the mujahideen. Spetsnaz and airborne troops were transported deep into mujahideen-held territory to eliminate mujahideen defensive positions or cut off their escape. On April 21, 1984, the mujahideen partially destroyed the Mattok Bridge over the Ghorband River, south of the Salang Tunnel. When the mujahideen concentrated for another attack on that structure, the Soviets launched a heliborne operation that killed the entire force of mujahideen, estimated to have been 1,500 to 2,000 strong.

Helicopters were also used to guard Soviet convoys. Whenever a Soviet troop column or supply convoy moved into mujahideen-held territory, it was accompanied by either Mi-24 Hind or Mi-8 Hip helicopters. While half of the helicopters circled overhead watching for mujahideen activity, the others landed troops ahead of the advancing column. The troops would provide security until the column passed, after which the process was repeated.

Helicopters, carrying Spetsnaz and airborne troops, were also used to help the Afghan government gain control over the eastern provinces of Afghanistan, to eliminate "liberated zones," as well as to relieve several government-held garrisons.

In 1985, the mujahideen first acquired the SA-7 Strela surface-to-air missile. Initial use of the SA-7 took the Soviets by surprise when eight Mi-8 Hip helicopters were shot down during one operation.

In 1986, the Soviets were able to counter the mujahideen's shoulder-held antiaircraft missiles. Soviet helicopters were equipped with ultra-red decoy flares and jamming equipment that neutralized the SA-7. To counter the Soviets' tactical advantage, the mujahideen then acquired from the West the more sophisticated British-made Blowpipe antiaircraft missile and the U.S.-made Stinger antiaircraft missile.

Soviet helicopter tactics changed and improved during the Soviet-Afghanistan War. Even though Soviet helicopter units were successfully employed against the mujahideen, the Soviets never had sufficient numbers of helicopters nor sufficient manpower to undertake all the missions necessary to destroy the resistance. Resources were often squandered on unnecessary missions or diverted to other purposes. Problems also occurred with the helicopters themselves. There were numerous reports of Hind rotors striking the tail during very low-altitude flight. Wear on airframes and systems increased dramatically, resulting in increased operational attrition. It is estimated that by the end of the war in 1989 the Soviets had lost 333 helicopters.

KEITH A. LEITICH

See also

Mujahideen, Soviet-Afghanistan War; Soviet-Afghanistan War

References

Collins, Joseph. "The Soviet-Afghan War: The First Four Years." *Parameters* 14(2) (Summer 1984): 49–62.

Dick, Charles J. *Mujahideen Tactics in the Soviet-Afghan War.* Camberley, Surrey, UK: Conflict Studies Research Centre, Royal Military Academy Sandhurst, 2002.

Grau, Lester W., ed. *The Bear Went over the Mountain: Soviet Combat Tactics in Afghanistan.* London: Frank Cass, 1998.

Kaplan, Robert D. *Soldiers of God: With Islamic Warriors in Afghanistan and Pakistan.* Boston: Houghton Mifflin, 1990.

Tanner, Stephen. *Afghanistan: A Military History from Alexander the Great to the Fall of the Taliban.* New York: Da Capo, 2003.

Aircraft, Manned Reconnaissance

Manned aircraft are some of the best platforms for reconnaissance gathering, thanks to their ability to peer into or fly across international borders. Reconnaissance aircraft are capable of carrying a variety of cameras as well as sensors that can locate and record electronic emissions from various communications and intelligence sources. The United States operated manned aircraft for these missions during the Middle East wars while completing a transition from planes dedicated exclusively to tactical photographic reconnaissance to a system of pods that could be added to any fighter. At the same time, the United States increased its use of unmanned airborne vehicles (UAV) for reconnaissance duties.

Operation DESERT STORM (1991) was possibly the last military engagement in which the United States employed manned aircraft variants dedicated exclusively to a tactical photographic reconnaissance role. The U.S. Air Force deployed one squadron of its aging but reliable McDonnell Douglas RF-4C Phantom II tactical reconnaissance aircraft to support operations over Kuwait and Iraq. The air force also flew the high-altitude Lockheed U-2 Dragon Lady in

U.S. Navy photographer's mate 3rd class Chris Pastol adjusts a digital camera's aperture in the Tactical Air Reconnaissance Pod System (TARPS) before taking it to the flight deck of the aircraft carrier *Independence* (CV-62) during a deployment to the Persian Gulf in support of Operation SOUTHERN WATCH, April 12, 1998. (U.S. Department of Defense)

support of photographic reconnaissance missions over Iraq. In the electronics intelligence (ELINT)–gathering role of reconnaissance, the air force utilized the Boeing RC-135 Rivet Joint aircraft, while the U.S. Navy flew the Lockheed Martin EP-3 Aries II. The navy entered Operation DESERT STORM without a manned aircraft variant dedicated exclusively for tactical photographic reconnaissance. However, naval aviators flying from aircraft carriers in the Persian Gulf did have access to the Grumman Tactical Reconnaissance Pod System (TARPS). Select navy Grumman F-14 Tomcats, often known as "Peeping Toms," carried the TARPS pods in the tactical photographic reconnaissance mission over Iraq.

Following the conclusion of Operation DESERT STORM, the United States maintained an air presence over Iraq in support of Operations NORTHERN WATCH and SOUTHERN WATCH. Manned tactical aircraft variants developed exclusively for photographic reconnaissance were not utilized in these missions over the no-fly zones. However, the U.S. Air Force did employ RC-135s in the ELINT reconnaissance role as well as U-2s in the ultrahigh-altitude photographic reconnaissance mission. The navy continued to fly F-14 aircraft with TARPS pods as well as EP-3s for ELINT gathering.

During Operation ENDURING FREEDOM in Afghanistan (2001), the U.S. Navy operated F-14 aircraft carrying TARPS pods as its primary manned tactical photographic reconnaissance platform and the EP-3 for ELINT missions, while the U.S. Air Force relied heavily on the U-2 for manned photographic reconnaissance and the RC-135 in the ELINT role.

The U.S. Navy introduced the Shared Reconnaissance Pod (SHARP) on McDonnell Douglas (now Boeing) F/A-18 Hornet aircraft as a replacement for TARPS during Operation IRAQI FREEDOM in 2003. The U.S. Air Force continued to rely on the U-2. Because of the lack of air force aircraft dedicated exclusively to manned tactical photographic reconnaissance, the British Royal Air Force assumed an important role in these lower-level missions. In 2004 the U.S. Air Force deployed the Theater Airborne Reconnaissance System (TARS) on General Dynamics F-16 Fighting Falcon aircraft supporting ongoing military operations in Iraq.

The two-seat McDonnell Douglas RF-4C Phantom II served as the primary tactical photographic reconnaissance aircraft of the U.S. Air Force since its introduction into the Vietnam War in the autumn of 1965. As a modification of the famous F-4 series of aircraft, the RF-4C was powered by two General Electric J79 turbojet engines that provided the plane with a maximum speed of more than 1,600 miles per hour and a range greater than 1,600 miles with external fuel tanks. The first models entered service with the U.S. Air Force in September 1964 and were committed in Vietnam a year later. The Persian Gulf War in 1991 was the last military engagement in which the air force operated its RF-4C workhorse. One Squadron, the 192nd Reconnaissance Squadron of the Nevada Air National Guard, had the distinction of flying the RF-4C in its last combat actions, including photographing the extent of the oil fires set by the Iraqis in Kuwait. The RF-4C was capable of carrying photographic equipment in three stations within the nose of the aircraft. One station could house a forward oblique or vertical camera. A low-altitude station could carry one of several different cameras designed specifically for taking photographs as the aircraft flew by quickly just above the treetops. A high-altitude station could be utilized for specialty cameras, with optics and film designed to record targets as the aircraft flew out of range of most antiaircraft weaponry. RF-4Cs employed optical and infrared film-based sensors during the Persian Gulf War. The U.S. Air Force retired the RF-4C, its last aircraft designed specifically for tactical photographic reconnaissance, in October 1995.

The General Dynamics F-16 Fighting Falcon entered service with the U.S. Air Force in 1978, and the service received its last Fighting Falcon from the manufacturer in 2005. The plane carried a single Pratt and Whitney F-100 engine that provided it with a speed of 1,500 miles per hour, a ceiling of 50,000 feet, and a range of 851 miles when fully loaded and carrying two fuel tanks. F-16s, carrying SHARP reconnaissance pods, were a manned alternative to the development of aircraft designed exclusively for tactical photographic missions such as the McDonnell Douglas RF-4C Phantom II, which was retired in 1995. In 2004 in Iraq, the U.S.

The U.S. Air Force Lockheed U-2 reconnaissance aircraft made its first flight in August 1955. (U.S. Air Force)

Air Force deployed the Theater Airborne Reconnaissance System (TARS) pods on Fighting Falcon aircraft supporting ongoing military operations over Iraq. TARS is an under-the-weather system housed in a pod that is attached to the center line underneath the aircraft. The system includes digital cameras that eliminate the need for film processing and that speed the process between taking the pictures and analyzing them. A recorder housed in the pod can store more than 12,000 images.

The Grumman F-14 Tomcat entered service with the U.S. Navy in 1974 and was retired in 2006. The aircraft was powered by two Pratt and Whitney TF-30P-414A jet engines that provided a maximum speed of more than 1,500 miles per hour and a maximum range of 1,600 miles. The U.S. Navy first employed the Grumman TARPS on F-14 aircraft in 1981 as a replacement for its fleet of North American RA-5C Vigilante and Chance-Vought RF-8G Crusader dedicated reconnaissance aircraft.

Select Navy F-14 Tomcats (some F-14A and F-14B as well as all F-14D models), often known as "Peeping Toms," were wired to carry TARPS. F-14s employed TARPS in tactical photographic reconnaissance missions over Iraq. TARPS, a 17-foot, 1,850-pound pod, houses three sensors including a KS-87 frame camera, a KA-99 low-altitude panoramic camera, and an AAD-5 infrared sensor. During Operation DESERT STORM, F-14s carrying TARPS flew from the aircraft carriers *Ranger, John F. Kennedy,* and *Theodore Roosevelt.*

The U.S. Navy introduced the F/A-18 Hornet to service in 1983. The aircraft are powered by twin General Electric F404-GE-402 engines and have a maximum speed of more than 1,100 miles per hour and a maximum range in excess of 2,000 miles without armament. During Operation IRAQI FREEDOM, the navy flew F/A-18s carrying the SHARP. The SHARP system, developed by Raytheon and mounted in a pod underneath the aircraft, houses medium- and high-altitude cameras. The pods are capable of transmitting real-time images directly from the aircraft to a monitoring station. Although designed primarily for the F/A-18 E and F models, the pod can be attached to other aircraft.

The Lockheed U-2 Dragon Lady, perhaps the most famous of the American reconnaissance aircraft ever developed, flew for the first time in 1955, and variations of the aircraft are still flying in the early 21st century. After 1994, the U.S. Air Force initiated an extensive modernization program for the U-2 series, resulting in the current designation of U2-S. The U-2 carries a single General Electric F-118-101 engine and has a reported speed of greater than 400 miles per hour and a range in excess of 7,000 miles. The aircraft provides photographic reconnaissance from very high altitudes. The Dragon Lady has seen service with the air force in Operation DESERT STORM, Operations NORTHERN WATCH and SOUTHERN WATCH, Operation ENDURING FREEDOM, and Operation IRAQI FREEDOM.

The Boeing RC-135 Rivet Joint, a modification of the C-135 airframe, entered service with the U.S. Air Force in 1964. The aircraft are powered by four CFM International F108-CF-201 engines and have a maximum range of 3,900 miles. RC-135s carry 21 to 27 crewmen and are designed to conduct ELINT and communications intelligence (COMINT) reconnaissance. The aircraft can provide extensive near real-time reconnaissance data to ground commanders in these two areas. The air force has employed these aircraft extensively during Middle East conflicts especially against Iraq, which had better-developed communications and other electronics-based systems than the Taliban and Al Qaeda in Afghanistan.

The U.S. Navy's Lockheed Martin EP-3 Aries II (Airborne Reconnaissance Integrated Electronics System) aircraft are based on the airframe developed for the P-3 Orion. Powered by four Allison T-56-A-14 turboprop engines, the EP-3 has a range of 3,000 miles. Although similar in mission to the U.S. Air Force's RC-135 Rivet Joint, the latter has a higher ceiling and can thus provide greater coverage with its sensors. Like its air force counterpart, the EP-3 has seen extensive service in the Middle East but especially against Iraq in Operation DESERT STORM, Operations NORTHERN WATCH and SOUTHERN WATCH, and Operation IRAQI FREEDOM due to the greater amount of electronics signals for collection compared to Afghanistan.

TERRY M. MAYS

See also

Aircraft, Bombers; Aircraft, Electronic Warfare; Aircraft, Fighters; Aircraft, Tankers; Aircraft, Transport; DESERT STORM, Operation; ENDURING FREEDOM, Operation; IRAQI FREEDOM, Operation; No-Fly Zones; United States Air Force, Afghanistan War; United States Air Force, Iraq War; United States Air Force, Persian Gulf War; United States Navy, Afghanistan War; United States Navy, Iraq War; United States Navy, Persian Gulf War

References

Birkler, John. *Competition and Innovation in the U.S. Fixed-Wing Military Aircraft Industry.* Santa Monica, CA: RAND Corporation, 2003.

Fredriksen, John C. *Warbirds: An Illustrated Guide to U.S. Military Aircraft, 1915–2000.* Santa Barbara, CA: ABC-CLIO, 1999.

Wilson, Charles P. *Strategic and Tactical Aerial Reconnaissance in the Near East.* The Washington Institute for Near East Policy Military Research Papers #1. Washington, DC: Washington Institute for Near East Policy, 1999.

Aircraft, Reconnaissance

Manned aircraft have proven to be some of the best platforms for reconnaissance gathering because of their ability to peer into, or fly across, international borders. Reconnaissance aircraft are capable of carrying a variety of cameras, as well as sensors that can locate and record electronic emissions from various communications and intelligence sources. This essay concentrates on manned aircraft employed in strategic photographic reconnaissance, tactical photographic reconnaissance, electronics intelligence (ELINT), and communications intelligence (COMINT) gathering roles.

Tactical photographic reconnaissance aircraft normally fly at low altitudes directly over their target areas while strategic photographic reconnaissance aircraft tend to operate from very high altitudes and often utilize oblique-angle cameras. The exact number of reconnaissance aircraft flown by a particular country often varies due to rotations in and out of the theater, and to stages of the conflict. Another problem in determining the number of aircraft arises after the 1991 Persian Gulf War, when most countries converted from aircraft designated specifically as reconnaissance platforms to reconnaissance pods that can be added to many aircraft in a particular series. Thus, many of the American Grumman F-14 Tomcats were capable of carrying a reconnaissance pod prior to the retirement of the F-14, but it may never be fully known how many reconnaissance pods were available to the various squadrons that flew the plane in combat at specific times.

Persian Gulf War

U.S. Air Force

The U.S. Air Force dispatched 24 of its McDonnell Douglas RF-4C Phantom II tactical photographic reconnaissance aircraft to the Middle East for the Persian Gulf War. Eighteen were based in Saudi Arabia and six in Turkey. The two-seat RF-4C Phantom II served as the primary tactical photographic reconnaissance aircraft of the air force since its introduction into the Vietnam War in the autumn of 1965. A modification of the famous F-4 series of aircraft, the RF-4C boasted two General Electric J79 turbojet engines that provided the plane with a maximum speed of more than 1,500 miles per hour (mph) and a range of more than 1,600 miles with external fuel tanks. A total of 503 RF-4Cs were produced by McDonnell Douglas. The first models entered service with the air force in September 1964 and deployed to Vietnam a year later. The 1991 Persian Gulf War was the last military engagement in which the air force employed its RF-4C workhorse. The RF-4C carried photographic equipment in three stations within the nose of the aircraft. One station housed a forward oblique or vertical camera. A low-altitude station could carry one of several different cameras designed specifically for taking photographs as the aircraft flew by quickly just above the treetops. A high-altitude station could be utilized for specialty cameras with optics and film designed to record targets as the aircraft flew out of range of most antiaircraft weaponry.

RF-4Cs employed optical and infrared film-based sensors during the Persian Gulf War. RF-4Cs were too few in number, did not adequately meet the tactical photographic needs of the U.S. military, and required armed escorts during the Persian Gulf War. Photographs taken by the aircraft required the pilot to return to base for the film to be processed, resulting in a time lag before commanders could evaluate them. The 192nd Reconnaissance Squadron of the Nevada Air National Guard claims the distinction of flying the RF-4C in its last combat actions, including photographing the extent of the oil fires set by the Iraqis in Kuwait. The air force retired the RF-4C, its last aircraft designed specifically for tactical photographic reconnaissance, in October 1995.

The U.S. Air Force Lockheed U-2R/TR-1 tactical reconnaissance aircraft in flight. (U.S. Department of Defense)

The air force also employed the Lockheed U-2 Dragon Lady, perhaps the most famous of the American reconnaissance aircraft ever developed, for high-level reconnaissance missions prior to and during the Persian Gulf War. The U-2 flew for the first time in 1955, and variations of the aircraft are still flying in the early 21st century. A U-2 carries a single General Electric F-118-101 engine and has a reported speed of more than 400 mph and a range of more than 7,000 miles. The aircraft provides photographic reconnaissance from very high altitudes and is often known as a strategic, rather than tactical, asset.

The air force also utilized the TR-1, a tactical version of the U-2, during the Persian Gulf War. The TR-1 first flew in August 1981 and carried a reconnaissance pod under each wing, permitting it to conduct standoff tactical missions. Winter cloud cover reduced the effectiveness of the TR-1 during many Gulf War photographic missions, however, causing the air force to rely heavily on the already overtaxed RF-4C aircraft. Six U-2 and six TR-1 aircraft supported the American effort, making the Persian Gulf War the largest U-2 operation conducted by the United States.

The Boeing RC-135 Rivet Joint provided the air force with an ELINT and COMINT collection asset during the Persian Gulf War. The RC-135, a modification of the C-135 airframe, entered service with the air force in 1964. The aircraft is powered by four CFM

International F108-CF-201 engines and has a maximum range of 3,900 miles. RC-135s carry a crew ranging from 21 to 27 in number and can collect extensive near real-time reconnaissance data for ground commanders. Prior to the opening of the air campaign, coalition fighters frequently flew directly toward Kuwaiti airspace before diverting. This procedure permitted RC-135 aircraft to gather intelligence on the electronic signals emitted by Iraqi radar systems along the border. Four RC-135 aircraft flew missions during the war.

Two Grumman E-8 Joint Surveillance Target Attack Radar System (JSTARS or Joint STARS) aircraft participated in the Persian Gulf War, although the system was still in the developmental stages and would not officially enter the air force inventory until 1996. JSTARS provided allied commanders with an airborne command and control system that produced "real time" images of targets on the ground, unlike "wet film" photographic reconnaissance planes such as the RF-4C and the European Tornado, which had to return to base for film development and delivery.

U.S. Navy

The U.S. Navy employed two reconnaissance aircraft during the Persian Gulf War. The first was the Lockheed Martin EP-3 Aries II. The navy's EP-3 Aries (Airborne Reconnaissance Integrated

Electronics System) aircraft is designed around the airframe developed for the P-3 Orion. Powered by four Allison T-56-A-14 turboprop engines, the EP-3 has a range of 3,000 miles. Although performing a similar ELINT mission as the U.S. Air Force's RC-135 Rivet Joint, the latter has a higher altitude ceiling and can, thus, provide greater coverage with its sensors.

The U.S. Navy also employed tactical reconnaissance pods on some of its Grumman F-14 Tomcat aircraft. The F-14 Tomcat entered service with the navy in 1974 and was retired in 2006. Grumman produced 583 F-14As between 1974 and 1988, and 55 F-14Ds for the navy from 1988 to 1992. The aircraft carried two Pratt and Whitney TF-30P-414A jet engines that provided the Tomcat with a maximum speed of more than 1,500 mph and a maximum range of 1,600 miles. The navy first employed the Grumman Tactical Reconnaissance Pod System (TARPS) on F-14 aircraft in 1981 as a replacement for its fleet of North American RA-5C Vigilante and Chance-Vought RF-8G Crusader dedicated reconnaissance aircraft.

Select navy F-14 Tomcats (some F-14A and B as well as all F-14D models), often known as "Peeping Toms," were wired to carry the TARPS pods. F-14s employed TARPS in tactical photographic reconnaissance missions over Iraq. TARPS, a 17-foot-long, 1,850-pound pod, houses three sensors, including a KS-87 frame camera, a KA-99 low-altitude panoramic camera, and an AAD-5 infrared sensor. During Operation DESERT STORM, F-14s carrying TARPS flew from the aircraft carriers *Ranger*, *John F. Kennedy*, and *Theodore Roosevelt*.

U.S. Marines

The U.S. Marine Corps faced a shortage of internal tactical reconnaissance aircraft during the Persian Gulf War. The marines still retained a few of their McDonnell Douglas RF-4B Phantom II tactical photographic reconnaissance aircraft (equivalent to the air force RF-4C aircraft). These aircraft were being phased out of service because of budget constraints and plans to acquire a newly designed reconnaissance pod for the McDonnell Douglas (now Boeing) F/A-18 Hornet aircraft. The marine corps finally made the decision not to deploy its remaining RF-4Bs due to concerns that they lacked sufficient spare-parts stocks and equipment to sustain the planes during combat operations. At the same time, the new F/A-18 reconnaissance pods were not ready for full production and acquisition. The combination of these two issues forced the marines to rely on other services for tactical reconnaissance assets.

Coalition

United Kingdom. The Royal Air Force (RAF) deployed six Panavia Tornado GR1A photographic reconnaissance aircraft to Saudi Arabia after the commencement of the Persian Gulf War air campaign in January 1991. The Tornado, built by a consortium from the United Kingdom, Germany, and Italy, carries two Turbo-Union RB199-34R Mark 103 afterburning turbofan jet engines that provide enough power for the aircraft to reach a maximum speed of 1,700 mph. The Tornado's maximum combat range is 870 miles. The RAF flew the Tornado GR1A aircraft for low-level tactical reconnaissance missions, including attempts to locate Scud missiles in western Iraq. On at least one of the latter night missions, Tornado reconnaissance aircraft captured photographs of Iraqi Scud missile sites, but delays related to returning to their bases, developing and processing the film, and delivering the intelligence permitted the Iraqis to move their missiles before coalition strike aircraft could arrive.

The RAF also deployed Sepecat Jaguar GR1A aircraft to Saudi Arabia for tactical reconnaissance missions. The Jaguar, introduced in 1973 and retired by the RAF in 2007, was powered by two Rolls-Royce/Turbomeca Adour Mark 102 turbofan jet engines. The aircraft could reach a maximum speed of 1,200 mph and a combat range of 335 miles. A total of 12 Jaguar aircraft of all variants flew missions during the Persian Gulf War.

The Royal Navy dispatched three BAe Systems Nimrod MR1 maritime patrol and reconnaissance aircraft to Oman during the Persian Gulf War. The aircraft patrolled the Persian Gulf and Gulf of Oman. The Nimrod, originally built by Hawker Siddeley, made its maiden flight in 1967. The MR1 was powered by four Rolls-Royce Spey turbofan jet engines with a maximum speed of approximately 530 mph and a range of up to 5,700 miles.

France. The French Armée de l'Air assets deployed to the Persian Gulf War included two aircraft models modified for tactical reconnaissance. France sent a small number of Jaguar aircraft to the theater in late 1990. While the majority of the 14 French Jaguar aircraft were strike planes, a couple of them were capable of conducting tactical reconnaissance missions similar to those of the RAF's GR1A models. On January 26, 1991, France introduced the Dassault Mirage F-1CR to the Persian Gulf War. The F-1CR is the reconnaissance version of the Dassault Mirage F-1 fighter introduced into the Armée de l'Air in 1973. Although Dassault designed many of its Mirage F-1 variants to carry external reconnaissance pods, the Armée de l'Air ordered a model specifically designed for the role with internal bays for the equipment. France flew 16 Mirage F-1s of all variants during the Persian Gulf War.

As a Mirage F-1 variant, each F-1CR carried a SNECMA Atar 9K-50 afterburning turbojet engine capable of reaching a maximum speed of 1,750 mph. The F-1CR flew at a combat range of 265 miles. The allies later grounded the French Mirage F-1CR aircraft, along with the Mirage F-1s, to avoid any possible confusion of these planes with Iraqi-operated Mirage F-1s.

Saudi Arabia. Saudi Arabia contributed to the coalition's tactical photographic reconnaissance missions with its 10 Northrop RF-5C Tigereye aircraft. Saudi Arabia is one of only two countries to have purchased the Tigereye, a modified version of the standard F-5 Freedom Fighter and Tiger II aircraft. Northrop first tested the F-5 in 1959, and it entered military service in 1962. Northrop envisioned the F-5 as a relatively inexpensive light fighter that could compete with and defeat larger Soviet-built aircraft of the Cold War. The RF-5C Tigereye aircraft is the reconnaissance version of the F-5E Tiger II, an improved variant of the F-5. Northrop elongated the nose of the aircraft to add space for camera equipment, which replaced the radar unit and one cannon. The RF-5C is powered by two General Electric J85-GE-21B turbojet engines with a maximum speed of 1,200 mph and a range of 870 miles.

United Arab Emirates. The United Arab Emirates (UAE) acquired eight Dassault Mirage 2000RAD tactical reconnaissance aircraft in 1989. The Mirage 2000RAD is an export reconnaissance variant flown only by the UAE and does not carry any internal camera bays, but instead carries reconnaissance pods, including the Thales SLAR 2000 radar pod, Dassault COR2 multicamera pod, and the Dassault AA-3-38 HAROLD telescopic long-range optical camera pod.

Australia. Australia dispatched a small contingent of air force photographic interpreters to Saudi Arabia to assist the coalition, but did not deploy any reconnaissance aircraft.

Iraq

The 1990 tactical photographic reconnaissance assets of the Iraqi Air force included five Mikoyan-Gurevich MiG-21RF Fishbeds and seven Mikoyan-Gurevich MiG-25RB Foxbats, as well as Dassault Mirage F-1EQs capable of carrying external reconnaissance pods. The Soviet Union officially fielded the MiG-21 with its air force in 1959 after four years of testing. More than 50 countries have acquired the MiG-21, and the plane is still being upgraded into new variants for continued service. The MiG-21RF, flown by the Iraqi Air Force and known in the West by the North American Treaty Organization (NATO) designation Fishbed-J, is the reconnaissance version of the MiG-21MF, an export variant of the Soviet/Russian-built aircraft. The MiG-21RF is powered by a Tumansky R-13-300 turbojet engine and contains internal bays for photographic and sensor equipment. All five of the Iraqi MiG-21RFs were no longer in service with the air force after the 1991 Persian Gulf War, and were either shot down by coalition aircraft or interned by Iran.

The Soviet Union introduced the MiG-25 in 1964 primarily as a high-altitude interceptor and reconnaissance aircraft. Iraq purchased both versions of this aircraft for its air force in 1979. The MiG-25 is a single-seat aircraft capable of reaching speeds of more than 2,200 mph utilizing its two Tumansky R-15B-300 afterburning turbojet engines, although pilots were warned not to exceed speeds of more than 1,900 mph. At the opening of the Persian Gulf War, the Iraqis possessed seven of the MiG-25RB reconnaissance aircraft, known in the West by the NATO designation Foxbat-B. Iraq lost two MiG-25RBs during the Persian Gulf War to either coalition aircraft or internment in Iran. Coalition fighters shot down two MiG-25s during the war, but it is not clear whether these were fighter or reconnaissance versions of the aircraft because they are nearly identical in appearance, differing only in the small openings for camera equipment in the reconnaissance plane.

Iraq had also purchased more than 60 of the French-manufactured Dassault Mirage F-1EQ aircraft in air defense and antishipping variations. The F-1EQs, a specially designated export version of the Mirage F-1 earmarked for Iraq, were capable of carrying an external tactical reconnaissance pod permitting any of the aircraft

to become a reconnaissance asset when flown by a pilot trained in the operation of the pod.

Operations NORTHERN WATCH and SOUTHERN WATCH
U.S. Air Force

Following the conclusion of Operation DESERT STORM, the U.S. Air Force maintained an air presence over Iraq in support of Operations NORTHERN WATCH and SOUTHERN WATCH, which sought to enforce the United Nations (UN)–mandated northern and southern no-fly zones over Iraq. Manned tactical aircraft variants developed exclusively for photographic reconnaissance were not utilized in these missions over the no-fly zones. The McDonnell Douglas RF-4C Phantom II aircraft employed during the Persian Gulf War were retired in 1995. The air force received its first reconnaissance pods for the General Dynamics F-16 Fighting Falcon aircraft as it phased out its last planes designated exclusively for low-altitude tactical photographic reconnaissance directly over the battlefield. The air force continued to fly the Boeing RC-135 Rivet Joint in the ELINT reconnaissance role, as well as the Lockheed U-2 Dragon Lady in the high-altitude photographic reconnaissance role. Some of the U-2 aircraft flown during this period carried the TR-1 nomenclature prior to 1992. After 1992 and the addition of a new engine, all U-2 and TR-1 aircraft were redesignated as U-2R, and later U-2S, aircraft. These planes frequently photographed their targets using oblique-angle cameras, even at lower altitudes.

U.S. Navy

The U.S. Navy continued to fly Grumman F-14 Tomcat aircraft with TARPS reconnaissance pods, as well as the Lockheed Martin EP-3 Aries II, for ELINT gathering during operations NORTHERN WATCH and SOUTHERN WATCH.

Coalition

United Kingdom. The United Kingdom flew aircraft in support of both Operation NORTHERN WATCH and Operation SOUTHERN WATCH. RAF assets with the former were based in Incirlik, Turkey, and included four Sepecat Jaguar GR3 tactical reconnaissance aircraft, which were upgrades of the GR1s flown during the Persian Gulf War. In Operation SOUTHERN WATCH, the RAF contribution included eight Panavia Tornado GR1 aircraft based in Kuwait and capable of carrying reconnaissance pods.

Turkey. The Turkish Air Force participated in Operation NORTHERN WATCH and provided basing for the United States and the United Kingdom. Turkish tactical photographic reconnaissance assets during this period included approximately 32 McDonnell Douglas RF-4E Phantom IIs, a reconnaissance variant of the RF-4E.

Iraq

Iraqi Air Force tactical reconnaissance assets included the five Mikoyan-Gurevich Mig-25RB Foxbats that survived the Persian Gulf War. These aircraft did not attempt any tactical reconnaissance missions against allied bases outside of Iraq.

A British Royal Air Force Jaguar during a mission supporting Operation NORTHERN WATCH, 2000. (U.S. Department of Defense)

Operation ENDURING FREEDOM

U.S. Air Force

For this conflict, the U.S. Air Force relied on the U-2 for manned photographic reconnaissance and the RC-135 in the ELINT role. U-2s supporting Operation ENDURING FREEDOM flew from the UAE, where one crashed while returning from a reconnaissance mission over Afghanistan in 2005. The number of these aircraft varied as planes rotated in and out of the theater.

U.S. Navy

During Operation ENDURING FREEDOM, the U.S. Navy utilized Grumman F-14 Tomcat aircraft carrying TARPS pods as its primary manned tactical photographic reconnaissance platform and the Lockheed Martin EP-3 Aries II for ELINT missions. The navy did remove the F-14 from its inventory in 2006 due to age and replaced its reconnaissance aircraft with F/A-18 Hornets carrying the Shared Reconnaissance Pod (SHARP).

Coalition

United Kingdom. The English Electric Canberra PR.9 of the RAF proved invaluable during Operation ENDURING FREEDOM until its retirement in 2006. The aircraft, the last RAF plane designated specifically for tactical photographic reconnaissance, flew its missions from Oman with a stopover in Kabul, Afghanistan, before returning to Oman the following day. The last three PR.9s in the British inventory flew this mission until retirement. One Nimrod R.1 ELINT aircraft has supported the allied effort in Afghanistan on a rotational basis. A Nimrod crashed in Afghanistan in September 2006, killing all 14 personnel aboard the plane.

France. France deployed both the Dassault Mirage F-1CR and the Dassault Mirage IV aircraft, both capable of carrying the CT-52 reconnaissance pod, to Afghanistan. The reconnaissance-capable Mirage IV's were retired from French service in 2005, leaving the Mirage F-1CR as that country's only aircraft operating with a tactical photographic reconnaissance pod. The French introduced a new generation reconnaissance pod for the Dassault Mirage 2000N variant, another aircraft that has seen service with France in Afghanistan. Dassault delivered the first planes of the Mirage 2000 series in 1984. The plane is powered by a SNECMA M53-P2 afterburning turbofan engine providing a maximum speed of 1,600 mph and a combat range of 770 miles.

Afghanistan

The Afghan Air Force under the Taliban regime maintained very few airworthy planes, and these were destroyed early during Operation ENDURING FREEDOM. The air force did include an unknown number of Sukhoi SU-20Rs reconnaissance aircraft, which were export versions of the SU-17R. The maiden flight of the SU-17 occurred in 1969. The Soviet-built aircraft underwent many modifications, and the SU-17R reconnaissance version emerged from the SU-17M. The SU-17 carried a single Lyulka AL-21F-3 afterburning turbojet engine that provided sufficient power for the aircraft to reach a maximum speed of 1,300 mph and a combat range of 620 miles. The Soviet Union provided 70 SU-17 aircraft to Afghanistan in 1982, but nearly all were out of commission by 2001. A few of the Afghan SU-17 aircraft were actually SU-20R reconnaissance models. These aircraft had been modified to carry reconnaissance pods rather than mount camera equipment within internal bays.

Operation IRAQI FREEDOM
U.S. Air Force

During Operation IRAQI FREEDOM, the U.S. Air Force deployed the Theater Airborne Reconnaissance System (TARS) pods on F-16 Fighting Falcon aircraft supporting ongoing military operations over Iraq. TARS is an "under the weather" system housed in a pod that is attached to the center line underneath the aircraft. The system includes digital cameras that eliminate the need for film processing and speed the process between taking the pictures and analyzing them. A recorder housed in the pod can store more than 12,000 images. The air force continued to rely on the U-2, and at least two U-2 aircraft supported the 2003 ground campaign of Operation IRAQI FREEDOM. In addition, the RC-135 Rivet Joint flew in support of coalition efforts in Iraq.

U.S. Navy

The U.S. Navy introduced the F/A-18 Hornet to service in 1983. The aircraft are powered by twin General Electric F404-GE-402 engines and have a maximum speed of more than 1,100 mph and a maximum range of more than 2,000 miles without armament. During Operation IRAQI FREEDOM, the navy flew F/A-18s carrying the SHARP system. Developed by Raytheon and mounted in a pod underneath the aircraft, the SHARP system houses medium- and high-altitude cameras. The pods are capable of transmitting real-time images directly from the aircraft to a monitoring station. Although designed primarily for the F/A-18 E and F models, the pod can be attached to other aircraft. The navy also flew the P-3 Orion in support of the coalition in Iraq.

U.S. Marines

The U.S. Marine Corps added the Advanced Tactical Airborne Reconnaissance System (ATARS) to some of its F/A-18D aircraft beginning in 1999, making them the long-awaited replacements for the RF-4Bs, retired in 1990. Each of the six F/A-18D squadrons has three aircraft modified for ATARS, located in the nose of the plane in lieu of a 20-mm cannon, and its accompanying reconnaissance pod. These were employed during Operation IRAQI FREEDOM.

Coalition

United Kingdom. The RAF flew at least one of its three Canberra PR.9s as well as six Tornado GR4As during tactical reconnaissance missions over Iraq. The latter aircraft is an upgrade of the GR1A utilized during the Persian Gulf War and can carry the Tornado Infra-Red Reconnaissance System (TIRRS). Other British assets have included one Nimrod R.1 and three Nimrod MR2 aircraft.

Australia. Australia provided two Lockheed AP-3 Orions for maritime reconnaissance during Operation IRAQI FREEDOM, but reduced the number to one after May 2003. The AP-3 is an Orion specifically modified to meet the ELINT reconnaissance requirements of Australia.

Iraq

In 2003 the Iraqi Air Force included the five Mikoyan-Gurevich Mig-25RB Foxbats that had survived the 1991 Persian Gulf War. Iraq did not fly any reconnaissance sorties against the coalition forces following the March 2003 invasion. At least two of the Mig-25RB aircraft were discovered buried in sand to hide them from allied troops.

TERRY M. MAYS

See also

Airborne Warning and Control System; DESERT STORM, Operation, Coalition Air Forces; ENDURING FREEDOM, Operation, U.S. Air Campaign; NORTHERN WATCH, Operation; Reconnaissance Satellites; SOUTHERN WATCH, Operation; United Kingdom, Air Force, Iraq War; United Kingdom, Air Force, Persian Gulf War; United States Air Force, Afghanistan War; United States Air Force, Iraq War; United States Air Force, Persian Gulf War

References

Fredriksen, John C. *Warbirds: An Illustrated Guide to U.S. Military Aircraft, 1915–2000.* Santa Barbara, CA: ABC-CLIO, 1999.

Jamieson, Perry D. *Lucrative Targets: The US Air Force in the Kuwaiti Theater of Operations.* Washington, DC: Air Force History and Museums Program, 2001.

Lake, Jon. "Canberra Finale." *Air Forces Monthly* 220 (July 2006): 41–47.

Lambeth, Benjamin S. *Air Power against Terror: America's Conduct of Operation Enduring Freedom.* Santa Monica, CA: RAND Corporation, 2005.

Nitschke, Stefan. "Recce Pods for Combat Aircraft." *Military Technology* 29(4) (April 2005): 38–45.

O'Ballance, Edgar. *The Second Gulf War: About the Liberation of Kuwait (August 1990–March 1991).* Bromley, UK: Galago Books, 1992.

Peters, John E., and Howard Deshong. *Out of Area or Out of Reach? European Military Support for Operations in Southwest Asia.* Santa Monica, CA: RAND Corporation, 1995.

Ripley, Tim. "US Ops in Afghanistan." *Air Forces Monthly* 220 (July 2006): 28–32.

Rockwell, David L. "Recce Pieces." *Journal of Electronic Defense* 25(6) (June 2002): 44–50.

Wilson, Charles P. *Strategic and Tactical Aerial Reconnaissance in the Near East.* Washington Institute for Near East Policy Military Research Papers #1. Washington, DC: Washington Institute for Near East Policy, 1999.

Aircraft, Suppression of Enemy Air Defense

The advent of integrated air defenses (IADs) involving a vast array of surface-to-air missiles (SAMs) and antiaircraft artillery has made suppressing an enemy's air defenses a critical component of any bombing campaign, particularly during the opening phases. The basic principle is that integrating fighter-interceptors, SAMs, and antiaircraft artillery provides defense in-depth and enables the air defense commander to employ his force components to comparative advantage. Fighters either engage incoming enemy aircraft beyond the range of SAMs or, if the enemy's fighters are more numerous, behind the SAMs to intercept targets of opportunity. The SAMs provide general area defense, primarily against high- and medium-altitude aircraft. Antiaircraft artillery is then employed for close-in and point defense to attack low-altitude enemy bombers flying along predicted routes or those diving to lower altitudes to escape SAM intercepts.

Theoretically, an integrated air defense forces the attacking aircraft to maneuver and evade nearly the entire time they are over enemy territory. During the Vietnam War, the Democratic Republic of Vietnam (DRV, North Vietnam) IAD system inflicted heavy losses on U.S. fighter-bombers operating over North Vietnam, while Egypt's IAD nearly halted Israeli air operations during the Yom Kippur (Ramadan) War in 1973. In both cases, the IADs inflicted such losses that Suppression of Enemy Air Defense (SEAD) missions now constitute nearly 30 percent of the sorties launched during an air campaign's first week and 5–10 percent of those employed throughout the campaign. They also gave rise to a class of aircraft and weapons specifically designed to suppress enemy air defenses.

There are two methods of suppressing enemy air defenses. One is through electronic warfare, often called the soft-kill option. Electronic warfare consists of jamming and deception of enemy communications networks and radars. The other means is the physical destruction or damage (i.e., hard kill) of those enemy systems. Aircraft engaged in hard-kill missions are known as SEAD aircraft. Typically, they are modified fighter or attack aircraft that have had their air intercept or bombing systems replaced by an onboard electronic sensor and targeting system that can detect, identify, and locate an enemy threat radar. In some cases, the aircraft simply carry wing pods with that capability. SEAD aircraft also carry antiradiation missiles (ARMs) designed to home in

An F-16C Fighting Falcon "Wild Weasel" aircraft, top left, and two F-4G Phantom II "Wild Weasel" aircraft from the U.S. Air Force 81st Tactical Fighter Squadron, 52nd Tactical Fighter Wing. The Fighting Falcon is armed with AIM-9 Sidewinder missiles and the lead Phantom II with an AGM-88 high-speed antiradiation missile (HARM). (U.S. Department of Defense)

on enemy radar emissions and fly down the beam to destroy the antenna and any nearby supporting equipment.

The U.S. F-4G Wild Weasel was the first SEAD aircraft known to enter combat service in the Middle East. Based on the McDonnell Douglas F-4C Phantom II, it entered service in 1966. It carried the AN/ALQ-131 and AN/ALQ-184 electronic warfare pods as well as four AGM-88 high-speed antiradiation missiles (HARMs) or AGM-65 Maverick missiles. The first variants were supplied to Israel in 1973 and saw extensive service in the closing days of the Yom Kippur War. U.S. Air Force F-4Gs were employed in every phase of Operations DESERT STORM, NORTHERN WATCH, and SOUTHERN WATCH. They were replaced by the Lockheed Martin F-16CJ beginning in 1988 and were retired from active service in 1995.

Derived from the Block 50 F-16C that entered production in 1994, the F-16CJ is a single-seat supersonic single-engine fighter that can carry the HARM targeting system in a wing pod and up to two HARM missiles. It first saw combat in Operations NORTHERN WATCH, SOUTHERN WATCH, and IRAQI FREEDOM. The U.S. Air Force retained two operational and one training squadron, each with 24 aircraft, in service through 2008.

The U.S. Navy modified its McDonnell Douglas (now Boeing) F/A-18 Hornet fighter, Grumman Aerospace A-6E Intruder attack, and EA-6B electronic warfare aircraft to carry the required targeting systems in wing pods and two AGM-65 Shrike (before 1985) or AGM-88 HARM (1985 onward) missiles. All three aircraft were employed in the SEAD role during Operations DESERT STORM and SOUTHERN WATCH, but the A-6Es were retired from service just after Operation ENDURING FREEDOM (2001). The navy's SEAD missions are now conducted either by F/A-18 or EA-6B aircraft. The aircraft operate in pairs with the hunter guiding the killer onto the target. The AF-18 will include SEAD missions among its capabilities once it enters service beginning in 2010. Once the EA-6B is retired, all U.S. SEAD-capable aircraft will be supersonic.

America's NATO allies also have SEAD aircraft and employed them during Operation DESERT STORM. The Royal Air Force used Panavia Tornado GR4s carrying four ALARM antiradiation missiles, while the Italian Air Force employed the Tornado ECR. The Tornado is a family of twin-engine aircraft jointly developed by the United Kingdom, Germany, and Italy. The Royal Air Force's GR4 is a modification of the reconnaissance variant of the Tornado in which electronic targeting pods replace the normal reconnaissance systems. The two-man crew consists of a pilot and sensor systems operator. The Royal Air Force acquired 30 GR4s, some of which are upgraded GR1s. The Italian Tornado ECR is unique in that it is the only European aircraft specifically designed for the SEAD mission. First entering service in 1990, it is equipped with an emitter-locator sensor system and can carry up to four AGM-88 HARMs. Italy employed 4 ECRs in DESERT STORM and acquired a total of 16.

Not all SEAD missions require aircraft specifically designed to attack enemy air defense systems. During Operations DESERT STORM and IRAQI FREEDOM, the United States employed Apache helicopters firing Hellfire missiles to take out Iraqi radars located along that country's border. Cluster bombs were also employed against Iraqi air defense systems. More recently, during Operation IRAQI FREEDOM U.S. Air Force and U.S. Navy attack aircraft employed the electro-optically guided GBU-15 bombs, laser-guided Paveway bombs, and the AGM-154 joint standoff weapons against air defense positions. Both weapons are accurate and provide the standoff distance required to ensure the attacking aircraft's survival.

As an air campaign progresses, SEAD aircraft increasingly are used in direct support of specific strikes or conduct area denial missions to attack any remaining air defense systems. Typically, if the air campaign's early SEAD operations are successful, mobile air defense systems are all that remain after the air campaign's first week.

A nation's ability to suppress enemy air defenses can spell the difference between success and failure in an air warfare operation or campaign. However, more often SEAD effectiveness determines the attackers' combat loss rate and bomber effectiveness. Even if the air defenses do not down many attacking aircraft, the need to evade engaging missiles and artillery and dedicate aircraft to SEAD missions reduces the number and accuracy of the weapons delivered on target. Thus, suppressing enemy air defenses probably will remain a critical mission for some time to come. The development of microminiaturization and high-speed and high-capacity computer systems suggests that future SEAD missions will involve fighter, attack, or electronic warfare aircraft equipped with plug-in or pod systems and standoff weapons. Barring the development of an air defense system requiring highly detailed and unique technologies to be defeated, the days of specialized SEAD aircraft may be at an end.

CARL OTIS SCHUSTER

See also

Aircraft, Attack; Aircraft, Electronic Warfare; Aircraft, Fighters; DESERT STORM, Operation; ENDURING FREEDOM, Operation; IRAQI FREEDOM, Operation; NORTHERN WATCH, Operation; SOUTHERN WATCH, Operation

References

Davies, Steve. *F-15E Strike Eagle Units in Combat, 1990–2005*. Oxford, UK: Osprey, 2005.

Gunston, Bill. *An Illustrated Guide to Spy Planes & Electronic Warfare Aircraft*. New York: Arco, 1983.

Hewson, Robert. *Jane's Air-Launched Weapons, 2001*. London: Jane's, 2002.

Jackson, Paul, et al. *Jane's All the World's Aircraft, 2005–06*. London: Jane's, 2005.

Knight, Michael, ed. *Operation Iraqi Freedom and the New Iraq*. Washington, DC: Washington Institute for Near East Policy, 2004.

Olsen, John. *Strategic Air Power in Desert Storm*. London: Frank Cass, 2003.

Tripp, Robert. *Lessons Learned from Operation Enduring Freedom*. Santa Monica, CA: RAND Corporation, 2004.

Aircraft, Tankers

Tankers are aircraft with the sole function of refueling other aircraft in midair. Aerial refueling extends the range or time on

A U.S. Air Force 401st Tactical Fighter Wing F-16C Fighting Falcon aircraft refuels from a KC-135 Stratotanker aircraft as another F-16 stands by during Operation DESERT STORM. (U.S. Department of Defense)

station of other aircraft and allows them to take off with a larger payload than would normally be possible. Two methods are employed for aerial refueling. In the first, the tanker aircraft's tail-mounted boom is guided into a receptacle on the receiver aircraft. In the other, the tanker aircraft trails a basketlike drogue on the end of a hose, and the receiver aircraft guides a probe into the drogue. Both methods are complex and require considerable training to execute safely.

Middle Eastern air forces have not purchased significant numbers of tankers because they are based sufficiently close to their opponents that they usually do not need this capability. The principal role of tankers in the Middle East wars has in fact been to support U.S. intervention. Refueling has enabled the United States to fly cargo and troops into the region, to ferry short-range aircraft from the United States to theater bases, and to conduct combat operations with bombers and tactical aircraft.

Numerous U.S. tankers have been employed in the Middle East wars. The Boeing KC-97 Stratotanker is a U.S. Air Force four-engine propeller-powered KC-97 used in the 1950s and 1960s. Israel operated nine KC-97s from 1965 to 1978. The KC-97 provided up to 60,000 pounds of fuel via a boom. It had a cruise speed of 483 miles per hour (mph), a ceiling of 30,200 feet, and a range of 4,300 miles.

Boeing converted a number of 707 transports into KC-707 tankers for foreign customers. During 1983–1999 Israel obtained five Boeing 707-320 aircraft and converted them to KC-707 tankers. Saudi Arabia bought eight KC-707 tankers from 1983 to 1998. Saudi tankers, sometimes designated KE-3, resemble the E-3 AWACS (Airborne Warning and Control System) aircraft but without rotodome or surveillance equipment. Iran has four KC-707-3J9C tankers, obtained in 1974. The KC-707 has four turbofans and can transfer 123,190 pounds of fuel via centerline boom and wing-mounted drogue pods simultaneously. Cruise speed is 550 mph, ceiling is 39,000 feet, and range is 5,755 miles.

Boeing modified three 747-100 aircraft as prototypes for the U.S. Air Force LC-747. Iran purchased them in 1975 and still operates them. They can transfer 330,000 pounds of fuel through a boom as well as carry cargo. They have four turbofans. Cruise speed is 565 mph, ceiling is 45,000 feet, and range is 6,333 miles.

Lockheed KC-130H

The Lockheed KC-130H is a variant of the C-130 Hercules transport that refuels fixed-wing aircraft or helicopters via two wing-mounted drogue pods. It has four turboprops. Fuel capacity is 86,000 pounds. Israel has operated 2 since 1976. Saudi Arabia has operated 8 since 1973. The U.S. Marine Corps employed 20 in

Operation DESERT STORM in 1991 and 22 in Operation IRAQI FREEDOM in 2003. They have a cruise speed of 362 mph, a ceiling of 30,000 feet, and a range of 1,150 miles.

The Boeing KC-135 Stratotanker replaced the KC-97 and took its name. Boeing's 367-80 design was the prototype for the KC-135 and the 707 commercial jetliner. The KC-135 thus superficially resembles the 707. Boeing built 732 KC-135 from 1956 to 1965, and 530 remain in service. The KC-135 has four turbofans and transfers up to 200,000 pounds of fuel via boom or drogue. Cruise speed is 530 mph, ceiling is 50,000 feet, and range is 3,450 miles.

In 1981 the U.S. Air Force began procuring the McDonnell Douglas KC-10 Extender, derived from the DC-10 passenger jetliner. Fifty-nine remain in service. The KC-10 can transfer up to 342,000 pounds of fuel via boom or drogue. Fifteen can provide fuel from centerline boom and two wingtip drogue pods simultaneously. All can carry cargo and passengers as well as fuel and can be refueled themselves, extending their time on station. They have three turbofans. Cruise speed is 619 mph, ceiling is 42,000 feet, and range is 4,400 miles.

Tankers are critical to American power projection. In Operations DESERT SHIELD and DESERT STORM, 302 tankers delivered 800 million pounds of fuel, flying 5,000 sorties during the prewar airlift and 17,000 sorties during the 43-day air campaign. In the first three months of Operation ENDURING FREEDOM in Afghanistan (2001), 60 tankers flew 13,625 sorties to support strike aircraft that often needed two refuelings each way to complete their missions. In Operation IRAQI FREEDOM (2003), 319 tankers offloaded 450 million pounds of fuel in 9,700 sorties. These operations would have been very different in nature, if they were possible at all, without aerial refueling.

The British operated their own tankers during various Middle East campaigns. The Royal Air Force procured six Lockheed L1011 Tristar tankers from 1985 to 1988. Two are pure tankers, and four can switch between tanker and cargo roles. Tristars have three turbofans. They transfer up to 260,500 pounds of fuel from two hose/drogue units mounted under the rear fuselage, only one of which can be used at a time. Cruise speed is 605 mph, ceiling is 42,000 feet, and range is 5,998 miles.

The Royal Air Force converted 27 Vickers VC10 transports into tankers between 1979 and 1996. Not all were in service simultaneously. The VC10 has four turbofans. Four K.3, 5 K.4, and 11 C.1K models are still in service today. The K.3 and K.4 tankers transfer fuel from three hose/drogue units (one unit in the centerline, two pods under each wing). The C.1K model has two underwing pods only. The C.1K and K.4 models transfer up to 155,000 pounds of fuel, and the K.3 transfers up to 176,000 pounds of fuel. Cruise speed is 580 mph, ceiling is 38,000 feet, and range is 4,720 miles.

British tankers served in Operations DESERT SHIELD, DESERT STORM, ENDURING FREEDOM, and IRAQI FREEDOM. The Royal Air Force intends to replace 20 of its tankers with a tanker based on the Airbus A330-200 airframe, which is a large commercial jetliner.

JAMES D. PERRY

See also
DESERT SHIELD, Operation; DESERT STORM, Operation; ENDURING FREEDOM, Operation; IRAQI FREEDOM, Operation

References
Angelucci, Enzo. *The Rand McNally Encyclopedia of Military Aircraft, 1914–1980.* New York: Military Press, 1983.
Fredriksen, John C. *Warbirds: An Illustrated Guide to U.S. Military Aircraft, 1915–2000.* Santa Barbara, CA: ABC-CLIO, 1999.
Gething, Michael, and Bill Sweetman. "Air to Air Refueling Provides a Force Multiplier for Expeditionary Warfare." *International Defence Review* (January 11, 2006): 5–11.

Aircraft, Transport

Transport aircraft move personnel, supplies, and weapons when speed is required or when ground or sea transport is impractical. Strategic airlifts use large aircraft to move troops and cargo over intercontinental distances. Tactical airlifts use smaller aircraft to move troops and cargo within a theater of operations. In the Middle East wars, the United States was the primary user of the strategic airlift. Middle Eastern nations tended to employ tactical airlifts.

U.S. Transports

Airlift is essential to U.S. power projection. Thus, in the October 1973 Yom Kippur (Ramadan) War, U.S. transports flew 566 missions to Israel and delivered 22,305 tons of tanks, ammunition, and supplies. From August 1990 to February 1991 during Operations DESERT SHIELD and DESERT STORM, U.S. aircraft moved 482,000 troops and 513,000 tons of cargo to Saudi Arabia. From 2001 to 2004 U.S. transports carried 464,239 tons of cargo and passengers to support Operation IRAQI FREEDOM in Iraq and Operation ENDURING FREEDOM in Afghanistan. Many Middle Eastern countries have acquired U.S. transport aircraft since 1945.

The U.S. Air Force operates 150 Boeing C-17 Globemaster III aircraft obtained after 1991. The C-17 carries 170,900 pounds of cargo, 102 paratroops, or an armored fighting vehicle. The C-17 has four turbofan engines. It has a cruising speed of 517 miles per hour (mph), a ceiling of 45,000 feet, and an unfueled range of 2,760 miles.

The four-turbofan Boeing 707-320 carries up to 215 passengers or 63,380 pounds of cargo. It cruises at 605 mph and has a 39,000-foot ceiling and a 5,755-mile range. Israel purchased 29 707-320 airliners beginning in 1973 and converted them to transports, tankers, and intelligence aircraft. Iran operates 14 707-3J9C transports acquired in the 1970s.

Boeing built more than 1,400 four-turbofan 747 Jumbo Jets from 1970 to 2006. They serve many airlines. The 747-100 carries up to 452 passengers or 30 pallets of cargo. Cruising speed is 555 mph at 35,000 feet, with a 6,100-mile maximum range. Iran operates 11 747 transports acquired in the 1970s (3 converted to tankers). Saudi Arabia operates 4 747s for communications and VIP transport.

U.S. Air Force staff sergeant David Pirie, a loadmaster with the 746th Expeditionary Airlift Squadron (EAS), helps prepare a Lockheed C-130J Super Hercules aircraft for takeoff on a mission in Southwest Asia, September 22, 2009. (U.S. Department of Defense)

The U.S. Air Force operates 126 Lockheed C-5 Galaxy aircraft acquired between 1969 and 1989. Each carries 270,000 pounds of cargo, including 73 passengers and a tank or armored fighting vehicle. The C-5 has four turbofan engines, a 500-mph cruising speed, a 41,000-foot ceiling, and a 2,473-mile unrefueled range.

Lockheed built more than 8,000 C-130 Hercules four-turbo-prop tactical transports in more than 40 variants from 1956 onward. The latest version (C-130J) carries 92 troops, 64 para-troops, 74 litters, or 42,000 pounds of cargo. The C-130J cruising speed is 417 mph, the ceiling is 28,000 feet, and the range with maximum payload is 2,382 miles. During the Persian Gulf War, 145 C-130s operated in-theater, flying 46,500 sorties and moving 209,000 personnel and 300,000 tons of supplies. In Operation IRAQI FREEDOM (2003), 124 C-130s flew 2,203 missions, moving 9,662 people and 12,444 tons of supplies.

Many foreign nations operate the C-130. Britain purchased 66 C-130K (equivalent to the C-130E) in 1966, 30 of which were "stretched" into the C-130H-30 configuration in 1980. Britain ordered 25 C-130J planes in 1994. British Hercules aircraft served in Operations DESERT STORM and DESERT SHIELD in 1990–1991, in Afghanistan (2001 to the present), and in Iraq from 2003 to the present. Today, 44 remain in service.

Israel acquired 13 C-130E and 11 C-130H Hercules from 1971 to 1976. Four C-130H serve as tankers, and two C-130E serve as electronic intelligence aircraft. Egypt purchased 23 C-130H trans-ports and 2 EC-130H electronic intelligence aircraft in 1974 and 3 C-130H-30 transports in 1990. Jordan bought 4 C-130B in 1972. Jordan also purchased 5 C-130H aircraft in 1978 that remain in service.

Iran purchased 20 C-130E and 40 C-130H planes during 1965–1974. Some 15 to 20 remain in service. Saudi Arabia received 54 C-130E/H from 1965 to 1992. Seven C-130E, 29 C-130H, 7 KC-130H, and 5 C-130H-30 planes remain in service. Kuwait bought 2 C-130E planes in 1970, 4 C-130H-30 planes in 1983, and 4 C-130J planes in 2004. C-130E cruising speed is 368 mph, ceiling is 23,000 feet, and range with a 45,000-pound maximum payload is 2,422 miles. The C-130H cruising speed is 374 mph, ceiling is 33,000 feet, and range with a 36,000-pound maximum payload is 2,356 miles.

Civil Reserve Air Fleet

The U.S. government has contracts with U.S. airlines that agree to provide airlift to the Defense Department during emergencies. The Civil Reserve Air Fleet (CRAF) consists of 1,364 aircraft, including the Boeing 707 and 747, Douglas DC-8 and DC-10, and Lockheed L-1011. The CRAF flew two-thirds of the passengers and one-fourth of the cargo to Saudi Arabia during Operation DESERT SHIELD. The CRAF moved 254,143 troops and 11,050 tons of cargo to Kuwait before Operation IRAQI FREEDOM.

The following American-built transports are no longer in U.S. service, but some still operate in Middle Eastern air forces.

The light twin-piston–engine Aero Commander transport first flew in 1948. The 690 model seated 7 to 11 passengers, with a 330-mph maximum speed, a 31,000-foot ceiling, and an 853-mile maximum range. The Iranian Air Force obtained 8 500, 6 680, and 15 690 Commanders in the 1970s. Some 10 690 models remain in service.

Beech produced the C-45 Expeditor, a twin-engine transport, from 1937 to 1970, including 4,000 C-45 models from 1940 to 1945. The Expeditor carried eight passengers and cruised at 185 mph. It has a 21,400-foot ceiling and a 1,530-mile range. Syria used 4 from 1949 to 1974. Iran employed 10 from 1950 to 1972.

The Boeing 377 Stratocruiser is a late 1940s design that served as a civilian airliner, military transport, and tanker (377/C-97/KC-97). Israel purchased five Stratocruisers from Pan Am Airlines in 1962 and converted them to military transports. Some were later converted into tankers. All were retired in 1978. Stratocruisers had four piston engines. They carried 96 troops or 20,000 pounds of cargo. Cruise speed was 300 mph, with a 30,200-foot ceiling and a 4,300-mile range.

Curtiss built 3,182 C-46 Commandos from 1942 to 1945. The C-46 had two piston engines. It carried 50 passengers and had a 173-mph cruising speed, a 24,500-foot ceiling, and a 3,150-mile range. Israel operated 5 from 1948 to 1949. Egypt operated 10 from 1945 to 1957.

Douglas built only five DC-5 airliners. Israel used one in 1948–1949. The DC-5 had two piston engines and carried 22 passengers. It cruised at 202 mph and had a 23,700-foot ceiling and a 1,600-mile range.

Douglas built an astounding 10,123 C-47 Skytrains after 1935. The civilian version is the venerable DC-3. Some remain in service today. The C-47, with two piston engines, carried 28 troops or 6,000 pounds of cargo. Cruising speed was 207 mph, with a 23,200-foot ceiling and a 2,125-mile range. Israel acquired 34 from 1948 to 1960 and retired them in 2001. Egypt operated 20 from 1945 to 1972. Syria used 6 from 1949 into the 1970s. Iran employed 23 from 1948 to 1976. Jordan owned 4 from 1966 to 1977.

Douglas manufactured 1,170 C-54 Skymasters during World War II. The C-54 had four piston engines and carried 50 passengers. It had a 227-mph cruising speed, a 22,300-foot ceiling, and a 2,500-mile range. Israel used 1 from 1948 to 1949. Iran had 6 from 1945 to 1976.

Fairchild produced more than 1,100 twin-engine C-119 Flying Boxcars from 1947 to 1955. The U.S. Air Force used them until 1975. They carried 62 troops or 10,000 pounds of cargo. Cruising speed was 200 mph, with a 30,000-foot ceiling and a 2,000-mile range. Jordan operated four surplus C-119Ks from 1972 to 1974.

Lockheed built only a few hundred Lodestars during World War II. Lodestars had two piston engines and carried 14 passengers. They had a 218-mph maximum speed, a 20,400-foot ceiling, and a 1,800-mile range. Israel employed one in 1948–1949, and Egypt utilized one during 1950–1951.

Lockheed built 846 Constellations from 1943 to 1956. They were quickly superseded by jet airliners in the early 1950s. The Constellation carried 60–100 passengers. They had four turbocompound engines, a 354-mph cruising speed, a 25,000-foot ceiling, and a 5,400-mile range. Israel employed 3 in 1948 and gave them to El Al, the Israeli airline, in 1951.

The U.S. Air Force procured 284 Lockheed C-141 Starlifters from 1964 to 1982, retiring the last in 2006. The C-141B carried 200 troops, 155 paratroops, 103 litters, or 68,725 pounds of cargo. With four turbofan engines, C-141 cruising speed was 500 mph, ceiling was 41,000 feet, and unrefueled range was 2,500 miles.

Soviet Transports

The Soviets employed their transports to supply the Arab states with weapons, ammunition, and equipment. For example, during the October 1973 Yom Kippur (Ramadan) War, Antonov An-12 and An-22 transports flew 930 sorties to deliver 15,000 tons of military cargo to Egypt and Syria. The Soviets also used airlift extensively during their war in Afghanistan from 1979 to 1989. In the initial invasion, 280 An-12, An-22, and Ilyushin Il-76 transports delivered three Guards Airborne divisions to Kabul. The Soviets also sold many transports to their Middle Eastern clients.

The Soviet Union and Poland built more than 17,000 Antonov An-2 single-engine transports from 1947 to 1992. The An-2 carried 12 passengers or 2,733 pounds of cargo. It had a 115-mph cruising speed, a 14,425-foot ceiling, and a 560-mile range. Egypt operated 10 from 1955 to 1999. Iraq used 20 from 1959 to 1990.

The Soviets produced some 900 Antonov An-12 aircraft between 1957 and 1973. The An-12 somewhat resembled the C-130. With four turboprops, it carried 90 troops or 44,000 pounds of cargo. It had a 342-mph cruising speed, a 33,465-foot ceiling, and a 2,113-mile range. Egypt operated 34 from 1956 to 1997. Syria flew 6 from 1975 to 1991. Iraq utilized 12 from 1962 to 1990, while Jordan flew 3 from 1981 to 1984.

The Antonov An-22 is an enlarged twin-tail An-12. Sixty-five were produced between 1965 and 1976. Some remain in service in Russia. It has four turboprops and carried 180,000 pounds of cargo and 29 passengers. Maximum speed is 460 mph, ceiling is 24,600 feet, and range is 3,100 miles.

The twin-turboprop Antonov An-24 carried 44 troops. Cruise speed was 280 mph, ceiling was 27,560 feet, and range was 342 miles. Egypt operated 3 from 1971 to 1994. Syria flew 5 from 1979 to 1998. Iraq employed 11 from 1969 to 1990.

The twin-turboprop Antonov An-26 carried 40 troops. Cruising speed was 270 mph, ceiling was 26,575 feet, and range was 559 miles. Syria used 6 from 1979 onward. Iraq flew 10 from 1973 to 1990.

A Soviet Antonov An-12 (NATO designation Cub) transport aircraft, photographed in 1985. (U.S. Department of Defense)

Antonov An-74

The Antonov An-74 is a twin-turbofan design that carries 52 passengers or 10 tons of cargo. Capable of short takeoff/landing (STOL) from rough airfields, the An-74 has a cruising speed of 440 mph, a ceiling of 33,136 feet, and a range of 2,980 miles. Iran ordered 10 An-74TK-200 planes in 1997.

The Ilyushin Il-14 is a twin-piston–engine transport that carried 25 passengers. Maximum speed was 259 mph, ceiling was 24,280 feet, and range was 811 miles. Egypt operated 70 from 1955 to 1994. Syria used 16 from 1957 to 1998. Iraq operated 70 from 1958 to 1990. Iran flew 1 from 1950 to 1976.

The Ilyushin Il-18 had four turboprop engines and carried 75 passengers. It cruised at 419 mph, with a 25,250-foot ceiling and 2,299-mile range. Syria operated five from 1972 to 1998.

Still in production, the Ilyushin Il-76 somewhat resembles the U.S. C-141. It has four turbofan engines and carries 88,185 pounds of cargo. Cruising speed is 497 mph, with a 50,850-foot ceiling and a 2,265-mile range. Syria purchased 4 in 1980 and still flies them. Iraq bought 33 from 1978 to 1984, but most were destroyed in the 1991 Persian Gulf War. Fifteen escaped from Iraq to Iran during that war, and Iran has operated them since.

The Yakovlev Yak-40 has three turbofans and carried 32 passengers. It cruised at 342 mph, with a 22,965-foot ceiling and a 901-mile range. Syria operated eight from 1976 onward.

The twin-turbofan Tupelov Tu-124 carried 44 passengers. It had a 603-mph maximum speed, 38,285 foot ceiling, and 758-mile range. Iraq operated two from 1965 to 1990.

The twin-turbofan Tupelov Tu-134 somewhat resembled the DC-9. The Tu-134 carried 72 passengers. Cruising speed was 550 mph, with a 39,010-foot ceiling and a 1,174-mile range. Iraq operated two from 1981 to 1990.

The twin-turbofan Tupelov Tu-143B-3 carries 72 passengers. Cruising speed is 550 mph, with a 39,010-foot ceiling and 1,174-mile range. Syria operated five from 1983 onward.

Royal Air Force Transports

During the 1956 Suez Crisis, British paratroops dropped on Port Said in Handley Page Hastings and Vickers Valetta transports. Royal Air Force (RAF) Tristar and VC10 transports supported Operations DESERT SHIELD/DESERT STORM in 1990–1991. Royal Air Force Tristar, VC10, and four leased C-17 transports operated in Afghanistan and Iraq from 2001 to 2006.

The Royal Air Force operates nine American-built Lockheed L1011 Tristars obtained between 1982 and 1989. Three C.2/2A models are pure cargo aircraft, two K.1 aircraft are tankers, and four KC.1 aircraft can switch between tanker and cargo roles. The C.2/2A transports 266 passengers, and the KC.1 in cargo mode transports 160 passengers or 44 tons of cargo. Tristars have three turbofans. Cruise speed is 605 mph, ceiling is 42,000 feet, and range is 5,998 miles.

The Royal Air Force operated 211 Vickers Valetta C.1, 11 C.2, and 40 T.3 twin-engine transports from 1947 to 1968. Valettas carried 34 troops, 20 paratroops, or 12,050 pounds of cargo. Maximum speed was 258 mph, with a 21,500-foot ceiling and 1,460-mile range.

The Royal Air Force obtained 14 Vickers VC10 C.1 transports during 1966–1968. Thirteen were converted into dual-capable cargo/tanker aircraft during 1992–1996, and 10 remain in service. In cargo mode, they carried 150 passengers or 45,000 pounds of cargo. The VC10 has four turbofans. Maximum speed is 580 mph, ceiling is 38,000 feet, and range is 7,210 miles.

Other Transports

Airspeed, a British company, built only 20 Airspeed Ambassadors, twin-piston–engine transports, in 1947. They carried 47 passengers. Cruising speed was 312 mph, with a 36,089-foot ceiling and 550-mile range. Jordan flew three from 1959 to 1963.

Israel operated two British-built Britten-Norman BN-2A Islander light transports from 1973 to 1994. They had two piston engines, carried nine passengers, cruised at 150 mph, and had a 14,600-foot ceiling and 870-mile range.

Israel purchased six Dornier Do-28D Skyservant twin-piston–engine transports from West Germany in 1975 and retired them in 1997. Skyservants carried 13 passengers or 2,205 pounds of cargo. They cruised at 202 mph, with a 25,195-foot ceiling and 399-mile range.

The Dutch-built Fokker F.27 Friendship twin-turboprop is widely used worldwide. It carries 28 passengers, with a 300-mph cruising speed, 32,600-foot ceiling, and 912-mile range. The Iranian military obtained 19 F.27-400M and 7 F.27-600 models from 1971 to 1983. Ten remain in service.

The Antonov-designed Iran-140 twin-turboprop is built in Iran. It carries 60 passengers or 13,000 pounds of cargo. It has a 328-mph cruising speed, 23,622-foot ceiling, and 1,304-mile range. The Iranian military now operates 45 of them.

The Israeli Air Force operated 10 Israeli Aircraft Industries Aravas from 1973 to 1997. Twin-piston–engine Aravas carried 19 passengers or 5,184 pounds of cargo, cruised at 193 mph, and had a 25,000-foot ceiling and 161-mile range.

Syria acquired seven examples of the Junkers Ju-52, the work-horse German transport of World War II, in 1949, using them until 1953. The Ju-52, with three piston engines, carried 18 troops. It had a 171-mph maximum speed, 19,360-foot ceiling, and 808-mile range.

Israel flew 20 Canadian-built Noorduyn Norsemen in 1948, retiring them in 1950. Powered by a single piston engine, the Norseman carried 8 passengers. It had a 155-mph cruising speed, 17,000-foot ceiling, and 1,150-mile range.

France's Nord Aviation built 425 N.2501 Noratlas transports from 1951 to 1961. Israel bought 24 in 1955 and retired them in 1976. They carried 15,000 pounds of cargo or 45 paratroops. The Noratlas had two piston engines, cruised at 273 mph, and had a 24,605-foot ceiling and 1,864-mile range. During the Suez Crisis, Israeli Noratlas dropped Israeli paratroops in the Sinai, while French Noratlas based in Cyprus dropped French paratroopers on Port Said.

JAMES D. PERRY

See also

Arab-Israeli Conflict, Overview; Aircraft, Tankers; DESERT SHIELD, Operation; DESERT STORM, Operation; ENDURING FREEDOM, Operation; IRAQI FREEDOM, Operation

References

Angelucci, Enzo. *The Rand McNally Encyclopedia of Military Aircraft, 1914–1980.* New York: Military Press, 1983.
Bickers, Richard Townshend. *Military Air Transport: The Illustrated History.* London: Osprey, 1998.
Donald, David. *The Complete Encyclopedia of World Aircraft.* New York: Orbis, 1997.
Williams, Nicholas M. *Aircraft of the Military Air Transport Service.* London: Midland, 1999.

Aircraft Carriers

Naval airpower has played an important role in the Middle East over the past decades. Although U.S., British, and French aircraft carriers played important roles in the 1956 Suez Crisis, in peace-keeping operations in Lebanon in the 1980s, in U.S. confrontations with Libya, and in Operation SOUTHERN WATCH against Iraq, discussion here is limited to their roles in Operations DESERT SHIELD, DESERT STORM, ENDURING FREEDOM, and IRAQI FREEDOM. All these saw extensive naval involvement, including naval airpower.

French and American aircraft carriers were traditional large-deck or conventional takeoff and landing (CTOL) carriers. That is, these aircraft were launched and recovered (landed on the carrier) by traditional or conventional means (e.g., steam-powered cata-pults for launch and recovered by using an arresting wire to stop the plane within the flight deck's length). The advantage of the system is that it enables the carrier to handle high-performance aircraft. The disadvantage is that it requires a large and expen-sive ship to do it. The French CTOL carriers displaced more than

32,000 tons to carry a 40-plane air wing, while U.S. aircraft carriers typically displace 94,000 (*Enterprise* [CVN-65]) to 104,000 tons full load (Nimitz-class) and have an air wing of up to 90 aircraft.

Both nations' CTOL carriers have four propellers and powerful propulsion systems, giving them top speeds exceeding 35 knots. Other allied nations deployed smaller vertical/short-takeoff and landing (V/STOL) carriers, displacing under 30,000 tons, with air wings of under 25 helicopters and lower-performance McDonnell Douglas/BAE/Boeing AV-8 Harrier V/STOL aircraft. Although their striking power was less than that of their CTOL counterparts, the V/STOL carriers were ideally suited for sea control and sanctions-enforcement missions in support of coalition naval operations before and during the outbreak of hostilities.

Two U.S. aircraft carriers, the *Independence* (CV-62) and *Dwight D. Eisenhower* (CVN-69) were within striking range of Iraq when Saddam Hussein's forces invaded Kuwait on August 2, 1990. The *Independence* was just south of the Arabian Sea and was the first to arrive in the Gulf of Oman, on August 4. The *Eisenhower* was in the eastern Mediterranean and transited the Suez Canal three days later. The air wing provided by the *Independence* served as the initial air cover for the deployment of coalition forces into the Persian Gulf, but several weeks would pass before it and the *Eisenhower* were joined by other carriers. By then, land-based airpower dominated the emerging anti-Hussein coalition's long-range striking power. Moreover, the U.S. Air Force's prepositioned weapons and equipment stockpiles enabled its units to be fully combat ready within hours of arrival. Coalition land-based aircraft provided the bulk of the coalition's airpower after August 7, 1990.

During Operation DESERT SHIELD, much of the U.S. Navy's air effort focused on maintaining air superiority over the Persian Gulf and supporting coalition sanctions-enforcement operations in those and surrounding waters as well as the Indian Ocean. As preparations for DESERT STORM advanced in late 1990, the navy quickly discovered that its command and control equipment was inadequate for involvement in large-scale air operations. Central Command's Air Tasking Order (ATO) was a comprehensive integrated air plan that incorporated all aspects of air operations, including tanking and cruise missiles. Disseminated daily in time for individual units to plan and prepare their flight operations, it was by necessity a large and complex electronic document. Air force units employed fiber-optic–linked computer systems to prepare and disseminate the ATO to ensure its rapid distribution and assimilation by tactical units. Unfortunately, the navy was still using narrowband command and control systems to support its deployed forces. To put it in a contemporary context, the ATO was transmitted over a high-speed broadband system, while the U.S. Navy employed the operational equivalent to Internet dial-up to receive it. It proved more practical to print out the ATO and deliver it to the aircraft carriers and cruise missile ships by helicopter. This was both a major inconvenience and an embarrassment for the navy.

Nonetheless, naval aircraft played an important role in DESERT STORM's combat operations, taking out coastal targets and air

The nuclear-powered aircraft carrier USS *Enterprise* (CVN 65) transiting the North Arabian Sea on November 11, 2007, while conducting flight operations with its embarked Carrier Air Wing 1. (U.S. Department of Defense)

defenses. Most of the carriers operated in the Gulf of Oman, with one forward deployed in the central/western Persian Gulf. Uncertainty about Iranian intentions influenced the carrier operations, particularly after the bulk of the Iraqi Air Force defected to Iran in February 1991. Although Iran never evinced any specific hostile intentions, its continued anti-Western rhetoric and hostility toward the United States led U.S. naval leaders to withhold a portion of their power to counter any potential Iranian threat. For example, the forward carrier dedicated nearly 50 percent of its sorties to fleet air defense, while those in the Gulf of Oman allocated 35 percent of their operations to that role.

At its peak, the U.S. Navy had six aircraft carriers deployed in the Persian Gulf and one supporting the coalition naval units enforcing the United Nations (UN) sanctions against the Hussein regime. At least one unit of every class of U.S. aircraft carrier participated at some point in either DESERT SHIELD or DESERT STORM. The oldest and smallest U.S. Navy carrier in the Persian Gulf War was the conventionally powered *Midway* (CV-41), the lead ship of a three-ship class and one of the two units of that class remaining in active service (the other being the *Coral Sea* [CV-41]). Originally commissioned in September 1945, the *Midway* had been modified extensively over the intervening 47 years, which had raised its displacement to over 70,000 tons, improved its command and control systems, increased the power of its catapults, and enlarged its flight deck. However, the ship had only two catapults, three instead of four elevators, and a much smaller air wing than the new carriers (60 planes versus 72–79). Its design was based on the lessons of World War II, making it one of the most damage-resistant ships ever built, but it was a difficult ship to move around in, carried less aviation fuel and ordnance than the other aircraft carriers, and was up to five knots slower. The *Midway* originally had been scheduled for decommissioning in 1991, but the war's outbreak extended its active service another year.

Four other classes of aircraft carriers served in DESERT SHIELD/DESERT STORM, two of which were single-unit classes: the nuclear-powered *Enterprise* (CVN-65) and the conventionally powered *John F. Kennedy* (CV-67). Commissioned on November 25, 1961, the *Enterprise* was America's first nuclear-powered aircraft carrier. Measuring more than 1,123 feet in length overall, it was powered by eight nuclear reactors generating more than 280,000 shaft horsepower. With 4,800 people, its crew complement and air wing were smaller than that of the carriers built since 1976, but the ship is expected to remain in service until 2012–2013.

The *John F. Kennedy* (CV-67) was America's last conventionally powered aircraft carrier (CV). Originally intended to be the navy's second nuclear-powered CV, Secretary of Defense Robert McNamara had directed that it be conventionally powered. As a result, the navy initiated its construction as the third Kitty Hawk-class unit but modified the design so extensively during construction that it

became a new class of unit and formed the basis for the nuclear-powered Nimitz class that has dominated the U.S. aircraft carrier inventory since the late 1980s. Displacing 82,000 tons full load, the *Kennedy* was commissioned in September 7, 1968, and had a crew of nearly 3,200 sailors and an air wing contingent that numbered nearly 2,500 personnel. Like all conventionally powered carriers, it had eight boilers driving four propellers, but it was the fastest of the conventional carriers, with a top speed exceeding 35 knots when it was new. The ship was decommissioned on August 1, 2007.

The other conventionally powered units that saw service in the Persian Gulf conflicts were the Forrestal and Kitty Hawk classes. The three-unit *James Forrestal* (CV-59) was the first class to follow the Midway-class units, the first carriers designed specifically to handle jet aircraft, and the first American carriers built with the angled flight deck found on all CTOL aircraft carriers. Displacing 81,000 tons full load, it was commissioned on October 1, 1955. The *Forrestal* itself never served in the Persian Gulf during any of the conflicts there, but its sisters ships, the *Saratoga* (CV-60), *Ranger* (CV-61), and *Independence* (CV-62) did. All three units were decommissioned by 1996. The follow-on three-ship Kitty Hawk class was slightly larger, displacing a little over 82,000 tons. All of them—the *Kitty Hawk* (CV-63), *Constellation* (CV-64), and *America* (CV-66)—served in DESERT SHIELD/DESERT STORM, but only

The British light aircraft carrier *Ark Royal*. Note the 12-degree ski-jump ramp forward to improve take off performance of its Harrier aircraft. (AP/Wide World Photos)

the *Kitty Hawk* participated in Operations ENDURING FREEDOM and IRAQI FREEDOM. Its sister ships were decommissioned by 1997, and the *Kitty Hawk,* which was commissioned on December 1, 1956, was decommissioned on May 12, 2009.

Commissioned in 1963, the French aircraft carrier *Clemenceau* was the only non-U.S. CTOL carrier involved in DESERT SHIELD and DESERT STORM. However, its participation was limited to sea control and sanctions-enforcement operations in the Mediterranean Sea and the Red Sea, protecting the transports that delivered French ground forces and delivering some of the army's helicopters to Saudi Arabia. It and its sister ship, the *Foch,* were decommissioned by 2000. The only other allied carrier involved in Operations DESERT SHIELD/DESERT STORM was the British V/STOL carrier *Ark Royal,* which conducted sanctions-enforcement operations in the eastern Mediterranean. The third of the Invincible-class carriers, it was commissioned in November 1985. It displaced 20,600 tons full load, and its four Rolls Royce Olympus gas turbines produced a top speed of more than 28 knots. Its air wing in 1991 consisted of six AV-8 Harriers and a dozen Westland Sea King helicopters. France did not provide naval assets for Operation ENDURING FREEDOM and did not participate in any capacity during Operation IRAQI FREEDOM.

The 10 years after DESERT STORM saw the United States decommission many of its older warships. As a result, the U.S. Navy was a much smaller fleet on September 11, 2001, when Al Qaeda conducted its terrorist attacks on the United States. However, the navy was much more technologically advanced. The three aircraft carriers that deployed to the Persian Gulf region for Operations ENDURING FREEDOM and IRAQI FREEDOM—the *Enterprise* (CVN-65), *John C. Stennis* (CVN-70), and *Theodore Roosevelt* (CVN-71)—constituted the primary strike element of coalition Task Force 50. They conducted long-range strike operations as part of the coalition strategic and operational air campaign.

The bulk of the U.S. Navy aircraft carriers supporting operations in the later wars were the Nimitz-class units. Their larger size enabled them to carry a larger crew (approximately 6,500 personnel total) and slightly larger air wing (90 versus 72) than the older carriers. The *John C. Stennis* (CVN-70) and *Theodore Roosevelt* (CVN-71) were commissioned on March 13, 1982, and October 25, 1986, respectively. Their propulsion system is powered by two nuclear reactors. In addition to their air wings, navy carriers carry extensive command, control, communications, computer, and intelligence (C4I) systems. These systems and their Tactical Flag Command Centers enable them to act as fleet flagships or, if need be, a floating headquarters for a joint task force commander. The ships' C4I capabilities were upgraded following Operation DESERT STORM. Prior to 1994, U.S. Navy ships' communications systems had a data-handling capacity of only eight kilobytes per second versus the multimegabyte speed of the U.S. Air Force's fiber-optic system. As a result, the ATO's 10-megabyte file size took several hours to be delivered to the naval ships participating in the air campaign.

The post–DESERT STORM upgrades eliminated this problem by expanding the ships' bandwidth capacity. As a result, they can support a strike group, navy task force, numbered fleet, or joint task force staff, which often adds another 100–300 personnel to the total aboard. The combination of ship's sensors, AWACS (Airborne Warning and Control System) aircraft, and capacity to integrate inputs from national and other service component assets enable these ships to monitor the battle space around them out to nearly 400 nautical miles.

Britain provided two V/STOL carriers to the later Middle East conflicts in the *Ark Royal* and *Illustrious,* while Italy deployed its V/STOL carrier the *Garibaldi.* The *Ark Royal* carried a contingent of Royal Marines and supported the invasion of Iraq in 2003, while the *Illustrious* conducted sea control missions with Task Force 50. Formally commissioned in June 1982, the *Illustrious* was the second of the three Invincible-class light aircraft carriers built for the Royal Navy. Like *Ark Royal,* it has a top speed of 28 knots and can carry a mix of up to 22 aircraft/helicopters and a nonaviation armament of three 30-millimeter (mm) Goalkeeper close-in weapons systems and two GAM-B01 20-mm close-range automatic cannon. At 14,000 tons, the smaller *Garibaldi* was commissioned in 1985 and can carry an air wing of 16 aircraft, usually an equal mix of AV-8 Harriers and helicopters. It is also equipped with eight OTOMAT long-range antiship cruise missiles and 48 Aspide short-range surface-to-air missiles as well as three 40-mm Oto Melara automatic cannon. A sonar suite and antisubmarine torpedo tubes round out its nonaviation armament. It can also carry a commando company and its supporting helicopters in lieu of a typical air wing. The primary role of these ships was sea control, a mission for which they were ideally suited. Their Harriers also proved to be useful quick-response attack assets. Although not as impressive as their larger American counterparts, the coalition carriers conducted vital sea control and littoral missions that freed the American carriers to concentrate on strike and close air support operations.

CARL OTIS SCHUSTER

See also

DESERT STORM, Operation, Coalition Naval Forces; ENDURING FREEDOM, Operation, Coalition Naval Forces; Iraq, Navy; IRAQI FREEDOM, Operation, Coalition Naval Forces; United Kingdom, Navy, Persian Gulf War; United States Navy, Afghanistan War; United States Navy, Persian Gulf War; United States Navy, Iraq War

References

Case Study. *Network Centric Warfare in the U.S. Navy's Fifth Fleet: Task Force 50 During Operation Enduring Freedom.* Washington, DC: Center for Naval Analysis, 2003.

Finlan, Alastair. *The Gulf War, 1991.* Oxford, UK: Osprey, 2003.

Freedman, Lawrence, and Efraim Karsh. *The Gulf Conflict, 1990–1991: Diplomacy and War in the New World Order.* Princeton, NJ: Princeton University Press, 1993.

Hallion, Richard P. *Storm over Iraq: Air Power and the Gulf War.* Washington, DC: Smithsonian Institution Press, 1997.

Holmes, Tony. *US Navy Hornet Units in Operation Iraqi Freedom.* 2 vols. Oxford, UK: Osprey, 2004–2005.

Saunders, Stephen, ed., *Jane's Fighting Ships, 2004–2005.* London: Jane's Information Group, 2005.

Air Defenses in Iraq, Iraq War

Before the U.S.-led invasion of Iraq in March 2003, the Iraqi air defense system was a major concern for coalition planners. The system included elements of the defenses used in the 1991 Persian Gulf War, during which 39 coalition aircraft were downed. Overall, however, the Iraqi air defenses proved to be largely ineffectual in the Persian Gulf War, and the coalition achieved rapid and complete air supremacy. The Iraqi air defense system was badly degraded by damage in 1991, an on-going arms embargo, and continued sporadic attacks by U.S. and British aircraft over more than a decade of enforcing the no-fly zones.

Following the 1991 Persian Gulf War, the arms embargo on Iraq made it difficult for Saddam Hussein to replace weapons that had been destroyed in the fighting or had become outmoded. Iraq's air defenses continued to be based on the Soviet model, with radar and observers providing information to a central command in real time. The central commanders were then able to determine the best mix of surface-to-air missiles (SAMs), antiaircraft artillery (AAA), and fighter aircraft to deal with the threat. The system was known as Kari, French for "Iraq," spelled backwards. The system employed technology from the 1980s, and had been developed by French companies. Computers and equipment came from both European and Soviet sources.

Iraq's central National Air Defense operations center was located in central Baghdad. It received data from four independent Sector Operations Centers (SOCs), which covered different parts of Iraq. The first sector, headquartered at Taji Military Camp in northern Baghdad, covered central and eastern Iraq, as well as the capital. This SOC controlled most of the SAMs and AAA. Prior to 2003, many weapons had been removed from other parts of Iraq and concentrated in the capital area. The region included the most sensitive targets, such as presidential palaces and factories where weapons of mass destruction could be produced. The SOC also controlled many individual radar sites and an electronic countermeasures unit.

The second SOC covered western Iraq, including the Jordanian and Syrian border. The third SOC was headquartered near Talil Airbase and covered southern Iraq. This SOC was most often in action against allied aircraft covering the southern no-fly zone. The fourth SOC was based near Kirkuk and covered the northern part of the country. Its SAM batteries engaged aircraft in the northern no-fly zone.

A separate SOC was also established during the 1990s in Baghdad. It was controlled by the Republican Guard and was armed with some of the most modern SAMs available. Other lightweight SAMs were employed by Republican Guard and regular Iraqi Army units, and were not integrated into the Kari system. Instead, these weapons were individually aimed and posed a deadly threat to coalition aircraft, especially those flying at low altitudes and relatively slow speeds. These weapons shot down a number of allied helicopters during the March 2003 invasion.

Most radar used by the Iraqis had been supplied by the Soviets, although some French, Italian, and Chinese radars had been integrated into the system. Different sets included such surveillance radars as the Soviet P-15 "Flat Face" (NATO designation) or P-15M(2) "Squat Eye," and the French Thompson-CSF Volex, which were not mobile. Other radars included target tracking and guidance radars, which were usually mounted on vans or trailers and could be moved to avoid coalition targeting. Some jamming and electronic countermeasure equipment was also available, along with thermal imaging telescopes and laser rangefinders that coalition countermeasures could not block. Even so, most of the equipment in 2003 was the same that had been in place in 1991.

Most of the SAMs available to Saddam Hussein's forces were introduced during the 1950s and 1960s. Some SA-2s and SA-3s were built by Iraqi factories, but most sources of missile replacements were cut off after the Persian Gulf War in 1991. More recent area defense SAMs included the SA-6, SA-8, SA-9, SA-13, and a few French-made Roland VIIs. While some had been upgraded since 1991, most remained obsolete. The SAMs were supplemented by over 4,000 antiaircraft guns ranging in size from 12.7-mm to 57-mm. Fighter aircraft from the Iraqi Air Force played little role in Iraq's air defenses.

During the 1991 Persian Gulf War, the coalition had attacked Kari's communications nodes. Since then, the Iraqis had improved communications with greater use of optical fiber links, along with continued use of underground bunkers to protect command and communication nodes.

Following the Persian Gulf War, the United States, Great Britain, and France established no-fly zones in southern and northern Iraq. Fighter planes patrolled these areas to prevent Iraqi aircraft from attacking Kurd and Shiite dissidents. After losing several fighters to the allies in 1992 and 1993, the Iraqi Air Force no longer sent aircraft to challenge the patrols. However, the Iraqi Air Defense Command periodically harassed allied patrols with SAM attacks, especially after Operation DESERT FOX in 1998. For the next five years, Iraq's radar and missile sites targeted allied aircraft and tried to shoot them down. In response, allied aircraft were allowed to respond with missiles and bombs. When the Iraqis learned to position their SAMs in population centers, the allies responded with attacks on fixed air defense installations, such as radar sites or communication centers.

Denied access to new technology, the Iraqis developed tactics to improve their chances against allied aircraft. By observing Serbian tactics in Kosovo that brought down several U.S. aircraft, they learned how to quickly turn radars on and off to prevent allied countermeasures from locking on, while still allowing a quick launch by SAMs. The Iraqis also improved their use of decoys and hidden deployment of weapons. More incidents of Iraq launching missiles and using radar to lock onto allied aircraft were reported after 1998.

Saddam encouraged attacks on allied aircraft by offering $5,000 to any unit that shot down a U.S. aircraft and $2,500 to any soldier who captured a downed pilot. In response, however, the allies began to target air defense targets in the no-fly zones more intensively, especially from late 2001 to early 2003. Although the number of Iraqi provocations declined, the number of air attacks on air defense sites increased dramatically during that time. In September 2002, for example, a raid by over 100 U.S. aircraft on air defense sites in western Iraq was not intended to protect aircraft patrolling the no-fly zone. Instead, it opened the way for U.S. Special Forces to fly from Jordan into northern Iraq. By the time U.S. and British forces moved into Iraq on March 20, 2003, Iraqi air defenses had already been seriously degraded.

The allies took Iraqi air defenses seriously during Operation IRAQI FREEDOM. The main targets of the early air strikes were the command centers in Baghdad. Tactics were similar to those used in 1991. Stealth aircraft and cruise missiles made up the first wave, to weaken air defenses at little risk to pilots. Extensive use of drones forced the Iraqis to turn on their radars, allowing allied aircraft to destroy them. Although the Iraqis fired over 1,660 radar-guided SAMs during the invasion, they failed to down any allied aircraft. Another 1,224 AAA "incidents" involving centrally controlled Iraqi batteries were reported by the allies, with no effect as well. A complete lack of involvement by Iraqi fighters pleasantly surprised the allies. Most Iraqi Air Force aircraft were hidden in residential or agricultural areas to prevent their destruction. After the first few days of the operation, strategic air defenses declined in activity. Allied suppression missions and the lack of SAMs had done their job.

The most effective Iraqi air defenses during the war were the individually aimed SAMs and AAA. These weapons were locally controlled and were most effective against low-altitude targets. On March 24, for example, the U.S. Army 11th Aviation Brigade attacked the Republican Guard Medina mechanized division deep behind Iraqi lines. One McDonnell Douglas/Boeing AH-64D Apache was shot down, and 33 were so badly shot up that they were rendered unserviceable for some time. A total of seven U.S. aircraft were shot down by locally controlled Iraqi air defenses.

In the end, Iraq's air defenses in 2003 were far too obsolete and limited to prevent the allies from striking at targets that they were determined to hit. Even so, however, the Iraqi defenses in certain areas, such as around Baghdad, were so dense that they continued to pose a threat to low-flying allied aircraft until the collapse of Saddam Hussein's regime. All of the aircraft lost to Iraqi defenses were helicopters or ground attack aircraft, indicating that determined Iraqi defenders remained dangerous.

TIM J. WATTS

See also

Air Defenses in Iraq, Persian Gulf War; Antiaircraft Guns; Antiaircraft Missiles, Iraqi; IRAQI FREEDOM, Operation, Air Campaign; Missiles, Surface-to-Air

References

Cordesman, Anthony H. *The Iraq War: Strategy, Tactics, and Military Lessons.* Westport, CT: Praeger, 2003.

Keegan, John. *The Iraq War: The Military Offensive, from Victory in 21 Days to the Insurgent Aftermath.* New York: Vintage, 2005.

Ripley, Tim. *Air War Iraq.* Barnsley, UK: Pen and Sword, 2004.

Air Defenses in Iraq, Persian Gulf War

Largely based on the network the Soviet Union had developed over the years, Iraqi air defenses during the Persian Gulf War (Operation DESERT STORM) in 1991 consisted of a layered system utilizing both Western- and Soviet-designed radars, missiles, antiaircraft artillery, and interceptor aircraft. The system utilized 7,000 optically-guided and radar-guided antiaircraft artillery pieces of various calibers. The network also included some 16,000 missiles that tracked targets by radar as well as by infrared technology. The system was designed to provide antiaircraft coverage from the ground level to an altitude of 40,000 feet with missiles, and from ground level to 15,000 feet with antiaircraft artillery.

The air defense network was coordinated by a French-built computer known as Kari (French for "Iraq," spelled backwards), which provided data management and coordination of information from the various radars and weapons' sites in the country. The system was used to provide coverage for three key areas. The first was the centralized national air defense system to provide protection for key airfields and the fixed surface-to-air missile

Aviation ordnancemen carry an AGM-88 High-Speed Anti-Radiation Missile (HARM) to an aircraft on the flight deck of the U.S. aircraft carrier *Independence.* The AGM-88 HARM is an air-to-surface missile designed to seek out and destroy enemy radar-equipped air defense systems. (U.S. Department of Defense)

U.S. military personnel examine a Soviet-made SA-2 surface-to-air missile launcher demolished in a coalition air attack during Operation DESERT STORM. (U.S. Department of Defense)

sites in the country. The next component of the system provided protection to the Iraqi Army's Republican Guard units, as well as nuclear, chemical, biological, and chemical weapon facilities. The final component of the network provided coverage for Iraqi battlefield units.

The system also provided protection in and around the capital city of Baghdad. The air defense network around Baghdad stretched from the center of the city to a distance of some 60 miles, and the concentration of antiaircraft artillery was also the densest in and around Baghdad.

The surface-to-air missiles used in the Iraqi air defense network came mostly from the Soviet Union with the exception of a few models from Western Europe. For high-altitude attacks, the Iraqi system relied on the Soviet SA-2 Guideline. It had been designed in the 1950s and was the same system used to shoot down the U.S. U-2 spy plane piloted by Gary Powers over the Soviet Union on May 1, 1960, and fired against U.S. aircraft involved in the bombing of North Vietnam (Operation ROLLING THUNDER) during the Vietnam War. The Guideline had a range of some 31 miles, was radar guided, and used fixed launchers. Two of the medium-range systems used by the Iraqi air defense network were also Soviet designs; the first, the SA-3 Goa, was a more mobile system than the SA-2 and had a range of 18 miles. It was also radar guided. The

other, the SA-6 Gainful, had a range of 37 miles and was a mobile system. The Goa and Gainful employed radar guidance to locate and engage targets.

The low-level systems used included the SA-7 Grail, a portable surface-to-air missile with a range of 7 miles. This system provided easy portability, but could only be employed against aircraft moving away from the operator. The SA-7 utilized infrared guidance, seeking heat generated by aircraft and helicopter engines. The SA-8 Geko and SA-13 Gopher were mobile, low-level surface-to-air missile systems that employed infrared guidance to locate targets. The Geko had a 7-mile range while the Gopher has a 5-mile range. The Roland mobile surface-to-air missile system was a European design with a 5-mile range, and was infrared guided.

These various missile systems were used in coordination with antiaircraft artillery ranging from 14.5-mm to 57-mm automatic cannon. These weapons were usually mounted on vehicles to provide mobility or made portable to allow crews to move them quickly. The larger fixed antiaircraft artillery systems utilized 85-mm to 130-mm projectiles. These guns were usually fixed and radar guided.

The planning for the air campaign by coalition forces took all available information on the Iraqi air defense network and exploited the weaknesses of the system. The United States had for years been running a covert program that collected information on various Soviet weapon systems and other electronic devices. The U.S. Air Force utilized that classified information on the Soviet air defense network, upon which the Iraqi system was closely based, and planned a campaign that would degrade and eventually render ineffective the Iraqi air defense network. The Special Technical Operations Center in the Pentagon coordinated information on the Soviet systems and provided that information to the planners readying air strikes on Iraq.

The degradation of the Iraqi air defense network during the opening phases of Operation DESERT STORM in January 1991 proved crucial in the coalition's success in driving Iraq from Kuwait in February 1991.

One of the tools used by the coalition to help destroy the Iraqi air defense network was the AGM-88 High Speed Anti-Radiation Missile (HARM). During the air campaign, approximately 1,000 of these missiles were fired, the majority of them by Navy and Marine aircraft. The missile and its explosive warhead can locate and hit targets emanating radar energy. The system also has the ability to strike targets that turn off their radars in hopes of fooling the missile.

The use of HARMs was coordinated by the use of tactical air-launched decoys (TALDs). These systems were rockets with electronic systems onboard that made the TALD look like an attacking bomber to the air defense network. The TALDs were launched ahead of striking aircraft, and when the Iraqi radar operators switched on their radars to engage what they thought were incoming planes, the attacking aircraft could strike the radars and missile sights.

Of course, the Iraqi air defense network also relied on fighter-interceptor aircraft to meet airborne threats. The air defense fighters consisted of 116 French-built Mirage F-1s and 120 Soviet-manufactured MiG-23, MiG-25, and MiG-29 fighters. Of the 750 total aircraft in the Iraqi Air Force at the beginning of the war, fewer then half were front-line combat aircraft. At the conclusion of the air campaign, the coalition forces had shot down 33 Iraqi aircraft, while many more were destroyed on the ground or by ground forces. At the end of the conflict, more than half of the entire Iraqi Air Force had been destroyed, had been captured, or had fled to neighboring Iran.

While the coalition air campaign did seriously degrade the effectiveness of the Iraqi air defense network, the threat from the Iraqis' man-portable missiles and optically-guided guns did force the coalition air forces to maintain a high state of readiness. During the campaign, 15 coalition aircraft were lost to antiaircraft artillery or surface-to-air missiles.

STEVEN F. MARIN

See also

Aircraft, Fighters; Antiaircraft Guns; Antiaircraft Missiles, Iraqi; DESERT STORM, Operation; DESERT STORM, Operation, Coalition Air Campaign; DESERT STORM, Operation, Coalition Air Forces; DESERT STORM, Operation, Planning for; Iraq, Air Force; Missile Systems, Iraqi

References

Friedman, Norman. *Desert Victory: The War for Kuwait*. Annapolis, MD: Naval Institute Press, 1991.

Hallion, Richard P. *Storm over Iraq: Air Power and the Gulf War*. Washington, DC: Smithsonian Institution Press, 1997.

Marolda, Edward, and Robert Schneller. *Shield and Sword: The United States Navy and the Persian Gulf War*. Annapolis, MD: U.S. Naval Institute Press, 2001.

AirLand Battle Doctrine

In the development of military doctrine, victory in war is usually followed by a period of complacency and stagnation, while defeat spurs a period of critical self-examination and robust internal debate that often leads to dramatic doctrinal innovations. This was true for the United States following the Vietnam War. For the U.S. military, the trauma of the loss in Vietnam was compounded by the unexpected lethality of modern weapons witnessed in the short but violent 1973 Yom Kippur (Ramadan) War. That in turn led to an increasing recognition that the North Atlantic Treaty Organization (NATO) could not rely on battlefield nuclear weapons to offset the overwhelming numerical advantage of the Warsaw Pact in any future war on the European continent.

Working through the problem, American military thinkers identified two types of wars that the United States could face in the future: a heavy mechanized war in Europe or a light infantry war in some other part of the world. Although the mechanized war in Europe was the least likely scenario, it was also the most dangerous. U.S. military doctrine had to be revised to be able to defeat America's strongest and most dangerous enemy.

Initially, the sights of the American military were fixed at the tactical level—"Win the First Battle"—with little consideration beyond that. There also was recognition that the next major conflict would be a "Come as You Are War." Under the direct guidance of General William E. DePuy, the first commander of the newly established U.S. Army Training and Doctrine Command (TRADOC), the initial expression of this doctrinal rethinking was the 1976 edition of *FM 100-5, Operations*. The new manual introduced the notion of active defense, a highly questionable substitute for the tested defensive concepts of mobile defense and defense in-depth. In focusing on the lethality of modern weapons, the new doctrine stressed the effects of firepower by devoting the preponderance of space to a discussion of its effects. The new *FM 100-5* did not ignore maneuver, but it did relegate that element of combat power to the mere function of movement to deliver firepower rather than gain positional advantage.

The 1976 edition of *FM 100-5* was wildly controversial even before it had been fully distributed to the field. The critics of DePuy's doctrine rejected it as too mechanical, too dogmatic, and too mathematically deterministic. Nonetheless, DePuy's efforts were a major contribution to the post–Vietnam War U.S. Army, because for the first time in many years, officers were again thinking and writing about doctrine. The resulting debate fueled a renaissance in American military thinking.

The immediate reactions to the 1976 edition resulted in the notion of follow-on forces attack (FOFA), which in turn led to recognition of the operational depth of the battlefield. That led directly to the final acceptance by the American military and NATO of the concept of the operational level of war, as distinct from the tactical or the strategic. The Soviets had formally recognized this level of warfare as early as the 1920s and had aggressively worked to define and expand the theory of operational art ever since. The West had long rejected the concept as little more than yet another crackpot element of Marxist thinking, but the Soviets had been right all along on this point.

The principal guiding force behind the development of Air-Land Battle Doctrine was General Donn A. Starry, who assumed command of TRADOC in July 1977. Working directly under Starry, Major General Donald R. Morelli, TRADOC's deputy chief of staff of doctrine, closely supervised the team of doctrine writers, which included lieutenant colonels Leonard D. Holder, Huba Wass de Czega, and Richard Hart Sinnerich. Classical German military thought had a great deal of influence on the development of the new doctrine. Even in the 1976 edition of *FM 100-5,* General DePuy had instructed the doctrine writers to study carefully the current capstone doctrinal manual of the West German Bundeswehr. That manual, *HDv 100/100, Truppenführung* (Command and Control in Battle), was based closely on the manual of the same name first introduced in 1932 with which the German Army fought World War II. Through the influence of the German manual, such standard German doctrinal concepts as *Auftragstaktik* (mission orders) and *Schwerpunkt* (center of gravity) became firmly embedded in American military thinking. Another major influence that was specifically mentioned in that edition was Basil Liddell Hart's book *Stragegy,* one of the most important books written about the indirect approach in warfare.

The 1982 edition of *FM 100-5* marked the U.S. military's first formal recognition of the operational level of war and introduced the concepts of AirLand Battle and Deep Battle. AirLand Battle Doctrine took a nonlinear view of combat. It enlarged the battlefield area, stressing unified air and ground operations throughout the theater. It recognized the nonquantifiable elements of combat power and restressed that maneuver was as important as firepower. Most significantly, the doctrine emphasized the human element of war, "courageous, well-trained soldiers and skillful, effective leaders." An undercurrent to this last theme, of course, was the fact that the United States had only recently abolished conscription and was then in the process of building an all-volunteer professional army. The AirLand Battle Doctrine identified the keys to success in war, which included indirect approaches, speed and violence, flexibility and reliance on the initiative of junior leaders, rapid decision making, clearly defined objectives and operational concepts, a clearly designated main effort, and deep attack.

Depth was one of the keys. A commander had to fight and synchronize three simultaneous battles: close, deep, and rear. The deep battle, of course, would be the enemy's rear battle, and vice versa. A well-coordinated attack deep in an enemy's rear area might in fact prove decisive. This marked the first recognition in American military doctrine that the battle might not necessarily be decided along the line of contact.

One of the most controversial features of the 1976 edition of *FM 100-5* had been the elimination of the venerable Principles of War, first adopted by the U.S. Army in the early 1920s. The 1982 edition restored the Principles of War but then went one step further by introducing the Four Tenets of AirLand Battle: initiative, depth, agility, and synchronization. Initiative is the ability to set the terms of the battle by action and was identified as the greatest advantage in war. Depth has components of time, space, and resources. Agility is the ability to act faster than the enemy to exploit his weakness and frustrate his plans. Synchronization ensures that no effort will be wasted, either initially or as operations develop.

Some critics complained that the Four Tenets of AirLand Battle were unnecessary additions to the Principles of War or were ultimately an attempt to replace them. But as other analysts pointed out, the Four Tenets were for the most part combinations of two or more of the Principles of War. Synchronization, for example, combined economy of force and unity of effort. Initiative combined offensive, maneuver, and surprise.

The 1982 *FM 100-5* was a major milestone in American military thought, but it was far from a perfect document. After its release to the field the debate continued, and the doctrine writers continued to refine the document. The 1986 edition of *FM 100-5* contained no significant changes or innovations, but it presented a far better discussion of the doctrine and corrected some of the minor errors in the 1982 edition. Some errors still remained, however. The 1986 edition used the German concept of *Schwerpunkt* interchangeably as either the center of gravity or the decisive point. As defined originally by 19th-century Prussian military strategist Carl von Clausewitz, however, the center of gravity and the decisive point (*Entscheidungsstelle*) were two distinct and separate concepts. The confusion was not corrected until the 1993 edition of *FM 100-5,* which stated clearly that "Decisive points are not centers of gravity, they are the keys to getting at the centers of gravity."

NATO never fully embraced the AirLand Battle Doctrine, and ironically neither did the U.S. Air Force. In any event, the new doctrine never had to be used in an actual war against the Warsaw Pact on the plains of Northern Europe. AirLand Battle, however, greatly concerned the Soviets and was just one more element of pressure in the 1980s that eventually contributed to the collapse of the Soviet Union. The overwhelmingly successful prosecution of the Persian Gulf War (Operation DESERT STORM) in 1991 was based on the 1986 edition of *FM 100-5,* which was arguably the single best official articulation of American war-fighting doctrine ever published.

AAV-7A1 amphibious assault vehicles of the 1st Combat Engineer Battalion (CEB), 1st Marine Division, advance toward Kuwait City during Operation DESERT STORM. An AH-1 Sea Cobra helicopter is flying in the background. (U.S. Department of Defense)

The 1993 edition of *FM 100-5* actually shifted the emphasis away from operations and conventional war fighting toward strategy and operations other than war (OOTW). Even the term "Air-Land Battle" was dropped in favor of "Army Operations," but that was more the result of bureaucratic infighting between the U.S. Army and the U.S. Air Force. A new edition of *FM 100-5* in 1998 was supposed to shift the emphasis back to the operational art, but the final coordinating draft caused considerable internal controversy. The new manual was finally issued in June 2001, under a new numbering system, as *FM 3-0 Operations*. Although the term "AirLand Battle" is no longer officially in use, the U.S. Army continues to train and operate in accordance with its principles, and its precepts were used again during the initial invasion of Iraq in 2003 during Operation IRAQI FREEDOM.

DAVID T. ZABECKI

See also

DESERT STORM, Operation; IRAQI FREEDOM, Operation; United States Air Force, Iraq War; United States Air Force, Persian Gulf War; United States Army, Iraq War; United States Army, Persian Gulf War

References

Naveh, Shimon. *In Pursuit of Military Excellence: The Evolution of Operational Theory*. London: Frank Cass, 1997.

Romjue, John L. *From Active Defense to AirLand Battle: The Development of Army Doctrine, 1973–1982*. Fort Monroe, VA: United States Army Training and Doctrine Command, 1984.

Zabecki, David T., and Bruce Condell, eds. and trans. *Truppenführung: On the German Art of War*. Boulder, CO: Lynne Rienner, 2001.

Akhund, Dadullah

See Kakar, Mullah

Al-Aqsa Intifada

See Intifada, Second

Albania, Role in Afghanistan and Iraq Wars

Balkan country located on the southeastern coast of the Adriatic Sea with a 2008 population of 3.620 million. Albania is bordered to the north and east by Serbia and Montenegro, due east by the former Yugoslavian republic of Macedonia, and to the southeast by Greece. A communist bloc nation since World War II, Albania experienced a difficult transition to democracy and free markets after the collapse of the Berlin Wall in 1989. In 1992 the communists were resoundingly defeated, and the country began its halting progress toward democracy. Since then, Albania has been governed by a parliamentary-style democracy featuring multiparty coalitions. Despite its internal difficulties and economic problems, Albania has firmly oriented itself toward the West.

Albania was a staunch supporter of the United States during Operation ENDURING FREEDOM and the 2003 Iraq War. After the end of the Cold War, the United States provided both economic and military aid to Albania and supported membership for the country in both the North Atlantic Treaty Organization (NATO) and the European Union (EU). Relations between the two countries became even closer following the 1999 NATO air campaign in Kosovo when the United States led allied nations in a campaign to protect ethnic Albanians in the Serbian province.

After the terrorist attacks of September 11, 2001, Albania offered diplomatic, intelligence, and military support for the U.S. Operation ENDURING FREEDOM. Albania granted the United States and other allied nations overflight rights during the 2001 invasion of Afghanistan and offered the coalition use of its bases and ports. Albania also deployed troops during the initial combat operations of ENDURING FREEDOM and later contributed more than 100 troops to the NATO-led International Security Assistance Force (ISAF). In 2002 Albania initiated a program to transfer excess military equipment to the Afghan National Army. Albanian forces also provided security in Kabul and were deployed in 2007 to Herat as part of an Italian-led rapid response force.

Albania endorsed the efforts by the George W. Bush administration to assemble a "coalition of the willing" against the Iraqi regime of Saddam Hussein in 2003 and offered to provide troops for the invasion of Iraq. On April 6, 2003, during Operation IRAQI FREEDOM, Albania dispatched elements of a commando company to Iraq, where the unit was deployed under U.S. command in Mosul. The initial deployment involved approximately 70 soldiers but was soon expanded to 120 troops. The contingent remained at that number until 2008, and the troops were deployed for six-month intervals before being rotated out. The Albanians engaged in general security operations to protect the Mosul airport and safeguarded coalition convoys in and around the city.

Albanian troops also participated in training exercises for Iraqi security forces. Meanwhile, Albanian staff officers served with the Multi-National Force in southern Iraq. Albania also offered the coalition use of its airspace and bases for operations in Iraq. In 2007 Albania began to transfer excess stockpiled ammunition to the Iraqi security forces.

In 2008 Albania deployed an additional company to Iraq, bringing its total troop strength to more than 200 personnel. The additional forces were stationed in Baghdad. However, in December 2008, as part of the general drawdown of foreign forces in Iraq, Albania withdrew its entire contingent from the country. Albania joined NATO on April 1, 2009.

TOM LANSFORD

See also

Afghanistan, Coalition Combat Operations in, 2002–Present; International Security Assistance Force; IRAQI FREEDOM, Operation, Coalition Ground Forces; Multi-National Force–Iraq; North Atlantic Treaty Organization in Afghanistan

References

Cockburn, Patrick. *The Occupation: War and Resistance in Iraq.* New York: Verso, 2007.
Feickert, Andrew. *U.S. and Coalition Military Operations in Afghanistan: Issues for Congress.* Washington, DC: Congressional Research Service, 2006.
Keegan, John. *The Iraq War: The Military Offensive, from Victory in 21 Days to the Insurgent Aftermath.* New York: Vintage, 2005.

Albright, Madeleine
Birth Date: May 15, 1937

Democratic Party foreign policy adviser, U.S. ambassador to the United Nations (UN) during 1993–1997, and secretary of state during 1997–2001. Madeleine Albright was born Marie Jana Korbel in Prague, Czechoslovakia, on May 15, 1937. Her father, Josef Korbel, was a diplomat, and he and his wife had converted to Catholicism from Judaism. In 1939 when the Germans took over Czechoslovakia, the Korbel family fled to Britain. Following the defeat of Germany the family returned to Prague, where Josef Korbel was appointed Czechoslovak ambassador to Yugoslavia and Albania. A few months after the February 1948 communist coup in Czechoslovakia the family again sought asylum, this time in the United States. In 1949 they settled in Denver, Colorado, where Korbel became a professor at the University of Colorado and developed an acclaimed program in international relations. He would become an adviser to two U.S. secretaries of state and his own daughter.

An excellent student, Madeleine Korbel graduated from Wellesley College in Massachusetts in 1959 and married Joseph Albright, a journalist from a distinguished family. Later they divorced. While rearing three daughters, Madeleine Albright earned a PhD in government and public law from Columbia University, where she worked with Professor Zbigniew Brzezinski, later the national security adviser to President Jimmy Carter.

Following extensive volunteer work for the Democratic Party, in 1976 Albright became chief legislative assistant to Maine senator Edmund Muskie. In 1982 she became a professor of international affairs and director of the Women in Foreign Service Program at Georgetown University's School of Foreign Service. Albright was active in the presidential campaigns of Walter Mondale (1984) and Michael Dukakis (1988), serving as chief foreign policy adviser to both candidates. Meanwhile, she built

U.S. secretary of state Madeleine Albright at a press conference regarding Middle East peace talks, September 19, 1997. (Najlah Feanny/Corbis Saba)

her reputation as an authority on foreign policy and women's issues while forming close personal ties with fellow Wellesley alumna Hillary Rodham Clinton. Upon his 1993 election to the presidency, William Jefferson Clinton appointed Albright U.S. ambassador to the UN, a post she took up in February 1994. Her extensive knowledge of foreign languages and Balkan ethnic politics served her well at the UN.

In January 1997 Clinton chose Albright to be secretary of state, the highest government post held to that time by an American woman. Her charm, sense of humor, and sharp wit garnered wide press attention. The exhilaration of Albright's first days in office were clouded by a journalist's revelation that three of her grandparents had perished in Nazi concentration camps and that Albright's immediate family had purposefully obscured their Jewish background. Albright, who had been baptized Roman Catholic at the age of five and had joined the Episcopal Church upon her marriage, knew nothing of her Jewish ancestry.

Early in Albright's term questions were raised about the effectiveness of a woman, especially one with a Jewish heritage, negotiating with Middle Eastern heads of state, but Albright soon established effective ties with Saudi Arabian officials and forged a strong friendship with King Hussein of Jordan. Still, the Israeli-Palestinian conflict proved intractable. The Clinton administration had made numerous efforts to bring both parties to the negotiating table, beginning with the 1993 Oslo Accords. In January 1998 Israeli prime minister Benjamin Netanyahu and Palestine Liberation Organization (PLO) chairman Yasser Arafat traveled to Washington for talks but showed little willingness to compromise on the status of Jerusalem, a release of prisoners, and Jewish settlements.

Albright and the administration persisted, however, sponsoring talks again in October 1998 at Wye River in Maryland. Albright was able to bring in King Hussein of Jordan and his wife, Queen Noor, as intermediaries. These talks ultimately resulted in the Wye River Memorandum, which pledged more cooperation in security for the Israelis and additional land rights for the Palestinians.

Any expectations that Albright and Clinton may have had for settling disputes in the Middle East were dashed in September 2000, when Israeli hard-line politician Ariel Sharon made a provocative visit to the Temple Mount (Haram al-Sharif), the site of the al-Aqsa Mosque and the Dome of the Rock, in Jerusalem. The visit not only dashed hopes of Palestinian-Israeli peace but also sparked a new wave of violence, known as the Second (al-Aqsa) Intifada. Albright's experience alerted her to the importance of understanding religious passions in framing global policy. After she left office in 2001, her writings and speeches stressed the importance of educating policy makers in the tenets of major world religions.

Albright also played a central role in the Balkans, which had descended into chaos and spasms of genocidal violence. She was influential in shaping policy during the Kosovo War (1996–1999), which ultimately resulted in the North Atlantic Treaty Organization (NATO) bombing campaign against Serbian-Yugoslavian targets during March–June 1999. The campaign forced Serbian strongman Slobodan Milosevic to the negotiating table. Albright also helped bring to an end the Bosnian War, culminating in the December 1995 Dayton Agreement.

By the end of her four-year term, Albright's critics charged that she dealt with problems on a case-by-case basis and lacked a coherent foreign policy doctrine. Many in the Republican Party also believed that the Clinton administration, basking in prosperous times and relative world peace, had neglected the growing problems of terrorism and collapsing economies in a world no longer held in check by the communist-capitalist rivalry.

But Albright could cite solid achievements. Her strong personality had generated wide public interest in foreign affairs, while her presence in high office had advanced women worldwide. As a refugee from European oppression, she had been an unquestioned American patriot and a strong proponent of worldwide democracy and human rights. She had pointedly warned of American smugness at the beginning of the new millennium, had identified a new world order, and had faced down aggression in the Balkans while maintaining cordial relations with Russia. And despite disappointments, she had kept Israeli-Palestinian peace negotiations from collapsing completely during the difficult tenures of Benjamin Netanyahu and Yasser Arafat.

Since leaving office, Albright has held a professorship at Georgetown University and has been active in numerous foundations. She has also sat on several boards, including that of the New York Stock Exchange. She has spoken and lectured widely, and in 2006 she attended two conferences at the White House with current and former foreign policy officials. She has spoken out against the Iraq War, claiming that among other things it has empowered Iran and North Korea to move forward with their nuclear weapons programs. In 2006 she asserted that the war may be "one of the worst disasters" in the history of U.S. foreign policy.

ALLENE PHY-OLSEN

See also

Arafat, Yasser; Clinton, William Jefferson; Hussein ibn Talal, King of Jordan; Intifada, Second; Netanyahu, Benjamin; Sharon, Ariel; United Nations

References

Albright, Madeleine. *Madam Secretary: A Memoir.* New York: Miramax, 2003.

———. *The Mighty and the Almighty: Reflections on America, God, and World Affairs.* New York: HarperCollins, 2006.

Dobbs, Michael. *Madeleine Albright: A Twentieth-Century Odyssey.* New York: Henry Holt, 1999.

Lippman, Thomas W. *Madeleine Albright and the New American Diplomacy.* Boulder, CO: Westview, 2000.

Alec Station

U.S. government-sanctioned Central Intelligence Agency (CIA) unit charged with the mission of hunting down and capturing or killing Al Qaeda leader Osama bin Laden. In late 1995 two members of the William J. Clinton administration, National Security Advisor Anthony (Tony) Lake and National Coordinator for Counterterrorism Richard Clarke, met with the head of the CIA's Counterterrorism Center (CTC) to discuss the need for a unit to concentrate solely on bin Laden. Soon afterward, CIA director George Tenet approved just such a unit. The plan called for Alec Station to run for only a couple of years before merging completely with the CTC, but as bin Laden became a greater and greater threat, Alec Station continued its operations for more than a decade.

When the CIA began Alec Station on January 8, 1996, bin Laden was mostly known as a financier of terrorism. Soon afterward, it became apparent that he had declared open warfare against the United States and its allies, and the campaign against bin Laden was then stepped up. Michael Scheuer, a veteran CIA agent, was placed in charge of the program when it was founded. Although the formal title of the program was the Usama Bin Laden Issue Station (UBL), it soon took the name Alec Station, after Scheuer's adopted Korean son, Alec.

Alec Station functioned as a subunit of the CIA's CTC. Sponsors of this program set it up as an interagency unit running agents from both the CIA and the Federal Bureau of Investigation (FBI). The plan was for this unit to fuse intelligence disciplines into one office that included operations, analysis, signals intercepts, overhead photography, and covert action.

As the unit developed, its strength lay in analysis. It began as a small unit with a staff of only about 15 analysts, mostly young women. Alec Station, not considered a choice assignment, was a low-profile operation and was at first housed outside Langley, Virginia, until it moved to the CTC.

By 1998 Scheuer was convinced that bin Laden posed an ongoing danger to the United States but had difficulty convincing his superiors, partly because of his difficult personality; he managed to alienate even those who agreed with him. After learning that bin Laden had attempted to acquire nuclear materials, Scheuer had difficulty convincing his superiors to accept the information and use it to inform others in the government. Scheuer, believing that bin Laden constituted a clear and present danger, became increasingly frustrated by the lack of action taken toward bin Laden.

Scheuer also had difficulties with the FBI. Although Alec Station had been set up as an interagency operation, the FBI often refused to share information with the CIA. The most intransigent member of the FBI in this regard was John O'Neill, the FBI's top counterterrorism expert. O'Neill possessed a notebook captured from an Al Qaeda operative that he refused for a year to turn over to Alec Station. In another instance, an FBI agent was caught raiding CIA files with the intent of taking their contents back to the FBI. Scheuer claimed that Alec Station sent 700–800 requests for information to the FBI but never received answers to any of them.

Alec Station planned to capture bin Laden after he moved to Afghanistan in May 1996. For the first time, the CIA knew where bin Laden and his family lived, in the Tarnak Farm compound 12 miles outside Kandahar. Beginning in 1997, plans were made with Afghan tribal leaders to kidnap bin Laden and take him to an Arab country or the United States for trial. The CIA even staged four rehearsals for the operation in late 1997 and early 1998. Then, on May 29, 1998, Tenet, the head of the CIA, called off the operation. Scheuer's reaction was swift. He complained that the CIA had enough intelligence against bin Laden and Al Qaeda to eliminate both, and he could not understand why the U.S. government had failed to take the chance to do so. The Clinton administration responded that it feared collateral damage and any negative publicity that might follow a less-than-perfect operation.

It was only after the bombings on August 7, 1998, of the two U.S. embassies in Tanzania and Kenya that the attention of the Clinton administration was redirected toward bin Laden. This resulted in the August 20, 1998, U.S. missile attacks on an Al Qaeda training camp in Afghanistan near Khost and on the El Shifa pharmaceutical plant in Khartoum, Sudan, in which 79 Tomahawk cruise missiles were fired from U.S. Navy ships in the Arabian Sea. However, warnings from Pakistani sources likely made certain that bin Laden escaped the missiles, and the Sudanese plant proved to be a harmless pharmaceutical factory. Several other plans were made to either capture or kill bin Laden, but they were cancelled each time because of one difficulty or another. Most cancellations were caused by a lack of confidence in intelligence sources and information.

The most promising opportunity came in February 1999. CIA agents learned that bin Laden was going to join a number of sheikhs from the United Arab Emirates at a desert hunting camp in Helmand Province, Afghanistan. Satellite pictures identified the camp on February 9. CIA operatives confirmed bin Laden's presence and requested a missile strike. Over the next several days the Clinton administration debated a missile strike before learning that members of the United Arab Emirates royal family were also present at the camp. Because of foreign policy complications with the United Arab Emirates (a provider of gas and oil supplies) nothing happened, and Scheuer was furious. His e-mails expressing his unhappiness traveled around government circles.

Tenet removed Scheuer from his position as head of Alec Station in the spring of 1999. The CIA claimed that Scheuer's inability to work with superiors and the FBI led to his dismissal. His critics within the agency claimed that he had a vendetta against bin Laden. CIA analysts at Alec Station blamed O'Neill for the firing of Scheuer because the dispute had reached the level of the agency heads of the CIA and FBI. Scheuer's replacement was a key assistant on Tenet's staff and a Middle East specialist, but he lacked Scheuer's drive. By this time, Alec Station had grown from 12 analysts to 25. Most of these analysts were women, something that

hurt their credibility in the male-dominated CIA. There was also a feeling in the CTC that others in the CIA ridiculed members of the Alec Station for their zeal in tracing the actions of bin Laden.

The status of Alec Station became more precarious after September 11, 2001. Some of the criticism directed against the CIA for failing to uncover the September 11 plot descended on Alec Station, and Scheuer reappeared as a senior analyst at the station after September 11. Members of Alec Station adamantly insisted that little if any connection existed between Iraqi dictator Saddam Hussein and Al Qaeda, something they communicated to Tenet. However, this stance made them enemies in the George W. Bush administration, which wanted the CIA to provide justification for the invasion of Iraq and the overthrow of Hussein. Those in the CIA who opposed the invasion became administration enemies. Personnel were soon transferred out of Alec Station until only 12 analysts remained. Scheuer protested this action, resigning from the CIA on November 12, 2004. Not long afterward, the CIA disbanded Alec Station entirely.

STEPHEN E. ATKINS

See also

Al Qaeda; Bin Laden, Osama; Bush, George Walker; Central Intelligence Agency; Clinton, William Jefferson; Counterterrorism Strategy; Tenet, George John

References

Anonymous. *Imperial Hubris: Why the West Is Losing the War on Terror.* New York: Brassey's, 2004.

Coll, Steve. *Ghost Wars: The Secret History of the CIA, Afghanistan, and Bin Laden, from the Soviet Invasion to September 10, 2001.* New York: Penguin, 2004.

Tenet, George. *At the Center of the Storm: My Years at the CIA.* New York: HarperCollins, 2007.

Wright, Lawrence. *The Looming Tower: Al-Qaeda and the Road to 9/11.* New York: Vintage Books, 2007.

Algerian War

Start Date: 1954
End Date: 1962

Unsuccessful eight-year military effort by France to maintain its hold on Algeria, its last, largest, and most important colony. For 130 years, Algeria had been at the core of the French Empire. France conquered Algiers in 1830 and expanded the territory. Algeria became the headquarters of the French Foreign Legion (at Sidi-Bel-Abbès) and home to the largest number of European settlers in the Islamic world. In 1960 there were 1 million Europeans (colons) in Algeria. Unique among French colonies, Algeria became a political component of France, as Algiers, Constantine, and Oran were made departments of the French Republic and had representation in the French Chamber of Deputies.

Nonetheless, Algeria was not fully three French departments, as only the European population enjoyed full rights there. The

French troops ready for action in the Bab-El-Oued District of the city of Algiers in Algeria, after the area had been sealed off by the military, March 26, 1962. (AP/Wide World Photos)

colon and Muslim populations lived separate and unequal lives, with the Europeans controlling the bulk of the wealth. During this time, the French expanded Algeria's frontiers deep into the Sahara.

The Great Depression of the 1930s affected Algeria's Muslims more than any experience since their conquest, as they began to migrate from the countryside into the cities in search of work. Subsequently, the Muslim birthrate climbed dramatically because of easier access to health care facilities.

While the colons sought to preserve their status, French officials vacillated between promoting colon interests and promoting reforms for the Muslims. Pro-Muslim reform efforts ultimately failed because of political pressure from the colons and their representatives in Paris. While French political theorists debated

between assimilation and autonomy for Algeria's Muslims, the Muslim majority remained largely resentful of the privileged status of the colons.

The first Muslim political organizations appeared in the 1930s, the most important of these being Ahmed Messali Hadj's Mouvement pour le Triomphe des Libertés Démocratiques (Movement for the Triumph of Democratic Liberties, MTLD). World War II brought opportunities for change that increasing numbers of Algerian Muslims desired. Following the Anglo-American landings in North Africa in November 1942, Muslim activists met with American envoy Robert Murphy and Free French general Henri Giraud concerning postwar freedoms but received no firm commitments. As the war in Europe was ending and the Arab League was forming, pent-up Muslim frustrations were vented in the Sétif Uprising of May 8, 1945. Muslim mobs massacred colons before colonial troops restored order, and hundreds of Muslims were killed in a colon reprisal.

Returning Muslim veterans were shocked by what they regarded as the French government's heavy-handed actions after Sétif, and some (including veteran Ahmed Ben Bella) joined the MTLD. Ben Bella went on to form the MTLD's paramilitary branch, the Organization Speciale, and soon fled to Egypt to enlist the support of President Gamal Abdel Nasser. Proindependence Algerian Muslims were emboldened by Ho Chi Minh's victory over French forces at Dien Bien Phu in Vietnam in May 1954, and when Algerian Muslim leaders met Ho at the Bandung Conference in April 1955, he told them that the French could be defeated.

Ben Bella and his compatriots formed the Front de Libération Nationale (National Liberation Front, FLN) on October 10, 1954, and the FLN revolution officially began on the night of October 31–November 1. The FLN organized its manpower into several military districts (*wilayas*). Its goal was to end French control of Algeria and drive out or eliminate the colon population. Wilaya 4, located near Algiers, was especially important, and the FLN was particularly active in Kabylia and the Aures Mountains. The party's organization was rigidly hierarchical and tolerated no dissent. In form and style it resembled Soviet bloc communist parties, although it claimed to offer a noncommunist and non-Western alternative ideology, articulated by Frantz Fanon.

As France increased the number of its military forces in Algeria to fight the growing insurgency, French officials sought support from North Atlantic Treaty Organization (NATO) partners in the Algerian War, arguing that keeping Algeria French would ensure that NATO's southern flank would be safe from communism. As a part of France, Algeria was included in the original NATO charter. Washington's position was nonetheless that European colonial empires were obsolete. Furthermore, U.S. officials believed that the United States could positively influence decolonization movements in the developing world.

The Arab League promoted Pan-Arabism and the image of universal Arab and Muslim support for the FLN. The French granting of independence to both Tunisia and Morocco in March 1956 further bolstered Algeria's Muslims. When France, Britain, and Israel invaded Egypt in the Suez Crisis of 1956, both the United States and the Soviet Union condemned the move, and the French, unable to topple Nasser, were forced to contend with an FLN supply base that they could neither attack nor eliminate.

On August 20, 1955, the FLN attacked colon civilians in the Philippeville Massacre, and colon reprisals resulted in the deaths of several thousand Muslims. The year-long Battle of Algiers began in September 1956 with FLN operative Saadi Yacef's terrorist-style bombing campaign against colon civilians. Meanwhile, other FLN leaders targeted governmental officials for assassination. The FLN movement faced a setback on October 22, however, when Ben Bella was captured.

Estimated Casualties during the Algerian War, 1954–1962

	French	Algerian
Military deaths	18,000	153,000 (including 12,000 from internal FLN purges)
Military wounded	65,000	Unknown
Civilian deaths	3,000	300,000–700,000

In December 1956 and January 1957, battle-tested French troops with combat experience in Indochina arrived in Algeria to restore order in Algiers. Among them were General Raoul Salan (commander in chief), paratrooper commander Major General Jacques Massu, and Colonels Yves Goddard and Marcel Bigeard, both of whom were adept at intelligence gathering and infiltration. Massu's men made steady headway, and Goddard himself captured Saadi Yacef in September 1957. The Battle of Algiers was now won. The French Army, however, employed torture to force FLN operatives to talk, while others were murdered in the process. The FLN, on the other hand, also routinely murdered captured French soldiers and colon civilians.

Despite victory in Algiers, French forces were not able to quell the Algerian rebellion or gain the confidence of the colons. Some colons were fearful that the French government was about to negotiate with the FLN. In the spring of 1958, colon Ultra groups began to hatch a plan to change the colonial government. Colon veteran Pierre Lagaillarde organized hundreds of Ultra commandos and began a revolt on May 13, 1958. Soon, tens of thousands of colons and Muslims arrived outside of the government building in Algiers to protest French government policy. Massu quickly formed the Committee of Public Safety, and Salan assumed leadership of the body. Salan then went before the throngs of protesters. Although the plotters would have preferred someone more frankly authoritarian, Salan called for the return to power of General Charles de Gaulle. Although de Gaulle had been out of power for more than a decade, on May 19, 1958, he announced his willingness to assume authority.

Massu was prepared to bring back de Gaulle by force if necessary, but military options were not needed. On June 1, 1958, the French National Assembly made de Gaulle premier, technically the last premier of the Fourth Republic. Algeria had managed to change the political leadership of the mother country.

De Gaulle visited Algeria five times between June and December 1958. At Oran on June 4 he said about France's mission in Algeria that "she is here forever." A month later he proposed a budget allocation of 15 billion francs for Algerian housing, education, and public works, and that October he suggested an even more sweeping proposal called the Constantine Plan. The funding for the massive projects, however, was never forthcoming, and true Algerian reform was never realized. In any case, it was probably too late for reform to impact the Muslim community of Algeria.

Algeria's new military commander, General Maurice Challe, arrived in Algeria on December 12, 1958, and launched a series of attacks on FLN positions in rural Kabylia in early 1959. Muslim troops loyal to the French guided special mobile French troops called Commandos de Chasse. An aggressive set of sorties deep in Kabylia made much headway, and Challe calculated that by the end of October his men had killed half of the FLN operatives in Kabylia. A second phase of the offensive was to occur in 1960, but by then de Gaulle, who had gradually eliminated options, had decided that Algerian independence was inevitable.

De Gaulle braced his generals for the decision to let go of Algeria in late August 1959 and then addressed the nation on September 19, 1959, declaring his support for Algerian self-determination. Fearing for their future, some Ultras created the Front Nationale Français (French National Front) and fomented another revolt on January 24, 1960, in the so-called Barricades Week. Mayhem ensued when policemen tried to restore order, and many people were killed or wounded. General Challe and the colony's governor, Paul Delouvrier, fled Algiers on January 28, but the next day de Gaulle, wearing his old army uniform, turned the tide via a televised address to the nation. On February 1, 1961, army units swore loyalty to the government. The revolt quickly collapsed. Early in 1961, increasingly desperate Ultras formed a terrorist group called the Secret Army Organization (OAS) that targeted colons whom they regarded as traitors.

The Generals' Putsch of April 20–26, 1961, seriously threatened de Gaulle's regime. General Challe wanted a revolt limited to Algeria, but Salan and his colleagues (Ground Forces chief of staff General André Zeller and recently retired inspector general of the air force Edmond Jouhaud) had all prepared for a revolt in France as well. The generals had the support of many frontline officers in addition to almost two divisions of troops. The Foreign Legion arrested the colony's commander in chief, General Fernand Gambiez, and paratroopers near Rambouillet prepared to march on Paris after obtaining armored support. The coup collapsed, however, as police units managed to convince the paratroopers to depart, and army units again swore loyalty to de Gaulle.

On June 10, 1961, de Gaulle held secret meetings with FLN representatives in Paris and then on June 14 made a televised appeal for the FLN's so-called Provisional Government to come to Paris to negotiate an end to the war. Peace talks during June 25–29 failed to lead to resolution, but de Gaulle's mind was already made up. During his visit to Algeria in December, he was greeted by large pro-FLN Muslim rallies and Muslim anticolon riots. The United Nations (UN) recognized Algeria's independence on December 20, and on January 8, 1962, the French public voted in favor of Algerian independence.

After the failed coup, a massive exodus of colons commenced. Nearly 1 million returned to their ancestral homelands (half of them went to France, and most of the rest went to Spain and Italy). Peace talks resumed in March at Évian, and both sides reached a settlement on May 18, 1962.

The formal handover of power occurred on July 4 when the FLN's Provisional Committee took control of Algeria. In September, Ben Bella was elected Algeria's first president. The Algerian War resulted in some 18,000 French military deaths, 3,000 colon deaths, and about 300,000 Muslim deaths. Some 30,000 colons remained behind, including the socialist mayor of Algiers, Jacques Chevallier. They were ostensibly granted equal rights in the peace treaty but instead faced official discrimination by the FLN government and the loss of much of their property. The FLN remained in power until 1989, practicing a form of socialism until changes in Algeria necessitated changes in internal affairs.

WILLIAM E. WATSON

See also

Arab League; Arab Nationalism; France, Middle East Policy; National Liberation Front in Algeria; Pan-Arabism and Pan-Arabist Thought

References

Horne, Alistair. *A Savage War of Peace: Algeria, 1954–1962.* New York: Viking, 1977.

Kettle, Michael. *De Gaulle and Algeria, 1940–1960.* London: Quartet, 1993.

Talbott, John. *The War without a Name: France in Algeria, 1954–1962.* New York: Knopf, 1980.

Watson, William E. *Tricolor and Crescent: France and the Islamic World.* Westport, CT: Praeger, 2003.

Algiers Agreement

Diplomatic accord between Iraq and Iran designed to settle outstanding issues between the two nations and avert war. The Algiers Agreement of March 6, 1975, known also as the Algiers Accord, was an agreement mediated by Algerian president Houari Boumedienne at a March 1975 meeting of the Organization of Petroleum Exporting Countries (OPEC). The accord was approved by Mohammad Reza Shah Pahlavi of Iran and President Saddam Hussein of Iraq.

Essentially, the agreement attempted to resolve territorial disputes between the two countries involving common borders as well as water and navigation rights. It provided for continuing Algerian participation in an ongoing Iranian-Iraqi dialogue that would occur at alternating meetings in Tehran and Baghdad. The Algiers Agreement also established an Iraqi-Iranian joint commission intended to refine and monitor the agreement's provisions and resolve any further disputes.

The agreement resulted in a formal treaty signed on June 13, 1975, which stipulated the Constantinople Protocol of 1913 and the Proceedings of the Border Delimitation Commission of 1914 as the basis of the determination of the Iranian-Iraqi border. Iran and Iraq agreed that the *thalweg,* or the median course of the Shatt al-Arab waterway, Iraq's only outlet to the sea, formed the river border between the two countries even though the shifting course of the Shatt al-Arab had given rise to some of the original disputes. They further consented to resolve ownership of disputed islands and other territories related to the waterway, to end subversive infiltrations of each other's country, and to resolve issues related to other border disputes, such as Khuzestan. Although not part of the agreement, the shah used the agreement's termination of subversive activities clause to withdraw Iranian support for the Kurdish rebellion against Iraq.

In the end, both parties failed to comply with the terms of the accord, and the festering unresolved territorial issues that it was designed to address led in part to the destructive Iran-Iraq War (1980–1988). This in turn led to a general destabilization in the Middle East.

RICHARD M. EDWARDS

See also

Hussein, Saddam; Iran-Iraq War; Iraq, History of, Pre-1990; Reza Pahlavi, Mohammad

References

Chubin, Shahram, and Charles Tripp. *Iran and Iraq at War.* Boulder, CO: Westview, 1988.

Coughlin, Con. *Saddam: His Rise and Fall.* New York: HarperCollins, 2002.

Hiro, Dilip. *The Longest War: The Iran-Iraq Military Conflict.* London: Routledge, 1991.

Ismael, Tariq. *Iraq and Iran: Roots of Conflict.* Syracuse, NY: Syracuse University Press, 1982.

Karsh, Efraim. *The Iran-Iraq War, 1980–1988.* Oxford, UK: Osprey, 2002.

Al Jazeera

The most popular news agency in the Arab world and its first large non–government-operated news network. Founded in 1996, Al Jazeera (al-Jazira) has become well known for its willingness to report on topics that are controversial in both the Middle East and in the Western media and to spark controversy through its inter-view format, in sharp contrast with state-controlled television. Al Jazeera is based in Qatar but is staffed by an international body of reporters. It claims to be the only uncensored news agency in the Middle East and, as a cable network, was available to viewers throughout the region. However, its commitment to presenting material that countered U.S. foreign policy in the Middle East and, at times, sharp criticism of Middle Eastern leaders or governments made it a focus of displeasure for the U.S. government, which banned its reporters from Iraq after the 2003 invasion.

The Arabic term *al-Jazeera* ("the island") is a colloquial refer-ence to the Arabian Peninsula. Its origins are rooted in a response to the censorship and control in the Arab media on the part of political commentators and reporters and the recognition of the new market available through satellite television.

Although popular with many in the region, the British Broad-casting Corporation (BBC) has discontinued much of its program-ming there in recent years. Many of the journalists employed by the BBC were eager to continue broadcasting and, together with Sheikh Hamad bin Thamer al-Thani, approached the emir of Qatar for money to establish a new network. Thani, a cousin of Emir Sheikh Hamad ibn Khalifa al-Thani, convinced the Qatari ruler to provide a grant of $150 million. This became the start-up money for Al Jazeera. The network continues to receive financial

assistance from Qatar and is further funded by advertising rev-enue and by distributing its exclusive news feeds.

Despite the subsidy from Qatar, Al Jazeera set out to maintain a strict independence from censorship, which was previously almost unknown in the region. Al Jazeera chose as its corporate motto "the right to speak up." It also proclaimed to the world that it sought in its reporting "objectivity, accuracy, and a passion for truth."

Broadcasting via satellite since November 1996, Al Jazeera quickly became the most-watched media outlet in the Arab world. Unfettered by the official censorship of government-sponsored news reporting, Al Jazeera has earned a reputation among its audience as a network committed to presenting multiple sides of any debate.

Al Jazeera became the first major news outlet in the Arabic-speaking Middle East to regularly present interviews with official Israeli spokesmen as well as with banned Islamist organizations and feminist groups. Al Jazeera has also been open in its critique of events that illustrate dictatorial or authoritarian actions by the governments of Saudi Arabia, Egypt, Syria, and Iraq. Such diversity of opinion and outspoken criticism of oppression made Al Jazeera a popular network in the latter part of the 1990s that became available to Arabic-speaking viewers worldwide. It was in 2001, however, that Al Jazeera captured the attention of news audiences far beyond the Arabic-speaking world. When the dramatic terror attacks of September 11, 2001, were carried out against the United States, Al Jazeera broadcast footage of Al Qaeda leader Osama bin Laden and Sulayman Abu Ghaith prais-ing the carnage. Al Jazeera subsequently broadcast tapes released by Al Qaeda in the interest of public knowledge. For many in the West who were otherwise unfamiliar with Al Jazeera, the net-work was now immediately seen as a mouthpiece for Al Qaeda. Al Jazeera vehemently rejected this charge, stating that it had merely presented news footage obtained in the interest of showing all sides in a major story. Nevertheless, the broadcast initiated a new barrage of attacks, particularly by the U.S. government, against Al Jazeera. These were exacerbated by Al Jazeera's coverage of Iraqi resistance activities to the American military presence, which the U.S. government presented as an insurgency carried out mainly by foreign elements.

Although news organizations around the world have pur-chased the rights to broadcast the footage from Al Jazeera, the George W. Bush administration was extremely critical of the net-work. The administration was outraged when Al Jazeera broadcast scenes of suffering experienced by Afghan civilians in the wake of the November 2001 invasion of their country by U.S. military forces, claiming that it sponsored the perpetuation of terrorist ideals. News organizations throughout the world, however, were impressed with the unparalleled quality of the Afghan war cov-erage by Al Jazeera. Indeed, its feeds were widely purchased for rebroadcast.

The stakes against Al Jazeera in the United States were raised even higher in early 2003. In the run-up to the March 2003 inva-sion of Iraq, Al Jazeera was accused of being connected to Iraqi

Al Jazeera English Channel staff prepare for a broadcast in the Doha newsroom in Qatar, November 14, 2006. (AP/Wide World Photos)

spies by a former Iraqi opposition organization known as the Iraqi National Congress. As a consequence, the U.S. Central Intelligence Agency (CIA) declared Al Jazeera to be an organ of anti-American propaganda. Al Jazeera's stock was banned from the New York Stock Exchange, and its reporters were ejected from the trading floor. Ironically, the Saddam Hussein regime had also tossed out of Iraq Al Jazeera's main reporter at the time, claiming that he was a spy for the United States. In response, Al Jazeera launched a searing editorial attack on an Iraqi government that tried at every turn to thwart free reporting from the country. Under attack from both the United States and Iraq in the days before the launch of the Iraq War, Al Jazeera became a symbol for what some see as hypocrisy in both Iraq and the United States in regard to a free press.

As the invasion of Iraq progressed in 2003 and the occupation of Iraq took hold, Al Jazeera continued to provide some of the world's most controversial and in-depth reporting, and its feeds were rebroadcast on every continent. Despite having its headquarters in Baghdad and Kabul bombed by U.S. forces and pressure being exerted by Washington on the Qatari government to shut it down, Al Jazeera's reporting on Afghanistan and Iraq continues to be the most comprehensive in the world. In fact, it is often the only reporting to focus on the heart-wrenching experiences of local people coping with disaster. Al Jazeera continued to broadcast controversial missives from insurgents, including footage of Westerners held

hostage, until the Iraqi interim government, with U.S. encouragement, banned the network from the country in September 2004.

The 2003 launch of Arabic- and English-language Web sites for Al Jazeera was plagued with controversy. Hackers repeatedly interrupted service on the English-language site, and several Internet service providers cancelled contracts with Al Jazeera when the network refused to remove controversial content. In 2005 an undeterred Al Jazeera planned to launch an international English-language satellite network based in Kuala Lumpur. In November 2006 Al Jazeera International, an English-language network, began its first broadcasts. Al Jazeera International's broadcasts are regularly picked up by the BBC and the U.S.-based Cable News Network (CNN), among others; its viewership is estimated to be 100 million households. Through extreme adversity and international controversy, Al Jazeera continues to be one of the most-watched news networks in the world, promoting itself as one of the only truly free voices in the Middle East.

NANCY STOCKDALE

See also
Terrorism; United States, Middle East Policy, 1945–Present

References
El-Nawawy, Mohammed, and Adel Iskander. *Al Jazeera: The Story of the Network That Is Rattling Governments and Redefining Journalism.* Boulder, CO: Westview, 2003.

Miles, Hugh. *Al Jazeera: How Arab TV News Challenges America*. New York: Grove, 2005.

Allah

Allah is the name of the one and only God, the very same One God worshipped by the Christians and the Jews. Indeed, the Arabic name "Allah" is likewise used by Arab Christians for "God." Prior to Islam, the Quraysh tribe who lived in Mecca believed in a deity they called simply *al-ilah*, or "the god"; however, they also worshipped other deities. The Prophet Muhammad's primary effort while still living in Mecca was to reform his fellow Quraysh by restricting their belief solely to Allah, or the One God, who was the God of Abraham just as surah 42:13 of the Qur'an states: "He has established for you the same religion that He enjoined on Noah, and which We revealed to you, and that He enjoined on Abraham, Moses, and Jesus—namely that you remain steadfast in the religion and make no divisions in it." The term "Allah" is a contraction of *al-ilah* (*al*, "the," and *ilah*, "god or deity"). Thus the *shahadah*, or Islamic statement of faith, states that there "is no *ilah* [god] but *Allah*," meaning the one and only god.

Elsewhere in the Qur'an, which Muslims believe to be Allah's divine message to men, sometimes the term for Allah is Rabb, meaning "Lord," or al-Rahman, meaning "the Merciful." From the Qur'an, Muslims later derived the 99 names of Allah, which are used as his characterizations, and the Sufi, or mystical Islamic type of prayer known as the *dhikr* ("remembrance of God"). As the Qur'an in surah 43:87 states, the Quraysh believed that Allah was the creator of the universe and the source of sustenance. However, the verse criticizes the additional deities of the pre-Islamic Arabs. In 630 CE when Mecca was conquered by the Muslim armies, the Kabah was cleansed of their idols. The Kabah, or sacred cube, was a structure that according to Islamic tradition was built by Abraham and his son Ishmael as the focal point of Allah's presence on earth.

Muhammad preached that Allah alone, without partners, was to be worshipped and served. Some historical sources allege that at one point during the Prophet's early ministry in Mecca, he struck a compromise with the Quraysh to allow the worship of Allah and these other three, which supposedly led to the inclusion of the controversial "Satanic Verses," or *gharaniq*, within the Qur'an. However, these verses were not included in the recension, or official edition of the Qur'an.

Allah is clearly described in the Qur'an, although many debates concerning Islamic theology arose later, especially in the medieval period. The Throne Verse (2:255), especially beloved to Muslims, declares Allah's omnipotence and uniqueness as compared to humankind: "Allah! There is no god but He, the Living, the Self-Subsistent. Slumber seizes Him not, no, nor sleep. To Him belong all that is in the heavens and upon earth. Who is there who intercedes with Him except with His permission? He knows what has appeared as past and as yet to come, and there is no share in His knowledge except by His will."

The Qur'an distinctly states that Allah is neither created nor begets a son or daughter with whom to share power. This belief challenged the Quraysh's belief in other deities but also the Christian conception of the Trinity.

Allah's corporeality and other aspects of his nature and functions were debated between theologians in what was called *kalam* and the group known as traditionists. Among their debates and those of others were the nature of the Qur'an, the battle between freewill and responsibility and Allah's omnipotence, and whether or not Allah had a face and hands (corporeality) as described in the Qur'an. On this last issue, the majority view was that belief in these matters must be maintained *bi-la kayfa* ("without asking how").

Allah is said to be omnipotent and aware of all and yet closer to man than "his jugular vein." His powerful and terrifying characteristics are stressed, as are His loving and tender aspects. Allah is the Creator of All. One of the most beautiful of Qur'anic surahs, The Bee, asks in a refrain throughout the chapter how any can doubt Allah, given the magnificence of his creations in nature.

The essential creed of Islam is known as *aqidah* and first consists of belief in Allah and His oneness, or *tawhid*. This is followed by belief in angels, prophets, scriptures, and the Last, or Judgment, Day.

More elaborate statements and discussions of Islamic faith began about 50 years after the death of the Prophet Muhammad. Many of these were in response to other philosophical questions, such as the balance between faith and works, the position of the Muslim sinner, the role of determinism, and the confrontations with Christian theology in its later stages.

The Sufi movements in Islam aim to develop the individual Muslim in order for the person to achieve a mystical union with Allah. This comes about through an end to individual ego. Vast amounts of literature and poetry focus on this process, expressed as love or longing for Allah. Various Sufi figures were controversial to institutional scholars; however, mystical Islam or Sufism shares with many ordinary Muslims the emphasis on *tawwakul*, or pronounced trust and reliance on Allah.

The Qur'an contains Allah's commandments for devout Muslims to follow His Sharia, or way. In addition to Islam's basic creed (or faith), the so-called five pillars of Islam, all basic commandments can be found within the Qur'an as pertain to relations between mankind and Allah and man's relations to his fellow men. Good and evil are clearly defined throughout the Qur'an, which consistently exhorts Muslims to follow the righteous path and abjure all evil, as commanded by Allah. Crimes against Allah are the most serious, followed by crimes against Muslims, or social crimes, that include failing to support the poor and orphans in the community.

Whereas there is no formula for atonement of sins as assigned in Catholicism, for example, Muslims believe that they can make up for sinful behavior by the adoption of righteous behavior, and certain substitutes are permitted for other actions. All souls will be judged and either condemned to hell, or *jahannam,* or released to *al-jannah,* or paradise. Many Muslims hope for intercession (*shafa*) with Allah to occur at this time of Judgment, as referred to above in the Throne Verse. They pray for that intercession to be enacted for them through holy figures, although fulfillment of basic Islamic duties is still required, and, as stated, this possibility is regulated by Allah.

RUSSELL G. RODGERS AND SHERIFA ZUHUR

See also

Martyrdom; Qur'an; Shia Islam; Sunni Islam

References

Goldziher, Ignacz. *Introduction to Islamic Theology and Law.* Translated by Ruth Hamori and Andras Hamori. Princeton, NJ: Princeton University Press, 1981.

Al-Hashimi, Muhammad Ali. *The Ideal Muslim Society: As Defined in the Qur'an and Sunnah.* Riyadh, Saudi Arabia: International Islamic Publishing House, 2007.

Ibrahim, I. A. *A Brief Illustrated Guide to Understanding Islam.* Houston, TX: Darussalam, 1997.

Philips, Abu Ameenah Bilal. *The Evolution of Fiqh: Islamic Law & the Madhhabs.* Kuala Lumpur, Malaysia: A. S. Noordeen, 2005.

Watt, W. Montgomery. *The Formative Period of Islamic Thought.* Edinburgh, UK: [Edinburgh] University Press, 1973.

Allawi, Iyad
Birth Date: May 31, 1944

Iraqi politician and prime minister of Iraq's appointed interim government that assumed the governance of Iraq on June 28, 2004; he held the premiership until April 7, 2005. Iyad Allawi was born into a well-to-do family in Baghdad on May 31, 1944. His father and uncle were physicians. His father was also a member of Iraq's parliament, and his grandfather had participated in the negotiations that granted Iraq its independence in 1932. His mother was Lebanese. The family had long-standing commercial and political ties to both the British and the Americans.

Allawi graduated from the American Jesuit's Baghdad College, an intermediate- and senior-level preparatory school, and entered the Baghdad University College of Medicine in 1961, the same year he joined the Baath Party, met future Iraqi dictator Saddam Hussein, and became active in the Iraqi National Students' Union. Allawi organized strikes and other activities against the government of Abd al-Karim Qasim. On February 8, 1963, Qasim was overthrown in a Baathist coup, which resulted in General Ahmad Hassan al-Bakr becoming prime minister. Allawi was eventually placed in charge of the central security office at the presidential palace and was given the nickname of the "palace doctor."

Although unproven, there are charges that Allawi participated in intense interrogations and torture that led to the deaths of trade union officials, students, and political leaders. Allawi was arrested on these charges, but he was released after Bakr intervened. Allawi participated in the July 17, 1968, coup that made Bakr president

and excluded all but Baathists from government positions. Bakr then pressured the minister of health, Ezzat Mustafa, to expedite Allawi's graduation from the college of medicine.

Opposition to Allawi grew within the government, and he was sent to Beirut in 1971 before moving to London in 1972 to head the Baath National Students Union and to pursue advanced medical studies. Allawi left the Baath Party in 1975 and supposedly began working for MI6, the British foreign intelligence service. In 1976 he earned a masters of science in medicine from London University. Allawi's name was placed on an assassination list in 1978 after Iraqi president Saddam Hussein failed to convince him to rejoin the Baathists. In February 1978 Allawi and his wife were attacked by an ax-bearing intruder in their Surrey home but escaped serious injury. Allawi earned a doctorate in medicine in 1979 from London University before being certified as a neurologist in 1982.

In 1979 Allawi had begun gathering alienated former Iraqi Baathists together into a group that grew into a Hussein opposition party. It was formalized in December 1990 as the Iraqi National Accord (INA). The INA received backing from Britain, the United States, Jordan, Saudi Arabia, and Turkey. It fomented dissent among the disaffected in Iraq and committed acts of terror and sabotage in that country in an attempt to bring down the Hussein regime. Allawi and the INA were recruited by the U.S. Central Intelligence Agency (CIA) after the 1991 Persian Gulf War

Iraqi prime minister Iyad Allawi, shown here attending a meeting of the European Union (EU) in Brussels on November 5, 2004. Allawi was critical of the EU over its lack of support for the U.S.-led coalition in the Iraq War. (Council of the European Union)

and were paid $5 million dollars in 1995 and $6 million in 1996. The CIA supported the INA's 1996 failed military coup, code-named DBACHILLES, which led to the execution of many Iraqis and to the confiscation or destruction of approximately $250 million of Allawi family assets.

The INA and Allawi gathered intelligence establishing the alleged existence of weapons of mass destruction (WMDs) in Iraq that formed the core of the MI6 dossier released in September 2002. This dossier formed a major part of the rationale for the 2003 U.S.- and British-led coalition invasion of Iraq in March 2003. On July 13, 2003, Allawi was appointed by Coalition Provisional Authority administrator L. Paul Bremer to the 25-member Iraqi Governing Council (IGC), where he served as minister of defense and assumed the rotating presidency for October 2003. He resigned as head of the IGC security committee in April 2004 over alleged concerns about U.S. tactics used to subdue the 2004 Fallujah insurgency.

The coalition-led IGC transferred authority to the Iraqi Interim Government, with Allawi as the appointed interim prime minister, on June 28, 2004. During his tenure in this position he created a domestic spy agency named the General Security Directorate to counter the Iraqi insurgency, closed the Iraqi office of the television network Al Jazeera, attempted to marginalize radical Shiite cleric Muqtada al-Sadr and his militia, and assumed the power to declare martial law. Allawi tried to draw Baathists who had not committed criminal acts during Hussein's rule into the government and considered pardoning insurgents who surrendered their weapons. Allawi stepped down as premier on April 7, 2005, the day the Islamic Dawa Party leader Ibrahim al-Jafari was elected to lead the transitional Iraqi National Assembly.

Allawi's INA won just 25 seats in the December 2005 elections establishing the permanent Iraqi National Assembly. This placed the party a distant third in the assembly, with only 14 percent of the vote. In 2007 the INA boycotted the Iraqi government altogether, and Allawi refused to take a cabinet position in it. He retains his dual British citizenship, and his wife and children reside in the United Kingdom for security reasons. In January 2009 Allawi excoriated the George W. Bush administration for its mismanagement of the Iraq War since 2003 and criticized Bush for his insistence on elections and democratic institutions in Iraq before first having achieved stability. Allawi was also highly critical of the Iraqi government led by Nuri al-Maliki.

RICHARD M. EDWARDS

See also

Al Jazeera; Baath Party; Bakr, Ahmad Hassan al-; Bremer, Jerry; Fallujah, Second Battle of; Hussein, Saddam; Iraq, History of, Pre-1990; Iraq, History of, 1990–Present; Iraqi Insurgency; Maliki, Nuri Muhammed Kamil Hasan al-; Qasim, Abd al-Karim

References

Allawi, Ali A. *The Occupation of Iraq: Winning the War, Losing the Peace.* New Haven, CT: Yale University Press, 2007.

Keegan, John. *The Iraq War: The Military Offensive, from Victory in 21 Days to the Insurgent Aftermath.* New York: Vintage, 2005.

Polk, William R. *Understanding Iraq: The Whole Sweep of Iraqi History, from Genghis Khan's Mongols to the Ottoman Turks to the British Mandate to the American Occupation.* New York: Harper Perennial, 2006.

Al-Manar Television

Official television station of the Lebanese Shiite movement and militia Hezbollah, which began broadcasting terrestrially in 1991 and via satellite in 2000. Al-Manar ("the beacon" in Arabic) played an important role in Hezbollah's 1984 to May 2000 campaign against the occupation of a large swath of southern Lebanon by the Israeli Army, which the Israelis dubbed the "security zone."

The station is a part of Hezbollah's sophisticated multimedia network, which also includes radio stations and print publications. Today, Al-Manar is carried by 7 major satellite companies and broadcasts programming 24 hours per day, 7 days a week. The station, which was partly funded by Iran in 1991, has an annual budget of $15 million and is a member of the Arab States Broadcasting Union.

Al-Manar's popularity spikes during times of crisis in southern Lebanon and is generally popular throughout the Arab and Muslim world. The station supplements its main Arabic language programming with broadcasts in French, English, and Hebrew. Based in Beirut, Al-Manar maintains bureaus in several countries, including Egypt, the United Arab Emirates (UAE), and Iran, and it has reporters stationed in numerous countries in Europe and the Middle East.

Al-Manar propaganda broadcasts had a significant effect throughout the Israeli occupation and again during the summer 2006 Hezbollah-Israeli conflict, particularly after the Israelis launched their major ground invasion of Lebanon. During the Israeli occupation of part of Lebanon, Hebrew broadcasts targeted Israeli units in Lebanon as part of Hezbollah's campaign of psychological warfare. A particularly effective series of broadcasts mixed images of slain Israeli soldiers followed by a question in Hebrew—"Who's next?"—with a blank profile cutout. Hezbollah filmed many of its attacks against the Israelis and their Lebanese allies, the South Lebanon Army (SLA), a militia made up predominantly of Maronite Catholics. These videos, which recorded ambushes of Israeli patrols, assaults on Israeli positions, and suicide attacks on Israeli and SLA military targets, were regularly broadcast on Al-Manar.

Today, Al-Manar's programming includes talk shows, television news magazines, religious programming, rousing propaganda music videos, documentaries, dramas, and news broadcasts. The station also broadcasts Hezbollah's rallies and public speeches and press conferences by its leaders. Religious and political music videos are included in its broadcasts. These videos serve different purposes—from commemorating the sacrifices of its guerrillas to supporting the Second (al-Aqsa) Palestinian Intifada against the Israeli occupation of the West Bank and blockade of the Gaza Strip. Some videos extol the party's military exploits against the Israelis, portraying Hezbollah as a defender of Lebanese, Arab, and Muslim honor against the Zionist Israelis and their U.S. backers. Al-Manar also includes news of particular issues of import, whether concerning the Arab-Israeli conflict, Iraq, or other events in the Islamic world. These measure up well against reportage by other media outlets.

Al-Manar was heavily watched during the summer 2006 war. Music videos are an attempt to bolster the party's support among Lebanese and Arabs, as well as within its own largely Shiite constituency. Images such as Lebanese flags, Lebanese cultural and historical sites and monuments, and religious symbols are integral parts of both types of music videos broadcast by Al-Manar.

Al-Manar has played a key role in the ongoing political disputes between Hezbollah and its political allies in the National Opposition coalition and the ruling March 14th Alliance, which currently controls the prime minister's office and a slight majority of Lebanon's parliamentary seats. The National Opposition also includes Lebanon's other large Shiite political party, Afwaj al-Muqawama al-Lubnaniyya (AMAL, the Lebanese Resistance Detachments), the Christian Free Patriotic Movement party of former Lebanese Army general Michel Aoun, a Maronite Catholic, and the Syrian Social Nationalist Party. The March 14th Alliance is controlled largely by three main parties: the Sunni Future Movement of Saad al-Hariri, the son of the assassinated prime minister Rafic al-Hariri; the Druze Progressive Socialist Party of Walid Jumblatt; and the Maronite Catholic Lebanese Forces party of Samir Ja'Ja. Al-Manar and other National Opposition media outlets were engaged in a propaganda and media war with March 14th media outlets, particularly Saad al-Hariri's Future Television station.

CHRISTOPHER ANZALONE

See also

Hezbollah; Lebanon; Lebanon, Armed Forces

References

Dallal, Jenine Abboushi. "Hizballah's Virtual Civil Society." *Television & New Media* 2 (2001): 367–372.

Hamzeh, Ahmad Nizar. *In the Path of Hizbullah.* Syracuse, NY: Syracuse University Press, 2004.

Harik, Judith Palmer. *Hezbollah: The Changing Face of Terrorism.* London: I. B. Tauris, 2005.

Jorisch, Avi. *Beacon of Hatred: Inside Hizballah's al-Manar Television.* Washington, DC: Washington Institute for Near East Policy, 2004.

Schleifer, Ron. "Psychological Operations: A New Variation on an Age Old Art: Hezbollah vs. Israel." *Studies in Conflict & Terrorism* 29 (2006): 1–19.

Al Qaeda

International radical Islamic organization, the hallmark of which is the perpetration of terrorist attacks against local governments or Western interests in the name of Islam. In the late 1980s members of Tanzim al-Qaida (Arabic for "base" or "foundation") fought with the mujahideen against the Soviet occupation of Afghanistan.

Al Qaeda, a salafi Sunni organization, was established around 1987–1988 by Sheikh Abdullah Azzam, a mentor to Osama bin Laden, the current leader of the group. Azzam was a professor at King Abdul Aziz University in Jeddah, Saudi Arabia. Bin Laden attended that university, where he met and was strongly influenced by Azzam.

Al Qaeda developed from the Mujahideen Services Bureau that Azzam established in Peshawar, Afghanistan. Bin Laden funded the organization and was considered the deputy director. This organization recruited, trained, and transported Muslim volunteers from any Muslim nation into Afghanistan to fight the jihad (holy war) against the Soviet armies in the 1980s.

Other elements in Al Qaeda arrived with members of radical groups from other countries, such as a faction of Egyptian Islamic Jihad, some of the members of which had been indicted and had fled Egypt. The credo of Al Qaeda came from its beliefs, based on ideas by many radical Islamist thinkers, including the practice of *takfir* (declaring that Muslim leaders who colluded with non-Muslim interests were apostates). Azzam adopted and expanded on these arguments, and bin Laden applied them to the government of Saudi Arabia, which he believed was too closely allied with the West. He proposed armed struggle to combat the far enemy as well as the near enemy in order to create a new Islamic society.

Following the mysterious death of Sheikh Azzam in November 1989, perhaps at bin Laden's behest, bin Laden took over the leadership of Al Qaeda. He has continued to work toward Azzam's goal of creating an international organization comprised of mujahideen who will fight the oppression of Muslims throughout the world. Al Qaeda aims to establish an authentic Islamic form of government, to fight against any government viewed as contrary to the ideals of Islamic law and religion, and to aid Islamic groups trying to establish an Islamic form of government in their countries.

No attacks by Al Qaeda are known to have occurred against Israel. The most damaging Al Qaeda attack by far has been the September 11, 2001, attack on the United States. The genesis of Al Qaeda's great antipathy toward the West—in particular the United States—can be traced back to the 1991 Persian Gulf War, precipitated by the Iraqi invasion of Kuwait on August 2, 1990. Bin Laden, originally a well-to-do Saudi Arabian, allegedly offered to commit Al Qaeda mujahideen to the defense of Saudi Arabia in case of an Iraqi invasion of that nation. The Saudi government declined the offer and permitted the stationing of hundreds of thousands of U.S. and coalition soldiers in Saudi Arabia during the run-up to the war (Operation DESERT SHIELD). This move enraged bin Laden, who perceived the presence of foreign troops in Saudi Arabia as a blatant acknowledgment of the political linkage between his government and the United States. He also portrayed this as a religious failing, for Saudi Arabia is home to both Mecca and Medina, the holiest of places in all of Islam, and the members of the Saudi royal family are the guardians of these. When he condemned the

Osama bin Laden (second from left) with his top lieutenant, Egyptian Ayman al-Zawahri (second from right), and two unidentified associates in an undisclosed location in this television image broadcast on October 7, 2001. (AP/Wide World Photos)

stationing of U.S. troops in Saudi Arabia, bin Laden was expelled from the kingdom and had his citizenship revoked. He then took up temporary residence in the Sudan.

Once in Sudan, bin Laden began training Al Qaeda fighters and is believed to have carried out an abortive assassination attempt against Egyptian president Hosni Mubarak in 1994. Under intense international pressure led by the United States, Sudan expelled bin Laden and Al Qaeda leadership in late 1996. From Sudan they traveled directly to Afghanistan, where the Islamic fundamentalist Taliban regime had already ensconced itself. The Taliban not only protected Al Qaeda but also in all probability helped arm it and by doing so gave to it an air of legitimacy, at least in Afghanistan. In 1998 bin Laden joined forces with leaders from the Egyptian Islamic Jihad, such as Ayman al-Zawahiri, and several other radical organizations, all of whom vowed to wage a holy war against Israel and its allies. In August of that year Al Qaeda carried out what is thought to be its first overseas attack against Western interests. That month saw the bombings of the U.S. embassies in Dar es Salaam, Tanzania, and Nairobi, Kenya. More than 200 people died in the attacks, and another 4,000 were wounded. In October 2000 Al Qaeda also carried out an attack on the U.S. Navy guided missile destroyer *Cole* in the Yemeni port of Aden in which 17 U.S. sailors perished.

The organization of Al Qaeda has a *majlis al-shura,* or consultative council. The *amir al-mu'minin* (commander of the faithful) is bin Laden, followed by several other generals and then additional leaders of related groups. Some sources say that there are 24 related groups as part of the consultative council. The council consists of four committees: military, religious-legal, finance, and media. Each leader of these committees has been selected personally by bin Laden and reports directly to him. All levels of Al Qaeda are highly compartmentalized, and secrecy is the key to all operations.

Al Qaeda's ideology has appealed to both Middle Eastern and non–Middle Eastern Muslim groups. There are also a number of radical Islamic terrorist groups, such as al-Qa'ida fi Bilad al-Rafhidayn ("in the land of the two rivers," meaning Iraq) and al-Qa'ida fi Jazirat al-Arabiyya ("of the Arabian Peninsula"), that initiated an association with Al Qaeda via public declarations. Nevertheless, Al Qaeda continues to be the central force of world terrorism because of the media attention given to its occasional pronouncements and the September 11 attacks.

Al Qaeda's most horrific deed has undoubtedly been the September 11, 2001, attacks on the United States. The attacks, which killed an estimated 2,976 people, were carried out by the hijacking of four commercial jetliners, two of which were flown into New York City's World Trade Center, destroying both towers. A third jetliner was crashed into the Pentagon outside Washington, D.C., while a fourth, supposedly bound for the White House or the U.S. Capitol, crashed in a western Pennsylvania field, killing all onboard. However, many Muslims and others demanded proof of a direct connection between bin Laden and the perpetrators of 9/11 and were unsatisfied with the results of the investigation into the terrorist attacks, believing instead that the event may have been staged.

It has been alleged that Al Qaeda inspired the March 2004 Madrid train bombings that killed nearly 200 and the July 2005 London subway bombings that killed 52. Although Al Qaeda took responsibility for the latter, there is no irrefutable evidence linking Al Qaeda to either attack; however, it is believed that the perpetrators borrowed Al Qaeda tactics to pull them off.

The Global War on Terror, initiated since the September 11 attacks, resulted in an invasion of Afghanistan and the toppling of the Taliban in late 2001 (Operation ENDURING FREEDOM). The Western presence in Afghanistan has kept Al Qaeda on the run ever since. Some of the leadership has been killed, but bin Laden has thus far apparently eluded capture or death. Since the 2003 Anglo-American invasion of Iraq, Al Qaeda was thought to have supported the growing insurgency in Iraq, which became a virtual full-blown civil war during 2006. Since 2007, U.S. and coalition forces have enjoyed some success in purging Iraq of Al Qaeda operatives. While most Arab and Muslim governments have tried to distance themselves from Al Qaeda and its operations, there can be little doubt that the group enjoys support among significant elements of the populations of these countries.

Bin Laden has been able to put most of the radical Islamic terrorist groups under the umbrella of Al Qaeda. Indeed, its leadership has spread throughout the world, and its influence penetrates many religious, social, and economical structures in most Muslim communities. Today, the upper-echelon leadership of Al Qaeda continues to elude American intelligence and Western armies in Afghanistan and Pakistan. The membership of Al Qaeda remains difficult to determine because of its decentralized organizational structure. By early 2005, U.S. officials claimed to have killed or taken prisoner two-thirds of the Al Qaeda leaders behind the September 11 attacks. However, some of these prisoners have been shown to have had no direct connection with the attacks.

Al Qaeda continues to periodically release audio recording and videotapes, some featuring bin Laden himself, to comment on current issues, exhort followers to keep up the fight, and prove to Western governments that it is still a force to be reckoned with.

HARRY RAYMOND HUESTON

See also

Afghanistan; Al Qaeda in the Arabian Peninsula; Al Qaeda in Iraq; Al Qaeda in the Islamic Maghreb; Bin Laden, Osama; Islamic Radicalism; Jihad; Mubarak, Hosni; Muslim Brotherhood; Salafism; Taliban; Terrorism

References

Bergen, Peter L. *Holy War, Inc.: Inside the Secret World of Osama bin Laden.* New York: Touchstone, 2002.

Gunaratna, Rohan. *Inside Al Qaeda: Global Network of Terror.* New York: Berkley Publishing Group, 2003.

Hueston, Harry R., and B. Vizzin. *Terrorism 101.* 2nd ed. Ann Arbor, MI: XanEdu, 2004.

Zuhur, Sherifa. *A Hundred Osamas: Islamist Threats and the Future of Counterinsurgency.* Carlisle Barracks, PA: Strategic Studies Institute, U.S. Army War College, 2006.

Al Qaeda in the Arabian Peninsula

Underground Muslim militant group based in Saudi Arabia that is loosely affiliated with Osama bin Laden's and Ayman al-Zawahiri's transnational Al Qaeda network. Al Qaeda in the Arabian Peninsula (al-Qaida fi Jazirat al-Arabiyya, AQAP) was organized in 2001–2002 and emerged publicly in 2003 when it carried out a series of deadly bombings against the Saudi government and expatriate residences in the kingdom's major cities, including the capital city of Riyadh and the key Red Sea port city of Jeddah. The group came under attack in 2004 and 2005 during a series of arrests and shootouts with Saudi police and soldiers. These shootouts resulted in the deaths of several top AQAP leaders and operatives including its founder, Yusuf Salah Fahd al-Uyayri (Ayiri) (d. 2003) and his two successors, Abd al-Aziz bin Issa bin Abd al-Muhsin al-Muqrin (d. 2004) and Salah al-Alawi al-Awfi (d. 2005).

AQAP's primary goal was to overthrow the House of Saud, the kingdom's ruling family, that is seen as corrupt and anathema to the "pure" society that the group's members and other unaffiliated and nonmilitant opponents of the monarchy seek to establish. The monarchy is harshly criticized by both the opposition and many of its own supporters among the ranks of the kingdom's official religious scholars (*ulama*) as being too closely aligned with foreign powers, such as the United States, to the detriment of Saudi interests and social values. AQAP members proved to be adept users of the Internet, creating Web sites and widely read online publications such as the Web magazine *Sawt al-Jihad* (Voice of Jihad).

Despite a series of small-scale attacks on Europeans and Americans in the kingdom during 2002 and early 2003, Saudi authorities did not acknowledge the existence of AQAP as a fully operational group until May 12, 2003. On that day, the group carried out three simultaneous suicide vehicle bombings at the Hamra, Vinnell, and Jedewahl housing compounds used by foreign (mainly Western) expatriates. The attacks killed 35 people, including 9 of the

A Saudi police vehicle in the al-Hamra compound, Riyadh, Saudi Arabia, on May 15, 2003. Three days earlier, three compounds housing foreigners were struck by Saudi terrorists, killing some 35 people and injuring more than 160. Nine attackers were also killed. Eight Americans were among the victims. (AP/Wide World Photos)

terrorists, and wounded 200 others. According to senior U.S. diplomats and Saudi intellectuals, this attack drove home to Crown Prince Abdullah (now King Abdullah) the need to vigorously combat homegrown Saudi radicalism.

In response to the attacks, hundreds of suspects were arrested by Saudi authorities, many of them with ties to AQAP and to the resistance in Iraq, although many were also probably figures from the nonmilitant religious opposition whom the authorities wished to silence under the guise of combating terrorism. Al-Uyayri (or Ayiri), AQAP's founder and first leader, was killed in June 2003 at the height of this sweep by Saudi authorities. He was succeeded by Abd al-Aziz al-Muqrin.

On November 3, 2003, Saudi security forces had a shootout with AQAP operatives in the city of Mecca, the location of the Kaba, Islam's holiest shrine, that resulted in the deaths of 2 militants and the capture of a large weapons cache. Five days later AQAP launched a successful suicide bombing attack against the Muhayya housing complex in Riyadh, which was home to many non-Saudi Arab expatriate workers; the attack killed 18 people and wounded scores of others.

The group continued to launch attacks on Saudi and foreign targets, including a Riyadh government building on April 21, 2004, and an oil company office in Yanbu on May 1, that resulted in the killing of five Western workers. AQAP suffered another setback on March 15, 2004, when Khalid Ali bin Ali al-Haj, a Yemeni national and senior AQAP leader, was killed in a shootout with Saudi police along with his companion, AQAP member Ibrahim al-Muzayni. The group retaliated with a host of deadly attacks on expatriates, killing Herman Dengel (a German, on May 22, 2004), BBC cameraman Simon Cumbers (on June 6), Robert Jacob (an American, on June 8), Kenneth Scroggs (an American, on June 12), Irish engineer Tony Christopher (on August 3), British engineer Edward Muirhead-Smith (on September 15), and Laurent Barbot (French, on September 26).

The most widely publicized attack, however, was the June 12, 2004, kidnapping and June 18 beheading of Paul M. Johnson Jr., an American employee of U.S. defense contractor Lockheed

Martin. His kidnappers demanded the release of all detainees held by Saudi authorities, which was denied. The beheading was filmed and released on Web sites associated with and sympathetic to AQAP. That same day, Muqrin was killed by Saudi security forces during a raid on an AQAP safe house. Meanwhile, on May 29 the group succeeded again in successfully carrying out attacks on three targets in the city of Khobar, taking hostages in oil business offices and housing complexes associated with foreign companies. Saudi police and soldiers stormed the buildings the next day and rescued many of the hostages but not before the attackers had killed 22 others. Shortly after this attack, the U.S. Department of State issued a statement that urged U.S. citizens to leave the kingdom. The year was capped off with a spectacular attack on December 6 on the U.S. consulate in Jeddah in which 5 consulate employees, 4 Saudi national guardsmen, and 3 AQAP members were killed.

The Saudi government waged a successful campaign against AQAP throughout 2004 and into 2005, killing dozens of the group's members and nearly wiping out its senior leadership. In April 2005 several senior operatives were killed in a shootout in Rass, and in August Saudi security forces killed Muqrin's successor and AQAP leader Salah al-Alawi al-Awfi in the holy city of Medina. Other members were arrested. After suffering dramatic setbacks, AQAP continued to organize and plan attacks through 2008.

The group's members remain at large, and Saudi and foreign intelligence agencies continue to warn that AQAP poses a threat. The Saudi government has responded with antiterrorist measures such as conferences and public pronouncements, a highly structured in-prison counseling program designed to de-radicalize detainees, and the Sakinah program that analyzes and engages Internet postings. In 2007 and 2008, Saudi security forces detained and imprisoned hundreds of people, some of them suspected militants and others in a variety of incidents, including those planning an attack during the hajj, the annual religious pilgrimage.

CHRISTOPHER ANZALONE

See also
Al Qaeda; Global War on Terror; Saudi Arabia; Terrorism

References
Al-Rasheed, Madawi. *Contesting the Saudi State: Islamic Voices from a New Generation.* Cambridge: Cambridge University Press, 2006.
Ambah, Faiza Saleh. "In Saudi Arabia, Fresh Recruits for Al Qaeda." *Christian Science Monitor,* April 16, 2004.
Cordesman, Anthony H., and Nawaf Obaid. *Al-Qaeda in Saudi Arabia: Asymmetric Threats and Islamist Extremists.* Washington, DC: Center for Strategic and International Studies, 2005.
Ghafour, P. K. "Death of Top Terrorists in al-Rass Gunbattle Confirmed." *Arab News,* April 10, 2005.
Murphy, Caryle. "Saudi Arabia Indicts 991 Suspected Al Qaeda Militants." *Christian Science Monitor,* October 22, 2008.
Riedel, Bruce, and Bilal Y. Saab. "Al Qaeda's Third Front: Saudi Arabia." *Washington Quarterly* 21 (2008): 33–46.
Zuhur, Sherifa. "Decreasing Violence in Saudi Arabia and Beyond." In *Home Grown Terrorism: Understanding and Addressing the Root Causes of Radicalisation among Groups with an Immigrant Heritage in Europe,* Vol. 60, edited by Thamas M. Pick, Anne Speckard, and B. Jacuch, 74–98. NATO Science for Peace and Security Series. Amsterdam: IOS Press, 2010.
———. *Saudi Arabia: Islamic Threat, Political Reform and the Global War on Terror.* Carlisle Barracks, PA: Strategic Studies Institute, 2005.

Al Qaeda in Iraq

Al Qaeda in Iraq (al-Qa'ida fi Bilad al-Rafhidayn, AQI) is a violent Sunni jihadist organization that has taken root in Iraq since the 2003 Anglo-American–led invasion of that nation. The U.S. government has characterized AQI, sometimes referred to as Al Qaeda in Mesopotamia, as the most deadly Sunni jihadist insurgent force now in Iraq. Other sources and experts argue that this designation is exaggerated, as the group is merely 1 of more than 40 similar organizations, and that the claim was made symbolically to rationalize the idea that coalition forces are fighting terrorism in Iraq and thus should not withdraw precipitously.

Opponents of the continuing U.S. presence in Iraq have argued that the 2003 invasion sparked the growth of salafi jihadism and suicide terrorism in Iraq and its export to other parts of the Islamic world. AQI first formed following the invasion and toppling of the Iraq regime, under the name Jama'at al-Tawhid wa-l Jihad (Group of Monotheism and Jihad) under Abu Musab al-Zarqawi.

Zarqawi had fought in Afghanistan in the 1980s and 1990s, and upon traveling to Jordan he organized a group called Bayt al-Imam with the noted Islamist ideologue Abu Muhammad al-Maqdisi (Muhammad Tahir al-Barqawi) and other veterans of the war in Afghanistan. Zarqawi was arrested and imprisoned but was released in 1999. Returning again to Afghanistan and setting up camp in Herat, he reportedly took charge of certain Islamist factions in Kurdistan, from there moving into Iraq and sometimes into Syria. Once Mullah Krekar, the leader of the Kurdish group Islamist Ansar al-Islam, was deported to the Netherlands in 2003, certain sources claim that Zarqawi led some 600 Arab fighters in Syria.

Tawhid wa-l Jihad was blamed for, or took credit for, numerous attacks, including bombings of the Jordanian embassy, the Canal Hotel that killed 23 at the United Nations (UN) headquarters, and the Imam Ali mosque in Najaf. It is also credited with the killing of Italian paramilitary police and civilians at Nasiriyah and numerous suicide attacks that continued through 2005. The group also seized hostages and beheaded them. A video of the savage execution of U.S. businessman Nicholas Berg, murdered in Iraq on May 7, 2004, reportedly by Zarqawi himself, was followed by other killings of civilians.

The group has targeted Iraqi governmental and military personnel and police because of their cooperation with the American occupying force. AQI's recruitment videos have highlighted American attacks and home searches of defenseless Iraqis and promise martyrdom. Estimates of AQI members have ranged from 850 to several thousand. Also under dispute have been the numbers of foreign fighters in relation to Iraqi fighters. Foreign fighters' roles were first emphasized, but it became clear that a much higher percentage (probably 90 percent) of fighters were Iraqi: members of the salafist jihadist, or quasi-nationalist jihadist, groups.

In October 2004 Zarqawi's group issued a statement acknowledging the leadership of Al Qaeda under Osama bin Laden and adopted the name al-Qa'ida fi Bilad al-Rafhidayn. The Iraqi city of Fallujah, in western Anbar Province, became an AQI stronghold. U.S. forces twice tried to capture the city, first in the prematurely terminated Operation VIGILANT RESOLVE from April 4 to May 1, 2004. The Fallujah Guard then controlled the city. U.S. military and Iraqi forces conquered the city in Operation PHANTOM FURY (code-named Operation FAJR) during November 7–December 23, 2004, in extremely bloody fighting.

Zarqawi formed relationships with other salafist jihad organizations, announcing an umbrella group, the Mujahideen Shura Council, in 2006. After Zarqawi was reportedly at a safe house in June 2006, the new AQI leader, Abu Ayyub al-Masri, announced a new coalition, the Islamic State of Iraq, that included the Mujahideen Shura Council.

Al Qaeda, along with other Sunni salafist and nationalist groups, strongly resisted Iraqi and coalition forces in Baghdad, Ramadi, and Baqubah and continued staging very damaging attacks into 2007. However, by mid-2008 U.S. commanders claimed dominance over these areas. Nevertheless, AQI was acknowledged to still be operative southeast of Baghdad in Jabour, Mosul, Samarra, Hawijah, and Miqdadiyah. The United States believes that AQI's diminished presence is attributable to the Anbar Awakening, which enlisted numerous tribes, including some former AQI members, to fight Al Qaeda. The Americans further believe that AQI has been diminished because of the troop-surge strategy that began in early 2007. Since then, bin Laden has urged the mujahideen to unify in the face of these setbacks.

AQI has strongly influenced other jihadist groups and actors, particularly through its Internet presence. In sparking intersectarian strife in Iraq, the group has also damaged Iraqi postwar reconstruction and has tapped into the intolerance of many salafi groups and voices as well as other Sunni Iraqis and Sunni Muslims outside of Iraq who have been threatened by the emergence of Shia political parties and institutions that had suffered under the Baathist regime under Saddam Hussein.

SHERIFA ZUHUR

See also

Al Qaeda; Anbar Awakening; Bin Laden, Osama; Iraq, History of, 1990–Present; Iraqi Insurgency; Salafism; Shia Islam; Sunni Islam; Surge, U.S. Troop Deployment, Iraq War

References

Associated Press. "In Motley Array of Iraqi Foes, Why Does U.S. Spotlight al-Qaida?" *International Herald Tribune,* June 8, 2007.
Burns, John, and Melissa Rubin. "U.S. Arming Sunnis in Iraq to Battle Old Qaeda Allies." *New York Times,* June 11, 2007.

Brisard, Jean-Charles, in collaboration with Damien Martinez. *Zarqawi: The New Face of al-Qaeda.* New York: Other Press, 2005.
Congressional Research Service, Report to Congress. *Iraq: Post-Saddam Governance and Security, September 6, 2007.* Washington, DC: U.S. Government Printing Office, 2007.

Al Qaeda in the Islamic Maghreb

An Algeria-based clandestine jihadi organization founded on January 24, 2007, that employs terrorist tactics in support of Islamist ideology. Al Qaeda in the Islamic Maghreb (Tanzim al-Qaida fi Bilad al-Maghrib al-Islamiyya, QIM) symbolizes Algeria's continuing political instability, North Africa's increasing vulnerability to militant Islam, and Al Qaeda's little-discussed ability to expand not by diffusing or splintering into local cells but rather by skillfully drawing established organizations into its sphere of influence.

QIM's origins lie in Algeria's modern history. The French-Algerian War (1954–1962) freed Algeria from French colonialism and led to rule under the wartime resistance movement, the National Liberation Front (Front de Libération Nationale, FLN). In 1989, however, militant Muslim opponents of the FLN regime formed the Islamic Salvation Front (Front Islamique du Salut, FIS). In the early 1990s the FLN manipulated and canceled elections to prevent the FIS from ascending to power, sparking a bloody civil war. This conflict radicalized and fragmented the opposition, with extremists gathering in the Armed Islamic Group (Groupe Islamique Armé, GIA), a faction bent on utterly destroying the FLN regime and installing a Muslim state under Sharia (Islamic law) through indiscriminate terrorist attacks against moderates and foreigners. The FLN weathered the storm, and as the civil war reached a horrendously violent stalemate, a new Islamist group—the Salafist Group for Preaching and Combat (Groupe Salafiste pour la Prédication et le Combat, GSPC)—superseded the GIA by denouncing the widely detested violence against civilians. Founded in 1998, the GSPC would adopt the Al Qaeda moniker a decade later.

The journey from GSPC to QIM was the result of a political dilemma facing Algerian Islamists and deft diplomacy by Al Qaeda operatives. The GSPC's first leader, Hassan Hattab (aka Abu Hamza), kept the popular promise to attack only government officials and forces, hoping to regain the far-reaching support for Muslim militancy enjoyed by the FIS. But building a broad backing was slow going, and time suggested that the FLN could withstand a conventional insurgency. Impatient elements within the GSPC forced Hattab's resignation in 2004. His successor, Nabil Sahraoui (aka Abu Ibrahim Mustafa), enjoyed only a brief reign before Algerian soldiers located and eliminated him in June 2004. Abdelmalek Droukdal (aka Abu Musab Abd al-Wadoud) has run the organization since, overseeing its radicalization, renaming, and return to GIA tactics.

Al Qaeda worked to influence the GSPC from its very inception. It helped to fund Muslim militants in Algeria in the early 1990s but refused to fully endorse the GIA despite experiences that so-called

Afghan Arabs in the two organizations shared while fighting the Soviets in Afghanistan in the 1980s. In 1998 Al Qaeda leader Osama bin Laden welcomed the advent of the GSPC, a group manned in part by Al Qaeda trainees who tied their renunciation of terrorism to an international jihadi agenda.

The new ideology harnessed the GSPC to Al Qaeda, and 12 days after the terror attacks of September 11, 2001, U.S. president George W. Bush labeled the GSPC a terrorist organization and froze its assets. This confrontation with the West—along with defections after 2000 of the halfhearted adherents, thanks to the Algerian government's amnesties for repentant civil war insurgents—further sharpened the GSPC's anti-Western extremist edge.

In 2002 Al Qaeda sent an emissary to Algeria for meetings with sympathetic figures within the GSPC. Two years later Chadian forces captured a key GSPC regional commander moving through the Sahara, and his colleagues decided to pressure Chad's ally, France, for his release. They reached out to Al Qaeda for assistance, and an obliging Abu Musab al-Zarqawi, head of Al Qaeda in Mesopotamia (Iraq), agreed to support the GSPC by kidnapping French citizens as bargaining chips. The plan did not materialize, but the congenial link remained, and after 2004 the GSPC's new hard-line leaders ultimately developed the link. Al Qaeda, for its part, grew increasingly interested in the GSPC after 2005 after the attempt to forge an affiliate terrorist network in Morocco had failed. Al Qaeda's strategists came to recognize that within North Africa, a critical region supplying long-standing Muslim immigrant communities to nearby Western Europe, only Algeria lacked a pervasive security apparatus capable of rooting out terrorist cells. The two organizations issued cordial statements throughout 2005, and by late 2006 a formal merger between Al Qaeda and the GSPC was announced, with the latter's name change coming the following year.

Since this merger, QIM has grown more powerful and dangerous. Al Qaeda is probably funneling resources into QIM, supplementing funds that the Algerian organization can gather on its own through the European financial network it inherited from the GIA. In return, QIM is internationalizing its purview. Some fear that it could make Europe an area of operations, and it has already forgone expansion—remaining at several hundred active members—in order to send newly trained North African recruits to fight in Iraq. The Al Qaeda–QIM alliance has been most pronounced in terms of tactics. The GSPC initially acquired conventional weaponry for guerrilla ambushes, false checkpoints, and truck bombs against military and government targets. With Al Qaeda's help and encouragement, QIM now executes impressive terrorist attacks featuring suicide bombers and civilian casualties. Since December 2006, QIM has bombed not only the Algerian prime minister's office and an army outpost but also foreign oil-services contractors and United Nations (UN) staff.

BENJAMIN P. NICKELS

See also

Al Qaeda; Al Qaeda in Iraq; Algerian War; Bin Laden, Osama; Global War on Terror; National Liberation Front in Algeria; Terrorism

References

Gunaratna, Rohan. *Inside Al Qaeda: Global Network of Terror*. New York: Berkley Publishing Group, 2003.

Hansen, Andrew, and Lauren Vriens. "Al-Qaeda in the Islamic Maghreb (AQIM) or L'Organisation Al-Qaïda au Maghreb Islamique (Formerly Salafist Group for Preaching and Combat or Groupe Salafiste pour la Prédication et le Combat)." Council on Foreign Relations, Backgrounder, Updated July 31, 2008. Available online at www.cfr.org/publication/12717.

Hunt, Emily. "Islamist Terrorism in Northwestern Africa: A 'Thorn in the Neck' of the United States?" Washington, DC: The Washington Institute for Near East Policy, Policy Focus #65, February 2007, www.washingtoninstitute.org/templateC04.php?CID=266.

Ibrahim, Raymond. *The Al Qaeda Reader*. New York: Doubleday, 2007.

Stora, Benjamin. *Algeria: A Short History*. Ithaca, NY: Cornell University Press, 2004.

Alusi, Mithal al-
Birth Date: 1954

Iraqi politician and member of the Iraqi parliament. Mithal al-Alusi was born into a prominent Sunni professorial family in Anbar Province in 1954. A Baath Party member who was not allied with Saddam Hussein's regime, in 1976 Alusi, while studying in Cairo, was sentenced to death in absentia for trying to organize a plot against Hussein's regime. Alusi lived in exile for a time in Syria and then settled in the Federal Republic of Germany (West Germany), where he became a businessman. Convicted of hostage taking by a Berlin court, he was sentenced to prison for three years but appealed the conviction and did not serve the full sentence.

Alusi returned to Iraq in 2003 following the overthrow of Hussein and was appointed the director of culture and media at the Higher National Commission for De-Baathification. Alusi is a strong proponent of close Iraqi ties with the United States, the United Kingdom, Turkey, and Israel. In September 2004 after a public visit to Israel, Alusi was expelled from his post and from the Iraqi National Congress of Ahmed Chalabi. Alusi was also indicted by the Central Criminal Court on a charge of having had contact with an enemy state.

Alusi then formed a new political party, the Democratic Party of the Iraqi Nation, to contest the January 2005 Iraqi elections. Receiving only 4,500 votes, it failed to win representation in the Council of Representatives. In February 2005 Alusi's car was ambushed in Baghdad. His two sons and a bodyguard were killed in the attack, although he escaped. Asad al-Hasimi, then minister of culture, was convicted of the crime and sentenced to death in absentia. In December 2005 the Mithal al-Alusi List coalition of small parties ran in the national elections and won only .3 percent of the popular vote. This was sufficient, however, to secure one seat, which Alusi took.

In September 2008 Alusi again visited Israel and spoke as a member of the audience at a conference on counterterrorism, during which he praised Israel and called for the normalization of relations with the Jewish state. On his return to Iraq, the National Assembly voted to revoke his parliamentary immunity and ban him from travel abroad. At the same time, a government minister threatened to indict Alusi again on the charge of having visited a country that is considered an enemy of Iraq. Alusi appealed to the Supreme Federal Court, which overturned the revocation of his immunity and declared that since no Iraqi law bars such travel, no crime had been committed.

SPENCER C. TUCKER

See also

Chalabi, Ahmed Abd al-Hadi; Iraq, History of, 1990–Present

References

Fox, Robert. *Peace and War in Iraq, 2003–2005.* Barnsley, UK: Leo Cooper, 2005.
"Iraq May Execute MP for Israel Visit." *Jerusalem Post,* September 22, 2008.
"Iraq Seeks to Prosecute Legislator for Israel Trip." *Reuters,* September 14, 2008.
Packer, George. *The Assassins' Gate: America in Iraq.* New York: Farrar, Straus and Giroux, 2005.

Amariyah Bunker or Shelter Bombing
Event Date: February 13, 1991

The U.S. military asserted that Public Shelter No. 25 in the Amariyah district of Baghdad was an Iraqi command shelter or backup communications bunker. It was, however, consistently publicized by the Iraqi government as the civilian air shelter for Amariyah. The bunker was bombed by the U.S. Air Force in the early morning hours of February 13, 1991, during INSTANT THUNDER, the air campaign component of Operation DESERT STORM. This attack, which occurred just 11 days before the allied ground offensive began, killed and wounded a large number of Iraqi civilians.

The coalition air war planners developed a plan for an air campaign that would destroy 84 strategic targets in Iraq in the opening week of the air campaign, which would begin on January 17, 1991. The planners believed that the destruction of these targets would paralyze Iraqi leadership, degrade its military and communications capabilities, and neutralize the Iraqi will to fight. Additionally, the air planners included other targets, such as Iraq's nuclear, biological, and chemical warfare facilities; ballistic missile production and storage facilities; key bridges; railroads and ports that enabled Iraq to supply its forces in Kuwait; and the Iraqi air defense system. Finally, at the insistence of General H. Norman Schwarzkopf Jr., the commander in chief of U.S. Central Command (CENTCOM), the air campaign envisaged attacks against Iraqi forces in Kuwait to reduce their effectiveness and compel their surrender or evacuation of Kuwait.

On January 17, 1991, coalition air forces opened Operation DESERT STORM with a massive air campaign, with more than 1,000 sorties launched per day. After several weeks the emphasis of the bombing moved from attacking Baghdad and leadership sites to other targets and Iraq's fielded military forces. Other priorities also intruded on the leadership focus, such as new intelligence on Iraq's weapons of mass destruction (WMDs) and tactical ballistic missiles that could carry chemical warheads and had the potential of provoking an Israeli overreaction to Iraqi missile attacks that in turn might cause Arab coalition partners to leave the fight. The initial attacks swept away much of Iraq's ability to defend against further air assaults including radar installations, command and control centers in Baghdad, air bases and hangars, and the Iraqi air defense system.

In early February 1991 U.S. war planners added what was alleged to be the "Al-Firdos command, control, and communications bunker" to the target list as a newly activated Iraqi command shelter. They claimed that they had intercepted signals traffic and that daytime satellite photography of limousines and trucks parked outside the bunker suggested "leadership" activity in the facility. On the evening of February 12 hundreds of Baghdad residents, possibly families of higher-ranking government and intelligence personnel, entered the bunker's upper levels to escape the nighttime bombing raids of Baghdad. In the early morning of February 13 two U.S. Air Force Lockheed F-117 Nighthawk stealth fighters dropped two 2,000-pound laser-guided bombs on the hardened shelter, piercing the concrete- and steel-reinforced roof. No warning had been issued.

Some 400 Iraqi civilians, mostly women and children, died in the attack. Another 200 were severely injured. The Department of Defense admitted that it knew the shelter had been used as a civilian air shelter during the Iran-Iraq war. Human Rights Watch conducted interviews with the neighborhood residents and affirmed that the facility was clearly marked as a civilian air shelter and that it was known to be operating in that capacity. Supposedly, a single human source claimed that the Iraqi military had begun using the facility, and this information had been previously considered credible. General Schwarzkopf and General Colin L. Powell, the chairman of the Joint Chiefs of Staff (JCS), considered the site a valid military objective and believed that the coalition had adhered to its legal obligations for limiting civilian casualties. Human Rights Watch, however, noted that bombing the facility without warning and knowing that civilians were housed there was a serious violation of international law. Schwarzkopf and Powell explained the attack as an unfortunate mistargeting problem and as an inevitable civilian tragedy brought on by wartime conditions. The attack brought an angry response from the Arab world.

The attack on the Amariyah shelter was the most glaring instance of civilian losses during the Persian Gulf War air campaign. The United States claimed that the great majority of the aerial attacks occurred against the Iraqi Army and took place in Kuwait and the southeastern portion of Iraq immediately adjacent to Kuwait. The Iraqi army in this area was located away from large populated areas with significant civilian populations, except for Kuwait City and its surrounding environment. The decision of the Iraqi Army to evacuate that city quickly after the start of the coalition ground attack limited the damage there. Other frequently attacked targets, such as Iraqi airfields and suspected Scud missile sites, were also situated away from population centers.

The impact of the Amariyah bombing was far-ranging. Although President George H. W. Bush had strong domestic backing for the war, he was still quite concerned about public opinion both at home and abroad and especially among the world's Muslim population. The Amariyah bombing sparked numerous anti-American demonstrations in the Arab world. In an effort to prevent similar incidents in the future, General Schwarzkopf received personal prebriefings on all daily target lists and took considerable time in deciding which targets would be attacked. Although he generally approved the targets, he did deny attack approval for some targets and ordered an end to bombing attacks on targets inside Baghdad following the Amariyah bombing.

This kind of higher-headquarters interference infuriated the CENTCOM air forces commander, Lieutenant General Charles A. Horner, as it reminded him and other air leaders of Washington's meddling control of the use of airpower during the Vietnam War.

ROBERT B. KANE

See also

Bombs, Precision-Guided; DESERT STORM, Operation, Coalition Air Campaign; Horner, Charles; Powell, Colin Luther; Schwarzkopf, H. Norman, Jr.

References

Conduct of the Persian Gulf War: Final Report to Congress, Washington, DC: Department of Defense, April 1992.

Davis, Richard G. *On Target: Organizing and Executing the Strategic Air Campaign against Iraq.* Washington, DC: U.S. Air Force History and Museums Program, 2002.

Human Rights Watch. *Needless Deaths in the Gulf War: Civilian Casualties during the Air Campaign and Violations of the Laws of War.* New York: Human Rights Watch, 1991.

Keaney, Thomas A., and Cohen, Eliot A. *Gulf War Air Power Survey Summary Report.* Washington, DC: Department of the Air Force, 1993.

Mann, Edward C., III. *Thunder and Lightning: Desert Storm and the Airpower Debates.* Maxwell Air Force Base, AL: Air University Press, 1995.

"Ambush Alley"

A stretch of road, including two bridges, located at the edge of Nasiriyah, Iraq. "Ambush Alley" gained its nickname in March 2003 during the initial stages of Operation IRAQI FREEDOM because of two incidents. The first was the ambush of the U.S. Army 507th Maintenance Company on March 23. A convoy element of the 507th blundered into an Iraqi ambush, resulting in several Americans being killed or wounded and several more, including Private Jessica Lynch, being captured.

The second more notable incident also occurred on March 23. In this engagement, Iraqi forces attacked a unit of U.S. marines seeking to capture two bridges over the Saddam Canal and the Euphrates River and the roadway between them. The ensuing battle became the costliest single engagement for American forces during the initial invasion of Iraq. It eventually involved the bulk of Task Force Tarawa, including the 1st and 3rd Battalions of the 2nd Marine Regiment; Alpha Company, 8th Tank Battalion; and Marine Aircraft Group 29.

The marine mission had seemed straightforward. Invasion planners recognized that the two bridges and the road between them represented a vital supply artery on the road to Baghdad. Once the bridges and the road were secured, the way would be open for the Americans to drive north toward Kut and, from there, to Baghdad.

Neither the marine field commanders entrusted with the capture of the bridges—Lieutenant Colonel Rick Grabowski, the commander of the 1st Battalion, 2nd Marine Regiment, and his immediate superior, Colonel Ronald Bailey, the commander of the regiment—nor the senior U.S. military leadership expected any difficulty here. Nasiriyah lay in one of the areas of Iraq considered by U.S. authorities to be less hostile to coalition forces. Senior U.S. commanders believed that the Shia population, traditionally hostile to the Iraqi regime, would welcome them. The U.S. leadership believed that the Iraqi regular army soldiers in the city, mostly from the 11th Infantry Division, were second rate and would flee or blend into the civilian population as soon as the Americans approached.

Based on these assumptions and the perceived need to capture the two bridges quickly, Grabowski planned to take the Southern Euphrates Bridge with Alpha Company. Bravo Company would then cross the bridge onto Route Moe ("Ambush Alley"), turn immediately to the east, and push to the Northern Saddam Canal Bridge with close artillery, air, and armored support. Charlie Company, 1st Battalion, 2nd Marines, was to move through Alpha and Bravo's lines and seize the Northern Saddam Bridge. The tank company was included in the initial attack, but some of its M1 Abrams tanks were refueling, so the initial attacks were launched without armored support.

As the marines approached the Southern Euphrates Bridge, Iraqi forces on both sides of the road opened fire on Alpha Company. Shortly thereafter, Charlie Company also reported that it was taking fire from the area around the Saddam Bridge. Bravo Company, following Alpha Company near the southern bridge, was soon pinned down by heavy fire from automatic weapons and rocket-propelled grenades. The marines were trapped in narrow streets surrounding the bridges, where it was difficult to bring their supporting arms to bear. Although they held the southern bridge, their foothold was tenuous.

The fighting involved U.S. efforts to relieve the embattled 1st Battalion and secure the road. The greatest difficulties proved to be getting armored support and reinforcements to the marines through the narrow streets and coordinating air support. The process proved to be costly. The marines faced a maze of Iraqi roadblocks. A field south of the Euphrates Bridge that seemed promising as a route for the tanks proved to be a sewage disposal bog that would not support heavy tanks. Mounting casualties made medical evacuation urgent, but it was impossible to get Medevac helicopters to the marine positions because of intense ground fire. In the early afternoon, an air strike by two Fairchild-Republic A-10 Thunderbolt II ground attack aircraft went awry and struck Charlie Company's position instead of the Iraqis.

By the evening of March 23 the 2nd Marine Regiment had seized both bridges, and the firing from the Iraqi positions had slackened. But the marines still had not completely secured Ambush Alley. It would take another two days to completely clear the roadway.

The events at Nasiriyah shook the marines. The official casualty count was 18 dead and 55 wounded, but many American officers privately thought that the count was much higher. Despite many acts of heroism, the "Ambush Alley" fight was not an impressive beginning to IRAQI FREEDOM. The intelligence on Iraqi strength and fortifications here was faulty, and the marine plan, which involved coordination among multiple commands, was too complicated. The tactics the Iraqis used at Nasiriyah indicated that they would not use conventional tactics but would fight using ambush and hit-and-run tactics. The Battle of Ambush Alley portended the nature of the fighting for the rest of the initial Iraq invasion and the ensuing Iraqi insurgency.

WALTER F. BELL

See also

Fedayeen; IRAQI FREEDOM, Operation; United States Marine Corps, Iraq War

References

Gordon, Michael R., and General Bernard E. Trainor. *Cobra II: The Inside Story of the Invasion and Occupation of Iraq.* New York: Pantheon Books, 2006.

Pritchard, Tim. *Ambush Alley: The Most Extraordinary Battle of the Iraq War.* New York: Ballatine Books, 2007.

Amos, James F.
Birth Date: ca. 1948

U.S. Marine Corps general and assistant commandant of the U.S. Marine Corps (2008–present). After graduating from the University of Idaho in 1970, James F. Amos joined the U.S. Marine Corps and qualified as an aviator. Assignments to fighter squadrons followed, where Amos flew the McDonnell Douglas F-4 Phantom. In 1985 he assumed command of Marine Air Base Squadron 24. After transitioning to the McDonnell Douglas/Boeing/Northrop F/A-18 Hornet, he joined Carrier Air Wing 8 on USS *Theodore Roosevelt.* In May 1996 Amos assumed command of Marine Aircraft Group 31. In August 2002 he took command of the 3rd Marine Aircraft Wing, and almost immediately he began planning for conflict in Iraq.

Amos's wing included more than 370 aircraft for operations against Iraq in Operation IRAQI FREEDOM and thus constituted a substantial part of the coalition air assets for the campaign. Marine

U.S. Marine Corps general James F. Amos. (U.S. Department of Defense)

aircraft were especially important in the ground support effort. Amos strongly supported the concept of the marine air-ground task force, which held that aircraft played an integral role in the support of ground forces. He was determined that his pilots do all they could to facilitate the ground advance.

To carry out the close support of marine ground forces, Amos worked closely with Major General James Mattis, commanding the 1st Marine Division. Amos also developed a good working relationship with U.S. Air Force lieutenant general Michael Moseley, the air component commander, who had wide latitude in the employment of his air assets. Amos also received naval cooperation.

Marine Bell AH-1 Cobra gunships were based on land, where they were closer to the fighting and able to support the marines quickly. The vertical takeoff and landing (VTOL) McDonnell Douglas/Boeing/BAE Systems AV-8B Harrier fighter-bombers were on amphibious ships offshore. These ships in effect became light aircraft carriers and provided support to the Harriers until they could be based ashore. The marine ground forces also relied on Amos's aircraft for much of their supplies. Mattis was determined to move fast and deep, and his vehicles could carry only a limited amount of ammunition, fuel, food, and water. For resupply, the marines depended on Amos's Lockheed C-130 Hercules transport planes.

When the invasion of Iraq began on March 20, 2003, Amos employed his aircraft aggressively. The Cobras were charged with destroying Iraqi units immediately in front of the marine spearheads, while the Harriers and Hornets were used in deeper missions to cut off Iraqi forces that might threaten the marine advance. To provide greater ability to respond to the needs of the ground forces, U.S. Marine Corps doctrine called for a combat pilot to be detailed to each infantry company as a forward air controller. Amos went even further and provided an extra flight officer to each battalion. As the troops advanced and captured Iraqi airfields, the Cobras were moved forward to decrease flight time.

The 3rd Marine Air Wing played an important role in the success of the marine advance on Baghdad. By the end of the organized fighting in late April, Amos's aircraft had flown 9,800 sorties. They had dropped 2,200 precision-guided munitions and 2,300 gravity (dumb) bombs, a total of 6.24 million pounds of ordnance. During the advance Amos was often near the front, inspecting the effectiveness of the air effort and gauging the needs.

In July 2004 Amos was advanced to command the II Marine Expeditionary Force based at Camp Lejeune, North Carolina. Once again he displayed an unconventional but logical approach to problem solving. He reorganized training facilities to be more like those encountered in Iraq and Afghanistan. He also built simulated forward-operating bases similar to those used by the marines in those countries. A road network suitable for training to deal with ambush and improvised explosive device (IED) attacks followed. Amos also worked on such projects as improving safety among marine motorcycle riders by organizing clubs and rodeos, and he provided recognition and support for wounded marines by sponsoring the Wounded Warriors Battalion.

Amos's achievements were recognized in July 2008, when he was selected as the 31st assistant commandant of the U.S. Marine Corps.

TIM J. WATTS

See also
Moseley, Teed Michael; United States Marine Corps, Iraq War

References
Gordon, Michael R., and General Bernard E. Trainor. *Cobra II: The Inside Story of the Invasion and Occupation of Iraq.* New York: Pantheon Books, 2006.
Murray, Williamson, and Robert H. Scales Jr. *The Iraq War: A Military History.* Cambridge, MA: Belknap, 2005.

Amphibious Assault Ships

U.S. Navy ship types whose aircraft-handling capabilities augment the traditional landing craft–based beach assault with their helicopter-borne troops and Harrier jets.

As early as 1955, the U.S. Navy sought to broaden the options in undertaking an amphibious assault, employing the helicopter to more widely disperse a landing force beyond the beachhead. To that end, between 1956 and 1961 a small escort carrier (the *Thetis Bay,* CVE-90) and three Essex-class aircraft carriers (the *Boxer,* CV-21; *Princeton,* CV-37; and *Valley Forge,* CV-45) were converted and redesignated as amphibious assault ships (LPH, originally

standing for Landing Ship, Personnel, Helicopter), each embarking a Marine battalion and its supporting helicopter squadron.

The seven purpose-built LPHs of the Iwo Jima (LPH-2) class began construction in 1959. The lead ship was commissioned in 1961, and all were completed by 1970. They resembled escort carriers but with higher freeboard, an improved hangar deck, and an enclosed rounded bow. About two-thirds the size of the Essex-class LPHs, the Iwo Jima class nonetheless was more efficient for its designed purpose in embarking an equal or greater number of troops. Each ship featured a large medical facility with a 300-bed capacity. The ships were the *Iwo Jima, Okinawa, Guadalcanal, Guam, Tripoli, New Orleans,* and *Inchon.*

Specifications were as follows: length, 602.25 feet; width, 104 feet; and draft, 26 feet. They displaced 11,000 tons (light) and 19,646 tons (full load), were capable of 23 knots, and had a range of 16,600 nautical miles at 11.5 knots or 10,000 nautical miles at 20 knots. They had a crew complement of 50 officers and 650 enlisted men. The Iwo Jima–class ships could carry 1,900 troops and 25 CH-46 Sea Knight and CH-53 Sea Stallion helicopters. The ships were armed with four 3-inch/76-millimeter (mm) guns, two 20-mm Phalanx CIWS, and two 8-tube Sea Sparrow missile mounts.

In addition to their primary role of amphibious helicopter assault, ships of this class acted as bases for CH-53 minesweeping helicopters during the Vietnam War and took part in operations to clear the Suez Canal following the 1967 Arab-Israeli war. During 1972–1974, the *Guam* embarked STOVL (short takeoff, vertical landing) Harriers and antisubmarine warfare (ASW) helicopters to evaluate the LPH as a sea control ship (SCS) in convoy escort and protection duties. All Iwo Jima–class ships contributed to Operation DESERT STORM. In December 1990 the *Tripoli* was deployed to the Persian Gulf as the flagship of the U.S. Navy mine countermeasures (MCM) group and a combined U.S. Navy and Royal Navy task force. On February 18, 1991, the ship struck a moored Iraqi contact mine, sustaining significant hull and internal damage. Excellent onboard damage control kept the *Tripoli* in operation and on station in support of further minesweeping activities until the U.S. Navy *LaSalle* (AGF-3) arrived to take over task force flagship duties nearly a week later. After a month of around-the-clock repairs in Bahrain, the *Tripoli* resumed flagship duties in the northern Gulf.

In the wake of the U.S. Navy's mine warfare experiences in the Persian Gulf War, in 1996 the *Inchon* was converted to a dedicated mine countermeasures command and support ship (MCS-12), capable of refueling minesweepers and mine hunters as well as embarking specially equipped MH-53E mine warfare helicopters. In 1997 the *Inchon* took part in mine countermeasures exercises in the Baltic and Mediterranean and, by the time of an Adriatic deployment during March–July 1999, in support of North Atlantic Treaty Organization (NATO) operations in Kosovo. The former LPH was the last serving member of the pivotal Iwo Jima–class. The *Inchon* was decommissioned in 2002.

The next iteration of the amphibious assault ship concept combined the successful features of the Iwo Jima–class LPH, basically a small helicopter carrier that could not deploy landing craft, with the in-hull well deck that defines both the dock landing ship (LSD) and the amphibious transport dock (LPD). The Tarawa (LHA-1) class matches the massive dimensions of an Essex-class aircraft carrier, and each ship can send an embarked marine battalion into action by means of both its helicopters and landing craft. In addition, its marine AV-8B Harrier jump-jets can activate quickly from the same flight deck to provide additional protection and ground attack measures.

The U.S. Navy's interest in blending the key aspects of the LPH and the LPD dates back to 1965. The ingenious design that would become the LHA was developed in 1968 by the naval engineer Reuven Leopold (responsible also for the Spruance [DD-963] class of destroyers) and was finally set in steel with the construction of the *Tarawa* commencing in 1971. It was launched in 1973 and commissioned in 1976.

Nine ships were planned, but in the end only five were approved and built. The LHA ships handle and store more helicopters than the LPH and can operate Harrier STOVL jets as well as OV-10 Bronco STOL (short takeoff and landing) observation aircraft. Nearly the same number of troops can be accommodated, and in a floodable docking well running nearly a third of the LHA's length from the stern, several types of landing craft can be transported

and deployed: four LCU (utility landing craft), 17 LCM (mechanized landing craft), or 45 AAVP (assault amphibian vehicles) in addition to the 35 AAVP that can be housed on a deck above. The docking well can accommodate one LCAC (landing craft air cushion). Like the LPH, each LHA has comprehensive medical facilities with three operating rooms and beds for 300.

The Tarawa-class ships were the *Tarawa, Saipan, Belleau Wood, Nassau,* and *Peleliu.* The ships' dimensions are as follows: length, 833.75 feet; width, 132 feet; and draft, 26 feet. Displacement is 33,536 tons (light) and 39,967 tons (full load). The ships are capable of 24 knots and have a range of 10,000 nautical miles at 20 knots. They have a crew complement of 1,103 (61 officers and 1,042 enlisted) and can transport 1,700 troops. Their normal aircraft complement is 6 AV-8B Harrier STOVL jets, 30 CH-46 Sea Knight and CH-53 Sea Stallion helicopters, and 3 UH-1N Huey and 4 AH-1W Super Cobra helicopters. Landing craft consist of 4 LCU 1610, or 7 LCM(8), or 17 LCM(6), or 45 AAV, and 1 LCAC. The Tarawa-class ships are armed with four 25-mm cannon, two 20-mm Phalanx CIWS, and two 21-cell RAM (rolling airframe missile) launchers.

The LHAs joined the fleet as the U.S. Marine Corps was making plans to deploy newly acquired AV-8A Harriers from VSTOL (vertical and/or short takeoff and landing) support ships (VSS). The VSS idea never reached fruition, but some aspects of it were

The U.S. Navy Tarawa-class amphibious assault ship *Saipan* (LHA-2). (U.S. Department of Defense)

fulfilled by the Tarawa-class ships as they carried out their primary amphibious assault role. In 1981 both the *Tarawa* and *Nassau* conducted trials operating the Harrier that were similar to the sea control ship (SCS) exercises undertaken earlier by the LPH *Guam*. The larger size of the LHA would eventually allow ships of this type to operate up to 20 Harriers in a sea-control role.

During the Persian Gulf War, the Tarawa-class ships joined the amphibious armada that, in the end, would not send its massive forces ashore. The *Tarawa* was the presumed target of a dud Iraqi Scud missile while moored in the Saudi harbor of Jubail on February 15, 1991. Five days later, the *Nassau's* Marine Harrier squadron flew into action against Iraqi ground forces in the first such sortie from a U.S. Navy amphibious assault ship. On February 24 the *Tarawa* launched a helicopter-borne expeditionary brigade as part of the Marine offensive moving into Kuwait. As Iraqi forces withdrew from Kuwait on February 26, the *Nassau's* helicopters joined those of the *Iwo Jima* and *Guam* in an elaborate amphibious feint targeting the coastal islands of Faylaka and Bubiyan. The *Peleliu* and *Saipan* were on station in the region from June 1991 and September 1991, respectively. The *Belleau Wood* underwent a shipyard refit from late 1990 into 1992.

All ships contributed to Operations ENDURING FREEDOM and IRAQI FREEDOM. The *Saipan*, notably, launched the first Harrier raids against Afghanistan in early November 2001. The *Belleau Wood* and *Saipan* were decommissioned in 2005 and 2006, respectively

Originally conceived as a slightly smaller and less costly version of the Tarawa-class LHA, the Wasp (LHD-1) class of amphibious assault ships as constructed actually became the world's largest amphibious ship type. The flight deck and hangar are larger than those of an LHA and can support more Harriers, while a reconfigured well deck increases the LCAC transport capacity from one to three. The internal redesign also yields a much-increased medical capacity over the LHA, doubling the care facilities to six operating rooms and 600 beds. Vehicle cargo space is slightly reduced, but troop accommodation remains on par with that of the LHA. The Wasp class comprises seven identical ships and one slight variant. The lead ship of the class, the *Wasp*, was launched in 1987 and commissioned in 1989. The other ships with date of commissioning are the *Essex* (1992), *Kearsarge* (1993), *Boxer* (1995), *Bataan* (1997), *Bonhomme Richard* (1998), *Iwo Jima* (2001), and *Makin Island* (2009). Dimensions are length, 844 feet; width, 140 feet; and draft, 26.6 feet. Displacement is 28,223 tons (light) and between 40,650 and 41,772 tons full load. The ships are capable of a speed of 24 knots (22 knots sustained). They have a range of 9,500 nautical miles at 20 knots. Their crew complement varies depending on the ship from 1,059 (65 officers and 994 enlisted) to 1,142 (62 officers and 1080 enlisted). They can transport 1,700–1,800 men. Aircraft consist of, for an amphibious role, 30 CH-46 Sea Knights and CH-53 Sea Stallion helicopters, 6 AV-8B Harrier STOVL jets, and 3 UH-1N Huey and AH-1W Super Cobra helicopters or, for a sea control/carrier role, 20 AV-8B STOVL Harrier STOVL jets and 6 SH-60 Seahawk ASW helicopters. Planning is under way for MV-22 Osprey VTOL tilt-rotor

and F-35B Joint Strike Fighter operations. They carry the following landing craft: 3 LCAC, or 12 LCM(6), or 6 LCM(8), or 2 LCU 1610. Armament consists of two RAM missile launchers, two NATO Sea Sparrow launchers, and two to three 20-mm Phalanx CIWS mounts.

USS *Makin Island,* which entered the fleet in October 2009, is something of a transitional step toward the realization of the LHA Replacement class, or LHA(R), proposed by the U.S. Navy to begin taking the place of the remaining LHAs by 2013. Otherwise identical to the other LHDs, *Makin Island's* funnels are canted outboard from the island structure to better disperse the hot gas turbine exhaust. Gas turbine propulsion is planned for these new ships, the first of which, the *America* (LHA-6, continuing the original LHA class hull numbers), will further divert from LHA/LHD characteristics by replacing the well deck with increased cargo and aviation support areas, and, like the original LPHs, by operating only aircraft.

LHDs have joined LHAs in both combat and humanitarian operations as they came on line, serving in Operations ENDURING FREEDOM and IRAQI FREEDOM as both forward Marine bases and medical facilities. Configured as "Harrier carriers" during the Iraq War, the *Bataan* and *Bonhomme Richard* sent their augmented fixed-wing jets on numerous sorties against Iraqi military targets.

GORDON E. HOGG

See also

Amphibious Command Ships; Dock Landing Ships, U.S. and Coalition; Hospital Ships; Landing Craft Air Cushion; United States Marine Corps, Iraq War; United States Marine Corps, Persian Gulf War; United States Navy, Iraq War; United States Navy, Persian Gulf War

References

Friedman, Norman. *U.S. Amphibious Ships and Craft: An Illustrated Design History*. Annapolis, MD: Naval Institute Press, 2002.

Marolda, Edward, and Robert Schneller. *Shield and Sword: The United States Navy and the Persian Gulf War*. Annapolis, MD: U.S. Naval Institute Press, 2001.

Polmar, Norman. *The Naval Institute Guide to the Ships and Aircraft of the U.S. Fleet*. 18th ed. Annapolis, MD: Naval Institute Press, 2005.

Saunders, Stephen, ed. *Jane's Fighting Ships, 2006–2007*. Coulsdon, Surrey, UK, and Alexandria, VA: Jane's Information Group, 2006.

Sharpe, Richard, ed. *Jane's Fighting Ships: 1991–1992*. London: Jane's Information Group, 1991.

Amphibious Command Ships

Naval ships specifically designed to facilitate the oversight and coordination of complex naval fleet activities by means of their enhanced C4I (command, control, communications, computer, and intelligence) capabilities.

Originally dedicated to the command of amphibious operations upon their commissioning in 1970 and 1971, the U.S. Navy *Blue Ridge* (LCC-19) and *Mount Whitney* (LCC-20) have expanded their roles to serve as fleet flagships, embarking admirals and their large command staff apparatus. The *Blue Ridge* was commissioned

The USS *Blue Ridge*, the only amphibious command ship in Operation DESERT STORM. Amphibious command ships provide logistical and combat support. (U.S. Department of Defense)

in 1970 and the *Mount Whitney* in 1971. Dimensions are length, 634 feet; beam, 108 feet; and draft, 29 feet. Their displacement is 16,790 tons (light) and 16,646 tons (full load). They are capable of 22 knots and have a range of 13,500 nautical miles at 16 knots. Crew complement is 842 (52 officers and 790 enlisted). They can accommodate a flag command staff of up to 296 (82 officers and 214 enlisted). They usually have one SH-60 Sea Hawk helicopter assigned. They are armed with two 25-millimeter (mm) Bushmaster cannon, two 20-mm Phalanx CIWS, and four .50-caliber machine guns. The ships are equipped with sophisticated radar, navigation, and electronic warfare systems.

The *Blue Ridge* and *Mount Whitney* are the only purpose-built large command ships in the U.S. Navy. Traditionally, flagships had been battleships and cruisers modified to accommodate a large flag staff and U.S. Marine Corps contingent and were outfitted with a powerful communications suite. Designers of the LCC model wished to avoid the topside clutter presented by existing flagships, so they chose the flat-decked aircraft carrier–like amphibious assault ships (LPH) of the Iwo Jima class as a starting point, placing a small superstructure block centrally and distributing a series of easily replaced or updated antennae masts on the

expansive decks forward and aft. A large helicopter landing area occupies the deck above the stern, and sponsons incorporating open gallery decks set on each side carry the ship's boats and provide underway replenishment access points.

The *Blue Ridge* was assigned as the U.S. Seventh Fleet command ship in 1979, home-ported at Yokosuka, Japan. In August 1990 the *Blue Ridge* became the flagship, in turn, of vice admirals Hank Mauz and Stanley Arthur, COMUSNAVCENT (Commander, U.S. Naval Forces Central Command), remaining on station in the Persian Gulf for Operations DESERT SHIELD and DESERT STORM until the end of April 1991. The *Mount Whitney*, under the aegis of U.S. Naval Forces Central Command/Fifth Fleet in November 2002, contributed to Operations ENDURING FREEDOM and IRAQI FREEDOM, becoming the lead command ship for the newly formed multinational Combined Joint Task Force (CTF-150) and conducting antiterrorism and antipiracy maritime security operations (MSO) patrols around the Horn of Africa and in the Arabian Sea, the Red Sea, and the Indian Ocean. The *Mount Whitney*, since 1981 the flagship of the U.S. Second Fleet at Norfolk, became in 2005 the Sixth Fleet flagship, home-ported at Gaeta, Italy. The *Blue Ridge* has operated in the Pacific and Indian oceans since 2002 in support of Operation ENDURING FREEDOM and has visited ports in China and Russia; Vladivostok has been a port of call three times since 1996. Both ships are reaching the limits of their service lives, and rather than replacing them with new ships, the U.S. Navy has contemplated the distribution of LCC-derived modules aboard several types of currently serving warships.

GORDON E. HOGG

See also

Arthur, Stanley; DESERT STORM, Operation, Coalition Naval Forces; ENDURING FREEDOM, Operation, Coalition Naval Forces; IRAQI FREEDOM, Operation, Coalition Naval Forces; Mauz, Henry H., Jr.; United States Navy, Iraq War; United States Navy, Persian Gulf War

References

Friedman, Norman. *U.S. Amphibious Ships and Craft: An Illustrated Design History.* Annapolis, MD: Naval Institute Press, 2002.

Marolda, Edward, and Robert Schneller. *Shield and Sword: The United States Navy and the Persian Gulf War.* Annapolis, MD: U.S. Naval Institute Press, 2001.

Polmar, Norman. *The Naval Institute Guide to the Ships and Aircraft of the U.S. Fleet.* 18th ed. Annapolis, MD: Naval Institute Press, 2005.

Schneller, Robert J., Jr. *Anchor of Resolve: A History of U.S. Naval Forces Central Command/Fifth Fleet.* Washington, DC: Naval Historical Center, 2007.

An Najaf, Battle of

See Najaf, First Battle of; Najaf, Second Battle of

An Nasiriyah, Battle of

See Nasiriyah, Battle of

ANACONDA, Operation
Start Date: March 1, 2002
End Date: March 18, 2002

A U.S.-led coalition campaign against the Taliban and Al Qaeda in Afghanistan during March 1–18, 2002. The offensive was part of Operation ENDURING FREEDOM and took place in the Shah-i-kot Valley in Paktia Province in eastern Afghanistan. Although the December 2001 Battle of Tora Bora had routed most of the Taliban and Al Qaeda from the region, by February 2002 insurgents and foreign fighters had begun to return to the Shah-i-Kot Valley and the Arma Mountains and were initiating new attacks on coalition forces. In response, the allies launched Operation ANACONDA in an effort to dislodge the insurgents and to prevent a more significant enemy offensive from unfolding in the spring. The coalition was also responding to reports that senior insurgent leaders, including Taliban leader Mullah Mohammed Omar and Al Qaeda leader Osama bin Laden, may have been present in the area.

Operation ANACONDA began on March 1, 2002, after special operations forces from the United States, Australia, Denmark, Germany, the Netherlands, New Zealand, and Norway had been inserted into the region and had established forward observation posts. These were followed by a ground assault that included elements of the U.S. Army's 10th Mountain Division and the 101st Airborne Division as well as the Canadian Army's Princess Patricia's Light Infantry, British Royal Marines, and Afghan National Army forces. The United States furnished about 1,200 troops, the Afghan National Army furnished 1,000 troops, and the other coalition partners furnished 200 troops. Aircraft from the United States, the United Kingdom, and France provided air support. U.S. Army major general Franklin Hagenbeck had command of the operation.

The difficult terrain in the region complicated the operation. The mountains ranged up to 12,000 feet and were dotted with caves and ravines, which provided hiding places for insurgent forces. The valley floor was between 7,000 and 8,000 feet in elevation. Temperatures during the offensive ranged from 60°F during the day to as low as 0°F at night.

The offensive suffered from a number of intelligence errors. Planners estimated the total number of insurgents at around 250; however, there were actually about 1,000, under the command of Saifur Rahman Monsoor of the Taliban. In addition, coalition officers underestimated their opponents' firepower. The insurgents were equipped with heavy machine guns, mortars, and artillery. One result was that the allied ground forces did not begin the operation with significant artillery support. Instead, they relied on mortars and airpower. Intelligence reports also falsely indicated that the majority of the enemy was on the valley floor, when most were actually in heavily fortified bunkers and caves in the mountains.

Reports also indicated the presence of some 800 civilians in the valley, although there were actually none. In an effort to minimize civilian casualties, the original plans called for the Afghan National forces to enter the valley from the west on March 2, supported by airpower and special operations forces, and help differentiate between the Taliban and Al Qaeda and the civilians. Planners expected the insurgents to flee before the advancing Afghans while U.S. and coalition conventional forces blocked their escape routes to the east and south. Most of the conventional forces were transported into the valley by helicopter.

The allied Afghan column was soon halted by heavy insurgent fire during its advance, and the coalition had to shift tactics. Allied special operations forces coordinated air strikes by bombers, Lockheed AC-130 Spectre gunships, and cruise missiles on Taliban and Al Qaeda positions. The coalition used more than 3,500 aerial bombs and cruise missiles during the offensive. The coalition also used 2,000-pound thermobaric bombs against caves and bunkers. Supported by airpower, the coalition ground forces were redeployed and advanced into the mountains. On March 4 a U.S. helicopter carrying Navy SEALs came under fire near the peak of Takur Ghar, and one SEAL fell from the aircraft; he was killed. The SEALs were to be inserted on the peak but found that the Taliban had a significant concentration of forces, including heavy machine guns and rocket-propelled grenades. During the subsequent rescue attempt, another helicopter was hit and crashed. In the ensuing firefight, seven U.S. troops were killed before the rescue mission was concluded. Although intense combat continued following the incident, the Taliban and Al Qaeda began to withdraw from the region.

On March 12 U.S. and Afghan forces initiated an advance through the valley and met little organized resistance. Operation ANACONDA officially ended on March 18, although there continued to be minor skirmishes in the region for the next month. During the operation, the coalition lost 15 killed and 82 wounded. The majority of the casualties were Americans, including 8 killed and 72 wounded. The Taliban and Al Qaeda lost between 300 and 400 killed; however, the majority of the enemy forces were able to escape.

TOM LANSFORD

See also

Afghan National Army; Afghanistan, Coalition Combat Operations in, 2002–Present; Aircraft, Helicopters; Al Qaeda; Bin Laden, Osama; Casualties, Operation ENDURING FREEDOM; ENDURING FREEDOM, Operation; North Atlantic Treaty Organization in Afghanistan; Omar, Mohammed; Takur Ghar, Battle of; Taliban; Taliban Insurgency, Afghanistan; Tora Bora; United Kingdom Forces in Afghanistan

References

Hersh, Seymour. *Chain of Command: The Road from 9/11 to Abu Ghraib.* New York: HarperCollins, 2004.

MacPherson, Malcolm. *Roberts Ridge: A Story of Courage and Sacrifice on Takur Ghar Mountain, Afghanistan.* New York: Bantam Dell, 2008.

Naylor, Sean. *Not a Good Day to Die: The Untold Story of Operation Anaconda.* New York: Berkley Trade, 2006.

Anbar Awakening

A U.S. operation to obtain or regain the loyalties of Sunni Arab tribes of Anbar Province, Iraq, that began in the provincial capital of Ramadi in September 2006. Tribal sheikhs who had been marginalized, or who sought revenge against Al Qaeda in Iraq (AQI) began cooperating with U.S. forces to root out the AQI network from the province. The Anbar Awakening restored a degree of order to a region that appeared on the verge of slipping irrevocably under insurgent control. It is credited as being a major factor in the diminution of violence in Iraq, which began in earnest in 2007.

That the Sunni tribes of Anbar would serve as the catalyst for such a transformative development was a carefully planned movement, based on the sentiments expressed by U.S. ambassador Zalmay Khalilzad and General David Patreus as well as others that the Sunni population must be granted a stake in the outcome. However, the province's recent engagement in violent opposition to the U.S.-led coalition and differences with the new Iraqi government were obstacles to be surmounted. Anbar, the largest of Iraq's 18 provinces with its predominantly Sunni population, became

a hotspot of insurgent activity following the fall of Baghdad in 2003. Disaffected sheikhs and their tribal followers gravitated to the insurgency, driven by anger at seeing their lands occupied by foreign soldiers, resentment over the loss of jobs and prestige, and distrust of the new Shiite-dominated political order, among other things. The porous border that Anbar shared with Syria at the far western end of the province also provided an easy point of entry for fighters from other nations, who filtered into Fallujah, Ramadi, and the smaller population centers along the upper Euphrates River. Many joined the organization founded by Jordanian extremist Abu Musab al-Zarqawi, which evolved into the AQI.

Tribal insurgents had formed an alliance of convenience with AQI jihadists in Anbar, and the AQI itself was actually an overwhelmingly Iraqi, not foreign, organization. By the middle of 2006, the insurgency had grown so strong that Anbar outpaced even Baghdad in terms of the number of violent incidents, with 30–40 attacks occurring daily in the province. Conditions in Ramadi were particularly grim: public services were negligible, and the Iraqi security presence was almost nonexistent, enabling insurgent fighters to operate freely in most sections of the city. A classified assessment completed by the U.S. Marine Corps in August 2006 concluded that the province was all but lost to the insurgency.

Yet the AQI laid the groundwork for its own demise by demanding control of the insurgency and reducing Anbar's tribal chiefs to subordinate status. AQI operatives punished in brutal fashion any who opposed them, with bombings and murders that targeted not only the sheikhs but also their family members and supporters. The vicious tactics used by the AQI to cow the tribes also alienated them and opened up a rift within the insurgency. In what in retrospect can be seen as a precursor to the Anbar Awakening movement, several tribes around Ramadi in January 2006 formed the al-Anbar People's Council, a breakaway group that sought to distance itself from the AQI while continuing to resist the coalition. The council collapsed soon thereafter after seven of its members were assassinated and a suicide bomber killed dozens at a police recruiting event.

The demise of the al-Anbar People's Council demonstrated that the Ramadi tribes lacked the strength and cohesion to stand up against the AQI on their own. A few months later, the sheikhs gained a powerful new benefactor when Colonel Sean MacFarland arrived with the U.S. Army's 1st Brigade Combat Team to take charge of Ramadi's security. MacFarland and his brigade had deployed first in January 2006 to Tal Afar, the city in northern Iraq that had been pacified the previous year by Colonel H. R. McMaster in what was widely hailed as a textbook counterinsurgency operation. Moving to Ramadi in June 2006, MacFarland was determined to apply some of the same counterinsurgency practices that had proven so effective at Tal Afar.

As one of the first steps in his plan to win back the city, MacFarland launched an outreach program aimed at gaining the trust and support of Ramadi's leaders. Among the earliest to respond was a charismatic young sheikh of relatively junior stature named Abd al-Sattar Buzaigh al-Rishawi. His record was far from clean, however: he was reputed to be a smuggler and highway bandit who had cooperated with the AQI in the past. More recently, however, he had lost his father and three brothers to the AQI's campaign of terror against the tribes, so he was receptive to American overtures. With Sattar's help in gathering recruits, MacFarland was able to begin the process of rebuilding Ramadi's embattled police force, which numbered only about 400 at the beginning of his tour. The sheikh also assisted with MacFarland's efforts to persuade other tribal leaders to shift their allegiance from the AQI to the coalition.

Sattar expanded his opposition to the AQI into a full-fledged movement after AQI agents bombed one of the new Iraqi police stations that had been set up in the city and murdered the sheikh whose tribesmen were staffing the post. In response, Sattar convened a meeting of over 50 sheikhs and MacFarland at his home on September 9, 2006. At the gathering, Sattar announced the launching of the Anbar Awakening, an alliance of tribes dedicated to expelling the AQI from the region. Initially, only a handful of tribes signed on to the movement. However, over the next few months the movement acquired new converts in and around Ramadi once those related to Sattar saw that MacFarland was committed to using his troops to protect the tribes that rejected the AQI. The American commander also supported the tribes' efforts to defend themselves through the organization of armed tribal auxiliary groups, later known as Concerned Local Citizens or Sons of Iraq. MacFarland arranged for militia members to receive training and ensured that as many as possible were incorporated into the Iraqi police force. By the end of 2006, some 4,000 recruits had been added to police ranks.

The AQI did not allow itself to be swept aside by the Anbar Awakening movement without a fight. Violence levels in Anbar peaked in October 2006 and remained high through March 2007. But the movement acquired its own momentum, spreading from Ramadi and gaining adherents in Fallujah and other parts of the province throughout 2007. Insurgent activity dropped sharply after March, a trend that reflected not only the diminishing strength of the AQI but also the fact that once sheikhs joined the Anbar Awakening, they directed their followers to cease all attacks on American troops. Sattar himself was killed in a bombing outside his Ramadi home on September 13, 2007, a mere 10 days after he had met with President George W. Bush at a military base in Anbar. Nonetheless, Sarrar's death did not reverse or slow the progress that had been made in the province, nor did it diminish local support for the Awakening Councils and their militia offshoots, which had sprouted up in Sunni areas outside of Anbar.

On September 1, 2008, Anbar completed its own remarkable turnaround from the most volatile region in Iraq to a more stable environment, and security for the province was officially transferred to the Iraqi government.

Growing tensions between the Awakening Councils and the government over late pay and a lack of jobs led in March 2009 to an uprising in the Sunni-dominated Fahdil section of Baghdad and the disarmament by Iraqi and U.S. troops of the Awakening Council there. The government retained a number of members of the Fahdi Council but subsequently announced that the 150 members of the council would be offered jobs in the Iraqi security forces.

JEFF SEIKEN

See also

Al Qaeda in Iraq; Iraq, History of, 1990–Present; Iraqi Insurgency

References

Lubin, Andrew. "Ramadi: From the Caliphate to Capitalism." *Proceedings* 134 (April 2008): 54–61.

McCary, John A. "The Anbar Awakening: An Alliance of Incentives." *Washington Quarterly* 32 (January 2009): 43–59.

Smith, Major Niel, and Colonel Sean MacFarland. "Anbar Awakens: The Tipping Point." *Military Review* (March–April 2008): 41–52.

West, Bing. *The Strongest Tribe: War, Politics, and the Endgame in Iraq.* New York: Random House, 2008.

Anglo-American Alliance

One of the most potent and enduring strategic partnerships of modern times, which evolved into a multifaceted strategic relationship based on the solid foundation of common heritage, culture, and language as well as shared values, vision, and interests. Because of its paramount strategic importance, the Middle East played an extremely important role in the evolution of the Anglo-American alliance. Despite sporadic disagreements, most notoriously during the 1956 Suez Crisis and the Yom Kippur (Ramadan) War of 1973 when American and British priorities diverged in the overall course of the Cold War and beyond, Anglo-American relations were generally harmonious, and both powers complemented each other's role in the region. This trend only gained momentum in the post–Cold War world, when new major challenges and threats, particularly the risk of the proliferation of the weapons of mass destruction and international terrorism, stimulated common Anglo-American security concerns and mutual recognition of the need for close strategic cooperation in the region.

There were also several other important factors dealing with the American and British postures in the Middle East and U.S.-UK relations that contributed to the further development of the alliance. Politically and diplomatically, both powers needed each other in the Middle East. For the United States, the solid and stable alliance with Britain had a special value in this volatile and unpredictable region where changing calculations of self-interest too often motivated many other American partners. Also, the alliance with Britain—one of the major powers and a permanent member of the United Nations (UN) Security Council—enhanced U.S. global leadership and gave American interests in the Middle East an additional international legitimacy. Moreover, despite their withdrawal from empire in the 1950s, 1960s, and 1970s, the British still retained close contacts with many regimes in the Middle East, and their expertise in local culture and traditions was of great advantage in dealing with Muslim countries, particularly during the 1991 Persian Gulf War, the Global

A pair of Royal Air Force GR4 Tornado aircraft peparing to refuel from a U.S. Air Force KC-135R Stratotanker during Operation IRAQI FREEDOM in 2003. (U.S. Department of Defense)

War on Terror, the Afghanistan War (since 2001), and the Iraq War (since 2003). These connections allowed a division of labor within the alliance: the British were indispensable at international coalition-building efforts, while the Americans could concentrate more on strategic and military planning and preparations.

Militarily, the alliance provided the British with critically important access to American high technology, particularly in reconnaissance and surveillance. At the same time, Britain's experiences of providing a long-term military presence in the Middle East, particularly in special operations, counterinsurgency, urban warfare, and pacification of hostile populations, were made available for the Americans.

Intelligence was another area of particularly fruitful cooperation between the United States and the United Kingdom. The degree of intelligence sharing and reciprocity in intelligence-gathering operations is unlikely equaled between any other two countries in the world. Recently, the intelligence services of both countries have been actively involved into gathering information about terrorist activities, particularly Al Qaeda, and the risk of the proliferation of weapons of mass destruction in the Middle East.

The close personal relations between American presidents and British prime ministers, who as a rule came to depend on each other, have also been of much importance for the development of the Anglo-American alliance. Many British prime ministers,

particularly Margaret Thatcher and Tony Blair, kept extraordinarily high profiles in Washington, frequently setting the very agenda of the alliance with much eloquence and persuasiveness and even personifying the alliance internationally. For example, just prior to the 1991 Persian Gulf War, Thatcher convinced President George H. W. Bush that he must not shy away from using military force if Iraqi president Saddam Hussein did not quit Kuwait within the time span set by the UN.

There was also a strong inclination in both capitals to reassert and solidify the special relationship in any international turmoil, including in the Middle East, on the basis of an almost axiomatic assumption that in case of crisis and/or war, both partners must stand shoulder to shoulder together. On the British side, that trend is frequently supplemented by the belief that a firm commitment to sharing military burdens with America and providing Washington open-ended unqualified support would make Britain the most trusted American ally. In so doing, London believes that it can influence the way in which America exercises its might, and this elevates Britain to the status of pivotal global power, greatly multiplying its real weight in international affairs.

The removal of the Taliban from power in Afghanistan in late 2001 and the rapid military overthrow of the Saddam Hussein regime in Iraq in 2003 signified the culmination of the ongoing Anglo-American strategy in the Middle East, which included the

British antiwar protesters carrying "NO" banners and passing by Big Ben in London's Parliament Square on February 15, 2003. The protesters were marching to Hyde Park to demonstrate against a possible war with Iraq. (AP/Wide World Photos)

victory in the Persian Gulf War and cooperation in policing of the no-fly zones in the Iraqi sky in its aftermath as well as military collaboration in Operation DESERT FOX in 1998. Diplomatically, the U.S.-UK partnership was instrumental in securing UN backing for the occupation and rebuilding of Iraq, in the promotion of the two-state solution for the Israeli-Palestinian problem, and in Libya's renunciation of its weapons of mass destruction program.

At the same time, the evolution of the Afghanistan War and the Iraq War into protracted insurgencies revealed some underlying problems and complexities in the Anglo-American alliance. Once more, these demonstrated the power asymmetry between the partners, where close security ties are of much more importance for London than for Washington. There are also differences in the decision-making process and in implementation of security policies in both countries as well as differences in the command and control systems and structures of their respective militaries. Moreover, the British Army found itself underequipped and overstretched by deployments in two very complex combat zones. Furthermore, the British public was not enamored of the alliance and protested their nation's involvement in Iraq, while Tony Blair was exceedingly unpopular in most parts

of the Middle East because of his close ties with American president George W. Bush.

Turning to the specific issues of the Anglo-American partnership, there were also some initial strategic disagreements between the parties on the priorities of the Global War on Terror. For example, the United States sought a military defeat of the terrorists and the states that support and harbor them, while Britain also suggested a continuing active search for the resolution of the Arab-Israeli conflict, which it believed was fanning the flames of terrorist sentiment. In setting the aims of the Iraq War, Britain's primary concern was to prevent Saddam Hussein from acquiring weapons of mass destruction, while the United States was also seeking immediate regime change in the country. The British also paid much more attention than the United States did to the efforts to secure UN sanctioning of the Iraq War and the Iraqi occupation and reconstruction efforts in the country. The British, concerned about the threat of chaos in Iraq after the victory, did not support the U.S.-promoted de-Baathification program.

In Afghanistan, the British supported the anti-Taliban factions among the dominating Pashtun tribes, while the United States supported the rival Northern Alliance. Additionally, there was a growing critique on the part of the U.S. military about British combat performance against the insurgencies in Iraq and Afghanistan. These included complaints about the institutional arrogance of the British military command, its overconfidence in its own counter-insurgency experiences, and its general inflexibility.

The aforementioned trends and developments have complicated the achievement of stability in the Middle East and within the alliance. Emphasizing Britain's modest military resources and its strong desire to achieve a UN mandate for military action, the most active proponents of interventions in Afghanistan and Iraq in the George W. Bush administration—Vice President Dick Cheney, Secretary of Defense Donald Rumsfeld, and Undersecretary of Defense Paul Wolfowitz—were rather skeptical about the values of British contributions to Afghanistan and Iraq. On the British side, there was wide and sustained popular and political criticism about following the American lead, particularly in Iraq. Indeed, the Iraq War has been hugely unpopular. Critics emphasized that the war isolated Britain from other European countries, damaged its international stance, and, instead of providing Britain with a voice in American decisions, turned the country into a de facto silent vassal and strategic hostage of the United States. In this atmosphere, Tony Blair maintained his desire to stay with America until the end by risking his own political future.

Regardless of these issues of contention, the British have proven to be an unfailing partner with the United States. Indeed, in all three conflicts—the Persian Gulf War, the Afghanistan War, and the Iraq War—Britain provided far more troops than any other nation besides the United States.

With the resignation of Blair in June 2007 and the coming to power of a new administration in Washington in January 2009, both sides have signaled their intention to review their respective policies in the Middle East, including the forms and scale of their military involvement in the region. Unavoidably, this will affect the Anglo-American alliance. At the same time, it is imperative to preserve and develop further the beneficial and multifaceted potential of the unique partnership, which has contributed so much to the shaping of the modern Middle East and the contemporary world.

PETER J. RAINOW

See also

Arab-Israeli Conflict, Overview; Blair, Tony; Brown, James Gordon; Bush, George Herbert Walker; Bush, George Walker; Suez Crisis; Thatcher, Margaret; United Kingdom; United States

References

Coughlin, Con. *American Ally: Tony Blair and the War on Terror.* New York: Ecco, 2006.

Dumbrell, John. *A Special Relationship: Anglo-American Relations from the Cold War to Iraq.* New York: Palgrave Macmillan, 2006.

Naughtie, James. *The Accidental American: Tony Blair and the Presidency.* New York: PublicAffairs, 2004.

Shawcross, William. *Allies: The U.S., Britain, and Europe in the Aftermath of the Iraq War.* New York: PublicAffairs, 2005.

Anglo-Iraqi Treaty

Agreement between the British government and the British mandate government of Iraq that went into force on November 16, 1930, giving to the British exclusive commercial and military rights in Iraq once that nation became independent in 1932. The Anglo-Iraqi Treaty of 1930 was in reality a redrafting of the Anglo-Iraqi Treaty of 1922. Neither agreement offered the Iraqis anything in return, and both engendered much antipathy in Iraq. The 1922 treaty was the result of the newly created British League of Nations mandate, which encompassed present-day Iraq, and political unrest among various Iraqi factions. Angered that Iraq was not to become independent but rather a British-administered mandate after World War I, a coalition of Shia and Sunni Muslims in Iraq precipitated a major revolt in 1920 against British occupation forces. The Kurds in northern Iraq also revolted against the British presence, hoping to form their own nation.

In 1921 Iraqi and British leaders convened in Cairo in an attempt to bring the Iraqi revolt to an end. There it was agreed to allow Iraq more (but still limited) autonomy under a newly installed Hashemite king, Faisal ibn Hussein. The arrangement was a clear compromise that was to allow for continued British influence in Iraq while appeasing—to a limited extent—the Iraqi nationalists who had fomented the 1920 uprising. The agreement resulted in the 1922 Anglo-Iraqi Treaty. The Iraqi Assembly, however, dragged its feet in ratifying the agreement, as many nationalists were displeased with the vague assurances of independence at some unspecified time in the future. Nor were they pleased by Britain's continuing influence in Iraqi affairs. Nevertheless, after British authorities threatened to circumvent the new Iraqi constitution and rule by decree, the Iraqis reluctantly acceded to the agreement in 1924.

Between 1924 and 1930 the situation in Iraq had stabilized, with King Faisal ruling in such a way as to keep the British contented and the nationalists from fomenting a revolt. Beginning in 1927, British-owned oil companies discovered massive petroleum reserves in Iraq, which made the nation all the more important to London. Because of this find and the impending end of the British mandate in 1932, London hoped to negotiate a new treaty with the Iraqis, building on the 1922 agreement, guaranteeing British control of Iraqi oil, and keeping out potential adversaries who might have viewed Iraq with strategic interest (Germany and the Soviet Union, in particular).

In a sop to Iraqi nationalists, the November 16, 1930, Anglo-Iraqi Treaty mapped a path toward independence after 1932. However, London clearly held most of the cards during the negotiations and insisted that it be granted wide-reaching commercial rights in Iraq, including ownership of Iraqi oil fields. Equally important, the treaty gave London extensive military rights in Iraq, allowing it to garrison troops there and/or use it as a base for future military operations.

Iraqi nationalists were incensed by the treaty, which appeared to offer the Iraqis nothing in return for the commercial and military concessions given to London. Critics were quick to point out that the 1930 agreement had essentially been dictated to the Iraq government and that the negotiations were a smokescreen designed to keep ardent nationalists from participating in them. Not surprisingly, the treaty was not looked upon with much favor in Iraq.

The Anglo-Iraqi Treaty of 1930 was invoked by the British in 1941 when they moved troops into Iraq and occupied it during much of World War II. This move had been necessitated by an Iraqi coup led by four nationalist generals. The British accused these leaders of allying themselves with the Axis powers. The British did not vacate Iraq until 1947. At that point, London attempted to foist another agreement on the Iraqis that would have given it even more influence in Iraqi affairs, but the Iraqis balked, and nothing came of it. The Anglo-Iraqi treaties of 1922 and 1930 clearly sowed the seeds of great nationalist-driven resentment in Iraq and helped set the stage for the Revolution of 1958 and the successive waves of political instability in Iraq that endure to the present.

PAUL G. PIERPAOLI JR.

See also

Iraq, History of, Pre-1990; United Kingdom, Middle East Policy

References

Abdullah, Thabit. *A Short History of Iraq.* London: Pearson, 2003.

Dodge, Toby. *Inventing Iraq: The Failure of Nation-Building and a History Denied.* New York: Columbia University Press, 2003.

Polk, William R. *Understanding Iraq: The Whole Sweep of Iraqi History, from Genghis Khan's Mongols to the Ottoman Turks to the British Mandate to the American Occupation.* New York: Harper Perennial, 2006.

Annan, Kofi
Birth Date: April 8, 1938

Ghanaian diplomat and seventh secretary-general of the United Nations (UN) from 1997 to 2006. Kofi Atta Annan was born on April 8, 1938, in the Kofandros section of Kumasi, Ghana, to a prominent chieftain of the Fante tribe. His father was the elected governor of the Ashanti Province of Ghana when it was a British colony known as the Gold Coast. Kofi Annan studied at the University of Science and Technology in Kumasi before going to the United States to attend Macalester College in Minnesota, where he earned a degree in economics in 1961. He attended graduate school in Geneva during 1961–1962 and received a master of science degree in management from the Massachusetts Institute of Technology in 1972. Annan first joined the UN in 1962 at the World Health Organization (WHO). Except for a brief stint from 1974 to 1976 as Ghana's director of tourism, Annan has spent his entire career with the UN, having been posted in Europe, Africa, and the United States. His admirers have described him as a man of quiet elegance with a powerful yet understated speaking style.

Kofi Annan served as United Nations (UN) secretary-general during 1997–2006. A native of Ghana, he was the first black African to hold that post. Annan opposed the U.S.-led invasion of Iraq and urged that the United States return to multilateralism in its dealings with other nations. (United Nations)

Annan had a remarkably varied UN career, focusing not only on management and administrative functions but also on refugee issues and peacekeeping. He rose steadily through the UN administrative hierarchy, first as the assistant chief of its programs planning, budget, and finance department and then as the head of human resources. He also served as security coordinator, director of the budget, chief of personnel for the High Commissioner for Refugees, and administrative officer for the Economic Commission for Africa. On March 1, 1993, he became the undersecretary-general for peacekeeping operations. Annan distinguished himself in that role as a clear-speaking diplomat and skillful negotiator despite the failure of a UN peacekeeping operation in Somalia in 1994 and the much-criticized decision not to intervene during the Rwandan genocide of the same year. Annan attracted U.S. attention by negotiating the release of Western hostages held by Iraq prior to Operation DESERT STORM and securing the safety of some 500,000 Asian workers trapped in Kuwait during the Persian Gulf War.

Annan was appointed secretary-general by the UN General Assembly on December 17, 1996, for a term that began on January 1, 1997. He was the first UN leader to have risen to the post through the UN organizational structure and was the first black African to serve in the post. As secretary-general, Annan emphasized his commitment to engaging UN member states in a dialogue about the best use of peacekeeping forces, preventive diplomacy, and postconflict peace building. He hoped to bring the UN closer to the world's people and achieve a consensus among member states as to the role the UN should play in its many fields of endeavor. The United States, the world organization's largest single contributor, hoped that with his administrative skills Annan would be able to reform the organization by cutting the budget, eliminating redundant suborganizations, and pioneering a new way to manage the UN in the post–Cold War era.

On June 29, 2001, Annan was reappointed secretary-general of the UN for another five-year term to begin officially in January 2002. In addition, on October 12, 2001, the Norwegian Nobel Committee announced that Annan and the UN were the 100th winners of the Nobel Peace Prize for their work in advancing world peace and security, which has included steps to eradicate international terrorism. The Nobel committee also praised Annan for his effective management of the UN and his continued dedication to eradicating AIDS.

Annan's tenure was not always free from controversy, however. When he publicly termed the March 2003 Anglo-American-led invasion of Iraq illegal and in violation of the UN charter on September 16, 2004, it strained his already testy relationship with the George W. Bush administration. In the run-up to the Iraq War, Annan had repeatedly urged that military force not be taken against Iraq. In addition, in December 2004, reports of graft and corruption in the UN's Oil-for-Food Programme affected Annan. In particular, Annan's son Kojo was alleged to have received payments from the Swiss company Cotecna Inspection SA, which had in turn received a lucrative contract in the program. Annan appointed an inquiry into the matter, and although he was personally exonerated of any illegal activity, the investigative committee found fault with the UN's management structure and recommended the appointment of a UN chief executive officer to prevent future financial oversights and potential conflicts of interest.

In addition to his regular UN posts, Annan also carried out a number of special assignments. He served as special representative of the UN secretary-general to the former Yugoslavia from November 1995 to March 1996, coordinating the UN's role in maintaining peace following the Dayton Agreement (1995). He has also contributed to the work of the Appointment and Promotion Board and the secretary-general's Task Force for Peacekeeping, and he has served as chairman of the Board of Trustees of the United Nations International School in New York and as governor of the International School in Geneva. In December 2006 Annan completed his second term as secretary-general of the UN and was succeeded by Ban Ki Moon in January 2007. In his last major speech as secretary-general on December 11, 2006, at the Harry S. Truman Presidential Library in Independence, Missouri, Annan urged the United States to return to the multilateralism typified by the Truman administration and asked that the United States maintain its commitment to human rights, even in the Global War on Terror. The Bush administration took a dim view of the speech.

Annan returned to Ghana in 2007, and some pundits have opined that he may become a candidate for head of state. He has been involved in numerous African and international organizations and was named president of the Global Humanitarian Forum in Geneva, Switzerland. He has also been engaged in efforts to quell civil unrest in Kenya and serves on the board of directors of the United Nations Foundation.

PAUL G. PIERPAOLI JR.

See also

Ban Ki Moon; Rwanda; Somalia, International Intervention in; United Nations

References

Meisler, Stanley. *Koffi Annan: A Man of Peace in a World of War.* New York: Wiley, 2007.

Traub, James. *The Best Intentions: Kofi Annan and the UN in the Era of American World Power.* New York: Farrar, Straus and Giroux, 2006.

Ansar al-Islam

A radical Kurdish Islamist separatist movement formed in 2001 in northern Iraq (Kurdistan). The U.S. government has held that the group was founded by Mullah Krekar, with assistance and funds from Al Qaeda leader Osama bin Laden. The complicated history of Ansar al-Islam (Supporters of Islam) dates back to the Islamic Movement in Kurdistan (IMK), formed in 1987 of various factions, some of whom had trained and fought in Afghanistan. Some others apparently returned to Kurdistan after the fall of the Taliban in late 2001, which was the basis of U.S. arguments that the group had links to Al Qaeda, a claim also made by its enemies in the larger Kurdish factions.

The IMK fought with the Popular Union of Kurdistan (PUK) and eventually had to retreat to the Iranian border before returning to its base in Halabja. In 2001 the group splintered, and various new groupings formed the Jund al-Islam in September of that year, declaring jihad on those Kurdish parties that had left the Islamic path. The PUK fought Jund al-Islam, which dissolved and renamed itself Ansar al-Islam in December 2001 under the leadership of Amir Mullah Krekar, also known as Najmuddin Faraj Ahmad. Since then, however, Krekar has been living in Norway and has faced various indictments and deferred deportation for supporting terrorism.

While still operating under the name of Jund al-Islam, Ansar al-Islam tried to quash non-Islamic practices. It banned music, television, and alcohol; imposed the veil on women and beards on men; closed schools and employment to women; and tried to force a minority religious group called the Ahl al-Haqq to convert and then drove its members out of their villages. Ansar al-Islam also cracked down on the Naqshabandi Sufis. The group also pursued individuals, and some were held and tortured. The group's strict salafi stance makes it akin to various Sunni nationalist resistance groups that developed after 2003 and accentuates its differences with the principal Kurdish political factions.

The struggle between the PUK and Ansar al-Islam has also involved human rights violations, the assassination of the governor of Arbil, and fighting that has continued for years. In December 2002 Ansar al-Islam forces took two PUK outposts and killed about 50 people; more than half of these reportedly died after they had surrendered. On the other hand, Ansar al-Islam prisoners have been mistreated by the PUK.

When the invasion of Iraq occurred in March 2003, Ansar al-Islam mounted various small attacks and carried out actions against those it called "collaborators" with the Americans, including civilians. The group carried out a much larger attack during 2004, when its suicide bombers attacked the PUK and Kurdistan Democratic Party (KDP) headquarters and killed 109 people, among them the KDP's deputy prime minister, Sami Abd al-Rahman. In 2005 Ansar al-Islam assassinated an aide to Grand Ayatollah Sayyid Ali Husayn al-Sistan, Sheikh Mahmud al-Madayini, in Baghdad.

In 2003 fighters from Ansar al-Islam joined with other Sunni salafi fighters in the central region of Iraq, forming Jamaat Ansar al-Sunna (formerly Jaysh Ansar al-Sunna). But the Ansar al-Islam elements returned to their earlier name in 2007. Also in 2007, the Ansar al-Sunna, along with Ansar al-Islam, the Islamic Army of Iraq, and the Army of the Mujahideen, formed a new grouping called the Jihad and Reformation Front. In any event, it remains unclear what links Ansar al-Islam has to Al Qaeda in Iraq, and there is some evidence to suggest that it might have received aid from Iran. The group continues to battle more secularist Kurdish groups, and in March 2009 it kidnapped and beheaded three Kurdish truck driver hostages to punish them for cooperating with the Americans.

SHERIFA ZUHUR

See also

Al Qaeda; Al Qaeda in Iraq; Bin Laden, Osama; Iraq, History of, 1990–Present

References

"Ansar al-Islam in Iraqi Kurdistan." Human Rights Watch Backgrounder, www.hrw.org/legacy/backgrounder/mena/ansarbk020503.htm.

Stansfield, Gareth R. V. *Iraqi Kurdistan: Political Development and Emergent Democracy.* New York: Routledge, 2003.

Wong, Edward. "The Reach of War: Violence, Militants Show the Beheading of 3 Kurdish Hostages." *New York Times*, March 22, 2009.

Antiaircraft Guns

During both Operation DESERT STORM and Operation IRAQI FREEDOM, Iraq's air defense system was based on the Soviet doctrine of integrating aircraft, surface-to-air missiles (SAMs), and antiaircraft guns. The guns took primary responsibility for point defense of key targets. Neither the United States nor its allies employed antiaircraft guns in a defensive capacity during either of the wars with Iraq. Also, because of the virtual absence of Afghan aircraft during Operation ENDURING FREEDOM, antiaircraft weapons were not deployed to Afghanistan.

Iraqi antiaircraft guns fell into two categories, artillery and small arms. The former had caliber exceeding 20 millimeters (mm), while the latter consisted of 14.5-mm and smaller guns. All were crew-served weapons and offered the advantages of being relatively cheap to purchase and required little training to operate. Most Iraqi antiaircraft guns were manned by conscripts. By 1990, Iraq had more than 7,500 antiaircraft artillery pieces and several hundred light antiaircraft weapons; when properly employed, they could be deadly for aircraft flying below 10,000 feet.

The largest Iraqi antiaircraft artillery piece was the Soviet-built KS-19 100-mm gun. Designed at the end of World War II and entering Soviet service in the late 1940s, the KS-19 served in four gun batteries. Some estimates claim that several hundred guns were placed around Baghdad alone from 1980 through 2003. The KS-19 fired a 33-pound shell out to a maximum range of 60,000 feet with a maximum ceiling of more than 42,000 feet. However, its slow rate of fire (8–12 rounds per minute) and traverse placed it at a disadvantage against high-speed maneuvering aircraft. Its primary purpose was to disrupt incoming air raids. Less than a dozen such batteries remained in Iraqi service in 1990.

Iraq's most numerous antiaircraft artillery piece was the 57-mm S-60, which was structured in six-gun batteries centered on a single Flap Wheel fire-control radar. The S-60 required a crew of six and theoretically fired up to 120 rounds per minute. However, as a practical matter, loader fatigue and barrel heating limited the rate of fire to 60 rounds per minute or less. Moreover, a typical engagement against a tactical jet aircraft was less than a minute. The S-60's maximum effective range and ceiling were 40,000 feet and 13,000 feet, respectively, but few engagements were initiated at ranges beyond 20,000 feet or altitudes above 5,000 feet. Although each weapon was capable of engaging targets independently, the most common practice was for all the battery's guns to fire on the target being tracked by the Flap Wheel radar (North Atlantic Treaty Organization [NATO] designation for this conical scan radar). Independent firing was conducted only when the fire-control radar was jammed or out of action. Moreover, the maximum effective range dropped to 13,000 feet when using optical fire control. The self-propelled variant, the ZSU-57/2, consisted of two 57-mm guns mounted on a tracked chassis. Lacking a data link or ability to receive fire-control radar inputs, each ZSU-57/2 fired independently.

Iraqi air defenses also included several hundred 37-mm guns and 23-mm guns. Organized into four gun batteries, the 37-mm used visual fire control, with each gun firing independently, although battery commanders could direct all guns to concentrate on a single target. The guns were loaded via 5-round clips, and a

A U.S. Army M163 Vulcan self-propelled antiaircraft gun system. (U.S. Department of Defense)

well-trained crew could fire up to 240 2-pound shells a minute, although the typical engagement against a jet aircraft lasted less than 30 seconds. The 37-mm had a maximum effective range of 2,500 yards and a theoretical ceiling of 10,000 feet, but tactically they rarely were used against targets flying above 3,500 feet and ranges beyond 4,000 feet.

The guns most feared by coalition pilots were the Soviet-built self-propelled ZSU-23/4 guns, which served with both Iraqi armored divisions and as mobile air defense platforms in and around critical facilities. Organized into four-unit platoons, each ZSU-23/4 was equipped with a jam-resistant fire-control radar, high rates of fire (1,000-plus rounds per minute per gun), and high traverse rates that enabled it to engage the fastest and most maneuverable tactical aircraft. The ZSU-23/4 consisted of a quadruple mount of 23-mm automatic cannon on a tracked carriage. Its relatively small size and mobility made it hard to detect prior to an engagement. However, the limited range (under 10,000 feet) and ceiling (under 8,200 feet) confined them to the point-defense role; furthermore, the advent of precision-guided ordnance allowed coalition fighters to attack from outside these weapons' effective range.

Iraqi forces were also equipped with ZPU-23/2, ZPU-14, and individual 14.5-mm guns. All fired individually and were most effective against slow-moving observation aircraft and helicopters.

The ZPU-23/2 consisted of two 23-mm guns installed on a collapsible towing mount that could be quickly transitioned into a firing platform. The ZPU-14 was lighter and consisted of four 14.5-mm machine guns mounted on a wheeled transport mount. The ZPU-14 had proven particularly effective against helicopters during the Vietnam War; however, it was all but useless against coalition aircraft employing fire-and-forget guided munitions fired from outside its maximum effective range of 2,000 yards.

In Operation DESERT STORM (1991) and Operation ENDURING FREEDOM (2001), the U.S. Arab allies were equipped with the same antiaircraft guns as the Iraqis except that they did not possess the 100-mm K-19. However, the United States and its other allies used few antiaircraft guns, assigning them to provide point air defense to ground units and mobile tactical headquarters. The only antiaircraft gun system employed by the U.S. Army was the M163 Vulcan system, which consisted of the Vulcan 20-mm Gatling cannon mounted on an M-113 chassis. The ammunition was delivered to the gun via 1,000-round powered belts. The Vulcan's rate of fire was 3,000 rounds a minute, and under optical fire control it could engage targets within a range of 8,000 feet range and an altitude of 3,000 feet.

The Saudi Arabian Army also employed the M-163 with its mobile units and the Bofors 40-mm L-70 around key facilities. Unlike the Vulcan, the Bofors could use radar fire control, which generally focused the fire of an entire 4-gun battery against a target. Its 2-pound shells came with a proximity and contact fuse to ensure target destruction, while the Vulcan's smaller 1-pound shell had only a contact fuse. The Bofors could engage incoming aircraft individually using optical fire control, but that was the exception, not the rule. The Bofors fired up to 240 rounds a minute and had a maximum engagement range of 11,500 feet and a ceiling of 8,000 feet. However, it could also be used against ground targets, which it could engage at ranges beyond 32,000 feet. The other gun in Saudi service was the Oerlikon-Buhrle twin 35-mm Skyguard system that the Royal Saudi Air Force used for airfield defense. Its rate of fire approaches 550 rounds per minute per barrel, and its maximum range against an incoming aerial target is approximately 13,000 feet. As with the Bofors, the Oerlikon can engage targets individually or via concentrated battery fire.

France was the only other coalition nation to employ antiaircraft guns. Its air mobile and airborne units had the GIAT towed 20-mm gun. Deployed in twin-gun mounts, the GIAT fired the same NATO-standard 20-mm round as the American Vulcan, but they were loaded via 60-round drums. The GIAT had the same maximum range and ceiling as its American counterpart, but the GIAT was helicopter-transportable, giving it better operational mobility. Nominal rate of fire was about 500 rounds a minute, but normally few engagements exceeded 10–20 seconds in length. The weapons engaged individually using optical fire control. The maximum range is 8,000 feet with a ceiling of 3,000 feet.

The virtual absence of an enemy air threat precluded the United States or its allies from employing their antiaircraft guns in an air defense role during any of the modern Middle East wars, but Iraq employed large numbers of antiaircraft guns to provide low-level point defense and attack-disruption defense of its tactical units and key facilities. They were integrated effectively into a complex air defense system that relied on SAMs for area and high-altitude air defense coverage, supplemented by interceptor aircraft. The system employed tactics and systems that had proven highly effective against Western air tactics during the Vietnam War, but the introduction of large numbers of precision standoff weapons and superior coalition electronic warfare tactics exposed the obsolescence of Iraq's tactics and systems. Aircraft deceived and evaded the SAMs and launched their weapons from outside the antiaircraft guns' effective range. Although their large numbers precluded coalition pilots from ignoring the guns' presence, new tactics and weapons had reduced them to a battlefield nuisance.

CARL OTIS SCHUSTER

See also

Air Defenses in Iraq, Iraq War; Air Defenses in Iraq, Persian Gulf War; Aircraft, Electronic Warfare; Aircraft, Fighters; Aircraft, Suppression of Enemy Air Defense; Antiaircraft Missiles, Iraqi; Bombs, Precision-Guided; Missiles, Air-to-Ground

References

Cooper, Toni, and Farzad Bishop. *Iran-Iraq War in the Air: 1980–1988.* Atglen, PA: Schiffer Military History, 2000.

Hallion, Richard P. *Storm over Iraq: Air Power and the Gulf War.* Washington, DC: Smithsonian Institution Press, 1997.

Isby, David. *Weapons and Tactics of the Soviet Army.* London: Arms and Armour Books, 1984.

Lynch, Kristin. *Supporting Air and Space Expeditionary Forces: Lessons from Operation Iraqi Freedom.* Washington, DC: RAND Corporation, 2004.

U.S. General Accounting Office. *Operation Desert Storm Evaluation of the Air War: Report to Congress.* Washington, DC: U.S. Government Printing Office, 1996.

Antiaircraft Missiles, Iraqi

Air defense missiles constituted the most significant component of Iraq's integrated air defense system during its three major conflicts since 1980. Iraq used radar-guided surface-to-air missiles (SAMs) for medium- to high-altitude and area air defense and man-portable infrared-guided SAMs for tactical air defense and to complement its antiaircraft artillery systems. Since the most common tactic to evade radar-guided SAMs involved a high-speed roll and dive to lower altitudes, the integration of guns, missiles, and fighter aircraft into a layered defense in-depth theoretically provided an almost impenetrable barrier to air attack. Aircraft that successfully avoided radar-guided SAMs found themselves flying through a gauntlet of intense antiaircraft fire supplemented by infrared-guided SAMs, the intensity of which increased as the attacking aircraft approached their target. Those that made it past the target pulled up into the sights of waiting fighter aircraft. Fighters escorting the attack aircraft had to penetrate the same gauntlet to engage enemy interceptors.

Although it did not lead to high scores among the defending pilots, it was a system that had inflicted heavy losses on U.S. aircraft over North Vietnam in the 1960s. The United States and its coalition allies learned from that conflict, however, and possessed the electronic warfare equipment and weapons to defeat the system during Operations DESERT STORM and IRAQI FREEDOM.

Most Iraqi air defense missiles were Soviet-built, with the venerable SA-2 Guideline (the missile and radar designations are those of the North Atlantic Treaty Organization [NATO]) and its supporting Fan Song radar being the oldest and longest-ranged weapon in service. Developed in the 1950s, the SA-2, with a range of 27 nautical miles, had enjoyed great success during the Vietnam War but was at best obsolete by 1990. Although it could engage aircraft operating at altitudes of up to 89,000 feet, its radar was easily defeated, and only a highly trained crew could employ its electro-optical guidance and electronic counter-countermeasures features effectively. Also, its minimum range of 4–5 nautical miles and its minimum altitude of 3,280 feet made it all but useless against low-flying targets. The SA-3 Goa was newer and longer-ranged. Introduced in Soviet service in 1963, the Goa, with a range of 22 nautical miles, used the Flat Face radar for guidance. It had an operational engagement ceiling of 59,000 feet and enjoyed better tactical mobility than the SA-2. The SA-2 and SA-3 were deployed around major Iraqi cities.

Iraq also deployed a wide range of Soviet mobile SAM systems, including the SA-6 Gainful, SA-9 Gaskin, and SA-12. Of these, the Gainful was the best known, having inflicted heavy losses on the Israeli Air Force when first employed during the October 1973 Yom Kippur War. Mounted on a tracked chassis, the Gainful was a medium-ranged SAM supported by a robust Straight Flush fire-control radar that was difficult to deceive. Introduced into Soviet service in 1970, the SA-6 deployed in four transporter-erector-launcher (TEL) batteries supported by a single fire-control radar. The missile has a maximum range of 13.2 nautical miles and an operational engagement ceiling of 39,000 feet.

The SA-9 Gaskin was a much shorter-ranged SAM mounted on a wheeled vehicle that carried two pairs of ready-to-fire missiles. The Gaskin was infrared-guided (IR), but unlike most IR missiles, it could engage an incoming target provided the aircraft was not obscured coming by the sun. Normally deployed in proximity to the ZSU-23/4 mobile antiaircraft gun, the SA-9 dated from 1966 and had a maximum range of 4.4 nautical miles and a ceiling of 20,000 feet. The SA-9 had little impact on allied air operations in either of the Persian Gulf conflicts.

The newest mobile SAM in the Iraqi inventory was the short-ranged radar-guided SA-8 Gecko. Carried in 6-missile canisters mounted atop a wheeled transporter-erector-launcher-and-radar (TELAR), the SA-8 was employed with Iraqi Army units in the field. Its six-wheeled TELAR was amphibious and was equipped with a frequency agile fire-control radar and alternate electro-optical guidance that made it particularly difficult to defeat electronically. Its normal engagement range was 1.1–5 nautical miles against targets flying between 100 and 16,500 feet. The most common tactics employed against the SA-8 were to use antiradiation missiles against its radar or fly above its engagement envelope.

The remaining SAMs in Iraqi service were man-portable. Of these, the Soviet-built IR-guided SA-7 Grail, SA-14 Gremlin, SA-16 Gimlet, and SA-18 Grouse were the most numerous. The SA-7 was the shortest ranged, reaching out only about 10,000 feet and effective only against slow-moving targets flying away at altitudes below 4,000 feet. The SA-14 was an improvement on the SA-7, providing greater range (3.7 nautical miles) and a limited capability for head-on engagements. The SA-16 incorporated an identification-friend-or-foe (IFF) feature and a more effective IR counter-countermeasures capability. The SA-18 was a simplified and more reliable improvement of the SA-16. The Gimlet and Grouse can engage a target from any aspect; they have a maximum range of 3.1 miles and a ceiling of 15,700 feet. Their performance is comparable to the U.S. FIM-92A Stinger.

The last SAM in Iraqi service was the French-built Roland. The Iraqis used the Roland for airfield defense. The radar-guided Roland had a maximum operational range of 5 nautical miles and an engagement ceiling of 17,100 feet. Its rapid acceleration and high speed made it an ideal air defense weapon. However, in the hands of inexperienced or poorly trained operators, it proved vulnerable to jamming and other electronic countermeasures. Also, the Iraqi missile crews had to operate the system from exposed positions, making them vulnerable to enemy attack, a factor that inhibited the weapon's effectiveness.

Coalition superiority, in terms of both numbers and technology, and superior tactics all but negated Iraq's integrated air defense system. Its SAMs achieved only limited success in the few opportunities that the air campaign presented to them. Allied air defense suppression systems, antiradiation missiles, and well-orchestrated electronic countermeasure operations blinded Iraqi radars, destroyed their command and control systems and communications networks, and inflicted heavy losses on SAM batteries. Although Iraq nominally possessed a modern integrated air defense system, its weapons, sensors, and communications networks were outdated, and its operators were poorly trained for war against a well-trained opponent equipped with third- and fourth-generation aircraft and precision-guided weapons.

CARL OTIS SCHUSTER

See also
Air Defenses in Iraq, Iraq War; Air Defenses in Iraq, Persian Gulf War; Aircraft, Electronic Warfare; Antiaircraft Guns; Antiradiation Missiles, Coalition; Bombs, Precision-Guided; DESERT STORM, Operation, Coalition Air Campaign; IRAQI FREEDOM, Operation, Air Campaign; Missiles, Surface-to-Air

References
Blake, Bernard, ed. *Jane's Weapons Systems, 1988–89 (Jane's Land-Based Air Defence)*. London: Jane's 1988.
Cooper, Toni, and Farzad Bishop. *Iran-Iraq War in the Air: 1980–1988*. Atglen, PA: Schiffer Military History, 2000.
General Accounting Office. *Operation Desert Storm: Evaluation of the Air War; Report to Congress*. Washington, DC: U.S. Government Printing Office, 1996.
Hallion, Richard P. *Storm over Iraq: Air Power and the Gulf War*. Washington, DC: Smithsonian Institution Press, 1997.
Lynch, Kristin. *Supporting Air and Space Expeditionary Forces: Lessons from Operation Iraqi Freedom*. Washington, DC: RAND Corporation, 2004.

Antiradiation Missiles, Coalition

Missiles designed chiefly to defeat enemy radar by homing in on and jamming or destroying radio emission sources. Antiradiation missiles (ARMs) constitute one of the most important weapons in any effort to suppress enemy air defenses (SEAD). ARMs rose out of the Vietnam War in response to North Vietnam's extensive use of surface-to-air missiles (SAMs). Early ARMs were modifications of existing air-to-air and air-to-ground missiles, with a receiver to home in on a SAM's acquisition or tracking radar. Early ARMs could be defeated by simply turning the radar off briefly, activating a similar radar nearby, or employing multiple radars against the target aircraft. However, by 1990 when Iraq invaded Kuwait, technology had advanced considerably, providing coalition forces with technologically advanced ARMs that could mask their launch, remember the radar's location, and in some cases effectively shut down an air defense sector by loitering over it for hours, waiting to attack the first SAM system to activate its radar. ARMs also now had the range to be launched from outside the SAM's engagement range. These weapons proved devastating to Iraq's integrated air defense networks, which many observers had considered one of the world's most effective.

The American-made Raytheon AGM-88 HARM (high-speed antiradiation missile) was the most widely employed of the coalition antiradiation missiles. Developed as a replacement for the Vietnam War–era AGM-45 Shrike and AGM-78 Standard ARM, the AGM-88 entered service in 1985. It was supersonic (Mach 2.5) and was equipped with inertial guidance and a computer that captured the enemy radar's location and characteristics. The aircraft's fire-control system fed the radar's information into the missile computer before launch, enabling the computer to guide the HARM onto the radar even if the operators turned it off or tried to draw the missile away by remote jamming or activating a similar radar nearby. A smokeless rocket engine made it all but impossible to detect HARMs visually, and a range of 57 nautical miles enabled the SEAD aircraft to launch HARMs from far outside the Iraqi SAM envelope. American Grumman A-6 Intruder, Ling-Temco-Vought A-7 Corsair II, Grumman EA-6 Prowler, McDonnell Douglas F-4 Phantom II, Lockheed-Martin F-16 Fighting Falcon, and Boeing A/F-18 Hornet aircraft employed HARMs during Operation DESERT STORM and, except for the F-4s, in Operation IRAQI FREEDOM as well. The HARM's most famous employment in DESERT STORM was its accidental use against a Boeing B-52 Stratofortress when the bomber's tail gunner mistakenly targeted a SEAD aircraft, which then engaged what it thought was an Iraqi antidefense radar. The B-52 suffered only slight damage to its tail, and there were no injuries.

British Aerospace's ALARM (air-launched antiradiation missile) was the only other antiradiation missile to see service in DESERT STORM and IRAQI FREEDOM. Employed by both the Royal Air Force and the Royal Saudi Air Force, ALARM entered service in 1990 and is carried by the Panavia GR4 Tornado and F3 Tornado aircraft. Like the HARM, it is a supersonic (Mach 2.1) missile that can be launched from outside most SAM envelopes (range of 50.1 nautical miles). However, it has a major advantage over HARM in that it can loiter over a target area, waiting for the enemy to activate their radars. Once it detects a radar, it ejects the warhead, which then makes a guided parachute descent onto the radar. ALARM proved particularly effective against mobile SAM systems because it could be employed almost as a search-and-destroy weapon over suspected SAM deployment areas. Unfortunately, ALARM's length (15 feet) limits its employment to larger tactical aircraft such as the Tornado, although some Sepecat Jaguar aircraft have been modified to carry it.

Antiradiation missiles are the ultimate in precision-guided weapons. With small warheads designed to destroy only the enemy's radar antennas, they inflict little to no collateral damage, and yet they cripple the enemy's ability to direct and employ their air defense system. The coalition's extensive use of antiradiation missiles all but destroyed Iraq's air defense commanders' ability to employ their SAMs, while allied jamming and strikes on Iraqi surveillance radars and command and control systems blinded those commanders. Within days of the start of both wars, Iraq's air defense forces could capture only glimpses of the coalition air campaign, forcing them to fire almost at random. Even then, engagements proved short-lived, as emanating a radar signal almost always resulted in antenna destruction by an ARM.

CARL OTIS SCHUSTER

See also

Aircraft, Bombers; Aircraft, Fighters; Aircraft, Electronic Warfare; Aircraft, Suppression of Enemy Air Defense; Antiaircraft Guns; DESERT STORM, Operation, Coalition Air Campaign; IRAQI FREEDOM, Operation, Air Campaign; Missiles, Air-to-Ground; Missiles, Surface-to-Air

References

Finlan, Alastair. *The Gulf War, 1991*. Oxford, UK: Osprey, 2004.

Hewson, Robert. *Jane's Air-Launched Weapons, 2001*. London: Jane's, 2002.

Knight, Michael, ed. *Operation Iraqi Freedom and the New Iraq*. Washington, DC: Washington Institute for Near East Policy, 2004.

Olsen, John. *Strategic Air Power in Desert Storm*. London: Frank Cass, 2003.

Tripp, Robert. *Lessons Learned from Operation Enduring Freedom*. Santa Monica, CA: RAND Corporation, 2004.

Antitank Weapons

Because of the large number of tanks and armored vehicles that saw service in both the Persian Gulf War and the Iraq War, antitank weapons played a critical role. Although initially equipped with large numbers of Soviet- and Russian-designed tanks and other weapons, the Iraqi Army only managed to knock out a small handful of American tanks. In the Iraq War, U.S. forces lost 9 tanks to friendly fire and 2 to mines, and 13 were damaged by various forms of Iraqi antitank fire (5 of those were severely damaged). Crew casualties from Iraqi fire were 1 killed and 13 wounded. The Iraqi Air Force played virtually no role in both wars, so whatever rotary and fixed-wing antitank aircraft they may have had in their inventory were largely irrelevant. The primary Iraqi antitank weapons were limited to antitank guided missiles (ATGMs) and shoulder-fired infantry weapons. In Afghanistan the Taliban had no armored vehicles, and their antitank weapons were limited primarily to shoulder-fired infantry weapons, recoilless rifles, and mines. The majority of the weapons considered here, therefore, are American systems.

Despite their armor and armament, tanks and other armored vehicles are not invulnerable. They can be defeated by land mines, aircraft, artillery, other tanks, rockets, guided missiles, and a wide range of infantry weapons. The various categories of tank kills are a function of the damage done to the tank combined with the tactical situation. A mobility kill, called an M-kill in current U.S. doctrine, occurs when the tank's power train or running gear have been damaged to the point where the tank cannot move. The tank may still be able to fire its weapons, but its inability to maneuver severely degrades its combat value. A firepower kill, called an F-kill, occurs when the tank's main gun or its fire-control optics and electronics have been severely damaged. A catastrophic kill, called a K-kill, occurs when the tank completely loses its ability to operate. It can neither move nor fire. A K-kill usually means that the tank has been totally destroyed and often also means that the tank crew has been killed.

Whether fired by artillery, aircraft, another tank, or infantry weapons, the warheads of all antitank rounds are classified as either kinetic energy or chemical energy. Most main battle tanks are capable of firing both types of rounds through their main guns. The three basic types of chemical energy (i.e., explosive) warheads are high explosive (HE), high-explosive antitank (HEAT), and high-explosive plastic (HEP).

Tanks can be defeated by a blast from conventional HEs, but only if the charge is large enough and close enough. HE projectiles delivered by artillery or air require a direct or very close hit, which usually exceeds the circular probable error of all but the most advanced precision-guided munitions (PGMs).

The most common and effective chemical energy projectile, the HEAT round, has a shaped-charge warhead that relies on the Munroe Effect to burn a hole through the tank's armor in the form of an expanding cone. What actually kills the tank crew is the semi-molten armor of their own tank. HEAT round detonations can also set off fuel and ammunition fires and secondary explosions.

HEP rounds, also called high-explosive squash head (HESH) rounds, carry a charge of plastic explosive that upon impact spreads over the outer surface of the armor before detonating. Unlike a HEAT round, the HEP round does actually penetrate the tank's armor. When the HEP charge explodes, it knocks off chunks of armor of a corresponding size, called spall, inside the tank, causing havoc for the crew and the internal components. HEP rounds are generally ineffective against most modern tanks because the internal compartments are equipped with spall liners, protecting the crew, ammunition, fuel, and equipment.

Nonexploding kinetic energy rounds are very heavy and dense and are fired at an extremely high velocity. The most common is some form of sabot round in which an outer casing falls away as soon as the round leaves the gun's muzzle. On impact the sabot punches its way through the target's armor. The effect inside the tank is usually even more catastrophic than that caused by a HEAT round. Tungsten and depleted uranium are two heavy and dense materials widely employed as sabots.

Because kinetic energy rounds require a flat line-of-sight trajectory and an extremely high velocity, they must be fired from a gun as opposed to a howitzer and from a very heavy platform. Thus, only tanks and antitank artillery can fire sabot rounds. A tank's most vulnerable area to a sabot round is at the slip ring, where the turret joins the main hull. Smaller nonsabot kinetic energy rounds are fired from rotary or fixed-wing aircraft armed with special antitank machine guns that deliver a high volume of fire to defeat the target's armor, usually from above, where the armor is the weakest.

Chemical energy rounds do not require a heavy launching platform and are thus ideal for infantry antitank weapons, which include rocket launchers, recoilless rifles, and antitank guided missiles (ATGMs). The best way to defeat a HEAT warhead is to cause it to detonate prematurely, which will prevent the Munroe Effect from forming properly on the outer skin of the tank's armor. Something as simple as a mesh outer screen mounted on the side of a tank with a few inches of standoff distance will cause that premature detonation. Reactive explosive armor, also called appliqué armor, mounted on the tank's integral armor is also relatively effective against HEAT rounds but not at all effective against sabot rounds. Each element of reactive armor contains a small explosive charge that detonates when it is hit, causing the impacting HEAT round to detonate prematurely and spoiling the Munroe Effect. Finally, the sloped surfaces of the tank's armor can cause the HEAT round to deflect, which also will spoil the Munroe Effect. Sloped armor surfaces can also deflect sabot rounds in certain instances.

Although common in World War II, purpose-built antitank artillery fell into disuse in the years following 1945. By the 1960s the Soviet Union, West Germany, and Sweden were among the few remaining countries still building antitank artillery. Most armies came to regard the tank itself as the premier, but certainly not the only, antitank weapon.

The antitank rifle first entered service in World War I. Today it is known as the antimaterial (antimatériel or equipment) rifle. Essentially a large-caliber high-velocity rifle firing special armor-piercing ammunition, it is designed to operate against enemy equipment, such as thin-skinned and lightly armored vehicles. The weapon may also be used for long-range sniping. Antimaterial rifles are often favored by special operations military units.

The U.S. Army Browning M-2 .50-caliber machine gun, which can be fired in single-shot mode, fits in this category. The Austrian Steyr 25-millimeter (mm) antimaterial rifle, with a claimed effective range of 1.2 miles, features both a muzzle brake and a hydro-pneumatic sleeve to reduce recoil. It has a bipod, and the weapon can be broken down for ease of transport by its crew. Among other such weapons is the South African Mechem NTW-20. This 20-mm bolt-action rifle features a 3-round side-mounted box magazine. There is also a 14.5-mm model. To reduce recoil, the NTW-20 uses a hydraulic double-action damper along with a double baffle muzzle brake. Among other such weapons are the U.S. Armalite AR-50 and Barretta M-82A1, both of which fire the 12.7-mm NATO (.50-caliber) round; the British Accuracy International AW50F, firing the 12.7-mm NATO (.50-caliber) round; the Hungarian Gerpard M-1(B) and M-2(B) 12.7-mm rifles, which with an interchangeable barrel can also fire the .50-caliber round; and the Russian KSVK 12.7-mm rifle. A number of these or similar weapons have been used in the various Middle East wars.

In the years following the Vietnam War, both the Americans and the Soviets developed special antitank machine guns for attack aircraft. Although the kinetic energy rounds fired by such weapons are far lighter than the sabot rounds fired from tanks, the high rate of fire from the machine guns produces multiple impacts in a concentrated area on the target that literally chews into the tank's armor. Attacking from above, the aircraft target the top of the tank, where the armor is generally the thinnest.

Entering service in 1977, the American GAU-8/A Avenger is a 30-mm seven-barrel electrically driven Gatling gun. It fires both armor-piercing incendiary (API) and high-explosive incendiary rounds, usually in a four-to-one mix. The API round weighs a little less than one pound and carries a depleted uranium penetrator. The GAU-8/A has a cyclic rate of fire of 3,900 rounds per minute. The Russian GSh-6-30 30-mm aircraft automatic cannon is a very similar weapon, except that it is gas-operated rather than electrically driven. Entering service in 1998, the U.S. M-230 Chain Gun also fires a 30-mm antitank round. Having only a single barrel, its rate of fire is only 625 rounds per minute, but it is considerably lighter than the GAU-8/A.

Purpose-built antitank mines first appeared in the last years of World War I and figured prominently during World War II. Most modern antitank mines use an HE charge to produce M-kills by blowing off the tread or damaging the road wheels. Some mines are designed to produce K-kills by attacking the underside of the tank, where the armor is thin. Although sometimes command detonated by either wire or remote control, most use pressure or magnetically triggered detonators that react to vehicles but not ground personnel.

The improvised explosive device (IED) is a variation on the antitank mine that has produced a high percentage of American and allied casualties during the Iraq War since 2003 and increasingly in Afghanistan. An IED is any locally fabricated explosive charge coupled with a detonating mechanism. Deadly to personnel, most IEDs initially could only damage unarmored and lightly armored vehicles. If the base explosive charge is large enough—for example, an artillery projectile buried in the road—the resulting explosion could do serious damage to a tank. In recent years, however, IEDs have become more sophisticated, especially with the appearance of explosively formed penetrators (EFPs). The EFP works on the same principle as the shaped charge, effectively transforming the IED from a simple HE to a HEAT weapon. An EFP has a cylindrical shaped charge capped by a concave metal disk pointed inward. When detonated, the metal disk, often made of copper, becomes a bolt of molten metal that can penetrate the armor on most vehicles in Iraq. An IED with an EFP is difficult to detect and counter because it is effective at standoff distances up to 164 feet.

Recoilless rifles and recoilless guns (smoothbore) were developed during World War II primarily as antitank weapons. Firing HE and HEAT projectiles similar to conventional artillery, a recoilless rifle is essentially a long tube, similar to a modern rocket launcher. Unlike the latter, however, the recoilless rifle has a breech mechanism. Also unlike conventional artillery, that breech has large exit vents, and the ammunition shell casings are perforated. When fired, almost all of the propellant blast escapes from the rear of the weapon. The resulting forward inertial force, however, is still sufficient to launch the projectile. The neutralization of almost all recoil eliminates the need for a standard gun carriage and a recoil system. Although most recoilless rifles are fired from some sort of vehicle or ground mount, some of the smaller calibers can be shoulder fired in the same manner as an infantry rocket launcher.

Recoilless rifles were widely used in Korea and Vietnam, but they were phased out of service in most armies as antitank rockets and guided missiles became more sophisticated from the 1970s on. Nonetheless, Taliban forces in Afghanistan have used a number of recoilless rifles, most of them captured from Soviet forces in the 1980s. The most common is the 82-mm B-10, which first entered service in 1950. Although it has a maximum range of 2.7 miles, its maximum effective range is only 1,640 feet. The most modern of the Taliban's recoilless antitank weapons is the 73-mm SPG-9. Designed initially for Soviet airborne units and entering service in 1962, it has a maximum effective range of 2,624 feet.

The first effective shoulder-fired infantry antitank weapons were free-flight rockets with HEAT warheads, entering service during World War II. All subsequent antitank rocket systems are derived from two basic designs, both introduced in 1942. The German Panzerfaust was an inexpensive single-shot lightweight weapon that could be fired by one man. The Panzerfaust consisted of a very simple small-diameter disposable launcher preloaded with a three-foot-long finned projectile with an oversized warhead that extended outside of the muzzle of the launching tube. The hollow tube concentrated the escaping gasses away from the gunner and made the firing recoilless. Pulling the trigger ignited a small charge of black powder inside the tube, driving the projectile toward its target. The projectile exploded on impact. The Panzerfaust was the prototype upon which the subsequent Soviet/Russian family of rocket-propelled grenade (RPG) antitank weapons was based.

The first U.S. antitank rocket was the 2.36-inch bazooka, which consisted of a rocket and launcher operated by a two-man crew of gunner and loader. The launcher was a reloadable aluminum tube with a shoulder stock and a hand grip that contained a trigger assembly with an electric generator. When the gunner squeezed the trigger, it generated an electric current through the wires to ignite the solid fuel in the rocket. Unlike the Panzerfaust, the entire antitank rocket was launched from inside the bazooka's firing tube. The Germans reversed-engineered captured bazookas to produce the significantly up-gunned 88-mm Panzerschreck. Except for the RPG family of weapons, the bazooka is the prototype for all other modern shoulder-fired infantry antitank rockets.

The Soviet RPG-7 is one of the most widely produced shoulder-fired infantry antitank weapons in the world. It is one of the

Demonstration of a Soviet-made RPG-7 portable antitank rocket launcher, similar to those employed by Iraqi forces in the Persian Gulf and Iraq wars. (U.S. Department of Defense)

principal weapons of choice of Afghan and Iraqi insurgents. It is also widely used by Afghan and Iraqi police and military forces loyal to the national governments. First entering service in 1961 and used extensively by the Viet Cong and the North Vietnamese Army against American armored vehicles in Vietnam, the RPG-7 consists of a steel launching tube 40-mm in diameter and 37 inches long. Depending on the exact type of projectile, the protruding warhead can be anything from 83-mm to 105-mm. Most RPG-7 ammunition has a range up to 2,952 feet, and the most effective warhead has a tandem HEAT charge capable of penetrating 600-mm to 700-mm of rolled homogeneous armor (RHA).

The only shoulder-fired free-flight rocket antitank weapon used by U.S. forces today is the Swedish-built AT-4. Similar in operating principle to the World War II–era bazooka, the AT-4 fires an 84-mm projectile with a HEAT warhead to a maximum effective range of 984 feet. The resulting blast can penetrate up to 400-mm of RHA. Unlike the earlier bazooka, the AT-4 is not reloadable. The launcher and projectile are manufactured and issued as a single unit of ammunition. The entire system weighs 14.75 pounds.

ATGMs first started to appear in the late 1960s and represented a vast improvement on the early unguided antitank rockets. ATGMs vary widely in size and type, from individual shoulder-fired missiles to crew-served missiles and to those launched from ground vehicles and from aircraft. Unlike unguided systems, missiles have the great advantage of standoff capability.

First-generation guided missiles were manually controlled during flight. Once the missile was fired, the gunner guided it to the target by means of a joystick or similar device. Second-generation antitank missiles only required that the gunner keep the sight on the target. Guidance commands for the missile were transmitted either by radio or by wire. Third-generation antitank missiles operate by laser painting or marking of the target on a nose-mounted TV camera. They are known as fire-and-forget missiles.

Antitank missiles generally carry a hollow-charge or shaped-charge HEAT warhead. Tandem warhead missiles are designed specifically to defeat reactive or spaced vehicle armor, while top-attack antitank missiles are designed to strike from above against the more lightly armored tops of tanks and armored fighting vehicles (AFVs).

The 9K11 Malyutka, known by its NATO designation as the AT-3 Sagger, was the Soviet Union's first man-portable ATGM and probably the most extensively produced ATGM in history. It was widely used by Iraqi forces in both the Persian Gulf War and the Iraq War. Entering service in September 1963, it was the standard model for all subsequent first-generation ATGMs. Some

25,000 Saggers were produced yearly by the Soviet Union alone in the 1960s and 1970s. It was also manufactured by other Soviet bloc countries as well as the People's Republic of China. The Sagger has been widely exported to the Middle East, including Afghanistan, Algeria, Egypt, Iran, Iraq, Libya, and Syria. Guided to its target by means of a joy stick and wire, the Sagger has a launch weight of some 24 pounds with a warhead of 5.5 pounds. It has a minimum range of 1,640 feet and a maximum range of 1.8 miles. At maximum range, it takes the missile about 30 seconds to reach its target. The Sagger can be fired from a portable suitcase launcher; from armored vehicles, such as the Soviet BMP-1 or BRDM-2; or from attack helicopters, including the Mi-2, Mi-8, and Mi-24.

The U.S.-made BGM-71 tube-launched optically tracked wire-guided (TOW) missile is a second-generation ATGM. TOWs were first produced by Hughes Aircraft Company and are now produced by Raytheon Systems Company. More than 500,000 TOWs have been manufactured, and they are employed by more than 45 nations. The TOW is designed to attack tanks, AFVs, bunkers and fortifications. First entering service in 1970, the TOW underwent a number of modifications, the most recent of which is the TOW-2B of 1991. The first use of the TOW in combat came in May 1972 during the Vietnam War. It also saw wartime service with the Israeli Army against Syrian forces and in the Iran-Iraq War (1980–1988). The TOW-2B first saw combat in 2003 during the Iraq War.

The TOW-2B missile weighs 49.8 pounds (64 pounds with carrier) and has an explosive filler of some 6.9 pounds. The missile is 5.8 inches in diameter and is 48 inches in length. It has a minimum range of 213 feet and a maximum range of 2.3 miles. TOW missiles can be ground fired from a tripod by a crew of four or, more usually, from both wheeled and tracked vehicles, including the M-1/M-3 Bradley, the M-966 HMMWV, and the M-1134 Stryker. TOWs also are mounted on attack helicopters. The missile operates on command line-of-sight guidance. The gunner uses a sight to locate the target and, once the missile is fired, continues to track the target through the sight, with guidance commands transmitted along two wires that spool from the back of the missile. The TOW-2B attacks the target from the top, and its double warheads explode downward when the missile is just above the target. A bunker-buster variant is designed to defeat bunkers, field fortifications, and buildings.

The Soviet Union's second-generation man-portable 9K111 Fagot (NATO designation AT-4 Spigot) ATGM entered service in 1972. Designed to replace the Sagger, the Spigot has a minimum range of 246 feet and a maximum range of 1.5 miles in a flight time of 11 seconds. Fired from a ground-mount folding tripod, the entire system in firing configuration weighs some 74 pounds, with the missile itself weighing 25.3 pounds and the warhead 5.5 pounds.

The M-47 Dragon was an American antitank infantry weapon that was fired from the gunner's shoulder but stabilized in front by a ground bipod. First fielded in 1975, it was used in the 1991 Persian Gulf War and was retired from service in the late 1990s. The improved Dragon II entered service in 1985, and the Super-Dragon entered service in 1990. At one time the Dragons were supplied to Iran, and the Iraqis captured some Dragons during the Iran-Iraq War and put them into service. The 140-mm wire-guided missile carried a HEAT warhead capable of penetrating 450-mm of RHA and defeating Soviet T-55, T-62, and T-72 tanks. The Dragon's maximum effective range was 3,280 feet. The launcher itself was expendable, but the sights could be removed after firing and reused. The Dragon's most significant drawback was that its tracking system required the gunner to remain kneeling and exposed to enemy fire while tracking the missile to the target.

The Dragon was replaced by the man-portable FGM-148 Javelin, a third-generation system. A joint venture of Texas Instruments (now Raytheon Missile Systems) of Dallas, Texas, and Lockheed Martin Electronics and Missiles (now Missiles and Fire Control) of Orlando, Florida, the Javelin entered service with the U.S. Army and U.S. Marine Corps in 1996. Designed for a two-man crew, the Javelin has a minimum range of 246 feet and a maximum effective range of 1.5 miles, more than twice that of the M-47 Dragon.

The Javelin system consists of a missile in a disposable launch tube, a reusable command launch unit (CLU) with triggering mechanism, an integrated day/night sighting device, and target-acquisition electronics. The missile weighs 49.5 pounds and is 5 feet 9 inches in length. Fins deploy when the missile is launched. The Javelin employs a small thermal imaging TV camera and sophisticated computer guidance system in its seeker section. To fire the missile, the gunner places a cursor over the selected target. The CLU then sends a lock-on-before-launch signal to the missile. The missile's infrared guidance system and onboard processing guide it after launch. The Javelin is designed for top attack and has a dual 8.5-pound warhead capable of defeating all known armor. U.S. forces have used the Javelin in both Afghanistan and Iraq since 2003, and British forces also fielded the Javelin in 2005.

The AGM-65 Maverick was an American air-to-ground missile designed to destroy not only armored vehicles but also ships, air defense and artillery emplacements, and logistics nodes. Entering service in 1972, the missile weighs between 462 and 670 pounds, depending on the warhead. The 125-pound shaped-charge warhead has a point-detonating fuse, and the 300-pound high-explosive penetrator has a delay-action fuse. The missile itself has a maximum effective range of 17 miles. The missile has an onboard infrared television camera, with which the aircraft pilot or weapons systems officer locks onto the target before firing. Once launched, the Maverick tracks its target automatically, making it a fire-and-forget system. Fired primarily from fixed-wing aircraft, the Maverick was used extensively in both the Persian Gulf War and the Iraq War.

The AGM-114 Hellfire entered service in 1984. It was designed specifically as an antitank weapon, primarily for launch from attack helicopters, although it can be fired from some fixed-wing attack aircraft and can even be ground launched. The missile weighs 106 pounds, including the 20-pound warhead. It has a maximum effective range of 4.9 miles. The initial versions of the Hellfire were laser-guided, but the more recent variants have been

The Dragon antitank/assault missile, developed for the U.S. Army in 1970, is a one-man antitank missile that was used against Iraqi tanks during the Persian Gulf War. (U.S. Department of Defense)

radar-guided. The Hellfire has been used in the Persian Gulf War, the Afghanistan War, and the Iraq War. Between 2001 and 2007 U.S. Forces have fired more that 6,000 Hellfires in combat.

Although direct-firing antitank artillery guns have been phased out of service by most armies since the 1950s, the increasing technical sophistication of artillery ammunition has given a new antitank role to indirect-firing field artillery. Most American antitank field artillery rounds are 155-mm, fired by either the M-198 towed howitzer or the M-109 family of self-propelled howitzers. Special antitank warheads also exist for the M-270 multiple launch rocket system (MLRS) and the army tactical missile system (ATACMS), which use the same self-propelled launcher system as the MLRS. The most current version of the M-109 howitzer, the Paladin M-109A6, entered service in 1999 and fires to a maximum range of 13.6 miles. The United States used the M-109A6 in the Iraq War, and the U.S., British, Egyptian, and Saudi armies all used earlier versions of the M-109 in the Persian Gulf War. The M-270 MLRS, which entered service in 1983, was developed jointly by the United States, Britain, Germany, and France. It fires 12 free-flight rockets to a maximum range of 26.1 miles. The MLRS launcher also can fire 2 MGM-140 ATACMS at a time. Operational in January 1991 and first fired in combat during the Persian Gulf War, the guided missiles have a range of 102 miles.

The improved conventional munitions (ICM) artillery round entered service for the U.S. 105-mm howitzer in 1961 and was first fired in combat in the Vietnam War. The projectile was a cargo-carrying round that burst in the air over the target, dispersing a number of unguided antipersonnel submunitions. In common terms, the ICM was an artillery version of a cluster bomb. In the early 1970s the United States developed a projectile for the 155-mm howitzer that carried submunitions designed to work against either personnel or tanks. Called a dual-purpose ICM (DPICM), the M-483 155-mm projectile carries 88 submunitions capable of penetrating 65-mm of RHA. Each M-42 or M-46 bomblet carries a HEAT shaped charge, designed to attack a tank's relatively thin top armor. The DPICM warhead for the MLRS rocket carries 644 M-77 submunitions, each capable of penetrating 100-mm of RHA. The ATACMS MGM-140 missile warhead carried 950 M-74 submunitions that are classified as antipersonnel/antimaterial (APAM). They are effective against thin-skinned tactical vehicles but not against armored vehicles. The most significant drawback to DPICMs is the 2–5 percent dud rate of the submunitions, which has caused unintended casualties as friendly forces have moved into a target area after the firing. During the 1991 Persian Gulf War, DPICMs acquired the nickname "Steel Rain."

Like DPICM artillery ammunition, family of scatterable mines (FASCAM) rounds are also cargo-carrying projectiles that burst in the air above the target area and disperse unguided submunitions. FASCAM rounds can be emplaced remotely, deep in an enemy's rear, by either field artillery or aircraft. FASCAM projectiles were initially developed for both the 155-mm and 8-inch howitzers and carried either antipersonnel mines (called area denial munitions [ADAMs]) or antitank mines (called remote antiarmor mines [RAAMs]). The 8-inch howitzer was retired from the American arsenal after the Persian Gulf War. The 155-mm M-741 projectile carries nine M-73 antitank mines, which are preset to self-destruct 48 hours after they have been emplaced. The M-741 projectile carries nine M-70 antitank mines, with a preset self-destruct time of 4 hours.

Unlike many antitank mines, the FASCAM RAAMs are designed to achieve a K-kill rather than just a M-kill. Each 3.75-pound M-70 and M-73 mine contains slightly more than 1 pound of RDX (cyclonite) explosive. When the mine is detonated by its magnetically induced fuse, a two-sided Miznay-Shardin plate creates a self-forging fragment that becomes a superdense molten slug that punches through the tank's relatively thin underarmor. The principle is very similar to that of the explosively formed penetrators used in some IEDs. The first artillery-delivered FASCAM minefield in combat was fired by the 5th Battalion, 11th Marines, during the Battle of Khafji (January 29–February 1, 1991).

The first PGM for field artillery weapons was the American M-712 Copperhead, a 155-mm fin-stabilized terminally guided projectile specifically designed to engage tanks and other hardened targets. In order for the Copperhead round to hit a tank directly, an observer must have the target under observation and be close enough to "paint" it with a laser-designator during the terminal leg of the projectile's trajectory. This requires that the round be below cloud cover long enough for it to lock on to the target and have sufficient time to maneuver to impact. The observer can be either a forward observer on the ground or an aerial in a helicopter. Unmanned aerial vehicles (UAVs) equipped with television cameras and laser designators can also be used to guide the Copperhead round to its target. The Copperhead was fired in combat for the first time during the Persian Gulf War.

The U.S. sense and destroy armor (SADARM) system is based in a cargo-carrying artillery round similar to the DPICM projectile except that it carries smart submunitions. The 155-mm M-898 round carries two submunitions that are released 3,280 feet above the target area. Specially designed parachutes slow the descent of the submunition and cause it to swing in a circle. As it descends, its millimeter wave radar and infrared telescope sensors sweep the area below about 492 feet in diameter. When the sensors acquire a target, the explosive charge triggers at the right time, sending an explosively formed penetrator through the top armor of the tank. SADARM rounds were fired in combat for the first time during the Iraq War. The divisional artillery of the U.S. 3rd Infantry Division fired 108 rounds and achieved 48 vehicle kills.

Purpose-built ground attack aircraft first appeared in the final year of World War I, and during World War II the British, Soviets, and Germans all developed fixed-wing aircraft specifically designed to attack tanks. During the Vietnam War the United States first started using helicopters in a ground-attack role, and during North Vietnam's 1972 Easter Offensives American helicopters firing TOW missiles attacked tanks for the first time.

The first American purpose-designed attack helicopter was the AH-1 Cobra, which entered service in 1967. The U.S. Army retired the Cobra in 1999, but the U.S. Marine Corps still flies the AH-1W Super Cobra, which can mount an antitank armament of eight TOW or eight Hellfire missiles. The U.S. Army's AH-64 Apache entered service in 1983 and saw significant service in the Persian Gulf War. It has also seen significant service in the Afghanistan War and the Iraq War. Specifically designed as a tank killer, the AH-64's primary armament is the M-230 Chain Gun. Depending on its specific mission, each AH-64 can carry up to 16 Hellfire antitank missiles and 1,200 rounds of 30-mm ammunition.

A number of American fixed-wing ground-support aircraft are capable of carrying antitank armament, but like the AH-64 Apache, the A-10 Thunderbolt II, universally known as the "Warthog," was specifically designed as a tank killer. Its primary armament is the GAU-8/A Gatling gun, which weighs 4,029 pounds and accounts for some 16 percent of the aircraft's unladen weight. The A-10 carries 1,174 rounds of 30-mm ammunition. When configured for a specific antitank mission, the A-10 can carry four AGM-65 Maverick missiles.

Unmanned aerial vehicles (UAVs) were initially designed as reconnaissance platforms. Their sophisticated onboard sensor systems and long dwell times over target areas made them critically valuable assets in finding enemy tanks. But some UAVs also have sufficient lift to carry 106-pound AGM-114 Hellfire missiles in addition to their sensor packages. Although not originally designed as attack platforms, both the MQ-1B Predator and the MQ-9 Reaper have carried and successfully launched Hellfires.

DAVID T. ZABECKI AND SPENCER C. TUCKER

See also

Armored Warfare, Persian Gulf and Iraq Wars; Improvised Explosive Devices

References

Gander, Terry J. *Anti-Tank Weapons*. Marlborough, UK: Crowood, 2000.
———. *The Bazooka: Hand-Held Hollow-Charge Anti-Tank Weapons*. London: PRC Publishing, 1998.
Ripley, Tim. *Tank Warfare*. Drexel Hill, PA: Casemate, 2003.
Weeks, John S. *Men against Tanks: A History of Anti-Tank Warfare*. New York: Mason/Charter, 1975.

Antiwar Movements, Persian Gulf and Iraq Wars

The antiwar movement during the 1991 Persian Gulf War was short-lived in large measure because overwhelming U.S. military power brought about a quick end to the hostilities. The Iraq War (2003–present), however, has seen substantial antiwar demonstrations and protests, including widespread use of the Internet. Anti–Iraq War demonstrations occurred in the United States, in Europe, and in the Middle East.

Months before Operation DESERT STORM commenced in January 1991, an antiwar movement had already manifested itself. On October 20, 1990, some 15,000 protestors marched in New York City and 15 other U.S. cities calling upon the George H. W. Bush administration to avoid war with Iraq. When the war was launched on January 16, 1991, more than 3,000 Bostonians turned out to protest the war as members of the Initiative for Peace led a rally at Boston Common. Protestors of the Persian Gulf War argued that it was a contest over oil and not one that involved other vital U.S. interests. On January 26, 1991, after 15,000 marchers demonstrated in Washington, D.C., another crowd assembled there a week later, with estimates of its size ranging from 70,000 to as high as 250,000 people. But the massive air campaign culminated in a rapid ground campaign, and in four weeks the war had ended, halting the protests as well.

Opposition to the Iraq War has seen the engagement of large numbers of protestors. Although lacking the types of civil disobedience tactics accompanying the Vietnam War, opposition has been no less intense. Antiwar groups began protests even before military action began in March 2003. Groups such as Americans Against War With Iraq, NOT IN OUR NAME, United for Peace and Justice, and ANSWER insisted that the George W. Bush administration's plans for war would lead to the killing of thousands of U.S. soldiers, Iraqi soldiers, and Iraqi civilians and would have a negative effect on Middle East stability. They also contended that the rush to war was generated by imperialistic

concerns based on oil interests, that it would violate international law without United Nations (UN) approval, that it would only breed more terrorism, that Iraqi president Saddam Hussein was not in consort with Al Qaeda, and that Iraq did not possess weapons of mass destruction (WMDs). Rallies and demonstrations continued prior to the war.

In the third week of January 2003 a group of 50 volunteers from various nations, led by former Persian Gulf War veteran Kenneth O'Keefe, headed to Baghdad to act as human shields against an impending U.S. air strike. Eventually, between 200 and 500 human shields made their way to Iraq and remained there during the shock-and-awe bombing campaign in March.

On February 15, 2003, between 100,000 and 250,000 people marched in New York City, making it the largest political demonstration the city had seen since the anti–nuclear proliferation movement of the early 1980s. On March 9 some 3,000 pink-clad women activists marched around the White House to oppose the impending war. This group called itself CODEPINK. On March 15 the last massive demonstrations before the war began occurred when tens of thousands of protestors participated in antiwar rallies from Portland, Oregon, to Los Angeles to Washington, D.C.

Once the war commenced on March 20, 2003, the antiwar protests grew in number. The antiwar coalitions that appeared were composed of people from all walks of life. They included the elderly, former veterans of past wars, school-age students, college students, and people of all races, ethnicities, and religious backgrounds. Indeed, opposition to the Iraq War cuts across race, gender, and economic lines. One of the more unique forms of protest later copied by other antiwar groups was initiated by a Quaker peace group, the American Friends Service Committee (AFSC).

Members of the Grandmothers for Peace organization stage a sit-in at an Armed Forces Recruiting Station in New York City during an anti–Iraq War rally in Times Square on October 17, 2005. Seventeen were arrested when they attempted to enter the facility and enlist. (AP/Wide World Photos)

Calling it "False Pretenses," the AFSC created a memorial by placing 500 pairs of boots at the Federal Building Plaza in Chicago to symbolize the number of soldiers who had been killed at that point in the war. Other antiwar activists built mock coffins and stretched out on busy streets.

One antiwar group that captured the national media's attention was Grandmothers against the War. Primarily a local coalition in New York City, 17 grandmothers, ranging in age from 49 to 90, were arrested on October 17, 2005, when they attempted to enlist in the military at the Times Square recruiting station. Their action inspired other elderly women to take up the cause in Chicago, San Francisco, and Los Angeles.

The actions of Cindy Sheehan also served as a lightning rod for the antiwar movement when, in August 2005, she conducted a 26-day vigil outside President Bush's ranch at Crawford, Texas. Sheehan's son was killed in Iraq in 2004. Her most dramatic act of civil disobedience occurred during the 2006 State of the Union Address, when she was forcibly removed from the House chamber sporting a T-shirt that read "2,245 Dead. How Many More?" In March 2006 Sheehan was arrested for allegedly blocking a door leading to the U.S. mission in the United Nations (UN) in New York City. She was also one of the founders of the Gold Star Families for Peace, an organization dedicated to helping families that had lost relatives in the Iraq War and to bringing an end to U.S. involvement in Iraq. Sheehan has since become the most recognizable antiwar protester in the United States and has appeared on numerous television programs and many rallies around the country.

From 2002 to 2007 large antiwar demonstrations took place in cities and towns throughout the nation. On January 28, 2007, an antiwar rally in the nation's capital saw thousands of peaceful protestors gathered to listen to Hollywood celebrities such as Jane Fonda, Sean Penn, Danny Glover, Susan Sarandon, and Tim Robbins condemn the war.

The current antiwar demonstrations have been remarkable for their discipline and adherence to the principle of nonviolent civil disobedience. In 2007, apart from visible protests, the National War Tax Resistance Coordinating Committee estimated that between 8,000 and 10,000 Americans refused to pay some or all of their federal taxes to support the war.

One of the unique aspects of the anti–Iraq War movement has been its online organization. Cyberactive antiwar groups such as Americans Against Escalation in Iraq, MoveOn.org, Win Without War, and WHY WAR? have effectively mobilized opposition at the grassroots level through use of the Internet. Use of online activism has emerged as a force for organizing, raising money, and influencing politicians through blogs (web logs) and e-mail messages. These organizations represent the new wave in protest movements, one aimed at influencing votes in Congress rather than just street theater and mass demonstrations. The Internet has also been responsible for increasing membership in antiwar organizations such as Veterans for Common Sense, Operation Truth, and Iraq Veterans against the War.

The strength of the current anti–Iraq War protests lies in its sophistication and perspective. Those joining the antiwar movement have done so because they perceive the war as a serious threat to the stability of the international order and the economic development of societies in need of global financial support. Media attention to the antiwar movements of the Middle East wars has not been as extensive as it was during the Vietnam War years, but the Internet has clearly aided its organization efforts and awareness of the issues. One important difference between the Iraq War protest movement and the protests during the Vietnam War is that those demonstrating against the Iraq War have avoided attacking or demonizing the troops but have rather concentrated their displeasure on the political leadership. This is seen in the slogan of "Support the Troops: Bring Them Home!"

The overwhelming antiwar sentiment in Europe—impossible to separate from a pervasive anti-American sentiment—was an important reason why only the United Kingdom, the Netherlands, and Poland of North Atlantic Treaty Organization (NATO) powers were making a major manpower commitment to Afghanistan.

CHARLES F. HOWLETT

See also

DESERT STORM, Operation; IRAQI FREEDOM, Operation; Sheehan, Cindy Lee Miller

References

Chomsky, Noam. *Hegemony or Survival: America's Quest for Global Dominance.* New York: Metropolitan Books, 2003.

Cortright, David. "The Movement and the 2003 War in Iraq." In *The Movement,* edited by Randy Scherer, 146–152. Farmington Hills, MI: Greenhaven, 2004.

Gardner, Lloyd, and Marilyn Young, eds. *Iraq and the Lessons of Vietnam: Or, How Not to Learn from the Past.* New York: New Press, 2007.

Johnson, Chalmers. *Nemesis: The Last Days of the American Republic.* New York: Henry Holt, 2007.

Miller, Christian T. *Blood Money: Wasted Billions, Lost Lives, and Corporate Greed in Iraq.* New York: Little, Brown, 2006.

Ryan, Claes G. *America the Virtuous: The Crisis of Democracy and the Quest for Empire.* New Brunswick, NJ: Transaction Books, 2003.

Sheehan, Cindy. *Peace Mom: A Mother's Journey through Heartache to Activism.* New York: Atria, 2006.

Spencer, Metta. "Anti-war Hawks and Prowar Doves in the Gulf War: Common Security versus Collective Security." *Peace & Change* 17 (April 1992): 172–197.

Arab-Israeli Conflict, Overview

Establishing precise parameters for the Arab-Israeli conflict is difficult. The wars are usually given as beginning with the Arab-Jewish Communal War (1947–1948) or the Arab-Israeli War of 1948–1949 (Israeli War of Independence). These wars in effect extend to the present, for some of the Arab confrontation states, most notably Syria, have yet to sign peace treaties with Israel.

Beginning the conflict in 1948 or even 1947 gives a false impression, as previously there had been episodes of violence and armed clashes between Arabs and Jews in Palestine, especially in the 1920s and 1930s. These events were sparked by Arab fears over significant Jewish immigration to Palestine and land purchases there. Animosity thus found expression in the Arab riots of 1920 and the Arab Revolt of 1936–1939.

Of course, strife was hardly new to this region. Palestine had been a battleground since the beginning of recorded history. History's first reliably recorded battle took place in 1457 BCE at Megiddo, at the head of present-day Israeli's Jezreel Valley. When Egyptian forces under the command of Pharaoh Thutmose III decisively defeated a Canaanite coalition under the king of Kadesh, the Canaanites withdrew to the city of Megiddo, which the Egyptians then brought under siege. Certain fundamentalist Christians identify Megiddo as the site of Armageddon, where according to the Book of Revelation the final great battle between good and evil will take place.

With its location on the eastern Mediterranean coast, ancient Palestine formed an important communication route between larger empires such as Egypt, Assyria, Babylon, and Persia. As such, it was destined for a stormy existence. These empires as well as Alexander the Great, the Seleucid Empire, the Romans, the Byzantines, the Abbasid caliphate, the Tartars, the Mongols, the Mamluks, the Ottoman Turks, and finally the British all fought for control of Palestine. Sometime around 1200 BCE the Jews established and then maintained an independent Jewish state there. Ultimately, more-powerful states prevailed, and the Jews were largely expelled from their own land by the occupiers in what became known as the Diaspora. Jews settled in most of the world's countries and on almost every continent.

In the 19th century, nationalism swept Europe. Sentiment for a national state also touched the Jews, many of whom longed for a state of their own, one that would be able to protect them from the persecutions (pogroms) that occurred in the late 19th and early 20th centuries, most notably in Russia. Zionism, or the effort to reestablish a Jewish state in Palestine, attracted a great many Jews—religious and nonreligious—and a number of them went to Palestine as immigrants.

During World War I, the British government endeavored to win the support of both Arabs and Jews in the war against the Central powers, including the Ottoman Empire. While at the same time supporting the Arab Revolt against Ottoman Turkey, the British government in the Balfour Declaration of November 1917 promised to work for the establishment of a Jewish homeland in Palestine. In retrospect, British policies were at once shortsighted and contradictory and helped sow the seeds of even more Arab-Jewish enmity when the war ended in 1918. Britain and France both secured League of Nations mandates in the Middle East after the war. France obtained Syria and Lebanon, while Britain took control of Palestine (which included what is today Israel/Palestine and Jordan) and Iraq.

Increasing Jewish immigration, however, as well as ongoing Jewish purchases of Arab land increasingly inflamed Arab leaders

in Palestine as well as leaders such as King Abdullah of Jordan and Ibn Saud of Saudi Arabia, who feared that if immigration could not be halted, the growing Jewish minority in Palestine would become a majority. In what became an increasingly violent atmosphere, the British government found it impossible to please both sides. London, worried about its overall position in the Middle East with the approach of a new world war, increasingly tended to side with the Arabs. This meant restrictions on both Jewish immigration and land purchases in Palestine, but this came at precisely the time when German leader Adolf Hitler challenged the post–World War I status quo in Europe and was carrying out a fervent anti-Semite policy.

Finding it impossible to secure agreement between the two sides, London announced plans for the partition of Palestine. The Arabs rejected this partitioning, insisting on independence for Palestine as one state under majority (Arab) rule. Concerned about their overall position in the Middle East, the British then withdrew from their pro-Zionist policy and in May 1939 issued a White Paper that severely restricted the immigration of Jews to Palestine and forbade the purchase of Arab lands in Palestine by Jews.

Following World War II, Jews in Palestine conducted a campaign against the British policy there that mixed diplomatic campaign with armed struggle. Finding it more and more difficult to contain the growing violence in Palestine, coupled with the support of President Harry S. Truman's administration in the United States for the Jewish position, London turned the future of Palestine over to the new United Nations (UN). On November 29, 1947, the UN General Assembly voted to partition the British mandate into Jewish and Arab states. The Arabs of Palestine, supported by the Arab League, adamantly opposed the partition, and the first of four major wars began following news of the UN vote. The first war of 1947–1949 contains two identifiably separate conflicts: the Arab-Jewish communal war of November 30, 1947–May 14, 1948, which included volunteer forces from other Arab states as well as Palestinian Arabs, and the Arab-Israeli War (Israeli War of Independence), which began on May 15, 1948, a day after the ending of the British mandate and with the founding of the State of Israel. The war ended with the last truce agreement with Syria on July 30, 1949. The three other conflicts ensued in 1956 (the Sinai War, or Suez Crisis), 1967 (the Six-Day War), and 1973 (the October War, Yom Kippur War, or Ramadan War). In these four conflicts, Israeli forces eventually triumphed. Each threatened to bring about superpower intervention, and the four wars also had profound implications throughout the Middle East and beyond. Beyond these wars, however, were ongoing terrorist attacks against Israel; cross-border raids, some of them quite large; a successful Israeli air strike on the Iraqi Osiraq nuclear reactor (1981); and large Israeli incursions into southern Lebanon in 1982 and in 2006.

The 1948 war began following the announcement of the UN General Assembly's endorsement of Resolution 181 on November 29, 1947, calling for the partition of Palestine into Jewish and Arab states. While Jewish authorities in Palestine accepted the

Barbed wire covers more than 100 yards of Princess Mary Avenue at Zion Square in Jerusalem on May 19, 1948. The wire is to separate Arabs and Jews. The Jewish state of Israel was proclaimed on May 15, and fighting immediately began. The Old City of Jerusalem appeared in imminent danger of being wrested from its Jewish defenders by the Arab Desert Legion. (AP/Wide World Photos)

resolution, the Arabs—including the Palestinians and the Arab League—rejected it. In response to passage of the UN resolution, Arabs began attacking Jews throughout Palestine, and the incidents expanded so that from December 1947 to April or May 1948 an intercommunal war raged between Jewish and Arab residents of Palestine.

The Jewish community in Palestine then numbered some 600,000 people, while the Palestinians consisted of more than 1.2 million. However, Palestinian numerical advantage counted for little on the battlefield. The Palestinians had no national institutions of any kind, let alone a cohesive military. They were fragmented with divided elites and were unprepared for the violence, expulsions, and loss of their property. Many Palestinians were reduced to starvation. Perhaps only 5,000 Palestinians took part in the fighting against the Jews. These essentially guerrilla forces were poorly trained, poorly equipped, and ineffectively organized.

The Arab League pledged support to the Palestinians but, through its Military Committee, actually usurped the conflict from the Palestinians. The Military Committee and the mufti Haj Amin al-Hussayni argued over the conduct of the war as each sought to control operations. The Military Committee failed, however, to provide the Palestinians with the money and weapons that the Arab rulers had pledged and sent its own commanders to Palestine to oversee the war. Such internal conflicts further weakened the overall Arab effort.

The Jews, on the other hand, were much better equipped and more organized. Jewish society was both Western and industrialized, having all the institutions of a modern state. In fact, structurally the establishment of the Jewish state required only the formal transformation of the prestatehood institutions to government entities, parliament, political parties, banks, and a relatively well-developed military arm, known as the Haganah. The Haganah was organized during the civil war as a full-fledged army, with 9 brigades with a total of some 25,000 conscripts. By May 1948 there were 11 brigades, with nearly 35,000 men. With the Jewish forces taking the offensive in early April 1948, the

Palestinians had no chance but to counterattack and by early May had been defeated.

During this time, and even before the Jews' final campaign, hundreds of thousands of Palestinians were driven from or fled their homes and became refugees. By the end of the war, there would be 750,000 to 1 million or more Palestinian refugees. Many of them escaped from the battle zone, but others were forcibly expelled and deported by Jewish forces during the actual fighting.

On May 15, 1948, with the formal establishment of the State of Israel, Israeli forces secured control over all the territory allocated to it by the UN in addition to a corridor leading to Jerusalem and the Jewish part of Jerusalem, which according to the Partition Resolution was to have been internationalized. With the official termination of British rule in Palestine on May 14, 1948, David Ben-Gurion, Israel's first elected prime minister, declared the establishment of the State of Israel. This declaration was followed by the advance of four Arab armies toward Palestine bent on a campaign to extinguish Israel.

The resulting war was, in many respects, primitive. Some 35,000 Israeli soldiers faced 35,000–40,000 Arab soldiers. Both sides were subjected to a UN Security Council arms embargo, but it was the Arabs who suffered the most from this. The Arab armies secured their weapons from Britain for Egypt, while Jordan and Iraq, which had no access to other markets, were forced into this arrangement under treaties with Britain. With the embargo in place, the Arabs were unable to replace damaged or destroyed weapons, and they had only limited access to ammunition. However, while the Jews received no military equipment from the West, they did manage in early 1948 to sign a major arms contract with the Czech government, thereby purchasing various weapons but mostly small arms and ammunition.

The strength of the Arab armies was in infantry. Their few tanks were mostly Egyptian. Even then, only a few dozen were operative. Despite an initial effort to create a unified command structure, the movements of the four Arab armies on Palestine were not coordinated. In April 1948 General Nur al-Din Mahmud, an Iraqi officer, was appointed by the Arab League to command the Arab forces. Mahmud submitted a plan that focused on northeastern Palestine, where the invading forces would try to sever eastern Galilee from the Hula Valley to Lake Kinneret (the Sea of Galilee) from Israel. That would be achieved through the coordinated advance of the Syrian, Lebanese, Iraqi, and Jordanian forces in the northern part of Palestine, while the Egyptian Army would move northward to Yibna, which was inside the designated Arab state. The Egyptians were not to advance into the Jewish state's territory, at least not in the first stage, but rather were to create a diversion that would lure Israeli forces into their sector and reduce Israeli pressure on the main Arab push in the north.

Jordan's King Abdullah had different plans for his army, however. He planned to occupy the area designated for the Palestinian Arab state, west of the Jordan River (the West Bank). For that reason he rebuffed Mahmud's plan and ordered the commander of the Arab Legion to act independently and occupy the West Bank. That was done, with the Arab Legion completing its mission in a few days. With that, each Arab army acted in isolation, while at the last minute Lebanon refrained from participation in the war. Syrian and Iraqi forces fought in the northern part of Israel, the Jordanian Arab League fought in the central sector, and the Egyptian Army fought in the southern sector.

The Egyptian government dispatched to Palestine 5,500 soldiers organized into two infantry brigades, accompanied by nearly 4,500 irregulars. Iraq dispatched to Palestine some 4,500 soldiers, while Syria sent 6,000. Jordan deployed almost all of its army, some 6,500 men. In addition, some 3,000 irregulars fought alongside the Arab armies.

At that time, Israel fielded more than 30,000 soldiers. The fighting was divided into two parts: the first from May 15 to June 10 and the second from July 9 to the end of the war. The first stage saw the Jews on the defensive, while in the second half of the war they took the offensive. In the indecisive first phase, small Iraqi and Syrian forces invaded Israel in the north but were repelled following a few days of fighting.

Jordanian forces concentrated on the occupation of the West Bank, while the main Egyptian expeditionary force moved northward along the coastline, reaching its final staging area near Yibna, within the area designated to the Arab state. Another part of the Egyptian force split from the main force. It crossed the Negev desert from west to east and moved toward Samaria through Hebron up to the southern outskirts of Jerusalem. Neither Egyptian force encountered any Israeli forces during their movements.

In the north, the Syrian and Iraqi armies tried to execute their part in Mahmud's plan, which was no longer valid. Acting in an uncoordinated manner, small forces of both armies invaded Israel in an area south of the Kinneret but were thwarted by the Israelis. The Syrian Army retreated, to return about a week later and attack two Israeli settlements near the Israeli-Syrian border and occupy them. Israeli counterattacks failed, and the Syrian forces withdrew only at the end of the war as part of the truce agreement between the two states. The Iraqi forces retreated too and returned to the Jordanian-occupied West Bank. The Iraqi troops acted in coordination with the Jordanian Army, allowing the Jordanian command to send troops from around Samaria, now held by the Iraqis, to the Israeli-Jordanian battlefield. Iraqi forces departed the West Bank at the end of the war, with Iraq refraining from signing a truce agreement with Israel.

In this initial stage, the Israelis were concentrated along the road to Jerusalem. Both the Jordanians and the Israelis completely misread the other's intentions. The Israelis assumed that the Arab Legion planned to invade Israel, and the Jordanians feared that the Israelis intended to drive the Arab Legion from the West Bank.

In fact, all the Israelis sought was to bring the Jewish part of Jerusalem under Israeli control and, toward that end, to gain control over the road from the coast to Jerusalem. The Israelis feared that the Arab Legion would cut the road to Jerusalem and occupy

Arab fighters pick their way through the rubble of the Tiferet Synagogue on May 21, 1948. Arab demolition squads blasted this structure in the Old City of Jerusalem, which was being used as a fortress by Haganah, the underground Zionist military organization, during the Israeli War of Independence. (AP/Wide World Photos)

all of Jerusalem, and to prevent this they reinforced Jerusalem. The Jordanians interpreted the dispatch of Israeli troops to Jerusalem as an attempt to build up a force to take the offensive against them. This mutual misunderstanding was the cause of the fierce fighting between Israeli and Jordanian forces that ended with the Jordanians repulsing the Israeli troops and holding on to bases in the Latrun area, the strategic site along the Tel Aviv–Jerusalem road.

Israeli-Jordanian fighting ended when the Israeli government acknowledged its inability to drive out Jordanian forces who blocked the road to Jerusalem and when the two governments realized that the other posed no risk. In November 1948 Jewish and Jordanian military commanders in Jerusalem concluded an agreement that formalized the positions established with the de facto cease-fire of the previous July.

With the end of the fighting with Jordan, the Israelis launched the final phase of the war. In a two-stage operation in October and December 1948, the Israeli Army drove the Egyptian forces from the Negev. The Israeli effort to force out the Egyptians along the coast was only partially successful, however. The Egyptians

remained in the Gaza Strip. Indeed, the Gaza Strip remained under Egyptian control until 1967.

Concurrent with the October operations in the south, other Israeli troops stormed the high ground in central Galilee, controlled by the Arab League's Arab Liberation Army. After brief fighting, the Israelis occupied all of Galilee. In early January 1949 a cease-fire came into effect, and shortly thereafter negotiations on armistice agreements began.

The second major confrontation between Israel and the Arabs was the Sinai War, or Suez Crisis, of October 1956. This time, France, Britain, Israel, and Egypt were involved in the fighting. The Israeli-Egyptian portion of the war, which in Israel was known as Operation KADESH, was part of a larger picture. During 1949–1956, there was constant unrest along the Israeli-Egyptian demarcation line as well as between Israel and Jordan. Infiltrators regularly crossed the border from the Egyptian-controlled Gaza Strip, from the Sinai, and from the West Bank. Some were Palestinian refugees seeking to return to their homes or to visit relatives who remained inside Israel, some hoped to harvest their fields on the Israeli side of the border, some came to steal, and a few went to launch terrorist attacks against Israeli targets.

These infiltrations had an enormous impact on Israel. Economic damage mounted, and border-area residents, many of them newly arrived immigrants, were unprepared for the challenge. Israel feared the political implications of the infiltrations, as estimates of their numbers were thousands per month. Consequently, Israeli security forces undertook harsh measures against the infiltrators, regardless of the motives for crossing the border. Israeli soldiers often ambushed infiltrators, killing them and launching reprisal attacks. As a result, tensions along the Israeli borders increased, chiefly along the frontiers with Jordan and Egypt.

While the cross-border tensions provided the background context, the war occurred for two main reasons. First, Egyptian president Gamal Abdel Nasser had absorbed a large number of Palestinian refugees into Egypt and was responsible in a legal sense for those in the Gaza Strip. Rather than allowing the Palestinians free rein to attack Israel, he sought to simultaneously support their cause yet limit the Israeli response to their actions in unspoken rules of engagement, which the Israelis hoped to overturn. Nasser was a fervent Arab nationalist who also aspired to lead and unite the Arab world, a potentiality that deeply troubled Prime Minister Ben-Gurion. Ben-Gurion attributed the Arab defeat in 1948 to a great extent to their divisions. Thus, he was fearful of a unified Arab world under Nasser's leadership. The third immediate reason for the war was the Egyptian-Soviet arms arrangement (normally referred to as the Czech Arms Deal), announced in September 1955. The agreement assured Nasser of the modern weapons that Ben-Gurion was certain Nasser intended to use in an all-out attack against Israel.

Israeli fears were mitigated by an Israeli-French arms agreement completed in June 1956 one month before Nasser nationalized the Suez Canal on July 26, provoking an acute international crisis that culminated with the 1956 war. Shortly after the beginning of the crisis, France invited Israel to take part in planning a joint military attack on Egypt.

For Israel, while there was no specific reason for such an offensive move, fear of Nasser's intentions seemed sufficient justification. Tensions between Israel and Egypt since 1949, and especially since 1954, had significantly diminished. In the summer of 1956 exchanges of fire along the armistice line had largely ceased. More importantly, Nasser, expecting a fierce Anglo-French reaction to the nationalization of the Suez Canal, reduced the Egyptian troop deployment along the Israeli-Egyptian border to reinforce the Suez Canal.

While Egypt had blockaded the Strait of Tiran, closing it to Israeli ships, that by itself could not be reason for war, as there was no Israeli commercial maritime transportation along that route. Nevertheless, Ben-Gurion feared that Nasser was planning to unite the Arab world against Israel, and thus the invitation from two major powers to take part in a combined military effort was too much to resist. In a meeting at Svres, France, during October

22–25, 1956, French, British, and Israeli negotiators worked out the details of the war.

According to the plan that was worked out, Israeli parachutists would land a few miles east of Suez. France and Britain would then issue an ultimatum to both parties to remove their military forces from the canal. Expecting an Egyptian refusal, French and British forces would then invade Egypt to enforce the ultimatum. In the meantime, Israeli forces would storm the Sinai peninsula. Their goal was to join up with the parachutists in the heart of the Sinai and to open the Strait of Tiran.

Israel deployed the 7th Armored Brigade, with two tank battalions; the 27th and 37th Mechanized brigades; the 202nd Parachute Brigade; and the 1st, 4th, 9th, 10th, 11th, and 12th Infantry brigades. The agreement with the British and French was the determining factor in the Israeli plan of attack. Instead of storming the Egyptian positions in front of them, a paratroop battalion was dropped on October 29, 1956, at the eastern gates of the Mitla Pass, some 30 miles east of the Suez Canal. Simultaneously, the paratroop brigade, commanded by Lieutenant Colonel Ariel Sharon, moved into the Sinai to join with the battalion waiting deep in the Sinai. The other Israeli forces had to wait until the Anglo-French attack on Egypt began.

Israeli commanders in the field were unaware of the agreement with the British and the French. Fearing for the parachute brigade and seeking a resolute and decisive victory over Egyptian forces, Major General Assaf Simhoni, commander of the southern command, ordered his forces to move ahead, with the armored brigade leading. The armored brigade stormed the Egyptian positions, with the remainder of the forces ensuring the defeat of the Egyptians. Israeli forces completed the occupation of the Sinai and the Gaza Strip within three days. During the fighting nearly 170 Israeli soldiers were killed, and 700 were wounded. The Egyptians suffered thousands of deaths, far more wounded, and more than 5,500 taken prisoner.

Israel did not enjoy for long the territorial achievements it gained in the war. Under enormous pressure from the United States and the Soviet Union, Israel was forced to remove its forces from the Sinai and the Gaza Strip. However, the terms of the Israeli evacuation of the Sinai aimed to provide it with the security it was lacking: UN observers were deployed along the armistice demarcation lines to ensure that they would not be crossed by infiltrators. One result of the stationing of UN forces was the nearly complete cessation of infiltration from the Gaza Strip to Israel. It was also agreed that the Sinai would be demilitarized, removing with that the threat of an Egyptian surprise attack against Israel. The Dwight D. Eisenhower administration provided assurances that it would no longer allow closure of the Strait of Tiran. Finally, the performance of Israeli forces in the war marked a dramatic change in the history of the Israel Defense Forces (IDF). The IDF went from being an unsophisticated infantry-based army to an efficient, modernized, and mechanized military force. The lessons of the Sinai War certainly paved the

Yugoslav troops of the United Nations Emergency Forces (UNEF) on patrol at El Arish, Egypt, in 1957. UNEF was established following the 1956 Suez Crisis to oversee the withdrawal of foreign forces. (Corel)

way toward the Israelis' impressive achievement in the Six-Day War of June 6–11, 1967.

While the immediate cause of the Six-Day War may be unclear, the long-term catalysts are more obvious. On May 15, 1967, Nasser sent his army into the Sinai. This set the stage for a dramatic three weeks that culminated in an Israeli attack and the total defeat of Egyptian, Jordanian, and Syrian forces. It also resulted in the loss of territories by these three Arab countries.

Tensions along the Israeli-Syrian and Israeli-Jordanian borders formed the long-term cause of the war. There were three issues of contention. The first was the Israeli-Syrian struggle over the sovereignty of several pieces of land along their mutual border. According to the Israeli-Syrian armistice agreements, these areas were demilitarized. The Syrians insisted that sovereignty of the areas was undecided, while the Israelis believed that because the areas were on their side of the international border, they were under Israeli sovereignty. Consequently, Israel insisted that it had the right to cultivate the controversial pieces of land, to Syria's dismay. In a number of instances the Syrians tried, by armed force, to prevent Israeli settlers from farming the land. The second point of controversy lay in Syrian attempts to prevent Israel from diverting water from the Jordan River. Encouraged by the Arab League, the Syrians had tried since 1964 to divert the headwaters of the Jordan River inside Syria. Israel reacted fiercely to this, and until

the Syrians finally abandoned the project, many clashes took place between the two nations' armed forces. The third issue was the continuing grievances of the Palestinians. Their desire to regain their land and find a solution for their displaced refugees was an ever-present theme in the politics of the neighboring Arab states and the Palestinian refugee community.

During 1957–1964 Palestinian engineer and nationalist Yasser Arafat established Fatah, a political organization dedicated to liberating Palestine within the rubric of the Palestine Liberation Organization (PLO), also established in that year by the Arab League to provide a political representative body for the Palestinians. Over the next few years other militant, political, and representative Palestinian organizations were established. In January 1965 Fatah planted a bomb near an Israeli water-pumping station. The Israelis defused the bomb, but Fatah celebrated this as the first Palestinian terrorist attack. Palestinian attacks continued throughout 1965, 1966, and 1967. Despite the relatively low scale of the attacks, Israel responded aggressively, blaming Jordan for funding the terrorists and Syria for harboring and encouraging them.

The extent and ferocity of Israeli-Syrian clashes increased during 1967, culminating in an aerial battle between Israeli and Syrian forces that took place in April 1967. Israeli pilots shot down six Syrian planes during one of the dogfights. In the course of a public address, IDF chief of staff Lieutenant General Yitzhak Rabin threatened war against Syria.

A month later, in May 1967, Nasser ordered his forces into the Sinai. The reasons for this action are in dispute. The common assumption is that Moscow warned both the Egyptian and Syrian governments that Israel was massing military forces along the Israeli-Syrian border and planning to attack Syria. Because Egypt and Syria were bound by a military pact signed on November 4, 1966, Nasser sent his army into the Sinai to force the Israelis to dilute their forces in the north and to forestall what he assumed was an imminent attack on Syria.

The Israelis responded to the entry of Egyptian forces into the Sinai with the calling up of IDF reserve forces. Nasser subsequently increased Israeli concerns when he ordered the UN observers along the Israeli-Egyptian border to concentrate in one location. UN secretary-general U Thant responded by pulling UN forces out of the Sinai altogether. Next, Nasser again closed the Strait of Tiran, yet another violation of the agreements that had led to the Israeli withdrawal from the Sinai in 1957. Besides that, Jordan and Egypt signed a military pact on May 30, 1967. This further increased the Israeli sense of siege.

Israeli military doctrine called for preemptive strikes in case of a concentration of Arab forces along its borders. All that was

necessary was U.S. permission, and the Lyndon B. Johnson administration gave that in early June. The war began at dawn on June 5, 1967, with preemptive Israeli air strikes on Egyptian and then Syrian, Jordanian, and Iraqi air bases. The purpose of the attack was to neutralize the Arab air forces and remove the threat of air strikes on Israel. This would also, at a later stage, allow the Israeli Air Force to provide close air support to its forces on the ground.

Catching the vast bulk of the Egyptian aircraft on the ground as their pilots were at breakfast, some 250 Israeli aircraft destroyed the backbone of the Arab air forces within an hour, and by the end of the day they had been almost completely wiped out. More than 300 of a total of 420 Egyptian combat aircraft were destroyed that day. The Israelis then turned to destroy the far smaller Jordanian and Syrian air forces.

About an hour after the start of the air raids against Egypt, at about 8:30 a.m. Israeli time, the IDF launched its ground offensive. Three Israeli divisions attacked Egyptian forces in the Sinai and within four days had destroyed the Egyptian army in the Sinai and occupied the Peninsula.

Israeli operational plans were initially restricted to the Egyptian front. The IDF high command had developed plans to take the fighting to the Jordanian and Syrian fronts, but on the morning of June 5 it had no wish to go to war with these two Arab states.

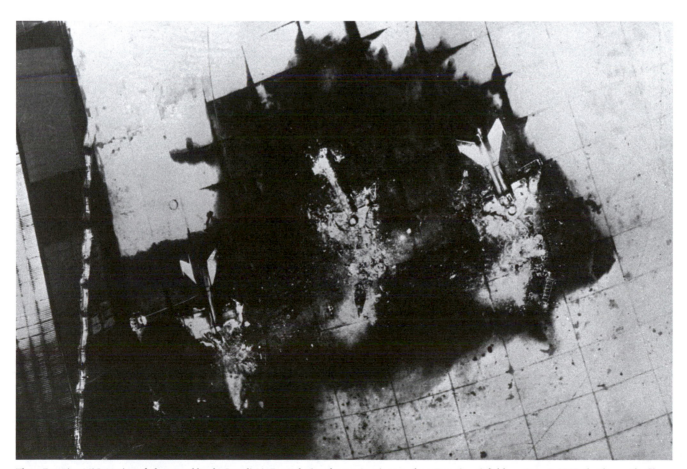

Three Egyptian MiG-21 aircraft destroyed by the Israeli Air Force during the preemptive attack on Egyptian airfields on June 5, 1967, that began the Six-Day War. (Israeli Government Press Office)

There were, however, unexpected developments. As the Israeli troops stormed into the Sinai, Jordanian artillery shelled the suburbs of Jerusalem and other targets in Israel. The Israeli government hoped that Jordan's King Hussein would stay out of the fray and refrain from engaging in serious fighting. That did not happen. Jordanian troops stormed the UN headquarters in Jerusalem, inducing fears that the next step would be an attempt to take over Israeli-held Mount Scopus, an enclave within eastern Jerusalem, a Jordanian-held territory. To prevent that, Israeli forces moved ahead to secure a road to Mount Scopus, and the Jerusalem area became a battlefield. In addition, Israeli troops moved into the northern West Bank, from which long-range Jordanian artillery was shelling Israeli seaside cities. A full-fledged war was now in progress that lasted two days and ended with the complete Israeli victory over Jordanian forces. Israel then occupied the West Bank and eastern Jerusalem.

In the north, Syrian forces began to move westward toward the Israeli border but did not complete the deployment and, for unknown reasons, returned to their bases. For five long days the Syrians shelled Israeli settlements from the Golan Heights overlooking the Jordan River Valley. Hoping to avoid a three-front war, the Israelis took no action against the Syrians, despite the heavy pressure imposed on them by the settlers who had come under Syrian artillery fire. It was only in the last day of the war, with the fighting in the south and center firmly under control, that Israeli troops stormed the Golan Heights, taking it after only a few hours of fighting.

The end of the war saw a new Middle East in which Israel controlled an area three times as large as its pre-1967 territory. It had also firmly established itself as a major regional power. Israel also found itself in control of nearly 2 million Arabs in the West Bank, many of whom were refugees from the 1948–1949 war. The 1967 Six-Day War, known as the Naksa in the Arab world, was considered an utter defeat not only for the Arab armies but also for the principles of secular Arab nationalism as embodied in their governments. The defeat led to a religious revival.

Militarily, the 1967 Six-Day War marked a major military departure. First, it was a full-fledged armor war in which both sides, but chiefly the Egyptians and Israelis, deployed hundreds of tanks. Second, Cold War imperatives were clearly evident on the battlefield, with Israel equipped with sophisticated Western weapons and enjoying the full political support of the United States, while the Egyptians and the Syrians had the military and political support of the Soviet Union.

The next major Arab-Israeli conflict occurred six years later: the 1973 Yom Kippur War, also known as the War of Atonement and the Ramadan War. The years between 1967 and 1973 were not peaceful ones in the Middle East. Nasser refused to accept the results of the Six-Day War and rejected Israeli terms for negotiations of direct peace talks that would end in a peace agreement in return for giving up the Sinai. The Jordanians and the Syrians, as well as the rest of the Arab world, also rejected Israel's terms, instead demanding compliance with UN Resolution 242

(November 22, 1967) that called for the "withdrawal of Israeli armed forces from territories occupied in the recent conflict" and the "termination of all claims or states of belligerency and respect for and acknowledgement of the sovereignty, territorial integrity, and political independence of every state in the area."

UN Resolution 242 became the main reference for any agreement in the region, but it has never been enforced. The Israelis argue that it called for the withdrawal of Israeli armed forces from "territories occupied" and not from "the territories occupied," and thus it need not return to all the pre–June 6, 1967, lines as the UN has instead argued. Tel Aviv held that this was a matter for discussion with the Arab states involved. In addition, the resolution was not tied to any demand for the parties to begin direct peace talks, as Israel consistently required. The result was stalemate.

Israel launched settlement endeavors and placed Jewish settlers in the occupied territories, seeking to perpetuate with that its hold on the territories, while the Arab side again resorted to violence. The first to endorse violence were the Palestinians. Disappointed by the Arab defeat and because of the stances of various Arab governments, some of the Palestinians changed their strategy, declaring a revolution or people's movement in 1968–1969. Prior to 1967 they had used terror attacks as a trigger that might provoke war, which they hoped would end in an Arab victory. Now they decided to take their fate into their own hands and launch their own war of liberation against what they called the Zionist entity. The result was a sharp increase in the extent and ferocity of Palestinian terrorist attacks on Israel and in increasing tensions between the Arab states and the Palestinians.

In 1968 the Palestinians internationalized their struggle by launching terrorist attacks against Israeli and Jewish targets all over the world. Nasser now also decided to take a path of aggression. Frustrated by his inability to bring about a change in Israel's position, he began a campaign under the slogan of "What was taken by force would be returned by force." Following low-level skirmishes along the Suez Canal and adjoining areas, from June 1968 Egyptian forces began shelling and raiding Israeli troop deployments across the canal. The Israelis responded with artillery fire and retaliatory attacks. The violence escalated as Israel struck deep inside Egypt with its air force. Before long, this mid-level-intensity conflict became known as the War of Attrition and continued until 1970.

With the growing intensity of Israeli air attacks on Egypt, pilots from the Soviet Union took an active part in the defense of Egypt. The increased involvement of the Soviet military in the conflict deeply worried both the Israelis and the United States. Through the mediation of U.S. secretary of state William Rogers, a cease-fire agreement was concluded in August 1970, and the fighting subsided. However, shortly after the signing of the agreement, the Egyptians began placing surface-to-air (SAM) batteries throughout the Suez Canal area.

During 1970–1973, Rogers and UN mediator Gunnar Jarring introduced peace plans that were rejected by both the Israelis and the Egyptians. Following Nasser's death in September 1970, his successor, Anwar Sadat, was determined to change the status quo. Toward that end, he acted on two fronts: he called for a gradual settlement that would lead to Israeli withdrawal from the Sinai without a full peace agreement, and he expelled the Soviet advisers brought in by Nasser and resumed negotiations with the United States, which Nasser had ended in 1955.

The failure of Sadat's diplomatic efforts in 1971 led him to begin planning a military operation that would break the political stalemate along the Israeli-Egyptian front. Sadat believed that even a minor Egyptian military success would change the military equilibrium and force a political settlement that would lead to a final settlement. In devising his plan, he carefully calculated Israeli and Egyptian strengths and weaknesses. He believed that Israel's strength lay in its air force and armored divisions, well trained for the conduct of maneuver warfare. Egyptian strengths were the ability to build a strong defense line and the new SAM batteries deployed all along the canal area and deep within Egypt. Sadat hoped to paralyze the Israeli Air Force with the SAMs and hoped to counter the Israelis' advantage in maneuver warfare by forcing them to attack well-fortified and well-defended Egyptian strongholds.

In an attempt to dilute the Israeli military forces on the Sinai front, Sadat brought in Syria. A coordinated surprise attack on both the Syrian and Egyptian fronts would place maximum stress on the IDF. But above anything else, the key to the plan's success lay in its secrecy. Were Israel to suspect that an attack was imminent, it would undoubtedly launch a preventive attack, as in 1967. This part of the plan was successful.

Israeli ignorance of effective deceptive measures undertaken by Egypt contributed to Israel's failure to comprehend what was happening. One deception consisted of repeated Egyptian drills along the canal that simulated a possible crossing. The Israelis thus became accustomed to large Egyptian troop concentrations at the canal and interpreted Egyptian preparations for the actual crossings as just another drill. Even the Egyptian soldiers were told that it was simply a drill. Only when the actual crossing was occurring were they informed of its true nature. Even with the actual attack, however, the real intent of Egyptian and Syrian forces remained unclear to the Israelis, and they initially refrained from action.

Beginning at 2:00 p.m. on October 6, 1973, Egyptian and Syrian artillery and aircraft, and later their ground forces, launched major attacks along the Suez Canal and the Golan Heights. On the Israeli-Egyptian front, Egypt amassed a force of nearly 800,000 soldiers, 2,200 tanks, 2,300 artillery pieces, 150 SAM batteries, and 550 aircraft. Egypt deployed along the canal five infantry divisions with accompanying armored elements supported by additional infantry and armored independent brigades. This force was backed by three mechanized divisions and two armored divisions. Opposing this force on the eastern bank of the Suez Canal was one Israeli division supported by 280 tanks.

This Israeli force was no match for the advancing Egyptian troops. The defenders lacked reinforcements, as reserves were called on duty only after the outbreak of the war. They also did not have air support, as Egyptian SAMs proved to be deadly effective against Israeli aircraft.

The attacking Egyptians got across the canal and swept over the defending Israelis. It took less than 48 hours for the Egyptians to establish a penetration three to five miles deep on the east bank of the Suez Canal. They then fortified the area with more troops. Two divisions held the seized area, which was defended also by the SAM batteries across the canal. With that, the Egyptians had achieved their principal aims and a psychological victory.

The Israelis rushed reinforcements southward and launched a quick counteroffensive on October 8 in an attempt to repel the invading Egyptians troops. Much to Israeli surprise, it was a failure. Undermanned, unorganized, and underequipped Israeli troops—largely a tank force insufficiently supported by infantry and artillery—moved against a far bigger and more well-organized and well-equipped force protected by highly effective handheld antitank missiles. The Egyptians crushed the Israeli counteroffensive.

Following this setback, the Israeli General Staff decided to halt offensive actions on the Suez front and give priority to the fighting in the north on the Golan Heights, where in the first hours of the war little stood between massive numbers of invading Syrian armor and the Jewish settlements. Syria deployed two infantry divisions in the first line and two armored divisions in the second. This force had 1,500 tanks against only two Israeli armored brigades with 170 tanks. The Syrian forces swept the Golan Heights, crushing the small Israeli forces facing them. The few Israeli forces there fought desperately, knowing that they were the only force between the Syrians and numerous settlements. The Israeli forces slowed the Syrians and bought sufficient time for reserves of men and tanks to be brought forward. The Syrians also had an ineffective battle plan, which played to Israeli strengths in maneuver warfare. After seven days of fighting, Israeli troops thwarted the Syrian forces beyond the starting point of the war, across the pre–October 1973 Purple Line, and then drove a wedge into Syrian territory. Only then did the IDF again turn to the Egyptian front, where the goal remained driving Egyptian troops from the Sinai.

Sadat also overruled his ground commander and continued the advance. This took his forces out of their prepared defensive positions and removed them from the effective SAM cover on the other side of the canal, working to the Israeli's advantage. Israeli troops also located a gap between the two Egyptian divisions defending the occupied area that had gone unnoticed by the Egyptian command. Israeli forces drove through the gap and crossed the canal. The IDF hoped to achieve two goals. The first and most immediate goal was to create a SAM-free zone over which Israeli aircraft could maneuver free from the threat of missile attack. The second goal was to cut off Egyptian troops east of the canal from their bases west of the canal. After nearly a week of fighting, the Israelis accomplished almost all of their objectives. Nonetheless, Soviet and U.S.

Israeli troops withdrawing from the Suez Canal area of Egypt in 1974 in accordance with an agreement reached by the United Nations Disengagement Observer Force following the Yom Kippur War. (Corel)

pressure led to a cease-fire before the Israelis could completely cut off the two Egyptian divisions in the east from their bases.

Neither the Soviets nor the Americans wanted to see the Egyptians completely defeated. They also assumed that the Egyptian achievement would allow progress in the political process, just as Sadat had wanted. As a result, the war ended with Israeli and Egyptian forces entangled, the latter on the eastern side of the canal and the former on Egyptian soil.

Syrian president Hafiz al-Asad's chief motivation in joining Sadat in the war against Israel was to recapture the Golan Heights. Asad had no diplomatic goals and no intention of using the war as leverage for a settlement with Israel. The fighting in the north with Syria ended with the IDF positioned only about 25 miles from Damascus, while no Syrian forces remained within Israeli-held territory. It was only in 1974, after a disengagement agreement, that Israeli forces withdrew from Syrian territory beyond the Purple Line.

The 1973 war in effect ended in 1977 when Sadat visited Israel and the consequent 1979 Israeli-Egyptian peace treaty was signed. Turmoil continued, however, chiefly from the unresolved Palestinian problem, which was at the root of the Arab-Israeli conflict. Militant Palestinians refused to recognize the existence of the State of Israel, while Israel refused to treat with the Palestinian leadership. Terrorist attacks against Israel continued, and with a sharp increase in such attacks against the northern settlements

from Lebanon, the Israeli government ordered IDF invasions of southern Lebanon in 1978 and 1982. The first invasion of 1978 was extremely costly in terms of civilian loss of life for the Lebanese, who were unable to mount an armed response to the Israelis. The Israelis also began to involve themselves in the ongoing civil war in Lebanon in order to further their own objectives.

Following increasing Palestinian rocket attacks from southern Lebanon, the Israelis began a large-scale invasion there on June 6, 1982. The stated goals of the operation were halting rocket attacks from that area against northern Israel and eliminating the Palestinian fighters there. Ultimately, Israel committed some 76,000 men and a considerable numbers of tanks, artillery, and aircraft to the operation. Minister of Defense Ariel Sharon and Prime Minister Menachem Begin had more ambitious goals, however. They hoped to also destroy the PLO and other Palestinian resistance in Lebanon altogether and to dismantle its political power. In addition, they sought to force Syria from Lebanon and to influence Lebanese politics.

Begin and Sharon informed the cabinet that their goal was merely to eradicate PLO bases in southern Lebanon and push back PLO and Syrian forces some 25 miles, beyond rocket range of Galilee. Once the operation began, however, Sharon changed the original plan by expanding the mission to incorporate Beirut. Within days, the IDF advanced to the outskirts of Beirut. The PLO merely withdrew ahead of the advancing IDF on West Beirut. Sharon now mounted a broader operation that would force the PLO from Beirut, and for some 10 weeks Israeli artillery shelled West Beirut, killing both PLO members and scores of civilians. Fighting also occurred with Syrian forces in the Bekáa Valley area, but most of this combat was in the air. Not until June 2000 did Israel withdraw all its forces from southern Lebanon.

Israel achieved none of its goals in the invasion of Lebanon except for the eviction of the PLO from Beirut to Tunis and the deaths of many Palestinians and Lebanese. The Lebanese political scene was more turbulent than ever, and the PLO was certainly not eliminated. The Lebanese saw Israel as an implacable enemy, and an even more radical Islamic resistance took up hostilities against Israeli occupying troops and their Lebanese allies. That resistance eventually grew into Hezbollah, backed by Syria and Iran.

In December 1987 Palestinians began a protest movement, now known as the First Intifada, against Israeli rule in an effort to establish a Palestinian homeland through a series of demonstrations, improvised attacks, and riots. This intifada produced widespread destruction and human suffering, yet it also helped strengthen the Palestinian sense of popular will and made

statehood a clear objective. It also cast much of Israeli policy in a negative light, especially with the deaths of Palestinian children, and thus helped rekindle international efforts to resolve the Arab-Israeli conflict. It also helped return the PLO from its Tunisian exile. Finally, it cost the Israeli economy hundreds of millions of dollars. The First Intifada ended in September 1993 with the signing of the historic Oslo Accords and the creation of the Palestinian National Authority (PNA).

Following torturous negotiations, the Israelis and Palestinians reached limited agreement at Oslo in September 1993 in the so-called Declaration of Principles. This eventually led to the establishment of the PNA and limited Palestinian self-rule in the West Bank and the Gaza Strip. Nonetheless, the agreement was not fully implemented, and mutual Palestinian-Israeli violence continued, placing serious obstacles in the path of a general Arab-Israeli peace settlement.

With the advent of rightist Likud Party governments in Israel in the late 1990s, the Israeli-Palestinian peace process was essentially put on hold. Many politicians in Likud—but especially Prime Minister Benjamin Netanyahu—rejected the so-called land-for-peace formula. In the summer of 2000, U.S. president Bill

Waving PLO flags and posters of Yasser Arafat, Palestinian residents of Jericho welcome home neighbors expelled from Israel at the time of the First Intifada in 1993. The First Intifada (literally, "shaking off") was a spontaneous protest movement by Palestinians against Israeli rule and an effort to establish a Palestinian homeland through a series of demonstrations, improvised attacks, and riots against Israeli rule. (Avi Ohayon/Israeli Government Press Office)

Clinton hosted talks at Camp David between Israeli prime minister Ehud Barak and PLO chairman Yasser Arafat in an attempt to jump-start the moribund peace process. After 14 days of intense negotiations, the summit ended in an impasse. The failure of the talks disheartened Clinton in the waning days of his presidency and led to bitter recriminations on both sides that the other had not negotiated in good faith.

Not surprisingly, the Palestinians lost hope in the negotiation process following the failure of the Camp David talks. Their frustration was heightened by their belief that Israel—and not the Palestinian side—had sabotaged the peace process. A new dimension to Palestinian outrage was added when Likud Party chairman Ariel Sharon visited the Temple Mount (Haram al-Sharif) on September 28, 2000. His presence there ignited Palestinian anger that began as a stone-throwing demonstration. Before long, a full-blown Palestinian uprising, known as the Second (Al-Aqsa) Intifada, was under way. The uprising resulted in the deaths of many Israelis and Palestinians.

In recent years, momentous changes within the PLO and the PNA have wrought more uncertainty for both the Palestinians and the Israelis. Arafat's death in November 2004 resulted in a sea change within the Palestinian leadership. Mahmoud Abbas was chosen to succeed Arafat. Like Arafat, Abbas was a member of Fatah. In January 2005 Abbas was elected president of the PNA. In the meantime, terror attacks against Israelis and Israeli interests continued, and Abbas seemed powerless to stop the violence. Just a year after he ascended to the presidency, he suffered a stinging reversal when the Islamist party and organization Hamas won a majority of seats in the January 2006 Palestinian legislative elections. This led to the appointment of a Hamas prime minister. The United States and certain European government entities refused to deal with the Hamas-led government and cut off all funding to the Palestinians. As violence continued to occur and the lack of foreign aid hobbled the PNA, Abbas threatened to call for early elections if Hamas would not submit to a coalition-led government. However, Abbas lacked the authority to do so under the PNA's own guidelines, and he was serving as president only because Hamas wanted a unity government.

With increasing violence that included the kidnapping of an Israeli soldier in Gaza and a cross-border raid mounted by Hezbollah from Lebanon in July 2006 that killed three IDF soldiers and captured two others, the cabinet of Israeli prime minister Ehud Olmert again attacked southern Lebanon as well as Gaza. The fighting along the Israel-Lebanese border raged for 32 days between mid-July and mid-August. The incursion was largely limited to artillery and to air strikes that nonetheless included sections of Beirut and key bridges and lines of communication. Finally, some IDF ground troops were also sent in. Hezbollah responded by launching thousands of rockets into Israel. A great deal of Lebanese infrastructure that had been rebuilt since 1982 was destroyed in the countering Israeli strikes, and Israeli's hopes that it might influence Lebanese politics again proved illusory.

Indeed, Hezbollah, whose ability to launch rockets into northern Israel appeared undiminished despite the strikes, appeared to have strengthened its position in Lebanese politics and also to have gained prestige in the Arab world for seemingly fighting toe-to-toe with the IDF.

In early 2007 and in 2008, there were renewed calls for a concerted effort to jump-start the peace process. Instead, a truce concluded between Israel and the Hamas government in Gaza in June 2008 broke down in November following Israeli assassinations of Hamas leaders in violation of the truce and Israeli's refusal to loosen the economic boycott. In December 2008 Israel launched an offensive against Gaza. This occurred just before the inauguration of new U.S. president Barack Obama and the holding of Israeli elections. The outgoing Olmert government claimed that it had to attack Gaza to control rocket fire into southern Israel, which had killed three civilians. The punishing Israeli attacks left much of the Gaza Strip in ruins, with damages estimated at $2 billion. Egypt has hosted talks between Hamas and Fatah aimed at a national unity government and a possible prisoner exchange with Israel, which demanded the release of hostage Gilad Schalit. Meanwhile, President Obama appointed former senator George Mitchell as U.S. special representative to the Middle East, but it was unclear if negotiations would be a priority for the new rightist Israeli government under Prime Minister Benjamin Netanyahu and Foreign Minister Avigdor Lieberman, who took office on April 1, 2009, and whether efforts at a lasting peace in the Middle East would be any more successful now than in the past.

DAVID TAL AND SPENCER C. TUCKER

See also

Arab League; Arafat, Yasser; Asad, Hafiz al-; Egypt; Hussein ibn Talal, King of Jordan; Israel; Jordan; Lebanon; Nasser, Gamal Abdel; Ottoman Empire; Sadat, Muhammad Anwar; Suez Crisis; Syria; World War I, Impact of; World War II, Impact of

References

Barker, A. J. *Arab-Israeli Wars.* New York: Hippocrene, 1980.

Bell, J. Bowyer. *The Long War: Israel and the Arabs since 1946.* Englewood Cliffs, NJ: Prentice Hall, 1969.

Hammel, Eric. *Six Days in June: How Israeli Won the 1967 Arab-Israeli War.* New York: Scribner, 1992.

Herzog, Chaim. *The Arab-Israeli Wars: War and Peace in the Middle East from the War of Independence to Lebanon.* Westminster, MD: Random House, 1984.

———. *The War of Atonement: October, 1973.* Boston: Little, Brown, 1975.

Oren, Michael B. *Six Days of War: June 1967 and the Making of the Modern Middle East.* Novato, CA: Presidio, 2003.

Taylor, Alan R. *The Superpowers and the Middle East.* Syracuse, NY: Syracuse University Press, 1991.

Arab League

The Arab League, also called the League of Arab States, is a voluntary organization of Arabic-speaking nations. It was founded at

Arab leaders pose during the Arab League Summit in the Sudanese capital of Khartoum, March 26, 2006. (Republic of Lebanon)

the end of World War II with the stated purposes of improving conditions in Arab countries, liberating Arab states still under foreign domination, and preventing the formation of a Jewish state in Palestine.

In 1943 the Egyptian government proposed an organization of Arab states that would facilitate closer relations between the nations without forcing any of them to lose self-rule. Each member would remain a sovereign state, and the organization would not be a union, a federation, or any other sovereign structure. The British government supported this idea in the hopes of securing the Arab nations as allies in the war against Germany.

In 1944 representatives from Egypt, Iraq, Lebanon, Yemen, and Saudi Arabia met in Alexandria, Egypt, and agreed to form a federation. The Arab League was officially founded on March 22, 1945, in Cairo. The founding states were Egypt, Iraq, Lebanon, Saudi Arabia, Transjordan, and Syria. Subsequent members include Libya (1953), Sudan (1956), Tunisia (1958), Morocco (1958), Kuwait (1961), Algeria (1962), South Yemen (1967, now Yemen), Bahrain (1971), Oman (1971), Qatar (1971), the United Arab Emirates (1971), Mauritania (1973), Somalia (1974), Djibouti (1977), and Comoros (1993).

The original goals of the Arab League were to liberate all Arab nations still ruled by foreign countries and to prevent the creation of a Jewish state in Palestine as well as to serve the common good, improve living conditions, and guarantee the hopes of member states. In 1946 Arab League members added to their pact a cultural

treaty under which they agreed to exchange professors, teachers, students, and scholars in order to encourage cultural exchange among member nations and to disseminate Arab culture to their citizens.

The Arab League's pact also stated that all members would collectively represent the Palestinians so long as Palestine was not an independent state. With no Palestinian leader in 1945, the Arab states feared that the British would dominate the area and that Jews would colonize part of Palestine. In response to these fears, the Arab League created the Arab Higher Committee to govern Palestinian Arabs in 1945. This committee was replaced in 1946 by the Arab Higher Executive, which was again reorganized into a new Arab Higher Executive in 1947.

The State of Israel was declared on May 14, 1948. The next day Egypt, Iraq, Lebanon, Saudi Arabia, Syria, and Transjordan responded with a declaration of war on Israel. Yemen also supported the declaration. Secretary-General Abdul Razek Azzam Pasha declared that the Arab League's goal was to conduct a large-scale massacre and extermination. Although King Abdullah of Jordan (he officially changed the name of Transjordan to Jordan in April 1949) claimed to be the legitimate power in Palestine, the Arab League did not wish to see Jordan in control of the area and thus established its own government on behalf of the Palestinians, the All-Palestine State of October 1, 1948. The mufti of Jerusalem, Haj Amin al-Husseini, was its leader, and Jerusalem was its capital. Although ostensibly the new government ruled Gaza, Egypt was the real authority there. In response, Jordan formed a rival

Member States of the Arab League

Date	Countries Admitted
March 1945	Egypt, Iraq, Jordan, Lebanon, Saudi Arabia, Syria, and Yemen
March 1953	Libya
January 1956	Sudan
October 1958	Morocco and Tunisia
July 1961	Kuwait
August 1962	Algeria
June 1971	United Arab Emirates
September 1971	Bahrain, Qatar, and Oman
November 1973	Mauritania
February 1974	Somalia
September 1976	Palestine Liberation Organization
April 1977	Djibouti
November 1993	Union of the Comoros

temporary government, the First Palestinian Congress, that condemned the government in Gaza. The Arab-Israeli War ended in 1949, with Jordan occupying the West Bank and East Jerusalem and Egypt controlling Gaza.

In 1950 the Arab League signed the Joint Defense and Economic Cooperation Treaty, which declared that the members of the league considered an attack on one member country to be an attack on all. The treaty created a permanent military commission and a joint defense council.

During the 1950s, Egypt effectively led the Arab League. In 1952 a military coup in Egypt nominally headed by General Muhammad Naguib overthrew King Faruq, but within two years Colonel Gamal Abdel Nasser assumed rule of the nation. A strong proponent of Arab unity, he called for a union of all Arab nations, including Palestine. Nasser ended the All-Palestine government in Palestine, formed the United Arab Republic with Syria, and called for the defeat of Israel.

In 1956 Nasser nationalized the Suez Canal, precipitating the Suez Crisis that brought an Israeli invasion of the Sinai followed by short-lived British and French invasions of Egypt. U.S. economic and political pressures secured the withdrawal of the invaders. Far from toppling Nasser as the British, French, and Israeli governments had hoped, these pressures both strengthened Nasser's prestige in the Arab world and raised the stature of Pan-Arabism and the Arab League.

In the 1960s the Arab League pushed for the liberation of Palestine, and in 1964 it supported the creation of the Palestine Liberation Organization (PLO), which was dedicated to attacks on Israel. Following the Six-Day War of 1967, which ended in extensive territory losses for Egypt, Jordan, and Syria, the Arab League met at Khartoum that August and issued a statement in which its members vowed not to recognize, negotiate with, or conclude a peace agreement with Israel. Egypt also agreed to withdraw its troops from Yemen.

The Arab League suspended Egypt's membership in 1979 in the wake of President Anwar Sadat's visit to Jerusalem and agreement to the 1978 Camp David Peace Accords. The league also moved its headquarters from Cairo to Tunis. When the PLO declared an independent State of Palestine on November 15, 1988, the Arab League immediately recognized it. Egypt was readmitted to the league in 1989, and the headquarters returned to Cairo.

During the prelude to the 1991 Persian Gulf War the Arab League condemned Iraq's invasion of Kuwait, passing a resolution on August 3 demanding that Iraq withdraw its troops. The league also urged that the crisis be resolved within the organization itself and warned that the failure to do so would invite outside intervention. Although somewhat ambivalent about forcing the Iraqis to withdraw by military force, the Arab League did vote—by the narrowest of margins—to allow Syrian, Egyptian, and Moroccan forces to send troops as part of building an international coalition. In the 1990s the Arab League also continued its efforts to resolve the Israeli-Palestine dispute in the Palestinians' favor.

More recently, in 2003 the Arab League voted to demand the unconditional removal of U.S. and British troops from Iraq. The lone dissenting voice was the tiny nation of Kuwait, which had been liberated by a U.S.-led coalition in the 1991 Persian Gulf War.

AMY HACKNEY BLACKWELL

See also

Egypt; Nasser, Gamal Abdel; Pan-Arabism and Pan-Arabist Thought

References

Hourani, Albert. *A History of the Arab Peoples.* Cambridge: Harvard University Press, 1991.

Smith, Charles D. *Palestine and the Arab-Israeli Conflict: A History with Documents.* 6th ed. New York: Bedford/St. Martin's, 2006.

Toffolo, Chris E., and Peggy Kahn. *The Arab League.* London: Chelsea House, 2008.

Arab Nationalism

Arab nationalism arose as a general response to European imperialism after World War I. Arab nationalism took different forms, from the desire for coordination and cooperation among Arab states to the realization of a single Arab nation, and also stressed unity of purpose among the Arab countries of the Middle East. While respectful of Islam, Arab nationalist movements recognized all Arab peoples, regardless of religion, as belonging to Arab civilization. In some cases, Arab nationalism combined with Arab socialism. Arab nationalism drew heavily upon socialist economic principles and anti-imperialist rhetoric and rejected the West in order to join with the nonaligned Third World bloc, and it also sought to secure Soviet political and military support. Still, Arab leaders sought to avoid domination by the Soviet Union, because their predominantly Muslim populations found communism anathema. Political and military opposition to the State of Israel also served as a focal point of Arab nationalist movements, although repeated Arab military defeats contributed to the decline of Arab nationalism. Nevertheless, Arab nationalist parties or rhetoric continue to play a dominant role in the politics of Syria, Egypt, Libya, Jordan, and, until recently, Iraq.

Arab nationalism has its roots in the late 19th century, when European ideas of nationalism affected the Ottoman Empire. Following World War I, as the British and French acquired mandate authority over various Arab territories of the former Ottoman Empire, Arab nationalist sentiment was divided between unifying notions of Pan-Arabism and individual independence movements. Such thinking contributed to the formation of the Arab League and the growth of numerous groups such as the Society of the Muslim Brothers (Muslim Brotherhood) in Egypt, which sought to organize Egyptian society on an Islamic basis, and the nationalist Étoile Nord-Africaine (North African Star) in Algeria. These and similar groups combined anti-imperialism with strong Islamic identity in their drive for independence from Britain and France.

In the years following World War II most Arab states had gained partial or full independence yet were ruled by governments sympathetic to the interests of the European powers. Political crises in the late 1940s and 1950s, including the Arab defeat in the first war with Israel (1948–1949), resulted in the overthrow of many of these governments and the establishment of new regimes that challenged the West, particularly in Egypt, Syria, and Iraq. These nations lay at the heart of the Arab nationalist movement during the Cold War. Ongoing conflict with Israel would play a major role in efforts toward Arab unity. The common Israeli enemy provided the Arab states with a greater cause that overshadowed their individual differences.

Opposition to Israel and support for Palestinian refugees also served to link the resources of the newly wealthy oil states of the Persian Gulf to the larger Arab cause. Finally, the conflict with Israel, combined with the importance of petroleum resources, made the Middle East a region of great strategic interest to the United States and the Soviet Union, and the two superpowers would have a substantial effect on the development and destiny of Arab nationalism.

Arab nationalism after World War II stressed Arab unity. It included experiments with unions of states, as in Egypt's union with Syria in the United Arab Republic. This effort and Egyptian sponsorship of republican forces in Yemen were part of a regional Arab Cold War between monarchies and more Western-oriented governments such as that of Lebanon and governments such as Egypt, Syria and Iraq. In addition, Arab nationalist movements fit into a broader picture of postcolonial political ideologies popular in the developing world. Such ideologies stressed national or cultural identity, along with Marxist, socialist, or merely populist ideas, as a counter to Western influence.

The two most important Arab nationalist movements that took root were Baathism and Nasserism. The Baath (or Resurrection) Party became prominent in Syria after World War II. One of its founders, Michel Aflaq, a Syrian Christian, conceived of a single Arab nation embracing all the Arab states and recapturing the glory of the Arabian past. This movement traced the sources of the Arab nation in history, civilization, and language. The policies of the two Baathist states, Iraq and Syria, incorporated Arab socialism to overthrow the power and holdings of the existing elites, support large and fairly poor populations, and enact protectionist and state-centered policies in order to exert more control. The Baath Party increased in influence in Syria and Iraq throughout the late 1950s and early 1960s but dominated politics from the end of the 1970s to 2003. In Syria, it came to control the country's turbulent politics by the early 1960s and continued to do so throughout the regime of Hafiz al-Asad and his son, Bashar al-Asad.

Nasserism reflected the agenda and the political prowess of Gamal Abdel Nasser, Egypt's leader during 1952–1970. Raised amid British domination in Egypt, Nasser combined his rejection of imperialist influence with Arab nationalism and socialist principles. Nasser stressed modernization, state ownership of industry, and the unity of the Arab people. He secured U.S. support for his ambitious economic project, the construction of a high dam at Aswan, but an arms deal with Czechoslovakia caused the United States to renege on the deal. Nasser then decided to secure the funds by nationalizing the Suez Canal. This brought a military intervention by British, French, and Israeli forces. Although Nasser survived the ensuing Suez Crisis, it resulted in a deep suspicion of the West.

Nasser also turned to state socialism in the Egyptian economy. While accepting Soviet military aid after 1955, he nonetheless avoided subservience to Moscow and supported the Non-Aligned Movement among developing nations. Considered the embodiment of the Arab unity movement, Nasser had supporters in many Arab countries. The short-lived union of Egypt and Syria in the United Arab Republic (1958–1961) illustrated his nationalist vision and the overlap of Nasserist and Baathist ideologies.

Israel, of course, served as a focal point for Nasser's brand of Arab nationalism; he viewed the defeat of Israel (never achieved) as a priority for the Arab nation and a rejection of imperialist interference in the Middle East. In addition, Egyptian leadership in the struggle with Israel contributed to his stature in the Arab world as a whole. Egypt's attempted military intervention in Yemen (1962–1967), however, brought Nasser's vision of Arab nationalism into conflict with the royalist Islamic views of Saudi Arabia and demonstrated the limits of his influence. Furthermore, Egypt's disastrous defeat in the Six-Day War with Israel in June 1967 dealt a crippling blow to his power and prestige. Nasser's authority survived the 1967 war, and the overwhelming rejection of his proffered resignation by ordinary Egyptians, who took to the streets, testified to the scope of his popular appeal, but the 1967 defeat ultimately signaled the end of the Nasserist vision of Arab unity. His successor, Anwar Sadat, abandoned some of Nasser's Arab nationalist rhetoric and policies. Sadat took the step—unpopular with Egyptians—of concluding peace with Israel and sought to emphasize Egyptian identity and national goals, although Egyptians continued to favor Arab nationalism in general. Sadat and his successor, Hosni Mubarak, moved Egypt out of the Soviet orbit while forging closer ties to the West, particularly the United States.

ROBERT S. KIELY AND SHERIFA ZUHUR

See also

Aflaq, Michel; Arab-Israeli Conflict, Overview; Arab League; Asad, Bashar al-; Asad, Hafiz al-; Baath Party; Egypt; Hussein, Saddam; Mubarak, Hosni; Muslim Brotherhood; Nasser, Gamal Abdel; Pan-Arabism and Pan-Arabist Thought; Suez Crisis; Syria

References

Dawisha, Adeed. *Arab Nationalism in the 20th Century.* Princeton, NJ: Princeton University Press, 2003.

Hourani, Albert. *A History of the Arab Peoples.* Cambridge: Harvard University Press, 1991.

Arabian Gulf

See Persian Gulf

Arafat, Yasser

Birth Date: August 24, 1929
Death Date: November 11, 2004

Palestinian nationalist, leader of the Palestine Liberation Organization (PLO), and first president of the Palestinian National Authority (PNA) during 1969–2004. Yasser Arafat was born Muhammad abd al-Rauf al-Qudwa al-Husayni on August 24, 1929. Arafat always stated that he was born in Jerusalem, but Israeli officials began to claim in the 1970s that he was born in Cairo to discredit him.

Arafat's father was a Palestinian Egyptian textile merchant. Neither Arafat nor his siblings were close to their father. His mother, Zahwa, also a Palestinian, was a member of a family that had lived in Jerusalem for generations. She died when Arafat was five years old, and he then lived with his mother's brother in Jerusalem. Arafat vividly remembered British soldiers invading his uncle's house one night, destroying possessions, and beating its residents. When Arafat was nine years old his father brought him back to Cairo, where his older sister raised him.

As a teenager in Cairo, Arafat became involved in smuggling arms to Palestine to aid those struggling against both the British authorities and the Jews living there. He attended the University of Fuad I (later Cairo University) but left to fight in Gaza against Israel in the Israeli War of Independence (1948–1949). When the Arabs lost the war and Israel was firmly established, Arafat was inconsolable. He briefly attended the University of Texas but then returned to Cairo University to study engineering. He spent most of his time with fellow Palestinian students spreading his hopes for a free Palestinian state.

Arafat became president of the Union of Palestinian Students, holding that position from 1952 to 1956. He graduated from college in 1956 and spent a short time working in Egypt. During the 1956 Suez Crisis he served as a second lieutenant in the Egyptian Army. In 1957 he moved to Kuwait, where he worked as an engineer and formed his own contracting company.

In 1957 Arafat founded the Fatah organization, an underground guerrilla group dedicated to the liberation of Palestine. In 1964 he quit his job and moved to Jordan to devote all his energies to the promotion of Palestinian nationhood and to organize raids into Israel. The PLO was founded that same year.

In 1968 the Israel Defense Forces (IDF) attacked Fatah at the small Jordanian village of Karameh. The Palestinians eventually forced the Israelis back, and Arafat's face appeared on the cover of *Time* magazine as the leader of the Palestinian movement. In consequence Palestinians embraced Fatah, and Arafat became a national hero. He was appointed chairman of the PLO the next year and within four years controlled both the military (the Palestine Liberation Army, or PLA) and political branches of the organization.

By 1970, Palestinians had assembled a well-organized unofficial state within Jordan. However, King Hussein of Jordan deemed them a threat to security and sent his army to evict them. Arafat enlisted the aid of Syria, while Jordan called on the United States for assistance. On September 24, 1970, the PLO agreed to a ceasefire and agreed to leave Jordan. Arafat and the fighters fled to Lebanon, where huge numbers of refugees were based. The PLO soon began launching occasional attacks across the Israeli border.

Arafat did not approve of overseas attacks because they gave the PLO a bad image abroad. He publicly dissociated the group from Black September, the organization that killed 11 Israeli athletes at the 1972 Munich Olympics. In 1974 he limited the PLO's attacks to Israel, the Gaza Strip, and the West Bank. Although Israel claimed that Arafat was responsible for the numerous terrorist attacks that occurred within the country during the 1970s, he denied responsibility. In 1974 he spoke before the United Nations (UN) General Assembly as the representative of the Palestinian people and condemned Zionism but offered peace, which won him praise from the international community.

During the Lebanese Civil War, the PLO initially sided with the Lebanese National Front against the Lebanese forces, who were supported by Israel and backed by Defense Minister Ariel Sharon. As such, when Israeli forces invaded southern Lebanon, the PLO ended up fighting against the Israelis and then the Syrian-sponsored Shia militia group Amal. Thousands of Palestinians, many of them civilians, were killed during the struggle, and the PLO was forced to leave Lebanon in 1982 and relocate to Tunisia, where it remained until 1993.

During the 1980s, Iraq and Saudi Arabia donated millions of dollars to Arafat to help him rebuild the PLO. The First Intifada (1987) broke out spontaneously against Israel. The leadership in Tunis was forced to support it, but the Israeli government charged Arafat with planning the uprising. In 1988 Palestinians declared Palestinian statehood at a meeting in Algiers. Arafat then announced that the Palestinians would renounce terrorism and recognize the State of Israel. The Palestinian National Council elected Arafat president of this new unrecognized state in 1989.

Arafat and the Israelis conducted peace negotiations at the Madrid Conference in 1991. Although negotiations were temporarily

From 1969 until his death in November 2004, Yasser Arafat was the leader of the Palestine Liberation Organization (PLO) and the most widely known Palestinian nationalist leader. (AP/Wide World Photos)

set back when the PLO supported Iraq in the 1991 Persian Gulf War, over the next two years the two parties held a number of secret discussions. These negotiations led to the 1993 Oslo Peace Accords in which Israel agreed to Palestinian self-rule in the Gaza Strip and the West Bank. This led to extreme divisions on the Arab and Palestinian side. Syria in particular regarded Arafat's secret negotiations with a dim eye. Arafat also officially recognized the existence of the State of Israel. Despite the condemnation of many Palestinian nationalists who viewed Arafat's moves as a sellout, the peace process appeared to be moving in a positive direction in the mid-1990s. Israeli troops withdrew from the Gaza Strip and Jericho in May 1994. Arafat was elected leader of the new PNA in January 1996 with 88 percent of the vote in elections that were by all accounts free and fair (but with severely limited competition because Hamas and other opposition groups refused to participate).

Later that same year Benjamin Netanyahu of the Likud Party became prime minister of Israel, and the peace process began to

unravel. Netanyahu, a hard-line conservative, condemned terrorism and blamed Palestinians for numerous suicide bombings against Israeli citizens. He also did not trust Arafat, whom he charged was supporting terrorists. Arafat continued negotiations with the Israelis into 2000. That July, with Ehud Barak having replaced Netanyahu as Israeli prime minister, Arafat traveled to the United States to meet with Barak and President Bill Clinton at the Camp David Summit. Despite generous concessions by Barak, Arafat refused to compromise, and a major chance at peace was lost.

When Ariel Sharon sought to assert Israeli authority over the Haram al-Sharif, or Temple Mount, then informally the territory of the PNA, the Second (al-Aqsa) Intifada began. From the beginning of the Second Intifada in September 2000, Arafat came under attack by Israeli forces, which destroyed much of the rebuilt areas of the West Bank and besieged him in his own compound. The Israelis held Arafat responsible for the waves of suicide and other attacks of the intifada. In declining health by 2004, Arafat also faced opposition from a new movement from within Fatah that attacked the considerable corruption in his government.

Flown to France for medical treatment, Arafat died on November 11, 2004, outside Paris, France. The exact circumstances of his death remain unclear, and many Palestinians contend that he was poisoned. Arafat's grave at the governmental compound at Ramallah is an important site for Palestinian nationalists.

AMY HACKNEY BLACKWELL

See also

Fatah; Clinton, William Jefferson; Hamas; Intifada, First; Intifada, Second; Lebanon; Muslim Brotherhood; Palestine Liberation Organization; Pan-Arabism and Pan-Arabist Thought; Terrorism

References

Aburish, Said K. *Arafat: From Defender to Dictator.* New York: Bloomsbury, 1998.

Gowers, Andrew. *Arafat: The Biography.* Rev. ed. London: Virgin Books, 1990.

Hart, Alan. *Arafat: A Political Biography.* Rev. ed. London: Sidgwick and Jackson, 1994.

Said, Edward W. *Peace and Its Discontents: Essays on Palestine in the Middle East Process.* New York: Vintage Books, 1995.

Arens, Moshe
Birth Date: December 27, 1925

Israeli Likud Party politician and diplomat who served as ambassador to the United States (1981–1983), defense minister (1983–1984, 1990–1992, 1999), foreign minister (1988–1990), and minister without portfolio (1984–1988). Moshe Arens was born on December 27, 1925, in Kovno (Kaunas), Lithuania. He immigrated with his family to the United States in 1939. During World War II he served in the U.S. Army Corps of Engineers and represented Betar, the youth organization of Vladimir Jabotinsky's Revisionist Zionism, in North America. Arens earned a bachelor's degree in mechanical engineering in 1947 from the Massachusetts Institute of Technology (MIT) and joined Menachem Begin's Irgun Tsvai Leumi (National Military Organization) at the beginning of the Israeli War of Independence (1948–1949). Afterward, Arens settled in the Mevo Betar area southwest of Jerusalem.

Arens returned to the United States in 1951 to complete a master's degree in aeronautical engineering (1953) and then worked in jet engine development in the United States before returning to Israel in 1957 as an associate professor of aeronautical engineering at the Technion-Israel Institute of Technology in Haifa. He joined Israel Aircraft Industries (IAI) in 1962 and as vice president for engineering was in charge of missile development and the Kfir and Lavi fighter jet projects.

Arens was one of the founding members of Begin's Herut (Freedom) Party in 1948. Herut merged into the conservative coalition Likud Party in 1973. In 1974 Arens was elected as a Likud member to the Knesset (Israeli parliament). Begin became the

prime minister (1977–1983) when Likud won the 1977 elections. Arens voted against the 1978 Camp David Accords but ultimately supported the Israel-Egypt Peace Treaty of 1979 as a fait accompli, notwithstanding his initial opposition to it as giving away too much. Although Arens was denied the position of defense minister in 1980 due in part to his opposition to the Camp David Accords, Begin appointed him Israel's ambassador to the United States, a post Arens held from 1981 to 1983. He served as defense minister from 1983 to 1984 after the Kahan Commission found his predecessor, Ariel Sharon, guilty of negligence in the massacres at Lebanon's Sabra and Shatilla refugee camps in 1982.

Arens served as a minister without portfolio during the national unity coalition under Shimon Peres (1984–1986) and again during the national unity coalition under Yitzhak Shamir (1986–1988). Arens then served as minister of foreign affairs from 1988 to 1990 and as minister of defense from 1990 to 1992.

Although Arens supposedly retired from politics after Likud's 1992 election loss, he wrote *Broken Covenant: American Foreign*

Israeli leader Moshe Arens, shown here during a press conference on April 27, 1999. Arens was Israel's ambassador to the United States (1981–1983), defense minister (1983–1984, 1990–1992, 1999), foreign minister (1988–1990), and minister without portfolio (1984–1988). (U.S. Department of Defense)

Policy and the Crisis between the U.S. and Israel (1994), was one of the chief opponents of the 1998 Wye River Agreement, and unsuccessfully challenged Prime Minister Benjamin Netanyahu, his former Washington ambassadorial assistant, for the leadership of Likud in 1999. Netanyahu, whose appointment as Israel's ambassador to the United Nations (UN) (1984–1988) had been arranged by Arens, appointed him defense minister from January to May 1999. Arens again retired from politics following Likud's loss in May 1999 to Ehud Barak's One Israel Party.

Since his retirement, Arens has served on the International Advisory Board of the Council on Foreign Relations, on the board of governors of the Technion-Israel Institute of Technology (1999–present), and as chairman of the board of governors at the College of Judea and Samaria (1999–present). He remains active in Likud and opposed the Gaza withdrawal of 2005 and Israel's broader disengagement policy with the Palestinian National Authority (PNA), believing Judea and Samaria (the Israeli designation for biblical rights to the West Bank) to be part of Israel. He supports Likud's Rebels faction led by Technion alumnus and Knesset member Dr. Uzi Landau and in the autumn of 2006 supported calls for an official state inquiry into the 2006 Lebanon War, which he termed a "defeat" for Israel.

RICHARD M. EDWARDS

See also

Camp David Accords; Lebanon; Shamir, Yitzhak

References

Arens, Moshe. *Broken Covenant: American Foreign Policy and the Crisis between the U.S. and Israel.* New York: Simon and Schuster, 1995.

Reich, Bernard, and Gershon R. Kieval. *Israel: Land of Tradition and Conflict.* 2nd ed. Boulder, CO: Westview, 1993.

Simon, Merrill. *Moshe Arens: Statesman and Scientist Speaks Out.* Middle Island, NY: Dean Books, 1988.

Arif, Abd al-Salam

Birth Date: 1921
Death Date: April 13, 1966

Iraqi military officer, Baath Party leader, and president of Iraq from 1963 to 1966. Abd al-Salam Arif was born in Baghdad in 1921, the son of a rug and clothing merchant. Arif attended Iraq's military college from 1938 to 1941 and trained for a time with British troops. He sided with the rebels during the pro-Axis rebellion in Iraq in 1941, which prompted a British intervention and occupation that lasted for the remainder of World War II.

In 1942 Arif first met his mentor, Abd al-Karim Qasim, who would go on to overthrow the British-installed Hashemite monarchy in 1958. By 1957, at the insistence of Qasim, Arif was a member of the Free Officers group, which was responsible for the 1958 revolution. Because Arif was an effective speaker and enjoyed more popular support than Qasim, this brought friction between the two men.

With the success of the 1958 Revolution, Arif, a Sunni Muslim, became Iraq's deputy prime minister and deputy supreme commander of the armed forces. Within months, however, Qasim ordered Arif into exile, possibly for his advocacy of Iraq's inclusion in Egyptian president Gamal Abdel Nasser's United Arab Republic of Egypt and Syria, which Qasim did not support. In November 1958 Arif was arrested and summarily sentenced to death, allegedly for trying to have Qasim assassinated. Arif was released from prison in 1961, and two years later he led a revolt that toppled Qasim's regime.

After solidifying his power and taking full charge of the Baath Party, Arif assumed the presidency, a position he held from 1963 to 1966. His power base came mainly from military officers with Pan-Arabist leanings. Arif signed a controversial agreement with Egyptian president Nasser in 1964 that called for the unification of Iraq and Egypt.

In keeping with his Baathist beliefs, Arif instituted a number of social and political reforms that were aimed at modernizing Iraq and were in keeping with Nasser's Pan-Arab visions. Included in these was the wholesale nationalization of Iraqi industries in an attempt to keep Western influence out of Iraq.

The planned unification of Iraq with Egypt was never realized, however, as Iraq went into a steep economic recession. Many Iraqis blamed Arif's aggressive Baathist policies and nationalizations for the downturn. At the same time, Arif was forced to deal with a Kurdish revolt in northern Iraq, the suppression of which was only partially successful.

On April 13, 1966, Arif was killed in a helicopter crash outside Baghdad. Given his unpopularity, some have posited that the accident was a successful assassination by disgruntled army officers and other high-ranking officials. Arif was succeeded in power by his older brother, Abd al-Rahman Arif. For all his mistakes, Abd al-Salam Arif had been a charismatic leader who helped bridge the gap between Iraq's Sunni and Shiite populations so that sectarian strife was kept to a minimum during his tenure in office. Arif's brother was ousted from power in July 1968 by General Ahmad Hassan al-Bakr.

PAUL G. PIERPAOLI JR.

See also

Baath Party; Bakr, Ahmad Hassan al-; Iraq, History of, Pre-1990; Nasser, Gamal Abdel; Pan-Arabism and Pan-Arabist Thought; Qasim, Abd al-Karim

References

Batatu, Hanna. *The Old Social Classes and the Revolutionary Movement of Iraq: A Study of Iraq's Old Landed and Commercial Classes and of Its Communists, Ba'athists, and Free Officers.* Princeton, NJ: Princeton University Press, 1978.

Tripp, Charles. *A History of Iraq.* Cambridge: Cambridge University Press, 2007.

Armenia, Role in Afghanistan and Iraq Wars

Nation located in Transcaucasia and a Soviet republic from 1920 to 1991. Armenia, a landlocked nation with a 2008 population of

2.969 million people, is bordered by Azerbaijan, Iran, Turkey, and Georgia. The land area of Armenia is 11,506 square miles. After Armenia declared its independence from the Soviet Union in August 1991, a brutal conflict broke out between Karabakh Armenians and neighboring Azerbaijan. A cease-fire was finally arranged by Russia in 1994, and despite the fact that Karabakh forces had gained most of the territory they sought, Armenia suffered crippling economic and political dislocations because of the war. A permanent peace deal between Armenia and Azerbaijan has yet to be reached. Armenia's government, a presidential-style parliamentary democracy, has made significant strides toward a fully free-market economy and has made numerous foreign policy overtures toward the West. Its government has been dominated by four major parties: the Republican Party (conservative), the Prosperous Armenia Party (a probusiness party), the Rule of Law Party (centrist), and the Armenia Revolutionary Federation (socialist-oriented).

Following the September 11, 2001, terrorist attacks on the United States, Armenia offered the United States and its allies the use of Armenian airspace and refueling capabilities during Operation ENDURING FREEDOM. The country did not, however, participate actively in the Afghanistan War.

Armenia was not an enthusiastic supporter of the Anglo-American–led invasion of Iraq in 2003, although it did send a staff contingent to U.S. Central Command in Florida in 2003 to ensure coordination with the coalition. Although this met with considerable domestic opposition, a deployment was undertaken as part of a broader effort by Armenia to improve relations with the United States. Armenian leaders hoped to counterbalance growing ties between Azerbaijan and the United States in light of Azerbaijan's contribution of troops to the U.S.-led coalition in Iraq. In addition, the United States had provided Armenia with approximately $1.5 billion in economic aid between 1991 and 2003, prompting government officials to argue that the deployment would be a sign of appreciation for the assistance.

In 2004 Armenian president Robert Kocharian planned to dispatch a small noncombat force to Iraq as part of the reconstruction and security efforts, but domestic opposition led the government to delay the deployment until January 2005. Armenia ultimately dispatched 46 personnel, including a medical team at Camp Echo, truck drivers on supply runs from Kuwait into the Polish sector, and ordnance disposal experts attached to the Salvadoran contingent. The Armenian forces undertook de-mining missions and conducted humanitarian operations. The troops were deployed in the Shia-dominated towns of Karbala and Hila in Diwaniyah Province and served as part of the Polish-led Multi-National Force in southern Iraq. The Armenian troops served in six-month rotations, and the number of personnel remained constant (a total of 322 Armenians served in Iraq). The mission had to be reauthorized by parliament each year, and the costs of the deployment were paid for by the United States. During the deployment, 1 Armenian soldier was wounded by an improvised explosive device (IED).

Approximately 20,000–30,000 ethnic Armenians resided in Iraq, and Armenian political leaders feared that greater participation in the "coalition of the willing" might undermine the community's safety and stability. Armenia agreed to accept approximately 1,000 Iraqi Armenian refugees in exchange for funding aid from the United Nations (UN).

In July 2007 coalition forces turned the security of Diwaniyah over to Iraqi security forces. This development along with the withdrawal of Polish forces from the region led to increased domestic pressure to end the Iraq mission. Meanwhile, during the 2007 parliamentary elections in Armenia, opposition candidates called for the withdrawal of the Armenian contingent in Iraq and argued that the deployment placed the Armenian Iraqi population at greater risk and that the effort to improve relations with the United States was harming the nation's traditional ties with Russia. Although the ruling Republican Party won the balloting, the government announced the withdrawal of Armenian forces, and the contingent left Iraq in October 2008. The Armenian government cited improved Iraqi security as the reason.

TOM LANSFORD

See also

IRAQI FREEDOM, Operation, Coalition Ground Forces; Multi-National Force–Iraq

References

Allawi, Ali A. *The Occupation of Iraq: Winning the War, Losing the Peace.* New Haven, CT: Yale University Press, 2007.

Cockburn, Patrick. *The Occupation: War and Resistance in Iraq.* New York: Verso, 2007.

Armored Warfare, Persian Gulf and Iraq Wars

The U.S. Army's overwhelming success against Soviet-equipped Iraqi divisions during the 1991 Persian Gulf War marked the culmination of a long-developed doctrine of armored warfare, the hallmarks of which were speed, maneuver, and high technology. With a few notable exceptions, U.S. armored doctrine following the 1950–1953 Korean War anticipated set-piece battles to defend the plains of Central Europe from a Soviet incursion. In the 1970s, catalyzed by the effectiveness of wire-guided antitank weapons used during the 1973 Yom Kippur (Ramadan) War and the burgeoning requirement to modernize and compete against new Warsaw Pact tanks, the U.S. armor community prepared to fully modernize its equipment, training, and doctrine. By 1982 the army had fielded the turbine-powered M-1 Abrams main battle tank; established a state-of-the-art desert training facility at Fort Irwin, California; and published the newly developed AirLand Battle Doctrine.

The 1991 Persian Gulf War (Operation DESERT STORM) served as a crucible to test the new doctrine. In particular, AirLand Battle focused on deep-attack offense to extend operational commanders' view of the modern battlefield in both distance and time. It viewed deep attack, the concept of engaging an enemy in close and rear actions simultaneously, as an indispensable requirement in defeating follow-on echelons in Europe. AirLand Battle also focused on the importance of maneuver and close coordination with heavy forces. Armored combined-arms teams became the key instruments of combat power: the M-1 and M-1A1 Abrams main battle tank would be supported by mechanized infantry, self-propelled artillery, and mechanized combat engineers. Additionally, AirLand Battle emphasized the importance of initiative, adapting the German Army principle of Auftragstaktik (mission tactics). Under this principle, American commanders were to continue to press an enemy on the offensive, even in the absence of higher orders, to take advantage of developing tactical situations.

U.S. armor units effectively employed AirLand Battle against the Iraqi Army in 1991. In the opening salvo of the war, an aerial bombing campaign that began in January and lasted more than a month attempted to destroy Iraqi command and control facilities and follow-on echelon forces. Armor units, supported by mechanized infantry, engineers, and coordinated indirect artillery fire, decisively destroyed Iraqi units during four days of offensive operations in February 1991. Massed coalition units conducted a frontal attack across the eastern edge of the Iraq-Saudi border while heavy elements of VII Corps engaged in a deep attack from the west, encircling rear and escaping Iraqi units in a maneuver later nicknamed the "Hail Mary." The M-1A1's advanced thermal targeting systems, capable of destroying targets at long ranges while on the move, provided mass firepower and shock effect.

The Battle of 73 Easting well exemplified armored employment of AirLand Battle concepts in the Persian Gulf War. On February 26, 1991, the 2nd Armored Cavalry Regiment, a reconnaissance element of the U.S. Army VII Corps, had been directed to find and fix elements of the Iraqi Tawakalnah Armored Division and halt at 70 Easting (a Global Positioning System [GPS] coordinate). Eagle Troop of the 2nd Armored Cavalry Regiment, commanded by Captain H. R. McMaster, was comprised primarily of M-1A1 tanks and M3 Bradley Fighting Vehicles. As the force reached 70 Easting during a late afternoon sandstorm and rainstorm, thermal targeting systems allowed it to identify an enemy battalion strong point visible about 1.8 miles away (73 Easting).

Despite earlier orders to hold his force's position, McMaster acted independently, aggressively attacking the Iraqi battalion while maintaining the elements of mass, surprise, and speed. Eagle Troop's tank platoons led the charge, supported by Bradley Fighting Vehicles to the rear. M-1A1 targeting systems decimated the Iraqi force while on the move, fixing and eventually destroying the battalion at 73 Easting. Bradley Fighting Vehicles then cleared dismounted infantry and assisted in holding off a counterattack.

In 1993 the U.S. Army developed a revised doctrine known as Full-Dimensional Operations to anticipate post–Cold War challenges and incorporate lessons learned from the Persian Gulf War. In it, the army attempted to enlarge the doctrinal scope of Air-Land Battle by including a section on operations other than war,

introducing joint terms, and expanding its scope to encapsulate strategic operations. The doctrine acted as the foundational document during peacekeeping operations in Bosnia and Kosovo and during the next eight years of the army's transformation.

As part of the armor community's force modernization, M-1A2 tanks and other vehicles were retrofitted with new digital battle command systems to increase situational awareness on the battlefield. However, the difficulties in deploying Task Force Hawk in the early days of the Kosovo conflict made clear the difficulty of deploying heavy Cold War equipment. Under the leadership of U.S. Army chief of staff General Eric Shinseki, the army established an immediate ready force in Europe and attempted to decrease reliance on tanks by establishing a lighter objective force capable of quick deployment using Stryker wheeled vehicles via Stryker Brigades. Commensurate with these objectives, in 2001 the army published a revised doctrine known as Full-Spectrum Operations, which provided the foundation for rapid deployment in response to global threats, sustained military campaigns, and revealed the growing importance of stability and support operations. This doctrine also anticipated that adaptive enemies would seek asymmetric advantages and attempt to pull troops into urban combat.

Strategic doctrine used during the Iraq War (Operation IRAQI FREEDOM) can be divided into two primary periods: the initial 2003 attack lasting from March 20 to May 1, 2003, and subsequent full-spectrum operations thereafter. While the operational strategy used in the 1991 Persian Gulf War can be described as overwhelming force, the 2003 action constituted overmatching power. Under the touted umbrella of shock and awe, American planners intended to overwhelm Iraqi military and government systems by conducting the main ground and air offensive at the same time rather than preparing objectives with a lengthy preinvasion air campaign. Thus, Iraqis were placed on the horns of a multipronged dilemma, defending against rear and forward attacks while maintaining command and control.

To counter the significantly fewer armored vehicles and soldiers employed during the 2003 invasion, American commanders increased combat power by augmented use of special operations forces, speed in movement, and electronic reconnaissance to precisely identify and target enemy locations. Rather than seizing and holding the entire theater, coalition units intended initially only to control key terrain and supply lines as armored U.S. Army V Corps units conducted a blitzkrieg-type movement to Baghdad.

Doctrinally, V Corps, commanded by Lieutenant General William Scott Wallace, adhered to conventional AirLand Battle tenets in executing its initial offensive operations in Iraq. Although the total number of coalition troops employed in 2003 was significantly smaller than in 1991, as directed by AirLand Battle principles, helicopter and artillery units engaged the enemy simultaneously in close and rear actions by conducting deep-strike attacks, while combined-arms units conducted offensive operations using fire and maneuver to seize Baghdad. This proven

U.S. Army armor moving into the Shiite neighborhood of Sadr City, Baghdad, Iraq, on May 10, 2004, after a U.S. air strike destroyed the Baghdad office of radical Shiite cleric Muqtada al-Sadr. (AP/Wide World Photos)

conventional doctrine allowed V Corps units to occupy Baghdad and remove the Baathist regime from power in just three weeks.

Under the army's 2001 Full-Spectrum Operations doctrine, coalition forces were capable of transitioning smoothly from combat to stability and support operations. Although army planners realized that the operation's posthostility phase would entail a rolling transition to stability and support operations, the coalition force's numbers were insufficient when compared historically with similar postconflict scenarios, including recent deployments in Bosnia and Kosovo. As sectarian and insurgent violence increased over the ensuing years, coalition troops were forced to counter asymmetric warfare to oppose amplified guerrilla and decentralized attacks. Increasingly, armored units were forced to fight in urban terrain alongside infantry and engineer units.

Actions to quell the 2004 Shia uprisings in Sadr City provide an example of armored employment within the Full-Spectrum Operations doctrine. In this suburban district of Baghdad, U.S. armor units negotiated the gridlike pattern of streets using a box pattern and moved slowly up streets, with weapon systems focused outside of the box. This formation created an artificial set of interior lines, allowing tanks and Bradleys to take advantage of independent thermal viewers to identify targets. Tankers moved with their hatches closed to prevent casualties from enemy sniper fire and removed unnecessary equipment from the top of the tanks to allow Bradleys to kill targets who attempted to climb onto the tanks. As insurgents increasingly used more powerful improvised explosive devices (IEDs) against coalition forces, tanks led the box formation to reduce casualties.

Commensurate with Full-Spectrum Operations, armored units in Iraq faced a wide variety of missions, including route clearance, reconnaissance and surveillance patrols, traffic control points, and raids. To enhance the Abrams' survivability and lethality in urban environments, Tank Urban Survivability Kits were fielded to add reactive armor tiles to counter antiarmor weapons, armored gun shields, and a tank infantry phone to communicate with ground troops. Despite disadvantages in urban terrain, including the Abrams' inability to elevate weapons far enough to fire at upper floors of buildings from close range and their vulnerability to light and medium antiarmor weapons when not supported by light infantry, tanks provided decisive support and protection throughout the spectrum of operations in Iraq.

WILLIAM E. FORK

See also

AirLand Battle Doctrine; Antitank Weapons; Bradley Fighting Vehicle; DESERT STORM, Operation, Ground Operations; IRAQI FREEDOM, Operation, Ground Campaign; M1A1 and M1A2 Abrams Main Battle Tanks; 73 Easting, Battle of; Stryker Brigades

References

Biddle, Stephen. "Victory Misunderstood: What the Gulf War Tells Us about the Future of Conflict." *International Security* 21(2) (Fall 1996): 139–179.

Blackwell, James A. "Professionalism and Army Doctrine: A Losing Battle?" In *The Future of the Army Profession,* edited by Don M. Snider and Lloyd J. Matthews, 325–348. Boston: McGraw-Hill, 2005.

Bourque, Stephen A. "Hundred-Hour Thunderbolt: Armor in the Gulf War." In *Camp Colt to Desert Storm: The History of U.S. Armored Forces,* edited by George F. Hofmann and Donn A. Starry, 497–530. Lexington: University Press of Kentucky, 1999.

Chiarell, Peter, Patrick Michaelis, and Geoffrey Norman. "Armor in Urban Terrain: The Critical Enabler." *Armor* (June–October 2004): 7–9.

DeRosa, John P. J. "Platoons of Action: An Armor Task Force's Response to Full-Spectrum Operations in Iraq." *Armor* (November–December 2005): 7–12.

Fontenot, Gregory, et al. *On Point: The United States Army in Iraqi Freedom.* Annapolis, MD: Naval Institute Press, 2005.

MacGregor, Douglas. *Warrior's Rage: The Great Tank Battle of 73 Easting.* Annapolis, MD: Naval Institute Press, 2009.

Murray, Williamson, and Robert H. Scales Jr. *The Iraq War: A Military History.* Cambridge, MA: Belknap, 2005.

Scales, Robert H. *Certain Victory: The U.S. Army in the Gulf War.* Washington, DC: Brassey's, 1994.

Swain, Richard M. "AirLand Battle." In *Camp Colt to Desert Storm: The History of U.S. Armored Forces,* edited by George F. Hofmann and Donn A. Starry, 360–402. Lexington: University Press of Kentucky, 1999.

Tucker, Terry. "Heavy Armor: The Core of Urban Combat." *Armor* (May–June 2005): 4, 49.

Arms Sales, International

Throughout the 20th century and into the 21st century, various world powers have used arms sales as a means to gain favor and influence in the Middle East. The immense wealth generated by oil sales in the aftermath of World War II accelerated this trend, as the region became one of the most heavily militarized areas of the world and accounted for the largest share of the world's arms trade. Ultimately, the high concentration of weapons heightened tensions and led to arms races between Israel and the Arab states.

During World War II, both the Axis and Allied powers tried to gain allies in the Middle East through military aid and arms sales. In the immediate aftermath of the war, the increasing importance of oil and the geostrategic importance of the area led the United States to grow increasingly involved in the region's security. The 1947 Truman Doctrine signaled a commitment by the United States to provide military aid to states facing communist insurgencies. By 1947, the United States had formal security commitments with regional states including Saudi Arabia, Iran, and Turkey. As the bipolar Cold War struggle progressed, the United States and the Soviet Union used arms sales as a means to secure allies and gain influence. The military conflict in 1948–1949 that accompanied the creation of Israel led that country and its Arab neighbors to seek ever-larger and more sophisticated weaponry.

Throughout the period of the Cold War, the United States and the Soviet Union and other Soviet-sphere countries such as Czechoslovakia were the main arms suppliers to the Middle East. Great Britain and France were also significant sellers, but after their participation, along with Israel, in the abortive 1956 invasion of the Sinai peninsula and the Suez Canal, Arab states led by Egypt boycotted sales from the former colonial powers. Meanwhile, the United States emerged as the main supplier of weapons to Israel and Iran. However, U.S. manufacturers often faced restrictions on arms sales. These constraints included prohibitions on the sale of the most advanced technology and limitations on sales to states likely to use the weapons against Israel. One result was that the Soviet Union came to be the chief supplier of weapons to such frontline states as Egypt and Syria.

In the 1970s, European states—mainly France, Italy, West Germany, and Britain—began to regain market share among the Arab states. In 1975 Egypt, Qatar, Saudi Arabia, and the United Arab Emirates each contributed $260 million to create the Arab Organization for Industrialization (AOI). The main goal of the AOI was to create a Pan-Arab body to coordinate weapons development and purchases as well as arms manufacturing. Arab leaders hoped that the AOI would give Arab states military and technological superiority over Israel. The AOI initiated a number of projects with European states, including Anglo-Arab joint manufacturing of Lynx helicopters and Franco-Arab production of parts for the Mirage and Alphajet aircraft. The AOI ceased to function when Egypt's partners withdrew from the organization in protest of the 1978 Camp David Accords and the 1979 Israel-Egypt Peace Treaty. Nevertheless, European states were able to

Arms Sales to Selected Middle Eastern Countries before and after the Persian Gulf War

Country	Deliveries (in millions of dollars)	
	1987–1990	*1991–1994*
Bahrain	$800	$300
Iran	$7,800	$3,900
Iraq	$16,600	none
Kuwait	$1,300	$2,500
Oman	$200	$300
Qatar	$300	none
Saudi Arabia	$26,300	$27,900
United Arab Emirates	$2,500	$1,300
Yemen	$2,800	$300

take advantage of their contacts and increase their share of the arms market in the Middle East.

U.S. arms sales were further undercut by the 1979 Iranian Revolution. Iran had been one of the top importers of U.S. arms, but after the overthrow of Mohammad Reza Shah Pahlavi, Iran turned to the Soviet Union to purchase arms and weapons. In the 1980s Saudi Arabia and Israel remained the main purchasers of U.S. weaponry. However, even the Saudis began to seek other suppliers during the period. In 1985 domestic supporters of Israel were able to block the sale of McDonnell Douglas F-15 Eagle fighter aircraft and Stinger missiles to Saudi Arabia. In response, the Saudis initiated a series of lucrative arms deals with Britain. The deals began with the 1986 al-Yamamah agreement in which the Saudis purchased $10 billion in arms, including 72 Panavia Tornado aircraft and 60 training aircraft. The al-Yamamah agreement was followed by a Saudi-French deal to purchase helicopters and missiles. The subsequent refusal of the United States to sell the latest version of the M-1 Abrams main battle tank led nations such as the United Arab Emirates to instead purchase French Leclerc main battle tanks.

By 1989, American and Soviet arms sales to the region were roughly equal (at about $2 billion annually), although U.S. sales remained concentrated on Israel, Egypt, and Saudi Arabia. Through the 1980s and 1990s, the United States supplied approximately 60 percent of Saudi arms imports and 90 percent of Israel's imported weapons. Combined West European sales were about two-thirds that of either of the superpowers. Between 1988 and 1991, U.S. sales to the Persian Gulf region alone amounted to $8.1 billion, while Soviet sales were $8.2 billion.

With the end of the Cold War and the collapse of the Soviet Union in 1991, the United States began to dominate arms sales and weapons transfers to the Middle East. Between 1992 and 1995, U.S. sales to the Middle East ballooned to $15.8 billion, while Russian sales were $1.9 billion. Throughout the 1990s, the United States supplied close to 50 percent of the arms and weapons imported into the Middle East. Other suppliers have been China, France, and other states.

The expansion of U.S. sales was mainly the result of the demise of the Soviet Union and the inability of the subsequent Russian arms industry to maintain production and develop new weapons and military technology. In addition, during the 1991 Persian Gulf War, there emerged the perception that U.S. weapons were superior to the Soviet-style weapons used by Iraqi forces. Consequently, many countries in the region, especially the Persian Gulf states, sought to replace Soviet-era weaponry with American-made weapons. Following the war, the United States negotiated large contracts to sell main battle tanks, aircraft, helicopters, and Patriot antimissile systems to Bahrain, Israel, Kuwait, Oman, Saudi Arabia, and the United Arab Emirates. However, restrictions on the sale of certain technology continued to constrain U.S. sales. For instance, the United States sold older M-60A3 main battle tanks to Bahrain and Oman instead of the newer M-1A2 Abrams.

Through the 1990s and early 2000s, the Middle East was one of the world's largest arms markets. During the late 1980s and early 1990s, the Middle East accounted for approximately 25 percent of the world's regional arms imports. Saudi Arabia alone purchased more than $68 billion in arms during the 1990s. Nevertheless, there was a significant decline in regional arms imports. Sanctions that prohibited sales to Iraq and Libya, combined with a diminution in oil revenues, contributed to the decline. In 1987 the region spent $30 billion on imported arms. By 1997, imports to the Middle East had dropped to $19.9 billion. Imports of main battle tanks and artillery pieces declined by half, while orders for aircraft and naval vessels were reduced by about one-third.

A percentage of U.S. arms sales to the Middle East is actually subsidized by the United States. For instance, between 1996 and 2003, Israel was the third-largest importer of American arms, with $9.4 billion in imports. However, a large portion of Israel's arms imports are financed through the U.S. Department of Defense's Foreign Military Financing (FMF) program and the U.S. Department of State's Economic Support Funds (ESF) initiative. These programs provide funds or credit to Israel. On average, the FMF provides $1.8 billion and the ESF $1.2 billion each year to support Israeli purchases of U.S. arms. Israel has received some $46 billion in aid to procure American weapons since the late 1970s. Egypt receives approximately $2 billion each year, $1.2 billion from the FMF and $815 million from the ESF. Since 1978, the United States has granted Egypt $38 billion to buy U.S. arms and weapons.

In contrast, wealthy oil nations such as Saudi Arabia do not receive FMF or other U.S. subsidies. Nevertheless, several states have negotiated a series of concessions from the United States or other suppliers. Saudi Arabia generally requires arms agreements to include clauses stipulating that 30–35 percent of the value of the contract has to be returned to the Saudi economy. This is usually accomplished through licenses that allow local manufacture of parts. Other forms of financial offsets include building production sites in recipient nations or licensing technology to the recipient country. In other cases, offsets involve economic investment in areas unrelated to the actual arms imports.

Israel is the only state in the Middle East with a highly developed domestic arms industry and significant arms exports of its own. Israel was able to develop its internal defense industrial base through support from the United States. As such, Israel is the only state that is allowed to use FMF funding to bolster its own arms industry and can use up to 27 percent of FMF funding for its domestic defense industrial base. By 2000, Israel recorded $2 billion in arms exports, which included 48 different countries ranging from Russia to Colombia to Ethiopia (although none to Arab states). Israeli exports of military technology have often placed the country at odds with the United States, especially over exports of sensitive technology to nations such as the People's Republic of China (PRC). In response, the United States has imposed, or threatened to impose, sanctions on the sale of arms to Israel.

American arms sales to the Middle East remain complicated by Washington's alliances with both Israel and other states in the region, including Egypt and Saudi Arabia. Policy makers in Washington often have to balance the sale or transfer of weapons to Arab states with similar sales to Israel and vice versa. For example, in the 1980s the U.S. Congress forbade the export of F-15E fighters to Saudi Arabia after intense lobbying by Israel and pro-Israeli groups. After the 1991 Persian Gulf War the restriction was relaxed, and the United States sold 48 F-15Es to the Saudis. However, in order to maintain Israel's superiority, the Americans sold an even more advanced version of the plane to Israel.

There has also been an expansion of European arms sales in the post–Cold War era. By 1995, the United States was the world's largest arms supplier to the developing world, with $3.8 billion in sales. But collectively, the four major European arms exporters had combined sales of $4 billion. The expansion of Europe's market share occurred as the European states, both individually and collectively, placed fewer restrictions on the sale of new technology. In some cases in which Arab countries were unable to buy the latest U.S. weapons, the same states were able to buy the latest European arms. Several European states have also proved more willing to engage in joint projects and approve offsets whereby some manufacturing or assembly of weapons systems is done in the Arab nations. France and Britain also emerged as leaders in the retrofit market. The two European countries gained highly valuable contracts to modernize aging Soviet equipment or make the weapons compatible with U.S. or Western defense systems. For example, France and Britain both secured contracts to replace the radar systems in Soviet- and Russian-made aircraft.

Iraq was one of the Soviet Union's largest arms importers. However, the end of the Cold War and the subsequent Persian Gulf War led to the cessation of sales to Baghdad. Between 1988 and 1991, Iraq bought $4.1 billion in arms from the Soviet Union. After the Persian Gulf War, United Nations (UN) sanctions meant that Russian sales stopped completely. In addition, Russia had been the main supplier of arms to Yemen. Russia had sold more than $2.1 billion in arms to Yemen in the period from 1988 to 1991, but sales dropped to zero by 1994. Russia did, however, significantly expand arms sales to Iran, but the more lucrative agreements were oil for arms. In 1991 in an agreement worth $10 billion, Russia transferred MiG-29 aircraft, Su-24 fighter-bombers, and SA-5 surface-to-air missiles (SAMs) to Iran in exchange for Iranian oil exports. Later Russian transfers included T-72 main battle tanks and even three Kilo-class diesel submarines.

During the 1990s, Russia regained market share in the Middle East because of the lower cost of its weaponry and the willingness

An Iraqi crew fires the main gun of their Soviet T-72 during a training exercise at the Besmaya Gunnery Range, Camp Besmaya, Iraq, some 25 miles east of Baghdad, on October 28, 2008. (U.S. Department of Defense)

of Moscow to sell all types of arms to almost any country. In 1994 the United Arab Emirates chose Russian personnel carriers over American and Western models because of the lower costs of the Russian vehicles. Russia was also able to gain new contracts with Kuwait, Oman, and the United Arab Emirates during the late 1990s and beyond.

TOM LANSFORD

See also

Arab-Israeli Conflict, Overview; Camp David Accords; Egypt; France, Middle East Policy; Germany, Federal Republic of, Middle East Policy; Iranian Revolution; Iraq, History of, Pre-1990; Iraq, History of, 1990–Present; Jordan; Kuwait; Russia, Middle East Policy, 1991–Present; Saudi Arabia; Soviet Union, Middle East Policy; Syria; United Arab Republic; United Kingdom, Middle East Policy; United States, Middle East Policy, 1917–1945; United States, Middle East Policy, 1945–Present

References

Cornish, Paul. *The Arms Trade and Europe.* London: Pinter, 1995.
Keller, William. *Arm and Arm: The Political Economy of the Global Arms Trade.* New York: Basic Books, 1995.
Krause, Keith. *Arms and the State: Patterns of Military Production and Trade.* New York: Cambridge University Press, 1992.
Laurance, Edward. *The International Arms Trade.* New York: Lexington Books, 1992.
Quandt, William B. *Decade of Decision: American Policy toward the Arab-Israeli Conflict, 1967–1976.* Berkeley: University of California Press, 1977.

Arnett, Peter
Birth Date: November 13, 1934

Acclaimed foreign correspondent and television journalist. Born on November 13, 1934, in Riverton, New Zealand, Peter Arnett left college to become a journalist. Subsequently, he worked for newspapers in New Zealand and Australia. On June 26, 1962, the Associated Press sent Arnett to Saigon. In August of that year, near the Mekong Delta, he first witnessed combat, an experience that led him to question U.S. involvement in the war.

Arnett's coverage of the Vietnam War established him as a high-profile reporter. His commitment to getting the real story, no matter the danger, won him the admiration of his peers and the respect of soldiers. Journalist David Halberstam once remarked that Arnett was the "gutsiest" man he had ever known, labeling him the consummate combat reporter.

Arnett's candor created controversy, however. In 1963 Premier Ngo Dinh Diem, who was upset with Arnett's coverage of the Republic of Vietnam (South Vietnam) government's treatment of Buddhist monks, threatened him with expulsion from the country. On July 23, 1963, members of the South Vietnamese secret police accosted Arnett on a Saigon street and began to beat him; a colleague interceded, saving Arnett from possible serious injury. The Diem regime then demanded that Arnett leave the country; only

after the John F. Kennedy administration intervened on his behalf was he allowed to remain in South Vietnam.

Arnett's forthright style also caused tension with the U.S. military establishment. On several occasions officials attempted to convince him to report a more sanitized version of the war. Because he refused to compromise the accuracy of his stories, Arnett was targeted by the Lyndon B. Johnson administration for surveillance. Military officials also sought to limit his access to combat, but Arnett's many connections with men in the field negated those efforts.

Arnett developed a penchant for covering difficult and revealing stories. In 1966 his dedication earned him a Pulitzer Prize for International Reporting. During the 1968 Tet Offensive, Arnett reported the now-infamous statement of an American officer who said that U.S. forces had to destroy the village of Ben Tre in order to save it. That same year Arnett quoted John Paul Vann, U.S. chief of the civilian pacification program, who opined that the initial U.S. troop withdrawals from Vietnam would consist of "nonessentials." That statement led readers to question the veracity of the Richard M. Nixon administration's promised troop reductions. In 1972 Arnett witnessed the release of the first American prisoners of war in Hanoi, and in 1975 he covered the fall of Saigon to communist forces.

Arnett believes that newsmen do not deserve much of the negative criticism they have received for their coverage of the war. He maintains that journalists merely report events and do not make policy decisions.

In 1981 Peter Arnett joined the Cable News Network (CNN); he was with the network until 1999. During the 1991 Persian Gulf War, Arnett became well known for his "Live from Baghdad" reports. In the opening hours of the war, he was the only Western reporter airing live as air raid sirens blared in the background and bombs exploded in the distance. Later, Arnett's reports on Iraqi civilian casualties from the fighting earned him the enmity of the U.S. military and the White House. One of the most controversial reports was about the bombing by coalition forces of the Abu Ghraib Infant Formula Production Plant. Arnett was insistent that it had produced only baby formula and that it was not associated with the production of biological weapons, as a U.S. Air Force spokesman and later even General Colin Powell claimed. Two weeks after the war began, Arnett conducted an uncensored interview with Iraqi president Saddam Hussein.

In 1994 Arnett published *Live from the Battlefield: From Vietnam to Baghdad, 35 Years in the World's War Zones,* about his wartime reporting. In late March 1997 in eastern Afghanistan, Arnett secured the first-ever television interview with Al Qaeda leader Osama bin Laden. In 1998 CNN fired Arnett under pressure from the U.S. Defense Department over Arnett's claim that the United States had employed Sarin nerve gas on American troops who had defected in Laos during the Vietnam War.

In late 2001 Arnett reported on the Afghanistan War (Operation ENDURING FREEDOM) for HDNet. In 2003, reporting for *National Geographic Explorer* and NBC television, Arnett covered the beginning of the Iraq War (Operation IRAQI FREEDOM). He again sparked controversy by giving an interview to state-controlled Iraqi television, in the course of which he stated, "The first war plan failed because of Iraqi resistance. Now they are trying to write another war plan. Clearly, the American war planners misjudged the determination of Iraqi forces." NBC and National Geographic promptly dismissed him for what they called a gross error in judgment. Less than 24 hours later Arnett was hired as a correspondent for the British tabloid *Daily Mirror,* which had opposed the invasion of Iraq.

DEAN BRUMLEY AND PAUL G. PIERPAOLI JR.

See also

CNN; Powell, Colin Luther; War Correspondents

References

Arnett, Peter. *Live from the Battlefield: From Vietnam to Baghdad, 35 Years in the World's War Zones.* New York: Simon and Schuster, 1994.

Halberstam, David. *The Best and the Brightest.* New York: Penguin, 1983.

Prochnaw, William. "If There's a War, He's There." *New York Times Magazine,* March 3, 1991.

Sheehan, Neil. *A Bright Shining Lie: John Paul Vann and America in Vietnam.* New York: Random House, 1988.

ARROWHEAD RIPPER, **Operation**
Start Date: June 19, 2007
End Date: August 19, 2007

Multi-National Force–Iraq (MNF-I) assault against Al Qaeda in Iraq and other insurgents in and around the Iraqi city of Baquba during June 19–August 19, 2007. Baquba is located about 30 miles northeast of Baghdad. As a result of the Baghdad Security Plan developed in early 2007 and the American troop surge that accompanied it, Al Qaeda in Iraq and other Sunni forces withdrew from some areas of Baghdad and began operating in Diyala Province.

The insurgents, who belonged to the Khalf al-Mutayibin group, established a strong presence in Diyala Province and especially in Baquba, a city of some half million people. They made it the capital of their self-proclaimed "Islamic State of Iraq." Al Qaeda was determined to create havoc for the newly formed government of Iraq and to kill coalition troops attempting to gain control of the province.

On June 19, 2007, 10,000 U.S. soldiers, along with more than 1,000 Iraqi police and Iraqi military personnel, launched ARROWHEAD RIPPER, an operation north of Baghdad to clear the region of Al Qaeda militants. Three U.S. brigades participated in the opening days of ARROWHEAD RIPPER: the 1st Cavalry Division's 3rd Brigade Combat Team, commanded by Colonel David Sutherland; the 2nd Infantry Division's 4th Stryker Brigade Combat Team, commanded by Colonel John Lehr; and the 2nd Infantry Division's 3rd Stryker Brigade Combat Team, commanded by Colonel Steven Townsend.

For security reasons, Iraqi leaders were not included in the initial planning of ARROWHEAD RIPPER, but as the operation progressed, the Iraqi 2nd Brigade and 5th Iraqi Army Division played sizable roles. By the operation's end, the Iraqi 5th Army Division had particularly distinguished itself.

The operation began with a night air assault by Colonel Townsend's 3rd Stryker Brigade Combat Team, which led the effort to clear Baquba. As the operation unfolded, it quickly became apparent that Al Qaeda units, estimated to number more than 1,000 fighters, had dug in to stay. However, news sources reported that the leadership had fled in advance of the operation. In addition to Iraqi security forces (army and police), "concerned citizens" groups—also referred to as Iraqi police volunteers—cooperated with U.S. military personnel and Iraqi security forces in rooting out insurgents. The citizens' movement hoped to restore a measure of peace to the war-torn region. It was instrumental in finding and exposing the safe houses where Al Qaeda militants were hiding.

Fighting was fierce throughout Diyala Province, but especially in Baquba, where Al Qaeda had essentially taken control of the city. Multinational troops, going house to house to capture or kill Al Qaeda insurgents, met heavy resistance in the early stages of the battle. As troops entered neighborhoods, they found schools, businesses, and homes booby-trapped with homemade improvised explosive devices (IEDs). The heaviest fighting during the operation occurred within the first four weeks.

American commanders had always believed that Al Qaeda was its own worst enemy, particularly in the way that it treated the locals. Thus, American leaders had anticipated help from citizens in the province, and when these citizens began to pass information as to the whereabouts of insurgents, it was clear that they were ready for Al Qaeda and its operatives to leave their province.

An important goal of ARROWHEAD RIPPER was to prevent insurgents fleeing Baquba from escaping and reorganizing elsewhere. The attacking forces, therefore, set up a series of blocking posts to the northwest of Baquba in the Khalis corridor and south of the city near Khan Bani Saad to deny insurgents passage through these areas.

Coalition and Iraqi forces also conducted operations to disrupt enemy lines of communication and deny Al Qaeda any areas of safe haven. Following the initial push that cleared Baquba of insurgents, coalition forces began to reposition and destroy Al Qaeda positions northeast of Baquba in the Diyala River Valley. In spite of their attempts to contain Al Qaeda forces inside the area to prevent them from reorganizing elsewhere, many of the insurgents escaped capture and fled.

During the operation, which ended on August 19, the Al Qaeda leader in Baquba was killed, along with more than 100 other insurgents. An additional 424 suspected insurgents were taken prisoner. A total of 129 weapons caches were captured or destroyed and some 250 IEDs were found and rendered inoperable, including 38 booby-trapped houses, which the military refers to as house-borne IEDs, and 12 vehicle-borne IEDs. Coalition casualties included 18 Americans killed and 12 wounded; 7 Iraqi army personnel killed and 15 wounded; 2 allied Iraqi militiamen killed; and 3 Iraqi police killed.

Civilian casualties in the province were not accurately recorded, but an estimated 350 were killed and many more were wounded. However, it was unclear if civilian casualties were a direct result of Multi-National Force–Iraq military actions, or Al Qaeda members simply killing civilians who had helped their enemies.

One reason for the success of the operation was the newly formed Diyala Operations Center, established to coordinate coalition activities in the province. Through it, coalition forces, local police, the Iraqi military, and citizen informants sympathetic to the American military were all linked to one headquarters location. This enabled planners and leaders of the operation to react quickly to any situation, a scenario that the insurgents had not anticipated.

The surge in American troop strength in Iraq combined with operations such as ARROWHEAD RIPPER forced Al Qaeda insurgents out of the cities of the Diyala Valley and broke their ability to sustain day-to-day attacks on coalition troops in the area. Success was also achieved in enabling government ministries to provide fundamental goods and services such as food, fuel, and displaced-persons services to Diyala Province. This enabled the local and national Iraqi governments to show that they could provide for their people and thus raise confidence in government authorities.

The U.S. troop surge begun in early 2007, and operations such as ARROWHEAD RIPPER had great success in the Diyala Valley, with normal life beginning to reemerge by the end of the offensive. Schools, hospitals, and businesses were reopened in the relatively safer environment that came about as a result of the operation.

RANDY J. TAYLOR

See also

Al Qaeda in Iraq; Iraqi Insurgency; Surge, U.S. Troop Deployment, Iraq War

References

Bensahel, Nora. *After Saddam: Prewar Planning and the Occupation of Iraq.* Skokie, IL: RAND Corporation, 2008.

Miller, Debra A. *The Middle East.* Detroit: Greenhaven, 2007.

Radcliffe, Woodrow S. *The Strategic Surge in Iraq: Pretense or Plan for Success?* USAWC Strategy Research Project. Carlisle Barracks, PA: U.S. Army War College, 2007.

Simon, Steven, and Council on Foreign Relations. *After the Surge: The Case for U.S. Military Disengagement from Iraq.* New York: Council on Foreign Relations, 2007.

Simons, G. L. *Iraq Endgame? Surge, Suffering and the Politics of Denial.* London: Politico's, 2008.

Woodward, Bob. *The War Within: A Secret White House History, 2006–2008.* New York: Simon and Schuster, 2008.

Arthur, Stanley
Birth Date: September 27, 1935

U.S. Navy officer who commanded coalition naval forces during Operation DESERT STORM in 1991. Born in San Diego, California, on September 27, 1935, Stanley Arthur entered the U.S. Navy through the NROTC program at Miami University, from which he graduated in 1957. He became a Grumman S-2 Tracker antisubmarine warfare aircraft pilot in 1958, then transitioned to Douglas A-4 Skyhawks in which he flew 513 combat missions over Vietnam and was awarded 11 Distinguished Flying Crosses. Arthur earned a BS degree in aeronautical engineering from the Naval Postgraduate School in 1964, and an MS in administration from George Washington University in 1974.

Promoted to captain in August 1976, Arthur commanded the *San Jose* (AFS-7) during July 1976–December 1977 and the *Coral Sea* (CV-43) during June 1978–December 1979; he then reported to staff duty in Hawaii, where he participated in planning the failed Iranian hostage rescue operation (Operation EAGLE CLAW) of April 24, 1980. A year later, as assistant chief of staff for plans and policy, to Admiral D. C. Davis, commander in chief, U.S. Pacific Fleet (CinCPac), Arthur assumed additional duty as the naval component commander of the Rapid Deployment Joint Task Force in July 1981, just prior to his promotion to rear admiral. When the U.S. Central Command (CENTCOM) was established on January 1, 1983, Rear Admiral Arthur became the first commander U.S. naval forces, Central Command (ComUSNavCent).

With neither Air Force nor Army units based in the region, CENTCOM depended on maritime prepositioning of equipment and supplies at Diego Garcia in the Indian Ocean and on board Military Sealift Command (MSC) ships of the Navy. In time of crisis, the Military Airlift Command (MAC) would fly personnel into the region to "marry up" with the vehicles and equipment landed from the MSC ships. Arthur had primary responsibility for establishing the system that would be activated during Operation DESERT STORM.

Promoted to vice admiral in February 1988, Arthur served as deputy chief of naval operations, logistics (N-4) before succeeding Vice Admiral Henry H. Mauz Jr. as commander of the U.S. Seventh Fleet and ComUSNavCent. He served in this position from December 1990 to July 1995. Viewing his role as a component force commander to be more important than that of a fleet commander, Arthur wished to shift his headquarters from his Seventh Fleet flagship to Central Command headquarters in Riyadh, Saudi Arabia, but feared combat operations for DESERT STORM would begin while the move was underway so put it off. Arthur quickly established more cordial relations with his cocommanders than his predecessor had achieved. Arthur acceded to most of the policies of his Air Force counterpart, Lieutenant General Charles Horner, the joint force air component commander (JFACC), but naval aviation was never fully integrated into the centralized system established to plan air operations in 24-hour units, 72 hours prior to execution.

Arthur considered the system of rigid preplanned detailed air tasking orders (ATOs) a violation of navy doctrine that called for decentralized air planning conducted on board each aircraft carrier, a system Arthur believed superior for reacting rapidly to strike and restrike needs. The requirement of aerial refueling by naval air units stationed on carriers in the Red Sea and northern Arabian Sea led to their closer integration into JFACC ATOs than operations conducted, especially over water, by the four aircraft carriers stationed in the Persian Gulf.

The flow of supplies into the war zone (95 percent of all supplies were delivered by sea), being primarily a navy operation directed from Seventh Fleet headquarters in Hawaii, proceeded without any serious problems.

Amphibious operations in the Persian Gulf were not as smooth. Concerned about Iraqi mines and potential missile attacks from neighboring Iran, Arthur believed that more time was needed for preparations than allotted by theater planning officers. Arthur came into conflict with theater commander General H. Norman Schwarzkopf when Arthur advocated leveling every high-rise building along the beach to protect marines scheduled to land in Kuwait City (Madinat al-Kuwayt). Schwarzkopf rejected such destruction and, with the concurrence of Lieutenant General Walter Boomer, commander of U.S. marines in the region, cancelled the amphibious landing that had been planned to provide logistical support for marine forces advancing along the coast into Kuwait from Saudi Arabia. Instead of an assault landing, the embarked marines carried out a feint designed to fix in place Iraqi coastal defense forces.

Following the successful conclusion of DESERT STORM, Arthur, promoted to admiral in July 1992, served as vice chief of naval operations from July 6, 1992 to April 30, 1995. His nomination to become commander in chief, U.S. Forces, Pacific was blocked by the U.S. Senate, which questioned Arthur's conduct during the investigation of sexual harassment allegations by a female student pilot in the aftermath of the 1991 Tailhook Incident. Many observers believed that Arthur had become a scapegoat and that the chief of naval operations, Admiral Jeremy Boorda, had not adequately supported Arthur, who retired from active duty in June 1995.

Arthur received the Admiral Arleigh A. Burke Leadership Award from the Navy League in 1996 and served as president of Lockheed Martin's Missiles and Fire Control Division from 1999 to 2004.

JAMES C. BRADFORD

See also

DESERT STORM, Operation, Coalition Naval Forces; Horner, Charles; Mauz, Henry H., Jr.; Military Sealift Command; Schwarzkopf, H. Norman, Jr.; United States Navy, Persian Gulf War; Warden, John Ashley, III

References

Kitfield, James. *Prodigal Soldiers: How the Generation of Officers Born of Vietnam Revolutionized the American Style of War.* Washington, DC: Brassey's, 1997.

Marolda, Edward, and Robert Schneller. *Shield and Sword: The United States Navy and the Persian Gulf War.* Annapolis, MD: U.S. Naval Institute Press, 2001.

Pokrant, Marvin. *Desert Shield at Sea: What the Navy Really Did.* Westport, CT: Greenwood, 1999.

Article 22, League of Nations Covenant

Provision in the covenant of the League of Nations, the predecessor agency to the United Nations (UN), passed on June 18, 1919. The League of Nations was a supranational organization formed in the aftermath of the Paris Peace Conference held at the end of World War I. Article 22 of the League of Nations Covenant called for the creation of a mandate system, which transferred the former colonies of Germany and the former territories of the Ottoman Empire to the custody of the League of Nations. Nations or regions falling under a mandate would be administered by a third-party nation upon the approval of the League of Nations. The principles of the mandate system have their legal precedent under the Roman principle of *mandatum,* which placed persons and property under the care of responsible parties. Newer precedents included the 1885 Berlin Conference, which established safeguards for the people of the Congo, and the 1892 Brussels Conference, which banned the import of alcohol and weapons to the Congo. At the convention of St. Germain in 1919, the signatories agreed to commit themselves to the protection and well-being of their colonies.

Under existing international law, colonies were considered to be "wards" under the responsibility of the colonial power. However, the question soon arose regarding to whom the colonial power was responsible. Through Article 22, the League of Nations was the authority that would oversee the conduct of the colonial powers in question. The former colonies and territories of Germany and the Ottoman Empire were distributed among the victorious Allied powers. Britain and France benefited the most by acquiring the majority of these territories as mandates. The British dominions of Australia and New Zealand were given mandates as rewards for their service in the war. In the Middle East proper, Britain gained a mandate over Palestine, while the French administered mandates in Syria and Lebanon.

The mandates were classified as either A, B, or C, according to the political and cultural development of the nations under mandate. The Middle Eastern mandates were classified as A mandates because they were on the brink of independence, and particularly because they had rebelled against the Turks during the war. The mandate powers in question were supposed to guide their mandates in the final steps toward statehood. The B mandates, consisting of the former German colonies in Central Africa, were considered to be at a lower developmental stage than the A mandates, and so it was the responsibility of the mandate powers to oversee their material needs and to prevent abuses such as slavery, exploitation of labor, and the importation of illicit liquor and drugs. They were also to allow access to other nations for trade purposes. The C mandates were deemed to be at the lowest level of development, for whom independence was not considered in the short term. The mandate system differed from old-fashioned colonialism in that the mandatory powers were required to make an annual report to the league. Ironically, Article 22 seemed to fly in the face of President Woodrow Wilson's call for self-determination, but the brainchild of the League of Nations had been forced to compromise to get the organization up and running.

Not surprisingly, problems arose from the creation of the mandate system. The question of whether the league or the mandate power held the final authority continued to bedevil officials throughout the existence of the mandate system. Also, international law did not have a mechanism for temporary sovereignty over a particular area. The league did not have enforcement powers within the mandates, and so mandate commission members could not visit a mandate to investigate problems. Issues of ascendant nationalism soon created tensions in Middle Eastern states, which ironically were supposed to be in the final stages of independence. Despite these problems, however, Article 22 helped change the face of colonialism and may have contributed to its ultimate demise after World War II. From the perspective of those people living in the mandates, however, especially in the Middle East, the situation seemed little different from the colonialism of the old order. In a sense, one might argue that League of Nations mandates in such places as the Middle East solved short-term difficulties, but only amplified long-term problems, which continue into the 21st century.

DINO E. BUENVIAJE

See also
Arab Nationalism; Mandates; United Nations

References
Nothedge, F. S. *The League of Nations: Its Life and Times 1920–1946.* Leicester, UK: Leicester University Press, 1986.
Ostrower, Gary B., and George Lankevich, eds. *League of Nations, 1919.* New York: Putnam, 1996.
Scott, George. *The Rise and Fall of the League of Nations.* New York: Macmillan, 1973.

Article 51, United Nations Charter

Self-defense clause contained in the charter of the United Nations (UN). Article 51 of the United Nations Charter guarantees the principle of self-defense by its members, whether through individual or collective security. The article falls under Chapter VII, which is titled "Actions with Respect to Threats to the Peace, Breaches of the Peace, and Acts of Aggression." It states: "nothing in the present charter shall impair the inherent right of individual or collective self-defense if an armed attack occurs against a Member of the United Nations, until the Security Council has taken measures necessary to maintain international peace and security." Further, it stipulates: "measures taken by Members in the exercise of this right of self-defense shall be immediately reported to the Security Council and shall not in any way affect the authority and responsibility of the Security Council under the present Charter."

The origins of Article 51 can be traced to the concerns shared by a number of Latin American countries in response to the veto power of the Security Council on actions taken by a regional body. In particular, the foreign ministers of Brazil, Colombia, and Cuba were concerned about the prospect of an outside power attacking the Western Hemisphere and then using the veto power of a Security Council member to prevent any collective action. The governments of Latin America were concerned that the Security Council might abrogate the 1945 Act of Chapultepec, which guaranteed the mutual defense of the Latin American republics in the event of an attack, whether by an outside power or by another state within the Western Hemisphere.

The Chapultepec agreement originally applied to concerns over Argentina, which had a military government that was sympathetic to the Axis powers. With World War II concluded, the concern now shifted to growing Cold War tensions. Not only did the Chapultepec agreement seem endangered, but it appeared that the long-standing Good Neighbor Policy and even the 1823 Monroe Doctrine would be swept away by the United Nations Charter. In particular, the Latin American nations were concerned about the infiltration of Soviet influence in the Western Hemisphere. Such concerns even reached prominent American officials like Senator Arthur Vandenburg, who worried that any provisions that would not protect the Western Hemisphere could lead to a Senate rejection of the United Nations Charter.

The problem of regionalism and regional defense was solved through the creation of three UN articles. Article 51 enshrined the principle of self-defense. Article 52 allowed the creation of regional bodies and defensive organizations, and Article 53 allowed the Security Council to work through regional agencies. Despite earlier fears, Article 51 maintained long-standing hemispheric agreements such as the Chapultepec agreement. Indeed, both individual and collective security were enshrined. Through Article 51, the United States and the Soviet Union were able to establish such regional security agreements as the North Atlantic Treaty Organization (NATO) and the Warsaw Pact.

In the Middle East, Article 51 permitted the creation and existence of such international defense organizations as the 1955 Baghdad Pact, which morphed into the Central Treaty Organization (CENTO) after the 1958 Baathist coup in Iraq that deposed the monarchy there. Iraq promptly withdrew from the Baghdad Pact and began to align itself with the Soviet bloc. After that, the organization adopted the name CENTO, and the United States became an associated partner in the organization. Throughout the various Middle East wars since the end of World War II, Article 51 has been invoked by a number of nations under attack. The Israelis have repeatedly referenced it in regard to defensive measures taken against outside aggression, whether it is from nation-states or nonstate entities. Indeed, in the Israeli-Hezbollah War that broke out in July 2006, Israel invoked Article 51 as its legal justification for attacking Hezbollah positions in southern Lebanon. Many nations have argued, however, that Israeli reprisals were out of proportion to the Hezbollah actions against Israel, and were therefore not within the legal scope of Article 51. Clearly, there seems to be sufficient room within Article 51 to allow support for either side of the issue.

DINO E. BUENVIAJE

See also
Baghdad Pact; Hezbollah; Israel; Lebanon; United Nations

References
Goodrich, Leland, and Edvard Hambro. *Charter of the United Nations: Commentary and Documents.* 2nd and rev. ed. Boston: World Peace Foundation, 1949.

Schlesinger, Stephen C. *Act of Creation: The Founding of the United Nations.* Boulder, CO: Westview, 2003.

Weiss, Thomas G., et al., eds. *The United Nations and Changing World Politics.* Boulder, CO: Westview, 1997.

Articles 41 and 42, United Nations Charter

Provisions that enable the United Nations Security Council to undertake specific measures to contain aggression and maintain peace. Articles 41 and 42 of the United Nations (UN) Charter established the enforcement power of the Security Council within the mechanism of the United Nations Charter. These articles are part of Chapter VII of the United Nations Charter, titled "Action with Respect to Threats to the Peace, Breaches of the Peace, and Acts of Aggression." Article 41 authorizes the Security Council to enact such nonmilitary measures to deter acts of aggression as "complete or partial interruption of economic relations and of rail, sea, air, postal, telegraphic, radio, and other means of communication and the severance of diplomatic relations." Should Article 41 prove inadequate, Article 42 authorizes the Security Council to enact such military measures as "demonstrations, blockade, and other operations by air, sea, or land forces of Members of the United Nations."

Articles 41 and 42 were a direct result of the shortcomings of the League of Nations, the predecessor organization to the United Nations. World War II essentially witnessed the complete failure of the League of Nations to preserve peace. There were two significant factors that contributed to the league's demise: the failure of the United States to ratify the League of Nations Covenant, and the organization's lack of enforcement powers. President Franklin D. Roosevelt, who had been an early supporter of the League of Nations, hoped to create an organization to succeed it that would not contain any of its flaws.

The United States had chosen not to join the League of Nations because of the language contained in Article 10 of the League of Nations Covenant, which obligated members "to undertake to respect and preserve, as against external aggression, the territorial integrity and existing political independence of all Members of the League." Some American officials believed that this concept of collective security appeared to endanger the sovereignty of the United States. Article 16 of the covenant furthermore enjoined its members to participate in protecting other members suffering from aggression. These two articles were soon proven meaningless, however, during Italy's invasion of Ethiopia in 1935. The invasion occurred with virtual impunity.

Unlike Articles 10 and 16 of the covenant, Articles 41 and 42 of the United Nations Charter gave the Security Council the sole prerogative of deciding what situations would involve the use of force. One reason the League of Nations failed was that it did not have any such mechanism for deliberating in situations that might have required the use of force. Second, the language of Article 16 proved to be the league's undoing by placing an obligation on its members to intervene with nonmilitary measures. Article 41 differs in language by using the words "call upon" rather than "obligate." By placing on the Security Council the responsibility for determining what kinds of measures should be taken, rather than allowing each individual member to decide what kinds of actions to take, the United Nations maintained its credibility.

Article 42 specifically placed military and other security measures in the hands of the Security Council. Under the League of Nations, it was impossible to find a consensus among the members to devote their armed forces toward enforcement. Thus, through Article 42, a system was devised whereby national military forces would be placed under international jurisdiction, but only for specified objectives. As a result of these measures, the United Nations has maintained a credibility that the league could not uphold.

The United Nations, largely through Articles 41 and 42, has been heavily involved in the Middle East since 1945. Most of its work has come in the form of peacekeeping, monitoring, and enforcement. Some of its actions there include the United Nations Observation Group in Lebanon, dispatched in 1958 to ensure that no illegal infiltrations of personnel or materials made their way into Lebanon after the uprising there that same year. In November 1956, following the Suez Crisis, the UN established the first United Nations Emergency Force (UNEF), whose job was to oversee the withdrawal of French, Israeli, and British forces from Egypt, and then to maintain a buffer zone between Egyptian and Israeli troops. This lasted until June 1967. In October 1973, following the Yom Kippur (Ramadan) War, the second United Nations Emergency Force was dispatched to the Middle East to enforce the cease-fire between Israel and Egypt. UN forces also created and maintained a buffer zone between the two nations, which lasted until July 1979. In August 1988, the UN established the UN Iran-Iraq Military Observer Group, which was charged with enforcing the terms of the cease-fire after the Iran-Iraq War (1980–1988). The UN Iraq-Kuwait Observation Commission, in operation from April 1991 to October 2003, was charged with deterring any aggression between the two nations and monitoring the demilitarized zone.

Ongoing UN activities in the Middle East include an observation force in the Golan Heights, first created in 1974, to supervise the cease-fire and withdrawal agreements made between Syria and Israel. The UN Interim Force in Lebanon, dispatched in 1978, continues the struggle to enable the Lebanese government to assert control over its territory and keep Israeli troops from occupying Lebanese lands. The UN Truce Supervision Organization, in existence since 1948, continues to monitor truces, observe military movements, enforce cease-fires, and perform other peacekeeping responsibilities in the region.

Articles 41 and 42 have also been invoked numerous times during Middle Eastern conflicts to effect embargoes, blockades, and economic sanctions against aggressor states. For example, after the Iraqi invasion of Kuwait in August 1990, the UN Security Council almost immediately passed Resolution 660, which condemned the Iraqi attack and demanded an immediate withdrawal. Just a few days later, the Security Council passed Resolution 661, which slapped international economic sanctions on Iraq. After more diplomatic wrangling while Iraq still occupied Kuwait, the UN passed Resolution 678 in November 1990. This resolution gave the Iraqis a firm deadline of January 15, 1991, to withdraw entirely from Kuwait. It also authorized "all necessary means" to implement and enforce Resolution 660, which was a de facto authorization of the use of force. When Iraq refused to leave Kuwait, an international coalition led by the United States forcibly expelled the invaders. Indeed, the 1991 Persian Gulf War was an almost textbook case of the effectiveness of the United Nations and of Articles 41 and 42.

The same cannot be said, however, of the 2003 Anglo-American–led coalition that invaded Iraq and ousted Iraqi dictator Saddam Hussein from office. Although the UN had passed a number of resolutions entreating Hussein to cooperate with UN weapons inspectors, it had not passed a clear-cut measure that specifically authorized force, as it had done in 1991. The United States continued to push the case for war, however, citing "clear" evidence that the Iraqis were concealing weapons of mass destruction. Thus, the United States and its allies went to war with Iraq in March 2003 lacking any pretense of UN authorization. This engendered bitter condemnations from many nations, including old allies of the United States and United Kingdom. UN secretary-general Kofi Annan termed the invasion "illegal" in September 2004. The lack of international support has bedeviled the Anglo-American war in Iraq, as have reports that no weapons of mass destruction were found in Iraq, even after many months of careful hunting by military professionals.

DINO E. BUENVIAJE AND PAUL G. PIERPAOLI JR.

See also

Arab-Israeli Conflict, Overview; DESERT STORM, Operation; Iran-Iraq War; IRAQI FREEDOM, Operation; Lebanon; Suez Crisis; United Nations; Weapons of Mass Destruction

References

Goodrich, Leland, and Edvard Hambro. *Charter of the United Nations: Commentary and Documents.* 2nd and rev. ed. Boston: World Peace Foundation, 1949.

Nothedge, F. S. *The League of Nations: Its Life and Times, 1920–1946.* Leicester, UK: Leicester University Press, 1986.

Riggs, Robert Egwon. *The United Nations: International Organization and World Politics.* Chicago: Wadsworth, 1993.

Roberts, Adam, and Benedict Kingsbury, eds. *United Nations, Divided World: The UN's Role in International Relations.* New York: Oxford University Press, 1994.

Schlesinger, Stephen C. *Act of Creation: The Founding of the United Nations.* Boulder, CO: Westview, 2003.

Artillery

Artillery used in the Arab-Israeli Conflict and Middle East wars has consisted of indirect fire and air defense weapons systems, including cannon, rockets, and missiles. Most of these weapons have been supplied to the region by the rival superpowers and regional powers. The indirect fire system, the most common method of delivering artillery fire on the modern battlefield, refers to a situation in which the target, typically several thousand meters distant, is not visible to the weapon firing an artillery projectile at it. Forward observers, either in the air flying above the battle zone or traveling with maneuver units on the ground, identify targets and communicate that information (usually in the form of map coordinates) to artillery unit fire direction centers that compute firing data and send the data to the guns. Forward observers send subsequent corrections from which fire direction centers compute new firing data that "adjust" the artillery projectiles' strike onto the target. This indirect fire system of observers, fire direction centers, and artillery weapons, linked by telephone or radio communications systems, was introduced during the 1904–1905 Russo-Japanese War, and has been refined over the past century to include computerized fire-control systems.

Artillery weapons deliver high lethality fires in support of maneuver units—armor and infantry—that close with the enemy and seize terrain. Some field artillery weapons are capable of shooting nuclear or chemical projectiles.

Field artillery cannon systems are either towed or self-propelled. A towed system consists of a cannon and a prime mover, usually a truck, that tows the cannon. Self-propelled weapons are cannons or rapid-fire antiaircraft guns mounted integrally on a motor carriage, usually tracked, to form self-contained gun platforms. Self-propelled artillery has a higher ground mobility and ability to keep pace with fast-moving mechanized formations. Lighter towed artillery has higher air mobility, especially when transported by helicopter.

Towed guns rely on their prime movers to carry ancillary equipment such as aiming stakes, tools, communications equipment, and other fire-control items. The prime mover also typically carries a small amount of ready ammunition, but the majority of the gun section's basic load of projectiles, propellant, and fuses is carried on a separate ammunition truck.

Self-propelled guns likewise carry only a few rounds of ready ammunition on-board, with the remainder of the basic load carried in a tracked ammunition vehicle. In many modern self-propelled systems, the specially designed ammunition vehicle is equipped with an automatic ammunition feed system that connects directly with the onboard hydraulic loader-rammer system of the self-propelled gun. This produces loading speed and efficiency far greater than the manual system on almost all towed guns.

Artillery ammunition is classified as fixed, semifixed, or separate-loading. Most direct fire guns, such as tank guns and antitank guns, fire fixed ammunition, where the projectile, fuse, propellant charge, and primer are supplied as a single unit. The propellant charge is packaged in a metal shell casing canister, made of brass or steel, which has a primer in its base and the projectile mounted on its top. After firing, the empty casing must be ejected from the firing chamber of the gun.

Semifixed ammunition is similar to fixed, except that it does not come prepackaged with a fuse, which gives the firing battery the flexibility of selecting the fuse to match the target. The point-detonating fuse produces a surface or delayed subsurface burst. The time and variable time (proximity) fuses produce air bursts over the target. The propellant inside the shell casing canister also comes packaged in separate increment bags, which the gun crew can remove as necessary to achieve the required charge for the range to the target. As with fixed ammunition, the empty shell casing canister must be removed from the gun after firing. Most light artillery, including the American-made M-101A1, M-102, and M-119 towed 105-millimeter (mm) howitzers, and some Soviet-made 122-mm guns, fire semifixed ammunition.

Almost all medium and heavy artillery pieces fire separate-loading ammunition, in which the projectile, fuse, propellant, and primer all come separately and are combined as required by the firing crew. Separate-loading propellant charges do not come packaged in a shell casing canister. The number of powder bags representing the required propellant charge is loaded directly into the cannon's breech chamber, immediately behind the projectile, and are completely consumed during the firing process.

Since World War II, surface-to-surface tactical artillery free-flight rockets and guided missiles have played increasingly larger roles in warfare. Free-flight rockets are generally fired from multiple launchers, which produces a massive surge effect at the target. Such weapons, however, come with heavy logistical requirements. Guided missiles are normally launched individually against precision targets. Almost all artillery-guided missile systems are capable of carrying conventional high-explosive, chemical, or nuclear warheads.

Air Defense Artillery (ADA) weapons are divided into antiaircraft guns and surface-to-air missiles (SAMs). The guns are rapid fire, usually radar-controlled, systems designed to engage aircraft at low and medium altitudes and close-in ranges. SAMs are radar controlled and/or heat-seeking systems that engage aircraft at higher altitudes and greater ranges. Man-portable air defense systems (MANPADS) are shoulder-fired, heat-seeking SAMs designed to protect friendly units from enemy ground attack aircraft at low altitudes and close-in ranges. When fired in mass, MANPADS can be especially lethal.

In 1948, the new state of Israel relied on artillery in place in Palestine. With hostilities imminent and the Jewish state facing an arms embargo by the Western powers, Israeli agents purchased from Czechoslovakia and other nations in Eastern Europe tons of surplus arms and ammunition left over from World War II. By necessity, many of those weapons were manufactured for the Third Reich. The Arab nations were initially equipped with British and French weapons, depending on which country had held the colony or mandate. During the course of the intervening years, the United States, France, and the Soviet Union were the principal arms suppliers in the states of the Middle East.

During the fighting in 1948 and 1949, the most common artillery pieces in the Arab arsenals were the towed 25-pounder gun/howitzer and the 17-pounder antitank gun, both mainstays of the British Army during World War II. The Israelis managed to capture many of these weapons and immediately put them into service with the Israeli Defense Forces (IDF). The Israelis also used 2-inch and 3-inch infantry mortars, captured directly from the British during the mandate period, as well as obsolete World War I vintage French 75-millimeter (mm) field guns and Austrian 65-mm mountain howitzers. The Israelis also introduced their own improvised heavy mortar, dubbed the "Davidka."

World War II artillery weapons still predominated on both sides by the time of the 1956 Suez fighting. Both sides, however, had begun to mount these systems on a wide variety of wheeled and tracked vehicles to produce locally fabricated self-propelled guns. The Israelis in particular were innovative in producing a wide range of variants mounted on American-made M-4 Sherman tank chassis or M-3 halftracks, which the IDF acquired in large numbers after 1949. The IDF also acquired AMX light tanks from France, on which they mounted 105-mm howitzers.

Following the Arab defeat in 1956, the Soviet Union increasingly became the principal arms supplier of Egypt, Syria, and Iraq. Along with Soviet weapons and military advisers, the Egyptians in particular adopted the Soviet doctrine of massed firepower. By the 1967 Six-Day War, Egyptian artillery units were armed with the Soviet 122-mm gun/howitzer and 130-mm gun, which outranged the American-made field artillery that increasingly made up the Israeli arsenal. The IDF had American-made 105-mm and 155-mm howitzers, towed and self-propelled in both calibers. The Israel Defense Forces (IDF), however, greatly preferred self-propelled systems that could keep pace with their highly mobile armored forces. The Israelis also used French-built 155-mm howitzers mounted on Sherman tank chassis in great numbers.

During the October 1973 Yom Kippur War, also known as the Ramadan War, the Israelis made extensive use of American-made 155-mm M-109 and 8-inch (203-mm) M-110A1 self-propelled howitzers. The Israelis also locally manufactured two versions of a self-propelled 155-mm howitzer with better range than the U.S. models. This allowed the IDF to counter the extended range of Arab artillery. The American-made 175-mm M-107 self-propelled gun also proved invaluable in countering the Arab's range advantage. Egypt, Syria, and their allies employed Soviet-built towed 122-mm gun/howitzers and 130-mm guns, as well as self-propelled 122-mm and 152-mm howitzers.

In later conflicts, Arab armies began using Soviet rocket and missile systems to achieve extended range and target saturation. The FROG 7 (NATO designation for Free Rocket Over Ground) was the Soviet version of the U.S. Honest John rocket. Soviet fire doctrine stressed the use of rockets to saturate a target area, enhance the psychological effect of fires, and multiply the volume of fires delivered by cannon systems.

The FROG 7A and 7B, which were capable of carrying conventional, chemical, or nuclear warheads, were extensively exported. The FROG's large circular probable error (CPE) of 550–750 yards

Soviet-made MAZ TEL (NATO designation SCUD) missile launcher. (U.S. Department of Defense)

and range of 42 miles made it a deep-strike system, rather than a weapon to influence the close battle.

The World War II Soviet Katyusha multiple rocket system was mounted on trucks used as prime movers and launch platforms and was fired in ripple salvos. American, British, and German forces used similar weapons. The most common multiple launch rocket systems fielded by the Soviets and their Middle Eastern client states included the BM-21, which carried 36 122-mm rockets in vehicular mounted pods with a range of 24 miles. The larger BM-27 mounted 16 220-mm rockets in launch configuration.

The Soviet SS-1 tactical ballistic missile (designated the Scud by NATO) had a mixed record in later Arab-Israeli and Middle East conflicts. Directly derived from the German V-2 of World War II, it is a surface-to-surface weapon with a relatively unsophisticated gyroscope guidance system that only controls the missile during the 80-second phase of powered flight. The resulting inaccuracy produces more of an area weapon than a precision weapon. The greatest potential threat from the Scud is its ability to carry chemical, biological, or nuclear warheads. Fortunately, all Scuds fired in actual war so far have carried only high-explosive warheads.

As the various armies in the Middle East evolved in their technical sophistication, all sides increased the use of close air support and long-range air strikes, which in turn increased the requirements

for ground-based air defense systems. The IDF used the U.S.-made Stinger MANPAD system and the time-tested U.S. M-2 .50-caliber heavy machine gun in a variety of air defense mountings.

The Arab forces employed a variety of Soviet gun and missile systems. The self-propelled, four-barreled, radar-controlled 23-mm ZSU 23/4 air defense system was especially devastating against low-flying Israeli attack aircraft. This Soviet-made gun had already proven itself in the Vietnam War, during which the North Vietnamese used it quite effectively against U.S. aircraft. The Arab forces also were well armed with the Soviet SA-2, SA-7, and SA-11 SAM systems, which created havoc for the IAF in the opening stages of the 1973 Yom Kippur (Ramadan) War.

During the 1948 and 1956 wars, the artillery doctrine of most of the Arab armies was patterned after that of the British. After 1956, Soviet artillery doctrine predominated, which stressed area fires by large numbers of artillery pieces. In the Yom Kippur (Ramadan) War, Egypt was able to commit massive numbers of artillery pieces to the operation to penetrate the Bar-Lev Line.

As the Egyptian and Syrian armies procured Soviet equipment on a large scale, one of the most lethal weapons in their arsenal became the AT-3 Sagger man-portable, wire-guided, antitank missile. Launched by a two-man crew, the Saggers devastated the massed Israeli armored formations in the early phases of the Yom Kippur War. The Israelis finally learned to neutralize the Sagger threat by using large concentrations of artillery fire to distract, obscure, or kill the Sagger gunners.

Israel continued to rely on American and British artillery procedures that focused on infantry and armor support through the use of direct support, general support, or reinforcing missions. An artillery unit with a direct support mission provides fires to a specific maneuver unit. Normally, one artillery battalion fires in support of one maneuver brigade. Firing units with general support missions answer calls for fire from the entire force and support the overall mission as defined by the maneuver commander, usually the division commander. Units with a reinforcing mission augment the fires of other artillery units, usually those with a direct support mission.

Because the Israelis prefer precision fire to area fire, they generally have eschewed the use of rockets, although the U.S. M-270 Multiple Launch Rocket System (MLRS) is currently in their arsenal. The doctrinal U.S. and NATO missions for the MLRS include the suppression of enemy air defense weapons, counterbattery missions, and the attack of fixed targets at extended ranges.

Because of Israel's numerical disadvantage against the Arab states, IDF tactical doctrine focuses on first achieving air superiority, and then committing its air force to attack deep targets, destroy enemy artillery, and engage air defense missile launchers as targets of opportunity. This leaves the bulk of the Israeli field artillery committed to providing close support to the armor and infantry maneuver units.

During 1980–1988, Iraq and Iran fought a conventional war over a combination of old border disputes and the Iranian intent to overthrow the Iraqi regime of Saddam Hussein. The initial Iraqi invasion netted some territorial gains from Iranian forces that the Iraqis calculated were in a state of chaos following the Iranian Revolution of 1979. Iranian patriotism and tenacity, however, regained lost territory and static war of attrition set in. The United States primarily supported Iraq, with the administration of President Ronald Reagan vowing that Hussein's government would not be allowed to fall.

After its initial stage, the Iran-Iraq War was fought predominantly on Iraqi territory, which allowed the smaller Iraqi military to defend in depth and extract large numbers of casualties from the Iranian attackers. Artillery played a key role during this fighting. Iraq purchased artillery weapons of all types from the international arms market, and had a 4-to-1 superiority over the Iranians in all types and calibers of weapons systems, both cannon and missile. The Iraqi numerical advantage was somewhat neutralized by Iran's aggressive use of attack helicopters and aircraft in a counterbattery role.

Both Iraq and Iran used Soviet artillery or copies of Soviet systems manufactured by the People's Republic of China, Egypt, and Czechoslovakia, including towed and self-propelled versions of the 122-mm gun/howitzer, the towed 130-mm gun, and the BM-21 122-mm multiple rocket launcher. France, South Africa, and Austria also supplied 155-mm towed howitzers to Iraq, especially the innovative extended-range systems designed by Dr. Gerald Bull. Iran preferred to equip its forces purely with Soviet bloc equipment, including surface-to-surface Scud missile variants, which it fired against Iraqi cities.

Both sides operated on the basis of Soviet artillery doctrine and tactics. Iraq frequently used massed artillery fire to defeat the more numerous Iranian human wave assaults, but there was never enough artillery or air power to fight a coordinated combined arms battle. Field guns, however, were in enough supply to wreak havoc on infantry and armor formations.

Iraq shocked the world when it fired chemical weapons against unprotected Iranian troops and dissident Kurd villages. Middle Eastern chemical companies operating in China, India, Singapore, Europe, and the United States supplied Iraq with the chemicals necessary to fabricate mustard (HD), Sarin (GB), and methylphosphonothioic acid (VX) warheads. Despite the universal ban on such weapons, the Iraqis used them in the manner outlined in classic Soviet doctrine for area denial and antipersonnel operations. But as demonstrated in World War I, nonpersistent agents, such as GB, have such a short duration that they generally do not produce significant tactical advantage. Against unprotected troops not in shelters, however, the initial strikes nonetheless produced devastating casualties.

When Iraq invaded Kuwait in August 1991, the United States and a multinational coalition of forces intervened militarily to eject Iraq and restore the international border. The United States and allied units employed mostly American and British artillery, including the self-propelled M-109A5 155-mm howitzer and the self-propelled M-110A2 8-inch howitzer. The U.S. Marine Corps artillery was equipped with the M-198 towed 155-mm howitzer.

The Persian Gulf War was also the combat debut of the American self-propelled M-270 Multiple Launch Rocket System (MLRS). Some Arab nations in 1991 were armed with the automated French AMX 155-mm self-propelled howitzer, and the French contingent was equipped entirely with French systems.

The United States and Great Britain were still using the same basic artillery weapons systems during the 2003 Iraq War, except that the standard version of the 155-mm howitzer had been upgraded to the M-109A6, known as the Paladin, and the venerable M-110 8-inch howitzer had been phased out of the American arsenal.

The United States in 1991 also used the Patriot air defense system, hastily modified to expand its intended role of shooting down enemy aircraft to the much more difficult task of intercepting missiles, in an attempt to defend key sites in Israel against Iraqi Scud missiles. While the Patriot received inflated praise in the American media at the time, postengagement analysis proved that the earlier version of the Patriot was something far short of a fully effective antimissile missile system. In 2006, when Israel again went to war in south Lebanon, Hezbollah hit various points in Israel with a large number of relatively inaccurate but nonetheless deadly surface-to-surface missiles based on the Soviet Katyusha design, which undoubtedly will lead Israel to increase its investments in antimissile technology.

Artillery is essential to success in modern war. Armies that deploy their weapons systems most effectively and adopt the ever-evolving new technologies, such as ground positioning systems based on satellite availability for target acquisition, will prevail on the battlefield. Although the predominant type of fighting in the Middle East since 2003 has been guerrilla and insurgency warfare, significant amounts of conventional weaponry remain in the region, and a return to larger-scale combat remains a potential threat for the foreseeable future. In that type of fighting, artillery is indispensable.

Jay A. Menzoff and David T. Zabecki

See also

Arab-Israeli Conflict, Overview; DESERT STORM, Operation; Iran-Iraq War; IRAQI FREEDOM, Operation; Israel; Lebanon; Suez Crisis

References

Gudmundsson, Bruce. *On Artillery.* Westport, CT: Praeger, 1993.

Hogg, Ian. *Twentieth-Century Artillery.* New York: Barnes and Noble, 2000.

Karsh, Efraim. *The Iran-Iraq War, 1980–1988.* Oxford, UK: Osprey, 2002.

ARTIMON, Operation

Start Date: August 2, 1990
End Date: March 1991

Code name/designation for France's maritime interception operations put in place after the August 2, 1990, invasion of Kuwait by Iraq. It lasted until March 1991. These operations were intended to prevent the export or import of certain materials to Iraq, Kuwait, and Jordan, as defined by sanctions enacted by the United Nations (UN) Security Council. The French Navy contributed the third-largest number of ships to interdiction operations off Kuwait, second only to the United States and Great Britain. The French were anxious to retain their national autonomy and requested their own area for maritime operations.

During the 1980s, France had become Iraq's largest trading partner. Iraqi president Saddam Hussein had grown uncomfortable relying strictly on the Soviet Union for his arms and military supplies, and so he looked to the West as an alternative. The French government, concerned about the possible spread of a fundamentalist Islamic revolution from Iran, was willing to help Iraq function as a counterbalance in the Persian Gulf. Also, because up to 30 percent of France's oil supply came from the region, regional stability was very important.

In 1980, Saddam had invaded Iran, hoping to take advantage of the disorder resulting from the Iranian Revolution. Besides providing weapons to the Iraqis in the ensuing long Iran-Iraq War (1980–1988), the French later sold additional weapons to the Iraqis and had also provided nuclear technology for Iraq's Osiraq reactor.

When Iraq invaded Kuwait, the French government was as surprised as the rest of the world. Despite its close economic and military relations with Iraq and the considerable sums owed France by Iraq, the French government immediately condemned the invasion and called for the removal of Iraqi troops. It also froze all Iraqi assets in the country. Within a week, the government had also placed restrictions on Iraqi diplomats and suspended any arms shipments to both Iraq and Kuwait. Perhaps just as important, France supported a European Community embargo and, on August 6, voted in favor of UN Security Council Resolution 661, which called for a complete military and economic embargo against Iraq except for food, medical supplies, and humanitarian aid. The goal of the sanctions was to force Saddam to withdraw his troops from Kuwait.

On August 9, France announced that it would send combat planes to Saudi Arabia to help defend that country against Iraqi aggression, and on August 25, France again voted with the United States, in support of UN Security Council Resolution 665. The resolution authorized member states to enforce the embargo against Iraq by stopping ships in the Persian Gulf, inspecting their cargo, and verifying their papers.

Meanwhile, the first French warships had been dispatched on August 6 to the Persian Gulf to begin maritime interdiction duties. The exercise was code-named Operation ARTIMON. The first group included the destroyers *Dupleix* and *Montcalm*. These Georges Leygues–class ships displaced 3,830 tons. They were armed with four Exocet antiship missiles and had the capacity to operate two Westland Lynx Mark 2 helicopters. Each had a crew of 219. Supporting the initial deployment of Operation ARTIMON was the tanker *Durance*.

On August 8, a military adviser to President François Mitterand's government suggested sending the aircraft carrier *Clemenceau* to a base in Saudi Arabia on the Red Sea. The move was intended as a political signal as much as a military one. The *Clemenceau* sailed on August 13, but it carried no combat aircraft. Instead, it acted as a fast transport. Forty combat helicopters and nearly 2,000 men from the Force d'Action Rapide were on board. The units involved were part of France's rapid reaction force and would be available to help protect Saudi Arabia, should that prove necessary. The French government denied that its deployment was part of an international military buildup in order to avoid placing French troops under foreign command. The *Clemenceau* was not part of Operation ARTIMON, however.

During the buildup in the Persian Gulf, the various navies at first had different rules of engagement for enforcing the maritime interdiction effort. Before Resolution 665 was passed on August 25, the French government argued that naval vessels had no legal authority to stop ships and search them. The very name given to the naval effort, "interdiction," had been a compromise to reduce opposition to the operations, because "blockade" indicated hostilities were already taking place.

On August 18, two Iraqi tankers tested the allies' interdiction effort. The *Khanaqin* and *Bab Gurgur* steamed past U.S. Navy ships patrolling in the Persian Gulf, their captains ignoring orders to stop. Even when two U.S. frigates fired warning shots across their bows, the ships refused to change course. American rules of engagement ordinarily authorized the next step to be an attempt to disable the ship without endangering its integrity. Although Vice Admiral Henry Mauz, commander of U.S. Central Command naval forces, had authorized his captains to disable ships, his orders were overridden by authorities in Washington.

After legal authority was granted on August 25 to stop and search ships, representatives of the various governments that had naval vessels in the region met to consider how to implement it. While most nations were willing to follow the U.S. lead, the French and Italian governments sought their own national areas of the Persian Gulf to patrol. The French remained leery of having their armed forces serve under another nation's military. To satisfy this requirement, Mauz assigned the French, British, Italian, and Dutch navies patrol areas off the United Arab Emirates and the Strait of Hormuz. The particular rules of engagement under which each nation's ships would operate were also left up to the national authorities. Most were content to follow the U.S. lead, as the U.S. Navy had extensive experience with blockades.

Despite some disagreements over how the interdiction was carried out, the French government proved it supported the concept by reinforcing its forces in Operation ARTIMON. In October 1990, the Georges Leygues–class destroyer *La Motte-Picquet* arrived to increase the French force in place. It was accompanied by the smaller *Du Chayla*, which was equipped with 40 surface-to-air missiles and three twin 57-millimeter (mm) guns. In December 1990, the *La Motte-Picquet* returned home, and was replaced with the destroyer *Jean de Vienne* and the frigate *Premier Maitre l'Her*. After the war ended, the *Jean de Vienne* was relieved in March

1991 by the *Latouche-Treville.* Other French naval ships that were assigned to Operation ARTIMON included the frigates *Cadet Bory, Doudart de Lagree,* and *Protet.* Also, the replenishment ship *Marne,* the maintenance ship *Jules Verne,* and the tug *Buffle* supported the warships of Operation ARTIMON at different times. Two French hospital ships, the *Rance* and the *Foudre,* operated in the Red Sea during this time.

Operation ARTIMON, as with the entire interdiction effort, should be considered a success. Between August 16, 1990, and March 1991, 7,675 merchant ships were intercepted in the Persian Gulf, the northern Arabian Sea, the Red Sea, and the Gulf of Aden. Of that number, 964 were boarded by coalition inspection teams. Fifty-one ships were turned back to other ports because they were carrying contraband forbidden by UN resolutions. Eleven warning shots were fired, but no disabling actions were taken.

TIM J. WATTS

See also

France, Role in Persian Gulf and Iraq Wars; Mauz, Henry H., Jr.; United Kingdom, Navy, Persian Gulf War; United States Navy, Persian Gulf War

References

Bennett, Andrew, Joseph Lepgold, and Danny Unger, eds. *Friends in Need: Burden Sharing in the Persian Gulf War.* New York: St. Martin's, 1997.

Marolda, Edward, and Robert Schneller. *Shield and Sword: The United States Navy and the Persian Gulf War.* Annapolis, MD: U.S. Naval Institute Press, 2001.

Pokrant, Marvin. *Desert Shield at Sea: What the Navy Really Did.* Westport, CT: Greenwood, 1999.

Asad, Bashar al-
Birth Date: September 11, 1965

President of the Syrian Arab Republic (2000–present) and head of the Syrian Baath Party. Bashar al-Asad was born in Damascus, Syria, on September 11, 1965. His father was Hafiz al-Asad, strongman and president of Syria from 1971 to 2000. The Alawi sect to which Asad belongs encompasses approximately 12 percent of the Syrian population. His older brother, Basil, was more popular among the Syrian public than was Bashar before he died in an automobile accident in 1994.

Beginning in the mid-1980s, the younger Asad studied medicine at the University of Damascus, training in ophthalmology at the Tishrin Military Hospital and then the Western Eye Hospital in London. After Basil's death, Bashar al-Asad enrolled in the military academy at Homs. He became a colonel in the Syrian Army in 1999.

Although Syria is a republic, President Hafiz al-Asad groomed Basil, then Bashar, as successor, although he never openly declared this intent. Bashar al-Asad's acquisition of both military and Baath Party credentials was imperative to his legitimacy, but most observers believed that the senior power brokers in the

Syrian president Bashar al-Asad inspects a guard of honor in New Delhi during a state visit to India, June 18, 2008. (AP/Wide World Photos)

Syrian government assented to Asad's succession as a matter of convenience. In 2000, he was elected secretary-general of the Baath Party and stood as a presidential candidate. The People's Assembly amended the Constitution to lower the minimum presidential age to 35, and Asad was duly elected president for a seven-year term. A general referendum soon ratified the decision.

A reform movement emerged during the first year of Asad's rule, which was dubbed the Damascus Spring. Some Syrians hoped that their young president—who had announced governmental reforms, an end to corruption, and economic liberalization—would open Syria to a greater degree. Indeed, reformers hoped to end the State of Emergency Law, which allows for the abuse of legal and human rights, and issued public statements in 2000 and 2001. Political prisoners were released from the notorious Mezze Prison, and certain intellectual forums were permitted. However, by mid-2001 the president reined in the reformists, some of whom were imprisoned and accused of being Western agents.

Under Bashar al-Asad, Syria has opened somewhat in terms of allowing more media coverage than in the past, although censorship remains a contentious issue. Cellular phones are now prevalent, and Syria finally allowed access to the Internet, whereas under Hafiz al-Asad, even facsimile machines were prohibited. Economic reform and modernization have received top priority under Bashar al-Asad. Job creation, the lessening of Syria's dependence on oil revenue, the encouragement of private capital investments, and the mitigation of poverty have been the key goals in the economic sphere. The government has created foreign investment zones, and private universities have been legally permitted, along with private banks. Employment centers were established after

2000, and Asad announced his support of an association with the European Union. However, these changes have been too gradual to instill much confidence in Syrian modernization.

Under Bashar al-Asad, Syria's relations with Iraq had improved prior to the change of regime in that country in April 2003, and Syrian-Turkish relations are also less tense than in the past. However, the United States showed great irritation with evidence that foreign fighters were crossing into Iraq from Syria and that former Iraqi Baathists were using Syria for funding purposes. The ensuing 2004 sanctions against Syria under the Syria Accountability Act, first enacted by the U.S. Congress in 2003, have discouraged investors and the modernization of Syria's banking systems. More importantly, this situation provided a lever to force Syria out of Lebanon, finally put in motion after the assassination of former Lebanese prime minister Rafic al-Hariri.

Syria adamantly and consistently opposed the American presence in Iraq after the Anglo-American invasion there in March 2003, and the country's own Islamist movement reemerged. President Asad also had to deal with a huge influx of Iraqi refugees to Syria, who posed an additional burden on the economy. Further, Asad did not wish to encourage radical Islamists in Syrian territory and made efforts to contain them.

In terms of the Arab-Israeli situation, Asad inherited a hardline position toward Tel Aviv along with sympathies toward the Palestinian cause during the Second (al-Aqsa) Intifada and its aftermath. Yet internally, the public saw the president as promoting an honorable peace for Syria, deemed necessary for further economic development. This did not mean that Syria and Israel were any closer to a peace agreement, but Syria would also most likely seek to avoid war, as during the Israeli invasion of southern Lebanon in 2006. Syria and Israel engaged in an exploration of peace talks, and by the end of 2008 there were signs that a Syria-Israeli rapprochement was in the offing, although Israel's war against Hamas in Gaza, which began in late 2008, threatened to suspend further negotiations.

Other important changes came with the shift in Syria's position in Lebanon. When Hariri was assassinated in a bombing in February of 2005, suspicions fell on Syria. Anti-Syrian Lebanese demonstrated as did such pro-Syrian groups as Hezbollah. The United Nations inquiry into Hariri's death, as well as comments by former Syrian vice president Abdul Halim Khaddam, implicated Syrians at the highest level and pro-Syrian elements in Lebanon intelligence services in the assassination. The Syrian government fought hard to postpone establishment of a tribunal to investigate Hariri's death, but to no avail. Syrian troops finally withdrew from Lebanon in April 2005, thereby ending a long period of direct and indirect influence over the country. Additional important Lebanese figures were assassinated, including Pierre Gemayel, founder of the Kataeb Party. Lebanon was a key economic asset for Syria because of highly favorable trade terms, smuggling, and the absorption of large numbers of Syrian laborers. The U.S. government continued to charge Asad with aiding

and bolstering Hezbollah in Lebanon, but Syria viewed the organization as a wholly Lebanese entity.

President Asad was reelected to another seven-year term in 2007. Nevertheless, many Western nations and some Arab nations continue to pressure Asad to curtail relations with Iran and to crack down on terrorism said to be funded or supported by various elements within Syria. Asad had taken pains to improve relations with his Arab neighbors, but his pro-Iranian policies and interference in Lebanese affairs have led to tensions with such countries as Saudi Arabia, and Syria has sided with a new group joined by Qatar. Although considerable differences remained over security issues and water rights, there was speculation in early 2009 that Asad was nearing a peace treaty with Israel that would result in the restoration of the Golan Heights to Syria. It is not clear if this endeavor will be pursued by the new Netanyahu-Lieberman Israeli government.

SHERIFA ZUHUR

See also

Arab Nationalism; Asad, Hafiz al-; Hezbollah; Iran; Israel; Lebanon; Syria; Syria, Armed Forces

References

Darraj, Susan Muaddi. *Bashar al-Assad*. New York: Chelsea House, 2005.
George, Alan. *Syria: Neither Bread Nor Freedom*. London: Zed Books, 2003.
Leverett, Flynt. *Inheriting Syria: Bashar's Trial by Fire*. Washington, DC: Brookings Institution Press, 2005.

Asad, Hafiz al-
Birth Date: October 6, 1930
Death Date: June 10, 2000

Syrian military officer, political leader, and president of Syria (1971–2000). Hafiz al-Asad was born in modest circumstance at Qardaha in western Syria on October 6, 1930. A member of the minority Alaite sect of Shia Islam, at age 16 he began his political career by joining the Baath Party. As a secular organization, the Baath Party actively recruited members from all sects and branches of Islam as well as from Christian groups. Baathism opposed imperialism and colonialism and espoused nonalignment, except with other Arab countries. As a youth, Asad participated in Baathist demonstrations against the French Occupation of Syria and for Syrian independence.

With no money to attend college, Asad secured a free education at the Syrian Military Academy. Graduating in 1955, he was commissioned an air force lieutenant pilot. He then received advanced fighter training and advanced to squadron leader in 1959.

Asad opposed the 1958 Union of Syria with Egypt in the United Arab Republic (UAR), for which he was exiled to Egypt during 1959–1961. In Cairo, Asad worked with other Syrian military officers committed to the resurrection of the Syrian Baath Party. Asad favored Pan-Arabism but he was opposed to the union with Egypt, which had concentrated most of the power in the hands of

Egyptian leader Gamal Abdel Nasser. Asad's outspoken opposition to the UAR led to his brief imprisonment in Egypt after the breakup of the UAR in 1961.

On March 27, 1962, the army seized power in Syria and abolished the parliament. Army leaders promised to introduce "just socialism." Then, on March 8, 1963, the Baath Party, supported by allies from within the military, toppled the previous regime. In 1964, Asad become commander of the Syrian Air Force. Although Amin al-Hafiz, a Sunni Muslim, was the nominal leader of Syria, in effect a group of young Alawites, including Asad, controlled affairs of the state.

Rivalries within the leadership of the state led to yet another coup, on February 23, 1966. The coup was led by General Saleh al-Jadid and entailed considerable bloodshed. Asad became one of the key members of the new government, as minister of defense (1966–1970). Asad's political position was considerably weakened by the disastrous Six-Day War of June 1967 that saw Syria lose the Golan Heights to Israel. A protracted power struggle then ensued between Asad and his mentor, Jadid, then chief of staff of the Syrian armed forces.

By the autumn of 1970, Jadid and Asad were locked in a struggle for control of power. Jadid then decided to intervene against King Hussein's government in Jordan, which had moved against the militant Palestinians there. Jordanian aircraft savaged the invading Syrian tanks, which then withdrew. This cleared the way for Jadid and his allies to be removed from power, attacked by Asad for the Jordanian fiasco. In the so-called corrective revolution, Asad forced Syrian president Nur al-Din al-Atasi to resign on October 17, 1970. This was followed by the arrest of Premier Yussuf Zuayyen and Foreign Minister Ibrahim Makhous. On November 21, Asad became prime minister. Atasi and Jadid were sent to prison.

Asad and his nationalist faction were more committed to Arab unity and the destruction of Israel than to socialism, while his rivals had concentrated on neo-Marxist economic reform. In 1971, Asad was elected president, the first of five terms. The previous regime had been a military dictatorship, and on coming to power Asad increased its repressive nature. Political dissenters were subject to arrest, torture, and execution, although usually the regime got its way through bribes and intimidation. The government became strongly totalitarian with a cult of personality buttressing the all-powerful leader, in part an effort to end the sharp fractures in Syrian society.

The only major internal threat to Asad's rule came in the form of a rebellion in the cities of Damascus, Hama, and Homs from 1979 until its denouement in Hama in February 1982. The rebels targeted the government and even tried to place suicide bombers on the Ministry of Defense. Suicide bombings took place in various parts of the capital of Damascus. Members of Syria's Islamist alliance purged the city of Hama of Baathists, killing perhaps 50 of them. Asad's reaction was out of all proportion to the actual events. He called up the army and special security forces and sent them into the city. Two weeks of fierce fighting followed,

Hafiz al-Asad, president of Syria from 1971 until his death in 2000. Asad ruled Syria with an iron hand and was a key figure in Middle East politics. (Courtesy: Embassy of the Syrian Arab Republic)

in which large parts of Hama were razed. Some 10,000 to 38,000 people died.

With Soviet support, Asad dramatically increased Syrian military strength. Syrian educational curriculums were revised to stress Asad's position that Syria was the champion of the Arab cause against Israel and Western imperialism. In his foreign policy, Asad employed a strange mix of diplomacy, war, and support of opposition movements in neighboring countries.

In foreign affairs, Asad's chief immediate aim was to regain the Golan Heights from Israel. Six years after the 1967 Six-Day War with no progress toward the return of that territory captured by the Jewish state, Asad and Egyptian president Anwar Sadat carefully planned and then initiated a surprise attack on Israel that would force it to fight simultaneously on two fronts. The conflict began on October 6, 1973. Known as the Yom Kippur (Ramadan) War, it caught Israel completely by surprise. Despite initial Egyptian and Syrian military successes, which included a Syrian drive into the Golan Heights and Egyptian crossing of the Suez Canal, Israel secured the initiative and was on the brink of a crushing victory over its two opponents when a United Nations (UN)–brokered cease-fire took effect on October 22. Asad then falsely sought to shift the blame for the defeat to Sadat and Egypt, resulting in lasting enmity between the two men. Asad's continued insistence on the unconditional return of the Golan Heights prevented any fruitful peace negotiations with Israel. Indeed, Asad opposed all peace accords between the Palestinians and the Israelis as well as Jordan's decision in 1994 to end the state of war between itself and Israel.

In 1976, Asad sent troops into Lebanon at the request of the West and the Arab League on a peacekeeping mission to end the civil war raging there. Israel's invasion and occupation of southern Lebanon (1982–1985) led Asad to impose some changes in the constitution of Lebanon that had been demanded by the Lebanese. These granted Muslims equal representation with Christians in the Lebanese government. Meanwhile, Syrian forces in Lebanon maintained a presence, which did not end until 2005.

Asad regularly supported radical Palestinian and Muslim terrorist groups based in Lebanon and allowed them to establish bases and offices in Syria. The United States routinely accused Syria of state-sponsored terrorism. Asad supported Iran in the Iran-Iraq War (1980–1988) and participated in the coalition formed to force Iraq from Kuwait in the Persian Gulf War (1991), but Asad and Iraqi dictator Saddam Hussein developed closer ties in 1998 when Israel began to develop a strategic partnership with Turkey.

Hafiz al-Asad died in Damascus of a heart attack on June 10, 2000. He was succeeded in power by his son, Bashar al-Asad.

RICHARD EDWARDS AND SPENCER C. TUCKER

See also
Arab-Israeli Conflict, Overview; Asad, Bashar al-; Baath Party; Egypt; DESERT STORM, Operation; Hussein, Saddam; Iran-Iraq War; Lebanon; Muslim Brotherhood; Pan-Arabism and Pan-Arabist Thought; Sadat, Muhammad Anwar; Syria; Terrorism; United Arab Republic

References
Patterson, Charles. *Hafiz Al-Asad of Syria.* Englewood Cliffs, NJ: Prentice Hall, 1991.
Seale, Patrick. *Asad: The Struggle for the Middle East.* Berkeley: University of California Press, 1990.

Aspin, Leslie, Jr.
Birth Date: July 21, 1938
Death Date: May 21, 1995

U.S. congressman (1971–1993) and secretary of defense (January 21, 1993–February 3, 1994) during the first administration of President William Jefferson "Bill" Clinton. Born on July 21, 1938, in Milwaukee, Wisconsin, Leslie "Les" Aspin Jr. earned a BA from Yale University in 1960, an MA from Oxford University in 1962, and a PhD in economics from the Massachusetts Institute of Technology (MIT) in 1965. A member of the U.S. Army from 1966 to 1968, Aspin was a systems analyst for Secretary of Defense Robert S. McNamara (1961–1967). Prior to being elected to Congress as a

representative from Wisconsin, he taught economics at Marquette University in Milwaukee.

An astute observer of U.S. military preparedness, and as such often at odds with Pentagon officials, Aspin became chairman of the House Committee on Armed Services in 1985. He was frequently criticized by fellow Democrats in the House because he supported President Ronald Reagan's policy of combating the Sandinistas in Nicaragua by providing aid to the Contras. Because of his support for the Contras, House Democrats were able to temporarily remove him from his chairmanship in 1987. In January 1991, he vocalized his support for President George H. W. Bush's plan to use military force to remove Iraqi occupation forces from Kuwait. Although his opinion was criticized by many House Democrats, his belief that the United States could rapidly achieve a military victory with minimal loss of American life proved to be correct.

Given Clinton's lack of military and foreign policy experience, Aspin, who emphasized the impact of U.S. national security on the national economy, and who had a firm grasp of U.S. defense issues, seemed to be a logical choice to lead the Pentagon. Immediately after being confirmed as defense secretary by the U.S. Senate, Aspin

U.S. congressman Les Aspin was a key supporter of President George H. W. Bush's policy of removing Iraqi troops from Kuwait by force in 1991. His subsequent tenure as secretary of defense during 1993–1994 was clouded by controversy, however. (Library of Congress)

pointed out the dangers that the end of the Cold War posed to U.S. national security. He was especially concerned about the potential proliferation of regional conflicts and their impact on U.S. national security. Notwithstanding a serious heart ailment, which resulted in the implantation of a pacemaker in March 1993, Aspin was immediately confronted with the politically explosive issue of homosexuals in the military. Although Clinton had promised to end discrimination against homosexuals in the military, in December 1993 Aspin unveiled the "don't ask, don't tell" policy, which pleased no one.

Aspin's development of a defense budget for fiscal year 1994 proved to be even more controversial than his handling of the issue of homosexuals in the military. Although Clinton had promised to reduce defense spending in the aftermath of the Cold War, Aspin's budget, which reduced defense spending by just $12 billion, was seen by many Democrats as a continuation of the Bush administration's high defense spending.

In September 1993, General Colin Powell, chairman of the Joint Chiefs of Staff, asked for tanks and armored vehicles for U.S. troops in Somalia; Aspin denied the request. Shortly thereafter, 18 U.S. troops were killed and dozens wounded in an ambush by Somali rebels. Following intense criticism in Congress, Aspin admitted that he had made a mistake. Several members of Congress then demanded Aspin's resignation. In December 1993, Clinton announced that Aspin was resigning for personal reasons. William J. Perry succeeded him as defense secretary. Following his resignation, Aspin taught at Marquette University until he died of a stroke on May 21, 1995, in Washington, D.C.

MICHAEL R. HALL

See also

Clinton, William Jefferson; DESERT STORM, Operation; Powell, Colin Luther; Somalia, International Intervention in

References

Aspin, Les. *The Aspin Papers: Sanctions, Diplomacy, and War in the Persian Gulf.* Washington, DC: Center for Strategic and International Studies, 1991.

Italia, Robert, and Rosemary Wallner. *Les Aspin: Secretary of Defense.* Edina, MN: Abdo and Daughters, 1993.

Association of Muslim Scholars

Iraqi organization established in 2003 to oppose the U.S. occupation of Iraq and to heal sectarian divisions there. The Association of Muslim Scholars (Hayat al-Ulama al-Muslimin) is a Sunni religious organization that has consistently opposed the American presence in Iraq based largely on a nationalistic, anti-imperialist, and religious perspective. It is able to exert some influence on Iraqi politics, and claims to reject terrorism and sectarian violence.

The association was established on April 14, 2003, just five days after the fall of Saddam Hussein's regime. Its headquarters are located in the immense Umm al-Qura mosque in Baghdad, built following the 1991 Persian Gulf War. The group claims to represent all Iraqis, including Arabs, Kurds, and Turks; however, it mainly numbers Sunni Arab imams and clerics of mosques and schools in the west and north of Iraq, and also in Sunni pockets in the predominantly Shia south.

The leader of the association, Sheikh Harith al-Dhari, is highly respected within the Sunni community. He is from the Zubay tribe, centered west of Baghdad in the Zaydun region. His grandfather and father both fought in the 1920 uprising against British colonial rule and played a role in the killing of Lieutenant Colonel Gerard Leachman on August 12, 1920. Dhari earned a degree from al-Azhar University in Cairo and taught Islamic law at Baghdad University until he fled Saddam Hussein's regime in the late 1990s. He returned when Hussein's regime fell in 2003. Currently, Dhari lives outside of Iraq, moving between Jordan and Egypt. Routinely, General David Petraeus, former commander of the Multi-National Force–Iraq (MNF-I), attempted to marginalize Dhari's importance for attaining stability in Iraq because of the association's opposition to the U.S. presence.

The association established its relevance for the Iraqi population in April 2004 when the Iraqi Governing Council, under U.S. pressure, supported American combat action in Fallujah. The association earned credibility among Iraqis because it was the most prominent Sunni organization to oppose the attack, known as the First Battle of Fallujah. It defended the Iraqi combatants there and rallied support from the wide network of Sunni mosques to collect food and aid for besieged inhabitants of the city. It also provided intellectual legitimacy for the rebels in their fight against the United States.

Subsequently, the association has maintained its relevance as a leading organization opposing American occupation of Iraq. It has tried to be a broker and sponsor of reconciliation between Sunni, Shia, and other faiths on the grounds of nationalist opposition to U.S. occupation. However, its attempts have almost always reflected its Sunni identity and have thus yielded little accomplishment to date in mending intersectarian conflict.

It is unknown if the association has provided aid (and if so, to what extent) to Al Qaeda in Iraq (AQI). In March 2007, AQI elements assassinated the grandnephew of Harith al-Dhari in an apparent warning that the association must maintain a hard-line anti-American approach and must not participate in any reconciliation measures then occurring. Although the assassination resulted in greater anti-AQI feeling, it did not result in any palpable change in the official policy line of the association. However, it is probable that some of its low-level supporters have participated in the anti-AQI Awakening movement.

The association's closest link with insurgent activity in Iraq is through the Revolutionary Brigades, named in honor of the uprising against British rule in 1920 and led by Muthanna al-Dhari, Sheikh Harith al-Dhari's son.

KARL RUBIS

See also

Al Qaeda in Iraq; Fallujah, First Battle of; Iraq, History of, 1990–Present; Petraeus, David Howell; Shia Islam; Sunni Islam

References

Gordon, Michael R., and General Bernard E. Trainor. *Cobra II: The Inside Story of the Invasion and Occupation of Iraq.* New York: Pantheon Books, 2006.

Ricks, Thomas E. *Fiasco: The American Military Adventure in Iraq.* New York: Penguin, 2006.

Aswan High Dam Project

The Aswan High Dam (al-Sadd al-Ali) was a major Egyptian development project and one of the largest engineering undertakings of the second half of the 20th century. Egyptian president Gamal Abdel Nasser, convinced that the dam would solve many Egyptian social and economic problems, made its construction a high priority. The plan involved building a new dam on the Nile River south of Aswan, the first cataract in southern Egypt.

The Nile River has rightly been called the lifeblood of Egypt. Each year, the river has flooded, depositing rich nutrients and aiding farmers, but this flooding has been uneven. In some years it nearly wiped out entire crops, while in drought years it often did not provide sufficient water. Heavy floods also brought misery for an expanding Egyptian population along the river. Construction of a new high dam on the Nile, it was believed, would provide a regular, consistent flow of water and prevent damaging floods.

Not only would such a dam end the regular flooding by the Nile, but it would also allow for the irrigation of 1.4 million acres of new land in the largely desert country and provide hydroelectric power to expand Egypt's industrial capacity, bringing jobs and increasing national prosperity. Nasser also saw the project as a hallmark of his regime and a model for economic development in the developing world.

This was not the first effort to dam the Nile. The British took control of Egypt in 1882, and during 1899–1902 they built a dam at Aswan. Later known as the Aswan Low Dam, it was nearly 2,000 yards long and some 75 feet high. Because its height was determined to be inadequate, the Low Dam was raised during 1907–1912 and again during 1929–1933.

The Low Dam nearly overflowed in 1946, and rather than raise it a third time the Egyptian government decided to build a new dam about four miles upriver. Planning for the new dam began in earnest in 1952 following the Egyptian Revolution of that year. Financing remained a problem, however, so Nasser approached the United States. President Dwight D. Eisenhower's administration was initially interested in the project, hoping to link financial support for the project to Western foreign policy initiatives. Eisenhower also hoped that the course of construction, predicted to take as long as 18 years, would see Egypt aligned with the United States and perhaps even provide sufficient leverage for Washington to prod the Egyptian government into making a peace agreement with Israel. Furthermore, funding through the U.S.-dominated World Bank might allow Washington to block Egyptian arms deals with the Soviet Union and economic policies deemed contrary to Western interests.

Nasser was reluctant to make any arrangement that would limit his freedom of action in foreign policy. Still, the Egyptians clearly preferred U.S. assistance to that of the Soviets. At the same time as he was pursuing the dam project, however, Nasser was seeking to build up and modernize the Egyptian military. Toward that end he sought to acquire modern weapons from the United States and other Western nations. When the U.S. and British governments refused to supply the advanced arms, which they believed might be used against Israel, in 1955 Nasser turned to the Soviet bloc. In September 1955, encouraged by Moscow, he reached a barter arrangement with Czechoslovakia for substantial quantities of modern weapons, including jet aircraft and tanks, in return for Egyptian cotton.

This arms deal affected the Aswan High Dam project. In December 1955, the Eisenhower administration announced that it was willing to lend $56 million for the dam construction, while Great Britain pledged $14 million and the World Bank $200 million. There were strings attached, however. Egypt had to provide matching funds and must not accept Soviet assistance.

Nasser was unhappy with the conditions and delayed accepting them. With the Egyptian president expecting a Soviet offer, the controlled Egyptian press launched a major propaganda campaign against the West, especially the United States. But when no Soviet offer was forthcoming, Nasser accepted the Western aid package on July 17, 1956. But only two days later, U.S. secretary of state John Foster Dulles announced that the offer had been withdrawn. The British government immediately followed suit. The official U.S. reasons were that Egypt had failed to reach agreement with the Sudan over the dam (much of the vast lake created by the dam would be in Sudanese territory) and that the Egyptian part of the financing for the project had become "uncertain." The real reasons for the rejection were quite different. In the U.S. Congress, strong opposition came from a number of powerful interests including fiscal conservatives skeptical about foreign aid, supporters of Israel concerned about Egyptian hostility toward the Jewish state, and Southerners who believed that expanded Egyptian cotton production resulting from new irrigated lands would undercut U.S. cotton growers. But Dulles was also determined to teach Nasser and other neutralist leaders a lesson. Dulles was angry over Nasser's demarche to the communist bloc and arms purchases but particularly was upset over Egypt's recent recognition of the People's Republic of China (PRC).

Nasser was furious and, a week later, took action. On July 26, he nationalized the Suez Canal Company, claiming that this revenue would pay for the construction of the cherished dam project. He had contemplated this step for some time, but the U.S. rejection of the funding for the dam prompted its timing. In 1955, the canal produced net revenues of nearly $100 million, of which Egypt received only $2 million. Seizure of the canal would not only provide funding for the Aswan High Dam project but would also raise Nasser's stature in the eyes of Arab nationalists.

Nasser's decision prompted what became known as the Suez Crisis and eventually led to collusion among the governments of Israel, Britain, and France. These three states then secretly planned

Soviet-Egyptian ceremonies at the Aswan High Dam, in the late 1950s. When the Western powers reneged on their pledge to assist in building the dam, the Soviet Union stepped in. (Bettmann/Corbis)

military intervention against Egypt with the aim of driving Nasser from power and returning the canal to control by the Suez Canal Company. Supposedly to protect the canal, Israel invaded Egypt at the end of October, and Britain and France followed suit in early November. This military intervention caught the United States by surprise, but within days heavy financial pressure from Washington, along with Soviet threats, brought about a withdrawal. The canal remained in Egyptian control.

Plans for the dam went forward, and in 1958 the Soviet Union agreed to assist with the project. Moscow provided technical and engineering assistance, including heavy equipment. The Soviet Zuk Hydroproject Institute designed the enormous rock and clay dam. Moscow, which saw this as an opportunity to gain a foothold in the Middle East, ultimately may have paid up to one-third of the cost of the project. Construction of the dam began in 1960. The first stage was completed in 1964 when the reservoir began filling. The dam was completed on July 21, 1970, and the reservoir reached capacity in 1976.

The United Nations Education, Scientific and Cultural Organization (UNESCO) raised concerns about the loss of historic sites from the rising waters, and an international effort was undertaken beginning in 1960 to move 24 major monuments, some of which were given to nations that had helped fund the relocation effort. One such example is the Nubian Temple of Dandur, given by Egypt to the United States and now located at the Metropolitan Museum of Art in New York City.

The Aswan High Dam is some 11,800 feet in length and 364 feet high. It is 3,200 feet wide at the base and 130 feet wide at its top. The reservoir behind the dam, Lake Nasser, is some 300 miles long and 10 miles across at its widest point. The dam's 12 generators are capable of producing 2.1 gigawatts of electricity. At first producing half of Egypt's power, the dam now produces perhaps 15 percent of the total.

The dam brought electricity to some Egyptian villages for the first time. It also mitigated damage from floods in 1964 and 1973 and from droughts during 1972–1973 and 1983–1984. It also led to the development of a new fishing industry on Lake Nasser. Unfortunately, much of the economic benefit promised by the dam has also been outstripped by the rapidly expanding Egyptian population.

The dam has also had negative impacts. More than 90,000 people had to be relocated because of the rising waters of Lake Nasser, and the fishing industry on Lake Nasser is remote from markets. Tremendous silting behind the dam lowers the water capacity of Lake Nasser and threatens the dam's generators, and restricting the flow of water on the Nile and its nutrients has adversely affected farming along the river and the fishing industry in the eastern Mediterranean. The dam has also led to erosion along the Nile Delta and the intrusion of salt water into areas used for the production of rice.

STEPHEN ZUNES AND SPENCER C. TUCKER

See also

Dulles, John Foster; Egypt; Eisenhower, Dwight David; France, Middle East Policy; Nasser, Gamal Abdel; Suez Crisis; United Kingdom, Middle East Policy

References

Lytle, Elizabeth Edith. *The Aswan High Dam.* Monticello, IL: Council of Planning Librarians, 1977.

Parks, Peggy J. *Aswan High Dam.* San Diego: Blackbirch, 2003.

Shibl, Yusuf A. *The Aswan High Dam Project.* Beirut, Lebanon: Arab Institute for Research and Publishing, 1971.

Atef, Muhammad
Birth Date: 1944
Death Date: November 18, 2001

Head of the terrorist organization Al Qaeda's military operations during the planning and implementation of the September 11, 2001, terror attacks on the United States. At that time, Atef was number three in the Al Qaeda hierarchy, behind Osama bin Laden and Ayman al-Zawahiri. Atef made numerous decisions about the planned attack of September 11 from the beginning, assisting Khalid Sheikh Mohammed in the final stages of the plot. Muhammad Atef was born in 1944 in Menoufya, Egypt, in the Nile Delta, about 35 miles north of Cairo. His birth name was Sobhi Abu Sitta. After graduating from high school, he served his required two years of military service in the Egyptian Army. Reports that Atef was a policeman in Egypt have been denied by the Egyptian government, but nearly all sources state that he was.

Atef became an Islamist extremist early in his career, and in the late 1970s, joined an Egyptian terrorist organization, the Egyptian Islamic Jihad. Evidently a low-ranking member, he did not meet with its leader, Ayman al-Zawahiri, while both were in Egypt. Despite his involvement in this group, he escaped arrest after the crackdown on extremists that followed the assassination of Egyptian president Anwar Sadat in 1981.

In 1983, Atef left Egypt for Afghanistan to fight with the mujahideen ("holy warriors," freedom fighters) against the Soviet forces. There he first met Zawahiri, who then introduced him to bin Laden. Atef and bin Laden became close friends. Atef also became acquainted with Abdullah Azzam and admired him greatly, but in the subsequent battle between Azzam and Zawahiri for bin Laden's support, Atef supported Zawahiri. In 1999,

Egyptian authorities sentenced Atef to a seven-year prison term in absentia for his membership in the Egyptian Islamic Jihad, but he never returned to Egypt.

Atef's close personal relationship with bin Laden made him an important member of Al Qaeda. When bin Laden founded Al Qaeda, Atef was a charter member. Ubaidah al-Banshiri was Al Qaeda's head of military operations, and Atef assisted him. He was active in organizing Somali resistance to the American military presence in 1992, but some evidence suggests that his stay there was not entirely successful. Atef also served as bin Laden's chief of personal security. Banshiri's death in a boating accident in Africa allowed Atef to replace him in 1996. From then until his death in 2001, Atef was in charge of military operations for Al Qaeda. All military operation came under his oversight, but he always remained subordinate to bin Laden, even after bin Laden's eldest son married one of Atef's daughters in January 2001.

Atef was aware of the September 11 plot from its beginning. Khalid Sheikh Mohammed had apparently outlined the plan to bin Laden and Atef as early as 1996. Bin Laden finally agreed on the basics of the plot in 1998, and it was Atef's job to search Al Qaeda's training camps for suitable candidates for a martyrdom mission that required operatives to live unnoticed in America. Once the members of the Hamburg cell were picked and recruited by bin Laden, Atef explained to Muhammad Atta, Ramzi Muhammad

Muhammad Atef, head of military operations for the Al Qaeda terrorist organization and considered the right-hand man to Osama bin Laden, is believed to have been killed in a U.S. air strike near Kabul in November 2001. (AP/Wide World Photos)

Abdallah ibn al-Shibh, Ziyad al-Jarrah, and Marwan al-Shehhi the outlines of the plot.

Al Qaeda avoided having its leaders at a single site except for particularly special occasions, a policy prompted by fears of American assassination of Al Qaeda's leaders. Bin Laden announced that in case of his death or capture, Atef would succeed him as head of Al Qaeda. Once the United States began military operations against the Taliban and Al Qaeda in Afghanistan in October 2001, it became even more important for Al Qaeda's leaders to be at separate locations. On November 18, 2001, Atef was at a gathering in Kabul when a U.S. Predator unmanned aerial vehicle fired Hellfire missiles, killing him and those with him—something for which the United States had been offering a $5 million reward. The loss of Atef was a blow to Al Qaeda, but he was soon replaced as military commander by Abu Zubaydah.

STEPHEN E. ATKINS

See also

Al Qaeda; Atta, Muhammad; Bin Laden, Osama; Hamburg Cell; Jarrah, Ziyad al-; September 11 Attacks; Shehhi, Marwan al-; Zawahiri, Ayman al-

References

Bergen, Peter L. *The Osama bin Laden I Know: An Oral History of Al Qaeda's Leader.* New York: Free Press, 2006.

Dawoud, Khaled. "Mohammed Atef: Egyptian Militant Who Rose to the Top of the al-Qaida Hierarchy." *Guardian* [London], November 19, 2001, 1.

Atta, Muhammad
Birth Date: September 1, 1968
Death Date: September 11, 2001

Commander of the Al Qaeda terrorist team that hijacked four American jetliners that were then used to attack the United States on September 11, 2001. Muhammad al-Amir Awad al-Sayyid Atta was born on September 1, 1968, in the village of Kafr el-Sheikh in the Egyptian Delta and had a strict family upbringing. His father was a middle-class lawyer with ties to the fundamentalist Muslim Brotherhood. Atta's family moved to the Abdin District of Cairo in 1978 when Atta was 10. His father, who had a dominating personality, insisted that his children study, not play; thus, Atta's family life allowed him few friends.

After attending high school, Atta enrolled in the Cairo University in 1986. At his graduation in 1990, his grades were not good enough to admit him to graduate school. On the recommendation of his father, he planned to study urban planning in Germany. In the meantime, he worked for a Cairo engineering firm.

Atta traveled to Hamburg, Germany, in July 1992 to begin studies there. During his courses he interacted very little with fellow students, earning a reputation as a loner. His classmates also noted his strong religious orientation. He traveled to Turkey and Syria in 1994 to study old Muslim quarters. After receiving a German grant, Atta and two fellow students visited Egypt to study the old section of Cairo, called the Old City. Up to this point in his life, Atta appeared to be an academic preparing for a career as a teacher at a university.

In 1995, however, Atta became active in Muslim extremist politics. After a pilgrimage to Mecca, he initiated contact with Al Qaeda recruiters. Atta was just the type of individual sought by Al Qaeda: intelligent and dedicated.

After returning to Hamburg to continue his studies, Atta attended the al-Quds Mosque, where his final recruitment to radical Islam took place. There Atta met radical clerics who steered him toward an Al Qaeda recruiter. Muhammad Haydar Zammar, a Syrian recruiter for Al Qaeda, convinced Atta to join that organization. Several of his friends, Ramzi Muhammad Abdallah ibn al-Shibh, Marwan al-Shehhi, and Ziyad al-Jarrah, also joined Al Qaeda at this time. Atta became the leader of the so-called Hamburg cell of radical Islamists.

In 1998 Atta left for Kandahar, Afghanistan, to receive military and terrorist training at the Al Qaeda training camp at Khaldan. He so distinguished himself during the training that Al Qaeda leaders decided to recruit him for a future suicide mission. Atta ranked high in all the attributes of an Al Qaeda operative—intelligence, religious devotion, patience, and willingness to sacrifice. Atta, Jarrah, and Shehhi met and talked with Osama bin Laden in Kandahar. Bin Laden asked them to pledge loyalty to him and accept a suicide mission. They agreed, and Muhammad Atef, Al Qaeda's military chief, briefed them on the general outlines of the September 11 operation. Then Atta and the others returned to Germany to finish their academic training.

Atta was a complex individual, deeply affected psychologically. He held the typical conservative Muslim view that relations with the opposite sex were not permitted outside of marriage. Atta also held strong anti-American views, disturbed as he was by the Americanization of Egyptian society.

After Atta finished his degree in 1999, Al Qaeda's leaders assigned him the martyrdom mission in the United States, a mission planned by Khalid Sheikh Mohammed. Atta arrived in the United States on June 2, 2000. His orders placed him in charge of a large cell, but he, Jarrah, and Shehhi were the only members of it who knew the details of his mission. Several times Atta flew back and forth between the United States and Germany and Spain to coordinate the mission. Members of his cell arrived in the United States at various times. Atta and key members of the cell received orders to take pilot lessons to fly large commercial aircraft.

Most of Atta's time was spent in pilot lessons in Florida. Before he could qualify for training on large commercial aircraft, Atta had to learn to fly small planes. Most of his flying instruction took place at Huffman Aviation in Sarasota, Florida. Next, he began to use simulators and manuals to train himself to fly the larger aircraft.

Atta gathered most of the members of his cell together in Florida for the first time in early June 2001. He organized the cell into four teams, each of which included a trained pilot. Throughout the

Two men, identified as hijackers Muhammad Atta, right, and Abdulaziz Alomari, center, pass through airport security in this September 11, 2001, photo from the surveillance tape at Portland International Jetport, Maine. (AP/Wide World Photos)

summer of 2001, each team rode as passengers on test flights in which they studied the efficiency of airline security and the best times to hijack an aircraft. They discovered that airline security was weakest at Boston's Logan International Airport and decided that the best day for hijacking would be a Tuesday. They also decided that first-class seats would give them better access to cockpits. Although the teams tried to remain inconspicuous, the film actor James Woods reported suspicious behavior by one of the teams on a flight. He reported his suspicions to the pilot and a flight attendant, who passed them on to the Federal Aviation Administration (FAA), but nothing came of his report.

Atta selected two airlines—American Airlines and United Airlines—that flew Boeing 757s and 767s, aircraft that hold the most aviation fuel because they are used for long flights. These aircraft were also equipped with up-to-date avionics, making them easier to fly.

Atta called for a leadership meeting in Las Vegas, Nevada, in late June 2001. Atta, Ziyad Jarrah, Hani Hanjour, and Nawaf

al-Hazmi then completed plans for the September 11 operation. Atta and Jarrah used a local Cyberzone Internet Café to send e-mails to Al Qaeda leaders abroad.

Atta then traveled to Spain via Zurich, Switzerland, to update his handlers on his final plans and receive last minute instructions. He met with Al Qaeda representatives in the resort town of Salou on July 8, 2001, receiving his final authorization for the September 11 mission. Atta was given final authority to determine the targets and date of the operation. Several times bin Laden had attempted to push the plan forward, but Atta had refused to carry out the mission before he was ready and was backed by Khalid Sheikh Mohammed in this decision. Atta flew back to the United States, and, despite an expired visa, had no trouble getting into the country.

Atta issued final instructions about the mission on the night of September 10, 2001. One-way tickets for flights on September 11 had been bought with credit cards in late August. Atta had made arrangements to have the cell's excess funds transferred back to Al

Qaeda on September 4. He traveled to Portland, Maine, with Abd al-Aziz al-Umari, and they stayed in South Portland. They caught a 5:45 a.m. flight out of Portland International Airport, but Atta's luggage arrived too late to make American Airlines Flight 11 from Logan International Airport. At 7:45 a.m., Atta and Umari boarded American Airlines Flight 11. Soon afterward, Atta phoned Marwan al-Shehhi, on board United Airlines Flight 175—also at Logan International Airport—to make sure everything was on schedule.

Atta commanded the first team. Approximately 15 minutes after takeoff, his team seized control of the aircraft using box cutters as weapons. Atta redirected the aircraft toward New York City and the World Trade Center complex, where it crashed into the North Tower of the World Trade Center at about 8:45 a.m. Members of the other teams carried out their attacks successfully, except for the one flight lost in Pennsylvania, where the passengers—informed of what had happened with the other three hijacked airplanes—fought the hijackers. Atta, along with the plane's entire crew and all passengers, died instantly when the airliner slammed into the North Tower of the World Trade Center. The North Tower collapsed less than two hours later.

STEPHEN A. ATKINS

See also

Bin Laden, Osama; Hamburg Cell; Jarrah, Ziyad al-; Mohammed, Khalid Sheikh; September 11 Attacks; Shehhi, Marwan al-; Shibh, Ramzi Muhammad Abdallah ibn al-

References

Fouda, Yosri, and Nick Fielding. *Masterminds of Terror: The Truth behind the Most Devastating Terrorist Attack the World Has Ever Seen.* New York: Arcade, 2003.

McDermott, Terry. *Perfect Soldiers: The 9/11 Hijackers: Who They Were, Why They Did It.* New York: HarperCollins, 2005.

Miller, John, Michael Stone, and Chris Mitchell. *The Cell: Inside the 9/11 Plot, and Why the FBI and CIA Failed to Stop It.* New York: Hyperion, 2002.

Sageman, Marc. *Understanding Terror Networks.* Philadelphia: University of Pennsylvania Press, 2004.

Australia, Role in Persian Gulf, Afghanistan, and Iraq Wars

Large, primarily English-speaking country located due south of Indonesia, surrounded by the Indian Ocean to the west and South Pacific to the east. Australia, including the island state of Tasmania and several smaller islands, comprises more than 2.97 million square miles. Founded as a penal colony for Great Britain in the 18th century, Australia's 2008 estimated population was 21 million. In 1901, the six former colonies on the continent formed the Commonwealth of Australia, with a constitution closely resembling that of the United States. Although it remains a commonwealth realm with strong ties to Great Britain, since 1945 Australia has developed close ties, particularly in the area of international affairs, with the United States.

Australia's government is a constitutional parliamentary democracy, with a prime minister and a governor-general at the federal level who represents Britain's Queen Elizabeth II. The governor-general normally acts only upon the advice of the prime minister. Two major political groups dominate Australian politics: the Australian Labor Party (a center-left, social democratic organization) and the Coalition, an amalgamation of center-right parties, chiefly the Liberal Party and the National Party. The Labor Party held power in Australia from 1983 to 1996; from 1996 to 2007, the Liberal Party held power. In December 2007, Labor again took the reins of government. The current prime minister, Kevin Rudd, has promised to implement a phased withdrawal of Australian troops from the Iraq War, which he began in June 2008.

At the time of the proclamation of the Federation of Australia in 1901, some Australian soldiers were engaged in fighting in the Boer War, and others had just returned from service in China's Boxer Rebellion. Since then, Australians have served in World War I, World War II, the Korean War, and the Vietnam War. They have also participated in the Persian Gulf War of 1991, Operation ENDURING FREEDOM in Afghanistan, and Operation IRAQI FREEDOM in Iraq.

The Australian Navy frigate HMAS *Toowoomba* (FFH-156) during coalition maritime operations in the Gulf of Oman on November 4, 2009. (U.S. Department of Defense)

Following the Iraqi invasion of Kuwait on August 2, 1990, the Australian government sharply condemned the actions of Iraq, and Australian prime minister Bob Hawke's government agreed to impose economic sanctions on Iraq if requested by the United Nations (UN), which occurred on August 6. With the implementation of UN sanctions against Iraq, Australia stopped wheat sales to the country and agreed with Canada to enforce the sanctions, which meant the commitment of naval vessels to that task.

Most members of Hawke's Australian Labor Party had opposed Australian participation in the Vietnam War, and indeed many of Hawke's own cabinet ministers had taken part in antiwar protests. After the passing of UN Resolution 678 on November 29, 1990, Hawke decided that in spite of the reservations of some of his colleagues, he would push for the commitment of Australian forces in a war with Iraq, Australia's first foreign troop deployment since the Vietnam War. Paul Keating, deputy prime minister, opposed the use of Australian service personnel in an Iraqi war, and John Button, the Senate leader, said that he opposed not only the use of Australian troops, but also the use of Australian ships to enforce sanctions, although he would not oppose government policy in public.

When it was clear that Hawke would obtain the necessary backing of the cabinet, he consulted the leaders of the Labor Party caucus, and urged them to support the sending of Australian forces into combat, as they would be acting at the behest of the United Nations and not simply the United States. By the late autumn of 1990, there were already some antiwar protests around Australia, which had at that point committed the DDG-2-class destroyer *Brisbane,* the Perry-class frigates *Adelaide, Darwin,* and *Sydney,* and two tankers—the *Success* and *Westralia.* The Australian ships were placed under U.S. tactical command, although the command and control center in Australia retained administrative control.

The *Adelaide* remained in the Persian Gulf region enforcing sanctions until December 1990; the *Darwin* departed later the same month. The *Success* remained in the area until late January 1991. The *Brisbane, Sydney,* and *Westralia* were the only three Australian vessels that remained in place for the duration of the war. The crew of all the ships underwent extensive training in preparation for potential chemical and biological weapons attacks, and Royal Australian Navy Clearance Diving Team CDT3 was prepared for work on ordnance demolition tasks.

During the Persian Gulf War, there were also a number of Australian military personnel who were attached to various British and U.S. air and ground force units. Also in service were Royal Australian Air Force photointerpreters and members of the Defense Intelligence Organization, stationed in Saudi Arabia.

Although Australian military support was small, the coalition made extensive use of the Pine Gap facility near Alice Springs, where much of the intelligence for the war was collected and processed. Australian ships in the area risked attack from the air, but their main worry was from mines, which the Iraqis had extensively employed.

There were no Australian casualties during Operation DESERT STORM. After the fighting had ended in February 1991, some 75 Australian personnel were posted to northern Iraq to aid the Kurds in humanitarian relief efforts. Opposition to the Persian Gulf War quickly dissipated in Australia following the rapid and easy victory of the United Nations forces. The Australian ships returned to their home ports amid wide celebrations.

Twenty-two Australian citizens died in the September 11, 2001, terror attacks on the World Trade Center and the U.S. Pentagon. Australian prime minister John Howard, leader of the Liberal Party, happened to be in Washington, D.C., that day, attending the 50th-anniversary commemoration of the Australia–New Zealand–United States (ANZUS) Treaty. He immediately declared his support for the U.S. military actions that followed September 11, and he committed Australian soldiers to the invasion of Afghanistan, known as Operation SLIPPER among the Australian armed forces.

Australia's initial support of the war against the Taliban and Al Qaeda included the deployment of a Special Forces task group (1 Squadron SAS, from October 2001 to April 2002; 2 Squadron SAS, from April to July 2002; and 3 Squadron SAS, from August to November 2002). The Australian Defence Force also dispatched two Royal Australian Air Force Boeing-707 air-to-air refueling aircraft, as well as four McDonell Douglas (now Boeing) F/A-18 Hornet fighter aircraft for the defense of the island of Diego Garcia. Subsequently, troops from the 1st Combat Engineer Regiment, the 5th/7th Battalion, the 6th Battalion from the Royal Australian Regiment, and the 2nd Cavalry Regiment were sent for humanitarian and reconstruction work in Oruzgan, alongside Dutch soldiers. As of June 2008, six Australians had been killed in operations in Afghanistan. Also, two Australians had been arrested over events in Afghanistan—one in Afghanistan and the other in Pakistan—and were being held by U.S. authorities at Guantánamo Bay, Cuba. One was released without charge, and the other pleaded guilty to supporting terrorism.

Although the commitment of soldiers to Afghanistan was received enthusiastically by Australian citizens, the deployment of military personnel to Iraq in 2003 was not. On March 21, 2003, Howard stated that his government had "decided to commit Australian forces to action to disarm Iraq because we believe it is right, it is lawful, and it's in Australia's national interest. We are determined to join other countries to deprive Iraq of its weapons of mass destruction." Apart from the United States and the United Kingdom, Australia was the only other country to deploy soldiers to the actual invasion of Iraq, which the Australians code-named Operation FALCONER.

Australia's commitment involved three Royal Australian Navy ships—HMAS *Anzac,* HMAS *Darwin,* and HMAS *Kanimbla.* In addition, it sent No. 75 Squadron, including 14 F/A-18 Hornet jet fighters, 3 Lockheed C-130H Hercules transport aircraft, and 2 Lockheed AP-3C Orion maritime patrol aircraft, along with associated ground crew and support personnel. The Australian Army supplied some 500 members of the Australian Special Forces. The soldiers were withdrawn after the invasion and replaced by combat troops who were deployed in the southern provinces of

Iraq and in air traffic control in Baghdad. Australian troops also assisted in the protection of the Australian embassy and Australian diplomatic and government personnel in Iraq.

During the federal election campaign in 2007, Labor Party leader Kevin Rudd announced that he would withdraw troops from Iraq if elected. His subsequent defeat of John Howard in December 2007 witnessed the beginning of the phased withdrawal of Australian soldiers from Iraq. In June 2008, he recalled 550 combat troops, leaving about 800 left in security details and aboard ships in the Persian Gulf. There were also a number of air force personnel left in the region. Of the 2,000 Australian troops deployed, 2 have died during active service in Iraq.

JUSTIN J. CORFIELD

See also

DESERT STORM, Operation; Diego Garcia; ENDURING FREEDOM, Operation; IRAQI FREEDOM, Operation

References

Evans, Gareth, and Bruce Grant. *Australia's Foreign Relations in the World of the 1990s.* Carlton, Victoria: Melbourne University Press, 1995.

Hawke, Bob. *The Hawke Memoirs.* Port Melbourne: William Heinemann Australia, 1994.

Horner, David. *The Gulf Commitment: The Australian Defence Force's First War.* Melbourne: Melbourne University Press, 1992.

Kirkland, Frederick, ed. *Operation Damask: The Gulf War—Iraq-Kuwait, 1990–1991.* Cremorne, New South Wales: Plaza Historical Services, 1991.

Nash, Greg, and David Stevens. *Australia's Navy in the Gulf: From Countenance to Catalyst, 1941–2006.* Sydney: Topmill, 2006.

AVALANCHE, **Operation**
Start Date: December 2, 2003
End Date: December 26, 2003

A joint U.S.-Afghan offensive undertaken in December 2003, and the largest coalition military operation in Afghanistan since the fall of the Taliban regime in late 2001. The campaign was designed to counter the growing threat by Taliban and Al Qaeda fighters to Afghan reconstruction efforts and end insurgent attacks on humanitarian and aid workers in the eastern and southern provinces of Afghanistan. Operation AVALANCHE was also to disrupt the cycle in which the Taliban and Al Qaeda insurgents used the winter months to regroup and reequip in order to launch offenses in the spring. In addition to identifying and destroying rebel bases, coalition forces sought to interdict supply and transport lines between Afghanistan and Pakistan. Finally, the Afghans were preparing for a broad-based political convention, known as a *loya jirga,* and there were concerns that the Taliban and Al Qaeda would launch strikes to disrupt the meeting.

Operation AVALANCHE involved about 2,000 U.S. troops and an equal number of Afghan National Army soldiers. On December 2, ground forces began moving into areas around Khost, supported by artillery units at forward operations base Salerno. The base received incoming rocket fire during the operation, but the eight 107-mm rockets failed to cause significant damage or casualties. On December 3, 500 airborne troops of the U.S. 501st Parachute Infantry Regiment were deployed outside of Khost near the border with Pakistan. There they conducted searches and interdiction operations. A second major assault was undertaken on a Taliban complex in Paktia on December 4. Following an aerial bombardment, U.S. forces captured a weapons cache, including small arms, mortars, howitzers, and ammunition, but they failed to apprehend Mullah Jalani, a local Taliban leader. Subsequent smaller operations throughout the region resulted in minor skirmishes and the capture of additional weapons and equipment.

During the operation, coalition forces killed 10 Taliban fighters and captured approximately 100 suspected insurgents. Coalition forces also uncovered dozens of weapons caches and seized small arms, ammunition, mines, rocket-propelled grenades, howitzers and explosive-making materials. Two Afghan National soldiers were killed during AVALANCHE, but no U.S. troops died. U.S. officials reported that their Afghan allies, part of the then 7,500-man Afghan National Army, exceeded expectations during the operation. The *loya jirga* began its deliberations on December 14, without incident.

Operation AVALANCHE was notable for the attention focused on civilian casualties caused by the coalition. For instance, during the bombing of Paktia, six Afghan children and two adults perished. The civilian casualties led to regional protests against coalition forces and warnings by Afghan officials that such losses undermined popular support for the government and its coalition allies. The following day, nine children were killed during a mission to capture the Taliban leader Mullah Wazir in Ghazni. The operation involved air units and about 100 ground forces. It failed to apprehend the leader, and led to further condemnation because of the loss of civilians, including a call by UN secretary-general Kofi Annan for a full investigation of the incident. The operation was essentially over by December 26.

TOM LANSFORD

See also

Afghan National Army; Afghanistan; Afghanistan, Coalition Combat Operations in, 2002–Present; Al Qaeda; Casualties, Operation ENDURING FREEDOM; North Atlantic Treaty Organization in Afghanistan; Taliban; Taliban Insurgency, Afghanistan

References

Feickert, Andrew. *U.S. and Coalition Military Operations in Afghanistan: Issues for Congress.* Washington, DC: Congressional Research Service, 2006.

Guistozzi, Antonio. *Koran, Kalashnikov and Laptop: The Neo-Taliban Insurgency in Afghanistan.* New York: Columbia University Press, 2008.

Jones, Seth G. *Counterinsurgency in Afghanistan: RAND Counterinsurgency Study No. 4.* Santa Monica, CA: RAND Corporation, 2008.

Awda, Muhammad Daoud

See Abu Daoud

"Axis of Evil"

Term coined by President George W. Bush in his January 29, 2002, State of the Union address to describe regimes that sponsor terrorism. Specifically, he identified the axis as consisting of Iran, Iraq, and North Korea, all of which he believed threatened the security of the United States. Conceived by presidential speechwriter David Frum, the phrase "axis of evil" was originally intended to justify the invasion of Iraq, but it came to be used by political neoconservatives to criticize Secretary of State Colin Powell's position on the Bush Doctrine. That doctrine, arising after the September 11, 2001, terror attacks, modified U.S. military policy to allow for a preemptive war against terrorists, unilateral military action against rogue states, and American measures to remain the sole military superpower in the world.

The origin of the phrase "axis of evil" can be traced to December 2001, when head speechwriter Mike Gerson tasked David Frum with articulating the case for ousting the government of Saddam Hussein in a few sentences, which were to be included in the 2002 State of the Union address. Frum originally intended to use the phrase "axis of hatred," but changed it to "axis of evil" to match the "theological" tone adopted by President Bush after September 11, 2001. Expecting his speech to be edited, Frum was surprised when his "axis of evil" was actually included, and the text of the speech was read nearly verbatim by President Bush, a controversial move that was seen in some quarters to be dangerously undiplomatic. Certainly, that speech, and particularly the term "axis of evil," was not well received in many of the world's capitals.

The usage of the phrase "axis of evil" was ultimately meant to suggest links between terrorists and nations that, according to neoconservatives, threatened the United States and its allies. Criteria for inclusion in the "axis of evil" were that the included nations be "rogue states," or that they allegedly support terrorist groups that sought to attack the United States or its allies, potentially with weapons of mass destruction.

President Bush's 2002 speech shocked people in many nations, but it was also viewed with considerable trepidation by America's stalwart allies. Not surprisingly, Iraqi president Saddam Hussein mocked and dismissed the talk as needless bluster. In Tehran, the fundamentalist regime there sharply denounced its inclusion in the "axis of evil." North Korean spokesmen bitterly rebuked Bush and his speech and vowed that any aggression toward North Korea would be met with withering military counterforce. In the longer term, Bush's incendiary language may have had the opposite effect intended; it likely induced Pyongyang and Tehran to be even less compliant with international rules of behavior.

KEITH LEITICH

See also
Bush, George Walker; Bush Doctrine; Hussein, Saddam; Iran; Powell, Colin Luther; Terrorism

References
Victor D. Cha. "Korea's Place in the Axis." *Foreign Affairs* 81(3) (May/June 2002): 79–92.
Frum, David. *The Right Man: The Surprise Presidency of George W. Bush.* New York: Random House, 2003.
Woodward, Bob. *Bush at War.* New York: Simon and Schuster, 2002.

Azerbaijan, Role in Afghanistan and Iraq Wars

Nation located in eastern Transcaucasia and a former Soviet republic until it gained independence in December 1991. Azerbaijan, with a 2008 population of 8.178 million, covers 33,436 square miles. Azerbaijan borders Russia, Georgia, Armenia, Iran, and the Caspian Sea. The country has a democratic, parliamentary-style government with a prime minister chosen by parliament to head government entities. Azerbaijan also has a popularly elected president who holds executive power, although he is not empowered to dissolve the government or parliament; he may only veto legislation passed by the National Assembly. He forms a cabinet that reports to him, which includes the prime minister. Currently, Azerbaijan's political landscape features multiple parties, although it has been heavily dominated by the New Azerbaijan Party, which has controlled both the legislative and executive branches.

Since 2001, Azerbaijan has endeavored to improve its relationship with the United States through successive deployments as part of U.S.-led coalitions in Afghanistan and Iraq. Following the end of the Cold War and independence, Azerbaijan sought to enhance its ties to the West as a means to counter Russian influence in the region and to improve its standing in relation to Armenia, with which Azerbaijan has had an ongoing border dispute. Meanwhile, the central Asian nation's oil and gas reserves drew attention and investment from the United States and other Western nations. In 1997, Azerbaijan created a peacekeeping battalion for deployment in multilateral humanitarian missions. The unit served in Kosovo as part of the North Atlantic Treaty Organization (NATO)–led peacekeeping mission following the 1999 air campaign.

After the September 11, 2001, terrorist strikes on U.S. soil, Azerbaijan offered a variety of assistance to the United States, including the use of its air space and bases to conduct operations against Al Qaeda and the Taliban regime in Afghanistan. In return, the United States provided about $3 million per year to Azerbaijan to support counterterrorism operations, including joint military exercises. Azerbaijan dispatched a small contingent of its peacekeeping battalion to Afghanistan in 2006 and increased its size to more than 100 troops in 2008. The forces were stationed there as part of a NATO-led provincial reconstruction team.

Following the invasion of Iraq in March 2003, Azerbaijan joined the U.S.-led "Coalition of the Willing" and deployed a company from its peacekeeping unit to Iraq in August 2003. It also offered to provide additional troops to support the United Nations (UN) mission in the Iraq; however, after the withdrawal of the bulk of UN personnel from the country in 2004 following a suicide attack, Azerbaijan withdrew the offer. The country became the first predominantly Muslim country to deploy troops to Iraq, and the presence of Azerbaijani troops was used by the George W. Bush administration to refute assertions that the invasion and occupation of Iraq was anti-Muslim. Azerbaijani troop strength remained steady at about 150 soldiers for the next five years (more than 1,000 Azerbaijanis served at least one six-months' tour of duty in Iraq), and the contingent was led by an army major. The troops were stationed at the Al-Haditha dam and water reservoir in Anbar Province and were under the operational command of the United States. The contingent was charged with providing security for the region's hydroelectric facility (the power plant supplied approximately 30 percent of Iraq's electricity). One Azerbaijani soldier was killed while serving in Iraq in 2008. Azerbaijan's deployment occurred during a period of dramatic increases in Azerbaijani military spending, fueled by increased energy revenues. The country's military budget increased from $146 million per year in 2004 to approximately $1 billion in 2007.

The deployment was scheduled to end with the termination of the United Nations mandate that recognized the U.S.-led coalition as the occupying power in Iraq. After consultations with the United States and the Iraqi government, Azerbaijani president Ilham Aliev asked Parliament to withdraw the nation's troops from Iraq in October 2008. Parliament approved the request on a vote of 86 to 1 the following month. Azerbaijani troops completed their withdrawal in December 2008.

Tom Lansford

See also

Afghanistan, Coalition Combat Operations in, 2002–Present; Iraqi Freedom, Operation, Coalition Ground Forces; Multi-National Force–Iraq; North Atlantic Treaty Organization in Afghanistan; Provincial Reconstruction Teams, Afghanistan

References

Cockburn, Patrick. *The Occupation: War and Resistance in Iraq.* New York: Verso, 2007.

Keegan, John. *The Iraq War: The Military Offensive, from Victory in 21 Days to the Insurgent Aftermath.* New York: Vintage, 2005.

Aziz, Tariq
Birth Date: April 1, 1936

Iraqi foreign minister (1983–1991) and deputy prime minister (1979–2003). Tariq Aziz was born on April 1, 1936, into a Chaldean Catholic family in Tell Kaif, Iraq. Originally named Michael Yuhanna, Aziz was the only Christian in a position of power during Saddam Hussein's 34-year-long dictatorship. While in college, he changed his name to Tariq Aziz, which means "glorious past," in order to avoid hostility regarding his religious heritage.

In 1957, Aziz joined the Baath Party and worked with Saddam Hussein to generate propaganda against the pro-Western Iraqi monarchy. After receiving his bachelor's degree in English literature in 1958 from the Baghdad College of Fine Arts, Aziz continued to produce Baath Party propaganda in addition to working as a journalist. From 1963 to 1966, Aziz was both editor in chief of the Baath Party's newspaper, *al-Thawra* [The Revolution], and director of the Arab Baath Socialist Party's press office in Damascus, Syria. When the British-imposed Hashimite monarchy came to an end in 1958, the Baath Party continued to seek power in Iraq. After an unsuccessful coup in 1963, the party finally gained power in 1968.

From 1974 to 1977, Aziz served as a member of the Regional Command, the Baath Party's highest governing unit. In 1979, Iraqi dictator Saddam Hussein named him deputy prime minister. His primary role was to explain and justify Iraq's policies to global audiences. With his effective communication skills, Aziz became known around the world for his eloquent diplomatic discourses.

Tariq Aziz became deputy prime minister of Iraq in 1979 and held that post until the fall of the Saddam Hussein government in the 2003 Iraq War. Although acquitted of other charges, in March 2009 Aziz was sentenced to 15 years in prison for his role in the executions of 42 merchants found guilty of profiteering in 1992. (AP/Wide World Photos)

In 1980, Aziz was wounded in an assassination attempt initiated by the Iranian-backed Shiite fundamentalist group al-Da'wah Islamiyyah (the Islamic Call). Members of the group threw a grenade at him in downtown Baghdad, killing several Iraqis in the process. The attack was one of several that Saddam Hussein blamed on the Iranian government, which was part of his justification for his September 1980 invasion of Iran that produced the Iran-Iraq War (1980–1988).

In 1984, just a year after being named foreign minister, Aziz secured the restoration of diplomatic relations with the United States after a 17-year-long interruption. The United States had chosen to support Iraq as a buffer to Iran's Islamic fundamentalist extremism.

When Iraq invaded Kuwait in August 1990, Aziz ardently supported the military action. He stated that the invasion was justified because of Kuwait's cheating on oil production quotas, which was driving down the price of oil, and because of Kuwait's alleged slant-drilling into Iraqi oil fields. During the subsequent Persian Gulf War (1991), Aziz enjoyed a substantial international profile, and was seen by the media as the chief Iraqi spokesperson. After the war, Aziz took on more responsibility as deputy prime minister, which forced him to relinquish the foreign ministry portfolio. Nevertheless, he retained a high profile in the government. Aziz now monitored the Iraqi media. In this position, Aziz also conducted Iraq's negotiations with United Nations (UN) weapons inspectors.

In his public remarks, Aziz blamed the United States, rather than the United Nations, for the economic sanctions that followed the Persian Gulf War, believing that they were implemented as a result of U.S. domestic policies. In 1997, he supported the expulsion of U.S. citizens from Iraq who were working for the United Nations Special Commission.

In February 2003, as tensions over Iraq's alleged illegal weapons programs were about to boil over into war, Aziz spoke with Pope John Paul II about the Iraqi government's desire to cooperate with the international community, notably on disarmament. In response, the pope insisted that Iraq respect and give concrete commitments to abide by United Nations Security Council resolutions. The Iraqis did not heed the advice. On March 19, 2003, at the beginning of the Anglo-American–led invasion of Iraq, there were reports that Aziz had been killed. They were proven false when Aziz later held a press conference. He surrendered to coalition forces on April 24, 2003.

Aziz, who is charged with crimes against humanity in connection with the murder of hundreds of Kurds in 1982, also testified as a defense witness before the Iraq Special Tribunal set up by the Iraq interim government in May 2006. He testified that the crackdown against the Kurds had been fully justified because of attacks against him and others in the regime. He also reiterated his loyalty to his old comrade Saddam Hussein.

Aziz is imprisoned at Camp Cropper in western Baghdad. On March 11, 2009, he was sentenced to 15 years in prison for his role in the 1992 summary executions of 42 merchants accused of fixing food prices.

CHARLENE T. OVERTURF

See also

Baath Party; Baker, James Addison, III; Baker-Aziz Meeting; DESERT STORM, Operation; Hussein, Saddam; Iraq, History of, Pre-1990; Iraq, History of, 1990–Present; IRAQI FREEDOM, Operation; John Paul II, Pope; Kurds; Kurds, Massacres of

References

Farouk-Sluglett, Marion, and Peter Sluglett. *Iraq since 1958: From Revolution to Dictatorship.* London: I. B. Tauris, 2001.

MacKey, Sandra. *The Reckoning: Iraq and the Legacy of Saddam Hussein.* New York: Norton, 2002.

B

B-2 Spirit

A multipurpose U.S. heavy bomber with stealth technology capable of deploying both conventional and nuclear weapons. The B-2 was designed specifically for penetrating air defense networks and disrupting command and control facilities. The Northrop Grumman B-2 Spirit stealth bomber played a vital role in delivering initial strikes during Operations ENDURING FREEDOM in Afghanistan (October 2001) and IRAQI FREEDOM (March 2003).

After flight testing at Edwards Air Force Base, California, the B-2 first saw combat action during the Kosovo War in 1999. Given its astronomical price tag of $1.2 billion per aircraft, the Pentagon has strictly limited its employment. Featuring a range of 6,000 nautical miles without refueling, the B-2 can reach any point around the globe within hours. Featuring a revolutionary "flying wing" construction designed to reduce radar cross-section, this Air Force platform has proven to be practically undetectable by radar in combat to date. Since its initial deployment, a new substance, known as alternate high-frequency material (AHFM), has been added to the plane to further enhance the radar-absorbent coating of its control surfaces. Engine intakes and exhausts are positioned low to the surface to minimize thermal detection. Designed ostensibly for daylight raids as well as night-time bombings, the B-2 is painted with a bluish-gray, anti-reflective paint that reduces optical visibility.

The bomber is aerodynamically unstable, which requires the use of a quadruple-redundant, fly-by-wire (FBW) system powered by a General Electric (GE) flight control computer. The aircraft flies with a two-man crew (pilot in the left seat and mission commander on the right), and all of its weapons are internally housed. The B-2 can carry up to 40,000 pounds of munitions, including conventional or nuclear weapons, precision-guided ordnance, gravity bombs, and a variety of maritime weapons. Two separate weapons bays are located in the center of the plane outfitted with a rotary launcher and two bomb-rack assemblies. Among the bombs compatible with the aircraft are the B61-11 earth-penetrating, nuclear bomb; the B83 free-fall, nuclear bomb; and the AGM-129 advanced cruise missile with a range of roughly 1,500 miles.

The military's Joint Direct Attack Munition (JDAM) missiles can also be deployed aboard a B-2 with the capacity expanded from 16 to 80 with the installation of new bomb racks in 2009. The aircraft can accommodate two massive ordnance penetrators (MOPs), which at 5,300 pounds apiece are potent weapons for eliminating hardened, buried targets with conventional explosives. The latest upgrade to the B-2 provided a generic weapons interface system (GWIS) that enables the aircraft to carry up to four different types of ordnance so that both stand-off strikes and direct attack munitions assaults are possible. Work has also begun on creating the means to engage moving targets. The B-2 is equipped with countermeasures and a J band multipurpose radar with terrain-following and terrain-avoidance modes. Also, Northrop Grumman received a contract in 2007 to develop an extremely high frequency (EHF) satellite communications capability and computer upgrade for the B-2.

The B-2 is 69 feet long with a wingspan of 172 feet. The aircraft is 17 feet in height, with landing gear, and weighs 158,000 pounds; its maximum allowable takeoff weight is 336,500 pounds. It is powered by four General Electric nonafterburning jet engines capable of achieving a maximum air speed of 604 miles per hour (mph). The B-2 has an operational ceiling of 50,000 feet.

The B-2's high operational ceiling has allowed it to maintain high sortie reliability rates. During the first three days of Operation ENDURING FREEDOM, six B-2s flew from Whiteman Air Force Base,

Missouri, to Afghanistan to complete the longest nonstop military aviation mission in history. They joined with Boeing B-52 Stratofortress bombers and Lockheed F-117 Nighthawk stealth ground attack aircraft to strike military training facilities, surface-to-air missile (SAM) sites, troop staging areas, and Al Qaeda infrastructure targets.

With the advent of a transportable hangar system, the B-2 was deployed to forward locations for the first time during Operation IRAQI FREEDOM in 2003. During that war, about 60 percent of the B-2s flew out of Whiteman while the remainder operated from the island of Diego Garcia in the Indian Ocean. On the evening of March 21, 2003, the inauguration of the shock-and-awe aerial campaign against Iraq, six B-2 sorties were assessed as having eliminated 92 targets. The extensive use of precision-guided weapons obviated the need for the sort of carpet bombing and elimination of civilian infrastructure (such as power stations) that had attracted much negative publicity during the 1991 Persian Gulf War. More than 1.5 million pounds of munitions were released by B-2 aircraft over Iraq, and the bomber was declared at full operational capability by December 2003.

To date, no B-2 has been shot down in the course of combat. In February 2008, one B-2 bomber crashed shortly after takeoff from Anderson Air Force Base, Guam. Investigations revealed moisture in the port transducer units that caused faulty information to be relayed to the air data system. Preventive maintenance has been developed to address the problem. This accident left 20 B-2 bombers in the U.S. arsenal.

Critics or the aircraft continue to note its very high cost, difficulty in reacting to pop-up threats, relatively slow speed, and often clumsy maneuverability. While new construction of a successor is unlikely in the near future, the B-2 bomber (with ongoing upgrades) remains in the vanguard of U.S. operational planning.

JEFFREY D. BASS

See also

Aircraft, Bombers; Bombs, Precision-Guided; ENDURING FREEDOM, Operation, U.S. Air Campaign; IRAQI FREEDOM, Operation, Air Campaign; Joint Direct Attack Munition and Small Diameter Bomb; United States Air Force, Afghanistan War; United States Air Force, Iraq War

References

Donald, David. *Black Jets: The Development and Operation of America's Most Secret Warplane.* Westport, CT: AIRtime Publishing, 2004.

Sweetman, Bill. *Northrop B-2 Stealth Bomber: The Complete History, Technology, and Operational Development of the Stealth Bomber.* St. Paul, MN: MBI Publishing, 1992.

Veronico, Nicholas, and Jim Dunn. *21st Century U.S. Air Power.* St. Paul, MN: MBI Publishing, 2004.

B-52 Stratofortress

U.S. long-range heavy bomber. Referred to by its crew of five as "BUFF," or (in polite terms) "big ugly fat fellow," the Boeing B-52 Stratofortress was first conceived in 1944 as a follow-on aircraft to the Boeing B-47 Stratojet. Development proceeded over the next decade. Two prototypes were built—the XB-52 and the YB-52. The XB-52 first flew in 1954. The B-52 entered service in 1955. Over the course of more than 50 years in service, a total of 744 B-52s have been built. The last model, the B-52H, was delivered to SAC in May 1961. Nearly 100 B-52s remain in service. The B-52H can carry up to 20 air-launched cruise missiles, along with numerous conventional and nuclear bombs.

Although built for the role of Cold War–era nuclear deterrence, the B-52's conventional capabilities make the plane a vital component of current U.S. Air Force operations. There are no plans to retire the B-52, which is certainly one of the greatest of all aircraft.

With a maximum speed of 595 miles per hour (mph) and ceiling of 55,000 feet, the B-52 has an initial flying range of about 8,800 miles. With aerial refueling, the aircraft has a virtually unlimited range, limited only by crew stamina. Powered by eight 17,000-pound thrust Pratt & Whitney TF33 turbofan jet engines, the B-52 is 157 feet 7 inches in length and has a wingspan of 185 feet. It is 40 feet 8 inches in height. It can weigh up to 488,000 pounds at takeoff. It is armed with a single 20mm Gatling gun and is capable of carrying up to 40,000 pounds of ordnance, both conventional and nuclear.

The B-52's conventional role was first demonstrated during the Vietnam War. B-52s flying from bases in Thailand and Guam dropped millions of tons of conventional ordnance, inflicting heavy losses on Communist troops and lines of communication. They even flew in close support of ground troops in South Vietnam, and in Operations LINEBACKER I and II, B-52s struck deep into North Vietnam.

B-52s performed highly effective service in both U.S. wars with Iraq, Operation DESERT STORM in 1991 and Operation IRAQI FREEDOM in 2003. During DESERT STORM, B-52s struck Iraqi troop concentrations and fixed targets, including bunkers, airfields, and radar installations. The longest strike mission in the history of aerial warfare occurred when a B-52H took off from Barksdale Air Force Base, Louisiana, and then launched cruise missiles in Iraq during a 35-hour, nonstop operation. Ultimately, B-52 bombers delivered 40 percent of all aerial-delivered coalition weaponry.

B-52s were responsible for taking out 13 percent of Iraq's electrical power production and almost 60 percent of Baghdad's electrical generation capability. The Persian Gulf War also highlighted the B-52's importance in destroying enemy ground forces. Its ability to carry internally 84 500-pound bombs made it a formidable weapons delivery platform. B-52s took a heavy toll of Iraqi ground formations and destroyed their morale. At least one Iraqi troop commander interrogated after the war stated that he had surrendered because of the threat of B-52 strikes.

B-52s also took part in Operation ALLIED FORCE as part of the joint North Atlantic Treaty Organization (NATO) operation in the Federal Republic of Yugoslavia (March–June 1999). They launched cruise-missile attacks and dropped general-purpose bombs and deadly cluster bombs on Serbian army positions and staging

A U.S. Air Force B-52 Stratofortress of the 40th Expeditionary Bomb Squadron heads toward Iraq on its mission to provide close air support for coalition troops during Operation IRAQI FREEDOM in April 2003. (U.S. Department of Defense)

locations in an effort to end the ethnic genocide taking place in the Balkans. However, fearful of collateral damage that might hinder peace negotiations, NATO air commanders limited the B-52's role.

B-52s provided close air support using precision-guided munitions during Operation ENDURING FREEDOM in Afghanistan. B-52s carried out massive bombing raids against suspected Al Qaeda positions in the mountains of Afghanistan, especially in the area of Tora Bora. B-52s have also played a role in Operation IRAQI FREEDOM (March 2003). During the early stages of the war, they provided close air support for U.S. ground troops and attacked selected targets with cruise missiles.

CHARLES FRANCIS HOWLETT

See also

DESERT STORM, Operation, Coalition Air Campaign; ENDURING FREEDOM, Operation, U.S. Air Campaign; IRAQI FREEDOM, Operation, Air Campaign; United States Air Force, Afghanistan War; United States Air Force, Iraq War; United States Air Force, Persian Gulf War

References

Andrews, William F. *Air Power against an Army: Challenge and Response in CENTAF's Duel with the Republican Guard.* Montgomery, AL: Air University Press, 1998.

Boyne, Walter J. *Boeing B-52: A Documentary History.* Washington, DC: Smithsonian Institution, 1984.

Dorr, Robert. *B-52 Stratofortress.* Oxford, UK: Osprey, 1995.

Lake, Jon. *B-52 Stratofortress Units in Operation Desert Storm.* Oxford, UK: Osprey, 2004.

Reynolds, Richard T. *Heart of the Storm: The Genesis of the Air Campaign against Iraq.* Montgomery, AL: Air University Press, 1995.

Baath Party

Political party that currently dominates Syria and which was the leading party in Iraq from 1968 to the end of Saddam Hussein's regime in 2003. The Baath Party (Hizb al-Baath al-Arabi al-Ishtiraki) also had branches in Lebanon, Jordan, the Sudan, Yemen, Mauritania, and Bahrain, and it enjoys support from some Palestinians. The Arabic word "Baath" means "renaissance" or "resurrection." The party's fundamental principles have been Arab unity and freedom from imperialist control for all Arab states; personal freedom for Arab citizens; and support for Arab culture. The party also supported Arab socialist policies intended to eliminate feudalism but not private property. The Arab Socialist Baath Party of Syria explains its ideology as "national (Pan-Arab), socialist, popular and revolutionary" and its founding charter and constitution identifies its commitment to the "Arab Nation, the Arab homeland, the Arab citizen, the Arab people's authority over their own land and the freedom of the Arab people."

The Arab Baath Party, as it was originally called, grew out of an ideological and political movement in Syria, founded in 1940 in Damascus with the goal of revitalizing the Arab nation and society. Syrian intellectuals Michel Aflaq, a Greek Orthodox Christian; Salah al-Din al-Bitar, a Sunni Muslim who studied at the Sorbonne in the early 1930s; and Zaki al-Arsuzi were the principal founders of the Baath movement and party. The Arab Baath Party accepted Arabs of all religious backgrounds and ethnic groups.

The first Arab Baath Party Congress was held on April 4–6, 1947. Abd al-Rahman al-Damin and Abd al-Khaliq al-Khudayri attended that congress and on their return to Iraq founded a branch of the party there. This evolved into a small group of about 50 individuals, mainly friends and associates of Fuad al-Rikabi, who took control of the group in 1951. The Baathists in Iraq joined with other organizations that were in opposition to the monarchy. Baathism spread more slowly in Iraq than in Syria, with its candidates losing out to Communists in many elections in the 1960s.

Meanwhile in Syria, in 1954 Aflaq and Bitar joined forces with Akram al-Hawrani, a populist leader who headed the Socialist Party. They adopted the name of Arab Socialist Baath Party. The Baath Party found its greatest strength in Syria and Iraq, although it had branches all over the Arab world.

The Baath Party came to power first in Iraq and then in Syria in coups d'état in 1963. The coup in Iraq did not last out the year, however, during which time 10,000 leftists, Marxists, and Communists were killed, 5,000 of these from the Iraqi Communist Party. Three years later, the Syrian and Iraqi parties split. Each was subsequently plagued by factionalism. Some disputes occurred as a result of Syria's union with Egypt in the United Arab Republic (UAR); others concerned a possible union of Syria and Iraq or ties with the Soviet Union and local Communist parties, as well as the Syrian Socialist Nationalist Party (SSNP) in Syria.

Rivalries between different factions of the Syrian Baath Party led to an interparty coup in 1966 followed by another one four years later that brought General Hafiz al-Asad to power. He headed a pragmatic faction that gained control of the military in contrast to a "progressive" faction that had pushed a more pervasive socialism and nationalizations and a harder-line regionally. Asad remained in office until his death in 2000. His son, Bashar al-Asad, assumed leadership of the Syrian Baath Party and remains the president of Syria.

Saddam Hussein joined the Iraqi Baath Party at the age of 21 in 1956 and steadily rose in the party's ranks, first as a consequence of the Iraqi Revolution of 1958, and then as an assassin in the U.S.-backed plot to do away with President Abd al-Karim Qasim. Later, after the Baath Party had regained power in a 1968 coup, Hussein served as vice-chairman of the Revolutionary Command Council and later as president and secretary-general of the Baath Party.

The Baath parties of Iraq and Syria operated in associations in schools, communities, and the army, and had workers' and women's associations, such as the General Association of Iraqi Women (al-Ittihad al-amm li-nisa al-Iraq). While the party ostensibly

Iraqi soldiers patrol Baghdad following a coup by the Arab Baath Socialist Party in 1963. Abd al-Karim Qasim, the deposed president, was executed. (AFP/Getty Images)

sought to expand membership to comprise a "mass party," in fact, membership was tightly controlled. Nonetheless, party members wielded considerable power. Average Syrians and Iraqis could hardly conclude any official business without the intercession of a party member. In the military and in academia, it was nearly impossible to advanced or be promoted without being a party member. In Iraq, the party claimed 1.5 million members or about 10 percent of the country's population in the late 1980s; however, only about 30,000 were bona fide party cadres. In Syria, Asad opened up membership so that by 1987, it was at about 50,000 people, and there were also some 200,000 probationary party members.

The Baath parties of both countries did not tolerate political challenges of any other group or party. They strongly opposed the Islamist movements that arose in each nation. Despite the dictatorial nature of the Iraqi governments in this period, one notable accomplishment, in part facilitated through the party, was the serious effort to modernize the economy and society by promoting literacy, education, and gender equality. As a result, by the 1970s, Iraq had a fairly high level of education. Hussein's disastrous war with Iran and then his invasion of Kuwait, which prompted war with the United States and a coalition of states, had a profoundly negative impact on the country and its economy.

The U.S.-led invasion of Iraq in March 2003 and the overthrow of Saddam Hussein led to an immediate ban of the Baath Party, the so-called de-Baathification, under U.S. and coalition occupation forces. Iraqis also attacked Baath Party offices all over the country. Some critics of the U.S. occupation policies in Iraq claim that U.S. administrator Paul Bremer's decision, approved by Washington, to bar all Baathists from government posts hopelessly hamstrung the government and fueled the Iraqi insurgency, which included some bitter and disenfranchised Baathists. Iraqi prime minister Nuri al-Maliki is still enforcing a ban on the Baath Party and has extended rehiring only to those who can show they were forced to join the party. A related controversy emerged over the transfer of the Baath Party records to the Hoover Institution at Stanford University via an agreement with the Iraq Memory Foundation and with permission of Maliki. The seizure of these documents (which could reveal the precise status of connections with the party) has been protested by, among others, the director of the Iraq National Library and Archive and the acting Iraqi minister of culture.

In Syria, the Baath Party has had a great impact. Changes in landholding and commercial policies in the 1960s displaced earlier elites, but suppression of the Sunni merchants and Islamists led, even after the Hama massacre, to an Islamist revival that challenged Baath Party primacy. Although President Bashar al-Asad promised democratic reforms in 2005, not much change has occurred. Asad's recent cooperation with the United States makes it less likely that he will be removed in favor of an alternative Baathist leader.

In Lebanon, Bahrain, and other countries, the Baath Party retains a small presence. In Lebanon, it held two seats in Parliament in the 1990s, and the Iraqi branch also had a link in a group within the Palestinian Fatah organization. The Sudanese Baath Party operates underground as part of the opposition to the Sudanese regime, and publishes a journal, *al-Hadaf*.

STEFAN M. BROOKS AND SHERIFA ZUHUR

See also

Aflaq, Michel; Arab Nationalism; Asad, Bashar al-; Asad, Hafiz al-; Hussein, Saddam; Iraq, History of, Pre-1990; Iraq, History of, 1990–Present; Pan-Arabism and Pan-Arabist Thought; Syria

References

Batatu, Hanna. *Old Social Classes and New Revolutionary Movements of Iraq.* London: Al-Saqi Books, 2000.

Committee Against Represssion and For Democratic Rights in Iraq, ed. *Saddam's Iraq: Revolution or Reaction?* London: Zed Books, 1986.

Devlin, John F. *The Ba'th Party: A History from Its Origins to 1966.* Stanford, CA: Hoover Institution Press, 1976.

Heydemann, Steven. *Authoritarianism in Syria: Institutions and Social Conflict, 1948–1970.* Ithaca, NY: Cornell University Press, 1999.

Hinnebusch, Raymond. *Syria: Revolution from Above.* Florence, NY: Routledge, 2001.

Ismael, Jacqueline S., and Shireen T. Ismael. "Gender and State in Iraq." In *Gender and Citizenship in the Middle East,* edited by Suad Joseph, 185–211. Syracuse, NY: Syracuse University Press, 2000.

Sallam, Qasim. *Al-Baath wal Watan Al-Arabi* [The Baath and the Arab Homeland]. Paris: EMA, 1980.

Tripp, Charles. *A History of Iraq.* Cambridge: Cambridge University Press, 2007.

Van Dam, Nikolaos. *The Struggle for Power in Syria: Sectarianism, Regionalism and Tribalism in Politics.* London: I. B. Tauris, 1979.

Badr Organization

Paramilitary wing of the Supreme Islamic Iraqi Council (SIIC), also referred to as the Supreme Islamic Council in Iraq, that was known for decades as the Supreme Council for the Islamic Revolution in Iraq (SCIRI), a Shia political party founded in Tehran, Iran, in November 1982 by Iraqi exiles led by Ayatollah Muhammad Baqir al-Hakim. The Badr Organization (Faylaq Badr), which is also commonly referred to as the Badr Corps, the Badr Brigade(s), and the Badr Army, was named after the Battle of Badr, fought between the Prophet Muhammad and the first Muslims against a larger and more well-equipped armed force commanded by his Meccan opponents. The Badr Organization is led by Hadi al-Amiri, a high-ranking SIIC official and an ally of its political leaders, Abd al-Aziz al-Hakim and his son, Sayyid Ammar al-Hakim. Abd al-Aziz is the youngest brother of Muhammad Baqr, who was assassinated by a massive car bombing probably carried out by the organization headed by the Jordanian Abu Musab al-Zarqawi (1966–2006), and a son of Grand Ayatollah Sayyid Muhsin al-Hakim (1889–1970), the most influential and widely followed Shia religious leader in Iraq from 1955 until his death.

The Badr Organization's origins lay in armed units, numbering several thousand men at most, made up of Iraqi Arab exiles trained and equipped with assistance from the Iranian government. These units were named after Ayatollah Sayyid Muhammad Baqr al-Sadr (1935–1980), a prominent Iraqi Arab Shia religious scholar and opposition leader who was executed by the ruling Iraqi Baath Party along with his sister, Amina bint Haydar al-Sadr (also known as Bint al-Huda), in April 1980. Both Muhammad Baqr and Abd al-Aziz al-Hakim were students of Baqr al-Sadr, who was a student of their father, Muhsin al-Hakim. The two brothers along with their other brother, Muhammad Mahdi, were early members of the Islamic Dawa Party (Hizb al-Da'wah al-Islamiyya), which was originally founded by Shia religious scholars (*ulama*) in the southern Iraqi shrine city of Najaf.

The Iranian Revolutionary Guard Corps (IRGC), an armed force dedicated to the protection and preservation of the Iranian revolutionary system, was the key source of training and military equipment for the SCIRI's paramilitary wing. This militia was renamed after the Battle of Badr (1982–1983) during the Iran-Iraq War. Badr drew its membership from the tens of thousands of Iraqi Arabs, the majority of them Shia political activists and anti-Baath operatives, who fled to Iran in the late 1970s and 1980s, particularly following the execution of Ayatollah Muhammad Baqr al-Sadr and his sister in April 1980.

After the start of the Iran-Iraq War (1980–1988) following Iraq's invasion of western Iran in September 1980, Badr also recruited members from among Iraqi prisoners of war, since many Iraqi soldiers were Shia conscripts who had no love or loyalty for Iraqi president Saddam Hussein. Prisoners of war who wished to join Badr were first required to repent for their membership in the Iraqi Army because it was regarded as an instrument not of the Iraqi nation but of the Iraqi Baath Party. Abd al-Aziz al-Hakim served as Badr's commander from its founding in 1982–1983 until he and his brother Muhammad Baqr returned to Iraq in May 2003 following the collapse of the Iraqi Baathist regime in the wake of the U.S.- and British-led invasion of the country. Despite its Iraqi identity and membership, Badr's leadership was split between Iraqi Arabs such as Abd al-Aziz al-Hakim and IRGC officers, who were largely responsible for the military training of Badr's recruits. Badr included infantry, armored, artillery, antiaircraft, and commando units and maintained ties to activists and small units in Iraq.

The Badr Organization was actively involved in the Iran-Iraq War, primarily in northern Iraq (Iraqi Kurdistan). Following the capture of Haj Omran, villages in northeastern Iraq, by Iranian forces in 1983, Badr units were stationed there, and Muhammad Baqr al-Hakim visited them and prayed on what was termed "freed Iraqi soil." The participation of Badr paramilitary fighters on the side of the Iranians during the war was not welcomed by all Iraqi Shia and was widely criticized by some of SCIRI's political rivals in the Iraqi Shia community.

Badr also carried out bombings and attacks on Iraqi Baath officials and offices during the 1980s and 1990s, and it sent units across the Iran-Iraq border in March–April 1991 to aid the uprisings in southern and northern Iraq among the Shia and Kurdish populations. These uprisings, encouraged by the U.S. government, were brutally crushed by Baath security forces and the Republican Guard after the United States refused to aid the rebels. The United States was reportedly fearful of empowering Iraq's Shia population, heeding alarmist talk from their Sunni Arab allies and reacting warily to the appearance of Badr fighters in southern Iraq, many of whom carried portraits of Iran's late revolutionary leader, Grand Ayatollah Ruhollah Khomeini, and banners calling for the formation of an Islamic republic in Iraq.

Following the collapse of the Iraqi Baath government in April 2003, the SCIRI and Badr leaderships returned to Iraq from exile, mainly from Iran, in May 2003. Muhammad Baqir al-Hakim was welcomed in southern Iraq by tens of thousands of his supporters. According to the Hakims and SIIC/Badr officials, the Badr Organization fielded some 10,000 paramilitary fighters upon their return to Iraq. Abd al-Aziz al-Hakim subsequently claimed that Badr, in addition to its regular fighters, could call upon tens of thousands of other reservists, although this claim seems to be highly exaggerated.

The United Iraqi Alliance (UIA), a loose coalition of mainly Shia political parties, was swept into power in the December 2005 national elections. The SCIRI and the Islamic Dawa Party were the two dominant political parties in the UIA. Bayan Jabr, a SCIRI official, was selected by Abd al-Aziz al-Hakim to head the Iraqi Ministry of the Interior in the 2005–2006 transitional government. Jabr oversaw the infiltration of the Iraqi security forces, police, and special commando units, all of which fall under the Interior Ministry. Badr members, both inside and outside of the national security forces, have engaged in gun battles with rival Shia parties, particularly the Sadr Movement led by Muqtada al-Sadr, and in a series of operations in Basra and other southern Iraqi cities and towns in the spring and summer of 2008, which were aimed at weakening the Sadr Movement's political and paramilitary structure in southern Iraq before the 2009 elections. Badr members have also been blamed for carrying out sectarian killings and ethnic cleansing of Sunni Arabs in southern and central Iraq as well as in the capital city of Baghdad.

CHRISTOPHER ANZALONE

See also

Baath Party; Hakim, Abd al-Aziz al-; Hakim, Muhammad Baqir al-; Hussein, Saddam; Iran; Iraq, History of, Pre-1990; Iraq, History of, 1990–Present; Islamic Dawa Party; Sadr, Muqtada al-; Shia Islam; Sunni Islam; Supreme Iraqi Islamic Council; United Iraqi Alliance

References

Jabar, Faleh A. *The Shi'ite Movement in Iraq*. London: Saqi Books, 2003.
Marr, Phebe. "Democracy in the Rough." *Current History* (January 2006): 27–33.
Samii, A. William. "Shia Political Alternatives in Postwar Iraq." *Middle East Policy* 10 (May 2003): 93–101.

Baghdad

The capital city of Iraq. Baghdad, established in 762 CE by Abbasid caliph al-Mansur, straddles the Tigris River and its tributary, the Diyala. The city is located at 33°18' North latitude and 44°36' East longitude in east-central Iraq. The city sits some 130 feet above sea level. Baghdad's climate typically consists of hot, dry summers and cool winters. With a 2003 population of 5.772 million people, Baghdad was the second-largest city in Southwest Asia (behind Tehran, Iran) and the second-largest city in the Arab world (behind Cairo, Egypt). For comparison, the next two largest cities in Iraq—Mosul and Basra—were estimated in 2003 at 1.74 million and 1.338 million people, respectively. The population of Baghdad constitutes about one-fifth of the country's people. The name "Baghdad" also refers to the small province that surrounds the city, one of 18 in Iraq. Iraq's capital city is ethnically Arab, with small Kurdish and Turkoman minorities.

Baghdad is the center of Iraq's power infrastructure, with power lines webbing outward in all directions. During the 1991 Persian Gulf War, this power infrastructure was severely damaged by the U.S.-led coalition's air strikes against the city in retaliation for Iraq's August 1990 annexation of Kuwait. Baghdad is also the air, road, and railroad center of Iraq, including Baghdad International Airport, several major highways, two primary railroads, two key oil pipelines, and one major gas pipeline. Baghdad is Iraq's foremost center of oil refining, food-processing plants, textile mills, tanneries and leather production, cement companies, metal-product manufacturers, and tobacco processing. The local economy is augmented by way of Baghdad's famous bazaars that showcase jewelry, utensils, rugs, cloth, leather, and felt.

Until the Anglo-American–led invasion of Iraq in March 2003, military installations in the area included air bases, barracks, bunkers, the Iraqi Air Force headquarters, the Republican Guard headquarters, and the Ministry of Defense. Key political buildings included various presidential palaces, the National Assembly, and the Baath Party headquarters. Baghdad is also home to three universities: the University of Baghdad, the University of Technology, and al-Mustansiriyah University.

Notable historical structures include the Abbasid Palace (1179 CE), the ruins of Bab al-Wastani, the Central Gate of Baghdad, and the Mirjan Mosque (1358 CE). The archaeological site of Ctesiphon is to the south, while the attractive domed mosque of Kazinayn is just to the north.

Portions of Baghdad were heavily damaged during the Persian Gulf War of 1991. Transportation, communication, sanitation, and power-generating centers were all affected to varying degrees. President George H. W. Bush halted coalition troops, however, and they never were allowed to proceed to Baghdad, a controversial decision that left Iraqi dictator Saddam Hussein in power.

In the war's aftermath Hussein, now far weaker militarily and economically, attempted to rebuild Baghdad. But the extent of the damage, international economic sanctions, and Hussein's own spending priorities meant that this proceeded only in piecemeal fashion. Spending on Hussein's palaces and on projects glorifying the regime and Hussein himself continued unabated, however.

In March and early April 2003 Baghdad was bombed heavily during the 2003 Iraq War (Operation IRAQI FREEDOM). By April 10, coalition forces had taken the city, and the widely televised toppling of Hussein's statue in Firdaws Square signaled the end of his oppressive regime. Baghdad saw more damage in the extensive looting immediately following the city's fall.

The conquerors soon established a Coalition Provisional Authority in a three-square-mile area (known as the Green Zone) in central Baghdad from which it governed the nation. Democratic elections commenced in 2004, and a new constitution was drafted. However, Baghdad experienced significant violence from both terrorist actions and Sunni-on-Shia sectarian violence. With Baghdad spiraling out of control in massive car bombings and scattered random executions and with the coalition military effort in Iraq seemingly in jeopardy, in January 2007 President George W. Bush authorized an increase of more than 20,000 troops in Baghdad to restore order. By the fourth quarter of 2007, Bush's troop surge had brought a reduction in violence in Baghdad, following the cordoning off of neighborhoods and sectarian designations of formerly mixed neighborhoods. The trend since then has been toward a gradual diminution in sectarian- and terrorist-inspired violence. Nevertheless, the city still remains a dangerous place in certain sectors, and periodic car and truck bombings continue to occur. Reconstruction efforts until 2008 had been modest because of the earlier unrest in the city, but there are signs that privately funded rebuilding projects are gathering momentum.

DYLAN A. CYR AND PAUL G. PIERPAOLI JR.

See also

Bush, George Herbert Walker; DESERT STORM, Operation; Hussein, Saddam; Iraq, History of, Pre-1990; Iraq, History of, 1990–Present; IRAQI FREEDOM, Operation

References

Cohen, Saul B., ed. *The Columbia Gazetteer of the World*, Vol. 1. New York: Columbia University Press, 1998.

Pax, Salam. *The Baghdad Blog*. London: Grove Atlantic, 2003.

The World Guide: An Alternative Reference to Countries of Our Planet, 2003/2004. Oxford, UK: New Internationalist Publications, 2003.

Baghdad, Battle for
Start Date: April 5, 2003
End Date: April 10, 2003

Climactic battle of the 2003 Anglo-American invasion of Iraq that ended with the fall of the Iraqi capital and the collapse of Saddam Hussein's government. American planners before the war operated under the assumption that removing Hussein from power would very likely require some kind of ground attack on Baghdad. What everyone, from President George W. Bush on down, wanted to avoid, however, was grueling urban warfare that would devastate the city and lead to heavy casualties on all sides, the civilian populace included. To avoid being drawn into a costly city fight, the U.S. Army developed a plan to isolate Baghdad first, with the 3rd Infantry Division encircling the city from the west and the I Marine Expeditionary Force enveloping it from the east. Once a rough cordon had been established around Baghdad, the Americans intended to employ a combination of air strikes, armored and mechanized infantry raids, special forces incursions, and other small-scale operations to whittle away at the city's defenses and Baath Party control of the government, ideally reducing one or both to the breaking point.

The army never got the opportunity to test its operational concept for taking Baghdad, however, as the plan was scrapped once elements of the 3rd Infantry Division reached the outskirts of Baghdad just a little over two weeks into the campaign. By April 4, 2003, the division had secured two of the three objectives on its half of the cordon west of the Tigris River: Saddam International Airport (Operation LIONS) and the crucial highway junction just south of the city (Operation SAINTS). The third area (Operation TITANS) controlled the roads heading northwest out of Baghdad and remained in Iraqi hands. Meanwhile, the 1st Marine Division, which had a more difficult approach to the capital through the populated center of the country, was involved in fierce fighting with Republican Guard armor, Iraqi militia, and foreign irregulars and had yet to reach either of the two objectives on its side

U.S. marines on a foot patrol in Baghdad prepare to rush a house believed to contain a weapons cache, April 18, 2003. (U.S. Department of Defense)

of the Tigris. Rather than wait for the encirclement of Baghdad to be completed, the 3rd Infantry Division commander, Major General Buford Blount, decided to begin probing the city's defenses immediately.

The recent battles on the approach to the city suggested to Blount that Iraqi resistance was beginning to crumble, while the latest intelligence reports indicated that Baghdad was not the heavily fortified, stoutly defended deathtrap that some were expecting. In fact, the opposite proved to be true, as Hussein's paranoia had played directly into American hands. His fears of a coup had prevented him from undertaking military preparations of any kind in Baghdad, and he had entrusted defense of the capital to a relatively small cadre of loyal troops—the three brigades of the Special Republican Guard—supported by the irregulars known as Fedayeen Saddam.

Blount launched his first foray into Baghdad on April 5, sending an armored battalion from the 2nd Brigade Combat Team on a thunder run (or reconnaissance in-force) from the SAINTS area into the city center and then out to the airport. The column of 29 Abrams tanks, 14 Bradley fighting vehicles, and assorted other vehicles met with a hail of small-arms fire, rocket-propelled grenades, and mortar fire from the many hundreds of Iraqi fighters who took up positions along its route. A lucky shot from a

rocket-propelled grenade disabled one of the American tanks, and it had to be abandoned. Otherwise, the thickly armored Abrams and Bradleys were able to withstand multiple hits, and while the crews were exhausted at the end of the 140-minute-long mission, the vehicles themselves needed only minor repairs before again being ready for action.

The outcome of the April 5 thunder run confirmed Blount's suspicion that Baghdad's defenses were brittle. While the members of the 2nd Brigade Combat Team battalion received a day to catch their breath, Blount employed the 3rd Brigade Combat Team to tighten his grip on the city perimeter. On April 6 the brigade advanced to take control of objective TITANS, an area that included the Highway 1 bridge across the Tigris, a crucial point of entry and exit from the capital. This move triggered an intense battle with Iraqi tanks and infantry seeking to regain control of the crossing. The Iraqi attack began on the evening of April 6 and continued into the next morning before it was finally broken up by a combination of concentrated artillery fire, direct fire, and low-level strafing attacks by Fairchild-Republic A-10 Thunderbolts flying close air support.

The conclusion of the battle for the Tigris bridge to the northwest coincided with the launching of the second thunder run. Intended to be a limited raid much like the first, the April 7

BATTLE FOR BAGHDAD, APRIL 5–10, 2003

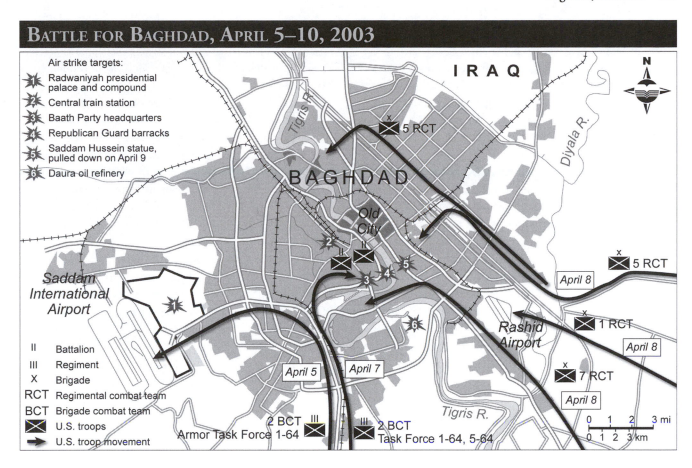

thunder run developed into something altogether different, an armored strike into the heart of downtown Baghdad. Colonel Dave Perkins, the commander of the 2nd Brigade Combat Team, took all three of his maneuver battalions on the mission. Blount and his superiors up the chain of command expected Perkins to pull back to the city's edge at the end of the thunder run. Instead, Perkins made the daring decision to lead his two armored battalions into the center of Baghdad and remain there. The battalions met with strong resistance on their drive into the city and afterward had to fend off repeated attacks by small bands of Iraqi fighters once they established their defensive perimeters in the downtown area. But it was the trailing infantry battalion, assigned the vital task of protecting the brigade's supply line into Baghdad, that found itself engaged in some of the heaviest and most desperate fighting. The battalion was assailed not only by Republican Guard and Fedayeen Saddam troops but also by hundreds of Syrian volunteers who had arrived in Iraq only days earlier. Despite some tense moments, the battalion kept the roadway open so that supply vehicles could reach the units parked downtown.

The thunder run of April 7 struck the decisive blow in the Battle for Baghdad. On the same day, the marines breached the Iraqi defenses along the Diyala River and began their advance into east Baghdad. Fighting continued on April 8, especially in the downtown area and in the 3rd Brigade Combat Team's sector at

TITANS. By April 9, however, resistance within the city had become generally disorganized and sporadic as increasing numbers of Iraqi fighters put down their weapons and melted into the general populace. The Baathist regime also dissolved, and some governing officials returned home. Others, most notably Saddam Hussein and his two sons, Uday and Qusay, slipped out of the capital and sought refuge elsewhere, leaving Baghdad to troops of the U.S. Army and the U.S. Marine Corps. Baghdad was considered secured by April 10.

Casualty figures are not terribly reliable, but it is believed that the coalition suffered 34 dead and at least 250 wounded. Iraqi dead have been given as 2,300 killed but were undoubtedly higher. There is no estimate of Iraqi wounded.

JEFF SEIKEN

See also

Baghdad; Blount, Buford, III; Hussein, Saddam; IRAQI FREEDOM, Operation; IRAQI FREEDOM, Operation, Ground Campaign

References

Fontenot, Gregory, et al. *On Point: The United States Army in Iraqi Freedom.* Annapolis, MD: Naval Institute Press, 2005.

Gordon, Michael R., and General Bernard E. Trainor. *Cobra II: The Inside Story of the Invasion and Occupation of Iraq.* New York: Pantheon Books, 2006.

Zucchino, David. *Thunder Run: The Armored Strike to Capture Baghdad.* New York: Grove, 2004.

Baghdad Pact

Treaty of mutual cooperation and mutual defense among the nations of Turkey, Iraq, Pakistan, Iran, and Great Britain agreed to in principle on February 4, 1955. The Baghdad Pact (also known as Central Treaty Organization [CENTO] or the Middle East Treaty Organization [METO]) was part of an effort by the United States and the West in general to establish regional alliances to contain the spread of Soviet influence.

The United States and Great Britain were the pact's chief sponsors. Each had different reasons for trying to lure Arab countries to join a defensive alliance. In the end, the Baghdad Pact failed because Arab leaders saw it as an attempt by the West to continue its colonial domination over the region. The Baghdad Pact in its different forms was the least effective of the anticommunist regional alliances sponsored by the United States.

As the Cold War developed in the late 1940s and early 1950s, the Harry S. Truman administration adopted a policy of communist containment. In Europe, the North Atlantic Treaty Organization (NATO) was formed in 1949 to prevent the expansion of Soviet control on that continent. The Dwight D. Eisenhower administration continued this process along other borders of the Soviet Union. The Middle East was viewed as a key area, in large part because it was the main source of oil for the West. The British government was expected to be the key to the formation of an alliance here, since it already had extensive relations with the Arab states. As such, British diplomats laid the groundwork for regional defense agreements. The first attempts included Egypt, but the government of President Gamal Abdel Nasser was more interested in Pan-Arabic agreements that excluded Britain. Indeed, Egypt refused to join a proposed Middle East Defense Organization in 1953, causing that initiative to collapse.

The United States and Britain therefore tried to create an alliance among the northern tier of Arab states. Turkey was already bound in an alliance to the West, thanks to NATO. Its status as a Muslim nation helped to encourage other Muslim countries to consider defensive alliances with the Western powers. In February 1954 Turkey and Pakistan signed a pact of mutual cooperation, one of the first in the region. Following much diplomatic activity, Iraqi prime minister Nuri al-Said announced that Iraq would sign a mutual defense pact with Turkey.

On February 24, 1955, Turkey and Iraq signed the Pact of Mutual Cooperation, which became better known as the Baghdad Pact, aimed at preventing Soviet aggression. The treaty included language inviting members of the Arab League as well as other interested nations to join. Britain signed the alliance on April 5, 1955. As a result, the Royal Air Force received the right to base units in Iraq and to train the Iraqi Air Force. Pakistan joined on September 23, 1955, and Iran joined on October 12, 1955. The United States remained a shadow member of the group but did not officially join. American relations with Israel were an obstacle that might have prevented Arab members from joining. A permanent secretariat and a permanent council for the alliance were created and headquartered in Baghdad.

Nasser viewed the Baghdad Pact as an attack on his own vision of Pan-Arabism, to be achieved under his leadership. He therefore immediately attacked the pact as Britain's way of continuing its colonial presence in the Middle East. He called it a hindrance to real Pan-Arab movements. At the time, Nasser had great prestige in the Arab world as a nationalist and opponent of Israel, and his condemnation of the treaty caused opposition to it among ordinary Arab peoples. Jordan had been expected to join the Baghdad Pact, but riots there convinced King Hussein I to withdraw his support for it. Syria refused to sign the treaty, instead forming a union with Egypt known as the United Arab Republic (UAR), to take effect on February 1, 1958. Even Lebanon, which requested Western assistance to help settle a civil war in 1958, refused to join the Baghdad Pact despite pressure from the United States and Britain to do so. Saudi Arabia also opposed the pact because it feared that Iraq would become the dominant regional power. The Saudis instead worked to persuade other members of the Arab League to establish closer contacts with Egypt.

The Baghdad Pact received a serious blow in October 1956 when Britain joined France and Israel in an invasion of Egypt in reaction to the Suez Crisis. The U.S. government opposed the attack and helped force its allies to withdraw. The action discredited Britain across the Middle East. To try to prop up the Western orientation of the Baghdad Pact, the United States joined the Military Committee of the organization in 1958 and funneled military assistance and other funds through the pact's organizations.

The gravest threat to the organization occurred on July 14, 1958, when Iraqi officers overthrew King Faisal II and the Iraqi monarchy. Popular sentiment in Iraq held that the Baghdad Pact simply modified Britain's colonial dominance of Iraq. Indeed, the alliance had weakened support for the government and the royal family. When Iraqi Army officers overthrew the government, few Iraqis were willing to defend the old order. The royal family was slaughtered, as was Said. The ruling officers, sympathetic to Nasser, withdrew Iraq from the Baghdad Pact on March 24, 1959. That same year, the United States officially joined the alliance, which changed its name to the Central Treaty Organization (CENTO).

The alliance proved to be weak, however. When Pakistan and Iran were involved in conflicts with India and Iraq, respectively, during the 1960s, they tried to invoke the alliance to involve Britain and the United States. Britain and the United States refused to be drawn into the regional conflicts, however, because they saw the alliance as one limited to stopping aggression on the part of the Soviet Union. As a result, Pakistan and Iran came to regard the alliance with considerable cynicism.

CENTO diminished in importance as British global influence continued to recede. In 1968 Britain decided to withdraw its forces from the Persian Gulf, making British bases on Cyprus the closest ones to the Middle East. In 1974 budget cutbacks forced Britain to withdraw specific troop commitments to CENTO. After that, CENTO became a chiefly symbolic structure rather than an effective defensive mechanism. In 1979 Iran withdrew from CENTO

Four premiers of nations belonging to the Baghdad Pact pose with British foreign secretary Harold MacMillan (second from right) at the inaugural meeting of the pact in Baghdad, Iraq, in November 1955. The pact, initially signed in 1955 by Iraq and Turkey, established a defense coalition between Iraq, Turkey, Pakistan, Iran, and the United Kingdom. Iraq withdrew from the pact shortly after the 1958 coup that brought down King Faisal II and put Abd al-Karim Qasim in power. (AP/Wide World Photos)

following the overthrow of Mohammad Reza Shah Pahlavi. On March 12, 1979, Pakistan withdrew as well. CENTO and the vestiges of the Baghdad Pact had now collapsed entirely.

TIM J. WATTS

See also

Arab League; Arab Nationalism; Egypt; Hussein ibn Talal, King of Jordan; Iran; Iraq, History of, Pre-1990; Nasser, Gamal Abdel; Nuri al-Said; Pan-Arabism and Pan-Arabist Thought; Turkey, Role in Persian Gulf and Afghanistan Wars; United Arab Republic; United Kingdom, Middle East Policy; United States, Middle East Policy, 1945–Present

References

CENTO Public Relations Division. *The Story of the Central Treaty Organization.* Washington, DC: CENTO, 1959.

Dann, Uriel. *Iraq under Qassem: A Political History, 1958–1963.* New York: Praeger, 1969.

Kuniholm, Bruce. *The Origins of the Cold War in the Near East.* Princeton, NJ: Princeton University Press, 1980.

Podeh, Elie. *The Quest for Hegemony in the Arab World: The Struggle over the Baghdad Pact.* New York: E. J. Brill, 2003.

Bahrain

Middle Eastern country consisting of an archipelago of more than 30 islands located in the Persian Gulf. As of 2008 no accurate count of the number of islands was possible, as Bahrain continues to create artificial islands off its coast for economic and tourism purposes. Bordered on the west by the Gulf of Bahrain and by the Persian Gulf on the north, east, and south, Bahrain is also about 20 miles from both Qatar to the south and Saudi Arabia to the west. A causeway connects Saudi Arabia with the Bahraini island of Umm al-Nasan. Bahrain's area is just 274 square miles, with only five of the islands being permanently inhabited. Bahrain's topography consists of low desert plains and a low central escarpment, with a climate ranging from hot and humid summers to temperate winters.

Officially known as the Kingdom of Bahrain, the nation's capital is Manama. Bahrain's population is approximately 709,000 people, with 63 percent of Bahraini descent, 19 percent Asian, 10 percent Arab, 8 percent Iranian, and a smattering of other nationalities. Islam is practiced by 85 percent of the population, and 70 percent of the Muslim population are Shia. The remaining 15 percent practice Bahai, Christianity, and other religions. Arabic, English, and Farsi are the most commonly spoken languages in Bahrain.

Politically, the country consists of a constitutional monarchy ruled by Emir Khalifa bin Hamad al-Thani. Bahrain is a member of the Gulf Cooperation Council (GCC), a collective security organization consisting of six countries on the western side of the Persian Gulf, the Arab League, the United Nations (UN), the Organization of Islamic Conference, the Organization of Arab Petroleum Exporting Countries, and other international organizations.

Although fixing the precise starting date of the Bahraini civilization is difficult, ancient civilizations such as Pakistan's Harappa and the Greeks traded their goods for Bahraini pearls in ancient times. Historically, Bahrain has been known as Dilmun, Tylos, and Awal. Pre-Islamic Bahrain's religions included both paganism and Nestorian Christianity, the latter having a bishopric located on the island and lasting until at least 835 CE. Bahrain adopted Islam during the Prophet Muhammad's lifetime, and it quickly grew to become the dominant religion in the country. The Ismaili al-Qaramita Islamic sect dominated Bahrain between 900 and 976 CE. Afterward, the Shia eventually became the dominant force in Bahraini Islam.

Throughout Bahrain's history various empires have occupied the country, including those of Babylon, Assyria, Portugal, and Safavid Iran. Portuguese forces captured Bahrain in 1521 and controlled the country until 1602, when Bahrainis overthrew Portuguese forces on the island. Iran's Safavid Empire quickly conquered Bahrain the same year and maintained control until 1717, a fact used by Iran to make repeated claims on Bahraini territory. In 1783 the al-Khalifa clan, led by Ahmad ibn Mohammed al-Khalifa, invaded and conquered Bahrain and has led the country since that time.

In 1820 Bahrain signed a treaty with Britain promising that it would not engage in piracy. Britain agreed to provide military protection for Bahrain and official recognition of the al-Khalifa family as the ruling party of Bahrain. In exchange, Bahrain agreed not to cede its territory to any country except Britain and not to establish foreign relations with other nations without British consent. Meanwhile, English advisers encouraged the al-Khalifa rulers to adopt a series of social reforms for the country.

Standard Oil Company of California's discovery of oil reserves in 1932 created significant changes, as Bahrain became an early leading exporter of petroleum. Bahrain allied itself with Britain during World War II, providing oil to the allies as well as serving as a staging point for protecting British colonies and oil-production facilities in Asia and Africa.

After India acquired its independence on August 15, 1947, British interests in the Persian Gulf region diminished, eventually leading to the decision in 1968 to withdraw from the treaties signed with Persian Gulf states during the 1800s. Initial attempts to unite Bahrain with other Persian Gulf states failed, and on August 15, 1971, Bahrain declared its full independence. By 1973 Bahrain's oil reserves were diminishing, while the price of oil was dramatically increasing. Looking for an alternative source of revenue, Bahrain established a robust banking industry to replace Lebanon's banking industry, which had suffered from the long Lebanese Civil War (1975–1990). Bahrain soon became the banking center of the Middle East.

Although a national assembly was elected in 1973, it quarreled with Emir Isa ibn Salman al-Khalifa, who ruled from 1961 through 1999, over implementation of a security law. He responded by dissolving the assembly in 1975 and passed the law by decree. Despite his actions, Bahrain is quite liberal and tolerant compared to most other Islamic nations in the region. In 1981 Iran attempted to encourage Bahrain's large Shia population to foment a revolution in Bahrain. Although some Bahraini Shias staged a coup d'état in 1981, it did not succeed. Iran's interference in Bahraini affairs encouraged the nation to establish collective security agreements that created the GCC and improved relations with the United States.

Violent acts against the government have included attacks by external and internal sources. The Islamic Front engaged in terrorist attacks against Bahraini targets in the county. Political dissent within the kingdom grew during 1980s and 1990s, as citizens lacked the opportunity to actively participate in the governing of the country. The Bahrain Freedom Movement (BFM), formed by Bahraini dissidents who wanted an Iranian-styled Islamic republic established, also engaged in bombings and other terrorist acts. Bahraini security forces reacted strongly against the BFM.

Manama City, Bahrain. (Orhancam/Dreamstime.com)

Emir Isa ibn Salman al-Khalifa's death in 1999 initiated a series of changes, as his son Khalifa bin Hamad al-Thani took a chance on reforming Bahraini society, initiating a series of social and political reforms, including the resumption of constitutional rule. Hamad al-Thani agreed to concessions limiting legislative power to the lower house of parliament in the National Action Charter that was designed to restore constitutional government yet reversed his decision with the 2002 constitution. In 2002 he agreed to hold parliamentary elections in which both men and women could vote and run for office, although no woman won a seat. Several parties, including the major religious party al-Wifaq National Islamic Society, boycotted the election.

Presently, there are 12 political parties in the country (6 are Islamic, and 6 are secular). The 2006 elections resulted in the Shia-associated Al-Wifaq National Islamic Society winning 17 seats, while the salafist al-Asalah party won 8 and the Sunni Al-Minbar Islamic Society won 7. The remaining parties and candidates won a combined 8 seats. Although 18 women ran, just 1 captured a seat in parliament.

Although the United States had sent ships to the region during the 1800s, Washington had little interest in Bahrain until 1949, when the United States began leasing British bases in Bahrain. The United States has maintained at least a minimal force in Bahrain since that time. Bahrain's role in America's conflicts in the Middle

East can be divided into two parts. The first is marked by its willingness to allow U.S. forces to use Bahraini territory and facilities for launching military operations against Iraq, first during the 1991 Persian Gulf War and next during Operation IRAQI FREEDOM. Bahrain was also used as a base during Operation ENDURING FREEDOM. The U.S. Naval Forces Central Command operates out of Manama. Army and air force units operating in Bahrain include the 831st Transport Battalion, located at Mina Sulman, and the Air Mobility Command, which has a detachment at Muharraq Airfield. Additionally, the Sheik Isa Air Base serves as a military airfield for various U.S. military aircraft.

Bahrain was also actively involved militarily in the Persian Gulf War and in providing limited military assistance in Operations ENDURING FREEDOM and IRAQI FREEDOM. In 1991 Bahrain sent a small contingent of 400 troops to serve in the coalition as part of the Joint Forces Command East. Additionally, the Bahraini Air Force, employing F-16 Fighting Falcon fighters and F-5 Tiger II fighters, engaged in defensive sorties in the region and launched offensives against Iraqi assets. The Bahraini Navy has sent forces to assist in ENDURING FREEDOM and in the larger Global War on Terror. Bahrain has also provided some limited forces in a support role for Operation IRAQI FREEDOM and to help the Iraqi government stabilize the country.

WYNDHAM WHYNOT

See also

Arab League; DESERT STORM, Operation; ENDURING FREEDOM, Operation;
    Gulf Cooperation Council; IRAQI FREEDOM, Operation; Khalifa, Isa bin
    Salman al-; Thani, Khalifa bin Hamad al-

References

Congressional Quarterly. *The Middle East.* 10th ed. Washington, DC: CQ
    Press, 2005.

Ochsenwald, William, and Sydney Nettleton Fisher. *The Middle East: A
    History.* 6th ed. New York: McGraw-Hill, 2004.

Palmer, Michael. *Guardians of the Gulf: A History of America's Expanding
    Role in the Persian Gulf, 1833–1992.* New York: Free Press, 1992.

Spencer, William J. *The Middle East.* 11th ed. Dubuque, IA: McGraw-
    Hill/Contemporary Learning Series, 2007.

Winkler, David. *Amirs, Admirals & Desert Sailors: Bahrain, the U.S.
    Navy, and the Arabian Gulf.* Annapolis, MD: Naval Institute Press,
    2007.

Baker, James Addison, III
Birth Date: April 28, 1930

U.S. politician, influential Republican adviser, secretary of the
treasury (1985–1988), and secretary of state (1989–1992). Born
on April 28, 1930, in Houston, Texas, to a wealthy local family,
James Addison Baker III studied classics at Princeton University,
graduating in 1952. After two years in the U.S. Marine Corps, he
went on to earn a law degree from the University of Texas at Austin

Prominent Republican James Baker III served as U.S. secretary of state
under President George H. W. Bush during 1989–1992. In 2006, Baker
cochaired the bipartisan Iraq Study Group. (U.S. Department of State)

U.S. Secretaries of State, 1989–Present

Name	Dates of Service
James A. Baker	January 25, 1989–August 23, 1992
Lawrence Eagleburger	August 23, 1992–January 20, 1993
Warren Christopher	January 20, 1993–January 17, 1997
Madeleine Albright	January 23, 1997–January 20, 2001
Colin Powell	January 20, 2001–January 26, 2005
Condoleezza Rice	January 26, 2005–January 20, 2009
Hillary Rodham Clinton	January 21, 2009–present

in 1957. That same year he began his legal career with a corporate
law firm in Houston, where he practiced until 1975.

Baker first entered politics in 1970, working for George H. W.
Bush's unsuccessful U.S. senatorial campaign. Beginning in 1975,
Baker spent a year as undersecretary of commerce in the Gerald
Ford administration. Baker then managed Ford's unsuccessful
1976 presidential campaign. After managing Bush's unsuccessful bid for the Republican presidential nomination in 1980, Baker
became a senior adviser to President Ronald Reagan's 1980 campaign after Bush withdrew from the race.

From 1981 until 1985, Baker served as White House chief of
staff. In 1984 he successfully engineered Reagan's reelection
campaign. Reagan subsequently appointed him secretary of the
treasury in 1985. In 1988 Baker resigned from the treasury and
managed Vice President George H. W. Bush's presidential campaign and was rewarded by being appointed secretary of state in
1989. In that role, Baker helped reorient U.S. foreign policy as the
Cold War ended. He was involved in negotiations that led to the
reunification of Germany and the dismantling of the Soviet Union.
Baker also presided over negotiations before and after the successful Persian Gulf War. In 1992 Bush named Baker White House
chief of staff and manager of his reelection campaign. Bush lost
that election to Democrat Bill Clinton.

After leaving government service in 1993, Baker joined the
Houston-based law firm of Baker Botts and become senior coun-
selor to the Carlyle Group, a corporate banking firm in Washington, D.C. In 2000 he served as President-elect George W. Bush's
transition adviser during the controversial Florida ballot recount
following the November presidential election. In 2004 Baker
served as the personal envoy of United Nations (UN) secretary-
general Kofi Annan in seeking to reach a peaceful solution to the
conflict over the western Sahara. In 2003 Baker was a special presidential envoy for President George W. Bush on Iraqi debt relief.

Beginning in March 2006, Baker cochaired, along with former
U.S. Democratic representative Lee Hamilton, the 10-person bipartisan Iraq Study Group, charged with recommending changes to
deal with the deteriorating situation in the Iraqi insurgency. The
group presented its report to President George W. Bush and Congress in early December 2006. Among its recommendations was a
strong call for a major drawdown of U.S. troops in Iraq. In January
2007 Bush did just the opposite, implementing a troop surge in Iraq
that began to show some signs of success late in the year. Baker

continued to advise the Bush administration on an ad hoc basis until the January 2009 inauguration of President Barrack Obama.

JOHN DAVID RAUSCH JR.

See also
Bush, George Herbert Walker; Bush, George Walker; DESERT STORM, Operation; Iraq Study Group; Reagan, Ronald Wilson

References
Baker, James A., III, with Thomas M. DeFrank. *The Politics of Diplomacy: Revolution, War, and Peace, 1989–1992*. New York: Putnam, 1995.
Gwynne, S. C. "James Baker Forever." *Texas Monthly* 31 (December 2003): 150–173.

Baker-Aziz Meeting
Event Date: January 9, 1991

Six-hour summit convened on January 9, 1991, between U.S. secretary of state James A. Baker III and Iraqi foreign minister Tariq Aziz. The Baker-Aziz meeting was ostensibly designed to head off a military attack against Iraq by American-led coalition forces, which were already massed in Saudi Arabia. The conference consisted of three rounds, all of which were held in the ballroom of the Hotel Intercontinental in Geneva, Switzerland. The high-level talks served as the last official U.S. demand for Iraqi military forces to withdraw immediately from Kuwait and avoid open hostilities in the Persian Gulf. Iraqi forces had invaded and occupied Kuwait since August 1990.

The meeting resulted from Iraqi president Saddam Hussein's noncompliance with United Nations (UN) Security Council Resolution 678. Approved on November 29, 1990, UN Resolution 678 had authorized the use of military force against Iraq should the nation not give up its occupation of Kuwait by January 15, 1991. Following a brief meeting with his advisers on the same day of the passage of the resolution, U.S. president George H. W. Bush directed Baker to enter into official negotiations with Iraqi diplomats. Seeking to show that they had done all they could diplomatically to avoid war, Bush administration officials also considered the meeting crucial for obtaining domestic support for war, silencing congressional opponents critical of the administration's diplomacy in the Middle East, and maintaining coalitional unity among 28 nations now allied against Iraq.

The Iraqi-American talks began when Baker presented Aziz with an official letter from President Bush addressed to President Hussein. Bush demanded that Hussein order Iraqi military forces to leave Kuwait and thus comply fully and unconditionally with UN Resolution 678 or face a military response led by the United States. Aziz rejected the letter, explaining that Iraq had invaded Kuwait to defend itself both against deflationary Kuwaiti oil policies and an Israeli-American alliance perceived by Baghdad as seeking to destroy Iraq. The remaining rounds of discussion centered on talking points prepared in Washington and Baghdad prior to the meeting.

Baker summarized American intelligence estimates of Iraqi military capabilities, figures that included the range and capabilities of Iraqi Scud missiles. Aziz assured Baker that the remaining American diplomatic personnel in Iraq would be allowed to leave by January 12 and also stated that Iraq would consider withdrawing its forces from Kuwait only after reaching a regional settlement that included an Israeli-Palestinian peace.

While the talks failed to persuade Hussein to withdraw his forces from Kuwait, the Baker-Aziz meeting nonetheless served the Bush administration well diplomatically.

JASON GODIN

See also
Aziz, Tariq; Baker, James Addison, III; Bush, George Herbert Walker; Carter, James Earl, Jr.; DESERT STORM, Operation; Hussein, Saddam; Iraq, History of, Pre-1990; Iraq, History of, 1990–Present; United Nations Security Council Resolution 678

References
Baker, James A., III, with Thomas M. DeFrank. *The Politics of Diplomacy: Revolution, War, and Peace, 1989–1992*. New York: Putnam, 1995.
Brands, H. W. *Into the Labyrinth: The United States and the Middle East, 1945–1993*. New York: McGraw-Hill, 1994.
Bush, George, and Brent Scowcroft. *A World Transformed*. New York: Knopf, 1998.
Lasensky, Scott B. "Friendly Restraint: U.S.-Israel Relations during the Gulf War Crisis of 1990–1991." *Middle East Review of International Affairs* 2 (June 1999): 24–35.

Baker-Hamilton Commission
See Iraq Study Group

Bakr, Ahmad Hassan al-
Birth Date: July 1, 1914
Death Date: October 4, 1982

Iraqi military officer, Baath Party leader, and president of Iraq from 1968 to 1979. Ahmad Hassan al-Bakr was born in Tikrit (then part of the Ottoman Empire) on July 1, 1914, and was an elder cousin of Iraqi dictator Saddam Hussein. After completing the equivalent of high school, Bakr taught secondary school for six years before enrolling in the Iraqi Military Academy in 1938.

Early in his military career, Bakr became involved with antigovernment activity that culminated in the 1941 Rashid Ali al-Gaylani Revolt. When that uprising was suppressed, he was arrested, jailed, and forced out of the army. Not until 1956, when he had sufficiently rehabilitated himself under the waning Hashemite monarchy, was he permitted to rejoin the Iraqi Army. That same year, he also clandestinely joined the Iraqi Baath Party.

In 1957 Bakr, now a brigadier general, was part of a military cabal known as the Free Officers group that successfully overthrew the monarchy during the July 14 Revolution. The coup d'état brought General Abd al-Karim Qasim to power, and he instituted Baathist reforms, withdrew Iraq from the Baghdad Pact, and cultivated ties with the Soviet Union.

In 1959 Bakr was once again purged from the military, this time for his alleged ties to an antigovernment rebellion in Mosul, the goal of which was to draw Iraq closer to the United Arab Republic. Nevertheless, he retained his prominent position within the Baath Party hierarchy and in 1963 helped foment a putsch against Qasim. With Qasim out, Bakr became prime minister and vice president but held these posts for only a few months before Abd al-Salam Arif launched another coup in November 1963. By January 1964 Bakr had been stripped of both government positions. In 1966 Arif's death brought his brother, Abd al-Rahman Arif, to power.

Bakr's power base within the Baath Party was still considerable, and he soon hatched a plan to oust Arif from power and return Baathist rule. With the help of the Egyptian government, in 1968 Bakr staged a coup that resulted in Arif's exile. That same year Bakr became president and prime minister of Iraq. Determined to implement his Baath Party platform, he named his cousin, Saddam Hussein, as his chief deputy and deputy head of the Revolutionary Command Council. Hussein was later made vice president and was essentially the second most powerful man in Iraq.

As president, Bakr nationalized Iraqi oil concerns and instituted a wide array of economic and social reforms. After 1973, when world oil prices skyrocketed, Bakr pursued an aggressive industrial expansion program and funded a panoply of public works projects and infrastructure improvements. Increased oil revenues also allowed his government to purchase large amounts of weapons and armaments from the Soviets and significantly augment Iraqi armed forces. During his period in power, Iraqi-Soviet relations improved dramatically. Bakr successfully suppressed a Kurdish uprising that had been financed in part by Iran, and when his government settled some long-standing differences with Iran in 1975, the Kurdish cause was dealt a crippling blow. In 1978 the Iraqi government banned all political parties except for the ruling Baath Party and made it a capital offense for any government or military official to belong to another party.

By the late 1970s Hussein had begun to consolidate his power, and as Bakr's health deteriorated, Hussein became the real power behind the throne. By early 1979 Bakr was leader in name only, and on July 16, 1979, he stepped down, allegedly because of health concerns. Hussein immediately took the reins of state and became the new president of Iraq. Bakr was allowed to live in quiet seclusion, but his paranoid cousin kept constant watch over him. On October 4, 1982, Bakr died, supposedly of natural causes, in Baghdad. Many have speculated that his death came not from natural causes but rather on the orders of Hussein.

PAUL G. PIERPAOLI JR.

See also

Arif, Abd al-Salam; Baath Party; Hussein, Saddam; Iraq, History of, Pre-1990; Qasim, Abd al-Karim

References

Marr, Phebe. *The Modern History of Iraq.* 2nd ed. Boulder, CO: Westview, 2003.

Tripp, Charles. *A History of Iraq.* Cambridge: Cambridge University Press, 2007.

Balfour Declaration

The Balfour Declaration was a promise by the British government to support the creation of a national homeland for the Jewish people. The British government issued the declaration in an effort to gain the support of Jews around the world for the Allied war effort. The promise apparently contradicted an earlier pledge by London to the Arabs to support the establishment of an independent Arab state after World War I. The Balfour Declaration helped encourage Jewish immigration to Palestine during the 1920s and 1930s, but it alienated Arabs from the British Mandate government. Indirectly, the Balfour Declaration led to the creation of the State of Israel and to ongoing conflict between Arabs and Jews in the Middle East that endures to the present day.

Before World War I, Palestine was a part of the Ottoman Empire and included the Sinai peninsula and parts of present-day Lebanon and Syria. A small number of Jewish settlements were located in Palestine, with a total population of approximately 50,000 people. The Zionist movement, developed in the 19th century, taught that Judaism was not only a religion but also a national group. Zionists called for Jewish immigration to traditional Jewish lands to establish a Jewish state for Jews from around the world. Zionism was formally organized in 1897 when smaller groups came together to create the World Zionist Organization (WZO) at Basel, Switzerland. Theodor Herzl became the group's first president. Supporters of Zionism included influential Jews and non-Jews throughout Europe and the United States.

When World War I began, Zionists urged the various governments to support their movement. The most fertile ground was in Great Britain. Although the total number of Jews in Britain was small, they included influential individuals such as Sir Herbert Samuel and the Rothschild banking family. The leader of the Zionists in Britain was Dr. Chaim Weizmann, chemistry professor at Manchester University. Weizmann had discovered a revolutionary method of producing acetone, important to the munitions industry. Members of the British government understandably held Weizmann in high esteem. Others believed that the West had a moral duty to Jews because of past injustices.

Events during the spring of 1917 aided Weizmann's campaign for British support for a Jewish homeland in Palestine. The first was the Russian Revolution in March (February by the Russian calendar). Some of the more prominent leaders of the revolution were Jews, and Weizmann argued that they were more likely to keep Russia in the war if an Allied goal was a Jewish homeland. Another important event was the entry of the United States into the war in April 1917. The large Jewish population in the United States could campaign for greater and more immediate U.S. contributions to the war effort. Jewish financial contributions toward the war effort might be increased with support for a homeland as well. Weizmann also told his friends in the British government that support for a Jewish homeland might prevent German Jews from giving their full support to Kaiser Wilhelm II's war effort.

Arthur James Balfour, British foreign secretary, supported a promise of a Jewish homeland after the war. On a trip to the United States, he conferred with Supreme Court justice Louis Brandeis, a Zionist. Brandeis was an adviser to President Woodrow Wilson and told Balfour that the president supported a homeland for the Jews. At the time, however, Wilson was reluctant to give it open support because the United States was not formally at war with the Ottoman Empire. Other prominent Americans, such as former presidential candidate William Jennings Bryan, supported a Jewish homeland, many because they believed that it would fulfill biblical prophecies.

Members of the Zionist movement in Britain helped draft a declaration that was approved by the British cabinet and released by Balfour on November 2, 1917. The key sentence in the document was "His Majesty's Government view with favour the establishment in Palestine of a national home for the Jewish people." The declaration went on to state that the civil and religious rights of the existing non-Jewish peoples in Palestine were not to be prejudiced. In response to fears by some Jews that a homeland in Palestine would harm their efforts to assimilate into other societies, the declaration also called for nothing that would harm those efforts. The French government pledged its support for the declaration on February 11, 1918. Wilson finally gave open approval in a letter to Rabbi Stephen Wise on October 29, 1918.

The declaration did indeed win Jewish support for the Allied war effort, but it had unintended effects as well. Correspondence between British high commissioner in Egypt Henry McMahon and Sharif Hussein of Mecca in 1915 had promised the establishment of an independent Arab state upon the defeat of the Ottomans. It was understood that this state would include Palestine. The declaration was also a violation of the Sykes-Picot Agreement between Great Britain and France that provided for joint rule over the area directly after the war. The apparent double-dealing by the British government alienated many Arabs and caused them to doubt whether they could trust British promises.

At the end of World War I, the League of Nations granted a mandate over Palestine to Great Britain. Language from the Balfour Declaration was incorporated into the mandate's wording. During the next 30 years, the Jewish population of Palestine increased from 50,000 to 600,000 people. This dramatic increase in immigration of Jews to Palestine led to numerous clashes with Palestinians already living there. Ultimately, the task of trying to keep conflicting promises to Arabs and Jews proved too much for the British. They gave up their mandate in 1948, and the State of Israel was created. The result has been hostility and sporadic wars between Jews and Arabs ever since.

TIM J. WATTS

See also

Mandates; Sykes-Picot Agreement; United Kingdom, Middle East Policy; World War I, Impact of

References

Lenczowski, George. *The Middle East in World Affairs.* 4th ed. Ithaca, NY: Cornell University Press, 1980.

Sanders, Ronald. *The High Walls of Jerusalem: A History of the Balfour Declaration and the Birth of the British Mandate for Palestine.* New York: Holt, Rinehart and Winston, 1983.

Stein, Leonard. *The Balfour Declaration.* New York: Simon and Schuster, 1961.

Bandar bin Sultan, Prince
Birth Date: March 2, 1949

Saudi Arabian military official, ambassador to the United States (1983–2005), and since October 16, 2005, secretary-general of the Saudi Arabian National Security Council. Prince Bandar bin Sultan bin Abdulaziz Al-Saud was born in Taif, Saudi Arabia, on March 2, 1949, the son of Crown Prince Sultan bin Abdul Aziz, the deputy prime minister, minister of defense and aviation, and inspector general of Saudi Arabia. Prince Bandar graduated from the Royal Air Force College at Cranwell, England, in 1968. He was then commissioned a second lieutenant in the Royal Saudi Air Force.

During the 1970s Bandar studied in the United States at the Air Command and Staff College at Maxwell Air Force Base in Montgomery, Alabama, and at the Industrial College of the Armed Forces at Fort McNair in Washington, D.C. Throughout the 1970s, Bandar commanded fighter squadrons at three different Saudi bases and held major responsibilities in the Royal Saudi Air Force's modernization program, known as Peace Hawk. In 1980 he earned a master's degree in international public policy from Johns Hopkins University.

During his military career, Bandar consistently strove to modernize the Royal Saudi Air Force. Intent on purchasing the most modern technology, in 1978 he successfully lobbied the U.S. Congress to approve the sale of F-15 fighter aircraft to Saudi Arabia. In 1981 he secured approval of the sale of the U.S. Airborne Warning and Control System (AWACS) to Saudi Arabia. In 1982 Bandar was assigned as the Saudi defense attaché to the United States at the rank of lieutenant colonel.

In 1983 Bandar became the ambassador to the United States. During his long tenure as Saudi ambassador to the United States, he rose to be the dean of the diplomatic corps in Washington, D.C. He strongly supported the Saudi Arabian government's decision to permit U.S. staging areas in Saudi Arabia during the 1991 Persian Gulf War. In the aftermath of the September 11, 2001, terrorist attacks on the United States, Bandar worked hard to convince the American public and government of Saudi Arabia's friendship with the United States and of its commitment to the Global War on Terror.

Bandar has repeatedly denied allegations that the Saudi government supports the activities of Osama bin Laden and other Islamic terrorists. Bandar also supported the U.S.-led offensive against Iraq's Saddam Hussein regime in March 2003. It is said that Bandar has promoted overtures to Israel and argued for the U.S.-urged harder line toward Hamas. Nevertheless, frequent criticism of Bandar and Saudi foreign policy has circulated in the American media, most notably by filmmaker Michael Moore. Since 2005, Bandar has presided over Saudi Arabia's national security apparatus.

MICHAEL R. HALL

See also

Bin Laden, Osama; Bush, George Herbert Walker; Bush, George Walker; DESERT STORM, Operation; *Fahrenheit 9/11;* Global War on Terror; IRAQI FREEDOM, Operation; Moore, Michael; Saudi Arabia; September 11 Attacks

References

Bond Reed, Jennifer. *The Saudi Royal Family.* New York: Chelsea House, 2002.

International Business Publications. *U.S.-Saudi Diplomatic and Political Relations Handbook.* Washington, DC: International Business Publications, 2005.

Posner, Gerald L. *Secrets of the Kingdom: The Inside Story of the Secret Saudi-U.S. Connection.* New York: Random House, 2005.

Ban Ki Moon
Birth Date: June 13, 1944

South Korean diplomat and eighth secretary-general of the United Nations (UN) (2007–present). Ban Ki Moon was born on June 13, 1944, in the village of Chungju in the province of North Chungcheong, in what is today the Republic of Korea (ROK, South Korea). As a teenager he spent several months in the United States. During that time he won a speech contest, and the grand prize was a trip to Washington, D.C., to meet President John F. Kennedy. Ban later credited the trip with sparking his interest in a diplomatic career. In 1970 he graduated from Seoul National University, where he earned a degree in international relations. He later studied public administration at Harvard University's John F. Kennedy School of Government, where he earned a master's degree in 1985.

At the time of his 2006 election as secretary-general, Ban's diplomatic career had spanned more than 30 years. His first position was as South Korea's vice-consul to New Delhi, India, in 1972. He also served at the UN as part of South Korea's permanent observer mission during 1978–1980. In 1980 he was promoted to director of the South Korean Foreign Ministry's UN division. He worked as director of the UN's International Organizations and Treaties Bureau in South Korea's capital, Seoul, and was consul-general at the South Korean embassy to the United States. In the 1990s Ban served in the South Korean government as director-general of the American Affairs Bureau and as an assistant to the foreign minister. He was also vice chair of the South-North Joint Nuclear Commission.

Ban returned to the UN in May 2001 to serve as chief of the UN General Assembly president's cabinet and as South Korea's UN ambassador. Then, in January 2004, South Korean president Roh Moo Hyun named Ban as the nation's foreign affairs and trade minister. Ban almost immediately faced several crises, most notably the kidnapping of a Korean worker by Iraqi terrorists in June 2004 and the deaths of many South Koreans in the tsunami of December 2004. In 2005 Ban successfully navigated meetings with the Democratic People's Republic of Korea (DPRK, North Korea) on nuclear disarmament. In September of that year, the two nations signed a joint statement on denuclearization. Ban remained foreign minister until taking his post at the UN in January 2007.

In February 2006 Ban announced his candidacy for UN secretary-general and traveled around the world to campaign for the

Ban Ki Moon. The South Korea diplomat was elected United Nations (UN) secretary-general on October 9, 2006. (AP/Wide World Photos)

post. Based on the UN's informal tradition of rotating the position of secretary-general among regions, outgoing secretary-general Koffi Annan's replacement was fairly certain to be an Asian. Ban faced competition from Shashi Tharoor of India and Prince Zeid al-Hussein of Jordan, but several factors made him the front-runner. First, South Korea is largely seen as a UN success, having emerged from the devastating Korean War into a democratized economic power. Second, many hoped that Ban's experiences in dealing with North Korea would aid the UN in resolving that nation's nuclear ambitions. And third, Ban had the support of the United States, one of the five permanent members of the UN Security Council with veto power over candidates for secretary-general. Ban's candidacy was approved by the Security Council's permanent members on October 9, 2006, and his name was then sent to the 192 members of the General Assembly, which officially elected him secretary-general on October 13. Ban was sworn in as secretary-general on December 14 and officially took over the post on January 1, 2007.

Ironically, the day of Ban's election witnessed the troubling announcement that North Korea had tested a nuclear weapon, prompting Ban to make denuclearization his first priority as secretary-general. Other prominent issues that he laid out included reform of the UN's vast bureaucracy, the cessation of continued warfare and famine in several regions of Africa, the international AIDS crisis, and unrest in the Middle East.

UN observers noted that Ban would most likely be "more secretary than general." Colleagues in the South Korean foreign service referred to him as "the bureaucrat" for his workaholic tendencies and facile administrative skill. Mild mannered, quiet, and modest, Ban has been criticized as uncharismatic. But Ban attributes his low-key personality to Asian culture, and he has defended his abilities. To many observers, Ban was the secretary-general candidate with whom Security Council members could live but who was not everyone's first choice. Either way, Ban has so far encountered little opposition in the UN, despite the certainly difficult first term he faces. Despite his continuing concern about North Korea's nuclear program and nuclear proliferation, he has generally deferred to the Security Council in these matters, just as he has with Iran's nuclear ambitions. He has urged the UN to take a larger role in Iraq to help the Iraqi people reinvigorate their social, political, and economic institutions and has pledged to do more to bring to an end the ongoing Palestinian-Israeli conflict. In March 2008, however, he criticized the Israeli government for its plans to build new housing in a West Bank settlement, calling these incompatible with Israel's earlier commitment to peace, including the so-called Road Map to Peace.

Ban oversees 9,000 employees and a budget of $5 billion. His five-year term ends in December 2012, when he will be eligible for reelection.

PAUL G. PIERPAOLI JR.

See also
Annan, Kofi; United Nations

References
Baehr, Peter R., and Leon Gordenker. *The United Nations: Reality and Ideal.* 4th ed. New York: Palgrave Macmillan, 2005.

Meisler, Stanley. *Koffi Annan: A Man of Peace in a World of War.* New York: Wiley, 2007.

Banna, Sabri Khalil al-

See Abu Nidal

Barno, David William
Birth Date: July 5, 1954

U.S. Army officer, commander of Combined Forces Command–Afghanistan, and the highest-ranking American commander in Afghanistan from October 2003 to May 2005. Born on July 5, 1954, in Endicott, New York, David William Barno attended the United States Military Academy, West Point, graduating in 1976. He earned a master's degree from Georgetown University in national security studies. During his army career, he also graduated from the United States Army Command and General Staff College and the United States Army War College.

Upon his commissioning in the U.S. Army in 1976, Barno served as a junior officer and company commander in the 25th Infantry Division. After attending the infantry officer advanced course, he assumed duties as a logistics officer in the 1st Battalion, 75th Ranger Regiment. During Operation URGENT FURY, the U.S. invasion that ousted the leftist government of Grenada in October 1983, Barno commanded a Ranger company. In Operation JUST CAUSE, the U.S. invasion of Panama to depose dictator Manuel Noriega in December 1989, Barno served as the operations officer for the 2nd Battalion, 75th Ranger Regiment. During his career, Barno served in Korea, Thailand, the Philippines, and New Zealand as well as in the continental United States.

During the 1990s Barno held several commands, including a parachute infantry battalion in the 82nd Airborne Division; the 2nd Battalion, 75th Ranger Regiment; and the Warrior Brigade. In July 1997 he served as the chief of the Joint Training and Doctrine Division at the Joint Warfighting Center. Following his promotion to brigadier general in 2000, he became the assistant division commander for operations for the 25th Infantry Division. Thereafter, he served as the deputy director for operations for the Untied States Pacific Command.

At the time of the September 11, 2001, terrorist attacks on the United States, Barno commanded the United States Army Training Center and Fort Jackson in South Carolina. In January 2003 Barno, now a major general, deployed to Tazar, Hungary, for three months, where he commanded Task Force Warrior. Task Force Warrior was an army training unit created to prepare free Iraqi forces before Operation IRAQI FREEDOM began in March 2003.

Working closely with the State Department, Task Force Warrior trained a small number of Iraqi volunteers to assist American and coalition civil-military units in their language skills and knowledge of Iraq.

In September 2003 Barno visited Afghanistan to receive briefings on what would become his next command. He assumed responsibility for U.S. military operations in Afghanistan in October 2003. Now a lieutenant general, he created a new military command structure, designated Combined Forces Command–Afghanistan, and established a counterinsurgency strategy for the country. Responsible for a region covering Afghanistan, southern Tajikistan and Uzbekistan, and parts of Pakistan, Barno worked closely with representatives from the U.S. Department of State, the United Nations (UN), the North Atlantic Treaty Organization (NATO), the International Security Assistance Force (Afghanistan), and the government of Afghanistan to coordinate counterinsurgency efforts across Afghanistan.

Barno shifted the focus of military operations from the primary goal of killing the enemy to reaching and aiding the Afghan people. His counterinsurgency strategy aimed to deny sanctuary to the enemy, support Afghan security forces, engage Afghanistan's neighbors, promote reconstruction and good governance, and create area "ownership" where military commanders could learn about and be responsible for specific regions.

Barno served as the assistant chief of staff for Installation Management before retiring from the army on June 1, 2006, as a lieutenant general. He subsequently accepted the position of director of the Near East South Asia Center for Strategic Studies at the National Defense University at Fort McNair in Washington, D.C. He also serves as a consultant on Afghanistan, counterinsurgency operations, and the Global War on Terror for government agencies and other organizations.

LISA M. MUNDEY

See also

Combined Forces Command, Afghanistan; ENDURING FREEDOM, Operation; International Security Assistance Force

References

Barno, David W. "Fighting 'The Other War': Counterinsurgency Strategy in Afghanistan, 2003–2005." *Military Review* (September–October 2007): 32–44.

Combat Studies Institute, Contemporary Operations Study Group. *A Different Kind of War: The United States Army Operation Enduring Freedom (OEF), September 2001–September 2005.* Fort Leavenworth, KS: Combat Studies Institute Press, 2009.

Rasanayagam, Angelo. *Afghanistan: A Modern History.* London: I. B. Tauris, 2005.

Basra

Major Iraqi port city. Basra (or al-Basrah), Iraq's main port, is located on the Shatt al-Arab waterway near the Persian Gulf (75 miles distant). With a present approximate population of 2.59 million, Basra is also Iraq's second-largest city and the capital of the Basra Governorate. Because of its geographically and economically strategic location, Basra has served as an important role in a number of conflicts.

In 636 Arab tribesmen who made up the armies of Emir Umar ibn al-Khattab formally established Basra. While fighting Sassanid forces, Muslim commander Utba ibn Ghazwan set up camp on the site of an old Persian settlement known as Vahestabad Ardasir, which ultimately became Basra. Al-Basrah, a name that means "the overwatcher," was given to the settlement because it served as a military stronghold against the Sassanid Empire. Basra served as a cultural center under Caliph Harun al-Rashid but eventually declined in influence with the fall of the Abbasid caliphate. Possession of Basra was long contested by both the Persians and the Turks because of its agricultural production and important geostrategic locale.

Basra and its environs hold significant petroleum resources, and the oil refinery at Basra has a daily production rate of approximately 140,000 barrels. Agricultural commodities also represent an important component to Basra's economy. Products such as millet, wheat, barley, dates, and corn are produced in the area's rich soil. Livestock are also an important part of the agricultural sector here. Basra's population is mainly of the Jafari Shia sect, but there are also many Sunni Muslims and some Christians. A pre-Islamic Gnostic sect known as the Mandaeans, who were based in the area formerly called Suk al-Shaykh, also contribute to Basra's population.

During World War I, the British occupied Basra and thoroughly modernized its port facilities. After the war, the construction of a rail line linking Basra to Baghdad and the establishment of a modern harbor made the city all the more important. In World War II, much of the military equipment and supplies sent to the Soviet Union by its Western allies via the Lend-Lease program moved through Basra.

Because of its location on the Shatt al-Arab waterway, Basra became a primary target for Iranian forces during the long and bloody Iran-Iraq War (1980–1988). The port at Basra also sustained heavy damage from bombing by coalition forces during the Persian Gulf War (Operation DESERT STORM) in 1991.

During the Persian Gulf War, a serious revolt against Iraqi dictator Saddam Hussein occurred in Basra, which was quelled by Iraqi military forces with much bloodshed. In 1999 a second revolt against the Hussein regime led to mass executions in the city. After this second uprising, the Iraqi government purposely diverted most of the country's sea-based commerce to Umm Qasr. Human rights abuses at Basra were among the many charges against Hussein that were considered by the Iraq Special Tribunal, which was established following the start of the 2003 Iraq War (Operation IRAQI FREEDOM) to try the former dictator for war crimes and crimes against humanity. He was eventually found guilty and executed in December 2006.

At the commencement of Operation IRAQI FREEDOM in March 2003, taking Basra was the first and primary goal for coalition troops during the 2003 Iraqi invasion. After a bruising battle, on April 7, 2003, British forces, led by the 7th Armored Brigade, took control of Basra. Nevertheless, from March to May 2003, Basra and its surrounding areas witnessed much of the heaviest combat in the war between Anglo-American–led coalition forces and Iraqi fighters. After the fighting stopped, the Multi-National Division under British command engaged in security and stabilization missions in the Basra Governorate and surrounding areas. Despite these pacification efforts, in mid-2006 Basra had seen several violent confrontations between secular Iraqis and Shiite Muslims in the area.

In September 2007 the British troops occupying Basra were withdrawn to the city's airport, part of a plan to gradually return occupied areas of Iraq over to Iraqi control. In December 2007 British troops withdrew entirely from Basra, including the airport. After receiving control of Basra, the Iraqi government stated that the city remains relatively stable and that violence has decreased in intensity and frequency.

CHARLENE T. OVERTURF

See also

Basra, Battle for; DESERT STORM, Operation; Hussein, Saddam; Iran-Iraq War; Iraq, History of, Pre-1990; Iraq, History of, 1990–Present; IRAQI FREEDOM, Operation; Persian Gulf; Shatt al-Arab Waterway; Umm Qasr, Battle of

References

Abbott, Delbert N. *Courage and Cowardice: The Liberation of Kuwait and the Rape of Basra.* Lincoln, NE: iUniverse, 2005.

Lyman, Robert, and Howard Gerrard. *Iraq 1941: The Battles for Basra, Habbaniya, Fallujah and Baghdad.* New York: Osprey, 2006.

Visser, Reidar. *Basra, the Failed Gulf State: Separatism and Nationalism in Southern Iraq.* Somerset, NJ: Transaction Publishers, 2006.

Basra, Battle for
Start Date: March 23, 2003
End Date: April 7, 2003

Battle fought between British and Iraqi forces during the Iraq War of 2003 at the Iraqi city of Basra (Basrah) in southeastern Iraq near the Shatt al-Arab waterway and the Persian Gulf. The battle began on March 23 and ended with the British capture of the city on April 7. At Basra, the British pursued a strategy considerably different from that followed by their American coalition partners during the invasion of Iraq. While this British strategy sharply limited loss of life, it also allowed many Iraqi soldiers and officials to escape and fight in the subsequent insurgency.

During the opening days of the Iraq War, British forces, supported by U.S. marines and offshore coalition naval units, seized

Iraqi civilians fleeing the city of Basra in southern Iraq during Operation IRAQI FREEDOM, March 28, 2003. (AP/Wide World Photos)

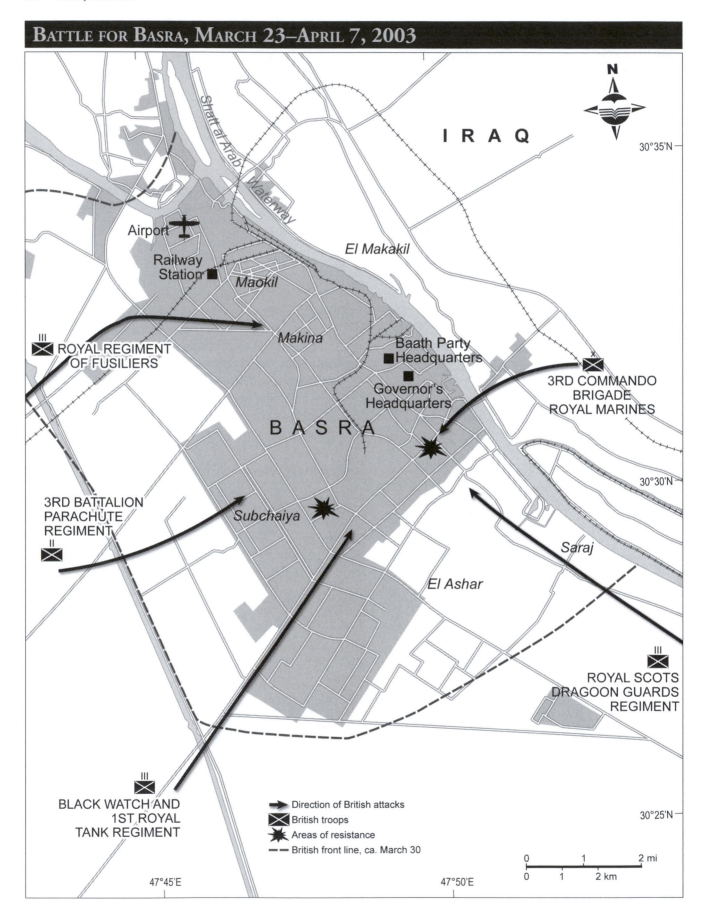

BATTLE FOR BASRA, MARCH 23–APRIL 7, 2003

the Faw peninsula and the deep-water port of Umm Qasr. British forces then took over occupation of the Rumaylah oil fields from American units that were needed elsewhere. The next major task for the British then became the capture of Basra, Iraq's second-largest city and its principal port, with an estimated population of more than 1.25 million people.

To achieve the capture of Basra, the British deployed the 1st Armored Division commanded by Major General Robin Brims. Iraqi forces in the city were commanded by General Ali Hassan al-Majid, otherwise known as "Chemical Ali" for his role in the Iraqi nerve gas attack on the Kurdish town of Halabja in 1988. Ali commanded a mixed force of Iraqi regulars and Baathist militia.

Brims decided upon a unique strategy for the taking of Basra, which would limit civilian deaths and mitigate physical damage to the city's buildings and infrastructure. The population of the city was made up primarily of anti–Saddam Hussein Shia. Basra had suffered greatly during President Hussein's suppression of the 1991 southern Shia rebellion that had followed the 1991 Persian Gulf War. Brims did not want to destroy the city and did not want to inflict needless casualties on the civilian population and thereby turn its people against the coalition.

Brims thus ordered the 1st Armored Division to surround Basra beginning on March 23, but he did not place the city under siege. He allowed anyone who wanted to leave Basra to do so, hoping to encourage desertion among Iraqi conscripts, which did occur. Brims also avoided the use of indirect artillery fire against Iraqi positions in Basra, thereby minimizing civilian casualties. Ali's strategy was to draw the British into battle in the narrow city streets of Basra where the British advantage in armor would be nullified, but Brims refused to engage in street fighting.

Frustrated, the Iraqis attempted to provoke the British into launching a major attack on the city. Ali sent out a column of Soviet-built T-55 tanks to attack the British on the evening of March 26. However, the T-55s were outranged by the 120-millimeter (mm) guns of the British Challenger tanks of the Royal Scots Dragoon Guards, resulting in the destruction of 15 T-55s without loss to the British.

On March 31 British reconnaissance, intelligence, and sniper teams began infiltrating the city, gathering intelligence, sniping at Iraqi officers and Baathist officials, making contact with anti-Hussein resistance circles, and directing artillery and air strikes. Beginning in early April, the British initiated a series of devastating yet limited raids against Iraqi positions using Warrior armored vehicles equipped with 30-mm cannon and capable of speeds of more than 50 miles per hour.

On April 5 an American F-16 fighter-bomber dropped two satellite-guided Joint Direct Attack Munition (JDAM) bombs on a building thought to be Chemical Ali's headquarters. The building was destroyed, and initially Ali was reported killed. Ali in fact survived the bombing and was not captured until after the war, but reports of his death were widely believed by Iraqi defenders, whose morale now plummeted.

A probe by the British into northern Basra on the morning of April 6 proved highly successful. Brims decided that the time had come to move into Basra in force. At 11:00 a.m. on April 6, he ordered British troops into the city. Despite heavy fighting, most of the city was under British control by nightfall. The British suffered only three soldiers killed. Some additional fighting continued the next day, but by the evening of April 7 the battle was officially over, and Basra was secure.

Because the British were not assigned the task of assaulting Baghdad and overthrowing Hussein's regime and because they were facing a population that they believed was sympathetic, the British could adopt a strategy at Basra that differed markedly from the strategy followed by the Americans in their drive to Baghdad. Loss of life was minimized, and further damage to the city's infrastructure was avoided. However, many of the Baathists who were allowed to escape from Basra must have certainly joined the postwar Sunni insurgency. Basra also experienced a wave of immediate postwar looting and violence similar to what also took place in Baghdad.

PAUL W. DOERR

See also

Basra; Brims, Robin; Hussein, Saddam; IRAQI FREEDOM, Operation; Kurds, Massacres of; Majid al Tikriti, Ali Hassan al-; Shia Islam; Sunni Islam

References

Gordon, Michael R., and General Bernard E. Trainor. *Cobra II: The Inside Story of the Invasion and Occupation of Iraq.* New York: Pantheon Books, 2006.

Keegan, John. *The Iraq War: The Military Offensive, from Victory in 21 Days to the Insurgent Aftermath.* New York: Vintage, 2005.

Battleships, U.S.

Periodically deemed anachronistic in an age of aircraft carriers, nuclear submarines, and long-range missiles, two of the four Iowa-class battleships, the *Missouri* (BB-63) and *Wisconsin* (BB-64), participated in Operation DESERT STORM during January–February 1991, again proving their usefulness in modern warfare.

In the 1980s the U.S. Navy recommissioned these World War II–era battleships to address a shortfall in deployable combatants within the U.S. fleet. Their reactivation and upgrades cost roughly the same as constructing a much smaller warship, such as a frigate. With a full displacement of more than 57,000 tons, the ships were 109 feet in width and 900 feet long. They were capable of a speed of 35 knots from eight boilers for steam propulsion. Their crews numbered 65 officers, more than 1,500 sailors, and a small contingent of marines. Primary firepower was provided by 9 Mark 7 16-inch/50-caliber guns with a range of more than 20 miles. Captains could choose between a 2,700-pound armor-piercing round capable of penetrating up to 30 feet of concrete or a 1,900-pound high-capacity projectile, the shrapnel from which could eliminate all soft targets within at least 60 yards of impact during shore bombardment. The ships' secondary battery consisted of 12 Mark 28 5-inch/38-caliber guns (originally 20 5-inch guns before refitting).

The ships were also refurbished with four quad cell launchers for the Harpoon antiship missile (range 65 nautical miles), eight armored-box launchers for a total of 32 Tomahawk Land-Attack Missiles (range 900 nautical miles), and four Falcon Phalanx Mark 15 20-millimeter (mm) Close-in Weapons System Gatling guns for air and missile defense. Although lacking a hangar, the battleships afforded sufficient deck space to accommodate up to four helicopters (either the Sikorsky Sea King SH-3 or Sikorsky SH-60 Seahawk).

The *Missouri* and *Wisconsin* accounted for 52 of the more than 300 Tomahawks launched against Iraqi targets during Operation DESERT STORM. When Iraqi units opened the ground campaign by engaging coalition forces near Khafji, Saudi Arabia, on January 29, the battleships initially proved of little use because of the threat of mines along the Kuwaiti coastline. Once minesweeping operations had cleared a zone by February 3, the *Missouri* went into action against Iraqi bunkers in southeastern Kuwait. The *Wisconsin* relieved its sister ship on February 6 and hurled shells at an artillery battery in its first combat firings since the 1950–1953 Korean War. The next day saw the *Wisconsin* destroy the Khawr al Mufattah marina, where Iraqi special forces had commandeered Kuwaiti craft. Unmanned aerial vehicles (UAVs) and marine spotters assisted in adjusting their fire. During the next two weeks as the U.S. Central Command (CENTCOM) prepared its ground assault, the battleships hit a variety of targets in southern Kuwait, including command bunkers, tanks, artillery, and troop concentrations.

The commanding presence of these capital ships helped deceive Iraqi leaders into expecting an amphibious assault on the shores of Kuwait instead of what actually ensued: a flanking attack spearheaded by armored forces in Saudi Arabia. On February 24 the two battleships commenced two days of naval gunfire support in conjunction with the much-anticipated coalition ground offensive. All told, during Operation DESERT STORM the *Missouri* and *Wisconsin* fired more than 1,000 shells against Iraqi positions in Kuwait in what constituted probably the last hurrah for these venerable platforms.

During these combat support missions, the 75 sailors in each 16-inch gun turret repeated a procedure dating back to World War II. Elevators provided propellant bags and shells from magazines below decks. The gun captain and rammer positioned these elements, while another crewman attached the primer. A gunner in the plot room pressed twin brass triggers that provided a brief warning bell to the crew before the subsequent blast recoiled each barrel by four feet and rattled the entire ship. A well-trained turret crew could put ordnance on target every 40 seconds.

The *Wisconsin* was decommissioned in September 1991 and was stricken from the Naval Vessel Register in January 1995. It is a museum ship in Norfolk, Virginia. Under congressional mandate, however, it is maintained so that if need be it could be returned to active service. The *Missouri,* once the site of the formal Japanese

surrender to end World War II in September 1945, was returned to retirement in 1992 and is a museum ship at Pearl Harbor.

JEFFREY D. BASS

See also

DESERT STORM, Operation; DESERT STORM, Operation, Coalition Naval Forces; United States Navy, Persian Gulf War

References

Marolda, Edward, and Robert Schneller. *Shield and Sword: The United States Navy and the Persian Gulf War.* Annapolis, MD: U.S. Naval Institute Press, 2001.

Morison, Samuel, and Norman Polmar. *The American Battleship.* St. Paul: MBI Publishing, 2003.

Muir, Malcolm. *The Iowa Class Battleships: Iowa, New Jersey, Missouri & Wisconsin.* Poole, Dorset, UK: Blandford, 1987.

Sumrall, Robert. *Iowa Class Battleships: Their Design, Weapons, and Equipment.* Annapolis, MD: U.S. Naval Institute Press, 1989.

Bazoft, Farzad
Birth Date: May 22, 1958
Death Date: March 15, 1990

Iranian-born British journalist who was accused of spying for Israel as he worked in Iraq as a reporter and was arrested and executed in 1990 in Iraq on the orders of the Saddam Hussein regime. Farzad Bazoft was born in Iran on May 22, 1958, and was educated in that country before relocating in 1985 to Great Britain, where he became a freelance journalist for the *Observer*. As a Middle Easterner, he was well suited to report on the region's news and occurrences, and he wrote a number of stories concerning Middle Eastern nations, including Iraq. In September 1989 Bazoft was invited to Iraq by the Hussein government, along with other international reporters, to report on that nation's rebuilding process following the destructive 1980–1988 Iran-Iraq War.

On September 19, 1989, just prior to Bazoft's departure for Iraq, a massive explosion ripped through an Iraqi military-industrial facility, located about 30 miles to the south of Baghdad. Several dozen Egyptian advisers and workers allegedly died in the blast, which the Hussein regime attempted to cover up. As it turns out, the explosion occurred in a clandestine rocket-manufacturing plant where the Iraqis were assembling medium-range ballistic missiles. Word of the incident soon leaked out, and Bazoft found out about it. He was determined to investigate the incident for himself when he reached Iraq.

After notifying the Iraqi government that he intended to do a story on the explosion and seemingly receiving approval for it, Bazoft traveled to the facility, took numerous photographs, interviewed workers, and left for Baghdad. While he was waiting to board a flight back to London, he was arrested, along with British nurse Daphne Parish, who had driven him to the missile plant. Both were charged with conducting espionage for the Israeli government and held in Iraq's infamous Abu Ghraib Prison.

Both vehemently denied any involvement in an Israeli espionage plot, and the arrest caused international consternation. The British government was especially vocal, demanding that the Iraqis release both Bazoft and Parish immediately.

On November 1, 1989, the Iraqis paraded Bazoft in front of reporters and television cameras as he admitted that he was an Israeli agent. In all likelihood, his captors had tortured him, or threatened torture, to exact the "confession." A trial was set for March 1990, before which Iraqi president Saddam Hussein had assured British prime minister Margaret Thatcher that Bazoft and Parish would receive a fair and impartial legal process.

No such trial occurred. The trial was held in secret, lasted less than one day, and found the two defendants guilty on March 10, 1990. That same day, Bazoft was sentenced to death; Parish was sentenced to 15 years behind bars. The summary convictions prompted more international condemnation, but on July 16 Parish was released following a plea of clemency by Zambian president Kenneth Kaunda. Other pleas to spare Bazoft poured into Iraq but were disregarded. Not permitted to file an appeal, Bazoft was executed by hanging in Baghdad on March 15, 1990. The execution prompted the Thatcher government to recall its ambassador to Iraq and cancel all ministerial visits. The affair brought with it international condemnation of Iraq and showcased the brutality of the Hussein regime. Less than five months later when Iraq invaded Kuwait, touching off the Persian Gulf War, much of the world recalled Bazoft's execution and took an even dimmer view of the Iraqi government.

In 2003 in the immediate aftermath of the invasion of Iraq, the *Observer* tracked down the Iraqi official who had arrested Bazoft, Colonel Kadhim Askar. He admitted that Bazoft was innocent and that he had known that when he arrested him. Askar also asserted that he was powerless to stop the proceedings against Bazoft because standing up to Saddam Hussein would have brought his own death and confirmed that Bazoft had been repeatedly and severely beaten during his interrogation.

PAUL G. PIERPAOLI JR.

See also

Media and Operation DESERT STORM; War Correspondents

References

Aburish, Said K. *Saddam Hussein: The Politics of Revenge.* New York: Bloomsbury, 2000.

Tripp, Charles. *A History of Iraq.* Cambridge: Cambridge University Press, 2007.

Beckwith, Charles Alvin
Birth Date: January 22, 1929
Death Date: June 13, 1994

U.S. Army officer and U.S. Army Special Forces leader. Charles Alvin Beckwith was born on January 22, 1929, in Atlanta, Georgia.

In high school he was an outstanding all-state football player, and he went on to play football at the University of Georgia. Beckwith also participated in the university's Reserve Officers' Training Corps (ROTC) program and upon graduation in 1952 was commissioned a second lieutenant.

In the mid-1950s Beckwith was assigned to the elite 82nd Airborne Division, where he was a support company commander of the 504th Parachute Infantry Regiment. In 1957 he joined the U.S. Army Special Forces (Green Berets), an unconventional warfare branch that became a high priority of the John F. Kennedy administration. Beckwith went to Southeast Asia in 1960 and served as military adviser in Laos and the Republic of Vietnam (ROV, South Vietnam). This was followed by a tour as an exchange officer in Great Britain with that nation's elite Special Air Service (SAS) in 1962–1963. Beckwith was impressed by both the antiterrorism focus of the SAS and the expertise and effectiveness of the unit.

Beckwith returned to Vietnam to command a Special Forces unit dubbed Project Delta, a 250-man force. In 1966 he was very seriously wounded in combat while flying in a helicopter. Medical personnel initially estimated the wound to his abdomen, caused by a large .50-caliber bullet, as fatal and determined that his condition was hopeless. Nevertheless, he recovered fully from the wound, a result credited to his iron will and superb physical condition.

After his service in Vietnam, Beckwith assumed command of the Florida component of the rigorous U.S. Army Ranger School. In this assignment he helped reform the school to address unconventional Vietnam War–style challenges and environments. The program previously had been based on the army's lessons from conventional military conflicts, in particular World War II.

Beckwith, promoted to colonel in 1976, played a principal role in the formation of Delta Force, formally known as the 1st Special Forces Operational Detachment–Delta (SFOD-D). This elite fighting unit, formally created in 1977, was in part inspired by and based generally on the British SAS antiterrorism unit. Beckwith had repeatedly sought to create an American version of the SAS, and his superiors finally gave in to his urgings in 1974. The unit focuses on countering terrorists, including hostage rescues, specialized reconnaissance, and other particularly demanding and irregular warfare missions.

Training for the unit is exceptionally rigorous, and Delta Force is highly selective in its membership. Members are termed "operators" and are divided into three squadrons. Delta Force is based at the U.S. Army base at Fort Bragg, North Carolina. Most details concerning the unit's full profile, characteristics, and operations are classified. Delta Force is one of two special elite units in the U.S. military focused on combating terrorism. The other is Dev Group, a U.S. Navy unit.

Beckwith became generally well known to the public as the commander of the unsuccessful Operation EAGLE CLAW in April 1980, a special interservice military task force that attempted to rescue

U.S. Army colonel Charles Beckwith, who led the unsuccessful attempt to rescue American hostages in Iran, attends the White House ceremony for the released hostages on January 27, 1981. (AP/Wide World Photos)

the American embassy hostages being held in Tehran, Iran. The embassy had been overrun and occupied on November 4, 1979, by Islamic student militants following the revolution that had overthrown Mohammad Reza Shah Pahlavi. American diplomatic personnel were taken captive at that time and held for 444 days.

The complex rescue effort involved a dangerous night flight across Iran by RH-53D helicopters and a rendezvous in a remote desert location in Iran with C-130 aircraft. Three of the eight helicopters on the mission experienced mechanical problems en route, leaving the mission one ship less than the minimum held necessary for success. The April 25, 1979, decision to end the hostage rescue mission was made by Beckwith himself at the rendezvous site. A collision in the dark between a helicopter and a Lockheed C-130 Hercules transport aircraft killed three marines and five airmen and seriously injured eight others.

The aftermath of the failed raid included some reorganization of the U.S. military, including the creation of the new Special Operations Command and the 160th Special Operations Aviation Regiment (the "Night Stalkers"). There were public accusations of fault by some members of the rescue operation, and Beckwith became engaged in this controversy. A panel of inquiry determined that lack of full coordination across service lines in

planning and training for the exercise along with simple bad luck lay behind the failure. Nevertheless, the affair ended Beckwith's military career, and he retired in 1981 at the rank of colonel. His book *Delta Force,* published in 1983, blamed the failure of the mission on the marines piloting the helicopters and on the helicopters themselves, which he argued were not designed for operation in adverse conditions such as those found in the Iranian desert.

Beckwith's principal legacy is his devotion to the development of unconventional warfare skills and techniques, primarily through the Special Forces and Delta Force. After leaving the service he formed his own security company, Security Assistance Services, in Austin, Texas, where he died suddenly on June 13, 1994.

ARTHUR I. CYR

See also

Delta Force; EAGLE CLAW, Operation; Iranian Revolution

References

Beckwith, Charlie A., and Donald Knox. *Delta Force: The Army's Elite Counterterrorist Unit.* New York: Avon, 2000.

Farber, David. *Taken Hostage: The Iran Hostage Crisis and America's First Encounter with Radical Islam.* Princeton, NJ: Princeton University Press, 2004.

Stanton, Shelby L. *Green Berets at War: U.S. Army Special Forces in Southeast Asia, 1956–1975.* Novato, CA: Presidio, 1985.

Bedouin

Nomadic and seminomadic tribal pastoral peoples generally located in the Arabian Peninsula, North Africa, the Levant, Jordan, Iraq, the Negev desert, and the Sinai peninsula. Bedouin live in present-day Jordan, Saudi Arabia, Kuwait, Yemen, Oman, the United Arab Emirates, Israel, Egypt, Sudan, Syria, Iraq, Lebanon, Algeria, Tunisia, Morocco, and Libya. Bedouin are of Arab origin and practice Islam. The Bedouin are organized by kinship clans into tribes. Individual households, or *bayts* ("tents"), may be comprised of two or more generations: a man and his wife or wives and his parents or siblings plus their children. A tribe (*qabila*) was traditionally presided over by a group of sheikhs, each a patrilinear position usually handed down from elder brother to younger brother and sometimes from father to son. On the other hand, not all sheikhs headed their families, and the term may simply be one of respect for an elder.

For centuries, the Bedouin have been nomads who engage in light agriculture and usually animal husbandry and live off the land. As they have been forcibly settled by governments since the 19th century, those retaining their traditional ways are mostly seminomadic. They move throughout their prescribed lands seasonally, following freshwater sources or moving to take advantage of various plant supplies. Many have herded sheep, goats, and camels. Traditionally, Bedouin move in groups containing several families and live in tents, which aid in their ability to pick up stakes and move when the situation warrants. However, ever since enforced settlement beginning in the first half of the 20th century or later, more and more Bedouin have given up their lifestyle to work and live in cities and towns throughout much of the region. Indeed, expanding population, urban sprawl, government policies, and the shrinking of suitable grazing lands have pushed many Bedouin into sedentary urban lifestyles. It is difficult to determine the precise number of Bedouin in the Middle East, although estimates vary from as few as 750,000 to well over 1 million. While Bedouin are noted for their generous hospitality, they are also fiercely territorial and do not take violations of their land rights lightly.

Bedouin culture is a complex and fascinating one and has been many centuries in the making. Bedouin tents are functional and well designed. One type could be divided in two by a cloth curtain (*ma'nad*), which separates the tent into a seating/living area for men and a place to entertain guests and another area (the *maharama*) in which women cook, socialize, and receive female guests. Bedouin have their own unique poetry, storytelling, music, and dance, much of which is reserved for the reception of guests, special occasions, and the like. Both Bedouin men and women wear traditional and prescribed clothing that can often indicate the status or age of the wearer. Clothing also varies depending upon the area or nation that the Bedouin inhabit. The Bedouin have their own tribal (or customary) law, and thus disputes may be solved

Bedouin camel camp, Sinai, Egypt. (Corel)

and punishment meted out according to those laws rather than resorting to civil courts in a state or locality.

Currently, Bedouin make up about 12 percent of the total Arab population in Israel. As part of the Arab minority, they face many of the same hurdles as their Arab brethren, including institutional and societal discrimination, reduced socioeconomic opportunities, substandard education, and poor health care. However, they have come under additional pressure as the Israeli government has tried to impose settlement policies on them and reduce or eliminate their traditional land areas. A fair number of Bedouin (5–10 percent of Bedouin males) serve in the Israeli military. Their intricate knowledge of the local terrain makes them valuable rangers and trackers.

Bedouin have faced similar pressures even in Arab states, however, as governments have purposely adopted land-use and settlement policies that are at odds with traditional Bedouin culture and lifestyle. Nevertheless, Bedouin have held fast to their tribal and cultural identities, even after they have settled and adopted modern urbanized lifestyles. For others, the restrictions and pressures on them have meant an abandonment of a truly nomadic way of life. For example, in the Egyptian Sinai peninsula, many Bedouin work on the coast in the tourist industry and in fishing, returning periodically to their families in the interior.

Bedouin have played important roles in the politics of various countries and have formed important portions of fighting forces such as in Sir John (Pasha) Glubb's Arab Legion, where they were known as Glubb's Girls for their long hair. Their transitional and rural status has also ensured their poor treatment on occasion such as in Israel, where they were not permitted to return after 1948 and had their grazing lands seized, or in Iraq, where various clans were decimated both in the western provinces and in the case of the Marsh Arabs.

PAUL G. PIERPAOLI JR.

See also

Egypt; Iraq, History of, Pre-1990; Iraq, History of, 1990–Present; Jordan; Kuwait; Lebanon; Libya; Oman, Role in Persian Gulf and Iraq Wars; Saudi Arabia; Sudan; Syria; United Arab Emirates; Yemen

References

Alotaibi, Muhammad. *Bedouin: The Nomads of the Desert.* Vero Beach, FL: Rourke, 1989.

Ingham, Bruce. *The Bedouin of Northern Arabia.* London: Kegan Paul International, 1986.

Losleben, Elizabeth. *The Bedouin of the Middle East.* Minneapolis, MN: Lerner, 2002.

Nevins, Edward, and Theon Wright. *World without Time: The Bedouin.* New York: John Day, 1969.

Begin, Menachem
Birth Date: August 16, 1913
Death Date: March 9, 1992

Prime minister of Israel (1977–1983). Menachem Wolfovitch Begin was born to an Ashkenazi Jewish family in Brest-Litovsk (Brisk), Russia (now Belarus), on August 16, 1913. He fled with his family to Vilnius, Poland, to escape the battling German and Russian armies in World War I. Begin's father was an ardent Zionist, and Begin was a member of the Hashomer Hatzair scout movement until age 13 and joined Vladimir Jabotinsky's Betar youth movement at age 16. Betar was a subset of the Zionist Revisionist movement committed to the creation of a Jewish state on both sides of the Jordan River. Begin took up the leadership of the Organization Department of Betar for Poland in 1932.

Begin graduated from the University of Warsaw with a law degree in 1935 and assumed the leadership of Betar Czechoslovakia in 1936. He returned to Warsaw in 1937 and was imprisoned for a short time because of his Zionist activities. He became head of Betar in Poland in 1938. Under his overall leadership, some 100,000 members engaged in self-defense, weapons, agricultural, and communications training. Members of Betar also transported to Palestine immigrants declared illegal by the British government. Begin advocated the establishment of a Jewish national homeland in Palestine by conquest and pushed this position at the 1938 Betar convention.

In 1939 Begin fled Warsaw when the Germans invaded Poland. He managed to cross into eastern Poland, which the Soviets invaded two weeks later, and thus avoided the roundup of Jews by

Menachem Begin was a militant Zionist guerrilla in Palestine who ultimately became the prime minister of Israel and a peacemaker. He is remembered for his part in the Camp David Peace Accords (1978), which brought peace between Egypt and Israel. (Sa'ar Ya'acov/Israeli Government Press Office)

the Nazis. Both his parents and a brother died in Nazi concentration camps during the war. In 1940 he was arrested by the Soviets and sent to a concentration camp in Siberia. He was released following the agreement establishing a Polish army to fight the Germans that followed the German invasion of the Soviet Union in June 1941.

Begin duly enlisted in the Free Polish Army in exile and was sent for training in 1942 to the British Mandate for Palestine. He left the army there in 1943 and joined the Jewish national movement in Palestine. He openly criticized the Jewish Agency for Palestine and worldwide Zionism as too timid in their approach to a Jewish state. In 1942 he had joined Irgun Tsvai Leumi (National Military Organization) and commanded the movement from 1943 to 1948. Under Begin's leadership, Irgun declared war on the British and resumed attacks on Palestinian Arab villages and British interests. The declaration came in February 1944.

The British had already classified Irgun as a terrorist organization. The Jewish Agency for Palestine, Haganah, and Histadrut had all declared its operations as terrorist acts. Nevertheless, Irgun's operations were so successful under Begin that the British launched an extensive manhunt for him. He avoided capture by disguising himself as an Orthodox rabbi. Meanwhile, he directed the Irgun bombing of the British military, police, and civil headquarters at Jerusalem's King David Hotel on July, 22, 1946, that killed 91 people. Begin and Irgun claimed to have issued three warnings in an attempt to limit casualties.

In anticipation of and following the partitioning of Palestine in 1947, Irgun and Haganah increasingly coordinated. Israel declared its independence on May 15, 1948, and announced the absorption of Haganah into its national military, the Israel Defense Forces (IDF), effective May 18, 1948. All other armed forces were banned. Irgun signed an agreement to be absorbed by the IDF on June 1, 1948, which formally occurred in September 1948. Begin also played a key role in the *Altalena* Incident of June 23, 1948.

After Israel's independence, Begin led Israel's political opposition from 1948 to 1977, reforming what remained of Irgun into the rightist Herut (Freedom) Party, with himself as its head. In 1965 Herut merged with the Liberal Party, creating the Gahal Party that formed the understructure of the future Likud (Unity) Party. Just prior to the June 1967 Six-Day War, Begin joined the National Unity government's cabinet as a minister without portfolio. The government was dissolved on August 1, 1970.

The Likud Party's May 17, 1977, victory in the national elections for the ninth Knesset allowed Begin, the chairman of Likud since 1970, to form the new government. On June 21 he became Israel's sixth (and first non-Labor) prime minister. Domestically, Begin moved to turn the Israeli economy away from the centralized, highly planned enterprise that characterized it under Labor. The prime minister also actively promoted immigration to Israel, especially from Ethiopia and the Soviet Union. Finally, he sought infrastructure improvements, advances in education, and the renewal of Israel's poorest neighborhoods.

Prime Ministers of Israel, 1945–Present

Name	Political Party	Term
David Ben-Gurion	Mapai	1948–1954
Moshe Sharett	Mapai	1954–1955
David Ben-Gurion	Mapai	1955–1963
Levi Eshkol	Mapai/Labour	1963–1969
Yigal Allon (interim)	Labour	1969
Golda Meir	Labour	1969–1974
Yitzhak Rabin	Labour	1974–1977
Menachem Begin	Likud	1977–1983
Yitzhak Shamir	Likud	1983–1984
Shimon Peres	Labour	1984–1986
Yitzhak Shamir	Likud	1986–1992
Yitzhak Rabin	Labour	1992–1995
Shimon Peres	Labour	1995–1996
Benjamin Netanyahu	Likud	1996–1999
Ehud Barak	Labour	1999–2001
Ariel Sharon	Likud/Kadima	2001–2006
Ehud Olmert	Kadima	2006–2009
Benjamin Netanyahu	Likud	2009–present

It was in the realm of foreign policy, however, that Begin most asserted himself. One of his first acts as prime minister was to challenge King Hussein of Jordan, President Hafiz al-Asad of Syria, and President Anwar Sadat of Egypt to meet with him to discuss peace. Sadat, but not the others, accepted the challenge and arrived in Israel on November 19, 1977. Following intermittent negotiations, Begin and Sadat met with U.S. president Jimmy Carter at Camp David, Maryland, and signed the Camp David Accords after nearly two weeks of negotiations (September 5–17, 1978).

The accords included two framework agreements that established guidelines for both the Israel-Egypt Peace Treaty and a potentially wider Middle East peace agreement. The bilateral treaty was signed in Washington, D.C., on March 26, 1979. Begin attended and participated in Sadat's funeral in Cairo after the Egyptian leader was assassinated by Muslim fundamentalists in October 1981.

Despite Begin's willingness to seek peace with Egypt, the other Arab states, including Syria and Jordan, remained hostile toward Israel. And Begin was uncompromising on the place of the West Bank and the Gaza Strip, seized by Israel during the Six-Day War, in the modern State of Israel. He considered them part of the historical lands given to Israel by God. Indeed, Begin promoted and oversaw the expansion of Jewish settlements in the West Bank and the Gaza Strip that continue to be an impediment to Palestinian-Israeli peace accords to the present day.

From May 28, 1980, to August 6, 1981, Begin served concurrently as Israel's prime minister and defense minister. When Israeli intelligence notified Begin that Iraq was close to producing weapons-grade nuclear fuel at its Osiraq/Tammuz nuclear reactor, he ordered the Israeli Air Force's successful destruction of the facility on June 7, 1981. Shortly thereafter he enunciated the Begin Doctrine, which held that Israel would act preemptively to counter any perceived threat from weapons of mass destruction (WMDs).

On June 30, 1981, Begin was reelected prime minister. It was soon apparent to the second Begin government that the Lebanese government was unable or unwilling to stop terrorist attacks launched from its soil. As such, in June 1982 Begin authorized Operation PEACE FOR GALILEE, the Israeli invasion of southern Lebanon. The operation was designed to drive Palestine Liberation Organization (PLO) Katyusha rockets out of the range of Israel's northern border and to destroy the terrorist infrastructure that had developed in southern Lebanon.

Although the PLO was driven from Lebanon, the Israeli presence in the country lasted for 18 years. Amplified in its impact through Lebanese proxy forces, it polarized Lebanese politics. The Israeli operation resulted in such a high number of Palestinian civilian deaths that worldwide public opinion turned against Israel. The failure of Operation PEACE FOR GALILEE to progress in the intended time frame and the large number of causalities on both sides weighed heavily on Begin. Tired and still mourning the recent death of his wife, he resigned as prime minister on September 15, 1983. Over the next 9 years he lived quietly, if not reclusively, in Tel Aviv. Begin died of heart failure on March 9, 1992, in Tel Aviv.

RICHARD EDWARDS

See also

Arab-Israeli Conflict, Overview; Camp David Accords; Carter, James Earl, Jr.; Lebanon; Sadat, Muhammad Anwar

References

Begin, Menachem. *The Revolt.* Los Angeles: Nash, 1972.

Perlmutter, Amos. *The Life and Times of Menachem Begin.* Garden City, NY: Doubleday, 1987.

Sofer, Sasson. *Begin: An Anatomy of Leadership.* New York: Blackwell, 1988.

Beharry, Johnson
Birth Date: July 26, 1979

British Army soldier awarded the Victoria Cross for actions during combat in Iraq. Born in Grenada on July 26, 1979, Johnson Beharry immigrated to the United Kingdom in 1999. In 2001 he joined the Princess of Wales's Royal Regiment. After training in Catterick, he served in both Kosovo and in Northern Ireland.

Assigned with his regiment to Iraq, on the night of May 1, 2004, Private Beharry was driving the lead Warrior Tracked Armoured Vehicle in a convoy of six sent to the aid of a foot patrol that had been ambushed in the town of Amarah. Beharry's vehicle was hit by a number of rocket-propelled grenades, wounding the platoon leader and a number of soldiers in the Warrior. The vehicle sustained serious damage and was soon on fire. The explosions had also destroyed the driver's periscope, and Beharry was forced to open the hatch to see, all the time exposing his head and shoulders to enemy small-arms fire. To escape the ambush he drove directly through it, deciding to crash through a barrier in the street while not knowing if there were improvised explosive devices there that

might destroy his vehicle. The five other Warriors followed after him to safety. During the escape, a bullet penetrated Beharry's helmet and lodged in its inner surface. Locating another Warrior, Beharry then carried the wounded from his still-burning vehicle to it, all the time while under enemy fire.

On duty on June 11, 2004, Beharry was again driving the lead Warrior in his platoon through Amarah when his vehicle was struck by a rocket-propelled grenade. Beharry suffered serious head injuries from shrapnel. Other rocket-propelled grenades also hit the vehicle, wounding the platoon leader and others in it. Despite his serious wounds, Beharry was able to retain control of the Warrior and drive it from the ambush area before losing consciousness. His wounds required brain surgery, and he was still recovering when he was awarded Britain's highest military decoration, the Victoria Cross, in March 2005.

Beharry was the first to win the Victoria Cross since the 1982 Falklands War and is the first living recipient since two Australians received it for actions during the Vietnam War. Since Beharry's award of the medal, a second Victoria Cross was awarded by Australia on January 16, 2009, to Trooper Mark G. Donaldson of Australia's Special Air Service Regiment for combat action in Afghanistan on September 2, 2008.

Beharry had said that he hoped to be able to return to active duty, but although he remained on the army payroll, his wounds would not allow this. In September 2006 Beharry was promoted to lance corporal. In 2005 he had signed a contract for a book about his experiences worth a reported £1 million. Written with the collaboration of Nick Cook, *Barefoot Soldier* was published in 2006. Beharry has made television appearances, including one in which he appealed for better care for military personnel suffering from mental health problems.

SPENCER C. TUCKER

See also

Bush, George Walker

References

Hunter, Chris. *Eight Lives Down.* London: Corgi Books, 2008.

"Iraq VC Hero Nets £1m Deal in Publishers' Bidding War." *Sunday Times,* September 18, 2005.

Johnson, Beharry, and Nick Cook. *Barefoot Soldiers.* Boston: Little, Brown, 2006.

Benedict XVI, Pope
Birth Date: April 16, 1927

Roman Catholic theologian, author, prelate, and pope (2005–present). Born on April 16, 1927, in Marktl am Inn, Bavaria, Germany, Joseph Alois Ratzinger, the son of a police officer, as a young boy exhibited a keen interest in becoming a Catholic priest. He attended local schools and in 1941 was compelled to join the Hitler Youth, a Nazi Party organization. Neither Ratzinger nor his family were at all sympathetic to the Nazi cause, however, and the young

German Catholic cardinal Joseph Ratzinger became Pope Benedict XVI on April 19, 2005. Benedict succeeded Pope John Paul II as the new leader of the 1.1 billion–member Roman Catholic Church. (Shutterstock)

Ratzinger remained as detached as possible from the organization. When he reached age 16, he was drafted into the German Army and trained as an infantryman, although illness precluded him from serving in combat. In early 1945 he was briefly interned by U.S. occupation forces as a prisoner of war but was soon released in the summer of 1945. That November, he entered St. Michael Seminary in Traunstein, Germany, and he subsequently studied at the Ducal Georgianum at Ludwig-Maximilian University in Munich. He was ordained a priest on June 29, 1951.

Well read, fluent in several languages, and dedicated to the study of theology and questions of the Catholic faith, Ratzinger began writing soon after his ordination and became a fixture in academe, earning his doctorate for a well-regarded study of St. Augustine's church doctrine. By 1959 Ratzinger had become a professor at the University of Bonn and was writing prolifically on theological matters, Church doctrine, and Catholic dogma. Four years later he joined the faculty of the University of Münster and was by then a theologian of international repute. In 1966 he moved to the University of Tübingen, where he held a chair in dogmatic theology. During this time, his writings portray a man who believed in Church reforms (he believed that the Roman Catholic Church had become too hierarchical). At the same time, the growing trends toward theological extremism and the insertion

of Marxist ideology into theology alarmed him greatly. By the late 1960s Ratzinger's writings and theological orientation had begun to take a more conservative tack, partly as a response to the social and academic upheavals of the decade. In 1969 he left Tübingen and took a faculty position at the University of Regensburg, where he founded an important theological journal titled *Communio*. During the Vatican II Conference (Second Vatican Council, 1962–1965), Ratzinger attended many meetings as an expert on theological and dogmatic matters.

In 1977 Pope Paul VI appointed Ratzinger archbishop of Munich and Freising. That same year Ratzinger became a cardinal. He continued his research and writing but became a central figure in the Vatican. In 1981 Pope John Paul II appointed him prefect of the Congregation of the Doctrine of the Faith and president of the Pontifical Biblical Commission and the International Theological Commission. This gave Ratzinger considerable influence within the Church, and his conservative theological positions and teachings were in perfect sync with those of Pope John Paul II, who was liberal on matters of social justice but conservative when it came to matters of faith and Church teaching.

In 1998 Ratzinger was elected vice dean of the College of Cardinals, and in 2002 he was elected dean. In the Roman Curia, he held numerous positions of leadership and authority. His writings are prolific and erudite, and he never disappointed those who sought theological positions that were at once conservative in nature and flawlessly argued. Prior to John Paul II's death in 2005, Ratzinger was without doubt the most powerful and influential man in the whole of the Roman Curia.

Following the death of John Paul II, Cardinal Ratzinger was elevated to the papacy on April 19, 2005. Although some pundits had viewed Ratzinger as too old (he was then 78), he was reported to be in good health, and his doctrinaire approach to Church teachings and his long and close relationship to his predecessor made him one of the most logical candidates for the papacy.

Since becoming pope and taking the name Benedict XVI, he has surprised few with his policies and stances on key issues. Like John Paul II, Benedict has decried war and called for a society that is less consumer- and pop-culture–driven and more attuned to God's words and good works toward others. He has also reformed and reduced in size the Roman Curia and has more recently signaled his agreement to convene a council to discuss the possible use of condoms to fight AIDS and HIV, although he steadfastly opposes their use as contraceptives alone, which would run counter to Church teaching. While he has embarked on a number of foreign visits, his travel schedule pales in comparison to his peripatetic predecessor. Benedict nevertheless continues John Paul's dedication to ecumenism but has angered some in both the Jewish and Muslim communities.

Benedict has made two official visits to Jewish synagogues and is only the second pope to do so (John Paul II was the first). But his meeting with a controversial Polish priest who was on record as having made disparaging remarks about Judaism and the Holocaust provoked a sharp response from the Jewish community. In September 2006 Benedict generated a storm of controversy during a talk he gave in Germany. In it, he quoted a controversial passage from a European work quoting a 14th-century Byzantine emperor who sharply rebuked the Prophet Muhammad by suggesting that his message was one of violence and "evil." The pope further amplified this statement with a critique of the Muslim practice of jihad throughout history and of aspects of the Qur'an, suggesting that both the Prophet and Muslim beliefs are inherently misguided and require reform. Benedict later apologized, but the damage had been done.

Benedict has also cautioned moderation in fighting terrorism, pointing out that it is immoral and counterproductive to kill innocent people in an effort to stamp out evil. Some have seen this as a subtle rebuke of aggressive foreign policy by the United States in recent years.

In May 2009 the pope visited the Middle East, where he celebrated Mass in Jordan and expressed his "deep respect" for Islam. He also called for more interfaith dialogue between Christians and Muslims in an attempt to mend fences following remarks he made in 2006 that were interpreted by many Muslims as insulting and inflammatory. Amid increased tensions between the Vatican and Tel Aviv, Pope Benedict next visited Israel and the Palestinian territories, where he acknowledged the horrors of the Holocaust and expressed deep regret for anti-Semitism but also called for a two-state solution to the ongoing Palestinian-Israeli conflict. Benedict's public endorsement of the two-state solution in his very first public appearance in Israel was seen as a clear prod to Prime Minister Benjamin Netanyahu, who has steadfastly refused to embrace the two-state compromise since he took office for the second time in March 2009.

Paul G. Pierpaoli Jr.

See also

John Paul II, Pope; Netanyahu, Benjamin

References

Sewald, Peter, ed. *Pope Benedict XVI: Servant of the Truth.* Ft. Collins, CO: Ignatius, 2006.

Weigel, George. *God's Choice: Pope Benedict XVI and the Future of the Catholic Church.* New York: HarperCollins, 2005.

Berger, Samuel Richard
Birth Date: October 28, 1945

Attorney, foreign policy expert, and national security adviser to President William J. Clinton from 1997 to 2001. Samuel (Sandy) Richard Berger was born on October 28, 1945, in Sharon, Connecticut. He grew up in nearby Millerton, New York, where his parents operated a store. Graduating with an undergraduate degree from Cornell University in 1967, he went on to earn a law degree at Harvard University in 1971. Interested in politics at a young age, Berger worked in Senator George McGovern's unsuccessful 1972 presidential campaign and met a young Bill Clinton; the two men became lifelong friends and political allies.

From 1973 to 1980, Berger held a series of political and government positions, including deputy director of policy planning for the U.S. State Department under Secretary of State Cyrus Vance from 1977 to 1980. After that, Berger became a partner at a leading Washington, D.C., law firm, where he greatly expanded its international law practice. He was heavily involved in trade issues with the Chinese government.

In 1992 Berger served as the senior foreign policy adviser to Governor Bill Clinton's presidential campaign. When Clinton won the November 1992 election, Berger served as the assistant director of transition for national security. From 1993 to 1997 Berger was Clinton's deputy national security adviser, working under National Security Advisor Anthony Lake. In 1997 Berger replaced Lake as national security adviser, a post he held until 2001.

Berger was a key player in numerous international endeavors and crises during his years in the West Wing, including the response to the 1996 Khobar Towers bombing in Saudi Arabia, the bombing of Iraq in December 1998 (Operation DESERT FOX), the response to the U.S. embassy bombings in Tanzania and Kenya in 1998, and the 1999 North Atlantic Treaty Organization (NATO) bombing campaign against the Federal Republic of Yugoslavia.

Berger also played a major role in the promulgation of trade and foreign policy with the People's Republic of China (PRC).

In late 1998 Berger gave a major speech in which he stated that the United States would eventually force Iraqi leader Saddam Hussein from power, using force if necessary. While Berger's speech put Hussein and other would-be aggressors on notice that their aggressive actions would not long be tolerated, it also compelled the U.S. military to begin drawing up plans for a potential invasion of Iraq. The result was OPLAN DESERT CROSSING, a thoughtful and detailed plan that laid out the potential pitfalls and opportunities involved with a ground invasion of Iraq and the removal of Hussein from power. Completed in the summer of 1999, DESERT CROSSING was not consulted when the George W. Bush administration drew up plans for the 2003 invasion of Iraq.

Berger's tenure was not without controversy. When it came to light that he had failed to immediately notify President Clinton of the PRC's acquisition of various designs for U.S. nuclear weapons via espionage (he waited 15 months to do so), numerous Republicans called for his resignation. In 2005 Berger was charged with having illegally removed classified information from the National Archives. He pled guilty to the charges and received a fine and two years' probation, and he lost his security clearance for three years and relinquished his law license.

Berger served as a foreign policy adviser to Democratic senator Hillary Clinton's failed 2008 presidential campaign and is currently involved with an international investment firm and provides advice to various international business organizations.

PAUL G. PIERPAOLI JR.

See also

Clinton, Hillary Rodham; Clinton, William Jefferson; Dar es Salaam, Bombing of U.S. Embassy; DESERT CROSSING, OPLAN; DESERT FOX, Operation; Nairobi, Kenya, Bombing of U.S. Embassy

References

Byman, Daniel, and Matthew C. Waxman. *Confronting Iraq: U.S. Policy and the Use of Force since the Gulf War.* Santa Monica, CA: RAND Corporation, 2002.

Clinton, Bill. *My Life.* New York: Knopf, 2004.

Bhutto, Benazir

Birth Date: June 21, 1953
Death Date: December 27, 2007

Pakistani politician and prime minister (1988–1990, 1993–1996). Benazir Bhutto, born in Karachi on June 21, 1953, was just 35 years old when she entered office in 1988 as the first female prime minister of a predominantly Muslim nation. Bhutto graduated from Harvard University's Radcliffe College in 1973 and then studied at Oxford University, where she pursued courses in economics, philosophy, and politics. In 1971 her father, Zulfikar Ali Bhutto, the leader of the Pakistan People's Party, was elected prime minister

of Pakistan. In 1977 he was overthrown by General Muhammad Zia-ul-Haq's military coup d'état. Zulfikar Bhutto was later executed following a two-year imprisonment.

Bhutto was herself subjected to repeated arrests between 1977 and 1986, a period of time interspersed with periods of exile in Great Britain. While abroad, she became a vocal critic of Pakistan's military regime, but in the wake of Zia's revocation of martial law in December 1985, she returned from exile the following year. Bhutto soon emerged as the leader of the Pakistan People's Party, cochairing the organization with Nusrat Bhutto, her mother. The party would win in the November 1988 democratic elections that followed Zia's death in a mysterious plane crash that previous August. Bhutto's first term of office as prime minister ran from 1988 to 1990; her second term lasted from 1993 to 1996.

Both of Bhutto's administrations were plagued by allegations of corruption, particularly on the part of her husband, Asif Zardari. Indeed, in 1990 President Ghulam Ishaq Khan dissolved Bhutto's government because of alleged corruption, and President Farooq Leghari dissolved her government in 1996 on similar grounds. She was also charged with having not ruled effectively and not being able to maintain law and order. In 1999 Zardari and Bhutto were convicted of corruption in a Lahore High Court (Pakistani superior court) case for inappropriate financial dealings with Swiss companies. As a result, they were fined $8 million and sentenced to five years in prison. Although the verdict was overturned in 2001 on the grounds of judicial bias, Swiss courts found the couple guilty of accepting bribes and laundering money in 2003. It was only on the condition that amnesty from corruption charges would be granted that Bhutto agreed to her final return to Pakistan in 2007.

Although Bhutto introduced social reform policies aimed at improving Pakistan's educational and health care systems, her legacy is tainted not only by accusations of corruption but also by the violence that pervaded her time in office. President Leghari, for instance, accused Bhutto of sanctioning extrajudicial executions as a means of quelling the violence that had gripped Karachi, Pakistan's largest city. Her government has also been implicated in the establishment of the Taliban in Afghanistan by the mid-1990s. While Bhutto would later come to denounce the ruthlessness of the Taliban regime, at the end of her second administration she initially welcomed its installment, believing that it would stabilize Afghanistan and the border areas. Despite her shortcomings, it should be noted that Bhutto had to contend with a powerful military establishment and a presidency that often overshadowed her. The former possessed the physical might necessary to impose its will, and the latter held the legal authority to dismiss administrations.

As with her homecoming in 1986, Bhutto returned in 2007 to a Pakistan governed by a military dictatorship; in this case, it was headed by General Pervez Musharraf, who at the time was both head of the military and president. Bhutto was again placed under house arrest, but she was nearly assassinated a day after her return on October 19 when terrorists launched a bombing attack against

Pakistani opposition leader Benazir Bhutto flashes victory signs to welcoming crowds shortly after her return from exile on April 10, 1986. (Reuters/Corbis)

her. As she prepared to launch another political bid, she was assassinated during a shooting and bombing in the city of Rawalpindi on December 27, 2007. Bhutto regarded the October 19 assassination attempt, which resulted in the slaying of 179 people, as the work of Al Qaeda, the Taliban, and members of Musharraf's government. Indeed, the latter's limited efforts to investigate the incident only served to confirm her suspicions of governmental complicity, which she wrote about in her book *Reconciliation: Islam, Democracy, and the West,* published posthumously in 2008.

Immediately following Bhutto's assassination, the Pakistani government named Baitullah Mahsud, a Taliban leader, as the key conspirator in her murder but has not made any significant attempts to capture him. As with the October 19 attack, suspicion has arisen concerning the role played by Musharraf's government in the assassination, and its handling of the affair has not sufficiently removed such sentiments. While Musharraf did invite Scotland Yard to assist in the investigation, he gave the organization a very limited mandate. Scotland Yard did confirm, however, the government's position that Bhutto died after hitting her head on the open roof of her car during the bomb blast and was not felled by gunfire. Despite the election of a new government with Bhutto's former party at its head, little new information on the assassination has emerged.

JASON R. TATLOCK

See also

Afghanistan; Al Qaeda; Musharraf, Pervez; Pakistan; Taliban

References

Baldwin, Louis. *Women of Strength: Biographies of 106 Who Have Excelled in Traditionally Male Fields, A.D. 61 to the Present.* Jefferson, NC: McFarland, 2006.

Bhutto, Benazir. *Reconciliation: Islam, Democracy, and the West.* New York: HarperCollins, 2008.

Bray, John. "Pakistan at 50: A State in Decline?" *International Affairs* 73(2) (1997): 315–331.

Gall, Carlotta. "Musharraf-Bhutto Accord Sets Stage for Pakistan Vote." *New York Times,* October 5, 2007, A15.

Hoogensen, Gunhild, and Bruce O. Solheim. *Women in Power: World Leaders since 1960.* Westport, CT: Praeger, 2006.

King, Laura. "Little Done in Bhutto Investigation. *Los Angeles Times,* July 4, 2008, A3.

Ziring, Lawrence. "Pakistan in 1990: The Fall of Benazir Bhutto. *Asian Survey* 31(2) (1991): 113–124.

Bible

The Bible is a compilation of ancient documents now accepted as the sacred canon for, among others, Christianity and Judaism. It has also served as the seed text for several other religions. The

Bible (from the Latin *biblia sacra,* or "holy books") is commonly divided into two sections, the 33 canonical works of the Hebrew Bible (Tanakh), or the Old Testamant, and the 27 books of the New Testament.

The Tanakh, or what Christians refer to as the Old Testament, is, to a Jew, the primary canonical scripture containing three main components. The Torah ("teaching" or "law") is the most important document of Judaism and is comprised of five books: Genesis, Exodus, Leviticus, Numbers, and Deuteronomy. These are often referred to as the Pentateuch (Greek for "five containers"). The Nevi'im ("Prophets") encompasses 17 books, which tell of the rise of the Jewish monarchy and the empowerment of the children of Israel. The Ketuvim ("writings") are made up of 11 books containing material ranging from the poetry of the Psalms to "The Five Scrolls," which include the prophecies of the book of Daniel.

The term "New Testament" was likely coined by Tertullian, an early Christian writer and polemicist, from the Latin phrase "Novum Testamentum" and implies "the new covenant." This refers to the belief that in the Tanakh, the first covenant was made between God and man through Moses. Jesus Christ established a new covenant, which was documented in a new set of scriptures that became the New Testament.

The New Testament is a collection of works by Christ's apostles. Despite their continuing discovery and use, it was not until the Council of Trent (1545–1563) that the various books, used by far-flung churches, began to be formalized into the canonical 27 books currently recognized as the New Testament. The King James Version of the Bible recognizes five divisions of New Testament works.

The first section is made up of the Gospels (Good News), and each of the four gospels (Matthew, Mark, Luke, and John) is comprised of one of Christ's apostles telling the life story and detailing the ministry of Christ. Next is the Acts of the Apostles where the narrative continues, detailing how each Apostle continued to spread Christ's ministry. The Pauline Epistles are 14 epistolary writings generally attributed to St. Paul. These letters provide instruction in moral guidance, church doctrine, and the nature of the church itself. The General Epistles, seven epistolary books written by apostles other than Paul, targeted a more universal audience of churches.

Revelation (also known as the Apocalypse of John) refers to its author, as John "of the Island which is called Patmos" (1:1, 9), whom early theologians believed was the Apostle John. Revelation's importance lies in the fact that the text has been interpreted by most Christians as prophesying a terrifying apocalyptic scenario known to them as the end-of-days or Armageddon.

The Bible remains relevant to the ongoing Arab-Israeli conflicts and the confrontations between fundamentalist Islam and the West for many reasons. One is ethnic monotheism, which holds that there is only one God who belongs only to His chosen people (Judaism). This concept creates a cultural dichotomy in that the world is automatically divided into the One God's chosen people in the Promised Land, leaving those on the outside to be either converted, saved, or destroyed.

The Bible also sowed the seeds for its own nemesis. The sacred text of Islam, the Qur'an, claims that Ishmael was the father of all Muslims. According to the Prophet Muhammad and based on Old Testament prophecy (Genesis 21:12), Muhammad draws a convincing argument that the children of Ishmael, the Arabs, are truly God's chosen people. Although Muslims view the Bible as a true narrative of the unfolding of God's revelation to His people, they also believe that parts of it became corrupted as it was handed down throughout the ages, especially the Old Testament. The Qur'an specifically refers to the Gospel in the New Testament numerous times, and Muslims acknowledge the existence of Jesus Christ but not as a divine entity or the son of God. Instead, they view him as a great prophet and God's final revelation to his people.

B. KEITH MURPHY

See also
Muhammad, Prophet of Islam; Qur'an

References
Asimov, Isaac. *Asimov's Guide to the Bible.* 2 vols. New York: Avenel Books, 1981.
Lamsa, George M. *Holy Bible: From the Ancient Eastern Text.* San Francisco: Harper and Row, 1957.
Nicholson, Adam. *God's Secretaries: The Making of the King James Bible.* New York: Perennial, 2004.
Panati, Charles. *Sacred Origins of Profound Things: The Stories behind the Rites and Rituals of the World's Religions.* New York: Arkana (Penguin), 1996.

Biden, Joseph Robinette, Jr.
Birth Date: November 20, 1941

Attorney, Democratic Party politician, U.S. senator representing Delaware (1973–2009), chairman of the powerful Senate Foreign Relations Committee (2001–2003, 2007–2009), and vice president of the United States (2009–present). Born in Scranton, Pennsylvania, on November 20, 1941, Joseph Robinette Biden Jr. was the first of four children born to Irish Catholic parents; his parents moved the family to Delaware during his childhood. Biden graduated from the University of Delaware in 1965 and earned a law degree at Syracuse University in 1968 before returning to Delaware to practice law in 1969.

In 1970 Biden was elected to a seat on the New Castle County Council in Delaware, and in 1972 he ran against Republican incumbent J. Caleb Boggs for the U.S. Senate from Delaware and won. Because Delaware is one of the few states small enough to have more senators than congressmen, Biden enjoyed an unusually rapid rise in his political career.

In the Senate Biden served on numerous committees, including Judiciary and Foreign Relations, and in time he would chair

As a U.S. senator from Delaware, Joseph Biden was a leading proponent of tougher crime and drug legislation and a major figure in the formulation of U.S. foreign policy. On January 20, 2009, Biden was sworn in as vice president of the United States. (U.S. Senate)

both on different occasions. He has adhered to a relatively moderate Democratic voting record, supporting industrial endeavors in Delaware and Amtrak and introducing legislation on anti-drug and domestic violence programs as well as college aid programs. In 1984, 1988, and 2008 he ran unsuccessfully to secure the Democratic nomination for president. Because Biden was a moderate and was well versed in national security issues, many considered him a serious contender who could reorient the party at the national level. In 1984 he quickly dropped out of the race, losing to the more liberal former vice president Walter Mondale. In the 1988 campaign his reputation was seriously damaged by the Michael Dukakis campaign, which accused him of plagiarizing a speech by Neil Kinnock, a British Labour Party leader. The accusation had validity in that Biden had not always given attribution to Kinnock when using some phrases from his speeches, although on many occasions he did indeed cite Kinnock.

These failed White House bids in 1984 and 1988 nonetheless raised Biden's profile, and he continued to advance in seniority in the Senate. He chaired the Judiciary Committee from 1987 to 1995 and the Foreign Relations Committee from 2001 to 2003 and again from 2007 to 2009. During William J. Clinton's presidency, Biden, as the ranking Democrat on the Foreign Relations Committee, was a proponent of lifting arms embargoes in the Balkans and using force to stop ethnic cleansing in Bosnia and Kosovo. Later,

Clinton adopted these positions and authorized the use of force by the North Atlantic Treaty Organization (NATO) against Serbia. Biden also supported the presence of U.S. troops in the Balkans, which had been dispatched there by Clinton.

During the early George W. Bush presidency, Biden supported the administration's effort against Afghanistan in the aftermath of the terror attacks of September 11, 2001. On October 11, 2002, Biden, still the ranking Democrat and chairman of the Senate Foreign Relations Committee, voted, along with 28 other Democratic Party senators, to authorize the use of military force against Iraq to oust President Saddam Hussein. Although initially supportive of the war, Biden soon became critical of the administration's handling of it and repeatedly called for the use of more troops (including those from the international community) in the occupation. He also urged the president to explain and reveal the full price of the commitment in Iraq to the American people.

In May 2006 Biden along with Leslie Gelb, a former president of the Council on Foreign Relations, outlined a plan for the future of Iraq in a *New York Times* op-ed piece prior to the release of the Iraq Study Group's Report. It called for a federalized Iraq that would allow for greater self-determination for the three largest ethnic groups in Iraq—the Shiites, Sunnis, and Kurds—while retaining a single state. Essentially, the central government would leave the three regions alone to determine their own affairs, restricting itself to foreign affairs, security, and the distribution of oil revenues. Such a plan, in the view of Biden and Gelb, would provide for stability while allowing for an American exit that would secure U.S. influence in the country. Critics of this plan, including Senator John McCain, have argued that in the long term this is little more than a three-state solution that would essentially destroy the nation of Iraq and lead to greater Iranian influence in the region, a claim that Biden hotly contests.

In 2004 Biden was a strong supporter of his friend Senator John Kerry's failed presidential campaign and was frequently mentioned as a potential running mate before Kerry's ultimate selection of Senator John Edwards. In 2007–2008 Biden once again was a contender for the Democratic presidential nomination, although he dropped out of the race in January 2008 after doing poorly in the Iowa primary. Biden subsequently was selected as Barrack Obama's running mate as the vice presidential candidate, and after victory in the November 2008 presidential election Biden became the 47th U.S. vice president on January 20, 2009. Biden's family is a force in Delaware state politics, with his oldest son, Beau, serving as the current attorney general.

Michael K. Beauchamp

See also
Biden-Gelb Proposal; Iraq, History of, 1990–Present; Iraq Study Group; United States Congress and the Iraq War

References
Biden, Joseph Robinette, Jr. *Promises to Keep: On Life and Politics.* New York: Random House, 2007.
Danchev, Alex, and John Macmillan, eds. *The Iraq War and Democratic Politics.* New York: Routledge, 2003.

Woodward, Bob. *State of Denial: Bush at War, Part III*. New York: Simon and Schuster, 2006.

Biden-Gelb Proposal

Proposal put forth by Senator Joseph Biden (D-Del.) and Leslie H. Gelb, celebrated journalist, former Defense Department and State Department official, and president emeritus of the Council on Foreign Relations. The proposal recommended the partitioning of Iraq as a way to end the insurgency there. Biden and Gelb revealed their plan in a joint-authored op-ed letter to the *New York Times* on May 1, 2006. The proposal came amid growing frustration with the Iraqi insurgency, which continued to claim the lives of many Iraqis as well as U.S. soldiers. At the time, antiwar sentiment in the United States had been sharply increasing, and the George W. Bush administration appeared unwilling—or unable—to change course in Iraq or devise a plan for an acceptable American exit strategy. Because Biden was already planning to run for the Democratic nomination for president in 2008, the Biden-Gelb Proposal was seen by some as political posturing. However, Biden had arrived at the proposal after long and careful deliberation and with many years of foreign policy experience in the U.S. Senate.

Gelb and Biden asserted that Iraq is essentially unworkable as a single nation with three highly divergent groups—the Kurds, Shiites, and Sunnis—competing for power and sharing only mutual animosity toward each other. Biden and Gelb held that the situation was not unlike the racial and religious tensions that plagued Yugoslavia after World War I. Only under Saddam Hussein's oppressive dictatorship was the country viable as a single entity, but one in which democracy was stifled.

Biden and Gelb proposed the formation of a nominally singular Iraq broken into three loosely organized autonomous federations: one each for the Kurds, Shiites, and Sunni Muslims. The centralized federal government of Iraq would be responsible for national defense and border security issues as well as oil concessions and revenues. The Sunnis, who do not occupy territory with any significant oil operations, would be guaranteed 20 percent of Iraqi oil revenue; in turn, the Sunnis would attempt to revitalize former Baath Party members who had not participated in Hussein's excesses. There individuals would help with defense and oil-related issues.

The Biden-Gelb Proposal also sought to engage other Middle Eastern powers (especially those with oil wealth) in a multilateral effort to provide more economic aid to a confederated Iraq, promote employment, discourage the formation or expansion of militias, and provide for the protection of minority rights within each of the three Iraqi sectors. The proposal also called for a regional summit between U.S. leaders and Middle Eastern leaders to advance the provisions of the proposal. Finally, Biden and Gelb urged the Pentagon to initiate a plan to withdraw most U.S. troops from Iraq by mid-2008, to hand over control to the centralized Iraqi defense force, and to maintain a small contingent of troops in Iraq to reinforce the settlement and conduct antiterror operations.

There was fairly broad and bipartisan support for the Biden-Gelb Proposal, although the plan was hardly without its detractors. The Bush administration rejected most of the Biden-Gelb prescriptions, arguing that portioning Iraq would not necessarily lessen sectarian violence and might, in fact, invite outside powers to wield undue influence in the autonomous areas. The administration also rejected any timetable to an American military withdrawal from Iraq. Others argued that Turkey would hardly support an autonomous Kurdish region along its southern border. Still others asserted that it was hardly likely that Iraq's Middle East neighbors would be willing or able to enter into a multilateral endeavor to secure a confederated Iraq, much less help fund such an entity. Some claimed that equitably splitting Iraq's oil revenues among three regions—one of which did not have access to oil facilities itself—would be an impossible task.

In the end, none of the prescriptions put forth in the Biden-Gelb Proposal was ever adopted as official policy. But its boldness, commonsense approach, and timing helped to inform the dialogue on the Iraq War and may well have been a factor in the Republicans' repudiation at the polls in the November 2006 midterm elections, which resulted in their loss of both houses of Congress. What Biden and Gelb had admitted to publicly—that Iraq in its current form is fraught with difficulty and is hardly a candidate for Western-style democracy—was the same criticism leveled at Great Britain's creation of modern Iraq in 1920, that a nation with disparate ethnic and religious groups with no history of cooperation is almost predisposed to fail or come under the spell of dictatorship. The proposal was also a viable alternative to allowing Iraq to plunge into full-scale civil war, which it was dangerously close to doing in the spring of 2006. Since that time, however, the situation in Iraq has greatly stabilized.

Paul G. Pierpaoli Jr.

See also

Biden, Joseph Robinette, Jr.; Iraq, History of, Pre-1990; Iraq, History of, 1990–Present; Iraqi Insurgency; Kurds; Shia Islam; Sunni Islam

References

Galbraith, Peter W. *The End of Iraq: How American Incompetence Created a War without End*. New York: Simon and Schuster, 2007.

Keegan, John. *The Iraq War: The Military Offensive, from Victory in 21 Days to the Insurgent Aftermath*. New York: Vintage, 2005.

Billiére, Sir Peter Edgar de la
Birth Date: April 29, 1934

British Army general and commander of British forces during Operation DESERT STORM in 1991. Peter Edgar de la Billiére was born on April 29, 1934, in Plymouth, England, the son of a naval doctor. Billiére attended Harrow, the elite British boarding school, and attempted to join the navy but was rejected because of color blindness. He then joined the army as a private in the King's Shropshire Light Infantry. While he was still a private, evaluation boards selected Billiére for officer training, and he was then commissioned a second lieutenant in the Durham Light Infantry. Billiére's first tours of duty sent him to Korea and then to Egypt.

In 1956 Billiére enrolled in the highly demanding Special Air Service (SAS) selection course, which put him through rigorous training in jungle fighting and parachuting in Malaya. He then went with the SAS to Oman, where his unit assisted the sultan of Oman's forces against rebel groups. Billiére saw combat in Oman and was awarded the Military Cross in 1959 for actions there. He then joined the Durham Light Infantry but was soon allowed to return to the SAS. In 1962 he and other British officers were attached to the Federal Army in Aden, where Billiére performed the same sort of missions as in Oman, helping Yemen put down rebellious tribes.

In 1964 Billiére became a commander of a squadron in the 22nd SAS, which was then assigned to Borneo until 1966. He again acquitted himself well and was awarded a Bar to his Military Cross. He went on to attend the Staff College and to train with Special Forces at Strategic Command.

Billiére soon returned to the SAS, serving as its second-in-command, and in this position he was sent to the Middle East. In 1972 he became the commanding officer of the 22nd SAS and headed up a training team in Khartoum. In 1978 he was advanced to brigadier and appointed director of the SAS. As the director, he oversaw the Iranian embassy crisis of 1980, counterterrorism activities in Northern Ireland, and SAS operations in the 1982 Falklands War. After he completed his turn as director, he was decorated as Commander of the British Empire (CBE) and promoted to major general in 1984. He commanded British forces in the Falklands during 1984–1985. Following this tour, he became the general officer commanding Wales. He was advanced to lieutenant general in 1987 and given command of the South East District.

Given Billiére's previous service in the Middle East, he seemed a natural choice for commander of British forces during the Persian Gulf War, and he lobbied hard for the posting. Despite some concerns about his age, he was assigned to the position and in essence served as the second-in-command of coalition forces under U.S. general H. Norman Schwarzkopf. British forces, second only to the United States in size, numbered some 43,000 troops, including the 1st Armoured Division, Royal Air Force squadrons, and Royal Navy frigates and destroyers in the Persian Gulf as well as an aircraft carrier stationed in the Mediterranean. Given Billiére's service record, Schwarzkopf placed him in command of all coalition special forces. These units played an important role in the war, despite Schwarzkopf's initial skepticism as to their effectiveness.

Billiére was able to convince Schwarzkopf to allow special forces to play a larger role in the conflict. As a result, Special Forces teams infiltrated Iraq six days prior to the invasion to disrupt Iraqi defenses and to serve as a potential diversion. They located Scud missile launchers and communications and radar sites and then called in air strikes.

Following the war, Billiére was advanced to full general in 1991 and served as an adviser on the Middle East to the British government. He was named Knight Commander of the Order of the Bath (KCB) as well as Knight Commander of the British Empire (KBE). Billiére retired from the military in June 1992. He has written an account of the Persian Gulf War and continues to be active as an author. In addition, he is active in promoting international aid and charitable causes in Britain.

MICHAEL K. BEAUCHAMP

See also

DESERT STORM, Operation; Schwarzkopf, H. Norman, Jr.; United Kingdom, Air Force, Persian Gulf War; United Kingdom, Army, Persian Gulf War; United Kingdom, Marines, Persian Gulf War; United Kingdom, Navy, Persian Gulf War

References

Billiére, Peter Edgar de la. *Looking for Trouble: From the SAS to the Gulf.* London: HarperCollins, 1994.

———. *Storm Command: A Personal Account of the Gulf War.* London: HarperCollins, 1992.

Schwarzkopf, H. Norman, with Peter Petre. *It Doesn't Take a Hero: General H. Norman Schwarzkopf, the Autobiography.* New York: Bantam Books, 1993.

Bin Laden, Osama
Birth Date: March 10, 1957

Islamic extremist and, as head of the Al Qaeda terrorist organization, the world's most notorious terrorist leader. Bin Laden has been linked most notoriously to the September 11, 2001, terrorist attacks on the United States but also to numerous other acts of terrorism throughout the world. Born on March 10, 1957, in Riyadh, Saudi Arabia, Usamah bin Muhammad bin 'Awa bin Ladin is most usually known as Osama bin Laden. The name Osama means "young lion" in Arabic. According to Arabic convention he should be referred to as bin Ladin, but in the West he is almost universally referred to as bin Laden.

Bin Laden's father, Muhammad bin Awdah bin Laden, was a highly successful and immensely wealthy construction manager from Yemen who prospered thanks to a close relationship with the Saudi royal family. His construction projects included first major highways and then also the reconstruction of the Muslim holy cities of Medina and Mecca. The elder bin Laden, who was also strongly opposed to Israel, reportedly had 21 wives and fathered 54 children. Osama was the 17th son but the only son of his father's 10th wife, Hamida al-Attas. The elder bin Laden died in a plane crash in 1967. He left an estate reported at $11 billion. Osama bin Laden's personal inheritance has been variously estimated at between $40 million and $50 million.

The family moved a number of times but settled in Jeddah, Saudi Arabia. There bin Laden attended al-Thagr, the city's top school. He had some exposure to the West through vacations in

Saudi Arabian Osama bin Laden is undoubtedly the world's most notorious terrorist. He is widely held to be responsible for approving the September 11, 2001, terrorist attacks on the United States, as well as many other acts of terrorism in the Middle East and elsewhere in the world. (AP/Wide World Photos)

Sweden and a summer program in English at Oxford University. At age 17 bin Laden married a 14-year-old cousin of his mother. In 1977 he entered King Abdulaziz University (now King Abdul Aziz University) in Jeddah, where he majored in economics and business management. Bin Laden was an indifferent student, but this was at least in part because of time spent in the family construction business. He left school altogether in 1979, evidently planning to work in the family's Saudi Binladin Group that then employed 37,000 people and was valued at some $5 billion. This plan was apparently blocked by his older brothers.

As a boy bin Laden had received religious training in Sunni Islam, but around 1973 he began developing a fundamentalist religious bent. This was sufficiently strong to alarm other family members. Bin Laden also developed ties with the fundamentalist Muslim Brotherhood that same year. While in the university he was mentored in Islamic studies by Muhammad Qutb, brother of the martyred Sayyid Qutb, leader of the Muslim Brotherhood, and by Sheikh Abdullah Yussuf Azzam, a proponent of jihad (holy war). Both men had a profound influence on bin Laden.

Two events also exacted a profound influence. The first was the seizure of the Grand Mosque in Mecca by Islamists led by Juhaynan ibn-Muhammad-ibn Sayf al-Taibi and the subsequent martyrdom of the group. The second was the Soviet Union's invasion of Afghanistan in 1979. It is safe to say that the latter marked a major turning point in bin Laden's life.

In 1979 bin Laden traveled to Pakistan and there met with Afghan leaders Burhanuddin Rabbani and Abdul Rasool Sayyaf. Bin Laden then returned to Saudi Arabia to organize resistance to the Soviets in Afghanistan. There was considerable sentiment in Saudi Arabia for assisting the Afghans against the Soviets, and reportedly some 10,000 Saudis volunteered. Bin Laden returned to Pakistan with construction equipment, such as bulldozers, to aid the Afghan mujahideen (freedom fighters, holy warriors) fighting the Soviet troops and allied Afghan government forces. This equipment was used to build roads, tunnels, shelters, and hospitals.

Bin Laden's organizational skills were more important than the equipment, however. He worked actively with Sheikh Abdullah Yussuf Azzau to recruit and train jihadists to fight in Afghanistan, much of the funding for which came from bin Laden's personal fortune. He also tapped his contacts in Saudi Arabia for additional funds. Azzam and bin Laden established the Mujahideen Services Bureau. Between 1985 and 1989, approximately 150,000 soldiers entered Afghanistan through training camps established in neighboring Pakistan by the Mujahideen Services Bureau.

In 1986 bin Laden, now having relocated to Peshawar, Pakistan, joined a mujahideen field unit and took part in actual combat. Notably, this included the 1987 Battle of the Lion's Den near Jaji. Such activity sharply increased bin Laden's prestige among the mujahideen.

The mysterious assassination of bin Laden's mentor Azzam on November 14, 1989, opened the way for bin Laden to assume a greater role in extremist Islamic politics. While he agreed with Azzam about the need for jihad against the enemies of Islam, bin Laden carried this philosophy a step further in insisting that it should be extended to a holy war on behalf of Islam around the world.

In the autumn of 1989 Azzam and bin Laden had founded the Al Qaeda ("the base" in Arabic) organization. On its announcement, those present were required to sign a loyalty oath (bayat). With Azzam's death, bin Laden, at the age of 32, became the undisputed leader of Al Qaeda.

With the end of the Soviet-Afghanistan War, bin Laden returned to Saudi Arabia. He was now acclaimed as a hero both by the Saudi people and the government. Bin Laden soon approached Prince Turki al-Faisal, head of the kingdom's intelligence services, offering to lead a guerrilla effort to overthrow the Marxist government of South Yemen, but Turki rejected the suggestion. Bin Laden then settled in Jeddah and worked in the family construction business until Iraqi president Saddam Hussein sent his army into Kuwait in August 1990.

The Iraqi military takeover of Kuwait directly threatened Saudi Arabia, and bin Laden again approached the Saudi government, offering to recruit as many as 12,000 men to defend the kingdom.

The Saudi government again rebuffed him. Instead, it allowed U.S. and other Western troops to be stationed in Saudi Arabia with the plan to drive the Iraqis from Kuwait by force if necessary. Incensed both at the rejection of his services and the injection of hundreds of thousands of infidels into his homeland, bin Laden bitterly denounced the Saudi government. Indeed, he demanded that all foreign troops leave at once. His vocal opposition to Saudi government policy brought him a brief period of house arrest.

Bin Laden's opposition to Saudi government policies and the Persian Gulf War led him to leave the kingdom. He moved with his family first to Pakistan and then to Sudan, where he had earlier purchased property around Khartoum. He also moved his financial assets there and became involved in a series of business ventures including a road-building company, all of which added considerably to his personal fortune. From Sudan, bin Laden also mounted verbal attacks on the Saudi royal family and the kingdom's religious leadership, accusing them of being false Muslims. These attacks led the Saudi government to strip him of his citizenship in April 1994 and freeze his financial assets in the kingdom (his share of the family business was then estimated to be about $7 million). Bin Laden also roundly denounced Israel.

In Sudan, bin Laden also organized the terrorist activities of Al Qaeda, which were in place by 1989. Its goals were to incite all Muslims to join in a defensive jihad against the West and to help overthrow tyrannical secular Muslim secular governments. Bin Laden established an Al Qaeda training camp at Soba, north of Khartoum, and in 1992 he sent advisers and equipment to Somalia to aid the fight against the Western mission to restore order in that country. He also began terrorist activities directed against Americans in Saudi Arabia. On November 13, 1995, a car bomb in Riyadh killed 5 Americans and 1 Saudi and wounded 60 others. Other similar actions followed.

Mounting pressure by the Saudi and U.S. governments forced the Sudanese government to ask bin Laden to leave that country. In May 1996 bin Laden relocated to Afghanistan. He left Sudan with little money; the Sudanese government settled with him for only a small fraction of his reported, but no doubt overestimated, $300 million in assets.

Afghanistan was a natural location for bin Laden. The Islamic fundamentalist Taliban had come to power, and bin Laden had established a close relationship with its head, Mullah Mohammed Omar. Although there was some unease among the Taliban leadership about the possible consequences of hosting the now-acknowledged terrorist, their scruples were overcome by bin Laden's promises of financial assistance from his Arab contacts. In return, the Taliban permitted bin Laden to establish a network of training camps and perpetrate worldwide terrorist activities. The alliance was firmly established when bin Laden directed Al Qaeda to join the fight against the Northern Alliance forces of General Ahmed Shah Massoud that were seeking to unseat the Taliban.

Now firmly established in Afghanistan, bin Laden began planning a series of attacks against the perceived worldwide enemies of Islam. His principal target was the United States, and on August 23, 1996, he issued a call for jihad against the Americans for their presence in Saudi Arabia. In February 1998 he broadened this to a global jihad against all enemies of Islam. Al Qaeda was in fact largely a holding organization with several dozen terrorist groups affiliated with it. Bin Laden's role was to coordinate, approve, and assist their various activities. Thus, when Khalid Sheikh Mohammed presented a plan to hijack large commercial airliners and crash them into prominent buildings in the United States, bin Laden approved the plan but left its implementation up to Mohammed.

Bin Laden expected that these attacks in the United States, if they were successful, would trigger a vigorous American response but that this, in turn, would produce an outpouring of support for his cause from within the Arab world. The first assumption proved correct. After the September 11, 2001, attacks on the World Trade Center in New York City and the Pentagon in Washington, D.C., the United States demanded that the Taliban turn over bin Laden and take action against Al Qaeda. When the leaders of the Taliban refused, U.S. forces, assisted by those of other Western nations, aided the Northern Alliance and attacked Afghanistan, driving the Taliban from power. The second assumption, that a forceful U.S. response would bring a Muslim backlash, proved false.

Bin Laden had also not expected the Taliban to be easily overthrown. When that occurred, he withdrew into his stronghold in Tora Bora, a cave complex in the White Mountains of eastern Afghanistan, where he remained until December 2001. U.S. efforts to capture him and his followers were botched, and he escaped, presumably into northwestern Pakistan. There Islamic fundamentalism and support for the Taliban and Al Qaeda is strong. Indeed, Western efforts to capture him have made him something of a hero in the Muslim world, where a significant percentage of people profess admiration for him. There are indications that he was wounded in the arm in the U.S. bombing of Tora Bora in late 2001, and there has been other speculation about the status of his health. Despite a reward of $50 million for his capture—dead or alive—Osama bin Laden continues to thwart efforts to bring him to justice.

HARRY HUESTON AND SPENCER C. TUCKER

See also

Afghanistan; Al Qaeda; Global War on Terror; Jihad; Pakistan; Taliban; Terrorism; Tora Bora

References

Atkins, Stephen E. *The 9/11 Encyclopedia*. Westport, CT: Praeger Security International, 2008.

Bergen, Peter L. *Holy War, Inc.: Inside the Secret World of Osama bin Laden*. New York: Touchstone, 2002.

———. *The Osama bin Laden I Know: An Oral History of Al Qaeda's Leader*. New York: Free Press, 2006.

Esposito, John. *Unholy War: Terror in the Name of Islam*. New York: Oxford University Press USA, 2003.

Gunaratna, Rohan. *Inside Al Qaeda: Global Network of Terror*. New York: Berkley Publishing Group, 2003.

Randal, Jonathan. *Osama: The Making of a Terrorist*. New York: Knopf, 2004.

Biological Weapons and Warfare

Biological weapons are forms of natural organisms that are used as weapons or modified versions of germs or toxins to kill or harm people or animals. The first type of biological weapon includes diseases such as anthrax or smallpox, while the second category includes toxins or poisons such as ricin or aflatoxin. Along with nuclear and chemical arms, biological weapons are considered to be weapons of mass destruction (WMDs).

Israel's advanced nuclear program prompted several Arab states to initiate biological weapons programs as a means to counter the Israeli nuclear arsenal. The proliferation of WMDs, including biological weapons, is one of the most serious security issues in the Middle East.

By the early 1970s, several Arab states had established biological weapons programs as a means to balance Israel's nuclear arsenal as they concurrently sought to develop their own nuclear and chemical weapons programs. Biological weapons were attractive to many states because they were perceived as being less expensive and easier to manufacture. Biological agents could also be developed far more quickly than nuclear or chemical programs.

The Middle Eastern country with the oldest biological weapons program is Israel. During the Israeli War of Independence (1948–1949), there were charges that Israeli units infected Arab wells with malaria and typhoid. Following independence, a biological weapons unit was created. Israel's program was designed to develop both offensive and defensive capabilities, and its successful nuclear program overshadowed its chemical and biological efforts. In the 2000s, Israel's biological and chemical weapons programs were increasingly focused on counterproliferation in the region and efforts to prevent bioterrorism.

Egypt began a wide-scale biological program in the 1960s and recruited European scientists to advance the program. By 1972, Egypt had an offensive biological weapons capability, a fact later confirmed by President Anwar Sadat in public addresses. In 1972 Egypt signed the Biological Weapons Convention (which bans the use of these arms) but did not ratify the convention. Among the Arab states, Egypt went on to develop one of the most comprehensive biological weapons programs, including anthrax, cholera, plague, botulism, and possibly smallpox. These agents were weaponized in such a fashion that they could be delivered in missile warheads. Beginning in the late 1990s, Egypt began working with the United States to develop more effective biological weapons defenses, ranging from decontamination plants to national contingency planning to stockpiles of personal gas masks.

Following the Yom Kippur (Ramadan) War of October 1973, evidence emerged from captured documents and equipment that Syria had a highly developed WMD program that included biological weapons such as anthrax, botulinum, and ricin. Syria's program proceeded with aid and products from Chinese and European firms. In the 1990s, Western intelligence agencies identified the town of Cerin as the center of Syria's biological weapons program. Toward the end of the decade, Syria also launched an effort to acquire missiles capable of delivering biological warheads into Israeli territory. Syria also developed a robust chemical weapons program. Syria's military planners hoped that their biological and chemical arsenals would deter Israel from using its nuclear weapons in the event of a conflict. For Israel and the United States, Syria's biological weapons program is especially troublesome because of the country's sponsorship of anti-Israeli groups such as Hezbollah and the fear that these weapons might be shared with terrorists.

Libya attempted to develop a broad WMD program in the 1970s that included biological weapons. However, international sanctions prevented that nation from acquiring significant biological arms. Instead, its program remained mainly at the research level. In 2003 Libyan leader Muammar Qaddafi renounced WMDs and pledged that his country would dismantle its WMD programs as part of a larger strategy to improve relations with the United States and Europe.

In 1974 the Iraqi government officially launched a biological weapons program, and within a year the country established facilities for research and development of biological agents. Through the 1970s and 1980s Iraq obtained cultures and biological agents from Western governments and firms through both legitimate and illicit means. Among the biological weapons that Iraq obtained were anthrax, salmonella, and botulinum. By 1983, Iraq began stockpiling biological warheads and accelerated its program, including efforts to develop new types of weapons.

During 1987–1988 Saddam Hussein's regime employed biological weapons against Iraq's Kurdish minority. There have been charges that this activity included rotavirus, a major killer of the young in developing countries. Iraq reportedly invested heavily in a rotavirus biological warfare program. Used either by itself or with other biological agents, rotavirus would produce major deaths and illness among children and infants.

Large-scale Iraqi production of anthrax and aflatoxin began in 1989, and that same year Iraqi scientists initiated field tests of biological weapons. In 1990 Iraq stockpiled some 200 bombs and 100 missiles capable of delivering biological agents.

Under the terms of the cease-fire that ended the 1991 Persian Gulf War, Iraq began destroying its biological weapons capability. Also in 1991, Iraq ratified the Biological Weapons Convention. United Nations (UN) weapons inspectors were granted limited access to biological weapons facilities and were able to verify the extent of the program and confirm that some materials had been destroyed. The belief by President George W. Bush's administration that Hussein's regime had not complied with UN resolutions to destroy its WMD programs was a major justification for the U.S.-led invasion in 2003. Following the occupation of Iraq, however, U.S. and international inspectors were unable to find any hidden WMDs.

The Iranian military worked with the United States during the 1960s and 1970s to develop defensive strategies against biological weapons. Iran signed the Biological Weapons Convention in 1972 and ratified it a year later. Following the Iranian Revolution in 1979, however, the country began a secret biological weapons program. The Iraqi use of chemical weapons in the war between the two countries during 1980–1988 accelerated the Iranian program. Throughout the 1980s and 1990s, Iranian agents and representatives attempted to acquire biological agents both legally and illicitly. The country also hired large numbers of scientists and experts on WMDs from the former Soviet Union. As a result, Iran has been able to develop small amounts of biological weapons. Iran has also developed the missile capabilities to deliver WMDs to Israeli territory.

TOM LANSFORD

See also

Arms Sales, International; Chemical Weapons and Warfare; DESERT STORM, Operation; Iran-Iraq War; IRAQI FREEDOM, Operation; Kurds, Massacres of; Missiles, Intermediate-Range Ballistic; Qaddafi, Muammar; Terrorism

References

Cordesman, Anthony. *Iran's Developing Military Capabilities.* Washington, DC: CSIS, 2005.

Guillemin, Jeanne. *Biological Weapons: From the Invention of State-Sponsored Programs to Contemporary Bioterrorism.* New York: Columbia University Press, 2005.

Walker, William. *Weapons of Mass Destruction and International Order.* New York: Oxford University Press, 2004.

Zubay, Geoffrey, et al. *Agents of Bioterrorism: Pathogens and Their Weaponization.* New York: Columbia University Press, 2005.

Blackman, Robert, Jr.
Birth Date: June 27, 1948

U.S. Marine Corps general and chief of staff to Lieutenant General David McKiernan as commander of Coalition Forces Land Component Command (CFLCC) during the Anglo-American–led invasion of Iraq in 2003 (Operation IRAQI FREEDOM). Robert "Rusty" Blackman Jr. was born in Orange, New Jersey, on June 27, 1948, and was commissioned in the U.S. Marine Corps upon graduation from Cornell University in June 1970. After completing Basic School, he served as a platoon commander and company executive officer. In March 1972 he reported to Marine Corps Recruit Depot, San Diego, where he served as a series commander and director of the Sea School until July 1975.

Blackman graduated from the Marine Corps Command and Staff College in June 1985. In May 1988 he assumed command of the 3rd Battalion, 8th Marines. Thereafter he was assigned to the Top Level School as a fellow in national security affairs at the John F. Kennedy School of Government. In August 1990 Blackman was assigned to the Operations Division at Headquarters Marine Corps. The next year he was reassigned as head of the Current Operations Branch, Headquarters Marine Corps.

In July 1991 Blackman reported to U.S. Central Command (CENTCOM) for duty as the commander in chief's executive officer. In March 1995 Blackman assumed duties as the military assistant to the secretary of the navy. In August 1996 he was made president of the Marine Corps University and was promoted to brigadier general on October 1, 1996. Upon promotion to major general in June 1999 Blackman assumed command of the 2nd Marine Division, a position he held until July 2001.

As the potential for war with Iraq grew in the autumn of 2002, U.S. Central Command began creating a headquarters staff to command the coalition ground forces. Accordingly, Lieutenant General David McKiernan assumed command of Third Army in September 2002 with headquarters at Camp Doha, north of Kuwait City. Most of the staff officers were from the army. However, a genuine joint and coalition headquarters could not be achieved by exclusively staffing it with army officers, and Blackman received the appointment as the chief of staff of Coalition Forces Land Component Command (CFLCC), which McKiernan commanded while also commanding Third Army.

At this time, Blackman was widely regarded within the U.S. Marine Corps as a thoughtful, quick-witted leader. He brought a wealth of experience to the CFLCC headquarter's team and amply demonstrated his skills as a leader. McKiernan wanted to move from the traditional staff structure of administrative, intelligence, operations, and logistics toward a staff organized around operational functions. In Blackman's view, this meant transitioning from a Napoleonic staff system to a functional staff system. These functions included operational maneuver, effects, intelligence, protection, and sustainment. The new organization required developing new staff organizations, coordination of boards and cells, and new processes, including digital architecture. To help meet these challenges, Blackman developed the Effects Synchronization Board that attempted to assess whether specific initiatives were achieving their intended outcomes.

On the eve of war in 2003, the Central Intelligence Agency (CIA) predicted that most Iraqis would greet the Americans as liberators. Blackman was skeptical. As he later recalled, "One of the towns where they said we would be welcomed was Nasiriyah, where marines faced some of the toughest fighting in the war."

One week after the capture of Baghdad—on April 10, 2003—senior American officers briefed President George W. Bush about future plans. To Blackman's amazement, General Tommy Franks predicted that U.S. forces could begin leaving the country within two months. Blackman knew that army and marine forces had yet to even enter several important cities, such as Fallujah, or to secure completely all of Baghdad. He cautioned that talk of withdrawal was overly optimistic.

Following the end of major combat operations in May 2003, Blackman was promoted to lieutenant general on October 1, 2003. He then left Iraq and was assigned to the U.S. Pacific Command. He subsequently led the Joint Task Force responsible for providing emergency relief following the Tsunami disaster in Asia in December 2004. Blackman retired from the U.S. Marine Corps on July 18, 2007.

JAMES ARNOLD

See also
Franks, Tommy Ray; IRAQI FREEDOM, Operation; McKiernan, David Deglan; United States Central Command

References
Cordesman, Anthony H. *The Iraq War: Strategy, Tactics, and Military Lessons.* Westport, CT: Praeger, 2003.

Gordon, Michael R., and General Bernard E. Trainor. *Cobra II: The Inside Story of the Invasion and Occupation of Iraq.* New York: Pantheon Books, 2006.

Murray, Williamson, and Robert H. Scales Jr. *The Iraq War: A Military History.* Cambridge, MA: Belknap, 2005.

Black Muslims

A term given to African American Muslims by C. Eric Lincoln in 1961. Black Muslims have mainly been members of the Nation of Islam, founded in the United States, although the group has avoided using the term to describe itself. They were generally the followers of Elijah Muhammad, a charismatic African American Black Muslim leader. In 1930 Wallace Fard founded the Lost-Found Nation of Islam in the Wilderness. He called for African Americans to embrace Islam, teaching them that they were being oppressed by whites, whom he labeled as "evil creatures." Because many African Americans were yearning for relief from oppression and discrimination, a sizable number embraced Fard's theology.

Fard preached to his followers that they were superior to whites, doing so in the name of Islam. In 1934 when Fard disappeared without any trace, Elijah Muhammad became the leader of the Nation of Islam and moved its headquarter to Chicago, where he built a successful movement that shaped the future of Islam in America. The term "Black Muslims" also applies to other African American Muslim organizations whether they are orthodox Muslims or not.

Under Elijah Muhammad, the Nation of Islam became a racist movement that preached the supremacy of blacks over whites. However, he also encouraged African Americans to free themselves of the "slave mentality" and to be financially independent. He established numerous companies, schools, and stores where many Black Muslims were employed, and he encouraged his followers to become industrious, educated, and well behaved. Although Elijah Muhammad worked hard to build the Nation of Islam, the roles that some of his followers—such as Malcolm X, Louis Farrakhan, and Warithu Deen Mohammed—played in sustaining the organization cannot be overlooked.

Indeed, it was Malcolm X who recruited many black youths into the Nation of Islam through his tireless effort and charisma. When Malcolm X joined the Nation of Islam, there were only a few thousand youth members and limited numbers of temples. Elijah Muhammad appointed him a minister, and through his eloquence and hard work Malcolm X brought thousands of blacks from all fields of life into the organization. As he became famous, however, tensions grew between himself and Elijah Muhammad.

Malcolm X was excommunicated in 1964 because of comments he made about the November 1963 assassination of President John Kennedy. Malcolm X eventually established a new organization, the Muslim Mosque Incorporation, after he left the Nation of Islam. He also traveled to Mecca and throughout Africa preaching black nationalism and Pan-Africanism and became a Sunni Muslim.

Early on Malcolm X became a vocal opponent of the Vietnam War, asserting that its sacrifices fell disproportionately to African Americans. He began to make such assertions even before the first major escalations of the Vietnam War began in mid-1965. Malcolm X was assassinated in February 1965 while giving a speech in New York. The murder plot has never been fully revealed, although many believe that he was killed on Elijah Muhammad's orders. Other Black Muslim groups similarly challenged the American establishment, especially after the major war escalations began in 1965, and Black Muslims played a notable role in the antiwar movement. Boxing great Muhammad Ali, who had become a Black Muslim in 1965, greatly raised the profile of the movement in 1966 when he refused to be inducted into the military on religious grounds, realizing that he would probably be sent to fight in Vietnam. In 1967 he was convicted of violating the Selective Service Act and was stripped of the heavyweight boxing title. Although the U.S. Supreme Court overturned his conviction in 1970, Ali forever linked antiwar sentiment and Black Muslims in the minds of most Americans.

Malcolm X left behind a lofty legacy of fighting for the rights of blacks all across the globe and emphasizing the pursuit of truth wherever it might be found. After Malcolm X's death, Elijah Muhammad appointed Louis Farrakhan to head New York's temple, where Malcolm X had previously preached.

When Elijah Muhammad died in 1975, his son, Warithu Deen Mohammed, succeeded him. He immediately introduced a deeper understanding of Islam and denounced many of his father's ideas of Islam and racism. He thus turned the Nation of Islam into a mainstream Islamic group and linked African American Muslims with universal Islam. He also flatly rejected the label "Black Muslims." That change of direction angered some of the older members of the organization, who did not like his new approach, but Imam Mohammed was convinced of the dire need for change and for a better understanding of Islam, which he insisted must be based on the Qur'an.

Eventually, Farrakhan broke with Imam Mohammed in 1978 and renewed the old racist ideologies of Elijah Muhammad. In 1985 Imam Mohammed decentralized his group and asked each imam to lead his own group. In October 2003 he resigned from the national leadership of the African American Muslims and encouraged each local mosque to be in charge of its own affairs.

Although many Americans during the 1960s decried the ideology and tactics of some Black Muslims, the movement did serve

Woman dressed in traditional garb at a gathering of the Nation of Islam. (National Archives)

to raise black consciousness and certainly fed into the emerging Black Power movement of the late 1960s. It also raised awareness of the civil rights movement, which marched in lockstep fashion with the antiwar movement after 1966. While it is true that Black Muslims generally embraced an ideology that was too extreme for most Americans both black and white, it did add a new dimension to the antiwar movement, especially with high-profile cases like that of Muhammad Ali.

Farrakhan remains the spiritual leader of the Nation of Islam. He is based in Chicago. At present, Black Muslims engage in community activities as well as local and national politics. Farrakhan launched the Million Man March in 1995 and 2005 to boost the morale of African Americans as he encouraged them to be industrious and to take care of their own lives and be responsible for their actions.

In recent years, Farrakhan has stirred up much controversy for comments and positions that many perceive as blatantly anti-Semitic. He dismisses such criticism, saying only that entrenched interests in the United States prevent a well-reasoned critique of Zionism and the State of Israel. Nevertheless, he strongly opposes U.S. government aid to Israel. Farrakhan also preaches that the United States is a racist oppressor nation that seeks world domination abroad and white supremacy at home. For that reason, he has sharply condemned the Global War on Terror and has excoriated the Iraq War, claiming that both are meant to be a war against Islam and nonwhite peoples. He has repeatedly urged his followers not to join the U.S. military in any form and to reject any proposed military draft.

YUSHAU SODIQ

See also
Antiwar Movements, Persian Gulf and Iraq Wars

References
Lincoln, C. Eric. *The Black Muslims in America.* Trenton, NJ: Africa
   World Press, 1994.
Marsh, Clifton E. *From Black Muslims to Muslims: The Transition from
   Separatism to Islam, 1930–1980.* Metuchen, NJ: Scarecrow, 1984.
Turrner, Richard Brent. *Islam in the African American Experience.*
   Bloomington: Indiana University Press, 1997.

Blackwater

Private U.S.-based security firm involved in military security operations in Afghanistan and Iraq. Blackwater USA (known as Blackwater Worldwide since October 2007) is one of a number of private security firms hired by the U.S. government to aid in security operations in Afghanistan and Iraq. The company was founded in 1997 by Erik D. Prince, a former Navy SEAL, wealthy heir to an auto parts fortune, and staunch supporter of the Republican Party. He serves as the firm's chief executive officer (CEO). The firm was named for the brackish swampy waters surrounding its 6,000-plus acre headquarters and training facilities located in northeastern North Carolina's Dismal Swamp.

Details of the privately held company are shrouded in mystery, and the precise number of paid employees is not publicly known. A good number of its employees are not U.S. citizens. Blackwater also trains upwards of 40,000 people per year in military and security tactics, interdiction, and counterinsurgency operations. Many of its trainees are military, law enforcement, or civilian government employees, mostly American, but foreign government employees are also trained here. Blackwater claims that its training facilities are the largest of their kind in the world. Nearly 90 percent of the company's revenues are derived from government contracts, two-thirds of which are no-bid contracts. It is estimated that since 2002 Blackwater has garnered U.S. government contracts in excess of $1 billion.

Following the successful ouster of the Taliban regime in Afghanistan in late 2001, Blackwater was among the first firms to be hired by the U.S. government to aid in security and law enforcement operations there. In 2003 after coalition forces ousted the regime of Iraqi president Saddam Hussein, Blackwater began extensive operations in the war-ravaged country. Its first major operation here included a $21 million no-bid contract to provide security services for the

Plainclothes members of Blackwater USA, the private security firm, take part in a firefight in Najaf, Iraq, on April 4, 2004, as Iraqi demonstrators loyal to Muqtada al-Sadr attempt to advance on a facility being defended by U.S. and Spanish soldiers. (AP/Wide World Photos)

Coalition Provisional Authority and its chief, L. Paul Bremmer. Since then, Blackwater has received contracts for several hundred million dollars more to provide a wide array of security and paramilitary services in Iraq. Some critics—including a number of congressional representatives and senators—took issue with the centrality of Blackwater in Iraq, arguing that its founder's connections to the Republican Party had helped it garner huge no-bid contracts.

Although such information has not been positively verified by either Blackwater or the U.S. government, it is believed that at least 30,000 private security contractors are in Iraq; some estimates claim as many as 100,000. Of that number, a majority are employees or subcontractors of Blackwater. The State Department and the Pentagon, which have both negotiated lucrative contracts with Blackwater, contend that neither one could function in Iraq without resorting to the use of private security firms. Indeed, the use of such contractors has helped keep down the need for even greater numbers of U.S. troops in Iraq and Afghanistan. After Hurricane Katrina smashed the U.S. Gulf Coast in 2005, the U.S. government contracted with Blackwater to provide security, law enforcement, and humanitarian services in southern Louisiana and Mississippi.

In the course of the Iraqi insurgency that began in 2003, numerous Blackwater employees have been injured or killed in ambushes, attacks, and suicide bombings. Because of the instability in Iraq and the oftentimes chaotic circumstances, some Blackwater personnel have found themselves in circumstances in which they felt threatened and had to protect themselves by force. This has led to numerous cases in which they have been criticized, terminated, or worse for their actions. Because they are not members of the U.S. military they often fall into a gray area, which can elicit demands for retribution either by the American government or Iraqi officials.

Loose oversight of Blackwater's operations has led to several serious cases of alleged abuse on the part of Blackwater employees. One of the most infamous examples of this occurred in Baghdad on September 16, 2007. While escorting a diplomatic convoy through the streets of the city, a well-armed security detail comprised of Blackwater and Iraqi police mistakenly opened fire on a civilian car that it claimed had not obeyed instructions to stop. Once the gunfire began, other forces in the area opened fired. When the shooting stopped, 17 Iraqi civilians lay dead, including all of the car's occupants. Included among the dead was a young couple with their infant child. At first there were wildly diverging accounts of what happened, and Blackwater contended that the car contained a suicide bomber who had detonated an explosive device, which was entirely untrue. The Iraqi government, however, faulted Blackwater for the incident, and U.S. Army officials backed up the Iraqi claims. Later reports state that the Blackwater guards fired on the vehicle with no provocation.

The Baghdad shootings caused an uproar in both Iraq and the United States. The Iraqi government suspended Blackwater's Iraqi operations and demanded that Blackwater be banned from the country. It also sought to try the shooters in an Iraqi court. Because some of the guards involved were not Americans and the others were working for the U.S. State Department, they were not subject to criminal prosecution. In the U.S. Congress, angry lawmakers demanded a full accounting of the incident and sought more detailed information on Blackwater and its security operations.

To make matters worse, just a few days after the shootings federal prosecutors announced that they were investigating allegations that some Blackwater personnel had illegally imported weapons into Iraq that were then being supplied to the Kurdistan Workers' Party, which has been designated by the United States as a terrorist organization.

These incendiary allegations prompted a formal congressional inquiry, and in October 2007 Erik Prince, Blackwater's CEO, was compelled to testify in front of the House Committee on Oversight and Government Reform. Prince did neither himself nor his company much good when he stonewalled the committee and told them that Blackwater's financial information was beyond the purview of the government. He later retracted this statement, saying that such information would be provided upon a "written request." Blackwater then struggled under a pall of suspicion, and multiple investigations were soon under way involving the incident in Iraq, incidents in Afghanistan, and the allegations of illegal weapons smuggling by company employees. In the meantime, Congress considered legislation that would significantly tighten government control and oversight of private contractors, especially those involved in sensitive areas such as military security.

In February 2009 Blackwater officials announced that the company would now operate under the name Xe, noting that the new name reflected a "change in company focus away from the business of providing private security." There is no meaning in the new name, which was decided upon after a year-long internal search.

In June 2009 the Central Intelligence Agency (CIA) disclosed to Congress that in 2004 it had hired members of Blackwater as part of a secret effort to locate and assassinate top Al Qaeda operatives. Reportedly Blackwater employees assisted with planning, training, and surveillance, but no members of Al Qaeda were captured or killed by them.

PAUL G. PIERPAOLI JR.

See also

Prince, Eric; Private Security Firms

References

Buzzell, Colby. *My War: Killing Time in Iraq*. New York: Putnam, 2005.
Engbrecht, Shawn. *America's Covert Warriors: Inside the World of Private Military Contractors*. Dulles, VA: Potomac Books, 2010.
U.S. Congress. *Private Security Firms: Standards, Cooperation, and Coordination on the Battlefield; Congressional Hearing*. Darby, PA: Diane Publishing, 2007.

Blair, Tony
Birth Date: May 6, 1953

British Labour Party politician and, as prime minister of the United Kingdom from May 2, 1997, to June 27, 2007, a major to use force to prevent genocide and widespread harm to innocent peoples.

After the September 11, 2001, attacks against the United States that led to the deaths of nearly 3,000 people, Blair quickly aligned Britain with the United States. He was convinced that the perpetrators of the act should be dealt with quickly and decisively to prevent setting in motion a series of events that might set Muslims against the Western world. He thus helped form the international coalition that carried out the 2001 intervention in Afghanistan (Operation ENDURING FREEDOM) that toppled the extremist Taliban Islamist group that ruled Afghanistan at the time and that was accused of supporting the terrorist group Al Qaeda. Al Qaeda, an organization whose objective was to bring down existing governments in the Middle East and impose radical Islamist rule on others around the world, became the top target in the Global War on Terror. Blair's government sent air, sea, and ground assets into Afghanistan during the initial thrust against the Taliban. The original deployment involved more than 5,700 British troops and then diminished to about 4,500.

In 2003 Blair enthusiastically supported President George W. Bush's call for an invasion of Iraq in order to overthrow the government of President Saddam Hussein. Blair argued that the Iraqi government, which had been ordered by the United Nations (UN) to dispose of its alleged weapons of mass destruction (WMDs), had not cooperated with UN weapons inspectors and was therefore subject to attack. When the United States invaded Iraq on March 20, 2003, Blair's government sent 46,000 British troops to assist with the invasion. Britain was by far the largest non-U.S. contingent in the coalition that supported Operation IRAQI FREEDOM. British troops remained in Iraq throughout the rest of Blair's premiership, which ended on June 27, 2007. The number of British troops in Iraq decreased significantly since the initial invasion, however, and about 7,000 British troops remained in that country when Blair left office.

Blair faced much criticism in Great Britain, even from members of his own party, for his support of the U.S. war effort. Critics accused him of spinning questionable evidence to galvanize support for the invasion of Iraq. At the heart of this criticism is the Iraq Dossier, nicknamed the "Dodgy Dossier" by many. The dossier was a briefing document given to reporters in hopes of justifying the British role in the Iraq War. Critics attacked the dossier not only because much of it had been plagiarized from a PhD dissertation available on the Internet but also because the claims that Iraq possessed WMDs were never proven. Indeed, to date no WMDs have been located in Iraq.

After resigning as prime minister on June 27, 2007, Blair was named an official Middle East envoy for the UN, the European Union, the United States, and Russia. He was succeeded as prime minister by his chancellor of the exchequer, Gordon Brown. Brown continued to support the United States in its reconstruction efforts in Iraq. Brown did, however, call for significant British troop reductions.

British politician Tony Blair led the Labour Party to a landslide victory in the 1997 general election. As prime minister, he strongly supported the use of force in Iraq in 2003. Blair, accused of too slavishly following U.S. president George W. Bush, left office in 2007 as Labour's longest-serving prime minister. (British Embassy)

supporter of U.S. and coalition efforts in both Afghanistan and Iraq. Anthony (Tony) Charles Lynton Blair was born on May 6, 1953, in Edinburgh, Scotland. He graduated from Oxford with a second-class honors BA in jurisprudence in 1976. Shortly thereafter, Blair joined the Labour Party and became a member of Parliament for Sedgefield in 1983. He became leader of the Labour Party in Great Britain a decade later, on July 21, 1994. When the Labour Party won the 1997 general election, Blair became the youngest person, at age 43, to become prime minister since Robert Jenkinson, Lord Liverpool, in 1812.

As prime minister, Blair lent strong support for the North Atlantic Treaty Organization (NATO) bombing campaign of Yugoslavia in 1999. He was among those urging NATO to take a strong line against Serbian strongman Slobodan Milosevic, the president of Yugoslavia, who was charged with violating human rights in his suppression of ethnic Albanians seeking secession from Yugoslavia, which precipitated the Kosovo War. Through his backing of the strong NATO response, Blair demonstrated that he would support the use of force in order to spread liberty and protect human rights. On April 22, 1999, in a speech in Chicago less than a month after the bombing campaign against Yugoslavia had commenced, he put forth what became known as the Blair Doctrine. In it he argued that it was sometimes necessary

Domestically, Blair has been both credited and criticized for having moved the Labour Party to the center of the political spectrum. His promarket policies seemed to boost the British economy and kept the Conservatives from questioning his motives. Blair successfully pushed for more funds for education and health care, and he oversaw the implementation of a national minimum wage act. Despite his domestic success, however, foreign affairs greatly overshadowed his premiership, none more so than the divisive Iraq War.

GREGORY W. MORGAN

See also

Brown, James Gordon; United Kingdom; United Kingdom, Middle East Policy

References

Coughlin, Con. *American Ally: Tony Blair and the War on Terror.* New York: Ecco, 2006.

Naughtie, James. *The Accidental American: Tony Blair and the Presidency.* New York: PublicAffairs, 2004.

Short, Clare. *An Honourable Deception? New Labour, Iraq, and the Misuse of Power.* London: Free Press, 2004.

Blix, Hans
Birth Date: June 28, 1928

Swedish diplomat, head of the United Nations (UN) International Atomic Energy Agency (IAEA) from 1981 to 1997, and head of the UN weapons inspection program in Iraq during the run-up to the 2003 Iraq War. Born in Uppsala, Sweden, on June 28, 1928, Hans Blix earned a degree in international law from the University of Stokholm in 1959 and also pursued studies at Trinity Hall, Cambridge University, from which he earned a doctorate in law. He was appointed associate professor of international law at the University of Stockholm in 1960.

Blix soon abandoned his academic career to pursue his passion for international politics. Between 1962 and 1978 he represented Sweden at the Disarmament Conference in Geneva, and from 1961 to 1981 he was a member of the Swedish delegation to the UN. During 1978–1979 he served as Swedish foreign minister in the government of the ruling Liberal Party.

In 1981 Blix was appointed to head the IAEA, a position he held until 1997. One of the major issues confronting the IAEA during Blix's tenure was monitoring the nuclear weapons program of the Iraqi regime of Saddam Hussein. Although Blix made several inspection visits to the Iraqi nuclear reactor at Osiraq before it was destroyed by an Israeli air strike in June 1981, the IAEA failed to discover the Iraqi clandestine nuclear weapons program initiated during the 1970s. The full extent of the Iraqi nuclear program was discovered only during the 1991 Persian Gulf War, and Blix was forced to acknowledge that the Iraqis had misled the IAEA. Following the loss of credibility for the IAEA, Blix tendered his resignation.

Less than three years later in 2000, however, UN secretary-general Kofi Annan lured the veteran diplomat out of retirement to head the United Nations Monitoring, Verification and Inspection Commission (UNMOVIC), a body assigned the responsibility of monitoring Iraqi weapons program following the Persian Gulf War. Because of Blix's perceived failures as head of the IAEA, Washington opposed the appointment.

Blix now attempted to build a diplomatic consensus for avoiding war and assuring the world that Iraq was compliant with UN resolutions regarding weapons development. Be that as it may, he chastised Saddam Hussein for playing "cat and mouse" games with weapons inspectors and seemed to realize that his inspectors were not getting the full story from Iraq. Blix nevertheless believed that UNMOVIC's monitoring of Iraq's weapons program could be employed to foster Iraqi disarmament. Critics in the George W. Bush administration, who seemed anxious for any pretense to wage war against Iraq, asserted that Blix was not sufficiently aggressive in searching for weapons of mass destruction (WMDs).

Following the invasion of Iraq by the United States and Great Britain in March 2003, Blix expressed considerable reservations regarding the war, asserting that the Bush administration had exaggerated the threat of WMDs in order to bolster its case for regime change in Iraq. In June 2003 Blix left UNMOVIC to chair the Weapons of Mass Destruction Commission, an independent body based in Stockholm. Blix elaborated on his criticisms of the rush to war in Iraq and the spurious intelligence reports upon which it was based in his 2004 memoir *Disarming Iraq.*

RON BRILEY

See also

Bush, George Walker; DESERT STORM, Operation; Hussein, Saddam; Iraq, History of, 1990–Present; IRAQI FREEDOM, Operation; Nuclear Weapons, Iraq's Potential for Building; United Nations; United Nations Weapons Inspectors; Weapons of Mass Destruction

References

Blix, Hans. *Disarming Iraq.* New York: Pantheon, 2004.

Williams, Ian. "Frustrated Neocons: Former U.N. Weapons Head Blix Assesses Year of War on Iraq." *Report on Middle East Affairs* 23 (May 1, 2004): 30–38.

Blount, Buford, III
Birth Date: September 15, 1948

U.S. Army general who commanded the successful assault on Baghdad during the 2003 Iraq War (Operation IRAQI FREEDOM) and who later became an outspoken critic of the U.S. war effort in Iraq. Buford "Buff" Blount III, born on September 15, 1948, in Travis County, Texas, was a career army officer who came from a family with a distinguished military background. In 1971 he graduated from the University of Southern Mississippi and was commissioned a second lieutenant in the U.S. Army. He later earned a master's degree in national security and strategic studies.

Throughout his career, Blount served primarily in armored and mechanized units. His command assignments included the

5th Infantry Division (Mechanized), Fort Polk, Louisiana; the 197th Infantry Brigade, Fort Benning, Georgia; commander, 3rd Battalion, 64th Armor, 3rd Infantry Division (Mechanized), USA-REUR, and Seventh Army, Germany; and commander, 3rd Brigade, 4th Infantry Division (Mechanized), Fort Carson, Colorado. He also served as armor plans and operations officer, Office of the Program Manager, Saudi Arabian National Guard Modernization Program, Saudi Arabia.

On the eve of the Iraq War, Blount, now a major general, was in command of the 3rd Infantry (Mechanized) Division; he had held that assignment since 2001 and had worked diligently to prepare the division for combat operations after it had been engaged in humanitarian and peacekeeping operations in the Balkans. Blount, who was a strong advocate of maneuver warfare, argued strongly that the original invasion plans for Iraq should be changed to allow his division to move to the west of the Tigris and Euphrates rivers and avoid the numerous river and stream crossings that would have delayed his advance. He was successful in convincing U.S. war planners of this more westerly advance toward Baghdad because the flat terrain was more conducive to armor.

When the war began on March 20, 2003, Blount's division of 19,000 troops and 8,000 vehicles was the lead unit of V Corps, the western column of the coalition's two-pronged advance on Baghdad. Blount's first major objective was capturing the airfield at Tallil, which allowed coalition forces to control several strategic bridges and two Iraqi highways. The ground attack began on March 21, and Blount's forces quickly took their main objectives and opened the main route to Baghdad.

Within three weeks Blount had moved his division 465 miles to the outskirts of the Iraqi capital in one of the most rapid armor advances in the history of modern warfare. During it, Blount coordinated his movements closely with air units to enforce close air support and concentrate maximum firepower against Iraqi forces, including elite Republican Guard units such as the Medina Division.

Blount rejected conventional military doctrine in laying siege to Baghdad, deciding instead to take the city in a succession of quick thrusts. Armored units usually do not perform well in urban combat because of the confines of streets and buildings and the potential for roadblocks and tank traps. Blount, however, believed that the rapid advance would not give the Iraqis time to establish substantial defenses and would demoralize the defenders. On April 5, 2003, he ordered a task force to conduct a reconnaissance of the Baghdad Airport in Operation THUNDER RUN. U.S. forces were able to capture the airport relatively quickly and also affirm weaknesses in the Iraqi defenses.

Blount was now convinced that the longer coalition forces waited to move on Baghdad, the more likely the Iraqis would be to reinforce the city and create a more robust defense. After a second thrust into Baghdad, Blount's division moved to capture government offices and presidential palaces. They met only minor and generally disorganized resistance. Meanwhile, elements of the I Marine Expeditionary Force, the eastern prong of the U.S.

advance, had arrived on the outskirts of Baghdad. By April 12, U.S. forces had virtual control of the Iraqi capital.

Blount's effective leadership in the Battle for Baghdad earned him praise from both subordinates and superiors. He led his division from the front, and he was generally in the lead units during the advance. This provided the division commander with an intimate sense of the ebb and flow of the advance. He also had a reputation for being calm and collected under fire, and he generally allowed his subordinates wide latitude in conducting tactical operations. He would set the objectives and the parameters of the mission but left it to his subordinates to develop the course of action to achieve these. Blount also embraced the new technology utilized during the campaign, including the command and control system, Force XXI Battle Command Brigade and Below/Blue Force Tracker (FBCB2/BFT). FBCB2/BFT provided soldiers with real-time awareness of coalition units and enhanced battlefield communications. Blount was able to accurately "see" the positions of his units at all times and make appropriate decisions based on that information.

After the capture of Baghdad, Blount found himself as the de facto mayor of the city, and he worked to maintain order with a limited number of troops. He opposed the decision to dismantle Iraqi security forces after their surrender, correctly forecasting that they would form the core of resistance to the U.S.-led occupation. He was also critical of the lack of planning to ensure the delivery of basic human services, food, and medicine in areas captured by the coalition. In October 2003 Blount was transferred to Washington, D.C., and became the U.S. Army's deputy chief of staff for operations and planning. He retired from active duty in 2004 as a major general. Since retirement he has publicly criticized the Iraq War effort, terming it "flawed" from the start. Observers have opined that his retirement was in part forced upon him because of his criticism of the war. Blount has steadfastly refused to comment on such observations, noting that he had generally supported the war plans in 2002 and 2003. Since 2004 Blount has taught at the university level and has given numerous speeches and interviews.

TOM LANSFORD

See also

Armored Warfare, Persian Gulf and Iraq Wars; Baghdad, Battle for; IRAQI FREEDOM, Operation, Coalition Ground Forces; Tallil Airfield; United States Army, Iraq War

References

Lacey, Jim. *Take Down: The 3rd Infantry's Twenty-one Day Assault on Baghdad*. Annapolis, MD: Naval Institute Press, 2007.
Zucchino, David. *Thunder Run: The Armored Strike to Capture Baghdad*. New York: Grove, 2004.

BLU-82/B Bomb

Bomb initially developed to clear helicopter landing areas. The BLU-82/B is a large high-altitude bomb developed for use in the Vietnam War. During that war the U.S. Air Force (USAF) at first employed

World War II–vintage M121 10,000-pound bombs to blast instant clearings in jungle and dense undergrowth from which helicopters could operate in connection with U.S. and South Vietnamese ground forces. With stocks of M121s diminishing, the USAF embarked on a replacement program and developed the Bomb Live Unit-82/B. Known as the "Daisy Cutter," the large (11'10" in length and 4'6" in diameter) BLU-82/B weighs 15,000 pounds. It is the heaviest bomb currently in use. The largest bomb of all time is the Grand Slam of 22,000 pounds, employed by the Royal Air Force Bomber Command against strategic targets in Germany during World War II. Some 225 BLU-82/Bs have been produced.

Contrary to reports that it is a fuel-air explosive device, the BLU-82/B is in fact a conventional bomb. It has a very thin .25-inch steel wall and is filled with 12,600 pounds of a GSX explosive slurry of ammonium nitrate, aluminum powder, and a binding agent. This filler has perhaps twice the power of TNT. As a result, the bomb can produce casualties among humans out to a radius of almost 400 yards from the point of detonation.

The Daisy Cutter has a minimum release altitude of 6,000 feet above the target. It relies on a cargo extractor/stabilization parachute to slow its descent to the target (approximately 27 seconds from a release point of 6,000 feet). A 38-inch fuse extender detonates the bomb just above ground level without producing a crater. At the point of blast, there is an overpressure of some 1,000 pounds per square inch.

The BLU-82/B was first utilized in combat during the Vietnam War on March 23, 1970. It found employment as a means to create helicopter landing zones and artillery fire bases in terrain covered by dense growth, to cause landslides for road interdiction, and to use against enemy troop concentrations. The BLU-82/B was also utilized during the rescue of the crew of the American merchant ship *Mayaguez* from the Cambodian Khmer Rouge in May 1975. The remaining bombs were then placed in storage. In air operations during Operation DESERT STORM the USAF 8th Special Operations Squadron employed Lockheed MC-130E Combat Talon aircraft to drop 11 BLU-82/Bs, first in an attempt to clear mines and then for both antipersonnel and psychological effects. The USAF also dropped several BLU-82/Bs in Afghanistan to attack Taliban and Al Qaeda strongholds.

SPENCER C. TUCKER

See also

Al Qaeda; Bombs, Gravity; DESERT STORM, Operation; ENDURING FREEDOM, Operation; Taliban; United States Special Operations Command

Reference

Doleman, Edgar D. *The Vietnam Experience: Tools of War*. Boston: Boston Publishing, 1984.

BMP-1 Series Infantry Fighting Vehicles

The BMP series of infantry fighting vehicles (IFVs) represented a revolutionary shift in doctrinal thinking not only for the Soviet military but also for other nations, including the United States. Prior to introduction of the BMP series in 1966, the predominant thinking about the use of mechanized infantry on the battlefield was that of the battlefield taxi, whereby the troops were moved to the combat area and then dismounted to fight on foot. The BMP dramatically changed this picture. While other nations such as the Federal Republic of Germany (West Germany) were working on their own IFVs, the BMP was the first to be fielded in any quantity.

Soviet doctrine in the 1950s was shifting to that of a nuclear battlefield, and to have infantry typically fighting on foot was a serious liability. The BMP was specifically designed with the nuclear battlefield in mind. The production model was armed with a 73-millimeter (mm) smoothbore gun that fired projectiles similar to those used in the handheld RPG-7 antitank launcher along with a rail to mount the new AT-3 Sagger 9M14M Malyutka wire-guided antitank missile (ATGM). The driver and vehicle commander were placed in tandem in the left-front of the hull, while the gunner for the 73-mm gun and AT-3 was alone in the small turret basket. The infantry squad of eight men sat in the rear, four on each side back-to-back and each with a firing port and vision block to allow them to fight from within the vehicle.

BMPs saw combat service in the October 1973 Yom Kippur (Ramadan) War as well as action in southern Lebanon in 1982 and the Iran-Iraq War of the 1980s. In the latter, BMPs were used by both sides. Crews liked the BMP's speed and maneuverability but discovered that the Sagger ATGM was virtually useless when fired from within the vehicle, mostly due to the inability of inexperienced gunners to guide the missile onto the target. Infantry also found it difficult to engage targets with any effectiveness from inside the vehicle. As a consequence, tactics began to develop that appeared to be a return to the battlefield taxi role of previous carrier designs.

The lessons learned from the Yom Kippur War led to an overhaul of the BMP design, culminating in the BMP-2 and BMP-3. As the Soviets continued to improve and modify the design, remaining BMP-1s were shipped off to client states such as Iraq. Thus, it was the BMP-1, constantly upgraded and modified, that continued to see the lion's share of combat service in Middle East wars. The Iraqis also received an unknown quantity of BMP-2s equipped with a 23-mm autocannon and the AT-4 Fagot 9M111 ATGM.

During the 1991 Persian Gulf War, coalition forces encountered a strange oddity. For years, British, French, and American tank and infantry personnel had engaged targets meant to look like Soviet tanks and infantry vehicles. Coalition forces were deployed along with Egyptian and Syrian units, equipped with large numbers of BMPs, and that created some initial confusion regarding vehicle identification, as it was sometimes hard to distinguish friendly BMPs from Iraqi vehicles. When the campaign began, it was deemed critical to keep forces properly organized and separated to limit allied fratricide. Combat units did engage BMPs only on limited occasions, as these were largely grouped with the Iraqi Republican Guard divisions that generally avoided

A Soviet-made BMP-1 infantry fighting vehicle near the village of Chagatai in Takhar Province in northern Afghanistan, 2001. (AP/Wide World Photos)

serious ground action. When coalition forces did manage to engage BMPs, they typically found them integrated with T-72 or T-62 Soviet-made tanks in combined arms company and battalion-sized groups. Some BMPs of the Medina Armored Division were destroyed by tankers from Colonel Montgomery Meigs's 2nd Brigade, 1st Armored Division, on February 27, 1991, but it would be the destruction of the Tawakalna Mechanized Division that saw one of the greatest losses of Iraqi BMPs in any one area.

The Tawakalna Mechanized Division was equipped with 220 T-72 tanks and more than 280 BMPs. It regularly trained in task-oriented battalion formations, and thus whenever tanks were encountered, BMPs were alongside. A typical formation was composed of 30–40 T-72 tanks and 12 BMP IFVs, with the infantry dug in around the vehicles. However, Soviet equipment was designed mostly for massed attack formations, not for flexible defensive tactics in small formations. The division was spread out over a large area and was hit by the concentrated power of the U.S. VII Corps, commanded by Lieutenant General Frederick Franks Jr. On February 26 in the Battle of 73 Easting, M1-A1 Abrams tanks and M3 Bradleys of the 2nd Armored Cavalry Regiment under Colonel Leonard Holder engaged and destroyed 37 T-72s and their escorting BMPs in a matter of six minutes, all in a swirling sandstorm at a range of more than 2,200 yards.

During the Iraq War of 2003 (Operation IRAQI FREEDOM), U.S. Army tanks and helicopters engaged some BMPs, again in mixed combined arms formations with tanks. Advancing elements of the 3rd Infantry Division encountered small combined arms groups attached to larger formations of Iraqi infantry during their drive north to Baghdad. On April 4, 2003, just south of the city at a crossroads marked "Objective Saints" on battle maps, American forces destroyed several dozen BMP-1s and BMP-2s that were part of the Medina Armored Division. The Iraqi forces had bravely resisted, and at one point a platoon of BMP-2s had engaged the advancing Americans with accurate fire from their 30-mm cannon before they were destroyed by tankers of the 4-64 Armored Battalion. Later, as American columns pushed into Baghdad, BMPs individually and in pairs attempted to ambush the Americans from the numerous narrow alleys of the city. As the Battle for Baghdad came to a close, there were numerous Iraqi tanks and BMPs littering the roadways. Unfortunately, precise loss statistics for the BMPs are not readily available for either the Persian Gulf War or the Iraq War of 2003. However, in the case of the former the losses may have been as high as 200.

Even though the BMP was outclassed by tanks and infantry vehicles of American and other Western nations, when used by smaller armies against comparable foes it proved itself an effective vehicle, as attested to by the Iraqi experience during the Iran-Iraq War. Therefore, BMPs of various configurations will likely be encountered on Middle Eastern battlefields into the foreseeable future.

Specifications of the BMP-1 are as follows:

Armament: 1 73-mm 2A28 smoothbore gun with a rate of fire of 7–8 rounds per minute; 1 coaxial 7.62-mm machine gun

Main Gun Ammunition: 40 Rounds

Armor: 23-mm maximum

Crew/Passengers: 3, with 8 infantry

Weight: 13.28 tons

Length: 22 feet 2 inches

Width: 9 feet 8 inches

Height: 7 feet 1 inch

Engine: V-6 diesel; 300 horsepower at 2,000 revolutions per minute

Speed: Road, 45 miles per hour

Range: 340 miles

RUSSELL G. RODGERS

See also

Baghdad, Battle for; DESERT STORM, Operation; Infantry Fighting Vehicles, Iraqi; Iran-Iraq War; IRAQI FREEDOM, Operation; 73 Easting, Battle of; T-62 Main Battle Tank; T-72 Main Battle Tank

References

Bourque, Stephen A. *Jayhawk! The VII Corps in the Persian Gulf War.* Washington, DC: Department of the Army, 2002.

Foss, Christopher, ed. *Jane's Armour and Artillery, 2007–2008.* Coulsdon Surrey, UK: Jane's Information Group, 2007.

Fontenot, Gregory, et al. *On Point: The United States Army in Iraqi Freedom.* Annapolis, MD: Naval Institute Press, 2005.

Gordon, Michael R., and General Bernard E. Trainor. *The Generals' War: The Inside Story of the Conflict in the Gulf.* New York: Little, Brown, 1995.

Hull, Andrew W., David R. Markov, and Steven J. Zaloga. *Soviet/Russian Armor and Artillery Design Practices: 1945 to Present.* Darlington, MD: Darlington, 1999.

Scales, Robert H. *Certain Victory: The U.S. Army in the Gulf War.* Washington, DC: Brassey's, 1994.

Zaloga, Steven J. *BMP Infantry Combat Vehicle.* New Territories, Hong Kong: Concord, 1990.

Bolton, John Robert, II
Birth Date: November 20, 1948

Attorney and U.S. representative to the United Nations (UN) during 2005–2006. John Robert Bolton II was born in Baltimore, Maryland, on November 20, 1948. He attended Yale University, graduating in 1970, and earned a law degree from Yale Law School in 1974, where he attended classes with future president Bill Clinton and future first lady Hillary Rodham Clinton as well as future U.S. Supreme Court justice Clarence Thomas. In 1970 Bolton joined the Maryland Army National Guard, seeking to avoid being sent to Vietnam because he believed that the antiwar lobby had already destined the nation to lose the war there. After graduating with his law degree, Bolton joined a Washington, D.C., law firm.

Bolton entered public service in 1981 as a counsel to the U.S. Agency for International Development (USAID), a post he held until 1982. From 1982 to 1983 he was assistant administrator of USAID. After several years back in private law practice, Bolton was

assistant U.S. attorney general during 1985–1989 and then assistant secretary of state for international organization affairs from 1989 to 1993. From 1993 to 1999 he again practiced law; from 1997 to 2001 he was senior vice president for public policy research at the American Enterprise Institute.

By 2001 Bolton had firmly established his bona fides as a neoconservative, on record as disdaining the UN and America's participation in it. Following the contested 2000 presidential election, James Baker III, George W. Bush's chief strategist, dispatched Bolton to Florida as part of the administration's effort to halt the recount there. In 2001 President George W. Bush named Bolton undersecretary of state for arms control and international security affairs, a post he held until 2005. Bolton was reportedly closely allied with Secretary of Defense Donald Rumsfeld and other neoconservatives who pushed aggressively for war against Iraq in 2003.

Bolton confronted Iran over its nuclear program, and in 2002 he accused Cuba of harboring a clandestine biological weapons program. Reportedly, he tried to fire several State Department biological warfare experts when their intelligence did not support his own position, although Bolton denied this. Bolton also went on record as stating that the United States would disavow entirely the International Criminal Court.

In March 2005 Bush nominated Bolton as U.S. ambassador to the UN, a strange nomination considering Bolton's earlier harsh comments about that international body. The nomination caused a firestorm in Washington, and a Democratic filibuster in the Senate stopped it. During the bruising nomination process, testimony claimed that Bolton had mistreated and bullied subordinates and had tried to fire those who did not agree with him. Bolton denied the accusations in what became a thoroughly partisan debate.

Angered by the rebuff of his nomination, Bush instead appointed Bolton permanent U.S. representative to the UN in what is called a recess appointment on August 1, 2005. This essentially circumvented Congress in the appointment process. Although Bolton could not claim the title of ambassador, he was in essence fulfilling that role. Democrats especially excoriated the Bush White House over the appointment. In 2006 Bush twice resubmitted Bolton's nomination, and each time the move was rebuffed. In December 2006, with the handwriting on the wall, Bolton announced his desire to step down from his temporary appointment and withdraw his name from nomination. Returning to private law practice, he is involved with numerous national and international organizations as well as conservative think tanks.

PAUL G. PIERPAOLI JR.

See also

Bush, George Walker; Neoconservatism; Rumsfeld, Donald Henry

References

Draper, Robert. *Dead Certain: The Presidency of George W. Bush.* New York: Free Press, 2008.

Lugar, Richard G., ed. *Nomination of John R. Bolton: Reports from the Committee on Foreign Relations, U.S. Senate.* Darby, PA: Diane Publishing, 2006.

Bombs, Cluster

Small explosive submunitions, or bomblets, dropped from aircraft or fired by artillery that are designed to detonate prior to, on, or after impact. In the 1930s, munitions experts in the Soviet Union developed early versions of cluster bomb technology. However, it was the Germans who first used cluster bombs operationally in World War II during the Battle of Britain in 1940. Called "Butterfly Bombs" by the Germans, their usage was not widespread because they were difficult to produce and were very fragile aboard aircraft. Despite these limitations, both British firemen and civilians viewed Butterfly Bombs as extremely dangerous because they did not explode upon impact but instead detonated later under the slightest vibration.

Cluster bombs quickly grew in popularity and are now produced in many countries thanks to their versatility on the battlefield. The United States first used cluster bombs in the 1950–1953 Korean War as an antipersonnel weapon. Since then, the U.S. military has employed cluster munitions in Laos, Cambodia, Vietnam, Iraq, Kosovo, and Afghanistan. During Operation DESERT STORM, the U.S. Air Force used the weapon extensively, dropping a total of 34,000 cluster bombs. U.S. warplanes dropped an estimated 1,100 cluster bombs during the North Atlantic Treaty Organization's 1999 Operation ALLIED FORCE in Kosovo, deploying roughly 222,200 submunitions. Fighter pilots flying the A-10 Thunderbolt II attack aircraft in Kosovo preferred using cluster bombs because they enabled them to neutralize targets without using precision-guided ordnance.

Cluster bombs remain a primary weapon among world military arsenals because of their wide variety of battlefield applications. Relatively inexpensive to make, cluster munitions offer a wide array of options in combat. They can be fired from the ground or dropped from the sky and afford numerous methods for delivery and employment. Ground-based deployments include the firing of cluster munitions with artillery or rocket launchers. Aircraft, meanwhile, are able to drop cluster munitions in a bomb-shaped container, or Cluster Bomb Unit (CBU), that breaks open at a predetermined height, scattering hundreds of bomblets over a wide area. Either delivery method results in a very effective weapon when used against personnel or armor. Cluster bombs are also frequently used on runways, electrical facilities, munitions dumps, and parked aircraft. Within the U.S. military, all four service branches use various forms of cluster munitions.

There are also many different types of cluster munitions. Some versions of cluster bombs are meant to be incendiary and ignite fires, while others are used as fragmentation bombs, designed to explode and scatter deadly pieces of metal in all directions.

Antitank versions of cluster munitions contain shaped-charge bomblets designed to penetrate armor more effectively. Sometimes the bomblets can be small mines, intended to function like regular land mines upon landing. Different types of submunitions may also be used together to increase lethality. These weapons, called Combined Effects Munitions (CEM), may implement incendiary, fragmentation, and armor-piercing bomblets in one

dispenser to maximize the level of damage against different enemy targets located in the same vicinity.

The most controversial type of cluster bomb involves the air-dropped mines meant to immobilize enemy movements and act as an area denial weapon. These versions are designed to land softly and detonate only when the internal battery runs out, when the internal self-destruct timer runs out, or when they are disturbed in any way. Mine-laying cluster bombs proved relatively effective when used against Scud missile launchers during Operation DESERT STORM in 1991. At the same time, these types of cluster bombs can cause many deaths and serious injuries to unsuspecting civilians who may run across them. A small percentage of the bomblets do not always explode or detonate as planned.

Mines deployed by cluster bombs pose a greater long-term threat to civilians living in a war zone. Roughly 1–10 percent of cluster submunitions do not explode on impact, becoming deadly to any nonmilitary personnel who may stumble upon them. Thousands of such civilian casualties have been reported in Iraq, Kosovo, Afghanistan, Lebanon, and Israel.

In 1999 the U.S. Department of Defense estimated that there were 11,110 unexploded bomblets in Kosovo after Operation ALLIED FORCE that caused an estimated 500 civilian deaths. Additionally, an estimated 1.2 million to 1.5 million unexploded submunitions still remained in Iraq after Operation DESERT STORM, claiming more than 4,000 civilian casualties.

While cluster munitions have caused controversy in many conflicts, their use in the summer 2006 war between Israel and Hezbollah was especially controversial. After the brief conflict, an estimated 1 million unexploded cluster bomb submunitions littered southern Lebanon and northern Israel. Thousands of artillery rounds carrying cluster munitions were fired between the two combatants, according to the United Nations (UN) Mine Action Coordination Center. Human rights organizations have accused both belligerents of deliberately targeting civilians during the conflict, as many of the bomblets fell into villages and towns where civilians were living. Human rights organizations also reported more than 1,600 deaths in Kuwait and Iraq stemming from unexploded submunitions dropped during the 1991 Persian Gulf War. Examples such as these have given rise to increased efforts to outlaw cluster bombs internationally.

Since the 1991 Persian Gulf War, the U.S. Defense Department reviewed its use of cluster munitions in an attempt to minimize collateral damage and reduce the noncombatant casualty rate. Thanks to the inaccuracy of certain types of cluster munitions, such as the CBU-87 used during Operation DESERT STORM, the U.S. Defense Department established a goal of reducing the dud rate among cluster submunitions to less than 1 percent by 2001.

In the mid-1990s the U.S. Air Force began experimenting with Wind Corrected Munitions Dispensers (WCMDs) in a further effort to reduce the noncombatant death rate. WCMD features include directional aerodynamic fins and an internal navigation system that adjusts for wind variations after its release.

Additionally, cluster bombs such as the CBU-105 have dispensers loaded with smart bomblets, designed to self-destruct if they do not hit their target. As an additional safety measure, these smart bomblets are designed to deactivate within minutes if they do not explode upon impact.

The U.S. military has also experimented with a new version of cluster munitions, substituting thousands of darts, or nails, for bomblets. When dropped from an aircraft or fired from the ground, these cluster munitions employ thousands of small nail-like pieces of metal that can destroy personnel and other soft targets. This method eliminates the possibility of duds, as there is no explosive submunition that could cause harm to an unsuspecting civilian.

During Operation IRAQI FREEDOM American forces made wide use of cluster bombs, much to the consternation of international human rights groups. It is estimated that in the opening weeks of the war, some 13,000 cluster munitions were employed in Iraq, and despite their careful use, the bombs caused considerable civilian deaths and casualties. Some human rights watch groups have alleged that as many as 240,000 cluster bombs have been used in Iraq after March 2003, a number that cannot be verified because the Defense Department does not provide such figures. In Operation IRAQI FREEDOM the United States also used the CBU-105 smart-guided cluster bomb, which was dropped from B-52 bombers. Cluster bombs were also employed during Operation ENDURING FREEDOM in Afghanistan. The collateral damage caused by these munitions raised international concern and may have unwittingly precipitated a backlash against U.S. operations there among many Afghan citizens.

After successful efforts to ban antipersonnel mines, many countries initiated efforts to implement policies curbing the use of cluster bombs or advocating their complete elimination. In February 2007 Norway invited interested countries to Oslo and began to push for an international ban on cluster bombs. More than 45 countries participated in the discussions and agreed to meet again in February 2008. Once again led by Norway, more than 80 countries signed the Wellington Declaration at the Cluster Munitions Conference in New Zealand. This meeting committed the participating countries to solving the humanitarian problems created by cluster bombs and their unexploded ordnance.

Continuing on in the goal of banning cluster munitions altogether, 111 countries met in Dublin, Ireland, in May 2008 and agreed on a treaty banning certain types of cluster munitions. Furthermore, the signatories agreed to eliminate stockpiled cluster ordnance by 2016. Signatories also promised not to develop, produce, use, obtain, stockpile, or transfer additional cluster munitions. British prime minister Gordon Brown was among the many diplomats calling for a total ban on the use of cluster bombs. However, representatives from the world's largest producers of cluster bombs, which include the United States, Russia, and the People's Republic of China, did not attend. Diplomats from Israel, India, and Pakistan raised objections about a total ban.

In lieu of an outright ban on cluster bombs, the UN and human rights organizations have begun new efforts to minimize damage to noncombatants. Education emphasizing the dangers associated with unexploded cluster bomb submunitions is being distributed to civilians living in war-torn areas around the world. The United States has opposed the ban because of the extreme utility of these weapons, preferring instead to improve the safety measures in cluster bomb technology.

MATTHEW R. BASLER

See also

Antitank Weapons; Artillery; DESERT STORM, Operation; ENDURING FREEDOM, Operation; Hezbollah; Israel, Armed Forces; Lebanon, Armed Forces; Mines, Sea, Clearing Operations, Persian Gulf and Iraq Wars; Mines, Sea, and Naval Mine Warfare, Persian Gulf and Iraq Wars; Mines and Mine Warfare, Land

References

Bailey, Jonathan B. A. *Field Artillery and Firepower.* Annapolis, MD: Naval Institute Press, 2004.

Bond, Horatio, ed. *Fire and the Air War.* Boston: National Fire Protection Association, 1946.

Conway, Simon. "Banning Bomblets." *The World Today* 64(5) (May 2008): 13–15.

Haave, Christopher E., and Phil M. Haun, eds. *A-10s over Kosovo: The Victory of Airpower over a Fielded Army as Told by the Airmen Who Fought in Operation Allied Force.* Maxwell Air Force Base, AL: Air University Press, 2003.

Hammick, Denise. "NZ Conference Paves Way for Cluster Munitions Treaty." *Jane's Defense Weekly* 45(10) (March 5, 2008): 7.

Hogg, Ian V. *Artillery 2000.* London: Arms and Armour Press, 1990.

Lennox, Duncan, ed. *Jane's Air-Launched Weapons.* Alexandria, VA: Jane's Information Group–Sentinel House, 1999.

Bombs, Gravity

Bombs and other explosive ordnance that do not contain internal guidance systems. Bombs were weapons utilized by aircraft to attack targets, whether on water or land. Today, bombs lacking a guidance system are called dumb bombs because they fall dumbly to the target by the force of gravity along a ballistic path, unable to adjust for errors in aiming, weather, wind, or visibility conditions. Dumb bombs are simple, consisting of an aerodynamically streamlined shape filled with high explosives. Up until Operation ENDURING FREEDOM in Afghanistan in 2001, dumb bombs constituted the vast majority of such weapons used in war and still remain the dominant bomb type in the arsenals of most Middle Eastern nations, including Israel.

On dumb bombs, stabilizing fins are attached at the back, and a detonating fuse is installed just before the bombs are loaded onto a plane. The bombs come in four types: high explosive or general purpose, cluster bombs, daisy cutter, and fuel air explosives (FAE). Of these bombs, the first is the most commonly used and comes in varying sizes based on weight, ranging from 220 pounds to 2,200 pounds. American and British bombs are designated by weight in pounds (250, 500, 1,000, 2,000), while most other countries use kilograms. For example, the former Soviet Union's bombs came in 100-, 200-, 500-, and 1,000-kilogram sizes. Fusing was determined by the mission. Proximity or variable-timed fuses, which detonate at various heights above the ground, were used against dug-in infantry. Quick fuses that detonated on impact were also used against surface targets to maximize blast effect. Delayed fuses were placed in the bomb's tail to hold up the detonation until the bomb had penetrated a predictable depth into the target to ensure destruction of armored targets such as bunkers.

Cluster bombs carried up to 100 smaller (50-kilogram) bombs within them that were released at a predetermined altitude above a target area about the size of a football field. They were used against moving targets such as tanks, armored personnel vehicles, and naval missile boats. Daisy cutters refer to the 15,000-pound bomb dropped from Lockheed MC-130 Hercules aircraft to clear out a landing area for helicopters, collapse tunnels, or destroy troop concentrations. Finally, FAEs differ from other bombs in that they employ an aerosol spray to create a mist of fuel that, when ignited, creates an overpressure followed immediately by a series of alternating underpressures and overpressures to flatten objects in an area (vehicles, aircraft) and inflict maximum personnel casualties.

Dumb bombs were employed in all of the various bombing missions executed during the Arab-Israeli wars, and more than 80 percent of all bombs dropped during Operation DESERT STORM (1991) were dumb bombs. Ten years later, that percentage had dropped to just 20 percent during Operation ENDURING FREEDOM (2001) and Operation IRAQI FREEDOM (2003). Nevertheless, dumb bombs still dominate the arsenals of the world's air forces. But the United States and most Western countries have guidance kits to install on them to convert them into smart bombs. Increasingly, dumb bombs are used only on battlefields located some distance from civilian populations. This trend will likely continue in the years ahead as bombs become more deadly and the international community places increasingly stringent standards against inflicting casualties on innocent civilians.

CARL OTIS SCHUSTER

See also

Bombs, Precision-Guided; DESERT STORM, Operation, Coalition Air Campaign; ENDURING FREEDOM, Operation, U.S. Air Campaign; IRAQI FREEDOM, Operation, Air Campaign

References

Frieden, David R. *Principles of Naval Weapons Systems.* Annapolis, MD: Naval Institute Press, 1985.
Werrell, Kenneth P. *Chasing the Silver Bullet: U.S. Air Force Weapons Development from Vietnam to Desert Storm.* Washington, DC: Smithsonian Institution Scholarly Press, 2003.
Yenne, Bill. *Secret Weapons of the Cold War.* New York: Berkley Publishing, 2005.

Bombs, Precision-Guided

Precision-guided munitions, commonly called smart bombs, refer to bombs that have integral guidance systems that compensate for environmental interference and poor aim and that ensure the bomb's accurate emplacement against the target. They differ from dumb or iron bombs in that they have an internal guidance system and a related power source. Typically, a modern smart bomb has a circular probable error of 20–94 feet. But even a highly trained pilot operating in an optimal environment can, at best, reliably place a dumb bomb within 300 feet of the aim point. Most modern smart bomb systems rely on a computer-based guidance system that accepts a target designated by the aircraft's pilot or weapons officer or a forward air or ground controller and guides the bomb onto it. The target's identification and designation are derived from electro-optical, infrared, or radar imaging. However, a growing number of guidance systems guide the bomb onto the target's geographic location using the target's and bomb's Global Positioning System (GPS) respective location. The bomb reverts to inertial guidance if the GPS link is lost. GPS-guided bombs are employed against fixed targets, while the others can be used against moving targets or those in which a specific entry point (e.g., ventilation shaft) is required.

The Germans employed the first guided bombs during World War II. The German Fritz bombs were radio-controlled bombs that the plane's bombardier glided into the target using a joy stick. He tracked the bomb's path via a flare in the bomb's rear. The Americans also employed a television-based guided bomb called the Azon bomb in 1945 and continued to pursue bomb-guidance systems after the war. The resulting AGM-62 Walleye relied on a TV camera installed in the bomb's nose that transmitted the target's image back to the aircraft's weapons officer. He steered the bomb to the target by keeping the aim in the TV crosshairs. The early Walleyes required so much operator attention, however, that they were primarily employed from crewed aircraft such as the navy's A-6 Intruder.

In 1968 during the Vietnam War, the U.S. Air Force introduced the Bolt-117, the first laser-guided bomb. These early bombs guided onto the reflected beam of a laser designator that illuminated the target. The early versions had to be illuminated by a second aircraft in the target area. By 1972, this system had given way to an automatic laser-tracking illuminator that enabled the bombing aircraft to illuminate the target as it withdrew. However, these early laser-based systems were vulnerable to smoke and poor visibility, which interfered with the laser beam.

By the late 1970s, the United States introduced improved laser, infrared, and electro-optical target-designation systems. Israel acquired some of these weapons and used them in strike missions over Lebanon in the mid-1980s, but the first significant large-scale use of smart bombs came in 1991, when the United States led a United Nations (UN) coalition to drive Iraqi troops out of Kuwait (Operation DESERT STORM). In that war, U.S. aircraft used precision weapons in approximately 20 percent of their strike missions over Iraq. They were employed primarily against high-priority targets located within population areas or in circumstances where the target's first-strike destruction had to be guaranteed (Scud surface-to-surface missile launchers, for example).

The lessons learned from that war drove the U.S. development of the Joint Direct Attack Munition (JDAM), Joint Standoff Weapon (JSOW), and GPS-based bomb-guidance systems. During Operation ENDURING FREEDOM (2001), more than 80 percent of the bombs dropped were smart bombs, and a similar percentage marked the air missions over Iraq in Operation IRAQI FREEDOM (2003).

Precision weapons will continue to gain ground in the years ahead as the world takes an increasingly harsh view of collateral damage and casualties inflicted on civilians. The introduction of cost-effective retrofit guidance kits has enabled many countries to convert their dumb bombs into smart bombs at little expense. Israel and most of the Arab frontline states are now acquiring guidance kits for their bomb arsenals. However, blast effects remain a problem regardless of the weapon's precision. For example, the Palestinian terrorists' strategic placement of their facilities within apartment blocks and housing areas has driven Israel away from the use of bombs. Israel increasingly employs short-range tactical missiles with small warheads (less than 30 kilograms) against terrorist targets in the occupied territories and southern Lebanon. Still, smart bombs will figure prominently in any future Middle Eastern conflict.

CARL OTIS SCHUSTER

See also

Aircraft, Bombers; Bombs, Gravity; DESERT STORM, Operation, Coalition Air Campaign; ENDURING FREEDOM, Operation, U.S. Air Campaign; IRAQI FREEDOM, Operation, Air Campaign

References

Allen, Charles. *Thunder and Lightning: The RAF in the Gulf; Personal Experiences of War.* London: Her Majesty's Stationery Office, 1991.

Drendei, Lou. *Air War Desert Storm.* London: Squadron Signal Publications, 1994.

Frieden, David R. *Principles of Naval Weapons Systems.* Annapolis, MD: Naval Institute Press, 1985.

Pollack, Kenneth M. *Arabs at War: Military Effectiveness, 1948–1991.* Lincoln: University of Nebraska Press, 2002.

Werrell, Kenneth P. *Chasing the Silver Bullet: U.S. Air Force Weapons Development from Vietnam to Desert Storm.* Washington, DC: Smithsonian Institution Scholarly Press, 2003.

Winnefeld, James A., Preston Niblack, and Dana J. Johnson. *A League of Airmen: U.S. Air Power in the Gulf War.* Santa Monica, CA: RAND Corporation, 1994.

Yenne, Bill. *Secret Weapons of the Cold War.* New York: Berkley Publishing, 2005.

Bonn Agreement

Agreement reached among Afghan leaders in Bonn, Germany, on December, 5, 2001, to create a governing authority for Afghanistan in the aftermath of the toppling of the Taliban regime several weeks earlier. Sponsored by the United Nations (UN), the Bonn Agreement produced the Afghan Interim Authority (AIA), a temporary governmental entity. The AIA was inaugurated on December 22, 2001. The Bonn Agreement was designed to stabilize Afghanistan and bring an end to the 20-year-long civil war there. Afghanistan had been plunged into chaos in 1989, when the last Soviet troops were withdrawn from the country. Between 1989 and 2001, Afghanistan was a nation besieged by internal strife and without an effective government that could provide its people basic needs and services. The U.S. government realized that before a permanent Afghan government could come to power, an interim governing body had to be established that could rally the Afghan people and work with the U.S. and allied forces. The Bonn Agreement was undertaken to accomplish these goals.

The AIA, which came into being on December 22, was comprised of 30 Afghans, to be headed by a chairman. The AIA would have a six-month mandate, to be followed by a two-year period under a Transitional Authority. At the end of the two years, national elections were to be held and a permanent Afghan government established. Hamid Karzai was chosen to chair the AIA; he became interim president after the convening of the *loya jirga* ("grand assembly") on June 22, 2002, and then president of Afghanistan in 2004. The Bonn Agreement also stipulated the

German chancellor Gerhard Schroeder, German foreign minister Joschka Fischer, United Nations (UN) envoy in Afghanistan Lakhdar Brahimi, rear from left, attend the Bonn Agreement signing ceremony with the delegation leaders, front from left, Houmayoun Jareer of the Cyprus delegation, Sayed Hamed Gailani of the Peshawar delegation and Abdul Sirat of the Rome delegation in Koenigswinter, near Bonn, in December 2001. (AP/Wide World Photos)

creation of the Afghan Constitution Commission, charged with drafting a new Afghan constitution that would be subjected to a future plebiscite. In the meantime, the AIA was asked to use the 1964 Afghan constitution until the new one could be drawn up. The agreement also established a judiciary commission to help rebuild Afghanistan's judicial system and specifically called for the creation of a national supreme court.

Another important accomplishment of the Bonn Agreement was a mandate to create a development and security mission to be led by the North Atlantic Treaty Organization (NATO). Approved by the UN Security Council on December 20, 2001, this mission became the NATO-led International Security Assistance Force (ISAF), charged with pacifying and stabilizing Afghanistan and continuing the hunt for Taliban and Al Qaeda insurgents there. Today, the ISAF continues its work in Afghanistan and is the umbrella command organization for all allied military efforts and operations in Afghanistan.

PAUL G. PIERPAOLI JR.

See also

Afghanistan; International Security Assistance Force; Karzai, Hamid; Loya Jirga, Afghanistan; North Atlantic Treaty Organization in Afghanistan

References

Abrams, Dennis. *Hamid Karzai.* Langhorne, PA: Chelsea House, 2007.

Rashid, Ahmed. *Descent into Chaos: The United States and the Failure of Nation-building in Pakistan, Afghanistan, and Central Asia.* New York: Viking, 2008.

Boomer, Walter
Birth Date: September 22, 1938

U.S. Marine Corps general and commander of Marine forces during Operations DESERT SHIELD and DESERT STORM. Walter Boomer was born on September 22, 1938, in Rich Square, North Carolina. He graduated from Duke University in 1960 and was commissioned a second lieutenant in the U.S. Marine Corps in January 1961. His initial assignments were with the 8th and 2nd Marine regiments at Camp Lejuene, North Carolina.

Shortly after his April 1965 promotion to captain, Boomer was ordered to South Vietnam, where he served as a company commander during the Vietnam War from 1966 to 1967. After returning from his first Vietnam tour, Boomer attended the Amphibious Warfare School. He was promoted to major in May 1968 and joined Marine Headquarters, Washington, D.C., as administrative assistant and aide-de-camp to the deputy chief of staff for plans and programs. Following that assignment, Boomer attended the Armed Forces Staff College.

In 1971, in preparation for his second Vietnam tour, Boomer attended the short adviser course at Fort Bragg, North Carolina. In August of that year he returned to Vietnam as adviser to a South Vietnamese Marine Battalion. Upon returning to the United States

in September 1972, Boomer attended American University in Washington, where he earned an MA degree in management technology. He was promoted to lieutenant colonel in September 1976 after a three-year stint at the United States Naval Academy, where he taught management. He then joined the 3rd Marine Regiment in Hawaii, where he served as regimental executive officer and as commander of its 3rd Battalion. He was promoted to colonel in November 1981 and became director of the 4th Marine District, Philadelphia, Pennsylvania, in June 1983. In February 1985 he took command of the Marine Security Battalion, Quantico. While serving in that post, he was appointed brigadier general in June 1986. Boomer earned advancement to major general in March 1989. In August 1990 he was promoted to lieutenant general and assigned to Saudi Arabia as commander of Marine Forces Central Command and I Marine Expeditionary Force (I MEF), posts he held throughout Operations DESERT SHIELD and DESERT STORM.

Throughout his military career, Boomer had staunchly advocated a separate U.S. Marine Corps combat doctrine. As with many Marine Corps officers, he had been influenced by experiences in Vietnam, where many marines believed that the army had misused them. The planning and execution of DESERT STORM gave Boomer and other Marine Corps commanders the chance to vindicate their views.

Initially, it did not appear that Boomer would get such an opportunity. Planning for the ground war, conducted in the summer and autumn of 1990, did not include the active use of the marines. The original plan developed by Central Command commander General H. Norman Schwarzkopf's staff called for an attack from western Saudi Arabia in which the I MEF would only breach the forward Iraqi defenses for the army's armored forces to exploit. When Boomer was finally invited to a planning meeting in early November 1990, he vigorously objected to the plan, arguing that the marines should not be used as a mere appendage to the army but instead that they should operate separately, although in support of army operations, and do their own planning. He wanted the marines deployed along the coast on the right flank, where their logistical base was tied to the navy. After a contentious debate, Schwarzkopf finally agreed.

Between November 1990 and the beginning of DESERT STORM in January 1991, Boomer and his I MEF staff formulated a plan that emphasized keeping the Iraqis off balance by attacking their command and control systems rather than trying to overwhelm them with superior numbers of tanks and artillery. Boomer believed that the Iraqi statistical superiority in tanks and men in southern Kuwait was deceptive and that the Iraqi force they faced was a hollow army. His assumptions proved correct, and the marines were able to concentrate their forces south of the Wafra oil fields where the Iraqis, with their command and control centers destroyed and their intelligence apparatus blinded by concentrated air and artillery strikes, did not expect them. As a result, the marines were able to overrun most of Kuwait and capture Kuwait City within two days of the start of the ground offensive on February 24, 1991.

Boomer's success and the marines' performance in the Persian Gulf War earned him considerable media attention and praise from the U.S. media as well as from General Schwarzkopf. Upon his return from the Gulf, Boomer was appointed assistant commandant of the U.S. Marine Corps. He served in that position until his retirement in 1994. In retirement, Boomer has been surprisingly critical of the quality of American intelligence prior to the Persian Gulf War and of the failure to move faster to cut off Iraqi forces remaining in Kuwait.

WALTER F. BELL

See also

Bush, George Herbert Walker; DESERT STORM, Operation; DESERT STORM, Operation, Ground Operations; Iraq, Army; Schwarzkopf, H. Norman, Jr.; United States Marine Corps, Persian Gulf War

References

Atkinson, Rick. *Crusade: The Untold Story of the Persian Gulf War.* New York: Mariner Books, 1994.

Boomer, Walter. "Ten Years After." *U.S. Naval Institute Proceedings* 127(1) (January 2001): 61–65.

Warren, James A. *American Spartans: The U.S. Marines; A Combat History from Iwo Jima to Iraq.* New York: Simon and Schuster, 2005.

Bosnia-Herzegovina, Role in Afghanistan and Iraq Wars

Confederation located in the Balkans in southeastern Europe. With a land area of 19,741 square miles, Bosnia-Herzegovina had a 2008 population of 4.59 million people. It is bordered by Croatia to the north, west, and south; Serbia to the east; and Montenegro to the south. Formerly one of six governmental units of the Socialist Federal Republic of Yugoslavia, the multiethnic confederation, comprised chiefly of Bosnians, Serbs, and Croats, is politically decentralized and is a federal parliamentary-style democratic republic with an economy that has been rapidly transforming itself into a free-market system. The presidency of the federation rotates among three popularly elected presidents (one representing each of the three major ethnic groups). Each person serves as president/chair for eight-month-long terms.

Bosnia-Herzegovina joined a number of other Central and East European countries in dispatching a small symbolic force as part of the U.S.-led coalition in Iraq after the 2003 invasion. Because of the role played by the United States in ending the nation's civil war and in ensuring Bosnian independence, relations between Sarajevo and Washington remained strong throughout the 1990s and 2000s. What is more, counterterrorism cooperation increased significantly in the aftermath of the September 11, 2001, terrorist attacks on the United States. As the United States prepared for the war with Iraq during the winter of 2002–2003, the George W. Bush administration particularly sought Muslim countries to serve as coalition partners. This was part of an effort to prevent the perception that the invasion was an anti-Muslim crusade.

Although Bosnia-Herzegovina remained a staunch ally of the United States, participation in the U.S.-led anti–Saddam Hussein coalition was unpopular among the populace. Negotiations between the two governments continued through 2003 and 2004 over a potential deployment before an agreement was finally reached in 2005. Bosnia-Herzegovina deployed a small contingent of troops in June 2005. The initial deployment involved 36 engineers who specialized in de-mining operations. The force was stationed outside Fallujah and undertook ordnance disposal operations in the area. The Bosnians were part of the Polish-led Multi-National Force. The Bosnians served six-month rotations and received training by U.S. personnel in Bosnia prior to their deployment. Significantly, the deployments included troops from both the Bosnian- and Croat-dominated Federation Army and the Serb-dominated Republic of Srpska Army. The deployment was the first joint operation outside of Bosnia-Herzegovina between the two forces. The joint mission was regarded as an important step in the government's effort to demonstrate to the European Union (EU) and other Western powers that progress was being achieved in ethnic reconciliation.

The example of Bosnia-Herzegovina was cited by scholars and policy makers as a potential model to resolve sectarian violence in Iraq at the height of the insurgency. Several proposals were developed that called for the division of Iraq, like Bosnia, into a federal system along ethnic lines, with a shared presidency. These included a nonbinding resolution by the U.S. Senate in 2007 to divide Iraq into three semiautonomous provinces, one for the Kurds, one for the Sunnis, and one for the Shiites. The Bush administration rejected the idea out of hand.

Bosnia-Herzegovina deployed 50 additional troops from its 6th Infantry Division in August 2008 under the command of a major. The new deployment was stationed at Camp Victory in Baghdad and provided base security and support operations for coalition forces stationed at the facility. The Bosnians were attached to U.S. forces. Between the two deployments, 290 Bosnian soldiers served tours in Iraq.

As other countries began to draw down their forces in Iraq, the Bosnian government announced that it would end its deployment in December 2008. Following the withdrawal of Bosnian forces from Iraq, the Bosnian government announced that it would deploy some 100 soldiers to Afghanistan as part of the mission led by the North Atlantic Treaty Organization (NATO) in 2009. Meanwhile, Bosnia-Herzegovina also began negotiations with NATO over eventual membership in that alliance.

TOM LANSFORD

See also

Afghanistan, Coalition Combat Operations in, 2002–Present; IRAQI FREEDOM, Operation, Coalition Ground Forces; Multi-National Force–Iraq; North Atlantic Treaty Organization in Afghanistan

References

Allawi, Ali A. *The Occupation of Iraq: Winning the War, Losing the Peace.* New Haven, CT: Yale University Press, 2007.

Cockburn, Patrick. *The Occupation: War and Resistance in Iraq.* New York: Verso, 2007.

Boutros-Ghali, Boutros
Birth Date: November 14, 1922

Egyptian diplomat and the sixth secretary-general of the United Nations (UN) during 1992–1997. The UN's first Arab leader, Boutros Boutros-Ghali was born on November 14, 1922, in Cairo to a well-regarded Coptic Christian family. One of his ancestors, Boutros-Ghali, had served as Egypt's prime minister. Boutros Boutros-Ghali was educated at Cairo University and received a degree in law in 1946. He also holds degrees in political science, economics, and public law from the University of Paris. In 1949 he earned his doctorate in international law, also from the University of Paris. He also holds a diploma in international relations from the Institute d'Études Politiques de Paris.

From 1949 to 1977 Boutros-Ghali was a professor of international law and international relations at Cairo University. During that time he was a Fulbright research scholar at Columbia University in New York (1954–1955), director of the Center of Research of The Hague Academy of International Law (1963–1964), and visiting professor of law at Sorbonne University (1967–1968). In 1977 he was appointed Egypt's minister of state for foreign affairs and served in that post until 1991. That same year, he became deputy prime minister for foreign affairs under President Hosni Mubarak.

Boutros-Ghali attended the historic September 1978 Camp David Summit Conference along with Egyptian president Anwar Sadat. During the negotiations Boutros-Ghali played a not insignificant role, and by 1979 Israel and Egypt had signed a peace accord. As a Christian in an overwhelmingly Muslim nation, Boutros-Ghali brought a unique vision to his role in Egyptian foreign policy. Nevertheless, he was a strong and loyal supporter of Egyptian sovereignty and frequently decried the heavy-handed approach to foreign affairs that Western nations, particularly the United States, often practiced. He was active in the Non-Aligned Movement as well as the Organization of African Unity (OAU).

In addition to his role in the Israeli-Egyptian peace process, Boutros-Ghali helped win the release in 1990 of South African anti-Apartheid leader Nelson Mandela from many years in jail as a political prisoner. That momentous occasion ultimately brought about the demise of South Africa's Apartheid regime. Boutros-Ghali is an expert on development in the Third World and believes that water conservation is a key to African and Middle Eastern political stability. He became the sixth secretary-general of the UN on January 1, 1992, commencing a five-year term.

Boutros-Ghali assumed his UN post at a time of tremendous crisis within the organization. It was also a period of considerable international tension, particularly in the Middle East. Enormous budgetary difficulties and greatly increased demands on the UN to increase international peacekeeping efforts combined with growing expectations and harsh criticism to create a nearly impossible leadership situation. When Boutros-Ghali became secretary-general, the UN had become highly in demand to help deal with myriad crises. These included extensive African drought

Boutros Boutros-Ghali of Egypt was secretary-general of the United Nations (UN) during 1992–1997. (Corel)

and starvation, global warming and pollution, Serbian ethnic-cleansing campaigns in Bosnia and Herzegovina, human rights abuses, terrorism and militant Islamic fundamentalism, violations of the Nuclear Non-Proliferation Treaty, various civil wars, and peace negotiations in Cambodia, Afghanistan, and Somalia.

During his term in office, Boutros-Ghali witnessed a potentially momentous peace-making effort between Israel and the Palestinians in the 1993 Oslo Accords. As a result, the Palestinian National Authority (PNA) was created, and Israel and the Palestinians formally recognized each other for the first time. In 1994 Israel and Jordan concluded a peace treaty. The 1995 assassination of Israeli prime minister Yitzhak Rabin seemingly derailed Arab-Israeli peace-making efforts, however.

Another Middle East conundrum haunted Boutros-Ghali's term as secretary-general: the aftermath of the 1991 Persian Gulf War. When that conflict ended in 1991, the UN came under considerable pressure—particularly by the Americans—to enforce the disarmament of Iraq by means of economic pressure and by UN-sponsored weapons inspections. Several times during Boutros-Ghali's tenure, the United States launched unilateral air attacks against Iraqi weapons and air facilities in retaliation for alleged violations of the terms of the cease-fire. By 1996, the United States had all but accused the UN's chief of abdicating his responsibility to monitor and enforce sanctions and inspections of Iraq.

Boutros-Ghali's time at the helm of the UN was not an altogether happy one. The United States made him out to be a controversial figure, and his perceived failures only added to his burden. Indeed, he came under fire for the UN's inability to deal with Rwanda's murderous genocide in 1994 and his inability to rally support for UN involvement in the ongoing Angolan Civil War. Meanwhile, the deepening enmity between American leaders and Boutros-Ghali left him open to criticism that he had allowed too much U.S. influence in the UN and that the very role of the UN had now been clouded in the post–Cold War world.

In 1996 Boutros-Ghali sought a second term in office. While 10 UN Security Council nations (including Egypt) backed his continuation as secretary-general, the United States adamantly objected. He eventually capitulated to U.S. pressure to step down but not before engineering a replacement from Africa, Ghana's Kofi Annan. When Boutros-Ghali stepped down in 1996, he became the first secretary-general not to be reelected. In 1997 he became secretary-general of La Francophonie, an organization of French-speaking nations. He remained there until 2002. Since that tune, he has served as the president of the Curatorium Administrative Council at The Hague Academy of International Law.

PAUL G. PIERPAOLI JR.

See also

Camp David Accords; Egypt; Iraq, History of, 1990–Present; Mubarak, Hosni; Oslo Accords; Rabin, Yitzhak; United Nations; United Nations Weapons Inspectors

References

Benton, Barbara, ed. *Soldiers for Peace: Fifty Years of United Nations Peacekeeping.* New York: Facts on File, 1996.

Boutros-Ghali, Boutros. *Egypt's Road to Jerusalem: A Diplomat's Story of the Struggle for Peace in the Middle East.* New York: Random House, 1997.

———. *Unvanquished: A U.S.-U.N. Saga.* New York: Random House, 1999.

Bradley Fighting Vehicle

Lightly armored tracked infantry and cavalry fighting vehicle. In 1975 the U.S. Army requested proposals for an armored mechanized vehicle to carry infantry on the battlefield for combined arms operations with the new M-1 Abrams tank. The new vehicle would gradually replace the M-113 armored personnel carrier, which the army did not believe could keep up with the new tank.

The Food Machinery Corporation, later United Defense and then BAE Systems, produced the XM-723 prototype in 1975, which differed slightly from the actual production models. It was an armored tracked vehicle with a 20-millimeter (mm) gun and a 7.62-mm machine gun in a turret. It had a crew of three and could carry eight infantrymen. A tracked vehicle with six road wheels, the original

Bradley was 21.5 feet long, 11.75 feet wide, and 8 feet 5 inches tall. Its 22.58 tons were moved by a 500-horsepower Cummins V-8 diesel, and it had a top speed of 41 miles per hour with a range of 300 miles. It was capable of crossing water at a speed of 4 miles per hour. Aluminum and spaced-laminated armor protected the hull.

The Bradley program evolved into the development of two vehicles, which in 1981 were named Bradley Fighting Vehicles and are produced by BAE Systems Land and Armaments. The M-2 is the infantry fighting vehicle, while the M-3 is designated as a cavalry fighting vehicle. The M-2 Bradley carries a crew of three—commander, driver, and gunner—as well as six infantrymen. The M-3 transports two cavalry scouts and additional radios and ammunition. Crew size remained unchanged at three. The interiors of the two models differed, and the only exterior difference were gun ports to allow the infantry to fire shoulder weapons from inside the M2.

Some Bradley production models began an upgrade to the M-2 and M-3 A2 models, which had engines capable of producing 600 horsepower and a stronger drive wheel allowing a top speed of 45 miles per hour. Internal armor and improved ammunition storage were also added in production.

Both models differed from the XM-723, as their upgraded turrets mounted a 25-mm Bushmaster chain gun and a 7.62-mm machine gun. The main gun automatically fired armor-piercing or high-explosive rounds as selected by the gunner, who could also select single or multiple shots for each fire mission. The bushmaster has a range of 1.2 miles. The vehicle could attack heavy armor with TOW (tube-launched, optically tracked, wire-guided) missile rounds, although it could not do so on the move but rather only after stopping for more than a minute and activating a collapsible launcher. Developers believed that the range of the TOW, 2.25 miles, and its ability to destroy any current armored vehicle with a missile that approached the speed of sound outweighed this drawback. The M-2 and M-3 also had smoke grenade launchers for concealment as well as the ability to generate their own smokescreen on the move. These models have a length of 21 feet 2 inches, a width of 10.5 feet, a height of 9.75 feet, and a weight of 25–33 tons, depending on the weight of additional armor for the A2 models.

The reduction in the number of infantrymen to six in the M-2 was controversial because of the impact on the force structure, but solid performance in the 1991 Persian Gulf War proved the viability of the reduced squad number. The U.S. Army's first order for the Bradley was in 1979 when 100 were to be produced, with subsequent orders for 600 yearly. By 1995, 6,375 vehicles had been delivered to the army, with 400 more produced for Saudi Arabia. About 2,200 Bradleys deployed for the 1991 Persian Gulf War, of which 1,619 were in maneuver units, with the rest at division level, in theater reserve, or declared excess.

Before the Persian Gulf War, work had already begun on upgrading the Bradleys, first to the A2 and then the A3 models. The A2 Bradleys had additional armor, which increased the weight

A Bradley fighting vehicle provides security as soldiers of the U.S. Army's 3rd Infantry Division conduct a joint clearing operation with local Abna'a Al Iraq (Sons of Iraq) through a group of small villages south of Salman Pak, Iraq, February 16, 2008. (U.S. Department of Defense)

to 30 tons and then an additional 3 tons with add-on tile armor. A 600-horsepower engine compensated for the additional weight.

Because of the threat of Iraqi tanks, the army rushed 692 A2s to the theater during Operation DESERT SHIELD in 1990, and by the time DESERT STORM began in early 1991, about half of the Bradleys involved were A2s. The Bradleys performed well during DESERT STORM. They had a reliability of 90 percent during the land war in spite of the fact that they traveled from 60 to 180 miles during the 100-hour land war. Twenty were destroyed, all but 3 from friendly fire, and only 12 were damaged, 4 of which were repaired quickly. The Bradleys kept pace with the Abrams tanks and accounted for more destroyed enemy armored vehicles than did the Abrams.

The conflict did reveal problems with the Bradleys, however. These led to further refinements, leading to the A3 model. Improvements included a position navigation system with GPS receiver. Coupled with sophisticated digital electronics and communications, the Bradley is now able to function in real time as an integral part of the combined arms team of tanks, attack helicopters, and other weapons systems. Better sights and a laser-range finder along with other digital upgrades allow for enhanced command and control as well as more lethal and reliable fire control. Upgrades to the identification of friend and foe (IFF) systems reduce the problem of friendly fire. Some crew functions were

automated, and the vehicle's speed in reverse increased to match that of the tanks. The vehicle armor was also improved, with the requirement to resist rounds up to 30-mm and the introduction of reactive armor. The TOW missile system was changed to add a hydraulic lift for the launchers, and the range finder allowed the system to fire on the move. The wear and tear of operating in a desert environment also required changes to various components to reduce damage from sand and dust.

These changes have since been tested in Operation IRAQI FREEDOM, launched in March 2003 to topple the rule of Saddam Hussein.

The Bradleys were an integral part of the mechanized infantry brigades in both the infantry and armored divisions deployed. The 100-hour ground war of DESERT STORM gave credence to the projection of a short conflict once the Iraqi capital was taken. That did not happen, however, and the conflict continues, thanks to a strong insurgency that began in earnest in 2004. Bradleys continued to be deployed, with units rotating to and from Iraq for 12- to 15-month deployments. By April 2006, some 50 Bradleys had been lost in combat, along with 20 Abrams tanks, 20 Stryker wheeled combat vehicles (deployed with some mechanized infantry units), and 20 M-113s, which continued to play a role in the conflict. The Bradleys performed well, but this conflict yielded many lessons learned, which will figure in further development of U.S. military forces.

Among these lessons is the impact of sustained combat on both men and matériel. Armored vehicles in the combat area operate at a tempo up to six times that in peacetime, with Abrams tanks driving 5,000 miles per year as opposed to 800 in peacetime. In spite of this, the army maintained an equipment readiness rate of 90 percent three years into the war in Iraq. Operation DESERT STORM validated the effectiveness of U.S. forces against a well-armed enemy in conventional unit-on-unit engagements. The conflict has also allowed evaluation of the tracked Bradley compared to the wheeled Stryker armored infantry vehicle in terrain that varies from desert sand to mountains and includes operations in large cities. More important will be the lessons learned from fighting militant insurgents who operate in a hit-and-run manner that includes use of improvised explosives capable of destroying armored vehicles.

As with the M-113 armored fighting vehicle, which is still in the inventory, the Bradley has been used as a platform for many functions. These include an air defense vehicle with Stinger rockets, an electronic fighting vehicle system, a fire-support team vehicle, an ambulance, and a platform for the stingray countermeasure system that detects enemy fire-control systems and destroys them with a laser transmitter. The multiple rocket launch system (MLRS) is based on the Bradley chassis.

DANIEL E. SPECTOR

See also

Infantry Fighting Vehicles, Iraqi; M1A1 and M1A2 Abrams Main Battle Tanks

References

Cordesman, Anthony H., and Abraham R. Wagner. *The Lessons of Modern War,* Vol. 4, *The Gulf War.* Boulder, CO: Westview, 1996.

Hogg, Ian V. *The Greenhill Armoured Fighting Vehicles Data Book.* London: Greenhill Books, 2002.

Scales, Robert H. *United States Army in the Gulf War: Certain Victory.* Washington, DC: U.S. Army, 1993.

Thompson, Loren B., Lawrence J. Korb, and Caroline P. Wadhams. *Army Equipment after Iraq.* Arlington, VA: Lexington Institute, Center for American Progress, 2006.

Bremer, Jerry
Birth Date: September 30, 1941

U.S. diplomat, career U.S. State Department official, and administrator of the Coalition Provisional Authority in Iraq (2003–2004). Lewis Paul "Jerry" Bremer was born in Hartford, Connecticut, on September 30, 1941. He received a BA from Yale University in 1963 and an MBA from Harvard University in 1966. Later that same year, he joined the Foreign Service and began his lengthy career as a diplomat.

Bremer's tenure with the State Department featured posts as an assistant to National Security Advisor and then Secretary of State Henry Kissinger (1972–1976), ambassador to the Netherlands

(1983), and ambassador-at-large for counterterrorism (1986). In 1981 Secretary of State Alexander Haig named Bremer executive secretary of the State Department, where he directed the country's round-the-clock crisis management and emergency response center.

In 2002 in the aftermath of the September 11, 2001, terrorist attacks, Bremer was appointed to the Homeland Security Advisory Council. Considered an expert on terrorism, Bremer spent much of his career advocating a stronger U.S. position against states that sponsor or harbor terrorists.

After Iraqi forces had been defeated in the March–May 2003 war, on May 6, 2003, President George W. Bush named Bremer U.S. presidential envoy in Iraq. In this role, Bremer became the top executive authority in Iraq as the administrator of the Coalition Provisional Authority. He was tasked with overseeing the beginning of the transition from the U.S.-led military coalition governing Iraq to Iraqi self-governance. Bremer was brought in to replace retired U.S. Army general Jay Garner, who had been put in

American Lewis Paul Bremer was director of reconstruction and humanitarian assistance in postwar Iraq (2003–2004). Among his controversial decisions accepted by the Bush administration was disbanding the Iraqi Army. (U.S. Department of Defense)

place only two weeks earlier. Bremer's job, which began just five days after Bush declared that major combat operations were completed, was to serve as the top civilian leader of Iraq until such time that the nation was stable enough to govern itself.

Garner's leadership has been generally praised but was not without its problems. Under Garner's watch, looting of commercial and government buildings had been rampant, including the alleged theft of priceless archaeological treasures from Iraqi museums. Iraqi citizens also faced growing problems with failing infrastructure and burgeoning street violence.

Bremer's first move was to increase the number and visibility of U.S. military police in Baghdad while making the reconstruction of the Iraqi police force a high priority. Bremer also pushed to speed up the rebuilding of Iraq's infrastructure and to make certain that government workers were being paid. Despite his efforts, however, violence—both sectarian and by insurgents—continued to mount, and Iraqis were becoming increasingly frustrated with the U.S.-led coalition. Bremer was also forced to postpone establishing an Iraqi-led transitional government.

Bremer is given credit for making some critically important decisions in his role as envoy. Among these were the removal of all restrictions against freedom of assembly, the suspension of the death penalty, and the establishment of a central criminal court. However, many were critical of some of Bremer's decisions, particularly his decision to disband the Iraqi Army and to remove members of Saddam Hussein's Baath Party from critical government positions. Bremer responds to his critics that there was, in truth, no Iraqi Army left for him to dissolve, as that task had already been accomplished by the war. He also claims that his Baath Party purge was directed at only the top 3 percent of the party leadership. During his tenure, Bremer was also the target of numerous failed assassination attempts. At one point, Al Qaeda leader Osama bin Laden placed a bounty of 10,000 grams of gold on the ambassador's head.

Despite the violence and the assassination attempts, Bremer was able to achieve many of his goals. On July 13, 2003, the Iraqi Interim Governing Council, chosen from prominent Iraqis, was approved. On March 8, 2004, the interim constitution was signed after being approved by the governing council. Then, on June 28, 2004, the U.S.-led coalition formally transferred limited sovereignty to the interim government. In a move that surprised many, Bremer left Iraq the same day. After his departure, U.S. ambassador to Iraq John Negroponte became the highest-ranking U.S. civilian in Iraq.

After leaving Iraq, Bremer embarked on several speaking tours and coauthored a book, *My Year in Iraq,* published in 2006. He is currently serving as chairman of the advisory board for GlobalSecure Corporation, a firm that deals with homeland security issues.

KEITH MURPHY

See also

Baath Party; Bin Laden, Osama; Garner, Jay Montgomery; IRAQI FREEDOM, Operation; Iraqi Insurgency; Terrorism

References

Bremer, L. Paul, ed. *Countering the Changing Threat of International Terrorism: Report from the National Commission on Terrorism.* Darby, PA: Diane Publishing, 2000.

Bremer, L. Paul, with Malcolm McConnell. *My Year in Iraq: The Struggle to Build a Future of Hope.* New York: Simon and Schuster, 2006.

Ricks, Thomas E. *Fiasco: The American Military Adventure in Iraq.* New York: Penguin, 2006.

Scheuer, Michael. *Imperial Hubris: Why the West Is Losing the War on Terror.* Washington, DC: Potomac Books, 2004.

Brims, Robin
Birth Date: June 27, 1951

British Army general. Born on June 27, 1951, Robin Brims was educated at Winchester College and the Royal Military Academy, Sandhurst, before receiving a short-service commission as a second lieutenant in the Light Infantry on October 31, 1970. His short-service commission was converted to a regular commission on June 27, 1972. While a junior officer, Brims served tours in England, West Germany, and Northern Ireland before attending the Staff College at Camberley. He was subsequently promoted to major and appointed chief of staff to the 8th Infantry Brigade in December 1983, a position he held until January 1986.

From January 1986 until December 1987, Brims commanded a company in the Light Infantry, after which he was promoted to lieutenant colonel. In December 1987 he was appointed military assistant to the military secretary, and during January 1989 to December 1991 he commanded the 3rd Battalion, Light Infantry. Brims was then promoted to full colonel and served in staff positions in the Ministry of Defence until December 11, 1994.

On December 12, 1994, Brims was promoted to brigadier and appointed brigade commander of the 24th Airmobile Brigade based in Colchester, a position he held until November 1996. With this command, he deployed to Bosnia as part of the United Nation (UN) Rapid Reaction Force in 1995. On November 18, 1996, he was appointed chief of staff, Headquarters Northern Ireland, where he remained until January 11, 1999, at which time he became director of Army Plans and Resources. On January 12, 2000, he was promoted to major general and appointed to command the North Atlantic Treaty Organization (NATO) Multi-National Division (South West) in Bosnia.

On November 11, 2000, Brims was appointed general officer in command of the 1st Armoured Division, a post he held until June 12, 2003. It was in this position that he was deployed to the Iraq War as part of Operation TELIC, the British component of Operation IRAQI FREEDOM. On the eve of the Iraq War, the 1st Armoured Division numbered some 20,000 men and women and represented a larger British contribution to the war effort than had been the case in the 1991 Persian Gulf War, accounting for almost one-third of the deployed allied land power. The division was composed of the 7th Armoured Brigade (the famed "Desert Rats"), the 16th Air Assault Brigade, and the 3rd Commando Brigade Royal Marines.

Brims's task in the Iraq War was to take and hold Basra, Iraq's second-largest city located in the southern part of the country, and to protect the oil fields and oil installations on the Faw (Fao) peninsula, which had been set on fire by Saddam Hussein's forces during the 1991 war. Beyond these general instructions, General Tommy Franks, the American commander of United States Central Command (CENTCOM), left the actual plan of battle to Brims's discretion.

Brims decided to have the 3rd Commando Brigade seize the Faw (Fao) peninsula and secure the oil fields while the 7th Armoured Brigade and 16th Air Assault Brigade lay siege to Basra, where they were later to be joined by the 3rd Commando Brigade. Despite making landfall in Iraq on the evening of March 20, 2003, Brims decided to be patient in the assault on Basra, inserting teams of Special Air Service (SAS) and Special Boat Service (SBS) snipers and reconnaissance squadrons into the city to gather intelligence but otherwise forming an impenetrable ring around the city without further advance.

On March 31 Brims ordered larger units to begin moving on the city, and on April 6 he ordered the main assault to begin. By that evening, the city was largely under British control. On April 7 members of the 16th Air Assault Brigade began to patrol the old portion of the city. The following day, Brims ordered his division to switch from combat operations to occupation mode. The Battle for Basra was over, but the battle for the hearts and minds of Iraq's Shia population was only just beginning.

On June 12, 2003, Brims was appointed deputy chief of operations at Permanent Joint Headquarters, Northwood, and left Iraq. Less than a month later, on July 11, 2003, the 1st Armoured Division handed over operations to the 3rd Mechanized Division, and it too departed Iraq. For his service in the Iraq War, Brims was awarded the Distinguished Service Order on October 31, 2003. He remained deputy chief of operations until March 2005, at which time he was promoted to lieutenant general and made commander of the Field Army. In this position, from April to October 2005, Brims again deployed to Iraq as the senior British military representative in Iraq and deputy commanding general of Multi-National Forces–Iraq. He held the post of commander of the Field Army until August 2007, at which time he retired from the army. Since then, Brims has served as the rector of Kurdistan University Hawler in the autonomous Kurdistani region of Iraq.

BENJAMIN GROB-FITZGIBBON

See also

Basra, Battle for; IRAQI FREEDOM, Operation; Multi-National Force–Iraq; United Kingdom, Army, Iraq War

References

The Army List, 2003. London: Her Majesty's Stationary Office, 2003.

Keegan, John. The Iraq War: The Military Offensive, from Victory in 21 Days to the Insurgent Aftermath. New York: Vintage, 2005.

Murray, Williamson, and Robert H. Scales Jr. The Iraq War: A Military History. Cambridge, MA: Belknap, 2005.

Brown, James Gordon
Birth Date: February 20, 1951

British Labour Party politician and chancellor of the exchequer (1997–2007) who succeeded Tony Blair as prime minister on June 27, 2007. James Gordon Brown was born on February 20, 1951, in Glasgow, Scotland, but grew up in Kirkcaldy. His father was a minister in the Church of Scotland. The younger Brown attended an accelerated program at Kirkcaldy High School and entered the University of Edinburgh at the age of 16. He studied history, eventually earning a doctorate in 1982. While a student, Brown served as rector and chair of the University Court. He briefly worked as a lecturer at Edinburgh and then taught politics at Glasgow College of Technology. Brown subsequently worked as a journalist and editor for Scottish Television during 1980–1983.

Brown first ran for Parliament in 1979 but lost to Michael Ancram. In 1983 Brown ran again and was elected to represent Dunfermline East (boundary changes later renamed this constituency Kirkcaldy and Cowdenbeath). He was also named chair of the Labour Party's Scottish Council. In the House of Commons, Brown shared an office with fellow Labourite Tony Blair, who was elected that year to represent Sedgefield. The two young, energetic politicians became fast friends, and their careers would be closely linked during their rise through government. Considered two leading modernizers, Brown and Blair set out to change the Labour Party. In 1987 Brown became the Labour Party's shadow chief secretary to the treasury, then controlled by the Conservative Party government. He served in that position until 1989, when he became shadow trade and industry secretary. He remained there until becoming opposition spokesperson on treasury and economic affairs (shadow chancellor) in 1992.

Brown reportedly wanted to run for the position of Labour Party leader in 1994, but he stood aside for Blair, who was elected that November. In 1997 the two achieved their goal of placing the Labour Party back in control after 18 years in the opposition. Rumors have since suggested that a deal between the two put Brown in charge of economic policy while Blair assumed the premiership, although that has never been confirmed. In May 1997 Brown was appointed chancellor of the exchequer, the equivalent of the U.S. treasury secretary. As chancellor, Brown presided over a long period of economic growth. He made the Bank of England independent and froze spending for two years. He controversially established five economic criteria that had to be met before allowing the public vote on joining the European Monetary Union. His methods were often called ruthless, but no one could argue with his record of high employment and low inflation.

By 2007, Brown was the longest-serving chancellor of the exchequer in modern British history. As Blair's popularity

British prime minister James Gordon Brown. (AP/Wide World Photos)

declined because of his support of the U.S.-led Iraq War, Brown appeared poised to assume the premiership. Indeed, Brown was the leading contender when Blair announced in May 2007 that he would step down on June 27. Brown formally announced his bid for leadership of the Labour Party on May 11, facing no opposition. He became prime minister on June 27 with the approval of Queen Elizabeth II.

Observers noted that Brown would not be a radical departure from Blair and the New Labour movement. However, he began to transfer several prime ministerial powers to Parliament and even some parliamentary powers to the general public. In the early days of his leadership, he faced an attempted terrorist attack on the airport in Glasgow and was praised for his handling of the incident. Although Brown pledged to address such issues as health care and housing during his leadership, he said that terrorism and the war in Iraq would remain at the forefront.

Although it was widely perceived that Brown was less enthusiastic about the Iraq War than Blair, Brown publicly remained staunchly loyal to the George W. Bush administration and the conflict in Iraq. At the same time, the prime minister has begun to draw down troops in Iraq, and he has more recently stated that he is becoming increasingly concerned about the Afghanistan War. The close relationship between London and Washington was reiterated in the very early days of the Barack Obama administration, especially by Secretary of State Hillary Clinton. Beginning in the last quarter of 2008, the Brown government became enveloped in the financial meltdown that began on Wall Street, and by early 2009 the British economy was mired in deep recession.

MELISSA STALLINGS

See also
Blair, Tony; United Kingdom; United Kingdom, Middle East Policy

References
Beckett, Francis. *Gordon Brown: Past, Present and Future*. London: Haus, 2007.

Bower, Tom. *Gordon Brown*. New York: Harper Perennial, 2005.

Routledge, Paul. *Gordon Brown: The Biography*. New York: Simon and Schuster, 1998.

Serfaty, Simon. *Architects of Delusion: Europe, America, and the Iraq War*. Philadelphia: University of Pennsylvania Press, 2008.

Brown, Monica Lin
Birth Date: May 24, 1988

U.S. Army soldier who was awarded the Silver Star. Monica Lin Brown was born in Lake Jackson, Texas, on May 24, 1988. Joining the army, she was trained as a medic and assigned to the 4th Squadron, 73rd Cavalry Regiment, 4th Brigade Combat Team, in Afghanistan. On April 25, 2007, Specialist Brown was in a convoy of four Humvees in eastern Paktia Province when insurgents set off a roadside bomb, hitting one of the Humvees and wounding five of its occupants. Brown braved hostile small-arms fire and mortar rounds to run to the wounded and attend to them, shielding their bodies with her own. For her bravery under fire, Brown was awarded the Silver Star in March 2008, only the second American woman to be so recognized since World War II. Four army nurses were awarded the Silver Star in that conflict, and Sergeant Leigh Ann Hester received the Silver Star for bravery under fire during the Iraq War in 2005.

SPENCER C. TUCKER

See also
Hester, Leigh Ann

Reference
Abrashi, Fisnik. "Medic Stationed in Afghanistan Becomes 2nd Woman to be Awarded Silver Star." Associated Press, cbsnews.com, March 9, 2008.

Brzezinski, Zbigniew
Birth Date: March 28, 1928

International relations scholar, diplomat, and U.S. national security adviser to the James (Jimmy) Carter administration during 1977–1981. Born the son of a Polish diplomat in Warsaw, Poland, on March 28, 1928, Zbigniew Brzezinski received his PhD from Harvard University in 1953 and became a U.S. citizen in 1958. Following his graduation, he joined the faculty of Harvard and then moved on to Columbia University in 1960, where he stayed until 1977.

Brzezinski served as a foreign policy adviser to U.S. president John F. Kennedy and as a member of the State Department's influential policy planning staff during the Lyndon B. Johnson administration. In 1968 Brzezinski resigned his State Department post in protest over U.S. Vietnam War policies. He subsequently returned to academia and directed the Trilateral Commission from 1973 to 1976. After serving as foreign policy adviser to Jimmy Carter in his successful 1976 presidential campaign, Brzezinski was named Carter's national security adviser in 1977.

As national security adviser, Brzezinski played a critical role in the normalization of relations with the People's Republic of China (PRC) as well as in the 1978 Camp David Accords and the resultant 1979 peace treaty between Israel and Egypt. He was also instrumental in providing covert aid to the mujahideen fighters in Afghanistan after the Soviet Union invaded that country in 1979. Most significant perhaps to both Carter and Brzezinski was the 1978 Iranian Revolution and the resultant hostage crisis that began on November 4, 1979, and endured for 444 days, not ending until Ronald Reagan was sworn in as president on January 20, 1981, at which time the U.S. hostages were released. The crisis dominated the Carter administration in its last year and likely cost Carter his reelection bid. Brzezinski worked closely with the president to end the crisis, including the abortive hostage rescue mission in April 1980, but to no avail.

Following Carter's defeat in the 1980 election, Brzezinski returned to Columbia University. In 1989 he joined the faculty of Johns Hopkins University. He has written and edited numerous books on international relations and has served on the boards of myriad council and advisory committees. Considered something of a hard-liner while in office—especially vis-à-vis communism and the Soviet Union—in more recent years Brzezinski has been a critic of the George W. Bush administration's Global War on Terror and the 2003 invasion of Iraq, which Brzezinski claims was a monumental error.

BRENT M. GEARY

See also
Camp David Accords; Carter, James Earl, Jr.; EAGLE CLAW, Operation; Mujahideen, Soviet-Afghanistan War

References
Andrianopoulos, Gerry Argyris. *Kissinger and Brzezinski: The NSC and the Struggle for Control of US National Security Policy.* New York: St. Martin's, 1991.
Brzezinski, Zbigniew. *Power and Principle: Memoirs of the National Security Adviser, 1977–1981.* New York: Farrar, Straus and Giroux, 1985.

Professor of international affairs Dr. Zbigniew Brzezinski served as a foreign policy adviser to Democratic presidents John F. Kennedy, Lyndon B. Johnson, and Jimmy Carter. He was Carter's national security adviser during 1977–1981. (Jimmy Carter Presidential Library)

BTR Series Armored Personnel Carriers

The Soviet/Russian-designed BTR series of armored personnel carriers (APCs) are some of the most ubiquitous armored transports on battlefields across the globe. The series includes several wheeled transports and one tracked version, as "BTR" is simply a designation given for any general infantry carrier. The BTRs followed the standard doctrinal practice of the "battlefield taxi," in which a modestly armored transport would bring infantry to the fight where they would then engage in combat dismounted. As a consequence, most BTR vehicles were lightly armed, primarily for protection against small-arms and artillery fire. Typical Soviet practice in the Cold War–era (1945–1991) was to ship obsolescent vehicles to client states, and thus many of these became part of the inventories of a number of Middle Eastern countries. This practice would change after the collapse of the Soviet Union and the downsizing of the Russian military, for state-run factories would then seek customers for their unsold inventories of more-modern equipment.

The earliest of these vehicles, the BTR-40, was a four-wheeled reconnaissance car based on the American White M-3 Scout Car that the Soviets had received via the Lend-Lease program during World War II. Numerous BTR-40s were exported to Soviet client states in the Middle East during the 1950s and 1960s, and they served mostly in reconnaissance roles and occasional infantry transport duties. However, this vehicle suffered from poor performance due largely to the inherent problems of cross-country mobility for a wheeled vehicle with just two axles.

A better cross-country armored transport was built in the early 1950s around the ZIL-157 chassis and was designated the BTR-152. It was an open-topped, six-wheeled vehicle that offered better mobility for a full infantry squad. The BTR-152 was a low-cost option that allowed the Soviets to motorize a large number of their units. These were shipped in large quantities to such countries as Egypt, Syria, Libya, and Iraq, and they saw extensive combat in the 1967 Six-Day War and 1973 Yom Kippur (Ramadan) War.

The BTR-152s were used not only as basic infantry carriers, but also as self-propelled antiaircraft platforms and tractors for towed artillery and antitank guns. Nevertheless, even a six-wheeled chassis was deemed insufficient to reduce the ground pressure on the tires and produce superlative cross-country performance. As a consequence, the Soviets embarked on an eight-wheeled transport program, which the Russians have maintained to this day.

The initial requirement for a new cross-country wheeled infantry carrier was initiated in 1959, and the resulting first vehicle, the BTR-60P, was delivered to Soviet forces by the end of 1960. By 1976, more than 25,000 BTR-60s had been produced by Soviet state factories, with many being exported to client states.

Iraqi national guardsmen move a BTR-80A armored personnel carrier into position in Baghdad to provide security for the Iraqi Democratic National Conference during Operation IRAQI FREEDOM in 2004. (U.S. Department of Defense)

Armored Personnel Carrier Specifications

	Armament	Armor	Crew/ Passengers	Weight (tons)	Length	Width	Height	Engine	Speed (mph)	Range (miles)
BTR-50P armored personnel carrier	1 12.7-mm machine gun	14-mm maximum	2/14	13.97	22'4"	10'1"	6'6"	V-6 diesel; 240 horsepower at 1,800 rpm	27	160
BTR-60PB armored personnel carrier	1 14.5-mm KPVT machine gun	9-mm maximum	2/14	10.20	24'10"	9'3"	7'7"	2 GAZ-49B 6-cylinder gasoline; 90 horsepower each	50 (road); 6 (water)	310

Two primary models were produced—one with an open top and the other with an armored roof and a small turret armed with a 14.5-millimeter (mm) KPVT heavy machine gun. This version became the standard model, but both were shipped to Middle East nations in the 1960s and 1970s. Although the BTR-60 was an eight-wheeled vehicle that was fast and had some unique features, such as adjustable tire pressure and several firing ports for the troops within, it encountered significant performance problems, especially in a harsh desert environment.

The most critical problem involved the two 90-horsepower GAZ-49B engines used to drive the wheels on either side. It was extremely difficult to synchronize the two engines, and therefore many crews simply disengaged one of them, causing a subsequent loss in performance. This was a serious problem in loose terrain, such as some of the sandy areas of the Sinai peninsula, where Egyptian forces would operate in 1967 and 1973. Nevertheless, the BTR-60 was the infantry carrier of choice for many Middle Eastern countries that were cash-poor, as it was relatively inexpensive, easy to maintain, and easy for crews to operate. It continued to operate with Middle Eastern armies into the 1990s, and was still being used by Iraq as late as the 2003 Iraq War. Its deficient cross-country ability and thin armor made it an easy target for coalition ground and air forces during Operation DESERT STORM (1991) and the 2003 Iraq War. However, against more modestly armed opponents, it performed reasonably well.

The BTR-50 was the tracked equivalent of the BTR-60 and was based on the chassis of the PT-76 light tank. It was designed initially as a more expensive alternative for mechanized units, carrying infantry attached to Soviet tank forces. It still retained the battlefield taxi philosophy, and it was thus lightly armed with a 12.7-mm machine gun for self-defense. It was introduced in 1954, and like the BTR-60, it was exported in large numbers to Middle Eastern armies, forming the backbone of their mechanized units designed to escort tank forces into battle.

As a tracked vehicle, the BTR-50's cross-country performance was markedly superior to that of a wheeled vehicle, but this reduced its road speed compared to the BTR-60, and it was more complex to maintain and operate. The infantry exited the vehicle by climbing over the sides, and in later closed-topped versions this became difficult, as the men had to exit a series of large hatches. A similar version of this vehicle was built by Czechoslovakia and was known as the OT-62 Topaz. It too was exported to Middle Eastern nations.

The combat performance of these vehicles was unspectacular but sufficiently good to warrant continued use. They performed as designed, fulfilling their role as battlefield taxis. Many were destroyed in the host of wars in the Middle East in which they were used, including some lost during the coalition invasion of Iraq in 2003.

Unfortunately, there is little data as to the actual numbers lost in either the 1991 Persian Gulf War or Iraq War. However, of the 6,000 BTRs available to Iraq during the Persian Gulf War, probably about 1,000 were destroyed or abandoned. Upgraded versions of the BTR-60, such as the BTR-80 and 90, have seen limited export, with BTR-80s going to Turkey and BTR-90s specifically designed to meet the demands of the export markets of Middle East countries. However, they have seen little combat action.

RUSSELL G. RODGERS

See also

DESERT STORM, Operation; IRAQI FREEDOM, Operation

References

Bourque, Stephen A. *Jayhawk! The VII Corps in the Persian Gulf War.* Washington, DC: Department of the Army, 2002.

Fontenot, Gregory, et al. *On Point: The United States Army in Iraqi Freedom.* Annapolis, MD: Naval Institute Press, 2005.

Foss, Christopher. *Armoured Fighting Vehicles of the World.* London: Ian Allan, 1974.

———, ed. *Jane's Armour and Artillery, 2007–2008.* Coulsdon Surrey, UK: Jane's, 2007.

Gordon, Michael R., and General Bernard E. Trainor. *The Generals' War: The Inside Story of the Conflict in the Gulf.* New York: Little, Brown, 1995.

Hull, Andrew W., David R. Markov, and Steven J. Zaloga. *Soviet/Russian Armor and Artillery Design Practices: 1945 to Present.* Darlington, MD: Darlington Publications, 1999.

Zaloga, Steven. *Modern Soviet Armor: Combat Vehicles of the USSR and Warsaw Pact Today.* Englewood Cliffs, NJ: Prentice Hall, 1980.

Bulgaria, Role in Afghanistan and Iraq Wars

A Balkan country with a land mass of 42,822 square miles. Bulgaria is bordered by Romania to the north, Greece and Turkey to the south, Macedonia and Serbia to the west, and the Black Sea to the east. Its estimated 2008 population was 7.263 million people. Bulgaria was dominated by the Bulgarian Communist Party (BCP) from 1946 to 1990, when free elections were held with the collapse of communism. The BCP held a one-party monopoly in the country, which was closely allied with the Soviet Union as a member of the Warsaw Pact.

Since 1990 and the collapse of communism, Bulgaria has been a parliamentary democracy with a prime minister as head of government. Also since 1990, Bulgaria has taken aggressive steps to privatize its industries and move toward free-market capitalism. The transition has not been without sacrifices, however, including high unemployment and a period of civil unrest and hyperinflation during 1996 and 1997. Until 2001, Bulgarian politics were dominated by the Bulgarian Socialist Party (BSP) and the Union of Democratic Forces (UDF). In June 2001 Simeon Saxe-Coburg-Gotha (Simeon II), son of Czar Boris III, became prime minister, which temporarily overturned the dominance of the BSP and UDF. He was in office until August 2005, when Sergey Stanishev of the BSP formed a coalition government. Despite internal struggles, political instability, and widespread corruption, Bulgaria sought close ties with the West.

Although Bulgaria did not participate in the 1991 Persian Gulf War, it did contribute to Operation ENDURING FREEDOM. Three months after assuming office and following the September 11, 2001, terrorist attacks against the United States, the Bulgarian government supported the United States and its allies in invading Afghanistan and toppling the Taliban regime, which had given Osama bin Laden's Al Qaeda terrorist organization sanctuary. Bulgaria granted the United States and North Atlantic Treaty Organization (NATO) forces overflight, landing, and refueling privileges, and it allowed U.S. KC-135 Stratotanker refueling aircraft and hundreds of U.S. personnel to be stationed at its Sarafovo airbase. In February, 2002, Bulgaria sent a 40-member nuclear, biological, and chemical decontamination unit to Afghanistan. Four years later, it deployed 350 soldiers to assist in guarding the Kabul airport. The total Bulgarian troop contingent climbed to 460 by the end of 2008.

Bulgaria strongly supported the United States in the run-up to the Iraq War in 2003. It again offered the United States the use of its airspace and territory in support of possible military action against Iraq, for which it reportedly received $9 million. Then, despite overwhelming public opposition, in July 2003 Prime Minister Saxe-Coburg-Gotha dispatched what he called "a peacekeeping force" of a battalion of 480 men to help with the stabilization and reconstruction of Iraq. The men were responsible for general security and guarding the city center of Diwaniyah.

Saxe-Coburg-Gotha's decision to send troops to Iraq and his continued support over the years for the Iraq War was motivated principally by an expectation of securing political and economic advantage from the United States and its allies. The Bulgarian leader saw participation in the Iraq War as a means to facilitate admission into NATO and demonstrate that Bulgaria would be a reliable NATO partner. Admission into NATO was also seen as a prerequisite for membership in the European Union (EU). Finally, Bulgaria expected to be rewarded by Washington in recovering the $2 billion debt owed by Iraq, by participating in lucrative Iraqi reconstruction projects, and by having new U.S. military bases built in Bulgaria. Indeed, Bulgaria secured membership in NATO on April 2, 2004, and membership in the EU on January 1, 2007.

Between 2003 and 2005, Bulgaria rotated five infantry battalions, averaging about 500 soldiers each, in and out of Iraq. During the two-year span, the Bulgarians suffered 13 soldiers killed; dozens of others were injured.

After 5 Bulgarian soldiers and another 26 were wounded in an attack on December 27, 2003, Saxe-Coburg-Gotha faced intense opposition to withdraw the men from Iraq. Then Abu Musab al-Zarqawi's Iraqi-affiliated Al Qaeda group executed two Bulgarian truck drivers who had been abducted near Mosul on July 8, 2004. This prompted large antiwar protests in Bulgaria, particularly given that the prime minister's unwillingness to negotiate with the terrorists coincided with the release of a group of Filipino hostages after the Philippine government had agreed to withdraw its troops from Iraq.

With parliamentary elections scheduled for August 2005, the death of another Bulgarian soldier in March 2005, and the April 2005 shooting down near Baghdad of a Bulgarian-owned civilian helicopter by insurgents, which resulted in the death of its three Bulgarian crewmembers, the National Assembly voted to withdraw all its troops from Iraq by the end of 2005. In August, the opposition BSP won a plurality of votes and formed a coalition government, headed by Prime Minister Sergei Stanishev.

As promised, by the end of 2005, Bulgaria's battalion departed Iraq, handing over control to an Iraqi unit it had trained. However, Defense Minister Veselin Bliznakov announced on December 11, 2005, that Bulgaria would deploy 155 "noncombat troops" for what he called a "peacekeeping and humanitarian mission." Beginning in March 2006, these men were first tasked with guarding the Ashraf refugee camp near the Iranian border. Following the closure of the camp in June of 2008, the troops were transferred to Camp Cropper near Baghdad International Airport, where they guarded detainees undergoing a social reintegration program.

On May 26, 2006, the Bulgarian National Assembly ratified an agreement authorizing the United States to use two Bulgarian airbases and an army training center for the next 10 years. On November 13, 2008, Prime Minister Stanishev announced that Bulgaria's 155 soldiers would leave Iraq, and on December 17, 2008, these troops returned home. In all, Bulgaria contributed 11 different contingents of troops and a total of 3,231 soldiers to the U.S.-led forces in Iraq. Bulgarian forces suffered in all 13 dead. Bulgaria also has troops in international military missions in Afghanistan, Kosovo, and Bosnia.

STEFAN M. BROOKS

See also

ENDURING FREEDOM, Operation; IRAQI FREEDOM, Operation; North Atlantic Treaty Organization

References

Fawn, Rick, and Raymond A. Hinnebusch, eds. *The Iraq War: Causes and Consequence.* Boulder, CO: Lynne Rienner, 2006.

Murray, Williamson, and Robert H. Scales Jr. *The Iraq War: A Military History.* Cambridge, MA: Belknap, 2005.

Bull, Gerald Vincent
Birth Date: March 2, 1928
Death Date: March 22, 1990

Aerophysicist engineer and arguably the 20th century's top artillery designer. Born in North Bay, Ontario, Canada, on March 2, 1928, Gerald Vincent Bull was raised by an aunt after his mother died. An outstanding student, Bull was the youngest person ever to earn a doctorate from the University of Toronto. A superb engineer, in 1951 he went to work for the Canadian Armament and Research Development Establishment (CARDE). There, he developed an innovative alternative to expensive wind tunnels, firing the model down a barrel and using high-speed cameras to record its behavior during flight. His engineering prowess brought rapid promotions, and in 1959 he became the chief of CARDE's Aerophysics Department.

Ballistics expert Gerald Bull, right, shown in 1965 with Premier of Quebec Jean Lesage inspecting one of Bull's giant guns, was found shot to death in Brussels in 1990. News reports linked his death to the effort by Iraq to construct a huge gun capable of firing nuclear or chemical shells some 600 miles. (AP/Wide World Photos)

Bull had little patience for bureaucracy, however. He left CARDE in 1961. The brilliant engineer had a stubborn personality and deep commitment to developing the best artillery. These would drive him to accept employment with any agency willing to fund his dreams; ultimately, this cost him his life.

Shortly after leaving CARDE, Bull convinced the U.S. government that large guns were potentially more cost-effective platforms than rockets for launching small satellites testing nose cones for orbital reentry. The resulting U.S.-Canadian High Altitude Research Project (HARP) enabled him to study and demonstrate his ideas. He built a small test center along the Vermont-Quebec border to conduct model testing and a launch range in Barbados for flight tests. There, he modified an old U.S. Navy 16-inch gun, extended its barrel to 36 meters and developed special propellants and projectiles to launch projectiles weighing nearly 400 pounds to altitudes of some 110 miles. The project's entire cost was $10 million, or about twice that of a single Atlas missile launch.

Despite the demonstrated economy of his project, his enemies in CARDE convinced the Canadian government to withdraw funding. However, Bull was able to transfer all the assets to the corporation he had founded to manage the project. He then became a consultant to any military willing to fund his research.

Using the knowledge he gained from HARP, Bull became the world's foremost expert at extending the range of artillery shells. His use of "base bleed" technology to reduce the drag of the projectiles enabled him to extend the range by as much as 50 percent without reducing the projectile's throw weight. Bull was first hired by South Africa to develop artillery that could outrange the Soviet M-46 field guns being supplied to Cuban forces the South Africans were fighting in Angola. The resulting 155-millimeter (mm) gun was the world's longest-ranged field gun until the late 20th century. However, a change in American administration made his once legal work for South Africa a criminal activity. Bull was convicted of illegal arms trafficking for selling the guns and ammunition to South Africa. Imprisoned for six months and bankrupt, on his release Bull moved to Brussels, Belgium, and began to work for the People's Republic of China and Iraq.

Iraq was then locked in a long war with Iran (1980–1988). Impressed with Bull's guns, which Baghdad had acquired from South Africa, Iraqi dictator Saddam Hussein hired Bull in 1981 to develop a "supergun" that Iraq could use for artillery purposes and to launch satellites into orbit. Bull designated the program Project Babylon. Although the international media and the Iraqi government reported that the gun was to be used to attack Israel, there was little to suggest that it might be a practical military weapon. The 150-mm long barrel was fixed along an embankment, and had a breech that exceeded 350 mm (14 inches) in breadth. The gun also weighed more than 2,100 tons. Reportedly, the gun was to be ready for test firing in 1991. Later media reporting indicates that Bull briefed both Israeli and British intelligence agencies on the project.

The supergun was not the only project he worked on for Iraq. Bull also agreed to assist Iraq in developing a multistage missile based on the Soviet-supplied Scud. Ostensibly designed to strike targets deep inside Iran, the missile also had the capacity to strike Israel. Given Iraq's possession and use of chemical agents in its war with Iran, the Israeli government viewed the missile project as a major strategic threat. Bull reportedly received warnings from the Israelis to abandon the project. If he did, he ignored them. On March 22, 1990, Bull was found in his Brussels apartment, dead from five bullet wounds to the head. None of his neighbors heard the shots and the assassin or assassins have never been identified. Although United Nations (UN) inspectors destroyed Bull's Iraqi supergun and its supporting equipment after the 1991 Persian Gulf War, the South African G-5 155-mm served the Iraqi Army through three wars, and derivative variants remain in service with the German, Italian, Dutch, and Greek armies today. In fact, virtually all long-range artillery pieces and extended range ammunition rounds introduced into service since 2000 are based on Bull's design principles.

CARL OTIS SCHUSTER

See also

Artillery; Hussein, Saddam; Iraq, History of, Pre-1990; Iraq, History of, 1990–Present; Project Babylon

References

Adams, James. *Bull's Eye: The Assassination and Life of Supergun Inventor Gerald Bull.* New York: Times Books, 1992.

Bull, Gerald V., and Charles H. Murphy. *Paris Kanonen: The Paris Guns (Wilhelmgeschütze) and Project HARP.* Bonn, Germany: Verlag E. S. Mittlre and Sohn, 1988.

Lowther, William. *Arms and the Man: Dr. Gerald Bull, Iraq and the Supergun.* Novato, CA: Presidio, 1991.

Burqan, Battle of
Event Date: February 25, 1991

Battle that occurred on February 25, 1991, the second day of ground combat during Operation DESERT STORM, between the U.S. 1st and 2nd Marine Divisions and elements of the Iraqi III Corps. Burqan is located in Kuwait, part of the vast Al Burqan oil fields. For the initial defense of occupied Kuwait, the Iraqis relied upon a defensive works known as the Saddam Line to stymie a coalition attack. Behind this, the Iraqis had placed infantry and mechanized divisions to contain any coalition breakthrough. Counterattacks would be carried out by divisions of the elite Republican Guard located farther to the north. However, the six-week coalition air offensive had significantly degraded Iraqi capabilities by the time the ground offensive was launched on February 24. The 1st and 2nd Marine Divisions broke through the Saddam Line that same day and headed for Kuwait City. Major General Salah Aboud Mahmoud, commander of the Iraqi III Corps, located in southeastern Kuwait, realized that the Marines had to be counterattacked in order to save the Iraqi army in Kuwait.

Mahmoud employed two brigades from the Iraqi 5th Mechanized Division with about 250 tanks and armored vehicles, along with smaller supporting units. These were to attack out of the cover of the Burqan oil field and catch the 1st Marine Division on its right flank as it advanced north, hopefully achieving surprise. The Iraqi attack was partially concealed by heavy morning fog and smoke from oil fields that the Iraqis had set ablaze to provide battlefield cover from coalition aircraft.

The Marines received some intelligence that an Iraqi attack could be expected, and began reorienting their defenses and calling in artillery during the early morning hours of February 25. The Iraqi attack materialized at 8:00 a.m., and the fighting continued for three hours. The attack had been preceded by the arrival of an Iraqi major at a U.S. Marine outpost, who rolled his T-55 tank up, surrendered, and then told his captors that the vehicles coming into view were about to open fire.

The Iraqi attack was furious, but the Marine positions held. Conditions were chaotic and the two sides often fought each other with minimal visibility. The Marines were assisted by the appearance of Cobra attack helicopters firing Hellfire missiles and directed from the ground. After the morning fog lifted, coalition fixed-wing aircraft were called in as well. The Marines were also helped by poor Iraqi tactical skills. The Iraqis attacked in predictable head-on patterns, made little effort to maneuver, and demonstrated abysmal marksmanship.

Marine casualties at the Battle of Burqan were negligible, although the Iraqis did manage to down a Marine OV-10 observation aircraft and a Harrier jet. The Marines destroyed 50 Iraqi tanks along with 25 armored personnel carriers and captured 300 prisoners. Additional Iraqi tanks and vehicles were destroyed in coalition air strikes. After the failure of Mahmoud's attack, the Iraqi General Staff ordered the III Corps to pull out of its positions in southeastern Kuwait, an order that precipitated a general rout of remaining Iraqi forces in Kuwait. While it ended in a decisive Iraqi defeat, the Battle of Burqan represents a rare example of the Iraqi Army taking an initiative during the Persian Gulf War.

PAUL W. DOERR

See also

DESERT STORM, Operation; DESERT STORM, Operation, Ground Operations; Kuwait, Liberation of; Mahmoud, Salah Aboud; Oil Well Fires, Persian Gulf War; Saddam Line, Persian Gulf War; United States Marine Corps, Persian Gulf War

References

Gordon, Michael R., and General Bernard E. Trainor. *The Generals' War: The Inside Story of the Conflict in the Gulf.* New York: Little, Brown, 1995.

Pollack, Kenneth M. *Arabs at War: Military Effectiveness, 1948–1991.* Lincoln: University of Nebraska Press, 2002.

Busayyah, Battle of
Event Date: February 26, 1991

The Battle of Busayyah, Iraq, occurred on February 26, 1991, between U.S. and Iraqi ground units during the critical opening phases of the ground campaign of Operation DESERT STORM. The engagement resulted in a victory for American forces, marked an important stage in the unfolding of the American strategic plan for fighting the ground campaign, and also generated a postwar controversy.

The Iraqi plan for the defense of occupied Kuwait was based on the belief that coalition forces had three possible invasion routes. The Iraqis expected an amphibious landing on the Kuwaiti coast; a direct attack from Saudi Arabia into southern Kuwait; or a movement through Wadi al-Batin, which delineated Kuwait's western border with Iraq. Coalition forces could possibly attack via any or all of these routes. The Iraqis believed, however, that coalition forces lacked the logistical and navigational capabilities to attack through Iraq's western desert, so their defenses did not extend much more than 100 miles to the west of Wadi al-Batin. The Iraqis built a line of static defenses and fortifications along Kuwait's southern border with Saudi Arabia, mined the Kuwaiti coast line, and amassed troops to defend the Wadi al-Batin. Iraqi infantry and motorized divisions were located behind the first line of defenses to contain potential coalition breakthroughs. Finally, the Iraqi Republican Guard was positioned farther north as a strategic reserve.

Aware of Iraqi intentions and expectations, coalition commanders drew up plans that would take advantage of Iraqi weaknesses. Two Marine divisions would storm into southern Kuwait to fix the Iraqi defenders in place. A diversionary attack would be launched in the Wadi al-Batin. But the main coalition attack would be carried out by the U.S. VII and VIII Corps, which would execute a giant left hook through the western Iraqi desert, designed to smash the Republican Guard divisions and encircle Iraqi troops in Kuwait. The tiny Iraqi crossroads town of Busayyah, located about 100 miles north of the Saudi-Iraqi border, was to be the pivot point on which the U.S. corps would turn. The town consisted of about 40 to 50 buildings located on a road oriented north to south. The Iraqi army was using the town as a corps logistical base and had positioned some 100 tons of ammunition there. Busayyah also served as headquarters for the Iraqi 26th Infantry Division, which was guarding the border opposite the U.S. VII Corps.

The ground phase of Operation DESERT STORM began on February 24, 1991. However, the Iraqi 26th Infantry Division, which was under strength and had endured heavy aerial and artillery bombardment, failed to offer any effective resistance to the VII Corps attack. Most surviving Iraqi troops quickly surrendered.

As VII Corps rolled northward, local Iraqi commanders reported only a small force of eight French tanks and four armored personnel carriers (APCs) headed for Busayyah. The inability to relay accurate information plagued the Iraqi effort during Operation DESERT STORM. In fact, Busayyah lay directly in the path of the VII Corps' 1st Armored Division, commanded by Major General Ronald H. Griffith. Iraqi headquarters dispatched just two armored brigades to reinforce Busayyah.

To defend Busayyah itself, the Iraqis had positioned only one infantry battalion, one commando battalion, and one company of T-55 tanks. The Iraqi defensive preparations included trenches ringing the town, defensive tank positions, and machine gun posts on rooftops. However, the Iraqi defenders were hopelessly outnumbered and outgunned. Their T-55 tanks, built in the 1970s, were simply no match for the technologically advanced U.S. M-1A1 Abrams tanks. Iraqi tanks were outranged by the Abrams, which could fire on the move and had vastly superior armor protection.

Forward units of the 1st Armored Division approached Busayyah late on the afternoon of February 25. The town had already been pummeled by U.S. Apache attack helicopters. Griffith decided to take the town rather than bypass it. Thus, the overall advance of VII Corps was accordingly delayed. The commander of VII Corps, Lieutenant General Frederick Franks Jr., approved Griffith's plan, a decision that caused friction with General H. Norman Schwarzkopf, who wanted the advance accelerated.

On the morning of February 26, Busayyah was subjected to a massive artillery bombardment. The 1st Armored Division fired 1,500 artillery shells and 350 rockets at the town, but a number of determined Iraqi survivors from the commando battalion continued to offer resistance. Unwilling to wait any longer, Griffith left behind a small task force to deal with the situation and ordered his division to resume the advance. VII Corps now headed east toward Iraqi Republican Guard positions for the decisive battles of the ground campaign. Iraqi forces dispatched the previous evening to assist in the defense of Busayyah had, meanwhile, been destroyed in transit by American air strikes. Iraqi resistance in Busayyah finally ceased later in the day of February 26.

Iraqi losses at Busayyah amounted to 11 T-55 tanks, 6 APCs, 11 trucks, 94 prisoners, and an undetermined number of soldiers killed. There were no American losses. Some critics allege that Busayyah was more of a skirmish than a proper battle and that Griffith used massive overkill to deal with a small, demoralized Iraqi garrison. Griffith rebutted that he had not wanted to leave an Iraqi force behind in Busayyah that could conceivably threaten his division's supply lines. After the war, Schwarzkopf alleged that the slow progress of VII Corps, including the delay at Busayyah, allowed units of the Iraqi Army to escape the coalition trap in Kuwait. Franks vigorously denied this charge. Overall, the seizure of the town allowed VII Corps to turn to the east and complete the final phase of the war.

PAUL W. DOERR

See also

DESERT STORM, Operation, Ground Operations; DESERT STORM, Operation; Franks, Frederick Melvin, Jr.; Griffith, Ronald Houston; M1A1 and M1A2 Abrams Main Battle Tanks; Schwarzkopf, H. Norman, Jr.; Wadi al-Batin, Battle of

References

Gordon, Michael R., and General Bernard E. Trainor. *The Generals' War: The Inside Story of the Conflict in the Gulf.* New York: Little, Brown, 1995.

Pollack, Kenneth M. *Arabs at War: Military Effectiveness, 1948–1991.* Lincoln: University of Nebraska Press, 2002.

Scales, Robert H. *Certain Victory: The U.S. Army in the Gulf War.* Washington, DC: Brassey's, 1994.

Schwarzkopf, H. Norman, with Peter Petre. *It Doesn't Take a Hero: General H. Norman Schwarzkopf, the Autobiography.* New York: Bantam Books, 1993.

Bush, George Herbert Walker
Birth Date: June 12, 1924

U.S. congressman, ambassador, director of the Central Intelligence Agency (CIA) during 1975–1976, vice president during 1981–1989, and president of the United States during 1989–1993. George Herbert Walker Bush was born on June 12, 1924, in Milton, Massachusetts, to a wealthy and patrician family. His father, Prescott Bush, was a prominent U.S. senator from Connecticut. Educated at the elite Phillips Andover Academy, on his 18th birthday the younger Bush enlisted in the U.S. Navy, becoming its youngest pilot and seeing service in the Pacific flying a torpedo bomber. He was shot down by Japanese aircraft and later rescued from the sea by an American submarine. After his World War II service, he married Barbara Pierce, graduated from Yale University with an economics degree, moved to west Texas, and embarked on a career in the oil business. Opening his own oil enterprise in 1950, by 1954 he was the president of Zapata Offshore Company. His oil dealings paid handsome dividends, and he had become wealthy in his own right in the span of a few years.

Bush entered electoral politics as a Republican in 1964, the year in which he lost a bid for the U.S. Senate. Undeterred, he won a seat in the U.S. House of Representatives in 1966. In 1970 he again ran unsuccessfully for the U.S. Senate. President Richard M. Nixon appointed Bush ambassador to the United Nations (UN) in 1971. In this post for two years, Bush fought to preserve Nationalist China's (Taiwan) seat in that organization, an effort that was ultimately unsuccessful.

During 1973–1974, Bush served as the chairman of the Republican National Committee (RNC) at the direct request of President Nixon. Bush's tenure with the RNC took place during the Watergate Scandal that ultimately forced Nixon to resign in August 1974. Bush steadfastly defended Nixon, to little avail.

Bush then served during 1974–1975 in President Gerald R. Ford's administration as chief of the U.S. liaison office to the People's Republic of China (PRC). Although the United States and the PRC had not yet established full and normal diplomatic relations, Bush nonetheless acted as the de facto ambassador to the PRC. In 1975 he took over the CIA. The agency was then reeling from a series of shocking and embarrassing revelations about its role in assassination plots, coups, and other covert operations conducted in the name of the Cold War. Bush tried to rehabilitate the CIA during his tenure, and his efforts met with some success. He left the agency in 1977 after Jimmy Carter defeated Ford in the 1976 presidential election. Bush then became chairman of the First International Bank of Houston.

George H. W. Bush, shown here in 1989, was president of the United States during 1989–1993. Bush assembled the highly successful international coalition that drove Iraqi forces from Kuwait in 1991. An economic downturn helped cost him reelection in 1992. (Library of Congress)

In 1980 Bush sought the Republican presidential nomination but lost to former California governor Ronald Reagan. During the primaries, Bush assailed Reagan's political agenda, referring to his economic prescriptions as "voodoo economics." Despite such rhetoric, Reagan named Bush his running mate in an attempt to balance the ticket and provide a moderating force to his conservative platform. The pair went on to win an overwhelming victory in the 1980 elections. As vice president Bush loyally backed Reagan's hard-line Cold War policies. Bush did not wield much power in the administration, however, and what effects he did have on policy were well disguised. During Reagan's first term, military spending increased dramatically, and the administration provided considerable aid to foreign governments and insurgents to combat communism.

Bush bolstered these measures by traveling around the globe soliciting support for Reagan's policies, particularly in Central America. Bush met with Panamanian strongman Manuel Noriega, who had allied himself with the anticommunist Nicaraguan Contras. The Contras were fighting the Sandinista government and receiving U.S. military and financial aid. After Congress voted to cut off assistance to the Contras in 1983, the Reagan administration began covertly aiding them. Members of the National Security Agency (NSA) concocted a plan by which proceeds from the illicit sale of weapons to Iran were diverted to the Contra rebels. When the Iran-Contra story broke in 1986, Bush denied any knowledge of the illegal operation. Questions remained about Bush's role in the Iran-Contra Affair when he ran for the presidency in 1988, but he nonetheless secured a sound victory that November over Massachusetts governor Michael Dukakis.

When Bush took office in January 1989, the Cold War was winding down. During Ronald Reagan's second term, relations between the United States and the Soviet Union had improved remarkably, and in Bush's first year as president he continued to negotiate with Soviet premier Mikhail Gorbachev. In November 1989, the momentous fall of the Berlin Wall ushered in the end of the Cold War. Bush's reactions to the changes in Eastern Europe were calculatingly restrained. He and his foreign policy advisers were wary of antagonizing the Soviet leadership and were fearful that the Soviet military might be employed to stanch the prodemocracy movements. But Soviet weakness and Gorbachev's promises not to intervene led to a peaceful revolution. By January 1992 the Soviet Union had been officially dissolved, and later that year President Bush and the new Russian leader, Boris Yeltsin, declared an official end to the Cold War.

Bush dealt with a series of foreign policy crises, including China's brutal crackdown against protesters in Tiananmen Square during May–June 1990. This event severely strained Sino-U.S. relations, although Bush's experience as liaison to China in the 1970s may have been a moderating factor in that impasse. In December 1989, Bush launched Operation JUST CAUSE, which saw a U.S. invasion of Panama that resulted in the capture and extradition of Panamanian president Manuel Noriega. Noriega, formally an ally of the United States and someone with whom Bush had once conducted diplomatic business, was taken to the United States and tried on a variety of drug and drug trafficking charges.

After Iraq invaded and occupied Kuwait in August 1990, Bush successfully mounted an international coalition force that liberated Kuwait and dealt a crippling blow to Iraqi dictator Saddam Hussein's military. Almost immediately, the Bush administration made it clear that the Iraqi takeover of Kuwait would not be permitted to stand. To pressure Hussein to withdraw and to protect Saudi Arabia, the United States embarked on Operation DESERT SHIELD. This operation saw the eventual positioning of nearly 500,000 U.S. troops in the region, mostly in Saudi Arabia. Meanwhile, Bush was carefully building an international coalition—which would include many Arab nations—that would ultimately expel Iraqi forces from Kuwait. The Bush administration was also building support in the UN, which on November 29, 1990, passed a resolution authorizing military action against Iraq if it did not withdraw by January 15, 1991. Bush's job in assembling such impressive international cooperation was undoubtedly made easier by the end of the Cold War. The Soviet Union did not interfere in the crisis and indeed gave its tacit support to the international coalition.

When the UN deadline passed and Hussein defiantly remained in Kuwait, the Persian Gulf War began, code-named Operation DESERT STORM. The conflict, which now had a 34-nation coalition arrayed against Iraq, began on January 17, 1991, with massive bombing raids against Iraqi targets by U.S. and coalition air assets. The next day, Hussein ordered Scud surface-to-surface missiles fired into Israel in an obvious attempt to draw the Israelis into the war and thereby break apart the unlikely multination coalition that included Arab states. The Bush administration implored Israel not to react to the attacks, which caused only light damage. It also sent Patriot air defense missile batteries to Israel that were intended to intercept and shoot down incoming Scuds. Although these had less success than was claimed at the time, the Patriots were a factor in Bush's success in keeping Israel out of the war. The Iraqis also fired Scuds into Saudi Arabia, but Hussein's ploy to split the coalition did not work.

On February 24, 1991, after sustaining a withering aerial bombardment campaign that destroyed much of Iraq's important infrastructure, the United States commenced the ground war to liberate Kuwait. It lasted less than 100 hours. On February 26, Iraqi troops were beating a hasty retreat from Kuwait. By February 27, with Iraqi forces badly beaten and with many surrendering, Bush, supported by Chairman of the Joint Chiefs of Staff Colin Powell, brought the war to a close. A cease-fire was declared, and the Persian Gulf War was officially ended on February 28, 1991. The conflict liberated Kuwait, protected Saudi Arabian and Middle Eastern oil supplies, and had not turned into a larger conflagration, despite Iraqi missile attacks against Israel. However, Hussein's repressive regime was left firmly in place. Presciently and certainly ironically, Secretary of Defense Dick Cheney defended the decision not to oust Hussein and invade Iraq because such a move would have "bogged [the United States] down in the quagmire inside Iraq."

Following the war, Bush enjoyed meteoric approval ratings. However, a deep economic recession combined with his inability to offer solutions to the downturn resulted in a near free fall in his popularity. In November 1992, he lost a close election to Democrat Bill Clinton. One of Bush's last significant accomplishments as president was the brokering of the North American Free Trade Agreement (NAFTA), which Clinton signed in 1993. Since leaving office, Bush has assembled his presidential library in Texas, has coauthored a book on foreign affairs, and has been involved in various humanitarian missions throughout the world. He remained largely silent on the difficulties his son, George W. Bush, faced as president between 2001 and 2009.

JUSTIN P. COFFEY AND PAUL G. PIERPAOLI JR.

See also

Baker, James Addison, III; Bush, George Walker; DESERT SHIELD, Operation; DESERT STORM, Operation; Iran-Contra Affair; JUST CAUSE, Operation; Nixon, Richard Milhous; Reagan, Ronald Wilson

References

Bush, George. *All the Best, George Bush: My Life in Letters and Other Writings*. New York: Scribner, 1999.

Bush, George, and Brent Scowcroft. *A World Transformed*. New York: Knopf, 1998.

Green, John Robert. *The Presidency of George Bush.* Lawrence: University of Kansas Press, 2000.

Parmet, Herbert S. *George Bush: The Life of a Lone Star Yankee.* New York: Scribner, 1997.

Bush, George Walker
Birth Date: July 6, 1946

Republican Party politician, governor of Texas (1995–2001), and president of the United States (2001–2009). George Walker Bush was born in New Haven, Connecticut, on July 6, 1946, and grew up in Midland and Houston, Texas. He is the son of George H. W. Bush, president of the United States during 1989–1993.

The younger Bush graduated from the exclusive Phillips Academy in Andover, Massachusetts, and from Yale University in 1968. He volunteered for the Texas Air National Guard after graduation and became a pilot, although questions later surfaced about his actual service. He earned an MBA from Harvard University in 1975 and returned to Texas, founding Arbusto Energy Company in 1977. He then served as a key staffer during his father's 1988 presidential campaign and later became one of the owners of the Texas Rangers baseball team.

In 1994, Bush was elected governor of Texas. As governor, he worked with the Democratic-dominated legislature to reduce state control and taxes. In 1996 he won reelection, by which time he had earned a reputation as an honest broker who could govern in a bipartisan manner.

In 2000, having set records for fund-raising and having campaigned as a "compassionate conservative," Bush easily won the 2000 Republican nomination for the presidency of the United States. His platform included tax cuts, improved schools, Social Security reform, and increased military spending. On foreign policy issues, he downplayed his obvious lack of experience but eschewed foreign intervention and nation-building.

The U.S. presidential election of November 2000 was one of the most contentious in American history. The Democratic candidate, Vice President Al Gore, won a slim majority of the popular vote, but the electoral vote was in doubt. Confusion centered on Florida. Eventually, after weeks of recounts and court injunctions, the issue reached the U.S. Supreme Court. On December 12, 2000, a deeply divided Court halted the recount in Florida, virtually declaring Bush the winner. For many Americans, Bush was an illegitimate and unelected president.

As president, Bush secured a large tax cut in hopes that this would spur the economy, and he pushed forward Social Security reform. He and the Republican-controlled Congress also enacted a tax rebate for millions of Americans in the late summer and early autumn of 2001. That same year, with prodding from the White House, Congress passed the No Child Left Behind Act, a standards-based reform measure designed to build more accountability into public education. Although the measure won broad

George W. Bush, son of President George H. W. Bush, was president of the United States during 2001–2009. His largely unilateral approach to foreign policy, as well as his decision to invade Iraq in 2003 and undertake it with inadequate troop resources have been widely criticized. (U.S. Department of Defense)

bipartisan support, it later was criticized for being too narrowly conceived and incapable of accounting for differences in the way children learn. Many also came to believe that the mandate was not properly funded, especially in poorer school districts. In 2003, Bush was successful in passing a prescription drug act for U.S. citizens over the age of 65, but the measure ended up being far more expensive than originally forecast. Many also criticized the plan for being too complicated and offering too many options.

Bush sent many mixed messages about his commitment to environmental issues. Although he seemed to support the Kyoto Protocol dealing with climate change and global warming while campaigning in 2000, once in office Bush withdrew American support for the pact, citing conflicting scientific evidence on global warming. He also stated that the protocol could hurt the U.S. economy and American industry because neither India nor China had signed on to the agreement. His rejection of the Kyoto Protocol angered many environmentalists and other nations of the world that had already embraced the accord. This in fact was the first of many policy decisions that caused consternation in the international community. Throughout its first term, the Bush administration repeatedly downplayed the extent of global warming and the role human activities play in it. In its second term, it seemed more accepting of the science on global warming, but took few steps to mitigate it. In 2002, Bush did sign legislation mandating the cleanup of the Great Lakes, but he also supported limited drilling for oil in Alaska's Arctic National Wildlife Refuge, which is anathema to environmentalists and conservationists.

The course of Bush's presidency was forever changed on September 11, 2001, when 19 hijackers associated with the Al Qaeda terrorist organization seized commercial airliners and crashed them into the World Trade Center and the Pentagon. The attacks killed nearly 2,700 Americans and 316 foreign nationals. Over the next few days, Bush visited the scenes of the attacks, reassuring the public and promising to bring those responsible to justice. The catastrophe of September 11 seemed to bring legitimacy and purpose to Bush's presidency, although it tilted the economy further into recession.

On September 20, 2001, Bush appeared before Congress and accused Al Qaeda of carrying out the attacks. He warned the American people that they faced a lengthy war against terrorism. He also demanded that the Taliban government of Afghanistan surrender members of Al Qaeda in their country or face retribution. When the Taliban failed to comply, U.S. and British forces began a bombing campaign on October 7. Initially, the United States enjoyed broad international support for the War on Terror and its campaign to oust the Taliban from Afghanistan. Indigenous Northern Alliance forces, with heavy American support—chiefly in the form of air strikes—handily defeated the Taliban and by November 2001 had captured the capital of Kabul. Taliban resistance continued thereafter, but the multinational coalition was nevertheless able to establish a new government in Afghanistan.

The Bush administration also sought to improve national security in the wake of September 11. A new Department of Homeland Security was created to coordinate all agencies that could track and defeat terrorists. In October 2001, at the behest of the Bush administration, Congress passed the so-called Patriot Act, giving the federal government sweeping powers to fight the War on Terror. Many Americans were uncomfortable with this legislation and feared that it might undermine American freedom and civil liberties.

In 2002, the Bush administration turned its attentions toward Iraq. Intelligence reports suggested that Iraqi dictator Saddam Hussein was continuing to pursue weapons of mass destruction (WMDs). When Bush demanded that he comply with United Nations (UN) resolutions seeking inspection of certain facilities, Hussein refused. Unfortunately, some of the intelligence dealing with Iraqi intentions and capabilities was faulty, and some have argued that the Bush White House pressured the Central Intelligence Agency (CIA) and other intelligence services to interpret their findings in a way that would support armed conflict with Iraq. Still others claim that the White House and Pentagon misled themselves and the public by reading into the intelligence reports more than what was actually there. By the end of 2002, the Bush administration had formulated a new policy of preemptive warfare (the Bush Doctrine) to destroy regimes that intended to harm the United States before they were able to do so.

In October 2002, Bush secured from Congress a bipartisan authorization to use military force against Iraq if necessary. Many in Congress had believed that all means of international diplomacy and economic sanctions would be exhausted before the United States undertook military action against the Iraqis. Such was not the case, however, for the White House seemed intent on war.

By the beginning of 2003, a military buildup against Iraq was already taking place. However, Bush's efforts to create a broad, multinational coalition failed to achieve the success of the Persian Gulf War coalition against Iraq in 1991. Nearly all of the forces were American or British, and the United Nations failed to sanction military action against Iraq, as it had done in 1990. The virtually unilateral U.S. approach to the situation in Iraq greatly angered much of the international community and even U.S. allies. Such longtime partners as France and Germany refused to sanction American actions in Iraq, and relations with those nations suffered accordingly. To much of the world, the Bush Doctrine smacked of heavy-handed intimidation and hubris that simply circumvented international law whenever the Americans believed unilateral action to be necessary.

Military operations commenced on March 19, 2001, and Baghdad fell on April 9. At that point, organized resistance was minimal, but manpower resources, while sufficient to topple Hussein, were clearly insufficient to maintain the peace. Rioting and looting soon broke out, and weapons stockpiles were pillaged by insurgents. Religious and ethnic tensions came to the fore between Sunnis, Shias, and Kurds. Far more American troops were killed trying to keep order in Iraq than had died in the overthrow of the regime.

Although Bush won reelection in November 2004 in large part because of his tough stance on the so-called War on Terror, support for the war in Iraq gradually waned, the consequence of mounting American military and Iraqi civilian dead, reports of American atrocities committed in Iraq, the war's vast expense, revelations that the White House trumped up or knowingly used questionable intelligence about Iraqi WMDs, and general mismanagement of the war effort. Meanwhile, large budget deficits and trade imbalances piled up. Clearly, the failure to find WMDs in Iraq undercut the stated reason for the attack, although Bush then claimed that the war was about overthrowing an evil dictatorship and bringing democracy to Iraq, a statement that was diametrically opposed to his insistence during the 2000 campaign that the United States should not undertake nation-building operations using the U.S. military.

The Bush administration was at first ambivalent toward the Arab-Israeli conflict, but with violence escalating, in August 2001 at the urging of Crown Prince Abdullah of Saudi Arabia, Bush issued a letter supporting the concept of a Palestinian state. September 11 and ensuing events in Iraq soon took precedence, however. Bush and his advisers realized that Arab support, or at least acquiescence, in his Iraq policies would be more likely if a peace process were under way.

On June 24, 2002, Bush publicly called for a two-state solution. He failed to outline specific steps but supported a process in which each side would meet certain criteria before moving to the next step. The result was called the Road Map to Peace. Bush agreed to work with the European Union (EU), the UN, and Russia in developing it. This so-called Quartet developed a series of steps intended to provide assurances for each side but without involving the Israelis or Palestinians in its development.

The Road Map to Peace was unveiled in March 2003, just before the invasion of Iraq, but no details were announced. In June of that year, Bush arranged a summit conference at Aqaba, Jordan, involving Prime Minister Ariel Sharon of Israel and Prime Minister Mahmoud Abbas of the Palestinian National Authority (PNA). Progress on the plan stalled. The Bush administration's push for elections in the Palestinian-controlled West Bank backfired in January 2006 when these were won by the radical Hamas organization, which has called for the destruction of Israel and has continued to harass Israelis with random rocket attacks from Gaza and the West Bank. The peace process then ground to a halt. The Bush administration, faced with mounting American public dissatisfaction over the continuing American troop presence in Iraq, concentrated on that issue to the exclusion of virtually all other foreign developments.

Meanwhile, Bush suffered stunning setbacks at home. The White House was roundly denounced for its poor handling of relief efforts following Hurricane Katrina in the autumn of 2005 in which hundreds died in Louisiana and along the Gulf Coast. In the November 2006 midterm elections, the Republicans lost both houses of Congress, and Bush was forced to fire Secretary of Defense Donald Rumsfeld, whose tenure had been rife with controversy. Many Americans placed the onus of blame for the Iraq debacle on his shoulders. The year before, Secretary of State Colin L. Powell had resigned because of sharp differences he had with the White House's foreign policy; he has since publicly regretted being taken in by faulty pre–Iraq War intelligence. By early 2007, Bush was besieged by bad news: plummeting approval ratings, a war gone bad in Iraq with no end in sight, and incipient signs that massive budget deficits fanned by Bush's spending and failure to veto appropriation bills were beginning to undermine the economy.

In January 2007, amid increasing calls for the United States to pull out of Iraq, Bush decided on just the opposite tack. His administration implemented a troop surge strategy that placed as many as 40,000 more U.S. soldiers on the ground in Iraq. Within six months, the surge strategy seemed to be paying dividends and violence in Iraq was down. At the same time, however, a growing Taliban insurgency in Afghanistan was threatening to undo many of the gains made there since 2001. Many critics, including a number of Republicans, argued that Bush's Iraq policies had needlessly diluted the U.S. effort in Afghanistan. But Bush was hard-pressed to send significantly more troops to Afghanistan because the military was already badly overstretched.

In the meantime, the White House's controversial policy of indefinitely detaining non-U.S. terror suspects, most of whom were being held at the Guantánamo Bay Detainment Camp in Cuba, drew the ire of many in the United States and international community. Although most of the detainees were supposed to be tried in secret, military tribunals, few were ever brought to trial. Some observers have alleged abuse and mistreatment at Guantánamo, which further eroded America's standing in the world. More recently, several U.S. courts have weighed in on the detainees' status and have ordered that they be tried or released. In June 2008, the U.S. Supreme Court ruled that terror detainees were subject to certain rights under the U.S. Constitution. Even more controversial has been the use of "coercive interrogation techniques" on terror suspects and other enemy combatants. A euphemism for torture, this has included waterboarding, which goes against prescribed international norms for the treatment of prisoners of war. The Bush administration at first insisted that it had not authorized coercive interrogation, but when evidence to the contrary surfaced, the administration claimed that waterboarding had been used on some suspects. The White House, and especially Vice President Dick Cheney, however, attempted to assert that the technique did not constitute torture.

Not all the news on the international scene was bad, however. After the departure of such neoconservatives as Rumsfeld and Deputy Secretary of Defense Paul Wolfowitz, Bush's foreign policy became more pragmatic and less dogmatic. Secretary of State Condoleezza Rice worked diligently to try to repair America's standing in the world, and she met with some success by the end of the administration. President Bush's 2003 Emergency Plan for AIDS Relief, a multibillion dollar aid package to African nations hit hard by the AIDS epidemic, drew much praise in the United States and abroad.

By 2008, Bush's approval ratings were as low for any U.S. president in modern history. In the fall, the U.S. economy went into a virtual free fall, precipitated by a spectacular series of bank, insurance, and investment house failures, necessitating a massive government bailout worth more than $800 billion. Other corporate bailouts followed as more and more businesses teetered on the brink of insolvency. Unemployment began to rise dramatically in the fourth quarter of 2008, and consumer spending all but collapsed. The only bright note was a precipitous drop in the price of oil and gas, which had risen to dizzying heights in July 2008. Bush, a formal oil man, and Vice President Cheney, who had also been in the petroleum-related business, had been excoriated for the run-up in energy prices, which certainly made the economic downturn even more severe. By the time Bush left office in January 2009 the nation was facing the worst economic downturn in at least 35 years.

Tim J. Watts and Paul G. Pierpaoli Jr.

See also

References

Bruni, Frank. *Ambling into History: The Unlikely Odyssey of George W. Bush.* New York: HarperCollins, 2002.

Daalder, Ivo H., and James M. Lindsay. *America Unbound: The Bush Revolution in Foreign Policy.* Washington, DC: Brookings Institution, 2003.

Schweizer, Peter. *The Bushes: Portrait of a Dynasty.* New York: Doubleday, 2004.

Singer, Peter. *The President of Good & Evil: The Ethics of George W. Bush.* New York: Dutton, 2004.

Woodward, Bob. *Bush at War.* New York: Simon and Schuster, 2002.

———. *Plan of Attack.* New York: Simon and Schuster, 2004.

———. *State of Denial: Bush at War, Part III.* New York: Simon and Schuster, 2006.

———. *The War Within: A Secret White House History, 2006–2008.* New York: Simon and Schuster, 2008.

Bush Doctrine

Foreign/national security policy articulated by President George W. Bush in a series of speeches following the September 11, 2001, terrorist attacks on the United States. The Bush Doctrine identified three threats against U.S. interests: terrorist organizations; weak states that harbor and assist such terrorist organizations; and so-called rogue states. The centerpiece of the Bush Doctrine was that the United States had the right to use preemptory military force against any state that is seen as hostile or that makes moves to acquire weapons of mass destruction, be they nuclear, biological, or chemical. In addition, the United States would "make no distinction between the terrorists who commit these acts and those who harbor them."

The Bush Doctrine represented a major shift in American foreign policy from the policies of deterrence and containment that characterized the Cold War and the brief period between the collapse of the Soviet Union in 1991 and 2001. This new foreign policy and security strategy emphasized the strategic doctrine of preemption. The right of self-defense would be extended to use of preemptive attacks against potential enemies, attacking them before they were deemed capable of launching strikes against the United States. Under the doctrine, furthermore, the United States reserved the right to pursue unilateral military action if multilateral solutions cannot be found. The Bush Doctrine also represented the realities of international politics in the post–Cold War period; that is, that the United States was the sole superpower and that it aimed to ensure American hegemony.

A secondary goal of the Bush Doctrine was the promotion of freedom and democracy around the world, a precept that dates to at least the days of President Woodrow Wilson. In his speech to the graduating class at West Point on June 1, 2002, Bush declared that "America has no empire to extend or utopia to establish. We wish for others only what we wish for ourselves—safety from violence, the rewards of liberty, and the hope for a better life."

The immediate application of the Bush Doctrine was the invasion of Afghanistan in early October 2001 (Operation ENDURING FREEDOM). Although the Taliban-controlled government of Afghanistan offered to hand over Al Qaeda leader Osama bin Laden if it was shown tangible proof that he was responsible for the September 11 attacks and also offered to extradite bin Laden to Pakistan where he would be tried under Islamic law, its refusal to extradite him to the United States with no preconditions was considered justification for the invasion.

The administration also applied the Bush Doctrine as justification for the Iraq War, beginning in March 2003 (Operation IRAQI FREEDOM). The Bush administration did not wish to wait for conclusive proof of Saddam Hussein's weapons of mass destruction (WMDs), so in a series of speeches, administration officials laid out the argument for invading Iraq. To wait any longer was to run the risk of having Hussein employ or transfer the alleged WMDs. Thus, despite the lack of any evidence of an operational relationship between Iraq and Al Qaeda, the United States, supported by Britain and a few other nations, launched an invasion of Iraq.

The use of the Bush Doctrine as justification for the invasion of Iraq led to increasing friction between the United States and its allies, as the Bush Doctrine repudiated the core idea of the United Nations (UN) Charter. The charter prohibits any use of international force that is not undertaken in self-defense after the occurrence of an armed attack across an international boundary or pursuant to a decision by the UN Security Council. Even more vexing, the distinct limitations and pitfalls of the Bush Doctrine were abundantly evident in the inability of the United States to quell sectarian violence and political turmoil in Iraq. The doctrine did not place parameters on the extent of American commitments, and it viewed the consequences of preemptory military strikes as a mere afterthought.

KEITH A. LEITICH

See also

Afghanistan; Al Qaeda; Bush, George Walker; ENDURING FREEDOM, Operation; Hussein, Saddam; IRAQI FREEDOM, Operation; September 11 Attacks; Taliban; Terrorism; Weapons of Mass Destruction

References

Buckley, Mary E., and Robert Singh. *The Bush Doctrine and the War on Terrorism: Global Responses, Global Consequences.* London: Routledge, 2006.

Dolan, Chris J. *In War We Trust: The Bush Doctrine and the Pursuit Of Just War.* Burlington, VT: Ashgate, 2005.

Gurtov, Melvin. *Superpower on Crusade: The Bush Doctrine in U.S. Foreign Policy.* Boulder, CO: Lynne Rienner, 2006.

Heisbourg, François. "Work in Progress: The Bush Doctrine and Its Consequences." *Washington Quarterly* 6(22) (Spring 2003): 75–88.

Jervis, Robert. *American Foreign Policy in a New Era.* New York: Routledge, 2005.

Schlesinger, Arthur M. *War and the American Presidency.* New York: Norton, 2004.

Cable News Network

See CNN

Camp David Accords
Start Date: September 5, 1978
End Date: September 17, 1978

Peace agreement reached between Egypt and Israel during talks held September 5–17, 1978, at Camp David, the U.S. presidential retreat in rural Maryland. During 1977 and 1978, several remarkable events took place that set the stage for the Camp David negotiations. In autumn 1977, Egyptian president Anwar Sadat indicated his willingness to go to Israel in the cause of peace, something that no Arab leader had done since the creation of the Jewish state in 1948. On November 19, 1977, Sadat followed through on his promise, addressing the Knesset (Israeli parliament) and calling for peace between the two nations. The Israelis welcomed Sadat's bold initiative but took no immediate steps to end the state of belligerency, instead agreeing to ministerial-level meetings in preparation for final negotiations.

In February 1978, the United States entered into the equation by hosting Sadat in Washington, D.C., with both President Jimmy Carter and Congress hailing the Egyptian president as a statesman and a courageous leader. American adulation for Sadat led to greater cooperation by the Israelis, and they thus agreed to a summit meeting in September at Camp David.

During September 5–17, 1978, Carter hosted a conference that brought together Sadat and Israeli prime minister Menachem Begin and their respective staffs at Camp David. Carter participated

as an active player in the resultant talks. As was expected, the discussions proved difficult. Begin insisted that Sadat separate the Palestinian issue from the peace talks, something that no Arab leader had been willing to do before. Israel also demanded that Egypt negate any former agreements with other Arab nations that called for war against Israel.

Sadat bristled at Begin's demands, which led to such acrimony between the two men that they met in person only once during the entire negotiation process. Instead, Carter shuttled between the two leaders in an effort to moderate their positions. After several days of little movement and accusations of bad faith directed mostly at Begin, however, Carter threatened to break off the talks. Faced with the possibility of being blamed for a failed peace plan, Begin finally came to the table ready to deal. He agreed to dismantle all Jewish settlements in the Sinai peninsula and return it in its entirety to Egypt. For his part, given Begin's absolute intransigence on it, Sadat agreed to put the Palestinian issue aside and sign an agreement separate from the other Arab nations. On September 15, 1978, Carter, Sadat, and Begin announced that an agreement had been reached on two frameworks, the first for a peace treaty between Egypt and Israel and the second for a multilateral treaty dealing with the West Bank and the Gaza Strip.

The framework regarding Egypt and Israel had 11 major provisions: (1) the two nations would sign a peace treaty within three months; (2) this treaty would be implemented within two to three years after it was signed; (3) Egypt would regain full sovereignty of the Sinai to its pre–Six-Day War (1967) borders; (4) Israel would withdraw its forces from the Sinai, with the first such withdrawal to occur nine months after signature of the treaty; (5) Israel was to have freedom of navigation through the Suez Canal and the Strait of Tiran; (6) a highway would be built between the Sinai

U.S. president Jimmy Carter stands between Egyptian president Anwar Sadat, left, and Israeli prime minister Menachem Begin, right, after the signing of the Camp David Accords on September 17, 1978. Forged during an unprecedented 13-day negotiating session at the presidential retreat at Camp David, Maryland, the accords established a framework for peace between Israel and Egypt. The formal agreement, the Camp David Peace Treaty, was signed on March 26, 1979. (Jimmy Carter Presidential Library)

and Jordan to pass near Eilat with the guarantee of free passage through Israeli territory for both nations; (7) Egyptian forces in the Sinai would be limited to one division in the area 30 miles (50 kilometers) east of the Gulf of Suez and the Suez Canal; (8) there would be no other Egyptian forces in the Sinai; (9) Israeli forces would be restricted to four infantry battalions in the area 1.8 miles (3 kilometers) east of the international border with Egypt; (10) United Nations (UN) forces would be positioned in certain areas; and (11) the peace between the two nations would be complete, including full diplomatic recognition and an end to any economic restrictions on the other nation's goods, with free movement of goods and people.

The second framework, officially known as the "Framework of Peace in the Middle East," was far more general and skirted major issues. It contained seven major provisions: (1) UN Security Council Resolutions 242 and 338 were recognized as holding "in all their parts" the basis for a peace settlement; (2) the peace settlement would be negotiated by Egypt, Israel, Jordan, and "the representatives of the Palestinian people"; (3) residents of the West Bank and Gaza would secure "full autonomy"; (4) Egypt, Israel, and Jordan were to agree on "modalities for establishing the elected self-governing authority" in these areas, and the Egyptian and Jordanian delegations "may include Palestinians from the West Bank and Gaza or other Palestinians as mutually agreed"; (5) a withdrawal of Israeli forces would occur, with remaining forces grouped in certain agreed-upon locations; (6) as soon as the self-governing authority ("administrative council") had been established, a five-year transitional period would begin, by the end of which the final status of the West Bank and Gaza would have been agreed to, understanding that there would be recognition of "the legitimate rights of the Palestinian people and their just requirements"; and (7) in the transitional period, representatives of Egypt, Israel, and Jordan as well as those of the self-governing authority "will constitute a continuing committee" to agree on "the modalities of admission of peoples displaced from the West Bank and Gaza in 1967."

Despite a feeling of euphoria in the United States and an upward spike in Carter's approval ratings, the agreement in fact was a retreat from the president's own program in 1977 that called for Israeli withdrawal from the occupied lands with only minor territorial adjustments and a homeland for the Palestinian people based on self-determination rather than on autonomy under Israeli administrative control. Much was also simply left out. There was no mention in the framework of the future of Jerusalem and the Golan Heights or about the 1948 Palestinian refugees, the Israeli settlements in the West Bank, or the future of the Palestine Liberation Organization (PLO), which the United States steadfastly refused to recognize.

Over the next several months, Secretary of State Cyrus Vance made numerous trips to the Middle East to finalize the agreement. The United States promised that it would help organize an international peacekeeping force to occupy the Sinai following the Israeli withdrawal. Washington also agreed to provide $2 billion to pay for the relocation of an airfield from the Sinai to Israel and promised economic assistance to Egypt in exchange for Sadat's signature on a peace treaty.

Finally, on March 26, 1979, in a White House ceremony, Sadat and Begin shook hands again and signed a permanent peace treaty, normalizing relations between their two nations. Hopes that other Arab nations, particularly the pro-Western regimes in Jordan and Saudi Arabia, would soon follow Egypt's lead and sign similar agreements with Israel were quickly dashed. Indeed, the Camp David Accords produced a strong negative reaction in the Arab world, where other states and the PLO denounced the agreement and condemned Sadat for having "sold out" the Arab cause. Egypt was expelled from the Arab League, and several Middle Eastern nations broke off diplomatic relations with Cairo. Not until the mid-1990s would another Arab nation, Jordan, join Egypt in signing a peace agreement with Israel. Nonetheless, the Camp David Accords were, without doubt, President Carter's greatest foreign policy success.

BRENT GEARY AND SPENCER C. TUCKER

See also

Arab-Israeli Conflict, Overview; Brzezinski, Zbigniew; Carter, James Earl, Jr.; Egypt; Palestine Liberation Organization

References

Brzezinski, Zbigniew. *Power and Principle: Memoirs of the National Security Adviser, 1977–1981*. New York: Farrar, Straus and Giroux, 1985.

Carter, Jimmy. *Keeping Faith: Memoirs of a President*. Fayetteville: University of Arkansas Press, 1982.

Lenczowski, George. *The Middle East in World Affairs*. 4th ed. Ithaca, NY: Cornell University Press, 1980.

Quandt, William. *Camp David: Peacemaking and Politics*. Washington, DC: Brookings Institution, 1986.

Telhami, Shibley. *Power and Leadership in International Bargaining: The Path to the Camp David Accords*. New York: Columbia University Press, 1990.

Canada, Role in Persian Gulf and Afghanistan Wars

Canada is a large North American nation comprising 3.855 million square miles. Larger in area than the United States (3.794 million square miles), Canada is bordered to the south by the continental United States, to the west by the Pacific Ocean and the U.S. state of Alaska, to the east by the Atlantic Ocean and Greenland, and to the north by the Arctic Ocean. Its 2008 population was estimated to be 33.21 million people.

Canada is a representative parliamentary democracy loosely tied to the British monarchy. Queen Elizabeth II's governor-general is acting head of state while the prime minister is head of government. Canada's principal political parties include the Conservative, Liberal, and New Democratic parties and the Bloc Québécois.

In the immediate aftermath of Iraq's invasion of Kuwait in August 1999, Canadian prime minister Brian Mulroney was among the world's first leaders to condemn the attack. Within days, he dispatched three Canadian destroyers—the *Terra Nova, Athabaskan,* and *Huron*—to the Persian Gulf to help enforce United Nations (UN)–imposed sanctions against Iraq via a trade blockade. During Operation DESERT SHIELD, the Canadian government also dispatched the supply ship *Protecteur.*

In November 1990, after the United Nations authorized the use of force against Iraq, if necessary, Ottawa signaled its willingness to participate directly in a potential military confrontation with Saddam Hussein. When the Persian Gulf War began in January 1991, two squadrons of Canadian McDonnell Douglas/Boeing CF-18 Hornets, including support personnel, were integrated into coalition air forces. Canada also established a large field hospital in Qatar that treated many wounded soldiers.

In all, 4,500 Canadian military personnel—including sea-, air-, and land-based forces—served in Operation DESERT STORM. The peak deployment came in January 1991, when there were 2,700 personnel in theater. Canada's code name for the operations against Iraq was Operation FRICTION. Canada suffered no casualties in the war. The Persian Gulf War marked the first time that Canadian forces were engaged in combat since the 1950–1953 Korean War.

Afghanistan has been Canada's major overseas military commitment since 2002. The Canadian government initially offered 1,000 troops to the UN peacekeeping force in Afghanistan in 2002. In 2005, the outgoing Liberal government decided to deploy a total of 2,500 troops to Afghanistan to strengthen anti-insurgency efforts in the province of Kandahar. Since then, Canadian forces have fought side-by-side with Americans, British, Dutch, and other allies in several parts of the country as part of the International Security Assistance Force (ISAF). In March 2006, Canada took command of the 6,000-strong multinational brigade that operates under North Atlantic Treaty Organization (NATO) rules of engagement. This force includes 100 commandos from the elite Joint Task Force 2 unit. By 2007, Canada's 2,500 soldiers constituted the fourth-largest contingent within the overall peacekeeping

A Canadian honor guard carries the remains of Canadian Army Private Sebastien Courcy during a ceremony at Kandahar Air Base, Afghanistan, July 17, 2009. Courcy was killed in action on July 16, 2009, during counterinsurgency operations in the Panjwaii District of Afghanistan. (U.S. Department of Defense)

force of 32,800 NATO-led troops in Afghanistan. Also in 2006, Canada assumed responsibility for the volatile southwestern province of Kandahar.

In 2004, Canadian forces in Afghanistan came under the command of Canadian general Rick Hillier, who was appointed a year later as chief of Canada's defense staff. The outspoken Hillier's experiences with the Taliban left him convinced that they are "detestable murderers." The fact that three generals with experience in irregular warfare in the Middle East and Afghanistan—chief of the defense staff General Hillier, his chief of strategic planning General Andrew Leslie, and Major General Walter Natynczyk—have risen to top positions within the Canadian forces brought fresh thinking about modern war fighting and about the need to reform Canada's military to be better suited for more robust requirements. Hillier refers to the Afghanistan conflict as the "three-block war," encompassing humanitarian assistance, peace support operations, and high-intensity conflict, all unfolding within a relatively small area.

Ottawa's Afghanistan deployment has had substantial domestic and international political significance for Canadians. As the most conspicuous contribution to the Global War on Terror, the Afghanistan operation is an opportunity to rebuild credibility in Washington after Canada's refusal to participate in the March 2003 invasion of Iraq and in the U.S. ballistic missile defense

program. The Afghan engagement has essentially enabled Canada to play its part in the post–September 11 world without appearing to be at the beck and call of the American president. As an integral part of the NATO force, which is acting with a UN mandate in Afghanistan, the Canadian army is establishing its competence in difficult anti-insurgency operations. For Canadian prime minister Stephen Harper, who took office in February 2006, Afghanistan is the defining element in Canada's new image in the world.

The Canadian government emphasizes that it is fighting in a multinational engagement, and not in an "American war." Nevertheless, Canada's interests correspond closely with those of other Western nations, and these are portrayed as global and threatened by extremist ideology. Engagement has proven to be a workable alternative to the traditional blue-bereted UN peacekeeping missions, and it is emblematic of what Ottawa calls "Three D" defense, which also includes development and diplomacy. Not since the 1950–1953 Korean War has Canada been involved in such an extensive military effort and suffered so many casualties—some 98 deaths and over 300 wounded by the end of 2008. This casualty rate is proportionally higher than those of other NATO countries, including the United States. In an increasingly two-tiered NATO alliance, Canada now occupies the fighting tier, alongside the United States, Great Britain, the Netherlands, and Denmark. In many respects, the Canadian military has transformed itself as a result of the conflict. Canada is also one of Afghanistan's largest donors, providing Can$650 million in aid through mid-2008 and pledging over $1 billion more. This assistance is the largest Canadian aid commitment ever made to a single country. In addition, it has been estimated that the total cost of the war, through 2011, will be between Can$14 billion–18 billion. By the end of 2008, the war's cost was estimated to be Can$10.5 billion.

By 2008, Canadian forces in Afghanistan consisted of one battle group, one strategic advisory team, one provincial reconstruction team, and a substantial number of special forces. The number of forces remained largely unchanged by year's end—approximately 2,800. Their equipment includes the German-made Leopard II main battle tank, the McDonnell Douglas (now Boeing) C-17 Globemaster strategic airlift aircraft, Lockheed Martin C-130J Hercules turbo-prop tactical lift aircraft, and numerous medium-lift helicopters. Canadians have been involved in multiple operations in Helmand and Kandahar provinces, and they engaged in intense combat at Pashmul in the summer of 2006.

Polls in 2007 revealed that about 50 percent of Canadians believe the mission in Afghanistan has failed and want it abandoned and their troops brought home. Many are appalled by the rising casualties and the sheer brutality of the fighting. One of the first political crises Prime Minister Harper faced in office involved the tradition of banning news media coverage of returning coffins from the war zone and the flying of flags at half-staff to mark the death of troops. Harper argued that the families should be able to grieve out of the limelight, but critics accused him of not honoring the dead by hiding their sacrifices. He was ultimately forced to back down.

The ensuing vigorous and emotional debates about Canadian involvement in the war merely underscored Canadians' uneasiness over their enhanced role in Afghanistan and the government's nervousness about unsteady public support for the conflict. Some Canadians see an Iraq-like quagmire, the wrong cause in the wrong place. Nevertheless, Canadians continue to debate what the appropriate global role should be for their country and military. Yet, realizing that the war in Afghanistan could go on for years, Harper ordered a substantial increase in military spending, to include the purchase of new transport helicopters, three new support ships, transport aircraft, and 2,300 supply trucks. His government hopes to increase the full-time military force from 62,000 to 75,000 and add 10,000 more reservists (who constitute 13 percent of the fighting forces in Afghanistan). Canada also dispatched a 216-soldier Disaster Assistance Response Team (DART) to Pakistan in late 2005 to provide emergency relief to Kashmir's earthquake victims.

DAVID M. KEITHLY

See also

Afghanistan; ENDURING FREEDOM, Operation; Global War on Terror; International Security Assistance Force; North Atlantic Treaty Organization

References

Hassan-Yari, Houchang. "Canada in Afghanistan: Continuity and Clarity." *Journal of Military and Strategic Studies* 9 (2006): 1–14.

Maloney, Sean M. "Blood on the Ground: Canada and the Southern Campaign in Afghanistan." *Defense and Security Analysis* 23 (2007): 405–417.

Thompson, Wayne C. *Canada 2008*. Harpers Ferry, WV: Stryker-Post, 2008.

Carl Gustav Recoilless Rifle

An 84-millimeter (mm) recoilless rifle antitank weapon produced by the Saab Bofors Arms Company in Sweden. The Carl Gustav, first introduced into Swedish Army service in 1948, has been steadily modified over the years and currently serves in a variety of functions in armies around the world. It has seen widespread service in the Middle East wars.

The Carl Gustav competed with such weapons as the U.S. Bazooka, British PIAT (Projector, Infantry, Anti-Tank), and the German *Panzershreck*. The Carl Gustav utilizes a rifled barrel for spin, as opposed to fins attached to the warhead in the other weapon types. Its projectile moves at a higher velocity because of its recoilless firing system. However, it is also much harder to conceal one's position because of the great back blast of the recoilless system.

The Carl Gustav is a two-man, portable weapon system, requiring a gunner and one loader/ammunition carrier. The M2 version weighed 31.2 pounds. Lighter materials in the upgraded version of the weapon, the M3, allow for greater mobility and applicability. The M3 weighs only 18.7 pounds.

The United States military has used the Carl Gustav to destroy enemy trucks and lightly armored vehicles. It has also been employed as a bunker-busting weapon.

The Carl Gustav has been used successfully by coalition forces in Afghanistan (Operation ENDURING FREEDOM) and Iraq (Operation IRAQI FREEDOM), primarily by the British Secret Air Service, U.S. Rangers and Special Forces, and Canadian infantry units. Nicknames given to the Carl Gustav include "Charlie G" by the British, "Carl G" by the Canadians, the Ranger Anti-Armor Weapon System (RAAWS) or "Goose" by the Americans, and "Charlie Gutsache" by the Australians.

The main round for the Carl Gustav is the high-explosive antitank (HEAT) round. The effective range of HEAT ammunition is about 2,500 yards, with penetration of up to 16 inches of armor. Newer HEAT rounds have been developed to counter reactive armor found on many modern tanks, but the primary use of the 84-mm HEAT round remains light armored vehicles. The High-Explosive Dual Purpose (HEDP) round is the round used mainly for the bunker-busting role. Maximum range for this round is some 1,100 yards, and it can penetrate up to 6 inches of armor. The Carl Gustav can also fire illumination rounds, smoke rounds, flechette (plastic dart) or Area Defense Munition (ADM) rounds, as well as many varieties of HEAT and HEDP rounds.

A Dutch marine demonstrates the 84-mm Carl Gustav recoilless rifle. (U.S. Department of Defense)

Many large-caliber recoilless rifles have been phased out of many armies around the world because of their weight and the availability of lighter, more powerful man-portable missile and rocket launchers. The Carl Gustav has repeatedly proven its versatility and will no doubt see battlefield service for many years to come.

JASON M. SOKIERA

See also

Antitank Weapons; ENDURING FREEDOM, Operation; IRAQI FREEDOM, Operation

References

Department of Defense. *21st Century U.S. Military Documents: World Weapons Guide—Army OPFOR Worldwide Equipment Guide—Infantry Weapons, Vehicles, Recon, Antitank Guns, Rifles, Rocket Launchers, Aircraft.* Washington, DC: Progressive Management, 2003.

Gander, Terry, ed. *Jane's Infantry Weapons, 2003–2004.* 29th ed. Alexandria, VA: Jane's Information Group, 2003.

Carter, James Earl, Jr.
Birth Date: October 1, 1924

U.S. Navy officer, Democratic Party politician, governor of Georgia (1971–1975), president of the United States (1977–1981), and Nobel laureate (2002). Born on October 1, 1924, in Plains,

Georgia, James "Jimmy" Carter was raised on his family's farm close to the town of Archery, Georgia. After having attended Georgia Southwestern College and the Georgia Institute of Technology, he graduated from the U.S. Naval Academy in 1946. He then pursued graduate work in physics at Union College and spent seven years as a naval officer working under Admiral Hyman Rickover in the nuclear submarine program. Carter eventually served on the nuclear submarine *Seawolf*.

Carter left the navy and returned to Georgia upon his father's death in 1953 to run the family farm, eventually building it into a large and prosperous enterprise. Carter entered state politics in 1962, serving two terms in the Georgia Senate. He also became a born-again Christian with a profound commitment to his Baptist faith. In 1966 he ran unsuccessfully for governor of Georgia. He spent the next several years tending to his booming agricultural concerns and methodically laying the groundwork for his planned 1970 gubernatorial campaign. He was elected governor of Georgia in 1970. As governor, he pursued a moderate approach. He also sought to bridge the racial divide by appointing African Americans to state offices, and he was the first governor from the Deep South to publicly denounce racial discrimination and segregation.

In December 1974, amid the fallout of the Watergate Scandal and an economy mired in a deep recession and plagued by high inflation, Carter decided to run for the presidency. Running as a

Washington outsider who promised to restore honesty and integrity to government, he secured the Democratic Party nomination. Attracted by his modesty, integrity, and moderate positions, many voters threw their support behind him. He went on to win the presidential election of November 1976 by a narrow margin.

Carter's first major act as president in January 1977 was to extend a pardon to draft evaders, military deserters, and others who had violated the Selective Service Act from 1964 to 1973 during the controversial Vietnam War. The psychic and political wounds from Vietnam had yet to heal, and the nation still remained deeply divided over its involvement in the war. Carter's move generated controversy among the public and elicited criticism from Congress, which contributed to a rift between it and the administration that only widened during the Carter presidency.

Carter was unable to inspire public confidence or to fulfill his election promise to end stagflation (rampant inflation coupled with economic recession). To solve the ongoing energy crisis, a contributory factor to economic stagnation, he proposed energy taxes, limits on imported oil, and greater reliance on domestic sources of energy. Congress largely stymied these plans. The Carter administration also deregulated the nation's airline industry, passed major environmental legislation to encourage cleanup of hazardous waste sites, revamped the civil service, and created the Departments of Energy and Education.

Carter frequently criticized other nations for human rights abuses, often linking economic and military cooperation to a country's commitment to the American ideals of freedom and equality. Such disapproval of the Soviets' treatment of political dissidents undermined détente and delayed Strategic Arms Limitation Treaty (SALT) II negotiations, which finally resulted in a 1979 treaty never ratified by Congress because of the Soviet invasion of Afghanistan that same year. In response to the Afghan situation, the administration enunciated the Carter Doctrine, which committed the United States to protecting oil interests in the Persian Gulf. Carter also imposed a controversial and ineffective American grain embargo on the Soviet Union and ordered a U.S. boycott of the 1980 Olympic Games in Moscow. In January 1979 he also extended full diplomatic recognition to the People's Republic of China (PRC), effectively cutting most American ties with Taiwan.

Perhaps Carter's singular achievement as president came in his brokering of a peace between Israel and Egypt. He invited Egyptian president Anwar Sadat and Israeli prime minister Menachem Begin to the presidential retreat at Camp David, Maryland, in September 1978. The meetings between the heretofore implacable enemies were tense and nearly broke down numerous times. When Sadat threatened to quit the talks, Carter personally implored him to stay, and Sadat agreed. Begin also wanted to end the talks at one point, and Carter prevailed upon him to see the negotiations through.

Following two weeks of intense negotiations, a deal was reached for a peace treaty between Israel and Egypt, known as the

In 1976, Jimmy Carter of Georgia was elected president of the United States. Carter served only a single term, undone by the Iranian hostage crisis. In 2002, Carter was awarded the Nobel Peace Prize for his accomplishments, including brokering a peace deal between Egypt and Israel. (Library of Congress)

Camp David Accords. The treaty was signed on March 26, 1979. The accords represented a true diplomatic breakthrough, provided a framework for future Middle East peace initiatives, and helped temporarily bolster Carter's sagging popularity.

In September 1977, Carter signed the controversial Panama Canal Treaties, ceding the canal to Panama and ensuring the neutrality of the waterway. Congress narrowly ratified the treaties in March 1978, but Carter nevertheless came under additional fire for having ceded an important U.S. strategic interest.

If the Camp David Accords and the prospects of a wider peace in the Middle East were the most important of Carter's legacies, another conflict in the Middle East ultimately brought about his downfall. Indeed, the 1979–1980 Iranian hostage crisis doomed Carter's presidency. The genesis of the crisis was the steadfast and long-standing U.S. support of Mohammad Reza Shah Pahlavi of Iran. Since 1953 when the U.S. Central Intelligence Agency (CIA) helped engineer the overthrow and house arrest of prime minister Mohammad Mosaddeq, which paved the way for the shah's autocratic rule, the United States had supported the shah and sold him billions of dollars' worth of weaponry. Despite the shah's blatant human rights abuses and increasingly dictatorial rule, the United States saw him as a key ally and an important stabilizing force in the volatile Middle East. The presidential administrations of Richard M. Nixon and Gerald R. Ford particularly sought to use the shah as a way to keep Soviet influence in the region to a minimum and to counteract Pan-Arabism. As protests and violence against the shah's rule increased in 1978 and early 1979, the Carter administration attempted to remain above the fray. Carter himself publicly praised the shah.

On January 16, 1979, however, a popular revolution forced the shah to flee Iran with his family. At first, Carter sought to recognize the new, interim revolutionary regime, but these efforts proved in vain. There was little chance that Carter's initiative would have lasted, however. In February, Ayatollah Ruhollah Khomeini arrived in Iran after years of exile. This fundamentalist cleric, who was rabidly anti-Western and anti-American, would establish an Islamic republic in Iran. A plebiscite in the spring of 1979 overwhelmingly endorsed such a step, and Khomeini's party assumed the leadership of Iran.

In October 1979, the Carter administration decided to admit the shah to the United States for badly needed cancer treatment. Although he remained in the country for only a few weeks, the move enraged radical Iranian militants, who were egged on by Khomeini. On November 4, 1979, a group of radical Iranian students seized the U.S. embassy in Tehran, taking the Americans there hostage. Carter struggled tirelessly to defuse the crisis through diplomacy, but the Iran hostage crisis dragged on for 444 days and ruined his presidency. In the meantime, the price of oil rose dramatically, adversely affecting the U.S. economy. Interestingly, Carter never invoked the Carter Doctrine to protect Middle East oil. Such a move probably would have invited disaster, given the Soviet Union's December 1979 invasion of Afghanistan and the resultant tense relations between Moscow and Washington. In April 1980, a U.S. hostage rescue attempt disastrously failed, and Secretary of State Cyrus R. Vance resigned in protest against the operation. The crisis and failure of the rescue attempt contributed greatly to Carter's defeat in the November 1980 presidential election. The hostages were released on January 20, 1981, only moments after Ronald Reagan was sworn in as president.

Carter has continued leading a vigorous public life following his presidency, acting as a mediator in international conflicts, working on the eradication of poverty, supervising elections in the developing world, promoting human rights, and writing books and memoirs. In 2002 he was awarded the Nobel Peace Prize for his accomplishments.

One of Carter's books, *Palestine: Peace Not Apartheid,* published in 2006, created considerable controversy. In it, Carter held Israel primarily responsible for the continuing Palestinian-Israeli conflict and criticized the system of segregation of Palestinians. Many praised Carter for his candor, while others condemned the book as one-sided and filled with misconceptions. Carter also sharply criticized the George W. Bush administration, terming it

"the worst in history" and has denounced former Britain prime minister Tony Blair's relationship with Bush, alleging that it is "blind (and) apparently subservient."

JOSIP MOCNIK AND PAUL G. PIERPAOLI JR.

See also

Camp David Accords; EAGLE CLAW, Operation; Iranian Revolution; Khomeini, Ruhollah; Reza Pahlavi, Mohammad

References

Brinkley, Douglas. *The Unfinished Presidency: Jimmy Carter's Journey beyond the White House.* New York: Viking, 1998.

Carter, Jimmy. *Keeping Faith: Memoirs of a President.* Fayetteville: University of Arkansas Press, 1982.

Kaufman, Burton I. *The Presidency of James Earl Carter, Jr.* Lawrence: University Press of Kansas, 1993.

Maga, Timothy P. *The World of Jimmy Carter: Foreign Policy, 1977–1981.* New Haven, CT: University of New Haven Press, 1994.

Strong, Robert A. *Working in the World: Jimmy Carter and the Making of American Foreign Policy.* Baton Rouge: Louisiana State University Press, 2000.

Carter Doctrine

U.S. foreign policy precept enunciated by President James "Jimmy" Carter in 1980 that pledged the nation to protect American and Allied interests in the Persian Gulf. By 1980, the Carter administration, which had been engaged in an ongoing debate over the direction of U.S. foreign policy as détente faded, declared its determination to use any means necessary, including military force, to protect American interests in the Persian Gulf. These interests mainly involved Persian Gulf oil and regional shipping lanes.

On January 23, 1980, Carter, in his State of the Union message, declared that "an attempt by any outside force to gain control of the Persian Gulf region will be regarded as an assault on the vital interests of the United States of America, and such an assault will be repelled by any means necessary, including military force." This emphasis on American military power marked a fundamental reorientation in Carter's foreign policy. Since 1977, in response to public disillusionment with the Vietnam War and disgust over the Watergate scandal, Carter had attempted to fight the Cold War with different weapons. While not ignoring the Soviet Union, he determined that U.S.-Soviet relations would not be allowed to dominate foreign policy formulation, a stance that he saw as having led to the costly containment policy and the tragedy of Vietnam. Instead, other nations, especially those in the developing world, would be considered in a regional rather than a global context. Additionally, the United States would assert its international predominance by emphasizing moral rather than military superiority by focusing on human rights and related humanitarian concerns.

By January 1980, however, the international climate had changed drastically. The Islamic Revolution in Iran had displaced America's longtime ally, Mohammad Reza Shah Pahlavi. On November 4, 1979, Iranian students seized the American embassy in Tehran and took 70 Americans hostage. This precipitated a 444-day crisis during which the Carter administration could do little to free the hostages. Also, on December 26, 1979, the Soviet Union invaded Afghanistan, sparking a bloody nine-year war there. Faced with these twin crises—religious fundamentalist terrorism and communist advancement by military force—during an election year, Carter reoriented his foreign policy. Although he did not abandon his commitment to human rights, the issue was accorded a much lower priority in policy formulation and was no longer used as a major weapon with which to wage the Cold War. Instead, the administration's official posture reflected a more customary Cold War policy that emphasized the projection of military power and communist containment. In addition, a globalist perspective began to supplant the regionalist outlook, with increased emphasis on East-West issues. These trends were accelerated considerably under President Ronald Reagan, Carter's successor. The Carter Doctrine is still operative in American foreign policy, almost three decades after it was enunciated. Indeed, it was used as a partial justification for the 1991 Persian Gulf War and the 2003 invasion of Iraq.

DONNA R. JACKSON

See also

Carter, James Earl, Jr.; Containment Policy; Iranian Revolution; Soviet-Afghanistan War; Soviet Union, Middle East Policy; United States, Middle East Policy, 1945–Present

References

Brzezinski, Zbigniew. *Power and Principle: Memoirs of the National Security Adviser, 1977–1981.* New York: Farrar, Straus and Giroux, 1985.

Carter, Jimmy. *Keeping Faith: Memoirs of a President.* Fayetteville: University of Arkansas Press, 1982.

Vance, Cyrus. *Hard Choices: Critical Years in America's Foreign Policy.* New York: Simon and Schuster, 1983.

Casey, George William, Jr.
Birth Date: July 22, 1948

U.S. Army general, commander of U.S. forces in Iraq (Multi-National Force–Iraq) during 2004–2007, and army chief of staff since 2007. George William Casey Jr. was born on July 22, 1948, in Sendai, Japan; his father, a career army officer, was serving with the army occupation forces there. (His father, Major General George William Casey Sr., died in Vietnam in 1970 in a helicopter crash.) Casey spent his early life on army posts throughout the United States and Europe and graduated from Georgetown University in 1970, where he was enrolled in the Army Reserve Officers' Training Corps (ROTC).

In August 1970, Casey was commissioned a second lieutenant in the army. During the next decade he served in a variety of command and staff positions. In 1980, he earned an MA in international relations from the University of Denver. Casey continued his military education at the Armed Forces Staff College, completing his studies there in July 1981.

Shortly thereafter, Casey was ordered to the Middle East where he worked with the United Nations (UN) Truce Observer Supervision Organization. From February 1982 to July 1987 he was assigned to the 4th Infantry Division based at Fort Carson, Colorado. In December 1989, he became a special assistant to the army chief of staff. He was then assigned as chief of staff of the 1st Cavalry Division at Fort Hood, Texas, where he later commanded that division's 3rd Brigade. In July 1996, he was promoted to brigadier general and sent to Europe, where he served as assistant commander for the 1st Armored Division in Germany and participated in the peacekeeping missions to Bosnia and Herzegovina.

In 1999, following his advancement to major general, Casey commanded the 1st Armored until July 2001. At the end of October 2001, he was appointed lieutenant general and took control of Strategic Plans and Policy for the Joint Chiefs of Staff. In January 2003 he became director, Joint Staff of the Joint Chiefs of Staff. That October, he became vice chief of staff of the Army and was advanced to four-star rank.

Casey became a major figure in planning for the U.S. response to the terrorist attacks of September 11, 2001, and for the 2003 invasion of Iraq. As director of the Joint Staff, he had been directly involved in the allocation of units and personnel for the Iraq operation. One of his assignments was the allocation of military personnel for administration in the occupied areas. In December 2002, with planning for the invasion in full swing, Casey ordered the formation of a follow-on headquarters for the postwar occupation but gave it few resources. It was in his capacity as director of the Joint Staff that Casey first encountered conflict over troop levels for the impending invasion, which occurred between the field commanders and Secretary of Defense Donald Rumsfeld.

Conditions in Iraq in the wake of the March 2003 invasion became central to Casey's fortunes. For all of his success, Casey had attracted little notice outside military circles. This changed when he was assigned to head the commission to investigate the abuse of prisoners by American guards at Abu Ghraib Prison in late 2003.

In the summer of 2004, Casey was appointed to command U.S. and coalition forces (Multi-National Force–Iraq). By the time Casey took command, the Iraqi insurgency was in full swing, but the coalition response had been hampered by fundamental conflicts over strategy and tactics between the civilian commissioner in Iraq, L. Paul Bremer, and the military commander, General Ricardo Sanchez. Casey soon established a cordial working relationship with the new American ambassador to Iraq, John Negroponte.

Such a relationship was needed in the desperate situation the two men faced in 2004. Casey was shocked to discover that there was no counterinsurgency strategy. He and Negroponte thus worked to develop a coherent approach to combating the growing attacks on American forces and the threat of civil war. Casey's strategy involved securing transportation infrastructure, containing insurgent violence by aggressively attacking insurgent bases, reaching out to Iraq's Sunni Muslims, and building up Iraqi security forces. Under Casey's direction, U.S. counterinsurgency operations took on a clearer direction, but violence in Iraq continued to escalate, and the war grew profoundly unpopular in the United States.

In March 2007, Casey turned over his command to Lieutenant General David Petraeus and returned to the United States to assume the post of U.S. Army chief of staff. Casey was cautious but noncommittal in his support of the troop surge implemented by the George W. Bush administration in January 2007. He also warned that U.S. Army resources were being stretched dangerously thin.

WALTER F. BELL

See also

Abu Ghraib; Bremer, Jerry; Bush, George Walker; Iraqi Insurgency; Negroponte, John Dimitri; Petraeus, David Howell; Rumsfeld, Donald Henry; Sanchez, Ricardo S.; Sunni Islam

References

Gordon, Michael R., and General Bernard E. Trainor. *Cobra II: The Inside Story of the Invasion and Occupation of Iraq.* New York: Pantheon Books, 2006.

Ricks, Thomas E. *Fiasco: The American Military Adventure in Iraq.* New York: Penguin, 2006.

Woodward, Bob. *State of Denial: Bush at War, Part III.* New York: Simon and Schuster, 2006.

Casualties, Operation DESERT STORM

Casualties for Operation DESERT STORM include those individuals killed, wounded, or captured in the operation that liberated Kuwait from Iraqi occupation and defeated Iraq during the 1991 Persian Gulf War. Operation DESERT STORM officially began on January 17, 1991, with an air campaign that lasted over a month, and ended on February 28, after a 100-hour ground offensive by coalition troops.

Given the number of troops engaged, casualties for the war were extremely low, at least for the coalition arrayed against Iraq. Controversy has dogged the question of casualties on two counts. First, the percentage of friendly-fire deaths has been debated; second, there is no agreement on the number of Iraqi soldiers and civilians killed.

The coalition against Iraq was made up of 34 nations, including the United States. Before the war began, some press reports predicted coalition casualties as high as 30,000. The U.S. Department of Defense reported 148 American battle deaths and 145 noncombat deaths. A total of 467 Americans were wounded in action, but more than 3,000 others were injured in noncombat-related accidents. Some statistics actually estimated that had American troops not been deployed, more would have died of natural causes and from accidents than those killed in the Persian Gulf combat

Air Force officers oversee the transport of coffins containing the remains of 20 U.S. servicemen killed during Operation IRAQI FREEDOM. Pursuant to a Pentagon order of 2003, it was forbidden to disseminate to the public images such as this scene at Dover Air Force Base. Requests filed in 2004 under the Freedom of Information Act resulted in the successful release of more than 300 such photographs of flag-draped coffins and the honor guards charged with their transport. (U.S. Air Force)

theater. The tactical use of air power, technological superiority, and efficient evacuation of the wounded to medical centers in Europe helped minimize U.S. combat deaths. The largest single loss of life was caused by an Iraqi Scud missile, which slammed into a U.S. military barracks in Dhahran, Saudi Arabia, on February 25, 1991. That incident killed 28 servicemen.

In addition to the official numbers of soldiers wounded in combat or accidents, the Department of Veterans Affairs has declared that more than 180,000 veterans of the Persian Gulf War were permanently disabled from mystery ailments, sometimes referred to as Gulf War Syndrome. One recent correction in U.S. casualty figures came in the case of U.S. Navy pilot Michael Scott Speicher, who was listed as killed in action (KIA) at the end of the conflict. Speicher's status was changed to missing in action (MIA), ironically the day after the U.S. Congress had authorized the use of military force in Iraq in October 2002.

In addition to U.S. losses, other coalition casualty figures include more than 300 wounded, as well as 24 British deaths, 2 French deaths, and 39 deaths among coalition Arab forces. An estimated 3,000 Kuwaitis died during the Iraqi occupation, some of whom were killed during coalition efforts to liberate the country in February 1991. To this number may be added 1 death and 78 wounded among the Israeli population, which had been subjected to Iraqi Scud missile attacks during the conflict.

A major question surrounds DESERT STORM casualties related to "friendly fire" incidents, a euphemism describing the accidental death of service personnel because of their own or allied fire. Considering the small number of overall coalition deaths, an extremely high proportion was lost to friendly-fire incidents. Indeed, an estimated 46 Americans died as a result of friendly fire, as did 9 British military personnel. This fact led to an ongoing and occasionally acrimonious debate after the conflict's end about why friendly-fire incidents were so prevalent in such a short war.

Initial estimates placed Iraqi military losses at 100,000 killed, in what Iraqi leader Saddam Hussein had promised would be the "mother of all battles." However, later estimates reduced this figure considerably, to no more than 35,000. A U.S. Air Force survey based on Iraqi prisoner of war (POW) testimony estimated that Iraqi military forces lost only 20,000–22,000 killed. More than 300,000 were also believed to have been wounded. More than 70,000 Iraqi soldiers were taken prisoner by coalition forces. The number of Iraqi civilian casualties, which is even harder to pinpoint, varies widely, from 2,300 to 200,000. The government of Iraq purposely inflated casualty rates during the war in an attempt to gain support from the Islamic world. Although most estimates place actual civilian casualty numbers closer to the lower end of the spectrum, this issue has remained highly politicized.

The issue of "collateral damage," a euphemism for unintended civilian deaths and injuries caused by attacking intended military targets, is also steeped in controversy. The Persian Gulf War was one of the first conflicts in which civilian targets were studiously avoided; nevertheless, civilian casualties ensued, particularly as a consequence of the air war. One especially gruesome example occurred on February 13, 1991, at the Amirya bunker, where many civilian dead were captured in images broadcast around the world. That day, the U.S. Air Force dropped two laser-guided bombs on what the Americans asserted was an Iraqi command and control bunker. As it turned out, however, the bunker was also filled with Iraqi civilians, and 314 were believed to have been killed, including 130 children. The United States government subsequently accused the Iraqi government of using its civilian population as human shields, which is considered a war crime. Iraq and its defenders, however, accused the United States of knowingly attacking a civilian shelter. The incident was perhaps the most troubling of all civilian casualty incidents in the war.

STEPHANIE TROMBLEY

See also

DESERT STORM, Operation; Friendly Fire; Gulf War Syndrome; Human Shields

References

Carlisle, Rodney P., and John Stewart Bowman. *Persian Gulf War.* New York: Facts on File, 2003.

Freedman, Lawrence, and Efraim Karsh. *The Gulf Conflict, 1990–1991: Diplomacy and War in the New World Order.* Princeton, NJ: Princeton University Press, 1993.

Human Rights Watch. *Needless Deaths in the Gulf War: Civilian Casualties during the Air Campaign and Violations of the Laws of War.* New York: Human Rights Watch, 1991.

Casualties, Operation ENDURING FREEDOM

The War on Terror was launched on October 7, 2001, in Afghanistan, a response to the terror attacks against the United States of September 11, 2001. In terms of coalition casualties, as of the end of 2009 there had been 1,567 U.S. and coalition military deaths in Afghanistan as part of Operation ENDURING FREEDOM and the International Security Assistance Force (ISAF). Americans have sustained the largest number of deaths, 946. The U.S. total includes Central Intelligence Agency (CIA) personnel. Not included among the number of American casualties are the deaths of armed American private security company personnel.

While American forces have suffered the most coalition casualties, other nations have also experienced a spike in the numbers killed in action in recent years, especially in 2009 when the total killed was double that of the previous year (520 vs. 295). Since 2006, after IASF expanded its jurisdiction to the southern regions of Afghanistan, which had previously been under U.S. military authority, the number of British and Canadian casualties increased. The highly volatile provinces of Helmand and Kandahar have been particularly dangerous for coalition forces. As of the end of 2009, British forces had suffered 245 killed. The war in Afghanistan has also resulted in the largest number of fatalities for any single Canadian military operation since the Korean War. As of the end of 2009, 118 Canadian troops had died.

Apart from the United States, the United Kingdom, and Canada, coalition deaths by country as of August 2009 were as follows: France, 36; Germany, 35; Spain, 26; Denmark, 30; Italy, 22; the Netherlands, 21; Poland, 16; Australia, 11; Romania, 11; Estonia, 7; Norway, 4; Sweden, 4; Czech Republic, 3; Latvia, 3; Hungary, 2; Portugal, 2; Turkey, 2; Belgium, 1; Finland, 1; Jordan, 1; Lithuania, 1; and South Korea, 1.

Since Operation ENDURING FREEDOM began, there have been numerous incidents involving civilians killed during military operations against the Taliban and Al Qaeda. U.S.-led coalition troops and North Atlantic Treaty Organization (NATO) forces have maintained that great efforts have been made to avoid civilian casualties in efforts to eliminate the insurgency. They have complained that insurgents often blend in with local populations when under attack, thus increasing the risk of more civilian casualties. Many civilians, as well as Afghan soldiers and security forces, were killed by insurgent attacks, especially in 2006 resulting from suicide bombings.

Casualties, by Branch, in the U.S. Armed Forces during Operation ENDURING FREEDOM **(through April 3, 2010)**

	U.S. Air Force	U.S. Army	U.S. Marines	U.S. Navy (including Coast Guard)	Total
Killed in action	20	454	92	32	598
Died of wounds	3	104	43	3	153
Nonhostile deaths	23	189	42	21	275
Wounded in action	142	4,057	1,207	104	5,510
Total casualties	188	4,804	1,384	160	6,536

As to exact numbers of civilians killed, the debate continues, with numbers varying markedly. Estimates of dead range as high as 50,000 in the invasion and ongoing war from all causes.

Beginning in 2007, insurgents launched attacks that were both more aggressive and greater in number. This has increased not only the number of collateral deaths but also the number of insurgent deaths. Casualties showed a dramatic increase in 2009. Afghan casualty totals are in dispute, but at least 5,500 Afghan security personnel had died through the end of 2009. Civilian deaths are even more difficult to ascertain. Insurgent losses are estimated at between 20,000 and 30,000, with 20,000 taken prisoner. The number of civilian deaths is very much in dispute. Through the end of 2009, they are believed to have numbered at least 25,000.

CHARLES F. HOWLETT AND SPENCER C. TUCKER

See also

Afghanistan; Al Qaeda; ENDURING FREEDOM, Operation; Taliban; Taliban Insurgency, Afghanistan

References

Goodson, Larry P. *Afghanistan's Endless War: State Failure, Regional Politics, and the Rise of the Taliban.* Seattle: University of Washington Press, 2001.

Kunkel, Thomas. "Casualties of War." *American Journalism Review* 24 (January 1, 2002): 4.

Casualties, Operation IRAQI FREEDOM

Casualties as a result of combat operations in Iraq during Operation IRAQI FREEDOM, which began on March 19, 2003, and continue to the present, have been a constant source of controversy, particularly in the United States. The quick and decisive victory won by the United States in the 1991 Persian Gulf War, which saw few American casualties, and the low initial American casualty count for the Afghanistan War, Operation ENDURING FREEDOM, had conditioned U.S. citizens and politicians to expect a speedy and relatively easy victory in Iraq. Although the initial combat phase (March 19–April 30, 2003) produced few U.S. and coalition combat deaths, the subsequent insurgency led to several thousand more, with the toll continuing to climb. Many responded to the mounting IRAQI FREEDOM casualty numbers with incredulity and calls for a full or total withdrawal of American troops from Iraq. Other nations with large troop deployments in Iraq—particularly Great Britain—experienced similar developments.

The U.S. Department of Defense provides a continuously running tally of American casualties. Its figures include numbers of American personnel killed in action (KIA) and wounded in action (WIA) in both official Operation IRAQI FREEDOM combat operations (March 19, 2003–April, 30, 2003) and postcombat operations (May 1, 2003–present). In the first phase of the war, 139 American military personnel were killed, and 545 were wounded. Total U.S. military deaths from both phases of IRAQI FREEDOM were 4,688 through the end of 2009, while the total number of American military personnel wounded in action during the same period is some 31,500. Of those wounded, a majority returned to active duty within 72 hours, classified as wounded in action, returned to duty (WIA RTD). Each fatality milestone has occasioned an outcry of opposition to the war, and when the casualty count topped 4,000 in spring 2008 and coincided with a particularly heated presidential primary campaign, these numbers became a source of even greater political controversy.

In addition to the U.S. casualties, through April 17, 2009, a total of 318 coalition troops had been killed, including 179 Britons. Also, the Iraq War has claimed the lives of 139 journalists. A total of 1,264 contractors have also been killed.

Although the Department of Defense makes information on U.S. casualties publicly available, precise figures documenting Iraqi casualties, both military and civilian, are more difficult to access, and nearly all figures come with caveats. Iraqi sources have reported that government agencies are not permitted to report the numbers of bodies buried daily. Credible sources indicate roughly 9,200 Iraqi combatant fatalities during the first phase of Operation IRAQI FREEDOM; estimates range from a low of 7,600 to a high of 10,800. According to the Iraq Coalition Casualty Count, an estimated 8,298 members of the Iraqi Security Forces (ISF) have been killed in combat, fighting Iraqi insurgents. The Iraq Coalition Casualty Count is one of the most thorough databases compiling this information, although the group does not provide numbers of wounded ISF personnel and its information is not considered reliable by European, Arab, or American academics. Current and credible estimates of the number of insurgents killed are among the hardest statistics to obtain, because membership in those groups is both fluid and clandestine. According to calculations made in September 2007, the number of insurgents killed after the fall of Baghdad in April 2003 was 19,492; casualties continue to accumulate, although a reliably sourced updated estimate has not been released.

Casualties, by Branch, in the U.S. Armed Forces during Operation IRAQI FREEDOM (through April 3, 2010)

	U.S. Air Force	U.S. Army	U.S. Marine Corps	U.S. Navy (including Coast Guard)	Total
Killed in action	29	1,910	664	63	2,666
Died of wounds	0	605	187	2	794
Died while missing	0	6	0	0	6
Died while captured	0	5	0	0	5
Nonhostile deaths	22	676	171	38	907
Wounded in action	444	22,067	8,624	635	31,770
Total casualties	495	25,269	9,646	738	36,148

The number of Iraqi civilians killed during IRAQI FREEDOM has been widely disputed. The Lancet study of 2006, so-called for its publication in the British medical journal of that name, was carried out by Iraqi and American physicians and researchers from al-Mustansiriyya University and Johns Hopkins University through a cluster-survey of households where respondents had to show death certificates. It estimated a total of 426,369 to 793,663 Iraqi deaths to that date.

A third study, by experts from the Federal Ministry of Health in Baghdad, the Kurdistan Ministry of Planning, the Kurdistan Ministry of Health, the Central Organization for Statistics and Information Technology in Baghdad, and the World Health Organization carried out the Iraq Family Health Survey Study (IFHS) Group (known as the WHO study in the media). The IFHS study estimated 151,000 Iraqi deaths from March 2003 to June 2006. The study actually presented a range of deaths from 104,000 to 223,000 for those years.

Other sources have estimated Iraqi civilian casualties from the war and sectarian violence from 600,000 to more than 1,000,000. The independent British-based Opinion Research Bureau estimated 1,220,580 Iraqis deaths by September 2007. Other than deliberate underreporting, some sources pointed to the suppression of statistics by the Iraqi government in the belief that to do so would compromise efforts to quell violence.

Although there is disagreement on the actual number of civilian deaths in Iraq, there is general agreement that the numbers have been very high. Generally speaking, those who supported the war have denied the higher civilian casualty counts, while those who opposed the war held them to be valid.

The Iraq Coalition Casualty Count serves as a thorough clearinghouse for information on all coalition fatalities. During the period of official IRAQI FREEDOM combat (March 19–May 1, 2003), 33 soldiers from the United Kingdom were killed; no other coalition nation suffered any fatalities during this phase of operations. As of the end of 2009, the Iraq Coalition Casualty Count cites the following fatality numbers for other coalition nations: Australia, 2; Azerbaijan, 1; Bulgaria, 13; Czech Republic, 1; Denmark, 7; El Salvador, 5; Estonia, 2; Fiji, 1; Georgia, 5; Hungary, 1; Italy, 33; Kazakhstan, 1; Latvia, 3; Netherlands, 2; Poland, 22; Romania, 3; Slovakia, 4; South Korea, 1; Spain, 11; Thailand, 2; Ukraine, 18; United Kingdom, 176. The group does not provide WIA casualty figures.

A high suicide rate among U.S. military and veterans has become a special matter of concern. Although no clear answers for this have emerged, it has been attributed to extended tours, too little time off between tours, the nature of the conflict, circumstances at home, and other factors.

Periodic lulls in violence and the achievement of certain strategic objectives have resulted in temporary decreases in the rates of injury and death, but the nature of the guerrilla-style, low-intensity conflict that has characterized the Iraq insurgency and the continuing sectarian conflicts mean that casualties on all sides will likely continue to accumulate.

REBECCA A. ADELMAN AND SHERIFA ZUHUR

See also

ENDURING FREEDOM, Operation; IRAQI FREEDOM, Operation; Iraqi Insurgency

References

Baker, James A., III, and Lee Hamilton. *The Iraq Study Group: The Way Froward, a New Approach.* New York: Vintage Books, USA, 2006.

Burnham, Gilbert, Riyadh Lafta, Shannon Doocy, et al. "Mortality after the 2003 Invasion of Iraq: A Cross-Sectional Cluster Sample Survey." *Lancet* 368(5945) (October 21, 2006): 1421–1429.

Capdevila, Luc, and Danièle Voldman. *War Dead: Western Society and Casualties of War.* Translated by Richard Veasey. Edinburgh, UK: Edinburgh University Press, 2006.

"Documented Civilian Deaths from Violence." Iraq Body Count, http://www.iraqbodycount.org/database.

Fischer, Hanna. "Iraqi Civilian Casualties Estimates." Washington DC: Congressional Research Service, January 12, 2009.

Iraq Family Health Survey Study Group. "Violence-Related Mortality in Iraq from 2002 to 2006." *New England Journal of Medicine* (January 31, 2008): 484–492.

Mueller, John. "The Iraq Syndrome." *Foreign Affairs* 84 (2005): 44–54.

Roberts, Les, Riyadh Lafta, Richard Garfield, et al. "Mortality before and after the 2003 Invasion of Iraq: Cluster Sample Survey." *Lancet* 364(9448) (October 29, 2004): 1857–1864.

United States Department of Defense. "Operation Iraqi Freedom (OIF) U.S. Casualty Status," http://www.defenselink.mil/news/casualty.pdf.

Wood, Trish. *What Was Asked of Us: An Oral History of the Iraq War by the Soldiers Who Fought It.* New York: Little, Brown, 2006.

Central Intelligence Agency

Primary civilian government agency charged with carrying out intelligence and espionage activities for the United States. The

Central Intelligence Agency (CIA), created by the National Security Act of 1947, exercised primary responsibility for intelligence collection and analysis, but also for the conduct of covert actions.

The agency is the direct successor of the World War II Office of Strategic Services (OSS). In January 1946, President Harry S. Truman signed an executive order forming a Central Intelligence Group (CIG) patterned after the OSS, and on July 16, 1947, Truman signed the National Security Act, replacing the CIG with the new CIA as an independent agency within the executive branch. The CIA was to advise the National Security Council (NSC) on intelligence matters and make recommendations regarding coordination of intelligence activities. Although the original intent was only to authorize espionage, broad interpretation of the act's provisions led to authorization of covert operations. The director of central intelligence (DCI) was charged with reporting on intelligence activities to the president and Congress.

Known to insiders as "the Agency" or "the Company," the CIA played a key role in the overthrow of allegedly radical governments in Iran in 1953 and Guatemala in 1954. It was also active in assisting the Philippine government in crushing the Hukbalahap uprising; in Southeast Asia, especially in Laos, it operated Air America to funnel U.S. aid to anticommunist forces. Notable failures included the Bay of Pigs fiasco in Cuba in April 1961 and attempts to assassinate or discredit Cuban leader Fidel Castro. The CIA played an important role in the 1962 Cuban Missile Crisis, and its agents penetrated key governmental agencies in the Soviet Union. The CIA-sponsored Phoenix Program in Vietnam for the assassination of communist operatives engendered considerable controversy, as did its role in helping to oust Chilean president Salvador Allende in 1973. The CIA's involvement in assassination plots and domestic spying led to the creation of the President's Intelligence Oversight Board, as well as an Intelligence Committee in each house of Congress. The CIA failed to predict the 1979 revolution overthrowing the Shah of Iran, Mohammad Reza Shah Pahlavi. It provided important assistance to Afghan rebels following the Soviet invasion of that country. It also took part in the secret sale of arms to Iran arranged with the hostage release and funneling of the proceeds to Contra rebels fighting Nicaragua's

President George W. Bush, right, and Central Intelligence Agency (CIA) director George Tenet, left, pose in the main entrance of agency headquarters in Langley, Virginia, on March 20, 2001. (AP/Wide World Photos)

leftist Sandinista government, the so-called Iran-Contra Affair. This activity led Congress in 1991 to pass a new oversight law to prevent a reoccurrence. The CIA did provide useful intelligence on the threat posed by Iraq to neighboring Kuwait, but it was caught off guard by the actual August 1990 invasion.

The sudden collapse of the Soviet Union beginning with the failed coup attempt against Mikhail Gorbachev in August 1991 came as a complete surprise to the agency. Although the CIA had warned that terrorists might attempt to seize control of civilian airliners and fly them into buildings, it failed to provide timely intelligence that might have prevented the September 11, 2001, terrorist attacks against the World Trade Center in New York City and the Pentagon in Washington, D.C.

In December 2004, President George W. Bush signed the Intelligence Reform and Terrorism Prevention Act. That legislation abolished the positions of director of central intelligence (DCI) and deputy director of central intelligence (DDCI) and created the positions of director of the Central Intelligence Agency (D/CIA) and director of national intelligence (DNI), which took over some of the responsibilities that had been formerly handled by the CIA. These reforms were in response to the lapses of intelligence over the preceding years, including the September 11, 2001, attacks, bogus reports of weapons of mass destruction (WMDs) in Iraq, and other incidents that called into question CIA credibility and effectiveness.

The D/CIA is nominated by the president and approved by the U.S. Senate. Working with numerous staffs, the D/CIA is responsible for managing the operations, staff, and budget of the CIA. The D/CIA also oversees the National Human Source Intelligence division (HUMINT) and interacts with the Department of Homeland Security (DHS) to monitor terrorist and extremist activities within the United States. The CIA is organized into four primary directorates: the National Clandestine Service; the Directorate of Intelligence; the Directorate of Science and Technology; and the Directorate of Support. All four directorates are supposed to work together to collect, analyze, and distribute intelligence that is deemed necessary to protect national security.

In 1999 CIA director George Tenet had developed plans to deal with the Al Qaeda terrorist organization, which was headquartered in Afghanistan. The CIA was soon involved in sending flights over Afghanistan with drones to gather intelligence information on the terrorist training camps there. Following the terror attacks on September 11, 2001, the CIA came under great pressure regarding its previous efforts to combat terrorism, which in turn prompted the 2004 changes described above to America's intelligence-gathering apparatus.

The CIA has also received considerable criticism for its role in the Iraq War. Indeed, the agency was blamed, rightly or wrongly, for the assertion that Iraq possessed WMDs, which was a key factor in the 2003 decision to invade the country. As it turned out, no WMDs were found, and public support for the war fell quickly after this was made public. Because the George W. Bush administration

used the threat of WMDs as a justification for the war, the CIA's reputation was badly tarnished. As the war in Iraq continued, more information regarding early CIA involvement was released. Since then, numerous people have come forward claiming that a large percentage of CIA officials did not support what the agency was claiming about WMDs in Iraq. Many claim the CIA was pressured by the Bush administration to produce reports with intelligence that the administration wanted the CIA to find, and not necessarily the actual intelligence collected. More recently, the CIA has come under sharp criticism for its connection to the torturing of terrorist suspects, especially the controversial technique of waterboarding. Harsh interrogation techniques were officially authorized by top CIA officials (and approved by Vice President Richard "Dick" Cheney and President George W. Bush).

ARTHUR M. HOLST

See also

Al Qaeda; Bin Laden, Osama; Bush, George Walker; Cheney, Richard Bruce; *Cole*, USS, Attack on; Counterterrorism Strategy; Dar es Salaam, Bombing of U.S. Embassy; Nairobi, Kenya, Bombing of U.S. Embassy; September 11 Attacks; Tenet, George John; Terrorism; Torture of Prisoners; Weapons of Mass Destruction

References

Blum, William, Larry Bleidner, and Peter Scott. *Killing Hope: U.S. Military and CIA Interventions since World War II*. Monroe, ME: Common Courage, 1995.

Jeffreys-Jones, Rhodri. *The CIA and American Democracy*. New Haven, CT: Yale University Press, 1998.

Kessler, Ronald. *Inside the CIA: Revealing the Secrets of the World's Most Powerful Spy Agency*. New York: Pocket Books, 1994.

Prados, John. *Presidents' Secret Wars: CIA and Pentagon Covert Operations from World War II through the Persian Gulf*. Chicago: Ivan R. Dee, 1996.

Theoharis, Athan, ed. *The Central Intelligence Agency: Security under Scrutiny*. Westport, CT: Greenwood, 2006.

Central Treaty Organization

See Baghdad Pact

Chalabi, Ahmed Abd al-Hadi
Birth Date: October 30, 1944

Prominent Iraqi dissident and founder and leader of the U.S.-funded Iraqi National Congress (INC) from 1992 to 1999. Born on October 30, 1944, in Baghdad, Iraq, Ahmed Abd al-Hadi Chalabi, a liberal Shiite Muslim, was a member of one of Iraq's wealthiest and most influential families. Prior to the 1958 revolution that overthrew the Iraqi monarchy, Chalabi's father, a prominent banker, was president of the Senate and an adviser to King Faisal II.

Although the entire royal family and many of its supporters were murdered by the revolutionaries, Chalabi's family managed to escape into exile, living primarily in England and the United States. Chalabi earned a BS in mathematics from the Massachusetts Institute of Technology in 1965. In 1969, he obtained a PhD in mathematics from the University of Chicago and subsequently taught mathematics at the American University in Beirut until 1977.

In 1977, Chalabi relocated to Jordan where he established the Petra Bank. Within two years, Petra Bank had become the second-largest bank in Jordan. In 1989, Jordanian Central Bank governor Mohammad Said Nabulsi ordered the 20 banks operating in Jordan to deposit 30 percent of their foreign exchange holdings with the Central Bank. When Petra Bank refused to comply with the order, the Jordanian government launched an investigation of the bank's holdings, which revealed that most of the bank's stated assets in fact did not exist. Chalabi then fled to the United Kingdom. Although Chalabi later claimed that the entire situation was the result of Iraqi dictator Saddam Hussein's chicanery, the Jordanian government was forced to pay $200 million to depositors to avert the complete collapse of the Jordanian banking system. In 1992, the Jordanian government sentenced Chalabi in absentia to 22 years in prison for bank fraud. Chalabi continues to proclaim his innocence in the affair.

In 1991, immediately following the Persian Gulf War, Chalabi began lobbying influential members of the U.S. Congress, the Central Intelligence Agency (CIA), and the Pentagon for funding to sponsor a coup against Saddam Hussein's government. In 1992, he formed the Iraqi National Congress. Between 1992 and 2004, Chalabi and the Iraqi National Congress received more than $30 million from U.S. government sources.

Many within the CIA and the U.S. State Department eventually became suspicious of Chalabi's ability to deliver on promises made concerning the opposition, and it attacked his veracity. But his close ties with former defense secretary and then-vice president Dick Cheney and Deputy Secretary of Defense Paul Wolfowitz enabled Chalabi to continue to receive funding until the eve of the 2003 Anglo-American invasion of Iraq. In 1999, Chalabi broke with the INC and established the National Congress Coalition, a group that considered itself a less Islamist alternative to other Iraqi opposition groups. During the U.S. occupation of Iraq, Chalabi served as one of the deputy prime ministers in Ibrahim al-Jafari's cabinet.

When it had become patently clear that there were no weapons of mass destruction (WMDs) in Iraq, the existence of which had been a major pretext of the 2003 war, the George W. Bush administration became more concerned about its connections with Chalabi. The information that he had been giving the administration since at least mid-2001 was either falsified or was unintentionally erroneous. Be that as it may, Chalabi steadfastly stood by the top-secret reports, much of which pointed to an illicit Iraqi program to build nuclear, chemical, and biological weapons. It is surprising that the Bush administration would have given so much credence to Chalabi's assertions, unless it was because they supported the administration's own conclusions.

On May 20, 2004, U.S. and Iraqi forces raided Chalabi's residence to determine the extent of his duplicity in his dealings with American officials. Charges were briefly drawn up against him, but these were later dropped. Nevertheless, in November 2005, Chalabi flew to Washington, D.C. to meet with high-level Bush administration officials.

From December 2005 to January 2006, Chalabi was Iraq's oil minister, and in April 2005 he was appointed deputy prime minister, a post he held from May 2005 to May 2006. In the December 15, 2005, elections, Chalabi suffered a humiliating defeat in his quest to become Iraqi prime minister. Allegations that Chalabi was bolstering his relations with Iranians and supposedly passed secret information to them in 2004 further tarnished his reputation in Washington. Paradoxically, his reputation in Iraq was troubled by his close relationship with the Americans.

Chalabi continues to lead the National Congress Coalition. In October 2007, Iraqi prime minister Nuri al-Maliki appointed Chalabi to head the Iraq Services Committee, a group that brings together eight government service ministries and several Baghdad municipal agencies that are at the forefront of the recovery and modernization effort in postwar Iraq. By all indications, Chalabi performed effectively in this position.

MICHAEL R. HALL

See also

Bush, George Walker; Cheney, Richard Bruce; DESERT STORM, Operation; Hussein, Saddam; Jafari, Ibrahim al-; Maliki, Nuri Muhammed Kamil Hasan al-; Wolfowitz, Paul Dundes

References

Fox, Robert. *Peace and War in Iraq, 2003–2005.* Barnsley, UK: Leo Cooper, 2005.
Packer, George. *The Assassins' Gate: America in Iraq.* New York: Farrar, Straus and Giroux, 2005.
Ricks, Thomas E. *Fiasco: The American Military Adventure in Iraq.* New York: Penguin, 2006.

Challenger Main Battle Tanks

British-designed main battle tank (MBT). The British Ministry of Defense placed its first order for the Challenger 1 series main battle tanks in 1978. The Challenger 1 was basically an improved Shir 2, modified to meet modern British Army requirements. The Shir 2 had originally been developed for export to Iran.

The Challenger 1's layout had the driver's compartment at the front, turret and fighting compartment in the center, and the engine and transmission in the rear. The Challenger 1 had a four-man crew. A Perkins Engines, Condor 12-volt, 1200 25-liter diesel engine developing 1,200 horsepower at 2,300 revolutions per minute powered the Challenger 1. Challenger 1 weighed 62 tons and measured 37.72 feet long (including the gun), 11.52 feet wide, and 9.68 feet high. It had an on-road range of 279 miles and a top speed of 37 miles per hour (mph).

Both the turret and hull incorporated Chobham armor, a classified mix of steel and ceramic layers that provided excellent protection against both conventional armor-piercing and high-explosive antitank rounds. The tank's original main weapon was a 120-millimeter (mm) rifled gun. Secondary armament included a 7.62-mm coaxial machine gun and an external 7.62-mm machine gun mounted at the commander's cupola. The Challenger 1 had a Marconi Command and Control Systems improved fire-control system (IFCS).

Challenger 1 tanks were deployed to Saudi Arabia in late 1990 as part of Operation DESERT SHIELD. The 7th Armoured Brigade deployed two regiments of Challenger 1 tanks, each equipped with 57 tanks. The 4th Brigade deployed one regiment of Challenger 1 tanks with 43 tanks. Both brigades were part of the British 1st Armoured Division. In early 1991, technicians upgraded the tanks by installing explosive reactive armor (ERA) on the nose and glacis plate of the Challenger 1, along with passive armor along the sides of the hull.

During Operation DESERT STORM, the British 1st Armoured Division protected the flank of the U.S. VII Corps. Its particular target was an Iraqi tank division, the 52nd Armored Division. The British armor decisively defeated the Iraqis during February 25–26, 1991. An Iraqi brigade commander later reported: "[I] did not know what a Challenger tank looked like until one showed up outside my bunker that morning." The Iraqis failed to knock out a single Challenger 1 during the entire campaign. Meanwhile, Challenger 1 crews were credited with destroying about 300 Iraqi main battle tanks. The American M1A1 Abrams tank and the British Challenger were the best tanks to fight in the Persian Gulf War. The Challenger's excellent long-range fire-control system achieved the longest confirmed kill of any tank during the war—a shot of more than three miles.

As with the American M1A1, the Challenger 1 was at least a generation ahead of any competing Iraqi tank. One of its main advantages was its ability to fire accurately while under way. Iraqi tanks could not do this. Also, compared to Iraqi tanks, Western tanks such as the Challenger 1 fired more lethal ordnance, depleted uranium shells, with far greater accuracy and at greater range.

In November 1986, Vickers Defense Systems began work on the design of the Challenger 2. The British government placed its first order for the Challenger 2 in June 1991. It featured a new turret design mounting a 120-mm rifled tank gun capable of firing a depleted uranium round. Its secondary armament was a coaxial 7.62-mm chain gun as well as an externally mounted 7.62-mm machine gun. The hull was almost identical to the hull of the Challenger 1. However, improvements in the chassis included more rugged steering controls and fire-retardant bag-type fuel tanks. The main engine featured 33 improvements in the electrical system, 11 improvements to the gearbox assembly, 11 improvements to the running gear, and 37 improvements to the vehicle electrics.

The Challenger 2 weighed 62.5 tons and measured 37.73 feet long (including gun), 11.48 feet wide (13.78 feet with armor appliqué), and was 8.2 feet high. Like its predecessor, the tank had a four-man crew. Its engine horsepower output is virtually identical, as are its performance statistics (range and speed). Compared to the Challenger 1, the main areas of improvement included a solid-state gun control equipment, more-modern fire-control equipment, a commander's gyro-stabilized panoramic day sight, rotor and mantlet gun mounting, gunner's gyro-stabilized sight, gunner's telescopic sight, thermal imager, and more-advanced Chobham armor. The superior fire-control equipment allowed the tank typically to engage a target in less than eight seconds.

During Operation IRAQI FREEDOM, the British included 116 Challenger 2 tanks in their deployed force. They operated in the 7th Armoured Brigade of the 1st (United Kingdom) Armoured Division. As had been the case in the Persian Gulf War, the Challenger 2s did not suffer much from hostile fire. The most serious damage to a Challenger 2 tank occurred on the night of March 25, 2003, during a series of contacts with Iraqi forces along the Shatt al-Basra Canal. A Challenger 2 attached to the Black Watch Battle Group mistakenly fired at a Challenger 2 serving in the Royal Regiment of Fusiliers Battle Group. The target's driver and tank commander were killed, and the other two crewmen were injured.

The Challenger 2 continues to be the United Kingdom's MBT, and will remain so for some time to come. Between 1993 and 2002, approximately 425 Challenger 2 tanks were manufactured.

JAMES ARNOLD

See also

Armored Warfare, Persian Gulf and Iraq Wars; Explosive Reactive Armor; M1A1 and M1A2 Abrams Main Battle Tanks

References

Cordesman, Anthony H. *The Iraq War: Strategy, Tactics, and Military Lessons.* Westport, CT: Praeger, 2003.

Jane's Armour and Artillery, 1990–1991. London: Jane's Information Group, 1990.

Jane's Armour and Artillery, 2001–2002. London: Jane's Information Group, 2001.

Chamoun, Camille Nimr
Birth Date: April 3, 1900
Death Date: August 7, 1987

Prominent Lebanese politician and premier. Camille Nimr Chamoun (Kamil Shamun) was born on April 3, 1900, into a prominent Maronite Christian family at Dayr al-Qamar in Lebanon. Although a Maronite Christian, he came from the Shuf district where many Muslim Druze lived, and he thus understood the principle of local support. The Druze, largely concentrated in Lebanon's Shuf Mountains and western Beirut, had once dominated Mount Lebanon and the Maronites. The latter gained social ascendancy. The Maronites, originally followers of St. Maroun, are Eastern-rite Catholics recognized by Rome in the sixth century and were largely concentrated in the Mount Lebanon district, eastern Beirut, and some areas of south Lebanon. Muslims, Druze, and Christians did

Lebanese president Camille Chamoun, photographed in 1953. (AP/Wide World Photos)

not seriously engage in violent conflict until 1860 in present-day Lebanon when Druze and Muslims clashed.

Lebanese political tensions between religious groups also had roots in economics, as some Maronites had become wealthy through commerce and their ties with European powers. They opposed the unification with Syria preferred by some Muslims and other Christian groups. Each sect possessed feudal lords who commanded the political loyalties of peasants or residents of urban areas.

Chamoun received his elementary education at a Catholic school in Dayr al-Qamar and graduated from high school in Beirut in a Francophone educational system. During World War I, the Chamoun family was exiled for anti-Turkish and Lebanese nationalist activities on the part of Chamoun's father. Following the war, Lebanon became a French mandate, and French colonialism thus became a target of Lebanese nationalists. Chamoun, meanwhile, immersed himself in his studies. Upon graduation from the Faculty of Law at the University of Saint Joseph in Beirut and obtaining his law license in 1923, he became a successful lawyer, businessman, and property holder. He also began expressing his political views in articles for the newspaper *Le Reviel.*

Although the economy had expanded during the French mandate, there was much about the system of French-dominated governance that the Lebanese disliked, including press censorship

and preference for French investors. Chamoun wanted this situation changed. In 1929 he won his first election campaign and became an elector, whose duty it was to help choose delegates to Lebanon's National Assembly. That year, he also married Zalfa Thabit, whose family had important connections in British social circles. Chamoun subsequently learned English and developed contacts with British politicians.

Chamoun's nationalism subsequently intensified, and upon winning election to the Chamber of Deputies in 1934 he sided with the Constitutional Bloc led by Sheikh Bishara al-Khuri, which sought an end to French domination. Chamoun won reelection in 1937 and was appointed minister of finance (although the Constitutional Bloc was a minority party). During World War II, he emerged as one of the crucial architects of Lebanese independence. In 1941, Free French and British forces invaded Lebanon and ousted the colonial government controlled by Vichy, which had collaborated with Nazi Germany. Britain supported Lebanese independence, a move that France opposed. Chamoun lobbied the British to ensure their continued support for nationhood. Such activities earned him the label from the French of "agent of British intelligence" and led to his arrest and imprisonment in November 1943, along with Khuri, and Riyadh al-Sulh. Massive public demonstrations, however, led to their release after only 11 days, on November 22, a day that has since been celebrated as Lebanon's Independence Day. The French government-in-exile agreed to allow Lebanon's independence.

Elections that year made the Constitutional Bloc the majority party in the National Assembly, and Khuri became president and Sulh prime minister. Chamoun became minister of finance. Then, because of his close ties to the British, Chamoun was made ambassador to Great Britain. He held this post during 1944–1946.

Chamoun's demonstrated political acumen helped bring British support for the withdrawal of French troops at a time when the French government had developed second thoughts about relinquishing total control of Lebanon. Chamoun also secured Lebanese membership in the United Nations (UN). Now enormously popular, he planned to become president, but Khuri moved to amend the Lebanese Constitution to allow himself another term. Chamoun subsequently resigned his ministerial post and cooperated with the opposition National Socialist Front Party led by Kamal Jumblat (Junblat), a Druze leader. Khuri remained president, but by 1951 his opponents gained a larger following, and widespread discontent over charges of corruption led to his resignation in 1952.

With Jumblat's support, Chamoun won election by the National Assembly as president. Chamoun now ran into a formidable problem. He had antagonized his Constitutional Bloc followers and many Maronites by having cooperated with Jumblat, and when he tried to win back these people, he antagonized Jumblat and many Druze, who opposed his pro-Western, conservative politics and alleged corruption. Nevertheless, Chamoun initiated several reforms: a change in the election system that weakened the domination of public office by landholding aristocrats and urban elites; suffrage for women; and an independent judiciary. The economy expanded under Chamoun, and he promoted a free exchange of ideas, including relative freedom of the press.

Yet many members of the politically disadvantaged Muslim communities objected to Chamoun's refusal to let Lebanon join the United Arab Republic (UAR) in 1958, and Pan-Arabists who favored Egyptian president Gamal Abdel Nasser held demonstrations that threatened to overthrow the government in June 1958. Chamoun believed that both his own power and Lebanese unity were imperiled. He claimed that the pro-Nasserists would make Lebanon socialist, and he called on the United States for assistance. President Dwight D. Eisenhower dispatched U.S. Marines to Beirut. This action brought charges that Chamoun was a tool of Western imperialism and was too close to the pro-Israeli United States. U.S. diplomat Robert Murphy helped persuade Chamoun to resign in 1958. He was succeeded by General Fuad Shihab, a Christian who nonetheless was popular with Lebanese Muslims.

Chamoun remained politically active. In 1959, he formed a new opposition organization, the National Liberal Party (al-Ahrar); he won election to the National Assembly in 1960 but was defeated in 1964 amid charges of gerrymandering. He again won election to the National Assembly in 1968 and 1972. He successfully maneuvered Sulayman Franjiyyah into the presidency in 1970. Chamoun held a succession of ministerial posts in the 1970s and 1980s.

In 1975, however, Lebanon's long-standing political and sectarian tensions erupted in civil war, and Chamoun obtained Israeli support for the Maronite forces. He helped found the Lebanese Front, heading it during 1976–1978. It was a mostly Christian grouping of different parties. Its united militia was known as the Lebanese Forces (LF). Chamoun was initially inclined toward Syria but then opposed the growing Syrian presence in Lebanon. In 1980 the LF was largely destroyed in a surprise attack by the Phalangists, the militia headed by Christian rival Bashir Jummayil.

The bloodshed in Lebanon continued. Following the Israeli invasion of Lebanon in 1982, Chamoun entered into tacit cooperation with Israel against Syria, which was then occupying much of Lebanon and controlling its affairs. In 1984 Chamoun entered the National Unity Government as deputy prime minister, but the civil war, which by the end of the decade had claimed some 130,000 lives, overwhelmed this effort. Chamoun died in office in Beirut on August 7, 1987. Four years later, a peace accord was signed, although it took several more years for peace to return to most of Lebanon. Chamoun was one of the most significant figures of modern Lebanese politics.

SPENCER C. TUCKER

See also
Eisenhower, Dwight David; Lebanon; Lebanon, U.S. Intervention in (1958); Lebanon, U.S. Intervention in (1982–1984); Murphy, Robert Daniel; Nasser, Gamal Abdel; United Arab Republic

References
Chamoun, Camille. *Crise au Liban*. Beirut: Imprimerie Catholique, 1977.

Cobban, Helena. *The Making of Modern Lebanon*. London: Hutchinson, 1985.
El-Khazen, Farid. *The Breakdown of the State in Lebanon, 1967–1976*. Cambridge: Harvard University Press, 2000.
Laffin, John. *The War of Desperation: Lebanon, 1982–1985*. London: Osprey, 1985.

Chemical Ali

See Majid al Tikriti, Ali Hassan al-

Chemical Weapons and Warfare

Chemical weapons use the toxic effects from man-made substances to kill or incapacitate enemy forces. Chemical weapons range from such riot control agents as tear gas and pepper spray, which cause short-term incapacitation, to lethal nerve agents such as tabun and sarin, which can kill humans with only a miniscule exposure. The use of living organisms, such as bacteria, viruses, or spores, is classified not as chemical warfare but as biological warfare. However, certain chemical weapons such as ricin and botulinum toxins use products created by living organisms.

Chemical weapons are typically described by the effects they have on victims. The major classes of chemical weapons are nerve agents, blood agents, vesicants, pulmonary agents, cytotoxic proteins, lachrymatory agents, and incapacitating agents. Nerve agents quickly break down neuron-transmitting synapses, resulting in the paralysis of major organs and quick death. Blood agents cause massive internal bleeding or prevent cells from using oxygen, leading to anaerobic respiration, seizures, and death. Vesicants, also known as blistering agents, burn skin and respiratory systems, either of which can be fatal. Pulmonary agents suffocate victims by flooding the respiratory system. Cytotoxic agents prevent protein synthesis, leading to the failure of one or more organs. Lachrymatory agents cause immediate eye irritation or blindness, although the effects are deliberately temporary. Incapacitating agents, also temporary, cause effects similar to drug intoxication.

The most important characteristics of an effective chemical weapon are its ability to be delivered accurately and its ability to persist as a danger to enemy troops. Throughout history, delivery methods for chemical weapons have evolved from simple dispersion, often by releasing a gas into the wind, to artillery shells or missile warheads containing chemical agents and to aerodynamic dispersal from aircraft. Since World War II, binary chemical weapons have been developed that contain two substances that are harmless by themselves but when combined form a weapons-grade chemical agent.

Primitive chemical weapons were used as early as the Stone Age, when hunter-gatherer societies used poison-tipped weapons for hunting. Sources of poisons included animal venoms and

A U.S. soldier training in protective clothing designed to protect against biological and chemical weapons, in Saudi Arabia during Operation DESERT SHIELD in 1990. (Derek Hudson/Sygma/Corbis)

States proposed the development of artillery shells containing toxic gasses.

During World War I (1914–1918), more chemical weapons were used than during any other war in history. At the Second Battle of Ypres (April 22, 1915), German troops opened canisters of chlorine gas and waited for the wind to push the gas into Allied trenches. Soon both sides were using artillery shells to deliver chemical attacks, incorporating a wide variety of chemical agents.

Although they caused a great deal of panic and disruption on the battlefield and caused more than 1 million mostly nonlethal casualties in World War I, chemical weapons were never decisive by themselves. The chemical weapons of the period were relatively weak by modern standards, and no army of the time had developed nerve agents. Although early gas masks and other countermeasures were relatively primitive, they did neutralize the chemical effects to some degree. The Germans, under the artillery genius Colonel Georg Bruchmüller, came the closest to achieving decisive breakthroughs with chemical weapons during the 1918 offensives, but the German Army didn't have the operational mobility to exploit the tactical advantage.

During World War II (1939–1945), chemical weapons were used in a few isolated instances, although both the Axis and the Allies had developed large arsenals of extremely toxic agents. Both sides feared retaliation by the enemy, and neither chose to use its massive stockpiles of chemical weapons.

In the Middle East, the first modern large-scale use of lethal chemical agents occurred during the Iran-Iraq War (1980–1988). Early in the war, Iraq dropped bombs containing mustard agent and tabun on Iranian troops, causing 100,000 casualties including 20,000 deaths. Iraq accused Iran of having used chemical weapons first, but the allegations were never confirmed by United Nations (UN) investigators. Near the end of the war, the Iraqi government used chemical weapons against rebellious Kurdish Iraqi citizens.

During the 1991 Persian Gulf War, Iraq was accused of launching Scud missiles with chemical warheads against Israel, although no traces of chemical weapons were found. Iraq did not strike the attacking coalition forces with chemical weapons. One possibility is that the Iraqis feared that the coalition would retaliate with its own chemical weapons or perhaps even tactical nuclear weapons. A more likely possibility, however, is that the Iraqis never had the planning and coordination time necessary to employ chemical

vegetable toxins. Undoubtedly, poison-tipped weapons were also used in intertribal warfare. Ancient writings describe efforts to poison water systems to halt invading armies. Chinese texts from approximately 1000 BC describe methods to create and disperse poisonous smoke in war. Ancient Spartan and Athenian armies both used chemical weapons by the fifth century BC. The Roman Army, however, considered the use of poisons abhorrent, and Roman jurists condemned enemies for poisoning water supplies. With the dawn of the gunpowder era, besieging armies launched incendiary devices and poisonous projectiles into enemy fortifications. By the 19th century, inventors in Britain and the United

Major Classes of Chemical Weapons

Class	Effects	Severity	Examples
Blistering agents	Burn skin and respiratory system	Mild to severe	Lewisite and mustard gas
Blood agents	Cause internal bleeding, prevent oxygen uptake	Moderate to severe	Cyanogen chloride and hydrogen cyanide
Cytotoxic agents	Prevent protein synthesis	Moderate to severe	Ricin
Incapacitating agents	Produce effects similar to intoxication	Mild to moderate	Agent 15, KOLOKOL-1, and LSD
Lachrymatory agents	Cause eye irritation or temporary blindness	Mild to moderate	Bromine, thiophene, and xylyl bromide
Nerve agents	Break down neural synapses causing paralysis	Moderate to severe	Sarin, soman, and tabun
Pulmonary agents	Cause suffocation	Mild to severe	Chlorine, diphosgene, and phosgene

weapons. Virtually every successful use of chemical weapons in the 20th century was in an offensive operation, where the attacker had the initiative and necessary time to plan and tightly control the use of such weapons and their effects. Being on the defensive from the start, the Iraqis never had that flexibility.

Chemical weapons in the hands of terrorist groups pose a significant potential threat. On March 20, 1995, Aum Shinrikyo, a Japanese apocalyptic cult, released sarin gas on a Tokyo subway, killing 12 commuters and injuring more than 5,000. In 2002 the terrorist organization Al Qaeda released a videotape purportedly showing the deaths of dogs from a nerve agent. Al Qaeda has repeatedly announced its intention to obtain chemical, biological, and nuclear weapons.

There have been many attempts to prohibit the development and use of chemical weapons. In 1874 the Brussels Declaration outlawed the use of poison in warfare. The 1900 Hague Conference banned projectiles carrying poisonous gasses, as did the Washington Arms Conference Treaty of 1922 and the Geneva Protocol of 1929. None of the prohibitions proved sufficient to eradicate chemical warfare, however. The most recent effort to eliminate chemical weapons was the multilateral Chemical Weapons Convention (CWC) of 1993. The CWC came into effect in 1997 and prohibited the production and use of chemical weapons. Numerous nations known to maintain or suspected of maintaining chemical weapons stockpiles refused to sign or abide by the treaty, including several in the Middle East. Egypt, Libya, and Syria, all known to possess chemical weapons, each refused to sign the CWC, although Libya acceded to the treaty in early 2004 and has vowed to dismantle its chemical weapons program.

Israel, long known to possess a sophisticated chemical weapons capability, signed the CWC but never ratified the agreement. Iran signed and ratified the CWC but refused to prove that it had destroyed known stockpiles of chemical weapons and does not allow international inspectors to examine its facilities.

In future Middle Eastern conflicts, chemical weapons are far less likely to be used in terrorist attacks than in large-scale military operations. Chemical weapons are not easy to use. They are difficult and awkward to store, transport, and handle; their use requires detailed and expensive planning and lead times; once they are released, their effects are difficult to predict and control; and one's own troops require specialized equipment and extensive training to operate in a chemical environment.

PAUL J. SPRINGER

See also

Al Qaeda; Biological Weapons and Warfare; DESERT STORM, Operation; Iran-Iraq War; Iraq, Army; Terrorism; Weapons of Mass Destruction

References

Butler, Richard. *The Greatest Threat: Iraq, Weapons of Mass Destruction and the Growing Crisis in Global Security.* New York: PublicAffairs, 2000.

Morel, Benoit, and Kyle Olson. *Shadows and Substance: The Chemical Weapons Convention.* Boulder, CO: Westview, 1993.

Solomon, Brian. *Chemical and Biological Warfare.* New York: H. W. Wilson, 1999.

Torr, James D. *Weapons of Mass Destruction: Opposing Viewpoints.* San Diego: Greenhaven, 2005.

Tucker, Jonathan B. *War of Nerves: Chemical Warfare from World War I to Al-Qaeda.* New York: Pantheon, 2006.

Cheney, Richard Bruce
Birth Date: January 30, 1941

Politician, businessman, secretary of defense (1989–1993), and vice president (2001–2009). Richard Bruce "Dick" Cheney was born on January 30, 1941, in Lincoln, Nebraska. He grew up in Casper, Wyoming, and was educated at the University of Wyoming, earning a BA in 1965 and an MA in political science in 1966. He completed advanced graduate study there and was a PhD candidate in 1968.

Cheney acquired his first governmental position in 1969 when he became the special assistant to the director of the Office of Economic Opportunity. He served as a White House staff assistant in 1970 and 1971 and as assistant director of the Cost of Living Council from 1971 to 1973. He briefly worked in the private sector as the vice president of an investment advisory firm. In 1974,

Republican Richard Cheney served as secretary of defense during the 1991 Persian Gulf War. A highly controversial yet powerful vice president of the United States during 2001–2009, he was a prime mover behind the decision to invade Iraq in 2003. (White House)

he returned to government service as President Gerald R. Ford's deputy assistant. In 1975, Ford appointed Cheney as White House chief of staff.

In 1978, Cheney was elected to the U.S. House of Representatives, serving six terms. He was elected House minority whip in December 1988. Cheney was known for his conservative votes: he opposed gun control, environmental laws, and funding for Head Start.

Cheney became secretary of defense on March 21, 1989, in the George H. W. Bush administration. In this position, Cheney significantly reduced U.S. military budgets and canceled several major weapons programs. In addition, in the wake of the Cold War he was deeply involved in the politically volatile task of reducing the size of the American military force throughout the world. Cheney also recommended closing or reducing in size many U.S. military installations, despite intense criticism from elected officials whose districts would be adversely impacted by the closures.

As secretary of defense, Cheney also provided strong leadership in several international military engagements, including the December 1989 Panama invasion and the humanitarian mission to Somalia in early 1992. It was Cheney who secured the appointment of General Colin Powell as chairman of the Joint Chiefs of Staff in 1989.

Cheney's most difficult military challenge came during the 1991 Persian Gulf War. He secured Saudi permission to begin a military buildup there that would include a United Nations (UN) international coalition of troops. The buildup proceeded in the autumn of 1990 as Operation DESERT SHIELD. When economic sanctions and other measures failed to remove the Iraqis from Kuwait, the Persian Gulf War commenced with Operation DESERT STORM on January 16, 1991. A five-week air offensive was followed by the movement of ground forces into Kuwait and Iraq on February 24, 1991. Within four days, the UN coalition had liberated Kuwait. Cheney continued as secretary of defense until January 20, 1993, when Democrat Bill Clinton took office.

Upon leaving the Pentagon, Cheney joined the American Enterprise Institute as a senior fellow. He also became president and chief executive officer of the Halliburton Company in October 1995 and chairman of its board in February 2000.

Only months later, Republican presidential candidate George W. Bush chose Cheney as his vice presidential running mate. After a hard-fought campaign, the Bush-Cheney ticket won the White House in December 2000, although only after a court fight and having lost the popular vote.

Arguably one of the more powerful vice presidents in U.S. history, Cheney endured much criticism for his hawkish views (he is believed to have strongly promoted the 2003 Iraq War) and his connections to the oil industry (Halliburton won several contracts for work in postwar Iraq). He also raised eyebrows by refusing to make public the records of the national energy task force he established to form the administration's energy initiatives.

Many people who knew Cheney personally have asserted that he became a changed man after the September 11 terrorist attacks. He became, they say, far more secretive, more hawkish than ever before, and, some say, even paranoid, seeing terrorists everywhere. As one of the principal promoters of the U.S. invasion of Iraq (Operation IRAQI FREEDOM), which began in March 2003, Cheney was well-placed to receive the burden of criticism when the war began to go badly in 2004. As the subsequent Iraqi insurgency increased in size, scope, and violence, Cheney's popularity plummeted. Following the 2006 mid-term elections, which caused the Republicans to lose control of Congress principally because of the war in Iraq, Cheney took a far lower profile. When his fellow neoconservative Donald Rumsfeld, the secretary of defense, resigned in the election's aftermath, Cheney was increasingly perceived as a liability to the Bush White House, which was under intense pressure to change course in Iraq or quit it altogether.

Cheney did not help his approval ratings when he accidentally shot a friend during a hunting trip in February 2006 and the information was slow to be released. Even more damaging to Cheney was the indictment and conviction of his chief of staff, I. Lewis "Scooter" Libby, for his involvement in the Valerie Plame-Joseph Wilson-CIA leak case. Some alleged that it was Cheney who first leaked the classified information to Libby and perhaps others, who in turn leaked it to the press. Cheney continued to keep a remarkably low profile. Beginning in 2007, a small group of Democrats in the House attempted to introduce impeachment proceedings against Cheney, but such efforts did not make it out of committee.

PAUL G. PIERPAOLI JR.

See also

Bush, George Walker; DESERT SHIELD, Operation; DESERT STORM, Operation; IRAQI FREEDOM, Operation; Libby, I. Lewis; Neoconservatism; Rumsfeld, Donald Henry; September 11 Attacks; Wilson, Joseph Carter, IV; Wilson, Valerie Plame

References

Nichols, John. *The Rise and Rise of Richard B. Cheney: Unlocking the Mysteries of the Most Powerful Vice President in American History.* New York: New Press, 2005.

Woodward, Bob. *Bush at War.* New York: Simon and Schuster, 2002.

———. *Plan of Attack.* New York: Simon and Schuster, 2004.

———. *State of Denial: Bush at War, Part III.* New York: Simon and Schuster, 2006.

Cherrie, Stanley
Birth Date: May 11, 1942

U.S. Army officer who played a major role in the planning and execution of Operations DESERT SHIELD and DESERT STORM. Born on May 11, 1942, in the Bronx, New York City, Stanley Cherrie later moved with his family to Mauricetown, New Jersey. He was commissioned a second lieutenant of armor upon graduation from Rutgers University in 1964.

After completing officer basic and airborne school, Cherrie was assigned to Fort Lewis, Washington. From there he attended rotary wing flight school, graduating in December 1966. In May 1967, after having formed the unit at Fort Bragg, North Carolina, he accompanied the 191st Assault Helicopter Company to Vietnam where he flew Bell UH-1C Huey gunships. In 1968, he returned to the United States and attended the Armor Officer Advanced Course at Fort Knox, Kentucky. In February 1971, Cherrie returned to Vietnam for his second combat tour. He served with H Troop, 17th Cavalry, 23rd Infantry Division in Chu Lai. In October of that year, he was seriously wounded when he stepped on a land mine; he lost his left leg below the knee and sustained other life-threatening injuries.

Following a lengthy period of rehabilitation, Cherrie successfully petitioned the army to remain on active duty in October 1972. He then served in successive assignments at Fort Benning, Georgia, and as a recruiter in New Orleans. He attended the U.S. Army Command and General Staff College, Fort Leavenworth, Kansas, after which he was assigned to the U.S. Retraining Brigade at Fort Riley, Kansas. In 1979, he was selected to attend the British Army Staff College in Camberley in England. Upon completion of that course, he was reassigned to the 11th Armored Cavalry Regiment in West Germany where he served as regimental executive officer and commanded the 3rd Squadron. Cherrie attended the U.S. Army War College in 1984–1985 and was subsequently assigned as Academic Division Chief in the Center for Army Tactics, U.S. Army Command and General Staff College.

In 1986, Cherrie, having been promoted to colonel, became the chief of staff of the 1st Armored Division, in Ansbach, West Germany. He then commanded the 3rd Brigade of the 2nd Armored Division (Forward) at Garlstedt.

After successful brigade command, Cherrie was assigned as the G3 Operations Officer for VII Corps in Stuttgart, West Germany, in June 1990. When Iraq invaded and occupied Kuwait in August 1990, President George H. W. Bush deployed U.S. forces to Saudi Arabia and directed that preparations be made for the ouster of Iraqi forces from Kuwait. As part of this deployment, Colonel Cherrie planned and oversaw the movement of VII Corps and its subordinate elements from Germany to Saudi Arabia. The corps consisted of 1st Armored Division, 3rd Armored Division, 1st Infantry Division, 1st Cavalry Division, British 1st Armoured Division, 11th Aviation Group, and 2nd Armored Cavalry Regiment. The corps formed part of the 34-nation coalition to prevent Iraq from invading Saudi Arabia: Operation DESERT SHIELD.

When Iraq failed to respond to United Nations (UN) Resolution 678, which gave the Iraqis a deadline of January 15, 1991, to withdraw from Kuwait, coalition forces launched the invasion of Kuwait code-named Operation DESERT STORM. Following the intensive air campaign that began on January 17, U.S. and coalition forces began the liberation of Kuwait on February 24.

VII Corps, commanded by Lieutenant General Frederick M. Franks Jr., having assembled its forces and occupied attack positions in the Saudi Arabian desert, launched a massive armored attack. Simultaneously, the U.S. XVIII Airborne Corps executed a sweeping "left-hook" attack across the largely undefended desert of southern Iraq. For the next five days, Lieutenant General Franks and Colonel Cherrie directed the corps attack against the Iraqi forces. The coalition ground forces quickly overwhelmed the Iraqi forces, and 100 hours after the ground campaign started, President Bush declared a cease-fire.

Upon return to the United States in late 1991, Colonel Cherrie was assigned as the director, Center for Army Tactics at Fort Leavenworth, Kansas. Cherrie was promoted to brigadier general in March 1993 and was reassigned as the deputy chief of staff G2/G3 of the Allied Command Europe Rapid Reaction Corps (ARRC) in Rheindahlen, Germany. In October 1994, Cherrie was reassigned to Baumholder, Germany, where he became the assistant division commander for maneuver of the 1st Armored Division. In December 1995, Cherrie and the division deployed to Bosnia as Task Force Eagle to conduct Operation JOINT ENDEAVOR, implementing the Dayton Peace Accords and enforcing the UN-mandated cease-fire. In June 1996, Cherrie returned to Fort Leavenworth, Kansas, where he assumed the duties as assistant deputy chief of staff for Training, U.S. Training and Doctrine Command, a billet he held until he retired from the army in February 1998. Upon retirement, he took a position as a defense contractor. He currently lives in Leavenworth, Kansas.

JAMES H. WILLBANKS

See also

Armored Warfare, Persian Gulf and Iraq Wars; DESERT SHIELD, Operation; DESERT STORM, Operation; DESERT STORM, Operation, Planning for; Franks, Frederick Melvin, Jr.

References

Atkinson, Rick. *Crusade: The Untold Story of the Persian Gulf War*. New York: Mariner Books, 1994.

Clancy, Tom, with General Fred Franks Jr. *Into the Storm: A Study in Command*. New York: Putnam, 1997.

Gordon, Michael R., and General Bernard E. Trainor. *The Generals' War: The Inside Story of the Conflict in the Gulf*. New York: Little, Brown, 1995.

Chertoff, Michael
Birth Date: November 28, 1953

Lawyer, judge, and secretary of Homeland Security from 2005 to 2009. Michael Chertoff was born on November 28, 1953, in Elizabeth, New Jersey. The son of a rabbi, he entered Harvard University in 1971 and graduated magna cum laude in 1975. He earned his law degree from Harvard in 1978. He then served as a clerk for appellate judge Murray Gurfein and then for U.S. Supreme Court justice William Brennan. He was admitted to the bar in the District of Columbia in 1980 and joined the law firm of Latham & Watkins.

In 1983, Chertoff began working in the U.S. attorney's office in New York City, and was soon working on an organized-crime investigation with then-U.S. attorney and future New York mayor

Secretary of the Department of Homeland Security Michael Chertoff, right, with Chief David Aguilar, left, of the Border Patrol, during a press conference to discuss the Secure Border Initiative, February 9, 2006. (U.S. Department of Homeland Security/James Tourtellotte)

Rudolph Giuliani. When Giuliani left that investigation to prosecute a case involving corruption in city government, Chertoff became lead prosecutor in the trials of several organized-crime bosses. With successful convictions of the leaders of the Genovese, Colombo, and Lucchese crime families, Chertoff earned his bona fides as a talented trial lawyer.

Chertoff next became an assistant prosecutor for the state of New Jersey in 1987 and, after serving as interim U.S. attorney for the state, was named by President George H. W. Bush to the position permanently in 1990. He stayed at the post until 1994, when he returned to the firm of Latham & Watkins as a partner.

Beginning in 1994, Chertoff was special counsel to the committee investigating President Bill Clinton and First Lady Hillary Rodham Clinton in what became known as Whitewater. In 2000, Chertoff investigated racial profiling as special counsel to New Jersey's state Senate Judiciary Committee. During the presidential campaign that year, he advised candidate George W. Bush on criminal justice issues. Beginning in 2001, Chertoff served in the new Bush administration as assistant attorney general in the criminal division of the Justice Department. During his tenure, he led prosecutions against suspected terrorist Zacarias Moussaoui, the "American Taliban" John Walker Lindh, and the accounting firm of Arthur Andersen, which was convicted of destroying documents related to the collapse of the Enron Corporation.

While Chertoff was with the Justice Department, the United States was attacked by terrorists on September 11, 2001. He was one of the first law officials to advocate treating terrorist suspects as "material witnesses" and detaining them without charging them with a crime, a stance he justified by claiming that because the nation was at war, it had a right and obligation to do whatever was necessary to keep the United States secure.

In 2003, President Bush nominated Chertoff to the post of judge for the Third Circuit U.S. Court of Appeals. Chertoff served as an appellate judge until his confirmation as secretary of the Department of Homeland Security (DHS) on February 15, 2005.

Chertoff was often criticized for some of his hard-line positions. He was opposed to allowing judges discretion in the imposition of sentences, and argued that there is no constitutional right for a defendant to be free of coercive questioning by police. His supporters, however, believed that he was well suited to serve in protecting the nation's homeland security. Indeed, they pointed out that he had been concerned with the threat of terrorism long before September 11, 2001. In 1996, he argued in "Tools Against Terrorism," an article in the *New Jersey Law Journal,* that officials must have leeway in the prosecution of suspected terrorists, even if it means restricting some civil liberties.

In assuming leadership of the DHS, Chertoff gave up a lifetime appointment as appellate judge on the Third Circuit. He faced the daunting task of overseeing some 22 separate agencies and over 170,000 employees. Chertoff's tenure became highly controversial after the government's bungled reaction to Hurricane Katrina, which struck the Gulf Coast—including New Orleans—in September 2005. Although the Federal Emergency Management Agency (FEMA) took the brunt of the criticism, Chertoff's sprawling agency included FEMA, and so blame was placed on his shoulders as well. Later, President Bush tasked Chertoff with helping usher comprehensive immigration reform through Congress, but when that failed in the summer of 2007, Chertoff's image was further tarnished. DHS includes the Immigration and Naturalization Service (INS). In 2008, Chertoff was criticized for having bypassed environmental protection laws during the hasty construction of a border fence between the United States and Mexico in the American Southwest. Those who believed that the Bush administration had not gone far enough to curb illegal immigration also cited Chertoff's weak and vacillating policies as part of the problem. After leaving office in January 2009, Chertoff planned to write and speak about his lengthy government experience.

PAUL G. PIERPAOLI JR.

See also

Patriot Act; Terrorism; United States Department of Homeland Security

References

McClellan, Scott. *What Happened: Inside the Bush White House and Washington's Culture of Deception.* New York: PublicAffairs, 2008.
Woodward, Bob. *The War Within: A Secret White House History, 2006–2008.* New York: Simon and Schuster, 2008.

Portrait of Jacques Chirac, president of France during 1995–2007. In foreign affairs, Chirac sought to restrain American hegemony and maintain French autonomy; he also promoted greater European integration. (Courtesy: Embassy of France; photo by Bettina Rheims)

Chirac, Jacques René
Birth Date: November 29, 1932

French politician who served as mayor of Paris (1977–1995), premier (1974–1976, 1986–1988), and president (1995–2007). Jacques René Chirac was born on November 29, 1932, in Paris to a middle-class Roman Catholic family. He attended the Lycées Carnot and Louis le Grand and both the Institut d'Études Politiques de Paris and the École Nationale d'Administration. Upon graduation from the latter in 1959, Chirac embarked on a civil service career. In 1962 he became Premier Georges Pompidou's chief of staff. In 1967 Chirac was elected to the French National Assembly as a center-right Gaullist. He then held a series of important governmental posts, including state secretary of the economy (1968–1971), minister of agriculture and rural development (1972–1974), and minister of the interior in 1974.

Throughout this period, Chirac was more aligned with Pompidou than with the Gaullists but nevertheless was among the inner sanctum of Gaullist political circles. When Valéry Giscard d'Estaing was elected president in 1974, Chirac became premier, helping reconcile the Gaullist leadership to more social spending. In 1974–1975 Premier Chirac met with Iraqi leader Saddam Hussein

to promote the interests of French businesses and oil companies in Iraq. Given the ties between the two nations, which were further advanced by Chirac, French companies sold the components necessary for the Iraqi nuclear reactor at Osiraq that was destroyed in an Israeli air strike in 1981. In the aftermath of the 1991 Persian Gulf War, documents seized suggested that the Iraqis had intended to use the facility as a means of constructing nuclear weapons.

Chirac resigned as premier in 1976, no longer able to bridge the gap between Giscard's policies and the more conservative Gaullists. In 1977 Chirac was elected mayor of Paris, a position he held until 1995 concurrently with the premiership. In 1981 he challenged d'Estaing for the conservative leadership, which may have contributed to socialist leader François Mitterrand's victory in the 1981 presidential election. As French patience with socialist economic prescriptions wore thin in 1986, the Right took control of the National Assembly, and Chirac again became premier.

In 1988 Chirac lost the presidential election to Mitterrand. This prompted Chirac to resign his post as premier, and some people began to write his political epitaph. Chirac was undeterred, however, and continued to set his sights on the presidency, announcing in 1993 that he had no desire to become premier in another government. He finally achieved the presidency in 1995, leading a center-right coalition that promised tax cuts and continued social spending. Chirac proved to be relatively popular, and he won reelection in 2002.

Domestically, Chirac's policies centered on job creation, tax cuts, and trimming government spending, certainly the hallmarks of modern conservative thinking. However, government-mandated austerity programs and the trimming of the very generous French welfare state created considerable friction with the Left and centrist parties and precipitated a series of major labor strikes. The Chirac government also endured its share of scandals, and in the president's second term challenges from the Far Right (such as Jean-Marie Le Pen's National Front party) and immigration issues that touched off nationwide rioting took up much of his administration's attention.

In foreign affairs, Chirac pursued a traditional Gaullist course by attempting to create a multipolar world capable of restraining American hegemony and maintaining French autonomy. However, he has differed from Gaullist foreign policy in his pursuit of greater European integration, generally along a French-German axis. In 1995 he created a national and international stir when he went forward with a nuclear test in French Polynesia, only to vow the next year that France would never again test a nuclear device. Chirac was a staunch proponent of the Constitution of the European Union (EU), and many viewed its defeat by referendum in France in 2005 as a personal failure for him.

Chirac was one of the first foreign leaders to condemn the September 11, 2001, terrorist attacks on the United States and offer French support. He also advocated invoking the North Atlantic Treaty Organization (NATO) charter, which stipulates that an attack on one signatory is an attack on them all. Chirac supported the U.S.-led effort to topple the Taliban regime in Afghanistan in 2001 and 2002, and France provided a small troop contingent as part of the NATO effort there. In January 2006 Chirac publicly warned would-be terrorists that France was able and willing to retaliate with tactical nuclear weapons for any large-scale terrorist attack on his country.

Yet for all his antiterrorist rhetoric and his early support of the George W. Bush administration, Chirac refused to support the preemptory attack on Iraq that began in March 2003. In this stance he was joined by the leaders of Germany, now France's closest ally. France, which had long maintained commercial ties to Iraq, along with many other nations opposed the U.S. proposals to invade Iraq in 2003. Within the United Nations (UN), France favored a two-step process. One resolution would have required further inspections of Iraq's weapons program, while the second resolution would have been required to authorize the use of force in the case of a breach of trust. The Americans, meanwhile, worded the first resolution such that war would be a necessary means of restoring stability.

Chirac adamantly opposed the Iraqi invasion, believing that there was not yet adequate justification to go to war. He was,

however, supportive of reconstruction efforts in Iraq. Chirac was also supportive of Saudi proposals to forestall the war by allowing Saddam Hussein to be exiled. Thus, Russia, the People's Republic of China (PRC), Germany, and France all issued statements calling for further inspections rather than war. Chirac also attempted to extend the weapons inspections for another 30 days, but the Americans chose to proceed.

Differences within Europe on Iraq disrupted one of the main pillars of the EU: a common foreign and security policy. This saw France and Germany heading a Europeanist bloc that acted with Russia and China on the UN Security Council to constrain the United States, while Great Britain, Italy, and many of the newer East European nations within the EU backed a more Atlanticist position that supported the United States in its war policy.

After deciding not to seek a third term as president, Chirac left office in May 2007. In retirement, he took up residence in a palatial apartment on the Quai Voltaire in Paris and joined the Constitutional Council of France, the nation's highest constitutional body. The council is charged with supervising national elections and referenda and upholding the statutes of the 1958 constitution.

Michael Beauchamp and Paul G. Pierpaoli Jr.

See also

Bush, George Walker; France, Middle East Policy; Hussein, Saddam; Nuclear Weapons, Iraq's Potential for Building; September 11 Attacks, International Reactions to; United Nations; United Nations Weapons Inspectors

References

Madelin, Philippe. *Jacques Chirac: Une Biographie* [Jacques Chirac: A Biogrpahy]. Paris: Flammarion, 2002.
Wright, Gordon. *France in Modern Times.* New York: Norton, 2002.

Civil Reserve Air Fleet

U.S. civilian passenger and cargo aircraft that are contractually obligated by the Department of Defense to augment the U.S. military's airlift capabilities in times of war and other emergencies. The Civil Reserve Air Fleet (CRAF), formed in 1952 during the Korean War, is designed to be activated on short notice when airlift requirements exceed the military's airlift capacity. Currently, the CRAF is comprised of three components: international operations, national operations, and aeromedical evacuation operations. International operations are subdivided into long-haul and short-haul flights, while national operations are subdivided into domestic flights and Alaskan operations. Aeromedical operations may encompass both national and international flights.

Long-range international operations are made up of both civilian cargo and passenger aircraft capable of supplying transoceanic air-lift capacity. These are chiefly large wide-body commercial jets. For short-haul international or domestic operations, medium to small cargo and passenger jets are employed. The aeromedical evacuation operations are designed to employ civilian aircraft to transport wounded individuals from specific combat theaters to regional military hospitals or military hospitals within the continental United States. These same aircraft can also be used to fly supplies and medical personnel into theater hospitals. The preferred aircraft for this purpose is the Boeing 767, for which the military has special kits that can quickly convert the plane's interior into a flying ambulance.

The Department of Defense maintains contracts with numerous civilian airlines that participate in the CRAF, and as an incentive for taking part in the program, the government promises airlines a certain amount of peacetime airlift business. As of 2008, CRAF contracts amounted to approximately $379 million, while additional peacetime business contracts amounted to more than $2.1 billion.

To qualify as a CRAF contractor, an airline must guarantee that a minimum of 30 percent of its CRAF-eligible passenger aircraft and 15 percent of its CRAF-eligible cargo planes will be maintained in ready status at all times. Ready status means that the aircraft and its crew must be ready to fly within 24–48 hours, depending on the type of aircraft. Four complete crews for each CRAF-designated aircraft must also be maintained on standby status at all times.

Currently, 37 civilian air carriers are involved in CRAF, with more than 1,300 aircraft designated for use by the military. That number includes 1,271 designated for international operations (990 long-haul aircraft and 282 short-haul aircraft), 27 aircraft for national/domestic purposes, and 50 for medical evacuation operations. These numbers are quite fluid and often change on a month-by-month basis. CRAF has a three-stage call-up system for eligible aircraft: Stage 1 is reserved for regional emergencies, Stage 2 is reserved for major conflicts overseas, and Stage 3 is reserved for full-scale national mobilization. The Air Mobility Command (AMC), supervised by the U.S. Air Force and part of the U.S. Transportation Command (TRANSCOM), regulates most of CRAF's operations and decides which stage should be implemented in the event of a conflict or emergency requiring additional airlift capabilities.

The AMC requires that all of its CRAF contractors meet Federal Aviation Administration (FAA) safety and operation guidelines and maintains its own team of airplane mechanics, engineers, and safety inspectors who conduct on-site inspections of airline equipment and facilities. Besides the aircraft themselves, AMC inspections scrutinize crew qualifications, training and instruction facilities, maintenance procedures, ground operations, and general quality-control procedures.

On August 17, 1990, the Department of Defense activated CRAF (Stage 1 and later Stage 2) for the first time in the history of the program. This was in response to the U.S. troop buildup in the Persian Gulf (Operation DESERT SHIELD), which began shortly after Iraq's invasion of Kuwait on August 2, 1990. Despite a few wrinkles early on, CRAF performed admirably well, helping to put in place more than 500,000 troops and many tons of supplies and military hardware. Between August 1990 and March 1991, CRAF aircraft flew two-thirds of all military personnel and one-quarter of all cargo to the Persian Gulf.

On February 8, 2003, in anticipation of the Anglo-American–led invasion of Iraq, CRAF was activated for the second time in its history, a Stage 1 mobilization. Stage 2 was implemented soon thereafter to augment the military's airlift capabilities. Once more, CRAF responded ably to the activation, using 51 commercial aircraft from 11 civilian airlines. CRAF flew some 1,625 missions during Operation IRAQI FREEDOM, transporting 254,143 troops to the front. Sixteen commercial air carriers also transported 11,050 short tons of cargo during the same time period. CRAF was deactivated on June 18, 2003.

PAUL G. PIERPAOLI JR.

See also

Aircraft, Transport; DESERT SHIELD, Operation; DESERT STORM, Operation; IRAQI FREEDOM, Operation; United States Transportation Command

References

Bickers, Richard Townshend. *Airlift: The Illustrated History of American Military Transport.* Botley, Oxford, UK: Osprey, 1998.
Wales, William S. "Civil Reserve Air Fleet Enhancement Program: A Study of Its Viability in Today's Environment." Master's thesis, Naval Postgraduate School, Monterey, CA, 1998.

Clark, William Ramsey
Birth Date: December 18, 1927

Lawyer, U.S. attorney general of the United States under President Lyndon B. Johnson (1967–1969), and outspoken critic of U.S. wars in the Middle East since 1991. Born in Dallas, Texas, on December 18, 1927, William Ramsey Clark served in the U.S. Marine Corps from 1945 to 1946. He received his undergraduate degree from the University of Texas in 1949 and his MA (history) and JD degrees from the University of Chicago in 1950. Clark then joined the Dallas law firm of Clark, Coon, Holt & Fisher, a firm founded by his grandfather, and worked there for 10 years, losing only one jury trial. Because his father Tom had become an associate justice of the U.S. Supreme Court in 1949, Ramsey avoided high court legislation except for one case in which his father recused himself.

Clark worked actively in Democratic Party politics, and in 1960 he campaigned for John F. Kennedy. In 1961 Kennedy appointed Clark assistant attorney general in charge of the Lands Division of the Justice Department (1961–1965). During his tenure, Clark instituted cost-cutting measures and reduced the backlog of cases. He also supervised other projects, mainly in the civil rights area. Clark headed federal civilian forces at the University of Mississippi after the 1962 riots there and served in Birmingham in 1963. He visited school officials throughout the South in 1963 to help them coordinate and implement desegregation plans. He also helped formulate the landmark 1964 Civil Rights Act.

As a consequence of his diligent work, Clark was appointed deputy attorney general in 1965. In this post he helped to draft the 1965 Voting Rights Act, and after the riots in the Watts section of Los Angeles in 1965 he headed federal forces sent to find solutions to the problems that led to the violence. When Attorney General Nicholas Katzenbach became undersecretary of state in 1966, President Lyndon B. Johnson appointed Clark acting attorney general. Five months later Johnson made the promotion permanent. Two hours after the official appointment, Justice Tom Clark announced his retirement from the Supreme Court to avoid any potential conflict of interest. On March 10, 1967, Ramsey Clark was sworn in as attorney general; his father administered the oath of office.

As attorney general from 1967 to 1969, Clark strongly supported civil rights for all Americans. He also opposed the death penalty, criticized police violence toward citizens and antiwar protesters, and steadfastly refused to use wiretaps except in cases of national security. These positions, in addition to his lenient stance on antiwar activities, attracted criticism from within the Johnson administration and from conservatives, who labeled Clark as soft on crime.

After leaving office in 1969, Clark actively opposed the Vietnam War, and in 1972 he visited North Vietnam to investigate American bombing of civilian targets. He also taught, first at Howard University (1969–1972) and then at Brooklyn Law School (1973–1981). Clark continued to practice law in New York City, and in 1974 he ran unsuccessfully for the U.S. Senate. In 1980 he led a group of private citizens to Teheran, Iran, during the hostage crisis there, and in 1982 he made a private fact-finding tour of Nicaragua. Clark also found time to write a book, *Crime in America* (1970), that examines the social and economic causes and potential solutions to crime.

In more recent years Clark has proven even more controversial, as he vigorously and publicly opposed the 1991 Persian Gulf War, the Global War on Terror, the Afghanistan War, and the Iraq War. In 1991 Clark accused the George H. W. Bush administration of crimes against humanity committed during the Persian Gulf War. Clark views the Global War on Terror as a war against Islam and believes that the conflict is eroding American's civil liberties. He has even gone so far as to propose that Al Qaeda was not behind the September 11, 2001, attacks; instead he blames the U.S. government, which he believed planned and staged the event in order to wage war against the Taliban and Iraq. From 2003 to 2009, Clark was active in the drive to bring impeachment proceedings against President George W. Bush and Vice President Dick Cheney. After the 1999 North Atlantic Treaty Organization (NATO) bombing campaign of Yugoslavia, Clark charged the organization with 19 counts of genocide.

Equally controversial have been the clients he has chosen to defend. They include Radovan Karadzic, Slobodan Milosevic, former Liberian strongman Charles Taylor, and former Iraqi president Saddam Hussein. Clark insisted that Hussein would be unable to receive a fair trial if it was held in Iraq.

LAURA MATYSEK WOOD

See also

Antiwar Movements, Persian Gulf and Iraq Wars; Bush, George Herbert Walker; Bush, George Walker; Cheney, Richard Bruce; Hussein, Saddam; September 11 Attacks

References

Clark, William Ramsey. *Crime in America: Observations on Its Nature, Causes, Prevention and Control.* New York: Simon and Schuster, 1970.

———. *The Fire This Time: U.S. War Crimes in the Gulf.* New York: Thunder's Mouth, 1994.

Who's Who in America, 1968–1969. New Providence, NJ: Marquis Who's Who, 1969.

Clarke, Richard Alan
Birth Date: October 1951

Longtime U.S. government employee, intelligence expert, and chief counterterrorism adviser on the U.S. National Security Council at the time of the September 11, 2001, terror attacks. Richard Alan Clarke was born in October 1951 in Boston, Massachusetts, to a working-class family. He earned an undergraduate degree from the University of Pennsylvania in 1972 and then attended the Massachusetts Institute of Technology (MIT), where he earned a degree in management. His first job, beginning in 1973, was with the U.S. Department of Defense as a defense analyst keeping tabs on the number of Soviet nuclear warheads. After a series of appointments, Clarke was promoted in 1985 to the post of assistant secretary of state for intelligence in the Ronald Reagan administration. By this time Clarke had earned a reputation as being blunt and on occasion abusive.

Clarke continued to work with the George H. W. Bush administration as an assistant secretary of state for politico-military affairs during 1989–1992, helping on security affairs during the 1991 Persian Gulf War. In 1992 Secretary of State James Baker fired Clarke for his apparent defense of Israel's transfer of U.S. technology to the People's Republic of China (PRC). Clarke then moved to the National Security Council, where he began to specialize in counterterrorism. Clarke was a holdover in the William J. Clinton and George W. Bush administrations, continuing as a member of the National Security Council from 1992 to 2003.

Clarke's preoccupation was with counterintelligence. Among his contentions was that Osama bin Laden's Al Qaeda terrorist organization was a growing threat to the United States. President Clinton agreed with this assessment, but he was not, after all, able to deal effectively with this threat. Clarke lobbied for a Counterterrorism Security Group to be chaired by a new national security official, the national coordinator for infrastructure protection and counterterrorism. Clinton approved this office by signing Presidential Decision Directive 62 on May 22, 1998.

Clarke then presided over a working group that included the counterterrorism heads of the Central Intelligence Agency (CIA),

Former White House counterterrorism adviser Richard Clarke testifies before the 9/11 Commission in Washington on March 24, 2004. Clarke's memoir *Against All Enemies* is highly critical of the George W. Bush administration for failing to recognize the dangers posed by Al Qaeda. (AP/Wide World Photos)

the Federal Bureau of Investigation (FBI), the Joint Chiefs of Staff, the Department of Defense, the Department of Justice, and the Department of State. But the national coordinator for infrastructure protection and counterterrorism had a limited staff of 12 and no budget; moreover, operational decision making could come only from the departments and agencies of the intelligence community. As Clarke has pointed out, he had the "appearance of responsibility for counterterrorism, but none of the tools or authority to get the job done."

Nevertheless, Clarke was in the middle of several counterterrorism operations. He was involved in decision making about the CIA's operation to apprehend Osama bin Laden in 1998. An Afghan team was to capture bin Laden at his residence at Tarnak Farms near Kandahar. This raid was called off because of a lack of confidence among CIA leadership, the White House, and Clarke that it would succeed.

Clarke continued his position on the National Security Council during the early years of the second Bush administration. Indeed, Clarke proposed a plan to combat Al Qaeda that included covert aid to the Afghan leader of the Northern Alliance, reconnaissance

flights by the new unmanned aerial vehicle Predator, and ways to eliminate bin Laden as a threat to the United States, but there was little enthusiasm for this report by the Bush administration. In the meantime, the events of September 11, 2001, transpired, changing the American political landscape dramatically.

On September 12, President Bush instructed Clarke to try to find evidence that Iraqi president Saddam Hussein was connected to September 11. Clarke sent a report to the White House stating categorically that Hussein had nothing to do with the terrorist attacks, but there is no evidence indicating that Bush read the report. It was sent back to be updated and resubmitted, but nothing came of it.

Clarke left government service in January 2003 and became an outspoken critic of the Bush administration and its policies prior to September 11. This led the White House to engage in a character assassination campaign against him. Clarke testified for 20 hours during the September 11 Commission hearings and made national headlines for his apology that the government had failed to prevent the September 11 attacks. In the middle of the commission hearings, Clarke published his book *Against All Enemies: Inside America's War on Terror,* which gives his side of the controversy.

In his book, Clarke was especially critical of the Bush administration's 2003 invasion of Iraq. Most of Clarke's criticism stems from his belief that by redirecting attention away from bin Laden and Al Qaeda, the Bush administration allowed Al Qaeda to reconstitute itself into an ongoing threat to the United States. In Clarke's view, the invasion of Afghanistan was so halfhearted in its commitment of low numbers of American troops that bin Laden and nearly all of the Al Qaeda and Taliban leaders easily escaped. By not committing the necessary resources to rebuild Afghanistan, Clarke wrote, the Bush administration had allowed both Al Qaeda and the Taliban to threaten the pro-American Afghanistan state, all to depose Saddam Hussein. Clarke now does consulting work, teaches, and has authored two works of fiction since 2005.

STEPHEN E. ATKINS

See also

Al Qaeda; Bin Laden, Osama; Bush, George Walker; Clinton, William Jefferson; Hussein, Saddam; September 11 Commission and Report; Taliban

References

Benjamin, Daniel, and Steven Simon. *The Age of Sacred Terror.* New York: Random House, 2002.

Clarke, Richard A. *Against All Enemies: Inside America's War on Terror.* New York: Free Press, 2004.

Coll, Steve. *Ghost Wars: The Secret History of the CIA, Afghanistan, and Bin Laden, from the Soviet Invasion to September 10, 2001.* New York: Penguin, 2004.

Naftali, Timothy. *Blind Spot: The Secret History of American Counterterrorism.* New York: Basic Books, 2005.

Cleland, Joseph Maxwell
Birth Date: August 24, 1942

U.S. Army officer, head of the Veterans Administration (1977–1981), Democratic Party politician, and U.S. senator (1997–2003). Born in Atlanta, Georgia, on August 24, 1942, Joseph Maxwell (Max) Cleland received a BA from Stetson University in Florida in 1964 and earned an MA in American history from Emory University the following year. Shortly thereafter he entered the U.S. Army, initially serving in the Signal Corps. After successfully completing Airborne School, in 1967 he volunteered for duty in Vietnam with the 1st Cavalry Division (Airmobile). The next year, near Khe Sanh, Captain Cleland lost both legs and his right arm as a result of a grenade blast. He received numerous citations, including the Bronze Star Medal and the Silver Star.

Not released from the hospital until 1970, Cleland wasted little time in resuming a productive life. In 1971 he won a seat in the Georgia Senate and used his position to promote issues related to veterans and the handicapped. From 1975 to 1977 he served on the professional staff of the U.S. Senate Veterans Affairs Committee.

In February 1977 President Jimmy Carter nominated his fellow Georgian to head the Veterans Administration (VA). Speedy Senate confirmation followed, and Cleland became at age 34 the youngest person to ever head the VA and the first Vietnam veteran to hold the position. He launched a vigorous expansion of VA programs, including drug and alcohol treatment and counseling services. He also worked to improve the public image of the VA and Vietnam veterans. His tenure at the VA ended in 1981 with the election of President Ronald Reagan. Returning to Georgia, Cleland became secretary of state, holding that position from 1982 to 1996. In 1996 he received the Democratic nomination to fill the Senate seat vacated by Democrat Sam Nunn and won the election that November, joining such prominent Vietnam veterans as John Kerry (D-Mass.), Robert Kerrey (D-Neb.), and John McCain (R-Ariz.). In 2003 Cleland was among 29 Senate Democrats to vote for the authorization for war with Iraq. Later, he announced that he deeply regretted his decision and admitted that his vote was in part influenced by his upcoming reelection bid.

In 2002 Cleland experienced a bruising reelection campaign, running against Republican Saxby Chambliss. The election made national news after the Chambliss campaign ran incendiary television commercials implicitly questioning Cleland's patriotism because he had failed to support some of the George W. Bush administration's homeland security decisions. The ads featured likenesses of Saddam Hussein and Osama bin Laden. The ads were pulled amid much uproar, and Republican senators John McCain and Chuck Hagel chastised Chambliss for his tactless and mean-spirited campaign. Nevertheless, Cleland lost the election to Chambliss, who had no military experience at all.

The smear campaign against Cleland has been seen by some as a precursor of the later campaign that raised troubling questions about the Vietnam service of Senator John Kerry, who ran for president on the Democratic ticket in 2004. Cleland campaigned vigorously for Kerry, and when the anti-Kerry Swift Boat Veterans for Truth organization ran ads questioning Kerry's patriotism, war record, and troubling details regarding his award of the Silver Star and Purple Heart medals, Cleland paid a personal visit to President George W. Bush's Texas ranch to protest the ads. Cleland's appeal had little effect, however. Kerry lost the election to the incumbent Bush.

Cleland has written extensively on veterans' issues and the plight of Vietnam veterans.

DAVID COFFEY

See also

Bush, George Walker; Kerry, John Forbes; McCain, John Sidney, III; Swift Boat Veterans for Truth; United States, National Elections of 2004

References

Cleland, Max. *Strong at the Broken Places.* Atlanta: Cherokee Publishing, 1989.

Cleland, Max, with Ben Raines. *Heart of a Patriot: How I Found the Courage to Survive Vietnam, Walter Reed, and Karl Rove.* New York: Simon and Schuster, 2009.

Who's Who in America, 1997. New Providence, NJ: Marquis Who's Who, 1996.

Cleveland, Charles T.
Birth Date: ca. 1956

U.S. Army general and longtime special operations officer with extensive experience in operations in Panama, El Salvador, and Bolivia in the decades before the 2003 Iraq War. Charles T. Cleveland was born around 1956 and is the son of a U.S. Army career enlisted man. Cleveland graduated from the U.S. Military Academy, West Point, in 1978. He had attended secondary school in Panama and had a good understanding of Latin American culture. By 1989, he was a captain and company commander in the 3rd Battalion, 7th Special Forces Group, in Panama. He was also the battalion operations officer. Besides sending teams into El Salvador to help the government there with an ongoing guerrilla war, Cleveland developed plans to train an antidrug police force in Bolivia. While inspecting a police camp in the drug-growing region of that nation, Cleveland helped defend it against an attack by guerrillas.

As relations between Panamanian president Manual Noriega and the U.S. government worsened during 1989, Cleveland developed plans and lists of targets for his unit in the event of a U.S. military intervention. When the U.S. invasion (Operation JUST CAUSE) was launched on December 19, 1989, Cleveland's plans were the basis for Special Forces operations in the country. The operations were successful, and Noriega was taken into custody in January 1991 to stand trial for drug trafficking in the United States. Cleveland displayed a keen ability to improvise and work with local populations to carry out operations and achieve results. During the 1990s, he continued to showcase his abilities during peacekeeping operations in the Balkans.

By early 2003, Cleveland was commanding the 10th Special Forces Group. When planning got under way for Operation IRAQI FREEDOM, Cleveland's group was assigned to northern Iraq. They were expected to help the 4th Infantry Division drive from Turkey to capture the major cities of Mosul and Kirkuk as well as the northern oil fields. When the government of Turkey refused to allow American forces across its territory, Cleveland's men were ordered to carry on. Subsequently, on the night of March 24 the entire 173rd Airborne Brigade, staging out of Italy, dropped into northern Iraq. Meanwhile, the Special Forces teams were to cooperate with local Kurdish forces to keep regular army and Republican Guard units in the area from reinforcing Baghdad. They also worked to destroy terrorist camps in the region.

Colonel Cleveland's command was code-named Task Force Viking and consisted of his 2nd and 3rd Battalions of the 10th Special Forces Group, supplemented by the 3rd Battalion of the 3rd Special Forces Group. Cleveland's men worked with 65,000 lightly armed Kurdish militiamen from different groups. While Cleveland was to use the Kurds to help defeat Iraqi president Saddam Hussein's supporters in northern Iraq, he was not to allow the Kurds to become so strong or independent that the Turks would fear an independent Kurdistan movement.

Cleveland's first objective when war broke out was to eliminate the Ansar al-Islam terrorist training camps in northeastern Iraq. Aided by Kurdish militiamen, the 3rd Battalion attacked on March 27. Ansar al-Islam positions were taken out by laser-guided bombs dropped by navy fighters, with direction from the Special Forces. Lockheed AC-130 Spectre gunships blasted those who tried to run. The camps were completely eliminated, although a number of fighters managed to flee.

Cleveland then concentrated his efforts on the four Iraqi corps defending the Green Line that separated the Kurdish territory from the remainder of Iraq. Again, the Special Forces teams employed airpower and advanced antiarmor missiles to weaken the Iraqi defenders. They punched holes through the Iraqi defenses, forcing the defenders to withdraw. On April 11, Cleveland, a few Special Forces troops, and about 100 Kurdish militiamen drove into Mosul, virtually ending the campaign in northern Iraq in complete victory.

Cleveland's accomplishment was recognized in his appointment as chief of staff of the Army Special Forces Command. He was also promoted to brigadier general and became commander of Special Operations Command South. In April 2008 Cleveland was appointed commander of Special Operations Command Central in the U.S. Central Command; he was promoted to major general in September 2008.

TIM J. WATTS

See also

IRAQI FREEDOM, Operation; JUST CAUSE, Operation; United States Special Operations Command

References

Murray, Williamson, and Robert H. Scales Jr. *The Iraq War: A Military History.* Cambridge, MA: Belknap, 2005.

Robinson, Linda. *Masters of Chaos: The Secret History of the Special Forces.* New York: PublicAffairs, 2004.

Climate

See Afghanistan, Climate of; Middle East, Climate of

Clinton, Hillary Rodham
Birth Date: October 26, 1947

Attorney, former first lady (1993–2001), U.S. senator (2001–2009), presidential candidate in 2008, and secretary of state (2009–present). Hillary Diane Rodham was born on October 26, 1947, in Chicago and was raised in Park Ridge, a prosperous Chicago suburb. Her family was staunchly Republican, and during the 1964 presidential campaign, while still a high school student, she actively campaigned for Republican nominee Barry Goldwater. She entered Wellesley College in 1965, and by 1968 she had become disenchanted with Republican politics and the Vietnam

Hillary Rodham Clinton, the wife of former president Bill Clinton, was a U.S. senator from New York during 2001–2009. In 2009, Clinton became the secretary of state in the Barack Obama administration. (U.S. Senate)

War. By 1968 she supported the Democratic antiwar presidential candidate Eugene McCarthy; the following year she graduated with a degree in political science.

Rodham enrolled at Yale Law School, where she met fellow student Bill Clinton, whom she would later marry. Graduating in 1973, she took a position with a child-advocacy group. The next year she served as a staff attorney for the House Committee on the Judiciary during the Watergate Scandal that caused President Richard Nixon to resign in 1974. In 1975, she wed Bill Clinton.

In 1976, Bill Clinton launched his political career when he was elected attorney general of Arkansas. The next year, Hillary Clinton joined the Rose Law Firm, the premier legal firm in Arkansas, where she specialized in intellectual property law and continued pro-bono child advocacy legal work. Bill Clinton became governor of Arkansas in January 1979, the same year that Hillary Clinton became a full partner in the Rose Law Firm, the first woman to achieve such status. In 1981 Bill Clinton lost a reelection bid but was reelected in 1982; Hillary Clinton was again the first lady of Arkansas, an informal post that she would hold until her husband became president in January 1993. She continued her legal work and was active on several boards, including those of Arkansas-based Wal-Mart as well as Lafarge and TCBY.

Taking a leave of absence from the Rose Law Firm to help her husband campaign for the presidency in 1992, Clinton proved to be a formidable campaigner, repeatedly weathering allegations that her husband had engaged in extramarital affairs. After Bill Clinton upset incumbent president George H. W. Bush in the November 1992 elections, Hillary Clinton became first lady in January 1993. She was an activist first lady, certainly more so than any of her immediate predecessors. Some pundits likened her to Eleanor Roosevelt, but it quickly became clear that Clinton would be a far more influential first lady than even Roosevelt.

Hillary Clinton's role in White House policy making was derided by the right wing of the Republican Party, and even some mainstream Democrats openly questioned her central role in decision making. In 1993 her husband named her chairperson of the Task Force on National Health Care Reform, a move that in retrospect was probably not a wise idea. Many questioned Hillary Clinton's motives, and the secrecy in which she conducted much of the task force's business only added to the public's skepticism. In the end, her health care plan was deemed too bureaucratic and too burdensome for business. The plan died in the Congress and became a major campaign boon to the Republicans in the 1994 elections, which saw the Democrats lose their control of Congress. Despite the setback, Clinton actively promoted certain national legislation, including the State Children's Health Insurance Program in 1997. She traveled widely, ultimately visiting 79 nations.

Clinton was at the epicenter of the fruitless Whitewater investigation, a Republican-inspired inquiry into a decade-old land deal in which the Clintons had been involved in Arkansas. As such, she became the only first lady to be subpoenaed by a federal grand jury. Although years of probing and $50 million of taxpayers' money went into the Whitewater inquiry, neither Clinton was found to have engaged in any illegal activity. Unfortunately, however, Whitewater revealed a sexual dalliance between Bill Clinton and a White House intern, Monica Lewinsky, that mortified Hillary Clinton and led to the president's impeachment in December 1998. While Mrs. Clinton's allegation that the persecution of her and her husband was the result of a "vast right-wing conspiracy" may have been hyperbole, there can be little doubt that the Clintons were subjected to endlessly harsh scrutiny and criticism, particularly by Republicans and other detractors.

In 2000 the Clintons purchased a home in New York, and Hillary Clinton ran for the state's senatorial seat being vacated by retiring U.S. senator Daniel Patrick Moynihan. Clinton was at first running against popular New York City mayor Rudolph Giuliani, and many believed that her chances of winning were not good. But after Giuliani dropped out of the race because of health problems, Clinton—now running against Rick Lazio, a relatively unknown congressman—was virtually assured a win. Clinton won the election by an impressive 12-point margin and took office in January 2001.

During her first term Clinton maintained a relatively low profile but garnered high marks for her intellect, excellent grasp of issues, and willingness to work in a bipartisan manner. Following the September 11, 2001, terror attacks on the United States, Clinton strongly backed the George W. Bush administration's response, including Operation ENDURING FREEDOM in Afghanistan and the 2001 Patriot Act. In October 2002 Clinton voted with the majority to grant the Bush administration authority to wage war in Iraq to enforce United Nations (UN) resolutions should diplomacy fail. She did not support an amendment that would have required another congressional resolution to invade Iraq. Meanwhile, Clinton visited both Afghanistan and Iraq to gauge the effectiveness of the U.S. war efforts there.

By 2005, already planning a run for the presidency in 2008, Clinton began to publicly criticize the Iraq war effort, noting the growing insurgency and the absence of firm plans to either extricate the United States from Iraq or quash the insurgents. She was careful to state, however, that a precipitous withdrawal was unwise if not dangerous, a position that chagrined many antiwar Democrats. Clinton did not back any of the Bush tax cuts, viewing them as economic grenades that would derail the economy, nor did she vote for Bush's two Supreme Court nominees, John Roberts and Samuel Alito.

In November 2006 Clinton, now quite popular with New York voters, won a landslide reelection. In early 2007 she began transferring leftover funds from her Senate race to her presidential campaign. On January 20, 2007, she announced her intention to form an exploratory committee for the 2008 presidential contest. That same year, she refused to support the Bush administration's troop surge in Iraq and backed unsuccessful legislation that would have forced the president to withdraw troops from Iraq based on a predetermined time line. Forced to deal with her affirmative vote for the Iraq War, Clinton now had to explain that she probably would have voted against the 2002 resolution had she been privy to accurate and reliable intelligence. Her position change left many wondering why she had taken so long to come to such a conclusion.

By the autumn of 2007, Clinton seemed the person to beat amid a large Democratic presidential field. Following a mediocre performance in a debate in October, Clinton's momentum began to slip. After placing third in the January 2008 Iowa caucus, Clinton's campaign began to slowly unravel as Senator Barack Obama made significant inroads with Democratic voters. After waging a well-run and valiant campaign, Clinton finally dropped out of the race on June 7, 2008, and endorsed Obama's candidacy. In 2009 Obama nominated Clinton as secretary of state, and she was subsequently confirmed in that position by the Senate. Since assuming the office, she has widely traveled the globe and has been particularly active in initiatives to repair U.S. relations with Western Europe and Russia that had deteriorated since the 2003 invasion of Iraq.

PAUL G. PIERPAOLI JR.

See also

Clinton, William Jefferson; Obama, Barack Hussein, II

References

Bernstein, Carl. *A Woman in Charge: The Life of Hillary Rodham Clinton.* New York: Knopf, 2007.

Clinton, Hillary Rodham. *Living History.* New York: Simon and Schuster, 2003.

Clinton, William Jefferson
Birth Date: August 19, 1946

U.S. Democratic Party politician and president of the United States (1993–2001). William "Bill" Jefferson Clinton was born William Blythe in Hope, Arkansas, on August 19, 1946. His early life was characterized by hardships and struggles that formed his character and attitudes throughout his public life. His biological father, William Blythe III, was killed in an automobile accident prior to his son's birth, and young Blythe was raised by his mother, Virginia Kelley. His mother's marriage to Roger Clinton prompted William's adoption and the changing of his name to William Clinton just prior to starting secondary school.

Clinton was a bright and astute student who hoped to pursue a medical career until he met President John F. Kennedy on a Boys' Nation trip to Washington, D.C. This experience led Clinton to focus his future career aspirations on public service and politics. He received an academic scholarship to attend Georgetown University, where he earned a bachelor of science degree in international affairs. During his time at Georgetown, he spent a year assisting Arkansas senator J. William Fulbright. Clinton's credentials as a progressive Democrat and social liberal were further developed under the tutelage of this prominent senator. In 1968 as the United States was being transformed by social changes and wracked by protests against the Vietnam War, Clinton was selected as a Rhodes Scholar. He spent 1968 to 1970 studying at Oxford University. On his return to the United States, he enrolled in the Yale University School of Law.

While studying at Yale, Clinton met his future wife Hillary Rodham, who shared many of the liberal and progressive ideas that would become the hallmark of Clinton's political career. They were married in 1975.

Clinton's initial foray into national politics occurred shortly after receiving his law degree. In 1974 he was defeated in a congressional race for Arkansas's Third District. After a brief career as a professor at the University of Arkansas (1974–1976), he was named state attorney general and was elected governor in 1978 at age 32, the youngest governor in the nation. In 1980 he suffered a humiliating reelection defeat, caused by widespread opposition to an automobile licensing tax. Clinton's resiliency and commitment were apparent when he successfully regained the Arkansas governorship in 1982, a post he held until his election as president in 1992.

In the summer of 1992 Clinton secured the Democratic Party nomination to run against incumbent president George Herbert Walker Bush, a Republican. Clinton was bedeviled, however, by questions regarding his marital fidelity and the emerging Whitewater real estate scandal in Arkansas. In the race, he benefited from an economic downturn and businessman H. Ross Perot's Independent Party candidacy.

Clinton won the November 1992 election with a minority of the popular vote. During his first term he balanced domestic issues

William Jefferson Clinton, shown here in 2000, was president of the United States during 1993–2001. The country enjoyed prosperity during his years in office, but Clinton was unable to realize his goal of securing Middle East peace. (U.S. Department of Defense)

and foreign policy in a highly effective manner. At home, he lobbied unsuccessfully for major health care reform. Clinton was successful, however, in raising taxes and reducing expenditures to reduce—and then eliminate—the federal deficit and in pushing through major welfare reforms. In foreign affairs, he promoted free trade agreements, brokered peace efforts in the Middle East, removed U.S. military personnel from Somalia, and restored diplomatic relations with the Socialist Republic of Vietnam.

The congressional elections of 1994, however, brought Republican majorities in both the House and Senate. The Republicans' "Contract with America," crafted chiefly by Republican congressman Newt Gingrich, called for reducing the role of government and continuing the conservative policies of Ronald Reagan and was a thorough repudiation of Clinton's presidency. A standoff between Clinton and congressional leaders led to a federal government shutdown in November and December 1995.

In the 1996 presidential campaign Clinton promised a tough approach to crime, supported welfare reform, called for reducing the federal deficit, and insisted on the need to continue affirmative action programs. Robert Dole, a respected senator and World War II veteran, was the Republican Party candidate. The booming

U.S. economy and suspicions regarding the Republicans' agenda ensured a respectable Clinton victory. He was the first Democrat to secure a second presidential term since Franklin D. Roosevelt.

In 1997 Clinton submitted to Congress the first balanced budget in nearly three decades. The cooperation of congressional Republicans and major compromises by Clinton generated significant budget surpluses during the remainder of his presidency. By decade's end, the American economy was more robust than at any time since the mid-1960s, unemployment stood at a historic low, and the stock market had reached new highs.

In addition to significant domestic accomplishments, Clinton responded effectively to a series of international crises. In 1998 in response to Iraqi president Saddam Hussein's noncompliance with United Nations (UN) weapons inspections, Clinton authorized air strikes in Iraq (Operation DESERT FOX), and sanctions significantly hurt Iraq's economy yet without producing any significant change in the Iraqi dictator's behavior. In 1999 Clinton prodded a North Atlantic Treaty Organization (NATO) military response to genocide conducted by Serbs against Albanians in Kosovo. He also worked mightily to secure a resolution to the Israeli-Palestinian conflict, a major Clinton administration goal.

Clinton constantly urged all sides to negotiate and come to an agreement, but his efforts were stymied by uncooperative leaders and events. The assassination of Israeli prime minister Yitzhak Rabin in November 1995 and the terrorist attacks by Islamic groups since 1994 were accompanied by a turn to the Right in Israeli public opinion, which led to a right-wing cabinet under hard-line prime minister Benjamin Netanyahu. Netanyahu promised to bring peace and security but also pledged that he would not return any of the occupied territories. He delayed in carrying out troop withdrawals in accordance with the 1993 Oslo Accords, in which Israel had agreed to give up land for peace, while the Palestinian side failed to crack down on terrorism. Netanyahu also demanded that Yasser Arafat and the Palestinian National Authority (PNA) move directly against the Hamas terrorist organization.

With tensions dramatically increasing, Clinton intervened directly and applied pressure on both sides. In October 1998 he succeeded in bringing together Netanyahu and Arafat at the Wye River estate in Maryland. Following days of difficult negotiations and sometimes bitter wrangling, Clinton secured agreement in what became known as the Wye River Accords. Israel agreed to withdraw from some additional 13 percent of West Bank territory, and the PNA renounced the use of terrorism and agreed both to suppress it and to eliminate the weapons that the PNA had stockpiled. The PNA also agreed to halt the most virulent anti-Israeli propaganda.

Netanyahu returned to Israel, however, to find strong opposition from within his ruling Likud coalition to the additional territorial concession. He nonetheless carried out a partial withdrawal. Meanwhile, although the PNA did crack down on militants, it failed to implement most of the provisions in the Wye River Accords, whereupon a month later Netanyahu suspended withdrawals.

Forced to call new elections, Netanyahu curried favor with the Israeli religious Right, alienating many secular Israelis. In the ensuing May 1999 elections, Netanyahu was defeated by the Labor coalition known as One Israel, headed by former Israeli Army chief of staff Ehud Barak.

Clinton reached out to Barak, whose premiership began with much promise but ended after only 17 months. Barak removed Israeli troops from southern Lebanon in May 2000, but negotiations with Arafat and the PNA ran afoul of right-wing charges that he was making too many concessions. Clinton again set up a meeting in the United States. During July 11–24, 2000, Clinton hosted a summit at the presidential retreat of Camp David, Maryland. Despite generous concessions by Barak the parties were unable to secure agreement, and a new wave of violence, the Second (al-Aqsa) Intifada, erupted. Clinton made one last try, this time at the White House during December 19–23, 2000. Both his and Barak's terms were nearing their ends. The U.S. plan, apparently endorsed by Barak, would have ceded to the Palestinians a greater percentage of the West Bank and Palestinian control of the Gaza Strip, with a land link between the two. Barak also agreed that Arab neighborhoods of East Jerusalem might become the capital of the new Palestinian state. Certain Palestinian refugees would also have the right of return to the Palestinian state and compensation from a fund raised by international donors. These concessions were anathema to the Likud Party and other Israeli rightists, but in the end, despite heavy pressure from Clinton, it was Arafat who rejected and torpedoed the agreement. Barak, who came under a storm of criticism for this process, was forced to step aside.

The Clinton White House also faced several foreign-inspired terrorist attacks on U.S. soil and on U.S. interests, the most serious of them being the 1993 World Trade Center bombing, the August 1998 truck bombing of two U.S. embassies in Kenya and Tanzania, and the bombing of USS *Cole* in Yemen in October 2000. The last two incidents were specifically linked to Al Qaeda, and the earlier attack was more than likely tied to the terrorist group. In retaliation for the 1998 embassy attacks, Clinton ordered cruise missile strikes against suspected Al Qaeda posts in Khartoum, Sudan, and in Afghanistan. The strikes were largely ineffective and engendered significant controversy in the United States and abroad. After leaving office and after the September 11, 2001, attacks by Al Qaeda, Clinton was insistent that his administration was fully aware of the danger that Al Qaeda posed to the United States but that it could not move quickly enough because neither the Central Intelligence Agency (CIA) nor the Federal Bureau of Investigation (FBI) was certain beyond all doubt as to Al Qaeda's complicity in the earlier attacks. He claimed that battle plans were already in place for an invasion of Afghanistan and a massive hunt for Al Qaeda leader Osama bin Laden, but the clock on his administration ran out before the plans could be put into motion.

Clinton's second term was also marked by personal scandal and legal problems. Kenneth Starr, the independent counsel investigating Whitewater, leveled against the president charges of sexual misconduct and lying to a federal grand jury. He did not, however, ever find evidence of wrongdoing in the Whitewater deal. In September 1998 the U.S. House of Representatives passed two articles of impeachment against the president, but in early 1999 the Senate acquitted Clinton on both counts along party lines. In order to end the Whitewater investigation, Clinton agreed to a five-year suspension of his law license and a $25,000 fine.

After leaving the presidency, Clinton assisted his wife in her successful senatorial campaign in New York and in her failed bid for the presidency in 2008, opened his own office in Harlem in New York City, and established a presidential library in Little Rock, Arkansas. He has also traveled extensively abroad and raised significant sums of money for charitable causes, including AIDS and, with former President George H. W. Bush, tsunami relief. Clinton also helped form the William J. Clinton Foundation, a global outreach enterprise that has helped millions of people around the world, and wrote his memoirs.

JAMES F. CARROLL AND SPENCER C. TUCKER

See also
Al Qaeda; Arafat, Yasser; Bin Laden, Osama; Clinton, Hillary Rodham; *Cole,* USS, Attack on; Dar es Salaam, Bombing of U.S.

Embassy; DESERT FOX, Operation; Hussein, Saddam; Iraq, History of, 1990–Present; Israel; Nairobi, Kenya, Bombing of U.S. Embassy; Netanyahu, Benjamin; Oslo Accords; Rabin, Yitzhak; Somalia, International Intervention in; Terrorism; World Trade Center Bombing

References

Clinton, Bill. *My Life*. New York: Knopf, 2004.

Maraniss, D. *First in His Class.* New York: Simon and Schuster, 1995.

Posner, R. A. *An Affair of State: The Investigation, Impeachment, and Trial of President Clinton.* Cambridge: Harvard University Press, 1999.

CNN

Twenty-four-hour U.S. cable television network dedicated to presenting domestic and international news and credited with having revolutionized the coverage of live events during the 1991 Persian Gulf War. The Cable News Network (CNN) was founded in 1980, when cable television was not much beyond its infancy, by media impresario Ted Turner in Atlanta, Georgia. It was part of his Turner Broadcast System (TBS), which owned a number of stations and networks that were broadcast throughout the United States. CNN is now owned by media giant Time Warner. In 1982 Turner launched a companion network to CNN, first called CNN-2 and then renamed Headline News, that broadcasts a short 30-minute all-inclusive news show designed to give viewers a brief overview of national and international events. Unlike CNN, it cycles much of its news program several times throughout the day. CNN was the first commercially viable network in the country dedicated solely to news and news-related shows. As such, it is credited for having begun the phenomenon of 24-hour news programming.

With a current viewership exceeding 90 million U.S. households plus households reached by its Canadian counterpart, CNN is known for its in-depth news reporting, various interview-style news shows, the use of experts to add more dimension to news stories, and reporting in real time on location during breaking news events. CNN caters more to U.S. news events, and its coverage of international events is not as extensive as that of the British Broadcasting System (BBC), which is perhaps its most direct foreign competitor. CNN's international coverage has been criticized in some quarters, especially in the Middle East where detractors claim that the network reports news events with an American perspective that can sometimes compromise fairness and accuracy.

It was not until the 1991 Persian Gulf War that CNN became a household word for American television viewers. When Operation DESERT STORM began in January 1991, CNN was the only news network capable of broadcasting out of Iraq, which it did with much fanfare and excitement in the opening hours of the air campaign in Baghdad. Holed up in Baghdad's Al-Rashid Hotel, CNN correspondents John Holliman, Peter Arnett, and Bernard Shaw reported live, first from cell phones and then on camera, as U.S. bombs and rockets exploded around them. At one point, bombs fell so close to the hotel that viewers saw the reporters scrambling for cover under desks in the makeshift studio. The coverage transfixed the American public and catapulted CNN and its reporters into the limelight. CNN also managed to scoop its then-more powerful competition, namely the big three networks of ABC, CBS, and NBC. Other CNN reporters saw their stars rise during the Persian Gulf War, including Wolf Blitzer and Christiane Amanpour.

CNN's on-the-scene real-time news coverage continued, including its coverage of the infamous October 3–4, 1993, Battle of Mogadishu; the September 11, 2001, terror attacks; and, of course, coverage of Operation IRAQ FREEDOM in 2003. By the mid-1990s, Pentagon officials and other war planners had begun to refer to the "CNN Effect," which was the public's reaction to the actual unfolding of news events as they occurred in front on the camera. This, they realized, added an entirely new dimension to the management of public opinion in times of war or crisis and also forced civilian leadership to react to events in a faster and more decisive manner. Some critics of the CNN Effect point out that coverage of events in real time can give viewers a skewed perception of occurrences because they see only what is being shown on television at any given time. Other critics point out that the advent of 24-hour news networks has led to less careful news reporting in order to stay abreast of the competition and has encouraged news outlets to create news stories from information that may not, indeed, be very newsworthy.

Despite its critics, CNN has had an extraordinary impact on broadcast news reporting and the shaping of public opinion. In 1995 CNN began its online news network (CNN.com), which has further revolutionized the reporting of news events. Since then, those seeking news information do not have to be near a television set, and with the recent advent of handheld computer devices, CNN can broadcast via cell phones, Blackberries, and the like.

PAUL G. PIERPAOLI JR.

See also

Media and Operation DESERT STORM; War Correspondents

References

Conroy, Thomas, and Jarice Hanson, eds. *Constructing America's War Culture: Iraq, Media, and Images at Home.* Lanham, MD: Lexington Books, 2007.

Greenberg, Bradley S., and Walter Gantz, eds. *Desert Storm and the Mass Media.* Cresskill, NJ: Hampton, 1993.

Smith, Hedrick, ed. *The Media and the Gulf War: The Press and Democracy in Wartime.* Washington, DC: Seven Locks, 1992.

Coalition Force Land Component Command–Afghanistan

Prior to September 11, 2001, the U.S. Third Army, commanded by Lieutenant General Paul T. Mikolashek, served as the Army Component (ARCENT) for U.S. Central Command (CENTCOM) and maintained a forward headquarters at Camp Doha, Kuwait. After the September 11, 2001, attacks on the World Trade Center and the Pentagon, CENTCOM—commanded by General Tommy Franks—responded to the new exigency.

Because ARCENT had already deployed to serve as the Coalition Force Land Component Command (CFLCC) for an exercise in Egypt, it did not assume control of land operations in the Afghanistan Joint Operational Area (JOA) as CFLCC-Afghanistan until November 20, 2001. Its mission as CFLCC was to direct land operations to destroy Al Qaeda and prevent the reemergence of international terrorist activities within JOA-Afghanistan and support humanitarian operations to create a peaceful and stable environment within Afghanistan. Mikolashek served as commander of CFLCC from November 20, 2001, until May 21, 2002, when command shifted to Lieutenant General Dan McNeil. At that point, CFLCC became a planning arm for the upcoming war in Iraq.

U.S. president George W. Bush ordered military action against the Taliban (Operation ENDURING FREEDOM) on October 7, 2001. CENTCOM developed two ground approaches into Afghanistan. On the northern approach, elements of the 10th Mountain Division deployed to provide security, with other army units providing logistical support, for Joint Special Operation Task Force–North. JSOTF-N, with air force and army special operations elements, established a forward operating base at Karshi-Kanabad (K2), Uzbekistan. Progress on the southern approach through two remote air bases in central Pakistan was secured initially by elements of the U.S. Marines Corps and later by elements of the 101st Air Assault Division. On November 20 the 10th Mountain Division established CFLCC-Forward headquarters at K2.

During November 25–26, 1,000 marines from the U.S. Fifth Fleet staged through Pakistan to a base near Kandahar to form the 1st Marine Expeditionary Brigade (MEB). Once it was firmly ashore, control over the 1st MEB shifted to the CFLCC. This permitted the CFLCC to expand its forces on the ground and, along with Southern Alliance and U.S. special operations units, to force the Taliban defenders of Kandahar to surrender the city on December 6.

In early December, ARCENT completed the CFLCC Operations Order for Land Operations in Afghanistan. Issued on December 11, 2001, this plan provided broad guidance for supervising the ongoing U.S. Army, Marine Corps, and Special Forces ground operations. Critical new tasks from CENTCOM, such as conduct detainee operations and sensitive site exploitation, created new unplanned requirements.

As many as 3,000 Taliban had surrendered to the Northern Alliance in November, and many had rioted as a result of their treatment. After processing, selected detainees would be held in temporary facilities constructed by the CFLCC at Kandahar and Bagram until they could be flown to the U.S. naval base at Guantánamo Bay for further interrogation or military tribunals. ARCENT deployed military police to augment the marines and army infantry units initially pressed into performing these missions and to conduct the detainee aerial escort mission. By August 2002, ARCENT had processed more than 4,500 detainees, transferred 377 to Cuba, repatriated 129 others, and held a further 167 in Afghanistan.

As operations continued around Kandahar, an estimated 1,200 Al Qaeda along with some Taliban, including Osama bin Laden, were detected in caves and tunnels along the Pakistan border in eastern Afghanistan. The offensive against Tora Bora began on December 1, 2001, with intense air strikes supporting Afghan forces advised by the JSOTF-N. Operations continued for several days, with an estimated 200 killed. The escape of large numbers of Al Qaeda indicated the risks of relying on Afghans to achieve U.S. operational goals and prompted General Franks to employ conventional ground forces as well.

Beginning in January 2002, the CFLCC replaced the 1st MEB with Task Force (TF) Rakkasans (3rd Brigade, 101st Airborne Division) and the 3rd Princess Patricia's Canadian Light Infantry Battalion. By the end of February, CFLCC forces had exploited 109 sensitive sites, inspected 59 suspected chemical sites, and delivered more than 1,000 tons of humanitarian assistance while also engaging numerous targets.

The CFLCC's next operation employed U.S. Army ground forces and Afghan allies against a buildup of Al Qaeda forces in the Shah-i-kot Valley. For better supervision, CFLCC-Forward, commanded by Major General Franklin L. Hagenbeck, relocated from Uzbekistan to Bagram on February 13 and became Coalition Joint Task Force (CJTF) Mountain.

Hagenbeck initiated Operation ANACONDA on March 2, 2002. Afghan forces maneuvered while two U.S. infantry battalions supported by army aviation established blocking positions on the slopes of the eastern ridge overlooking the valley. Because of the high altitude and weather, army helicopters would be operating at the outer limit of performance, and only Boeing CH-47 Chinooks would be used to lift the infantry. The assaulting troops suffered numerous wounded casualties on the first day in sharp firefights with Al Qaeda immediately after landing. U.S. infantry once again engaged the enemy in classic close combat, employing organic small arms and mortars. With Al Qaeda fighters so near that air support was often impossible, Hughes/McDonnell Douglas/Boeing AH-64 Apaches became the most effective fire support available to ground commanders despite withering small-arms fire that damaged all seven of the helicopters.

After the initial engagement, CJTF Mountain obtained additional ground and air assets. The battle continued for several days as the allied air forces worked with Apaches to engage and destroy the determined Al Qaeda fighters. Marine helicopters, flown from ships in the Arabian Sea, and additional Apaches deployed directly from Fort Campbell provided reinforcements. The CFLCC committed the 2nd Brigade, 10th Mountain, with two additional army infantry battalions as well as the Canadians. By March 10, CENTCOM estimated that allied ground and air forces had killed more than 500 of the enemy.

After ANACONDA, the CFLCC shifted its conventional and special operations forces south of Gardez and elsewhere in eastern Afghanistan against remaining Al Qaeda and Taliban enclaves. In mid-April 2002, the CFLCC received additional multinational support from TF Jacana, with 1,700 British personnel drawn from the 3rd Commando Brigade.

At the end of April 2002, ARCENT conducted an assessment of its initial performance as CFLCC-Afghanistan. General Mikolashek observed that because of an imposed force cap of 7,000 personnel in country and unanticipated missions, the CFLCC had not been able to properly employ its units. However, the CFLCC had successfully and creatively integrated air, naval, marine, Special Operations, allied, and interagency forces in the conduct of a complex and unusual operation. In a move indicative of a long-term U.S. military commitment, XVIII Airborne Corps under Lieutenant General Dan McNeil deployed to Bagram on May 31, 2002, as Combined Joint Task Force 180 and assumed control of U.S. and coalition operations in JOA-Afghanistan. The total number of personnel under the CFLCC by the end of May 2002, at which time the command changed name and focus, was approximately 20,000. This change allowed ARCENT to refocus on the conduct of potential land operations against Iraq.

JOHN A. BONIN

See also

Al Qaeda; ANACONDA, Operation; Combined Joint Task Force 180; ENDURING FREEDOM, Operation; ENDURING FREEDOM, Operation, Initial Ground Campaign; Franks, Tommy Ray; McNeill, Dan K.; United States Central Command

References

Bonin, John A. *U.S. Army Forces Central Command in Afghanistan and the Arabian Gulf during Operation Enduring Freedom, 11 September 2001–11 March 2003.* Carlisle, PA: Army Heritage Center Foundation, 2003.

Briscoe, Charles H., Richard L. Kiper, James A. Schroder, and Kalev I. Sepp. *Weapon of Choice: U.S. Army Special Operations Forces in Afghanistan.* Ft. Leavenworth, KS: Combat Studies Institute Press, 2003.

Mikolashek, Paul T. "'Patton's Own' Third U.S. Army: Always First, Versatile, Ready, Warfighting Command." *Army* (October 2002): 201–208.

Coercive Interrogation

Methods of interrogation meant to compel a person to behave in an involuntary way or reveal information by use of threat, intimidation, or physical force or abuse. In particular, coercive interrogation has been used during the U.S. Middle East wars to obtain information from prisoners, especially those being held as terrorists. Coercive interrogation has been labeled by numerous individuals and organizations as inhumane torture and war crimes that violate international law. In addition, coercive interrogation has been criticized by many for being ineffective; critics contend that it leads to false confessions.

There are various techniques of interrogation that can be described as coercive, including, but not limited to, sleep deprivation, food deprivation, ceaseless noise, sexual abuse, forced nakedness, cultural humiliation, exposure to extreme cold, prolonged isolation, painful postures, beating, and waterboarding. Waterboarding, a highly controversial interrogation method, involves positioning a victim on his back, with the head in a downward position, while pouring water over the face and head. Soon, as water enters the nasal passages and mouth, the victim believes that drowning is imminent. Waterboarding is a favored interrogation technique because it leaves no visible marks on the victim and can be very effective in extracting confessions.

During the 1991 Persian Gulf War, records indicate that the U.S. military generally abided by international law concerning treatment of civilian and military detainees. However, there is ample evidence that Iraqis tortured American prisoners of war (POWs) by employing numerous coercive interrogation techniques. Coercive interrogation became a much larger issue during the George W. Bush administration after the Global War on Terror began in 2001. Although many international agreements signed by the United States forbid torture, President Bush, Vice President Richard Cheney, and his administration have supported the use of coercive interrogation in the Global War on Terror, the Afghanistan War, and the Iraq War. After the September 11, 2001, terrorist attacks on the United States, the Bush administration acknowledged a need for new interrogation techniques.

Shortly after the September 11 attacks, the Bush administration worked to gain support for coercive interrogation techniques and began to change the definition of torture to better suit its needs. Numerous senior officials believed that the Central Intelligence Agency (CIA) had to employ coercive interrogation techniques to deal with Al Qaeda suspects and other terrorists. The administration now began to devise arguments for going against prevailing prescriptions vis-à-vis torture. First, Bush believed that as commander in chief he could use the inherent powers given to him in the U.S. Constitution to stretch U.S. policy to best protect the citizens of the United States. The administration had argued repeatedly that terrorism is a major threat that cannot be fought with conventional means. Also, the White House repeatedly stated that coercive interrogation is not torture in the strict sense of the word. Most legal scholars on the subject disagree with this assessment.

Beginning in 2004, accounts surfaced of Iraqi prisoners being abused by U.S. soldiers in the Abu Ghraib Prison in Iraq. Pictures showing U.S. military personnel abusing and violating prisoners by various means proved highly incendiary. Some methods used included urinating on prisoners, punching prisoners excessively, pouring phosphoric acid on prisoners, rape, forcing prisoners to strip nude and attaching electrodes to their genitals, or photographing prisoners in compromising positions to humiliate them. Eventually, 17 soldiers and officers were removed from duty because of the Abu Ghraib scandal; some eventually faced criminal charges and trial.

The situation was compounded when the CIA was accused of having destroyed evidence of the torture of civilian detainees in 2005. There were apparently two videotapes (subsequently destroyed) that contained images of Al Qaeda suspects being tortured. By 2007, the CIA admitted to some use of coercive interrogation. However, the agency admitted that this had happened rarely and that techniques such as waterboarding were used fewer than five times. In a television interview in December 2008, Vice President Cheney admitted that he has supported the use of waterboarding. More allegations of CIA-sponsored torture surfaced, but the Bush administration stuck to its support of coercive interrogation techniques, asserting that they were not cruel and unusual and therefore did not constitute torture. Nevertheless, under considerable pressure, Bush signed an executive order in July 2007 forbidding the use of torture against terror suspects; it did not, however, specifically ban waterboarding.

In early 2008, waterboarding was again a hot topic as Congress considered an antitorture bill designed largely to limit the CIA's use of coercive interrogation. The bill, which was passed in February 2008, would have forced the CIA to abide by the rules found in the *Army Field Manual on Interrogation* (FM 34-52). The manual forbids the use of physical force and includes a list of approved interrogation methods; waterboarding is not among them.

Arizona senator John McCain, who had been brutally tortured as a POW during the Vietnam War and had already engaged in a war of words with the Bush White House over the use of torture, voted against the bill. McCain, in defending his vote, argued that the CIA should have the ability to use techniques that are not listed in the *Army Field Manual of Interrogation*. He argued that there are other techniques available that are effective and not cruel and unusual. He continued to claim, however, that waterboarding is torture and illegal. Bush vetoed the February 2008 bill, and its proponents did not have the requisite votes to override it.

ARTHUR M. HOLST

See also

Abu Ghraib; Al Qaeda; Bush, George Walker; Central Intelligence Agency; McCain, John Sidney, III; Torture of Prisoners

References

Bellamy, Alex J. "No Pain, No Gain? Torture and Ethics in the War on Terror." *International Affairs* 82 (2006): 121–148.

Dershowitz, Alan M. *Is There a Right to Remain Silent: Coercive Interrogation and the Fifth Amendment after 9/11.* Oxford: Oxford University Press, 2008.

Guiora, Amos N. *Constitutional Limits on Coercive Interrogation.* New York: Oxford University Press, 2008.

Posner, Eric A., and Adrian Vermeule. *Terror in the Balance? Security, Liberty, and the Courts.* New York: Oxford University Press, 2007.

Cohen, William Sebastian
Birth Date: August 28, 1940

Republican politician, U.S. senator, and secretary of defense (1997–2001). William Sebastian Cohen was born in Bangor, Maine, on August 28, 1940, to Russian immigrant parents. He attended Bowdoin College, graduating in 1962, and received a law degree from Boston University in 1965. After law school, he returned to Maine to practice law. Cohen subsequently became assistant county attorney for Penobscot and also served on the Bangor school board. In 1969 he was elected to the Bangor City Council, and during 1971–1972 he was mayor of Bangor.

In 1972 Cohen ran as a Republican to succeed Democratic congressman William Hathaway, who became a U.S. senator from Maine. Cohen won election to the U.S. House of Representatives and was reelected twice. In 1978 he ran against Hathaway for a Senate seat and won. During his three terms in the Senate (1979–1997) Cohen focused on national security issues, serving on the Senate Armed Services Committee and the Senate Intelligence Committee. He also served on the Governmental Affairs Committee. Cohen announced his retirement from the Senate in 1996 ostensibly to pursue other career objectives.

Later that year, however, after President Bill Clinton won reelection, Cohen was nominated to become secretary of defense. Although a Republican, Cohen was considered a moderate, and Clinton believed that his presence in the post would help to build a bipartisan consensus around his foreign policy. Cohen subsequently accepted the nomination, which sailed unanimously through the Republican-controlled Senate.

As defense secretary, Cohen focused on developing a lighter and more mobile and modernized fighting force and investing in

William Cohen, secretary of defense under President Bill Clinton during 1997–2001, speaks at Ramstein Air Base in Germany on April 8, 1999. (U.S. Department of Defense)

new weapons systems. He did this while continuing to maintain the "two regional wars" template that had been part of Pentagon planning for many years. That is, U.S. forces were to be kept ready to wage two regional wars simultaneously. Cohen also drew increasing attention to the dangers posed by the proliferation of weapons of mass destruction (WMDs), and he oversaw the expansion of the North Atlantic Treaty Organization (NATO) into Eastern Europe.

Cohen remained uneasy over troop commitments in the Balkans made during Clinton's first term, fearing that protracted humanitarian and peacekeeping missions might endanger U.S. forces. Cohen was also concerned that money expended on such endeavors might be better spent elsewhere. These monetary issues were real concerns for Cohen, given the budgetary constraints under which he had to work. Indeed, because of the Clinton administration's determined plan to erase decades-long budget deficits and pay down some of the national debt, spending more on defense during a time of peace was not a viable option.

Cohen oversaw U.S. operations in the Balkans during his tenure in office. When Serbian forces began ethnic cleansing against Albanian Muslims from Kosovo, the United States, in concert with NATO, responded with a bombing campaign to force the Serbs to the peace table. This operation began on March 24, 1999, and ended on June 10, 1999, when the Yugoslav government agreed to return to the negotiating table. A number of nay-sayers believed that the bombing campaign was folly, but the relatively quick success of it silenced many of Clinton's critics who had derided his Balkans policy. The low point of the operation occurred when faulty intelligence led to the mistaken bombing of the Chinese embassy in Belgrade on May 7, 1999. Despite his reservations about troop deployments to the Balkans, Cohen nevertheless hoped to stop Serbian aggression. His public disagreement with General Wesley Clark, NATO's supreme allied commander who insisted that ground troops might be needed in Kosovo, led to the general's early retirement in 2000.

When Al Qaeda bombed U.S. embassies on August 7, 1998, in Dar es Salaam, Tanzania, and Nairobi, Kenya, Cohen oversaw the American response on August 20, 1998. Operation INFINITE REACH saw U.S. cruise missile attacks on sites in Afghanistan and Sudan. Much controversy surrounded the operation, however, as the Sudanese target in all likelihood was not a chemical weapons facility but rather a pharmaceutical plant. Some of President Clinton's detractors charged that the attacks were designed to take the public's attention off the Monica Lewinsky scandal, which was then being fully revealed.

Cohen also oversaw American military operations in Iraq. In 1998 after the consistent Iraqi failure to comply with United Nations (UN) weapons inspectors and Security Council resolutions, the United States and Great Britain authorized Operation DESERT FOX, which resulted in the bombing of Iraqi targets during December 16–19, 1998. Targets were chosen so as to disrupt the Iraqi regime but also to degrade the ability of the regime to produce WMDs. Some Republicans attacked the timing of the largely ineffective operation as politically motivated, as it occurred at the same time as House impeachment hearings. In the aftermath of the September 11, 2001, terror attacks, many commentators criticized these responses as too tepid.

Since leaving office Cohen has been generally supportive of the Global War on Terror, although he has consistently argued that the nation should do more to gird itself for such an effort, including making shared sacrifices and instituting some form of compulsory national service. He currently presides over the Cohen Group, an international business consulting firm based in Washington, D.C., and has authored several books and many articles and essays. One of his latest writings is *Dragon Fly*, a novel published in 2006.

MICHAEL K. BEAUCHAMP

See also

Al Qaeda; Clinton, William Jefferson; DESERT FOX, Operation; INFINITE REACH, Operation

References

Halberstam, David. *War in a Time of Peace: Bush, Clinton, and the Generals*. New York: Scribner, 2001.

Harris, John F. *The Survivor: Bill Clinton in the White House*. New York: Random House, 2005.

Cold War

The ideological-political-military confrontation between the East, led by the Soviet Union, and the West, led by the United States, that lasted for nearly half a century, from shortly after the end of World War II until shortly before the collapse of the Soviet Union at the end of 1991. Cold War considerations strongly influenced U.S. policy toward the Middle East after World War II. The deadlock between East and West was the single most momentous development in the post–World War II period and dominated the next half century. Put in its simplest terms, the Cold War was the ideological, military, and political rivalry that developed between the Soviet Union and the United States as each sought to fill the power vacuum left by the defeat of Germany and Japan. Profound differences in ideology and political philosophy, exacerbated by misunderstandings, bluff, pride, personal and geopolitical ambitions, and simple animosity between the two sides, grew until this contest became the Cold War.

At the end of World War II, a power vacuum existed throughout much of the world. In the defeat of Germany and Japan, the Allies had in fact destroyed traditional bulwarks against communist expansion. In Western Europe there was no single continental state sufficiently strong to block Soviet expansion. In the Far East there was only China, but it had been badly weakened by the long war with Japan and was in any case about to plunge into full-scale civil war.

Most Americans naively assumed that wars ended with the shooting, and domestic political considerations compelled the rapid demobilization of the U.S. armed forces before the situation abroad had stabilized. Although the Soviet Union was actually much weaker in 1945 than was assumed at the time, British prime minister Winston Churchill expressed the view that only the U.S. nuclear monopoly prevented Soviet forces from overrunning war-devastated Western Europe.

In 1945 the Soviet Union had just emerged from a desperate struggle for survival. The German and Soviet armies had fought back and forth across and laid waste to vast stretches of the western Soviet Union. Twenty-five million people were left homeless, and perhaps one-fourth of the total property value of the country had been lost. The human costs were staggering, and there were as many as 27 million Soviet military and civilian dead. Certainly for the indefinite future, whatever government held power in Moscow would be obsessed with security; one led by the paranoid dictator Joseph Stalin was particularly vulnerable to such an obsession. This, rather than expansion, was the Kremlin's paramount concern in the immediate postwar years.

Despite all the destruction, the Soviet Union emerged from the war in the most powerful international position in its history. Soviet leader Stalin, who had seen the Western powers after World War I erect a cordon sanitaire in the form of a string of buffer states against communism, now sought to do the same in reverse: to erect a cordon sanitaire to keep the West out and not incidentally extend Soviet influence. This was for security reasons, but it was also to prevent the spread of Western ideas and political notions. To Western leaders the Kremlin seemed to have reverted to 19th-century diplomacy, establishing spheres of influence, bargaining for territory, and disregarding the United Nations (UN). Western leaders did not appreciate the extent to which concerns over security and xenophobia drove this policy.

Finally, there was an ideological dimension. Although its leaders had soft-pedaled it during World War II, Soviet leaders had never abandoned the goal of furthering international communism, and the Kremlin was ideologically committed to combating capitalism. It is thus inconceivable that Stalin would not have sought to take full advantage of the opportunities that presented themselves at the end of the war.

As with the United States, Soviet foreign policy was closely tied to domestic needs. Soviet leaders saw the advantage of confrontation with the United States as an excuse for enforcing authority and cooperation at home. The communist world had to appear to be threatened by encircling enemies. Millions of Soviet soldiers had been in the West and had seen, even in ruined Germany, a higher quality of life. They found their own system sadly wanting by comparison and expected improvements in their standard of living with the victory over fascism. Only a new announced threat from abroad would cause them now to close ranks behind the Soviet leadership. Playing the nationalist card would enable the Kremlin to mobilize public effort and suffocate dissent.

Although for different reasons, U.S. president Franklin Roosevelt shared with Stalin a strong antipathy toward European colonialism, and Washington encouraged the disintegration of these empires, including in the Middle East. While idealistic and correct morally, this stance nonetheless reduced the strength of U.S. allies and ensured that ultimately the United States would have to carry most of the defense burden for the noncommunist world.

Roosevelt gambled his place in history in part on the mistaken assumption that he could arrange a détente with the Soviet Union. His optimism regarding Stalin was ill-founded. By the spring of 1945 it was obvious, even to Roosevelt, that the Soviets were taking over Poland and Romania and violating at least the spirit of the Yalta Conference (February 1945) agreements regarding multiparty systems and free elections. Roosevelt died that April. His successor, Harry S. Truman, insisted on honoring wartime agreements and also insisted that U.S. forces withdraw from areas they had occupied deep beyond the lines assigned to the Soviets for the occupation of Germany. The American public clearly did not want confrontation or a global economic and political-military struggle with the Soviet Union. Americans were limited internationalists who merely wanted to return to domestic concerns and economic prosperity.

The Soviets, however, were angry over Washington's abrupt termination of Lend-Lease aid in August 1945. Ill will was also generated by the smooth cooperation of the Anglo-Saxon powers and Moscow's belief that the two constantly combined against the Soviet Union. The U.S. monopoly on the atomic bomb also aroused fear in the Soviet Union. Soviet concerns increased when the United States retained bomber bases within striking distance of Soviet industrial areas and undertook naval maneuvers in the Mediterranean Sea. The Soviet Union, however, rejected a plan put forth by the United States to bring nuclear weapons under international control; instead, the Soviet Union proceeded with its atomic research (aided by espionage) and exploded its own bomb in September 1949. The atomic arms race was under way.

Certainly American and British attitudes toward Soviet activity in Eastern Europe and the Balkans exasperated Moscow. Initially, Moscow permitted political parties other than the communists there, and now it seemed to the Kremlin as though the West was encouraging these parties against Soviet interests. At a minimum the Soviet Union required security, while the United States wanted democratic parties in a Western-style democracy. In only one country, Finland, did the Soviet Union and the West achieve the sort of compromise implicit in the Yalta agreements. In countries such as Poland and Hungary, noncommunist parties were highly unlikely to assure the Soviet Union of the security it desired, and Western encouragement of these groups seemed to Moscow to be a threat.

On the American side, the Russian moves kindled exasperation and then alarm as the Soviet Union interfered in the democratic processes of one East European state after another. In addition, the UN seemed paralyzed, for the Soviet Union, in order to protect its interests, made increasing use of its veto power in the UN Security Council. Despite this, Western pressure in the UN did help secure a Soviet withdrawal from northern Iran in 1946.

U.S. president Franklin D. Roosevelt and Soviet leader Joseph Stalin during the Tehran Conference in Iran, November 28–December 1, 1943. (Library of Congress)

The Western powers were hardly unified. In Britain, left-wing Labourites criticized American capitalism and wanted to work with the Soviets. The French, especially interim president Charles de Gaulle, made vigorous efforts to build a third force in Europe as a counterbalance to the Anglo-Saxon powers and the Soviet Union. It is thus tempting to conclude that only Moscow could have driven the West to the unity achieved by 1949 by founding the North Atlantic Treaty Organization (NATO).

The British bore the brunt of the initial defense against communism. But for a variety of reasons, chiefly financial, Britain eventually had to abandon its role as world policeman. Nevertheless, Churchill, now out of power, sounded the alarm regarding the Soviet Union in a March 5, 1946, speech at Westminster College in Fulton, Missouri. In what became known as the "Iron Curtain Speech," he warned that the Soviet Union had created an "iron curtain" from "Stettin on the Baltic to Trieste on the Adriatic," and he called for a "special relationship" between Britain and the United States to meet the challenge. Americans were not enthusiastic.

In early 1947 peace treaties were finally signed in Paris with many of the defeated states, but the Big Powers deadlocked over

arrangements for Austria and Germany. By the spring of 1947 East and West were approaching a complete break over the German question. The Soviets were stripping their zone of everything they could move and failing to supply food to the three western zones as promised. Facing increasing costs and difficulties caused by a lack of Soviet cooperation, the British and Americans merged their zones economically at the beginning of 1947.

In addition to its demands on Iran, Moscow had pressured Turkey to return land lost by Russia at the end of World War I and also to permit the Soviet Union a share in the defense of the straits connecting the Black Sea to the Mediterranean. There was also trouble in Greece, where communist guerrillas opposed the royalist government. Fighting flared at the end of 1946, and the Greek communists secured material support from the three neighboring communist states of Yugoslavia, Albania, and Bulgaria.

In February 1947 the British government, which had been propping up the Greek government, informed the United States that it could no longer afford to do so. In response, on March 12, 1947, President Truman announced what came to be known as the

Truman Doctrine, stating that the United States would "support free peoples who are resisting attempted subjugation by armed minorities or by outside pressures." The United States had taken up the burden of the world's policeman.

In a remarkably short time, the U.S. Congress appropriated $400 million for Greece and Turkey. This U.S. attempt to draw a line against communist expansion was successful, and by the end of 1949 the Greek insurrection had been contained. The Truman Doctrine led directly to the Marshall Plan and NATO. On June 5, 1947, Secretary of State George Catlett Marshall announced a plan for the reconstruction of Europe in a speech at Harvard University. He promised that the United States would undertake financial assistance to Europe if the nations of Europe united, devised assistance plans for economic recovery, and concentrated on self-help and mutual assistance.

Behind this initiative lay the fear that continued economic troubles would weaken the resistance of the surviving Western nations to communism. Continued American prosperity was also tied to a European economic revival. The plan was deliberately drawn so as to be rejected by the Soviet Union, which insisted that other governments in Eastern and Central Europe under its sway also refuse to participate.

In December 1947 the U.S. Congress passed an Interim Act for $522 million in aid; the following April it appropriated $6.8 billion for the first 15 months of a program slated to run for four years. The aid came just in time to influence crucial elections in Italy, where the communists were making a bid for power. In four years Congress appropriated $13.15 billion in aid plus an additional sum for Asia, bringing the total to $14.2 billion.

Both the Truman Doctrine and the Marshall Plan were early manifestations of the so-called containment policy against communist expansion. U.S. diplomat George Kennan, writing in the July 1947 issue of the *Journal of Foreign Affairs,* called for "a long-term, patient but firm and vigilant containment of Russian expansive tendencies." Even Kennan did not visualize as total an implementation as occurred, however.

Containment and the Marshall Plan compelled the Kremlin to take more proactive measures to guarantee its hold on power and to rearm militarily. In October 1947 the Soviets established the nine-nation Communist Information Bureau, known as the Cominform. It took the place of the old Communist International (Comintern), which had been abolished in 1943 in order to show solidarity with the Soviet Union's allies. The new agency had as its goal the promotion of world communism.

In January 1949 Moscow established the Council for Mutual Economic Assistance (COMECON). It was intended as an organization parallel to the Marshall Plan for integrating the national economies of the satellite nations with that of the Soviet Union. The Kremlin also announced its own program of economic assistance, known as the Molotov Plan, but under it the Soviet Union received more than it gave, as raw materials were often exchanged for shoddy and unwanted Soviet products.

In late November and early December 1947, the Council of Foreign Ministers (United States, Soviet Union, Britain, and France) made a final attempt at resolving the deadlock over Germany. It ended in impasse. The lines had hardened, and the Soviets tightened their control in their satellite states. One by one, surviving opposition leaders were purged. In February 1948 the communists seized power in Czechoslovakia. This sent a shock wave through Western Europe but also marked the zenith of communist expansion in Europe.

The first major confrontation of the Cold War occurred over Berlin. In early 1948 the three Western powers began discussing the establishment of a German government for their combined zones. The Western zones of the city of Berlin seemed vulnerable, an island deep within the Soviet zone of Germany. The Kremlin reasoned that if it could seize West Berlin, this might dishearten and intimidate the West. Angered by the planned Western currency reform for their zones, the Soviets began slowly cutting off surface access to the city on April 1, 1948. A week later the Western governments introduced new currency for their zones. This was the signal for the Soviet blockade to begin in earnest, and by early August it was complete. In this crisis, the Truman administration opted for a massive airlift operation. The Berlin Airlift went on for nearly a year. With a counterblockade hurting the Soviets, they finally backed down and lifted the siege.

By its pressure the Soviet Union had forced the West Europeans to confront the necessity of greater unity, prompting a series of treaties and organizations such as the Council of Europe and the European Common Market. Militarily, the Berlin emergency quickly brought about the Brussels Pact and the formation of NATO.

In June 1948 there was a significant break with tradition in American foreign policy. Powerful Republican senator Arthur H. Vandenburg drafted a resolution that was approved by the Senate. The resolution reaffirmed the U.S. policy of working with the UN. It was the sense of the Senate that the veto should be removed from all questions involving international disputes and the admission of new members. The resolution also associated the United States "with such regional and other collective arrangements as are based on continuous and effective self-help and mutual aid, as affect the national security." This ran counter to President George Washington's admonition against "entangling alliances," which had been heeded since 1796.

On April 4, 1949, the North Atlantic Pact was signed in Washington by 10 European nations as well as the United States and Canada, binding them to a collective military security pact. The resultant NATO went into effect on August 24, 1949.

For the time being Europe enjoyed a breathing spell, but the status quo was about to change. In late August 1949 the Soviet Union exploded its first atomic bomb, an event that shocked Washington and ended the U.S. atomic monopoly. In October 1949 the communists were victorious in China, and on June 25, 1950, the Cold War entered a dangerous new phase when forces of

Berliners watch a Douglas C-54 Skymaster aircraft landing at Tempelhof Airport in 1948 during the Berlin Airlift. The airlift was a massive lift of essential supplies flown into the Western zones of the city during 1948–1949. (Library of Congress)

the Democratic People's Republic of Korea (DPRK, North Korea) invaded the Republic of Korea (ROK, South Korea), touching off the Korean War (1950–1953).

North Korean leader Kim Il Sung had conferred twice with Stalin, securing his approval for the invasion as well as the support of the People's Republic of China (PRC) leader, Mao Zedong. Stalin and Mao evidently believed Kim's confident assurances that the war would be over before the United States could mount an effective response. Fearful that South Korean leader Syngman Rhee might unleash hostilities in an attempt to reunify Korea, the United States had provided only defensive weapons to South Korea, while North Korea possessed a wide range of offensive weapons systems including tanks, heavy artillery, and aircraft. U.S. leaders had assumed that because the United States possessed the atomic bomb, North Korea would never invade South Korea.

In what Truman later characterized as the most difficult decision of his presidency, he decided to fight for Korea. U.S. forces arrived just in time and in sufficient numbers to stave off defeat. The UN also intervened, thanks to the poorly timed Soviet boycott of the Security Council. Following the Inchon invasion of September 1950 and the concurrent United Nations Command (UNC) breakout from the Pusan Perimeter, UNC forces invaded North

Korea in an effort to reunify the nation. The Truman administration ignored Chinese warnings of possible intervention. As UNC forces drove to the Yalu River, the Chinese entered the war in force, and in November they smashed a UNC offensive and pushed south of the 38th Parallel. Gradually the lines stabilized, and the Chinese were driven north again.

The war then changed from a contest of movement to one of position and stalemate. The Western powers, and especially the United States, concluded that restoration of the prewar status quo would be sufficient and that reuniting Korea was not worth the risk of wider conflict. Armistice talks dragged on, hampered by the issue of prisoner exchanges. The fighting finally ended in an armistice agreement in July 1953, although no peace treaty has ever been signed in Korea. Throughout the rest of the Cold War and beyond, Korea remained one of the world's flash points.

The Korean War affected the Cold War in a number of ways. It led to the institutionalizing of the military-industrial complex in the United States and raised fears that the nation was morphing into a garrison state. After all its previous wars, the United States had disarmed. The U.S. military underwent a massive expansion during the Korean War, however, and remained militarily strong thereafter. The Korean War also led the Truman administration to extend direct military assistance to the French in Indochina, where they had been fighting the communist-led Viet Minh since 1946.

The Korean War fed anticommunist paranoia in the United States and had a pronounced impact on developments in Europe, especially the rearmament of the Federal Republic of Germany (FRG, West Germany) because many professed to see parallels between a divided Korea and a divided Germany.

Both the Soviet Union and the United States had new leadership in 1953. Dwight D. Eisenhower took office in January as president of the United States, with John Foster Dulles as his secretary of state. Stalin died in March and was followed by a collective leadership that ultimately gave way to rule by Nikita Khrushchev.

Fear of thermonuclear war dominated the 1950s. The Soviet Union exploded its first hydrogen bomb in 1953, and Americans worried that the Soviets might strike the American heartland with long-range bombers. On the Soviet side, leaders were deeply concerned about the proven strategic bombing capability of the United States and the ring of U.S. overseas bases that surrounded the Soviet Union. A diplomacy of stalemate, based on mutual fear of destruction through nuclear weapons, held sway.

In January 1954 Dulles announced the Eisenhower administration's policy of massive retaliation, with heavy reliance on nuclear weapons in the event of a Soviet attack. This greatly concerned America's European allies, as the most likely location for a military confrontation was the European continent. Throughout the Cold War, Washington professed to believe in monolithic communism, the idea that all communist states moved together in lockstep, with Moscow calling the shots. This proved to be a mistaken notion, but it permeated American policy making.

In 1954 France suffered a resounding military defeat at Dien Bien Phu in northeastern Vietnam. The Indochina War had grown increasingly unpopular in France, and this defeat enabled the French politicians to extricate their nation from the war. Not coincidental to the timing of the battle, a conference was under way at Geneva to discuss problems in Asia. The resulting Geneva Accords of July 1954 provided for the independence of Laos, Cambodia, and Vietnam. Vietnam was temporarily divided at the 17th Parallel, with elections to take place in 1956 to reunify the country.

Ngo Dinh Diem, president of the Republic of Vietnam (ROV, South Vietnam), refused to permit the elections, however, and the Eisenhower administration firmly supported him in this stance. Washington pointed out that communists ruled the Democratic Republic of Vietnam (DRV, North Vietnam) and that communists, once in power, had never allowed truly free elections that might unseat them. Nevertheless, Diem's decision led to a renewal of the struggle to unify Vietnam that became the Vietnam War (1957–1975).

Meanwhile, French Army regulars found themselves immediately transported from Indochina to fight in Algeria, where nationalist agitation led to violence in November 1954. The Algerian War simmered for a time but then grew in intensity and claimed increasing numbers of French soldiers. Ultimately, fears among the French settlers in Algeria and professional army officers that they were again going to be sold out by the Paris government led to a military putsch that brought the end of the French Fourth Republic in May 1958 and the return to power of General Charles de Gaulle, who established the Fifth Republic with a greatly strengthened presidency.

In the 1950s a group of nations was emerging as a self-proclaimed neutralist or nonaligned bloc, also known as the Third World or developing world to distinguish it from the Western powers and the communist bloc. Indian prime minister Jawaharlal Nehru became its leader, but other prominent spokesmen were Josip Broz Tito of Yugoslavia—a communist leader who had broken with and successfully defied Stalin—and Gamal Abdel Nasser of Egypt. For Washington at least, this brand of neutralism—laced with a strong condemnation of colonialism and imperialism promoted by leaders of the developing world—often seemed to favor the Soviet Union.

In Europe, the major problem was the ongoing impasse over the settlements with Germany and Austria. The United States insisted on free elections throughout Germany, while the Soviet Union preferred direct talks between West Germany and the German Democratic Republic (GDR, East Germany). The Soviets also made it clear to their Western counterparts that the price for the reunification of Germany and Austria would be the permanent demilitarization of both states. Washington, however, firmly supported the creation of a West European army that would include West Germany. When that failed to materialize, a formula was then found for it to rearm within NATO.

In 1955 the Soviet government made a number of moves to ease the Cold War. Moscow established diplomatic relations with West Germany and agreed to release the last German POWs from World War II. Finland received the territory of Porkkala near Helsinki, which the Soviet Union had secured at the end of World War II. The Soviets also evacuated their naval base at Port Arthur in the Far East. Finally, the Soviets agreed to the Treaty of Belvedere that ended the occupation of Austria and restored it to full sovereignty, on the pledge of permanent Austrian neutrality and economic concessions. Leaders from the United States, the Soviet Union, Great Britain, and France met in Geneva in July 1955 in an effort to resolve the impasse over Germany. Both sides refused to budge from their previous positions regarding Germany, however, resulting in continued impasse.

The continuing threat posed by the Soviet Union greatly boosted the movement toward European unification. The Council of Europe had been established in 1949. It was followed by the 1953 European Coal and Steel Community, and although efforts by the West European states to create a European army had failed, the European Economic Community (EEC) came into being in 1957.

The year 1956 saw two watershed events of the Cold War occur simultaneously: the Suez Crisis and the Hungarian Revolution. To meet a perceived growing threat by the Soviet Union in the Middle East, the United States had promoted the formation of the

Baghdad Pact in 1955. Iraq and Turkey were the original signatories, soon followed by Britain, Pakistan, and Iran. Many in the Arab world, especially the Egyptian leader Nasser, saw this treaty as nothing less than an attempt by the West to reassert its old colonial control over the Middle East.

In 1956 Nasser sought funding for a high dam at Aswan on the upper Nile. He saw this as a means of improving the Egyptian standard of living and strengthening his standing in the Middle East. At the same time, however, Nasser sought to secure new weapons that would place the Egyptian military on a par with that of Israel. Dulles promised U.S. assistance for the dam, but when he refused the Egyptian request for advanced weaponry, Egypt turned to the Soviet bloc. This incensed Dulles, who then withdrew the offer to help finance the dam. To pay for the project, Nasser therefore nationalized the Suez Canal.

Nasser's actions led to the formation of a coalition of Britain, France, and Israel against him. The British government had the largest stake in the Suez Canal Company and in its operations, and Prime Minister Anthony Eden developed an almost pathological hatred of Nasser and was determined to topple him. The French believed that Egypt was actively supporting the Algerian rebels, while the Israelis were angry over Nasser's decision to blockade the Gulf of Aqaba as well as Egyptian sponsorship of fedayeen (Arab commando) raids against the Jewish state. Leaders of the three powers therefore determined that Israel would invade the Sinai, giving Britain and France the excuse to intervene militarily to "protect" the canal.

The Israelis moved at the end of October, and the French and British governments demanded the right to occupy the canal zone. When the Egyptian government rejected the ultimatum, French and British forces invaded and occupied Port Said on November 5, 1956.

Both the Soviet Union and the United States demanded a withdrawal from Egyptian territory. While the Soviet Union threatened to send "volunteers," it was the United States that was critical. President Eisenhower put heavy economic pressure on Britain, obliging the allied forces to withdraw.

The Suez Crisis was a major event in the Cold War. Israel and Egypt were the chief winners. Although the blockade of the Gulf of Aqaba was ended, Nasser found himself a hero in the Arab world. The Suez Crisis marked the effective end of Britain as a world power and shattered the solidarity of the major Western powers.

Unfortunately for the West, the crisis came at the worst possible time, diverting attention from the concurrent Soviet action in Hungary. The Hungarian Revolution of late October and early November 1956 was one of the most dramatic events of the Cold War. Khrushchev's moves toward de-Stalinization in early 1956 had led to unrest in Poland in June 1956. Similar protests in Hungary that October became revolution. Encouraged by events in Poland and by the limited reforms subsequently introduced there, student demonstrators in Budapest protested the wide gulf between the stated goals of the communist regime and the reality

British troops advance through Port Said, Egypt, as oil tanks burn in the background during the Anglo-French invasion of the Suez Canal area, November 10, 1956. (Bettmann/Corbis)

of its rule. This demonstration led to widespread demands for democratic reform, an end to the hated security police and censorship, and Hungary's withdrawal from the Warsaw Pact. Hungarian premier Imre Nagy, brought to power in an effort to accommodate the reformists, was swept along by a revolutionary tide. He announced a host of changes that included free elections, an end to press censorship, and reform of the hated security police. The Soviets decided to intervene, finding Nagy's commitment to democratic reforms unacceptable, for if the situation in Hungary was allowed to stand, Soviet leaders feared that the movement would surely spread to other satellites.

On November 4, 1956, Khrushchev sent 200,000 Soviet troops and 2,000 tanks into Hungary. Nagy called for resistance, and the Hungarians fought as best they could. Thousands of people died, and 200,000 Hungarians fled to neighboring Austria.

There was nearly universal condemnation of the Soviet action, but no action was taken, in part because the Soviet move was made while the Western powers were embroiled in the Suez Crisis. The lesson of the Hungarian Revolution for the peoples of the Soviet bloc was that the Kremlin could do as it pleased within its existing sphere of influence.

The Cold War appeared to spread in the late 1950s with increasing Soviet challenges in the Middle East, Africa, and Asia, especially in its support for so-called wars of national liberation. In an effort to reassert U.S. influence in the Middle East, the American president announced the Eisenhower Doctrine in early 1957. The doctrine pledged the United States to support the independence of Middle Eastern countries against the threat of communism. The Eisenhower administration also continued to send significant economic and military aid to support South Vietnam.

The Soviet challenge also spread to space, as Khrushchev was keenly interested in his nation's space program. On August 17, 1957, the Soviets fired the first intercontinental ballistic missile (ICBM)—the United States did not fire its first ICBM until the next year—and on October 4, 1957, the Soviets launched the first satellite into Earth's orbit. Sputnik 1 was especially embarrassing to the United States, as it was seen as a sign of Soviet scientific prowess and became more so when in December a much smaller U.S. rocket exploded on the launch pad. The United States did not place its first satellite into orbit until January 1958, and it was still far smaller than those launched by the Soviets. Sputnik 1 also marked the start of the Space Race between the two superpowers.

Many in the West questioned whether the United States still held an edge in military technology, and the notion spread that there was a so-called missile gap in which the Soviets held a sizable lead. Although Eisenhower knew, thanks to U-2 reconnaissance flights over the Soviet Union, that no missile gap existed, he could not make this information public. Democratic presidential candidate John F. Kennedy's charges of a missile gap therefore helped sway a close presidential election in November 1960, lost by Republican Richard Nixon, Eisenhower's vice president.

For NATO, the Soviet missiles posed serious problems. In order to offset its far smaller manpower strength, NATO members agreed to the placing of missiles on their soil. This elicited fears in Europe that a Soviet preemptive strike or counterstrike might wipe out sizable population centers. At the same time, other Europeans questioned whether the United States would actually risk nuclear attack on its own soil in order to defend Western Europe.

The irony was that at the same time Khrushchev trumpeted peaceful coexistence, he also embarked on a period of missile rattling, threatening on at least 150 different occasions the use of nuclear weapons against the West. Many feared that the unpredictable Khrushchev might precipitously launch a catastrophic war.

In 1958 Khrushchev ushered in a period of acute tension when he resumed the pressure on the Western powers over Berlin. Believing that he was dealing from strength, he attempted to secure a Western withdrawal from Berlin. Because the autobahn leading across East Germany to the Western zones of Berlin was the one place in the world where armed Soviet and U.S. forces faced one another, the situation was very tense indeed.

In November 1958 the Soviets simply informed the Western occupying powers that they considered the agreements governing postwar Germany to be null and void. Khrushchev demanded that Berlin be turned into a demilitarized free city, and he gave a deadline of six months—to May 27, 1959—for resolving the situation. In February 1959 he threatened to sign a separate peace treaty with East Germany that would give it control of access

routes into the divided city. East Germany might then choose to close the routes, setting up the possibility of war should the West attempt to reopen them.

To Western leaders, Khrushchev's threats and posturing seemed reminiscent of those of Adolf Hitler before World War II, and they were determined not to yield to such pressure. In May 1959 the foreign ministers of the Soviet Union, the United States, Britain, and France met in Geneva, where they endeavored to find a solution. Again there was no common meeting ground, but the three Western powers stood united, which may have given the Soviets pause. Khrushchev let his May deadline pass without taking action. The world breathed a collective sigh of relief as the Soviet leader probably lost his one chance for nuclear blackmail.

Khrushchev was somewhat mollified by an invitation from Eisenhower to visit the United States. The Soviet leader arrived in September 1959, just as the Soviets landed a probe on the moon. Khrushchev and Eisenhower held extensive talks and actually cultivated a cordial, friendly atmosphere, the so-called Spirit of Camp David. Khrushchev, for his part, denied that there was ever any deadline over settling the Berlin issue. The two leaders also agreed to hold a summit in Paris in May 1960 to discuss Germany. Eisenhower was scheduled to visit the Soviet Union shortly thereafter.

This thaw in the Cold War proved short-lived, if indeed it existed at all. It was formally broken by the Kremlin following the May 1, 1960, U-2 Crisis, in which the Soviets shot down one of the U.S. reconnaissance aircraft that had been making regular overflights of the Soviet Union. An angry Khrushchev stormed out of Paris, torpedoing the summit only a few hours after it began.

Neutralist leaders such as Nasser, Nehru, and Sukarno of Indonesia attacked the West in the UN. Khrushchev also delivered a speech before that body in September 1960. Strangely, he attacked the authority of the UN and particularly Secretary-General Dag Hammarskjöld. In the end, Khrushchev's bizarre behavior ended up alienating the neutralists.

Khrushchev's frantic leadership also created friction within the communist bloc. By 1960, a simmering dispute between the Soviet Union and the PRC erupted into full-blown antagonism: the Sino-Soviet split. Chinese leader Mao Zedong had dutifully followed Moscow's lead during the first decade of the Cold War, but cracks then began to appear in the relationship. For one thing, following the death of Stalin in 1953, Mao believed that he and not the new Kremlin leader was the logical leader of international communism. Mao was also much more confrontational toward the West than were the new leaders of the Soviet Union. Also, the Soviets had refused to share advanced nuclear technology with China and expand military aid. Then there was their 2,000-mile frontier border—the longest in the world—and disputes over Mongolia.

In the confrontation between the two communist giants, most of the other communist states lined up behind Moscow. In Europe, Beijing enjoyed the support only of Albania. By the spring of 1961 the split was sufficiently pronounced for the Soviet Union to cut off assistance to the PRC.

U.S. president Dwight D. Eisenhower and Soviet leader Nikita Khrushchev at the presidential retreat at Camp David, Maryland, during Khrushchev's vist to the United States in 1959. (U.S. Navy/Dwight D. Eisenhower Presidential Library)

While this might have benefited the United States, leaders in Washington were in no position to take advantage of the split in the communist world. President Kennedy, who took office in January 1961, almost immediately faced a series of international challenges. The first was the outbreak of fighting in Laos, where communist, neutralist, and rightist factions vied for power. Then in April 1961, U.S.-trained and -sponsored Cuban exile forces landed on that island in an attempt to overthrow its now avowedly communist leader, Fidel Castro. The operation, conceived and largely planned under Eisenhower, was incredibly botched. Without air cover, which Kennedy refused to provide, the Bay of Pigs invasion was doomed to failure, and Kennedy was forced to take responsibility.

An apparently weakened Kennedy met with Khrushchev in June 1961 in Vienna, where the Soviet leader renewed his pressure on Berlin. Attempting to test the new U.S. administration, Khrushchev intimated that he wanted the issue settled by the end of the year. Yet Khrushchev merely trotted out the same demands, with the sole concession that Berlin might be garrisoned by UN or neutralist troops. This time the Soviets began harassment of some allied air traffic into the city, and the East German–West German border was for a brief period almost completely closed. Again, the Soviet leader threatened the use of nuclear weapons.

Khrushchev was determined to stabilize East Germany, which was fast hemorrhaging its population. By the summer of 1961,

some 3.5 million people, among them the young and best educated, had fled to West Germany. The communist response came on August 13 with the erection of the Berlin Wall. The escape hatch of West Berlin was at last closed, and East Germans were now walled in.

Kennedy called for a sizable increase in defense spending and mobilization of some reserve and National Guard air transport units. The only military action undertaken by the United States, however, was to send 1,500 reinforcing troops along the autobahn and into West Berlin. The ugly concrete barrier remained, symbolizing both the failure of communism and the unwillingness of the West to take action.

In the autumn of 1961 the Soviet Union broke a three-year moratorium on nuclear testing to explode a series of large hydrogen bombs. This set the stage for the Cuban Missile Crisis of October 1962, the single most dangerous confrontation between the Soviet Union and the United States of the Cold War and the closest the two sides ever came to thermonuclear war.

Castro had come to power in Cuba in early 1959 and soon transformed the island into a communist state. Increasingly dire conditions on the island, in large part the consequence of U.S. economic policies designed to unseat Castro, forced the Cuban leader to turn to the Soviet Union for economic and military aid. Anxious to secure his ally and buttress his own popularity at home, Khrushchev responded. Cuba, so close to the United States, appeared to Khrushchev in the spring of 1962 as the ideal means by which to offset the heavy advantage in long-range nuclear weaponry enjoyed by the United States. Placing Soviet medium-range missiles in Cuba 90 miles from U.S. shores, they suddenly became, in effect, intercontinental missiles.

The high-rolling Khrushchev ordered the secret placement of Soviet missiles on the island, hoping to present Kennedy with a fait accompli. Despite the contrary opinion of some key Soviet military officers, Kremlin leaders persisted in the belief that this could be accomplished without American detection. U.S. U-2 surveillance flights over Cuba, however, soon discovered the operation.

On October 22, 1962, in a dramatic television address, Kennedy revealed the presence of the missiles and demanded that they be removed. He ignored certain of his advisers who urged a preemptive military strike on the island, announcing a naval quarantine of Cuba instead. Peace hung in the balance for a week as Soviet ships carrying missiles continued toward the island nation.

On October 27 a U-2 was downed over Cuba by a surface-to-air missile. This event shocked even Khrushchev and may well have marked a watershed in his thinking. U.S. contingency plans called for an air strike if a U-2 was shot down, but Kennedy countermanded the order just in time.

Khrushchev's hand was weak, for the Soviet Navy was in no position to run the blockade. Convinced that the United States was about to invade Cuba, the Soviets arranged a face-saving compromise in which Castro, who had sought a preemptive Soviet nuclear strike on the United States, was all but ignored. Khrushchev agreed to remove the missiles along with jet bombers and some Soviet troops from Cuba. In return, the United States pledged not to invade Cuba and agreed to withdraw older Jupiter missiles from Turkey. Massive Soviet economic assistance to Cuba continued, however. Khrushchev's misstep here was one of the chief causes of his ouster from power less than two years later, but it greatly strengthened Kennedy's hand and encouraged a stronger response to communist aggression elsewhere.

The United States became increasingly involved in Vietnam, supporting South Vietnam against an insurgency supported by North Vietnam that aimed to reunify Vietnam under communist rule. U.S. strategy here was prompted by both the containment policy and by the domino theory: the mistaken belief that if South Vietnam fell to the communists, the rest of South Asia would automatically follow. With the communist Viet Cong apparently on the brink of winning the war in 1961–1962, Kennedy increased American involvement in the conflict by dispatching both helicopters and additional American advisers. Both the PRC and the Soviet Union supported North Vietnam, although at considerably lower levels than the assistance provided by the United States to South Vietnam.

As each side raised the stakes, the Vietnam conflict slowly escalated. In 1965 President Lyndon B. Johnson, Kennedy's successor, began bombing North Vietnam and introduced U.S. ground troops into South Vietnam. Troop numbers steadily increased as North Vietnam escalated in turn, sending its regular forces south. Following the costly but ultimately unsuccessful communist Tet Offensive of January 1968 and a sharp drop in American public support for the war, Washington sought a way out.

The war cost Johnson the presidency. Facing sharp challenges from within his own party, he decided not to run again in 1968. That November Republican Richard Nixon won a very close race against Johnson's vice president, Hubert Humphrey.

Nixon, who was president from 1969 to 1974, carried out the policy of Vietnamization, or turning over more of the war to the South Vietnamese. But Vietnamization required time, and the war dragged on, with more U.S. casualties under Nixon than during the Johnson years, until a peace settlement was reached at Paris in January 1973 that enabled the United States to quit Vietnam "with honor." South Vietnam, largely abandoned by the United States, fell to a communist offensive in April 1975, however.

Even as the war in Vietnam wound down, other events were moving the Cold War from confrontation to cooperation, or détente. The latter policy originated with de Gaulle's return to power in France in 1958. Uncertain that the United States would risk nuclear retaliation on its own soil to defend Europe, de Gaulle sought to develop a French nuclear deterrent and the means to deliver it (the Force de Frappe). He also wanted to organize Europe as a third force between the United States and the Soviet Union. De Gaulle negotiated independently with the Soviets and made well-publicized trips to Poland and Romania appealing for European unity. Soviet leaders were quite content with de Gaulle's attacks on the United States, but they had no intention of giving up their hold

on their satellites. In 1966, angry because the United States and Britain would not share control of nuclear weapons within NATO, de Gaulle withdrew France from the NATO military command.

West Germany was the next country to venture into détente. In the late 1960s, Foreign Minister Willy Brandt instituted what became known as Ostpolitik. This reflected a shift in attitude in West Germany regarding relations with East Germany. Under Chancellor Konrad Adenauer, West Germany had refused diplomatic relations with any nation that recognized East Germany. This policy had in part isolated West Germany as well as East Germany, however, and had cost West Germany trading opportunities with East Germany. Brandt believed that trade and recognition would help facilitate rather than impede German reunification.

The Czech government also attempted to take advantage of the new, more flexible attitudes brought by détente in 1968. Under the leadership of Alexander Dubçek, the regime introduced socialism with a human face, a host of reforms that ultimately included free elections and an end to censorship. Dubçek, himself a communist, claimed that these steps would in fact preserve communism.

The Soviet reaction was swift and decisive. In August 1968 an estimated 500,000 Warsaw Pact troops invaded Czechoslovakia, where they met only minimal resistance from a stunned population. The so-called Prague Spring was over. The Czechs did not fight, for to do so would have been futile.

To justify the action, Soviet leader Leonid Brezhnev announced what became known as the Brezhnev Doctrine. This held that whenever a communist regime was threatened, other communist

A Soviet tank rolls on despite the efforts of protesters who attempt to stop it during the Warsaw Pact invasion of Czechoslovakia to end the Prague Spring, August 21, 1968. (Libor Hajsky/CTK/AP/Wide World Photos)

states had the right and indeed the obligation to intervene. This doctrine would later be invoked to justify the Soviets' 1979 invasion of Afghanistan as well.

The Brezhnev Doctrine understandably alarmed the PRC. Strictly interpreted, the Brezhnev Doctrine could be applied against the PRC itself. Indeed, at the end of the 1960s the Soviets assembled considerable forces along their long common border with China, and Moscow did nothing to dampen rumors that it was contemplating a preemptive nuclear strike against China. In 1969 and 1970 there were actually armed clashes along the border that easily could have escalated into full-scale war.

Such Chinese concerns were a key factor leading to a thaw in relations with the United States. Since the communist victory in China in 1949, the PRC, even more so than the Soviet Union, had been the bëte noire of the conservative Right in the United States, which regarded the loss of China as nothing short of a sellout. The United States and the PRC did not have formal diplomatic ties, and their only talking ground was the UN or through third parties. That ended in February 1972 with the dramatic state visit of President Nixon to Beijing. Nixon, with impeccable Cold Warrior credentials from the 1950s, was perhaps the only U.S. president of the era who could have carried this off. The United States nonetheless moved cautiously, fearful of alarming the Soviet Union and disturbing détente. U.S. negotiators also ran up against the wall of Chinese insistence on the return of Taiwan, which Washington had regarded, since the Chinese Civil War, as the true representative of China. Finally, in 1978 under President Jimmy Carter, the United States established full diplomatic ties with the PRC. The U.S.-PRC thaw was one of the more interesting events of the Cold War and served somewhat to inhibit Soviet aggressive behavior.

Another significant part of détente was the extension of Ostpolitik by Brandt. When he became chancellor of West Germany in 1969, he decisively changed relations with the Soviet bloc nations. In 1970 he concluded a treaty with Moscow whereby West Germany recognized the existing border between East Germany and Poland, implicitly recognizing East Germany itself.

At the same time, even as the war in Vietnam continued, U.S. presidents Johnson and Nixon endeavored to engage the Soviets in a range of discussions. They even raised the possibility of improved relations with the Soviets, to include access to Western technology, if the Vietnam War could be settled. Nixon and Secretary of State Henry Kissinger went so far as to declare the world to be multipolar, with East-West relations no longer the central issue in international affairs.

Nixon did not let substantial Soviet aid to North Vietnam interfere with efforts to strengthen détente. Traveling to Moscow in May 1972, he signed two major agreements with Brezhnev: the Strategic Arms Limitation Treaty, which came to be known as SALT I, and an agreement of principles to regularize relations between the two superpowers. The document held that as each power possessed the capability to destroy the other and much of the rest of the world besides, there was no alternative to the two powers conducting their relations on the basis of peaceful coexistence. The two powers pledged to do their "utmost to avoid military confrontations and to prevent the outbreak of nuclear war." They also pledged to resolve their differences "by peaceful means."

To no one's surprise, this agreement did not usher in an era of perpetual peace. The Soviets, for one thing, had entered into the agreement in the hopes of securing Western trade, investment, and badly needed technology. In the new era of détente, Moscow hoped to achieve its ends while also supporting communist expansion in the developing world by means of proxy forces. Nixon, for his part, announced the Nixon Doctrine in 1973, a rough parallel to Soviet policy whereby the United States would assist other nations in defending themselves against communist aggression but would no longer commit American troops to this effort.

Following the end of the Vietnam War, the United States reduced defense spending to about 5 percent of gross national product (GNP)—from a high of about 9 percent during the war—while the Soviet Union's defense expenditures rose to more than 15 percent of GNP. The Soviet Union also obtained less for its defense spending than the United States and thus was less able to bear the burden of this expense. Certainly, the heavy claim of defense spending played a role in the ultimate collapse of the Soviet Union, but it is by no means clear that this alone brought an end to the Cold War.

Détente led to a tremendous increase in trade between Western nations and the Soviet bloc and greatly aided the communist bloc economies. West European nations and Japan gave extensive loans to the Soviet bloc, most of which were used to prop up communist regimes with short-term spending on consumer goods rather than to invest in long-term economic solutions. Much Western technology also flowed to the Soviet Union. The hope of those supporting détente was that improved trade and economic dependence on the West would discourage aggressive actions by the communist states.

While direct diplomatic confrontation between the Soviet Union and the United States decreased in the period of the 1970s, both sides pursued the same goals by supporting proxy states especially in the Middle East and in Africa, the scene of a number of civil wars, including one in Namibia. The late 1970s saw not only an Angolan civil war fueled by support from both the Soviets and from the West but also the actual intervention of Cuban troops in that African nation. The Soviets also benefited from the overthrow of key American ally Mohammad Reza Shah Pahlavi of Iran in 1979. Soon the new Iranian regime had seized as hostages U.S. embassy personnel, beginning a protracted standoff with the United States.

Although President Carter met with Brezhnev in Moscow to approve yet another strategic arms reduction agreement (SALT II) in June 1979, Soviet leaders sent troops into Afghanistan to protect the pro-Moscow communist government there only five months later, sending U.S.-Soviet relations plummeting. Ultimately the Soviets dispatched to Afghanistan some 150,000 men as well as substantial numbers of aircraft and tanks.

Instead of rolling to victory, however, the Soviets came up against tough Afghan guerrilla fighters, the mujahideen, who received modest aid from the United States through Pakistan. It seemed a close parallel with Vietnam, where the Soviets kept an insurgency going against the United States and its allies for more than two decades with only a modest outlay of its own. Relations between the two superpowers suffered further when, to punish the Soviet Union for its actions in Afghanistan, President Carter imposed a U.S. boycott of the 1980 Moscow Olympics and then began a substantial U.S. military buildup that was continued under his successor.

The cost of globalism for the Soviet Union was also high. With the strain of Afghanistan, international aid commitments, and massive defense spending brought on by the large U.S. buildup and the Strategic Defense Initiative (SDI, nicknamed "Star Wars") initiated by President Ronald Reagan, the Soviets simply could not keep up. Soviet premier Mikhail Gorbachev, who took power in March 1985, therefore had to deal with the consequences of decades of economic mismanagement.

Debate over the basing of the upgraded Pershing II missiles in Europe almost split NATO, but in the end the deployment of these missiles was one of the tipping points that put the Soviet Union on the slippery downward slope of an arms race that it could not win and that ultimately brought their economy to the brink of collapse.

A committed communist, Gorbachev nonetheless believed that the Soviet Union would have to reform itself if it was to compete with the West. His programs of glasnost (openness) and perestroika (transformation) were designed to rebuild the Soviet economy while maintaining communist control over the political life of the state. Unfortunately, his economic reforms produced scant improvement, and his moves to ease censorship often led to civil unrest and ethnic strife as well as national and regional independence movements.

Even as the Soviet Union slid toward chaos domestically, however, Gorbachev scored successes in foreign policy. In the course of two summit meetings with Reagan, he offered concessions and proposed sometimes striking solutions in a manner that led to improved U.S.-Soviet relations and agreements on the reduction of nuclear weapons, including the first agreement in history to eliminate an entire class of nuclear weapons. In 1988 Gorbachev ordered the unilateral withdrawal of Soviet troops from Afghanistan. He also promised publicly to refrain from military intervention in Eastern Europe, and he encouraged open elections in the states of the Soviet empire in Central and Eastern Europe.

After the surprising collapse of the government of East Germany and the dismantling of the Berlin Wall in the autumn of 1989, Gorbachev also agreed to the reunification of Germany and the inclusion in NATO of the new united Germany. Many observers credit Gorbachev, who was awarded the Nobel Peace Prize in 1990, with being the driving force behind the end of the Cold War. Others cite weaknesses inherent in the Soviet system that had plagued it since its inception. Certainly, Gorbachev deserves great

U.S. president Ronald Reagan with Soviet president Mikhail Gorbachev in Red Square, Moscow, on May 31, 1988. (Ronald Reagan Presidential Library)

credit for managing the Soviet Union's implosion in a way that avoided significant bloodshed.

Although the Soviet leader's foreign policy was widely hailed abroad, the situation within the Soviet Union continued to deteriorate. Old-line communists considered Gorbachev's policies equivalent to treason. In 1990 several Soviet republics, including the Russian Soviet Federal Republic led by Boris Yeltsin, declared their independence. Gorbachev tried to stem this tide but was unsuccessful. Talks between Soviet authorities and the breakaway republics resulted in the creation of a new Russian federation (or confederation) in August 1991.

Also in August 1991, a number of high-ranking officials representing the rightist faction in the Communist Party placed Gorbachev under house arrest and attempted to seize power. Faced with Yeltsin's courageous intervention on behalf of opposition groups, the coup collapsed after two days. Gorbachev returned to Moscow but was now dependent on Yeltsin, who banned the Communist Party from the new Russian republic. Gorbachev resigned as general secretary of the Communist Party in August 1991.

In December 1991 the presidents of Russia, Ukraine, and Belarus created a loose confederation known as the Commonwealth of Independent States (CIS). Eight other republics subsequently joined, and the CIS formally came into being that same month. Gorbachev resigned as president on December 31, 1991, and the Soviet Union was officially dissolved.

The Cold War was over. Fortunately, it ended with a whimper rather than a bang. Few knowledgeable observers predicted that it would occur as it did. Most assumed that the Soviet Union was incapable of reforming itself and saw the Cold War ending only after the military defeat of the Soviet Union or if some sort of internal violent revolution were to occur in there. Almost no one had perceived the fragility and weakness of the economic and social structures in one of the world's superpowers that ultimately led to its demise.

Of course, the end of the Cold War did not extinguish international tensions and bloodshed. Problems in the Middle East remained unresolved, and the Russian aim to control its former satellite buffer states somewhat continued the Cold War, as in Ukraine and Georgia. Yugoslavia broke apart in bloodshed that threatened to erupt into wider conflict and eventually triggered armed NATO intervention; civil war and famine remained endemic on the African continent already being ravaged by AIDS; nuclear proliferation widened, intensifying the danger of terrorists securing nuclear weapons; and North Korea's dalliance with nuclear weapons remained an ongoing source of concern. If anything, the breakup of the bipolar world increased, rather than lessened, challenges facing the world's diplomats.

SPENCER C. TUCKER

See also

Arab-Israeli Conflict, Overview; Carter, James Earl, Jr.; Carter Doctrine; Eisenhower, Dwight David; France, Middle East Policy; Germany, Federal Republic of, Middle East Policy; Gorbachev, Mikhail; Kennedy, John Fitzgerald; Nasser, Gamal Abdel; Nixon, Richard Milhous; Reagan, Ronald Wilson; Soviet-Afghanistan War; Soviet Union, Middle East Policy; Truman, Harry S.; United Kingdom, Middle East Policy; United Nations; United States, Middle East Policy, 1945–Present; Yeltsin, Boris Nikolayevich

References

Ball, Simon J. *The Cold War: An International History, 1947–1991.* New York: St. Martin's, 1998.
Beschloss, Micahel R., and Strobe Talbott. *At the Highest Levels: The Inside Story of the End of the Cold War.* Boston: Little, Brown, 1993.
Fontaine, Andre. *History of the Cold War, 1917–1966.* 2 vols. New York: Pantheon, 1968.
Gaddis, John Lewis. *The Long Peace: Inquiries into the History of the Cold War.* New York: Oxford University Press, 1989.
———. *We Now Know: Rethinking Cold War History.* New York: Oxford University Press, 1997.
Kennan, George F. *Memoirs, 1925–1950.* Boston: Little, Brown, 1967.
McCormick, Thomas J. *America's Half-Century: United States Foreign Policy in the Cold War and After.* Baltimore: Johns Hopkins University Press, 1995.
Painter, David S. *The Cold War: An International History.* New York: Routledge, 1999.
Thomas, Hugh. *Armed Truce: The Beginnings of the Cold War, 1945–1946.* New York: Atheneum, 1987.
Yergin, Daniel H. *Shattered Peace: The Origins of the Cold War.* New York: Penguin, 1990.

Cold War Peace Dividend, U.S. Troop/Force Structure Reductions

In the aftermath of the Cold War, the administrations of U.S. presidents George H. W. Bush and William J. Clinton sought to reduce military expenditures to secure a peace dividend whereby spending previously devoted to defense could be redirected to social programs, internal infrastructure improvements, etc. As early as the 1970s, U.S. officials had sought an elusive peace dividend from savings following the Vietnam War, which ended for the United States in January 1973.

In the late 1980s as Cold War tensions eased substantially, the George H. W. Bush administration developed plans to reduce the nation's force structure while also cutting spending on advanced weaponry, including weapons of mass destruction (WMDs). The administration pursued a three-track strategy that included reductions in standing troops and the redeployment of forces, consolidation of military bases and facilities, and arms control and disarmament efforts. All three tracks were interrelated. As arms control measures such as the 1990 Treaty on Conventional Forces in Europe mandated significant cuts in standing military forces in Europe, the United States was able to redeploy and reduce troop strength and eliminate both foreign and domestic bases. The United States was also able to decommission sizable numbers of nuclear missile forces, a result of historic arms-reduction efforts begun under Bush's predecessor, President Ronald Reagan.

Under the Bush administration, the number of active duty U.S. military personnel was reduced from 2.24 million in 1989 to 1.92 million by 1992. The number of U.S. forces deployed overseas was also reduced significantly. For example, U.S. forces in Europe declined from 300,000 in 1989 to 150,000 by 1993. U.S. military expenditures fell from 5.5 percent of gross domestic product (GDP) to 4.8 percent from 1989. Overall, defense spending fell from $303.4 billion in 1989 to $273.3 billion in 1991 before rising again to $298.4 billion in 1992 with the costs associated with the 1991 Persian Gulf War. Bush reoriented U.S. defense policy so that the nation's military was no longer mandated to be prepared to fight two major military campaigns simultaneously (for instance, a World War II–style campaign in Europe and a similar effort in Asia). Instead, the Pentagon was required to be ready to fight simultaneously two regional conflicts of the size and scale of the 1991 Persian Gulf War. The administration also initiated a series of military facility closures and consolidations under the Base Realignment and Closure Commission (BRAC). Throughout the 1990s there were four rounds of cuts under BRAC, including the closure of 97 major domestic bases and 55 realignments. Overseas, more than 960 facilities were closed. BRAC produced $16 billion in savings during the 1990s, with annual savings thereafter of at least $6 billion.

In 1993 the Clinton administration launched the Bottom-Up Review (BUR) of U.S. defense needs and capabilities. BUR kept the requirement to fight two simultaneous regional conflicts but suggested a new approach, the win-hold-win strategy in which the country would maintain the capability to win one regional war while preventing defeat in the second (the hold strategy). After victory in the first conflict, forces would be redeployed to the second to gain victory. BUR also recommended $105 billion in defense cuts through 1999. These recommendations became the basis for the Clinton administration's defense policy.

By 2000 U.S. forces had been reduced to 1.49 million, while defense expenditures had been cut to 3 percent of GDP. Defense spending declined from 1993 through 1998, falling from $291.1 billion in 1993 to $268.5 billion in 1998; however, spending did increase in 1999 and 2000, rising to $294.5 billion the last full year Clinton was in office (2000).

A range of problems emerged with the Cold War peace dividend. The first was that the reduction in defense expenditures contributed to the 1992–1993 recession, as defense firms cut research and production and laid off approximately one-third of all their civilian workers by the late 1990s. Especially hard hit were California, Massachusetts, and Texas, which were home to significant numbers of high-tech and defense-related firms. There was also a wave of mergers and consolidations among military contractors, resulting in an industry dominated by several large firms including Boeing, General Dynamics, Haliburton, Northrop Grumman, and Lockheed Martin. By 1998, more than 500 smaller defense firms had gone out of business or had been acquired by larger competitors.

In addition, the BRAC closings had a significant impact on many communities that had come to depend on military facilities to power the local economy. While some localities were able to recover quickly by using the former military facilities in new and often innovative ways, other towns and cities were hard-pressed to replace the impact of federal outlays. One result was increased political opposition to BRAC's recommendations. The cuts in military personnel were not accompanied by significant alterations in force structures in that the U.S. military continued to emphasize conventional forces designed to counter Cold War–style threats instead of transitioning to lighter, more mobile forces. Troop reductions also created future problems by increasing the reliance on military reserve units and National Guard forces. This became a major problem after 2003, when the George W. Bush administration attempted to wage two wars simultaneously without making any arrangements for a larger standing force.

TOM LANSFORD

See also

Bush, George Herbert Walker; Bush, George Walker; Clinton, William Jefferson; Cold War; National Defense Authorization Act for Fiscal Years 1992 and 1993; United States Department of Defense, Military Reform, Realignment, and Transformation

References

Braddon, Derek. *Exploding the Myth? The Peace Dividend, Regions and Market Adjustment.* Amsterdam: Oversees Publishers Association, 2000.

Hogan, Michael J., ed. *The End of the Cold War: Its Meaning and Implications.* New York: Cambridge University Press, 1992.

Markusen, Ann, Peter Hall, Scott Campbell, and Sabrina Deitrick. *The Rise of the Gunbelt: The Military Remapping of Industrial America.* New York: Oxford University Press, 1991.

Cole, USS, Attack on
Event Date: October 12, 2000

The attack on USS *Cole* in Yemen on October 12, 2000, marked the first time a modern U.S. Navy warship was successfully targeted by terrorists. On October 12, 2000, the 8,600-ton displacement (full load), 506-foot-long U.S. Navy destroyer *Cole* (DDG-67) was docked in the Yemeni port of Aden for a refueling stop. At 11:18 a.m. local time, 2 suicide bombers in a small harbor skiff pulled alongside the anchored ship and detonated explosives. The blast killed both bombers and 17 members of the *Cole*'s crew; another 39 were injured.

The explosives blew a gaping hole in the ship's hull that measured 35 feet high and 36 feet long. Crew members aboard the *Cole* clearly recollect having seen the 2 men as they approached the ship. The bombers, however, made no untoward moves and indeed appeared friendly. Several aboard the *Cole* believed that the men were workers for the harbor services, collecting trash or performing some other kind of routine task. When the skiff neared the ship, there was no warning of trouble until the explosion.

Three days later, the stricken destroyer was taken aboard the Norwegian ship *Blue Marlin* off Yemen and transported to the United States. It reached its home port of Norfolk, Virginia, in December and continued on to Pascagoula, Mississippi, for extensive renovations. Repairs took approximately one year and cost more than $240 million. While still undergoing repair, the ship was towed a short distance to a mooring at Ingalls Shipbuilding in southern Mississippi on September 16, 2001, in a symbolic message of the nation's resolve following the September 11, 2001, World Trade Center and Pentagon attacks.

U.S. and Yemeni officials stated on the day after the bombing that key suspects in the affair had fled to safety in Afghanistan. There was no immediate credible claim of responsibility, but American officials made Al Qaeda and Osama bin Laden as the focus of their investigation. Still, however, some military and national security officials faulted the Bill Clinton and George W. Bush administrations for failing to take appropriate retaliatory measures after the bombing.

The *Cole* bombing prompted an investigation into the ease with which the attackers were able to approach the ship. An initial Pentagon inquiry found that the commanding officer had acted reasonably and that the facts did not warrant any punitive action against him or any other member of the *Cole*'s crew.

Coordination between U.S. and Yemeni officials investigating the incident was aided by a counterterrorism agreement signed by Yemen and the United States in 1998, and the trial of 12 suspects

The U.S. Navy destroyer *Cole* being towed from the port city of Aden, Yemen, by the oceangoing tug USNS *Catawba* following the attack on the destroyer on October 12, 2000, that badly damaged the *Cole* and killed 17 members of its crew. (U.S. Department of Defense)

formally commenced in June 2004. In late September 2004, Abd al-Rahim al-Nashiri and Jamal Mohammed al-Badawi both received the death penalty for their participation in the terrorist act. Four other participants were sentenced to 5–10 years in jail.

Paul G. Pierpaoli Jr.

See also

Al Qaeda; Bin Laden, Osama; Terrorism; Yemen

References

Williams, Paul. *The Al Qaeda Connection: International Terrorism, Organized Crime, and the Coming Apocalypse.* Amherst, NY: Prometheus Books, 2005.

Wright, Lawrence. *The Looming Tower: Al-Qaeda and the Road to 9/11.* New York: Vintage Books, 2007.

Combined Forces Command, Afghanistan

The highest-level U.S. military command in Afghanistan for Operation ENDURING FREEDOM from November 2003 to February 2007. By the spring of 2003, combat operations in Afghanistan had scaled down. As a result of the relatively stable environment in the country and to conserve manpower, which was now crucial with the beginning of Operation IRAQI FREEDOM in March 2003, the headquarters in Afghanistan shifted from a three-star corps-level command

down to that of a two-star division level, designated Combined Joint Task Force 180 (CJTF-180). Overwhelmed with too many tasks, however, the CJTF focused on issues relating directly to military operations rather than on larger political and strategic concerns.

In the summer of 2003 the commanding general of U.S. Central Command (CENTCOM), General John Abizaid, decided that Afghanistan required a different and more effective headquarters organization that could focus on political-military efforts. In September 2003 Abizaid ordered the creation of a new three-star–level coalition headquarters in Afghanistan to take over high-level political, military, and strategic planning, which would permit the divisional headquarters to focus on combat operations. Newly promoted lieutenant general David W. Barno took command in October 2003.

Barno moved the new headquarters out of Bagram Air Base, which was the headquarters for CJTF-180, into the Afghan capital of Kabul. He began with a staff of six and had to borrow facilities and personnel from CJTF-180 to operate. Staff also came from active-duty personnel from all U.S. military services and from the U.S. reserve forces as individual ready reservists and individual mobilization augmentees, service members serving separately from rather than with a unit. Coalition partners also contributed personnel. Great Britain, for example, filled the deputy commander position. In early 2004 the new headquarters was designated Combined Forces Command–Afghanistan (CFC-A). By 2005, the CFC-A had grown to a staff of more than 400 personnel, about 10 percent of whom were from coalition nations including France, South Korea, and Turkey. The CFC-A provided needed continuity because rotations of the staff were staggered to keep some personnel with knowledge and experience in the command at all times; meanwhile, combat units rotating through Afghanistan stayed for a year or less and were replaced with units often unfamiliar with conditions on the ground.

The CFC-A was responsible for Afghanistan as well as southern Uzbekistan, southern Tajikistan, and Pakistan, with the exception of Jammu and Kashmir. CFC-A commanders regularly traveled and coordinated with senior leadership in these countries. During the command's duration, Afghan and Pakistani leaders met with the CFC-A commander for a quarterly conference to coordinate border security and other issues. Under Barno's command, the CFC-A also had a close working relationship with the U.S. embassy in Kabul, headed by Ambassador Zalmay Khalilzad. Taking a few staff members with him, Barno moved into an office in the embassy and lived in a trailer complex within the embassy compound. Barno and Khalilzad coordinated and integrated military and civilian efforts throughout Afghanistan.

In early 2004 Barno established regional commands, designated Regional Command East, Regional Command South, and Regional Command West. The regional commanders assumed responsibility for all military forces in their areas of operation. Before this change military units stayed on large bases, went out into the countryside to conduct an operation for a week or two, and then returned to their bases. The new organization allowed commanders to become more familiar with their areas of operation, work in them for the duration of their tours of duty in Afghanistan, and build relationships with local Afghans as part of a counterinsurgency campaign to prevent the reemergence of the Taliban and other insurgent groups.

One of the first tasks of the CFC-A was to create a campaign plan for Afghanistan to address security, stability, and reconstruction issues. Begun by the British director of planning, this campaign plan evolved into a counterinsurgency approach supported by the U.S. embassy, the Afghan government, and the international community. It required keeping the Afghan people the central focus of the campaign rather than killing the enemy. The strategy included a broad range of activities meant to defeat terrorism and deny the enemy safe sanctuary, enable the Afghans to provide their own security, promote good local and provincial governments, and encourage reconstruction.

During his tenure, Barno had to respond to accusations that American military personnel acted too aggressively and used firepower too heavily when conducting military operations. As a result, the CFC-A created a list of guidelines for American military personnel to follow during operations in order to reduce tensions with the Afghan people. One guideline, for example, required service members to ask locals to open locked doors whenever possible instead of forcing entry.

Lieutenant General Karl W. Eikenberry took over command of the CFC-A in May 2005, shifting the emphasis of operations back to fighting enemy forces. He also moved back into the military compound located at Bagram Air Base. Eikenberry oversaw the transition of Operation ENDURING FREEDOM from an American-led operation to an effort led by the international community. In mid-2005 the North Atlantic Treaty Organization (NATO) began to take responsibility for military operations in Afghanistan, beginning in the north and moving into the west and south. In late 2006 NATO assumed command of all operations throughout Afghanistan except for an area along the Pakistan border, which U.S. forces still control. With this shift in responsibility to NATO, Eikenberry supervised the closure of the CFC-A, which was deactivated in February 2007. Combined Joint Task Force 76, a division-level command based on the U.S. Army's Southern European Task Force and 173rd Airborne Brigade, both deployed from Italy, assumed responsibility for all U.S. forces in Afghanistan, while the Combined Security Transition Command–Afghanistan, another division-level command, retained the mission to train the Afghan National Army and police forces. Before the dissolution of the CFC-A, General John Abizaid presented the command with three Joint Meritorious Unit Awards.

LISA M. MUNDEY

See also

Abizaid, John Philip; Afghanistan; Barno, David William; Combined Joint Task Force 180; Combined Security Transition Command–Afghanistan; Eikenberry, Karl W.; North Atlantic Treaty Organization; United States Central Command

References

Barno, David W. "Fighting 'The Other War': Counterinsurgency Strategy in Afghanistan, 2003–2005." *Military Review* (September–October 2007): 32–44.

Combat Studies Institute, Contemporary Operations Study Group. *A Different Kind of War: The United States Army Operation Enduring Freedom (OEF), September 2001–September 2005*. Fort Leavenworth, KS: Combat Studies Institute Press, 2009.

Rasanayagam, Angelo. *Afghanistan: A Modern History*. London: I. B. Tauris, 2005.

Stewart, Richard W. *The United States Army in Afghanistan: Operation Enduring Freedom, October 2001–March 2002*. Washington, DC: U.S. Government Printing Office, 2003.

Combined Joint Task Force 180

The highest-level U.S. military organization in Afghanistan during Operation ENDURING FREEDOM from May 2002 to November 2003. The Combined Joint Task Force (CJTF) included the two-star divisional command from November 2003 to February 2007 and one of the two division-level U.S. military headquarters from February 2007 onward.

In December 2001 Major General Franklin L. Hagenbeck established a military headquarters to command U.S. Army forces operating in Afghanistan. In accordance with standard operations, it was designated Coalition Forces Land Component Command Forward, or CFLCC (Forward). Located in Karshi Kandabad, Uzbekistan, CFLCC (Forward) oversaw combat operations and logistics during the early phases of Operation ENDURING FREEDOM, which had begun in October 2001. While CFLCC (Forward) commanded U.S. Army forces, other military units, such as air assets, special operations forces, and coalition troops, all reported through separate chains of command and to different commanders.

A new three-star corps-level headquarters was created to bring U.S. military forces in Afghanistan under one senior commander, who reported directly to United States Central Command (CENTCOM), the organization that has overall authority for U.S. military operations in the Middle East. In May 2002 Lieutenant General Daniel K. McNeill took command of the new headquarters, designated Combined Joint Task Force 180 (CJTF-180). It was established at Bagram Air Base, close to Afghanistan's capital, Kabul. Personnel for CJTF-180 came from the XVIII Airborne Corps Headquarters as well as from the U.S. Marine Corps, the U.S. Air Force, and coalition forces. A brigadier general from the U.S. Air Force acted as both the deputy commander for CJTF-180 and the commander for the air component. Aviation, logistics, Special Forces, and civil-military operations all reported to CJTF-180.

Hagenbeck's command, now renamed Coalition Task Force Mountain, became subordinate to CJTF-180. Coalition Task Force Mountain served as the tactical headquarters directing ground forces. The CJTF-180's mission focused on hunting down the remnants of the Taliban and Al Qaeda terrorist organization. Combat operations centered on the Afghanistan-Pakistan border and included air assaults into areas of suspected enemy activity, the use of aerial bombardment against enemy compounds, the capture of Al Qaeda and Taliban fighters and leaders, and the interception of enemy forces along the border. In 2002 the 82nd Airborne took over responsibility for CJTF-180, and the 10th Mountain Division returned for another rotation leading CJTF-180 in 2003.

American and coalition military operations successfully disrupted Al Qaeda and Taliban forces. By the spring of 2003 the military scaled back combat operations to focus on stability and reconstruction efforts. With this shift in focus and to save on manpower with a new war beginning in Iraq in March 2003, CJTF-180 was downsized to a two-star division. The smaller CJTF-180 continued to have responsibility for tasks usually given to three-star commands as well as the duties assigned to two-star headquarters. Overwhelmed with too many missions, CJTF-180 focused on issues relating directly to combat operations rather than the larger strategic concerns of a corps-level headquarters. To address this issue, CENTCOM ordered the creation of a new three-star headquarters in October 2003, designated Combined Forces Command–Afghanistan (CFC-A). While the CFC-A took over strategic and political efforts, CJTF-180 served as the two-star division-level command for combat operations. CJTF-180 then initiated a series of campaigns to fight the growing Taliban insurgency and clear the Afghanistan-Pakistan border of enemy forces. In December 2003 CJTF-180 forces also provided security for the Afghan *loya jirga* ("grand assembly") that chose a constitution.

When the 25th Infantry Division rotated into Afghanistan in April 2004, it took over responsibility for CJTF-180, which was renamed CJTF-76. CJTF-76 conducted combat and presence patrols in villages, air assault operations into suspected enemy strongholds, and cordon and search operations to cut off and surround suspected enemy compounds. It also provided security for national elections, supporting reconstruction efforts and tightening border security. By 2004 the Taliban had changed tactics from fighting coalition forces in large numbers to targeting soft nonmilitary targets, such as civilian aid agencies. As a response, the coalition adopted a counterinsurgency strategy to develop relationships with the Afghan people rather than focusing exclusively on combat operations to kill and capture enemy forces. In May 2005 the Southern European Task Force replaced the 25th Infantry Division as the CJTF-76.

In mid-2005 the North Atlantic Treaty Organization (NATO) began to take over responsibility for combat operations in Afghanistan, assuming full control in late 2006. With this change in command authority, the CFC-A was inactivated in February 2007, elevating CJTF-76 to the highest U.S. combat command in Afghanistan. The Combined Security Transition Command is the other divisional command and has the responsibility for training Afghan security forces. The CJTF controls Regional Command East, which encompasses 14 provinces along the Afghanistan-Pakistan border. Its mission is to provide security along the border, support the Afghan Army and police forces, remove corrupt or ineffective provincial leaders, and continue to seek out and destroy Al Qaeda and Taliban forces.

The designation for the CJTF changed with each new rotation. During 2006–2007 the 82nd Airborne named it CJTF-82, and the 101st Airborne named it CJTF-101 during the next rotation. Although the CJTF has continued to search for suspected insurgents and has conducted combat operations to deny sanctuary to enemy forces, the Taliban regained strength and numbers during 2007 and 2008. As a result, the CJTF has refocused it efforts on killing enemy forces and an aggressive use of airpower.

LISA M. MUNDEY

See also

Afghanistan; Coalition Force Land Component Command–Afghanistan; Combined Forces Command, Afghanistan; Combined Security Transition Command–Afghanistan; ENDURING FREEDOM, Operation; Hagenbeck, Franklin L.; North Atlantic Treaty Organization; Taliban Insurgency, Afghanistan; United States Central Command

References

Barno, David W. "Fighting 'The Other War': Counterinsurgency Strategy in Afghanistan, 2003–2005." *Military Review* (September–October 2007): 32–44.

Combat Studies Institute Contemporary Operations Study Group, *A Different Kind of War: The United States Army Operation Enduring Freedom (OEF), September 2001–September 2005.* Fort Leavenworth, KS: Combat Studies Institute Press, 2009.

Rasanayagam, Angelo. *Afghanistan: A Modern History.* London: I. B. Tauris, 2005.

Stewart, Richard W. *The United States Army in Afghanistan: Operation Enduring Freedom, October 2001–March 2002.* Washington, DC: U.S. Government Printing Office, 2003.

Combined Security Transition Command–Afghanistan

The mission of the Combined Security Transition Command–Afghanistan (CSTC-A) is to assist in the development of a stable Afghanistan, strengthen the rule of law, and combat terrorism by working in partnership with the government of the Islamic Republic of Afghanistan and other elements of the international community that are engaged in coordinated activities. As a primary component of this mission, the CSTC-A provides plans and programs and implements reforms for the Afghan National Security Forces (ANSF), which consists of the Afghan National Army (ANA) and the Afghan National Police (ANP). On April 4, 2006, the Office of Security Cooperation–Afghanistan (OSC-A) was redesignated as the CSTC-A and headquartered at Camp Eggers in Kabul. The CSTC-A is a joint military services organization that draws military personnel from several coalition partners and employs thousands of civilian contract personnel.

The CSTC-A provides military and civilian personnel to help both the Afghan Ministry of Defense and the Ministry of the Interior organize, train, equip, employ, and support the ANSF in its war against the Taliban and Al Qaeda insurgency and its allied functions of providing internal security, fostering conditions for economic development, and gaining the support of Afghanistan's populace. The goal is to create an ANSF that is professional, literate, representative of the ethnic diversity of the country, and competent to perform its security functions.

Examples of specific tasks include recruiting soldiers and policemen; providing training both for the personnel and the recruiters; organizing the Ministry of Defense and Ministry of the Interior; mentoring the military general staff and civilian political leaders; acquiring weapons, uniforms, and equipment; and developing policies and processes required by a modern army and police force. The CSTC-A also assists the ANSF in establishing matériel acquisition systems, personnel systems, and other internal infrastructure needed for effective security forces and operations.

The CSTC-A, which is under the organizational control of the United States Central Command (CENTCOM), has several thousand military personnel and thousands of civilian contract personnel directly attached to it. It also has operational control over the Combined Joint Task Force–Phoenix (CJTF-Phoenix), which has a military strength of more than 6,000 personnel. CJTF-Phoenix concentrates directly on training, mentoring, and advising the ANA and the ANP. The CSTC-A also coordinates with other international groups that are engaged in similar tasks, such as the European Police Mission in Afghanistan (EUPOL Afghanistan).

The CSTC-A is a prime example of the evolving and changing administrative structures dedicated to developing and assisting Afghanistan in assuming responsibility for its own destiny.

Joe P. Dunn

See also

Afghanistan; Combined Forces Command, Afghanistan; International Security Assistance Force; Taliban Insurgency, Afghanistan; Task Force Phoenix; United States Central Command

References

Barno, David W. "Fighting 'The Other War': Counterinsurgency Strategy in Afghanistan, 2003–2005." *Military Review* (September–October 2007): 32–44.

Combat Studies Institute, Contemporary Operations Study Group. *A Different Kind of War: The United States Army Operation Enduring Freedom (OEF), September 2001–September 2005.* Fort Leavenworth, KS: Combat Studies Institute Press, 2009.

Jalali, Ali A. "The Future of Afghanistan." *Parameters* (Spring 2006): 4–19.

Maloney, Sean M. *Enduring the Freedom: A Rogue Historian in Afghanistan.* Washington, DC: Potomac Books, 2007.

Sundquist, Leah R. *NATO in Afghanistan: A Progress Report.* Carlisle Barracks, PA: U.S. Army War College, 2008.

Cone, Robert
Birth Date: March 19, 1957

U.S. Army officer who assumed command of the Combined Security Transition Command–Afghanistan (CSTC-A) on July 16, 2007. The CSTC-A employs military personnel from a number of coalition nations and civilian contract agents in a wide range of activities to assist in the development of a stable Afghanistan. At the heart of this development is the building, training, mentoring, and professionalization of the Afghanistan National Security Forces (ANSF), which consists of the Afghan National Army (ANA) and the Afghan National Police (ANP). The CSTC-A reports to the United States Central Command (CENTCOM).

Robert Cone was born on March 19, 1957, in Manchester, New Hampshire, and was commissioned as a second lieutenant in the armor branch upon graduation from the United States Military Academy, West Point, in 1979. He earned a master of arts degree in sociology from the University of Texas at Austin in 1987 and a master of arts degree in national security and strategic studies from the Naval War College in 1988. He was promoted to brigadier general on May 1, 2004, and to major general on August 8, 2007.

Cone's previous command assignments included 1st Squadron, 3rd Armored Cavalry Regiment, III Corps, at Fort Bliss, Texas, and later at Fort Carson, Colorado, and 2nd Brigade, 4th Infantry Division (Mechanized), at Fort Hood, Texas. His staff positions included executive officer, 11th Armored Cavalry Regiment, Fulda, Germany; operations officer, 4th Infantry Division, Fort Hood, Texas; director, Joint Advanced Warfighting Program, Institute for Defense Analysis, Alexandria, Virginia; and director, Joint Center for Operation Analysis, U.S. Joint Forces Command, Operation IRAQI FREEDOM. Cone has also served as an instructor and an assistant professor at the U.S. Military Academy. His immediate previous assignment before becoming commanding general of CSTC-A was commanding general, U.S. Army National Training Center and Fort Irwin in California.

At an October 2008 ceremony to celebrate the inauguration of a sleeve insignia patch for the CSTC-A, Major General Cone reflected that over the last year during his command, the ANA had fielded 2 brigade headquarters and 24 battalions; 26 units had received a military competency rating to operate on their own; ANA units had led 62 percent of operations, which constituted a 14 percent increase over the previous year; the Afghanistan Army Air Corps was flying 90 percent of the missions to support the ANA; and 20,000 new ANP soldiers were in the field in 24 districts under reform.

JOE P. DUNN

See also

Afghan National Army; Afghanistan; Combined Security Transition Command–Afghanistan; United States Central Command

References

Lambeth, Benjamin S. *Air Power against Terror: America's Conduct of Operation Enduring Freedom*. Santa Monica, CA: RAND Corporation, 2005.

Rashid, Ahmed. *Descent into Chaos: The United States and the Failure of Nation-building in Pakistan, Afghanistan, and Central Asia*. New York: Viking, 2008.

Conscientious Objection and Dissent in the U.S. Military

Conscientious objection—the refusal to wage war because of religious, ethical, moral, philosophical, or humanitarian convictions—is a basic human right confirmed by the Universal Declaration of Human Rights (1948) and other United Nations (UN) conventions, including the nonbinding 1998 General Assembly resolution that explicitly asserts the right for soldiers already performing military service to claim conscientious objector status. In international law, conscientious objection is complemented by Article 4 of the Nuremberg Principles established after World War II, which mandates that following orders does not relieve one from responsibility for war crimes. Although bona fide conscientious objector status has been a part of the American identity since the Revolutionary War, conscientious objection by members of the U.S. armed forces since 2001 has frequently proven controversial, with many conscientious objectors imprisoned or driven into exile. Issues surrounding conscientious objector status and

dissent during the 1991 Persian Gulf War were extremely limited in scope because of the very short duration of that conflict.

The U.S. Department of Defense Directive 1300.6 (revised 2007) provides a narrowed definition of conscientious objection. Conscientious objectors may be officially recognized if claimants establish "sincere objection to participation in war in any form, or the bearing of arms, by reason of religious training and/ or belief." While the Defense Department guidelines do encompass "moral and ethical beliefs" outside traditional religion, they exclude "selective" conscientious objection to specific conflicts or modes of warfare. Each armed service has regulations codifying the processing of conscientious objector claimants (e.g., chaplain and psychiatrist interviews, a hearing before an investigating officer, Defense Department review board, etc). In accordance with inactive Selective Service guidelines for conscription, bona fide conscientious objectors are to be discharged from the military or reassigned to noncombatant duties.

Between 2002 and 2006, the Pentagon reported 425 requests for conscientious objector status, with 224 (53 percent) approved, covering both the Afghan War and the Iraq War. However, in September 2007 the U.S. Government Accountability Office acknowledged a potential underreporting of applicants. Meanwhile, a consortium of churches, veterans, and peace groups networked in the GI Rights Hotline has reported counseling thousands of soldiers who have experienced a crisis of conscience. Alleging that many conscientious objection claims are not represented in official figures because they never reach the Pentagon, the Center for Conscience and War has lobbied Congress for new legislation that would streamline conscientious objector processing and recognize the "selective" objection encompassed by UN guidelines and many religious doctrines. At the same time, dissenting soldiers have continued to manifest objection to the wars in Afghanistan and Iraq in other ways.

Echoing similar actions by the GI Movement against the Vietnam War, these demonstrations of opposition to U.S. war policies are rooted in isolated acts of individual conscience. However, the current all-volunteer U.S. armed forces means that today's conscientious objectors are in an entirely different situation than those in the Vietnam War–era, when the draft brought hundreds of thousands into the armed forces involuntarily. Since today's conscientious objectors volunteered to join the armed forces, implying their willingness at least at the time of enlistment to engage in combat, the Defense Department understandably carefully examines each petition for conscientious objector status today.

The first soldier to publicly oppose Operation IRAQI FREEDOM was Marine Reserve lance corporal Stephen Funk, who learned of the possibility of claiming conscientious objector status just before his unit was activated in February 2003, a month before the war began. After missing deployment to prepare his conscientious objection claim, Funk turned himself in and explained that he went public with his claim to allow others to realize that conscientious objector status was an option. Because of his unauthorized absence, Funk's conscientious objection claim was not processed, and he was sentenced to six months' imprisonment and a bad conduct discharge.

In the months that followed, as public criticism of the George W. Bush administration's justifications for the Iraq War intensified and American occupation policies drew international censure, more U.S. service members became disillusioned. By the beginning of 2006, according to a Zogby Poll, almost 30 percent of American troops in Iraq wanted the United States to withdraw immediately, and 72 percent believed that American forces should leave the country within a year. An *Army Times* poll conducted later that same year revealed that only 41 percent of soldiers believed the war should have occurred. Press reports have noted increased alcohol and drug abuse, and one out of three combat veterans has sought psychological counseling. Also, between 2002 and 2008, the U.S. Army suicide rate nearly doubled. Although other factors related to military service, such as more frequent overseas deployments, multiple combat tours, the pressures of family separations, etc., are more likely contributing factors in the rise in the negative statistics, opposition to the war should not be ruled out.

Meanwhile, roughly 150 members of the U.S. military have publicly refused to fight, resulting in criminal charges, imprisonment, and bad conduct discharges. Some of them were declared as prisoners of conscience by the human rights organization Amnesty International. The more highly publicized cases include Staff Sergeant Camilo Mejia, an army squad leader who refused to return to Iraq from leave in 2003 and sentenced to 12 months in prison; Kevin Benderman, an army sergeant and Iraq War veteran who resisted redeployment in 2005 and was sentenced to 15 months in prison; U.S. Navy petty officer 3rd Class Pablo Paredes, who abandoned ship in 2004 and was sentenced to 3 months' hard labor without confinement; and Texas Army National Guard specialist Katherine Jashinski, who after her conscientious objector

U.S. Army sergeant Kevin Benderman, center, is led away by military police on July 28, 2005, following his court-martial at Fort Stewart, Georgia. Benderman refused deployment to Iraq and had sought conscientious objector status. Acquitted of desertion, Benderman was found guilty of a lesser charge and sentenced to 15 months in prison. (AP/Wide World Photos)

claim was denied following 18 months of processing was court-martialed in 2006 for refusing weapons training in preparation for deployment to Afghanistan and was sentenced to 120 days of confinement. These cases unfolded amid the climate of a threefold increase, between 2002 and 2006, in the number of army soldiers court-martialed for desertion, defined by the military as being absent without leave (AWOL) for more than 30 days. Most deserters were to be serving in Iraq; desertion rates for those serving in Afghanistan have been considerably lower.

While tens of thousands of service members have gone AWOL since 2001, such absences range from as short as a few hours to as long as weeks and months. It is impossible to know for certain service members' individual reasons for being AWOL; however, some 200 have sought sanctuary in Canada, where more than three dozen have formally applied for political asylum. Refusing to consider the legality of the Iraq War, the sitting Conservative government refused to grant any of the AWOL Americans official refugee status. However, on June 3, 2008, the Canadian Parliament passed a nonbinding resolution asking the prime minister to allow conscientious objectors from wars not sanctioned by the UN to become Canadian residents. Canadian courts have stayed a number of threatened deportations.

Questions concerning the Iraq War's legality as well as the limited Defense Department definition of conscientious objection have also been highlighted in the prosecution of First Lieutenant Ehren Watada, a U.S. Army infantry officer who asserted in June 2006 that it was his "command responsibility" to refuse participation in "war crimes." In February 2007 a court-martial judge declared a mistrial, ruling that the legality of Watada's deployment orders was a "nonjusticiable political question." That October, the army's attempt at another court-martial was declared unconstitutional double jeopardy by a U.S. District Court, which ruled that Watada could not be tried on three of the five counts with which he was charged. At the end of 2008 Watada remained on active duty at Fort Lewis, Washington, as the Defense Department decided whether to appeal the case further or to try him on the two remaining counts of conduct unbecoming an officer.

The contested nature of active service members' First Amendment right to free speech provided the context for another high-profile development in military dissent. Knowing that soldiers are explicitly permitted by law to contact their congressional representatives, in late 2006 U.S. Navy seaman Jonathan Hutto instigated an "Appeal for Redress," an Internet statement and organizing tool that by the end of 2008 had mobilized more than 2,200 service members, including some 100 field officers, to publicly declare that "As a patriotic American proud to serve the nation in uniform, I respectfully urge my political leaders in Congress to support the prompt withdrawal of all American military forces and bases from Iraq. Staying in Iraq will not work and is not worth the price. It is time for U.S. troops to come home."

Hutto has sought assistance from and has been supported by David Cortright, a Vietnam War veteran and author of *Soldiers in Revolt,* an account of military dissent during that war; Courage to Resist, a San Francisco–based coalition of activists that originated in community support mobilized during Lance Corporal Funk's court-martial in 2003; and Iraq Veterans against the War (IVAW), the 1,200-member organization eventually joined by most of today's military objectors.

Modeled after the influential Vietnam Veterans Against the War (VVAW) group established in 1967, the IVAW was founded in 2004 at the annual convention of Veterans for Peace, a national peace group encompassing all veterans who have embraced nonviolence. Like the "Appeal for Redress," these organizations have capitalized on the credibility gained by their members having served their country in uniform to legitimate their antiwar message.

It is unknown what effect the new U.S. administration of President Barack Obama will have on the wars in Afghanistan and Iraq or the military policies related to conscientious objection and the growth of military dissent. It is clear, however, that the realities of combat will not change and that the legacy of America's Global War on Terror will continue to shape American society and its military for years to come.

The point needs to be emphasized that the vast majority of the members of the all-volunteer U.S. Armed Forces (as of 2009, this represents 1.5 million active component personnel and 850,000 in the reserve components), regardless of how they might personally feel about the Afghanistan War and the Iraq War, continue to perform their duties as they signed on to do. Despite several high-profile instances of war resistance and of military personnel claiming conscientious objector status, the impact of such actions has apparently not had an appreciable effect on armed forces recruiting or on reenlistment rates, both of which remain high.

JEFF RICHARD SCHUTTS

See also

Abu Ghraib; ENDURING FREEDOM, Operation; IRAQI FREEDOM, Operation; Weapons of Mass Destruction

References

Hutto, Jonathan W., Sr. *Antiwar Soldier: How to Dissent within the Ranks of the Military.* New York: Nation Books, 2008.

Iraq Veterans against the War and Aaron Glantz. *Winter Soldier Iraq and Afghanistan: Eyewitness Accounts of the Occupations.* Chicago: Haymarket Books, 2008.

Lauffer, Peter. *Mission Rejected: U.S. Soldiers Who Say No to Iraq.* White River Junction, VT: Chelsea Green, 2006.

Containment Policy

Key U.S. foreign policy strategy during the Cold War that was also applied in the Middle East. It is impossible to understand the origins and course of the Cold War without comprehending the policy, or doctrine, of containment. The concept can be traced back to February 1946 when George F. Kennan, deputy head of the U.S. mission in Moscow, sent an 8,000-word telegram to

Secretary of State James F. Byrnes. In the message, dubbed the "Long Telegram," Kennan provided both an analysis of Soviet behavior and a diplomatic strategy to deal with Moscow. Arguing that "at the bottom of the Kremlin's neurotic view of world affairs is the instinctive Russian sense of insecurity," Kennan went on to suggest that Soviet leader Joseph Stalin required a hostile international environment to legitimize his autocratic rule. Kennan also asserted that the Marxist-Leninist ideology upon which Stalin had built his regime contained elements of a messianism that envisioned the spread of Soviet influence and conflict with capitalism. The only way to stop the communist contagion, Kennan opined, was to strengthen Western institutions, apply appropriate counterforce when needed, and wait for the Soviet system to either implode under its own weight or sufficiently mellow so that it could be rationally bargained with. In short, the Soviets were to be contained. Kennan, however, was not at all specific as to how containment was to be achieved.

Although U.S. policy toward the Soviets had already begun to take on elements of containment, Kennan's missive struck like a lightning bolt in Washington. Indeed, Secretary of the Navy James Forrestal immediately took note of the telegram and used it as further justification for his own hard-line views of the Soviet Union. Kennan returned to Washington something of a hero to anti-Soviet hawks in the Harry Truman administration and became the first director of the U.S. State Department's policy planning staff. Kennan served in that capacity during April 1947–December 1949.

In the meantime, the containment policy continued to gain traction. The first public invocation of the strategy came in March 1947. Concerned about the communist insurgency in the Greek Civil War and instability in neighboring Turkey, Truman addressed a joint session of Congress, ostensibly to request aid money for Greece and Turkey. Clearly echoing Kennan's Long Telegram, Truman stated in what became known as the Truman Doctrine that we must "support free peoples who are resisting attempted subjugation by armed minorities or by outside pressures." The United States had now taken on the responsibility of helping any nation fighting against communism.

Next came the June 1947 announcement of the Marshall Plan (of which Kennan was the chief architect). The Marshall Plan aimed at fostering European reconstruction. But it was also a program clearly aimed at containing Soviet influence and keeping it out of Western Europe. In July 1947 Kennan anonymously wrote an article for the influential journal *Foreign Affairs*. Dubbed the "X" article for its supposed anonymity, it went even further than Kennan's earlier telegram. Using somewhat alarmist language, Kennan asserted that U.S. policy toward the Soviets must be a "patient but firm vigilant containment of Russian expansive tendencies." The "X" article gave full voice to containment, although Kennan would soon argue that policy makers had unnecessarily militarized the idea.

In November 1948 Truman approved a top-secret memo (NSC-20/4) from the National Security Council (NSC) that made the

U.S. president Harry Truman addresses Congress on March 12, 1947. Truman spelled out what became known as the Truman Doctrine, a program whereby the United States would provide assistance to those countries resisting pressures from communism. It became the cornerstone of the U.S. containment policy. (Harry S. Truman Presidential Library)

containment of Soviet influence a key precept of American foreign policy. The formation of the North Atlantic Treaty Organization (NATO) in April 1949 further entrenched containment. But up until 1950, containment had been largely limited to economic and institutional mechanisms. The Korean War changed that forever. In April 1950 the NSC had produced what is considered one of the seminal documents of the early Cold War. This report, known as NSC-68, was a call to arms. It presented in stark terms the low level of U.S. military capabilities while playing up Soviet motives and capabilities. The NSC claimed 1954 to be the "year of maximum danger," a time during which the Soviet Union would possess sufficient nuclear and conventional military capacity to launch a catastrophic strike against the United States. The only way to avoid such a possibility was to embark on a massive rearmament program. Truman shelved the project because the political environment would not have tolerated such an expensive program.

After the Korean War began in June 1950, however, the political climate had indeed changed. Truman approved NSC-68 in September, and the nation undertook a massive and permanent mobilization, allowing it to react to crises anywhere in the world. Containment was now fully militarized and would remain so (although defense budgets would wax and wane) until the end of the Cold War. Containment not only produced a permanent and large military establishment—not to mention a constantly expanding nuclear arsenal—but also informed policy makers' thinking toward all type of foreign threats. Indeed, the domino theory, a corollary of sorts to containment, can be traced to the

Truman years, although it became de rigueur under Dwight Eisenhower and his immediate successors. Concerned that communist insurgencies in Indochina would result in a domino effect in which one nation after the other would fall to what was incorrectly assumed to be a monolithic communist empire controlled by Moscow, U.S. policy makers decided to hold the line in Vietnam. Ultimately, this thinking helped bring the long and tortuous debacle of the Vietnam War. The domino theory was also applied in other areas where communist advances were feared, including Africa, Central and South America, and the Middle East.

As the U.S. containment policy matured, critics from both sides of the political spectrum attacked it. Many on the Left, epitomized by Franklin D. Roosevelt's former vice president, Henry Wallace, attacked the policy from a moral standpoint, arguing that the United States was acting hypocritically by seeking to impose a stringent moral code on the Soviet Union that America itself often did not live up to. In effect, Wallace argued that the United States was not good enough to hold the Soviet Union to a standard of behavior that the United States was unwilling to apply to its own actions. Critics on the Far Right were just as vocal but argued that containment did not go far enough in rolling back communist global gains. Merely containing the spread of communism, many on the Right claimed, was a totally defensive measure that gave tacit acceptance by Washington of the status quo. Those espousing this position demanded that the United States instead take offensive action to roll back communism, regardless of the risks involved. Even somewhat more moderate critics, such as Walter Lippman, criticized the containment policy, predicting that the vast expenditure of economic and military resources that must be committed in the attempt to contain communism everywhere in the world would only weaken the United States more than it would harm the Soviet Union. Although these various arguments against containment waxed and waned during the nearly half century of the Cold War, they never completely disappeared.

During the 1970s as détente between the United States and the Soviet Union flourished and with the aftermath of the Vietnam War still fresh in Americans' minds, containment appeared less attractive. During President Ronald Reagan's tenure in office (1981–1989), containment was virtually abandoned. In its place was the belief that the Soviet Union should be defeated rather than merely contained. Reagan attempted to do this by engaging the United States in a major military buildup, announcing his controversial Strategic Defense Initiative (SDI) and signaling his intention to employ American nuclear might against any Soviet advance. The theory behind the approach was that the United States would force the Soviets into bankruptcy by forcing them to keep up with U.S. military advances. In the end the Soviet Union did fall, although it is inaccurate and overly simplistic to suggest that Reagan's policies alone caused the collapse. The Soviet system had within it the seeds of its own destruction. Kennan made that clear 50 years ago. And since Truman's time, every president employed all or part of containment to hasten the demise of the Soviet Union.

While not specifically formulated for the Middle East, the containment policy nevertheless informed U.S. policy in the region. Indeed, between the late 1940s and the end of the Cold War in 1991, the United States built alliances with various Middle Eastern nations in an attempt to check or contain Soviet influence in the region. An example of this was the Baghdad Pact, a treaty of mutual cooperation and mutual defense among the nations of Turkey, Iraq, Pakistan, Iran, and Great Britain agreed to in February 1955. Also known as the Central Treaty Organization (CENTO) or the Middle East Treaty Organization (METO), it was part of a wider effort by the United States and the West in general to establish regional alliances to contain the spread of Soviet influence.

Until the 1979 Iranian Revolution, Iran was the strongest Middle Eastern U.S. ally and the recipient of hundreds of millions of U.S. dollars in aid and military hardware. Saudi Arabia and Israel have also been longtime U.S. allies in the region. The Carter Doctrine, enunciated in January 1980 by President Jimmy Carter, was a direct offshoot of containment. The doctrine held that the United States would employ military force if needed to forestall any threats to shipping or oil supplies in the region. Carter's declaration came at a time in which the Cold War had once more become active and détente had all but collapsed. The Soviets had just invaded Afghanistan, and it was quite clear that Carter was putting the Kremlin on notice that the United States would not permit further Soviet encroachments into the Middle East.

Paul G. Pierpaoli Jr.

See also

Baghdad Pact; Carter, James Earl, Jr.; Carter Doctrine; Cold War; Eisenhower, Dwight David; Reagan, Ronald Wilson; Reagan Administration, Middle East Policy; Truman, Harry S.

References

Acheson, Dean. *Present at the Creation: My Years at the State Department.* New York: Norton, 1969.

Gaddis, John Lewis. *Strategies of Containment: A Critical Appraisal of Postwar American National Security Policy.* New York: Oxford University Press, 1982.

———. *We Now Know: Rethinking Cold War History.* New York: Oxford University Press, 1997.

Hixson, Walter. *George F. Kennan: Cold War Iconoclast.* New York: Columbia University Press, 1989.

Lafeber, Walter. *America, Russia and the Cold War, 1945–2002.* Updated 9th ed. New York: McGraw-Hill, 2004.

Yergin, Daniel H. *Shattered Peace: The Origins of the Cold War.* New York: Penguin, 1990.

Conway, James Terry
Birth Date: December 26, 1947

U.S. Marine Corps officer, veteran of Operations DESERT STORM and IRAQI FREEDOM, and the 34th commandant of the U.S. Marine Corps since November 2006. James Terry Conway was born in Walnut Ridge, Arkansas, on December 26, 1947. His family moved back and forth between St. Louis, Missouri, and Walnut Ridge before finally settling in St. Louis in 1958. Conway graduated from Southeast Missouri State University in 1969 and was commissioned a second lieutenant in the U.S. Marine Corps in 1970. His first duty station was Camp Pendleton, California. He then served aboard the aircraft carrier *Kitty Hawk*. Conway next served in the 2nd Marine Regiment and as operations officer for the 31st Marine Amphibious Unit with sea duty in the western Pacific and in operations off the coast of Beirut, Lebanon, in 1983. Returning to the United States, he was for two years senior aide to the chairman of the Joint Chiefs of Staff (JCS). After completing further U.S. Marine Corps schooling in 1990, Conway took command of the 3rd Battalion, 2nd Marines. The next year he commanded the Battalion Landing Team during its eight-month deployment to Southwest Asia as a diversionary unit during Operation DESERT STORM.

In 1993 Conway assumed command of the Marine Basic School at Quantico, Virginia. He was promoted to brigadier general in December 1995. Conway's next assignment was to the JCS. In 1998 he served as president of the Marine Corps University at Quantico. Advanced to major general in 2000, he served as commander of the 1st Marine Division and was deputy commanding general of Marine Forces Central. In 2002 he was promoted to lieutenant general and assumed command of the I Marine Expeditionary Force, serving two combat tours in Operation IRAQI FREEDOM. In Iraq, Conway's 60,000 men included not only U.S. marines but also U.S. Army troops, U.S. Navy personnel, and British Special Forces. His I Marine Expeditionary Force was among the first U.S. forces to enter Baghdad in March 2003 and also formed a key component in Operation VIGILANT RESOLVE in the First Battle of Fallujah in Iraq during April 4–May 1, 2004.

Conway was advanced to the rank of full general and assumed his current post as commandant of the U.S. Marine Corps on November 13, 2006. Upon assuming his post, he stated that he hoped to provide the nation with a U.S. Marine Corps fully prepared to meet any contingency in keeping with his motto, "Be most ready when the nation is least ready." He also set out to improve the quality of life for marines and their families and to reinstill the core values and warrior ethics that have served the U.S. Marine Corps so well in past conflicts.

RANDY J. TAYLOR

See also

DESERT STORM, Operation; IRAQI FREEDOM, Operation; United States Marine Corps, Iraq War; United States Marine Corps, Persian Gulf War

References

Anderson, Jon Lee. *The Fall of Baghdad*. New York: Penguin, 2004.
Franks, Tommy, with Malcolm McConnell. *American Soldier*. New York: Regan Books, 2004.
Keegan, John. *The Iraq War: The Military Offensive, from Victory in 21 Days to the Insurgent Aftermath*. New York: Vintage, 2005.
West, Bing, and Ray L. Smith. *The March Up: Taking Baghdad with the 1st Marine Division*. New York: Bantam, 2003.
Brady, James. *Why Marines Fight*. New York: Thomas Dunne Books/St. Martin's, 2007.

Reynolds, Nicholas E. *Basrah, Baghdad, and Beyond: The U.S. Marine Corps in the Second Iraq War*. Annapolis, MD: Naval Institute Press, 2005.

Cook, Robin
Birth Date: February 28, 1946
Death Date: August 6, 2006

British Labour Party politician, secretary of state for foreign and commonwealth affairs (1997–2001), and leader of the House of Commons (2001–2003) who refused to support British prime minister Tony Blair's decision to go to war with Iraq in March 2003 and resigned his post as a result. Robin Cook was born on February 28, 1946, in Bellshill, Scotland, to a lower middle-class family. Cook studied at the University of Edinburgh, ultimately earning a master's degree in English there in 1968. Following in his father's footsteps, he taught school for a brief time before entering politics in 1971, at which time he became a councilman (councilor) in Edinburgh on the Labour Party ticket. In February 1974 he was elected to the British House of Commons, representing Edinburgh's central district. In 1983 his district changed to Livingston. Cook remained in Parliament until his untimely death in 2006.

Cook was in the left wing of the Labour Party and was especially critical of Britain's Conservative governments during the 1980s and into the 1990s. He only tepidly backed Labour leader Blair's attempt to modernize the Labour Party in the 1990s, believing it to be too rightist-leaning. Cook soon earned a reputation for his formidable debating skills and fiery oratory. He was also an excellent parliamentarian, effectively using the rules of the House of Commons to his own and his party's benefit. By the late 1980s Cook had risen through the ranks of the leadership, and in 1987 he began holding shadow cabinet posts (unofficial parliamentary posts that shadow official government posts held by the opposition party, in this case the Conservative Party). He was the shadow social services secretary (1887–1989), shadow health secretary (1989–1992), shadow trade secretary (1992–1994), and shadow foreign secretary (1994–1997).

In 1997 after many years in Britain's political wilderness, an invigorated Labour Party came to power, with Blair as prime minister. Cook was not entirely enamored with Blair, whom he found too conservative for his own taste, but Cook nevertheless welcomed Labour's ascendancy and sought out the highly coveted cabinet post of chancellor of the exchequer. Blair had apparently already promised that position to another Labourite, however, so Cook was offered the post of secretary of state for foreign and commonwealth affairs, which he readily accepted. Upon assuming office, he promised to return an "ethical dimension" to the United Kingdom's foreign policy, a statement that was viewed with considerable skepticism by many Britons.

Cook's tenure was marked chiefly by the British intervention—along with the North Atlantic Treaty Organization (NATO)—in the Kosovo War in 1999, which witnessed an air campaign that lasted for more than two months. The Kosovo intervention brought considerable criticism to both Blair and Cook because many Britons were uncomfortable with a military action that had not been officially blessed by the United Nations (UN).

After the June 2001 general elections, Blair and other Labour leaders implored Cook to return to the House of Commons, where they believed his leadership was now sorely needed. Cook reluctantly gave up his cabinet post and began serving as leader of the House of Commons and lord president of the council later that month. Cook immediately set about reorganizing Parliament, taking particular pains to bring about reform in the House of Lords. After the September 11, 2001, terror attacks against the United States when the Blair government began to move in unison with the George W. Bush administration, Cook found himself in the uneasy position of defending Britain's pro-American foreign policy initiatives. This became more and more difficult, however, as the United States and Great Britain moved closer and closer to a preemptive war against Iraq.

By early 2003, Cook was on record publicly and privately for his opposition to war against Iraq. He reportedly had numerous meetings with Blair and prepared several memoranda in which he implored the Labour government not to follow the United States in lockstep fashion toward war. When war looked inevitable, Cook resigned his position as leader of Parliament on March 17, 2003, just three days before the war began. His speech announcing his resignation made clear his opposition to a war in Iraq. Reportedly, Cook's speech was the first to receive a standing ovation in the House of Commons.

Cook remained in Parliament working quietly behind the scenes, but there can be no doubt that his dramatic resignation demonstrated how split the British electorate was on the subject of the Iraq War. Cook died suddenly from a massive heart attack while hiking near Sutherland, Scotland, on August 6, 2006.

PAUL G. PIERPAOLI JR.

See also

Blair, Tony; United Kingdom, Middle East Policy

References

Cook, Robin. *The Point of Departure.* New York: Simon and Schuster, 2004.

Stephens, Phillip. *Tony Blair: The Making of a World Leader.* New York: Viking Books, 2004.

Cornum, Rhonda
Birth Date: October 31, 1954

Physician, U.S. Army brigadier general, and one of two American servicewomen captured by Iraqi forces during the 1991 Persian Gulf War. During her captivity, Cornum was sexually assaulted by an Iraqi guard. This revelation and the way in which Cornum handled it helped change American attitudes toward women in combat roles and opened more duties to women. Rhonda Cornum was born on October 31, 1954, in Dayton, Ohio. She earned a PhD in biochemistry from Cornell University in 1978.

Cornum joined the U.S. Army that same year and conducted medical-related research in San Francisco. Later, she went to medical school at the Uniformed Services, University of the Health Sciences, in Bethesda, Maryland, earning an MD in 1987. Later that year she was a finalist for selection as an astronaut. Although she was disappointed when she was not selected, Cornum became a flight surgeon at Fort Rucker, Alabama.

In 1990 Cornum deployed to Saudi Arabia as a flight surgeon with the 101st Airborne Division as part of Operation DESERT SHIELD. On February 27, 1991, three days after the commencement of ground operations in DESERT STORM during fighting near Basra, a Lockheed Martin F-16 Fighting Falcon, flown by Captain William Andrews, was shot down. Andrews successfully ejected, although he suffered a broken leg. An initial rescue attempt failed to locate Andrews, however. A second rescue mission by the 101st Airborne including Cornum flew in a Sikorsky UH-60 Black Hawk helicopter to Andrews's last reported position.

Despite the overall destruction of Iraq's air defenses, Iraqi ground forces still retained significant antiaircraft capabilities. The Black Hawk in which Cornum was flying was shot down and crashed. Five of the eight team members were killed in the crash, and Cornum was severely injured. She had taken a bullet in one shoulder, and both her arms were broken. Iraqi soldiers pulled Cornum and other survivors from the wreck and threatened to shoot them. Instead, the Iraqis placed them in a truck and drove them to a prison in Basra. During the transit, Cornum was sexually assaulted by one of the Iraqi soldiers guarding her. Because of her injuries, Cornum was unable to resist the assault.

For the next eight days, Cornum was held prisoner. She later reported that she was treated well by the other Iraqi guards; they helped her with personal hygiene and other matters that she was not able to perform for herself because of her injuries. Although she was interrogated, she was not tortured or physically beaten, as were some other American prisoners of war (POWs). Cornum and the other American POWs were released on March 5, 1991. Cornum and Melissa Rathbun-Nealy, an army enlisted woman, were the only female POWs in the group.

The experiences of Cornum and Rathbun-Nealy as POWs were cited by some people who opposed American women in combat as reasons why women did not belong on the battlefield. In the spring of 1992 a congressional committee held hearings on the question of women's roles in the military. Cornum testified and revealed that she had been sexually assaulted. Although this experience was precisely what those who did not want women in combat warned about, Cornum's testimony helped convince most Americans that women could and should play a more central role in the military.

She argued that military women should be treated according to their talents and abilities. The fact that she had been sexually assaulted, she declared, was not relevant. According to Cornum, everything that happens to a POW is essentially nonconsensual, so her sexual assault was only one part of the experience.

Cornum's arguments helped sway opinion in favor of greater opportunities for women in the military. In April 1993 Secretary of Defense Les Aspin announced that more duties in the military, including some that might include combat, would be opened to women. That policy has continued to the present, as more and more tasks and roles have been opened to both genders.

Cornum remained in the army. Promoted to colonel, she subsequently commanded a medical unit in Tuzla, Bosnia. She also trained in urology and was named a staff urologist at the Eisenhower Medical Center in 1998. In 2003 she assumed command of the Landstuhl Military Hospital in Germany, the largest American military facility outside the United States. During her tenure, the hospital treated many American soldiers wounded in the 2003 invasion of Iraq. Cornum was often found working with the wounded, encouraging them and treating their wounds. She has since been promoted to brigadier general and was appointed assistant surgeon general for force protection.

TIM J. WATTS

See also
Aspin, Leslie, Jr.; Women, Role of in Afghanistan and Iraq Wars; Women, Role of in Persian Gulf War

References
Cornum, Rhonda, as told to Peter Copeland. *She Went To War: The Rhonda Cornum Story*. Novato, CA: Presidio, 1992.
Stiehm, Judith. *It's Our Military, Too! Women and the U.S. Military*. Philadelphia: Temple University Press, 1996.

Counterinsurgency

A warfare strategy employed to defeat an organized rebellion or revolutionary movement aimed at bringing down and replacing established governmental authority. Among the more confusing terms relating to the practice of warfare, the term "counterinsurgency" implies both the purpose of military operations and methods selected. U.S. interest in counterinsurgency soared in 2005 as it became increasingly apparent that an insurgency was gravely undermining the efforts of the United States and its allies to establish a new regime in Iraq after the 2003 Anglo-American–led invasion and occupation. To a lesser degree, a revived Taliban movement has also hindered U.S. progress in nation building in Afghanistan, and counterinsurgency tactics are being employed there as well.

Understanding the term "counterinsurgency" requires an appreciation of its logical opposite, insurgency. Counterinsurgency originated as a conceptual response to the spread of insurgencies, particularly as carried out by anticolonialist or communist movements during the Cold War from the late 1940s to the 1980s. Insurgents typically lacked key sources of power, such as financial wealth, a professional military, or advanced weaponry, that were available to established regimes or governments. Consequently, insurgents adopted asymmetric tactics and strategies that focused on avoidance of direct combat until such time as governmental power had been gravely weakened. Instead, skillful insurgents blended an array of methods including propaganda, attacks on public institutions and infrastructure, the creation of secret support networks, and use of unconventional or guerrilla combat tactics. By these means, insurgents could whittle away at the strength of existing regimes or occupying powers while slowly increasing their own capabilities.

U.S. interest in counterinsurgency, sometimes referred to as counterrevolutionary warfare, grew during the Vietnam War. Efforts to defeat the Viet Cong guerrillas in South Vietnam were considered important but more often than not took a back seat to the conduct of conventional military operations against the People's Army of Vietnam (PAVN, North Vietnamese Army). With the American withdrawal from Vietnam in 1973, however, the U.S. military resumed focusing on conventional war, and the study of counterinsurgency by the U.S. Army waned. Even with the end of the Cold War in 1991, the U.S. military did not regard the study of counterinsurgency as equally important to the mastery of conventional combat.

To many, Operation DESERT STORM in Iraq in 1991 justified the American focus on conventional combat. The Persian Gulf War provided an awesome demonstration of U.S. military proficiency and technology. Indeed, American dominance was so compelling that it may have dissuaded future potential opponents from attempting to challenge American might on any conventional battlefield. One result of this was perhaps to encourage adversaries to attack U.S. interests by asymmetric means, such as guerrilla insurgency tactics or terror. There was also a growing perception among enemies of the United States that American politicians and military leaders were extremely uncomfortable in situations in which they could not bring superior conventional military power to bear. The deaths of 18 U.S. Army soldiers on October 3–4, 1993, during a raid against a renegade warlord in Somalia may have been the exception that proved the rule. Largely a product of events in Somalia, Bill Clinton's casualty-averse posture of U.S. forces in subsequent peacekeeping missions in Haiti, Bosnia, and Kosovo during the 1990s tended to reinforce the view that Americans were reluctant to suffer any casualties in scenarios short of unconstrained conventional combat.

The startling terror attacks on U.S. soil on September 11, 2001, led to a swift reorientation in American military thinking. The immediate American response was to strike against the Taliban regime in Afghanistan that had provided refuge for Al Qaeda terrorists claiming responsibility for the attacks. Informed by its own support for the mujahideen guerrilla resistance to the Soviet occupation of Afghanistan during the 1980s, the United States decided

Afghan president Hamid Karzai, right, listens as U.S. defense secretary Donald Rumsfeld, left, responds to a reporter's question at the Presidential Palace in Kabul, Afghanistan, on May 1, 2003. During the press conference, Rumsfeld announced the end of major U.S. military operations in Afghanistan and that the U.S. commitment would shift from combat to reconstruction assistance. Rumsfeld's statement proved premature. (U.S. Department of Defense)

to rely as much as possible on small teams of special operations forces, which would support allied indigenous forces with cutting-edge technologies, rather than on massed conventional forces. The fall of the Taliban regime within three months now placed American forces in the position of stabilizing a fledgling regime under Hamid Karzai.

Very soon the tools of counterinsurgency would prove most relevant in Afghanistan against surviving remnants of the Taliban that found sanctuary along the Pakistani frontier. One important measure taken was the creation and deployment of Provincial Reconstruction Teams (PRTs) beginning in 2003. These combined a small number of military specialists with representatives of various U.S. or other foreign governmental agencies possessing expertise in diplomacy, policing, agriculture, and other fields relevant to the process of fostering security and development. Found to be effective in Afghanistan in extending governmental reach to remote areas, the concept soon found application in Iraq as well.

In the meantime, the invasion of Iraq in March 2003, while initially marking another triumph of conventional operations, did not result in a smooth transition to a stable civilian government. Indeed, coalition forces in Iraq soon faced a formidable counterinsurgency challenge for which neither military nor civilian officials

had fully prepared. In fact, many critics maintain that the early failure to establish public order, restore services, and identify local partners provided the insurgency, which Iraqis term "the resistance," with an interval of chaos that enabled it to organize and grow. Since Iraqi politics had consistently shown wave after wave of resistance, purges, and new coups, such a challenge could reasonably have been expected. Sectarian leaders and their militias began to assert influence, and Al Qaeda fighters infiltrated key provinces in anticipation of a new struggle to come.

By 2005, spreading ethnic and religious violence in Iraq resulted in the deaths of many civilians as well as local governmental and security personnel. Suicide bombings as well as the remote detonation of improvised explosive devices (IEDs) became signature tactics of the Iraqi insurgency. Furthermore, repeated attacks on United Nations (UN) personnel and foreign relief workers caused a virtual suspension of outside aid to the Iraqi people.

Recognition of the need to focus on counterinsurgency methods led to a vitally significant effort to publish a military doctrinal manual on the subject. An initial indicator of the official shift in U.S. military thinking was the release of Department of Defense Directive 3000-05 on November 28, 2005, which specifically acknowledged responsibility for planning and carrying out so-called support and stability operations essential to any counterinsurgency campaign. Under the leadership of Lieutenant General David Petraeus during his tenure as commander, Combined Arms Center, and commandant of the U.S. Army Command and General Staff College at Fort Leavenworth, Kansas, in 2006–2007, a team of writers and practitioners with experience in Iraq and Afghanistan undertook a crash project to draft, revise, and publish the new manual.

In his opening address to the Combat Studies Institute Military History Symposium on August 8, 2006, Petraeus set forth several points of emphasis of the soon-to-be-published U.S. Army Field Manual 3-24 (also known as U.S. Marine Warfighting Publication No. 3-33.5), titled *Counterinsurgency*. Asserting that T. E. Lawrence (of Arabia) had figured out the essentials of counterinsurgency during World War I, Petraeus contended that any prospect of success depended upon identifying capable local leaders, providing them necessary assistance without doing the hard work for them, fostering the development of public institutions, forming a partnership with existing security forces, and maintaining a flexible and patient outlook. In other words, counterinsurgency would require far more of military leaders than the performance of traditional and familiar combat tasks. Petraeus himself had practiced these principles in Iraq, where in late 2004 he served as the first commander of the Multi-National Security Transition Command–Iraq, which focused on the training of local personnel to become civilian and military leaders in Iraq.

Officially released in December 2006, *Counterinsurgency* attracted great attention in the press and conveyed the impression that the military was not stuck in an outmoded mind-set. Rather, U.S. Army and U.S. Marine Corps leaders on the ground in Afghanistan and Iraq became increasingly adaptive and creative in the search for improved solutions to the problem of combating insurgency where nation building was still very much in progress. *Counterinsurgency* devoted a majority of its eight chapters and five appendices to tasks other than war fighting. Lengthy sections also related to ethics, civilian and military cooperation, cultural analysis, linguistic support, the law of war, and ethical considerations.

Of course, the U.S. Army and the U.S. Marine Corps had not ignored the principles of counterinsurgency before the new doctrine was published. However, publication signaled to the American public and the U.S. Congress that the military was wholly committed to the implementation of counterinsurgency principles. Since the end of 2007, it would appear that the implementation of this new counterinsurgency doctrine was beginning to bear fruit, as there was a sizable diminution in violence in most parts of Iraq beginning in the fourth quarter of the year.

ROBERT BAUMANN

See also
Al Qaeda; Al Qaeda in Iraq; DESERT STORM, Operation; ENDURING FREEDOM, Operation; Improvised Explosive Devices; IRAQI FREEDOM, Operation; Iraqi Insurgency; Karzai, Hamid; Mujahideen, Soviet-Afghanistan War; Petraeus, David Howell; Somalia, International Intervention in; Taliban

References
Keegan, John. *The Iraq War: The Military Offensive, from Victory in 21 Days to the Insurgent Aftermath.* New York: Vintage, 2005.
Kitson, Frank. *Low Intensity Operations: Subversion, Insurgency and Peacekeeping.* London: Faber and Faber, 1971.
Nagl, John A. *Learning to Eat Soup with a Knife: Counterinsurgency Lessons from Malaya and Vietnam.* Chicago: University of Chicago Press, 2005.

Counterterrorism Center

U.S. government agency designed to combat terrorism. In 1985, the Central Intelligence Agency (CIA) decided to create a new section to fight international terrorism. This decision came shortly after intelligence failures in Lebanon had led to the deaths in October 1982 of 241 U.S. marines when their barracks was bombed and the kidnapping and killing of CIA section chief William Buckley in 1982. President Ronald Reagan pressed CIA director William J. Casey to do something about terrorism.

Casey soon approached Duane R. "Dewey" Clarridge, a respected veteran field officer, to make a recommendation as to how the CIA could most effectively fight terrorism. Clarridge recommended an interdisciplinary center in the CIA that had an international reach and could utilize all the capabilities of the agency. Part of its mission was to launch covert action against known terrorists, so the Special Operations Group (SOG) was transferred to the Counterterrorism Center. It was to be a section staffed by 100 persons with representation from the Federal Bureau of Investigation (FBI). Casey accepted Clarridge's recommendation and appointed him as its head. Instead of the original plan for a staff of 100, however, Casey authorized it at a staffing of 250. The Counterterrorism Center became operational in February 1986.

Clarridge's first target as head of the Counterterrorism Center was the Abu Nidal Organization (ANO). In the 1970s and 1980s the ANO, named after its leader, was the most violent terrorist group in operation and had become the number one terrorist threat. The CIA was able to recruit a source within the ANO, and this individual provided inside information. Much of it appeared in a State Department publication, *The Abu Nidal Handbook*. After this information became public, Abu Nidal became so concerned about penetration of his organization that he ordered the execution of a large number of his followers in Libya. This purge ended the effectiveness of the ANO.

The next target was Hezbollah (Party of God) in Lebanon. Hezbollah, which the United States considers a Shia terrorist organization, was blamed for complicity in the bombing of the U.S. Marine Corps barracks in Beirut, and factions that became a part of Hezbollah had taken hostage a number of Westerners. Among these was William Buckley, the CIA agent in Lebanon, who had died from harsh treatment. The campaign against Hezbollah was less successful, although it involved attempted assassinations of the leadership. Efforts to launch covert operations were also hampered by the Lebanese position that the organization was no more terrorist than any other during the Lebanese Civil War period and was the only effective force in battling the Israeli and Israeli-proxy occupation of southern Lebanon.

Clarridge soon became frustrated by the lack of support for the Counterterrorism Center. His role in the Iran-Contra Affair also led his superiors in the CIA to question his judgment. He maintained that Lieutenant Colonel Oliver North had misled him in the exchange of hostages from Iran for weapons to be used by the opposition Contras to fight against the Sandinista government in Nicaragua. Clarridge's goal had been to make the center a proactive force against terrorism. Instead, he found that his new boss, CIA director William Webster, who had assumed control of the CIA on May 26, 1987, was averse to risk. This lack of support led Clarridge to leave the Counterterrorism Center later in 1987.

Clarridge's successor, Fred Turco, picked the next major target for the Counterterrorism Center as the Peruvian Shining Path organization. Abimael Guzman, a philosophy professor, had founded the Maoist terrorist group in 1970, and it had opened a war against the Peruvian government. The Counterterrorism Center provided the Peruvian police with sophisticated electronic surveillance equipment and training that enabled them to capture Guzman in a Lima suburb in September 1992.

The Counterterrorism Center's activities assumed more importance in 1993. By this time the new head of the Counterterrorism Center was Winston Wiley, who had assumed the position in November 1992. Two events mobilized this activity. First was the murder of two CIA employees in Langley, Virginia, by Mir Amal Kasi on January 25, 1993. Believing the CIA responsible for countless Muslim deaths, Kasi opened fire with an AK-47 assault rifle just outside of CIA headquarters, killing the CIA employees in their automobiles. Kasi was from Baluchistan, and he managed to escape back to Pakistan, where he promptly disappeared. A special CIA unit was set up to locate and capture him; he was finally apprehended on June 15, 1997.

An even bigger task was investigation of the conspiracy behind the February 23, 1993, World Trade Center bombing. While the domestic investigation was left up to the FBI, the Counterterrorism Center established a subunit to gather intelligence about the bombing. Information was slow to surface, and at first the Counterterrorism Center suspected that it had been a state-sponsored terrorist operation, with Iraq, Libya, and Iran as the prime suspects. Over time, the intelligence analysts came to realize that it was an independent operation led by Ramzi Yousef. In a combined CIA-FBI operation, Yousef was captured in Islamabad, Pakistan, on February 7, 1995.

The Counterterrorism Center continued to target terrorist groups. First under Geoff O'Connell and then under J. Cofer Black, the center planned counterterrorist operations. Black's target was Osama bin Laden and Al Qaeda. Black was also able to count on an expanded Counterterrorism Center. The center had grown from

Wanted poster for Ramzi Yousef, presumed mastermind of the 1993 World Trade Center bombing. (Sygma/Corbis)

only 20 analysts in 1986 to 340 people, of whom more than a dozen were FBI agents, by early 2001. Despite the additions, the staffing of the Counterterrorism Center was too low to handle the volume of information flowing into it. Not surprisingly, the leaders and the staff of the Counterterrorism Center were caught unawares on September 11, 2001.

American pressure on Sudan had led bin Laden to move from Sudan to Afghanistan in 1996. Bin Laden, his family, and retainers traveled to Afghanistan by aircraft on May 18, 1996. The staff of the Counterterrorism Center thought that this presented a golden opportunity to capture bin Laden in transit. A proposal to do so was given to President William J. Clinton, but it never received presidential approval. Members of the Counterterrorism Center were furious over this lost opportunity.

Throughout the late 1990s, analysts in the Counterterrorism Center monitored bin Laden's activities from sources within Afghanistan. The problem was that bin Laden was constantly moving, so tracking him was almost impossible. There was also an ongoing and unresolved debate in the Clinton administration about whether it was legal to assassinate bin Laden. Attorney General Janet Reno made it plain to George Tenet, head of the CIA, and Geoff O'Connell, head of the Counterterrorism Center, that any attempt to kill bin Laden was illegal. All schemes thus involved capturing bin Laden first and killing him only in self-defense.

Another problem was the issue of collateral damage in an attack on bin Laden. Isolating bin Laden from civilians was almost impossible. Members of the Counterterrorism Center wanted to proceed with covert action regardless of the likelihood of collateral civilian losses.

In the middle of the debate over bin Laden, the U.S. Navy destroyer *Cole* was attacked while anchored in the harbor in Aden, Yemen, on October 12, 2000. The attack killed 17 American sailors and wounded scores more. This incident caught the Counterterrorism Center by surprise. It thus took a while for the analysts to find the evidence connecting this attack with Al Qaeda, but the evidence was indeed found. Counterterrorism Center staffers sought retaliation, but the American military was reluctant to undertake any such operations and so advised the White House. To the leadership of the Counterterrorism Center, the only option was to support the Afghan leader General Ahmad Shah Massoud and his war against the Taliban. But the Clinton administration was reluctant to do this and forbade the Counterterrorism Center from increasing aid to him. The Clinton administration left office in 2001 with the problem of bin Laden and Al Qaeda unresolved.

Counterterrorism analysts continued to be frustrated by the inaction of the George W. Bush administration toward terrorism. Reports indicated increased activity by Al Qaeda, but the problem was that there was no evidence of what kind of operation it might undertake or where. A series of warnings came out of the Counterterrorism Center that Tenet took to President Bush and other prominent administration figures. These warnings coincided with similar warnings from the FBI. Some of them even made the case that Al Qaeda operatives might carry out an operation in the United States. What weakened these frequent warnings was the lack of specific details. The Bush administration listened to the warnings, noted the lack of specifics, and took no action. Bush wanted more specific intelligence before he would authorize any action.

Tenet now ordered the CIA to round up suspected Al Qaeda members to gather information on what Al Qaeda was planning. This tactic had two purposes: to gather intelligence and to delay Al Qaeda missions. Several Al Qaeda plots were uncovered, and a massive amount of intelligence material arrived at the Counterterrorism Center. The problem was that there were not enough translators and analysts to handle the mass of material. Frustration was high among the intelligence analysts because they were fearful that important information was being overlooked. In mid-July 2001 Tenet ordered the Counterterrorism Center analysts to search back in its files and its current information on bin Laden's

major plots. He was suspicious that bin Laden might be targeting the United States for a terrorism mission. Tenet took what information the Counterterrorism Center had uncovered and presented the report titled "Bin Laden Determined to Strike in United States" to President Bush at his Crawford, Texas, ranch on August 6, 2001. In early September the Bush administration began to consider a plan to attack terrorism, especially bin Laden and Al Qaeda, but there was no sense of haste.

Following the September 11, 2001, terror attacks, resources poured into the Counterterrorism Center. By the summer of 2002 Tenet had expanded its staff to 1,500. This number of workers was able to handle 2,500 classified electronic communications a day, and it could produce 500 terrorist reports a month.

The Counterterrorism Center was also given the responsibility for the interrogations of important Al Qaeda prisoners. A series of secret interrogation centers was established in friendly countries. Meanwhile, top Al Qaeda prisoners were kept at an interrogation center, Bright Lights, the location of which was not known even to analysts in the Counterterrorism Center. These interrogations are ongoing, with some of the information making it back to intelligence circles. There have also been reports of CIA interrogators using questionable interrogation techniques and torture, including the controversial waterboarding process. The FBI refuses to have anything to do with these interrogations. Several news reports have confirmed this information, and CIA agents have become increasingly uncomfortable about their legal position over these interrogations. This nervousness about interrogation techniques led to controversy in December 2007 when news surfaced that the secret tapes of CIA interrogations had been destroyed in 2005. This action was defended by the then-head of the CIA, Michael V. Hayden, but there have been congressional efforts to hold hearings on whether this action was illegal.

Stephen A. Atkins

See also

Abu Nidal; Al Qaeda; Alec Station; Bin Laden, Osama; Bush, George Walker; Central Intelligence Agency; Clinton, William Jefferson; Coercive Interrogation; Counterterrorism Strategy; Hezbollah; Iran-Contra Affair; Tenet, George John; Terrorism

References

Coll, Steve. *Ghost Wars: The Secret History of the CIA, Afghanistan, and Bin Laden, from the Soviet Invasion to September 10, 2001.* New York: Penguin, 2004.

Kessler, Ronald. *The CIA at War: Inside the Secret Campaign against Terror.* New York: St. Martin's Griffin, 2003.

Miller, John, Michael Stone, and Chris Mitchell. *The Cell: Inside the 9/11 Plot, and Why the FBI and CIA Failed to Stop It.* New York: Hyperion, 2002.

Naftali, Timothy. *Blind Spot: The Secret History of American Counterterrorism.* New York: Basic Books, 2005.

Risen, James. *State of War: The Secret History of the CIA and the Bush Administration.* New York: Free Press, 2006.

Tenet, George. *At the Center of the Storm: My Years at the CIA.* New York: HarperCollins, 2007.

Counterterrorism Strategy

A general approach toward the struggle against terrorism that involves the selection, distribution, and application of all resources and means available to achieve the desired aims (i.e., the prevention and/or eradication of terrorism). A successful counterterrorism strategy must target the vital dimensions of terrorism; address its current and prospective trends; reflect its rapidly changing nature, complexity, and flexibility; and employ a wide array of military, political, economic, social, ideological, cultural, law enforcement, and other means in often intermingled offensive and defensive efforts.

Terrorist activity, especially from Islamic extremists based in the Middle East, has in recent years demonstrated significantly increasing diversity and complexity. There is a wide range of participants with a diverse set of motivations, goals, structures, and strategies. Despite the destruction of the Al Qaeda sanctuaries in Afghanistan after the September 11, 2001, terror attacks, this global terrorist clearinghouse network continues to operate and, utilizing global information technology, continues to recruit and train supporters, share experiences, coordinate activities of various widely dispersed terrorist cells, and advance its ideological and strategic goals. These include the eradication of Western influence and presence in the region and the overthrow of existing regimes that accommodate the Western powers.

More structured than Al Qaeda, Hezbollah, headquartered in Lebanon, retains some potential for regional and even overseas terrorist activity but currently is concentrating its efforts on securing additional political influence within Lebanon and is not engaging in violence within Lebanon against Lebanese. The Palestinian terrorist organization Islamic Jihad has continued sporadic terrorist activities, mainly within the framework of the Israeli-Palestinian confrontation. Syria and Iran view support for organizations such as Hamas and Hezbollah as a means to promote their own national interests and ambitions in the region.

The successful expansion of transnational terrorism, according to American analysis under President George W. Bush, owes much to the emergence of so-called failed states such as Afghanistan, where such terrorism was able to prosper, virtually unchecked, due to the combination of political and social disintegration, fierce civil strife, and a lack of interest and support from the international community. The concept of a failed state is, however, disputed in the region, where underdevelopment and incomplete political control are commonplace. According to the Western ideas about transnational terrorists, the latter use the paramount anarchy in the failed states as well as weak governmental control over some portions of territory to obtain safe haven and to set up their training camps and communication centers, exploiting the remains of local infrastructure. In the late 1990s Al Qaeda managed to secure a close alliance with the Taliban in Afghanistan. The Taliban, after being driven from power in Afghanistan in 2001, has managed to reestablish itself in certain areas, including the remote Afghanistan-Pakistan border.

Any effective counterterrorism strategy must also take into account new developments in strategy and tactics of the terrorist actors. The terrorists have constantly tried to acquire more lethal weapons. This is particularly true with respect to weapons of mass destruction (WMD). Until 2001 Al Qaeda, using sanctuaries in Afghanistan, planned to launch chemical or biological attacks on U.S. and European targets. In addition to the continuous pursuit of more deadly weapons, the terrorists persistently employ suicide bombings to increase the lethality of their attacks.

Terrorist leaders have also demonstrated their ability to adjust to changing conditions. The decentralized, loose organizational structure of Al Qaeda allowed it to continue to operate even after the loss of Afghanistan in 2001. This has been amply demonstrated in its terrorist attacks in Yemen, Tunisia, Saudi Arabia, Jordan, and Kuwait as well as in Istanbul, Madrid, and London. The U.S. government had argued that Al Qaeda operated a network that recruited and operated in the Muslim communities of Britain, Spain, France, Germany, Italy, Spain, the Netherlands, and Belgium. Current thinking, however, sees Al Qaeda more as an inspiration to and clearinghouse for local groups who are autonomous of it. By active participation in the Iraqi insurgency since 2003, the terrorist networks have also acquired experience in urban warfare and enhanced their skills in ambush tactics, assassinations, and kidnappings.

The profound transformation, both in the scale and the complexity of operations that terrorists could undertake, allowed powerful, well-organized, and devoted groups and associations as well as smaller ones to evade state powers and to obtain global-reach capability. These terrorists are able to endanger the international security profoundly. Because the terrorist challenge amounts to a new form of warfare, successful counterterrorism strategy must constantly realign itself with the developments of the threats. Conventional military force has played a strong role in the struggle against alleged terrorism, as the long history of Israeli military campaigns against the Palestine Liberation Organization (PLO), the Israeli-Hezbollah War of 2006, and the Gaza War of 2009 demonstrate. Israel's strategy of heavy punishment of a neighboring state for permitting and/or abetting terrorism, while inflicting disproportionate loss of life and property damage, does not seem to have ended terrorist activity, which its proponents regard as rightful and necessary resistance, and has led to serious criticism of the Jewish state, even from its traditional allies.

Special operations forces play an important role in the struggle against terrorism. While capable of a global reach, military operations against terrorists need to be pinpointed and limited in scale to avoid civilian and collateral damage. This is particularly important because of the inability or reluctance of particular governments to attack the terrorist leadership and cells directly. Special operations transcend national boundaries and reflect the transnational character of the struggle against terrorism. The Israeli experience of deep-penetration commando raids and targeted assassinations of terrorist leaders reveals the ability of special operations to undermine the morale and disrupt activities of terrorist organizations and to violate state sovereignty as well as the terms of truces concluded with the enemy, although there are limits to what special operations can accomplish. Primarily, these special operations have angered the local population, making the resistance, or terrorism, that much more difficult to uproot.

Conventional military approaches retain their importance in dealing with state-sponsored terrorism, namely to wage wars against nations and achieve regime change, surely denying safe haven for the terrorists. At the same time, as the U.S.-led campaigns in Afghanistan after 2001 and Iraq after 2003 demonstrated, even victorious conventional campaigns can be complicated by ensuing insurgencies, which demand much greater flexibility on the part of the military. Here again, special operations come into play.

While the achievement of a decisive military victory remains elusive because of the dispersed and decentralized organizational structure of modern terrorism and while the use of military means resembles an endless war of attrition, the readiness to apply overwhelming and destructive military force can work to some extent. As recent changes in the policies of the Palestinian National Authority (PNA) and Libya suggest, providing government bodies with enticements to stop terrorist activities can also work to curb terrorist activity. These include economic, territorial, and governing incentives.

Diplomacy is another essential tool in fighting terrorism. International cooperation is vital in collecting information on terrorist cells, which includes the tracking and disrupting of financial transactions, recruitment, and propaganda activities of the terrorists. It is also of paramount importance in seeking to isolate regimes that sponsor terrorism.

Intelligence gathering is essential in any successful counterterrorist strategy. Simply gathering the information is not sufficient; it must be properly disseminated and coordinated within government agencies. The failure of the U.S. intelligence community to provide early warning about the September 11 terrorist attacks demonstrates this all too clearly.

Defensive efforts within the framework of counterterrorism strategy focus predominantly on homeland security and encompass enhanced border security. This includes monitoring and protecting likely terrorist targets (transportation, communication systems, and other elements of infrastructure as well as high-profile objects and places of significant concentration of populations) using intelligence, law enforcement, and military means. While Israel over the years has dealt with existential threats by developing comprehensive, integrated, and highly effective systems of territorial defense, the United States and European countries remain vulnerable to terrorist attacks because of porous borders and/or the ability of the Islamic terrorists to strike from inside, mobilizing militants from the Muslim diaspora, particularly in Western Europe. While the Western democracies' domestic counterterrorism strategies have improved vastly since September 11, 2001, they still remain deficient compared to those of Israel.

Comprehensive and multifaceted counterterrorism strategies must also involve political efforts to mobilize domestic support, social and cultural efforts to resist extremist propaganda efforts, and a determination to resolve problems and issues that terrorists often use for their own advantage. This is perhaps the most challenging aspect of any successful counterterrorism strategy. Political activities should include the resolution of the regional disputes, especially the Israeli-Palestinian issue; the advancement of economic development; addressing economic inequality and poverty; the promotion of democracy; high-quality governance; and the rule of law.

PETER J. RAINOW

See also

Al Qaeda; Central Intelligence Agency; Democratization and the Global War on Terror; Failed States and the Global War on Terror; Global War on Terror; Hamas; Hezbollah; Islamic Jihad, Palestinian; Martyrdom; Narcoterrorism; Taliban; Terrorism

References

Berntsen, Garry. *Human Intelligence, Counterterrorism, and National Leadership: A Practical Guide.* Washington, DC: Potomac Books, 2008.

Davis, Paul K. *Deterrence and Influence on Counterterrorism: A Component in the War on al-Qaeda.* Santa Monica, CA: RAND Corporation, 2002.

Forrest, James J. F. *Countering Terrorism and Insurgency in the 21st Century.* 3 vols. Westport, CT: Praeger Security International, 2007.

Freedman, George. *America's Secret War: Inside the Worldwide Struggle between America and Its Enemies.* New York: Broadway Books, 2004.

Guiora, Amos N. *Global Perspectives on Counterterrorism.* New York: Aspen Publishers, 2007.

Rubin, Barry, and Judith Colp Rubin, eds. *Anti-American Terrorism and the Middle East.* New York: Oxford University Press, 2002.

Crocker, Ryan Clark
Birth Date: June 19, 1949

Career U.S. diplomat. Ryan Clark Cocker was born on June 19, 1949, in Spokane, Washington. He attended University College Dublin and Whitman College in Walla Walla, Washington, from which he received his bachelor's degree in 1971. That same year he entered the U.S. Foreign Service. Crocker became a specialist in Middle East affairs, learning Persian and holding a wide variety of posts in the region. During 1984–1985 he studied at Princeton University, concentrating on Near East studies. Articulate, intelligent, and effective, Crocker moved quickly up the State Department's career ladder.

Crocker held diplomatic posts in Iran, Iraq, Egypt, Qatar, and Lebanon, among other nations, in addition to stints in Washington, D.C. He served as the U.S. ambassador to Lebanon (1990–1993), Kuwait (1994–1997), Syria (1998–2001), and Pakistan (2004–2007). From August 2001 to May 2003 he held the position of deputy assistant secretary of Near East affairs in the George

W. Bush administration. In January 2002 after the defeat of the Taliban regime in Afghanistan, the Bush administration sent Crocker to Kabul as interim U.S. envoy to Afghanistan. Crocker was charged with reopening the U.S. embassy there.

After the major fighting was declared over in the 2003 invasion of Iraq, Crocker went to Baghdad in May 2003 where he served as the director of governance for the new Coalition Provisional Authority. He stayed in Iraq until August 2003. In September 2004 President Bush granted Crocker the rank of career ambassador, the highest-ranking ambassadorial position in the U.S. State Department. After being nominated for the position of U.S. ambassador to Iraq, Crocker was confirmed and assumed his new duties in Baghdad on March 29, 2007.

According to Karen De Young's biography of Colin L. Powell, in the autumn of 2002 Secretary of State Powell tasked Crocker and another official with drafting a memorandum outlining the potential risks of launching a war against Iraq. The result was a six-page report that stated unambiguously that ousting Saddam Hussein from power would likely lead to sectarian and ethnic turmoil. It also posited that the United States would face a long and expensive reconstruction effort in a postwar Iraq. The memorandum proved quite prescient.

In September 2007 Crocker was called upon to testify—along with General David H. Petraeus, commander of the Multi-National Force in Iraq—before the U.S. House and Senate on the progress of the war in Iraq. While carefully avoiding any politically charged rhetoric, Crocker reported that Iraq remained a troubled and traumatized nation. He also stated that he believed that Iraqi officials would eventually take control of their own affairs but that this would likely take longer than anyone had envisioned or desired. Crocker continues in his role as ambassador to Iraq and has expressed his pleasure with the progress made in Iraq since September 2007.

PAUL G. PIERPAOLI JR.

See also

Afghanistan; Iraq, History of, 1990–Present; Iraqi Insurgency; Petraeus, David Howell; Powell, Colin Luther

References

De Young, Karen. *Soldier: The Life of Colin Powell.* New York: Knopf, 2006.

Keegan, John. *The Iraq War: The Military Offensive, from Victory in 21 Days to the Insurgent Aftermath.* New York: Vintage, 2005.

Cruise Missiles, Employment of, Persian Gulf and Iraq Wars

Cruise missiles are unmanned aircraft launched from the air, sea, or land that cruise at various altitudes and speeds until they hone onto their targets. Cruise missiles can carry an explosive warhead (nuclear or conventional) or other lethal payloads, such as chemical or biological warheads. During the 1991 Persian Gulf War (Operation DESERT STORM) and the 2003 Iraq War (Operation IRAQI FREEDOM), coalition cruise missiles proved reliable, accurate, and effective. They were launched from the land, air, and sea. In flight, they were difficult to detect and could fly indirect routes (low or high) to avoid heavily defended areas and could attack from any direction.

During DESERT STORM, the U.S. Navy's version of the cruise missile was the powerful Tomahawk land-attack missile (TLAM). The Tomahawk combined two new technologies: a small turbojet engine that powered the missile up to a speed of around 500 knots and a terrain-contour-matching system. This guidance system enabled it to navigate over land by matching its onboard radar's picture of the terrain below against a computer-developed map of its flight route to the target. Over water, it used a Global Positioning System (GPS) for navigation. The Tomahawks were particularly useful against well-defended targets. Instead of risking pilots and planes against such targets, they could be attacked with cruise missiles. However, technicians required about three days to reprogram a Tomahawk's guidance software. Consequently, the Tomahawks were not flexible enough to use in a rapidly changing environment. A variety of naval ships, ranging from destroyers and cruisers to nuclear-powered submarines as well as the renovated battleships *Missouri* and *Wisconsin,* carried TLAMs.

The 1991 Persian Gulf War saw the first major employment of land-attack cruise missiles. The anti-Iraq coalition opened Operation DESERT STORM by launching 122 of the U.S. Navy's Tomahawk missiles against key Iraqi air defense posts, radar systems, and communications facilities. Western cameramen operating in Baghdad filmed the low-flying slow-moving Tomahawks maneuvering through the city's streets to strike targets with amazing precision. During the entire Persian Gulf War, U.S. naval forces fired about 300 Tomahawks.

The first nighttime bombing mission of the Persian Gulf War began when seven Boeing B-52G Stratofortress bombers took off from a base in Louisiana. The bombers flew for 15 hours before releasing from their bomb bays the U.S. Air Force's version of the cruise missile, the AGM-86C ALCM (air-launched cruise missile). The bombers released about 35 ALCMs. Each of these missiles carried a 1,000-pound warhead. They also struck their targets with great accuracy. An estimated 89 percent of these cruise missiles hit their targets.

The success of U.S. cruise missile operations in the Persian Gulf War led to increased interest in these systems and spurred worldwide developments throughout the 1990s. By the late 1990s the original Tomahawk system aboard the U.S. Navy's vessels was replaced by a module that guided the missile by using the GPS. GPS navigation made the missile accurate to within three to six feet. Additionally, a Digital Scene Matching Area (DSMA) correlation feature was added to ensure that the missile would select the right target as it entered the target area by matching either a digital image of the target scene (radar, optical, or infrared or a combination of them) against an onboard image data base. DSMA was particularly useful against mobile targets. Compared to those in the Persian Gulf War, these more sophisticated cruise missiles could be reprogrammed much faster, in three hours or less and sometimes in a matter of minutes. This allowed planners to act upon the most recent intelligence in an effort to target and kill the enemy.

Overall, the U.S. Navy's Tomahawks featured improved accuracy, reliability, and destructive capacity along with special anti-jamming features. They had an estimated range of 600 miles carrying a 1,000 pound warhead at a speed of 550 miles per hour. These improvements were first exhibited in Bosnia in 1995 and were confirmed during Operation ENDURING FREEDOM in 2001, when some 70 Tomahawks attacked Taliban and Al Qaeda targets. By the time of the Iraq War, the U.S. Navy also had a much larger inventory of cruise missiles compared to its inventory on the eve of the Persian Gulf War.

The world at large became fully aware of the effectiveness of the improved cruise missiles during the 2003 Iraq War. On March 19, 2003, some 20 minutes after the expiration of the U.S. ultimatum demanding that Iraqi dictator Saddam Hussein leave Iraq, U.S. Navy ships launched an estimated 40 BGM-109 TLAMs against selected targets, including a leadership compound used by senior Iraqi officers. The attack occurred about three hours after an intelligence report suggested that Hussein and his two sons were present at a specific leadership compound. The U.S. hoped that this so-called decapitation strike would kill Hussein, but it did not. On April 7 intelligence again thought that it had located Hussein. The ensuing failed effort to kill him again featured cruise missiles. The missiles performed perfectly; however, the intelligence was faulty. In total, the United States probably conducted about 156 time-sensitive strikes against Iraqi leadership, missile, and weapons of mass destruction (WMD) targets. Many of these strikes involved cruise missiles. The ability to reprogram the cruise missiles rapidly allowed planners to include cruise missiles in their strike packages.

On March 21, 2003, the air campaign component of Operation IRAQI FREEDOM intensified. Hundreds of air and cruise missile strikes attacked regime leadership and military targets in Baghdad and other major cities. About 500 U.S. Navy Tomahawks and 100 U.S. Air Force air-launched cruise missiles were fired. Two British submarines also fired cruise missiles.

March 21 also marked the combat introduction of the Royal Air Force's Storm Shadow missiles. The Matra Bae Dynamics Storm Shadow was a stealth cruise missile of about 2,860 pounds and carried a powerful conventional warhead. Storm Shadows were air-launched conventionally armed long-range standoff precision weapons, deployable during night or day in most weather and operational conditions. They were used to give British aircraft such as the Panavia Tornado Interdictor and the AV-8B Harrier long-range firepower so that they would not have to fly into heavily defended air space to attack high-value targets.

During ensuing operations, U.S. forces alone fired close to 20,000 guided weapons. They included 802 sea-launched BGM-109 TLAMs and 153 air-launched AGM-86 C and D CALCMs (conventional air-launched cruise missiles). An estimated 35 of the 140 U.S. Navy vessels operating in the Persian Gulf, the Red Sea, and the Mediterranean were capable of firing the Tomahawks. The British also employed Tomahawks, including submarine-launched missiles, but the number fired remains classified.

Through the course of the Iraq War, the U.S. Air Force employed CALCMs against military command and control installations, structures, and buildings. They carried a heavier warhead (estimated at between 1,500 and 3,000 pounds, and there may have been two versions) than their naval counterparts and could be fitted with a hard-target penetrator, which made them particularly useful against heavily fortified Iraqi command and control centers.

The CALCMs featured advanced navigation software and a special GPS electronics module and antenna to prevent jamming from hostile electronic transmissions. The CALCMs also had the capacity to dive onto a target at an almost vertical plane or to attack from a shallow angle. This versatility increased the number of targets they could attack.

Compared to the 1991 Gulf War, the cruise missiles used in the Iraq War performed much better. The use of global positioning technology gave the cruise missiles greater accuracy and allowed them to fly more complicated missions. Other improvements increased their operational range to more than 1,000 miles, double the range of the cruise missiles used in DESERT STORM.

There were still some inevitable, and embarrassing, misses with cruise missiles plunging out of control and landing in Turkey or Saudi Arabia. The claimed failure rate was about 2 percent.

JAMES ARNOLD

See also

Missiles, Cruise; Tomahawk BGM-109 Land Attack Missile

References

Cordesman, Anthony H. *The Iraq War: Strategy, Tactics, and Military Lessons.* Westport, CT: Praeger, 2003.

Dunnigan, James F., and Austin Bay. *From Shield to Storm: High-Tech Weapons, Military Strategy, and Coalition Warfare in the Persian Gulf.* New York: William Morrow, 1992.

Jane's Armour and Artillery, 1990–1991. London: Jane's Information Group, 1990.

Jane's Armour and Artillery, 2001–2002. London: Jane's Information Group, 2001.

Knight, Michael, ed. *Operation Iraqi Freedom and the New Iraq.* Washington, DC: Washington Institute for Near East Policy, 2004.

Marolda, Edward, and Robert Schneller. *Shield and Sword: The United States Navy and the Persian Gulf War.* Annapolis, MD: U.S. Naval Institute Press, 2001.

Cruisers, U.S.

Cruisers are warships possessing moderate armament and yet are capable of high speed. The ancestor of the cruiser is the 18th-century frigate, which was detached from a battle fleet to cruise in search of enemy forces. The Ticonderoga class (CG-47) formed the backbone of the U.S. Navy's cruiser force during wars in the Middle East. Designed for versatility, these warships have performed a wide range of missions within carrier battle groups and amphibious assault groups and through independent operations.

Incorporating the hull design of the Spruance destroyer class (DD 963), the Ticonderoga class was initially conceptualized as a guided missile destroyer until redesignation in 1980. Displacing 9,600 tons with a beam of up to 55 feet and powered by four General Electric LM-2500 gas turbine engines, these cruisers can exceed 30 knots, with a range of 6,000 nautical miles at 20 knots. The crew consists of 24 officers and 334 sailors, although berthing is available for several dozen more.

The Ticonderoga class inaugurated the use of the Aegis weapons system for the most integrated and automated war-fighting capability on surface vessels worldwide. A central advantage to Aegis is the AN/SPY-1 phased-array radar that allows for continuous detection and tracking functions in all directions.

Ticonderoga-class cruisers, like the subsequently designed Arleigh Burke–class destroyers, enjoy an unparalleled degree of efficiency in managing a multithreat combat environment through Aegis. Twenty-two of the cruisers are equipped with the vertical launching system (VLS) for a more rapid employment of the Tomahawk land-attack missile (TLAM) with a range of at least 700 nautical miles, the standard missile (SM) for air targets, and the antisubmarine rocket (ASROC). The five pre-VLS cruisers relied upon two twin Mark 26 Mod 5 launcher systems. Two Mark 45 5-inch/54-caliber gun mounts provide naval gunfire support, antiship capabilities, and a limited antiair option. All Ticonderoga-class cruisers sport two launchers with a total of eight Harpoon antiship missiles with a range of better than 60 nautical miles. The combination of the SQS-53 hull-mounted and SQR-19 passive towed-array sonars give this class the ability to hunt submarines more effectively than any previous cruiser. Two Mark 32 Mod 14 torpedo launchers provide short-range protection against submarines. Two Mark 15 Mod 2 Falcon Phalanx close-in weapons system Gatling guns utilize depleted uranium or tungsten shells to deal with attacking aircraft and missiles at close quarters. All but the first two of the cruisers built have an embarked crew and maintenance team for the Sikorksy SH-60B Seahawk helicopter. The last ship in the class, *Port Royal* (CG-73) was commissioned in 1994.

In 1996, the *Yorktown* (CG-48) was selected as the pilot vessel for the U.S. Navy's Smart Ship Project to enhance automation in order to reduce manning requirements. Innovations such as fiber optic technology and wireless communications helped reduce the ship's crew by 4 officers and 44 sailors. The normal watch standing team on the bridge dropped from 70 to 3, with only 4 personnel necessary to monitor the entire engineering plant. As an outgrowth of the Smart Ship initiative, most of the Ticonderoga class has participated in the Integrated Ship Controls (ISC) program to cut costs through modernization without compromising mission readiness. In 2005, the *Cape St. George* (CG-71) initiated the practice of using digital navigation charts in place of roughly 12,000 paper charts.

Nine Ticonderoga-class cruisers participated in Operation DESERT STORM (January–February 1991); together they launched more than 300 Tomahawk missiles against Iraqi targets. This early neutralization of air defense and command and control centers helped isolate Iraqi units and facilitated a rapid and successful ground offensive. The *Normandy* (CG-60) became the first warship since 1945 to face combat on its maiden cruise and, in the process, fired more cruise missiles than any other vessel of its type. Other cruisers in theater were two Virginia-class nuclear-powered warships and one apiece from the Leahy and Belknap classes. The navy decommissioned all non-Aegis cruisers shortly thereafter.

Operation ENDURING FREEDOM (October 2001) included an entirely Aegis-equipped cruiser contingent of 15 warships. Since the Persian Gulf War, their targeting cycle for the Tomahawk had dropped from 101 minutes to 19 minutes. Operation IRAQI FREEDOM (March–April 2003) saw 11 Ticonderoga-class cruisers in action that played a major role in the firing of more than 800 Tomahawks. In February 2008 the *Lake Erie* (CG-70) used an SM-3 missile to down a U.S. satellite in orbital decay at a range of 133 miles. Speculation ensued that the operation served as a de facto experiment in reviving the Strategic Defense Initiative (SDI) of space-based weapons that stalled during the 1990s.

The five pre-VLS cruisers have been decommissioned, and the U.S. Navy's plan for the remainder of the class is a gradual phaseout during 2018–2029. The Cruiser Conversion program has been implemented to provide nearly all of these assets with the upgrades necessary to remain competitive. Among other things, missile defense capabilities will be enhanced, and larger-caliber guns will be added with extended range-guided munitions. The navy is considering design options (including a nuclear propulsion plant) for a CG(X) cruiser class to be constructed as multimission warships with augmented air and missile defense potential. The program is currently on pace to complete the first vessel in 2017.

JEFFREY D. BASS

See also

Tomahawk BGM-109 Land Attack Missile; United States Navy, Afghanistan War; United States Navy, Iraq War; United States Navy, Persian Gulf War

References

Marolda, Edward, and Robert Schneller. *Shield and Sword: The United States Navy and the Persian Gulf War*. Annapolis, MD: U.S. Naval Institute Press, 2001.

Murray, Williamson, and Robert H. Scales Jr. *The Iraq War: A Military History*. Cambridge, MA: Belknap, 2005.

Silverstone, Paul. *The Navy of the Nuclear Age, 1947–2007*. New York: Routledge, 2008.

Cultural Imperialism, U.S.

The term cultural imperialism refers to the process of imposing cultural values onto another culture or entity, often for the purposes of assimilation and political domination or long-term economic ties. It is also seen in policies that assume that the cultural values of the dominant country are the norm, while those of another culture are deviant, traditional, or less desirable. The ambiguity in defining this term in relation to the Middle East stems from the highly politicized attitudes of the West toward the Middle East, coupled with an almost total ignorance of the region's cultures. A similar Middle Eastern lack of sustained contact with and knowledge of the United States and distrust of its political motives in the region exists, as well as a long-standing embrace and defense of traditionalism.

Imperialism implies the extension of power over another entity for exploitative purposes. Typically, this term is used in reference to empires, colonies, nations, and states. Culture generally refers to patterns of human activities and symbolic expressions. So, while imperialism takes the forms of military hostilities, political dominance, or economic leverage, cultural imperialism is a more subtle process achieved mainly through symbolism, language, education, and meaning via consumer products, civil institutions, and the media.

Since at least the turn of the 20th century, some have labeled the United States a cultural hegemon that practices the transmittal of cultural imperialism through both government-sponsored means as well as private enterprise. Indeed, the concept of "American exceptionalism," the idea that the U.S. democratic political system represents not only the best of all systems but should stand as an example, a "shining city on a hill" for other countries to emulate, dates back to the founding of the Republic. Much of this American attitude was embodied in President Woodrow Wilson's Fourteen Points, his plan to remake the post–World War I world by calling for self-determination of peoples and representative institutions. Nationalists throughout the Middle East embraced Wilson's program. At the same time, they saw no need to give up their own cultures.

Most Middle Eastern populations, while they had had little contact with Americans, had experienced extensive cultural imperialism accompanied by political manipulation at the hands of French, British, Italian, and other European nations. Thus in the case of Egypt, everything that was native Egyptian, or *baladi,* was degraded, whereas that which was foreign, of Turko-Circassion origin or Levantine, French, or British, was prized. Those who embraced the occupying foreigners and their cultures secured special legal and economic privileges through the capitulatory treaties.

The impact of Western cultural influences in the Middle East accelerated rapidly after World War II with the advent of modern communication and transportation technologies that figuratively shrunk the world. The sheer size and dominance of the U.S. economy in the decades after World War II ensured that American cultural values would spill into all corners of the globe, mainly through the media and consumerism. In the Middle East, as in other parts of the Third World, this influence mostly impacted the upper elites, but it also coincided with new governmental policies and national pride in indigenous language, customs, traditions, and the arts. Many countries in the region sought to overcome disadvantageous balances of trade, which accompanied colonial suppression of native industries. Many people saw and wanted American products and tried to buy them whenever possible. However, these came with heavy tariffs, as certain governments, such as Egypt until 1974, or Syria, applied protective policies so as to bolster indigenous industries and agricultural products. Western foods and customs of eating more protein foods, such as red meat and chicken, often displaced local consumption patterns as Western-style one-stop supermarkets replaced traditional markets.

As far as social culture was concerned, the worlds of the Middle East and United States and other Western nations were at polar opposites. Many in the Middle East did not understand or wish to replicate American individualism and societal independence, in which people live at great distances from their relatives, may marry or not as they choose, have relationships outside of marriage without censure, and are not expected to care for their parents in old age.

Many young people in the Middle East, however, embraced American popular culture, products, and business methods. In a number of countries, the United States Information Service offered English classes and general programs about the United States and American culture, which were very popular. At the same time, however, Arab populations were in general critical of U.S. Middle East foreign policy that appeared to offer unconditional support to Israel or that, even though principally intended to counter Soviet influence in the region during the Cold War, seemed intended to secure American dominance in the region.

In the 1970s the rise of more militant Islamist movements and groups coincided with economic changes that saw a greater influx of imported consumer goods, such as cars and electronic items, from the West, which not all could afford. Conservative and new Islamist groups were specifically critical of the way their nations' elites and youth aped Western styles and overspent to acquire the latest products. Many were highly suspicious of U.S. motives and saw American culture as antithetical to their own basic values.

This theme was the subject of a book in prerevolutionary Iran by Jalal-e Ahmad, which identified *gharbzadeghi,* or Westoxification, as a primary problem. Islamists elsewhere complained of women dressing in Western styles, and Islamic businesses and banks responded to consumers' desire to spend where they would not be contributing to usury.

U.S. cultural imperialism in the Middle East has been most evident in political campaigns and efforts to influence Islamic beliefs and societies since both the September 11, 2001 (9/11) terrorist attacks against America and the commencement of the Iraq War of 2003. It has manifested itself in a battle "to win the hearts and minds" of the Muslim world, specifically in Iraq and Afghanistan, but also to pressure the broader Islamic world to refrain from and reject militant Islamic policies. In this, the so-called Global War on Terror was used as a vehicle for promoting American culture in the region that had given birth to the 9/11 terrorists. The basic logic of U.S. cultural imperialism followed that if American values could be brought to bear in radical Islamic societies, then potential terrorists would not hate America.

The official campaigns that involved winning "hearts and minds" claimed that the United States invaded Iraq in 2003 to overthrow an evil dictator and to establish democracy there. However, it was clear to most people in the Middle East that this was a war of choice, waged for other reasons, and many believed that securing Iraq's oil industry was a primary reason.

Americans had promoted democracy, although not its attendant cultural aspects, in a region historically dominated by authoritarian rulers and repressive regimes. However, in the case of key allies, U.S. foreign policy in the region had often downplayed democratization in favor of stability. Thus the United States had not promoted democracy in Saudi Arabia, nor did it insist that the Shah of Iran democratize or that the Egyptian and Syrian governments do so.

The Middle East was bombarded in the years following 2001 with Western critiques of its culture and deeply held religious beliefs. Such messages of cultural superiority were ill-timed, coming as they did after decades of programs aimed to build pride in national and religious identity.

Various U.S. organizations engaged in "Information Warfare," "Information Campaigns," or "Information Operations" and understood that such programs could be the strongest weapons in the Global War on Terror. The processes of this cultural imperialism are manifested primarily through media outlets, with the basic goal of the United States being to expunge the enemy's civil and governmental media and replace it with its own. For example, Iraqi radio and television stations were one of the first U.S. targets at the beginning of the March 2003 invasion. Iraqis laughed at many of these programs because they had extensive experience with official propaganda under Hussein's regime. The bright side was a mushrooming of many smaller news publications, even though many have been censored.

There were various tangible applications of what results in cultural imperialism by several branches of the U.S. government. The Public Diplomacy and Public Affairs Office conceived of promoting positive images of the United States to the Arab/Muslim world after 9/11. The Office of Global Communications was also created immediately after 9/11 by the White House to synchronize official opinion among various organizations like the Central Intelligence Agency (CIA), the Department of Defense, and the State Department. The Advertising Council of America, a World War II creation, formulated positive television advertisements for the White House. As per military operations, press agencies called "Coalition Information Centers" were created in November 2001 by the U.S. government to ensure that official opinions were aired during Operation ENDURING FREEDOM in Afghanistan.

During the Iraq War, coalition air forces dropped leaflets with the intention of warning civilians of upcoming military dangers or to threaten Iraqi military forces of the dire consequences of resisting. The U.S. Department of Defense converted all Iraqi television stations into the al-Iraqiyya Network, while the State Department created a satellite and cable network, known as 911, for promoting American-friendly programming. Many other organizations also performed information operations funded annually by the federal government.

A more extensive example of an American information operation can be seen through Radio Sawa (Sawa meaning "together"). This station broadcasts in FM and medium-wave frequencies, day and night, to Middle Eastern and North African countries. It replaced the Voice of America in the region, which was never as popular as the BBC radio service. It took advantage of new rules that permitted establishment of private FM radio stations; in the past, all were state controlled. Syria and Saudi Arabia have not yet liberalized their radio station practices.

Listeners can also tune in to Radio Sawa via the Internet. Its stations are located in Washington, D.C., and Dubai, United Arab Emirates (UAE). In addition, Radio Sawa has several news centers in the region. The broadcast language is Arabic, and the content consists of information and entertainment programs friendly to American culture. It broadcasts a strange mix of Arabic, American, and Spanish music. It is a service of U.S. International Broadcasting, which is organized, managed, and funded by the Broadcasting Board of Governors, an agency of the State Department under supervision of the U.S. Congress. The station is meant to counterbalance the frequently anti-American Arabic news organizations. However, its impact is minimal in much of the region, where, like the decidedly unpopular American-created Alhurra (al-Hurra) television satellite channel, it is regarded as a propaganda outlet. Actually, far more popular than Radio Sawa are many smaller radio stations, some of which focus on Arabic musical heritage and now broadcast hard-to-find recordings, more popular types of music, or controversial news programs.

Despite American efforts, positive Arab sentiments toward the United States decreased with exposure to information warfare. Prior to 9/11, the Arab world was already resentful of American financial and moral support of Israel. However, immediately after 9/11, most moderate Arabs expressed genuine sympathy for American suffering and support for the Global War on Terror. This did not last long, however, as antipathy toward the United States skyrocketed in the wake of the 2003 Iraq War and the occupation and pacification campaign there. In the absence of a United Nations (UN) resolution calling for armed intervention in Iraq, many in the Arab world viewed the U.S.-led war as illegal, and the mere existence of Iraq's large oil reserves created skepticism toward the motives behind the American-led invasion amid U.S. calls for democracy and freedom. When no weapons of mass destruction (WMDs) were discovered in Iraq, many Muslims became even more cynical of U.S. motives. In Iraq, impatience with the continuing presence of American troops has also served to disillusion many who initially welcomed the action.

Kuwaiti merchant Mohammed Said listens to Radio Sawa on his portable radio in a vegetable market in Kuwait City. The U.S.-funded Radio Sawa uses music to help promote U.S. views with Arab listeners. (AP/Wide World Photos)

Many Arabs feared that the U.S. attempt to shape Iraq into a democracy would merely be the opening step in a U.S. effort to transform the entire region. Indeed, some U.S. officials, such as Paul Wolfowitz, had long asserted this to be a U.S. objective. People in the region do not object to democracy, but rather a pseudo-democracy set up by a foreign government by military means that imposes a particular set of foreign policies on the new government.

Many of the new political leaders in Iraq support the imposition of Islamic law, rather than the Iraqi civil code. Indeed, the Iraqi constitution sets out the role of Islamic law in Iraq. With the intensely Islamist atmosphere in Afghanistan and Pakistan, many American programs, products, and movies are highly controversial and are banned by Islamist conservatives throughout the region. Tying the creation of markets to democratization tends to confuse the issue of cultural imperialism in the Middle East.

Americans tend to believe in the universality of their goods, ideas, and culture, and that, deep within every Iraqi or Afghan, there is an American waiting to leap out. This is not the case.

DYLAN A. CYR AND SHERIFA ZUHUR

See also

Bush Doctrine; ENDURING FREEDOM, Operation; IRAQI FREEDOM, Operation; Radio Baghdad

References

Eckes, Alfred, and Thomas Zeiler. *Globalization and the American Century.* Cambridge: Cambridge University Press, 2003.

Harding, Jim. *After Iraq: War, Imperialism and Democracy.* Black Point, Nova Scotia: Fernwood, 2004.

Said, Edward. *Culture and Imperialism.* New York: Knopf, 1999.

Schiller, Herbert. *Communication and Cultural Domination.* New York: M. E. Sharpe, 1976.

Tatham, Steve. *Losing Arab Hearts and Minds: The Coalition, Al-Jazeera and Muslim Public Opinion.* London: Hurst, 2006.

Czech Republic, Role in Persian Gulf, Afghanistan, and Iraq Wars

Central European nation that was created on January 1, 1993, out of the former Czechoslovakia. The Czech Republic, which covers

30,450 square miles, had a 2008 population of 10.221 million people. It is bordered by Poland to the northeast, Germany to the west, Austria to the south, and Slovakia to the east. The government of the Czech Republic features a multiparty parliamentary democracy with a prime minister, who is head of the government, and a president, selected by both houses of parliament, who is head of state. The president's powers are more limited than those of the prime minister, at least on domestic issues. Recently, Czech politics have been dominated by three parties: the Civil Democratic Party (a rightist organization), the Czech Social Democratic Party (centrist-left), and the Communist Party of Bohemia and Moravia (leftist).

The Czech Republic supported the U.S.-led coalitions in the 1991 Persian Gulf War, the 2001 Afghanistan War, and the 2003 Iraq War. After gaining freedom from Soviet domination at the end of the Cold War in 1990, Czechoslovakia (and later the Czech Republic) engaged in a broad effort to integrate itself into the institutions of the West, including the North Atlantic Treaty Organization (NATO), which it joined in 1999, and the European Union (EU), which it joined in 2004. Following the August 1990 invasion of Kuwait by Iraq, Czechoslovakia deployed elements of a chemical weapons battalion as part of the anti–Saddam Hussein coalition. The unit received significant praise from coalition partners for identifying and disposing of Iraqi chemical weapons stockpiles. The Czech government also granted permission for coalition forces to use its airspace and bases. Approximately 200 troops served in DESERT STORM.

The Czech Republic offered the U.S.-led coalition the use of its chemical weapons unit during the invasion of Afghanistan in late 2001. Elements of the unit were subsequently deployed to Afghanistan to support specific operations or missions. The Czech Republic also undertook three deployments of special operations forces between 2004 and 2008, staffed a field hospital in Kabul beginning in 2007, and dispatched a range of other units. In 2008 the Czechs established a provincial reconstruction team with 200 troops in Logar Province as part of the NATO-led International Security Assistance Force (ISAF). That same year, the Czech Republic also deployed an additional 65-member security force, bringing the Czech contribution to ISAF to more than 400 troops. The Czech

Republic also donated military equipment, including helicopters, to the Afghan National Army.

The Czech Republic supported the U.S. effort to develop a coalition to overthrow Hussein's regime in Iraq in 2003, although it faced diplomatic pressure from France and Germany to oppose military action. In December 2003 the Czech Republic began participation in the Multi-National Force in Iraq. The Czech contribution to the coalition peaked at 300 troops, and various units were deployed, ranging from infantry forces to medical personnel. Czech forces were stationed mainly in the area in and around Basra and served within the British area of operations. Czech personnel served as trainers for the Iraqi security forces, both as part of the U.S.-led coalition and under the auspices of the NATO-led training mission to Iraq. The Czech trainers were stationed at the Iraqi armor training facility at Taji and in Baghdad. Beginning in 2007 about 100 Czech troops were stationed at a British base outside of Basra, where they provided base security and undertook reconnaissance missions.

Czech forces served six-month rotations. One Czech soldier was killed during the nation's deployment in Iraq. Although the government staunchly supported the coalition, public opinion in the Czech Republic opposed the nation's involvement in the Iraq War. Thus, as other nations began to draw down their forces or end their missions in late 2008, the government announced that it would withdraw its forces in December. The last troops left on December 30, 2008.

TOM LANSFORD

See also

Afghanistan, Coalition Combat Operations in, 2002–Present; DESERT STORM, Operation, Coalition Nations' Contributions to; IRAQI FREEDOM, Operation, Coalition Ground Forces; Multi-National Force–Iraq; North Atlantic Treaty Organization in Afghanistan

References

Cockburn, Patrick. *The Occupation: War and Resistance in Iraq.* New York: Verso, 2007.

Feickert, Andrew. *U.S. and Coalition Military Operations in Afghanistan: Issues for Congress.* Washington, DC: Congressional Research Service, 2006.

Keegan, John. *The Iraq War: The Military Offensive, from Victory in 21 Days to the Insurgent Aftermath.* New York: Vintage, 2005.

D

Dahlan, Muhammad Yusuf
Birth Date: September 29, 1961

Palestinian politician and important figure in both Fatah and the Palestinian National Authority (PNA). Muhammad Yusuf Dahlan was born on September 29, 1961, in the Khan Yunis Refugee Camp in the Gaza Strip. His family had fled from Hammama, Palestine (now Nitzanim, Israel). Dahlan became politically active as a teenager in Khan Yunis, recruiting other youngsters for civic projects. He earned a degree in business administration from the Islamic University of Gaza, where he was also a student leader, and expanded his earlier activities to include charitable work such as the delivery of food and medicine but also the spreading of Palestinian nationalist propaganda. The organization he founded became the Fatah Youth Movement (Fatah Shabiba) in 1981.

By the time he was 25 years old, Dahlan had been arrested by the Israeli authorities on 11 separate occasions. Altogether he spent six years in Israeli prisons, becoming fluent in Hebrew in the process. One of the leaders of the First Intifada (1987–1994) in which the Fatah Youth Movement was very much involved, he was again arrested by the Israeli authorities in 1988 and deported to Jordan. He then went to Tunis, where he worked with the leaders of the Palestine Liberation Organization (PLO).

A protégé of PLO chairman Yasser Arafat, Dahlan returned to Gaza with Arafat in July 1994. Arafat appointed him to head the Preventive Security Service (PSS) for the Gaza Strip, a PLO security force, as well as to head Fatah in Gaza. The two posts made Dahlan one of the most powerful figures in the new PNA. With a police force of 20,000 men, Dahlan also became the most powerful figure in Gaza, which some came to refer to as Dahlanistan. To enforce his authority, Dahlan's associates reportedly used strong-arm methods, including torture. As with many other Fatah leaders, Dahlan became wealthy through PLO monopolies such as oil and cement and kickbacks on building contracts. The fact that he had been born in a refugee camp and had been imprisoned by the Israelis and had the loyalty of other such prisoners helped shield him from some Palestinian criticism, however.

As head of the PSS in Gaza, Dahlan was responsible for ensuring support from all members of Hamas for the 1993 Oslo Accords. Reportedly, he met regularly with Israeli security officials and U.S. Central Intelligence Agency (CIA) representatives to coordinate security issues. In 1995 following a number of Hamas suicide attacks, Dahlan, reportedly on the orders of Arafat, ordered the PSS to crack down on Hamas militants, arresting some 2,000 of them. The PSS also raided Islamic charities, schools, and mosques. Dahlan was able to succeed in such activities in large part because of the initial Palestinian support for the Oslo Accords and his tough methods. Because the Likud government of Prime Minister Benjamin Netanyahu in Israel was obstructionist toward the peace process, however, the PNA crackdown on militants soon lost support, and Dahlan himself backed off from it.

Dahlan was a regular member of negotiations with Israeli government officials on a variety of issues. He was also a participant in the Wye River negotiations (1999), and he took part in the Camp David Summit (2000) and the Taba negotiations (2001). Reportedly, he tried hard to secure a peace agreement at Camp David.

Dahlan's relationship with Israeli authorities cooled considerably with the beginning of the Second (al-Aqsa) Intifada in September 2000. Although he claimed that he remained committed to the peace process, Israeli officials blamed him for some of the violence in the Gaza Strip, and he was suspected of being involved in a November 2000 attack on an Israeli school bus. In May 2001

Muhammad Yusuf Dahlan, Palestinian politician and important Fatah and Palestinian National Authority (PNA) figure. (AP/Wide World Photos)

his motorcade came under attack from the Israel Defense Forces (IDF) in Gaza, and four of his bodyguards were wounded. Israeli prime minister Ariel Sharon denied that Dahlan was deliberately targeted and expressed regret for what the Israeli government later called an unfortunate mistake.

Dahlan reportedly offered to resign from the PSS in November 2001 in protest of the PNA's policy of arresting members of the Popular Front for the Liberation of Palestine (PFLP) and Islamic Jihad. Arafat supposedly refused the resignation. Anticipating that Arafat would be forced to unify his security forces, Dahlan began to expand his authority among low-level commanders in the West Bank PSS, seeking to undermine the authority of its commander, Jibril Rajob. Reportedly enjoying the support of U.S. president George W. Bush's administration, Dahlan also began to see himself as the possible successor to Arafat. Expecting to be named to head the security service, Dahlan resigned as head of the PSS. Arafat, however, resisted U.S. pressure to unify the security services. Although in July 2002 Arafat appointed Dahlan as his national security adviser, the position was devoid of any real power, let alone control of security services.

When Arafat was pressured into naming Mahmoud Abbas as the PNA's first prime minister in February 2003, Abbas sought to name Dahlan as the minister of the interior. Arafat opposed this, and after considerable turmoil within the PNA leadership Arafat agreed in April that Abbas would retain that post as well as the

prime ministership, while Dahlan would become minister of state for security affairs. Abbas then authorized Dahlan to restructure the PNA's Ministry of the Interior with a view toward cracking down on militants opposed to the peace process. In effect, Dahlan controlled some 20,000 security personnel but without having the title of interior minister. It proved an impossible situation, with a Likud government in Israel and Hamas militants both opposing the U.S.-sponsored Road Map to Peace. Dahlan instead proposed negotiations with Hamas to achieve a cease-fire, which was reached in July 2004. The cease-fire collapsed soon thereafter following the Israeli assassinations of Hamas and Islamic Jihad leaders.

Abbas resigned on September 6, 2003, and the new prime minister, Ahmed Qurei, dropped Dahlan from his cabinet. This decision led to protest demonstrations, especially in Khan Yunis, supporting Dahlan in Gaza and to Dahlan's posturing as a reformer when he called for elections in Fatah organizations that would bring in new leadership, although Dahlan was careful not to attack Arafat personally. Dahlan was seen as a prime mover in a wave of intra-Palestinian violence between his supporters and those favoring the Fatah old guard in the summer of 2004 in the Gaza Strip.

Appointed Palestinian minister for civil affairs, Dahlan had charge of coordinating with Israeli minister of defense Shaul Mofaz the Israeli pullout from Gaza. In January 2006 Dahlan narrowly won election to the Palestinian Legislative Council in the general elections as a representative of Khan Yunis.

In March 2007, over Hamas objections, Palestinian president Mahmoud Abbas named Dahlan to head the newly reestablished Palestinian National Security Council, which had control of all security services in the Palestinian territories. Dahlan resigned from this post in July 2007, but the National Security Council had already been dissolved following the Hamas takeover of Gaza in mid-June. Many in Fatah held Dahlan responsible for that easy Hamas victory, during which time he and key lieutenants were absent from Gaza. In the course of the fighting Dahlan's Gaza residence, which many Palestinians had come to view as a symbol of Fatah corruption, was seized by Hamas militants and then demolished.

SPENCER C. TUCKER

See also

Arafat, Yasser; Fatah; Intifada, First; Intifada, Second; Islamic Jihad, Palestinian; Netanyahu, Benjamin; Oslo Accords; Palestine Liberation Organization; Sharon, Ariel

References

Pappe, Ilan. *A History of Modern Palestine: One Land, Two Peoples.* Cambridge: Cambridge University Press, 2003.
Parsons, Nigel Craig. *The Politics of the Palestinian Authority: From Oslo to Al-Aqsa.* London: Routledge, 2003.
Rubin, Barry. *Revolution until Victory? The Politics and History of the PLO.* Cambridge: Harvard University Press, 1996.
Sayigh, Yezid. *Armed Struggle and the Search for State: The Palestine National Movement, 1949–1993.* New York: Oxford University Press, 2000.

Daisy Cutter Bomb

See BLU-82/B Bomb

Damascus Agreement

Agreement signed on December 28, 1985, that was designed to end the Lebanese Civil War (1975–1990) by revising the Lebanese political system in favor of a more equitable distribution of power on behalf of Lebanese Muslims as compared to the Lebanese Christian representatives. In addition, the Damascus Agreement was meant to bring Lebanon into a closer relationship with Syria and to achieve the expulsion of Israeli forces from southern Lebanon. The agreement failed to end the civil strife within Lebanon, although in some ways it prefigured the more successful Taif Accords of 1989, which eventually brought an end to the lengthy civil war.

When Lebanon achieved its independence in 1943, the unwritten National Pact (*mithaq al-watani*) governed the political arrangement among the various Lebanese religious groups, including Maronite Christians, Greek and Syrian Orthodox Christians, Sunni and Shiite Muslims, the Druze, and other smaller sects. In essence, Lebanese Muslims agreed that their nation would be an affiliated Arab nation but would not seek annexation or intervention by Syria. The Maronite Christians in turn agreed not to seek annexation or intervention by European or other Western powers, as had occurred in the past. In addition, the government would be ordered so that the president would always be a Christian, the prime minister a Sunni Muslim, and the president of the National Assembly a Shia Muslim. Parliamentary seats were to be distributed on a 6:5 Christian-to-Muslim ratio because at the time of the last census in 1932, the Christian population was larger than the Muslim population. However, the ratio shifted, and the Shia community became the largest group in Lebanon. By the late 1950s, as a consequence of other political circumstances, Muslims demanded a change in the ratio in Parliament as well as other changes.

In 1948 the establishment of the State of Israel resulted in thousands of Palestinian refugees fleeing to Lebanon, further increasing the Muslim population. By 1975 the demographic changes in Lebanon had created growing frustration with the political status quo on the part of Muslims, who called for new arrangements based on the demographic changes. The Maronite Christians refused, and tensions increased especially after demonstrations by Palestinians and killings of Palestinian and Christian groups that, together with the other Lebanese disputes, resulted in a civil war. It lasted off and on until 1990, after the conclusion of the Taif Accords. The Palestinian Resistance Movement had been conducting attacks on Israel from southern Lebanon since 1969. Israel, however, charged that these actions had increased, and in the absence of a viable central government the Israelis invaded in 1978.

Israeli troops again invaded southern Lebanon in 1982. The invasion was initially successful, and the Israelis then moved against Beirut, which resulted in substantial civilian casualties.

The Israelis also allowed Christian militias, with whom it was allied, to slaughter innocent Palestinian refugees within the refugee camps. In response, the United States, France, and Italy introduced peacekeeping forces into Lebanon. The American mission was short-lived, however. In October 1983 an Islamic suicide bomber drove a truck full of explosives into the U.S. Marine Corps barracks at the Beirut airport, killing 241 servicemen. As a result, in 1984 the Ronald Reagan administration maintained its peacekeeping force offshore on U.S. naval vessels, which greatly reduced its effectiveness.

The Israeli invasion served only to stir up Lebanon's seething ethnic and religious tensions. In addition, the Israeli invasion provided a pretext for Syria to inject its own forces into eastern Lebanon, ostensibly to protect the Lebanese from Israel but also to exert Syrian influence in Lebanon.

In 1985 the Israelis withdrew from Beirut and back into southern Lebanon, retaining about 10 percent of Lebanese territory as a buffer zone to reduce further attacks on their territory. The withdrawal of Israeli forces and the U.S. troops changed the balance of forces within the civil war. The Syrian-backed president, Amin Gemayel (Jumayyil), sought Syrian support in his war against Shia and Druze armed militias. The Syrians then moved troops into Lebanon to support him. Consequently, Syria was able to cajole the Lebanese factions to agree to a return to the peace table, which resulted in the Damascus Agreement of December 28, 1985.

The Damascus Agreement called for continued resistance to Israeli occupation in Lebanon and outlined the basic constitutional form of government for Lebanon, which was to continue to be republican and democratic. The agreement did address the basic demographic problem that had bedeviled the previous National Pact. The Damascus Agreement reduced the power of the Christian president by requiring the approval of the Muslim prime minister for most major decisions. In addition, the agreement expanded the Chamber of Deputies and called for equality among the sects there. Most importantly, at least from the Syrian perspective, it outlined a close relationship between Lebanon and Syria. In essence, it called for the mutual coordination of military strategy, foreign policy, security measures, economic relations, and education policy. Syria thus gained unparalleled power within Lebanon. The agreement was achieved in the face of immense Syrian pressure, for Syria then had some 40,000 troops stationed in Lebanon. The Damascus Agreement was thus designed to bind Lebanon to Syria while ending the civil war.

The Damascus Agreement failed to bring peace to Lebanon, however. Militias throughout the country continued their conflicts with one another and the government. After the end of Gemayel's presidency, his successor, General Michel Aoun, turned against the Syrians in 1989, resulting in conflict between Aoun's Christian forces and the Syrians and their militias and in Aoun's defeat. A workable peace plan would not emerge until 1989 under the auspices of the Arab League at Taif in Saudi Arabia. The Taif Accords built on much that had been contained in the Damascus

Agreement. The Taif Accords weakened the presidency and strengthened the premiership, expanded the Chamber of Deputies, and delivered more power to the Muslim majority by shifting the old 6:5 ratio to equal representation for both Christians and Muslims. The Taif Accords differed from the Damascus Agreement most dramatically by requiring a two-thirds vote by the Council of Ministers needed to change the implementation of the agreement, providing protection for minority rights, and omitting much of the language binding Lebanon to Syria.

Even after Taif, however, Syria continued to be immensely influential in Lebanese affairs and a major stumbling block to stability in Lebanon. Subsequent governments have implemented many elements of the Taif Accords without ending sectarianism, as the accords had demanded. A combination of pressures forced Syria to withdraw in 2005. Israel likewise has disrupted Lebanese efforts toward stability, most recently with its invasion into southern Lebanon in the summer of 2006.

MICHAEL K. BEAUCHAMP

See also

Hezbollah; Israel; Lebanon; Lebanon, U.S. Intervention in (1982–1984); Palestine Liberation Organization; Syria; Taif Accords

References

Cleveland, William L. *A History of the Modern Middle East*. 3rd ed. Boulder, CO: Westview, 2004.

Deeb, Marius. *Syria's Terrorist War on Lebanon and the Peace Process*. New York: Palgrave Macmillan, 2003.

Long, David E., and Bernard Reich. *The Government and the Politics of the Middle East and North Africa*. Boulder, CO: Westview, 2002.

Picard, Elizabeth. *Lebanon, a Shattered Country: Myths and Realities of the Wars in Lebanon*. New York: Holmes and Meier, 2002.

Damluji, Maysoon Salem al-
Birth Date: 1962

Liberal Iraqi politician and women's rights activist. Maysoon (Maysun) Salem al-Damluji was born in Baghdad in 1962 to a prominent family of doctors and political figures. Damluji moved to London in 1962 when she and her family were forced to leave Iraq because they would not join the Baath Party. Settling in Britain, she graduated from the Architectural Association in London in 1985 and began a successful practice as an architect in West London. Despite residing in Britain, Damluji retained a keen interest in her homeland, at first promoting the arts among Iraqi exiles in Britain and, after 1990, becoming involved in active political opposition to the Saddam Hussein regime.

Within a few weeks of the end of the Hussein regime in 2003, Damluji returned to Baghdad. Soon she was active in women's rights there, forming the Iraqi Independent Women's Group. She became president of that organization and also edited its magazine, *Noon*. In late 2003 she accepted the post of deputy minister of culture in the new Iraqi administration and continued in that

position with the transfer of Iraqi sovereignty. Damluji worked to save works of art produced during the period of Baath rule because these are considered to be the best art of the period, and often the artists had no connection with Hussein's regime. Many Shiite religious groups have opposed this approach, preferring to start afresh with purely Islamic art.

In February 2006 Damluji gave up her government post to become a member of the Iraqi parliament representing the city of Mosul. In the parliament, she has spoken out in favor of preserving human rights in the face of Sharia (Islamic law). Her stance on these issues has produced frequent threats on her life.

SPENCER C. TUCKER

See also

Iraq, History of, 1990–Present

References

Al-Ali, Nadje, and Nicola Pratt. *What Kind of Liberation: Women and the Occupation of Iraq*. Berkeley: University of California Press, 2009.

Al-Jawaheri, Yasmin Husein. *Women in Iraq: The Gender Impact of International Sanctions*. Boulder, CO: Lynne Rienner, 2008.

Dar es Salaam, Bombing of U.S. Embassy
Event Date: August 7, 1998

Bombing of the U.S. embassy in Dar es Salaam, Tanzania, by Al Qaeda terrorists. Early on the morning of August 7, 1998, Al Qaeda operatives, using a truck bomb, attacked the U.S. embassy, killing 12 people and injuring 86 others. U.S. Federal Bureau of Investigation (FBI) investigators concluded that the bomb was most likely planted in a refrigeration truck. The building suffered major damage and was deemed unusable. A year prior to the attack there had been a warning of a possible terrorist attack on the embassy, but it had been ignored because the source could not be verified.

The attack on the embassy in Dar es Salaam caused far fewer casualties than the nearly simultaneous attack on the U.S. embassy in Nairobi, Kenya, also targeted by Al Qaeda. In fact, none of the Dar es Salaam personnel inside the building were killed in the attack. The Tanzanian embassy was located farther from the city center, which helped to minimize civilian casualties. According to reports, the truck bomber was unable to penetrate the outer wall of the embassy because a water tanker had blocked its path. When the bomb detonated, the tanker absorbed much of the blast that otherwise would undoubtedly have caused greater damage to the chancery building.

The investigators concluded that Osama bin Laden, leader of Al Qaeda, had masterminded the embassy attacks. As a result, the U.S. government issued indictments against him and offered a $5 million dollar reward for his capture. In 2001 four men were convicted in U.S. federal courts and sentenced to life in prison for their role in the bombings of the U.S. embassies in Kenya and Tanzania. However, to this date bin Laden remains at large.

In response to the attacks on the U.S. embassies, President Bill Clinton pledged to wage a war against international terrorism. In retaliation for the bombings, on August 20, 1998, the United States launched cruise missiles against three terrorist camps in Afghanistan and a suspected chemical weapons plant in Sudan. The operation was code-named INFINITE REACH. The attacks on the camps in Afghanistan killed 24 people but failed to kill bin Laden. The attack on the plant in Sudan came under great criticism because there was no corroborating evidence to justify the attack, and many believe that the plant produced pharmaceuticals rather than chemical weapons. That attack killed the night watchmen at the plant.

In the United States, some cynics accused President Clinton of mounting the retaliatory attacks to distract the public's attention from the still-unfolding Monica Lewinsky scandal. The cruise missile attacks precipitated massive protests around the world, mostly in Muslim countries. In addition, bin Laden pledged to strike the United States again, a threat that he made good on with the devastating attacks in New York and Washington, D.C., on September 11, 2001.

DANIEL KUTHY

See also

Al Qaeda; Bin Laden, Osama; Clinton, William Jefferson; INFINITE REACH, Operation; Nairobi, Kenya, Bombing of U.S. Embassy; Terrorism

References

Ferguson, Amanda. *The Attack against the U.S. Embassies in Kenya and Tanzania*. New York: Rosen Publication Group, 2003.

Labévière, Richard. *Dollars for Terror: The United States and Islam*. New York: Algora Publishing, 2000.

Obwogo, Subiri. *The Bombs That Shook Nairobi & Dar es Salaam: A Story of Pain and Betrayal*. Nairobi: Obwogo and Family, 1999.

Debecka Pass, Battle of
Event Date: April 6, 2003

Engagement that unfolded in northern Iraq on April 6, 2003, during Operation IRAQI FREEDOM. U.S. strategy for the Iraq War called for the major thrust against Iraq to come from the south. A secondary offensive featuring the 4th Infantry Division would move through Turkey and invade northern Iraq. When Turkey refused permission for the 4th Division to transit across its territory, however, strategists revised the plan for a northern thrust. The new plan called for a joint force consisting of the 173rd Airborne Brigade, the 26th Marine Expeditionary Unit, and U.S. Army Special Forces operating in cooperation with Kurdish fighters known as Peshmerga ("those who face death").

The 10th Special Forces Group, commanded by Colonel Charlie Cleveland, opened the second front in northern Iraq. Its mission was to destroy training camps used by Ansar al-Islam terrorists and to prevent Iraqi forces in northern Iraq from reinforcing the units defending Baghdad. The particular objectives of the 10th

Special Forces Group were the cities of Mosul and Kirkuk and the northern oil fields near these cities.

The basic unit of the Special Forces was the Operational Detachment-A, or A-Team. A captain commanded the 12-man A-Team with a warrant officer serving as second in command. Noncommissioned officers composed the balance of the team, with two each possessing specialty training in one of the five Special Forces functional areas: weapons, engineering, medical, communications, and operations and intelligence.

For the push into northern Iraq, the Special Forces utilized specially modified Humvees (high-mobility multipurpose wheeled vehicles). The Humvees served as a mobile headquarters and fighting platform, and they had sophisticated communications equipment to enable the men to call in air strikes. Each vehicle carried several machine guns, Mark 19 grenade launchers, sniper rifles, side arms, Stinger shoulder-fired antiaircraft missiles, and the new Javelin fire-and-forget antitank missile. The Stinger launcher and missile weighed about 50 pounds. Consequently, a single soldier could carry and operate it. The Javelin had a range of about 2,750 yards. The missile used an internal guidance system to fly to the target and then dive down to strike the top of an armored vehicle, its most vulnerable spot because top armor was thinner than front or side armor. The Javelins figured prominently in the April 6, 2003, Battle of Debecka Pass.

Two Special Forces A-Teams and forward air controllers (26 personnel in all) were given the task of securing a key intersection on Highway 2 near the town of Debecka in northern Iraq between the cities of Irbil to the north and Kirkuk to the south. Accompanied by as many as 80 Peshmerga fighters, the team deployed to block Iraqi troop movements along Highway 2 in either direction. However, a surprise Iraqi counterattack featuring some 150 infantry, eight armored personnel carriers, and four T-55 tanks with 100-millimeter (mm) main guns struck the Special Forces, forcing them to withdraw to a nearby ridge line.

From their new position the Americans engaged the approaching Iraqi armored forces with Javelin antitank missiles, .50-caliber machine guns, and Mark 19 40-mm grenade launchers. One Javelin destroyed an armored personnel carrier from a distance of 2,950 yards, 200 yards beyond the rated maximum engagement range. During this phase of the battle, of eight Javelins fired by the Special Forces, seven struck their intended targets, destroying five armored personnel carriers and two trucks. The Javelin strikes stopped the momentum of the Iraqi attack. The Iraqis then moved the tanks behind an earthen berm where they could not be targeted by the Javelins because the Javelins required the operator to have a clear line of sight to the target. The Iraqis did not know that the Americans had only three Javelins remaining.

Meanwhile, a request for air support brought U.S. Navy Grumman F-14 Tomcat fighters. U.S. Air Force forward air controllers operating with the Special Forces directed the Tomcats to attack the Iraqi armor at the intersection. In a case of mistaken identify, an F-14 Tomcat bombed friendly Kurdish fighters operating behind the Special Forces, killing 16 Kurds and wounding another 45. A British Broadcasting Corporation (BBC) film crew was present and broadcast a description of this incident as it occurred.

The Special Forces were holding their position until an Iraqi battery of D-20 towed 152-mm howitzers opened fire. The Special Forces had no answer to this fire and were again compelled to relocate. In their new position they received a resupply of Javelin missiles. The Americans were also able to see more clearly the Iraqi T-55 tanks as well as the surviving armored personnel carriers. The Special Forces again opened fire with the Javelins. When an Iraqi tank tried to change positions it emerged into the open, where it was promptly destroyed by a Javelin. This event broke the morale of the Iraqi forces.

At 12:45 p.m. local time, about 15 Iraqi soldiers appeared from a ravine indicating that they wished to surrender. Suddenly, two white Toyota Land Cruisers appeared and disgorged Iraqi security personnel, who began shooting down the surrendering Iraqi soldiers. A laser-guided bomb dropped from an American airplane then destroyed the Land Cruisers. During the final phase of the combat, another Javelin missile destroyed another Iraqi T-55 tank. The remaining Iraqi soldiers abandoned their vehicles and fled.

In a telephone interview in the autumn of 2003, one of the Special Forces sergeants in the battle attributed the American victory to the Javelin missiles. Without them, the Special Forces would not have been able to hold off the Iraqi tanks. The Americans suffered no casualties, but the Peshmerga sustained 16 dead and 45 wounded from the friendly fire incident; 1 civilian was also killed. Iraqi killed and wounded are unknown, but 20 were taken prisoner. The Iraqis also lost at least two T-55 tanks, eight armored personnel carriers, and four trucks. The Battle of Debecka Pass was an example of how small highly trained well-led units with sophisticated weaponry can defeat larger conventional units.

JAMES ARNOLD

See also

Antitank Weapons; High Mobility Multipurpose Wheeled Vehicle; IRAQI FREEDOM, Operation; Peshmerga; T-54/55 Series Main Battle Tank

References

Antenori, Frank, and Hans Halberstadt. *Roughneck Nine-One: The Extraordinary Story of a Special Forces A-team at War.* New York: St. Martin's, 2006.

Gordon, Michael R., and General Bernard E. Trainor. *Cobra II: The Inside Story of the Invasion and Occupation of Iraq.* New York: Pantheon Books, 2006.

Murray, Williamson, and Robert H. Scales Jr. *The Iraq War: A Military History.* Cambridge, MA: Belknap, 2005.

Stilwell, Alexander. *Special Forces Today: Afghanistan, Africa, Balkans, Iraq, South America.* Dulles, VA: Potomac Books, 2007.

Defense Intelligence Agency

Formally established at the direction of Secretary of Defense Robert McNamara on October 1, 1961, the Defense Intelligence Agency (DIA) is the leading intelligence agency for the Department of Defense. The DIA is directly responsible for meeting the intelligence requirements of the secretary of defense, the Joint Chiefs of Staff (JCS), and each of the Combatant Commands. Prior to the agency's establishment, each of the military services collected and analyzed its own intelligence separately and disseminated the intelligence to its own service chiefs, components, and the Unified and Specific Commands (now called Combatant Commands).

The Defense Reorganization Act of 1958, which gave birth to the DIA, sought to reduce the duplication and uncoordinated efforts that derived from those separate efforts. It also hoped to provide integrated intelligence analysis and support to the JCS and secretary of defense. The DIA acquired the mandate for all aspects and phases of the Defense Department's intelligence production except those intelligence-collection platforms and activities specifically assigned to the individual military services.

The 1962 Cuban Missile Crisis was the first major test for the DIA. That crisis was followed almost immediately by the Berlin Crisis. For a new agency, the DIA performed surprisingly well in both instances.

The Vietnam War saw the DIA become the primary authority and coordinating agency for military intelligence related to facilities and infrastructure. In the late 1970s the DIA also became the coordinating agency for any Defense Department relationships with foreign military intelligence organizations. By the 1980s the DIA became the Defense Department's coordinating agency for national collection assets as well as its spokesman before Congress on budgeting and national intelligence production priorities.

Defense Intelligence Agency (DIA) Directors, 1988–Present

Name	Rank	Branch	Dates of Service
Harry E. Soyster	Lieutenant general	U.S. Army	December 1988–September 1991
Dennis M. Nagy (interim)	None	Civilian	September 1991–November 1991
James R. Clapper	Lieutenant general	U.S. Air Force	November 1991–August 1995
Kenneth Minihan	Lieutenant general	U.S. Air Force	August 1995–February 1996
Patrick M. Hughes	Lieutenant general	U.S. Army	February 1996–July 1999
Thomas R. Wilson	Vice admiral	U.S. Navy	July 1999–July 2002
Lowell E. Jacoby	Vice admiral	U.S. Navy	July 2002–November 2005
Michael D. Maples	Lieutenant general	U.S. Army	November 2005–March 2009
Ronald Burgess	Lieutenant general	U.S. Army	March 2009–present

A Defense Intelligence Agency (DIA) photograph of Iraqi military headquarters. The DIA is the primary producer of strategic intelligence within the Department of Defense. (U.S. Department of Defense)

Driven by the lessons learned from the Persian Gulf War (Operation DESERT STORM, 1991), the DIA's authority and mission expanded in consonance with America's increasing integration of its military forces into a joint structure and operations. Combatant Command intelligence centers now report their production requirements to and acquire their operating funds from the DIA. Although dissenting intelligence analysis is included in the DIA's coordinated national intelligence assessments, the DIA's assessment has become the dominant one.

The September 11, 2001, terror attacks on the United States perpetrated by Al Qaeda and the sequella from these have placed a spotlight on the DIA and its activities. The September 11 Commission, charged with evaluating America's response to the 9/11 attacks, was critical of the DIA's inability to thwart them and called into question its ability to effectively compile and disseminate intelligence information to prevent another such terrorist attack.

Similarly, the DIA has been criticized by the Weapons of Mass Destruction (WMDs) Commission for its role in the faulty intelligence surrounding Iraq's alleged WMD program prior to the Anglo-American invasion of Iraq in March 2003. The George W. Bush administration was later embarrassed when no WMDs were found in Iraq. Their presence had been one of the key reasons for the invasion. Indeed, both commissions cited the DIA's failure to use open-source and human intelligence sources effectively. In all fairness, however, other intelligence agencies were criticized in similar fashion. The intelligence-gathering reforms based on the commission's recommendations began in 2005 but may not be fully implemented until the end of the decade. In 2005 a new cabinet-level intelligence position was created: director of national intelligence. The director serves as the president's chief intelligence adviser and also serves as principal adviser to the National Security Council and the Department of Homeland Security. As such, the post calls upon the director to coordinate information from the DIA and other intelligence-gathering agencies.

CARL OTIS SCHUSTER

See also

Bush, George Walker; IRAQI FREEDOM, Operation; Nuclear Weapons, Iraq's Potential for Building; September 11 Attacks; September 11 Commission and Report; Terrorism; Weapons of Mass Destruction

References

Richelson, Jeffrey T. *The U.S. Intelligence Community.* 4th ed. Boulder, CO: Westview, 1999.

Roberts, Pat, ed. *Report on U.S. Intelligence Community's Prewar Intelligence Assessments on Iraq: Conclusions.* Washington, DC: Diane Publishing, 2004.

United States. *21st Century Complete Guide to American Intelligence Agencies.* Washington, DC: U.S. Government Printing Office, 2002.

Defense Meteorological Satellite Program

A satellite program developed by the U.S. Department of Defense to provide worldwide meteorological, oceanographic, and solar-geophysical data and imagery to the U.S. military for use in planning and executing military operations. The U.S. Air Force Space and Missile Systems Center (SMC), Los Angeles Air Force Base, California, designed, built, and launched the Defense Meteorological Satellite Program (DMSP) satellites. Since the launch of the first DMSP satellite in 1965, the air force has launched 34 more. In December 1972 the Department of Defense made DMSP data available to civil and scientific communities. In June 1998 the air force transferred the control of the satellites to the National Oceanographic and Atmospheric Administration (NOAA), but the SMC retained responsibility for the development and acquisition of future DMSP satellites.

DMSP satellites send images and data to tracking stations in New Hampshire, Greenland, Alaska, and Hawaii. These sites in turn send the images to the U.S. Air Force Weather Agency (AFWA), Offutt Air Force Base, Nebraska; the 55th Space Weather Squadron, Falcon Air Force Base, Colorado; and the U.S. Navy's Fleet Numerical Meteorology and Oceanography Center (FNMOC), Monterey, California. The AFWA and the FNMOC process the images and data into a product that is then sent to military installations, where meteorologists develop up-to-date weather observations and forecasts for use by unit commanders in scheduling and planning military operations.

During the Vietnam War, early DMSP satellites supplied cloud-cover information to military headquarters in Saigon and to aircraft carriers in the Gulf of Tonkin for more precise planning of tactical air missions. DMSP imagery provided highly accurate weather forecasting that operational commanders used to plan air strikes over the Democratic Republic of Vietnam (DRV, North Vietnam) and close air support over the Republic of Vietnam (ROV, South Vietnam), determine air-to-air refueling tracks, and plan rescue operations. The DMSP weather data eliminated the need for weather reconnaissance aircraft in Southeast Asia.

For Operations DESERT SHIELD/DESERT STORM from August 1990 to February 1991, the SMC procured the Rapid Deployment Imagery Terminal, which, supplemented by older weather terminals, provided DMSP data and images directly to the commanders of fielded forces in the Persian Gulf region. The terminals provided commanders with high-resolution nearly real-time weather information that allowed them to select targets and munitions, especially laser-guided weapons that required clear weather for accurate targeting, during the air campaign.

Commanders also used weather data and images to plan and redirect aerial and ground missions and optimize night-vision equipment and night-capable targeting systems. DMSP satellites also provided information to alert troops to sandstorms and to predict the possible use and spread of chemical agents.

In December 1990 the U.S. Air Force launched a third DMSP satellite to augment coverage in the Persian Gulf area. With the additional capability of detecting areas of moisture and standing water, DMSP imagery helped coalition ground forces plan movement routes into Kuwait during Operation DESERT STORM. DMSP and other weather satellites also provided extensive imagery and data of the oil fires, ignited by the Iraqi Army as it fled Kuwait in February 1991. The fires produced large smoke plumes, causing significant environmental effects on the Persian Gulf region.

There have been some problems with the terminals and dissemination networks, however. For example, the incompatibility of the four different types of terminals delayed the receipt of timely weather data. With rapidly changing weather conditions, field units often did not have the latest target-area weather data, and high-quality satellite imagery did not get to the flyers. Some navy ships could not receive DMSP data at all. These problems emphasized the need for more compatible and user-friendly systems. During Operations ENDURING FREEDOM and IRAQI FREEDOM some of these problems had been eliminated, and DMSP provided badly needed weather data to troops in both theaters of war.

ROBERT B. KANE

See also

DESERT SHIELD, Operation; DESERT STORM, Operation; ENDURING FREEDOM, Operation; IRAQI FREEDOM, Operation; Oil Well Fires, Persian Gulf War

References

Hall, R. Cargill. *A History of the Military Polar Orbiting Meteorological Satellite Program.* Chantilly, VA: National Reconnaissance Office History Office, 2001.

History Office, Space and Missile Systems Center, Los Angeles Air Force Base. *Historical Overview of the Space and Missile Systems Center, 1954–2003.* Los Angeles: Missile Systems Center, 2003.

Peeples, Curtis. *High Frontier: The United States Air Force and the Military Space Program.* Washington, DC: Air Force History and Museum Program, 1997.

Spires, David N. *Beyond Horizons: A Half Century of Air Force Space Leadership.* 2nd ed. Maxwell Air Force Base, AL: Air Force Space Command and Air University Press, 2007.

Defense Satellite Communications System

A constellation of nine satellites in geosynchronous orbit 22,300 miles above the earth that provides high-volume secure voice and data communications among the White House, senior U.S. defense officials, and U.S. military forces in the field worldwide. The U.S. Air Force launched the first Defense Satellite Communications

System (DSCS) satellite in 1966. In 1967 DSCS I satellites transmitted reconnaissance photographs and other data from military headquarters in the Republic of Vietnam (ROV, South Vietnam) to Hawaii and from Hawaii to Washington, D.C. In 1968 the air force declared the satellite system, along with 2 fixed and 34 mobile ground terminals, to be operational and changed the system's name to the Initial Defense Satellite Communication System (IDCS).

After having launched 26 IDCS satellites, the U.S. Air Force renamed the program the Defense Satellite Communications System (DSCS). In 1971 the air force began launching a more sophisticated satellite, DSCS Phase II (DSCS II). DSCS II, the first operational military communications satellite system to occupy a geosynchronous orbit, became fully operational in early 1979. By 1989 the air force had launched 16 DSCS II satellites.

In 1982 the U.S. Air Force launched the first DSCS III, the only current model of the DSCS family still operational, and achieved a full constellation of five satellites in 1993. The DSCS III satellites carry multiple beam antennas that provide flexible coverage over six communication channels and resistance to jamming.

The U.S. Air Force Space Command's Space and Missile Systems Center, Los Angeles Air Force Base, California, contracted with Martin Marietta to build the DSCS III satellites and ground segment. The Electronics Systems Center, Hanscom Air Force Base, Massachusetts, developed the air force portion of the terminal segment. The 3rd Space Operations Squadron, 50th Space Wing, Schriever Air Force Base, Colorado, provides command and control of the DSCS satellites.

During Operations DESERT SHIELD and DESERT STORM (August 1990–February 1991), satellite communications provided essential command and control of deployed coalition forces. Although military communications were very tenuous at the start of DESERT SHIELD, U.S. military forces within the first 90 days established more military communications connectivity to the Persian Gulf than they had achieved in Europe over the previous 40 years.

Operation DESERT SHIELD forces communicated through a U.S. Navy Fleet Satellite Communications satellite (FLTSATCOM), a Leased Satellite (LEASAT) program satellite, and two DSCS satellites over the Indian Ocean. In addition, the U.S. Department of Defense

An illustration of a Defense Satellite Communications System (DSCS) satellite. (U.S. Air Force)

used FLTSATCOM satellites over the Atlantic Ocean and DSCS satellites over the eastern Atlantic to facilitate communications between the U.S. Central Command (CENTCOM) headquarters in the Persian Gulf and various headquarters in the United States.

DSCS III satellites also provided long-haul communications for U.S. military forces during Operations DENY FLIGHT (1993–1995) and ALLIED FORCE (1999) in the Balkans and Operations ENDURING FREEDOM and IRAQI FREEDOM in the Middle East since 2001. Throughout these operations, communications requirements steadily grew, reaching the capacity of the DSCS satellites to provide for the increasing needs. For Operation ENDURING FREEDOM, the U.S. Air Force reconfigured the DSCS satellites to provide added bandwidth. The introduction of unmanned aerial vehicles (UAVs, or drones) and increased use of digital imagery and data in Middle Eastern combat operations contributed to the growing demand for large communications networks.

Since 2000 the U.S. Air Force, through the DSCS Service Life Enhancement Program (SLEP), has upgraded the last four DSCS III satellites prior to launch to extend the usable lifetime of the DSCS III satellites. In addition, the air force has incorporated several technology upgrades to increase the capabilities of the DSCS satellites prior to launch into orbit.

ROBERT B. KANE

See also

DESERT SHIELD, Operation; DESERT STORM, Operation; ENDURING FREEDOM, Operation; IRAQI FREEDOM, Operation; Satellites, Use of by Coalition Forces; United States Central Command; Unmanned Aerial Vehicles

References

History Office, Space and Missile Systems Center, Los Angeles Air Force Base. *Historical Overview of the Space and Missile Systems Center, 1954–2003.* Los Angeles: Missile Systems Center, 2003.

Levis, Alexander H., John C. Bedford (Colonel, USAF), and Sandra Davis (Captain, USAF), eds. *The Limitless Sky: Air Force Science and Technology Contributions to the Nation.* Washington, DC: Air Force History and Museums Program, 2004.

Peeples, Curtis. *High Frontier: The United States Air Force and the Military Space Program.* Washington, DC: Air Force History and Museum Program, 1997.

Spires, David N. *Beyond Horizons: A Half Century of Air Force Space Leadership.* 2nd ed. Maxwell Air Force Base, AL: Air Force Space Command and Air University Press, 2007.

Dellums et al. v. Bush
Event Date: 1990

Lawsuit brought against President George H. W. Bush by U.S. representative Ronald V. Dellums and some 50 other members of Congress concerning the massive buildup of U.S. forces in the Persian Gulf that began in August 1990. The lawsuit, decided on December 13, 1990, by the U.S. District Court for the District of Columbia, sought to limit the president's ability to wage war without the explicit consent of Congress.

After Iraqi president Saddam Hussein sent his troops into Kuwait on August 2, 1990, quickly defeating and occupying the small oil-rich nation, the United States, working in concert with numerous other nations, began to assemble an international coalition in Saudi Arabia to force the Iraqis from Kuwait. The troops, part of Operation DESERT SHIELD, would number more than 550,000 by late 1990 and were also being used as a deterrent to a potential Iraqi incursion into Saudi Arabia.

Bush ordered the massive buildup without seeking any congressional authorization, but given that the deployments were at that point defensive in nature, he was not required to do so. What is more, it was not entirely clear in the autumn of 1990 that the troops would actually be involved in a war against Iraqi forces. International diplomacy and economic sanctions were still being applied to the Hussein regime in an attempt to force him from Kuwait without resorting to military action. Be that as it may, many in Congress, especially the Democrats, were wary of Bush's actions and hoped to force the White House to seek an up or down vote on the use of force in Iraq. Dellums and his colleagues thus filed the suit in a U.S. District Court, citing the 1973 War Power Act and Article I of the U.S. Constitution as the basis for the action.

Dellums, a left-of-center Democratic U.S. representative of California's Ninth District, was a rabid opponent of the Vietnam War and had a long voting record that demonstrated his abhorrence of large military budgets. He actively opposed development of the MX Missile and the B-2 Stealth bomber and consistently supported the agendas of big labor and environmental groups. It came as no surprise, then, that he would have objected to Operation DESERT SHIELD. By bringing suit against the president, Dellums and his coplaintiffs hoped to prevent Bush from employing troops in any sort of offensive capacity before receiving the explicit consent of Congress.

On December 13, 1990, the presiding judge in the case, Harold Greene, essentially threw the case out of court, asserting that the timing of the case was premature and that the issue had not become "ripe" for review. His ruling was based on a 1979 U.S. Supreme Court case, *Goldwater v. Carter,* in which Senator Barry Goldwater had brought suit against President Jimmy Carter for having abrogated a previously ratified treaty with Taiwan. The Supreme Court dismissed the case, claiming that it had not been brought at the appropriate time. Furthermore, Greene opined that there was not a viable case against Bush unless or until a majority of Congress demanded that Bush's troop deployments be stopped or reversed. Unless branches of government—in this case the Executive and Legislative branches—arrive at a complete impasse, the Judicial branch should not intervene, Greene continued.

Dellums et al. v. Bush would have been rendered moot even if Judge Greene had sided with the plaintiffs in the case. Indeed, in early January when armed confrontation with Iraq appeared almost certain, the Bush administration sought a vote on the use of military force by the U.S. Congress. It specifically requested an up or down vote by both the Senate and the House of Representatives, which is essentially what Dellums and his coplaintiffs had demanded in the lawsuit. Fearful of fighting a large war far from American shores with no congressional authorization, Bush gambled that he had amassed enough support to request—and obtain—an authorization to wage war against Iraq if necessary. On January 12, 1991, the U.S. Senate gave its authorization in a 52 to 47 vote; the House voted 250 to 183 in favor of authorization. Four days later, on January 16, Operation DESERT STORM began. The case set precedents that were used again in the 1990s when the William Jefferson Clinton administration took action in Bosnia and after September 11, 2001, when the George W. Bush administration sought approval for Operation IRAQI FREEDOM.

PAUL G. PIERPAOLI JR.

See also

Bush, George Herbert Walker; DESERT SHIELD, Operation; DESERT STORM, Operation; United States Congress and the Iraq War; United States Congress and the Persian Gulf War

References

Graff, Henry Franklin. *The Presidents: A Reference History.* New York: Macmillan, 1997.

Sheffer, Martin S. *The Judicial Development of Presidential War Powers.* Westport, CT: Praeger, 1999.

Delta Force

U.S. Army counterterrorism unit. The 1st Special Forces Operational Detachment–Delta (Airborne), officially known as the Combat Applications Group (CAG) and known commonly to the general public as Delta Force, is a Special Operations force of the U.S. Army Special Operations Command (USASOC).

Although the force has diverse capabilities, Delta Force's main task is counterterrorism. Delta Force is widely known for its activities during Operations DESERT SHIELD and DESERT STORM in the Persian Gulf War (1990–1991), Operation RESTORE HOPE (1993) in Somalia, Operation ENDURING FREEDOM (2001), and the U.S.-led Iraqi invasion in March 2003 (Operation IRAQI FREEDOM). It is modeled on other elite counterterrorism forces worldwide, such as the British Special Air Service (SAS), the Australian Special Air Service Regiment (SASR), the Israeli Sayeret Matkal, and Germany's GSG-9.

Delta Force was established in 1977 in response to numerous terrorist incidents that had occurred in the 1970s. Its first commander was Colonel Charles Beckwith. From its inception, Delta Force was heavily influenced by the British SAS, a result of Colonel Beckwith's one-year-long exchange tour with that unit.

The force is organized into three operating squadrons (A, B, and C), which are subdivided into small groups known as troops. Each troop specializes in either HALO (high-altitude low-opening parachute insertion), HAHO (high-altitude high-opening parachute insertion), or scuba (self-contained underwater breathing apparatus) insertion. The troops can be further divided into smaller units as needed. Delta Force maintains support units that handle selection and training, logistics, finance, and the unit's medical requirements. Within these units is a vital technical unit responsible for maintaining covert eavesdropping equipment.

The Department of Defense doggedly protects detailed information about Delta Force and publicly refuses to comment on specifics about the unit. Delta Force is able to deploy anywhere in the world with 18 hours' notice. Delta Force capabilities include airborne operations; direct action operations; raids; infiltrating and exfiltrating by sea, air, or land; intelligence collection; recovery of personnel and special equipment; and support of general purpose forces.

Delta Force recruits its members solely from the U.S. Army, usually from the army Special Forces, specifically the Green Berets and Rangers. Headquartered in a remote facility at Fort Bragg, North Carolina, Delta Force's compound holds numerous shooting facilities, both for close-range and longer-range sniping; a dive tank, an Olympic size swimming pool; a climbing wall; and a model of an airliner.

Delta Force operatives are granted an enormous amount of flexibility and autonomy. They do not maintain a general uniformed presence and usually wear civilian clothing while on or off duty at Fort Bragg in order to conceal their identity. Hair styles and facial hair are also allowed to grow to civilian standards to allow for greater anonymity. In addition, Delta Force soldiers carry highly customized weapons. While the unit's weapon of choice is the M4 carbine, operatives often carry foreign weapon systems that are used by the enemy in the area of operation. This allows them to remain inconspicuous and to employ the ammunition from slain enemy fighters if necessary.

While Delta Force specializes in counterterrorism operations, it also engages in hostage rescue. For example, the unit took part in Operation EAGLE CLAW, the failed attempt to rescue the American hostages from the U.S. embassy in Iran in April 1980. The mission failed when a severe sandstorm clogged engine intakes on several U.S. helicopters, forcing them to abort the mission and leaving too few helicopters to successfully complete it. The mission ended in disaster when one of the remaining helicopters and a Lockheed C-130 Hercules transport plane had a midair collision that killed 8 servicemen. After the failure of EAGLE CLAW, the U.S. Army established the 160th Special Operations Aviation Regiment to specialize in the type of air support necessary for special operations.

At the beginning of Operation DESERT STORM in 1991, Delta Force was deployed to the Persian Gulf to serve as bodyguards for senior army officials and to work with British SAS units to search for and destroy mobile Scud missile launchers in Iraq's northern deserts. The primary mission for both the SAS and Delta Force, however, was to locate and designate targets for destruction by coalition warplanes. This contributed immensely to the quick and relatively painless victory of coalition forces in the Persian Gulf War.

Delta Force was also involved in Operation GOTHIC SERPENT in Somalia. That operation led to the Battle of Mogadishu and was later detailed in Mark Bowden's *Black Hawk Down: A Story of*

Modern War (2000). In 2001 the unit also played an important role in overthrowing the Taliban regime in Afghanistan in Operation ENDURING FREEDOM, the U.S. military response to the September 11, 2001, terrorist attacks. Two years later Delta Force played a vital role in Operation IRAQI FREEDOM, the Anglo-American operation to oust Iraqi dictator Saddam Hussein from power. Accompanied by Navy SEALS from DEVGRU (the U.S. Navy Special Warfare Development Group), the unit entered Baghdad in advance of the attack to build networks of informants while eavesdropping on and sabotaging Iraqi communication lines.

CHARLENE T. OVERTURF

See also

DESERT SHIELD, Operation; DESERT STORM, Operation; EAGLE CLAW, Operation; ENDURING FREEDOM, Operation; IRAQI FREEDOM, Operation; Somalia, International Intervention in; United States Army, Afghanistan War; United States Army, Persian Gulf War; United States Army, Iraq War

References

Beckwith, Charlie A., and Donald Knox. *Delta Force: The Army's Elite Counterterrorist Unit.* New York: Avon, 2000.

Bowden, Mark. *Black Hawk Down: A Story of Modern War.* 1st ed. New York: Atlantic Monthly Press, 1999.

Haney, Eric. *Inside Delta Force: The Story of America's Elite Counterterrorist Unit.* New York: Dell, 2003.

Democratization and the Global War on Terror

The link between democratization and the Global War on Terror has been one of the most controversial elements of post–September 11, 2001, U.S. foreign policy. However, democratization has also been a consistent plank of U.S. foreign policy, especially in the Middle East, although more often stated than fully supported. Democratization is the complex process whereby a democracy replaces a nondemocratic political regime or pluralism is increased. Free elections for government control, the participation of a legal opposition or multiple parties, the application of equal rights, and the extension of liberal rules of citizenship and laws are typically considered minimum requirements of democratization. In turn, the term "Global War on Terror" may take either of two meanings. First, it may refer to a general state of conflict against violent radicalism, broadly defined. In this sense, the George W. Bush administration contends that democratization is the key to winning the Global War on Terror, especially in the Middle East. Second, the term "Global War on Terror" may refer to a bundle of unilateralist and often forceful security strategies initiated by the United States after the September 11 terror attacks. This interpretation of the Global War on Terror is also closely associated with an assertive promotion of democracy, including by military imposition, as seen in the U.S.-led invasions of Afghanistan (2001) and Iraq (2003). This entry focuses on the second meaning of the term "Global War on Terror."

The notion that democratization enhances national and global security is deeply rooted in the study of international relations as well as U.S. foreign policy. The liberal (sometimes called idealist) approach to international relations views nondemocratic governments as a primary cause of war. Eighteenth-century German philosopher Immanuel Kant proposed that "perpetual peace" requires an alliance of liberal states. Such governments, he reasoned, need the consent of citizens who are averse to the risks of war. In 1917 President Woodrow Wilson justified the U.S. intervention in World War I by condemning traditional balance-of-power politics as the undemocratic "old and evil order" that pushed nations toward war. Future world peace, Wilson asserted, must be founded upon political liberty. When he spelled out U.S. war aims in his Fourteen Points speech of January 8, 1918, Wilson made an international organization of nations one of them. The representatives at the Paris Peace Conference of 1919 set up the League of Nations called for by Wilson, and its covenant was very much along the lines he proposed. While the U.S. Senate failed to ratify the treaty that would have brought U.S. membership in the League of Nations—and indeed the United States never joined that organization—liberal Wilsonian internationalism continues to influence U.S. foreign policy. President Franklin Roosevelt was a firm believer in Wilsonian principles and continued this approach. Roosevelt was an ardent champion of the successor to the League of Nations, the United Nations (UN), which came into being after World War II.

In recent years, scholars have turned to historical evidence to test whether or not democracies are indeed more pacific than undemocratic regimes. Proponents of the democratic peace theory argue that similar liberal institutions, cultures, laws, and linked economies make democracies especially unwilling to fight each other. Consequently, Michael Doyle argues that liberal democracies have reached a separate peace among themselves, although they remain insecure and conflict-prone toward nations that are not democratic.

Liberal theorists therefore expect that an increase in the number of democracies will expand existing zones of the democratic peace. Not all agree, however, on the full implications to the world system. For example, John Owen argues that a peaceful union of liberal countries would still need nondemocratic states against which to define themselves.

Many notable scholars, particularly those working in the dominant realist tradition of international relations, vigorously dispute the premises of democratic peace theory. They maintain, for example, that the theory neglects how peace among Western democracies during the Cold War was induced by a shared Soviet threat. Moreover, Edward Mansfield and Jack Snyder conclude that emerging democracies are historically more, not less, war-prone than other states.

Such criticisms aside, democratic peace theory's impact on U.S. policy makers since the 1980s is hard to exaggerate. Proponents, including both Republican and Democratic presidents, presented the 1989 fall of the Berlin Wall, the 1991 collapse of the Soviet Union, and a roughly concurrent rise in the global number of democracies as bellwethers of a freer, more secure international order. Political theorist Francis Fukuyama's famous thesis on the emergence of Western liberal democracy (*The End of History and the Last Man*) as "the final form of government" captured liberalism's optimistic, even triumphal, spirit at the start of the post–Cold War era.

Complicating the picture, however, was the distinctive neoconservative political philosophy that also gained influence in the 1980s, especially within the Republican Party. With the Soviet collapse, neoconservatives contend that the proper role of the United States as the sole remaining superpower is to forge and maintain a benevolent world order. Neoconservatives share liberals' confidence that democracies do not fight each other, but they depart from traditional liberalism by arguing that the United States should shun reliance on international organizations—including the UN, toward which they have much antipathy—in promoting democracy overseas. Rather, the United States should be willing to use unilateral force if necessary to bring democracy to steadfastly nondemocratic states and regions.

Significantly, a public letter from associates of the neoconservative think tank Project for the New American Century urged President William J. Clinton to consider removing Iraqi dictator Saddam Hussein militarily more than three years before the 2001 terror attacks. The 1998 letter was signed by numerous individuals who would go on to occupy top foreign and national security policy posts in the first and second George W. Bush administrations, including Secretary of Defense Donald Rumsfeld, Deputy Secretary of Defense Paul Wolfowitz, Undersecretary of Defense for Policy Douglas Feith, and U.S. representative to the UN John Bolton.

Neoconservative influence became most pronounced after September 11, which the Bush administration framed as an attack on liberal democracy around the world. Shortly after the invasion of Afghanistan, neoconservative speechwriter David J. Frum coined the phrase "Axis of Evil" to describe undemocratic Iran, Iraq, and North Korea for the president's January 2002 State of the Union address. This address was widely seen as setting the stage for further U.S. military action overseas. Other aspects of the Global War on Terror strategy reflect neoconservative precepts, including the Bush Doctrine of preemptive war, the decision to invade Iraq despite strong international and UN opposition, the belief that a lack of democracy in the Middle East fosters terrorism, and the argument that democratization justifies military action.

The ideas of Israeli politician and former Soviet dissident Natan Sharansky also align with neoconservative priorities. In 2005 President Bush praised Sharansky's recent work, which argues that the United States must lead the drive for democratization, as "a great book" that validated his own policies. However, observers note a decline in the more forceful aspects of the administration's prodemocracy rhetoric after Egyptian Islamists made notable gains in

U.S. president George W. Bush delivers his first State of the Union Address to a joint session of Congress at the U.S. Capitol Building in Washington, D.C., on January 29, 2002. In his speech, Bush outlined his plan to fight the war against terrorism and characterized the nations of Iran, Iraq, and North Korea as forming an "Axis of Evil." (AP/Wide World Photos)

2005 parliamentary elections and the armed Hamas movement won the Palestinian parliamentary elections of January 2006.

Policy makers continue to debate both the desirability of an alliance of democracies and the U.S. role in promoting democracy abroad. Critics of the current strategy linking democratization to national security and the Global War on Terror reflect a number of ideological and theoretical approaches and include former Bush administration officials. They can be divided into three major camps, with frequent overlap. One camp emphasizes pragmatism and feasibility. These critics see efforts to propel democracy via military invasion and occupation as unworkable, fed by false analogies to post–World War II Germany and Japan. They may also judge the strategy counterproductive, arguing that it heightens anti-Americanism and hurts the legitimacy of local prodemocracy groups in target countries. A second camp is rooted in ethical or nationalistic concerns. While some critics label the democratization strategy hypocritical in light of close American ties to Saudi Arabia and other undemocratic states, others assert that neoconservatives in the Bush administration have crafted a Global War on

Terror strategy that privileges Israeli over U.S. security concerns. A third camp argues that the Global War on Terror is a veiled and fundamentally antidemocratic attempt to enhance U.S. power in regions rich in important natural resources, such as oil.

The difficulty of installing stable, workable, and effective governments in Afghanistan and Iraq offer a prime example of the problems associated with linking democratization to the Global War on Terror. In nations that have no history of democratic organizations, imposing democracy—even by use of force—is rife with difficulties and contradictions. Furthermore, in nations in which the economic system was either nonexistent (such as Afghanistan) or badly damaged (such as Iraq), the cultivation of democracy is not as important as survival for the great majority of the citizenry. Democracy and widespread poverty and economic and social inequalities do not often go together very well.

RANJIT SINGH

See also

"Axis of Evil"; Bolton, John Robert, II; Bush, George Walker; Bush Doctrine; Failed States and the Global War on Terror; Feith, Douglas; Global War on Terror; Neoconservatism; Rice, Condoleezza; Rumsfeld, Donald Henry; Terrorism; Wolfowitz, Paul Dundes

References

Doyle, Michael W. "Liberalism and World Politics." *American Political Science Review* 80 (December 1986): 1151–1169.

Fukuyama, Francis. *The End of History and the Last Man.* New York: Free Press, 1992.

Kant, Immanuel. *Perpetual Peace, and Other Essays on Politics, History, and Morals.* Translated by Ted Humphrey. Indianapolis: Hackett, 1983.

Mansfield, Edward D., and Jack Snyder. *Electing to Fight: Why Emerging Democracies Go to War.* Cambridge, MA: MIT Press, 2005.

Owen, John M., IV. *Liberal Peace, Liberal War: American Politics and International Security.* Ithaca, NY: Cornell University Press, 1997.

Sharansky, Natan, and Ron Dermer. *The Case for Democracy: The Power of Freedom to Overcome Tyranny and Terror.* New York: PublicAffairs, 2004.

Woodward, Bob. *State of Denial: Bush at War, Part III.* New York: Simon and Schuster, 2006.

Dempsey, Martin E.
Birth Date: 1954

U.S. Army general and acting commander of the U.S. Central Command (CENTCOM) during March–December 2008. Born in 1954, Martin E. Dempsey began his army career when he was commissioned a second lieutenant upon graduation from the United States Military Academy, West Point, in June 1974. His first posting, from June 1975 to June 1978, was as a scout and platoon leader in the 2nd Armored Cavalry Regiment. In August 1982 Dempsey earned an MA degree in English from Duke University, and in 1984 he returned to West Point to teach English. After earning a master's degree in military art and science in 1988 from the Command and General Staff College (Fort Leavenworth,

Kansas), Dempsey served as a battalion executive officer in the 3rd Armored Division in Friedburg, Germany. As operations officer and then executive officer for the 3rd Brigade, he deployed with the 3rd Armored Division to Saudi Arabia in Operations DESERT SHIELD and DESERT STORM (1990–1991).

In 1993 Dempsey was assigned as chief of the Armor Branch at the U.S. Total Army Personnel Command in Arlington, Virginia. He then earned another master's degree, in national security and strategic studies, at the National War College in Washington, D.C., in 1995, the same year he was promoted to colonel. The next year Dempsey took command of the 3rd Armored Cavalry Regiment at Fort Carson, Colorado. He has served in numerous leadership positions at all levels, including assistant deputy director for Politico-Military Affairs Europe and Africa J5. From July 1998 to September 2001 he was a special assistant to the chairman of the Joint Chiefs of Staff (JCS) in Washington, D.C.

In 2001 Dempsey was promoted to brigadier general, and from September 2001 to June 2003 he served in Riyadh, Saudi Arabia, as a program manager and headed a U.S. effort to modernize the elite Saudi force assigned to protect the kingdom's royal family. From June 2003 to July 2005 Dempsey commanded the 1st Armored Division, and from June 2003 to July 2004 he served in Iraq in support of Operation IRAQI FREEDOM. During his time in Iraq he had charge of the Task Force Iron command, consisting not only of the 1st Armored Division but also, attached to it, the 2nd Armored Cavalry Regiment and a brigade of the 82nd Airborne Division. It was one of the larger divisional-level commands in the history of the U.S. Army. Dempsey's command tour coincided with the dramatic growth of the Sunni insurgency. He had charge of the Baghdad Area of Operations and received high marks for his handling of a difficult situation.

Dempsey redeployed his division to Germany and completed his command tour in July 2005. From August 2005 until the spring of 2007, he commanded the Multi-National Security Transition Command–Iraq with responsibility for recruitment, training, and equipment of the Iraqi Security Forces. Promoted to lieutenant general on March 27, 2007, Dempsey became deputy commander of CENCTOM at MacDill Air Force Base, Florida. He served in that post until March 28, 2008, when he was named acting commander of CENTCOM, temporarily replacing General David Petraeus. On December 8, 2008, Dempsey was promoted to full (four-star) general and assumed command of the U.S. Army Training and Doctrine Command.

GARY KERLEY

See also

Fallujah; Iraqi Insurgency; Petraeus, David Howell; United States Central Command

References

Ricks, Thomas E. *Fiasco: The American Military Adventure in Iraq.* New York: Penguin, 2006.

Schwartz, Anthony J. "Iraq's Militias: The True Threat to Coalition Success in Iraq." *Parameters* 37(1) (2007): 55–58.

Zelnick, Robert. "Iraq: Last Chance." *Policy Review* 140 (2006): 3–6.

Denmark, Role in Persian Gulf, Afghanistan, and Iraq Wars

North European nation covering 16,639 square miles. Denmark also included the Faroe Islands (540 square miles) and Greenland (839,900 square miles). Denmark proper is bordered by Germany to the south; the remainder is surrounded by the North Sea to the west, north, and east and the Baltic Sea to the southeast. With a 2008 population of 5.485 million people, Denmark is a constitutional monarchy with a parliamentary-style government. The monarch, Queen Margrethe II, who has reigned since 1972, is head of state. The head of government is the prime minister, although that individual undertakes significant executive responsibilities in the name of the queen. Danish politics have largely been dominated by multiparty coalitions, ranging from socialist-oriented parties to rightist conservative parties.

Denmark provided troops, equipment, and diplomatic support for the American-led coalitions during Operations DESERT STORM, ENDURING FREEDOM, and IRAQI FREEDOM. Denmark is generally considered one of the more Atlantic-oriented states of Europe, and the country has a long history of close security cooperation with the United States. Following the August 1990 Iraqi invasion of Kuwait, Denmark provided modest naval assets as part of the Multi-National Force that enforced the United Nations (UN) sanctions against the regime of Saddam Hussein. Denmark subsequently contributed air, naval, and ground forces to the U.S.-led coalition that liberated Kuwait the following year. They numbered about 100 personnel in all. Partially in response to its experiences during the Persian Gulf War and to ensure that Denmark had the capability to quickly deploy forces in future conflicts, in 1995 the Ministry of Defense created a 4,500-member rapid reaction force, the Danish International Brigade. Units of the brigade would subsequently be deployed in peacekeeping operations in the Balkans as well as subsequent conflicts in the Middle East.

Denmark offered a variety of intelligence and security cooperation to the United States after the September 11, 2001, terrorist attacks. Danish air crews were part of the North Atlantic Treaty Organization (NATO) airborne early warning force that was deployed to the United States following the attacks, and a Danish frigate was stationed in the Eastern Mediterranean as part of the NATO naval force that supported the U.S.-led coalition in Afghanistan. During Operation ENDURING FREEDOM, Denmark deployed a small military unit to support operations against the Taliban and Al Qaeda in Afghanistan. In 2002 Denmark dispatched six Lockheed Martin F-16 Fighting Falcons to the region. It also undertook successive deployments of select special operations forces, the Jaegerkorpset, to Afghanistan. Denmark also participated in the NATO-led International Security Assistance Force (ISAF) in Afghanistan. By the end of 2008 Denmark's contribution to the ISAF numbered approximately 700 troops, stationed mainly in Kandahar and Helmand Province. There were also small contingents in Kabul and in Ghowr as part of a provincial reconstruction team. Between 2002 and January 2009, Denmark had lost 21 soldiers killed in Afghanistan.

At the beginning of Operation IRAQI FREEDOM, Denmark dispatched a submarine and a frigate to support the initial invasion of Iraq. Meanwhile, on March 21, 2003, Denmark created Dancon/Irak (Danish Contingent Iraq) for deployment as part of the U.S.-led coalition that invaded and occupied Iraq. The unit was dispatched to Iraq in June 2003. Its peak strength was 545 troops. Dancon/Irak included armored reconnaissance units, a medical detachment, ordnance disposal troops, and various staff and logistics personnel. The Danish troops served six-month deployments and were stationed in the southern areas of Iraq, where they served in the British area of operations. Following the publication of cartoons of the Prophet Muhammad in Danish newspapers, Iraq temporarily broke off relations with Denmark in 2006, although Danish troops continued to serve as part of the international coalition. In August 2007 Dancon/Irak was withdrawn, although Denmark continued to maintain a small contingent of about 50 soldiers in Iraq to protect its embassy and to operate a helicopter reconnaissance unit. Denmark lost 7 soldiers killed in Iraq.

TOM LANSFORD

See also

Afghanistan, Coalition Combat Operations in, 2002–Present; DESERT STORM, Operation; IRAQI FREEDOM, Operation, Coalition Ground Forces; Multi-National Force–Iraq; North Atlantic Treaty Organization in Afghanistan

References

Cockburn, Patrick. *The Occupation: War and Resistance in Iraq.* New York: Verso, 2007.

Feickert, Andrew. *U.S. and Coalition Military Operations in Afghanistan: Issues for Congress.* Washington, DC: Congressional Research Service, 2006.

Keegan, John. *The Iraq War: The Military Offensive, from Victory in 21 Days to the Insurgent Aftermath.* New York: Vintage, 2005.

Deptula, David A.
Birth Date: June 11, 1952

U.S. Air Force officer and one of the chief planners of the Persian Gulf War air campaign, first as a member of Colonel John Warden's Checkmate group and then as part of the U.S. Central Command's (CENTCOM) offensive air campaign planning group, known as the "Black Hole." Born in Dayton, Ohio, on June 11, 1952, David A. Deptula graduated from the University of Virginia with a bachelor's degree in astronomy in 1974 and earned a master's degree from the same institution in systems engineering in 1976. Having been enrolled in the U.S. Air Force ROTC as an undergraduate, Deptula entered the air force and completed flight training in 1977. He ultimately logged more than 3,000 flying hours, including 400 in combat in the Cessna T-37 Tweet, Northrop T-38 Talon, and McDonnell Douglas/Boeing F-15A/B/C/D Eagle. Deptula has been involved in operations, planning, and joint war fighting at unit, major command, service headquarters, and combatant-command levels.

U.S. Air Force lieutenant general David Deptula, deputy chief of staff for intelligence, talks to the press on July 23, 2009, during an unmanned aircraft systems briefing at the Pentagon. (U.S. Department of Defense)

When the Iraqi Army invaded and occupied Kuwait in August 1990, Lieutenant Colonel Deptula was assigned to the staff group supporting U.S. Air Force secretary Donald Rice. After General John Loh, the air force vice chief of staff, directed Colonel Warden to develop an air campaign plan for Central Command commander General H. Norman Schwarzkopf, Warden requested that Deptula be added to the Checkmate group. Deptula had previously worked for Warden and shared many of his airpower concepts.

Working with other like-minded officers, Warden developed the initial air campaign plan, which Warden called INSTANT THUNDER as a counter to the ROLLING THUNDER campaign of the Vietnam War. The plan won approval from both Schwarzkopf and Joint Chiefs of Staff (JCS) chairman General Colin L. Powell.

General Schwarzkopf then directed Colonel Warden to brief Lieutenant General Charles Horner, the Joint Air Forces Component commander (JFACC) in Riyadh, Saudi Arabia, on the air campaign plan. Warden selected lieutenant colonels Bernard Harvey, Ronald Stanfill, and Deptula to accompany him. When the Checkmate planners presented the INSTANT THUNDER briefing to Horner on August 20 they received a chilly reception, as Horner held to more traditional ideas on airpower employment. Because of these differences, Horner asked Warden to return to Washington but kept with him the three lieutenant colonels, including Deptula, who had accompanied Warden.

These former Checkmate planners now became the core of an offensive air campaign planning group, directed by then-Brigadier General Buster Glosson, formerly the commander of Joint Task Force (JTF) Middle East. Working with Glosson, Deptula guided the air campaign planning, blending the basic ideas of Warden's original plan with more operational reality. In two weeks of intensive efforts, the planning group, soon known as the "Black Hole," had developed the plan that Horner ultimately presented to General Schwarzkopf. Its central concept was to allocate the limited air assets that CENTCOM had available to specific target groups simultaneously and render them unable to function instead of attempting to destroy them, as had been doctrine in the past.

In late December 1990 General Horner created the Directorate of Campaign Plans by combining the former Black Hole with portions of the Central Command's Air Force (CENTAF) Combat Operations Planning Staff that performed D-Day defensive planning in case of an Iraqi offensive, the Air Tasking Order (ATO) staff that prepared the daily training ATO, and the Airborne

Combat Element (ACE) staff that manned the Airborne Warning and Control System (AWACS) aircraft. The new organization had three elements: the Guidance, Apportionment, and Tasking (GAT) Division; the ATO Division; and the ACE Division. The GAT Division consisted of the Kuwait theater of operations, the Iraq (strategic), and the electronic combat, Scud, nuclear, biological, and chemical planning cells.

Working within the GAT Division, Deptula reviewed, selected, and assembled the completed targeting recommendations into a final Master Attack Plan (MAP). Deptula then reviewed the MAP with General Glosson and handed over the approved MAP to the GAT division night shift, which transcribed the MAP onto target-planning worksheets that, in turn, the ATO Division used to create the daily ATO. When the air campaign began in January 1991, the GAT division became the overseer of last-minute updates to the MAP and ATO to ensure overall execution of the plan. The coalition air campaign was highly effective and was credited with bringing the war to a quick conclusion with few allied casualties.

Following the Persian Gulf War, Deptula graduated from the National War College in 1994. He served as the JTF commander, Operation NORTHERN WATCH (1998–1999) and as director of the Combined Air Operations Center for Operation ENDURING FREEDOM in 2001. He was promoted to brigadier general in September 1999, major general in June 2002, and lieutenant general in October 2005. In December of that same year he became the JFACC for Operation UNIFIED ASSISTANCE, the South Asia tsunami relief effort, and in 2006 he was the standing JFACC for the Pacific Command. Thereafter, he served as commander of the General George C. Kenney Warfighting Headquarters and vice commander, Pacific Air Forces. Currently, Deptula is the deputy chief of staff for Intelligence, Surveillance, and Reconnaissance, Headquarters U.S. Air Force, in Washington, D.C., where he is responsible for formulating policies and plans for and evaluates U.S. Air Force intelligence, surveillance, and reconnaissance capabilities.

ROBERT B. KANE

See also

DESERT STORM, Operation, Coalition Air Campaign; DESERT STORM, Operation, Coalition Air Forces; DESERT STORM, Operation, Planning for; Glosson, Buster C.; Horner, Charles; INSTANT THUNDER, Plan; NORTHERN WATCH, Operation; Schwarzkopf, H. Norman, Jr.; Warden, John Ashley, III

References

Davis, Richard G. *On Target: Organizing and Executing the Strategic Air Campaign against Iraq.* Washington, DC: U.S. Air Force History and Museums Program, 2002.

Jamieson, Perry D. *Lucrative Targets: The U.S. Air Force in the Kuwaiti Theater of Operations.* Washington, DC: U.S. Air Force History and Museums Program, 2001.

Keaney, Thomas A., and Eliot A. Cohen. *Gulf Air Power Survey Summary Report.* Washington, DC: Department of the Air Force, 1993.

Reynolds, Richard T. *Heart of the Storm: The Genesis of the Air Campaign against Iraq.* Montgomery, AL: Air University Press, 1995.

DESERT CROSSING, OPLAN

A plan developed in June 1999 to stabilize Iraq in the event of the death or overthrow of Iraqi president Saddam Hussein. Following the liberation of Kuwait in 1991 during Operation DESERT STORM, the United States adopted a Middle East policy based, in part, on dual containment. Dual containment sought to restrain both further adventurism by Iraq and Iran's exportation of its Islamic fundamentalist revolution. With respect to Iraq, Hussein's actions and threats in the years immediately after the Persian Gulf War prompted the United States and its allies to react at least annually with several options—from low-end shows of force to the four-day intensive bombing campaign of December 1998 known as Operation DESERT FOX. For seven years, the Iraqi part of dual containment consisted of a cycle of provocation and response.

Late in 1998, U.S. National Security Advisor Samuel R. "Sandy" Berger stated in a speech that the United States would eventually remove Hussein from power and would do so with force if necessary. That speech effectively replaced dual containment with a policy of containing Iran while preparing for Iraqi regime change at a time and place of U.S. choosing. Following the speech, commentators and pundits focused on what it meant and how regime change might be accomplished.

The impact on the United States Central Command (CENTCOM) was somewhat different. One of the U.S. regional combatant commands, CENTCOM was responsible for U.S. military peacetime operations as well as combat operations in a geographic area that encompasses most of the Middle East, including Iraq.

In CENTCOM'S daily planning directorate staff meeting following the Berger speech, an epiphany of sorts occurred. The question that the planners believed should have been considered long before was what would happen to Iraq absent Hussein (for any number of reasons, including a coup, an accident, or regime-replacement operations) and consequently what would be the command's responsibilities in a potentially unstable situation. Key concerns were how unstable would Iraq be after two decades of centralized repression and what kind of response would be required to reestablish stability and prevent the potential crisis from spreading beyond Iraq's borders. Thus began a planning effort that resulted in a planning document or operation plan (OPLAN). An OPLAN provides broad concepts of operations versus operational detail. CENTCOM's effort in this regard came to be code-named DESERT CROSSING.

As DESERT CROSSING was developed over the next few months, it became evident that a true interagency response would be required. Intelligence estimates indicated that a post-Hussein Iraq would indeed be highly and dangerously unstable. Probable scenarios included ethnic strife fueled by the emergence of the majority Shia population and disenfranchisement of the ruling but minority Sunnis, retribution against the Sunni Baath Party, and efforts to secure autonomy or even independence by the Kurds in the north. Other possibilities included the emergence of one or more Hussein-like strongmen, interference by outside entities, fierce competition among players within each of the three major Iraqi groups, and the expansion of a separate Kurdish state into Turkey and Iran. Stabilization would require not only military and police forces to provide security but also the application of numerous instruments of international power, including diplomacy; humanitarian, financial, and technical assistance; facilitation of a rational Iraqi political process; and coordination of the contributions that could be made by nongovernmental organizations (NGOs).

While CENTCOM planners could lay down broad concepts, the best product would result from an interagency effort. CENTCOM leaders believed that the most efficient approach would be a two- to three-day tabletop simulation to test the planners' assumptions and concepts. The resulting DESERT CROSSING seminar, held during June 28–30, 1999, brought together senior officials from the State Department, the Defense Department, the National Security Council, the Central Intelligence Agency, and senior officers from the Joint Staff, the CENTOM staff, and the army, navy, air force, and marine commands subordinate to Central Command.

The seminar participants were organized into four groups: two replicated the U.S. interagency process, one represented Iraq, and one represented the international community. The two U.S. groups acted as the principals' committee (cabinet-level officials providing direct advice to the president) and deputies' committee (principals' deputies charged with considering alternative courses of action and making recommendations to the principals). Each of the four groups was presented with information that they would be likely to have in a real-world scenario and was asked to evaluate their options given the ideas contained in the draft OPLAN.

The simulation proved highly successful in developing valuable insights that helped to refine the plan. The key points considered included triggering events that would require U.S. and international intervention; reactions by neighboring states and what should be done about them; the assembling and maintenance of a military coalition; humanitarian concerns involved in an invasion of Iraq; the disposition of the Iraqi military postinvasion; the avoidance of a fragmented Iraq; the synchronization of humanitarian, military, and civilian activities in a postwar environment; and the development of an exit strategy.

The seminar exercise reached the following goals: the end result should be a stable, unified Iraq with effective governance in place and a military capable of defending Iraq's borders but not threatening to Iraq's neighbors; Turkish and Iranian interests must be understood, addressed, and managed, primarily through effective diplomacy; an international coalition would best be built around humanitarian considerations and a stable outcome; NGOs must be included; military and police forces would be required in large numbers to achieve and maintain the long-term broad-based security; and the actual interagency process, in accordance with standing presidential directives, should commence immediately to plan for the eventuality of regime change in Iraq.

OPLAN DESERT CROSSING was modified and refined as a result of the seminar. A planned follow-on seminar did not occur, however, and the revised plan was shelved to be used as a starting point should real-world events dictate an Iraqi invasion or regime change. When Operation IRAQI FREEDOM commenced in March 2003, DESERT CROSSING was largely ignored and was not utilized in the George W. Bush administration's planning.

JOHN F. SIGLER

See also

Berger, Samuel Richard; DESERT FOX, Operation; Hussein, Saddam; IRAQI FREEDOM, Operation; IRAQI FREEDOM, Operation, Planning for; United States, Middle East Policy, 1945–Present; United States Central Command

References

Byman, Daniel, and Matthew C. Waxman. *Confronting Iraq: U.S. Policy and the Use of Force since the Gulf War.* Santa Monica, CA: RAND Corporation, 2002.

Clancy, Tom, with Anthony Zinni and Tony Kolz. *Battle Ready.* New York: Putnam, 2004.

Ricks, Thomas E. *Fiasco: The American Military Adventure in Iraq.* New York: Penguin, 2006.

DESERT FOX, **Operation**
Start Date: December 16, 1998
End Date: December 19, 1998

American and British air campaign against Iraq during December 16–19, 1998, conducted in response to Iraqi resistance to United Nations Special Commission (UNSCOM) weapons inspectors carrying out their duties in searching for weapons of mass destruction (WMDs). The UNSCOM visits were being held under agreements reached at the end of Operation DESERT STORM in 1991.

President William J. (Bill) Clinton ordered the attacks with the objectives of degrading Iraqi development and delivery capabilities of WMDs, limiting the Iraqi ability to threaten neighboring states, and punishing President Saddam Hussein's regime for not supporting the United Nations (UN) inspection requirements. The DESERT FOX strikes occurred within the context of Operations NORTHERN WATCH and SOUTHERN WATCH, which had imposed no-fly zones in Iraq north of the 36th Parallel and south of the 33rd Parallel (originally the 32nd Parallel). These operations began after Operation DESERT STORM in February 1991 and lasted until the commencement of Operation IRAQI FREEDOM in March 2003. U.S. Marine Corps general Anthony Zinni, commander in chief of U.S. Central Command (CENTCOM), planned and commanded Operation DESERT FOX, using U.S. Air Force, U.S. Navy, and U.S. Marine Corps resources as well as assets from the British Royal Air Force.

Operation DESERT FOX consisted of a brief, intense, and highly focused series of strikes against a carefully selected set of 100 targets in Iraq, including sites capable of producing and delivering WMDs, command and control centers, intelligence service and Republican Guard facilities, airfields, components of the integrated air defense system, and a petroleum site associated with illegal exports under the existing UN sanctions.

U.S. Army general Henry H. Shelton, chairman of the Joint Chiefs of Staff, briefs reporters regarding bomb damage assessment of selected Iraqi targets during Operation DESERT FOX, December 1998. (U.S. Department of Defense)

The attack force included 325 sea-launched Tomahawk cruise missiles, 90 conventional air-launched cruise missiles fired from American B-52 bombers, and 600 bomb strikes conducted by B-1 bombers (carrying out their first combat operation) and fighter aircraft flown from aircraft carriers and bases in Kuwait and neighboring Persian Gulf states. Saudi Arabia chose not to support direct combat missions against Iraq, and the French Air Force, which had been participating in the no-fly zone enforcement, also did not participate and subsequently withdrew from the theater.

The strikes were an impressive tactical success, with substantial target damage and no allied aircraft lost. However, the strategic results were less conclusive, and the impact of the strikes was debated until the issue of Iraqi WMDs was resolved by the invasion and occupation of Iraq during Operation IRAQI FREEDOM.

Some critics have charged that the operation was designed by President Clinton as a distraction from the impeachment process stemming from the Monica Lewinsky affair, which was then under way in the U.S. Congress, but no conclusive evidence has been discovered to support such an allegation. Additionally, some analysts believe that the operation was not a strong enough blow to achieve substantial results, and others noted that it created diplomatic challenges for the United States with selected diplomatic partners.

Although Operation DESERT FOX did not force Iraq to resume cooperation with the UNSCOM inspection program, it nonetheless significantly damaged elements of the targeted Iraqi capabilities, and although Saddam Hussein remained highly belligerent in his public comments, the strikes demonstrated American resolve and in general contributed to a strengthened containment of Iraq.

JEROME V. MARTIN

See also

Clinton, William Jefferson; DESERT STORM, Operation; Iraq, History of, 1990–Present; IRAQI FREEDOM, Operation; NORTHERN WATCH, Operation; SOUTHERN WATCH, Operation; United Nations Special Commission; United Nations Weapons Inspectors; United States Central Command; Weapons of Mass Destruction; Zinni, Anthony Charles

References

Byman, Daniel, and Matthew C. Waxman. *Confronting Iraq: U.S. Policy and the Use of Force since the Gulf War.* Santa Monica, CA: RAND Corporation, 2002.

Clancy, Tom, with Anthony Zinni and Tony Kolz. *Battle Ready.* New York: Putnam, 2004.

Cordesman, Anthony H. *The Military Effectiveness of Desert Fox: A Warning about the Limits of the Revolution in Military Affairs and Joint Vision, 2010.* Washington, DC: Center for Strategic and International Studies, 1999.

Ricks, Thomas E. *Fiasco: The American Military Adventure in Iraq.* New York: Penguin, 2006.

DESERT SHIELD, Operation
Start Date: August 1990
End Date: January 1991

Defensive staging operation from August 1990 to January 1991 that served as the vital precursor to Operation DESERT STORM, also known as the 1991 Persian Gulf War. Following the Iran-Iraq War (1980–1988), Iraq found itself in a perilous situation economically and strategically. Iraqi president Saddam Hussein had financed his war by loans on the anticipated revenue from oil production but by 1989 was more than $40 billion in debt to various Western lenders. In the postwar era, concerned by threats from a resurgent Iran and a powerful Israeli military, Hussein continued to expend enormous resources on his armed forces. By 1990 Iraq was hard-pressed financially, with only three months' cash reserves and a domestic inflation rate of almost 50 percent. Neighboring Kuwait and Saudi Arabia were essentially unsympathetic to Hussein's concerns for financial assistance and a downward adjustment in oil production to drive up the price of oil. Kuwait, especially, rebuffed the Iraqi leader's efforts to acquire Bubiyan Island and continued to pump oil from the al-Rumaylah oil field area on the Iraq-Kuwait border. High Kuwaiti oil production was also helping to keep oil prices low, exacerbating Iraqi financial problems. Following unsuccessful diplomatic maneuvering by Egyptian president Hosni Mubarak to diffuse the crisis and receiving mixed signals from the George H. W. Bush administration through U.S. ambassador to Iraq April Glaspie regarding U.S. intentions, Hussein moved his forces to the Kuwait border.

On August 2, 1990, two armored and one mechanized division of the Iraqi Republican Guard Forces Command crossed the border and invaded Kuwait. Simultaneously, Iraqi commando units attacked government installations in Kuwait City by helicopter. After only very limited Kuwaiti resistance, the Iraqis swept across Kuwait and moved toward the Saudi Arabian border.

Incorporating Kuwait as its "19th province," the Iraqi Baathist regime began a systematic program of absorbing the small kingdom's wealth and population. Iraq now controlled or threatened a major portion of the world's supply of oil. The Iraqis appeared to be poised to move militarily farther south against Saudi Arabia. The most likely objectives of such an attack would be the Saudi ports of Jubayl and Dhahran on the coast of the Persian Gulf. A successful strike there would end the kingdom's export of oil from the eastern provinces and directly threaten all oil producers on the Arabian Peninsula. At the very least, Iraq appeared to be able to pressure Saudi Arabia and the other Gulf states regarding oil production. Such a strategic situation was unacceptable to the Bush administration.

The same day of the Iraqi attack, the commander of United States Central Command, General H. Norman Schwarzkopf, briefed President Bush, Secretary of Defense Richard B. Cheney, and chairman of the Joint Chiefs of Staff (JCS) General Colin Powell on military options available to the United States. Bush decided

that if invited by the government of Saudi Arabia, the United States would send troops to the region to defend that kingdom. Three days later, characterizing the Iraqi invasion as "naked aggression" that would not stand unanswered, Bush demanded that Hussein withdraw all of his forces from Iraq.

President Bush also sent a small delegation led by Cheney to confer with King ibn Abd al-Aziz Fahd of Saudi Arabia on a possible response. Shown satellite imagery of Iraqi divisions arrayed along his kingdom's border, King Fahd agreed to receive American forces. His decision set in motion Operation DESERT SHIELD, which had four major objectives: to develop a defensive capability to deter Iraq from attacking Saudi Arabia, to defend Saudi Arabia if deterrence failed, to build a military coalition to participate in regional defense, and to enforce economic sanctions against Iraq as prescribed by the United Nations (UN) Security Council.

Between August 2 and November 29, 1990, the UN Security Council passed 12 separate resolutions concerning the Iraqi invasion of Kuwait. These resolutions, generally passed unanimously or by overwhelming majorities, condemned both the invasion and Iraq's conduct of the occupation. In addition, the resolutions authorized an embargo of most imports to Iraq other than food and humanitarian aid supplies. Finally, Resolution 678 of November 29 authorized UN members to use "all means necessary" to enforce previous resolutions. It became the basis for military operations during Operation DESERT STORM.

Schwarzkopf determined that his first requirement was to deter Hussein from continuing his offensive south. The means of accomplishing this task was to introduce combat forces into the area of operations as quickly as possible. Immediately after the Iraqi invasion, the Defense Department ordered two aircraft carrier battle groups to move to the region, one in the eastern Mediterranean and the other in the Gulf of Oman. Saudi Arabian forces also established a screen line along the kingdom's northern border.

On August 7 U.S. Air Force F-15C fighter aircraft from the 1st Tactical Fighter Wing deployed to Saudi Arabia and began flying combat patrols along the border two days later. As in all DESERT SHIELD military deployments, these were highly publicized. U.S. aircraft departing Langley Field (near Washington, D.C.), landing in Dhahran and other locations in the kingdom, and taking off for combat patrols were constant images on international television. The goal was to impress senior Iraqi Army commanders and lead them to believe that there were more American forces in the region than were actually in place.

Ground forces, led by the 82nd Airborne Division from Fort Bragg, North Carolina, began arriving on August 9. This division had only a limited antitank capability, and soldiers joked that they were "speed bumps" in the path of a determined Iraqi assault. Certainly, there was not enough serious combat power on the ground during those first few weeks to defend the eastern portion of the kingdom. The first heavy ground forces arrived in late August when a brigade of the I Marine Expeditionary Force

Members of the U.S. Army's 82nd Airborne Division watch a CH-47 Chinook helicopter as it touches down during Operation DESERT SHIELD. (U.S. Department of Defense)

was ready for operations in the vicinity of Jubayl. On August 20 the lead units of the 101st Airborne (Airmobile) Division and the 24th Infantry (Mechanized) Division, all under the command of Lieutenant General Gary Luck's XVIII Airborne Corps, began arriving near Dhahran. The arrival of these two army units, with their Apache attack helicopters, M2 Bradley fighting vehicles, and M1A1 Abrams tanks, along with the large quantity of fighter and bomber aircraft in the theater, represented a significant counterweight to Iraqi forces along the border.

An important element of the diplomatic response to the Iraqi invasion of Kuwait was the development of a military coalition willing and able to defend Saudi Arabia. These forces were assigned to two separate major commands, one American and the other Saudi Arabian. Schwarzkopf's Central Command commanded all U.S. forces and had operational control of all military units from the United Kingdom. Saudi lieutenant general Khaled Bin Sultan commanded the Joint Forces Command. This included command of Saudi Arabian military units, operational control of all Arab and Muslim forces in theater, and coordinating authority for French military forces. Schwarzkopf and Sultan managed operations through a coordination and communications integration center in Riyadh. Major coalition forces included the Egyptian

3rd Mechanized Division, the British 7th Armored Brigade, and the Syrian 9th Armored Division. All were in position by December 1990. In addition, more than 30 other nations contributed smaller contingents of ground, naval, and air units as well as large quantities of military and medical supplies.

By the end of October, Schwarzkopf had sufficient forces on hand to decisively defeat and destroy any potential Iraqi invasion. The U.S. Third Army was in place to control American army forces in Saudi Arabia. The XVIII Airborne Corps now had two heavy divisions (24th Mechanized and 1st Cavalry divisions), the 82nd Airborne Division, the 101st Airmobile Division, and the 3rd Armored Cavalry Regiment deployed in a defense in-depth along the eastern flank of the kingdom. The I Marine Expeditionary Force and the British 7th Armored Brigade reinforced these forces along the main avenue of approach toward Jubayl. In the Persian Gulf, the 4th Marine Expeditionary Brigade remained afloat and prepared to reinforce ground operations or conduct amphibious operations. Saudi Arabian mechanized forces acted as a covering force for this powerful force. To the west of the American defensive zone, Lieutenant General Khaled deployed almost five divisions of Saudi, Kuwaiti, Egyptian, and Syrian forces along the Saudi border with Kuwait and Iraq, blocking the avenue of approach along the

Wadi al-Batin. To the far west, the 6th French Light Armored Division protected the coalition's left flank in the Arabian Desert.

At sea, coalition naval units conducted extensive maritime intercept operations. Coalition warships challenged 7,500 merchant ships, carried out 964 boardings, and forced 51 ships to divert. These all but stopped the flow of supplies into Iraq. In the Persian Gulf and the Red Sea, the coalition arrayed an impressive force of combat ships including six aircraft carriers, Aegis missile cruisers, and, for the last time in combat, the battleships *Wisconsin* and *Missouri* with their 16-inch guns and Tomahawk cruise missiles.

In the air, by mid-September 1990 the coalition deployed more than 2,400 aircraft, the bulk of these from the United States. Air units included the U.S. Air Force 4th, 37th and 48th Tactical Fighter Wings as well as several hundred navy and marine aircraft and fighter-bombers from many coalition partners.

As impressive as this assembled combat power was, Hussein seemed unmoved and refused to leave Kuwait. At the beginning of November, the Iraqi Army had committed in the Kuwait area 36 combat divisions of an estimated 400,000–450,000 men, some 4,000 tanks, 3,000 artillery pieces, and 2,800 armored personnel carriers. The Iraqi Army arrayed these forces in a series of defensive sectors along the border and extending in-depth back to the Euphrates River. In the center of the sector, the Republican Guard Forces Command deployed three heavy and several light divisions poised to counterattack any allied thrust into Kuwait. Iraq also possessed some 800 aircraft.

Generals Powell and Schwarzkopf therefore let Secretary Cheney know that they would require significant reinforcement if the president wished to eject the Iraqis from Kuwait. On November 8 President George H. W. Bush notified the world that the United States had decided to array sufficient forces in the Gulf region to wage an offensive campaign. The centerpiece of this reinforcement would be the U.S. VII Corps from Stuttgart, Germany. The 1st and 3rd Armored divisions, the 2nd Armored Division (Forward), and the 2nd Armored Cavalry Regiment from Germany would join the 1st Infantry Division (Mechanized) from the United States in making up the corps' combat power.

The final phase of DESERT SHIELD was the movement of Lieutenant General Frederick M. Franks Jr.'s VII Corps units from Germany and the United States to Saudi Arabia. This was a massive undertaking because this was a heavy corps consisting almost entirely of armored and mechanized infantry forces. For example, each of the armored or mechanized infantry divisions had more than 22,000 soldiers, 1,940 tracked vehicles (such as tanks, infantry fighting vehicles, and self-propelled artillery), and 7,234 wheeled vehicles. Add to these totals the hundreds of helicopters and logistics units at division and corps, and the experience was similar to moving a small American city to a new location 8,000 miles away. Because of the offensive plans developing at Central Command, this entire deployment had to be accomplished in only 90 days.

The transportation figures indicate the scale of this deployment. More than 150 ships delivered a daily average of 4,200 tons of combat equipment and supplies. Civilian-chartered aircraft deposited 25 plane loads of soldiers a day, primarily at King Fahd Airport west of Dhahran. By the end of DESERT SHIELD in January 1991, more than 107,000 VII Corps soldiers and 51,000 vehicles and aircraft had been off-loaded at the ports and moved to a large assembly area in the Arabian Desert, just south of the Kuwait border. By the middle of January, more than 90 percent of VII Corps was in the area of operations. In addition to the American forces, the British, Egyptians, and Syrians contributed additional forces, bringing the coalition's overall military strength to approximately 650,000 men. With that impressive military force, General Schwarzkopf was ready to evict the Iraqi Army from Kuwait. At 2:38 a.m. on January 17, 1991, army Apache helicopters destroyed an Iraqi early warning radar system, initiating Operation DESERT STORM.

Operation DESERT SHIELD was an impressive undertaking. In less than a month after Iraq's invasion of Kuwait, Schwarzkopf had assembled a multinational coalition of land, air, and maritime forces in Southwest Asia robust enough to defeat an invasion by the world's fourth-largest army. With the deployment of VII Corps, the American government, in astounding short order, moved a second army corps into assembly areas and set the conditions for rapid military success of Operation DESERT STORM. It was a dramatic demonstration of the political and military capabilities of the United States at the end of the Cold War.

STEPHEN A. BOURQUE

See also

Bush, George Herbert Walker; Cheney, Richard Bruce; DESERT STORM, Operation; Dhahran; Fahd, King of Saudi Arabia; Hussein, Saddam; Iran-Iraq War; Iraq, Air Force; Iraq, Army; Iraq, History of, Pre-1990; Iraq, History of, 1990–Present; Iraq, Navy; Kuwait; Kuwait, Armed Forces; Powell, Colin Luther; Saudi Arabia; Saudi Arabia, Armed Forces; Schwarzkopf, H. Norman, Jr.; United Nations Security Council Resolution 678; United States, Middle East Policy, 1945–Present; United States Army, Persian Gulf War; United States Coast Guard, Persian Gulf War; United States Marine Corps, Persian Gulf War; United States Navy, Persian Gulf War

References

Bourque, Stephen A. *Jayhawk! The VII Corps in the Persian Gulf War.* Washington, DC: Department of the Army, 2002.
Bush, George, and Brent Scowcroft. *A World Transformed.* New York: Knopf, 1998.
Cordesman, Anthony H., and Abraham R. Wagner. *The Lessons of Modern War,* Vol. 4, *The Gulf War.* Boulder, CO: Westview, 1996.
Franconia, Rick. *Ally to Adversary: An Eyewitness Account of Iraq's Fall from Grace.* Annapolis, MD: Naval Institute Press, 1999.
Freedman, Lawrence, and Efraim Karsh. *The Gulf Conflict, 1990–1991: Diplomacy and War in the New World Order.* Princeton, NJ: Princeton University Press, 1993.
Khalid ibn Sultan, Prince, with Patrick Seale. *Desert Warrior: A Personal View of the Gulf War by the Joint Forces Commander.* New York: HarperCollins, 1995.
Knights, Michael. *Cradle of Conflict: Iraq and the Birth of Modern U.S. Military.* Annapolis, MD: Naval Institute Press, 2005.
Marolda, Edward, and Robert Schneller. *Shield and Sword: The United States Navy and the Persian Gulf War.* Annapolis, MD: U.S. Naval Institute Press, 2001.

Matthews, James K., and Cora J. Holt. *So Many, So Much, So Far, So Fast: United States Transportation Command and Strategic Deployment for Operation Desert Shield/Desert Storm.* Washington, DC: Joint History Office, Office of the Chairman of the Joint Chiefs of Staff and Research Center, United States Transportation Command, 1996.

Menarchik, Douglas. *Powerlift-Getting to Desert Storm: Strategic Transportation and Strategy in the New World Order.* Westport, CT: Praeger, 1993.

Schwarzkopf, H. Norman, with Peter Petre. *It Doesn't Take a Hero: General H. Norman Schwarzkopf, the Autobiography.* New York: Bantam Books, 1993.

United States, Department of Defense. *Conduct of the Persian Gulf War: Final Report to Congress.* Washington, DC: U.S. Government Printing Office, 1992.

DESERT STORM, **Operation**

The combat phase of the 1991 Persian Gulf War, pitting a multinational coalition led by the United States against Iraq. Operation DESERT STORM began on January 17, 1991, and ended on February 28, 1991. It followed on the heels of Operation DESERT SHIELD, a defensive and staging operation that began on August 7, 1990. The primary objective of DESERT STORM was to liberate the emirate of Kuwait, which had been invaded by Iraq on August 2, 1990.

This was the first major conflict of the post–Cold War era. As such, it showcased U.S. technical and military superiority. It also marked the end of the so-called Vietnam Syndrome in the United States, whereby the United States had been reluctant to commit troops in a foreign conflict.

From August 1990, the United States and its allies steadily built up their military assets in the Middle East. On November 8, President George H. W. Bush announced that he would increase the number of forces to enable an offensive capability. On November 29 the United Nations (UN) Security Council voted 12 to 2 in favor of Resolution 678 that authorized "all necessary means" to effect an Iraqi withdrawal from Kuwait by January 15, 1991. This provided the legal justification for the use of military force against Iraq after January 15.

On the eve of Operation DESERT STORM, Iraq appeared to have a formidable military machine. It had emerged from the Iran-Iraq War (1980–1988) with the fourth-largest army in the world. Closer inspection, however, clearly gave a considerable advantage to coalition forces. Iraq deployed in the desert facing Saudi Arabia some 36 divisions of 400,000–450,000 men. The Iraqis possessed some 4,000 tanks and 3,000 artillery pieces. On paper, their air force capability seemed impressive also: some 1,000 aircraft and a Soviet-style integrated air defense system that included 7,000 antiaircraft guns and 10,000 antiaircraft missiles. The Iraqis also possessed several hundred Scud intermediary-range ground-to-ground missiles, capable of mounting chemical and biological as well as high-explosive warheads.

But the Iraqi troops were mostly young and relatively untrained conscripts, and much of their equipment was in fact second-rate.

Thus, more than three-quarters of the Iraqi tanks were outdated Soviet T-55 and T-62 types. Even the newer T-72 models were still no match for the U.S. M-1 Abrams or the British Challenger. The T-72's main gun was inaccurate over 4,921 feet (1,500 meters); the U.S. M-1 could bring the Iraqi tanks under accurate fire at twice that range.

Ultimately, the coalition deployed some 650,000 men and women—of whom three-quarters were Americans—in Southwest Asia against Iraq. General H. Norman Schwarzkopf, head of the U.S. Central Command, had command of the U.S. and Western troops, while Saudi Arabia's Lieutenant General Khalid ibn Sultan ibn Abd al-Aziz al-Saud controlled the Arab forces. As of January 17, the coalition had 3,600 tanks and 2,400 aircraft. While the Iraqi Navy consisted of 13 fast-attack boats armed with surface-to-surface missiles and some small motor boats, the coalition boasted 230 ships from 20 nations. The United States alone supplied 6 carrier task forces (*America, John F. Kennedy, Midway, Ranger, Saratoga,* and *Theodore Roosevelt*) and 2 battleship task forces (*Wisconsin* and *Missouri*).

On January 15, 1991, the UN Security Council deadline expired. At 2:38 a.m. on January 17, U.S. Army Apache helicopters destroyed an Iraqi early warning radar system, initiating Operation DESERT STORM. It was the first day of what would be a 38-day aerial bombardment of targets inside Iraq. At the beginning of the war, chairman of the Joint Chiefs of Staff (JCS) General Colin Powell summarized the coalition strategy succinctly, which was "to cut [the Iraqi army] off and . . . to kill it." That meant that there would be two phases to the war. The first phase was defeating the Iraqi military by destroying its command and control centers, military communications, and logistical supplies such as food, fuel, and ammunition. Airpower accomplished the coalition goal.

The second phase consisted of defeating the Iraqi military through direct attacks during the ground campaign. Planners estimated that to accomplish these ends would require 32 days. Iraqi strategy meanwhile was based largely on the Iran-Iraq War experience. For the most part the strategy involved the construction of a network of trenches and berms across Kuwait and Iraq that were

Comparative Cost of America's Wars

War	Cost*
American Revolutionary War	$1.8 billion
War of 1812	$1.2 billion
Mexican-American War	$1.8 billion
Civil War (Union)	$45 billion
Civil War (Confederacy)	$15 billion
Spanish-American War	$6.8 billion
World War I	$253 billion
World War II	$4.1 trillion
Korean War	$320 billion
Vietnam War	$686 billion
Persian Gulf War	$96 billion
Wars in Iraq and Afghanistan (as of May 2009)	$942 billion

* Wars in Iraq and Afghanistan in 2009 dollars; all other wars in 2008 dollars.

designed to slow down any coalition advance. The Iraqis undertook only very limited offensive ground action, the most notable being a spoiling attack against the Saudi town of Khafji, just across the border. It was without major effect.

The first objective of the air campaign was to knock out Iraq's air defenses, especially the radar network and communication grids. The air attack commenced on January 17, and during the first 24 hours of the aerial campaign U.S. B-52 bombers had launched 35 Tomahawk cruise missiles, while U.S. Navy ships launched 106. The 1,300 sorties in the first day of combat equaled two weeks of those flown over Hanoi in North Vietnam during the two-week Christmas bombing campaign in 1972. The United States unleashed most of its impressive air arsenal, particularly the F-117 stealth bomber with radar-defeating characteristics that made it invisible at night. In response, Iraq launched numerous Scud missiles against Saudi Arabia and Israel. Coalition efforts to hunt down and destroy the Scuds were largely unsuccessful. The United States rushed Patriot antimissile batteries to Israel, and these and others in Saudi Arabia scored some kills, although they were not as effective as claimed at the time.

Between January 17 and February 23, the U.S. Air Force flew nearly 1,000 missions a day; the U.S. Navy added another 1,800 total, while the Royal Air Force flew 6,000. Nearly half of these were against Iraqi ground forces, with the loss of only 38 coalition aircraft, the lowest loss rate per sortie of any air combat in history and less than the normal accident rate per sortie in combat training. By the end of the war, coalition airplanes had dropped 88,500 tons of ordnance, of which 6,500 tons were new precision-guided weapons. A quarter of Iraq's electricity-generating capability was destroyed, and half of it was damaged. Night after night B-52s dropped massive bomb loads in attrition warfare; many Iraqi defenders were simply buried alive.

Schwarzkopf also mounted an elaborate deception to convince the Iraqis that the coalition would mount an amphibious assault against Kuwait. This feint pinned down a number of Iraqi divisions. In reality, Schwarzkopf planned a return to large-scale maneuver warfare.

On February 24, with the air campaign having accomplished its ends, the coalition launched the ground assault. Schwarzkopf's plan involved three thrusts. On the far left 200 miles from the coast, XVIII Airborne Corps of the 82nd Airborne Division and the 101st Airborne Division (Airmobile), supplemented by the French 6th Light Armored Division and the U.S. 24th Infantry Division (Mechanized) and 3rd Armored Cavalry Regiment, would swing wide and cut off the Iraqis on the Euphrates from resupply or retreat.

The center assault, the mailed fist of VII Corps, was mounted some 100 miles inland from the coast. It consisted of the heavily armored coalition units: the U.S. 1st and 3rd Armored divisions, 1st Cavalry Division, the 1st Infantry (Mechanized) Division, and the British 1st Armored Division. VII Corps's mission was to thrust deep, engage, and destroy the elite Iraqi Republican Guard divisions.

The third thrust occurred on the Kuwaiti border on the coast. It consisted of the U.S. I Marine Expeditionary Force of two divisions, a brigade from the U.S. 2nd Armored Division, and allied Arab units. It would drive on Kuwait City, with the job of liberating it from the Iraqis.

On February 24 coalition forces executed simultaneous drives along the coast, while the 101st Airborne Division established a position 50 miles behind the border. As the marines moved up the coast toward Kuwait City, they were hit in the flank by Iraqi armor. In the largest tank battle in U.S. Marine Corps history, the marines, supported by coalition airpower, easily defeated this force in a battle that was fought in a surrealist day-into-night atmosphere caused by the smoke of burning oil wells set afire by the retreating Iraqis. As the marines prepared to enter Kuwait City preceded by a light Arab force, Iraqi forces laden with booty fled north in whatever they could steal. Thousands of Iraqi vehicles were caught in the open on Highway 80 from Kuwait City and there were pummeled by air and artillery along what became known as the "highway of death." In the major opening engagement, these divisions came up against an Iraqi rear guard of 300 tanks, covering for the withdrawal north toward Basra of four Republican Guard divisions. The U.S. tankers were able to take the Iraqi armor under fire at twice the effective range for their opponents. The high muzzle velocity of the M1s enabled them to destroy the Iraqi tanks well beyond the range at which they could engage their opponents. In perhaps the most lopsided massed tank battle in history, the Iraqi force was wiped out at a cost of only one American dead.

Lieutenant General Frederick Franks Jr., commander of VII Corps to the west, enraged General Schwarzkopf by insisting on halting on the night of the February 24 and concentrating his forces rather than risk an advance through a battlefield littered with debris and unexploded ordnance and the possibility of casualties from friendly fire. When VII Corps resumed the advance early on February 25, its problem was not the Iraqis but rather an adequate supply of fuel; the M1s needed to be refueled every eight to nine hours.

The afternoon of February 27 saw VII Corps engaged in some of its most intense combat. Hoping to delay the coalition advance, an armored brigade of the Iraqi Medina Republican Guard Division established a six-mile-long skirmish line on the reverse slope of a low hill, digging in their T-55 and T-72 tanks there. The advancing 2nd Brigade of the 1st Armored Division came over a ridge, spotted the Iraqis, and took them under fire from 2,500 yards. The American tankers used sabot rounds to blow the turrets off the dug-in Iraqi tanks. The battle was the largest armor engagement of the war. In only 45 minutes, U.S. tanks and aircraft destroyed 60 T-72 tanks, 9 T-55 tanks, and 38 Iraqi armored personnel carriers. As VII Corps closed to the sea, XVIII Corps to its left, which had a much larger distance to travel, raced to reach the fleeing Republican Guards divisions before they could escape the trap to Baghdad.

At this point, before the elite Republican Guards divisions could all be destroyed, President Bush halted the war. Combat ended at

DISPOSITION OF FORCES AFTER THE PERSIAN GULF WAR, MARCH 1991

Black Sea

SOVIET UNION

SOVIET UNION

Caspian Sea

Amu R.

N

40°N

Ankara

T U R K E Y

Incirlik

Nicosia

CYPRUS

Euphrates R.

Kurds and other religious and ethnic groups resist Iraqi government

Arbıl

Mosul

SYRIA

Tigris R.

Kirkuk

Tehran

LEBANON

Mediterranean Sea

Damascus

Beirut

ISRAEL

Amman

Baghdad

I R A Q

Amarah

I R A N

JORDAN

Shabakah

Nasiriyah

Abadan

Ar Ar

Jaliba

Neutral Zone

Kuwait

KUWAIT

PAKISTAN

Cairo

Tabuk

Hafar al-Batin

Persian Gulf

AFGHANISTAN

30°N

E G Y P T

Manama

QATAR

OMAN

Dhahran

BAHRAIN

Doha

Medina

S A U D I

Riyadh

Abu Dhabi

Muscat

A R A B I A

UNITED ARAB EMIRATES

Taif

Mecca

O M A N

20°N

Khamis Mushayt

Red Sea

Nile R.

SUDAN

Khartoum

Sanaa

Y E M E N

Arabian Sea

Blue Nile

White Nile R.

ETHIOPIA

Socotra (YEMEN)

DJIBOUTI

Djibouti

10°N

Addis Ababa

S O M A L I A

UN coalition country

Neutral country

✈ Allied air base

✈ Iraqi air base

40°E

50°E

0   150   300 mi

0   150   300 km

midnight Washington time on February 27 (8:00 a.m., February 28, in the Persian Gulf region). The ground war had lasted only 100 hours. This had a nice ring to it, but Bush had stopped the war because he feared the cost of an assault on Baghdad and also feared that Iraq might then break up into a Kurdish north, a Sunni Muslim center, and Shiite Muslim south. In addition, the president wanted to keep Iraq intact against a resurgent Iran. Powell called continued combat against a beaten foe "un-American."

The war was among the most lopsided in history. Iraq lost 3,700 tanks, more than 1,000 other armored vehicles, and 3,000 artillery pieces. In contrast, the coalition lost 4 tanks, 9 other combat vehicles, and 1 artillery piece. Of 600 M1 Abrams tanks that saw combat, none were penetrated by an enemy round; 3 were struck by depleted uranium shells fired from other M1s, but none of the 3 were permanently disabled, and there were no crew fatalities. This reflected the casualty rate. The coalition sustained combat deaths of only 211 (148 Americans, 47 British, 2 French, and 14 Egyptians), many of these from friendly fire. Iraqi military casualties totaled between 25,000 and 100,000 dead, but the actual figure is unknown. Some 2,278 Iraqi civilians died, hundreds of them in the Amiriyyah civilian air shelter. The coalition also took perhaps 86,000 Iraqis prisoner.

Iraq was allowed to escape with its best Republican Guard troops largely intact. At the time Schwarzkopf declared himself satisfied with the decision. But he also erred in allowing the beaten Iraqis as part of the cease-fire agreement to fly their armed helicopters; this along with other measures enabled the Iraqi government to crush resistance to Hussein's government.

The war was a remarkable renaissance of American military power from the ashes of Vietnam in the mid-1970s. It was an amazingly successful yet also unsatisfying war, for Saddam Hussein still held power in Iraq and remained there for another 12 years until a new war against Iraq was waged in 2003, that one under entirely different circumstances.

DINO E. BUENVIAJE AND SPENCER C. TUCKER

See also

Bush, George Herbert Walker; DESERT SHIELD, Operation; Hussein, Saddam; Iran-Iraq War; Iraq, Air Force; Iraq, Army; Kuwait; Kuwait, Armed Forces; Kuwait, Liberation of; Powell, Colin Luther; Saudi Arabia; Saudi Arabia, Armed Forces; Schwarzkopf, H. Norman, Jr.; United Kingdom; United Kingdom, Air Force, Persian Gulf War; United Kingdom, Army, Persian Gulf War; United Kingdom, Marines, Persian Gulf War; United Kingdom, Navy, Persian Gulf War; United States; United States Air Force, Persian Gulf War; United States Army, Persian Gulf War; United States Marine Corps, Persian Gulf War; United States Navy, Persian Gulf War; Vietnam Syndrome

References

Bin, Alberto, Richard Hill, and Archer Jones. *Desert Storm: A Forgotten War.* Westport, CT: Praeger, 1998.

Bourque, Stephen A. *Jayhawk! The VII Corps in the Persian Gulf War.* Washington, DC: Department of the Army, 2002.

Bush, George, and Brent Scowcroft. *A World Transformed.* New York: Knopf, 1998.

Cordesman, Anthony H., and Abraham R. Wagner. *The Lessons of Modern War,* Vol. 4, *The Gulf War.* Boulder, CO: Westview, 1996.

Francona, Rick. *Ally to Adversary: An Eyewitness Account of Iraq's Fall from Grace.* Annapolis, MD: Naval Institute Press, 1999.

Freedman, Lawrence, and Efraim Karsh. *The Gulf Conflict, 1990–1991: Diplomacy and War in the New World Order.* Princeton, NJ: Princeton University Press, 1993.

Khalid ibn Sultan, Prince, with Patrick Seale. *Desert Warrior: A Personal View of the Gulf War by the Joint Forces Commander.* New York: HarperCollins, 1995.

Knights, Michael. *Cradle of Conflict: Iraq and the Birth of Modern U.S. Military.* Annapolis, MD: Naval Institute Press, 2005.

Marolda, Edward, and Robert Schneller. *Shield and Sword: The United States Navy and the Persian Gulf War.* Annapolis, MD: U.S. Naval Institute Press, 2001.

Matthews, James K., and Cora J. Holt. *So Many, So Much, So Far, So Fast: United States Transportation Command and Strategic Deployment for Operation Desert Shield/Desert Storm.* Washington, DC: Joint History Office, Office of the Chairman of the Joint Chiefs of Staff and Research Center, United States Transportation Command, 1996.

Menarchik, Douglas. *Powerlift-Getting to Desert Storm: Strategic Transportation and Strategy in the New World Order.* Westport, CT: Praeger, 1993.

Pokrant, Marvin. *Desert Storm at Sea: What the Navy Really Did.* Westport, CT: Greenwood, 1999.

Schwarzkopf, H. Norman, with Peter Petre. *It Doesn't Take a Hero: General H. Norman Schwarzkopf, the Autobiography.* New York: Bantam Books, 1993.

United States, Department of Defense. *Conduct of the Persian Gulf War: Final Report to Congress.* Washington, DC: U.S. Government Printing Office, 1992.

DESERT STORM, Operation, Coalition Air Campaign
Start Date: January 17, 1991
End Date: February 25, 1991

Called by British air vice marshal R. A. "Tony" Mason the "apotheosis of twentieth-century airpower," the stunningly successful coalition air campaign prompted many to claim that Operation DESERT STORM may well be the first time in history in which a war was won from the air. As brilliant as subsequent land operations proved to be, the powerful Iraqi forces had already sustained devastating blows delivered by combined air operations of the coalition forces before the ground campaign commenced. This success resulted from both effective planning and skill in execution.

The precise execution of some of the air strikes during the campaign, presented so effectively on television, made it look too easy, almost facile. The public failed to grasp that such expertise was the result of long years of careful effort, superb training, and a brilliant procurement effort that had been under siege for many years.

Following the Iraqi occupation of Kuwait on August 2, 1990, Iraqi president Saddam Hussein rejected demands from the world community that he withdraw his troops. Acting under the authority of United Nations (UN) resolutions, U.S. president George H. W.

A U.S. Navy F-14A Tomcat flies over burning Kuwaiti oil wells during Operation DESERT STORM in February 1991. (U.S. Department of Defense)

Bush then put together a grand coalition, including Arab states, to oust the Iraqi Army from Kuwait by force.

The buildup of U.S. forces there, first to protect Saudi Arabia and then to allow offensive operations against Iraq, known as Operation DESERT SHIELD, began on August 7, 1990. The most visible and immediate measure of support came in the form of airpower when the U.S. Air Force dispatched 48 McDonnell F-15C/D Eagles from Langley Air Force Base, Virginia, to Dhahran, Saudi Arabia. The longest operational fighter deployment in history, this non-stop flight required about 17 hours and seven en route in-flight refuelings. It proved to be the first step in the largest buildup of airpower in the history of the Middle East. By September 2 more than 600 aircraft were in place, buttressed by U.S. Navy and U.S. Marine Corps forces and by the deployed ground forces of Great Britain, France, and the Arab coalition nations. Iraq was effectively ringed by airpower, with two carrier battle groups operating in the Red Sea and four others operating in the Persian Gulf.

Despite this show of force, coalition forces did not arrive in the Persian Gulf with an air war plan in hand. The creation of the plan is still a matter of debate. Briefly, maverick colonel John Warden III, author of *The Air Campaign: Planning for Combat* (1988), was called upon to furnish an air war plan to Lieutenant General Charles A. Horner, commander of both U.S. Central Command (CENTCOM) air forces and the Joint Force Air Component.

Warden and 20 colleagues in the Pentagon put forward what they called INSTANT THUNDER (so-named to signal its difference from the attenuated and ineffective Operation ROLLING THUNDER of the Vietnam War). Horner believed that INSTANT THUNDER was insufficiently detailed. Warden was then sent home, and Brigadier General Buster C. Glosson was ordered to transform the plan into a usable document. Ironically, as developed, the plan followed the broad brush strokes of Warden's ideas.

From Glosson's efforts, aided by Warden's Pentagon group, a new plan emerged from which the daily Air Tasking Order (ATO) could be created. Targets were selected and apportioned to the constituent air elements of the coalition forces, along with recommendations for aircraft types, numbers, and weapons to be used.

Ultimately the air plan called for securing and maintaining air superiority; attacking Iraqi political and military leadership by destroying the command and control networks; severing Iraqi supply lines; destroying all Iraqi chemical, biological, and nuclear capabilities; and destroying the elite Republican Guard units. In essence, the plan required history's most intensive air battlefield preparation prior to a land offensive.

Iraq appeared to be a formidable opponent, with the typical effective Soviet-style integrated air defense system. This latter included almost 1,000 aircraft, many of them flown by pilots with combat experience gained in the war with Iran; 7,000 antiaircraft guns; 16,000 surface-to-air missiles (SAMs); and a surprisingly modern command, control, and communications system.

The United States and its coalition allies possessed a powerful strike force of 2,614 aircraft. The countries represented in the air war and the number of aircraft they supplied were as follows: United States, 1,990; Saudi Arabia, 339; Great Britain, 73; France, 66; Kuwait, 43; Canada, 28; Bahrain; 24; Qatar, 20; United Arab Emirates, 20; Italy, 8; and New Zealand, 3. Of the total, 1,838 were fighters, bombers, or attack aircraft, and 312 were tankers.

Some crucial elements of the strike force were as yet unproven, particularly one of the key aircraft in the developed air plan, the Lockheed F-117A stealth fighter. It had been employed in Operation JUST CAUSE, the U.S. intervention in Panama, without notable success. Furthermore, there was no way of knowing whether or not the Iraqis and their military suppliers had crafted a defense against a stealthy aircraft.

Military operations against Iraq, known as Operation DESERT STORM, commenced on January 17, 1991. To achieve maximum surprise, air operations actually began on the morning of January 16, when seven Boeing B-52Gs departed Barksdale Air Force Base, Louisiana, carrying AGM-86Cs, nonnuclear versions of the cruise missile. These were reinforced by some 100 Tomahawk land-attack missiles (TLAMs) launched by battleships, cruisers, and destroyers stationed in the Red Sea and the Persian Gulf. The missile combination coincided with a stealthy but piloted attack force. The latter consisted first of 10 F-117As, which took off from Khamis Mushayt in southern Saudi Arabia at 12:22 a.m. on January 17. Also in action were the sophisticated U.S. Air Force MH-53J Pave Low and U.S. Army AH-64 Apache helicopters, the latter using their withering firepower in a direct attack on Iraqi early-warning radar systems. The stealth bombers dropped laser-guided bombs to cripple Iraq's air defense system, their success verified by the sudden end of Iraqi television transmissions. A lethal array of bombers, fighters, tankers, electronic warfare aircraft, and Wild Weasels (suppression of enemy air defense aircraft) were soon airborne in an attack that completely overwhelmed Iraqi defenses.

Thus began a savage campaign that devastated Iraqi air defenses and decisively defeated the Iraqi Air Force. The value of the F-117As had been firmly established; these aircraft had not been detected by the Iraqi radar, nor had any succumbed, as statistically they might have, to any one of many antiaircraft shells illuminating the night sky over Baghdad.

The air campaign proceeded flawlessly. Every one of coalition commander General H. Norman Schwarzkopf's requirements and every feature of General Glosson's plan was met. The coalition forces scored 41 air-to-air victories during the war and 2 more in the following month. The United States suffered 35 losses in combat, while coalition forces lost eight aircraft, six of the latter being Royal Air Force Tornados lost in low-level attacks on heavily defended airfields. Twenty-two U.S. aircraft were also lost in noncombat accidents.

Sandstorms proved to be a significant deterrent to air operations, but the single most important factor that distracted planners from executing the air war plan as originally conceived was the emphasis given to the elimination of the Iraqi Scud threat. The Scud was a Soviet-developed tactical ballistic missile widely sold abroad. Iraq possessed some 600 Scuds, and these posed a strategic rather than a tactical threat. The Scud was not accurate but had the great advantage of being easily dispersed, and many were on mobile missile launchers. The principal coalition worry was the certainty of an Iraqi Scud attack on Israel and military response by the Jewish state that would unhinge the coalition. Iraq had carefully surveyed Israel for just such an attack for that exact reason.

The United States applied great pressure on Israel not to intervene in the war, but if Scuds caused significant damage to the Jewish state, it would be difficult for the Israeli government to resist public pressure for retaliation. Iraq fired its first two Scuds against Israel on January 17, followed by seven more the next day. In return for Israeli restraint, the United States supplied U.S. Army Patriot PAC-2 missiles and prepared an intensive Scud hunt that consumed an immense amount of time and resources. Iraq also fired Scuds against Saudi Arabia. Ultimately, the coalition flew some 2,500 sorties against the Scuds and their missile launchers, detracting from the other aerial effort but effectively diminishing the Scud threat so that firings dropped to one or less per day.

The coalition air campaign gutted the fighting strength of the Iraqi forces. In the 43-day war, the coalition flew some 110,000 sorties (a sortie being 1 flight by an individual aircraft). This effort placed an immense demand on aerial refueling capacity, with U.S. Air Force tankers refueling just under 46,000 aircraft (including U.S. Air Force, U.S. Navy, U.S. Marine Corps, and coalition units) and off-loading an incredible 110 million gallons of aviation fuel.

The coalition flew more than 44,000 combat sorties and dropped more than 84,000 tons of bombs. Of this amount, some 7,400 tons changed the shape of warfare, for they were precision-guided munitions (PGMs) with a much greater capability than those that had debuted in the Vietnam War. U.S. Air Force F-117s dropped more than 6,600 tons of PGMs, with U.S. Navy and U.S. Marine Corps aircraft dropping the remainder. Although fewer than 10 percent of the total tonnage expended, PGMs accounted for more than 75 percent of the damage inflicted on key Iraqi

AIR CAMPAIGN DURING THE PERSIAN GULF WAR, JANUARY 17, 1991

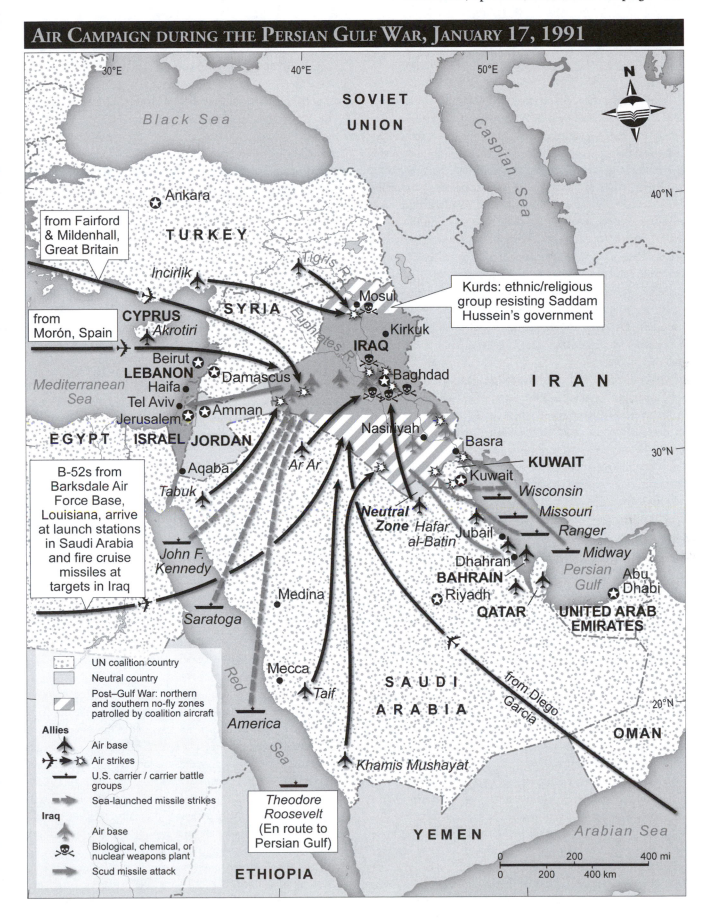

targets. The inventory of PGMs include Paveway bombs and Maverick, Hellfire, Tomahawk, and AGM-86C missiles as well as high-speed antiradiation missiles (HARMs) and a few other missile types.

Interestingly, the very success of the PGM may have sown the seeds of future difficulties in the Persian Gulf. The incredible accuracy of the PGM permitted F-117As to completely dislocate Iraqi command and control capability while inflicting only minor damage on the Iraqi capital. This led to a general perception that the value of the PGM lay not only in its lethality but also in its ability to avoid collateral damage. The PGM made warfare much more refined and much easier on the civilian populace. In the subsequent Iraq War (Operation IRAQI FREEDOM), the even more extensive use of PGMs inflicted decisive damage on Iraq's military capability, but this did not convince the populace that it was—or indeed could be—defeated. The situation was unique in modern warfare. As successful as the air campaign was in destroying the Iraqi electrical grid, fuel economy, and transport system and the Iraqi Air Force, it did not make a lasting impression on Saddam Hussein or the Iraqi people.

Nevertheless, the air campaign had a catastrophic effect upon the Iraqi military's ability to resist. Schwarzkopf had stipulated the requirements for the degradation of Iraqi effectiveness that would be necessary before an attack was begun. He later reported that this had been achieved, for when he made his land attack, intelligence estimates claimed that one-third of the Iraqi divisions were at 50 percent or lower strength, one-third at 50–75 percent, and one-third at full strength.

The considerable Iraqi armored force was decimated by tank plinking by A-10s and helicopters. The Warthog's performance rescued it from retirement and launched an entirely new career in U.S. Air Force service.

On February 24, 1991, the ground campaign began, its key being a massive armor attack on the western flank of the Iraqi Army, with the goal of cutting off and destroying Iraqi Republican Guard divisions in Kuwait. The ground forces were able to accomplish this assembly and execution in complete security, for the Iraqi forces were bereft of airpower, had no insight into coalition action, and were for the most part immobile. American and coalition forces were thus able to achieve a ground victory with only the most minor losses. The decimated Iraqi forces crumbled before the coalition ground offensive, and a cease-fire was granted after only 100 hours of ground warfare.

The great coalition victory was thus accomplished largely as a consequence of airpower's pummeling of the Iraqi Army in the weeks before the ground war began. The U.S. Air Force and U.S. Navy had put together a force of aircraft varying in age from more than 40 years (the B-52) to just a few years (the F-117A). The U.S. Air Force had labored under funding shortages and procurement limits for decades, yet it managed to field an intricate system of satellites, airborne command and control, stealth fighters, air superiority fighters, tankers (also 40 years old), and airlift so as

to create a force that was unbeatable. Much was owed to the crews who operated the weapons. Satellites were tweaked to provide an optimum result for the combat theater. Ancient aircraft reached new reliability standards. Obsolete aircraft such as the Fairchild (later Boeing) A-10, Boeing B-52, and McDonnell Douglas F-4G Wild Weasels suddenly assumed new stature. Both stealth munitions and PGMs proved themselves. All of this effort and its resultant validation prepared the U.S. Air Force for the coming years of almost continuous combat but completely failed to convince the U.S. Congress and the public of the requirement to update aging systems.

WALTER J. BOYNE

See also

Air Defenses in Iraq, Persian Gulf War; DESERT STORM, Operation; DESERT STORM, Operation, Coalition Air Forces; Iraq, Air Force; United Kingdom, Air Force, Persian Gulf War; United States Air Force, Persian Gulf War

References

Boyne, Walter J. *Operation Iraqi Freedom: What Went Right, What Went Wrong and Why.* New York: Forge Books, 2003.

Hallion, Richard P. *Storm over Iraq: Air Power and the Gulf War.* Washington, DC: Smithsonian Institution Press, 1997.

McFarland, Stephen L. *A Concise History of the United States Air Force.* Washington, DC: Air Force History and Museum Program, 1997.

Warden, John A., III. *The Air Campaign: Planning for Combat.* Washington, DC: National Defense University Press, 1988.

DESERT STORM, Operation, Coalition Air Forces

Allied air force components committed to the military effort against Iraqi military forces in the campaign to liberate Kuwait in January and February 1991 (Operation DESERT STORM). The air effort was dominated by the aviation assets of the U.S. Air Force and the U.S. Navy as well as fixed-wing and rotary-wing aviation resources of the U.S. Army and the U.S. Marine Corps. Additional air assets were provided by North Atlantic Treaty Organization (NATO) states and from regional Arab states.

Overall planning and the command and control of coalition air operations for the defense of Saudi Arabia and for the offensive operations against the Iraqi military were led by the commander of U.S. Central Command Air Forces (CENTAF), Lieutenant General Charles A. Horner, who served as the joint air force component commander (JFACC) under U.S. Central Command (CENTCOM) commander in chief General H. Norman Schwarzkopf. The Arab air forces were formally assigned to Saudi lieutenant general Prince Khalid ibn Sultan al-Saud, appointed as the Joint Forces commander by the Saudi government.

The integration of the NATO member forces—from the British Royal Air Force, the French Air Force, the Italian Air Force, and the Royal Canadian Air Force—was facilitated by long-standing shared tactics, techniques, and procedures and extensive training in the European environment as well as by general equipment interoperability based on NATO standards. The integration of regional air forces was also facilitated by established bilateral relationships between the U.S. military and local forces, which included regular exercises. The intense planning, training, and preparation that occurred from the initial deployment of outside forces to Saudi Arabia in the autumn of 1990 to the implementation of Operation DESERT STORM in January 1991 allowed the allies to refine their strategic and operational concepts and ensure a well-coordinated tactical effort.

U.S. airpower was certainly the dominant component of the air campaign against Iraq in 1991. U.S. aircraft flew some 83 percent of the sorties (88 percent of the attack sorties and 66 percent of the air defense sorties) in the operation to free Kuwait from Iraqi control. However, the contributions by other allied air forces were operationally significant and were even more important as symbols of the broad international political support for the coalition.

The United Kingdom provided the largest deployed combat contribution apart from the U.S. forces, including 36 ground attack Tornados, 12 reconnaissance Tornados, 18 air superiority Tornados, 6 Jaguar ground attack aircraft, and 12 Buccaneer attack aircraft that provided laser designation for Tornados using precision-guided weapons. British Royal Air Force aircraft flew 5.1 percent of the combat sorties during the campaign.

The French Air Force provided 12 Mirage 2000 air superiority fighters, 12 Mirage F-1 attack and reconnaissance fighters, and 24 Jaguar ground attack aircraft. Additionally, Italy provided 10 ground attack Tornados, and Canada contributed 18 CF-18 dual-role fighters. The NATO member air forces as well as several other countries also contributed a range of other capabilities, including transport aircraft, helicopters, air refueling tankers, electronic reconnaissance platforms, and maritime patrol aircraft.

The Royal Saudi Air Force (RSAF) provided the largest component of the non-U.S. air forces, having an inventory of 69 F-15C air superiority fighters, 24 air superiority and 24 ground attack Tornados, 87 F-5 attack and reconnaissance fighters, and 24 Hawk attack (and trainer) aircraft. The RSAF also operated 5 E-3 AWACS (Airborne Warning and Control System), which were integrated into the coalition's air defense system. The RSAF flew 6.5 percent of the sorties during the operation. Remnants of the Kuwait Air Force that escaped the Iraq invasion also participated in the liberation campaign, flying 15 Mirage F1s and 20 Skyhawks. Other Arab aircraft available for the defense of Saudi Arabia were provided by the Gulf Cooperation Council states, including 12 F-5s and 12 F-16s from Bahrain, 14 Mirage F1s from Qatar, and 14 Mirage IIIs and 12 Mirage 5s from the United Arab Emirates.

The biggest challenge in the air operation was coordinating and properly integrating the large numbers of aircraft from different countries and services to ensure an effective application of available force and, especially, to ensure that fratricide (shooting down friendly forces) was avoided in the heat of battle. As an example, fratricide concerns caused the coalition to limit the use of the Mirage F1 early in the conflict because the Iraqis also operated that fighter. However, as complete air supremacy was quickly established over the Iraqi Air Force, the Mirage F1s were fully integrated into the air operations.

Coordination was established by the centralized control role of General Horner as the JFACC and the use of a Master Attack Plan and the daily Air Tasking Order (ATO) that detailed all of the planned air missions for each day of combat operations. The coalition air campaign proved to be extremely effective, providing the foundation for the ground offensive and the liberation of Kuwait.

JEROME V. MARTIN

See also

DESERT STORM, Operation; DESERT STORM, Operation, Coalition Air Campaign; Horner, Charles; Saud, Khalid ibn Sultan ibn Abd al-Aziz al-; Schwarzkopf, H. Norman, Jr.

References

Cohen, Eliot A., and Thomas A. Keaney. *Gulf War Air Power Survey: Summary Report.* Washington, DC: United States Department of the Air Force, 1993.

Friedman, Norman. *Desert Victory: The War for Kuwait.* Annapolis, MD: Naval Institute Press, 1991.

Leyden, Andrew. *Gulf War Debriefing Book: An After Action Report.* Grants Pass, OR: Hellgate, 1997.

Morse, Stan, ed. *Gulf Air War Debrief.* Westport, CT: Airtime Publishing, 1991.

Murray, Williamson. *Air War in the Persian Gulf.* Baltimore: Nautical and Aviation Publishing Company of America, 1995.

DESERT STORM, Operation, Coalition Ground Forces

In response to the August 1990 Iraqi invasion and occupation of Kuwait, the United States assembled a 34-nation coalition that ultimately freed Kuwait in Operation DESERT STORM in February 1991. A number of states contributed forces. Overall coalition strength totaled some 956,600 personnel. Precise strength figures are difficult to ascertain for a number of nations, as is breaking these down among land, air, and naval forces. Thus, Saudi Arabia claims on occasion to have committed as many as 100,000 troops to coalition forces, but because it was the principal host country, it is difficult to tell the number of Saudi troops actually taking part in Operations DESERT SHIELD and DESERT STORM.

The United States supplied in its army and marine forces the bulk of the ground strength. Total U.S. strength on February 22, 1991, was 533,608 personnel, with some 333,565 of these in army ground combat forces, chiefly the U.S. VII Corps and XVIII Airborne Corps. The U.S. Central Command, commanded by General H. Norman Schwarzkopf, had overall direction of the war.

U.S. Army general John Yeosock was the U.S. Central Command army ground forces commander (ARCENT). The bulk of his forces were in the XVIII Airborne Corps and VII Corps. The principal components of the XVIII Airborne Corps were the

Coalition forces drive a T-72 main battle tank along a channel cleared of mines during Operation DESERT STORM in 1991. (U.S. Department of Defense)

101st Airborne Division (Air Assault), commanded by Major General Binford Peay; the 82nd Airborne Division under Major General James Johnson; the 24th Infantry Division (Mechanized) under Major General Barry McCaffrey; and the French 6th Light Armored ("Dauget") Division (heavily reinforced), commanded by Brigadier General Bernard Janvier.

VII Corps was commanded by Lieutenant General Frederick M. Franks. Its principal units were the 1st Armored Division, commanded by Major General Ronald H. Griffith, with the 3rd Brigade of the 3rd Infantry Division attached; the 3rd Armored Division, commanded by Major General Paul E. "Butch" Funk; and the 1st Infantry Division (Mechanized), commanded by Major General Thomas Rhame, with the 3rd Brigade of the 2nd Armored Division attached. VII Corps also had the 2nd Armored Cavalry Regiment. Also attached was the United Kingdom's 1st Armoured Division, under Major General Rupert Smith.

Lieutenant General Walter Boomer commanded Marine Forces, Central Command (MARCENT). His forces included the I Marine Expeditionary Force composed of the 1st Marine Division under Major General James M. "Mike" Myatt, the 2nd Marine Division under Major General William Keys, and the 5th Marine Expeditionary Brigade. Attached to the marines to provide additional punch to the mostly M-60 tanks operated by the marines

against the anticipated Iraqi armor threat was Colonel John Sylvester's 1st ("Tiger") Brigade of the U.S. Army 2nd Armored Division. At sea off the Kuwaiti coast as an amphibious threat to pin Iraqi coastal defense forces in place was the II Marine Expeditionary Force (afloat), commanded by Major General Harry W. Jenkins.

The Theater Reserve (or other forces under direct control of Schwarzkopf) included the 1st Armored Division. Deployed with the XVIII Airborne Corps, it was transferred to theater reserve by Schwarzkopf and then was released to control of the VII Corps on February 26, 1991. The U.S. Army 3rd and 5th Special Forces Groups were assigned deep-insertion missions as well as search and rescue for downed pilots.

Saudi Arabia provided the next largest contingent of forces, numbering between 52,000 and 100,000 troops. Saudi lieutenant general Prince Khalid ibn Sultan al-Saud headed the Joint Forces Command of all Arab forces in the war.

Britain contributed 43,000–45,400 troops. Its ground forces were under overall command of Lieutenant General Sir Peter de la Billiére. Britain initially deployed to the Persian Gulf the 7th Armoured Brigade (the "Desert Rats" of World War II fame). Later that deployment was increased to include a full division, designated the 1st Armoured Division, that was formed of different British divisions deployed in Germany. It was equipped with the excellent Challenger 1 main battle tank. The British also brought with them the Warrior infantry fighting vehicle and the Scorpion and Scimitar light fighting vehicles.

Egypt had the next largest contingent: some 33,600–35,000 troops formed into the Egyptian II Corps under the command of Major General Salah Mohamed Attiya Halaby. It consisted of the 3rd Mechanized Division, the 4th Armored Division, and the 1st Ranger Regiment.

French forces numbered some 14,600–18,000 troops. The bulk of these were in the French 6th Light Armored ("Dauget" for the code name the French gave to the entire operation) Division (heavily reinforced), commanded by Brigadier General Bernard Janvier. The French relied on the somewhat outmoded AMX-30 B2 tank and the AMX-10P infantry combat vehicle.

Syria contributed 14,500 troops in its 9th Armored Division and 45th Commando Brigade, but its Soviet equipment presented problems in terms of distinguishing friendly forces from those of the foe. Morocco provided 13,000 troops, Kuwait provided 9,900, Oman provided 6,300, Pakistan provided 4,900–5,500, Canada provided 2,700 (4,500 total in theater), the United Arab Emirates provided 4,300, Qatar provided 2,600, Bangladesh provided 2,200, Australia provided 1,800, and Italy provided 1,200. Smaller numbers still were contributed by the Netherlands (600), Niger (600), Senegal (500), Spain (500), Bahrain (400), Belgium (400), the Republic of Korea (314), Afghanistan (300), Argentina (300), Norway (280), Czechoslovakia (200), Poland (200), the Philippines (200), Denmark (100), and Hungary (50). The aforementioned totals include naval and air units, and many, if not most, of the smaller forces did not see action during the war. Coalition major ground units were situated east to west, as follows. On the far east flank next to the sea was Joint Forces Command–East. Next came the Marine Expeditionary Force of the 1st and 2nd Marine Divisions, 5th Marine Expeditionary Brigade, and the attached U.S. Army's 1st Brigade of the 2nd Armored Division. To its immediate west was the Joint Forces Command–North (even though it was in the west) of additional Arab nation allied forces under bin Sultan's command. Farther west was the U.S. VII Corps, and then came the U.S. XVIII Airborne Corps, with the French taking up blocking positions to prevent any Iraqi force from threatening the coalition left flank.

Coalition ground forces fielded some 3,850 artillery pieces. While the coalition boasted 3,318 tanks, the Iraqis had an estimated 4,500. Yet it soon became apparent during Operation DESERT STORM that Iraqi tanks, even their newest, the Soviet T-72 Ms, were no match for the British Challenger 1 or American M-1 Abrams, which could engage their opponents at far greater range and with deadly accuracy. Modern navigation and night-vision equipment also allowed coalition ground forces to operate anywhere at any time. Morale in the coalition ground forces was far better than among the Iraqis, many of whom had suffered considerable losses during the preceding air campaign and units of which sought to desert at the first opportunity, often led by their commanding

officers. Coalition ground forces not only had superior equipment but were also better trained in its use and were far better led.

SPENCER C. TUCKER

See also

Billiére, Sir Peter Edgar de la; Boomer, Walter; Franks, Frederick Melvin, Jr.; Funk, Paul Edward; Griffith, Ronald Houston; Keys, William Morgan; McCaffrey, Barry Richard; Myatt, James Michael; Peay, Binford James Henry, III; Saud, Khalid ibn Sultan ibn Abd al-Aziz al-; Schwarzkopf, H. Norman, Jr.; Yeosock, John J.

References

Friedman, Norman. *Desert Victory: The War for Kuwait*. Annapolis, MD: Naval Institute Press, 1991.

Office of the Secretary of Defense. *The Conduct of the Persian Gulf War, Final Report to Congress Pursuant to Title V of the Persian Gulf Conflict Supplemental Authorization and Personnel Benefits Act of 1991 (P.L. 102-25)*. Washington, DC: Office of the Secretary of Defense, 1993.

Pollack, Kenneth M. *Arabs at War: Military Effectiveness, 1948–1991*. Lincoln: University of Nebraska Press, 2002.

Ripley, Tim. *Land Power: The Coalition and Iraqi Armies*. London: Osprey Military, 1991.

Scales, Robert H. *Certain Victory: The U.S. Army in the Gulf War*. Washington, DC: Brassey's, 1994.

Schubert, Frank N., and Theresa L. Kraus, eds. *The Whirlwind War: The United States Army in Operations Desert Shield and Desert Storm*. Washington, DC: U.S. Government Printing Office, 1995.

Swain, Richard. *Lucky War: The Third Army in Desert Storm*. Fort Leavenworth, KS: U.S. Army Command and General Staff College Press, 1999.

DESERT STORM, Operation, Coalition Nations' Contributions to

The massive forces readied to expel Iraqi forces from Kuwait during Operation DESERT SHIELD and DESERT STORM numbered 737,000 troops, 190 naval vessels, and 1,800 aircraft. In its broadest definition, coalition forces encompassed 50 nations, each of which contributed military forces, funds, or logistical support. The United States provided the bulk of these resources—532,000 troops, 120 ships, and 1,700 aircraft—but it also was dependent upon and received strong coalition support. Coalition nations other than the United States provided 205,000 troops, 70 warships, 100 aircraft, and 1,200 tanks. In addition, monetary contributions brought the $61.1 billion cost of the war to the United States to a mere $7.2 billion. Other nations also aided the effort. For example, Turkey helped tie down significant Iraqi forces on its border and allowed European forces to use its air bases.

Militarily, the United States drew heavily upon its European allies, with the next largest contributors being the United Kingdom and France. These were significant. Britain, for example, provided 45,000 troops, 9 ships, and 5 fighter squadrons and 18 helicopters. Additionally, British air tankers refueled American aircraft en route to Saudi Arabia. Poland, Czechoslovakia, Sweden, the Netherlands, and Hungary each sent medical teams, while Bulgaria opened its airspace to coalition aircraft. Germany provided $6.5 billion to the coalition while agreeing to take up the slack of defending Western Europe in the transfer of significant U.S. forces from there to the Persian Gulf. While most of the nations assisting the United States were part of the North Atlantic Treaty Organization (NATO), Operation DESERT STORM was not an official NATO action. Luxembourg and Italy placed aircraft in their national airlines in coalition hands to aid in the logistical support of combat forces.

Besides forces arrayed under the United States Central Command (CENTCOM), there was also the Saudi-led Joint Force Command (JFC). It allowed Muslim/Arab nations to join the effort without placing their forces under direct U.S. control. Led by Saudi lieutenant general Khalid ibn Sultan, these forces from 24 nations helped defend Saudi Arabia as well as cover the flanks of the I Marine Expeditionary Force.

Saudi Arabia, fearing further Iraqi aggression, was a no-cost host to coalition forces. It provided 4,800 tents, 20 million meals, 20 million gallons of fuel per day, and bottled water to the entire theater. This was in addition to its contributing $16.8 billion to the coalition. The Royal Saudi Air Force (RSAF) was the second largest in the coalition and flew more than 12,000 sorties. This strong Saudi leadership allowed the Gulf Cooperation Council (Kuwait, Bahrain, Qatar, Oman, and the United Arab Emirates) and other nations such as Syria, Egypt, Morocco, Niger, Senegal, and Pakistan to commit military forces to the fight.

The United Arab Emirates (UAE), like Saudi Arabia, opened its ports and air bases to coalition forces while operating its 50 French-made Mirage jet fighters during the air campaign. In addition, the UAE contributed $4 billion to the coalition. Refugees from Kuwait constituted five brigades, two of which were mechanized. Pakistan sent its 7th Armored Brigade and an infantry battalion, while small Bahrain and Qatar sent 3,500 soldiers and a 7,000-man mechanized task force, respectively.

The African nation of Sierra Leone sent a medical team, while Niger sent a 480-man battalion and Senegal managed an entire infantry battalion. All of these forces were split into the JFC-East and JFC-North Army Corps, which helped cover the marine force that pushed into Kuwait. The JFC-East forces were the first to enter Kuwait City.

One nation conspicuously absent from the coalition was Israel, which was pressured by the United States not to intervene even after Iraqi Scud missiles rained down on the country. An assortment of nations, including Italy, Greece, Norway, Portugal, Argentina, Denmark, and Spain, provided naval ships. Many of these took part in the blockade of Iraq and conducted mine-clearing operations.

Other nations provided monetary support alone. Although the Republic of Korea (South Korea) sent a medical team, its major support came in the form of $355 million to the effort.

Japan practiced checkbook diplomacy. Initially giving $10 billion because constitutional constraints militated against the use of its military forces as part of an aggressive assault, Japan later sent several minesweepers to solidify its commitment. Afghanistan sent 300 mujahideen fighters to assist coalition ground forces in their attacks into Iraq.

ROBERT H. CLEMM

See also

DESERT SHIELD, Operation; DESERT STORM, Operation; Gulf Cooperation Council; September 11 Attacks; United States Central Command

References

Blair, Arthur. *At War in the Gulf.* College Station: Texas A&M University Press, 1992.

Hutchinson, Kevin Don. *Operation Desert Shield/Desert Storm: Chronology and Fact Book.* Westport, CT: Greenwood, 1995.

Summers, Harry. *Persian Gulf War Almanac.* New York: Facts on File, 1995.

DESERT STORM, Operation, Coalition Naval Forces

Multinational naval force that helped prosecute the 1991 Persian Gulf War and that assembled in the Middle East after Iraq invaded Kuwait in August 1990. Both Operation DESERT SHIELD and Operation DESERT STORM utilized coalition naval assets. Although U.S. Navy ships comprised most of the force that supported DESERT STORM and DESERT SHIELD, ships from 23 nations, including Argentina, Australia, Belgium, Canada, Denmark, France, Germany, Greece, Italy, Japan, the Netherlands, Norway, Saudi Arabia, Kuwait, Spain, and the United Kingdom, also contributed naval assets. Altogether, 60 vessels from other coalition nations worked with the U.S. Navy (which utilized some 115 ships) to implement an effective blockade that intercepted thousands of merchant ships, conducted mine countermeasure missions, detected almost two dozen antiship mines, and supported the eventual military ground thrust that routed Iraqi forces.

By January 15, 1991, the deadline imposed by the United Nations (UN) for Iraq to withdraw from Kuwait, U.S. Navy vice admiral Stanley R. Arthur, chief of the Central Command's (CENTCOM) naval forces, controlled an impressive fleet of more than 100 ships from his headquarters onboard the amphibious command ship *Blue Ridge.* The most potent of these were aircraft carriers. The *Saratoga, John F. Kennedy,* and *Midway* were in the theater with their escorts weeks before hostilities commenced, and the *America, Ranger,* and *Theodore Roosevelt* carrier groups joined them in January. The air wings of the six American carriers represented a substantial 20 percent of all coalition aircraft in the theater. The *Saratoga, John F. Kennedy, and America* comprised the core of Battle Force Yankee (also known as Red Sea Battle Force), which operated throughout the conflict in the Red Sea. Some additional ships, including platforms that could fire cruise missiles, were stationed in the eastern Mediterranean Sea.

Battle Force Zulu, operating in the central Persian Gulf, was the largest and most powerful naval fleet. It consisted of the *Ranger,*

Midway, and *Theodore Roosevelt* (and the reassigned *America* by mid-February); the battleships *Missouri* and *Wisconsin;* the *Tarawa* and *Nassau* as the core of an amphibious task force consisting of about 17,000 marines, 141 helicopters, and 25 planes; the Aegis-class cruisers *Bunker Hill* and *Mobile Bay;* and numerous smaller ships that served as escorts, supply ships, and hospital ships. These included ships from the United Kingdom, the Netherlands, Canada, and Australia, placed under the tactical command of U.S. Navy rear admiral Daniel P. March, commander of the force. One of the Royal Navy ships, the *Gloucester,* served with American warships in the van of the fleet. This group screened for possible air, surface, and underwater threats to the capital ships positioned farther south.

The initial missions of the coalition naval forces revolved around securing control of the waters of the Persian Gulf. This included engaging Iraqi warships and attacking oil platforms. For instance, Surface Action Group Alfa, consisting of three American ships and three Kuwaiti fast-attack craft, patrolled the northern areas of the Persian Gulf. British ships carrying helicopters that could be outfitted with air-to-surface weaponry were particularly valuable in this effort. Supporting the air campaign and feigning an attack on the Iraqi forces' flank in Kuwait represented the primary missions of the naval forces within the overall war strategy.

U.S. Navy and U.S. Marine Corps aircraft flew hundreds of sorties against a wide variety of targets once the aerial attacks began on January 17, 1991. Eighteen ships in the theater fired almost 300 Tomahawk cruise missiles at Iraqi targets during the first two weeks of the conflict. As the coalition successfully prosecuted the aerial campaign, the Zulu force moved closer to Iraqi-held territory, and the battleships bombarded coastal areas for the first time in early February. Defending the multinational fleet was a top priority. Within the first month of fighting, 21 American, British, Australian, and Italian ships were tasked partially or fully to a multilayered air defense scheme. Five British minesweepers operated within range of the Iraqis' Silkworm missiles during the first two days of the ground assault, as did the battleship *Missouri* and its three escorts, two of which were also British. In a dramatic turn, the *Gloucester* shot down one of the antiship weapons fired at the fleet. The coalition's naval force also supported the decisive ground campaign, as when the *Wisconsin* shelled areas to support advances by U.S. marines.

MATTHEW J. KROGMAN

See also

Arthur, Stanley; DESERT SHIELD, Operation; DESERT STORM, Operation; United Kingdom, Navy, Persian Gulf War; United States Navy, Persian Gulf War

References

Marolda, Edward, and Robert Schneller. *Shield and Sword: The United States Navy and the Persian Gulf War.* Annapolis, MD: U.S. Naval Institute Press, 2001.

Millett, Allan R., and Peter Maslowski. *For the Common Defense: A Military History of the United States of America.* New York: Free Press, 1994.

Palmer, Michael A. *On Course to Desert Storm: The United States Navy and the Persian Gulf.* Washington, DC: Naval Historical Center, 1992.

Pokrant, Marvin. *Desert Storm at Sea: What the Navy Really Did.* Westport, CT: Greenwood, 1999.

DESERT STORM, **Operation, Ground Operations**
Start Date: February 24, 1991
End Date: February 28, 1991

On August 2, 1990, Iraqi forces invaded Kuwait and speedily overran that small country. When Hussein rejected demands that he recall his troops, the George H. W. Bush administration took action. Washington feared that an unchecked Iraq would threaten Saudi Arabia, which possessed the world's largest oil reserves, and thus could control both the price and flow of oil to the West. Bush, a veteran of World War II, also saw Hussein as a new Adolf Hitler and was determined that there would be no "Munich-like appeasement" of aggression.

On paper, Iraq appeared formidable. Its army numbered more than 950,000 men, and it possessed some 5,500 main battle tanks (MBTs)—of which 1,000 were modern T-72s—along with 6,000 armored personnel carriers (APCs) and about 3,500 artillery pieces. Hussein ultimately deployed 43 divisions to Kuwait, positioning most of them along the border with Saudi Arabia.

In Operation DESERT SHIELD, designed to protect Saudi Arabia and prepare for the liberation of Kuwait, the United States put together an impressive coalition of 34 nations that included Syria, Egypt, and Saudi Arabia as well as Britain, France, and many other states. Altogether, coalition forces grew to 665,000 men and 3,600 tanks plus substantial air and naval assets.

Hussein remained intransigent but also quiescent, allowing the buildup of coalition forces in Saudi Arabia to proceed unimpeded. When the deadline for Iraq to withdraw from Kuwait passed on January 15, 1991, coalition commander U.S. Army general H. Norman Schwarzkopf unleashed Operation DESERT STORM the next day. It began with a massive air offensive, striking targets in Kuwait and throughout Iraq, including Baghdad. In only a few days the coalition had established absolute air supremacy over the battlefield. The air campaign destroyed important Iraqi targets along the Saudi border. Night after night B-52s dropped massive bomb loads in classic attrition warfare; many Iraqi defenders were simply buried alive.

At the same time, Schwarzkopf mounted an elaborate deception to convince the Iraqis that the coalition was planning an amphibious assault against Kuwait. This feint pinned down a number of Iraqi divisions. In reality, Schwarzkopf had planned a return to large-scale maneuver warfare, which tested the U.S. Army's new AirLand Battle concept.

Schwarzkopf's campaign involved three thrusts. On the far left, 200 miles from the coast, the XVIII Airborne Corps of the 82nd Airborne Division and the 101st Airborne Division (Air Assault), supplemented by the French 6th Light Armored Division and the U.S. 24th Infantry Division (Mechanized) and 3rd Armored Cavalry Regiment, were to swing wide and cut off the Iraqis on the Euphrates River, preventing resupply or retreat. The center assault, the mailed fist of VII Corps, was to be mounted some 100 miles inland from the coast. It consisted of the following heavily armored coalition divisions: the U.S. 1st and 3rd Armored divisions, the 1st Cavalry Division, the 1st Infantry (Mechanized) Division, and the British 1st Armored Division. VII Corps's mission was to thrust deep, engage, and then destroy the elite Iraqi Republican Guard divisions. The third and final thrust was to occur on the coast. It consisted of the U.S. I Marine Expeditionary Force of two divisions, a brigade from the U.S. Army 2nd Armored Division, and allied Arab units and was to drive on Kuwait City.

On February 24 coalition forces executed simultaneous drives along the coast, while the 101st Airborne Division established a position 50 miles behind the border. As the marines moved up the coast toward Kuwait City, they were hit in the flank by Iraqi armor. In the largest tank battle in the history of the U.S. Marine Corps, the marines, supported by coalition airpower, easily defeated the Iraqis. The battle was fought in a surrealist day-into-night atmosphere caused by the smoke of oil wells set afire by the retreating Iraqis.

As the marines, preceded by a light Arab force, prepared to enter Kuwait City, Iraqi forces fled north with whatever they could steal. Thousands of vehicles and personnel were caught in the open on Highway 80 from Kuwait City and were pummeled by air and artillery along what became known as the "highway of death." Although media images of the destruction were dramatic, coalition troops found only about 200 Iraqi corpses amid the vehicle wreckage but did round up several thousand Iraqi prisoners hiding nearby in the desert.

The coalition now came up against an Iraqi rear guard of 300 tanks covering the withdrawal north toward Basra of four Republican Guard divisions. In perhaps the most lopsided tank battle in history, the Iraqi force was defeated at a cost of only one American death.

Lieutenant General Frederick Franks Jr., commander of VII Corps to the west, angered Schwarzkopf by insisting on halting on the night of February 24 and concentrating his forces rather than risking an advance through a battlefield littered with debris and unexploded ordnance and the possibility of casualties from friendly fire. When VII Corps resumed the advance early on February 25, its problem was not the Iraqis but rather the supply of fuel; because of the speed of the advance, the M1 Abrams tanks needed to be refueled every eight to nine hours.

The afternoon of February 27 saw VII Corps engaged in some of its most intense combat. Hoping to delay the coalition, an armored brigade of the Medina Republican Guard Division established a six-mile-long skirmish line on the reverse slope of a low hill, digging in their T-55 and T-72 tanks. The advancing 2nd Brigade of the 1st Armored Division came over a ridge, spotted the Iraqis, and took them under fire from 2,500 yards. The American tankers used sabot rounds to blow the turrets off the dug-in Iraqi tanks. The battle was the single-largest armor engagement of the war. In only 45 minutes, U.S. tanks and aircraft destroyed 60 T-72 and 9 T-55 tanks as well as 38 Iraqi armored personnel carriers.

Coalition tanks, especially the M1A1 Abrams and the British Challenger, proved their great superiority over their Soviet counterparts, especially in night fighting. Of 600 M1A1 Abrams that saw combat, not one was penetrated by an enemy round. Conversely, the M1A1's 120-millimeter gun proved lethal to Iraqi MBTs. It could engage the Iraqi armor at 1.86 miles (3,000 meters), twice the Iraqis' effective range, and its superior fire-control system could deliver a first-round hit while on the move. Overall, the coalition maneuver strategy bound up in the AirLand Battle worked to perfection. As VII Corps closed to the sea, XVIII Corps to its left, with a much larger distance to travel, raced to reach the fleeing Republican Guards' divisions before they could escape to Baghdad.

In only 100 hours of ground combat, coalition forces had liberated Kuwait. On February 28 President Bush stopped the war. He feared the cost of an assault on Baghdad and also feared that Iraq might then break up into a Kurdish north, a Sunni Muslim center, and a Shiite Muslim south. Bush wanted to keep Iraq intact to counter a resurgent Iran.

The war was among the most lopsided in history. Iraq lost 3,700 tanks, more than 1,000 other armored vehicles, and 3,000 artillery pieces. In contrast, the coalition lost 4 tanks, 9 other combat vehicles, and 1 artillery piece. In human terms, the coalition sustained 500 casualties (150 dead), many of these from accidents and friendly fire. Iraqi casualties are estimated at between 25,000 and 100,000 dead, but the true figure is unknown. The coalition also took 80,000 Iraqis prisoner. Perhaps an equal number simply deserted.

Following the cease-fire, Saddam Hussein reestablished his authority. In a controversial decision, Schwarzkopf had agreed in the cease-fire terms to permit the Iraqis to fly helicopters. This enabled Hussein to put down revolts against him by the Shiites in the south and the Kurds in the north, at great cost to the civilian population. Hussein also went on to defy United Nations (UN) inspection teams by failing to account for all of his biological and chemical weapons, the so-called weapons of mass destruction (WMDs). Ultimately, President George W. Bush would use the alleged presence of WMDs as an excuse to send U.S. and allied forces to invade and occupy Iraq in another war in March 2003.

SPENCER C. TUCKER

See also
AirLand Battle Doctrine; Bush, George Herbert Walker; DESERT SHIELD, Operation; DESERT STORM, Operation; Franks, Frederick Melvin, Jr.; Hussein, Saddam; Kurds; Kurds, Massacres of; Kuwait, Liberation of; Powell, Colin Luther; Schwarzkopf, H. Norman, Jr.; Weapons of Mass Destruction

A column of Iraqi prisoners captured on February 26, 1991, march to a processing center in Kuwait. A total of 86,743 Iraqis were held by coalition forces as prisoners of war (POWs) as a consequence of Operation DESERT STORM. (AP/Wide World Photos)

References

Dunnigan, James F., and Austin Bay. *From Shield to Storm: High-Tech Weapons, Military Strategy, and Coalition Warfare in the Persian Gulf.* New York: William Morrow, 1992.

Romjue. John L. *American Army Doctrine for the Post–Cold War.* Washington, DC: Military History Office and U.S. Army Training and Doctrine Command, 1997.

Scales, Robert H. *Certain Victory: The U.S. Army in the Gulf War.* Washington, DC: Brassey's, 1994.

Schubert, Frank N., and Theresa L. Kraus, eds. *The Whirlwind War: The United States Army in Operations Desert Shield and Desert Storm.* Washington, DC: U.S. Government Printing Office, 1995.

Schwarzkopf, H. Norman, with Peter Petre. *It Doesn't Take a Hero: General H. Norman Schwarzkopf, the Autobiography.* New York: Bantam Books, 1993.

DESERT STORM, **Operation, Planning for**

On August 2, 1990, Iraqi forces invaded and then occupied neighboring Kuwait. By the beginning of September 1990, some 40,000 U.S. troops had already arrived in the Persian Gulf, a force deemed sufficient to defend Saudi Arabia from potential Iraqi aggression. At that point, American leaders began seriously considering offensive options. President George H. W. Bush and some of his advisers, notably national security adviser General Brent Scowcroft, were growing increasingly skeptical that economic sanctions would compel an Iraqi withdrawal from Kuwait. However, senior U.S. military leaders, including the commander in chief of U.S. Central Command, General H. Norman Schwarzkopf, emphasized that deployments suitable for the defense of Saudi Arabia were ill-suited for offensive operations. Indeed, in the beginning of October when Bush requested a detailed briefing regarding offensive options, U.S. Army planners were unready.

Then and thereafter, the army took the lead in planning a ground offensive. Army briefers described the hastily prepared first plan to Bush and his senior advisers on October 11, 1990. It involved four overlapping phases, beginning with a series of air strikes against Iraqi command and control facilities and culminating with a U.S. corps-sized attack into the teeth of the Iraqi defenses. Scowcroft questioned the wisdom of a frontal assault and wondered why the Iraqis could not be outflanked by a wide envelopment movement. Although this option had always been an obvious choice, only after this meeting did both the Pentagon and Schwarzkopf's staff begin to consider it in detail.

On October 31 Bush convened a meeting of the National Security Council (NSC) to resolve the question of whether or not to continue the buildup of forces in the Middle East. Thereafter, Bush authorized the deployment of more units to the region, including the tank-heavy VII Corps, then based in Europe. The additional ground forces permitted planners to conceive of a two-corps instead of a one-corps offensive. Terrain analysis indicated that a flanking move was feasible, particularly if it took place before seasonal rains began. The favorable weather window was between January 1 and February 15.

To deceive Iraqi intelligence, Schwarzkopf ordered several rehearsals of major amphibious landings designed to convince Iraqi president Saddam Hussein that an amphibious assault against Kuwait was pending. Simultaneously, Pentagon planners seriously considered—but ultimately rejected—offensive operations to be launched from Turkey, Syria, and Jordan.

Meanwhile, army planners drew upon the AirLand Battle doctrine of maneuver warfare, originally developed to confront the Warsaw Pact in Europe, to perfect the ground plan. In its final form, the plan called for attracting Iraqi attention to the east and then launching a deep, wide sweep from the west that would enter southern Iraq and sever the main roads linking Iraq and Kuwait, thus isolating the Iraqi forces in Kuwait. One day before the flanking attack was to begin, the marines and multinational coalition forces were to attack along the coast to pin Iraqi forces in place. However, Schwarzkopf gave U.S. Marine Corps planners considerable freedom to develop their own plan of operations. Initially, the U.S. Marine Corps wanted to conduct an amphibious assault into Kuwait. The next U.S. Marine Corps plan called for an attack in-depth on a one-division front. Late in the planning, the U.S. Marine Corps shifted to an attack along a two-division front. Moreover, U.S. Marine Corps commander Lieutenant General Walter E. Boomer anticipated that the marines would reach Kuwait City within three days from the beginning of the attack. In other words, although no one realized it at the time, the U.S. Marine Corps planned for a breakthrough assault rather than Schwarzkopf's notion of a pinning attack. The net effect of this failure of communication between the two services was to drive the Iraqis rapidly in the direction they needed to move if they were to escape from the projected trap created by the U.S. Army's deep envelopment.

The U.S. Air Force took the lead in developing the air campaign. U.S. Air Force general Charles Horner selected Brigadier General Buster Glosson to develop the air campaign. Glosson and most air force officers were completely convinced that a decapitating strike against Hussein's government would possibly eliminate Hussein and his senior command and certainly prevent him from communicating effectively with his people or his military forces. The air plan took into account powerful Iraqi air defense systems, particularly around Baghdad. Consequently, the initial attack on Baghdad would feature stealth Lockheed F-117 Nighthawk aircraft and Tomahawk cruise missiles fired from U.S. Navy surface ships aimed at Iraqi command and control facilities, including the Baath Party headquarters, the International Communications Center, the Presidential Palace, the Government Control Center, and the Telecommunications Center. Subsequent attacks would target the Iraqi power grid. Meanwhile, U.S. Air Force McDonnell Douglas/Boeing F-15 Eagles would attack stationary Scud missile launchers in western Iraq. U.S. General Dynamics F111 Aardvarks, British- and Saudi-operated Panavia Tornados, and Boeing B-52

Stratofortress bombers would target Iraqi airfields. Air force and navy fighter-bombers and Grumman A-6 Intruders were tasked with attacking Republican Guard positions. Subsequent missions would assault an expanded target list, to include Iraq's military-industrial base, bridges, rail yards, and television transmitters.

Overall, the war plan successfully deceived the Iraqis, with the air assault achieving initial tactical surprise and the disposition of allied ground forces remaining concealed from Iraqi intelligence. However, planners failed to coordinate adequately marine, army, and air force strategy. Consequently, the rapid marine advance toward Kuwait City inadvertently contributed to the escape of Hussein's best formations, his Republican Guards. The survival of the Republican Guards later allowed Hussein to crush Shiite and Kurdish rebels and maintain his hold on power inside Iraq in the immediate aftermath of the war.

JAMES ARNOLD

See also

AirLand Battle Doctrine; Boomer, Walter; DESERT STORM, Operation; Glosson, Buster C.; Horner, Charles; Schwarzkopf, H. Norman, Jr.; Scowcroft, Brent

References

Freedman, Lawrence, and Efraim Karsh. *The Gulf Conflict, 1990–1991: Diplomacy and War in the New World Order.* Princeton, NJ: Princeton University Press, 1993.

Gordon, Michael R., and General Bernard E. Trainor. *The Generals' War: The Inside Story of the Conflict in the Gulf.* New York: Little, Brown, 1995.

Scales, Robert H. *Certain Victory: The U.S. Army in the Gulf War.* Washington, DC: Brassey's, 1994.

DESERT THUNDER I, **Operation**
Event Date: 1998

U.S. plan to deploy more troops and equipment to the Persian Gulf in 1998 to deter Iraqi belligerency and to force Iraq to comply with United Nations (UN) weapons inspectors. In late 1997 Iraq had begun to take aggressive action that threatened to destabilize the region. Worse, Iraq continued to interfere with UN weapons inspection teams. In response, the United States initiated Operation DESERT THUNDER I to increase its military presence during negotiations between the UN and Iraq over its alleged weapons of mass destruction (WMDs) program.

Initially DESERT THUNDER referred to potential military operations against Iraq, but it later became the nomenclature for several troop deployments during 1998. Ultimately there were two main DESERT THUNDER deployments (DESERT THUNDER I and DESERT THUNDER II), with DESERT VIPER designated as the actual strike plan if one were to occur.

Early in 1998, U.S. Central Command (CENTCOM) commenced the dispatch of land, sea, and air assets, including more than 35,000 U.S. and coalition forces, to the Persian Gulf region. Concurrently, General Anthony C. Zinni, CENTCOM commander, established a permanent Coalition Joint Task Force–Kuwait (CJTF-KU) based at Camp Doha, Kuwait, commanded by Lieutenant General Tommy R. Franks, commander of Army Central Command's (ARCENT) Third Army.

Even as these forces took up positions, officials deployed a brigade task force from the 3rd Infantry Division at Fort Stewart, Georgia, to Kuwait. On January 18, 1998, that contingent left Hunter Army Airfield, Georgia, with 4,000 personnel and 2,900 short tons of equipment on 120 aircraft. They landed at Kuwait City International Airport 15 hours later. Having drawn prepositioned equipment, they were in their desert battle positions 48 hours afterward.

By February 28, 1998, 9,000 troops of the CJTF-KU were in fortified positions ready to defend Kuwait. Allies including Argentina, Australia, Canada, the Czech Republic, Hungary, New Zealand, Poland, Romania, the United Kingdom, and Kuwait rounded out the CJTF with liaison teams, aircraft support, special operations elements, chemical and biological units, base defense units, and field medical personnel and facilities.

Offshore in the Persian Gulf, a Maritime Preposition Force waited with equipment sufficient for one army and one marine brigade. Plans called for soldiers and marines to obtain their equipment from the ships near shore and deploy to the front if necessary. In addition, U.S. Navy, U.S. Air Force, and coalition air assets were stationed at ground bases and on aircraft carriers nearby.

During a three-week period in February and March, United States Transportation Command (USTRANSCOM) personnel supported the deployment by flying more than 300 airlift missions and nearly 200 air-refueling missions, transporting 10,000 passengers and 11,000 short tons of cargo. Simultaneously, the U.S. Navy aircraft carrier *George Washington* (CVN-73) arrived in the Gulf to join the carrier *Nimitz* (CVN-68) battle group. Later in the spring, the Forrestal-class *Independence* (CV-62) battle group relieved the *Nimitz,* leaving two carrier battle groups in the region. These Fifth Fleet assets joined coalition ships such as the British carrier *Invincible* (R-05), an antisubmarine warfare carrier, and the *Illustrious* (R-06), an Invincible-class light aircraft carrier, for a total of 50 ships and submarines and 200 naval aircraft.

During February as the 366th Air Expeditionary Wing (AEW) from Mountain Home Air Force Base, Idaho, prepared to deploy to Bahrain, the 347th Air Expeditionary Wing from Moody Air Force Base, Georgia, deployed to Bahrain as the first true Air Expeditionary Wing in the U.S. Air Force. After 120 days in theater, the 347 AEW was replaced by the 366th AEW on April 1, 1998. As this initial deployment wound down, the Third Army ARCENT moved its headquarters to Riyadh, Saudi Arabia, establishing ARCENT-SA. It had moved thousands of troops, civilian technicians, and more than $1 billion of equipment. Members of the 11th Signal Brigade also deployed to the region to provide long-haul communications services to the CJTF headquarters. In addition, 175 soldiers from the 86th and 504th Signal battalions deployed from Fort Huachuca, Arizona, to Riyadh.

During the buildup, UN secretary-general Kofi Annan flew to Baghdad to meet with Iraqi president Saddam Hussein. Annan convinced Hussein to allow uninterrupted weapons inspections. This meant an end to tensions for the time being. In June 1998 the *Independence* battle group returned to Yokosuka, beginning a deliberate drawdown of most of the U.S. forces.

DESERT THUNDER I had been the largest multinational force assembled in the Persian Gulf region since the conclusion of the 1991 Persian Gulf War. It demonstrated allied resolve and an ability to rapidly deploy combat troops when and where needed in short order. If an actual attack had been ordered, it would have been code-named Operation DESERT VIPER.

November 11, 1998, Iraq again refused to allow UN weapons inspections, resulting in the initiation of Operation DESERT THUNDER II. Again, CENTCOM moved its forces into position to initiate strikes into Iraq. During this operation an additional 2,300 troops were deployed, and once more Hussein backed down.

By December 1998, however, continued Iraqi intransigence prompted Operation DESERT FOX, during which allied forces destroyed several important Iraqi facilities during this brief engagement. DESERT FOX reportedly set back the Iraqi ballistic missile program by several years.

WILLIAM P. HEAD

See also

DESERT FOX, Operation; DESERT THUNDER II, Operation; DESERT VIPER, Operation; Franks, Tommy Ray; United Nations Weapons Inspectors

References

Clancy, Tom, with Anthony Zinni and Tony Kolz. *Battle Ready.* New York: Putnam, 2004.

Raduege, Major General Harry D., Jr., USAF, and Lt. Col. Jerry L. Pippins Jr., USAF. "Operation DESERT THUNDER: New Dimensions for C4I in Expeditionary Warfare." In *New Dimensions for C4I in Expeditionary Warfare.* Washington, DC: Chief of Information, Department. of the Navy, 1999.

Woodward, Bob. *Plan of Attack.* New York: Simon and Schuster, 2004.

DESERT THUNDER II, **Operation**
Event Date: 1998

U.S.-led troop buildup begun in November 1998 in the Persian Gulf designed to end Iraqi intransigence regarding United Nations (UN) weapons inspections. Less than three months after the end of Operation DESERT THUNDER I, Iraqi president Saddam Hussein again refused to allow UN weapons inspectors to conduct unhindered inspections of Iraqi weapons development facilities. This refusal to abide by UN Security Council resolutions led to the initiation of Operation DESERT THUNDER II on November 11, 1998. At the direction of the National Command Authorities (NCA), U.S. Central Command (CENTCOM) began the deployment of forces and positioned in-theater assets in expectation of strike operations.

Specifically, DESERT THUNDER II was the U.S. deployment of an additional 2,300 troops to Kuwait, including advance parties from the 3rd Infantry Division and two marine expeditionary units, in mid-November in support of the Central Command Joint Task Force–Kuwait. By November 13, 1998, there were 23,500 troops in the area, including 2,600 soldiers, 14,300 sailors and marines, 5,600 air force personnel, and joint headquarters and other joint units comprising some 1,000 people.

Toward the end of November officials decided to halt the buildup, which left aircraft scattered between the continental United States, the Middle East, and various locations in Europe. The deployment also encountered administrative problems as well as mechanical failures that waylaid a number of aircraft. Eventually, those aircraft that did not reach bases in the Persian Gulf returned to their home stations.

By the beginning of December, senior Defense Department officials reported that there were about 25,000 military personnel in the area. U.S. Air Force personnel had increased to 7,600. Air assets included 267 land and carrier-based aircraft with air-to-air, air-to-ground, dual-role, and support capabilities as well as attack helicopters and fixed-wing gunships.

Other units comprised a cruise missile force, surface warships, a marine expeditionary unit, a Patriot missile battalion, a mechanized battalion task force, and a mix of special operations forces deployed in support of CENTCOM operations. To ensure in-theater force protection, military security personnel were also deployed.

In late November the impact of this second deployment resulted in Iraq's eventual, albeit short-lived, compliance with the UN weapons inspections. After only two weeks, however, the situation worsened again, and between December 16 and 19, 1998, Operation DESERT FOX occurred, during which actual military attacks were carried out. In it U.S. Air Force, U.S. Navy, and U.S. Marine Corps aircraft as well as British Royal Air Force aircraft and Tomahawk cruise missiles were employed against military targets in Iraq. The attacks were designed to force a recalcitrant Iraq to allow the inspection of its weapons research facilities as provided for in UN Security Council Resolution 687, agreed upon at the end of the 1991 Persian Gulf War.

Operation DESERT THUNDER II officially came to an end on December 22, 1998. A number of U.S. Defense Department officials were critical of the reluctance by the William J. Clinton administration to pursue a more aggressive military option in the seemingly endless conflict with the Iraqi dictator. Yet the immense difficulties involved with invading and occupying Iraq would later be revealed during Operation IRAQI FREEDOM.

WILLIAM P. HEAD

See also

DESERT FOX, Operation; DESERT THUNDER II, Operation; United Nations Weapons Inspectors

References

Clancy, Tom, with Anthony Zinni and Tony Kolz. *Battle Ready*. New York: Putnam, 2004.

Raduege, Major General Harry D., Jr., USAF, and Lt. Col. Jerry L. Pippins Jr., USAF. "Operation DESERT THUNDER: New Dimensions for C4I in Expeditionary Warfare." In *New Dimensions for C4I in Expeditionary Warfare*. Washington, DC: Chief of Information, Department. of the Navy, 1999.

DESERT VIPER, **Operation**
Event Date: 1998

Aborted military operation planned against Iraq in late 1998, part of the ongoing effort to coerce Iraq to adhere to arms inspections agreements. Based on Iraqi dictator Saddam Hussein's constant harassment of United Nations (UN) weapons inspectors and his on-again, off-again acceptance of UN resolutions in late 1997, the United States and its key allies deployed sizable forces to the region twice in 1998. The first deployment was code-named Operation DESERT THUNDER I; the second was Operation DESERT THUNDER II. The strike plan against Iraq was designated Operation DESERT VIPER. It should be noted that the Task Force 2-70 Armor After-Action Report also employed the designation Operation DESERT VIPER as the coalition's February 24–March 1, 1991, ground assault into Iraq and southern Kuwait during Operation DESERT STORM. This was not the official name of that operation, however, and there remains only one truly correct DESERT VIPER designation.

General Anthony Zinni, commander in chief of the U.S. Army's Central Command (CENTCOM), had previously asserted that because of Iraq's constant harassment of UN inspectors, the United States planned to bomb what American intelligence determined were the key Iraqi facilities involved in weapons of mass destruction (WMDs) production. For more than a year, from October 1997 to November 1998, Hussein continually interfered with UN inspectors. In response, the United States, supported by some other states, deployed forces to the area to coerce him to live up to his agreements. Each time UN forces came close to attacking, however, Hussein backed down. Both Operation DESERT THUNDER I and Operation DESERT THUNDER II were undertaken in preparation for an actual attack (DESERT VIPER).

The initial 1998 DESERT THUNDER buildup was scheduled to conclude with cruise missile attacks and air strikes directed against Iraq's ballistic missile program and other key military targets. However, on December 19 within eight minutes after the U.S. firing of BGM-109 Tomahawk land-attack missiles (TLAMs) at Iraqi targets, U.S. president Bill Clinton called off the attack upon assurances from Hussein that he would abide by the UN resolutions.

Although the first operation was halted in August, on November 11, 1998, UN inspectors were once again forced out of Iraq, and the United States undertook renewed preparations to launch Tomahawk cruise missiles. DESERT THUNDER II increased the number of forces in preparation for the DESERT VIPER assault. However, only minutes from launch time Hussein once more agreed to terms. The missiles were shut down, and the assigned aircraft returned to base.

DESERT VIPER was never carried out. In mid-November 1998, chairman of the Joint Chiefs of Staff (JCS) General Hugh Shelton expressed his belief that the United States needed to "outfox the fox." The United States would launch the next attack with the forces in theater without the usual buildup. Hussein would thus have no advance warning and no chance to move his WMDs. On December 16 when the UN inspectors were again forced out of Iraq, the Americans initiated a 24-hour attack clock. Only 4 hours after the inspectors landed in Bahrain, coalition cruise missiles and attack aircraft began operations.

As General Zinni recalled, even though the Iraqis "had suspicions that we would hit them when the inspectors walked out, it turns out that the absence of visible preparations for the strike and the approach of Ramadan seems to have lulled them into a lackadaisical approach to their own preparations." Indeed, the Iraqis were caught unprepared.

Coalition forces attacked suspected WMD targets and other weapons development facilities over a three-day span. They bombed command and control centers, communication facilities, and Republican Guard targets. In addition, Third Army again deployed forces to defend Kuwait, and by late December the Joint Task Force in Kuwait numbered more than 6,000 troops.

Officially, the attacks ended on December 19, and DESERT THUNDER ended on December 22. DESERT VIPER ended with it. For a time, Hussein remained more malleable after DESERT THUNDER II was terminated.

WILLIAM H. HEAD

See also

DESERT THUNDER I, Operation; DESERT THUNDER II, Operation

References

Clancy, Tom, with Anthony Zinni and Tony Kolz. *Battle Ready*. New York: Putnam, 2004.

Woodward, Bob. *Plan of Attack*. New York: Simon and Schuster, 2004.

Destroyers, Coalition

Destroyers from other nations joined with the U.S. Navy to serve in the 1991 Persian Gulf War and the ongoing conflicts in Afghanistan and Iraq as well as the wider Global War on Terror. Since early autumn 1990, numerous destroyers and frigates (and some smaller corvettes) from a variety of nations have been patrolling the waters of the greater Middle East as part of task groups, North Atlantic Treaty Organization (NATO) standing forces, antiterrorism units, and even U.S. aircraft carrier battle groups (CVBG). These ships as well as their U.S. Navy counterparts are, for the most part, descendants of early 20th-century torpedo boat destroyers. They are relatively small and fast warships designed to run down and destroy enemy motor torpedo boats that, by the years of World War I, presented a proven threat to capital ships.

Nimble enough to give plausible chase yet also of a size that provided an effective platform for heavier longer-range weapons, torpedo boat destroyers by the mid-20th century had metamorphosed into an indispensable new class of warship called upon to escort convoys, hunt submarines, stand guard around aircraft carriers, and provide additional antiaircraft firepower to task forces centered around cruisers, battleships, and carriers.

By the last three decades of the 20th century, destroyers and frigates in some navies grew in size from the essential World War II standard of a ship approximately 370 feet in length and about 2,200 tons in displacement to the singular dimensions of the U.S. Navy's Kidd class of cruiser-size 1980s missile destroyers, stretching 564 feet in length and displacing up to 9,600 tons at full load.

Among European and other coalition navies, destroyers and frigates did not quite match this level of size expansion, but both types became decidedly larger than their earlier counterparts. Destroyers and frigates came to be less and less differentiated by relative size and instead were differentiated by mission and capabilities. In the Royal Navy, frigates of the Type 22 "Batch 3" group of the Broadsword class of the late 1980s (486 feet, 4,900 tons) were larger than any Royal Navy destroyer type until the new Daring class began to enter service in 2008.

Because of many years of experience with joint operations, standing NATO force exercises, United Nations (UN) deployments, and cooperative humanitarian responses, the navies of the United States and the coalition nations had developed an effective level of interoperability by the time of the Persian Gulf War, and this certainly has been maintained as the protracted operations centered on the wars in Afghanistan and Iraq have progressed. In response to UN Security Council Resolution 665 of August 1990, destroyers and escorts from the coalition navies joined with U.S. Navy units to execute the naval blockade against Iraq. Some 60 coalition warships of different types undertook patrols, interception, and inspection of merchant ships bound to and from Iraq. Representing the navies of Argentina, Australia, Belgium, Canada, Denmark, France, Greece, Italy, the Netherlands, Norway, Spain, and the United Kingdom, these destroyers and frigates became the mainstay of maritime security in the region.

As Operations ENDURING FREEDOM and IRAQI FREEDOM continue, so does the rotation of U.S. and coalition naval units in and out of the theater. Following this paragraph is a representative sampling of the coalition destroyers and escorts participating in Operations DESERT SHIELD, DESERT STORM, ENDURING FREEDOM, and IRAQI FREEDOM as well as in antiterrorism campaigns and the more recent antipiracy initiatives in and around the Middle East. Emblematic of the wider focus necessarily employed since 2001 by the cooperating naval forces in this region was the establishment late in 2002 of three Combined Task Forces (CTF-150, CTF-152, and CTF-158) to ensure maritime security in the waters of the Gulf of Aden, the Gulf of Oman, the Arabian Sea, the Red Sea, the Persian Gulf, and the Indian Ocean. Coming under the command of the U.S. Fifth Fleet and typically operating with a dozen or more destroyer types, a U.S. cruiser, and a replenishment ship, these task forces have come to include escort vessels from Portugal, Turkey, Bahrain, Pakistan, and New Zealand in addition to the familiar core navies of the coalition forces.

A roster sampling summarizing the variety of coalition naval activities involving destroyer types follows:

Argentina: The Argentine Navy deployed the destroyer *Almirante Brown* (D-10) and the frigate *Spiro* (P-43) to the Persian Gulf in late September 1990 for blockade duty until their return to Argentina in April 1991.

Australia: The destroyer *Brisbane* (41) and the frigates *Adelaide* (01), *Sydney* (03), and *Darwin* (04) were very closely integrated with U.S. Navy units during DESERT SHIELD and DESERT STORM. Built in the United States, they were siblings of the U.S. Navy Charles F. Adams class and the Oliver Hazard Perry class, respectively. As such, their defense and communications systems were highly compatible, so both the *Brisbane* and the *Sydney* were tasked in late January 1991 with providing a radar picket and antiaircraft shield for U.S. Battle Group Zulu as it moved deep into the northern Gulf. The Australian naval presence has continued during the Afghanistan War and the Iraq War, including the frigates *Anzac* (F-150), *Arunta* (F-151), *Stuart* (F-153), and *Parramatta* (F-154) in Combined Task Force (CTF) rotations.

Bahrain: The frigate *Sabha* (FFG-90) in 2008 became the flagship of CTF-152.

Belgium: The frigate *Wandelaar* (F-912) served in the Persian Gulf during December 1990 and January 1991.

Brazil: In 2008 the frigate *Greenhalgh* (F-46) became the first Brazilian Navy warship to be integrated into exercises with a U.S. Navy strike group.

Canada: The destroyer *Athabaskan* (DDH-282) and the frigate *Terra Nova* (DD-259) provided logistics coordination in the central Gulf during DESERT SHIELD, and the *Athabaskan* escorted the U.S. mine-damaged cruiser *Princeton* (CG-59) to safety at Bahrain in the midst of hostilities on February 18, 1991. Since 1997, a number of Halifax-class frigates, due to their compatibility, have been integrated into U.S. carrier battle groups operating in the Middle East, including the *Regina* (FFH-334), *Ottawa* (FFH-341), *Calgary* (FFH-335), *Charlottetown* (FFH-339), and *Winnipeg* (FFH-338). In August 2008 the *Iroquois* (DDH-280) and *Calgary* became components of CTF-150.

France: Part of the French naval force clustered around the aircraft carrier *Clemenceau* (R-98); the destroyers *Suffren* (D-602), *Dupleix* (D-641), and *Montcalm* (D-642); and the frigates *Protet* (F-748) and *Commandant Ducuing* (F-795), all operated primarily in the Red Sea during the Persian Gulf War. The frigates *Guepratte* (F-714) and *Commandant Birot* (F-796) have recently operated with CTF-150.

Germany: The frigates *Emden* (F-210), *Koln* (F-211), *Augsburg* (F-213), *Bayern* (F-217), *Mecklenburg-Vorpommern* (F-218), and *Augsburg* (F-213) have been in rotation with others of their type in the Bremen and Brandenburg classes as components of Operation ENDURING FREEDOM.

Greece: The frigates *Psara* (F-454), *Limnos* (F-451), and *Elli* (F-450) have been in rotation during ENDURING FREEDOM in recent years, while *Adrias* (F-459) foiled a pirate skiff attack in the Persian Gulf in October 2002.

India: The destroyer *Delhi* (D-61), with the frigates *Godavari* (F-20) and *Talwar* (F-40), established a presence in 2008 off East Africa and visited area ports. The frigate *Tabar* (F-44) was active in antipiracy patrols in the Gulf of Aden in November 2008.

Italy: The frigates *Orsa* (F-567), *Libeccio* (F-572), *Zeffiro* (F-577), and *Aviere* (F-583) and the corvettes *Minerva* (F-551) and *Sfinge* (F-554) all were deployed in the Persian Gulf War. The *Euro* (F-575) took up Gulf of Aden patrols in 2003, and the destroyer *Luigi Durand de la Penne* (D-560) operated with Standing NATO Maritime Group 2 (SNMG2) off Somalia on antipiracy duty from October 2008.

Japan: In the first Japan Maritime Self-Defense Force (JMSDF) deployment during hostilities since World War II, the Japanese government in 2002 approved the rotating presence of a JMSDF replenishment ship in support of Indian Ocean–based coalition forces. The *Towada* (AOE-422) and *Tokiwa* (AOE-423) were escorted in turn by, among others, the destroyers *Yudachi* (DD-103), *Ikazuchi* (DD-107), *Inazuma* (DD-105), and *Sawakaze* (DDG-170). In November 2007 the *Kirisame* (DD-104), providing logistics support for the *Tokiwa* (AOE-423), received word from Japanese officials that both ships were to be withdrawn from their supporting role in ENDURING FREEDOM.

Netherlands: The frigates *Jacob van Heemskerck* (F-812), *Witte de With* (F-813), *Philips van Almonde* (F-823), and *Pieter Florisz* (F-826) were on hand during the Persian Gulf War; more recently the *De Zeven Provincien* (F-802) and *Evertsen* (F-805) have been in rotation with CTF-150, concentrating on pirate activities around the Horn of Africa.

New Zealand: In 2008 the frigate *Te Mana* (F-111) joined the units of CTF-152 in patrols and exercises in the Persian Gulf.

Pakistan: CTF-150 came under Pakistani command in 2006; the *Shahjahan* (D-186) became the force's flagship. The *Tippu Sultan* (D-185) joined CTF-150 in 2008.

Spain: The frigates *Numancia* (F-83), *Diana* (F-32), *Infanta Cristina* (F-34), *Vencedora* (F-36), *Descubierta* (F-31), and *Cazadora* (F-35) were in the Persian Gulf during DESERT SHIELD and DESERT STORM. The *Victoria* (F-82) patrolled the Gulf of Aden in 2002, and in 2003 the *Navarra* (F-85) became the CTF-150 flagship. The frigate *Juan de Borbon* (F-102) joined Standing NATO Maritime Group 1 (SNMG1) for an unprecedented 2008 foray into the Black Sea.

The French Navy destroyer *Dupleix* and the U.S. Navy destroyer *Preble* in the Arabian Sea, 2007. (U.S. Department of Defense)

United Kingdom: The Type 42 destroyers *Cardiff* (D-108), *York* (D-98), and *Gloucester* (D-96) as well as the Type 22 frigates *Battleaxe* (F-89) and *London* (F-95) and the Leander-class frigate *Jupiter* (F-60) were all on hand in the Persian Gulf War. On February 25, 1991, the *Gloucester*'s Sea Dart air defense system shot down an Iraqi Silkworm missile about to strike the U.S. battleship *Missouri* (BB-63). Among the many Royal Navy assets in rotation during ENDURING FREEDOM and IRAQI FREEDOM have been the destroyers *Liverpool* (D-92), *Edinburgh* (D-97), and *York* (D-98) and the frigates *Portland* (F-79), *Campbeltown* (F-86), *Chatham* (F-87), *Lancaster* (F-229), and *Montrose* (F-236).

GORDON E. HOGG

See also

DESERT STORM, Operation, Coalition Naval Forces; Destroyers, U.S.; ENDURING FREEDOM, Operation, Coalition Naval Forces; IRAQI FREEDOM, Operation, Coalition Naval Forces; North Atlantic Treaty Organization; Standing Naval Force Atlantic

References

Gardiner, Robert, ed. *Warship 1991*. London: Conway Maritime, 1991.

Germond, Basil. *Les Forces Navales Européennes dans la Periode Post-Guerre Froide*. Paris: Harmattan, 2008.

Marolda, Edward, and Robert Schneller. *Shield and Sword: The United States Navy and the Persian Gulf War*. Annapolis, MD: U.S. Naval Institute Press, 2001.

Proceedings of the United States Naval Institute. Annapolis, MD. 1874–. Annual "International Navies" issue (March) 1990–.

Saunders, Stephen, ed. *Jane's Fighting Ships 2008–2009*. Coulsdon, Surrey, UK, and Alexandria, VA: Jane's Information Group, 2008.

Schneller, Robert J., Jr. *Anchor of Resolve: A History of U.S. Naval Forces Central Command/Fifth Fleet*. Washington, DC: Naval Historical Center, 2007.

Sharpe, Richard, ed. *Jane's Fighting Ships: 1991–1992*. London: Jane's Information Group, 1991.

Destroyers, U.S.

Originally known as torpedo boat destroyers and designed to protect the battle fleet against torpedoes, destroyers were utilized in hunting submarines, escorting convoys, and providing gunfire support in amphibious landings. Modern destroyers have grown more versatile to meet the demands of a smaller navy. In the wars in the Middle East, destroyers have routinely launched long-range missiles against targets while guarding against air, surface, and subsurface threats.

As Operation DESERT STORM commenced in January 1991, the Spruance class of 31 warships (6 in theater) served as the backbone of the U.S. Navy's destroyer force. Displacing 9,100 tons and carrying a crew of 30 officers and 352 sailors, these ships had a primary mission of antisubmarine warfare but also provided naval gunfire support as well as antiship and antiair capabilities. Over the years the ships have undergone a variety of upgrades to enhance their effectiveness. Twenty-four Spruance-class destroyers received the installation of a 61-cell vertical launching system (VLS) capable of deploying the Tomahawk land-attack missile (TLAM) and the Harpoon antiship missile with ranges in excess of 700 and 60 nautical miles, respectively. The remaining complement of weapons includes two 5-inch/54 Mark 45 guns, two Mark 32 torpedo tubes, and the vertically launched ASROC (antisubmarine rocket). Twin hangars allow for the maintenance and operation of two LAMPS (Light Airborne Multi-Purpose System) Mark III helicopters outfitted with sonobuoys and torpedoes.

Both a hull-mounted and a towed-array sonar rendered the Spruance class ideal for pursuing submarines. They relied upon the two 20-millimeter (mm) Mark 15 Phalanx close-in weapons systems (CIWS) and the North Atlantic Treaty Organization (NATO) Sea Sparrow Point Defense Missile System for enemy aircraft and antiship cruise missiles.

The Spruance class also represented the navy's first attempt at using gas turbine power for warships. Four LM-2500 General Electric gas turbine engines (GTEs) give them a top speed of 33 knots and a range of 6,000 nautical miles at 20 knots. Their hulls and physical plant configuration were copied in the subsequent Kidd-class destroyers (DDG-93), and the hull of the Ticonderoga-class cruisers (CG 47) reflects a variation upon the Spruance-class design. Six Spruance-class destroyers fired 112 Tomahawks during the opening phase of Operation DESERT STORM.

Destroyers played only a very minor role in the Afghanistan War. Just nine participated in Operation ENDURING FREEDOM (October 2001), when they launched Tomahawks against Taliban and Al Qaeda targets. Seven joined Operation IRAQI FREEDOM (March–April 2003) for Tomahawk strikes and other missions. The entire Spruance class was decommissioned in 2005 in favor of Aegis destroyers.

The Arleigh Burke–class destroyer (DDG-51) has been regarded as the navy's most capable and survivable surface combatant since its introduction to the fleet in 1991. This class displaces 8,300 tons, is capable of a peak speed of more than 30 knots, and has a cruising range of 4,400 nautical miles at 20 knots. A new hull design allows for better seakeeping at high speeds and in rough conditions. These warships are visually distinctive thanks to their "V" shape at the waterline and a tilted mast for reduced radar cross-section. Each Burke-class destroyer has a crew of some 30 officers and 302 sailors. Since 1994, they have been constructed with a hangar to house two LAMPS Mark III helicopters. Flight I of this class contained only a flight deck without permanently housed helicopters.

All Burke-class destroyers are equipped with the Aegis air defense system, featuring the SPY-1D phased array radar. Older rotating radars are only capable of registering a target once during each 360-degree cycle of their antenna. A separate tracking radar must then engage each contact. Aegis combines these functions with beams of electromagnetic energy transmitted simultaneously in all directions. Moreover, Aegis integrates the various weapons and sensor suites like no other system currently found in world navies. The Burke class employs a 90-cell vertical launching system (VLS) for missile launches (either standard, Tomahawk, or ASROC) against surface, air, and land targets. Antisubmarine warfare is facilitated through both hull-mounted (AN/SQS-53C) and towed array (AN/SQR-19) sonars. The latter is particularly effective, as its depth can be altered to place a sensor in the same temperature and acoustic conditions as a submarine to increase the likelihood of detection and tracking. The ships' antisubmarine warfare (ASW) helicopters can drop sonobuoys to help pinpoint target locations before torpedoes or the ASROC are brought to bear. The Aegis fire-control system also works in tandem with the Harpoon antiship cruise missile launcher and the 5-inch/54 gun. Engagement parameters can be preset such that Aegis can strike targets without further operator interface. The Block 1 upgrade to the Phalanx CIWS supplies the last line of defense against air threats by directing depleted uranium or tungsten shells through a Gatling gun.

The engineering plant features the latest in GTE technology with a high degree of plant automation through an interconnected system of control consoles. Four General Electric LM2500 GTEs supply propulsion, with three gas turbine generator sets (GTGs) providing 450 VAC, three-phase, 60-hertz power.

Survivability was a prime consideration in the planning for this class. The destroyer's internal spaces can be sealed off from the weather decks and further compartmentalized into several zones using the Collective Protective System (CPS) in the event of a chemical, biological, or nuclear attack. Dedicated facilities are available to decontaminate personnel exposed to harmful agents. The ships' all-steel construction with additional armor around vital systems offers enhanced protection against fragments from weapons detonations. The class is also equipped to withstand electromagnetic pulse damage. Sound isolators in machinery spaces have reduced noise output substantially. Halon firefighting systems that can be locally or remotely activated protect the engineering plant.

Fifteen Burke-class destroyers participated in Operation ENDURING FREEDOM. Eleven joined the carrier battle groups engaged in Operation IRAQI FREEDOM. During the latter conflict, they supported ground operation with Tomahawk launches.

Although the Burke-class has been hampered by cost overruns and poor performance by shipbuilders and subcontractors, the navy's goal is to produce 84 Aegis-capable surface combatants (including Ticonderoga-class cruisers) by 2010. By roughly 2020, the Burke class will require replacement. One possibility is the DDG-1000 *Zumwalt* DD(X) destroyer, which remains a controversial option debated within Congress and the Pentagon.

JEFFREY D. BASS

The destroyer USS *Spruance* in the Persian Gulf. A total of 31 of these ships served with the U.S. Navy beginning in 1975. Equipped with 5-inch guns and cruise missiles, the last Spruance-class ship was decommissioned in 2005. (U.S. Department of Defense)

See also

Cruisers, U.S.; Destroyers, Coalition; Tomahawk BGM-109 Land Attack Missile; United States Navy, Afghanistan War; United States Navy, Iraq War; United States Navy, Persian Gulf War

References

Crawford, Steve. *Twenty-first Century Warships: Surface Combatants of Today's Navies.* St. Paul, MN: MBI Publishing, 2002.

Sanders, Michael. *The Yard: Building a Destroyer at Bath Iron Works.* New York: Harper Perennial, 2001.

Tomajczyk, Steve. *Modern U.S. Navy Destroyers.* St. Paul, MN: MBI Publishing, 2001.

Destroyer Tenders, U.S.

Large depot vessels capable of tending to the supply, rearmament, and repair needs of destroyers, frigates, or cruisers. The last purpose-built destroyer tenders of the U.S. Navy were the six ships of the Samuel Gompers and Yellowstone classes. The *Samuel Gompers* (AD-37) was commissioned in 1967; its sister ship, the *Puget Sound* (AD-38), was commissioned in 1968. The *Yellowstone* (AD-41) was commissioned in 1980. Its sister ships, the *Acadia* (AD-42), *Cape Cod* (AD-43), and *Shenandoah* (AD-44), were commissioned in 1981, 1982, and 1983, respectively.

Dimensions were a length of 644 feet, a beam of 85 feet, and a draft of 22.5 feet. Maximum speed was 20 knots. The crew complement was 630 (45 officers, 585 enlisted). The ships were armed with two 40-millimeter (mm) grenade launchers and four 20-mm cannon.

Despite their being built in two phases, separated by more than a decade, these two classes were essentially of the same design and were planned to complement and replace the aging destroyer tenders of the World War II–era Dixie class. They share a common massive hull design with the seven submarine tenders of the Simon Lake, L. Y. Spear, and Emory S. Land classes, built between the mid-1960s and the early 1980s. Their intended clientele consisted of the Spruance-class destroyers, the nuclear-powered cruisers of the California and Virginia classes, and the Oliver Hazard Perry–class frigates, but these destroyer tenders could effectively support most other warship types, including amphibious vessels and aircraft carriers, auxiliaries, smaller patrol craft, and units of the coalition navies. Their two 6.5-ton cranes and a pair of heavy capacity 30-ton cranes gave them increased lift capability over the still-serving general repair ships of the Vulcan class (contemporaries of the Dixie class), whose duties the destroyer tenders were steadily supplementing—if not acquiring—by the 1980s and 1990s. Beyond stocking the huge range of supplies and victuals necessary to sustain multiple alongside combatants' crews, each tender was a veritable arsenal of the ordnance and missile weaponry required to rearm ships in the combined force.

It was the *Acadia* that came to the aid of the *Stark* (FFG-31) at Bahrain after the U.S. Navy frigate was struck by two Iraqi Exocet missiles on May 17, 1987, while escorting reflagged oil tankers in the Persian Gulf. The *Acadia* fed the displaced crew of the *Stark* and conducted round-the-clock repairs to prepare both the ship and its complement for safe passage to the Bath Iron Works shipyard in the United States by late June 1987. During Operation DESERT SHIELD, both the *Acadia* and the *Yellowstone* were stationed in the troubled region beginning in the early autumn of 1990. As Operation DESERT STORM got under way, the *Puget Sound* and the *Cape Cod* joined the other two tenders in late February 1991 to enhance forward-deployed rearmament and repair capabilities for the coalition naval forces. After the cruiser *Princeton* (CG-59) was crippled by Iranian mines on February 18, 1991, in the Persian Gulf, the tender *Acadia* stood by and provided heavy repairs while the damaged ship was dry docked at Dubai. The *Yellowstone* joined the repair ship USS *Vulcan* (AR-5) in the Red Sea in tending to coalition naval units' repair and rearmament needs, basing these operations at Jeddah, Saudi Arabia, during DESERT SHIELD and DESERT STORM. The destroyer tenders also featured substantial medical facilities, supplementing the care available from the hospital ships *Mercy* (T-AH-19) and *Comfort* (T-AH-20).

By the mid-1990s the U.S. Navy's approach to fleet support turned from dependence on forward-deployed vessels such as repair ships, destroyer tenders, and submarine tenders to a model that called on special repair teams to be flown in from the United States or the use of dry docks and facilities in friendly ports. All six tenders were decommissioned between 1994 and 1996.

GORDON E. HOGG

See also

Cruisers, U.S.; DESERT STORM, Operation, Coalition Naval Forces; Destroyers, Coalition; Destroyers, U.S.; Repair Ships, U.S.; *Stark* Incident; Support and Supply Ships, Strategic; United States; United States Navy, Persian Gulf War

References

Marolda, Edward, and Robert Schneller. *Shield and Sword: The United States Navy and the Persian Gulf War.* Annapolis, MD: U.S. Naval Institute Press, 2001.
Polmar, Norman. *The Naval Institute Guide to the Ships and Aircraft of the U.S. Fleet.* 18th ed. Annapolis, MD: Naval Institute Press, 2005.
Saunders, Stephen, ed. *Jane's Fighting Ships 2002–2003.* Coulsdon, Surrey, UK, and Alexandria, VA: Jane's Information Group, 2002.
Sharpe, Richard, ed. *Jane's Fighting Ships: 1991–1992.* London: Jane's Information Group, 1991.

Dhahran

Located in Saudi Arabia's Eastern Province, Dhahran is the headquarters of Saudi Aramco (Arabian American Oil Company), the national oil company of Saudi Arabia and the largest oil company in the world. Dhahran is a fenced-in company compound for Saudi Aramco employees and their dependants. Founded in 1938, the compound consists of two main divisions: Dhahran proper and the newer Dhahran Hills, which are separated by a 27-hole golf course. As of 2004, there were 11,300 people residing in the Aramco compound. Although there are residents from various European nations, Arab nations, non-Western nations, and Saudi Arabia, more than half of the residents in 2004 were from the United States. As of 2008, however, Saudis constituted 85 percent of the Aramco workforce, with expatriates numbering only 15 percent.

Dhahran is frequently used to refer to the municipality of Dhahran as well as a metropolitan area that includes Dhahran, Khobar, Dammam, and surrounding communities. Metropolitan Dhahran has a population of some 1 million people. It is also home to King Fahd Petroleum and Minerals University and the largest airbase in Saudi Arabia.

Dhahran's origins can be traced back to 1933, when the Saudi Arabian government, encouraged by recent oil discoveries in neighboring Bahrain, signed a land concession agreement with Standard Oil of California (Socal). This agreement allowed the American company to search for oil in the Saudi kingdom. A Socal subsidiary, the California–Arabian Standard Oil Company, eventually discovered oil near Dhahran in 1938. That company, which changed its name to the Arabian American Oil Company (Aramco) in 1944, was purchased by the Saudi government in 1980. In 1988 the Saudis changed the name of the company to Saudi Aramco.

To house the many foreign oil workers, Aramco built Dhahran, the first and largest of the four fenced-in company compounds in Saudi Arabia. After oil was discovered at Dammam Well Number 7 in 1938, the company decided to construct its headquarters on two barren hills in the area. The two hills, which were known in Arabic as *dhahran* ("two backs"), provided the name for the new community. Although the community is primarily made up of foreigners, the percentage of Saudi nationals has increased since 1980. Regardless, the compound is culturally and linguistically American. English is the common language, and Saudi Arabia's Islamic laws are not applicable, less strictly applied, or ignored within the compound. For example, women are allowed to drive in the compound, and there are no Islamic clothing restrictions. During the 1991 Persian Gulf War, the coalition utilized Dhahran's King Abdul Aziz Air Base in the fighting against Iraq.

Saudi Aramco's Industrial Security Department is responsible for traffic, security, and law enforcement within the compound. A terrorist attack occurred not far away on June 25, 1996, when terrorists bombed the U.S. military complex at Khobar Towers. Another attack killed 22 people at the Oasis Compound at Khobar in May 2004. Fears about attacks on the compound increased on February 25, 2006, when Saudi security forces interrupted two cars trying to enter the side gate of the Abqaiq oil facility. The guards opened fire, and the vehicles, which had been packed with explosives, blew up and killed the 2 suicide-bomber drivers.

MICHAEL R. HALL

See also

DESERT STORM, Operation; Saudi Arabia

References

Brown, Anthony Cave. *Oil, God, and Gold: The Story of Aramco and the Saudi Kings.* New York: Houghton Mifflin, 1999.

Nolte, Richard H. *A Tale of Three Cities: Dhahran, Riyadh, Jedda.* Riyadh: American Universities Field Staff, 1977.

Pledge, Thomas A. *Saudi Aramco and Its People: A History of Training.* Dhahran: Saudi Arabian Oil Company, 1998.

Dhahran, Scud Missile Attack on
Event Date: February 25, 1991

Iraqi Scud missile attack on a U.S. Army installation on February 25, 1991, at Dhahran, Saudi Arabia, during Operation DESERT STORM. The missile strike killed 28 soldiers, seriously injured 110 others, and lightly injured an additional 100 people. The Scud missile that hit the barracks and warehouse in Dhahran, located in eastern Saudi Arabia, was one of 46 such missiles launched from Iraq into Saudi Arabia during the Persian Gulf War. The Iraqis also fired 42 Scud missiles into Israel.

The Dhahran barracks at the time housed soldiers attached to the 475th Quartermaster Group. Iraq targeted Dhahran not only because of the army barracks located there but also because the city was the administrative headquarters for the lucrative Saudi oil industry and a significant seaport.

At 8:32 p.m. on February 25, 1991, the Scud warning sirens began to sound in Dhahran. This was by no means the first Scud missile attack on the area, and so by now the army personnel were well acquainted with the air raid procedures. Thirteen minutes later a Scud missile slammed into the compound, killing and injuring soldiers by its blast and affecting still others who were crushed to death or trapped by debris. The nearby surface-to-air Patriot missile batteries, six in all, recently redesigned from their originally intended antiaircraft role and deployed to Saudi Arabia to provide U.S. forces with at least some ability to intercept and destroy missiles before they could reach their targets, had failed to track and intercept the Scud missile. By this time in the conflict, the Patriot had a mixed track record of successfully intercepting Scuds both in Israel and in Saudi Arabia. This was in spite of media reports during the course of the preceding eight weeks indicating that the Patriot system was highly accurate, an impression that the U.S. Defense Department seemed in no hurry to correct.

A postattack investigation found that the Patriot's software system, which helped track the trajectory of incoming missiles, had malfunctioned. This, in combination with the army's inexperience using the Patriot as a missile interceptor, led to the failure to intercept the Iraqi missile at Dhahran and to prevent the great loss of life caused by the Scud. Indeed, prior to DESERT STORM, the Patriot system had never before been used to intercept Scud missiles, and it was not designed to be operated continuously for many hours at a time. This extended operation may have been a contributing factor to the failure of its software guidance system.

The Scud attack at Dhahran represented the single greatest loss of life for U.S. or coalition forces during all of Operation DESERT STORM and has spurred Defense Department efforts to develop purpose-designed antimissile systems.

PAUL G. PIERPAOLI JR.

See also

Dhahran; Missile Systems, Iraqi; Patriot Missile System; Saudi Arabia; Saudi Arabia, Armed Forces

References

Brenner, Elliott, and William Harwood, eds. *Desert Storm: The Weapons of War.* London: Orion Books, 1991.

Editors of *Time* Magazine. *Desert Storm: The War in the Persian Gulf.* Boston: Little, Brown, 1991.

Zaloga, Steven J. *Scud Ballistic Missile and Launch Systems, 1955–2005.* New York: Osprey, 2006.

Diego Garcia

British-held atoll in the Indian Ocean and site of a jointly controlled American and British naval air base. Diego Garcia is located in the southern Indian Ocean about 1,000 miles south of the Indian coast and 7 degrees north of the equator. The atoll is part of the Chagos Archipelago and is the largest atoll of the Chagos chain, which stretches from 4 degrees to 7 degrees north latitude. Because of its location, Diego Garcia has a tropical climate characterized by hot humid summers and warm wet winters. It receives upwards of 100 inches of rain per year. The island is also subject to tropical cyclones but only infrequently, and it has not been hit by a serious tropical storm in more than 40 years. Diego Garcia, which is relatively flat, comprises 66 square miles, only 12 of which are landmass; the remainder is coral reef and a huge lagoon, which is approximately 48 square miles in area. The land area almost completely surrounds the lagoon except for an opening in the north that leads to open ocean. Because of this, it is quite easy to limit marine access to Diego Garcia.

Portuguese mariners discovered the atoll in the early 1500s. It is presumably named after a Portuguese sea captain or explorer. Diego Garcia was uninhabited until the 1700s, at which time the French took control of the island and introduced slave labor to cultivate and process copra, which is the kernel of a cocoanut, used for cocoanut meat and highly prized cocoanut oil. Diego Garcia passed into British possession in 1814 at the conclusion of the Napoleonic Wars. It has remained under British control since. The British continued to use the atoll for its rich cocoanut yields, although slave labor was abolished when Britain took control.

In the late 1960s the British and U.S. governments began to make plans to turn Garcia Diego into a naval and air force base. Beginning in 1967, the British began relocating the small native population on the island to the Seychelles and Mauritius. By 1971 the last of the copra plantations was phased out, and the atoll had been depopulated. Per previous agreements, London leased the use of Diego Garcia to the U.S. government, which began to construct a joint naval and air force base there. Although Great Britain retains sovereignty over the island, the U.S. government controls the military base. By the 1990s, Diego Garcia was home to 16 different sea- and air-based commands, including the important U.S. Navy Support Facility. The Support Facility's function is to provide forward-deployed logistical support to operational forces in the Persian Gulf and the Indian Ocean. The Military Sealift Command located on Diego Garcia is also an important forward-based command.

There are presently about 40 British and 1,000 U.S. military personnel on Diego Garcia and an additional 2,500 support workers. Access to the atoll is limited, and it is not open to the general public. Because of its great isolation and restricted access, it is believed that the U.S. government is using the island as a small detention facility for captured members of Al Qaeda. The U.S. government has declined to verify this.

Outfitted with facilities and runways to accommodate the largest military aircraft, Diego Garcia was used during the 1991 Persian Gulf War as a staging area for American B-52 long-range bombers that conducted the aerial bombing campaign of Operation DESERT STORM in January and February 1991. It was also used as a refueling base during the conflict. In December 1998 during Operation DESERT FOX, B-52s based at Diego Garcia launched nearly 100 cruise missiles at Iraqi targets after Iraq refused to cooperate with international weapons inspectors. In 2001 during Operation ENDURING FREEDOM in Afghanistan, the island served as a forward base for B-52 and B-1 bombers.

In Operation IRAQI FREEDOM, which commenced in March 2003, Diego Garcia once more played a critical role in the bombing campaign. It served as a base for B-1, B-2, and B-52 bombers, which were among the first to assault Baghdad in the opening hours of the campaign. Because Turkey forbade the United States from using its territory to attack Iraq in 2003, Diego Garcia played an even larger role than it had in the 1991 Persian Gulf War.

Diego Garcia was first built as a forward base of operations in case of war with the Soviet Union during the Cold War. The United States also wished to maintain a base relatively close to India, which at the time was tilting toward the Soviet orbit. However, after the Cold War when U.S.-Indian relations dramatically improved, both nations have used Diego Garcia as a staging area for joint naval exercises. This will likely maintain Diego Garcia's great strategic importance well into the 21st century as long as American priorities in the Middle East and the Persian Gulf region remain high. The National Aeronautics and Space Administration (NASA) also claims the atoll as an alternate landing area for the space shuttle; in fact, it is the only designated landing facility in the Indian Ocean.

PAUL G. PIERPAOLI JR.

See also
Al Qaeda; DESERT FOX, Operation; DESERT STORM, Operation; ENDURING FREEDOM, Operation; IRAQI FREEDOM, Operation; United States Navy, Afghanistan War; United States Navy, Iraq War; United States Navy, Persian Gulf War

References
Bandjunis, Vytautas. *Diego Garcia: Creation of the Indian Ocean Base.* Chestnut Hill, MA: Writer's Showcase, 2001.
Gerson, Joseph, and Bruce Birchard. *The Sun Never Sets: Confronting the Network of Foreign U.S. Military Bases.* Cambridge, MA: South End Press, 1991.

Dock Landing Ships, U.S. and Coalition

Amphibious ships designed to transport and launch landing craft from a floodable internal dock through a gate at the stern. The dock landing ship (LSD) shares essential features with the amphibious transport dock (LPD).

Like the tank landing ship (LST), the LSD was a joint development project between the U.S. Navy and the Royal Navy during the early years of World War II. While the LST was easily built in great numbers and proved remarkably sturdy and adaptable in service, a blunt bow with large doors kept its speed down to 10 or 12 knots under even the best sea conditions, preventing the LST's integration into faster amphibious convoys. A U.S.-British design team proposed a larger ship displacing 9,200 tons at full load and extending 458 feet (compared to the LST at 4,000 tons and 328 feet), capable of 15 to 17 knots, with a conventional bow and forward superstructure that would carry two to three tank landing craft (LCT) in a partially covered well deck extending four-fifths the length of the ship. Unlike the LST, which thrust its bow upon the beach and discharged its tanks and trucks by means of a ramp to the shore, the LSD stood some distance offshore and launched its vehicle cargo aboard LCTs via the flooded well deck for the transfer to the beach. The LSDs, while not built in the same quantity as the LST, could carry and deploy the heaviest tanks in service.

Twenty-five ships of the Ashland class were built between 1942 and 1946, including 4 for the Royal Navy. Despite their relatively small numbers when compared to the more than 1,000 LSTs produced in U.S. shipyards, the fast dock landing ships may be the most important amphibious ships designed during World War II. By the end of 1970, all of the Ashland class had left U.S. Navy service.

The first postwar LSD construction program was prompted by the U.S. naval experience during the Korean War and by the desire to prevent a near-future LSD gap. The eight ships of the Thomaston class (LSD-28 through LSD-35) were built during 1953–1957 and were improved better-armed enlargements of their Ashland-class forebears. The hulls of Thomaston-class ships extended to an overall length of 510 feet, and the ships displaced 12,150 tons at full load. After decades of almost constant service that taxed both their structure and machinery, the Thomaston-class LSDs were decommissioned by 1989.

As the veteran Ashland class approached the end of its career, construction was begun on the five ships of the Anchorage class (LSD-36 through LSD-40) in 1967. Joining the fleet between 1970 and 1972, they had improved cargo, troop, and landing craft capacity over the Thomaston class. Their successors of the current Whidbey Island class (LSD-41 through LSD-48) were specifically designed and configured around the effective transport and operation of the advanced air cushion landing craft (LCAC) and increased cargo loads (the Harpers Ferry–class variants of this class, LSD-49 through LSD-52). Specifications for the Anchorage-class, Whidbey Island–class, and Harpers Ferry–class LSDs follow.

The Anchorage class (five ships, LSD-36 through LSD-40) was built by Ingalls Shipbuilding and General Dynamics during 1967–1972. Their dimensions were length, 553.3 feet; beam, 84 feet; and draft, 19.5 feet. Displacement was 8,600 tons (light) and 13,700 tons (full load). Speed was 22 knots (20 knots sustained). They had a crew complement of 374 (25 officers and 349 enlisted). They could carry 366 troops and 3 LCAC or 3 LCU landing craft in the well deck (430 feet by 50 feet). They had a vehicle cargo capacity of 15,800 square feet. There was also a helicopter pad fitted over the well deck but no hangar. They were armed with three twin 3-inch (76-millimeter [mm]) guns and two 20-mm Phalanx CIWS.

The Whidbey Island class of eight ships (LSD-41 through LSD-48) was built by Lockheed Shipbuilding and Avondale Industries, during 1981–1992. Their dimensions were length, 609.5 feet; beam, 84 feet; and draft, 20.5 feet. Displacement was 12,434 tons (standard) and 15,939 tons (full load). Speed was 22 knots, and range was 8,000 nautical miles at 20 knots. Crew complement was 310 (19 officers and 291 enlisted). They could carry 560 troops. Landing craft were 4 LCAC, 3 LCU, 10 LCM(8), 21 LCM(6), or 64 amphibious assault vehicles (AAVs) in their well deck (440 feet by 50 feet). Cargo capacity was 5,000 cubic feet marine cargo or 12,500 square feet vehicle space. There was a helicopter deck over the docking well but no hangar. The ships were armed with two 21-cell RAM (Rolling Airframe Missile) launchers, two 25-mm Bushmaster cannon, and two 20-mm Phalanx CIWS.

The Harpers Ferry class of four ships (LSD-49 through LSD-52) was built by Avondale Industries during 1991–1998. Dimensions were as for the Whidbey Island class. Displacement was 11,894 tons (light) and 16,740 tons (full load). Speed and range were the same as for the Whidbey Island class. Complement was 307 (19 officers and 288 enlisted). They could transport 400 troops. Landing craft capacity was 2 LCAC, 1 LCU, 4 LCM(8), or 9 LCM(6) in the well deck (180 feet by 50 feet). Cargo was 67,600 cubic feet

USS *Tortuga* (LSD-46) is a Whidbey Island–class dock landing ship. Commissioned in November 1990, it remains in active service. (U.S. Department of Defense)

marine cargo or 20,200 square feet vehicle space. There was a helicopter deck over the docking well but no hangar. Armament was the same as for the Whidbey Island class.

The United States originally planned to build 12 ships in the Harpers Ferry class, but with the unexpectedly precipitous dissolution of the Soviet Union late in 1991 and the de facto end of the Cold War, the order was reduced to 4. The move toward a blended cargo transport–dock landing ship in this development of the later Whidbey Island–class ships in any case reflected a U.S. Navy design trend first begun as early as 1957, which paralleled the plans for the Iwo Jima (LPH-2) class of amphibious helicopter assault ships. The U.S. Marine Corps, in fact, had hoped for more: an assault ship that could handle marine cargo, launch large landing craft such as LCUs, and function as a helicopter carrier, a wish that eventually would come true with the appearance of the Tarawa (LHA-1) class in the 1970s. At the time, however, such ships were simply out of reach financially, so the new amphibious transport dock (LPD), which would embark more than 900 troops, carry more than 2,000 tons of cargo, operate helicopters from a permanent deck, and still be able to launch heavy landing craft, was derived from the dock landing ship, coming into its own with the launching of the *Raleigh* (LPD-1) in 1962 and persisting

prominently as a viable amphibious ship type into the 21st century. The specifications of the Raleigh class and the Austin class (the second group of original LPDs) are below. In 2000, construction began on the third and current iteration of the LPD, the San Antonio (LPD-17) class, the particulars of which also follow.

The Raleigh class of three ships (LPD-1 through LPD-3; *La Salle*, LPD-3, became command ship AGF-3 in 1972) was built by New York Naval Shipyard during 1960–1964. Dimensions were length, 521.5 feet (overall); beam, 84 feet; and draft, 22 feet. Displacement was 8,491 tons (light) or 14,865 tons (full load). Speed was 21.6 knots (20 knots sustained) and range was 16,500 nautical miles at 10 knots and 9,600 nautical miles at 16 knots. Complement was 397 (24 officers and 373 enlisted). They could carry 1,140 troops. Landing craft capacity was 1 LCU and 3 LCM(6), 9 LCM(6), 4 LCM(8), or 28 AAVs in well deck (168 feet by 50 feet). Cargo capacity was 12,500 square feet vehicle space. There was a helicopter deck over the docking well but no hangar. The ships were armed with three twin 3-inch (76-mm) guns and two 20-mm Phalanx CIWS.

The Austin class of 12 ships (LPD-4 through LPD-15) was built by New York Naval Shipyard, Ingalls Shipbuilding, and Lockheed Shipbuilding during 1963–1971. Dimensions were length, 570 feet; beam, 84 feet; and draft, 23 feet. Displacement was 11,050

The Landing Craft, Air Cushioned 58, assigned to Assault Craft Unit 5, prepares to enter the well deck of the amphibious dock landing ship USS *Harpers Ferry* (LSD-49) on September 23, 2009. (U.S. Department of Defense)

tons (light) or 17,595 tons (full load). Speed was 21 knots, and range was 7,700 nautical miles at 20 knots. Complement was 402 (28 officers and 374 enlisted). They could transport 840 to 930 troops. Landing craft carried were 1 LCU and 3 LCM(6), 9 LCM(6), 4 LCM(8), or 28 AAVs in the well deck (168 feet by 50 feet). Cargo capacity was 40,000 cubic feet marine cargo or 12,000 square feet vehicle space. They also carried 6 CH-46 Sea Knight helicopters. They were armed with two 25-mm Bushmaster cannon and two 20-mm Phalanx CIWS.

The San Antonio class of nine ships (LPD-17 through LPD-25) was begun by Northrop Grumman/Avondale in 2000, and the last ship is expected to join the fleet in 2014. Dimensions are length, 684 feet; beam, 105 feet; and draft, 23 feet. Displacement is 25,885 tons (full load). Speed is 25 knots (maximum) and 22 knots (sustained). Complement is 361 (28 officers and 333 enlisted). They can carry 720 to 800 troops. Landing craft are 2 LCAC, 1 LCU, or 14 AAVs in the well deck. Cargo capacity is 34,000 cubic feet marine cargo or 24,000 square feet vehicle space. Aircraft number 2 CH-53E Sea Stallion helicopters, 2 MV-22 Osprey tilt-rotors, or 4 CH-46 Sea Knight helicopters. They are armed with two 8-cell Sea Sparrow surface-to-air missiles (SAMs), two RAM missile launchers, and two 30-mm Bushmaster II CIWS.

Considerably larger than the predecessor Austin-class LPDs, the San Antonio–class ships all will feature fully integrated helicopter hangars that can store a single CH-53E Sea Stallion, two CH-46 Sea Knights, or one MV-22 Osprey. Two LCAC craft can be accommodated in the docking well, and a 24-bed medical facility also includes two operating rooms. These are the first U.S. Navy ships to employ the tall and pyramidal Advanced Enclosed Mast System, similar to mast structures on new European destroyers and frigates, giving them a distinctive almost futuristic profile when compared to the pole or lattice masts common on other U.S. warships. In a unique construction gesture acknowledging these ships' role in the Global War on Terror, the *New York* (LPD-21) incorporates steel salvaged from the ruins of the World Trade Center in its bow structure. According to U.S. Navy information on the San Antonio class, these ships constitute the functional replacement of more than 41 older ships, including the Austin-class LPDs, the Anchorage-class LSDs, the Newport-class LSTs, and amphibious cargo ships (LKA) of the Charleston class.

Somewhat before their projected retirements and especially during operations DESERT SHIELD and DESERT STORM, these amphibious ships constituted part of the huge naval force gathered as part of the preparations for a massive northern Persian Gulf landing campaign—in the end a brilliant and persuasive feint—that never materialized. Nonetheless, most of the ships in these classes of LSDs and LPDs—excepting the San Antonio–class LPDs still under construction—contributed to Operations DESERT SHIELD/DESERT STORM, ENDURING FREEDOM, and IRAQI FREEDOM and, in some cases, to all three campaigns. The veteran Anchorage class was represented by the *Anchorage* (LSD-36), *Portland* (LSD-37), *Pensacola* (LSD-38), and *Mount Vernon* (LSD-39) during DESERT SHIELD/DESERT

STORM, which also saw the participation of the Whidbey Island–classships *Germantown* (LSD-42), *Fort McHenry* (LSD-43), and *Gunston Hall* (LSD-44). LPDs joining in these Persian Gulf War operations were the *Raleigh* (LPD-1), *Vancouver* (LPD-2), *Ogden* (LPD-5), *Duluth* (LPD-6), *Dubuque* (LPD-8), *Denver* (LPD-9), *Juneau* (LPD-10), *Shreveport* (LPD-12), and *Trenton* (LPD-14).

An amphibious force as large as this aggregation was not deployed in such concentration for the subsequent Operations ENDURING FREEDOM and IRAQI FREEDOM, but the effectiveness and versatility of these amphibious ships has made their rotating availability a mainstay of the U.S. naval presence in this theater. Of the above-named LSDs and LPDs, returning to the region for these campaigns were the *Anchorage, Portland, Gunston Hall, Ogden, Duluth, Dubuque, Shreveport,* and *Trenton.* The *Austin* (LPD-4), *Cleveland* (LPD-7), and *Ponce* (LPD-15) have deployed in support of both recent campaigns, as have the *Whidbey Island* (LSD-41), *Comstock* (LSD-45), *Tortuga* (LSD-46), *Rushmore* (LSD-47), *Ashland* (LSD-48), *Oak Hill* (LSD-51), and *Pearl Harbor* (LSD-52). As the more capable LPDs of the San Antonio class join the U.S. Navy, they will replace a number of these long-serving and versatile amphibious vessels.

Despite the U.S. Navy's primacy in amphibious warfare, other coalition navies have contributed analogous vessels in the region during ongoing operations. During Operation DESERT STORM, the French Navy in late January 1991 dispatched the specially fitted LPD *Foudre* (L-9011) to augment medical facilities and capabilities in Kuwait. The Falklands War veteran HMS *Fearless* (L-10), an LPD type of the Royal Navy, participated from the beginning of Operation ENDURING FREEDOM until relieved by the LPH HMS *Ocean* (L-12) in February 2002. The *Fearless* was decommissioned the following month; the new LPDs *Albion* (L-14) and *Bulwark* (L-15) replaced both the *Fearless* and the earlier-decommissioned sister ship *Intrepid* (L-11) as they joined the fleet in 2003 and 2005. Construction or acquisition of the LPD type has continued in Europe and elsewhere. The Argentine Navy acquired the French predecessors to the *Foudre,* the LSDs *Ouragan* and *Orage,* during 2006–2007; Spain completed two LPDs in 1998 and 2000; and the Netherlands, Portugal, and South Korea have recently built or will shortly commission examples of the type in their shipyards.

GORDON E. HOGG

See also

Amphibious Assault Ships; Amphibious Command Ships; DESERT STORM, Operation, Coalition Naval Forces; ENDURING FREEDOM, Operation, Coalition Naval Forces; IRAQI FREEDOM, Operation, Coalition Naval Forces; Tank Landing Ships, U.S.; United States Navy, Iraq War; United States Navy, Persian Gulf War

References

Dictionary of American Naval Fighting Ships, Vol. 4, Appendix I, *Amphibious Warfare Ships.* Washington, DC: Naval Historical Center, 1969.

Friedman, Norman. *The Naval Institute Guide to U.S. Amphibious Ships and Craft: An Illustrated Design History.* Annapolis, MD: Naval Institute Press, 2002.

Marolda, Edward, and Robert Schneller. *Shield and Sword: The United States Navy and the Persian Gulf War*. Annapolis, MD: U.S. Naval Institute Press, 2001.

Polmar, Norman. *The Naval Institute Guide to the Ships and Aircraft of the U.S. Fleet*. 18th ed. Annapolis, MD: Naval Institute Press, 2005.

Saunders, Stephen, ed. *Jane's Fighting Ships, 2006–2007*. Coulsdon, Surrey, UK, and Alexandria, VA: Jane's Information Group, 2006.

Sharpe, Richard, ed. *Jane's Fighting Ships: 1991–1992*. London: Jane's Information Group, 1991.

Donkey Island, Battle of
Start Date: June 30, 2007
End Date: July 1, 2007

Minor military engagement between U.S. forces and Al Qaeda in Iraq insurgents during June 30–July 1, 2007. The Battle of Donkey Island occurred on the banks of a canal leading from Ramadi to Lake Habbaniyah near the city of Tash, south of the city of Ramadi, in Anbar Province, Iraq. The island is named for the wild donkeys native to the region. This skirmish pitted elements of the U.S. Army Task Force 1–77 Armor Regiment and the 2nd Battalion, 5th Marines, against a force of Al Qaeda in Iraq insurgents, who outnumbered the Americans.

The insurgent force had gathered in the area to launch a planned assault on Ramadi, employing daytime suicide attacks to break the shaky peace that had been recently established in the city. American forces discovered the company-sized insurgent force while conducting a routine patrol in Humvee vehicles on the evening of June 30. The insurgents had opened fire on the convoy. Despite being outnumbered, a U.S. platoon-sized element, along with the original patrol group, counterattacked with superior firepower a short while later and defeated the insurgent group after what turned out to be a 23-hour on-again, off-again gun battle. Although a clear military victory for the American forces, the engagement demonstrated that Al Qaeda in Iraq, along with other insurgent groups, still had the ability to organize forces effectively in an attempt to destabilize the Anbar region.

American forces suffered 2 dead and 11 wounded, while an estimated 32 insurgents were killed out of an estimated force of 40–70 fighters. U.S. forces also managed to destroy two trucks operated by the insurgents that had carried considerable numbers of arms and ammunition.

RICHARD B. VERRONE

See also
Al Qaeda in Iraq; Iraqi Insurgency

References
Cockburn, Patrick. *Muqtada: Muqtada al-Sadr, the Shia Revival, and the Struggle for Iraq*. New York: Scribner, 2008.

Ricks, Thomas E. *The Gamble: General David Petraeus and the American Military Adventure in Iraq, 2006–2008*. New York: Penguin, 2009.

Dostum, Abd al-Rashid
Birth Date: 1954

Uzbek warlord, chief of staff to the commander in chief of the Afghan Army (2003–2008), and leader of the National Islamic Movement of Afghanistan. Born in Khwaja Dukoh in Jowzjan Province, Afghanistan, in 1954, Abd al-Rashid Dostum completed his national service as a paratrooper before commencing work in a state-owned gas refinery in 1970. During his employment he engaged in union politics and emerged as a communist union boss, a position he retained until 1978 when he joined the Afghan military in the fight against the Soviet Union's 1979 invasion.

In the early 1980s, however, Dostum began a six-year battle against the Afghan mujahideen as a regional commander of his own militia. By the mid-1980s his aptitude for rallying Uzbek and Turkmen mujahideen soldiers to both government and personal causes proved fruitful. With approximately 20,000 men under his command, he pacified the northern provinces and established control there. While his force recruited throughout his native Jowzjan Province and had a relatively broad base, the majority of his initial troops and commanders originated from Dostum's home village, Khwaja Dukoh, and represented the core of the force both during the civil war and upon the force's reconstitution in 2001. Despite his military prowess, Dostum's predilection for meting out merciless punishments on the enemy as well as his own men cemented his reputation as a skilled military tactician and a ferocious, uncompromising leader.

Initially allied with the government of President Mohammed Najibullah, in 1992 Dostum switched allegiance as the Soviet-backed government crumbled amid economic woes and internal strife. Despite his communist past, Dostum joined the moderate Tajik leader of the Northern Alliance, Ahmad Shah Massoud, in toppling the Afghan communist government and fought in a coalition against Gulbuddin al-Hurra Hekmetyar, the Kharuti Pashtun leader of the Islamic Party of Afghanistan (Hezb-e-Islami Afghanistan) in 1992.

Between 1992 and 1997 Dostum ran a secular fiefdom based in Mazar-e Sharif and the surrounding provinces. Under his watch, women enjoyed the freedom to attend school, ventured outside without burqas, and were permitted to wear high-heeled shoes; Mazar-e Sharif's university had 1,800 female students. Boasting the last academic institution in Afghanistan, Mazar-e Sharif was the final bastion untouched by the oppression exercised by the Taliban regime.

As the Taliban forces of Mullah Mohammed Omar approached his stronghold, Dostum assumed a defensive stance and led his Turkmen and Uzbek forces into an ill-fated battle. In May 1997 Dostum's Uzbek commander in Faryab, Abd al-Malik, switched allegiance to the Taliban midway through a skirmish as the Pashtun leader of Balkh and Mazar-e Sharif, Juma Khan Hamdard, attacked from the east and obliterated Dostum's forces. By 1998, with the gates to Mazar-e Sharif now open, Hamdard flowed into the secularized city with his Pashtun Taliban brothers, and Sharia law was enforced. Dostum went into self-imposed exile in Turkey, where he remained until April 2001. In 2000 he suffered an additional blow to his reputation upon the publication of Ahmed Rashid's book, *Taliban: Militant Islam, Oil, and Fundamentalism in Central Asia,* in which the author related the gruesome tale of a soldier being punished by Dostum for stealing.

In the aftermath of the September 11, 2001, terror attacks, Dostum moved to redeem his reputation as a leader, and he offered his services to the United States in its quest to defeat the Taliban. With a small company comprising 2,000 horse-mounted rangers, Dostum and U.S. Special Forces secured a pivotal victory over the Taliban in the Hindu Kush Mountains in November 2001, thereby liberating much of northern Afghanistan.

Serving first as deputy defense minister to Afghani president Hamid Karzai, in 2003 Dostum also assumed the position of chief of staff to the commander in chief of the Afghan Army. In 2004 he entered the presidential race but captured only 10 percent of the vote. In response to this loss, Dostum resurrected the Uzbek militia force, much to the chagrin of President Karzai. In a bid to thwart his political endeavors, Karzai urged the commander who had defied Dostum, Abdul Malik, to return to the north and there establish a rival political party, Hezb-e Azadi-ye Afghanistan (Afghan Liberation Party). Karzai also placed a governor in Faryab who called for Dostum's indictment for war crimes. The measures were neatly countered, however, when pro-Dostum supporters rioted and drove the appointed governor out of Faryab later that year.

Because the north is one of the few areas of Afghanistan in which relative stability has been maintained, government opposition to Dostum has been more recently muted, and his authority prevails for the time being. Holding the northern provinces of Jowzjan, Saripul, Balkh, Faryab, Baghlan, and Kunduz, Dostum also assisted in the establishment of the Islamic National Party (Jumbesh-e-Milli Islami Afghanistan). In February 2008 Dostum reportedly ordered the kidnapping of a political rival, Akbar Bai. In the process, Bai's son and several associates were beaten and injured. Government forces subsequently surrounded Dostum's home, demanding that he be held accountable for the Bai incident. Dostum claimed that he had not ordered the kidnapping and refused to cooperate with a government investigation. As a result, he was stripped of his army position.

K. Luisa Gandolfo

See also

Afghanistan; Karzai, Hamid; Soviet-Afghanistan War; Taliban; Warlords, Afghanistan

References

Ewans, Martin. *Afghanistan: A Short History of Its History and Politics.* New York: Harper Perennial, 2002.

Rashid, Ahmed. *Taliban: Militant Islam, Oil, and Fundamentalism in Central Asia.* New Haven, CT: Yale University Press, 2001.

Saikal, Amin. *Modern Afghanistan: A History of Struggle and Survival.* London: I. B. Tauris, 2004.

Tanner, Stephen. *Afghanistan: A Military History from Alexander the Great to the Fall of the Taliban.* New York: Da Capo, 2003.

Downing, Wayne Allan
Birth Date: May 10, 1940
Death Date: July 18, 2007

U.S. Army officer, commander of U.S. Special Forces in Saudi Arabia during the 1991 Persian Gulf War, and acknowledged expert on terrorism and counterterrorism. Wayne Allan Downing was born on May 10, 1940, in Peoria, Illinois. He graduated from the U.S. Military Academy, West Point, in 1962. Assigned to the 173rd Airborne Brigade, he served two tours of duty during the Vietnam War, during which he was wounded.

In May 1977 Lieutenant Colonel Downing took command of the 2nd Battalion, 75th Infantry (Ranger) Regiment, beginning a lengthy career in special operations forces. Downing believed that training should be rigorous and that Rangers should learn how to deal with the unexpected. He quickly earned a reputation as a hands-on commander who could participate alongside his men in any operation they undertook.

In December 1989 Downing, now a major general, took command of the Joint Special Operations Command, under the U.S. Special Operations Command. That same month, U.S. forces invaded Panama in Operation JUST CAUSE to overthrow dictator Manuel Noriega. JUST CAUSE was the largest American military operation since Vietnam, and each branch of the military wanted to show that it had corrected deficiencies exposed in that earlier conflict. The Rangers and other Special Operations Forces (SOF) performed well in Panama, and although Noriega escaped the first attempts to capture him, he finally emerged from the Vatican compound and surrendered personally to Downing.

When Iraq invaded Kuwait in August 1990, Downing's SOF hoped to join the action against Iraqi dictator Saddam Hussein's forces. That autumn, they trained in Florida for Operation PACIFIC WIND, a plan to rescue American diplomats trapped in Kuwait City. U.S. Air Force Lockheed F-117 Nighthawk and McDonnell Douglas/Boeing F-15 Eagle strike aircraft would have blocked roads into the city by precision bombing while Downing's forces dropped into the embassy compound, freed the diplomats, and escaped. However, General H. Norman Schwarzkopf, commanding general of Operation DESERT SHIELD/DESERT STORM, opposed the plan; fortunately, Hussein soon released the diplomats.

Schwarzkopf did not think particularly highly of SOF and gave them important—but not essential—jobs during DESERT SHIELD. They were employed mostly as liaisons to allied forces but undertook no combat missions. Downing continually proposed operations to take advantage of his men's capabilities, such as attacking the Iraqi leadership, but Schwarzkopf rejected each suggestion.

At the beginning of DESERT STORM in January 1991 when Iraqi Scud missiles were launched from western Iraq against Israel, however, Schwarzkopf could no longer ignore the SOF. U.S. leaders feared that Israel would retaliate against Iraq for the missile attacks, causing Arab members of the coalition to pull out. British special forces had already begun operating in western Iraq, so Schwarzkopf authorized Downing to organize a joint force to hunt for and destroy Scuds and their launchers.

On January 30 Downing and 400 SOF troops arrived in Arar, a town in western Saudi Arabia. Beginning on February 7, the unit spent three weeks trying to find Scuds and destroy them or calling in air strikes. SOF teams swept through the region, and although they claimed the destruction of a number of Scuds, most experts now believe that these were decoys. The teams did destroy some of the Iraqi infrastructure, however, including electrical cables and communications. Even if they had not destroyed actual Scuds, Downing believed that his forces had disrupted Iraqi operations. The number of Scuds launched after SOF troops had entered Iraq during February 24–28, 1991, dropped dramatically.

Following DESERT STORM, Downing, now a lieutenant general, served as commander of the U.S. Army Special Operations Command, headquartered at Fort Bragg, North Carolina. He held this post during August 1991–April 1993. Promoted to full (four-star) general, he then became commander in chief of the joint U.S. Special Operations Command and held that post from May 1993 to February 1996, at which point he retired.

Thereafter, Downing lobbied for U.S. support of an indigenous Iraqi revolt against Saddam Hussein. Downing also served on task forces that investigated terrorist threats to the United States. For example, in 1997 he war-gamed a scenario in which terrorists used crop dusting planes to release chemical agents against U.S. targets. In 1996 immediately after retirement, he supervised the investigation of the terrorist bombing at the Khobar Towers in Saudi Arabia that killed 19 U.S. servicemen. On October 9, 2001, in the immediate aftermath of the September 11 terror attacks, Downing came out of retirement to serve as deputy national security adviser for combating terrorism. He also organized an office within the National Security Council to combat terrorism and gather information about terrorists. Downing retired again from government service on June 26, 2002. From 2003 to 2007 he held the distinguished chair at West Point's Combating Terrorism Center. He was also a sought-after security consultant and a fixture on numerous television news programs. Downing died suddenly of bacterial meningitis on July 18, 2007, in Peoria, Illinois.

TIM J. WATTS

See also

DESERT STORM, Operation; JUST CAUSE, Operation; Schwarzkopf, H. Norman, Jr.; Scud Missiles, U.S. Search for during the Persian Gulf War; September 11 Attacks; Terrorism

References

Atkinson, Rick. *Crusade: The Untold Story of the Persian Gulf War.* New York: Mariner Books, 1994.

Gordon, Michael R., and General Bernard E. Trainor. *The Generals' War: The Inside Story of the Conflict in the Gulf.* New York: Little, Brown, 1995.

Dulles, John Foster

Birth Date: February 25, 1888
Death Date: May 24, 1959

Lawyer, briefly U.S. senator, staunch anticommunist, and U.S. secretary of state (1953–1959). Born in Washington, D.C., on February 25, 1888, John Foster Dulles graduated in 1908 from Princeton University, where he studied under Woodrow Wilson. In 1911 Dulles earned a law degree from George Washington University and joined the prestigious Wall Street law firm of Sullivan and Cromwell. Appointed to the U.S. delegation at the 1919 Paris Peace Conference, Dulles unsuccessfully sought to restrain Allied reparations demands on Germany.

Active between the wars in internationalist organizations, Dulles initially opposed American intervention in World War II. Once American belligerency seemed probable, however, he focused intensely on postwar planning. He also became prominent in Republican politics, advising 1944 presidential candidate Thomas E. Dewey on international affairs. President Harry S. Truman, seeking to secure bipartisan political support for his foreign policy, included Dulles in virtually all major international meetings beginning with the 1945 San Francisco Conference that drafted the final United Nations (UN) Charter. Briefly appointed Republican senator for New York in 1948–1949, Dulles strongly supported creation of the North Atlantic Treaty Organization (NATO). He also supported European integration as a means of strengthening the continent's economies and militaries.

By the late 1940s Dulles had become a dedicated anticommunist. When the Chinese communists won control of the mainland in 1949, he advocated American backing for Jiang Jieshi's (Chiang Kai-shek) Guomindang (Kuomintang, Nationalist) regime on Taiwan. In June 1950 when the Democratic People's Republic of Korea (DPRK, North Korea) invaded the Republic of Korea (ROK, South Korea), Dulles urged U.S. intervention and the extension of protection to Taiwan. As a foreign affairs adviser to Dwight D. Eisenhower's Republican presidential campaign in 1952, Dulles argued that the Truman administration had been timorous in merely containing Soviet communism when it should have moved to roll back Soviet influence.

Named secretary of state by Eisenhower in 1953, Dulles deferred to the president's leadership. A supporter of Eisenhower's New Look defense policy of heavy reliance on nuclear weapons, Dulles rhetorically threatened to wreak massive retaliation against American enemies, tactics nicknamed "brinkmanship." In practice, however, he was often far more cautious. Although

Staunch anticommunist John Foster Dulles was U.S. secretary of state in the Dwight D. Eisenhower administration during 1953–1959. (Library of Congress)

Dulles's bellicose anticommunist rhetoric alarmed many European leaders, his policies proved pragmatic.

Dulles and Eisenhower presided over the end of the Korean War in July 1953, pressuring both sides to accept an armistice. They also established a series of military alliances in Asia. When possible Eisenhower avoided direct major military interventions, preferring to rely on covert operations orchestrated by the Central Intelligence Agency (CIA), headed by Dulles's younger brother Allen. The CIA played key roles in coups that overthrew Left-leaning governments in Iran in 1953 and Guatemala in 1954.

Indeed, the U.S.-sponsored coup in Iran that ousted Mohammad Mossadegh and strengthened Mohammad Reza Shah Pahlavi's hand showcased Dulles's approach to Middle East politics. Dulles believed that to advance American interests in Iran, the region had to remain free of major Soviet influences, free of leftist or communist regimes, and free of Pan-Arabism. Mossadegh's socialist policies and references to imperialism and Western exploitation did not sit well with Dulles or Eisenhower. In the Middle East, Dulles's ardent anticommunism was mixed with considerable concerns that the region's oil supplies would be compromised by instability or Soviet advances. The 1953 coup in Iran, while accomplishing its goals in the short term, served only to create significant long-term problems. As the shah of Iran became more autocratic throughout the 1960s and 1970s, many Iranians would hold the United States responsible for the excesses of his

regime. When he was ousted by an Islamic fundamentalist revolution in 1979, U.S.-Iranian relations were severed.

In Indochina in 1954, Dulles and Eisenhower withstood pressure from U.S. military leaders and—after Britain had declined to assist—refused to authorize air strikes to rescue French troops surrounded by Viet Minh forces at Dien Bien Phu. Nevertheless, Dulles and Eisenhower ended up backing noncommunist South Vietnam by 1956.

Dulles and Eisenhower considered strengthening the U.S. West European allies as their first priority. Thus Dulles, seeking to reinforce NATO, also backed proposals for a multinational European Defense Community (EDC), a plan that France vetoed in 1954. While Dulles sought to help U.S. allies in Europe, however, he nevertheless deplored British and French imperialism.

Dulles's relations with Britain and France reached their nadir in 1956. Following the 1952 revolution, Gamal Abdel Nasser became Egypt's leader in 1954. Initially, Nasser sought military aid from the United States. The powerful Israeli lobby, however, prevented such assistance. Nasser then obtained arms from the Soviet bloc. This in turn led Dulles in 1956 to rescind an earlier American pledge to provide Nasser with funding for his project to build a dam on the Nile south of Aswan.

Believing he had been betrayed, Nasser nationalized the Suez Canal, which was co-owned by the British and French governments. While openly joining Dulles in negotiations with Egypt, British and French leaders covertly intrigued with Israeli leaders for an Israeli attack against Egypt that would enable Britain and France to intervene militarily in Egypt and regain the canal. The invasion began in early November 1956, just before the U.S. presidential election. Dulles and Eisenhower strenuously pressured all three powers to withdraw, which occurred in a matter of weeks. Nevertheless, the episode soured Anglo-American relations.

Although Dulles hoped to align the United States with nationalist forces around the world, the open growth of Soviet interest in the Middle East brought the January 1957 announcement of the Eisenhower Doctrine. Authored chiefly by Dulles, the doctrine conferred upon the United States the right to intervene militarily (if requested) against indigenous or external communist threats in the region. This provoked significant anti-Americanism throughout the world. Just four months after Eisenhower had enunciated the Eisenhower Doctrine and believing that Jordan's King Hussein faced a significant threat from indigenous communists, Dulles and Eisenhower responded by offering Hussein $10 million in economic aid.

The Eisenhower administration also responded to reported threats of Nasserists and political opposition to Lebanese president Camille Chamoun by dispatching the Sixth Fleet to the eastern Mediterranean. Anti-Chamoun demonstrators had attacked the Lebanese president's palace in May. A regional threat seemed more credible when the coup in Iraq in July 1958 brought down the monarchy and a second coup had been attempted in Jordan, although it failed. A British force arrived on July 17, 1958, at Hussein's invitation.

Two days earlier, on July 15, 1958, the first wave of nearly 15,000 U.S. troops landed in Lebanon to restore order. Many arrived without orders, and as they met no opposition and could not identify the rebels, they acted as a peacekeeping force and deterrent to other Middle Eastern countries. The crisis in Lebanon was soon over, and American troops departed Lebanon in the early autumn.

The emergence of Nikita Khrushchev as top Soviet leader in the mid-1950s seemed to promise a relaxation of Soviet-American tensions. As such, the Eisenhower administration hoped to conclude substantive disarmament agreements with Khrushchev. In practice, however, Khrushchev was often far from accommodating. The Soviets' success in launching the first space satellite (Sputnik) in 1957, Soviet possession of nuclear and thermonuclear weapons, and Khrushchev's seeming readiness from late 1958 onward to provoke an international crisis over Berlin all alarmed American leaders, including the ailing Dulles, diagnosed in 1957 with cancer.

Although American nation-building efforts in both Taiwan and South Vietnam enjoyed apparent success, during the Second Taiwan Strait Crisis in 1958 Dulles was notably more cautious about gratuitously challenging either communist China or possibly, by extension, the Soviets. When his cancer worsened, he resigned as secretary on April 15, 1959. Dulles died in Washington, D.C., on May 24, 1959.

PRISCILLA ROBERTS

See also

Chamoun, Camille Nimr; Egypt; Eisenhower, Dwight David; France, Middle East Policy; Nasser, Gamal Abdel; Reza Pahlavi, Mohammad; Russia, Middle East Policy, 1991–Present; Soviet Union, Middle East Policy; Suez Crisis; United Kingdom, Middle East Policy; United States, Middle East Policy, 1945–Present

References

Hoopes, Townsend. *The Devil and John Foster Dulles.* Boston: Little, Brown, 1973.

Immerman, Richard H. *John Foster Dulles: Piety, Pragmatism, and Power in U.S. Foreign Policy.* Wilmington, DE: Scholarly Resources, 1999.

Louis, Wm. Roger, and Roger Owen, eds. *A Revolutionary Year: The Middle East in 1958.* London: I. B. Tauris and Woodrow Wilson Center Press, 2002.

Marks, Frederick W., III. *Power and Peace: The Diplomacy of John Foster Dulles.* Westport, CT: Praeger, 1993.

Dumb Bombs

See Bombs, Gravity

Dunham, Jason

Birth Date: November 10, 1981
Death Date: April 22, 2004

U.S. marine and posthumous Medal of Honor recipient. Born in Scio, New York, on November 10, 1981, Jason Dunham joined the U.S. Marine Corps in 2000. In early 2004 he deployed to Iraq, where he served with the 3rd Battalion, 7th Marine Regiment. On April 14 Corporal Dunham was leading a patrol near Husaybah in reaction to an insurgent attack on a marine convoy. His patrol soon became engaged with insurgents in cars. One insurgent left his vehicle and engaged Dunham in hand-to-hand combat, in the course of which the insurgent dropped a hand grenade. In an attempt to save his patrol from injury, Dunham threw himself on the grenade, using his helmet to try to shield himself and his comrades. Severely wounded in the ensuing explosion, Dunham was evacuated from Iraq. He died at the Naval Medical Center, Bethesda, Maryland, on April 22, 2004.

On November 10, 2006, President George W. Bush announced on the occasion of the dedication of the National Museum of the Marine Corps at Quantico, Virginia, that Dunham had been awarded the Medal of Honor. Bush formally presented the medal to Dunham's family in a ceremony at the White House on January 22, 2007. Dunham was the first marine to receive the medal in the Iraq War and the first marine to be so honored since the Vietnam War. The U.S. Navy's newest Arleigh Burke–class destroyer (DDG-109), which is scheduled to enter service in 2010, has been named in his honor.

SPENCER C. TUCKER

See also

Bush, George Walker

References

Fuentes, Gidget. "Medal of Honor is First for a Marine since Vietnam." *Marine Corps Times,* November 20, 2006.

Phillips, Michael M. "In Combat, Marine Put Theory to Test, Comrades Believe Col. Dunham's Quick Action in Face of Grenade Saved 2 Lives." *Wall Street Journal,* May 25, 2004.

———. *The Gift of Valor: A War Story.* New York: Broadway Books, 2005.

Dunwoody, Ann E.

Birth Date: 1953

U.S. Army general, the first woman to hold full general (four-star) rank, and currently the commanding general of the U.S. Army Materiel Command. Ann E. Dunwoody was born at Fort Belvoir, Virginia, in 1953. Her family has a long record of military service extending back five generations (her father, Harold H. Dunwoody, was a professional army officer who retired as a brigadier general). Dunwoody grew up on military installations in Germany and Belgium, where her father was stationed. She attended State University of New York College at Cortland and graduated in 1975 with a degree in physical education.

Dunwoody entered the army on graduation through the Reserve Officers' Training Corps (ROTC) program as a second lieutenant. Originally planning only to honor her two-year commitment, she found the service to her liking and decided to make it a career. Dunwoody's service has been entirely with the Quartermaster Corps. It began as a platoon leader with a maintenance company at Fort Sill, Oklahoma. Subsequent assignments took her to Kaiserlautern in Germany, Fort Bragg in North Carolina, and Fort Drum in New York, among other places. She earned an MS degree in logistics management from the Florida Institute of Technology in 1988 and an MS degree in national resource strategy from the Industrial College of the Armed Forces in 1995.

Staff assignments include service in the Office of the Chief of Staff of the Army; executive officer to the director, Defense Logistics Agency; and deputy chief of staff for logistics. Among notable command assignments have been that of the first woman to command a battalion in the 82nd Airborne Division (Dunwoody holds the Master Parachutist Badge). As executive officer and later division parachute officer for the 407th Supply and Transportation Battalion, 82nd Airborne Division, she deployed to Saudi Arabia during Operation DESERT SHIELD/DESERT STORM. In 2001 she commanded the I Corps Support Command in support of Operation ENDURING FREEDOM in Afghanistan, and she had charge of establishing the Joint Logistics Command in Uzbekistan. In 2004 Dunwoody was the first woman to head the Combined Arms Support Command at Fort Lee, Virginia.

In 2005 Dunwoody became the army's top-ranking woman when she was promoted to lieutenant general and became deputy chief of staff of the army for logistics. Nominated to serve as the commander of the U.S. Army Materiel Command, she was confirmed by the U.S. Senate on July 23, 2008. She received her fourth star on November 14, 2008. Dunwoody married Craig Brotchie in 1990; he is now a retired air force colonel.

SPENCER C. TUCKER

See also

Logistics, Persian Gulf War; Women, Role of in Afghanistan and Iraq Wars; Women, Role of in Persian Gulf War

References

Swarns, Rachel L. "Commanding a Role for Women in the Military." *New York Times,* June 30, 2008.

———. "A Step up for Women in the U.S. Military." *International Herald Tribune,* November 22, 1908.

Tyson, Ann Scott. "Army Promotes Its First Female Four-Star General." *Washington Post,* November 15, 2008.

White, Josh. "Army General's Nomination Called Historic." *Washington Post,* June 24, 2008.

Williams, Kayla, and Michael E. Staub. *Love My Rifle More than You: Young and Female in the U.S. Army.* New York: Norton, 2005.

Ziegler, Sara L., and Gregory G. Gunderson, eds. *Moving beyond G.I. Jane: Women and the U.S. Military.* Lanham, MD: University Press of America, 2005.

Durant, Michael
Birth Date: July 23, 1961

U.S. Army chief warrant officer and pilot whose helicopter was shot down over Mogadishu on October 3, 1993, and who was held captive by a Somali warlord faction for 11 days. Michael Durant

was born in Berlin, New Hampshire, on July 23, 1961. He enlisted in the army in August 1979 and trained as a helicopter pilot. He earned a BS degree in professional aeronautics and an MBA degree in aviation management from Embry-Riddle Aeronautical University.

On August 1, 1988, Durant joined the 160th Special Operations Aviation Regiment, known as the "Night Stalkers." The unit has the mission of providing rotary-wing air support to special operations forces. Its mission includes organizing, equipping, training, resourcing, and employment of army special operations aviation forces worldwide. Durant participated in combat operations such as the invasion of Panama in 1989 and the liberation of Kuwait in 1991.

In the late summer of 1993, Durant was sent to Mogadishu as part of a United States Special Forces mission code-named Operation GOTHIC SERPENT, the primary goal of which was to capture the leaders of the United Somali Congress/Somali National Alliance (USC/SNA), including warlord Mohammed Farrah Aidid (Aideed). These individuals had been accused of staging attacks on United Nations (UN) peacekeeping forces on June 5, 1993, which resulted in the deaths of dozens of Somalis and Pakistani UN peacekeepers.

On the afternoon of October 3, 1993, Chief Warrant Officer-3 Durant was piloting his Sikorsky MH-60 Black Hawk helicopter as part of a special operations raid to capture USC/SNA leaders who were located in a house in the southern part of Mogadishu. The raiding forces included approximately 150 U.S. soldiers. The original plan was to enter the targeted house, capture the men, and drive them in armored vehicles and trucks back to the U.S. base located at Mogadishu Airport.

The plan came apart when hundreds of Somalis fired on U.S. soldiers in the streets of Mogadishu. Outgunned and exposed, the American forces suffered significant casualties. The fighting worsened after two Black Hawks providing air support to the forces on the ground were shot down. Durant was in the second helicopter.

An American search and rescue team reached the first helicopter but failed to get to Durant's aircraft before the Somalis captured him. U.S. forces were entangled in a pitched fight throughout the night and into the dawn of October 4.

Durant suffered severe back and thigh injuries during the crash. His three crew members were also badly injured. The helicopter's crew members were to be aided by two Delta Force snipers, Master Sergeant Gary Gordon and Sergeant First Class Randy Shughart, who volunteered for the rescue mission and were airlifted into the area near the crash site. Both died from enemy fire, however, and the remainder of Durant's crew also perished. Durant, the sole survivor, was then captured. Gordon and Shughart posthumously received the Medal of Honor for their bravery.

Durant was held captive by the USC/SNA militia for 11 days. Although he was badly injured, he showed steely resolve and did not divulge any information to his captors. He was released on October 14 following intense American pressure on the USC/

BATTLE FOR MOGADISHU, OCTOBER 3–4, 1993

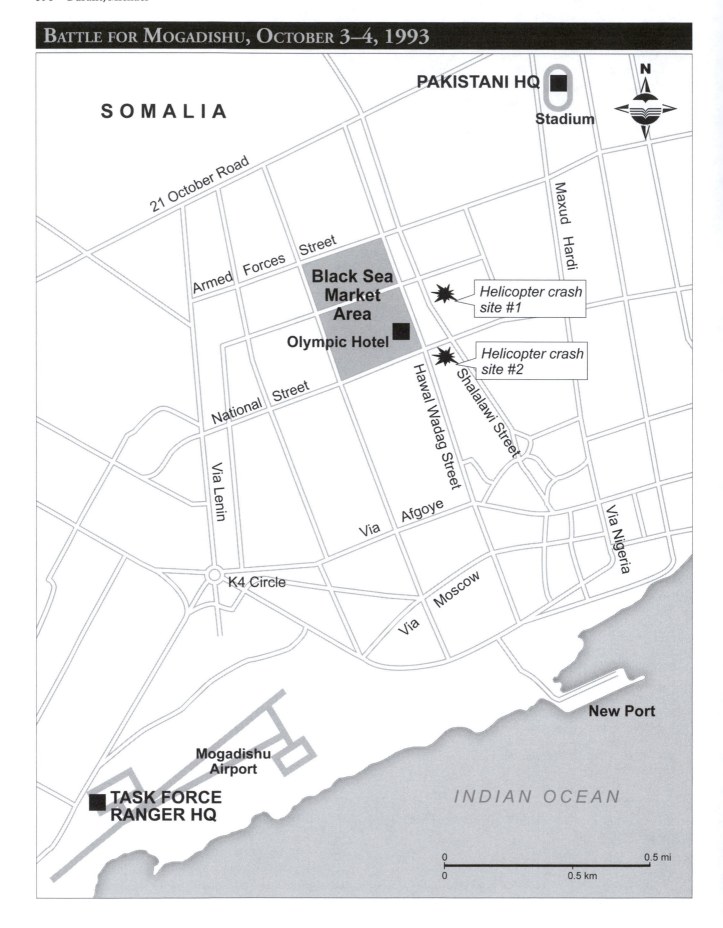

SNA. After his return, Durant's picture was published on the covers of *Time, Newsweek, U.S. News and World Report,* and many newspapers.

Durant returned to active duty after recovering from his injuries. He retired from the army in 2001 as a chief warrant officer-4. He logged approximately 3,700 flight hours, 1,400 of them while wearing night-vision goggles. In 2003 Durant published a book titled *In the Company of Heroes* in which he described his years of service, with an emphasis on his 11 days of captivity in Mogadishu. The book appeared on the *New York Times* Bestseller List.

Durant is now CEO and president of Pinnacle Solutions, Inc., an engineering services company located in Huntsville, Alabama.

CHEN KERTCHER

See also

Delta Force; Somalia, International Intervention in

References

Bowden, Mark. *Black Hawk Down: A Story of Modern War.* 1st ed. New York: Atlantic Monthly Press, 1999.

Durant, Michael, with Steven Hartov. *In the Company of Heroes.* New York: New American Library, 2003.

Index

Dostum, Abd al-Rashid, **384–385**, 416
Doudart de Lagree (FS), 161
Downing, Wayne Allan, **385–386**, 1380
DRAGON FURY, Operation, 22
Dubçek, Alexander, 303
Dugan, Michael, 656
DuLaney, Robert, 915
Dulles, John Foster, **386–388**, 387 (image), 1317
　Central Intelligence Agency (CIA) and, 409, 410
　death of, 388
　education of, 386
　Eisenhower Doctrine and, 387
　relationship with Britain and France, 387
　as secretary of state, 386–388
　Suez Crisis and, 387, 1168–1169
Dulverton (HMS), 821
Dumb bombs. *See* Bombs, gravity
Dunham, Jason, **388**
Dunlavey, Michael, 501
Dunwoody, Ann E., **388–389**
A Durable Peace: Israel and Its Place among the Nations (Netanyahu), 895
Durant, Michael, **389–390**, 1125
Dutton, Jim, 1280
Dwight D. Eisenhower (USS), 416

EAGLE ASSIST, Operation, 908
EAGLE CLAW, Operation, 201–202, 343, **394–395**, 395 (image)
　consequences of, 394–395
　failure of, 394, 395, 1380
　reason for, 394
Eagleburger, Lawrence Sidney, **393–394**
EARNEST WILL, Operation, **395–397**, 396 (image)
　capture of *Iran Ajr*, 396
　minesweeping operations, 396
　reasons for, 395–396
　special forces operations in, 396–397
　start date of, 396
　success of, 397
　U.S. retaliatory actions in, 397
　vessels damaged in, 396, 397
EASTERN EXIT Operation, **397–398**
　plans for, 397
　purpose of, 397
　start/end dates of, 398
　success of, 398
Eberly, David William, **398–399**
Economic effects of the Persian Gulf War, **399–400**, 399 (image)
Economic impact of the September 11, 2001 attacks, **400–401**
Eden, Anthony, 300, 1168, 1170, 1171
Edwards, Mickey, 1355
Egypt, **401–404**, 402 (image)
　Arab Cold War and, 403
　Arab Socialist Union party, 403
　biological weapons and, 217
　Civil War in Yemen and, 1445–1446
　climate of, 794

Corrective Revolution (May 1971), 1145
Egyptian-Israeli armistice, 404–405
Free Officers Movement, 1056
Gaza Strip and, 403, 404
geographic size and population of, 401
Hamas and, 404
Hosni Mubarak and, 403, 406
Israel-Egypt Peace Treat (1979) y, 406
Moslem Brotherhood, 402, 519
Operation HARD SURFACE and, **523–524**
recognition of the People's Republic of China (PRC), 409
Suez Canal and, 401–402, 1530–1532**Doc.**
War of Attrition (1969), 405, 640, 1145
Yom Kippur (Ramadan) War, 132–134, 403, 406
See also Aswan High Dam project; Nasser, Gamal Abdel; Suez Crisis
Egypt, armed forces of, **404–407**, 405 (image)
　Air Force of, 406–407, 586
　annual expense of, 407
　conscription and, 404 (table), 406
　decision making of, 406
　equipment of, 406–407
　first-line armored and mechanized forces, 406
　against Israel, 405–406
　military handicap of, 406
　navy of, 407
　number of personnel in, 406
　paramilitary groups and, 407
　ties with U.S., 406, 407
Eight (VIII) Airborne Corps (United States), 248, 271, 667, 1448
Eighteenth (XVIII) Airborne Corps (United States), 353, 363–364, 365, 368, 1055, 1345, 1346, 1448
Eikenberry, Karl W., 309, **407–408**, 925
Eiland, Giora, 1358
Eisenhower, Dwight D., **408–410**, 409 (image), 1255 (image)
　address to the nation concerning landing of Marines in Lebanon, 1575–1578**Doc.**
　Central Intelligence Agency (CIA) and, 409, 410, 1317
　deploying troops to Lebanon, 720, 733–734
　domino theory of, 410
　education of, 408
　Middle East policy, 409
　military career of, 408
　New Look strategy of, 408
　overthrow of the Shah of Iran, 1317
　response to U-2 incident, 887
　Southeast Asia and, 410
　Suez Crisis and, 300, 409, 1318
　Taiwan Strait crisis and, 410
Eisenhower Doctrine, 301, 387, 409, **410–411**, 734, 736, 1567–1571**Doc.**
　Arab states reaction to, 411
　first significant test of, 409–410
　Soviet reaction to, 411, 1571–1573**Doc.**
Ekéus, Rolf, 1302, 1303

El Salvador, role in Iraq War, **412–413**, 413 (image)
ElBaradei, Muhammad Mustafa, **411–412**, 411 (image), 559
Electronic warfare, 61
Elijah Muhammad, 219
Elizabeth II, Queen of the United Kingdom, 1271
Endara, Guillermo, 667
ENDURING FREEDOM, Operation, 22, 27, 28, **413–415**, 414 (image), 1249
　aircraft in, 53, 59, 415, 420 (image)
　Battle of Mazar-e Sharif, **776–778**
　Battles of Najaf, **871–872**, **872–874**
　cluster bombs in, 230
　components of, 415
　countries contributing to, 415
　expansion of, 415
　first phrase of, 414
　Kandahar fighting, 414
　Northern Alliance and, 912, 913
　objectives of, 1231
　search for Osama bin Laden, 414
　success of, 414–415
　Ukraine and, 1261, 1262
ENDURING FREEDOM, Operation, coalition naval forces, **415–416**
ENDURING FREEDOM, Operation, initial ground campaign, **416–417**
　Combined Forces Land Component Command (CFLCC), 416
　general strategy of, 416
　Joint Special Operation Task Force Dagger, 416
　Kunduz siege, 417
　Pashtun heartland campaign, 417–418
　success of, 418
　Tora Bora campaign, 418
ENDURING FREEDOM, Operation, planning for, **418–421**
　Afghan strategic conditions, 418–419
　British/Australian assistance in, 419
　completed plan, 419–420
　declared strategic goals of, 418
　general strategic scheme, 419
　logistics problems, 419
　low-risk retaliatory options, 418
　phases of, 420
　political dimension in, 419
ENDURING FREEDOM, Operation, U.S. air campaign, 421
Enterprise (USS), 1374
Environmental effects of the Persian Gulf war, **421–422**
Epstein, Giora, 638
Erhard, Ludwig, 483
Escobar, Pablo, 875
Estonia, role in Afghanistan and Iraq Wars, **422–423**
Euphrates (Nahr al-Furat) River, 1238, 1239
Euphrates Valley. *See* Tigris and Euphrates Valley

Two (II) Marine Expeditionary Force (MEF), 1369–1370

U-2 Crisis, 301
U-2 Crisis (May 1, 1960), 301
Ukraine
geographic position and size of, 1261
political system of, 1261
population of, 1261
relations with the U.S., 1261, 1262
Ukraine, role in Afghanistan and Iraq Wars
in Afghanistan, **1261–1262**
in Iraq, 1262
Operation ENDURING FREEDOM, 1261, 1262
Umm Qasr, **1262–1263**
Umm Qasr, Battle of, **1263–1264**, 1263 (image)
Underway replenishment ships (UNREP), **1264–1267**
ammunition ships (AE), 1265
Cimarron (AO-22) class of, 1264
combat stores ships (AFS), 1265
fast combat support ship (AOE), 1264
Henry J. Kaiser (T-AO-187) class, 1264
Kilauea (AE-26) class, 1265, 1266
Mars (T-AFS-1) class, 1265
Mispillion (T-AO-105) and Neosho (T-AO-143) classes, 1264
in Operation ENDURING FREEDOM, 1266–1267
in Operation IRAQI FREEDOM, 1266, 1267
in Operations DESERT SHIELD/DESERT STORM, 1266
purpose of, 1264
replenishment techniques, 1264
Sacramento (AOE-1) class, 1264
Sirius (T-AFS-8) class, 1265
Supply (AOE-6) class, 1265
Suribachi (AE-21) class, 1265–1266
Wichita (AOR-1) class, 1264–1265
Unfit for Command (O'Neil and Corsi), 1190
United Arab Alliance, **1270–1271**
makeup of, 1270–1271
number of political parties in, 1271
results of December 2005 Iraqi legislative election, 1271, 1271 (table)
United Arab Emirates, 58, **1267–1269**, 1268 (image)
emirates in, 1267
geographic position of, 1267
history of, 1267
Iran-Iraq War (1980–1988) and, 1268
Iraq War (2003) and, 1268–1269
Persian Gulf War and, 1268
population of, 1267
previous name of, 1267
relations with Iran, 1268
wealth of, 1267
United Arab Republic (UAR), **1269–1270**, 1269 (image)
Baath Party and, 1269
breakup of, 1270
Gamal Abdel Nasser and, 1269, 1270

motivation for formation of, 1269
start/end dates of, 1269
United Iraqi Alliance (UIA), 650, 651
United Kingdom, **1271–1275**, 1272 (image), 1273 (image)
composition of, 1271
enforcing no-fly zone in northern Iraq, 1273
intervention in Iraq, 1272–1274
Iraq war casualties of, 1274
main political parties of, 1271
Muslim population of, 1274
population of, 1271
response to September 11, 2001 attacks, 1272
size of, 1271
terrorism in, 1274
United Kingdom, Air Force (RAF), Iraq War, **1275–1276**, 1275 (image)
aircraft involved in, 1275
commander of, 1275
friendly fire loss in, 1276
squadrons employed by, 1275
United Kingdom, Air Force (RAF), Persian Gulf War, **1276–1277**
aircraft involved in, 1276
JP233 runway-cratering bomb delivery, 1276
number of helicopter sorties flown, 1277
number of personnel and equipment lost in, 1277
number of troops involved in, 1276
United Kingdom, Army, Iraq War, **1277–1278**, 1277 (image)
commanders of, 1277
number of dead and wounded in, 1278
Operation SINBAD, 1278
operational command of, 1277
operations of, 1277–1278
units involved in, 1277
See also Special Air Service, United Kingdom; Special Boat Service, United Kingdom
United Kingdom, Army, Persian Gulf War, **1278–1279**, 1279 (image)
commanders of, 1278
number of dead and wounded in, 1279
number of Iraqi prisoners taken, 1279
units involved in, 1278–1279
United Kingdom forces in Afghanistan, **1288–1289**, 1288 (image)
International Security Assistance Force (ISAF) and, 1289
number of casualties of, 1289
number of personnel involved in, 1289
training the Afghan National Security Forces (ANSF), 1288
United Kingdom, Marines, Iraq War, **1280**
United Kingdom, Marines, Persian Gulf War, **1280–1281**
United Kingdom, Middle East policy, **1281–1287**, 1283 (image), 1284 (image), 1286 (image)

Anglo-American Committee of Inquiry, 1285
Anglo-Iranian Oil Company (AIOC) crisis, 1285
control of Egypt, 1281–1283
displaced persons (DPs) and, 1284–1285
of Ernest Bevin, 1284
influence of oil on, 1282
military disengagement, 1285–1286
of Neville Chamberlain, 1283
Ottoman Empire war, 1282
in Palestine, 1282–1283
prior to 1914, 1281–1282
St. James Conference (1939), 1283
Suez Canal and, 1282, 1285–1286
support for Israel, 1285, 1286
Transjordan and, 1285, 1540–1542**Doc.**
Treaty of Portsmouth (1946), 1285
White Paper(s) and Jewish immigration, 1283, 1284
World War I and, 1434–1437
World War II and, 1283–1285, 1438–1439
See also Baghdad Pact; Balfour Declaration; Sykes-Picot Agreement
United Kingdom, Navy, Persian Gulf War, **1287**
United Nations (UN), **1289–1291**, 1290 (image)
Article 41 of, 1298
Article 51 of, **154**
Articles 41 and 42 of, **155–156**
authority of secretary-general, 1291
International Court of Justice (ICJ), 1289, 1290
Iraqi letter (on weapons inspectors) to the United Nations, September 25, 1991, and the Security Council's official reply, September 27, 1991, 1687–1688**Doc.**
Iraqi letters of capitulation to, February 27, 1991, 1662–1663**Doc.**
partition of Palestine (1947), 125, 633
principal bodies of, 1289
sanctions against Iraq, 592, **598–599**
Secretariat of, 1289, 1290
secretaries-general of during Middle East wars, 1290
Security Council of, 1289
Trusteeship Council of, 1289, 1290
United Nations Assistance Mission for Afghanistan, **1291–1292**, 1291 (image)
United Nations Convention against Torture (1987), 1249
United Nations Draft Resolution, **1292–1293**
United Nations Economic and Social Council (ECOSOC), 1289
United Nations Educational, Scientific and Cultural Organization (UNESCO), **1293–1294**, 1293 (image)
United Nations Emergency Force (UNEF), 130 (image), 155, 405